2011 North American

Coins & Prices

A GUIDE TO U.S., CANADIAN AND MEXICAN COINS

20th Edition

David C. Harper, Editor

Harry Miller & Thomas Michael, Market Analysts

The World's Best-Selling Coin Books

Published by

Krause Publications, a division of F+W Media, Inc.
700 East State Street • Iola, WI 54990-0001
715-445-2214 • 888-457-2873
www.krausebooks.com

To order books or other products call toll-free 1-800-258-0929
or visit us online at www.shopnumismaster.com

ISSN 1935-0562
ISBN-13: 978-1-4402-1286-4
ISBN-10: 1-4402-1286-4

Cover Design by Donna Mummery
Designed by Sandi Carpenter
Edited by Debbie Bradley

Printed in the United States of America

Contents

≈ **Preface** ≈

Providing coin collectors with accurate, independently produced pricing information on collectible coins has become a trademark of Krause Publication's numismatic division in its 55 years of publishing. Visit our Web site at www.krausebooks.com for more information about us. We employ a full-time staff of market analysts who monitor auction results, trading on the Internet and trading at major shows.

This information is compiled by our analysts and they determine what price most accurately reflects the trading that has occurred for each date and mintmark in each grade listed in *North American Coins & Prices.* By studying this information and referring back to it repeatedly, a collector can arm himself with the necessary knowledge to go out in the market and make wise purchasing decisions. It must be remembered that these prices are intended solely as a guide. They are neither offers to buy or sell. Because prices do fluctuate, those that appear in this book may be in some cases obsolete by the time of publication. By checking the more than 40 price charts in the U.S. section, you can get a feel as to how price swings have occurred since 1972.

U.S. coins are the most popularly collected issues in the world. This is attributable in part to the popularity of coin collecting in the United States, but collectors in many other countries also covet collectible U.S. coins. After collecting U.S. coins for a while, many collectors in the United States branch out into issues of Canada and Mexico. These coins also enjoy a popular following in their countries of origin.

Thus, *North American Coins & Prices* brings together pricing information on all three of these countries. But this book also takes the price-guide concept a step further by providing information on the nuts and bolts of collecting coins: acquiring coins, grading them, organizing them into a collection, storing them properly and much more. Novice collectors can gain the necessary knowledge to collect coins enjoyably; veterans can pick up some pointers to add to their knowledge.

"A Small Beginning"
The U.S. Mint grew from a modest start

By Robert R. Van Ryzin

It was a "small beginning" but a significant one. In July 1792, a site for the new U.S. Mint not yet having been secured, 1,500 silver half dismes were struck on a small screw press nestled in the cellar of a Philadelphia building owned by sawmaker John Harper. Though some have since categorized these early emissions of the fledgling U.S. Mint as patterns, it is clear that first President George Washington – who is said to have deposited the silver from which the coins were struck – considered this small batch of half dismes the first official U.S. coins.

It is true that this limited coinage, the first since passage of the act establishing the Mint on April 2, 1792, pales by comparison to modern U.S. Mint presses. Today's machines can churn out up to 750 coins a minute, striking as many as four coins at a time and boasting yearly mintages in the billions. But it is also true that these first small pieces – struck from silver and stamped with a plump Liberty on the obverse and a scrawny eagle in flight on the reverse – have tremendous historical importance.

For within what Washington would declare in his 1792 address to Congress as a "small beginning" were the seeds of a monetary system that has lasted more than 200 years and has become the study and admiration of many.

Before the U.S. Mint

Collectors today can trace much of the nation's development and learn of its struggles and growth through its coinage: from a cumbersome system first proposed by Robert Morris, a Revolutionary War financier and first superintendent of finance, to the refinements tendered by Thomas Jefferson and Alexander Hamilton, which firmly placed the nation on an easily understood decimal system of coinage.

At first there was little coinage in circulation, except for foreign coins that arrived through trade or in the purses of the first settlers. Despite a dire need for coinage in the Colonies, Great Britain considered it a royal right and granted franchises sparingly. Much of the Colonial economy, therefore, revolved around barter, with food staples, crops, and goods serving as currency. Indian wampum or bead money also was used, first in the fur trade and later as a form of money for Colonial use.

Copper pieces were produced around 1616 for the Sommer Islands (now Bermuda), but coinage within the American Colonies apparently didn't begin until 1652, when John Hull struck silver threepence, sixpence and shillings under authority of the General Court of Massachusetts. This coinage continued, with design changes (willow, oak and pine trees), through 1682. Most of the coins were dated 1652, apparently to avoid problems with England.

In 1658 Cecil Calvert, second Lord Baltimore, commissioned coins to be struck in England for use in Maryland. Other authorized and unauthorized coinages – including those of Mark Newby, John Holt, William Wood, and Dr. Samuel Higley – all became part of the landscape of circulating coins. In the 1780s this hodgepodge of coinage was augmented by influxes of counterfeit British halfpenny coins and various state coinages.

In terms of the latter, the Articles of Confederation had granted individual states the right to produce copper coins. Many states found this to be appealing, and merchants in the mid-1780s traded copper coins of Vermont, Connecticut, Massachusetts, New Jersey, and New York. Not all were legal issues; various entrepreneurs used this as an invitation to strike imitation state coppers and British halfpence. Mutilated and worn foreign coins also circulated in abundance. Included among these were coins of Portugal, Great Britain and France, with the large majority of the silver arriving from Spain.

The accounting system used by the states was derived from the British system of pounds, shillings and pence. Each state was allowed to set its own rates at which foreign gold and silver coins would trade in relation to the British pound.

In 1782 Robert Morris, newly named superintendent of finance, was appointed to head a committee to determine the values and weights of the gold and silver coins in circulation. Asked simply to draw up a table of values, Morris took the opportunity to propose the establishment of a federal mint. In his Jan. 15, 1782, report (largely prepared by his assistant, Gouverneur Morris), Morris noted that the exchange rates between the states were complicated.

He observed that a farmer in New Hampshire would be hard-pressed if asked to determine the value of a bushel of wheat in South Carolina. Morris recorded that an amount of wheat worth four shillings in his home state of New Hampshire would be worth 21 shillings and eightpence under the accounting system used in South Carolina.

Robert Morris devised a complicated plan for a national coinage based on a common denominator of 1,440.

Morris claimed these difficulties plagued not only farmers, but that "they are perplexing to most Men and troublesome to all." Morris further pressed for the adoption of an American coin to solve the problems of the need for small change and debased foreign coinages in circulation.

In essence, what he was advocating was a monometallic system based on silver. He said that gold and silver had fluctuated throughout history. Because these fluctuations resulted in the more valuable metal leaving the country, any nation that adopted a bimetallic coinage was doomed to have its gold or silver coins disappear from circulation.

Gouverneur Morris calculated the rate at which the Spanish dollar traded to the British pound in the various states. Leaving out South Carolina, because it threw off his calculations, Gouverneur Morris arrived at a common denominator of 1,440. Robert Morris, therefore, recommended a unit of value of 1/1,440, equivalent to a quarter grain of silver. He suggested the striking of a silver 100-unit coin, or cent; a silver 500-unit coin, or quint; a silver 1,000-unit coin, or mark; and two copper coins, one of eight units and the other of five units.

On Feb. 21, 1782, the Grand Committee of Congress approved the proposal and directed Morris to press forward and report with a plan to establish a mint. Morris had already done so. Apparently feeling confident that Congress would like his coinage ideas, Morris (as shown by his diary) began efforts at the physical establishment prior to his January 1782 report. He had already engaged Benjamin Dudley to acquire necessary equipment for the mint and hoped to have sample coins available to submit with his original report to Congress.

Things went awry, however.

By Dec. 12, 1782, 10 months after Congress had approved his plan, Morris still could not show any samples of his coins. He was forced, ironically, to suggest that Congress draw up a table of rates for foreign coins to be used until his report was ready. It was not until April 2, 1783, that Morris was able to note in his diary that the first of his pattern coins were being struck.

"I sent for Mr. Dudley who delivered me a piece of Silver Coin," he wrote, "being the first that has been struck as an American Coin."

He also recorded that he had urged Dudley to go ahead with production of the silver patterns.

It wasn't until April 23, 1783, that Morris was able to send his Nova Constellatio patterns to Congress and suggest that he was ready to report on establishing a mint. Apparently nothing came of Morris' efforts. Several committees looked into the matter, but nothing was accomplished. Dudley was eventually discharged as Morris' hopes dimmed.

Thomas Jefferson was the next to offer a major plan. Jefferson liked the idea of a decimal system of coinage, but disliked Morris' basic unit of value. As chairman of the Currency Committee, Jefferson reviewed Morris' plan and formulated his own ideas.

To test public reaction, Jefferson gave his "Notes on Coinage" to The Providence Gazette, and Country Journal, which published his plan in its July 24, 1784, issue. Jefferson disagreed with Morris' suggestion for a 1/1,440 unit of value and instead proposed a decimal coinage based on the dollar, with the lowest unit of account being the mil, or 1/1,000.

"The most easy ratio of multiplication and division is that by ten," Jefferson wrote. "Every one knows the facility of Decimal Arithmetic."

Jefferson argued that although Morris' unit would have eliminated the unwanted fraction that occurred when merchants converted British farthings to dollars, this was of little significance. After all, the original idea of establishing a mint was to get rid of foreign currencies.

Morris' unit, Jefferson said, was too cumbersome for use in normal business transactions. According to Jefferson, under Morris' plan a horse valued at 80 Spanish dollars would require a notation of six figures and would be shown as 115,200 units.

Jefferson' coinage plan suggested the striking of a dollar, or unit; half dollar, or five-tenths; a double tenth, or fifth of a dollar, equivalent to a pistereen; a tenth, equivalent to a Spanish bit; and a one-fifth copper coin, relating to the British farthing. He also wanted a gold coin of $10, corresponding to the British double guinea; and a copper one-hundredth coin, relating to the British halfpence.

In reference to his coinage denominations, Jefferson said, it was important that the coins "coincide in value with some of the known coins so nearly, that the people may by quick reference in the mind, estimate their value."

Thomas Jefferson proposed that the United States adopt a decimal system of coinage.

More than a year, however, passed without any further action on his plan or that proposed by Morris. In a letter to William Grayson, a member of the Continental Congress, Washington expressed concern for the establishment of a national coinage system, terming it "indispensably necessary." Washington also complained of the coinage in circulation: "A man must travel with a pair of scales in his pocket, or run the risk of receiving gold at one-fourth less than it counts."

A plan at last

On May 13, 1785, the 13-member Grand Committee, to whom Jefferson's plan had been submitted, filed its report, generally favoring Jefferson's coinage system. The committee did, however, make slight alterations, including the elimination of the gold $10 coin, the addition of a gold $5 coin, and the dropping of Jefferson's double tenth, which it replaced with a quarter dollar. The committee also added a coin equal to 1/200th of a dollar (half cent). On July 6, 1785, Congress unanimously approved the Grand Committee's plan. It failed, however, to set a standard weight for the silver dollar or to order plans drawn up for a mint.

These two factors led to new proposals.

On April 8, 1786, the Board of Treasury, which had been reinstated after Morris' resignation as superintendent of finance two years prior, tendered three distinct coinage proposals based on varying weights and bimetallic ratios for the silver dollar. The first of these three plans (the one passed by Congress on Aug. 8, 1786) required the silver dollar to contain 375.64 grains of pure silver. The board's proposal varied from earlier coinage plans in that it advocated a higher bimetallic ratio of 15.256-to-1 and differing charges to depositors for coining of gold and silver. It called for minting of gold $5 and $10 coins, and silver denominations of the dime, double dime, half dollar, and dollar. In copper were a cent and half cent. The proposal came during the peak of state coinages and influxes of debased coppers, which, as the board reported, were being "Imported into or manufactured in the Several States."

Concerned over the need to control state coinages and foreign coppers, the board suggested that, within nine months of passage of its proposal, the legal-tender status of all foreign coppers be repealed and that values be set at which the state coppers would circulate. The board obviously expected immediate action and ordered a supply of copper that was being stored in Boston to be brought to New York in the hope that it might soon be coined. Their hopes, however, rested on the positive and quick action of Congress, something that hadn't occurred with the other proposals and would not occur this time.

Opposition to the mint was beginning to surface. Several members of Congress expressed their belief that the supply of foreign gold and silver coins in circulation was sufficient to preclude any need for a mint. They also argued that the problem with debased coppers could be solved by contracting with private individuals to strike the nation's cents and half cents.

Several proposals were offered for a contract coinage. On April 21, 1787, the board accepted a proposal by James Jarvis to strike 300 tons of copper coin at the federal standard. Jarvis, however, delivered slightly less than 9,000 pounds of his contract. The contract was voided the following year for his failure to meet scheduled delivery times, but helped to delay further action on a mint. Concerted action on a coinage system and a mint would wait until the formation of the new government.

Alexander Hamilton, named in September 1789 to head the new Treasury, offered three different methods by which the new nation could achieve economic stability, including the funding of the national debt, establishment of the Bank of North America, and the founding of the U.S. Mint. On Jan. 21, 1791, Hamilton submitted to Congress a "Report on the Establishment of a Mint." It was compiled through his study of European economic theories and the earlier works of Morris and Jefferson, along with the 1786 report of the Board of Treasury.

Hamilton agreed with Jefferson that the dollar seemed to be best suited to serve as the basic unit, but believed it necessary to establish a proper weight and fineness for the new coin. To do so, Hamilton had several Spanish coins assayed to determine the fine weight of the Spanish dollar. He also watched the rate at which Spanish dollars traded for fine gold (24 3/4 grains per dollar) on the world market.

From his assays and observations he determined that the Spanish dollar contained 371 grains of silver. He then multiplied 24 3/4 by 15 (the gold value of silver times his suggested bimetallic ratio) and arrived at 371 1/4 as the proper fine silver weight for the new silver dollar.

In regard to his findings, Hamilton admitted that Morris had made similar assays and had arrived at a weight of 373 grains for the Spanish dollar. Hamilton attributed the discrepancy to the differing equipment used in making the assays. He failed, however, to observe that silver coins were traded in the world market at actual weight rather than the weight at time of issue. The Spanish dollar contained 376 grains of pure silver when new, 4 3/4 grains more than Hamilton's proposed silver dollar.

Hamilton also wanted a bimetallic ratio of 15-to-1, in contrast to the Board of Treasury's 15.6-to-1 ratio. Hamilton said his ratio was closer to Great Britain's, which would be important for trade, and Holland's, which would be important for repaying loans from that country.

His report suggested the striking of a gold $10; gold dollar; silver dollar; silver tenth, or disme; and copper one-hundredth and half-hundredth. Hamilton felt the last of these, the half cent, was necessary because it would enable merchants to lower their prices, which would help the poor.

Congress passed the act establishing the U.S. Mint in April 1792. It reinstated several coin denominations left out by Hamilton and dropped his gold dollar. In gold, the act authorized at $10 coin, or "eagle"; a $5 coin, or "half eagle"; and a $2.50 coin, or "quarter eagle." In silver were to be a dollar, half dollar, quarter dollar, disme, and half disme, and in copper a cent and half cent.

Though it established a sound system of U.S. coinage, the act failed to address the problem of foreign coins in circulation. It was amended in February 1793 to cancel their legal-tender status within three years of the Mint's opening.

Coinage begins

Coinage totals at the first mint were understandably low. Skilled coiners, assayers and others who could handle the mint's daily operations were in short supply in the United States. Also in want were adequate equipment and supplies of metal for coinage. Much of the former had to be built or imported. Much of the latter was also imported or salvaged from various domestic sources, including previously struck tokens and coins, and scrap metal.

Coinage began in earnest in 1793 with the striking of half cents and cents at the new mint located at Seventh Street between Market and Arch streets in Philadelphia. Silver coinage followed in 1794, with half dimes, half dollars and dollars. Gold coinage did not begin until 1795 with the minting of the first $5 and $10 coins. Silver dimes and quarters and gold $2.50 coins did not appear until 1796.

Production at the first U.S. mint, in Philadelphia, was minuscule by today's standards.

Under the bimetallic system of coinage by which gold and silver served as equal representations of the unit of value, much of the success and failure of the nation's coinage to enter and remain in circulation revolved around the supply and valuation of precious metals. One need only to gain a cursory knowledge of such movements to understand what role precious metals played in development of U.S. coinage. That role, to a large extent, determined why some coins today are rare and why some passed down from generation to generation are still plentiful and of lower value to collectors.

From the Mint's beginning, slight miscalculations in the proper weight for the silver dollar and a proper bimetallic ratio led gold and silver to disappear from circulation. The U.S. silver dollar traded at par with Spanish and Mexican dollars, but because the U.S. coin was lighter, it was doomed to export.

A depositor at the first mint could make a profit at the mint's expense by sending the coins to the West Indies. There they could be traded at par for the heavier Spanish or Mexican eight reales, which were then shipped back to the United States for recoinage. As a result, few early silver dollars entered domestic circulation; most failed to escape the melting pots.

Gold fared no better. Calculations of the bimetallic ratio by which silver traded for gold on the world market were also askew at first and were always subject to fluctuations. Gold coins either disappeared quickly after minting or never entered circulation, languishing in bank vaults. These problems led President Jefferson to halt coinage of the gold $10 and silver dollar.

The gold $10 reappeared in 1838 at a new, lower-weight standard. The silver dollar, not coined for circulation since 1803, returned in 1836 with a limited mintage. Full-scale coinage waited until 1840.

Nor was the coinage of copper an easy matter for the first mint. Severe shortages of the metal led the Mint to explore various avenues of obtaining sufficient supplies for striking cents and half cents.

Witness, for example, the half-cent issues of 1795 and 1797 struck over privately issued tokens of the New York firm of Talbot, Allum & Lee because of a shortage of copper for the federal issue. Rising copper prices and continued shortages forced the Mint to lower the cent's weight from 208 grains to 168 grains in 1795.

By that same year Congress had begun to investigate the Mint. Complaints about high costs and low production had been raised. Suggestions that a contract coinage might be more suitable for the new nation surfaced again, despite bad experiences with previous attempts.

The Mint survived this and another investigation, but the problems of fluctuating metal supplies continued to plague the nation. In 1798, because of the coinage shortage, the legal-tender status of foreign coins was restored. Several more extensions were given during the 1800s, ending with the withdrawal of legal-tender status for Spanish coins in 1857.

In the 1830s great influxes of silver from foreign mints raised the value of gold in relation to silver, which made it necessary for the Mint to lower the standard weight of all gold coins in 1834. It also led to the melting of great numbers of gold coins of the old specifications.

By the 1850s discovery of gold in California had again made silver the dearer metal. All silver quickly disappeared from circulation. Congress reacted in 1853 by lowering the weight of the silver half dime, dime, quarter, and half dollar, hoping to keep silver in circulation. A new gold coin of $20 value was introduced to absorb a great amount of the gold from Western mines.

Not long after, silver was discovered in Nevada. By the mid-1870s the various mines that made up what was known as the Comstock Lode (after its colorful early proprietor, Henry P. Comstock) had hit the mother lode. Large supplies of silver from the Comstock, combined with European demonetization, caused a severe drop in its value, which continued through the close of the 19th century.

It was believed that the introduction of a heavier, 420-grain silver dollar in 1873, known as the Trade dollar, would create a market for much of the Comstock silver, bolster its price, and at the same time wrest control from Great Britain of lucrative trade with the Orient. It didn't. Large numbers of Trade dollars eventually flooded back into the United States, where they were, ironically, accepted only at a discount to the lesser-weight Morgan dollars.

The latter had been introduced in 1878 as a panacea to the severe economic problems following the Civil War. Those who proudly carried the banner of free silver contended that by taking the rich output of the Comstock mines and turning it into silver dollars, a cheaper, more plentiful form of money would become available. In its wake, they believed, would be a much needed economic recovery.

The Free Silver Movement gained its greatest support during the late 19th century when William Jennings Bryan attempted to gain the White House on a plank largely based on restoration of the free and unlimited coinage of the standard 412.5-grain silver dollar. He failed. Silver failed. Shortly thereafter the United States officially adopted a gold standard.

Silver continued to be a primary coinage metal until 1964, when rising prices led the Mint to remove it from the dime and quarter. Mintage of the silver dollar had ended in 1935. The half dollar continued to be coined through 1970 with a 40-percent-silver composition. It, too, was then debased.

Gold coinage ended in 1933 and exists today only in commemorative issues and American Eagle bullion coins with fictive face values. A clad composition of copper and nickel is now the primary coinage metal. Even the cent is no longer all copper; a copper-coated zinc composition has been used since 1982.

Precious-metal supplies were also linked to the opening of additional mints, which served the parent facility in Philadelphia. The impact of gold discoveries in the 1820s in the southern Appalachian Mountains was directly tied to the construction of branch mints in Dahlonega, Ga., and Charlotte, N.C., in 1838. These new mints struck only gold coins. New Orleans also became the site of a branch mint in the same year as Dahlonega and Charlotte. It took in some of the outflow of gold from Southern mines, but also struck silver coins.

Discovery of gold in California in the late 1840s created a gold rush, and from it sprang a great western migration. Private issues of gold coinage, often of debased quality, were prevalent, and the cost of shipping the metal eastward for coinage at Philadelphia was high. A call for an official branch mint was soon heard and heeded in 1852 with the authorization of the San Francisco Mint, which began taking deposits in 1854.

The discovery of silver in the Comstock Lode led to yet another mint. Located only a short distance via Virginia & Truckee Railroad from the fabulous Comstock Lode, the Carson City mint began receiving bullion in early 1870.

Denver, also located in a mineral-rich region, became the site of an assay office in 1863 when the government purchased the Clark, Gruber & Co. private mint. It became a U.S. branch mint in 1906. In addition to the Denver and Philadelphia mints, San Francisco and a facility in West Point, N.Y., continue to serve as U.S. mints, but the others have left behind a rich legacy.

The collector taking a more extended journey into the history of U.S. coinage can find plenty of interesting tales – some as tall as the day is long and others factually based – all of which are part of the rich and ever-changing panoply of U.S. coinage history. There are stories of denominations that failed, great discoveries, great rarities, great collectors, and, for those with an artistic bent, a rich field of pattern coins to be explored and a wealth of much-heralded designs by famous sculptors such as Augustus Saint-Gaudens, Adolph Weinman, James Earle Fraser, and others.

For those who are drawn to the hobby by the allure of age-old relics of days gone by, or by coins handed down through the family, or even by dreams of great wealth, coin collecting has much to offer. The history of the U.S. Mint, with its small but ever so important beginning, is the starting point.

The Grading Factor
How to classify a coin's condition

By Arlyn G. Sieber

Grading is one of the most important factors in buying and selling coins as collectibles. Unfortunately, it's also one of the most controversial. Since the early days of coin collecting in the United States, buying through the mail has been a convenient way for collectors to acquire coins. As a result, there has always been a need in numismatics for a concise way to classify the amount of wear on a coin and its condition in general.

A look back

In September 1888, Dr. George Heath, a physician in Monroe, Mich., published a four-page pamphlet titled *The American Numismatist*. Publication of subsequent issues led to the founding of the American Numismatic Association, and *The Numismatist*, as it's known today, is the association's official journal. Heath's first issues were largely devoted to selling world coins from his collection. There were no formal grades listed with the coins and their prices, but the following statement by Heath indicates that condition was a consideration for early collectors:

"The coins are in above average condition," Heath wrote, "and so confident am I that they will give satisfaction, that I agree to refund the money in any unsatisfactory sales on the return of the coins."

As coin collecting became more popular and The Numismatist started accepting paid advertising from others, grading became more formal. The February 1892 issue listed seven "classes" for the condition of coins (from worst to best): mutilated, poor, fair, good, fine, uncirculated, and proof. Through the years, the hobby has struggled with developing a grading system that would be accepted by all and could apply to all coins. The hobby's growth was accompanied by a desire for more grades, or classifications, to more precisely define a coin's condition. The desire for more precision, however, was at odds with the basic concept of grading: to provide a concise method for classifying a coin's condition.

For example, even the conservatively few classifications of 1892 included fudge factors.

"To give flexibility to this classification," *The Numismatist* said, "such modification of fine, good and fair, as 'extremely,' 'very,' 'almost,' etc., are used to express slight variations from the general condition."

The debate over grading continued for decades in *The Numismatist*. A number of articles and letters prodded the ANA to write grading guidelines and endorse them as the association's official standards. Some submitted specific suggestions for terminology and accompanying standards for each grade. But grading remained a process of "instinct" gained through years of collecting or dealing experience.

A formal grading guide in book form finally appeared in 1958, but it was the work of two individuals rather than the ANA. *A Guide to the Grading of United States Coins* by Martin R. Brown and John W. Dunn was a breakthrough in the great grading debate. Now collectors had a reference that gave them specific guidelines for specific coins and could be studied and restudied at home.

The first editions of Brown and Dunn carried text only, no illustrations. For the fourth edition, in 1964, publication was assumed by Whitman Publishing Co. of Racine, Wis., and line drawings were added to illustrate the text.

The fourth edition listed six principal categories for circulated coins (from worst to best): good, very good, fine, very fine, extremely fine, and about uncirculated. But again, the desire for more precise categories were evidenced. In the book's introduction, Brown and Dunn wrote, "Dealers will sometimes advertise coins that are graded G-VG, VG-F, F-VF, VF-XF. Or the description may be ABT. G. or VG plus, etc. This means that the coin in question more than meets minimum standards for the lower grade but is not quite good enough for the higher grade."

When the fifth edition appeared, in 1969, the "New B & D Grading System" was introduced. The six principal categories for circulated coins were still intact, but variances within those categories were now designated by up to four letters: "A," "B," "C" or "D." For example, an EF-A coin was "almost about uncirculated." An EF-B was "normal extra fine" within the B & D standards. EF-C had a "normal extra fine" obverse, but the reverse was "obviously not as nice as obverse due to poor strike or excessive wear." EF-D had a "normal extra fine" reverse but a problem obverse.

But that wasn't the end. Brown and Dunn further listed 29 problem points that could appear on a coin – from No. 1 for an "edge bump" to No. 29 for "attempted re-engraving outside of the Mint." The number could be followed by the letter "O" or "R" to designate whether the problem appeared on the obverse or reverse and a Roman numeral corresponding to a clock face to designate where the problem appears on the obverse or reverse. For example, a coin described as "VG-B-9-O-

X" would grade "VG-B"; the "9" designated a "single rim nick"; the "O" indicated the nick was on the obverse; and the "X" indicated it appeared at the 10 o'clock position, or upper left, of the obverse.

The authors' goal was noble – to create the perfect grading system. They again, however, fell victim to the age-old grading-system problem: Precision comes at the expense of brevity. Dealer Kurt Krueger wrote in the January 1976 issue of *The Numismatist*, "Under the new B & D system, the numismatist must contend with a minimum of 43,152 different grading combinations! Accuracy is apparent, but simplicity has been lost." As a result, the "New B & D Grading System" never caught on in the marketplace.

The 1970s saw two important grading guides make their debut. The first was *Photograde* by James F. Ruddy. As the title implies, Ruddy uses photographs instead of line drawings to show how coins look in the various circulated grades. Simplicity is also a virtue of Ruddy's book. Only seven circulated grades are listed (about good, good, very good, fine, very fine, extremely fine, and about uncirculated), and the designations stop there.

In 1977 the longtime call for the ANA to issue grading standards was met with the release of *The Official A.N.A. Grading Standards for United States Coins*. Like Brown and Dunn, the first edition of the ANA grading guide used line drawings to illustrate coins in various states of wear. But instead of using adjectival descriptions, the ANA guide adopted a numerical system for designating grades.

The numerical designations were based on a system used by Dr. William H. Sheldon in his book *Early American Cents*, first published in 1949. He used a scale of 1 to 70 to designate the grades of large cents.

"On this scale," Sheldon wrote, "1 means that the coin is identifiable and not mutilated – no more than that. A 70-coin is one in flawless Mint State, exactly as it left the dies, with perfect mint color and without a blemish or nick." (Sheldon's scale also had its pragmatic side. At the time, a No. 2 large cent was worth about twice a No. 1 coin; a No. 4 was worth about twice a No. 2, and so on up the scale.)

With the first edition of its grading guide, the ANA adopted the 70-point scale for grading all U.S. coins. It designated 10 categories of circulated grades: AG-3, G-4, VG-8, F-12, VF-20, VF-30, EF-40, EF-45, AU-50, and AU-55. The third edition, released in 1987, replaced the line drawings with photographs, and another circulated grade was added: AU-58. A fourth edition was released in 1991.

Grading circulated U.S. coins

Dealers today generally use either the ANA guide or Photograde when grading circulated coins for their inventories. (Brown and Dunn is now out of print.) Many local coin shops sell both books. Advertisers in *Numismatic News*, *Coins* magazine, and *Coin Prices* must indicate which standards they are using in grading their coins. If the standards are not listed, they must conform to ANA standards.

Following are some general guidelines, accompanied by photos, for grading circulated U.S. coins. Grading even circulated pieces can be subjective, particularly when attempting to draw the fine line between, for example, AU-55 and AU-58. Two longtime collectors or dealers can disagree in such a case.

But by studying some combination of the following guidelines, the ANA guide, and Photograde, and by looking at a lot of coins at shops and shows, collectors can gain enough grading knowledge to buy circulated coins confidently from dealers and other collectors. The more you study, the more knowledge and confidence you will gain. When you decide which series of coins you want to collect, focus on the guidelines for that particular series. Read them, reread them, and then refer back to them again and again.

AU-50

AU-50 (about uncirculated): Just a slight trace of wear, result of brief exposure to circulation or light rubbing from mishandling, may be evident on elevated design

Indian cent   Lincoln cent

Buffalo nickel   Jefferson nickel

Mercury dime

Standing Liberty quarter

Washington quarter

Walking Liberty half dollar

Morgan dollar

Barber coins

areas. These imperfections may appear as scratches or dull spots, along with bag marks or edge nicks. At least half of the original mint luster generally is still evident.

XF-40

Indian cent

Lincoln cent

Buffalo nickel

Jefferson nickel

Mercury dime

Standing Liberty quarter

Washington quarter

Walking Liberty half dollar

Morgan dollar

Barber coins

XF-40 (extremely fine): The coin must show only slight evidence of wear on the highest points of the design, particularly in the hair lines of the portrait on the obverse. The same may be said for the eagle's feathers and wreath leaves on the reverse of most U.S. coins. A trace of mint luster may still show in protected areas of the coin's surface.

VF-20

Indian cent

Lincoln cent

Buffalo nickel

Jefferson nickel

Mercury dime

Standing Liberty quarter

Washington quarter

Walking Liberty half dollar

Morgan dollar

Barber coins

VF-20 (very fine): The coin will show light wear at the fine points in the design, though they may remain sharp overall. Although the details may be slightly smoothed, all lettering and major features must remain sharp.

Indian cent: All letters in "Liberty" are complete but worn. Headdress shows considerable flatness, with flat spots on the tips of the feathers.

Lincoln cent: Hair, cheek, jaw, and bow-tie details will be worn but clearly separated, and wheat stalks on the reverse will be full with no weak spots.

Buffalo nickel: High spots on hair braid and cheek will be flat but show some detail, and a full horn will remain on the buffalo.

Jefferson nickel: Well over half of the major hair detail will remain, and the pillars on Monticello will remain well defined, with the triangular roof partially visible.

Mercury dime: Hair braid will show some detail, and three-quarters of the detail will remain in the feathers. The two diagonal bands on the fasces will show completely but will be worn smooth at the middle, with the vertical lines sharp.

Standing Liberty quarter: Rounded contour of Liberty's right leg will be flattened, as will the high point of the shield.

Washington quarter: There will be considerable wear on the hair curls, with feathers on the right and left of the eagle's breast showing clearly.

Walking Liberty half dollar: All lines of the skirt will show but will be worn on the high points. Over half the feathers on the eagle will show.

Morgan dollar: Two-thirds of the hair lines from the forehead to the ear must show. Ear should be well defined. Feathers on the eagle's breast may be worn smooth.

Barber coins: All seven letters of "Liberty" on the headband must stand out sharply. Head wreath will be well outlined from top to bottom.

F-12

Indian cent

Lincoln cent

Buffalo nickel

Jefferson nickel

Mercury dime

Standing Liberty quarter

Washington quarter

Walking Liberty half dollar

Morgan dollar

Barber coins

F-12 (fine): Coins show evidence of moderate to considerable but generally even wear on all high points, though all elements of the design and lettering remain bold. Where the word "Liberty" appears in a headband, it must be fully visible. On 20th century coins, the rim must be fully raised and sharp.

VG-8

Indian cent

Lincoln cent

Buffalo nickel

Jefferson nickel

Mercury dime

Standing Liberty quarter

Washington quarter

Walking Liberty half dollar

Morgan dollar

Barber coins

VG-8 (very good): The coin will show considerable wear, with most detail points worn nearly smooth. Where the word "Liberty" appears in a headband, at least three letters must show. On 20th century coins, the rim will start to merge with the lettering.

G-4

Indian cent

Lincoln cent

Buffalo nickel

Jefferson nickel

Mercury dime

Standing Liberty quarter

Washington quarter

Walking Liberty half dollar

Morgan dollar

Barber coins

G-4 (good): Only the basic design remains distinguishable in outline form, with all points of detail worn smooth. The word "Liberty" has disappeared, and the rims are almost merging with the lettering.

About good or fair: The coin will be identifiable by date and mint but otherwise badly worn, with only parts of the lettering showing. Such coins are of value only as fillers in a collection until a better example of the date and mintmark can be obtained. The only exceptions would be rare coins

Collectors have a variety of grading services from which to choose. This set of Arkansas half dollars that appeared in an Early American History Auctions sale used two of the services.

Grading uncirculated U.S. coins

The subjectivity of grading and the trend toward more classifications becomes more acute when venturing into uncirculated, or mint-state, coins. A minute difference between one or two grade points can mean a difference in value of hundreds or even thousands of dollars. In addition, the standards are more difficult to articulate in writing and illustrate through drawings or photographs. Thus, the possibilities for differences of opinion on one or two grade points increase in uncirculated coins.

Back in Dr. George Heath's day and continuing through the 1960s, a coin was either uncirculated or it wasn't. Little distinction was made between uncirculated coins of varying condition, largely because there was little if any difference in value. When *Numismatic News* introduced its value guide in 1962 (the forerunner of today's *Coin Market* section in the *News*), it listed only one grade of uncirculated for Morgan dollars.

But as collectible coins increased in value and buyers of uncirculated coins became more picky, distinctions within uncirculated grade started to surface. In 1975 *Numismatic News* still listed only one uncirculated grade in *Coin Market*, but added this note: "Uncirculated and proof specimens in especially choice condition will also command proportionately higher premiums than these listed."

The first edition of the ANA guide listed two grades of uncirculated, MS-60 and MS-65, in addition to the theoretical but non-existent MS-70 (a flawless coin). MS-60 was described as "typical uncirculated" and MS-65 as "choice uncirculated." *Numismatic News* adopted both designations for *Coin Market*. In 1981, when the second edition of the ANA grading guide was released, MS-67 and MS-63 were added. In 1985 *Numismatic News* started listing six grades of uncirculated for Morgan dollars: MS-60, MS-63, MS-65, MS-65+, and MS-63 prooflike.

Then in 1986, a new entity appeared that changed the nature of grading and trading uncirculated coins ever since. A group of dealers led by David Hall of Newport

Beach, Calif., formed the Professional Coin Grading Service. For a fee, collectors could submit a coin through an authorized PCGS dealer and receive a professional opinion of its grade.

The concept was not new; the ANA had operated an authentication service since 1972 and a grading service since 1979. A collector or dealer could submit a coin directly to the service and receive a certificate giving the service's opinion on authenticity and grade. The grading service was the source of near constant debate among dealers and ANA officials. Dealers charged that ANA graders were too young and inexperienced, and that their grading was inconsistent.

Grading stability was a problem throughout the coin business in the early 1980s, not just with the ANA service. Standards among uncirculated grades would tighten during a bear market and loosen during a bull market. As a result, a coin graded MS-65 in a bull market may have commanded only MS-63 during a bear market.

PCGS created several innovations in the grading business in response to these problems:

1. Coins could be submitted through PCGS-authorized dealers only.

2. Each coin would be graded by at least three members of a panel of "top graders," all prominent dealers in the business. (Since then, however, PCGS does not allow its graders to also deal in coins.)

3. After grading, the coin would be encapsulated in an inert, hard-plastic holder with a serial number and the grade indicated on the holder.

4. PCGS-member dealers pledged to make a market in PCGS-graded coins and honor the grades assigned.

5. In one of the most far-reaching moves, PCGS said it would use all 11 increments of uncirculated on the 70-point numerical scale: MS-60, MS-61, MS-62, MS-63, MS-64, MS-65, MS-66, MS-67, MS-68, MS-69, and MS-70.

The evolution of more uncirculated grades had reached another milestone.

Purists bemoaned the entombment of classic coins in the plastic holders and denounced the 11 uncirculated grades as implausible. Nevertheless, PCGS was an immediate commercial success. The plastic holders were nicknamed "slabs," and dealers couldn't get coins through the system fast enough.

In subsequent years, a number of similar services have appeared. Among them, one of the original PCGS "top graders," John Albanese, left PCGS to found the Numismatic Guaranty Corp (NGC). The ANA grading service succumbed to "slab mania" and introduced its own encapsulated product.

There now are numerous other reputable private third-party grading services. PCGS and NGC are the oldest and remain the leaders. In 1990 the ANA sold its grading service to a private company. It operates under the ANACS acronym.

How should a collector approach the buying and grading of uncirculated coins? Collecting uncirculated coins worth thousands of dollars implies a higher level of numismatic expertise by the buyer. Those buyers without that level of expertise should cut their teeth on more inexpensive coins, just as today's experienced collectors did. Inexperienced collectors can start toward that level by studying the guidelines for mint-state coins in the ANA grading guide and looking at lots of coins at shows and shops.

Study the condition and eye appeal of a coin and compare it to other coins of the same series. Then compare prices. Do the more expensive coins look better? If so, why? Start to make your own judgments concerning relationships between condition and value.

According to numismatic legend, a collector walked up to a crusty old dealer at a show one time and asked the dealer to grade a coin the collector had with him. The dealer looked at the coin and said, "I grade it a hundred dollars." Such is the bottom line to coin grading.

Grading U.S. proof coins

Because proof coins are struck by a special process using polished blanks, they receive their own grading designation. A coin does not start out being a proof and then become mint state if it becomes worn. Once a proof coin, always a proof coin.

In the ANA system, proof grades use the same numbers as circulated and uncirculated grades, and the amount of wear on the coin corresponds to those grades. But the number is preceded by the word "proof." For example, Proof-65, Proof-55, Proof-45, and so on. In addition, the ANA says a proof coin with many marks, scratches or other defects should be called an "impaired proof."

Grading world coins

The state of grading non-U.S. issues is similar to U.S. coin grading before Brown and Dunn. There is no detailed, illustrated guide that covers the enormous scope and variety of world coins; collectors and dealers rely on their experience in the field and knowledge of the marketplace.

The *Standard Catalog of World Coins* gives the following guidelines for grading world coins, which apply to the Canadian and Mexican value listings in this book:

In grading world coins, there are two elements to look for: (1) overall wear and (2) loss of design details, such as strands of hair, feathers on eagles, designs on coats of arms, and so on. Grade each coin by the weaker of the two sides. Age, rarity or type of coin should not be considered in grading.

Grade by the amount of overall wear and loss of detail evident in the main design on each side. On coins with a moderately small design element that is prone to early wear, grade by that design alone.

In the marketplace, adjectival grades are still used for Mexican coins. The numerical system for Canadian coins is now commonplace:

Uncirculated, MS-60: No visible signs of wear or handling, even under a 30X microscope. Bag marks may be present.

Almost uncirculated, AU-50: All detail will be visible. There will be wear on only the highest points of the coin. There will often be half or more of the original mint

SELL YOUR COINS & CURRENCY TO AN EXPERT!

Gary Adkins

Gary Adkins Associates, Inc. is one of the premier numismatic firms in the country. Our goal is to be the best company in the rare coin business. Not the biggest, but the best! We do that by providing personalized service and attention to every customer. Gary Adkins, our senior numismatist, has over 40 years in the business. As a board member & president of the Professional Numismatic Guild, he brings qualifications and credentials that insure our most important goal ... your complete satisfaction. We are proud to have a staff of very experienced numismatists who are qualified to help you with your coin purchases or sales, find coins that you need to complete your collection, and answer any of your numismatic questions.

We work with clients to provide whatever is best for each individual and we never lose sight of the fact that coins are not a necessity of life. They are a luxury meant to be enjoyed as objects of beauty, history, and pride of ownership. You can be assured that we will make every effort to give you the finest quality coins at the best possible price level for the grade you select. Our desire is to assist you in obtaining your objectives, both in portfolio selection and in the purchase or sale of your coins. Our company motto is, "If we wouldn't put it in our collection, we wouldn't ask you to put it in yours." We are here to build long-term relationships and help you enjoy your collecting to the fullest.

Visit Our Website: www.coinbuys.com

---

luster present.

Extremely fine, XF-40: About 95 percent of the original detail will be visible. Or, on a coin with a design that has no inner detail to wear down, there will be light wear over nearly the entire coin. If a small design is used as the grading area, about 90 percent of the original detail will be visible. This latter rule stems from the logic that a smaller amount of detail needs to be present because a small area is being used to grade the whole coin.

Very fine, VF-20: About 75 percent of the original detail will be visible. Or, on a coin with no inner detail, there will be moderate wear over the entire coin. Corners of letters and numbers may be weak. A small grading area will have about 60 percent of the original detail.

Fine, F-12: About 50 percent of the original detail will be visible. Or, on a coin with no inner detail, there will be fairly heavy wear over the entire coin. Sides of letters will be weak. A typically uncleaned coin will often appear dirty or dull. A small grading area will have just under 50 percent of the original detail.

Very good, VG-8: About 25 percent of the original detail will be visible. There will be heavy wear on the entire coin.

Good, G-4: Design will be clearly outlined but with substantial wear. Some of the larger detail may be visible. The rim may have a few weak spots of wear.

About good, AG-3: Typically only a silhouette of a large design will be visible. The rim will be worn down into the letters, if any.

Where to write for more information

American Numismatic Association: 818 N. Cascade Ave., Colorado Springs, CO 80903-3279.

Independent Coin Grading Co.: 7901 E. Belleview Ave., Suite 50, Englewood, CO 80111.

Numismatic Guaranty Corp: P.O. Box 4776, Sarasota, FL 34230.

NTC (Numistrust Corp.): 2500 N. Military Trail, Suite 210, Boca Raton, FL 33431.

Professional Coin Grading Service: P.O. Box 9458, Newport Beach, CA 92658.

Sovereign Entities Grading Service: 401 Chestnut St., Suite 103, Chattanooga, TN 37402-4924.

Visit the Krause Publications website
www.numismaster.com

Get a Map
How to organize a collection

By David C. Harper

Do you have a jar full of old coins? Did a favorite relative give you a few silver dollars over the years? Or did you just come across something unusual that you set aside?

All three circumstances make good beginnings for collecting coins. It may surprise you, but this is how just about everybody starts in the hobby. It is a rare collector who decides to start down the hobby road without first having come into a few coins one way or another.

What these random groupings lack is organization. It is organization that makes a collection. But think about it another way: Organization is the map that tells you where you can go in coin collecting and how you can get there.

Have you ever been at a large fair or a huge office building and seen the maps that say "you are here"? Did you ever consider that, over time, thousands of other people have stood on the same spot? This is true in numismatics also. Figuratively, you are standing on the same spot on which the writers of this book stood at some point in their lives.

At a fair, the map helps you consider various ways of seeing all the sights. In coin collecting, too, there are different ways to organize a collection. The method you choose helps you see the hobby sights you want to see.

It should be something that suits you. Remember, do what you want to do. See what you want to see. But don't be afraid to make a mistake; there aren't any. Just as one can easily retrace steps at a fair, one can turn around and head in another direction in the coin-collecting hobby. Besides, when you start off for any given point, often you see something along the way that was unplanned but more interesting. That's numismatics.

There are two major ways to organize a collection: by type, and by date and mintmark. These approaches work in basically the same fashion for coins of the United States, Canada and Mexico. Naturally, there are differences. But to establish the concepts, let's focus first on U.S. coins.

United States

Let's take collecting by type first. Look at your jar of coins, or take the change out of your pocket. You find Abraham Lincoln and the Lincoln Memorial on most cents and four commemorative reverse designs in 2009. You find Thomas Jefferson and his home, Monticello, on most nickels, but special reverse designs were produced in 2004 and 2005 and a new obverse began in 2006. Franklin D. Roosevelt and a torch share the dime. George Washington and an eagle (or since 1999, designs honoring states and the District of Columbia and territories) appear on the quarter. John F. Kennedy and the presidential seal are featured on the half dollar. Sacagawea paired with an eagle or a woman planting and Presidents paired with the Statue of Liberty are on dollars.

Each design is called a "type." If you took one of each and put them in a holder, you would have a type set of recent coins.

With just these six denominations, you can study various metallic compositions. You can evaluate their states of preservation and assign a grade to each. You can learn about the artists who designed the coins, and you can learn of the times in which these designs were created.

As you might have guessed, many different coin types have been used in the United States over the years. You may remember seeing some of them circulating. These designs reflect the hopes and aspirations of people over time. Putting all of them together forms a wonderful numismatic mosaic of American history.

George Washington did not mandate that his image appear on the quarter. Quite the contrary. He would have been horrified. When he was president, he headed off those individuals in Congress who thought the leader of the country should have his image on its coins. Washington said it smacked of monarchy and would have none of it.

Almost a century and a half later, during the bicentennial of Washington's birth in 1932, a nation searching for its roots during troubled economic times decided that it needed his portrait on its coins as a reminder of his great accomplishments and as reassurance that this nation was the same place it had been in more prosperous days.

In its broadest definition, collecting coins by type requires that you obtain an example of every design that was struck by the U.S. Mint since it was founded in 1792. That's a tall order. You would be looking for denominations like the half cent, two-cent piece, three-cent piece, and 20-cent piece, which have not been produced in more than a century. You would be looking for gold coins ranging in face value from $1 to $50 and current bullion coins.

But even more important than odd-sounding denominations or high face values is the question of rarity. Some of the pieces in this multi-century type set are rare and expensive. That's why type collectors often divide the challenge into more digestible units.

Type collecting can be divided into 18th, 19th, 20th and 21st century units. The 21st century set is rapidly growing. Starting type collectors can focus on 20th century coin designs, which are easily obtainable. The fun and satisfaction of putting the 20th century set together then creates the momentum to continue backward in time.

In the process of putting a 20th century type set together, one is also learning how to grade, learning hobby jargon, and discovering how to obtain coins from dealers, the U.S. Mint, and other collectors. All of this knowledge is then refined as the collector increases the challenge to himself.

This book is designed to help. How many dollar types were struck in the 20th century? Turn to the U.S. price-guide section and check it out. We see the Morgan dollar, Peace dollar, Eisenhower dollar, and Anthony dollar. Hobbyists could also add the Ike dollar with the Bicentennial design of 1976 and the silver American Eagle bullion coin struck since 1986. One can also find out their approximate retail prices from the listings.

The beauty of type collecting is that one can choose the most inexpensive example of each type. There is no need to select a 1903-O Morgan when the 1921 will do just as well. With the 20th century type set, hobbyists can dodge some truly big-league prices.

As a collector's hobby confidence grows, he can tailor goals to fit his desires. He can take the road less traveled if that is what suits him. Type sets can be divided by denomination. You can choose more than two centuries of one-cent coins. You can take just obsolete denominations or copper, silver or gold denominations.

You can even collect by size. Perhaps you would like to collect all coin types larger than 30 millimeters or all coins smaller than 20 millimeters. Many find this freedom of choice stimulating.

Type collecting has proven itself to be enduringly popular over the years. It provides a maximum amount of design variety while allowing collectors to set their own level of challenge.

The second popular method of collecting is by date and mintmark. What this means, quite simply, is that a collector picks a given type – Jefferson nickels, for example – and then goes after an example of every year, every mintmark, and every type of manufacture that was used with the Jefferson design.

Looking at this method of collecting brings up the subject of mintmarks. The "U.S. Mint" is about as specific as most non-collectors get in describing the government agency that provides everyday coins. Behind that label are the various production facilities that actually do the work.

In the more than two centuries of U.S. coinage, there have been eight such facilities. Four are still in operation. Those eight in alphabetical order are Carson City, Nev., which used a "CC" mintmark to identify its work; Charlotte, N.C.

A basic type set of 20th century dollar coins would consist of (from top) a Morgan type, Peace type, Eisenhower type and Anthony type.

("C"); Dahlonega, Ga. ("D"); Denver (also uses a "D," but it opened long after the Dahlonega Mint closed, so there was never any confusion); New Orleans ("O"); Philadelphia (because it was the primary mint, it used no mintmark for much of its history, but currently uses a "P"); San Francisco ("S"); and West Point, N.Y. ("W").

A person contemplating the collecting of Jefferson nickels by date and mint-mark will find that three mints produced them: San Francisco, Denver and Phila-delphia. Because the first two are branch mints serving smaller populations, their output has tended over time to be smaller than that of Philadelphia. This fact, repeated in other series, has helped give mintmarks quite an allure to collectors. It provides one of the major attractions in collecting coins by date and mintmark.

The key date for Jeffersons is the 1950-D when using mintages as a guide. In that year, production was just 2.6 million pieces. Because collectors of the time

Jefferson nickels have been produced at the (from top) Philadephia, Denver and San Francisco Mints. Note the Denver and San Francisco mintmarks to the right of Monticello.

The wartime nickels of 1942-1945 marked the first time a "P" mintmark, for Philadelphia, was used.

were aware of the coin's low mintage, many examples were saved. As a result, prices are reasonable.

The Depression-era 1939-D comes in as the most valuable regular-issue Jefferson nickel despite a mintage of 3.5 million – almost 1 million more than the 1950-D. The reason: Fewer were saved for later generations of coin collectors.

Date and mintmark collecting teaches hobbyists to use mintage figures as a guide but to take them with a grain of salt. Rarity, after all, is determined by the number of surviving coins, not the number initially created.

The Jefferson series is a good one to collect by date and mintmark, because the mintmarks have moved around, grown in size, and expanded in number.

When the series was first introduced, the Jefferson nickel was produced at the three mints previously mentioned. In 1942, because of a diversion of certain metals to wartime use, the coin's alloy of 75 percent copper and 25 percent nickel was changed. The new alloy was 35 percent silver, 56 percent copper, and 9 percent manganese.

To denote the change, the mintmarks were moved and greatly enlarged. The pre-1942 mintmarks were small and located to the right of Monticello; the wartime mintmarks were enlarged and placed over the dome. What's more, for the first time in American history, the Philadelphia Mint used a mintmark ("P").

The war's end restored the alloy and mintmarks to their previous status. The "P" disappeared. This lasted until the 1960s, when a national coin shortage saw all mintmarks removed for three years (1965-1967) and then returned, but in a different location. Mintmarks were placed on the obverse, to the right of Jefferson's portrait near the date in 1968. In 1980 the "P" came back in a smaller form and is still used.

Another consideration arises with date and mintmark collecting: Should the hobbyist include proof coins in the set? This can be argued both ways. Suffice to say that anyone who has the desire to add proof coins to the set will have a larger one. It is not necessary nor is it discouraged.

Some of the first proof coins to carry mintmarks were Jefferson nickels. When proof coins were made in 1968 after lapsing from 1965 to 1967, production occurred at San Francisco instead of Philadelphia. The "S" mintmark was placed on the proof coins of that year, including the Jefferson nickel, to denote the change. Since that time, mintmarks used on proof examples of various denominations have included the "P," "D," "S," and "W."

In 1968 the mintmarks reappeared on U.S. coins and production of proof coins resumed, this time at the San Francisco Mint. On the nickels, the mintmark moved from the reverse to the obverse below the date.

For all of the mintmark history that is embodied in the Jefferson series, prices are reasonable. For a first attempt at collecting coins by date and mintmark, it provides excellent background for going on to the more expensive and difficult types. After all, if you are ever going to get used to the proper handling of a coin, it is far better to experiment on a low-cost coin than a high-value rarity.

As one progresses in date and mintmark collecting and type collecting, it is important to remember that all of the coins should be of similar states of preservation. Sets look slapdash if one coin is VG and another is MS-65 and still another is VF. Take a look at the prices of all the coins in the series before you get too far, figure out what you can afford, and then stick to that grade or range of grades.

Sure, there is a time-honored practice of filling a spot with any old example until a better one comes along. That is how we got the term "filler." But if you get a few placeholders, don't stop there. By assembling a set of uniform quality, you end up with a more aesthetically pleasing collection.

The date and mintmark method used to be the overwhelmingly dominant form of collecting. It still has many adherents. Give it a try if you think it sounds right for you.

Before we leave the discussion of collecting U.S. coins, it should be pointed out that the two major methods of organizing a collection are simply guidelines. They are not hard-and-fast rules that must be followed without questions. Collecting should be satisfying to the hobbyist. It should never be just one more item in the daily grind. Take the elements of these collecting approaches that you like or invent your own.

It should also be pointed out that U.S. coinage history does not start with 1792, nor do all of the coins struck since that time conform precisely to the two major organizational approaches. But these two areas are good places to start.

There are coins and tokens from the American Colonial period (1607-1776) that are just as fascinating and collectible as regular U.S. Mint issues. There are federal issues struck before the Mint was actually established. See the Colonial price-guide section in this book.

There are special coins called commemoratives, which have been struck by the U.S. Mint since 1892 to celebrate some aspect of American history or a contemporary event. They are not intended for circulation. There was a long interruption between 1954 and 1982, but currently annual commemoratives are being offered for sale directly to collectors by the Mint.

Collecting commemoratives has always been considered something separate from collecting regular U.S. coinage. It is, however, organized the same way. Commemoratives can be collected by date and mintmark or by type.

Current commemoratives can be purchased from the U.S. Mint. Check the U.S. Mint Web site at www.usmint.gov. Hobbyists who order from the U.S. Mint's Web site receive notices of product availability by e-mail. Hobbyists will get the various solicitations for not only commemoratives, but regular proof sets and mint sets and proof American Eagle bullion coins. Buying coins from the Mint can be considered a hobby pursuit in its own right. Some collectors let the Mint organize their holdings for them. They buy complete sets and put them away. They never buy anything from anywhere else.

Admittedly, this is a passive form of collecting, but there are individuals around the world who enjoy collecting at this level without ever really going any deeper. They like acquiring every new issue as it comes off the Mint's presses.

Once done, there is a certain knowledge that one has all the examples of the current year. Obviously, too, collectors by date and mintmark of the current types would have to buy the new coins each year, but, of course, they do not stop there.

Varieties and errors make up another area. Under this heading come the coins the Mint did not intend to make. There are all kinds of errors. Many of them are inexpensive. Check out the U.S. Minting Varieties and Errors section in the price guide. If you want to pursue it further, there are specialty books that deal with the topic in more detail.

Canada

Starting point for the national coinage of Canada is popularly fixed at 1858. In that year a large cent was first produced for use in Upper and Lower Canada (Ontario and Quebec). These prices were intended to supplant local copper coinage, which in turn had been attempts to give various regions a medium of exchange.

What was circulating in Canada at the time was a hodgepodge of world issues. The large cent predates a unified national government by nine years, but it is considered the beginning of national issues nevertheless.

There are many similarities between the United States and Canada and their respective monetary systems. Both continent-sized nations thought in terms of taming the frontier, new settlements, and growth. Both came to use the dollar as the unit of account because of the pervasiveness of the Spanish milled dollar in trade. For each, the dollar divides into 100 cents.

However, Canada had a far longer colonial history. Many of its residents resisted the tide that carried the United States to independence and worked to preserve their loyalties to the British crown. As a result, Canada was firmly a part of the British Empire. So even today with its constitution (the British North America Act transferred from Westminster to Ottawa in 1982), parliamentary democracy, and a national consciousness perhaps best symbolized by the maple leaf, Canada retains a loyalty to the crown in the person of Queen Elizabeth II of the United Kingdom. Canada is a member of the British Commonwealth of Nations.

*Canadian coins
have depicted (from
top) Queen Victoria,
King Edward VII,
King George V,
King George VI and
Queen Elizabeth II.*

The effect of this on coins is obvious. Current issues carry the queen's effigy. How Canada got its coins in the past was also influenced. The fledgling U.S. government set about creating its own mint as one of its earliest goals, despite that better-quality pieces could be purchased abroad at lower cost. Canada found that ties to mints located in England were logical and comfortable.

The Royal Canadian Mint was not established until 1908, when it was called the Ottawa branch of the British Royal Mint, and it was not given its present name until 1931. Both events are within living memory. Canadian coins, therefore, have a unique mixture of qualities. They are tantalizingly familiar to U.S. citizens yet distinctly different.

The coinage of a monarchy brings its own logic to the organization of a collection. Type collecting is delineated by the monarch. United Canada has had six. The first was Queen Victoria, whose image appeared on those large cents of 1858. Her reign began in 1837 and lasted until 1901.

She was followed by Edward VII, 1901-1910; George V, 1910-1936; Edward VIII, 1936; George VI, 1936-1952; and Queen Elizabeth II, 1952-present. All but Edward VIII had coins struck for circulation in Canada. The collectible monarchs, therefore, number five, but the longer reigns inspired changes of portraits over time to show the aging process at work. Legends also changed. When George VI ceased being emperor of India, Canada's coins were modified to recognize the change.

Like U.S. coins, sizes and alloys were altered to meet new demands placed on the coinage. However, the separateness of each nation might best be summed up this way: Though the United States abolished its large cent in 1857, Canada's was just getting under way in 1858. The United States put an end to the silver dollar in 1935, the very year Canada finally got its series going.

And Canada, the nickel-mining giant, used a small-sized silver five-cent coin until 1921, almost 50 years after the half dime was abolished in the United States. But whereas the Civil War was the major cause of the emergence of modern U.S. coinage as specified by the Coinage Act of 1873, World War I influenced the alterations that made Canada's coins what they are today.

It might be assumed that change in the monarch also signaled a change in the reverse designs of the various denominations. A check of the Canadian price guide section shows this is not necessarily the case. Current designs paired with Queen Elizabeth II basically date back to the beginning of her father's reign. The familiar maple-leaf cent, beaver five-cent piece, schooner 10-cent, caribou 25-cent, and coat-of-arms 50-cent have been running for more than 50 years. Significant changes were made to the 50-cent coin in 1959, but the reverse design remains the coat of arms.

So where does that leave type collectors? It puts them in a situation similar to categorizing the various eagles on U.S. coins. They can be universalists and accept the broadest definitions of type, or they can narrow the bands to whatever degree suits them best.

By checking the price-guide section, date and mintmark collectors will quickly note that their method of organization more or less turns into collecting by date. Though currently there are three mints in Canada – Hull, Quebec; Ottawa, Ontario; and Winnipeg, Manitoba – they don't use mintmarks. Historically, few mintmarks were employed.

Ottawa used a "C" on gold sovereigns of 1908-1919 and on some exported colonial issues. The private Heaton Mint in Birmingham, England, used an "H" on coins it supplied to Canada from 1871 to 1907.

But the coins supplied to Canada by the British Royal Mint and later by its Ottawa branch did not carry any identifying mark. Collectors who confine their activities to the more recent issues need never think about a mintmark.

It would be easy to slant a presentation on Canadian issues to stress similarities or differences to U.S. issues. One should remember that the monetary structures of each evolved independently, but each was always having an impact on the other.

Common events, such as World War II, had a similar impact. For example, the Canadian five-cent coin changed in much the same way as the U.S. nickel. In Canada, nickel was removed and replaced first by a tombac (brass) alloy and then by chromium-plated steel. Peace brought with it a return to the prewar composition.

To see an example of differences between the United States and Canada, take the Canadian approach to the worldwide trend of removing silver from coinage. Canada made its move in 1968, three years after the United States. Instead of choosing a copper-nickel alloy as a substitute for silver, Canada looked to its own vast natural resources and employed pure nickel.

Canada also seems more comfortable with its coinage than the United States. Whereas the United States often feared confusion and counterfeiting from making the least little changes in its coins, Canada has long embraced coinage to communicate national events, celebrations and culture. Its silver-dollar series actually began as a celebration of George V's 25 years on the throne.

Succeeding years saw additional commemorative $1 designs interspersed with the regular Voyageur design. When the centennial of national confederation was observed in 1967, all of the denominations were altered for one year. The United States only reluctantly tried out the idea on three of its denominations for the nation's Bicentennial.

Ultimately, Canada began an annual commemorative dollar series in 1971. It issued coins for the 1976 Montreal Olympic Games and again in 1988 for the Calgary Olympic Games. Bullion coins were created to market its gold, silver and platinum output. A commemorative series of gold $100 coins was also undertaken. Canada, too, issues special proof, prooflike and specimen sets, similar to the United States.

Hobbyists who would like to be informed of new issues should write Royal Canadian Mint, P.O. Box 457, Station A, Ontario K1A 8V5, Canada. The mint also main-

Like the U.S. Mint, the Royal Canadian Mint offers sets of coins in a variety of finishes to the collector market.

tains special toll-free lines. In the United States, hobbyists may telephone the Royal Canadian Mint at 1-800-268-6468. In Canada, the number is 1-800-267-1871. You can get on the mailing list by using these numbers and you can buy currently available coins. (See Chapter 6 for Web information.)

When collecting Canada, another thing to remember is the importance varieties play in the nation's various series. Certainly, a type collector has no need to dwell on this information, but the date and mintmark collector may puzzle over the many extra identifying abbreviations in the price guide for certain coins. These varieties should not be confused with the U.S. variety-and-error category.

Here the varieties are not mistakes; they are deliberately created and issued variations of the standard design. We see Voyageur dollars on which the number of water lines changes. Other dollars count the number of beads.

These differences are minor. Though they were deliberately done to meet varying mint needs, they were not intended to be set apart in the public mind. The hobby, however, likes to look at things under a microscope.

Some varieties were indeed intended to be deliberately and noticeably different. An example of this occurs with 1947-dated issues. A maple leaf was placed on the 1947-dated cent through 50-cent issues. This indicated the coin was struck after George VI lost his title of emperor of India, as proclaimed in the Latin legend, but that the design had not yet been altered to reflect this. All of these varieties are considered integral parts of the Canadian series, and they are listed as such.

Do not construe any of this to mean there is no collecting of varieties and errors of the type common in the United States. There is. Collecting Royal Canadian Mint mistakes is just as active, just as interesting, and just as rewarding. After all, mint errors are universal. The methods of manufacture are the same. So the mistakes can be classified in the same manner.

Canada's numismatic listings also include items from various provinces issued before they were part of the confederation. The largest portion of this section is devoted to Newfoundland, because it retained a separate status far longer than the other provinces – until 1949, in fact.

Advice given to collectors of U.S. coins also applies to collectors of Canadian coins: Do what interests you. Do what you can afford. Create sets of uniform grade.

The rules of rarity transcend national boundaries. The only thing to keep in mind is the relative size of the collecting population. Because Canada has only a tenth of the U.S. population, it stands to reason that the number of collectors in that nation is but a fraction of the U.S. number. A mintage that seems to indicate scarcity for U.S. coin, therefore, could indicate something quite common in Canada. Don't forget that mintage is just a guide. The same factors that caused loss of available specimens or preserved unusually large quantities were at work in Canada, too.

Mexico

Coinage produced in Mexico dates to the establishment of a mint in Mexico City in 1536, more than 250 years before a federal mint was set up in the United States and more than 300 years before Canada circulated its own coins. The output of those extra centuries alone would make organizing a Mexican coin collection more challenging than a collection of U.S. or Canadian coins. But there are numerous other factors involved.

You say you like the kings and queens on Canada's coins? Mexico has kings, too – nearly 300 years' worth, plus a couple of emperors. You say the ideals of liberty embodied by the great men and women on U.S. coins is more your cup of tea? Mexico's coins also feature men and women committed to liberty.

In addition, Mexico is the crossroads of civilizations and empires. The great pyramid-building society of southern Mexico and Central America met its end at the hands of the Spanish conquistadors led initially by Hernando Cortez. The great Aztec empire was looted and overturned in 1519-1521 in the name of Spain.

The great natural resources of the area then supported successive Spanish kings in their grand dreams of dominating Europe. Through the doors of the Mexico City Mint and later facilities scattered about the country passed legendary quantities of silver. Even today the country ranks at the top of the list of silver producers.

But while Spain could dominate Mexico for a long time, the basic ideals of liberty and human dignity eventually motivated the people to throw off the foreign yoke. Unfortunately, victory was often neither complete nor wisely led. And in more recent years, the scourge of inflation had exacted a high toll on the currency itself. The numismatic consequences of a long history punctuated by periods of turmoil are an abundance of denominations, metals and types.

It is tempting for a would-be collector of Mexican coins to forget about anything that happened in the country prior to its monetary reform of 1905. By starting at that point, a hobbyist can happily overlook anything other than a decimal monetary system in which 100 centavos equal 1 peso. That system is as modern as any. The coins' striking quality is high. Legends are easy to read and understand, and the variety of issues is wide but not overwhelming.

There always is a certain logic to begin the collecting of any country with recent issues. The costs of learning are minimized, and as one becomes comfortable, a level of confidence can be built up sufficient to prompt diving further into the past.

One thousand of these equaled one new peso as 1993 began.

The issues of 1905 to date also more easily fit into the mold of type collecting and collecting by date and mintmark. To take type collecting, for example, let's look at the peso. In 1905 it was a silver-dollar-sized coin with a silver-dollar-sized quantity of bullion in it, 0.786 ounces. In 1918 it was reduced to 0.4663 ounces; in 1920, 0.3856 ounces; in 1947, 0.2250 ounces; 1950, 0.1285 ounces; 1957, 0.0514 ounces; and in 1970 silver was eliminated completely in favor of a copper-nickel alloy.

At almost every one of those steps, the design changed, too. After sinking to 3,300 to the U.S. dollar, monetary reform dropped three zeroes in 1993. The new peso, equal to 1,000 old ones, is now about 14 to the U.S. dollar.

By beginning with 1905, a date and mintmark collector misses out on issues of the various branch mints that were located around the country. Regular issues were all struck in Mexico City. Yearly output was reasonably regular for the various denominations, so date sets are extensive.

There have been rumblings since the early 1980s that Mexico would abandon the peso because of its greatly reduced value. The government, however, has been working hard to retain it since the monetary reform. So far it has succeeded.

One thing the government cannot do, however, is turn the clock back to a time when the fractional denominations of 1, 2, 5, 10, 20, 25, and 50 centavos were relatively high face values. However, it is stimulating to assemble sets because they offer a range of rarities. They are neither so expensive that it would prevent a collector from acquiring them at some point, but neither are they so common that you can walk into a shop, write a check, and come away with all of the 20th century sets complete. Check out the price guide section and see.

Gold in the post-1905 era is basically so much bullion. There are some scarcer pieces and some strikingly beautiful designs, such as the Centenario, a gold 50-peso coin containing 1.2 ounces of bullion. It was first struck in 1921 to mark 100 years of independence. Because Mexico actively restruck its gold coins, however, it is virtually impossible to tell an original issue from the newer version.

The result is a retail price structure based on metallic content. Gold, however, does not conjure up the images that silver does. Silver is the magic word for Mexico. That, of course, means the peso.

The modern Mexico City Mint also strikes commemoratives and collector sets from time to time. These are generally marketed to collectors through private firms,

Mexico also strikes commemorative coins for the collector market. They are available through private firms in the United States.

details of which are published in hobby newspapers like World Coin News. Mexico, like the United States and Canada, also issues gold and silver bullion coins.

These also are marketed through arrangements with private firms. Interestingly, Mexico's many gold-coin restrikes were the bullion coins of their day. They had the advantage of ready identification, and they were legally tradable according to gold-coin regulations that existed in the United States from 1933 through 1974.

It is appropriate that we conclude discussion of the modern period on the concept of bullion, because bullion is at the root of Mexico's numismatic history. That is a period to which we now turn.

When Cortez toppled the Aztec Empire, for a time the wealth returning to Spain was merely that taken by the victors from the vanquished. But the business of permanently administering a vast area in the name of the Spanish king, exploiting its natural resources, and funneling the proceeds to Spain quite soon involved the establishment of a mint in Mexico City. This was undertaken in 1536, just 15 years after the end of Aztec dominion.

At first, the authorized coins were low denominations: silver quarter, half, 1, 2, 3, and 4 reales, and copper 2 and 4 maravedis. To understand their face values and how they related to each other, let's take the common reference point of a silver dollar. The silver dollar is 8 reales, and you might recognize the nickname for the denomination of "piece of eight" from pirate lore. The eighth part, the silver real, was divided into 34 copper maravedis. That means the 8 reales was worth 272 copper maravedis.

The copper coinage was hated and soon abolished, not to reappear until 1814. The silver coins were fine as far as they went. When the mines of Mexico began producing undreamed of quantities of metal, however, it was the 8 reales that took center stage. This occurred after 1572. The piece of eight became the standard form for shipping silver back to Spain.

Mexico City's output was prodigious. Minting standards were crude. All denominations produced are called "cobs," because they are basically little more than irregular-looking lumps of metal on which bits and pieces of design can be seen. The only constant was weight, fineness, and the appearance of assayer's initials (which guaranteed the weight and fineness). Not showing those initials was cause for severe punishment.

Designs showed the arms of the monarch on one side, a cross on the other, appropriate legends, and an indication of denomination. The period of cob issues lasted until 1732. Rulers of the period start with Charles and Johanna, 1516-1556; Philip II, 1556-1598; Philip III, 1598-1621; Philip IV, 1621-1665; Charles II, 1665-1700; Philip V, 1700-1724 and 1724-1746; and Luis I, 1724.

Modern mint machinery began turning out coins in 1732. Quality was similar to today. The arms design was continued. It was not until 1772 that the monarch's portrait began appearing. The honor of this numismatic debut belongs to Charles III. Kings of this period are Ferdinand VI, 1746-1759; Charles III, 1760-1788; Charles IV, 1788-1808; and Ferdinand VII, 1808-1821. *The Standard Catalog of Mexican Coins* by Colin R. Bruce II and Dr. George W. Vogt is recommended to those who want to study this period in greater depth.

The revolutionary period begins in 1810, when a parish priest, Miguel Hidalgo y Costilla, issued the call for independence. The first attempts to achieve this were violently suppressed. Hidalgo was executed, but independence did come in 1821.

With revolt against central authority came a dispersal of the right to strike coins. Mexico City continued as the major facility, but other operations began. The list of these over the next century is lengthy. Mintmarks and assayer initials proliferated.

The old colonial coinage standard survived the period. The 8 reales and its parts carried on. A slight reduction in bullion content had been ordered by the king in 1760, but otherwise things continued as they were. Gold was coined during the colonial period beginning in 1679 based on an 8-escudo piece, which divided into eighths just like the 8 reales. Gold, however, was not as important as silver.

Mexico's first emperor came shortly after independence. He was a leader in the struggle that set Mexico free from Spain. Augustin de Iturbide, originally an officer in the service of Spain, was proclaimed emperor in 1822. He abdicated in 1823 and was executed in 1824.

The second emperor had a reign almost as short as the first. Maximilian I, emperor only because he had a French army to secure the throne, reigned from 1863 to 1867. He was shot by a firing squad when the French left.

He is remembered numismatically because he decided to decimalize the coinage. The centavo and peso were born. Soon afterward, the republic was re-established. Further monetary changes were minor thereafter until 1905.

Collectors focusing on Mexico can devote much time to the study of the quasi-official issues of rebels during the periods of instability. They can look at hacienda tokens, which were issued by large farms or ranches that employed hundreds or thousands of people. Or they can pick whichever period in Mexico's history that fascinates them most. Whatever collectors of Mexico eventually settle on, they will find it rewarding.

Where to write for more information:

World Coin News: 700 E. State St., Iola, WI 54990.

Caring for coins
How to store and preserve your collection

By Alan Herbert

From the day you acquire your first collectible coin, you have to consider where and how to store your collection. Often a shoebox or a small cardboard or plastic box of some kind will be the principal storage point as you start to gather coins, even before they can be considered a collection. Sooner or later you will outgrow that first box and need to think seriously about what to do with your coins to protect and preserve them.

All too often security takes precedence over preservation. We're more worried that the kids will dip into the coins for candy or ice cream or that burglars will somehow learn about your "valuable" collection and pay a visit. It often isn't until years later when you suddenly notice that your once beautiful coins are now dingy and dull, with spots and fingerprints all over them, that preservation becomes a primary consideration.

Learning good storage habits should be one of the first things to do right along with acquiring those first coins. There are a multitude of storage products on the market that are intended for more or less specific situations, so learning which to use and how to use them is vital to the health of your collection. Most if not all of the products mentioned here should be available at your nearest coin shop or hobby store.

Safe storage methods

The common impulse is to use what's available around the house; never allow that impulse to control your collecting. Plastic wrap, aluminum foil, cardboard, stationery envelopes, and other common household products are not designed for coin storage and never should be used for your collection. The same goes for soaps and cleansers found around the home.

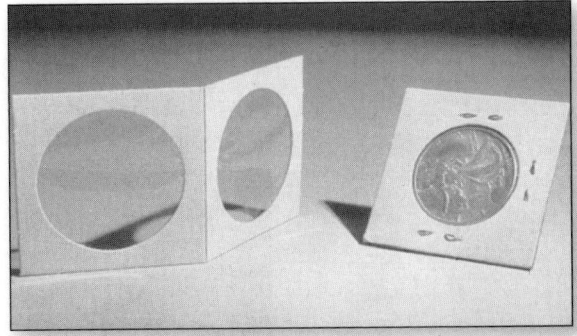

Two-by-two cardboard holders are a common form of short-term, inexpensive coin storage.

Many dealers sell coins in 2-by-2 plastic "flips," but these should not be used for long-term storage.

There are specific products that have been designed, tested and found safe to use for coins. These are the media your collection deserves. The slight added expense will pay a thousand dividends years from now when you sell you collection or pass it on to your heirs.

The most common storage media are 2-inch by 2-inch cardboard holders with Mylar windows, 2-by-2 plastic "flips," coin tubes, hard-plastic holders, coin boards, and coin albums.

The 2-by-2 cardboard holders are the cheapest and most commonly used storage method. They are usually folded and stapled around the coin. They are intended for short-term general storage. They are not airtight or watertight, and staples driven too close to the coin can ruin it.

The 2-by-2 plastic flips come in good and bad varieties. The old, usually soft flips are made of plastics that contain polyvinyl chloride, a chemical found in many plastics. Over time it breaks down into substances that put a green slime on your coins, which attacks the surface and ruins them.

The good flips are made of Mylar, but they are brittle and prone to splitting. So they should not be used to mail coins or when the coins are moved about frequently. Mylar flips, too, are for short-term general storage.

Often you will find coins in PVC holders when you buy them from a dealer. Remove them immediately and put them in some better storage medium.

Coin tubes are often used for bulk storage, but there is a proper technique to placing the coins in the tube.

Coin tubes come in clear and cloudy, or translucent, plastic. These are made of an inert plastic that will not harm your coins. Tubes are intended for bulk, medium- to long-term storage, with one caution: Use care when inserting the coins. Merely dropping one coin onto another in a tube can damage both coins. The best technique is to make a stack or pile of the coins, then slide the pile carefully into the tube while holding it at an angle.

Hard-plastic holders are the elite items for storing your collection. There are a number of varieties, some of which come in three parts that are screwed together. Some come in two pieces that fit together. Some of these are airtight and watertight. They are more expensive, but they deserve to be used for any really valuable coins in your collection.

Coins processed by the third-party grading services come in hard-plastic holders, most of which are at least semi-airtight. The hard-plastic holders used by the U.S. Mint for proof sets since 1968 are not airtight, so coins should be watched carefully for signs of problems. In recent years these holders have been improved, but you should check your proof sets periodically.

Any stored coins should be checked regularly, at least twice a year. Check coins for signs of spotting or discoloration. Check the storage media for any signs of deterioration, rust, mildew, or other problems.

The older mint sets and proof sets – issued from 1955 to 1964 – come in soft-plastic envelopes that are not intended for long-term storage. Coins in these envelopes should be put in better storage media for the long term. In recent years the Mint has switched to an inert, stiffer plastic for the mint sets. This plastic is safe.

A coin folder is frequently the first piece of equipment the beginning collector buys. It is simply a piece of cardboard with holes to hold the coins. The holder folds up for storage. It is intended for inexpensive circulated coins only.

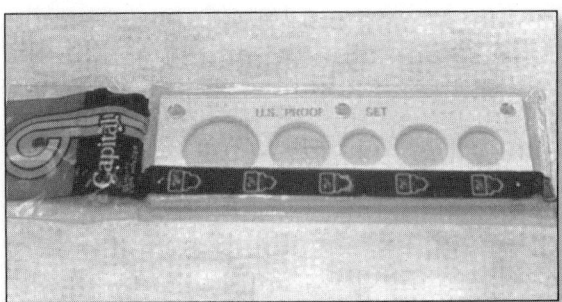

Hard-plastic holders are the top of the line in coin storage.

Coin albums also provide attractive storage for inexpensive circulated coins.

They give no protection from contamination or fingerprints. Worn coins will often fall out of the holes, which leads some novice collectors to tape the coins in the album. This is another example of misuse of a household product; tape can permanently damage a coin's surface.

Pride of ownership and the desire to show off a collection are the moving forces behind the sale of thousands of coin albums. They should also be used for inexpensive circulated coins only, with a couple of exceptions.

Some albums are merely coin boards mounted between covers. Others have pages with sliding plastic strips on both sides of the page so both sides of the coin can be seen.

The open-face albums are subject to fingerprints and contamination. Sneezing on your coins can do as much damage as gouging them with a knife. The

Placing coins in folders can bring generations together.

slides will rub on your coins, damaging the high points of the design over time. These two types of albums should never be used for expensive uncirculated or proof coins, although they are fine for circulated coins that you want to display.

Fairly new on the market are albums designed for coins in inert, airtight holders. This allows you to display your coins and still keep them safe from handling and contact with the atmosphere.

One more storage medium that deserves mention is the clear-plastic notebook page that has pockets for 2-by-2 holders or flips. Here again there are good and bad. Most old pocket sheets contain PVC, so they cannot be used to hold coins in non-airtight holders because the gases will migrate into the holders and damage the coins. The newer Mylar pages are brittle but will not generate damaging gases or liquids.

When buying storage media, make sure the dealer guarantees that his products are safe for coins. Many of the old albums, flips and pocket pages are still around, especially at flea markets. If you are in doubt, don't buy.

There are also thin, two-piece, inert plastic holders that many collectors use to protect coins put in flips or 2-by-2 cardboard holders, especially to protect them from moving about against the holder and getting scratched. They are virtually airtight, so they do offer some protection.

Coins need to be protected from burglars. A box under the bed or in the closet offers no protection. If you must keep coins at home, a good, fireproof safe is a must. Otherwise, rent a safe-deposit box at a bank, but read the fine print on your box contract to make sure a coin collection is covered.

Most homeowner's insurance policies will not cover a coin collection or will cover only a fraction of its value. Special riders are expensive, but if you keep most of your coins at the bank, this will cut costs. For details, consult your insurance agent. The American Numismatic Association also offers collection insurance to its members.

Where to store coins is often a problem. The commonest solution is to put them in the attic or basement. Those are the two worst places for your collection. Attics are notoriously hot. Heat can damage almost any storage media, and if there is the slightest hint of PVC, you've got trouble.

Basements are equally bad. They can flood, and humidity is high. Mildew can attack holders and other material stored with your coins.

So what's left? Ideally coins should be treated like a family member. They should be stored in some part of the house where temperature and humidity are relatively constant year round. If it's comfortable for you, it's probably much more comfortable for your coins than the basement or attic.

Protecting coins from humidity is always a good idea, even in areas where it is not a major health problem. For your coins, too much dampness can become a serious problem, often before you realize it. A good solution is to get several good-sized packets of silica gel and store them with your coins in your safe or a container of some kind that will isolate them from the general climate in the home.

To clean or not to clean

Before you store your coins, you should be aware that coins are like dishes: They should never be put away dirty. Ah, but you've probably already heard or read that you should never clean a coin. If you haven't, I'll say it now: Never clean a coin.

OK, so there are exceptions, but be careful of those exceptions and for good reason. Ignoring the exception can be excruciatingly and embarrassingly expensive.

Coins get dirty, just like anything else. The impulse is to shine them up – polish them to a brilliance that will dazzle the viewer. If you've already succumbed to the temptation to clean even a single coin, stand up, kick yourself, then sit back down and read on. The one exception is loose dirt, grease, oil, or something similar, and there are even exceptions to that rule.

Use a neutral solvent to dissolve the grease and oils that usually coat uncirculated coins as they come from the mint. Follow the instructions on the container exactly, and if the directions say to use the product outdoors, they mean it.

For circulated coins, lighter fluid will often dissolve the accumulated "gunk" that sticks to them, but I don't recommend it for uncirculated coins, especially copper alloy coins. Air dry the coins; don't rub or wipe them. Even the softest cloth or paper towel can pick up sharp-edged particles that will ruin a coin's surface. Proof coins are clean when they are packaged, so this should not be necessary and should be done only as a last resort if they have somehow picked up oil in handling.

Using dips, household cleansers, metal polish, and even soap can permanently damage a coin. Avoid acid-based cleaners at all costs. They work by eating away the coin's surface to remove the embedded dirt or discoloration. Cleaning a coin with any of these products will sharply reduce its collectible value. To put it simply, collectors do not want cleaned coins, so they are heavily discounted.

One of the reasons for this is that once a coin has been cleaned, it will discolor much more quickly, requiring fresh cleaning. Each time it is cleaned, the surface is further dulled, reducing the coin's appeal and reducing its value.

Obviously this advice applies especially to uncirculated and proof coins, but it applies to any coin that is or has the potential to become valuable. But if you clean it, its career ends right there.

There are products specifically designed for removing the green PVC slime from coins. They do not contain acid, so they are safe. They will stop but cannot reverse the damage that the PVC has already done to the coin. Read the label, and use exactly as directed.

I frequently am asked about ultrasonic cleaners. They fall under the same heading as the various cleaning products I've described. In other words, the apparatus should not be used for uncirculated, proof, or other valuable coins. If you do use one, do one coin at a time so there is no chance for the vibration to rub two coins together. Change or filter the cleaning solution frequently to keep abrasive particles from coming in contact with the vibrating coin.

Like anything else, cleaning can be carried to an extreme, so I'll give you one horror story and just such a mistake: Years ago I had a collector fly several hundred miles to bring his collection for me to sell for him. When he laid out the coins on the table, I was shocked to discover that the hundreds of coins had all been harshly cleaned.

When I questioned him he calmly recounted that he had decided that the coins needed cleaning, so he dumped them all into a rock tumbler and left it on for several hours. It ruined all his coins, reducing them to face value. With his passion for cleanliness he had destroyed several thousand dollars worth of collectible value, plus air fare, a rental car, and a motel bill.

The key to a long-term collection that might appreciate in value is to learn what not to do to your coins and what care they need to survive years of waiting in the wings. Learning to protect your coins with the best available storage methods and media is a key first step toward enjoying your collection for years to come.

A private firm, Numismatic Conservation Services, LLC, will clean coins that need it for a fee. The firm's Web site address is www.ncscoin.com.

Where to write for more information

American Numismatic Association: 818 N. Cascade Ave., Colorado Springs, CO 80903-3279. Web address is http://www.money.org.

New Quarter Series starts
Will mintage totals continue dropping?

By David C. Harper

The down trend in 2009 U.S. quarter production that seemed highly likely to continue as the 2010 edition of this book went to press is a confirmed fact now that the 2011 edition is heading to the printer. Each of the six District of Columbia and Territories quarters had a lower mintage than the prior design. Where the Philadelphia Mint produced 83,600,000 of the first design, which honored the District of Columbia, by the time the Northern Mariana Islands issue rolled off the presses at year end, the total mintage from Philadelphia was just 35,200,000 pieces. Denver mintage figures sank in similar fashion. See the chart below for details.

Is it any wonder that many collectors have yet to see some of the 2009 quarters in their change?

In 2010, the 12-year, 56-design America the Beautiful quarter program began in April with the Hot Springs National Park issue. With no sign that demand for new coinage is picking up, the first five designs in this series might rival the 2009 quarters for low mintage honors.

The order of issuance for the America the Beautiful coins is different. Where the state quarters were released in the order each state was admitted to the Union, the America the Beautiful coins are issued in the order the parks and other national sites were recognized by Congress. That puts Arkansas at the head of the list. There the schoolroom lesson that Yellowstone was the first National Park in 1872 gets trumped by the fact that Congress designated Hot Springs

2009 Quarter Production		
LOCATION	PHILADELPHIA	DENVER
District of Columbia	83,600,000	88,800,000
Puerto Rico	53,000,000	86,000,000
Guam	45,000,000	42,600,000
American Samoa	42,600,000	39,600,000
U.S. Virgin Islands	41,000,000	41,000,000
Northern Mariana Islands	35,200,000	37,600,000

The first five designs in the America the Beautiful series begin in April 2010 with Arkansas and conclude with Oregon.

a special reservation in 1832.

Some of the parks to be honored are very well known. Some, such as Yosemite in California and Mount Rushmore in South Dakota, were also the state quarter themes.

Other sites are less well known and will provide an ongoing geography lesson for collectors. Because not every state and territory has a national park, other national sites such as forests and wildlife refuges make it into the mix.

Will the new series prove to be as

America the Beautiful quarters

America the Beautiful quarters will be issued at the rate of five per year 2010-2021 in the order the sites gained congressional recognition.

STATES	SITE
Arkansas (2010)	Hot Springs National Park
Wyoming	Yellowstone National Park
California	Yosemite National Park
Arizona	Grand Canyon National Park
Oregon	Mount Hood National Park
Pennsylvania (2011)	Gettysburg National Park
Montana	Glacier National Park
Washington	Olympic National Park
Mississippi	Vicksburg National Military Park
Oklahoma	Chickasaw National Recreation Area
Puerto Rico (2012)	El Yunque National Forest
New Mexico	Chaco Culture National Historical Park
Maine	Acadia National Park
Hawaii	Hawai'i Volcanoes National Park
Alaska	Denali National Park
New Hampshire (2013)	White Mountain National Forest
Ohio	Perry's Victory and Internat'l Peace Memorial
Nevada	Great Basin National Park
Maryland	Fort McHenry National Monument
South Dakota	Mount Rushmore National Memorial
Tennessee (2014)	Great Smokey Mountains Nat. Park
Virgina	Shenandoah National Park
Utah	Arches National Park
Colorado	Great Sand Dunes National Park
Florida	Everglades National Park

exiting as the first state quarters? Probably not. But that just might be a good thing. Because once the initial excitement of the state quarters wore off, collectors began to see that the mintages for many of them are awfully large. Where the entire 2009 quarter output for the District of Columbia and Territories adds up to 636,200,000 pieces, that total falls short of many individual state quarter issues. The Philadelphia Mint alone produced 688,744,000 Connecticut quarters in 1999. Collectors will notice the lower mintages for the 2009 quarters, and if 2010 quarters continue on the low mintage path, collectors will notice them as well.

One thing is sure. The lowest mintages for the 12-year America the Beautiful quarters will come in the first year. It isn't often that a set of this kind begins when the down economy needs so few new coins from the Mint. This is just the opposite of economic conditions for the state quarter set where the first years of issue saw very high mintage totals followed by declining totals through the end of the series.

That could mean opportunity for alert collectors.

America the Beautiful quarters

Here is the order of issue for the years 2015 to 2021. The final year of 2021 features just one quarter design.

States	Site
Nebraska (2015)	Homestead National Monument
Louisiana	Kisatchie National Forest
North Carolina	Blue Ridge Parkway
Delaware	Bombay Hook Nat. Wildlife Refuge
New York	Saratoga National Historic Park
Illinois (2016)	Shawnee National Forest
Kentucky	Cumberland Gap Nat. Historic Park
West Virginia	Harpers Ferry Nat. Historic Park
North Dakota	Theodore Roosevelt National Park
South Carolina	Ft. Moultrie (Ft. Sumter) Nat. Monument
Iowa (2017)	Effigy Mounds National Monument
District of Columbia	Frederick Douglass Nat. Historic Site
Missouri	Ozark National Scenic Riverways
New Jersey	Ellis Island Nat. Monument (Statue of Liberty)
Indiana	George Rogers Clark Nat. Historical Park
Michigan (2018)	Pictured Rocks National Lakeshore
Wisconsin	Apostle Islands National Lakeshore
Minnesota	Voyageurs National Park
Georgia	Cumberland Island National Seashore
Rhode Island	Block Island Nat. Wildlife Refuge
Massachusetts (2019)	Lowell National Historical Park
N, Mariana Islands	American Memorial Park
Guam	War in the Pacific Nat. Historical Park
Texas	San Antonio Missions Nat. Historical Park
Idaho	Frank Church River of No Return Wilderness
American Samoa (2020)	National Park of American Samoa
Connecticut	Weir Farm National Historic Site
U.S. Virgin Islands	Salt River Bay Nat. Historical Park
Vermont	Marsh-Billings-Rockefeller Nat. Historical Park
Kansas	Tallgrass Prairie National Preserve
Alabama (2021)	Tuskegee Airmen Nat. Historic Site

What's Hot in 2011?

Cent looks for TRIFECTA

By David C. Harper

Who would have thought modern collectors could stay focused on Lincoln cents for three years in a row? With the aid of yet another new design in 2010 – the Union Shield – collectors now have five new designs that have proven uncommonly hard to acquire in circulation, as well as record prices being recorded in auction sales for the classic rarities in the century-long Lincoln series.

A Proof-68 1909 VDB cent sold for over $200,000 as this edition of *North American Coins and Prices* was being prepared. It was such an incredible figure that some in the hobby asked whether the 1909-S VDB had been replaced as the key coin to the set. However, as interesting as that high price was, most collectors stayed concerned about, and were even mad about, the difficulty of obtaining the four designs of 2009 in change or in rolls at their local banks. Most just couldn't get them. The result was to remain out of luck or to turn to the U.S. Mint to buy two-roll sets for $8.95. If they wanted to get the 2009 cents that were struck in the old copper-based alloy, well, then they had to buy the regular 2009 proof set, the special four-coin Lincoln proof set and regular uncirculated coin set.

Bad feelings aside, collector interest caused a feeding frenzy. The value of Lincoln cent rolls in online auctions was such that if anybody was fortunate enough to get some at their local bank, he or she either kept them or sold them online. Spending some so others might get them in change

2009 Lincoln cents

Birthplace Philadelphia	284,400,000
Brithplace Denver	350,400,000
Formative Years Philadelphia	376,000,000
Formative Years Denver	363,600,000
Professional Life Philadelphia	316,000,000
Professional Life Denver	336,000,000
Presidency Philadelphia	129,600,000
Presidency Denver	198,000,000

Final mintage figures for Lincoln cents struck for circulation in the standard copper-coated zinc alloy.

Birthplace and Formative Years designs are at left. Below from left, is the Professional Life design, Presidency design, and the Union Shield.

was the last thing anyone wanted to do. At first glance, this might seem strange, because the mintage figures in the table look fairly large. There is enough so that virtually every American who wants one could have one of each design. However, with people saving them by the 50-coin roll or in larger quantities, the math quickly turns against most people ever getting one. Also fostering the sense of scarcity was the fact that the economic crisis caused many banks to ignore their basic function of supplying coins to the public. They simply did not order any, or if they did, the armored car companies that supplied them would give them older issues that were backed up in inventory rather than the new ones. Unfairly or not, the U.S. Mint was blamed for the overall lack of supply.

When the 2010 Union Shield design was released in January of 2010, many people had not even seen one of the 2009 cents. The 2010 design proved equally elusive in circulation, at least in the first few months. First reports of them in circulation originated from vacationers in Puerto Rico, adding a little exotic allure to the ongoing question of cent scarcity.

Experiencing the release of multiple new designs in a short period of time will make collectors of the future envy us. However, knowledge of that fact does not soften the pang of unfulfilled desire to get the new coins quickly – but that is a collector's life. It is history to boot.

2009 Lincoln cents

Birthplace two-roll set:	*96,000
Formative Years two-roll set:	*300,000
Professional Life two-roll set:	278,911
Presidency two-roll set:	240,200
2009 Lincoln Proof Set:	*200,000

The numbers with the asterisk were final sales totals for each of the offerings. The two totals without were still being sold to collectors as this edition went to press. Cents in proof set made of 95 percent copper alloy.

Glossary of Coin Terms

Adjustment marks: Marks made by use of a file to correct the weight of overweight coinage planchets prior to striking. Adjusting the weight of planchets was a common practice at the first U.S. Mint in Philadelphia and was often carried out by women hired to weigh planchets and do any necessary filing of the metal.

Altered coin: A coin that has been changed after it left the mint. Such changes are often to the date or mintmark of a common coin in an attempt to increase its value by passing to an unsuspecting buyer as a rare date or mint.

Alloy: A metal or mixture of metals added to the primary metal in the coinage composition, often as a means of facilitating hardness during striking. For example, most U.S. silver coins contain an alloy of 10 percent copper.

Anneal: To heat in order to soften. In the minting process planchets are annealed prior to striking.

Authentication: The act of determining whether a coin, medal, token or other related item is a genuine product of the issuing authority.

Bag marks: Scrapes and impairments to a coin's surface obtained after minting by contact with other coins. The term originates from the storage of coins in bags, but such marks can occur as coins leave the presses and enter hoppers. A larger coin is more susceptible to marks, which affect its grade and, therefore, its value.

Base metal: A metal with low intrinsic value.

Beading: A form of design around the edge of a coin. Beading once served a functional purpose of deterring clipping or shaving parts of the metal by those looking to make a profit and then return the debased coin to circulation.

Blank: Often used in reference to the coinage planchet or disc of metal from which the actual coin is struck. Planchets or blanks are punched out of a sheet of metal by what is known as a blanking press.

Business strike: A coin produced for circulation.

Beading

Cast copy: A copy of a coin or medal made by a casting process in which molds are used to produce the finished product. Casting imparts a different surface texture to the finished product than striking and often leaves traces of a seam where the molds came together.

Center dot: A raised dot at the center of a coin caused by use of a compass to aid the engraver in the circular positioning of die devices, such as stars, letters, and dates. Center dots are prevalent on early U.S. coinage.

Chop: A mark used by Oriental merchants as a means of guaranteeing the silver content of coins paid out. The merchants' chop, or stamped insignia, often obliterated the original design of the host coin. U.S. Trade dollars, struck from 1873 through 1878 and intended for use in trade with China, are sometimes found bearing multiple marks.

Chop

Clash marks: Marks impressed in the coinage dies when they come together without a planchet between them. Such marks will affect coins struck subsequently by causing portions of the obverse design to appear in raised form on the reverse, and vice versa.

Clipping: The practice of shaving or cutting small pieces of metal from a coin in circulation. Clipping was prevalent in Colonial times as a means of surreptitiously extracting precious metal from a coin before placing it back into circulation. The introduction of beading and a raised border helped to alleviate the problem.

Coin alignment: U.S. coins are normally struck with an alignment by which, when a coin is held by the top and bottom edge and rotated from side-to-side, the reverse will appear upside down.

Collar: A ring-shaped die between which the obverse and reverse coinage dies are held during striking. The collar contains the outward flow during striking and can be used to produce edge reeding.

Commemorative: A coin issued to honor a special event or person. United States commemorative coins have historically been produced for sale to collectors and not placed in circulation, though the 50-states quarters are circulating commemoratives.

Copy: A replica of an original issue. Copies often vary in quality and metallic composition from the original. Since passage of the Hobby Protection Act (Public Law 93-167) of Nov. 29, 1973, it has been illegal to produce or import copies of coins or other numismatic items that are not clearly and permanently marked with the word "Copy."

Counterfeit: A coin or medal or other numismatic item made fraudulently, either for entry into circulation or sale to collectors.

Denticles: The toothlike pattern found around a coin's obverse or reverse border.

Die: A cylindrical piece of metal containing an incuse image that imparts a raised image when stamped into a planchet.

Die crack: A crack that develops in a coinage die after extensive usage, or if the die is defective or is used to strike harder metals. Die cracks, which often run through border lettering, appear as raised lines on the finished coin.

Device: The principal design element.

Double eagle: Name adopted by the Act of March 3, 1849, for the gold coin valued at 20 units or $20.

Eagle: Name adopted by the Coinage Act of 1792 for a gold coin valued at 10 units or $10. Also a name used to refer to gold, silver, and platinum coins of the American Eagle bullion coinage program begun in 1986.

Edge: The cylindrical surface of a coin between the two sides. The edge can be plain, reeded, ornamented, or lettered.

Electrotype: A copy of a coin, medal, or token made by electroplating.

Exergue: The lower segment of a coin, below the main design, generally separated by a line and often containing the date, designer initials, and mintmark.

Face value: The nominal legal-tender value assigned to a given coin by the governing authority.

Fasces: A Roman symbol of authority consisting of a bound bundle of rods and an axe.

Field: The flat area of a coin's obverse or reverse, devoid of devices or inscriptions.

Galvano: A reproduction of a proposed design from an artist's original model produced in plaster or other substance and then electroplated with metal. The galvano is then used in a reducing lathe to make a die or hub.

Glory: A heraldic term for stars, rays or other devices placed as if in the sky or luminous.

Grading: The largely subjective practice of providing a numerical or adjectival ranking of the condition of a coin, token, or medal. The grade is often a major determinant of value.

Gresham's law: The name for the observation made by Sir Thomas Gresham, 16th century English financier, that when two coins with the same face value but different intrinsic values are in circulation at the same time, the one with the lesser intrinsic value will remain in circulation while the other is hoarded.

Half eagle: Name adopted by the Coinage Act of 1792 for a gold coin valued at five units or $5.

Hub: A piece of die steel showing the coinage devices in relief. The hub is used to produce a die that, in contrast, has the relief details incuse. The die is then used to produce the final coin, which looks much the same as the hub. Hubs may be reused to make new dies.

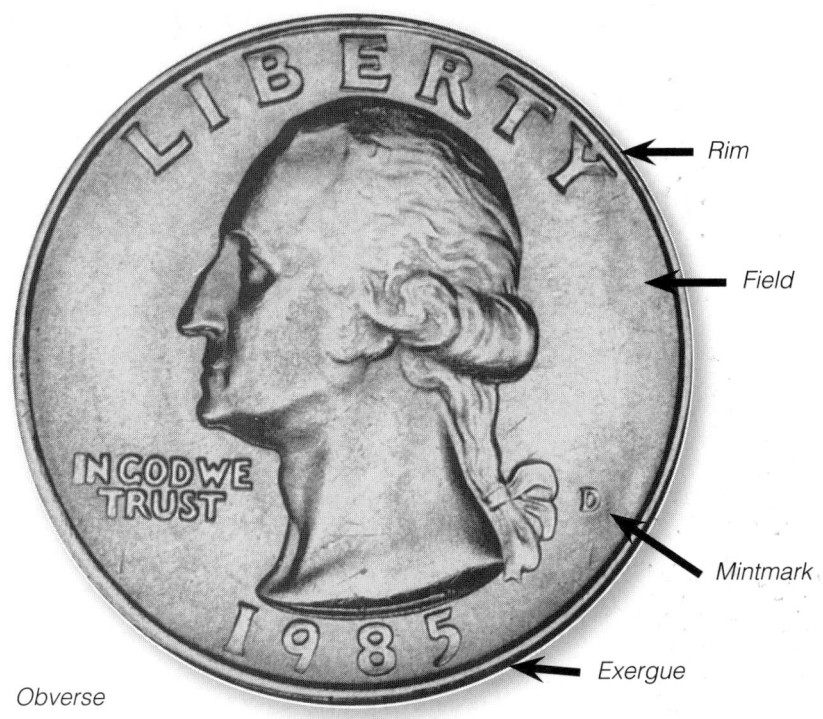

Rim

Field

Mintmark

Exergue

Obverse

Legend

Reverse

Legend: A coin's principal lettering, generally shown along its outer perimeter.

Lettered edge: Incuse or raised lettering on a coin's edge.

Matte proof: A proof coin on which the surface is granular or dull. On U.S. coins this type of surface was used on proofs of the early 20th century. The process has since been abandoned.

Magician's coin: A term sometimes used to describe a coin with two heads or two tails. Such a coin is considered impossible in normal production due to physical differences in obverse and reverse die mountings, though as of 2001 two have been certified as genuine by professional coin authenticators. The vast majority are products made outside the Mint as novelty pieces.

These Canadian Olympic commemoratives have lettered edges.

Medal: Made to commemorate an event or person. Medals differ from coins in that a medal is not legal tender and, in general, is not produced with the intent of circulating as money.

Medal alignment: Medals are generally struck with the coinage dies facing the same direction during striking. When held by the top and bottom edge and rotated from side-to-side, a piece struck in this manner will show both the obverse and reverse right side up.

Mintage: The total number of coins struck during a given time frame, generally one year.

Mintmark: A letter or other marking on a coin's surface to identify the mint at which the coin was struck.

A medal usually commemorates an event but has no monetary value. It can be issued by a private entity or a government.

Mule: The combination of two coinage dies not intended for use together.

Numismatics: The science, study or collecting of coins, tokens, medals, paper money, and related items.

Obverse: The front or "heads" side of a coin, medal, or token.

Overdate: Variety produced when one or more digits of the date are repunched over an old date on a die at the Mint, generally to save on dies or correct an error. Portions of the old date can still be seen under the new one.

Overmintmark: Variety created at the Mint when a different mintmark is punched over an already existing mintmark, generally done to make a coinage die already punched for one mint usable at another. Portions of the old mintmark can still be seen under the new one.

Overstrike: A coin, token or medal struck over another coin, token, or medal.

Pattern: A trial strike of a proposed coin design, issued by the Mint or authorized agent of a governing authority. Patterns can be in a variety of metals, thicknesses, and sizes.

Phrygian cap: A close-fitting, egg-shell-shaped hat placed on the head of a freed slave when Rome was in its ascendancy. Hung from a pole, it was a popular symbol of freedom during the French Revolution and in 18th century United States.

Planchet: A disc of metal or other material on which the image of the dies are impressed, resulting in a finished coin. Also sometimes called a blank.

Proof: A coin struck twice or more from specially polished dies and polished planchets. Modern proofs are prepared with a mirror finish. Early 20th century proofs were prepared with a matte surface.

Prooflike: A prooflike coin exhibits some of the characteristics of a proof despite having been struck by regular production processes. Many Morgan dollars are found with prooflike surfaces. The field will have a mirror background similar to that of a proof, and design details are frosted like some proofs.

Quarter eagle: Name adopted by the Coinage Act of 1792 for a gold coin valued at 2.5 units or $2.50.

Reeding: Serrated (toothlike) ornamentation applied to the coin's edge during striking.

Relief: The portion of a design raised above the surface of a coin, medal, or token.

This U.S. Trade dollar has a reeded edge.

A token is issued by a private entity and can be redeemed for its face value in trade or service.

Restrike: A coin, medal or token produced from original dies at a later date, often with the purpose of sale to collectors.

Reverse: The backside or "tails" side of a coin, medal or token, opposite from the principal figure of the design or obverse.

Rim: The raised area bordering the edge and surrounding the field.

Series: The complete group of coins of the same denomination and design and representing all issuing mints.

Token: A privately issued piece, generally in metal, with a represented value in trade or offer of service. Tokens are also produced for advertising purposes.

Type coin: A coin from a given series representing the basic design. A type coin is collected as an example of a particular design rather than for its date and mintmark.

Variety: Any coin noticeably different in dies from another of the same design, date and mint. Overdate and overmintmarks are examples of varieties.

Wire edge: Created when coinage metal flows between the coinage die and collar, producing a thin flange of coin metal at the outside edge or edges of a coin.

Introduction to Pricing

The following value guide is divided into six sections:
1. U.S. minting varieties and errors.
2. Colonial coins, issued prior to the establishment of the United States
3. U.S. issues of 1792.
4. U.S. issues of 1793-present.
5. Canadian coins.
6. Mexican coins.

Value listings

Values listed in the following price guide are average retail prices. These are the approximate prices collectors can expect to pay when purchasing coins from dealers. They are not offers to buy or sell. The pricing section should be considered a guide only; actual selling prices will vary.

The values were compiled by Krause Publications' independent staff of market analysts. They derived the values listed by monitoring auction results, business on electronic dealer trading networks, and business at major shows, and in consultation with a panel of dealers. For rare coins, when only a few specimens of a particular date and mintmark are known, a confirmed transaction may occur only once every several years. In those instances, the most recent auction result is listed.

Grading

Values are listed for coins in various states of preservation, or grades. Standards used in determining grades for U.S. coins are those set by the American Numismatic Association. See Chapter 2 for more on grading.

Dates and mintmarks

The dates listed are the individual dates that appear on each coin. The letter that follows the date is the mintmark and indicates where the coin was struck: "C" — Charlotte, N.C. (1838-1861); "CC" — Carson City, Nev. (1870-1893); "D" — Dahlonega, Ga. (1838-1861), and Denver (1906-present); "O" New Orleans (1838-1909); "P" — Philadelphia (1793-present); "S" San Francisco (1854-present); and "W" — West Point, N.Y. (1984-present). Coins without mintmarks were struck at Philadelphia.

A slash mark in a date indicates an overdate. This means a new date was engraved on a die over an old date. For example, if the date is listed as "1899/8," an 1898 die had a 9 engraved over the last 8 in the date. Portions of the old numeral are still visible on the coin.

A slash mark in a mintmark listing indicates an overmintmark (example: "1922-P/D"). The same process as above occurred, but this time a new mintmark was engraved over an old.

See the "U.S. Minting Varieties and Errors" section for more information on overdates and overmintmarks.

Price charts

Pricing data for the selected charts in the U.S. section were taken from the January issues of *Coin Prices* for the years indicated.

Mexican coin mintages

Quantities minted of each date are indicated when that information is available.

Precious-metal content

Throughout this book precious-metal content is indicated in troy ounces. One troy ounce equals 480 grains, or 31.103 grams.

Abbreviations

AGW. Actual gold weight.

APW. Actual platinum weight.

ASW. Actual silver weight.

BV. Bullion value. This indicates the coin's current value is based on the amount of its precious-metal content and the current price for that metal.

Est. Indicates the exact mintage is not known and the figure listed is an estimate.

G. Grams.

Inc. Abv. Indicates the mintage for the date and mintmark listed is included in the previous listing.

KM#. Indicates "Krause-Mishler number." This sequential cataloging numbering system originated with the *Standard Catalog of World Coins* and provides collectors with a means for identifying coins.

Leg. Legend.

Mkt value. Market value.

MM. Millimeters.

Obv. Obverse.

P/L. Indicates "prooflike," a type of finish used on some Canadian coins.

Rev. Reverse.

Spec. Indicates "specimen," a type of finish used on some Canadian coins.

U.S. Minting Varieties and Errors

Introduction

By Alan Herbert

The P.D.S. cataloging system used here to list minting varieties was originally compiled by Alan Herbert in 1971. PDS stands for the three main divisions of the minting process, "planchet," "die" and "striking." Two more divisions cover collectible modifications after the strike, as well as non-collectible alterations, counterfeits and damaged coins.

This listing includes 445 classes, each a distinct part of the minting process or from a specific non-mint change in the coin. Classes from like causes are grouped together. The PDS system applies to coins of the world, but is based on U.S. coinage with added classes for certain foreign minting practices.

Price ranges are based on a U.S. coin in MS-60 grade (uncirculated.) The ranges may be applied in general to foreign coins of similar size or value although collector values are not usually as high as for U.S. coins. Prices are only a guide as the ultimate price is determined by a willing buyer and seller.

To define minting varieties, "A coin which exhibits a variation of any kind from the normal, as a result of any portion of the minting process, whether at the planchet stage, as a result of a change or modification of the die, or during the striking process. It includes those classes considered to be intentional changes, as well as those caused by normal wear and tear on the dies or other minting equipment and classes deemed to be "errors."

The three causes are represented as follows:
1. (I) = Intentional Changes
2. (W) = Wear and Tear
3. (E) = Errors
Note: A class may show more than one cause and could be listed as (IWE).

Rarity level

The rarity ratings are based on the following scale:
1 - Very Common. Ranges from every coin struck down to 1,000,000.
2 - Common. From 1,000,000 down to 100,000.
3 - Scarce. From 100,000 down to 10,000.
4 - Very Scarce. From 10,000 down to 1,000.
5 - Rare. From 1,000 down to 100.
6 - Very Rare. From 100 down to 10.
7 - Extremely Rare. From 10 down to 1.

Unknown: If there is no confirmed report of a piece fitting a particular class, it is listed as Unknown. Reports of finds by readers would be appreciated in order to update future presentations.

An Unknown does not mean that your piece automatically is very valuable. Even a Rarity 7 piece, extremely rare, even unique, may have a very low collector value because of a lack of demand or interest in that particular class.

Classes, definitions and price ranges are based on material previously offered in Alan Herbert's book, The Official Price Guide to Minting Varieties and Errors and in Coin Prices Magazine.

Pricing information has also been provided by John A. Wexler and Ken Potter, with special pricing and technical advice from Del Romines.

Also recommended is the Cherrypicker's Guide to Rare Die Varieties by Bill Fivaz and J.T. Stanton. Check your favorite coin shop, numismatic library or book seller for availability of the latest edition.

For help with your coin questions, to report significant new finds and for authentication of your minting varieties, include a loose first class stamp and write to Alan Herbert, 700 E. State St., Iola, WI 54990-0001. Don't include any numismatic material until you have received specific mailing instructions from me.

Quick check index

If you have a coin and are not sure where to look for the possible variety:

If your coin shows doubling, first check V-B-I.

Then try II-A, II-B, II-C, II-I (4 & 5), III-J, III-L, or IV-C.

If part of the coin is missing, check III-B, III-C, or III-D.

If there is a raised line of coin metal, check II-D, II-G.

If there is a raised area of coin metal, check II-E, II-F, or III-F.

If the coin is out of round, and too thin, check III-G.

If coin appears to be the wrong metal, check III-A, III-E, III-F-3 and III-G.

If the die appears to have been damaged, check II-E, II-G. (Damage to the coin itself usually is not a minting variety.)

If the coin shows incomplete or missing design, check II-A, II-E, III-B-3, III-B-5 or III-D.

If only part of the planchet was struck, check III-M.

If something was struck into the coin, check III-J and III-K.

If something has happened to the edge of the coin, check II-D-6, II-E-10, III-I, III-M and III-O.

If your coin shows other than the normal design, check II-A or II-C.

If a layer of the coin metal is missing, or a clad layer is missing, check III-B and III-D.

If you have an unstruck blank, or planchet, check I-G.

If your coin may be a restrike, check IV-C.

If your coin has a counterstamp, countermark, additional engraving or apparent official modifications, check
IV-B and V-A-8.

Do not depend on the naked eye to examine your coins. Use a magnifying lens whenever possible, as circulation damage, wear and alterations frequently can be mistaken for legitimate minting varieties.

Division I: planchet varieties

The first division of the PDS System includes those minting varieties that occur in the manufacture of the planchet upon which the coins will ultimately be struck and includes classes resulting from faulty metallurgy, mechanical damage, faulty processing, or equipment or human malfunction prior to the actual coin striking.

Planchet alloy mix (I-A)

This section includes those classes pertaining to mixing and processing the various metals which will be used to make a coin alloy.

I-A-1 Improper Alloy Mix (WE), Rarity Level: 3-4 . . . . .Values: $5 to $10
I-A-2 Slag Inclusion Planchet (WE), Rarity Level: 5-6. . . . . .Values: $25 up

Damaged and defective planchets (I-B)

To be a class in this section the blank, or planchet, must for some reason not meet the normal standards or must have been damaged in processing. The classes cover the areas of defects in the melting, rolling, punching and processing of the planchets up to the point where they are sent to the coin presses to be struck.

I-B-1 Defective Planchet (WE), Rarity Level: 6 . . . . Values: $25 up
I-B-2 Mechanically Damaged Planchet (WE), Rarity Level: – . . . . Values: No Value
    (See values for the coin struck on a mechanically damaged planchet.)
I-B-3 Rolled Thin Planchet (WE), Rarity Level: 6 - *(Less rare on half cents of 1795, 1797 and*
    restrikes of 1831-52.) . . . . Values: $10 up
I-B-4 Rolled Thick Planchet (WE), Rarity Level: 7 - *(Less rare in Colonial copper coins. Notable examples occur*
    on the restrike half cents of 1840-52.) . . . . Values: $125 up
I-B-5 Tapered Planchet (WE), Rarity Level: 7 . . . . Values: $25 up
I-B-6 Partially Unplated Planchet (WE), Rarity Level: 6 . . . . Values: $15 up
I-B-7 Unplated Planchet (WE), Rarity Level: 6-7 . . . . Values: $50 up
I-B-8 Bubbled Plating Planchet (WE), Rarity Level: 1 . . . . Values: No Value
I-B-9 Included Gas Bubble Planchet (WE), Rarity Level: 6-7 . . . . Values: $50 up
I-B-10 Partially Unclad Planchet (WE), Rarity Level: 6 . . . . Values: $20 up
I-B-11 Unclad Planchet (WE), Rarity Level: 6-7 . . . . Values: $50 up
I-B-12 Undersize Planchet (WE), Rarity Level: 7 . . . . Values: $250 up
I-B-13 Oversize Planchet (WE), Rarity Level: 7 . . . . Values: $250 up
I-B-14 Improperly Prepared Proof Planchet (WE), Rarity Level: 7 . . . . Values: $100 up
I-B-15 Improperly Annealed Planchet (WE), Rarity Level: - . . . . Values: No Value
I-B-16 Faulty Upset Edge Planchet (WE), Rarity Level: 5-6 . . . . Values: $10 up
I-B-17 Rolled-In Metal Planchet (WE), Rarity Level: 6-7 . . . . Values: $50 up
I-B-18 Weld Area Planchet (WE), Rarity Level: Unknown . . . . Values: No Value Established
    (See values for the coins struck on weld area planchets.)
I-B-19 Strike Clip Planchet (WE), Rarity Level: 7 . . . . Values: $150 up
I-B-20 Unpunched Center-Hole Planchet (WE), Rarity Level: 5-7 . . . . Values: $5 and up
I-B-21 Incompletely Punched Center-Hole Planchet (WE), Rarity Level: 6-7. . . . . Values: $15 up
I-B-22 Uncentered Center-Hole Planchet (WE), Rarity Level: 6-7 . . . . Values: $10 up
I-B-23 Multiple Punched Center-Hole Planchet (WE), Rarity Level: 7 . . . . Values: $35 up
I-B-24 Unintended Center-Hole Planchet (WE), Rarity Level: Unknown . . . . Values: -
I-B-25 Wrong Size or Shape Center-Hole Planchet (IWE), Rarity Level: 5-7 . . . . Values: $10 up

Clipped planchets (I-C)

Clipped blanks, or planchets, occur when the strip of coin metal fails to move forward between successive strokes of the gang punch to clear the previously punched holes, in the same manner as a cookie cutter overlapping a previously cut hole in the dough. The size of the clip is a function of the amount of overlap of the next punch.

The overlapping round punches produce a missing arc with curve matching the outside circumference of the blanking punch. Straight clips occur when the punch overlaps the beginning or end of a strip which has had the end sheared or sawed off. Ragged clips occur in the same manner when the ends of the strip have been left as they were rolled out.

The term "clip" as used here should not be confused with the practice of clipping or shaving small pieces of metal from a bullion coin after it is in circulation.

I-C-1 Disc Clip Planchet (WE), Rarity Level: 3-5 . . . . Values: $5 up
I-C-2 Curved Clip Planchet - (To 5%) (WE), Rarity Level: 5-6 . . . . Values: $5 up
I-C-3 Curved Clip Planchet - (6 to 10%) (WE), Rarity Level: 6 . . . . Values: $10 up
I-C-4 Curved Clip Planchet - (11 to 25%) (WE), Rarity Level: 5-6 . . . . Values: $15 up
I-C-5 Curved Clip Planchet - (26 to 60%) (WE), Rarity Level: 6-7 . . . . Values: $25 up
I-C-6 Double Curved Clip Planchet (WE), Rarity Level: 6 . . . . Values: $10 up
I-C-7 Triple Curved Clip Planchet (WE), Rarity Level: 5-6 . . . . Values: $25 up
I-C-8 Multiple Curved Clip Planchet (WE), Rarity Level: 6-7 . . . . Values: $35 up
I-C-9 Overlapping Curved Clipped Planchet (WE), Rarity Level: 6-7 . . . . Values: $50 up
I-C-10 Incompletely Punched Curved Clip Planchet (WE), Rarity Level: 6 . . . . Values: $35 up
I-C-11 Oval Curved Clip Planchet (WE), Rarity Level: 6-7 . . . . Values: $50 up
I-C-12 Crescent Clip Planchet - (61% or more) (WE), Rarity Level: 7 . . . . Values: $200 up

I-C-13 Straight Clip Planchet (WE), Rarity Level: 6. . . . . .Values: $30 up
I-C-14 Incompletely Sheared Straight Clip Planchet (WE), Rarity Level: 6 . . . . .Values: $50 up
I-C-15 Ragged Clip Planchet (WE), Rarity Level: 6-7 . . . . .Values: $35 up
I-C-16 Outside Corner Clip Planchet (E), Rarity Level: - . . . . Values: No Value
I-C-17 Inside Corner Clip Planchet (E), Rarity Level: - . . . . Values: No Value
I-C-18 Irregularly Clipped Planchet (E) Rarity Level: - . . . . .Values: Value not established
I-C-19 Incompletely Punched Scalloped or Multi-Sided Planchet (E), Rarity Level: 7 . . . . .Values: $25 up

Laminated, split, or broken planchet (I-D)

For a variety of reasons the coin metal may split into thin layers (delaminate) and either split completely off the coin, or be retained. Common causes are included gas or alloy mix problems. Lamination cracks usually enter the surface of the planchet at a very shallow angle or are at right angles to the edge. The resulting layers differ from slag in that they appear as normal metal.

Lamination cracks and missing metal of any size below a split planchet are too common in the 35 percent silver 1942-1945 nickels to be collectible or have any significant value.

I-D-1 Small Lamination Crack Planchet (W), Rarity Level: 4-5 . . . . .Values: $1 up
I-D-2 Large Lamination Crack Planchet (W), Rarity Level: 3-4 . . . . .Values: $5 up
I-D-3 Split Planchet (W), Rarity Level: 5-6 . . . . .Values: $15 up
I-D-4 Hinged Split Planchet (W), Rarity Level: 6-7 . . . . .Values: $75 up
I-D-5 Clad Planchet With a Clad Layer Missing (W), Rarity Level: 5-6 .Values: $35 up
I-D-6 Clad Planchet With Both Clad Layers Missing (W), Rarity Level: 6-7 . . . . .Values: $75 up
I-D-7 Separated Clad Layer (W), Rarity Level: 5 . . . . .Values: $25 up
I-D-8 Broken Planchet (WE), Rarity Level: 3-4 . . . . .Values: $5 up

Wrong stock planchet (I-E)

The following classes cover those cases where the wrong coin metal stock was run through the blanking press, making blanks of the correct diameter, but of the wrong thickness, alloy or metal or a combination of the wrong thickness and the wrong metal.

I-E-1 Half Cent Stock Planchet (IE), Rarity Level: Unknown . . . . .Values: No Value Established
I-E-2 Cent Stock Planchet (IE), Rarity Level: Unknown . . . . .Values: No Value Established
I-E-3 Two Cent Stock Planchet (E), Rarity Level: Unknown .Values: No Value Established
I-E-4 Three Cent Silver Stock Planchet (E), Rarity Level: Unknown. . . . . .Values: No Value Established
I-E-5 Three Cent Nickel Stock Planchet (E), Rarity Level: Unknown . . . . .Values: No Value Established
I-E-6 Half Dime Stock Planchet (E), Rarity Level: Unknown . . . . .Values: No Value Established
I-E-7 Dime Stock Planchet (E), Rarity Level: 7 . . . . .Values: $200 up
I-E-8 Twenty Cent Stock Planchet (E), Rarity Level: Unknown. . . . . .Values: No Value Established
I-E-9 Quarter Stock Planchet (E), Rarity Level: Unknown . . . . .Values: No Value Established
I-E-10 Half Dollar Stock Planchet (E), Rarity Level: Unknown. . . . . .Values: No Value Established
I-E-11 Dollar Stock Planchet (E), Rarity Level: 7. . . . . .Values: $300 up
I-E-12 Token or Medal Stock Planchet (E), Rarity Level: Unknown . . . . .Values: No Value Established
I-E-13 Wrong Thickness Spoiled Planchet (IWE), Rarity Level: Unknown. . . . . . . .Values: No Value Established
I-E-14 Correct Thickness Spoiled Planchet (IWE), Rarity Level: Unknown . . . . . . .Values: No Value Established
I-E-15 Cut Down Struck Token Planchet (IWE), Rarity Level: Unknown . . . . .Values: No Value Established
I-E-16 Experimental or Pattern Stock Planchet (IE), Rarity Level: Unknown . . . . . .Values: No Value Established
I-E-17 Proof Stock Planchet (IE), Rarity Level: Unknown . . . . .Values: No Value Established
I-E-18 Adjusted Specification Stock Planchet (IE), Rarity Level: 7. . . . . .Values: $25 up
I-E-19 Trial Strike Stock Planchet (IE), Rarity Level: Unknown . . . . .Values: No Value Established
I-E-20 U.S. Punched Foreign Stock Planchet (E), Rarity Level: 7 . . . . Values: $75 up
I-E-21 Foreign Punched Foreign Stock Planchet (E), Rarity Level: 7. . . . . .Values: $75 up
I-E-22 Non-Standard Coin Alloy Planchet (IE), Rarity Level: 7 . . . . Values: Unknown

Extra metal on a blank, or planchet (I-F)

True extra metal is only added to the blank during the blanking operation. This occurs as metal is scraped off the sides of the blanks as they are driven down through the thimble, or lower die in the blanking press. The metal is eventually picked up by a blank passing through, welded to it by the heat of friction.

A second form of extra metal has been moved to this section, the sintered coating planchet, the metal deposited on the planchet in the form of dust during the annealing operation.

I-F-1 Extra Metal on a Type 1 Blank (W), Rarity Level: 7 . . . . .Values: $50 up
I-F-2 Extra Metal on a Type 2 Planchet (W), Rarity Level: 6-7 . . . . .Values: $75 up
I-F-3 Sintered Coating Planchet (W), Rarity Level: 7 . . . . .Values: $75 up

Normal or abnormal planchets (I-G)

This section consists of the two principal forms – the blank as it comes from the blanking press – and in the form of a planchet after it has passed through the upsetting mill. It also includes a class for purchased planchets and one for planchets produced by the mint.

I-G-1 Type I Blank (IWE), Rarity Level: 3-5 . . . . .Values: $2 up
I-G-2 Type II Planchet (IWE), Rarity Level: 3-4 . . . . .Values: 50 up
I-G-3 Purchased Planchet (I), Rarity Level: 1 . . . . Values: No Value
I-G-4 Mint Made Planchet (I), Rarity Level: 1 . . . . Values: No Value
I-G-5 Adjustment-Marked Planchet (I), Rarity Level: Unknown . . . . .Values: No Value
I-G-6 Hardness Test-Marked Planchet (I), Rarity Level: - .Values: No Value Established
Note: There are no classes between I-G-6 and I-G-23
I-G-23 Proof Planchet (IE), Rarity Level: 6-7 . . . . .Values: $1 up

Coin metal strip (I-H)

When the coin metal strip passes through the blanking press it goes directly to a chopper. This cuts the remaining web into small pieces to be sent back to the melting furnace. Pieces of the web or the chopped up web may escape into the hands of collectors.

I-H-1 Punched Coin Metal Strip (IWE), Rarity Level: 4-6 . . . . Values: $5 up,
   depending on size, denomination and number of holes showing
I-H-2 Chopped Coin Metal Strip (IE), Rarity Level: 3-5 . . . . .Values: $5 up

The die varieties

Division II

Die varieties may be unique to a given die, but will repeat for the full life of the die unless a further change occurs. Anything that happens to the die will affect the appearance of the struck coin. This includes all the steps of the die making:

- Cutting a die blank from a tool steel bar.
- Making the design.
- Transferring it to a model.
- Transferring it to the master die or hub.
- The hubbing process of making the die.
- Punching in the mintmark.
- Heat treating of the die.

The completed dies are also subject to damage in numerous forms, plus wear and tear during the striking process and repair work done with abrasives. All of these factors can affect how the struck coin looks.

Engraving varieties (II-A)

In all cases in this section where a master die, or master hub is affected by the class, the class will affect all the working hubs and all working dies descending from it.

Identification as being on a master die or hub depends on it being traced to two or more of the working hubs descended from the same master tools.

II-A-1 Overdate (IE), Rarity Level: 1-7 . . . . .Values: $1 up
II-A-2 Doubled Date (IE), Rarity Level: 1-7 . . . . .Values: $1 up
II-A-3 Small Date (IE), Rarity Level: 2-5 . . . . .Values: $1 up
II-A-4 Large Date (IE), Rarity Level: 2-5 . . . . .Values: $1 up
II-A-5 Small Over Large Date (IE), Rarity Level: 4-6 . . . . .Values: $15 up
II-A-6 Large Over Small Date (IE), Rarity Level: 3-5 . . . . .Values: $10 up
II-A-7 Blundered Date (E), Rarity Level: 6-7 . . . . .Values: $50 up
II-A-8 Corrected Blundered Date (IE), Rarity Level: 3-5 . . . . .Values: $5 up
II-A-9 Wrong Font Date Digit (IE), Rarity Level: 5-6 . . . . .Values: Minimal
II-A-10 Worn, Broken or Damaged Punch (IWE), Rarity Level: 5-6 . . . . .Values: $5 up
II-A-11 Expedient Punch (IWE), Rarity Level: 5-6 . . . . .Values: $10 up
II-A-12 Blundered Digit (E), Rarity Level: 4-5 . . . . .Values: $50 up
II-A-13 Corrected Blundered Digit (IE), Rarity Level: 3-6 . . . . .Values: $10 up
II-A-14 Doubled Digit (IWE), Rarity Level: 2-6 . . . . .Values: $2 up
II-A-15 Wrong Style or Font Letter or Digit (IE), Rarity Level: 3-5 . . . . .Values: Minimal
II-A-16 One Style or Font Over Another (IE), Rarity Level: 4-6 .Values: $10 up
II-A-17 Letter Over Digit (E), Rarity Level: 6-7 . . . . .Values: $25 up
II-A-18 Digit Over Letter (E), Rarity Level: 6-7 . . . . .Values: $25 up
II-A-19 Omitted Letter or Digit (IWE), Rarity Level: 4-6 . . . . .Values: $5 up
II-A-20 Blundered Letter (E), Rarity Level: 6-7 . . . . .Values: $50 up
II-A-21 Corrected Blundered Letter (IE), Rarity Level: 1-3 . . . . .Values: $10 up
II-A-22 Doubled Letter (IWE), Rarity Level: 2-6 . . . . .Values: $2 up
II-A-23 Blundered Design Element (IE), Rarity Level: 6-7 . . . . .Values: $50 up
II-A-24 Corrected Blundered Design Element (IE), Rarity Level: 3-5 . . . . .Values: $10 up
II-A-25 Large Over Small Design Element (IE), Rarity Level: 4-6 . . . . .Values: $2 up
II-A-26 Omitted Design Element (IWE), Rarity Level: 5-7 . . . . .Values: $10 up
II-A-27 Doubled Design Element (IWE), Rarity Level: 2-6 . . . . .Values: $2 up
II-A-28 One Design Element Over Another (IE), Rarity Level: 3-6 . . . . .Values: $5 up
II-A-29 Reducing Lathe Doubling (WE), Rarity Level: 6-7 . . . . .Values: $50 up
II-A-30 Extra Design Element (IE), Rarity Level: 3-5 . . . . .Values: $10 up
II-A-31 Modified Design (IWE), Rarity Level: 1-5 . . . . .Values: No Value up
II-A-32 Normal Design (I), Rarity Level: 1 . . . . .Values: No Extra Value
II-A-33 Design Mistake (IE), Rarity Level: 2-6 . . . . .Values: $1 up
II-A-34 Defective Die Design (IWE), Rarity Level: 1 . . . . Values: No Value
II-A-35 Pattern (I), Rarity Level: 6-7 . . . . .Values: $100 up
II-A-36 Trial Design (I), Rarity Level: 5-7 . . . . .Values: $100 up
II-A-37 Omitted Designer's Initial (IWE), Rarity Level: 3-7 . . . . .Values: $1 up
II-A-38 Layout Mark (IE), Rarity Level: 5-7 . . . . .Values: Minimal
II-A-39 Abnormal Reeding (IWE), Rarity Level: 2-5 . . . . .Values: $1 up
II-A-40 Modified Die or Hub (IWE), Rarity Level: 1-5 . . . . .Values: No Value up
II-A-41 Numbered Die (I), Rarity Level: 3-5 . . . . .Values: $5 up
II-A-42 Plugged Die (IW), Rarity Level: 5-6 . . . . .Values: Minimal
II-A-43 Cancelled Die (IE), Rarity Level: 3-6 . . . . .Values: No Value up
II-A-44 Hardness Test Marked Die (IE), Rarity Level: 7 . . . . .Values: $100 up
II-A-45 Coin Simulation (IE), Rarity Level: 6-7 . . . . Values: $100 up, but may be illegal to own
II-A-46 Punching Mistake (IE), Rarity Level: 2-6 . . . . .Values: $1 up
II-A-47 Small Over Large Design (IE), Rarity Level: 4-6 . . . . .Values: $5 up
II-A-48 Doubled Punch (IE), Rarity Level: 5-7 . . . . .Values: $5 up
II-A-49 Mint Display Sample (I) Rarity Level: 7 . . . . Values not established
II-A-50 Center Dot, Stud or Circle (IE) Rarity Level: 7, much more common on early cents. . Values not established

Hub doubling varieties (II-B)

Rotated hub doubling   *Hub break*

This section includes eight classes of hub doubling. Each class is from a different cause, described by the title of the class. At the latest count over 2,500 doubled dies have been reported in the U.S. coinage, the most famous being examples of the 1955, 1969-S and 1972 cent dies.

II-B-I Rotated Hub Doubling (WE), Rarity Level: 3-6. . . . . .Values: $1 up
II-B-II Distorted Hub Doubling (WE), Rarity Level: 3-6 . . . . .Values: $1 up
II-B-III Design Hub Doubling (IWE), Rarity Level: 3-6. . . . . Values: $1 up to five figure amounts
II-B-IV Offset Hub Doubling (WE), Rarity Level: 4-6 . . . . .Values: $15 up
II-B-V Pivoted Hub Doubling (WE), Rarity Level: 3-6 . . . . .Values: $10 up
II-B-VI Distended Hub Doubling (WE), Rarity Level: 2-5. . . . . .Values: $1 up
II-B-VII Modified Hub Doubling (IWE), Rarity Level: 2-5 . . . . .Values: $1 up
II-B-VIII Tilted Hub Doubling (WE), Rarity Level: 4-6 . . . . .Values: $5 up

Mintmark varieties (II-C)

Double   *Triple*

Mintmarks are punched into U.S. coin dies by hand (Up to 1985 for proof coins, to 1990 for cents and nickels and 1991 for other denominations). Variations resulting from mistakes in the punching are listed in this section. Unless exceptionally mispunched, values are usually estimated at 150 percent of numismatic value. Slightly tilted or displaced mintmarks have no value.

II-C-1 Doubled Mintmark (IE), Rarity Level: 2-6 . . . . Values: 50 cents up
II-C-2 Separated Doubled Mintmark (IE), Rarity Level: 5-6. . . . . .Values: $15 up
II-C-3 Over Mintmark (IE), Rarity Level: 3-6 . . . . .Values: $2 up
II-C-4 Tripled Mintmark (IE), Rarity Level: 3-5 . . . . .Values: 50 up
II-C-5 Quadrupled Mintmark (IE), Rarity Level: 4-6 . . . . .Values: $1 up
II-C-6 Small Mintmark (IE), Rarity Level: 2-5 . . . . Values: No Extra Value up
II-C-7 Large Mintmark (IE), Rarity Level: 2-5 . . . . Values: No Extra Value up
II-C-8 Large Over Small Mintmark (IE), Rarity Level: 2-5 . . . . .Values: $2 up
II-C-9 Small Over Large Mintmark (IE), Rarity Level: 3-6 . . . . .Values: $5 up
II-C-10 Broken Mintmark Punch (W), Rarity Level: 5-6 . . . . .Values: $5 up
II-C-11 Omitted Mintmark (IWE), Rarity Level: 4-7. . . . . .Values: $125 up
II-C-12 Tilted Mintmark (IE), Rarity Level: 5-7 . . . . .Values: $5 up
II-C-13 Blundered Mintmark (E), Rarity Level: 4-6 . . . . .Values: $5 up

II-C-14 Corrected Horizontal Mintmark (IE), Rarity Level: 4-6 . . . . .Values: $5 up
II-C-15 Corrected Upside Down Mintmark (IE), Rarity Level: 4-6 . . . . .Values: $5 up
II-C-16 Displaced Mintmark (IE), Rarity Level: 4-6 . . . . .Values: $5 to $10
II-C-17 Modified Mintmark (IWE), Rarity Level: 1-4 . . . . Values: No Extra Value up
II-C-18 Normal Mintmark (I), Rarity Level: 1 . . . . .Values: No Extra Value
II-C-19 Doubled Mintmark Punch (I), Rarity Level: 6-7 . . . . Values: No Extra Value up
II-C-20 Upside Down Mintmark (E) Rarity Level 6-7 . . . . .Values: $5 up
II-C-21 Horizontal Mintmark (E) Rarity Level 6-7 . . . . .Values: $5 up
II-C-22 Wrong Mintmark (E) Rarity Level 6-7 . . . . Values $15 up
(Example has a D mintmark in the date, but was used at Philadelphia.)

Die, collar and hub cracks (II-D)

Die cracks

Cracks in the surface of the die allow coin metal to be forced into the crack during the strike, resulting in raised irregular lines of coin metal above the normal surface of the coin. These are one of the commonest forms of die damage and wear, making them easily collectible.

Collar cracks and hub cracks are added to this section because the causes and effects are similar or closely associated.

Die cracks, collar cracks and hub cracks are the result of wear and tear on the tools, with intentional use assumed for all classes.

II-D-1 Die Crack (W), Rarity Level: 1-3 . . . . .Values: 10 to $1, $25 up on a proof coin
  with a rarity level of 6-7
II-D-2 Multiple Die Cracks (W), Rarity Level: 1-3 . . . . Values: 25 cents to $2
II-D-3 Head-To-Rim Die Crack (Lincoln Cent) (W), Rarity Level: 2-6 . . Values: 25 to $10 for multiple die cracks
II-D-4 Split Die (W), Rarity Level: 5-6 . . . . .Values: $10 up
II-D-5 Rim-To-Rim Die Crack (W), Rarity Level: 2-5 . . . . .Values: $1 up
II-D-6 Collar Crack (W), Rarity Level: 4-6 . . . . .Values: $10 up
II-D-7 Hub Crack (W), Rarity Level: 3-5 . . . . .Values: $1-$2

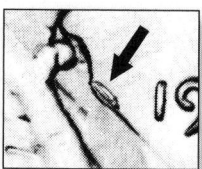

Small die break II-E-2

Clogged letter II-E-1

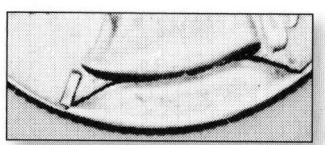

Major die break, date missing, II-E-5

Rim die break II-E-4

Die breaks (II-E)

Breaks in the surface of the die allow coin metal to squeeze into the resulting holes, causing raised irregular areas above the normal surface of the coin. Die chips and small die breaks are nearly as common as the die cracks, but major die breaks, which extend in from the edge of the coin, are quite rare on the larger coins.

If the broken piece of the die is retained, the resulting design will be above or below the level of the rest of the surface.

II-E-1 Die Chip (W), Rarity Level: 1-2 . . . . .Values: 10 to $1
II-E-2 Small Die Break (W), Rarity Level: 1-3 . . . . .Values: 10 to $2
II-E-3 Large Die Break (W), Rarity Level: 3-5 . . . . Values: $1 to $50 and up
II-E-4 Rim Die Break (W), Rarity Level: 2-3 . . . . Values: 25 cents to $5
II-E-5 Major Die Break (WE), Rarity Level: 3-6 . . . . .Values: $5 to $100 and up
II-E-6 Retained Broken Die (W), Rarity Level: 3-5 . . . . .Values: $1 to $10 and up
II-E-7 Retained Broken Center of the Die (W), Rarity Level: 6-7 . . . . .Values: $100 up
II-E-8 Laminated Die (W), Rarity Level: 3-5 . . . . Values: 10 cents to $5
II-E-9 Chipped Chrome Plating (W), Rarity Level: 4-5 . . . . .Values: $10 to $25 on proofs
II-E-10 Collar Break (W), Rarity Level: 4-6 . . . . Values: $5 to $25 and up
II-E-11 Broken Letter or Digit on an Edge Die (W), Rarity Level: 4-6 . . . . Values: Minimal.
II-E-12 "Bar" Die Break (W), Rarity Level: 3-5 . . . . .Values: 25 to $20
II-E-13 Hub Break (W), Rarity Level: 4-6 . . . . Values: 50 to $10 and up

"BIE" varieties (II-F)

A series of small die breaks or die chips in the letters of "LIBERTY" mostly on the wheat-reverse Lincoln cent are actively collected. The name results from the resemblance to an "I" between the "B" and "E" on many of the dies, but they are found between all of the letters in different cases. Well over 1,500 dies are known and cataloged. Numerous more recent examples are known.

II-F-1 ILI Die Variety (W), Rarity Level: 4-5 . . . . Values: 25 cents to $10
II-F-2 LII Die Variety (W), Rarity Level: 3-5 . . . . Values: 50 cents to $15
II-F-3 IIB Die Variety (W), Rarity Level: 3-5 . . . . Values: 50 cents to $15
II-F-4 BIE Die Variety (W), Rarity Level: 3-5 . . . . .Values: $1 to $20
II-F-5 EIR Die Variety (W), Rarity Level: 3-5 . . . . .Values: 50 to $15
II-F-6 RIT Die Variety (W), Rarity Level: 4-5 . . . . .Values: $2 to $25
II-F-7 TIY Die Variety (W), Rarity Level: 4-5 . . . . .Values: $5 to $30
II-F-8 TYI Die Variety (W), Rarity Level: 4-5 . . . . .Values: $2 to $25

Worn and damaged dies, collars and hubs (II-G)

Many dies are continued deliberately in service after they have been damaged, dented, clashed or show design transfer, since none of these classes actually affect anything but the appearance of the coin. The root cause is wear, but intent or mistakes may enter the picture.

II-G-1 Dented Die, Collar or Hub (IWE), Rarity Level: 3-5 . . . . .Values: 25 to $5
II-G-2 Damaged Die, Collar or Hub (IWE), Rarity Level: 3-5 . . . . .Values: 25 to $5
II-G-3 Worn Die, Collar or Hub (IWE), Rarity Level: 2-3 . . . . .Values: No Extra Value to Minimal Value
II-G-4 Pitted or Rusted Die, Collar or Hub (IWE), Rarity Level: 3-4 . . . . .Values: No Extra Value, marker only
II-G-5 Heavy Die Clash (IWE), Rarity Level: 4-5 . . . . Values: $1 to $10 and up
II-G-6 Heavy Collar Clash (IWE), Rarity Level: 3-4 . . . . Values: $1 to $5 and up
II-G-7 Heavy Design Transfer (IWE), Rarity Level: 3-4 . . . . Values: 10 cents to $1

Die progressions (II-H)

The progression section consists of three classes. These are useful as cataloging tools for many different die varieties, but especially the die cracks and die breaks which may enlarge, lengthen or increase in number.

II-H-1 Progression (W), Rarity Level: 3-5 . . . . .Values: $1 up

II-H-2 Die Substitution (IW), Rarity Level: 2-4 . . . . Values: No Extra Value to Minimal Value
II-H-3 Die Repeat (I), Rarity Level: 2-4 . . . . Values: No Extra Value to Minimal Value

Die scratches, polished and abraded dies (II-I)

This section consists of those classes having to do with the use of an abrasive in some form to intentionally polish proof dies, or repair the circulating die surface. Several classes that previously were referred to as "polished" now are listed as "abraded."

II-I-1 Die Scratch (IW), Rarity Level: 1-2 . . . . .Values: No Extra Value to 10 cents to 25 cents, as a marker
II-I-2 Polished (proof) Die (IW), Rarity Level: 1. . . . . .Values: No Extra Value
II-I-3 Abraded (Circulation) Die (IW), Rarity Level: 1-2. . . . . .Values: No Extra Value up to $10
II-I-4 Inside Abraded Die Doubling (IW), Rarity Level: 1-3 . . . . Values: No Extra Value to $1
II-I-5 Outside Abraded Die Doubling (IW), Rarity Level: 1-3. . . . . Values: No Extra Value to $1
II-I-6 Lathe Marks (IW), Rarity Level: 5-7 . . . . .Values: No Extra Value, marker only

Striking varieties
Division III

Once the dies are made and the planchets have been prepared, they are struck by a pair of dies and become a coin. In this division, we list the misstrikes resulting from human or mechanical malfunction in the striking process. These are one-of-a-kind varieties, but there may be many similar coins that fall in a given class.

Multiples and combinations of classes must be considered on a case by case basis. The first several sections match the planchet sections indicated in the title.

Struck on defective alloy mix planchets (III-A)

This section includes those classes of coins struck on planchets that were made from a defective alloy.

III-A-1 Struck on an Improper Alloy Mix Planchet (IE), Rarity Level: 2-3 . . . . Values: 10 cents to $2
III-A-2 Struck on a Planchet With Slag Inclusions(IE), Rarity Level: 5-6 . . . . .Values: $10 up

Struck on damaged, defective or abnormal planchet (III-B)

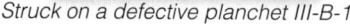

Struck on a defective planchet III-B-1   *Struck on a tapered planchet III-B-5*

Coins get struck on many strange objects. The more common, of course, are planchets that have been damaged in some way in the production process. In most of the classes in this section, intent is at least presumed, if not specifically listed as a cause.

III-B-1 Struck on a Defective Planchet (IWE), Rarity Level: 4-6. . . . . .Values: $5 to $10 and up
III-B-2 Struck on a Mechanically Damaged Planchet (IWE), Rarity Level: 5-6. . . . . . .Values: $10 to $20 and up
III-B-3 Struck on a Rolled Thin Planchet (IWE), Rarity Level: 5-6. . . . . .Values: $2 to $5 and up
III-B-4 Struck on a Rolled Thick Planchet (IWE), Rarity Level: 5-6 . . . . Values: $35 to $50 and up
III-B-5 Struck on a Tapered Planchet (WE), Rarity Level: 4-6 . . . . .Values: $2 to $5 and up
III-B-6 Struck on a Partially Unplated Planchet (WE), Rarity Level: 5 . . . . .Values: $10 up
III-B-7 Struck on an Unplated Planchet (WE), Rarity Level: 6-7 . . . . .Values: $100 up
III-B-8 Struck on a Bubbled Plating Planchet (IWE), Rarity Level: 1 . . . . Values: No Value
III-B-9 Struck on an Included Gas Bubble Planchet (WE), Rarity Level: 5-6 . . . . .Values: $5 up
III-B-10 Struck on a Partially Unclad Planchet (WE), Rarity Level: 5-6 .Values: $5 up

III-B-11 Struck on an Unclad Planchet (WE), Rarity Level: 4-5 . . . . Values: $5 and up
III-B-12 Struck on an Undersize Planchet (WE), Rarity Level: 4-6 . . . . .Values: Minimal
III-B-13 Struck on an Oversize Planchet (WE), Rarity Level: 6-7 . . . . Values: Minimal
III-B-14 Struck on an Improperly Prepared Proof Planchet (IWE), Rarity Level: 3-5 . . . . .Values: $5 up
III-B-15 Struck on an Improperly Annealed Planchet (IWE), Rarity Level: 4-5 . . . . .Values: $5 up
III-B-16 Struck on a Faulty Upset Edge Planchet (IWE), Rarity Level: 4-5 . . . . .Values: $1 to $2
III-B-17 Struck on a Rolled In Metal Planchet (WE), Rarity Level: 4-6 . . . . .Values: $2 up
III-B-18 Struck on a Weld Area Planchet (WE), Rarity Level: 6 . . . . .Values: $25 to $50
III-B-19 Struck on a Strike Clip Planchet (W), Rarity Level: 6-7 . . . . .Values: $25 up
III-B-20 Struck on an Unpunched Center Hole Planchet (WE), Rarity Level: 4-6 . . . . Values: $1 and up
III-B-21 Struck on an Incompletely Punched Center Hole Planchet (WE), Rarity Level: 6-7 . . . . . Values: $5 up
III-B-22 Struck on an Uncentered Center Hole Planchet (WE), Rarity Level: 6-7 . . . . .Values: $10 up
III-B-23 Struck on a Multiple Punched Center Hole Planchet (WE), Rarity Level: 7 . . . . .Values: $25 up
III-B-24 Struck on an Unintended Center Hole Planchet (WE), Rarity Level: 6-7 . . . . Values: $25 and up
III-B-25 Struck on a Wrong Size or Shape Center Hole Planchet (WE), Rarity Level: 5-7 . . . . .Values: $5 up
III-B-26 Struck on Scrap Coin Metal (E), Rarity Level: 4-6 . . . . .Values: $10 up
III-B-27 Struck on Junk Non Coin Metal (E), Rarity Level: 4-6 . . . . .Values: $15 up
III-B-28 Struck on a False Planchet (E), Rarity Level: 3-5 . . . . .Values: $35 up
III-B-29 Struck on Bonded Planchets (E), Rarity Level: 6-7 . . . . .Values: $50 up

Struck on a clipped planchet (III-C)

Ragged edge clip III-C-15

Multiple clip III-C-8

Incomplete curved clip III-C-10

Coins struck on clipped blanks, or planchets, exhibit the same missing areas as they did before striking, modified by the metal flow from the strike which rounds the edges and tends to move metal into the missing areas. Values for blanks will run higher than planchets with similar clips.

III-C-1 Struck on a Disc Clip Planchet (WE), Rarity Level: 4-5 . . . . Values: $1 on regular coins,
    $20 and up for clad coins
III-C-2 Struck on a Curved Clip Planchet - to 5% (WE), Rarity Level: 3-5 . . . . Values: 50 cents up
III-C-3 Struck on a Curved Clip Planchet - (6 to 10%) (WE), Rarity Level: 4-5 . . . . .Values: $1 up
III-C-4 Struck on a Curved Clip Planchet - (11 to 25%) (WE), Rarity Level: 4-5 . . . . .Values: $2 up
III-C-5 Struck on a Curved Clip Planchet - (26 to 60%) (WE), Rarity Level: 4-6 . . . . .Values: $10 up
III-C-6 Struck on a Double Curved Clip Planchet (WE), Rarity Level: 3-4 . . . . .Values: $2 up
III-C-7 Struck on a Triple Curved Clip Planchet (WE), Rarity Level: 4-5 . . . . .Values: $5 up
III-C-8 Struck on a Multiple Curved Clip Planchet (WE), Rarity Level: 4-6 . . . . .Values: $5 up
III-C-9 Struck on an Overlapping Curved Clipped Planchet (WE), Rarity Level: 5-6 . . . . .Values: $15 up
III-C-10 Struck on an Incomplete Curved Clip Planchet (WE), Rarity Level: 4-5 . . . . .Values: $10 up
III-C-11 Struck on an Oval Clip Planchet (WE), Rarity Level: 5-6 . . . . .Values: $20 up
III-C-12 Struck on a Crescent Clip Planchet - (61% or more) (WE), Rarity Level: 6-7 . . . . .Values: $100 up
III-C-13 Struck on a Straight Clip Planchet (E), Rarity Level: 4-6 . . . . .Values: $10 up

III-C-14 Struck on an Incomplete Straight Clip Planchet (WE), Rarity Level: 5-6 . . . . .Values: $20 up
III-C-15 Struck on a Ragged Clip Planchet (E), Rarity Level: 4-6 . . . . .Values: $15 up
III-C-16 Struck on an Outside Corner Clip Planchet (E), Rarity Level: 7 . . . . .Values: $100 up
III-C-17 Struck on an Inside Corner Clip Planchet (E), Rarity Level: Unknown outside mint. . . . . .Values:
III-C-18 Struck on an Irregularly Clipped Planchet (E), Rarity Level: 6-7 . . . . Values: $20 up.
III-C-19 Struck on an Incompletely Punched Scalloped or Multi-Sided Planchet (E), Rarity Level: 7
. . . . Values: $20 up.

Struck on a laminated, split or broken planchet (III-D)

Lamination crack III-D-1   *Layer peeled off III-D-2*   *Split planchet III-D-3*

This section has to do with the splitting, cracking or breaking of a coin parallel to the faces of the coin, or at least very nearly parallel, or breaks at right angles to the faces of the coin.

Lamination cracks and missing metal of any size below a split planchet are too common in the 35-percent silver 1942-1945 nickels to be collectible or have any significant value.

III-D-1 Struck on a Small Lamination Crack Planchet (W), Rarity Level: 3-4. . . . . .Values: 10 up
III-D-2 Struck on a Large Lamination Crack Planchet (W), Rarity Level: 3-6. . . . . .Values: $1 up
III-D-3 Struck on a Split Planchet (W), Rarity Level: 4-6. . . . . .Values: $5 up
III-D-4 Struck on a Hinged Split Planchet (W), Rarity Level: 5-6. . . . . .Values: $35 up
III-D-5 Struck on a Planchet With a Clad Layer Missing (W), Rarity Level: 4-5. . . . . .Values: $15 up
III-D-6 Struck on a Planchet With Both Clad Layers Missing (W), Rarity Level: 4-5 . . . . .Values: $25 up
III-D-7 Struck on a Separated Clad Layer or Lamination (W), Rarity Level: 6-7. . . . . .Values: $75 up
III-D-8 Struck on a Broken Planchet Before the Strike (W), Rarity Level: 3-5 . . . . .Values: $10 up
III-D-9 Broken Coin During or After the Strike (W), Rarity Level: 4-6 . . . . .Values: $20 up
III-D-10 Struck Coin Fragment Split or Broken During or After the Strike (W), Rarity Level: 3-5. . .Values: $5 up
III-D-11 Reedless Coin Broken During or After the Strike (W), Rarity Level: Unknown . . . . .Values: -

Struck on wrong stock planchets (III-E)

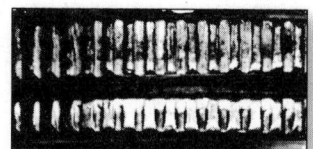

Quarter on dime stock
III-E-7 (lower coin edge)

These classes cover those cases where the wrong stock was run through the blanking press, making planchets of the correct diameter, but of the wrong thickness, alloy or metal or a combination of incorrect thickness and metal.

III-E-1 Struck on a Half Cent-Stock Planchet (IE), Rarity Level: Unknown. . . . . . . .Values: No Value Established
III-E-2 Struck on a Cent-Stock Planchet (IE), Rarity Level: Unknown . . . . .Values: No Value Established
III-E-3 Struck on a Two-Cent-Stock Planchet (E), Rarity Level: Unknown . . . . .Values: -
III-E-4 Struck on a Three-Cent-Silver Stock Planchet (E), Rarity Level: Unknown . . . . .Values: -
III-E-5 Struck on a Three-Cent-Nickel Stock Planchet (E), Rarity Level: Unknown . . . . .Values: -
III-E-6 Struck on a Half Dime-Stock Planchet (E), Rarity Level: Unknown. . . . . .Values: -
III-E-7 Struck on a Dime-Stock Planchet (E), Rarity Level: 5-6 . . . . .Values: $20 up

III-E-8 Struck on a Twenty-Cent-Stock Planchet (E), Rarity Level: Unknown.....................Values: -
III-E-9 Struck on a Quarter-Stock Planchet (E), Rarity Level: 6 ....Values: $50 up
III-E-10 Struck on a Half Dollar-Stock Planchet (E), Rarity Level: 6-7....................Values: $100 up
III-E-11 Struck on a Dollar-Stock Planchet (E), Rarity Level: 6-7 ....Values: $300 up
III-E-12 Struck on a Token/Medal-Stock Planchet (E), Rarity Level: 7..........Values: No Value Established
III-E-13 Struck on a Wrong Thickness Spoiled Planchet (IWE), Rarity Level: 7...............Values: $50 up
III-E-14 Struck on a Correct Thickness Spoiled Planchet (IWE), Rarity Level: Unknown. Values: No Value Established
III-E-15 Struck on a Cut Down Struck Token (IWE), Rarity Level: 6-7 ....Values: $50 up
III-E-16 Struck on an Experimental or Pattern-Stock Planchet (IE), Rarity Level: 7 ....Values: $50 up
III-E-17 Struck on a Proof-Stock Planchet (IE), Rarity Level: 7 ....Values: $100 up
III-E-18 Struck on an Adjusted Specification-Stock Planchet (IE), Rarity Level: 3-7. Values: No Value to $5 and up
III-E-19 Struck on a Trial Strike-Stock Planchet (IE), Rarity Level: Unknown......Values: No Value Established
III-E-20 U.S. Coin Struck on a Foreign-Stock Planchet. (E), Rarity Level: 5 ....Values: $35 up
III-E-21 Foreign Coin Struck on a Foreign-Stock Planchet (E), Rarity Level: 5-6 ....Values: $25 up
III-E-22 Struck on a Non-Standard Coin Alloy (IE), Rarity Level: 4-7 ....Values: $20 up

Extra metal (III-F)

Extra metal on a
struck coin (III-F-2)

Sintered coating III-F-3

The term "extra metal" for the purpose of this section includes both extra metal added to the blank during the blanking operation and metal powder added to the planchet during the annealing operation.

III-F-1 Struck on a Type 1 Blank With Extra Metal (W), Rarity Level: Unknown..................Values: -
III-F-2 Struck on a Type 2 Planchet With Extra Metal (W), Rarity Level: 4-5 ....Values: $10 up
III-F-3 Struck on a Sintered Coating Planchet (W), Rarity Level: 6-7 ....Values: $35 up

Struck on normal or abnormal blanks, or planchets (III-G)

Half on dime
planchet III-G-10

Cent on dime
planchet III-G-10

Half on quarter
planchet III-G-10

This section includes coins struck on either a blank, as it comes from the blanking press, or as a planchet that has passed through the upsetting mill. Added to this section are those planchets that are normal until they are struck by the wrong dies. These differ from the wrong stock planchets because the wrong stock planchets are already a variety before they are struck.

III-G-1 Struck on a Type 1 Blank (IWE), Rarity Level: 4-6 ....Values: $10 up
III-G-2 Struck on a Type 2 Planchet (I), Rarity Level: 1 ....Values: No Extra Value
III-G-3 Struck on a Purchased Planchet (I), Rarity Level: 1 ....Values: No Extra Value
III-G-4 Struck on a Mint-Made Planchet (I), Rarity Level: 1 ....Values: No Extra Value
III-G-5 Struck on an Adjustment-Marked Planchet (I), Rarity Level: 4-7 .... Values: Minimal, and may
   reduce value of coin in some cases
III-G-6 Struck on a Hardness Test-Marked Planchet (I), Rarity Level: 6-7..................Values: $10 up

III-G-7 Wrong Planchet or Metal on a Half Cent Planchet (IE), Rarity Level: 5-7............Values: $100 up
III-G-8 Wrong Planchet or Metal on a Cent Planchet (IE), Rarity Level: 3-6 ....Values: $25 up
III-G-9 Wrong Planchet or Metal on a Nickel Planchet (E), Rarity Level: 4-6.................Values: $35 up
III-G-10 Wrong Planchet or Metal on a Dime Planchet (E), Rarity Level: 4-6 ....Values: $50 up
III-G-11 Wrong Planchet or Metal on a Quarter Planchet (E), Rarity Level: 4-6.............Values: $100 up
III-G-12 Wrong Planchet or Metal on a Half Dollar Planchet (E), Rarity Level: 6-7 ....Values: $500 up
III-G-13 Wrong Planchet or Metal on a Dollar Planchet (E), Rarity Level: 7 ....Values: $500 up
III-G-14 Wrong Planchet or Metal on a Gold Planchet (E), Rarity Level: 7 ....Values: $1000 up
III-G-15 Struck on a Wrong Series Planchet (IE), Rarity Level: 6-7......................Values: $1500 up
III-G-16 U.S. Coin Struck on a Foreign Planchet (E), Rarity Level: 5-7.....................Values: $35 up
III-G-17 Foreign Coin Struck on a U.S. Planchet (E), Rarity Level: 6-7.....................Values: $50 up
III-G-18 Foreign Coin Struck on a Wrong Foreign Planchet (E), Rarity Level: 6-7 ....Values: $50 up
III-G-19 Struck on a Medal Planchet (E), Rarity Level: 6-7 ....Values: $100 up
III-G-20 Medal Struck on a Coin Planchet (IE), Rarity Level: 3-5 ....Values: $10 up
III-G-21 Struck on an Official Sample Planchet (IE), Rarity Level: Unknown......Values: No Value Established
III-G-22 Struck Intentionally on a Wrong Planchet (I), Rarity Level: 6-7 .. Values: Mainly struck as Presentation
    Pieces, full numismatic value
III-G-23 Non-Proof Struck on a Proof Planchet (IE), Rarity Level: 6-7 ....Values: $500 up

Struck on coin metal strip (III-H)

Pieces of the coin metal strip do manage at times to escape into the coin press.
III-H-1 (See I-H-1 Punched Coin Metal Strip), Rarity Level: Impossible........................Values: -
III-H-2 Struck on Chopped Coin Metal Strip (E), Rarity Level: 6-7 ....Values: $25 up

Die adjustment strikes (III-I)

As the dies are set up and adjusted in the coin press, variations in the strike occur until the dies are properly set. Test strikes are normally scrapped, but on occasion reach circulation.
III-I-1 Die Adjustment Strike (IE), Rarity Level: 5-6....................................Values: $35 up
III-I-2 Edge Strike (E), Rarity Level: 5-6 ....Values: $10 to $20 and up
III-I-3 Weak Strike (W), Rarity Level: 1 ....Values: No Extra Value
III-I-4 Strong Strike (IWE), Rarity Level: 1.......................Values: No value except for the premium
    that might be paid for a well struck coin
III-I-5 Jam Strike (IE), Rarity Level: 7 ....Values: $50 up
III-I-6 Trial Piece Strike (I), Rarity Level: 6-7.....................................Values: $100 up
III-I-7 Edge-Die Adjustment Strike (I), Rarity Level: 5-7 ....Values: $5 up
III-I-8 Uniface Strike (I), Rarity Level 7 ....Values: $50 up

Indented, brockage and counter-brockage strikes (III-J)

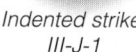

| Indented strike | Counter-brockage strike | Capped die strike |
| III-J-1 | III-J-11 | III-J-15 |

Indented and uniface strikes involve an extra unstruck planchet between one of the dies and the planchet being struck. Brockage strikes involve a struck coin between one of the dies and the planchet and a counter-brockage requires a brockage coin between one of the dies and the planchet.

A cap, or capped die strike results when a coin sticks to the die and is squeezed around it in the shape of a bottle cap.
III-J-1 Indented Strike (W), Rarity Level: 3-6..Values: $5 up
III-J-2 Uniface Strike (W), Rarity Level: 3-5 ....Values: $15 up
III-J-3 Indented Strike By a Smaller Planchet (WE), Rarity Level: 5-7.....................Values: $100 up

III-J-4 Indented Second Strike (W), Rarity Level: 3-5 . . . . Values: $10 up, about the same as a regular double strike of comparable size
III-J-5 Partial Brockage Strike (W), Rarity Level: 3-6. . . . . Values: $15 up
III-J-6 Full Brockage Strike (W), Rarity Level: 3-6. . . . . Values: $5 up
III-J-7 Brockage Strike of a Smaller Coin (WE), Rarity Level: 6-7 . . . . Values: $200 up
III-J-8 Brockage Strike of a Struck Coin Fragment (WE), Rarity Level: 4-6 . . . . Values: $5 up
III-J-9 Brockage Second Strike (WE), Rarity Level: 3-5. . . . . Values: $5 up
III-J-10 Partial Counter-Brockage Strike (WE), Rarity Level: 3-5. . . . . Values: $10 up
III-J-11 Full Counter-Brockage Strike (WE), Rarity Level: 5-7. . . . . Values: $100 up
III-J-12 Counter-Brockage Second Strike (WE), Rarity Level: 4-6. . . . . Values: $10 up
III-J-13 Full Brockage-Counter-Brockage Strike (WE), Rarity Level: 6-7. . . . . Values: $150 up
III-J-14 Multiple Brockage or Counter-Brockage Strike (WE), Rarity Level: 5-7 . . . . Values: $100 up
III-J-15 Capped Die Strike (WE), Rarity Level: 6-7 . . . . Values: $500 up
III-J-16 Reversed Capped Die Strike (WE), Rarity Level: 7 . . . . Values: $1,000 up

Struck through abnormal objects (III-K)

Struck through cloth
III-K-1

Struck through a filled die
III-K-4

Struck through a
dropped filling III-K-5

This section covers most of the objects or materials that might come between the planchet and the die and be struck into the surface of the coin. Unless noted, the materials - even the soft ones - are driven into the surface of the coin.

III-K-1 Struck Through Cloth (IWE), Rarity Level: 3-6. . . . . Values: $35 up
III-K-2 Struck Through Wire (IWE), Rarity Level: 3-6 . . . . Values: $5 up
III-K-3 Struck Through Thread (IWE), Rarity Level: 3-6. . . . . Values: $5 up
III-K-4 Struck Through Dirt-and-Grease-Filled Die (IWE), Rarity Level: 1-4
. . . . Values: 10 cents to 25 cents up, but no value on a worn or circulated coin
III-K-5 Struck Through a Dropped Filling (IWE), Rarity Level: 5-6 . . . . Values: $10 up
III-K-6 Struck Through Wrong Metal Fragments (IWE), Rarity Level: 4-6 . . . . Values: $1 up
III-K-7 Struck Through an Unstruck Planchet Fragment (IWE), Rarity Level: 3-5 . . . . Values: $1 up
III-K-8 Struck Through a Rim Burr (IWE), Rarity Level: 3-5. . . . . Values: $1 to $2 and up
III-K-9 Struck Through plit-Off Reeding (IWE), Rarity Level: 5-6. . . . . Values: $25 up
III-K-10 Struck Through a Feed Finger (IWE), Rarity Level: 5-7 . . . . Values: $25 to $50 and up
III-K-11 Struck Through Miscellaneous Objects (IWE), Rarity Level: 4-6 . . . . Values: $1 up
III-K-12 Struck Through Progression (IWE), Rarity Level: 4-6 . . . . Values: $1 up
Note: Some 1987 through 1994 quarters are found without mintmarks, classed as III-K-4, a Filled Die. Values depend on market conditions. Filled dies have value ONLY on current, uncirculated grade coins.

Double strikes (III-L)

Only coins that receive two or more strikes by the die pair fall in this section and are identified by the fact that both sides of the coin are affected. Unless some object interferes, an equal area of both sides of the coin will be equally doubled.

The exception is the second strike with a loose die, which will double only one side of a coin, but is a rare form usually occurring only on proofs. A similar effect is flat field doubling from die chatter.

III-L-1 Close Centered Double Strike (WE), Rarity Level: 4-6 . . . . Values: $15 up
III-L-2 Rotated Second Strike Over a Centered First Strike (WE), Rarity Level: 4-6 . . . . Values: $15 up
III-L-3 Off-Center Second Strike Over a Centered First Strike (WE), Rarity Level: 4-6 . . . . Values: $15 up

Off-center second strike over
centered first strike III-L-3

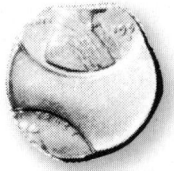

Non-overlapping
double strike III-L-8

Multiple strike III-L-16

Chain strike III-L-10

III-L-4 Off-Center Second Strike Over an Off-Center First Strike (WE), Rarity Level: 4-6. . . . . . . .Values: $10 up
III-L-5 Off-Center Second Strike Over a Broadstrike (WE), Rarity Level: 5-6. . . . . .Values: $20 up
III-L-6 Centered Second Strike Over an Off-Center First Strike (WE), Rarity Level: 5-6. . . . . .Values: $50 up
III-L-7 Obverse Struck Over Reverse (WE), Rarity Level: 5-6. . . . . .Values: $25 up
III-L-8 Nonoverlapping Double Strike (WE), Rarity Level: 5-6. . . . . .Values: $20 up
III-L-9 Struck Over a Different Denomination or Series (WE), Rarity Level: 6 . . . . Values: $300 and up
III-L-10 Chain Strike (WE), Rarity Level: 6 . . . . . Values: $300 up for the pair of coins that were struck together
III-L-11 Second-Strike Doubling From a Loose Die (W), Rarity Level: 6-7 . . . . .Values: $200 up
III-L-12 Second-Strike Doubling From a Loose Screw Press Die (W), Rarity Level: 5-6 . . . . . .Values: $100 up
III-L-13 Second Strike on an Edge Strike (WE), Rarity Level: 5-6 . . . . .Values: $20 up
III-L-14 Folded Planchet Strike (WE), Rarity Level: 5-7. . . . . .Values: $100 up
III-L-15 Triple Strike (WE), Rarity Level: 6-7 . . . . .Values: $100 up
III-L-16 Multiple Strike (WE), Rarity Level: 6-7. . . . . .Values: $200 up
III-L-17 U.S. Coin Struck Over a Struck Foreign Coin (WE), Rarity Level: 6-7 . . . . .Values: $300 up
III-L-18 Foreign Coin Struck Over a Struck U.S. Coin (WE), Rarity Level: 6-7 . . . . .Values: $400 up
III-L-19 Foreign Coin Struck Over a Struck Foreign Coin (WE), Rarity Level: 7 . . . . .Values: $500 up
III-L-20 Double Strike on Scrap or Junk (E), Rarity Level: 6 . . . . .Values: $50 up
III-L-21 Struck on a Struck Token or Medal (E), Rarity Level: 5-6 . . . . .Values: $100 up
III-L-22 Double-Struck Edge Motto or Design (E), Rarity Level: 6-7 . . . . .Values: $200 up
III-L-23 One Edge Motto or Design Struck Over Another (E), Rarity Level: 7. . . . . .Values: $300 up
III-L-24 Flat Field Doubling (W), Rarity Level: 2-3 . . . . .Values: $1 to $5
III-L-25 Territorial Struck over Struck U.S. Coin: (I) Rarity Level: 6-7 .Values: $200 up
III-L-26 Pattern Struck over Struck U.S. Coin: (I) Rarity Level: 6-7 . . . . .Values: $200 up
III-L-27 Pattern Struck over Struck Pattern:(I) Rarity Level 6-7 . . . . .Values: $200 up
III-L-28 Pattern Struck Over Foreign Coin:(I) Rarity Level 6-7 . . . . Values - $200 up

Collar striking varieties (III-M)

The collar is often referred to as the "Third Die," and is involved in a number of forms of misstrikes. The collar normally rises around the planchet, preventing it from squeezing sideways between the dies and at the same time forming the reeding on reeded coins.

If the collar is out of position or tilted, a partial collar strike results; if completely missing, it causes a broadstrike; if the planchet is not entirely between the dies, an off-center strike.

Flanged partial collar III-M-1

Struck off center
10 to 30 percent III-M-7

Struck off center
31 to 70 percent III-M-8

Struck off center
71 percent or more
III-M-9

III-M-1 Flanged Partial Collar Strike (WE), Rarity Level: 5-6. . . . . .Values: $20 up
III-M-2 Reversed Flanged Partial Collar Strike (WE), Rarity Level: 6-7 . . . . .Values: $35 up
III-M-3 Tilted Partial Collar Strike (WE), Rarity Level: 5-6 . . . . .Values: $20 up
III-M-4 Centered Broadstrike (WE), Rarity Level: 5-6 . . . . .Values: $5 up
III-M-5 Uncentered Broadstrike (WE), Rarity Level: 5 . . . . .Values: $3 up
III-M-6 Reversed Broadstrike (WE), Rarity Level: 6 . . . . .Values: $10 up
III-M-7 Struck Off-Center 10-30% (W), Rarity Level: 3-6 . . . . .Values: $3 up
III-M-8 Struck Off-Center 31-70% (W), Rarity Level: 4-6 . . . . .Values: $5 up
III-M-9 Struck Off-Center 71% or More (W), Rarity Level: 3-5 . . . . .Values: $2 up
III-M-10 Rotated Multi-sided Planchet Strike (W), Rarity Level: 5-6 . . . . .Values: $10 up
III-M-11 Wire Edge Strike (IWE), Rarity Level: 1-2 . . . . .Values: No Extra Value
III-M-12 Struck With the Collar Too High (WE), Rarity Level: 6-7. . . . . .Values: $20 up
III-M-13 Off-Center Slide Strike (W), Rarity Level: 3-6 . . . . .Values: $4 up

Misaligned and rotated (die) strike varieties (III-N)

Misaligned die III-N-1

Normal rotation

90 degrees

180 degrees

One (rarely both) of the dies may be Offset Misaligned, off to one side, or may be tilted (Vertically Misaligned). One die may either have been installed so that it is turned in relation to the other die, or may turn in the holder, or the shank may break allowing the die face to rotate in relation to the opposing die.

Vertical misaligned dies are rarely found, and, like rotated dies, find only limited collector interest. Ninety- and 180-degree rotations are the most popular. Rotations of 14 degrees or less have no value. The 1989-D Congress dollar is found with a nearly

180-degree rotated reverse, currently retailing for around $2,000. Only about 30 have been reported to date.

III-N-1 Offset Die Misalignment Strike (WE), Rarity Level: 3-5 . . . . .Values: $2 up
III-N-2 Vertical Die Misalignment Strike (WE), Rarity Level: 4-6. . . . . .Values: $1 up
III-N-3 Rotated Die Strike - 15 to 45 Degrees (IWE), Rarity Level: 4-6 . . . . .Values: $2 up
III-N-4 Rotated Die Strike - 46 to 135 Degrees (IWE), Rarity Level: 5-6 . . . . .Values: $10 up
III-N-5 Rotated Die Strike - 136 to 180 Degrees (IWE), Rarity Level: 5-6 . . . . .Values: $25 up

Lettered and design edge strike varieties (III-O)

Overlapping edge letters III-O-1

Early U.S. coins and a number of foreign coins have either lettered edges or designs on the edge of the coin. Malfunctions of the application of the motto or design to the edge fall in this section.

III-O-1 Overlapping Edge Motto or Design (WE), Rarity Level: 3-4 . . . . Values: $5 to $10 and up
III-O-2 Wrong Edge Motto or Design (WE), Rarity Level: 5-6-7 . . . . .Values: $50 up
III-O-3 Missing Edge Motto, Design or Security Edge (IWE), Rarity Level: 5-6-7 . . . . .Values: $50 up
III-O-4 Jammed Edge Die Strike (W), Rarity Level: 6. . . . . .Values: $10 up
III-O-5 Misplaced Segment of an Edge Die (E), Rarity Level: 4-7 . . . . .Values: $25 up
III-O-6 Reeded Edge Struck Over a Lettered Edge (IE), Rarity Level: 3-6 . . . . Values: No Extra Value up

Defective strikes and mismatched dies (III-P)

The final section of the Striking Division covers coins that are not properly struck for reasons other than those in previous classes, such as coins struck with mismatched (muled) dies. The mismatched die varieties must be taken on a case by case basis, while the other classes presently have little collector demand or premium.

III-P-1 Defective Strike (WE), Rarity Level: 1. . . . . .Values: No Extra Value
III-P-2 Mismatched Die Strike (E), Rarity Level: 4-7 . . . . .Values: $25 up
III-P-3 Single-Strike Proof (WE), Rarity Level: 4-5 . . . . .Values: Minimal
III-P-4 Single Die-Proof Strike (IE), Rarity Level: 5-6 . . . . .Values: $100 up
III-P-5 Reversed Die Strike (I), Rarity Level: 4-5 . . . . .Values: No Extra Value to Minimal

Official Mint modifications
Division IV

Several mint-produced varieties occur after the coin has been struck, resulting in the addition of the fourth division to my PDS System. Since most of these coins are either unique or are special varieties, each one must be taken on a case by case basis. All classes listed here are by definition intentional.

I have not listed values as the coins falling in these classes, which are sold through regular numismatic channels, are cataloged with the regular issues or are covered in specialized catalogs in their particular area.

Matte proofs (IV-A)

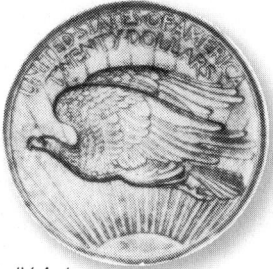

Matte proofs IV-A-1

Matte proofs as a section include several of the forms of proof coins that have the striking characteristics of a mirror proof but have been treated AFTER striking to give them a grainy, non-reflective surface.

IV-A-1 Matte Proof (I), Rarity Level: 3-5 . . . . .Values: Normal Numismatic Value
IV-A-2 Matte Proof on One Side (I), Rarity Level: 7 .Values: Normal Numismatic Value
IV-A-3 Sandblast Proof (I), Rarity Level: 4-6 . . . . .Values: Normal Numismatic Value

Additional engraving (IV-B)

Counterstamp IV-B-3

This section includes any added markings that are placed on the struck coin and struck coins that later were cut into pieces for various purposes. The warning is repeated: Anything done to a coin after the strike is extremely difficult t o authenticate and is much easier to fake than a die struck coin.

IV-B-1 Counterstamp and Countermark (I), Rarity Level: 3-6 . . . . .Values: Normal Numismatic Value
IV-B-2 Perforated and Cut Coins (I), Rarity Level: 4-6 . . . . .Values: Normal Numismatic Value

Restrikes (IV-C)

Restrike with new dies IV-C-7

Restrikes cover a complicated mixture of official use of dies from a variety of sources. Whether or not some were officially sanctioned is always a problem for the collector.

IV-C-1) Restrike on the Same Denomination Planchet (I), Rarity Level: 4-6. . .Values: Normal Numismatic Value
IV-C-2 Restrike on a Different Denomination or Series Planchet (I), Rarity Level: 4-6
. . . . .Values: Normal Numismatic Value
IV-C-3 Restrike on a Foreign Coin (I), Rarity Level: 6-7 . . . . .Values: Normal Numismatic Value
IV-C-4 Restrike on a Token or Medal (I), Rarity Level: 5-6 . . . . .Values: Normal Numismatic Value
IV-C-5 Restruck With the Original Dies (I), Rarity Level: 4-6 . . . . .Values: Normal Numismatic Value
IV-C-6 Restruck With Mismatched Dies (I), Rarity Level: 4-6 . . . . .Values: Normal Numismatic Value
IV-C-7 Copy Strike With New Dies (I), Rarity Level: 3-5 . . . . .Values: Normal Numismatic Value
IV-C-8 Fantasy Strike (I), Rarity Level: 4-6 . . . . .Values: Normal Numismatic Value

After strike modifications

Division V

This division includes both modifications that have value to collectors – and those that don't. I needed a couple of divisions to cover other things that happen to coins to aid in cataloging them. This avoids the false conclusion that an unlisted coin is quite rare, when the exact opposite is more likely to be the case.

Collectible modifications after strike (V-A)

Mint modification V-A-8

This section includes those classes having to do with deliberate modifications of the coin done with a specific purpose or intent that makes them of some value to collectors. Quite often these pieces were made specifically to sell to collectors, or at least to the public, under the guise of being collectible.

V-A-1 Screw Thaler, Rarity Level: 5-6 . . . . .Values: Normal Numismatic Value
V-A-2 Love Token, Rarity Level: 3-6 . . . . .Values: $10 up
V-A-3 Satirical or Primitive Engraving, Rarity Level: 6-7 . . . . .Values: $5 up
V-A-4 Elongated Coin, Rarity Level: 2-7 . . . . Values: 50 cents to $1 and up
V-A-5 Coin Jewelry, Rarity Level: 2-5 . . . . .Values: $1 up
V-A-6 Novelty Coin, Rarity Level: 1-3 . . . . .Values: No Value up to $5 to $10
V-A-7 Toning, Rarity Level: 3-6 . . . . Values: No value up, depending on coloration. Easily faked
V-A-8 Mint Modification, Rarity Level: 4-7 . . . . Values: $5 up. Easily faked
V-A-9 Mint Packaging Mistake, Rarity Level: 5-7 . . . . Values: Nominal $1. Very easily faked

Alterations and damage after the strike (V-B)

Machine doubling damage V-B-1

This section includes those changes in a coin that have no collector value. In most cases, their effect on the coin is to reduce or entirely eliminate any collector value - and in the case of counterfeits they are actually illegal to even own.

V -B-1 Machine Doubling Damage: *NOTE: Machine doubling damage is defined as: "Damage to a coin after the strike, due to die bounce or chatter or die displacement, showing on the struck coin as scrapes on the sides of the design elements, with portions of the coin metal in the relief elements either displaced sideways or downward, depending on the direction of movement of the loose die."* Machine doubling damage, or MDD, is by far the most common form of doubling found on almost any coin in the world. Rarity Level: 0 . . . . Values: Reduces the coin's value
V-B-2 Accidental or Deliberate Damage, Rarity Level: 0 . . . . Values: Reduces the coin's value
V-B-3 Test Cut or Mark, Rarity Level: 0. . . . . Values: Reduces value of coin to face or bullion value
V-B-4 Alteration, Rarity Level: 0 . . . . .Values: Reduces value to face or bullion value
V-B-5 Whizzing, Rarity Level: 0. . . . . . Values: Reduces value sharply and may reduce it to face or bullion value
V-B-6 Counterfeit, Copy, Facsimile, Forgery or Fake, Rarity Level: 0 . . Values: No Value and may be illegal to own
V-B-7 Planchet Deterioration. Very common on copper-plated zinc cents. Rarity level: 0 . . . . .Values: No Value

Pricing Section

COLONIAL COINAGE
MARYLAND
Lord Baltimore

PENNY (DENARIUM)

KM# 1 • **Copper** • **Obv. Legend:** CAECILIVS Dns TERRAE MARIAE

Date	Good	VG	Fine	VF	XF	Unc
(1659) 5 known	—	—	—	—100,000	—	

Note: Stack's Auction 5-04, proof realized $241,500

4 PENCE (GROAT)

KM# 2 • **Silver** • **Obv:** Large bust **Obv. Legend:** CAECILIVS Dns TERRAE MARIAE **Rev:** Large shield

Date	AG	Good	VG	Fine	VF	XF
(1659)	1,250	1,850	3,500	6,250	13,500	20,000

KM# 3 • **Silver** • **Obv:** Small bust **Obv. Legend:** CAECILIVS Dns TERRAE MARIAE **Rev:** Small shield

Date	Good	VG	Fine	VF	XF	Unc
(1659) unique	—	—	—	—	—	—

Note: Norweb $26,400

6 PENCE

KM# 4 • **Silver** • **Obv:** Small bust **Obv. Legend:** CAECILIVS Dns TERRAE MARIAE **Note:** Known in two other rare small-bust varieties and two rare large-bust varieties.

Date	AG	Good	VG	Fine	VF	XF	Unc
(1659)	850	1,400	2,400	4,900	9,000	15,000	—

SHILLING

KM# 6 • **Silver** • **Obv. Legend:** CAECILIVS Dns TERRAE MARIAE **Note:** Varieties exist; one is very rare.

Date	AG	Good	VG	Fine	VF	XF	Unc
(1659)	1,100	1,800	3,000	5,750	13,500	20,000	—

MASSACHUSETTS
New England

3 PENCE

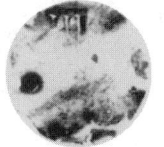

KM# 1 • **Silver** • **Obv:** NE **Rev:** III

Date	AG	Good	VG	Fine	VF	XF
(1652) Unique	—	—	—	—	—	—

Note: Massachusetts Historical Society specimen

6 PENCE

KM# 2 • **Silver** • **Obv:** NE **Rev:** VI

Date	Good	VG	Fine	VF	XF
(1652) 8 known	25,000	50,000	90,000	175,000	—

Note: Garrett $75,000

SHILLING

KM# 3 • **Silver** • **Obv:** NE **Rev:** XII

Date	AG	Good	VG	Fine	VF	XF
(1652)	—	35,000	65,000	100,000	200,000	—

Oak Tree

2 PENCE

KM# 7 • Silver • Note: Small 2 and large 2 varieites exist

Date	AG	Good	VG	Fine	VF	XF	Unc
1662	—	500	900	2,000	3,850	6,500	15,000

3 PENCE

KM# 8 • Silver • Note: Two types of legends.

Date	AG	Good	VG	Fine	VF	XF	Unc
1652	350	600	1,000	2,500	5,500	9,000	—

6 PENCE

KM# 9 • Silver • Note: Three types of legends.

Date	AG	Good	VG	Fine	VF	XF	Unc
1652	400	900	1,100	2,700	6,400	9,500	25,000

SHILLING

KM# 10 • Silver • Note: Two types of legends.

Date	AG	Good	VG	Fine	VF	XF	Unc
1652	350	650	1,100	2,600	5,400	8,800	25,000

Pine Tree

3 PENCE

KM# 11 • Silver • Obv: Tree without berries

Date	AG	Good	VG	Fine	VF	XF	Unc
1652	250	500	700	1,650	3,000	5,600	17,500

KM# 12 • Silver • Obv: Tree with berries

Date	AG	Good	VG	Fine	VF	XF	Unc
1652	250	500	700	1,650	3,200	5,750	18,500

6 PENCE

KM# 13 • Silver • Obv: Tree without berries; "spiney tree"

Date	AG	Good	VG	Fine	VF	XF	Unc
1652	400	700	1,400	2,000	3,750	6,500	20,000

KM# 14 • Silver • Obv: Tree with berries

Date	AG	Good	VG	Fine	VF	XF	Unc
1652	300	500	800	1,750	3,500	6,250	18,000

SHILLING

KM# 15 • Silver • Note: Large planchet. Many varieties exist; some are very rare.

Date	AG	Good	VG	Fine	VF	XF	Unc
1652	350	600	950	2,000	4,350	7,500	20,000

KM# 16 • Silver • Note: Small planchet; large dies. All examples are thought to be contemporary fabrications.

Date	AG	Good	VG	Fine	VF	XF	Unc
1652	—	—	—	—	—	—	—

KM# 17 • Silver • Note: Small planchet; small dies. Many varieties exist; some are very rare.

Date	AG	Good	VG	Fine	VF	XF	Unc
1652	285	525	800	1,700	3,750	6,950	22,500

Willow Tree

3 PENCE

KM# 4 • Silver •

Date	AG	Good	VG	Fine	VF	XF
1652 3 known	—	—	—	—	—	—

6 PENCE

KM# 5 • Silver •

Date	AG	Good	VG	Fine	VF	XF
1652						
14 known	9,000	17,500	30,000	57,500	125,000	200,000

SHILLING

KM# 6 • Silver •

Date	AG	Good	VG	Fine	VF	XF
1652	9,800	18,000	34,000	80,000	150,000	225,000

NEW JERSEY
St. Patrick or Mark Newby

FARTHING

KM# 1 • Copper • Obv. Legend: FLOREAT REX **Rev. Legend:** QUIESCAT PLEBS

Date	AG	Good	VG	Fine	VF	XF	Unc
(1682)	70.00	125	285	700	2,250	4,500	—

Note: One very rare variety is known with reverse legend: QUIESAT PLEBS

KM# 1a • Silver • Obv. Legend: FLOREAT REX **Rev. Legend:** QUIESCAT PLEBS

Date	AG	Good	VG	Fine	VF	XF	Unc
(1682)	800	1,500	2,200	4,500	8,000	12,500	—

HALFPENNY

KM# 2 • Copper • Obv. Legend: FLOREAT REX **Rev. Legend:** ECCE GREX

Date	AG	Good	VG	Fine	VF	XF	Unc
(1682)	180	365	850	1,650	4,000	10,500	—

EARLY AMERICAN TOKENS
American Plantations

1/24 REAL

KM# Tn5.1 • Tin • Obv. Legend: ET HIB REX

Date	AG	Good	VG	Fine	VF	XF	Unc
(1688)	125	200	300	450	750	2,000	—

KM# Tn5.3 • Tin • Rev: Horizontal 4

Date	AG	Good	VG	Fine	VF	XF	Unc
(1688)	275	400	900	1,500	2,700	5,000	—

KM# Tn5.4 • Tin • Obv. Legend: ET HIB REX

Date	AG	Good	VG	Fine	VF	XF	Unc
(1688)	—	250	450	750	1,400	2,650	9,000

KM# Tn6 • Tin • Rev: Arms of Scotland left, Ireland right

Date	AG	Good	VG	Fine	VF	XF	Unc
(1688)	450	750	1,250	2,000	3,000	6,500	—

KM# Tn5.2 • Tin • Obv: Rider's head left of "B" in legend **Note:** Restrikes made in 1828 from two obverse dies.

Date	AG	Good	VG	Fine	VF	XF	Unc
(1828)	75.00	110	175	275	500	1,000	—

Elephant

KM# Tn1.1 • 15.5500 g., Copper • Note: Thick planchet.

Date	AG	Good	VG	Fine	VF	XF	Unc
(1664)	125	200	300	500	1,000	1,750	3,850

KM# Tn1.2 • Copper • Note: Thin planchet.

Date	AG	Good	VG	Fine	VF	XF	Unc
(1664)	175	300	500	850	3,000	5,500	11,750

KM# Tn2 • Copper • Rev: Diagonals tie shield

Date	AG	Good	VG	Fine	VF	XF	Unc
(1664)	250	450	650	2,250	6,500	10,000	17,500

KM# Tn3 • Copper • Rev: Sword right side of shield

Date	AG	Good	VG	Fine	VF	XF
(1664) 3 known	—	—	—	—	12,500	

Note: Norweb $1,320

KM# Tn4 • Copper • Rev. Legend: LON DON

Date	AG	Good	VG	Fine	VF	XF	Unc
(1684)	340	650	1,000	2,250	4,000	7,000	17,500

KM# Tn7 • Copper • Rev. Legend: NEW ENGLAND

Date	AG	Good	VG	Fine	VF	XF
(1694) 2 known	—	—	50,000	75,000	95,000	140,000

Note: Norweb $25,300

KM# Tn8.1 • Copper • Rev. Legend: CAROLINA (PROPRIETORS)

Date	AG	Good	VG	Fine	VF	XF
(1694) 5 known	—	—	4,750	6,500	14,000	22,500

Note: Norweb $35,200

KM# Tn8.2 • Copper • Rev. Legend: CAROLINA (PROPRIETORS, O over E)

Date	AG	Good	VG	Fine	VF	XF	Unc
1694	1,300	2,500	4,000	6,000	12,000	17,500	—

Note: Norweb $17,600

Gloucester

KM# Tn15 • Copper • Obv. Legend: GLOVCESTER COVRTHOVSE VIRGINIA **Rev. Legend:** RIGHAVLT DAWSON.ANNO.DOM.1714.

Date	AG	Good	VG	Fine	VF	XF
(1714) 2 known	—	—	—	—	—	—

Note: Garrett $36,000

Hibernia-Voce Populi

FARTHING

KM# Tn21.1 • Copper • Note: Large letters

Date	AG	Good	VG	Fine	VF	XF	Unc
1760	125	200	325	600	1,600	3,000	8,500

KM# Tn21.2 • Copper • Note: Small letters

Date	AG	Good	VG	Fine	VF	XF	Unc
1760	—	650	1,250	2,750	7,500	13,500	—

Note: Norweb $5,940.

HALFPENNY

KM# Tn22 • Copper •

Date	AG	Good	VG	Fine	VF	XF	Unc
1700 Extremely rare	—	—	—	—	—	—	—

Note: Date is in error; ex-Roper $575. Norweb $577.50. Stack's Americana, VF, $2,900.

1760	40.00	70.00	135	175	365	675	2,500
1760	50.00	80.00	135	195	425	775	3,500

Note: legend VOOE POPULI

1760 P below bust	65.00	100.00	185	350	700	1,750	8,000
1760 P in front of bust	55.00	90.00	170	325	600	1,400	6,500

Higley or Granby

KM# Tn16 • Copper • Obv. Legend: CONNECTICVT **Rev. Legend:** THE VALVE OF THREE PENCE

Date	AG	Good	VG	Fine	VF	XF
1737	—	10,000	18,000	40,000	80,000	—

Note: Garrett $16,000

KM# Tn17 • Copper • Obv. Legend: THE VALVE OF THREE PENCE **Rev. Legend:** I AM GOOD COPPER

Date	AG	Good	VG	Fine	VF	XF
1737 2 known	—	11,000	20,000	40,000	85,000	—

Note: ex-Norweb $6,875

KM# Tn18.1 • Copper • Obv. Legend: VALUE ME AS YOU PLEASE **Rev. Legend:** I AM GOOD COPPER

Date	AG	Good	VG	Fine	VF	XF
1737	6,500	10,000	18,000	40,000	80,000	—

KM# Tn18.2 • Copper • Obv. Legend: VALVE.ME.AS.YOU.PLEASE. **Rev. Legend:** I AM GOOD COPPER.

Date	AG	Good	VG	Fine	VF	XF
1737 2 known	—	—	—	—	—	275,000

KM# Tn19 • Copper • Rev: Broad axe

Date	AG	Good	VG	Fine	VF	XF
(1737)	—	10,000	18,000	35,000	125,000	—

Note: Garrett $45,000

1739 5 known	—	—	—	—	—	—

Note: Eliasberg $12,650. Oechsner $9,900. Steinberg (holed) $4,400.

KM# Tn20 • Copper • Obv. Legend: THE WHEELE GOES ROUND **Rev:** J CUT MY WAY THROUGH

Date	AG	Good	VG	Fine	VF	XF
(1737) unique	—	—	—	150,000	—	—

Note: Roper $60,500

New Yorke

KM# Tn9 • Brass • Obv. Legend: NEW.YORK.IN.AMERICA

Date	AG	Good	VG	Fine	VF	XF	Unc
1700	1,800	3,500	5,500	13,000	22,500	35,000	—

KM# Tn9a • White Metal • Obv. Legend: NEW.YORK.IN.AMERICA

Date	AG	Good	VG	Fine	VF	XF
1700 4 known	—	—	6,000	15,000	28,000	50,000

Pitt

FARTHING

KM# Tn23 • Copper •

Date	AG	Good	VG	Fine	VF	XF
1766	—	—	—	7,500	22,000	35,000

HALFPENNY

KM# Tn24 • Copper •

Date	AG	Good	VG	Fine	VF	XF	Unc
1766	140	250	400	700	1,500	2,750	7,500

KM# Tn24a • Silver Plated Copper •

Date	AG	Good	VG	Fine	VF	XF	Unc
1766	—	—	—	—	2,250	5,000	12,000

ROYAL PATENT COINAGE
Hibernia

FARTHING

KM# 20 • Copper • Note: Pattern.

Date	AG	Good	VG	Fine	VF	XF	Unc
1722	135	235	375	500	1,000	2,600	7,750

KM# 24 • Copper • Obv: 1722 obverse **Obv. Legend:** ...D:G:REX.

Date	AG	Good	VG	Fine	VF	XF	Unc
1723	20.00	40.00	60.00	90.00	150	350	—

KM# 25 • Copper • Obv. Legend: DEI • GRATIA • REX •

Date	AG	Good	VG	Fine	VF	XF	Unc
1723	25.00	45.00	60.00	180	300	550	950
1724	—	90.00	125	225	600	1,350	3,500

KM# 25a • Silver •

Date	AG	Good	VG	Fine	VF	XF	Unc
1723	—	—	1,600	2,250	4,000	5,500	10,000

HALFPENNY

KM# 21 • Copper • Obv: Bust right **Obv. Legend:** GEORGIUS • DEI • GRATIA • REX • **Rev:** Harp left, head left **Rev. Legend:** • HIBERNIA • 1722 •

Date	AG	Good	VG	Fine	VF	XF	Unc
1722	50.00	90.00	110	160	325	700	1,750

KM# 22 • Copper • Obv: Bust right **Obv. Legend:** GEORGIVS D: G: REX **Rev:** Harp left, head right **Rev. Legend:** • HIBERNIÆ • **Note:** "Rocks Reverse" pattern.

Date	AG	Good	VG	Fine	VF	XF	Unc
1722	—	—	—	2,750	3,850	8,500	—

KM# 23.1 • Copper • Rev: Harp right

Date	AG	Good	VG	Fine	VF	XF	Unc
1722	35.00	60.00	80.00	120	285	600	1,400
1723	20.00	35.00	45.00	75.00	190	280	800
1723/22	35.00	60.00	80.00	150	375	750	1,750
1724	25.00	50.00	90.00	160	360	825	2,000

KM# 23.2 • Copper • Obv: DEII error in legend

Date	AG	Good	VG	Fine	VF	XF	Unc
1722	75.00	125	160	325	750	1,400	2,750

KM# 26 • Copper • Rev: Large head **Note:**
Rare. Generally mint state only. Probably a pattern.

Date	AG	Good	VG	Fine	VF	XF	Unc
1723	—	—	—	—	—	—	—

KM# 27 • Copper • Rev: Continuous legend
over head

Date	AG	Good	VG	Fine	VF	XF	Unc
1724	45.00	80.00	150	300	900	1,500	3,500

Rosa Americana

HALFPENNY

KM# 1 • Copper • Obv. Legend: D • G • REX •

Date	AG	Good	VG	Fine	VF	XF	Unc
1722	20.00	50.00	140	250	525	1,050	4,000

KM# 2 • Copper • Obv: Uncrowned rose **Obv.
Legend:** ... • DEI • GRATIA • REX • **Note:** Several
varieties exist.

Date	AG	Good	VG	Fine	VF	XF	Unc
1722	50.00	90.00	135	250	450	950	3,500
1723		385	700	850	1,750	3,600	—	—

KM# 3 • Copper • Rev. Legend: VTILE DVLCI

Date	AG	Good	VG	Fine	VF	XF	Unc
1722		250	450	850	2,200	3,800	7,500	—

KM# 9 • Copper • Rev: Crowned rose

Date	AG	Good	VG	Fine	VF	XF	Unc
1723	45.00	85.00	110	165	425	1,000	4,500

PENNY

KM# 4 • Copper • Rev. Legend: UTILE DULCI
Note: Several varieties exist.

Date	AG	Good	VG	Fine	VF	XF	Unc
1722	60.00	100.00	135	240	450	950	3,750

KM# 5 • Copper • Note: Several varieties exist.
Also known in two rare pattern types with long hair
ribbons, one with V's for U's on the obverse.

Date	AG	Good	VG	Fine	VF	XF	Unc
1722	18.00	35.00	150	275	750	1,350	5,600

KM# 10 • Copper • Note: Several varieties exist.

Date	AG	Good	VG	Fine	VF	XF	Unc
1723	40.00	75.00	110	175	425	900	3,600

KM# 12 • Copper • Note: Pattern.

Date	AG	Good	VG	Fine	VF	XF
1724 2 known	—	—	—	—	—	—

KM# 13 • **Copper** • **Rev. Legend:** ROSA: SINE: SPINA •

Date	AG	Good	VG	Fine	VF	XF
(1724) 5 known	—	—	—	—	—	—
Note: Norweb $2,035						

KM# 14 • **Copper** • **Obv:** George II **Note:** Pattern.

Date	AG	Good	VG	Fine	VF	XF
1727 2 known	—	—	—	—	—	—

2 PENCE

KM# 6 • **Copper** • **Rev:** Motto with scroll

Date	AG	Good	VG	Fine	VF	XF	Unc
(1722)	80.00	150	200	425	700	1,200	6,250

KM# 7 • **Copper** • **Rev:** Motto without scroll

Date	AG	Good	VG	Fine	VF	XF
(1722) 3 known	—	—	—	—	—	—

KM# 8.1 • **Copper** • **Obv. Legend:** ...REX • **Rev:** Dated

Date	AG	Good	VG	Fine	VF	XF	Unc
1722	70.00	125	175	275	750	1,500	5,500

KM# 8.2 • **Copper** • **Obv. Legend:** ...REX

Date	AG	Good	VG	Fine	VF	XF	Unc
1722	70.00	125	175	275	775	1,600	6,000

KM# 11 • **Copper** • **Obv:** No stop after REX **Rev:** Stop after 1723 **Note:** Several varieties exist.

Date	AG	Good	VG	Fine	VF	XF	Unc
1723	65.00	120	160	285	550	1,200	3,500

KM# 15 • **Copper** • **Note:** Pattern. Two varieties exist; both extremely rare.

Date	AG	Good	VG	Fine	VF	XF	Unc
1724	—	—	—	—	—	—	—
Note: Stack's 5-05 choice AU realized $25,300. Ex-Garrett $5,775. Stack's Americana, XF, $10,925							

KM# 16 • **Copper** • **Obv:** Bust left **Rev:** Crowned rose **Note:** Pattern.

Date	AG	Good	VG	Fine	VF	XF
1733 4 known	—	—	—	—	—	—
Note: Norweb $19,800						

Virginia Halfpenny

KM# Tn25.1 • **Copper** • **Rev:** Small 7s in date. **Note:** Struck on Irish halfpenny planchets.

Date	Good	VG	Fine	VF	XF	Unc	Proof
1773	—	—	—	—	—	—	—22,000

KM# Tn25.2 • **Copper** • **Obv. Legend:** GEORGIVS •... **Rev:** Varieties with 7 or 8 strings in harp

Date	AG	Good	VG	Fine	VF	XF	Unc
1773	30.00	50.00	70.00	110	235	425	1,000

KM# Tn25.3 • Copper • Obv. Legend:
GEORGIVS... **Rev:** Varieties with 6, 7 or 8 strings
in harp

Date	AG	Good	VG	Fine	VF	XF	Unc
1773	35.00	60.00	75.00	135	275	500	1,250

KM# Tn25.4 • Copper • Obv. Legend:
GEORGIVS... **Rev:** 8 harp strings, dot on cross

Date	AG	Good	VG	Fine	VF	XF	Unc
1773	—	—	—	—	—	—	—

Note: ex-Steinberg $2,600

KM# Tn26 • Silver • Note: So-called "shilling"
silver proofs.

Date	AG	Good	VG	Fine	VF	XF	Unc
1774 6 known	—	—	—	—	—	—	—

Note: Garrett $23,000

REVOLUTIONARY COINAGE
Continental "Dollar"

KM# EA1 • Pewter • Obv. Legend:
CURRENCY.

Date	AG	Good	VG	Fine	VF	XF	Unc
1776	—	7,500	9,350	12,000	21,000	32,500	70,000

KM# EA2 • Pewter • Obv. Legend:
CURRENCY, EG FECIT.

Date	AG	Good	VG	Fine	VF	XF	Unc
1776	—	8,000	10,500	13,500	25,000	36,000	75,000

KM# EA2a • Silver • Obv. Legend:
CURRENCY, EG FECIT.

Date	AG	Good	VG	Fine	VF	XF
1776 2 known	—	—	—	300,000	450,000	—

KM# EA3 • Pewter • Obv. Legend:
CURRENCEY

Date	AG	Good	VG	Fine	VF	XF
1776 extremely rare	—	—	—	—	—	100,000

KM# EA4 • Pewter • Obv. Legend:
CURRENCY. **Rev:** Floral cross.

Date	AG	Good	VG	Fine	VF	XF
1776 3 recorded	—	—	—	—	—	400,000

Note: Norweb $50,600. Johnson $25,300

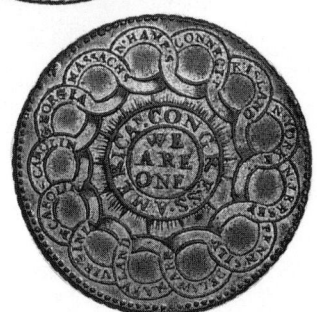

KM# EA5 • Pewter • Obv. Legend: CURENCY.

Date	Good	VG	Fine	VF	XF	Unc
1776	7,500	9,500	12,000	22,500	33,000	65,000

KM# EA5a • Brass • Obv. Legend:
CURENCY. **Note:** Two varieties exist.

Date	AG	Good	VG	Fine	VF	XF
1776	—	22,500	28,500	36,000	70,000	110,000

KM# EA5b • Silver • Obv. Legend:
CURENCY.

Date	AG	Good	VG	Fine	VF	XF
1776 unique	—	—	—	300,000	450,000	—

Note: Romano $99,000

STATE COINAGE
CONNECTICUT

KM# 1 • Copper • Obv: Bust facing right.

Date	AG	Good	VG	Fine	VF	XF	Unc
1785	35.00	55.00	90.00	200	650	1,750	—

KM# 2 • Copper • Obv: "African head."

Date	AG	Good	VG	Fine	VF	XF	Unc
1785	55.00	85.00	150	600	1,500	3,800	—

KM# 3.1 • Copper • Obv: Mailed bust facing left.

Date	AG	Good	VG	Fine	VF	XF	Unc
1785	125	220	375	750	1,800	3,850	—
1786	30.00	50.00	90.00	175	475	1,200	—
1787	30.00	50.00	85.00	160	450	1,350	—
1788	30.00	50.00	80.00	160	435	1,100	—

KM# 3.3 • Copper • Obv: Perfect date. **Rev. Legend:** IN DE ET.

Date	AG	Good	VG	Fine	VF	XF	Unc
1787	50.00	80.00	125	350	750	1,500	—

KM# 3.4 • Copper • Obv. Legend: CONNLC.

Date	AG	Good	VG	Fine	VF	XF	Unc
1788	44.00	60.00	120	240	650	1,850	—

KM# 4 • Copper • Obv: Small mailed bust facing left. **Rev. Legend:** ETLIB INDE.

Date	AG	Good	VG	Fine	VF	XF	Unc
1786	45.00	75.00	150	350	900	2,100	—

KM# 5 • Copper • Obv: Small mailed bust facing right. **Rev. Legend:** INDE ET LIB.

Date	AG	Good	VG	Fine	VF	XF	Unc
1786	60.00	100.00	175	450	2,000	4,250	—

KM# 6 • Copper • Obv: Large mailed bust facing right.

Date	AG	Good	VG	Fine	VF	XF	Unc
1786	55.00	90.00	160	400	1,750	3,750	—

KM# 7 • Copper • Obv: "Hercules head."

Date	AG	Good	VG	Fine	VF	XF	Unc
1786	60.00	110	220	600	2,500	5,800	—

KM# 8.1 • Copper • Obv: Draped bust.

KM# 8.2 • Copper • Obv: Draped bust. **Note:** Many varieties.

Date	AG	Good	VG	Fine	VF	XF	Unc
1787	28.00	42.00	70.00	115	325	750	—

KM# 8.3 • Copper • Obv. Legend: AUCIORI.

Date	AG	Good	VG	Fine	VF	XF	Unc
1787	30.00	55.00	90.00	175	450	1,000	—

KM# 8.4 • Copper • Obv. Legend: AUCTOPI.

Date	AG	Good	VG	Fine	VF	XF	Unc
1787	35.00	65.00	110	200	650	1,650	—

KM# 8.5 • Copper • Obv. Legend: AUCTOBI.

Date	AG	Good	VG	Fine	VF	XF	Unc
1787	35.00	65.00	110	200	625	1,550	—

KM# 8.6 • Copper • Obv. Legend: CONNFC.

Date	AG	Good	VG	Fine	VF	XF	Unc
1787	32.00	60.00	90.00	160	475	1,000	—

KM# 8.7 • Copper • Obv. Legend: CONNLC.

Date	AG	Good	VG	Fine	VF	XF	Unc
1787	50.00	75.00	150	300	650	1,850	—

KM# 8.8 • Copper • Rev. Legend: FNDE.

Date	AG	Good	VG	Fine	VF	XF	Unc
1787	35.00	55.00	80.00	160	475	1,400	—

KM# 8.9 • Copper • Rev. Legend: ETLIR.

Date	AG	Good	VG	Fine	VF	XF	Unc
1787	32.00	50.00	75.00	150	440	1,175	—

KM# 8.10 • Copper • Rev. Legend: ETIIB.

Date	AG	Good	VG	Fine	VF	XF	Unc
1787	35.00	50.00	75.00	150	450	1,200	—
Date	AG	Good	VG	Fine	VF	XF	Unc
1786	50.00	90.00	175	475	1,150	2,750	—

KM# 9 • Copper • Obv: Small head. **Rev. Legend:** ETLIB INDE.

Date	AG	Good	VG	Fine	VF	XF	Unc
1787	65.00	110	180	375	1,500	3,750	—

KM# 10 • Copper • Obv: Small head. **Rev. Legend:** INDE ET LIB.

Date	AG	Good	VG	Fine	VF	XF	Unc
1787	75.00	135	200	450	2,000	4,000	—

KM# 11 • Copper • Obv: Medium bust. **Note:** Two reverse legend types exist.

Date	AG	Good	VG	Fine	VF	XF	Unc
1787	60.00	90.00	150	350	1,500	3,000	—

KM# 12 • Copper • Obv: "Muttonhead" variety. **Note:** Extremely rare with legend INDE ET LIB.

Date	AG	Good	VG	Fine	VF	XF	Unc
1787	60.00	90.00	175	500	2,200	4,500	—

KM# 13 • Copper • Obv: "Laughing head"

Date	AG	Good	VG	Fine	VF	XF	Unc
1787	35.00	60.00	120	240	650	1,800	—

KM# 14 • Copper • Obv: "Horned head"

Date	AG	Good	VG	Fine	VF	XF	Unc
1787	30.00	50.00	80.00	165	450	1,200	—

KM# 15 • Copper • Rev. Legend: IND ET LIB

Date	AG	Good	VG	Fine	VF	XF	Unc
1787/8	50.00	85.00	170	450	1,500	4,000	—
1787/1887	85.00	150	225	600	1,750	4,500	—

KM# 16 • Copper • Obv. Legend: CONNECT. **Rev. Legend:** INDE ET LIB. **Note:** Two additional scarce reverse legend types exist.

Date	AG	Good	VG	Fine	VF	XF	Unc
1787	35.00	50.00	120	240	550	1,500	—

KM# 20 • Copper • Obv: Mailed bust facing right.

Date	AG	Good	VG	Fine	VF	XF	Unc
1788	28.00	40.00	85.00	180	550	1,450	—

KM# 21 • Copper • Obv: Small mailed bust facing right.

Date	AG	Good	VG	Fine	VF	XF	Unc
1788	850	1,500	2,950	4,150	9,500	18,500	—

KM# 22.1 • Copper • Obv: Draped bust facing left. **Rev. Legend:** INDE ET LIB.

Date	AG	Good	VG	Fine	VF	XF	Unc
1788	45.00	70.00	125	285	675	1,650	—

KM# 22.2 • Copper • Rev. Legend: INDLET LIB.

Date	AG	Good	VG	Fine	VF	XF	Unc
1788	55.00	80.00	175	375	800	1,750	—

KM# 22.3 • Copper • Obv. Legend: CONNEC.
Rev. Legend: INDE ET LIB.

Date	AG	Good	VG	Fine	VF	XF	Unc
1788	58.00	85.00	190	400	875	1,850	—

KM# 22.4 • Copper • Obv. Legend: CONNEC.
Rev. Legend: INDL ET LIB.

Date	AG	Good	VG	Fine	VF	XF	Unc
1788	58.00	85.00	190	400	875	1,850	—

MASSACHUSETTS

HALFPENNY

KM# 17 • Copper •

Date	AG	Good	VG	Fine	VF	XF
1776 unique	—	—	—	200,000	—	—

Note: Garrett $40,000

PENNY

KM# 18 • Copper •

Date	AG	Good	VG	Fine	VF	XF
1776 unique	—	—	—	—	—	—

HALF CENT

KM# 19 • Copper • Note: Varieties exist; some
are rare.

Date	AG	Good	VG	Fine	VF	XF	Unc
1787	60.00	90.00	140	210	550	1,000	3,250
1788	70.00	110	175	260	585	1,100	3,500

CENT

KM# 20.1 • Copper • Rev: Arrows in right talon

Date	Good	VG	Fine	VF	XF	Unc
1787 7 known	9,000	22,500	45,000	—	—	—350,000

Note: Ex-Bushnell-Brand $8,800. Garrett $5,500

KM# 20.2 • Copper • Rev: Arrows in left talon

Date	AG	Good	VG	Fine	VF	XF	Unc
1787	60.00	90.00	165	240	650	1,250	6,800

KM# 20.3 • Copper • Rev: "Horned eagle" die break

Date	AG	Good	VG	Fine	VF	XF	Unc
1787	70.00	110	190	275	775	1,500	7,750

KM# 20.4 • Copper • Rev: Without period after Massachusetts

Date	AG	Good	VG	Fine	VF	XF	Unc
1788	70.00	105	190	260	675	1,600	6,250

KM# 20.5 • Copper • Rev: Period after Massachusetts, normal S's

Date	AG	Good	VG	Fine	VF	XF	Unc
1788	60.00	90.00	170	235	600	1,375	5,750

KM# 20.6 • Copper • Rev: Period after Massachusetts, S's like 8's

Date	AG	Good	VG	Fine	VF	XF	Unc
1788	50.00	75.00	135	200	575	1,250	5,400

NEW HAMPSHIRE

KM# 1 • Copper •

Date	AG	Good	VG	Fine	VF	XF
1776 extremely rare	—	—	75,000	—	—	—

Note: Garrett $13,000

NEW JERSEY

KM# 8 • Copper • Obv: Date below draw bar.

Date	AG	Good	VG	Fine	VF	XF
1786 extremely rare	—	—	48,000	110,000	—	

Note: Garrett $52,000

KM# 9 • Copper • Obv: Large horse head, date below plow, no coulter on plow.

Date	AG	Good	VG	Fine	VF	XF	Unc
1786	450	750	1,450	2,350	7,500	20,000	—

KM# 10 • Copper • Rev: Narrow shield, straight beam.

Date	AG	Good	VG	Fine	VF	XF	Unc
1786	38.00	60.00	140	210	550	1,350	—

KM# 11.1 • Copper • Rev: Wide shield, curved beam. **Note:** Varieties exist.

Date	AG	Good	VG	Fine	VF	XF	Unc
1786	45.00	75.00	150	225	600	2,000	—

KM# 11.2 • Copper • Obv: Bridle variety (die break). **Note:** Reverse varieties exist.

Date	AG	Good	VG	Fine	VF	XF	Unc
1786	45.00	70.00	145	235	650	2,400	—

KM# 12.1 • Copper • Rev: Plain shield. **Note:** Small planchet. Varieties exist.

Date	AG	Good	VG	Fine	VF	XF	Unc
1787	35.00	55.00	110	200	500	1,050	—

KM# 12.2 • Copper • Rev: Shield heavily outlined. **Note:** Small planchet.

Date	AG	Good	VG	Fine	VF	XF	Unc
1787	38.00	60.00	120	215	550	1,150	—

KM# 13 • Copper • Obv: "Serpent head."

Date	AG	Good	VG	Fine	VF	XF	Unc
1787	55.00	85.00	200	375	1,500	3,750	—

KM# 14 • Copper • Rev: Plain shield. **Note:** Large planchet. Varieties exist.

Date	AG	Good	VG	Fine	VF	XF	Unc
1787	45.00	60.00	135	240	750	1,650	—

KM# 15 • Copper • Rev. Legend: PLURIBS.

Date	AG	Good	VG	Fine	VF	XF	Unc
1787	85.00	150	275	450	1,000	2,800	—

KM# 16 • Copper • Obv: Horse's head facing right. **Note:** Varieties exist.

Date	AG	Good	VG	Fine	VF	XF	Unc
1788	42.00	60.00	115	190	700	1,275	—

KM# 17 • Copper • Rev: Fox before legend. **Note:** Varieties exist.

Date	AG	Good	VG	Fine	VF	XF	Unc
1788	75.00	135	285	550	1,750	4,400	—

KM# 18 • Copper • Obv: Horse's head facing left. **Note:** Varieties exist.

Date	AG	Good	VG	Fine	VF	XF	Unc
1788	235	400	850	1,500	4,800	13,000	—

NEW YORK

Nova Eboracs

KM# 1 • Copper • Obv: Bust right **Obv. Legend:** NON VI VIRTUTE VICI. **Rev. Legend:** NEO-EBORACENSIS

Date	AG	Good	VG	Fine	VF	XF
1786	3,250	5,000	7,500	15,000	35,000	—

KM# 2 • Copper • Obv: Eagle on globe facing right. **Obv. Legend:** EXCELSIOR **Rev. Legend:** E. PLURIBUS UNUM

Date	AG	Good	VG	Fine	VF	XF	Unc
1787	1,400	2,250	3,850	7,000	17,500	32,500	—

KM# 3 • Copper • Obv: Eagle on globe facing left. **Obv. Legend:** EXCELSIOR **Rev. Legend:** E. PLURIBUS UNUM

Date	AG	Good	VG	Fine	VF	XF
1787	1,250	2,000	3,500	6,500	16,500	32,000

KM# 4 • Copper • Obv. Legend: EXCELSIOR **Rev:** Large eagle, arrows in right talon. **Rev. Legend:** E. PLURIBUS UNUM

Date	AG	Good	VG	Fine	VF	XF
1787	—	4,500	9,000	16,500	35,000	55,000

Note: Norweb $18,700

KM# 5 • Copper • Obv: George Clinton. **Rev. Legend:** EXCELSIOR

Date	AG	Good	VG	Fine	VF	XF
1787	4,500	7,500	14,500	26,000	48,500	125,000

KM# 6 • Copper • Obv: Indian. **Obv. Legend:** LIBERNATUS LIBERTATEM DEFENDO **Rev:** New York arms. **Rev. Legend:** EXCELSIOR

Date	AG	Good	VG	Fine	VF	XF	Unc
1787	4,500	7,000	10,000	17,500	40,000	90,000	—

KM# 7 • Copper • Obv: Indian. **Obv. Legend:** LIBERNATUS LIBERTATEM DEFENDO **Rev:** Eagle on globe. **Rev. Legend:** NEO EBORACUS EXCELSIOR

Date	AG	Good	VG	Fine	VF	XF
1787	6,000	11,000	15,000	27,500	55,000	120,000

KM# 8 • Copper • Obv: Indian. **Rev:** George III.

Date	AG	Good	VG	Fine	VF	XF
1787 3 Known	—	— 60,000		—	—	—

KM# 9 • Copper • Obv: Bust right **Obv. Legend:** NOVA EBORAC. **Rev:** Figure seated right. **Rev. Legend:** VIRT.ET.LIB.

Date	AG	Good	VG	Fine	VF	XF	Unc
1787	75.00	115	220	360	1,150	2,700	—

KM# 10 • Copper • Obv: Bust right **Obv. Legend:** NOVA EBORAC **Rev:** Figure seated left. **Rev. Legend:** VIRT.ET.LIB.

Date	AG	Good	VG	Fine	VF	XF	Unc
1787	60.00	100.00	200	325	825	1,750	—

KM# 11 • Copper • Obv: Small head, star above. **Obv. Legend:** NOVA EBORAC. **Rev:** Figure seated left **Rev. Legend:** VIRT.ET.LIB.

Date	AG	Good	VG	Fine	VF	XF	Unc
1787	2,450	3,500	5,200	7,500	20,000	55,000	—

KM# 12 • Copper • Obv: Large head, two quatrefoils left. **Obv. Legend:** NOVA EBORAC. **Rev:** Figure seated left **Rev. Legend:** VIRT.ET.LIB.

Date	AG	Good	VG	Fine	VF	XF	Unc
1787	350	600	1,250	2,250	7,500	15,000	—

Machin's Mill

KM# 13 • Copper • Note: Crude, lightweight imitations of the British Halfpenny were struck at Machin's Mill in large quantities bearing the obverse legends: GEORGIVS II REX, GEORGIVS III REX, and GEORGIUS III REX, with the BRITANNIA reverse. There are many different mulings. Plain

crosses in the shield of Britannia are noticeable on high grade pieces, unlike common British made imitations, which usually have outlined crosses in the shield. Some Machin's Mill varieties are very rare.

Date	AG	Good	VG	Fine	VF	XF
(1747-1788)	40.00	70.00	120	250	750	2,200

Note: Prices are for most common within date ranges. Examples are dated: 1747, 1771, 1772, 1774, 1775, 1776, 1777, 1778, 1784, 1785, 1786, 1787 and 1788. Other dates may exist

KM# 1 • Copper • Obv: Bust right **Obv. Legend:** NON VI VIRTUTE VICI. **Rev. Legend:** NEO-EBORACENSIS

Date	AG	Good	VG	Fine	VF	XF	Unc
1786	3,250	5,000	7,500	15,000	35,000	—	—

KM# 2 • Copper • Obv: Eagle on globe facing right. **Obv. Legend:** EXCELSIOR **Rev. Legend:** E. PLURIBUS UNUM

Date	AG	Good	VG	Fine	VF	XF
1787	1,400	2,250	3,850	7,000	17,500	32,500

KM# 3 • Copper • Obv: Eagle on globe facing left. **Obv. Legend:** EXCELSIOR **Rev. Legend:** E. PLURIBUS UNUM

Date	AG	Good	VG	Fine	VF	XF	Unc
1787	1,250	2,000	3,500	6,500	16,500	32,000	—

VERMONT

KM# 4 • Copper • Obv. Legend: EXCELSIOR
Rev: Large eagle, arrows in right talon. **Rev.**
Legend: E. PLURIBUS UNUM

Date	AG	Good	VG	Fine	VF	XF
1787	—	4,500	9,000	16,500	35,000	55,000

Note: Norweb $18,700

KM# 5 • Copper • Obv: George Clinton. **Rev.**
Legend: EXCELSIOR

Date	AG	Good	VG	Fine	VF	XF
1787	4,500	7,500	14,500	26,000	48,500	125,000

KM# 6 • Copper • Obv: Indian. **Obv. Legend:**
LIBERNATUS LIBERTATEM DEFENDO **Rev:** New
York arms. **Rev. Legend:** EXCELSIOR

Date	AG	Good	VG	Fine	VF	XF
1787	4,500	7,000	10,000	17,500	40,000	90,000

KM# 7 • Copper • Obv: Indian. **Obv. Legend:**
LIBERNATUS LIBERTATEM DEFENDO **Rev:**
Eagle on globe. **Rev. Legend:** NEO EBORACUS
EXCELSIOR

Date	AG	Good	VG	Fine	VF	XF
1787	6,000	11,000	15,000	27,500	55,000	120,000

KM# 8 • Copper • Obv: Indian. **Rev:** George III.

Date	AG	Good	VG	Fine	VF	XF
1787 3 Known	—	—	60,000	—	—	—

KM# 1 • Copper • Rev. Legend: IMMUNE
COLUMBIA

Date	AG	Good	VG	Fine	VF	XF	Unc
(1785)	3,750	5,500	9,000	12,750	32,000	—	—

KM# 2 • Copper • Obv: Sun rising over field with
plow **Obv. Legend:** VERMONTIS. RES. PUBLICA.
Rev: Eye, with rays and stars **Rev. Legend:**
QUARTA. DECIMA. STELLA.

Date	AG	Good	VG	Fine	VF	XF	Unc
1785	120	290	650	1,450	4,500	11,000	—

KM# 3 • Copper • Obv: Sun rising over field with
plow **Obv. Legend:** VERMONTS. RES. PUBLICA.
Rev: Eye, with rays and stars **Rev. Legend:**
QUARTA. DECIMA. STELLA.

Date	AG	Good	VG	Fine	VF	XF	Unc
1785	150	275	600	1,250	3,100	7,500	—

KM# 4 • Copper • Obv: Sun rising over field with
plow **Obv. Legend:** VERMONTENSIUM.
RES.PUBLICA **Rev:** Eye, with pointed rays and
stars **Rev. Legend:** QUARTA. DECIMA. STELLA.

Date	AG	Good	VG	Fine	VF	XF	Unc
1786	140	235	400	750	2,000	4,400	—

KM# 5 • Copper • Obv: "Baby head." **Obv. Legend:** AUCTORI: VERMON: **Rev:** Seated figure left **Rev. Legend:** ET:LIB: INDE

Date	AG	Good	VG	Fine	VF	XF	Unc
1786	200	350	650	1,750	4,800	12,500	—

KM# 6 • Copper • Obv: Bust facing left. **Obv. Legend:** VERMON: AUCTORI: **Rev:** Seated figure left **Rev. Legend:** INDE ETLIB

Date	AG	Good	VG	Fine	VF	XF
1786	115	175	350	800	2,800	4,750
1787 extremely rare	—	—	4,500	11,000	27,500	44,000

KM# 7 • Copper • Obv: Bust facing right. **Obv. Legend:** VERMON. AUCTORI. **Rev:** Seated figure left **Rev. Legend:** INDE ETLIB **Note:** Varieties exist.

Date	AG	Good	VG	Fine	VF	XF	Unc
1787	—	150	260	575	1,450	3,000	—

KM# 8 • Copper • Obv: Bust right **Obv. Legend:** VERMON AUCTORI **Rev:** Seated figure left **Note:** Britannia mule.

Date	AG	Good	VG	Fine	VF	XF	Unc
1787	65.00	110	150	275	650	1,650	—

KM# 9.1 • Copper • Obv: Bust right **Obv. Legend:** VERMON. AUCTORI. **Rev:** Seated figure left **Rev. Legend:** INDE . ET LIB. **Note:** Varieties exist.

Date	AG	Good	VG	Fine	VF	XF	Unc
1788	200	325	625	1,350	4,000	11,500	—

KM# 9.2 • Copper • Obv: Bust right. "C" backward in AUCTORI. **Rev:** Seated figure left

Date	AG	Good	VG	Fine	VF	XF
1788 extremely rare	—	4,200	7,000	17,500	38,000	—

Note: Stack's Americana, Fine, $9,775

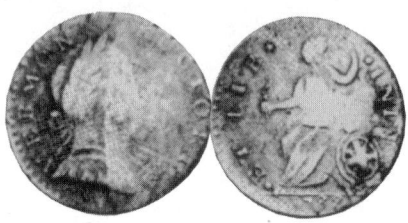

KM# 10 • Copper • Obv: Bust right **Rev:** Seated figure left. **Rev. Legend:** .ET LIB. .INDE.

Date	AG	Good	VG	Fine	VF	XF	Unc
1788	200	325	625	1,250	4,000	13,500	—

KM# 11 • Copper • Obv: Bust right **Rev:** Seated figure left **Note:** George III Rex mule.

Date	AG	Good	VG	Fine	VF	XF	Unc
1788	300	550	900	2,250	4,500	12,000	—

EARLY AMERICAN TOKENS

Albany Church "Penny"

KM# Tn54.1 • Copper • Obv: Without "D" above church. **Note:** Uniface.

Date	AG	Good	VG	Fine	VF	XF
5 known	—	—	10,000	25,000	75,000	—

KM# Tn54.2 • Copper • Obv: With "D" above church. **Note:** Uniface.

Date	AG	Good	VG	Fine	VF	XF
rare	—	—	9,000	22,500	67,500	—

Auctori Plebis

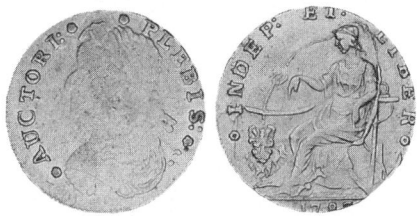

KM# Tn50 • Copper • Obv: Bust left **Obv. Legend:** AUCTORI: PLEBIS: **Rev:** Seated figure left **Rev. Legend:** INDEP. ET. LIBER

Date	AG	Good	VG	Fine	VF	XF	Unc
1787	—	100.00	165	340	800	2,100	15,000

Bar "Cent"

KM# Tn49 • Copper • Obv: USA monogram **Rev:** Horizontal bars

Date	Good	VG	Fine	VF	XF	Unc
(1785)	1,400	1,750	3,100	6,250	9,500	27,500

Castorland "Half Dollar"

KM# Tn87.1 • Silver • Obv. Legend: FRANCO.AMERICANA COLONIA **Edge:** Reeded.

Date	AG	Good	VG	Fine	VF	XF	Unc
1796	—	—	—	—	—	5,000	13,500

KM# Tn87.1a • Copper • Obv. Legend: FRANCO.AMERICANA COLONIA **Edge:** Reeded.

Date	AG	Good	VG	Fine	VF	XF
1796 3 known	—	—	—	—	—	2,850

KM# Tn87.1b • Brass • Obv. Legend: FRANCO.AMERICANA COLONIA **Edge:** Reeded.

Date	AG	Good	VG	Fine	VF	XF	Unc
1796	—	—	—	—	—	200	650

KM# Tn87.2 • Copper • Obv. Legend: FRANCO.AMERICANA COLONIA **Edge:** Plain. **Note:** Thin planchet.

Date	AG	Good	VG	Fine	VF	XF
1796 unique	—	—	—	—	—	—

KM# Tn87.3 • Silver • Obv. Legend: FRANCO.AMERICANA COLONIA **Edge:** Reeded. **Note:** Thin planchet. Restrike.

Date	Good	VG	Fine	VF	XF	Unc	Proof
1796	—	—	—	—	—	500	—

KM# Tn87.3a • Copper • Obv. Legend: FRANCO.AMERICANA COLONIA **Edge:** Reeded. **Note:** Thin planchet. Restrike.

Date	Good	VG	Fine	VF	XF	Unc	Proof
1796	—	—	—	—	—	450	—

KM# Tn87.4 • Silver • Obv. Legend: FRANCO.AMERICANA COLONIA **Edge:** Lettered. **Edge Lettering:** ARGENT. **Note:** Thin planchet. Restrike.

Date	Good	VG	Fine	VF	XF	Unc	Proof
1796	—	—	—	—	—	200	—

KM# Tn87.5 • Copper • Obv. Legend: FRANCO.AMERICANA COLONIA **Edge:** Lettered. **Edge Lettering:** CUIVRE. **Note:** Thin planchet. Restrike.

Date	Good	VG	Fine	VF	XF	Unc	Proof
1796	—	—	—	—	—	150	—

Chalmers

3 PENCE

KM# Tn45 • Silver •

Date	AG	Good	VG	Fine	VF	XF
1783	650	1,100	1,750	3,250	6,500	13,500

6 PENCE

KM# Tn46.1 • Silver • Rev: Small date

Date	AG	Good	VG	Fine	VF	XF
1783	900	1,600	2,500	6,000	12,500	22,500

KM# Tn46.2 • Silver • Rev: Large date

Date	AG	Good	VG	Fine	VF	XF
1783	775	1,450	2,250	6,000	11,500	18,500

SHILLING

KM# Tn47.1 • Silver • Rev: Birds with long worm

Date	AG	Good	VG	Fine	VF	XF
1783	450	750	1,250	2,400	5,500	10,000

KM# Tn47.2 • Silver • Rev: Birds with short worm

Date	AG	Good	VG	Fine	VF	XF
1783	450	750	1,250	2,350	5,000	10,000

KM# Tn48 • Silver • Rev: Rings and stars

Date	AG	Good	VG	Fine	VF	XF
1783 4 known	—	—	—	—	200,000	—

Note: Garrett $75,000

Copper Company of Upper Canada

HALFPENNY

KM# Tn86 • Copper • Obv. Legend: BRITISH SETTLEMENT KENTUCKY

Date	Good	VG	Fine	VF	XF	Unc	Proof
1796	—	—	—	—	—	—	—10,500

Franklin Press

KM# Tn73 • Copper • Obv: Printing press **Obv. Legend:** SIC ORITUR DOCTRINA SURGETQUE LIBERTAS **Edge:** Plain.

Date	AG	Good	VG	Fine	VF	XF	Unc
1794	30.00	75.00	110	150	250	425	1,350

Kentucky Token

KM# Tn70.1 • Copper • Obv. Legend: UNANIMITY IS THE STRENGTH OF SOCIETY **Rev. Legend:** E. PLURIBUS UNUM **Edge:** Plain.
Note: 1793 date is circa.

Date	AG	Good	VG	Fine	VF	XF	Unc
(1793)	12.00	25.00	40.00	150	200	375	1,210

KM# Tn70.2 • Copper • Obv. Legend: UNANIMITY IS THE STRENGTH OF SOCIETY **Rev. Legend:** E. PLURIBUS UNUM **Edge:** Engrailed.

Date	AG	Good	VG	Fine	VF	XF	Unc
(1793)	35.00	75.00	125	200	500	950	3,400

KM# Tn70.3 • Copper • Obv. Legend: UNANIMITY IS THE STRENGTH OF SOCIETY **Rev. Legend:** E. PLURIBUS UNUM **Edge:** Lettered. **Edge Lettering:** PAYABLE AT BEDWORTH.

Date	AG	Good	VG	Fine	VF	XF
(1793) unique	—	—	—	—	—	1,980

KM# Tn70.4 • Copper • Obv. Legend: UNANIMITY IS THE STRENGTH OF SOCIETY **Rev. Legend:** E. PLURIBUS UNUM **Edge:** Lettered. **Edge Lettering:** PAYABLE AT LANCASTER.

Date	AG	Good	VG	Fine	VF	XF	Unc
(1793)	14.00	28.00	45.00	65.00	225	400	1,250

KM# Tn70.5 • Copper • Obv. Legend: UNANIMITY IS THE STRENGTH OF SOCIETY **Rev. Legend:** E. PLURIBUS UNUM **Edge:** Lettered. **Edge Lettering:** PAYABLE AT I.FIELDING.

Date	AG	Good	VG	Fine	VF	XF
(1793) unique	—	—	—	—	—	—

KM# Tn70.6 • Copper • Obv. Legend:
UNANIMITY IS THE STRENGTH OF SOCIETY
Rev. Legend: E. PLURIBUS UNUM **Edge:**
Lettered. **Edge Lettering:** PAYABLE AT W.
PARKERS.

Date	AG	Good	VG	Fine	VF	XF
(1793) unique	—	—	—	— 20,000	—

KM# Tn70.7 • Copper • Obv. Legend:
UNANIMITY IS THE STRENGTH OF SOCIETY
Rev. Legend: E. PLURIBUS UNUM **Edge:**
Ornamented branch with two leaves.

Date	AG	Good	VG	Fine	VF	XF
(1793) unique	—	—	—	—	—	—

Mott Token

KM# Tn52.1 • Copper • Obv: Clock **Rev:** Eagle
with shield **Note:** Thin planchet.

Date	AG	Good	VG	Fine	VF	XF	Unc
1789	50.00	80.00	150	250	400	750	1,750

KM# Tn52.2 • Copper • Obv: Clock **Rev:** Eagle
with shield **Note:** Thick planchet. Weight generally
about 170 grams.

Date	AG	Good	VG	Fine	VF	XF	Unc
1789	60.00	95.00	175	325	550	1,250	—

KM# Tn52.3 • Copper • Obv: Clock **Rev:** Eagle
with shield **Edge:** Fully engrailed. **Note:** Specimens
struck with perfect dies are scarcer and generally
command higher prices.

Date	AG	Good	VG	Fine	VF	XF	Unc
1789	90.00	160	325	450	700	1,750	4,800

Myddelton Token

KM# Tn85 • Copper • Obv. Legend: BRITISH
SETTLEMENT KENTUCKY **Rev. Legend:**
PAYABLE BY P.P.P.MYDDELTON.

Date	Good	VG	Fine	VF	XF	Unc	Proof
1796	—	—	—	—	—	—	37,500

KM# Tn85a • Silver •

Date	Good	VG	Fine	VF	XF	Unc	Proof
1796	—	—	—	—	—	—	12,000

New York Theatre

KM# Tn90 • Copper • Obv: Theater building
Obv. Legend: THE.THEATRE.AT.NEW.YORK.
AMERICA **Rev:** Ships at sea, viewed from dock
Rev. Legend: MAY.COMMERCE.FLOURISH
Note: 1796 date is circa.

Date	AG	Good	VG	Fine	VF	XF	Unc
1796	—	—	—	—	7,000	9,500	25,000

North American

HALFPENNY

KM# Tn30 • Copper • Obv: Seated figure left,
with harp **Obv. Legend:** NORTH AMERICAN
TOKEN **Rev:** Ship **Rev. Legend:** COMMERCE

Date	AG	Good	VG	Fine	VF	XF	Unc
1781	32.00	50.00	65.00	130	300	750	3,250

Rhode Island Ship

KM# Tn27a • Brass • Obv: Without wreath
below ship.

Date	AG	Good	VG	Fine	VF	XF	Unc
1779	—	—	325	550	1,000	2,000	7,500

KM# Tn27b • Pewter • Obv: Without wreath
below ship.

Date	AG	Good	VG	Fine	VF	XF	Unc
1779	—	—	—	—	5,000	8,500	18,500

KM# Tn28a • Brass • Obv: Wreath below ship.

Date	AG	Good	VG	Fine	VF	XF	Unc
1779	—	—	—	675	1,100	2,100	7,750

KM# Tn28b • Pewter • Obv: Wreath below ship.

Date	AG	Good	VG	Fine	VF	XF	Unc
1779	—	—	—	—	5,500	9,000	20,000

KM# Tn29 • Brass • Obv: VLUGTENDE below ship

Date	AG	Good	VG	Fine	VF	XF
1779 unique	—	—	—	—	—	35,000

Note: Garrett $16,000

Standish Barry

3 PENCE

KM# Tn55 • Silver • Obv: Bust left **Obv. Legend:** BALTIMORE.TOWN.JULY.4.90. **Rev:** Denomination **Rev. Legend:** STANDISH BARRY.

Date	AG	Good	VG	Fine	VF	XF
1790	—	—	15,000	22,500	50,000	—

Talbot, Allum & Lee

CENT

KM# Tn71.1 • Copper • Rev: NEW YORK above ship **Edge:** Lettered. **Edge Lettering:** PAYABLE AT THE STORE OF

Date	AG	Good	VG	Fine	VF	XF	Unc
1794	32.00	50.00	85.00	165	275	550	2,000

KM# Tn71.2 • Copper • Rev: NEW YORK above ship **Edge:** Plain. **Note:** Size of ampersand varies on obverse and reverse dies.

Date	AG	Good	VG	Fine	VF	XF
1794 4 known	—	—	—	—	10,000	24,000

KM# Tn72.1 • Copper • Rev: Without NEW YORK above ship **Edge:** Lettered. **Edge Lettering:** PAYABLE AT THE STORE OF

Date	AG	Good	VG	Fine	VF	XF	Unc
1794	200	375	600	3,500	6,500	10,500	22,000

KM# Tn72.2 • Copper • Edge: Lettered. **Edge Lettering:** WE PROMISE TO PAY THE BEARER ONE CENT.

Date	AG	Good	VG	Fine	VF	XF	Unc
1795	30.00	50.00	75.00	135	240	375	1,200

KM# Tn72.3 • Copper • Edge: Lettered. **Edge Lettering:** CURRENT EVERYWHERE.

Date	AG	Good	VG	Fine	VF	XF
1795 unique	—	—	—	—	—	—

KM# Tn72.4 • Copper • Edge: Olive leaf.

Date	AG	Good	VG	Fine	VF	XF
1795 unique	—	—	—	—	—	15,000

Note: Norweb $4,400

KM# Tn72.5 • Copper • Edge: Plain.

Date	AG	Good	VG	Fine	VF	XF
1795 plain edge; 2 known	—	—	—	—	—	—
1795 Lettered edge; unique	—	—	—	—	—	15,000

Note: Edge: Cambridge Bedford Huntington.X.X.; Norweb, $3,960

Washington Pieces

KM# Tn35 • Copper • Obv. Legend: GEORGIVS TRIUMPHO.

Date	AG	Good	VG	Fine	VF	XF	Unc
1783	—	95.00	125	260	325	750	—

KM# Tn36 • Copper • Obv: Large military bust. **Note:** Varieties exist.

Date	AG	Good	VG	Fine	VF	XF	Unc
1783	—	—	50.00	85.00	180	450	2,600

KM# Tn37.1 • **Copper** • **Obv:** Small military bust. **Edge:** Plain.

Date	AG	Good	VG	Fine	VF	XF	Unc
1783		—	70.00	95.00	220	525	3,600

Note: One proof example is known. Value: $25,000

KM# Tn37.2 • **Copper** • **Obv:** Small military bust. **Edge:** Engrailed.

Date	AG	Good	VG	Fine	VF	XF	Unc
1783	—	75.00	110	150	300	750	4,250

KM# Tn38.1 • **Copper** • **Obv:** Draped bust, no button on drapery, small letter.

Date	AG	Good	VG	Fine	VF	XF	Unc
1783	—	40.00	60.00	90.00	180	400	2,200

KM# Tn38.2 • **Copper** • **Obv:** Draped bust, button on drapery, large letter.

Date	AG	Good	VG	Fine	VF	XF	Unc
1783	—	85.00	110	150	325	600	4,000

KM# Tn38.4 • **Copper** • **Edge:** Engrailed. **Note:** Restrike.

Date	Good	VG	Fine	VF	XF	Unc	Proof
1783	—	—	—	—	—	—	800

KM# Tn38.4a • **Copper** • **Note:** Bronzed. Restrike.

Date	Good	VG	Fine	VF	XF	Unc	Proof
1783	—	—	—	—	—	—	—

KM# Tn83.3 • **Copper** • **Obv:** Large modern lettering. **Edge:** Plain. **Note:** Restrike.

Date	Good	VG	Fine	VF	XF	Unc	Proof
1783	—	—	—	—	—	—	900

KM# Tn83.4b • **Silver** • **Note:** Restrike.

Date	Good	VG	Fine	VF	XF	Unc	Proof
1783	—	—	—	—	—	—	1,600

KM# Tn83.4c • **Gold** AGW • **Note:** Restrike.

Date	AG	Good	VG	Fine	VF	XF
1783 2 known	—	—	—	—	—	—

KM# Tn60.1 • **Copper** • **Obv. Legend:** WASHINGTON PRESIDENT. **Edge:** Plain.

Date	AG	Good	VG	Fine	VF	XF	Unc
1792	850	1,450	3,000	7,500	16,000	—	—

Note: Steinberg $12,650. Garrett $15,500

KM# Tn60.2 • **Copper** • **Obv. Legend:** WASHINGTON PRESIDENT. **Edge:** Lettered. **Edge Lettering:** UNITED STATES OF AMERICA.

Date	AG	Good	VG	Fine	VF	XF	Unc
1792	—	—	—	—	—	—	—

KM# Tn61.1 • **Copper** • **Obv. Legend:** BORN VIRGINIA. **Note:** Varieties exist.

Date	AG	Good	VG	Fine	VF	XF	Unc
(1792)	500	1,000	2,000	4,000	7,500	12,000	—

KM# Tn61.1a • **Silver** • **Edge:** Plain.

Date	AG	Good	VG	Fine	VF	XF
(1792) 4 known	—	—	—	—	—	200,000

Note: Roper $16,500

KM# Tn61.2 • **Silver** • **Edge:** Lettered. **Edge Lettering:** UNITED STATES OF AMERICA.

Date	AG	Good	VG	Fine	VF	XF
(1792) 2 known	—	—	—	—	—	—

KM# Tn62 • **Silver** • **Rev:** Heraldic eagle. 1792 half dollar. **Note:** Mule.

Date	AG	Good	VG	Fine	VF	XF
(1792) 3 known	—	—	—	—	50,000	75,000

KM# Tn77.1 • Copper • Obv. Legend:
LIBERTY AND SECURITY. **Edge:** Lettered. **Note:** "Penny."

Date	AG	Good	VG	Fine	VF	XF	Unc
(1795)	70.00	110	165	300	525	1,100	3,500

KM# Tn77.2 • Copper • Edge: Plain. **Note:** "Penny."

Date	AG	Good	VG	Fine	VF	XF
(1795) extremely rare	—	—	—	—	—	—

KM# Tn77.3 • Copper • Note: "Penny." Engine-turned borders.

Date	Good	VG	Fine	VF	XF	Unc
(1795) 12 known	275	450	650	1,250	2,400	7,500

KM# Tn78 • Copper • Note: Similar to "Halfpenny" with date on reverse.

Date	AG	Good	VG	Fine	VF	XF
1795 very rare	—	—	—	—	—	—

Note: Roper $6,600

HALFPENNY

KM# Tn56 • Copper • Obv. Legend:
LIVERPOOL HALFPENNY

Date	AG	Good	VG	Fine	VF	XF	Unc
1791	40.00	70.00	1,000	125	300	550	3,250

KM# Tn66.1 • Copper • Rev: Ship Edge: Lettered.

Date	AG	Good	VG	Fine	VF	XF	Unc
1793	20.00	30.00	60.00	200	425	800	3,400

KM# Tn66.2 • Copper • Rev: Ship **Edge:** Plain.

Date	AG	Good	VG	Fine	VF	XF
1793 5 known	—	—	—	— 15,000	—

KM# Tn75.1 • Copper • Obv: Large coat buttons **Rev:** Grate **Edge:** Reeded.

Date	AG	Good	VG	Fine	VF	XF	Unc
1795	—	— 70.00	110	200	400	900

KM# Tn75.2 • Copper • Rev: Grate **Edge:** Lettered.

Date	AG	Good	VG	Fine	VF	XF	Unc
1795	90.00	140	210	275	400	800	2,800

KM# Tn75.3 • Copper • Obv: Small coat buttons **Rev:** Grate **Edge:** Reeded.

Date	AG	Good	VG	Fine	VF	XF	Unc
1795	50.00	75.00	120	190	275	585	2,650

KM# Tn76.1 • Copper • Obv. Legend:
LIBERTY AND SECURITY. **Edge:** Plain.

Date	AG	Good	VG	Fine	VF	XF	Unc
1795	18.00	35.00	60.00	160	350	700	3,250

KM# Tn76.2 • Copper • Edge: Lettered. **Edge Lettering:** PAYABLE AT LONDON ...

Date	AG	Good	VG	Fine	VF	XF	Unc
1795	40.00	65.00	90.00	140	300	625	2,850

KM# Tn76.3 • Copper • Edge: Lettered. **Edge Lettering:** BIRMINGHAM ...

Date	AG	Good	VG	Fine	VF	XF	Unc
1795	55.00	85.00	115	165	340	775	3,600

KM# Tn76.4 • Copper • Edge: Lettered. **Edge Lettering:** AN ASYLUM ...

Date	AG	Good	VG	Fine	VF	XF	Unc
1795	18.00	35.00	60.00	275	600	1,600	6,500

KM# Tn76.5 • Copper • Edge: Lettered. **Edge Lettering:** PAYABLE AT LIVERPOOL ...

Date	AG	Good	VG	Fine	VF	XF
1795 unique	—	—	—	—	—	—

KM# Tn76.6 • Copper • Edge: Lettered. **Edge Lettering:** PAYABLE AT LONDON-LIVERPOOL.

Date	AG	Good	VG	Fine	VF	XF
1795 unique	—	—	—	—	—	—

KM# Tn81.1 • Copper • Rev. Legend: NORTH WALES **Edge:** Plain.

Date	AG	Good	VG	Fine	VF	XF	Unc
(ca.1795)	60.00	110	175	265	625	1,750	—

KM# Tn82 • Copper • Rev: Four stars at bottom **Rev. Legend:** NORTH WALES

Date	AG	Good	VG	Fine	VF	XF	Unc
(1795)	1,250	2,000	4,500	7,500	21,000	—	—

KM# Tn81.2 • Copper • Rev. Legend: NORTH WALES **Edge:** Lettered.

Date	AG	Good	VG	Fine	VF	XF	Unc
	350	550	1,150	1,750	5,500	9,500	—

CENT

KM# Tn39 • Copper • Obv: Draped Bust left **Obv. Legend:** WASHINGTON & INDEPENDENCE **Rev:** Denomination in wreath **Rev. Legend:** UNITY STATES OF AMERICA

Date	AG	Good	VG	Fine	VF	XF	Unc
1783	30.00	50.00	70.00	100.00	250	500	2,250

KM# Tn40 • Copper • Note: Double head.

Date	AG	Good	VG	Fine	VF	XF	Unc
(1783)	25.00	45.00	60.00	90.00	225	450	2,750

KM# Tn41 • Copper • Obv: "Ugly head." **Note:** 3 known in copper, 1 in white metal.

Date	AG	Good	VG	Fine	VF	XF	Unc
1784	—	90,000	—	—	—	—	—

Note: Roper $14,850

KM# Tn57 • Copper • Obv: Military bust left **Obv. Legend:** WASHINGTON PRESIDENT. **Rev:** Small eagle

Date	AG	Good	VG	Fine	VF	XF	Unc
1791	—	—	350	500	725	1,000	4,750

KM# Tn58 • Copper • Obv: Military bust left **Obv. Legend:** WASHINGTON PRESIDENT **Rev:** Large eagle

Date	AG	Good	VG	Fine	VF	XF	Unc
1791	—	200	325	475	650	900	2,850

KM# Tn65 • Copper • Obv: "Roman" head **Obv. Legend:** WASHINGTON PRESIDENT.

Date	AG	Good	VG	Fine	VF	XF	Unc
1792	—	—	—	—	—	—	—

HALF DOLLAR

KM# Tn59.1 • Copper • Edge: Lettered. **Edge Lettering:** UNITED STATES OF AMERICA

Date	AG	Good	VG	Fine	VF	XF
1792 2 known	—	—	—	—	—	75,000

Note: Roper $2,860. Benson, EF, $48,300

KM# Tn59.1a • Silver • Edge: Lettered. **Edge Lettering:** UNITED STATES OF AMERICA

Date	AG	Good	VG	Fine	VF	XF	Unc
1792 rare	—	—	—	—	40,000	65,000	—

Note: Roper $35,200

KM# Tn59.1b • Gold AGW • **Edge:** Lettered. **Edge Lettering:** UNITED STATES OF AMERICA

Date	AG	Good	VG	Fine	VF	XF
1792 unique	—	—	—	—	—	—

KM# Tn59.2 • Copper • Edge: Plain.

Date	Good	VG	Fine	VF	XF
1792 3 known	—	—	—	125,000	200,000

KM# Tn59.2a • Silver • Edge: Plain.

Date	AG	Good	VG	Fine	VF	XF	Unc
1792 rare	—	—	—	—	—	—	—

KM# Tn63.1 • Silver • Rev: Small eagle **Edge:** Plain.

Date	AG	Good	VG	Fine	VF	XF
1792	—	—	—	—	200,000	300,000

KM# Tn63.1a • Copper • Edge: Plain.

Date	AG	Good	VG	Fine	VF	XF
1792	—	4,000	6,500	12,500	32,000	65,000

Note: Garrett $32,000

KM# Tn63.2 • Silver • Edge: Ornamented, circles and squares.

Date	VG	Fine	VF	XF	Unc
1792 5 known	—	—	100,000	175,000	400,000

KM# Tn63.3 • Silver • Edge: Two olive leaves.

Date	AG	Good	VG	Fine	VF	XF
1792 unique	—	—	—	—	—	—

KM# Tn64 • Silver • Rev: Large heraldic eagle

Date	AG	Good	VG	Fine	VF	XF
1792 unique	—	—	—	—	100,000	—

Note: Garrett $16,500

EARLY AMERICAN PATTERNS
Confederatio

KM# EA22 • Copper • Obv: Standing figure with bow & arrow **Obv. Legend:** INIMICA TYRANNIS • AMERICANA • **Rev:** Small circle of stars **Rev. Legend:** • CONFEDERATIO •

Date	AG	Good	VG	Fine	VF	XF	Unc
1785	—	—	—	—	50,000	95,000	—

KM# EA23 • Copper • Obv: Standing figure with bow & arrow **Obv. Legend:** INIMICA TYRANNIS • AMERICANA • **Rev:** Large circle of stars **Rev. Legend:** • CONFEDERATIO • **Note:** The

Confederatio dies were struck in combination with 13 other dies of the period. All surviving examples of these combinations are extremely rare.

Date	Good	VG	Fine	VF	XF
extremely rare	—	—	—	50,000	100,000

Immune Columbia

KM# EA17 • Copper • Obv. Legend: IMMUNE COLUMBIA. **Rev:** Eye, with pointed rays & stars **Rev. Legend:** NOVA • CONSTELLATIO

Date	AG	Good	VG	Fine	VF	XF	Unc
1785	—	—	—	—	22,500	40,000	—

KM# EA17a • Silver • Obv. Legend: IMMUNE COLUMBIA • **Rev:** Eye, with pointed rays & stars **Rev. Legend:** NOVA CONSTELLATIO

Date	AG	Good	VG	Fine	VF	XF	Unc
1785	—	—	—	—	45,000	90,000	—

KM# EA18 • Copper • Obv. Legend: IMMUNE COLUMBIA • **Rev:** Eye, with pointed rays & stars. Extra star in reverse legend **Rev. Legend:** NOVA • CONSTELLATIO *

Date	AG	Good	VG	Fine	VF	XF
1785	—	—	—	—	22,500	40,000

Note: Caldwell $4,675

KM# EA19 • Copper • Obv. Legend: IMMUNE COLUMBIA • **Rev:** Blunt rays **Rev. Legend:** NOVA CONSTELATIO

Date	AG	Good	VG	Fine	VF	XF
1785 2 known	—	—	—	—	—	100,000

Note: Norweb $22,000

KM# EA19a • Gold AGW • **Obv. Legend:** IMMUNE COLUMBIA • **Rev:** Blunt rays **Rev. Legend:** NOVA CONSTELATIO •

Date	AG	Good	VG	Fine	VF	XF
1785 unique	—	—	—	—	—	—

Note: In the Smithsonian Collection

KM# EA20 • Copper • Obv: George III **Obv. Legend:** GEORGIVS III • REX • **Rev. Legend:** IMMUNE COLUMBIA •

Date	AG	Good	VG	Fine	VF	XF	Unc
1785	3,500	5,000	7,500	9,500	22,500	—	—

KM# EA21 • Copper • Obv: Head right **Obv. Legend:** VERMON AUCTORI **Rev. Legend:** IMMUNE COLUMBIA •

Date	AG	Good	VG	Fine	VF	XF	Unc
1785	—	5,500	8,500	11,500	35,000	—	—

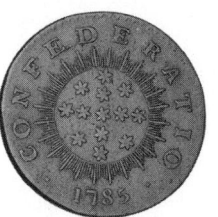

KM# EA24 • Copper • Obv: Washington **Rev:** Stars in rayed circle **Rev. Legend:** • CONFEDERATIO •

Date	AG	Good	VG	Fine	VF	XF
1786 3 known	—	—	—	—	50,000	—

Note: Garrett $50,000. Steinberg $12,650

KM# EA25 • Copper • Obv: Eagle, raw shield **Obv. Legend:** * E • PLURIBUS UNUM • **Rev:** Shield **Rev. Legend:** * E * PLURIBUS * UNUM *

Date	AG	Good	VG	Fine	VF	XF
1786 unique	—	—	—	—	—	—

Note: Garrett $37,500

KM# EA26 • Copper • Obv: Washington **Obv. Legend:** GEN • WASHINGTON • **Rev:** Eagle

Date	AG	Good	VG	Fine	VF	XF
1786 2 known	—	—	—	—	—	—

KM# EA27 • Copper • Obv. Legend: IMMUNIS
COLUMBIA **• Rev:** Shield **Rev. Legend:** * E *
PLURIBUS * UNUM *

Date	AG	Good	VG	Fine	VF	XF
1786						
extremely rare	—	—	—	—	40,000	—

Note: Rescigno, AU, $33,000. Steinberg, VF, $11,000

KM# EA28 • Copper • Obv. Legend: IMMUNIS
COLUMBIA **Rev:** Eagle **Rev. Legend:** * E *
PLURIBUS * UNUM *

Date	AG	Good	VG	Fine	VF	XF
1786 3 known	—	—	—	—	50,000	90,000

Nova Constellatio

KM# EA6.1 • Copper • Obv: Pointed rays **Obv.
Legend:** NOVA • CONSTELATIO **• Rev:** Small
"U•S"

Date	AG	Good	VG	Fine	VF	XF	Unc
1783	50.00	70.00	100.00	225	440	950	3,750

KM# EA6.2 • Copper • Obv: Pointed rays **Obv.
Legend:** NOVA • CONSTELATIO **• Rev:** Large "US"

Date	AG	Good	VG	Fine	VF	XF	Unc
1783	55.00	75.00	110	250	600	1,400	6,000

KM# EA7 • Copper • Obv: Blunt rays **Obv.
Legend:** NOVA • CONSTELATIO •

Date	AG	Good	VG	Fine	VF	XF	Unc
1783	50.00	75.00	110	250	575	1,300	5,000

KM# EA8 • Copper • Obv: Blunt rays **Obv.
Legend:** NOVA • CONSTELATIO •

Date	AG	Good	VG	Fine	VF	XF	Unc
1785	50.00	75.00	110	260	625	1,500	6,500

KM# EA9 • Copper • Obv: Pointed rays **Obv.
Legend:** NOVA • CONSTELATIO •

Date	AG	Good	VG	Fine	VF	XF	Unc
1785	—	—100.00	225	450	1,000	3,600

KM# EA10 • Copper • Note: Contemporary
circulating counterfeit. Similar to previously listed
coin.

Date	AG	Good	VG	Fine	VF	XF
1786						
extremely rare	—	—	—	—	—	—

5 UNITS

KM# EA12 • Copper • Obv: Eye, with pointed
rays & stars **Obv. Legend:** NOVA

CONSTELLATIO **Rev. Legend:** • LIBERTAS • JUSTITIA •

Date	AG	Good	VG	Fine	VF	XF
1783 unique	—	—	—	—	—	—

100 (BIT)

KM# EA13.1 • **Silver** • **Obv:** Eye, with pointed rays & stars **Obv. Legend:** NOVA CONSTELLATIO **Rev. Legend:** • LIBERTAS • JUSTITIA • **Edge:** Leaf.

Date	AG	Good	VG	Fine	VF	XF
1783 2 known	—	—	—	—	—	—

Note: Garrett $97,500. Stack's auction, May 1991, $72,500

KM# EA13.2 • **Silver** • **Obv:** Eye, with pointed rays & stars **Obv. Legend:** NOVA CONSTELLATIO **Rev. Legend:** • LIBERTAS • JUSTITIA • **Edge:** Plain

Date	AG	Good	VG	Fine	VF	XF
1783 unique	—	—	—	—	—	—

500 (QUINT)

KM# EA14 • **Silver** • **Obv:** Eye with pointed rays & stars **Obv. Legend:** NOVA CONSTELLATIO **Rev. Legend:** • LIBERTAS • JUSTITIA •

Date	AG	Good	VG	Fine	VF	XF
1783 unique	—	—	—	—	—	250,000

Note: Garrett $165,000

KM# EA15 • **Silver** • **Obv:** Eye, with rays & stars, no legend **Rev. Legend:** • LIBERTAS • JUSTITIA •

Date	AG	Good	VG	Fine	VF	XF
1783 unique	—	—	—	—	75,000	—

Note: Garrett $55,000

1000 (MARK)

KM# EA16 • **Silver** • **Obv:** Eye, with pointed rays & stars **Obv. Legend:** NOVA CONSTELLATIO **Rev. Legend:** • LIBERTAS • JUSTITIA •

Date	AG	Good	VG	Fine	VF	XF
1783 unique	—	—	—	—	—	350,000

Note: Garrett $190,000

EARLY FEDERAL COINAGE

Brasher

KM# Tn51.1 • **Gold** AGW • **Obv:** Sunrise over mountains. **Rev:** Displayed eagle with shield on breast, EB counterstamp on wing.

Date	AG	Good	VG	Fine	VF	XF
1787 6 known	—	—	—	—	—	—

Note: Heritage FUN Sale, January 2005, AU-55, $2.415 million.

KM# Tn51.2 • **Gold** AGW • **Obv:** Sun rise over mountains **Rev:** Displayed eagle with shield on breast. EB counterstamp on breast.

Date	AG	Good	VG	Fine	VF	XF
1787 unique	—	—	—	—	—	—

Note: Heritage FUN Sale, January 2005, XF-45, $2.99 million. Foreign gold coins with the EB counterstamp exist. These are valued at over $5,000, with many much higher.

Fugio "Cent"

KM# EA30.1 • Copper • Obv: Club rays, round ends.

Date	AG	Good	VG	Fine	VF	XF
1787	225	325	450	850	2,000	3,850

KM# EA30.2 • Copper • Obv: Club rays, concave ends.

Date	AG	Good	VG	Fine	VF	XF
1787	1,500	2,500	3,500	8,000	20,000	—

KM# EA30.3 • Copper • Obv. Legend: FUCIO.

Date	AG	Good	VG	Fine	VF	XF
1787	—	2,000	3,000	7,000	25,000	35,000

KM# EA31.1 • Copper • Obv: Pointed rays. **Rev:** UNITED above, STATES below.

Date	AG	Good	VG	Fine	VF	XF
1787	600	950	1,400	3,000	7,750	10,000

KM# EA31.2 • Copper • Rev: UNITED STATES at sides of ring.

Date	AG	Good	VG	Fine	VF	XF	Unc
1787	110	175	275	550	850	1,600	3,500

KM# EA31.3 • Copper • Rev: STATES UNITED at sides of ring.

Date	AG	Good	VG	Fine	VF	XF	Unc
1787	110	190	275	550	800	1,500	3,500

KM# EA31.4 • Copper • Rev: Eight-pointed stars on ring.

Date	AG	Good	VG	Fine	VF	XF	Unc
1787	150	285	450	650	1,200	2,500	9,000

KM# EA31.5 • Copper • Rev: Raised rims on ring, large lettering in center.

Date	AG	Good	VG	Fine	VF	XF	Unc
1787	185	325	500	900	2,400	5,250	17,500

KM# EA32.1 • Copper • Obv: No cinquefoils, cross after date. **Obv. Legend:** UNITED STATES.

Date	AG	Good	VG	Fine	VF	XF	Unc
1787	300	485	750	1,450	3,500	6,500	—

KM# EA32.2 • Copper • Obv: No cinquefoils, cross after date. **Obv. Legend:** STATES UNITED.

Date	AG	Good	VG	Fine	VF	XF	Unc
1787	—	—	750	1,500	3,750	6,800	—

KM# EA32.3 • Copper • Obv: No cinquefoils, cross after date. **Rev:** Raised rims on ring.

Date	AG	Good	VG	Fine	VF	XF	Unc
1787	—	—	—	—22,500	—	—

KM# EA33 • Copper • Obv: No cinquefoils, cross after date. **Rev:** With rays. **Rev. Legend:** AMERICAN CONGRESS.

Date	AG	Good	VG	Fine	VF	XF
1787						
extremely rare	—	—	—	—	275,000	—

Note: Norweb $63,800

KM# EA34 • Brass • Note: New Haven restrike.

Date	AG	Good	VG	Fine	VF	XF	Unc
1787	—	—	—	—	—	450	1,000

KM# EA34a • Copper • Note: New Haven restrike.

Date	AG	Good	VG	Fine	VF	XF	Unc
1787	—	—	—	—	450	750	1,000

KM# EA34b • Silver • Note: New Haven restrike.

Date	Good	VG	Fine	VF	XF	Unc
1787(ca.1858)	—	—	—	—	1,500	4,000

KM# EA34c • Gold AGW • Note: New Haven restrike.

Date	AG	Good	VG	Fine	VF	XF
1787(ca.1858)						
2 known	—	—	—	—	—	—

Note: Norweb (holed) $1,430

ISSUES OF 1792

CENT

KM# PnE1 • Bi-Metallic, Silver center in Copper ring •

Date	Good	VG	Fine	VF	XF
1792 12 known	—	—	175,000	300,000	450,000

Note: Norweb, MS-60, $143,000

KM# PnF1 • Copper • Note: No silver center.

Date	Good	VG	Fine	VF	XF
1792 8 known	—	—	250,000	500,000	750,000

Note: Norweb, EF-40, $35,200; Benson, VG-10, $57,500

KM# PnG1 • Copper • Edge: Plain **Note:**
Commonly called "Birch cent."

Date	AG	Good	VG	Fine	VF	XF
1792 unique	—	—	—	—	—	500,000

KM# PnH1 • Copper • Obv: One star in edge
legend **Note:** Commonly called "Birch cent."

Date	Good	VG	Fine	VF	XF
1792 2 known	—	—	150,000	350,000	450,000

Note: Norweb, EF-40, $59,400

KM# PnI1 • Copper • Obv: Two stars in edge
legend **Note:** Commonly called "Birch cent."

Date	AG	Good	VG	Fine	VF	XF
1792 6 known	—	—	—	—	—	—

Note: Hawn, strong VF, $57,750

KM# PnJ1 • White Metal • Rev: "G.W.Pt." below
wreath tie **Note:** Commonly called "Birch cent."

Date	AG	Good	VG	Fine	VF	XF
1792 unique	—	—	—	—	—	550,000

Note: Garrett, $90,000

HALF DISME

KM# 5 • Silver •

Date	AG	VG	Fine	VF	XF	Unc
1792	25,000	35,000	55,000	90,000	125,000	450,000

KM# PnA1 • Copper •

Date	AG	Good	VG	Fine	VF	XF
1792 unique	—	—	—	—	—	—

DISME

KM# PnB1 • Silver •

Date	Good	VG	Fine	VF	XF
1792 3 known	—	—	—	700,000	1,000,000

Note: Norweb, EF-40, $28,600

KM# PnC1 • Copper • Edge: Reeded

Date	VG	Fine	VF	XF	Unc
1792 14 known	—	—	150,000	250,000	500,000

Note: Hawn, VF, $30,800; Benson, EF-45, $109,250

KM# PnD1 • Copper • Edge: Plain

Date	Good	VG	Fine	VF	XF
1792 2 known	—	—	—	450,000	750,000

Note: Garrett, $45,000

QUARTER

KM# PnK1 • Copper • Edge: Reeded **Note:**
Commonly called "Wright quarter."

Date	AG	Good	VG	Fine	VF	XF
1792 2 known	—	—	—	—	—	—

KM# PnL1 • White Metal • Edge: Plain **Note:**
Commonly called "Wright quarter."

Date	AG	Good	VG	Fine	VF	XF
1792 2 known	—	—	—	—	—	—

Note: Norweb, VF-30 to EF-40, $28,600

KM# PnM1 • White Metal • Note: Commonly
called "Wright quarter."

Date	AG	Good	VG	Fine	VF	XF
1792 die trial	—	—	—	—	—	—

Note: Garrett, $12,000

UNITED STATES

CIRCULATION COINAGE

HALF CENT

Liberty Cap Half Cent
Head facing left obverse

KM# 10 • 6.7400 g., **Copper**, 22 mm. • **Designer:** Henry Voigt

Date	Mintage	G-4	VG-8	F-12	VF-20	XF-40	MS-60
1793	35,334	3,250	5,350	8,500	15,500	24,500	60,000

Head facing right obverse

KM# 14 • **Copper**, 6.74 g. (1794-95) and 5.44 g. (1795-97), 23.5 mm. • **Designer:** Robert Scot (1794) and John Smith Gardner (1795) **Notes:** The "lettered edge" varieties have TWO HUNDRED FOR A DOLLAR inscribed around the edge. The "pole" varieties have a pole upon which the cap is hanging, resting on Liberty's shoulder. The "punctuated date" varieties have a comma after the 1 in the date. The 1797 "1 above 1" variety has a second 1 above the 1 in the date.

Date	Mintage	G-4	VG-8	F-12	VF-20	XF-40	MS-60
1794 Normal Relief Head	81,600	485	750	1,200	2,250	5,000	27,500
1794 High Relief Head	Inc. above	550	900	1,450	2,850	6,400	—
1795 lettered edge, pole	25,600	525	735	1,060	1,760	4,150	—
1795 plain edge, no pole	109,000	455	665	990	1,675	3,750	21,500
1795 lettered edge, punctuated date	Inc. above	525	750	1,500	2,500	6,500	—
1795 plain edge, punctuated date	Inc. above	440	650	975	1,675	3,750	21,500
1796 pole	5,090	20,000	24,500	37,500	55,000	75,000	170,000
1796 no pole	1,390	37,500	75,000	140,000	125,000	—	—
1797 plain edge	119,215	465	675	1,025	1,760	3,850	24,500
1797 lettered edge	Inc. above	1,500	3,500	4,500	8,000	—	—
1797 1 above 1	Inc. above	455	665	975	1,675	4,850	21,500
1797 gripped edge	Inc. above	22,000	39,500	58,500	—	—	—

Draped Bust Half Cent
Draped bust right, date at angle below obverse
Value within thin wreath reverse

Stemless   Stems

KM# 33 • 5.4400 g., **Copper**, 23.5 mm. • **Obv. Legend** LIBERTY **Rev. Legend:** UNITED STATES OF AMERICA **Designer:** Robert Scot **Notes:** The wreath on the reverse was redesigned slightly in 1802, resulting in "reverse of 1800" and "reverse of 1802" varieties. The "stems" varieties have stems extending from the wreath above and on both sides of the fraction on the reverse. On the 1804 "crosslet 4" variety, a serif appears at the far right of the crossbar on the 4 in the date. The "spiked chin" variety appears to have a spike extending from Liberty's chin, the result of a damaged die. Varieties of the 1805 strikes are distinguished by the size of the 5 in the date. Varieties of the 1806 strikes are distinguished by the size of the 6 in the date.

Date	Mintage	G-4	VG-8	F-12	VF-20	XF-40	MS-60
1800	211,530	60.00	90.00	125	185	500	5,500
1802/0 rev. 1800	14,366	15,000	55,000	30,000	—	—	—
1802/0 rev. 1802	Inc. above	800	1,400	5,750	6,500	17,000	—
1803	97,900	70.00	95.00	105	575	950	7,000
1804 plain 4, stemless wreath	1,055,312	55.00	80.00	90.00	150	550	1,400
1804 plain 4, stems	Inc. above	55.00	90.00	155	550	1,500	15,000
1804 crosslet 4, stemless	Inc. above	60.00	90.00	100.00	175	550	1,350
1804 crosslet 4, stems	Inc. above	57.00	90.00	125	195	300	1,500
1804 spiked chin	Inc. above	70.00	105	155	195	355	1,500
1805 small 5, stemless	814,464	60.00	90.00	105	175	400	3,500
1805 small 5, stems	Inc. above	800	1,500	5,400	4,500	8,000	—
1805 large 5, stems	Inc. above	60.00	85.00	100.00	160	400	3,000
1806 small 6, stems	356,000	500	355	600	1,000	5,750	—
1806 small 6, stemless	Inc. above	60.00	85.00	100.00	195	535	1,350
1806 large 6, stems	Inc. above	60.00	85.00	100.00	195	550	1,500
1807	476,000	60.00	95.00	155	200	300	1,400
1808/7	400,000	300	400	600	1,500	6,000	57,500
1808	Inc. above	60.00	85.00	105	195	350	5,000

Classic Head Half Cent
Classic head left, flanked by stars, date below obverse
Value within wreath reverse

KM# 41 • 5.4400 g., **Copper**, 23.5 mm. • **Rev. Legend:** UNITED STATES OF AMERICA **Designer:** John Reich **Notes:** Restrikes listed were produced privately in the mid-1800s. The 1831 restrikes have two varieties with different sized berries in the wreath on the reverse. The 1828 strikes have either 12 or 13 stars on the obverse.

Date	Mintage	G-4	VG-8	F-12	VF-20	XF-40	MS-60
1809/6	1,154,572	60.00	80.00	110	150	250	850
1809	Inc. above	58.00	78.00	87.00	100.00	135	650
1809 circle in 0	—	65.00	93.00	87.00	140	285	800
1810	215,000	65.00	103	150	500	600	3,550
1811	63,140	255	375	750	1,800	4,000	—
1811 restrike, reverse of 1802, uncirculated	—	—	—	—	—	—	57,500
1825	63,000	55.00	73.00	82.00	110	500	950
1826	234,000	50.00	68.00	79.00	90.00	500	750
1828 13 stars	606,000	50.00	68.00	72.00	75.00	88.00	225
1828 12 stars	Inc. above	60.00	78.00	122	175	550	850
1829	487,000	50.00	71.00	79.00	100.00	150	500
1831 original	2,200	—	—	—	—	65,000	—
1831 1st restrike, lg. berries, reverse of 1836	—	—	—	—	—	—	6,500
1831 2nd restrike, sm. berries, reverse of 1840, proof	—	—	—	—	—	—	55,000
1832	154,000	50.00	68.00	72.00	75.00	88.00	225
1833	120,000	50.00	68.00	72.00	75.00	88.00	225
1834	141,000	50.00	68.00	72.00	75.00	88.00	225
1835	398,000	50.00	68.00	72.00	75.00	88.00	225
1836 original, proof	—	—	—	—	—	—	6,000
1836 restrike, reverse of 1840, proof	—	—	—	—	—	—	50,000

HALF CENT

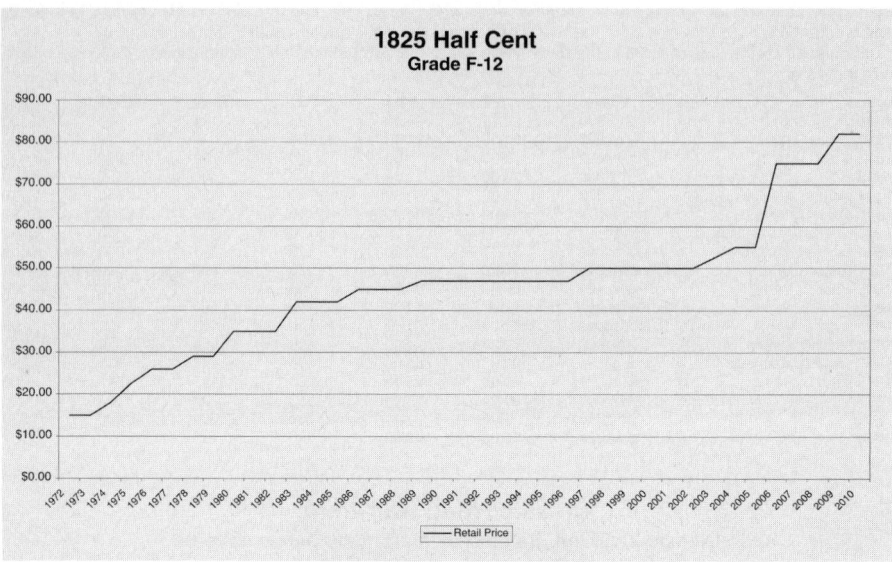

1825 Half Cent
Grade F-12

Braided Hair Half Cent
Head left, braided hair, within circle of stars, date below obverse
Value within wreath reverse

KM# 70 • 5.4400 g., **Copper**, 23 mm. • **Rev. Legend:** UNITED STATES OF AMERICA **Designer:** Christian Gobrecht **Notes:** 1840-1849 and 1852 strikes, both originals and restrikes, are known in proof only; mintages are unknown. The small-date varieties of 1849, both originals and restrikes are known in proof only. The restrikes were produced clandestinely by Philadelphia Mint personnel in the mid-1800s.

Date	Mintage	G-4	VG-8	F-12	VF-20	XF-40	MS-60	Prf-60
1840 original	—	—	—	—	—	3,000	—	3,250
1840 1st restrike	—	—	—	—	—	3,000	—	3,250
1840 2nd restrike	—	—	—	—	—	3,000	—	5,500
1841 original	—	—	—	—	—	3,000	—	3,250
1841 1st restrike	—	—	—	—	—	3,000	—	3,250
1841 2nd restrike	—	—	—	—	—	3,000	—	6,000
1842 original	—	—	—	—	—	3,000	—	3,250
1842 1st restrike	—	—	—	—	—	3,000	—	3,250
1842 2nd restrike	—	—	—	—	—	3,000	—	6,000
1843 original	—	—	—	—	—	3,000	—	3,250
1843 1st restrike	—	—	—	—	—	3,000	—	3,250
1843 2nd restrike	—	—	—	—	—	3,000	—	6,500
1844 original	—	—	—	—	—	3,000	—	3,250
1844 1st restrike	—	—	—	—	—	3,000	—	3,250
1844 2nd restrike	—	—	—	—	—	3,000	—	6,000
1845 original	—	—	—	—	—	3,000	—	6,000
1845 1st restrike	—	—	—	—	—	3,000	—	3,250
1845 2nd restrike	—	—	—	—	—	3,000	—	6,000
1846 original	—	—	—	—	—	3,000	—	3,250
1846 1st restrike	—	—	—	—	—	3,000	—	3,250
1846 2nd restrike	—	—	—	—	—	3,000	—	6,000
1847 original	—	—	—	—	—	3,000	—	3,250
1847 1st restrike	—	—	—	—	—	5,500	—	3,250
1847 2nd restrike	—	—	—	—	—	3,000	—	6,000
1848 original	—	—	—	—	—	3,000	—	6,000
1848 1st restrike	—	—	—	—	—	3,000	—	3,250
1848 2nd restrike	—	—	—	—	—	3,000	—	6,000
1849 original, small date	—	—	—	—	—	3,000	—	3,250

Date	Mintage	G-4	VG-8	F-12	VF-20	XF-40	MS-60	Prf-60
1849 1st restrike small date	—	—	—	—	—	3,000	—	3,250
1849 large date	39,864	56.00	75.00	80.00	90.00	110	300	—
1850	39,812	56.00	75.00	80.00	90.00	110	340	—
1851	147,672	52.00	70.00	75.00	82.00	96.00	195	—
1852 original	—	15,000	55,000	30,000	35,000	40,000	—	90,000
1852 1st restrike	—	1,000	1,500	1,500	3,000	5,000	—	5,000
1852 2nd restrike	—	1,000	1,500	1,500	3,000	5,000	—	7,000
1853	129,694	52.00	70.00	75.00	82.00	96.00	195	—
1854	55,358	52.00	70.00	75.00	82.00	96.00	195	—
1855	56,500	52.00	70.00	75.00	82.00	96.00	195	3,250
1856	40,430	52.00	70.00	75.00	82.00	96.00	195	3,250
1857	35,180	57.00	77.00	85.00	100.00	126	270	3,250

CENT

Flowing Hair Cent
Chain reverse

KM# 11 • 13.4800 g., **Copper**, 26-27 mm. • **Designer:** Henry Voigt

Date	Mintage	G-4	VG-8	F-12	VF-20	XF-40	MS-60
1793 "AMERI"	36,103	8,950	13,750	25,500	45,500	86,000	245,000
1793 "AMERICA"	Inc. above	6,950	10,500	17,750	36,500	61,500	140,000
1793 periods after "LIBERTY"	Inc. above	7,850	11,250	18,850	38,500	63,500	147,000

Flowing Hair Cent
Wreath reverse

KM# 12 • 13.4800 g., **Copper**, 26-28 mm. • **Designer:** Henry Voigt

Date	Mintage	G-4	VG-8	F-12	VF-20	XF-40	MS-60
1793 vine and bars edge	63,353	1,950	2,950	4,750	7,500	12,500	30,000
1793 lettered edge	Inc. above	2,100	3,250	5,200	8,000	14,000	—
1793 strawberry leaf; 4 known	—	350,000	450,000	875,000	—	—	—

Liberty Cap Cent

KM# 13 • **Copper**, 13.48 g. (1793-95) and 10.89 g. (1795-96), 29 mm. • **Designer:** Joseph Wright (1793-1795) and John Smith Gardner (1795-1796) **Notes:** The heavier pieces were struck on a thicker planchet. The Liberty design on the obverse was revised slightly in 1794, but the 1793 design was used on some 1794 strikes. A 1795 "lettered edge" variety has ONE HUNDRED FOR A DOLLAR and a leaf inscribed on the edge.

CENT

Date	Mintage	G-4	VG-8	F-12	VF-20	XF-40	MS-60
1793 cap	11,056	3,500	6,500	11,500	36,500	67,500	—
1794 head '93	918,521	1,350	2,600	4,000	8,450	20,000	—
1794 head '94	Inc. above	550	750	1,000	18,505	3,750	9,000
1794 head '95	Inc. above	475	675	900	1,650	3,350	—
1794 starred rev.	Inc. above	10,500	17,500	35,000	—	—	—
1795 plain edge	501,500	400	650	900	1,750	3,850	4,750
1795 reeded edge	Inc. above	350,000	700,000	—	—	—	—
1795 Jefferson head	Inc. above	24,500	49,500	95,000	150,000	—	—
1795 Jefferson head lettered edge	Inc. above	75,000	—	175,000	—	—	—

Liberty Cap Cent

KM# 13a • 10.8900 g., **Copper**, 29 mm. • **Designer:** Joseph Wright (1793-1795) and John Smith Gardner (1795-1796)

Date	Mintage	G-4	VG-8	F-12	VF-20	XF-40	MS-60
1795 lettered edge, "One Cent" high in wreath	37,000	400	550	900	1,750	4,000	15,000
1796	109,825	350	500	800	1,400	3,750	21,000

Draped Bust Cent

Draped bust right, date at angle below obverse   Value within wreath reverse

Stemless   Stems

KM# 22 • 10.9800 g., **Copper**, 29 mm. • **Obv. Legend** LIBERTY **Rev. Legend:** UNITED STATES OF AMERICA **Designer:** Robert Scot **Notes:** The 1801 "3 errors" variety has the fraction on the reverse reading "1/000," has only one stem extending from the wreath above and on both sides of the fraction on the reverse, and UNITED in UNITED STATES OF AMERICA appears as "linited."

Date	Mintage	G-4	VG-8	F-12	VF-20	XF-40	MS-60
1796 Rev. of 1794	363,375	300	450	900	2,800	6,850	—
1796 Rev. of 1796	Inc. above	260	375	700	3,250	9,500	—
1796 Rev. of 1797	Inc. above	240	350	650	1,500	3,250	—
1796 Liberty error	Inc. above	300	750	1,500	5,500	13,500	—
1797 reverse of 1796 plain edge	897,510	165	300	600	3,450	5,500	—
1797 reverse of 1796 gripped edge	Inc. above	185	375	550	1,350	4,750	—
1797	Inc. above	130	175	250	335	1,150	3,300
1797 stemless	Inc. above	300	495	600	910	3,200	—
1798/7	1,841,745	200	300	375	1,200	3,900	—
1798 reverse of 1796	Inc. above	—	—	—	—	—	—
1798 1st hair style	Inc. above	90.00	130	200	350	1,300	3,100
1798 2nd hair style	Inc. above	—	—	—	—	—	—
1799	42,540	2,750	4,650	10,000	24,500	58,500	—
1799/98	Inc. above	2,600	4,300	9,200	21,000	46,000	—
1800	2,822,175	50.00	95.00	200	400	1,750	—
1800/798	Inc. above	—	—	—	—	—	—
1800/79	Inc. above	—	—	—	—	—	—
1801	1,362,837	60.00	85.00	195	375	850	—
1801 3 errors	Inc. above	225	500	925	1,750	5,500	—
1801 1/000	Inc. above	—	—	—	—	—	—
1801 100/000	Inc. above	—	—	—	—	—	—
1802	3,435,100	60.00	85.00	185	360	780	2,250
1802 stemless	Inc. above	68.00	95.00	200	350	—	—
1802 fraction 1/000	Inc. above	—	—	—	—	—	—
1803 small date, small fraction	2,471,353	60.00	85.00	185	350	750	2,250

CENT

Date	Mintage	G-4	VG-8	F-12	VF-20	XF-40	MS-60
1803 small date, large fraction	Inc. above	60.00	85.00	185	360	800	—
1803 large date, small fraction	Inc. above	4,600	6,950	14,500	26,500	75,000	—
1803 large date, large fraction	Inc. above	—	—	—	—	—	—
1804	96,500	1,400	2,000	2,600	3,200	7,000	—
1804 Restrike of 1860	—	—	—	650	750	800	1,000
1805	941,116	60.00	90.00	160	300	875	2,450
1806	348,000	70.00	100.00	150	375	1,100	4,700
1807 small fraction	727,221	60.00	80.00	160	300	800	2,250
1807 large fraction	Inc. above	—	—	—	—	—	—
1807/6 large 7/6	Inc. above	60.00	80.00	160	350	1,275	—
1807/6 small 7/6	Inc. above	1,900	2,900	4,200	6,000	19,000	—

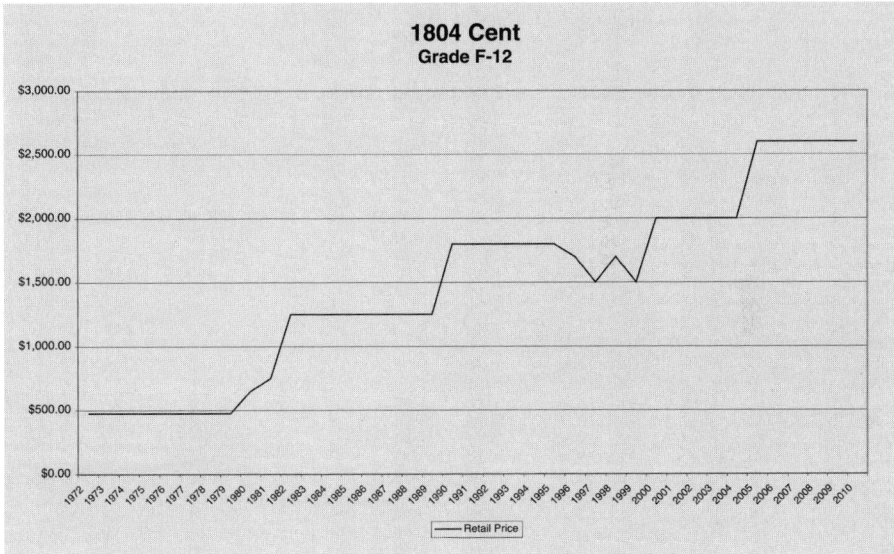

1804 Cent
Grade F-12

Classic Head Cent
Classic head left, flanked by stars, date below obverse
Value within wreath reverse

KM# 39 • 10.8900 g., **Copper**, 29 mm. • **Rev. Legend:** UNITED STATES OF AMERICA **Designer:** John Reich

Date	Mintage	G-4	VG-8	F-12	VF-20	XF-40	MS-60
1808	1,109,000	85.00	150	250	575	1,450	3,600
1809	222,867	135	250	450	1,050	2,650	6,300
1810/09	1,458,500	—	—	—	—	—	—
1810	Inc. above	75.00	95.00	210	550	1,100	3,850
1811/10	218,025	130	200	440	1,200	2,200	—
1811	Inc. above	110	175	400	1,000	1,500	7,000
1812 small date	1,075,500	54.00	88.00	215	550	975	2,800
1812 large date	—	—	—	—	—	—	—
1813	418,000	60.00	175	400	800	1,200	—
1814 Plain 4	357,830	54.00	93.00	225	530	975	2,800
1814 Crosslet 4	Inc. above	54.00	88.00	215	550	975	—

Coronet Cent

Coronet head left, within circle of stars, date below obverse
Value within wreath reverse

KM# 45 • 10.8900 g., **Copper**, 28-29 mm. • **Rev. Legend:** UNITED STATES OF AMERICA **Designer:** John Reich

Date	Mintage	G-4	VG-8	F-12	VF-20	XF-40	MS-60
1816	2,820,982	31.00	37.00	51.00	98.00	175	420
1817 13 obverse stars	3,948,400	29.00	34.00	45.00	75.00	145	500
1817 15 obverse stars	Inc. above	35.00	44.00	70.00	163	550	1,600
1818	3,167,000	29.00	33.00	40.00	72.00	125	270
1819	2,671,000	29.00	33.00	40.00	72.00	120	285
1820	4,407,550	29.00	33.00	40.00	72.00	120	300
1821	389,000	40.00	75.00	250	400	1,500	6,000
1822	2,072,339	31.00	35.00	45.00	100.00	195	750
1823	—	90.00	200	310	690	2,750	—
1823/22	—	80.00	110	300	675	2,450	—
1823 Restrike	—	600	750	850	1,000	1,200	2,000
1824	1,262,000	31.00	35.00	38.00	160	350	950
1824/22	Inc. above	40.00	49.00	90.00	375	1,000	9,850
1825	1,461,100	30.00	35.00	50.00	110	300	960
1826	1,517,425	30.00	35.00	40.00	84.00	175	750
1826/25	Inc. above	30.00	40.00	75.00	175	600	2,000
1827	2,357,732	29.00	33.00	40.00	91.00	125	750
1828	2,260,624	29.00	33.00	40.00	81.00	150	450
1829	1,414,500	29.00	33.00	40.00	91.00	130	475
1830	1,711,500	25.00	29.00	36.00	68.00	120	400
1831	3,359,260	25.00	29.00	36.00	68.00	115	315
1832	2,362,000	25.00	29.00	36.00	68.00	120	380
1833	2,739,000	25.00	29.00	36.00	68.00	113	300
1834	1,855,100	25.00	29.00	36.00	68.00	125	375
1834 Large 8 & stars, small letters	Inc. above	75.00	120	145	250	625	—
1835	3,878,400	25.00	29.00	36.00	68.00	105	300
1836	2,111,000	25.00	29.00	36.00	68.00	105	350
1837	5,558,300	25.00	29.00	36.00	68.00	105	300
1838	6,370,200	25.00	29.00	36.00	68.00	105	300
1839	3,128,661	29.00	33.00	40.00	72.00	110	350
1839/36	Inc. above	300	600	1,250	2,450	4,900	—

Braided Hair Cent

Head left, braided hair, within circle of stars, date below obverse
Value within wreath reverse

KM# 67 • 10.8900 g., **Copper**, 27.5 mm. • **Rev. Legend:** UNITED STATES OF AMERICA **Designer:** Christian Gobrecht **Notes:** 1840 and 1842 strikes are known with both small and large dates, with little difference in value. A slightly larger Liberty head and larger reverse lettering were used beginning in 1843.

Date	Mintage	G-4	VG-8	F-12	VF-20	XF-40	MS-60
1840	2,462,700	25.00	28.00	31.00	36.00	69.00	475
1841	1,597,367	25.00	28.00	31.00	39.00	79.00	440
1842	2,383,390	25.00	28.00	31.00	36.00	69.00	425
1843	2,425,342	25.00	28.00	31.00	36.00	69.00	445
1843 obverse 1842 with reverse of 1844	Inc. above	27.00	30.00	33.00	38.00	79.00	400
1844	2,398,752	25.00	28.00	31.00	36.00	69.00	300

Date	Mintage	G-4	VG-8	F-12	VF-20	XF-40	MS-60
1844/81	Inc. above	40.00	50.00	60.00	100.00	225	700
1845	3,894,804	25.00	28.00	31.00	36.00	69.00	250
1846	4,120,800	23.00	26.00	29.00	34.00	69.00	250
1847	6,183,669	23.00	26.00	29.00	34.00	69.00	250
1847/7	Inc. above	32.00	50.00	90.00	150	385	1,350
1848	6,415,799	25.00	28.00	31.00	36.00	61.00	250
1849	4,178,500	25.00	28.00	31.00	36.00	61.00	325
1850	4,426,844	25.00	28.00	31.00	36.00	61.00	250
1851	9,889,707	23.00	26.00	29.00	34.00	59.00	165
1851/81	Inc. above	36.00	45.00	55.00	85.00	175	600
1852	5,063,094	23.00	26.00	29.00	34.00	59.00	165
1853	6,641,131	23.00	26.00	29.00	34.00	59.00	165
1854	4,236,156	23.00	26.00	29.00	34.00	59.00	165
1855 Slanted 5's	1,574,829	43.00	56.00	66.00	71.00	96.00	200
1855 Upright 5's	Inc. above	23.00	26.00	29.00	34.00	59.00	165
1855 Slanted 5's Knob on Ear	Inc. above	29.00	34.00	41.00	52.00	99.00	—
1856 Slanted 5	2,690,463	23.00	26.00	29.00	34.00	59.00	165
1856 Upright 5	Inc. above	43.00	56.00	69.00	—	—	—
1857 Large date	333,456	125	150	175	235	310	600
1857 Small date	Inc. above	85.00	110	140	190	265	—

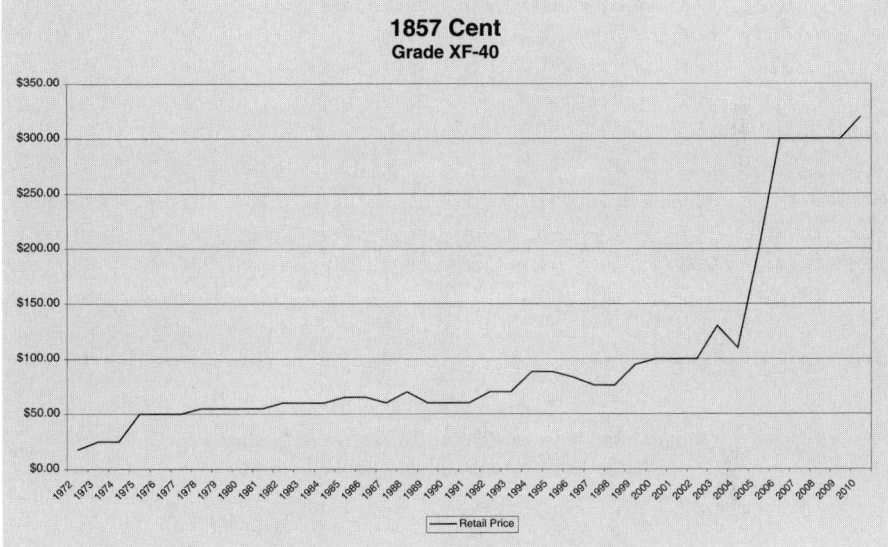

1857 Cent
Grade XF-40

Flying Eagle Cent
Flying eagle above date obverse
Value within wreath reverse

Large letters AM touch at bottom

Small letters Space between AM

KM# 85 • 4.6700 g., **Copper-Nickel**, 19 mm. • **Obv. Legend** UNITED STATES OF AMERICA **Designer:** James B. Longacre **Notes:** On the large-letter variety of 1858, the "A" and "M" in AMERICA are connected at their bases; on the small-letter variety, the two letters are separated.

Date	Mintage	G-4	VG-8	F-12	VF-20	XF-40	AU-50	MS-60	MS-65	Prf-65
1856	Est. 2,500	6,250	7,250	9,000	10,750	12,850	13,500	16,500	65,000	28,500
1857	17,450,000	27.50	39.00	40.00	47.00	125	165	320	3,500	29,000
1858/7	Inc. below	65.00	92.50	175	380	760	1,500	3,300	60,000	—
1858 large letters	24,600,000	27.50	41.00	43.50	56.00	150	220	340	3,850	24,500
1858 small letters	Inc. above	26.00	39.00	42.00	47.00	135	175	320	3,650	30,000

Indian Head Cent
Indian head with headdress left above date obverse
Value within wreath reverse

KM# 87 • 4.6700 g., **Copper-Nickel**, 19 mm. • **Obv. Legend** UNITED STATES OF AMERICA **Designer:** James B. Longacre

Date	Mintage	G-4	VG-8	F-12	VF-20	XF-40	AU-50	MS-60	MS-65	Prf-65
1859	36,400,000	13.00	16.00	22.50	48.00	100.00	175	230	3,650	5,200

Indian Head Cent
Indian head with headdress left above date obverse
Value within wreath, shield above reverse

KM# 90 • 4.6700 g., **Copper-Nickel**, 19 mm. • **Obv. Legend** UNITED STATES OF AMERICA **Designer:** James B. Longacre

Date	Mintage	G-4	VG-8	F-12	VF-20	XF-40	AU-50	MS-60	MS-65	Prf-65
1860 Rounded Bust	20,566,000	11.00	15.00	22.00	46.00	68.00	110	190	965	3,600
1860	1,000	—	—	—	—	—	—	—	—	—
1860 Pointed Bust	Inc. above	20.00	30.00	42.00	60.00	100.00	160	300	6,000	—
1861	10,100,000	20.00	30.00	42.00	58.00	95.00	160	180	975	7,250
1862	28,075,000	11.00	11.50	12.50	15.00	28.00	60.00	80.00	1,050	2,350
1863	49,840,000	7.50	9.25	11.00	12.50	25.00	58.00	75.00	1,050	3,100
1864	13,740,000	16.50	28.50	35.00	72.00	125	175	220	1,350	3,200

Indian Head Cent
Indian head with headdress left above date obverse
Value within wreath, shield above reverse

1864 "L"

KM# 90a • 3.1100 g., **Bronze**, 19 mm. • **Obv. Legend** UNITED STATES OF AMERICA **Designer:** James B. Longacre **Notes:** The 1864 "L" variety has the designer's initial in Liberty's hair to the right of her neck.

Date	Mintage	G-4	VG-8	F-12	VF-20	XF-40	AU-50	MS-60	MS-65	Prf-65
1864	39,233,714	8.00	20.00	25.00	45.00	70.00	80.00	110	335	10,500
1864 L pointed bust	Inc. above	52.50	72.50	139	185	275	325	410	1,700	200,000
1865 plain 5	35,429,286	7.00	11.00	20.00	25.00	45.00	60.00	90.00	485	6,750
1865 fancy 5	Inc. above	6.00	10.50	18.50	23.00	40.00	55.00	85.00	465	—
1866	9,826,500	46.00	66.00	80.00	115	195	240	280	1,350	4,500
1867	9,821,000	52.00	72.00	110	120	195	240	285	1,350	6,100
1867/1867	Inc. above	60.00	85.00	130	190	275	385	565	1,950	—
1868	10,266,500	37.50	50.00	77.00	120	180	245	265	985	5,750
1869/9	6,420,000	145	280	495	660	825	1,000	1,250	2,350	—
1869	Inc. above	90.00	125	230	335	450	560	625	1,750	3,100
1870	5,275,000	62.00	118	225	285	410	510	600	1,400	2,650
1871	3,929,500	88.00	125	280	310	420	510	610	2,400	2,500
1872	4,042,000	90.00	180	390	425	625	750	840	3,850	4,250
1873 closed 3	11,676,500	30.00	52.00	95.00	135	235	300	400	2,850	2,950
1873 open 3	Inc. above	20.00	34.00	65.00	82.00	175	215	250	1,300	—
1873 Double Liberty die 1	Inc. above	275	450	950	1,500	2,400	4,250	7,500	—	—
1873 Double Liberty die 2	Inc. above	—	—	450	900	1,650	2,800	4,500	—	—
1874	14,187,500	15.00	22.50	46.00	65.00	112	150	225	700	2,850
1875	13,528,000	16.00	29.00	56.00	72.00	120	165	215	800	8,500

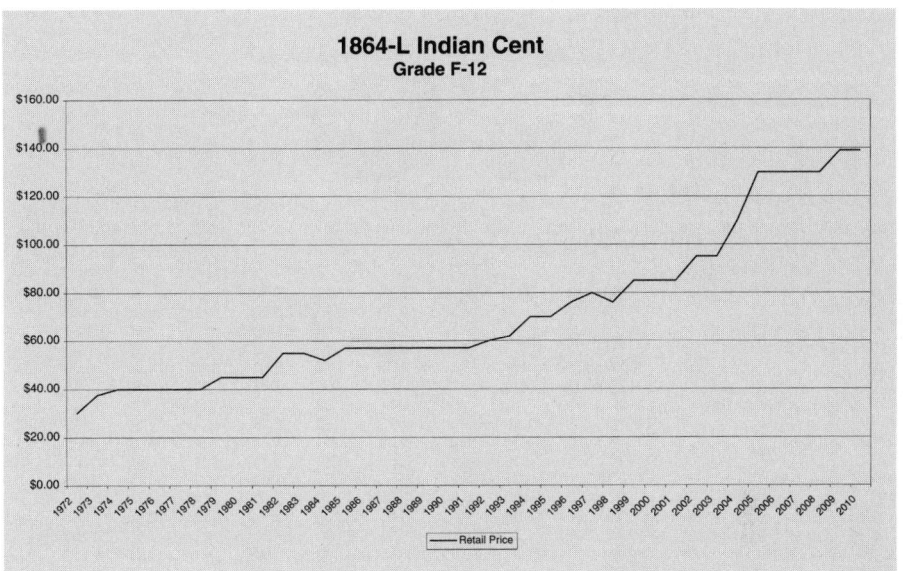

1864-L Indian Cent
Grade F-12

Date	Mintage	G-4	VG-8	F-12	VF-20	XF-40	AU-50	MS-60	MS-65	Prf-65
1876	7,944,000	27.00	38.50	74.00	130	230	295	335	975	2,600
1877	852,500	985	1,190	1,600	2,050	2,650	3,000	3,450	13,000	12,500
1878	5,799,850	26.00	35.00	68.00	135	245	290	350	875	1,375
1879	16,231,200	7.00	10.00	16.50	33.00	75.00	90.00	100.00	365	1,250
1880	38,964,955	3.50	5.50	6.50	11.00	28.00	48.00	66.00	360	1,250
1881	39,211,575	3.50	4.25	6.50	8.00	22.00	30.00	43.00	325	1,250
1882	38,581,100	3.50	4.25	5.00	10.00	22.00	30.00	40.00	325	1,450
1883	45,589,109	3.00	4.00	4.50	7.50	17.50	30.00	42.00	325	1,600
1884	23,261,742	3.50	4.50	7.00	12.50	29.00	40.00	60.00	460	1,250
1885	11,765,384	6.75	8.00	12.00	27.00	62.00	82.00	105	725	1,500
1886 Type 1 obverse	17,654,290	3.75	6.60	19.80	56.00	148	170	190	1,250	2,650
1886 Type 2 obverse	Inc. above	7.00	10.00	35.00	90.00	200	250	325	2,500	7,500
1887	45,226,483	2.50	3.00	4.00	7.00	19.00	28.00	50.00	400	6,200
1888	37,494,414	2.75	3.25	5.00	8.00	21.00	28.00	48.00	900	5,400
1889	48,869,361	2.25	2.75	3.50	6.00	12.00	26.00	40.00	400	1,900
1890	57,182,854	2.10	2.50	3.00	5.50	10.00	23.00	37.50	400	1,800
1891	47,072,350	2.25	2.75	3.25	5.50	13.00	23.00	37.00	400	2,150
1892	37,649,832	2.40	3.25	4.40	6.00	18.50	25.00	35.00	400	1,325
1893	46,642,195	2.10	2.75	3.25	5.50	10.00	22.00	30.00	340	1,250
1894	16,752,132	5.00	6.00	13.00	20.00	50.00	65.00	85.00	375	1,350
1894/94	Inc. above	24.00	34.00	80.00	150	275	440	800	8,000	—
1895	38,343,636	2.10	2.40	3.50	4.50	11.00	22.00	32.00	200	1,275
1896	39,057,293	1.95	2.50	3.25	4.75	13.00	26.00	34.00	225	1,900
1897	50,466,330	1.95	2.40	2.75	4.00	10.00	22.00	30.00	195	1,600
1898	49,823,079	1.95	2.40	2.75	4.00	10.00	22.00	30.00	195	1,275
1899	53,600,031	1.95	2.20	2.60	4.00	10.00	22.00	30.00	165	1,275
1900	66,833,764	1.95	2.20	2.50	4.00	12.00	23.00	30.00	175	1,275
1901	79,611,143	1.85	2.20	2.50	4.00	11.00	22.00	29.00	165	1,275
1902	87,376,722	1.85	2.20	2.50	4.00	10.00	22.00	28.00	165	1,325
1903	85,094,493	1.85	2.20	2.50	4.00	10.00	21.00	28.00	165	1,275
1904	61,328,015	1.75	2.20	2.50	4.00	10.00	21.00	28.00	165	1,275
1905	80,719,163	1.75	2.20	2.50	3.50	9.00	20.00	28.00	165	1,350
1906	96,022,255	1.75	2.20	2.50	3.50	9.00	21.00	28.00	165	1,275
1907	108,138,618	1.75	2.20	2.50	3.50	8.50	20.00	28.00	165	1,950
1908	32,327,987	1.75	2.30	2.50	3.50	9.00	20.00	28.00	165	1,275
1908S	1,115,000	77.00	82.00	105	122	166	195	285	2,650	—
1909	14,370,645	14.00	14.80	15.50	15.90	18.50	30.00	38.00	155	1,275
1909S	309,000	590	655	720	825	900	950	1,000	2,250	—

Lincoln Cent
Wheat Ears reverse

KM# 132 • 3.1100 g., **Bronze**, 19 mm. • **Designer:** Victor D. Brenner **Notes:** The 1909 "VDB" varieties have the designer's initials inscribed at the 6 o'clock position on the reverse. The initials were removed until 1918, when they were restored on the obverse • MS60 prices are for brown coins and MS65 prices are for coins that are at least 90% original red.

Date	Mintage	G-4	VG-8	F-12	VF-20	XF-40	AU-50	MS-60	MS-65	Prf-65
1909 VDB	27,995,000	12.50	13.00	13.25	13.50	14.00	16.00	25.00	195	12,500
1909 VDB Doubled Die Obverse	Inc. above	—	—	55.00	75.00	100.00	120	150	4,650	—
1909S VDB	484,000	765	1,010	1,235	1,395	1,500	1,650	1,825	6,850	—
1909	72,702,618	365	3.85	4.35	4.75	5.50	12.00	14.50	85.00	950
1909S	1,825,000	115	120	142	185	245	265	350	1,275	—
1909S/S S over horizontal S	Inc. above	115	120	135	180	255	280	350	1,600	—
1910	146,801,218	.50	.60	.75	1.00	4.25	10.00	17.50	250	800
1910S	6,045,000	16.50	20.00	21.00	27.50	47.50	72.00	98.00	825	—
1911	101,177,787	.60	.80	2.00	2.50	6.75	11.00	18.50	350	765
1911D	12,672,000	4.75	5.85	9.50	22.50	50.00	70.00	88.00	1,450	—
1911S	4,026,000	49.00	53.00	55.00	60.00	75.00	105	175	2,850	—
1912	68,153,060	1.60	1.85	2.35	5.50	13.50	26.00	32.00	520	975
1912D	10,411,000	6.50	9.75	11.00	26.00	69.00	105	160	2,350	—
1912S	4,431,000	24.00	26.00	29.00	42.00	78.00	115	175	4,150	—
1913	76,532,352	.90	1.10	1.65	3.25	18.50	28.00	34.00	385	750
1913D	15,804,000	2.75	3.25	3.60	10.50	49.00	61.50	90.00	2,650	—
1913S	6,101,000	13.50	16.50	20.00	32.00	57.00	105	190	6,350	—
1914	75,238,432	.60	.95	2.10	6.00	18.00	40.00	52.00	415	775
1914D	1,193,000	205	245	395	450	945	1,475	2,000	24,500	—
1914S	4,137,000	25.00	27.50	31.00	39.00	88.00	175	300	9,350	—
1915	29,092,120	1.65	2.90	4.00	18.00	60.00	68.00	82.00	1,300	775
1915D	22,050,000	1.75	2.85	4.50	6.85	24.00	44.00	70.00	1,250	—
1915S	4,833,000	21.00	24.50	28.00	32.00	72.00	90.00	185	4,650	—
1916	131,833,677	.45	.60	1.10	2.40	8.50	14.50	18.50	385	2,450
1916D	35,956,000	1.35	2.00	3.25	6.50	17.50	38.00	72.00	3,150	—
1916S	22,510,000	1.85	3.25	4.40	9.50	27.50	48.00	102	7,450	—
1917	196,429,785	.35	.40	.55	1.85	4.75	13.00	16.00	475	—
1917 Doubled Die Obverse	Inc. above	90.00	110	175	350	900	1,750	2,500	27,500	—
1917D	55,120,000	1.15	1.60	2.85	5.00	36.50	44.00	70.00	2,900	—
1917S	32,620,000	.65	1.00	1.50	2.50	11.50	25.00	63.00	6,500	—
1918	288,104,634	.35	.40	.50	1.00	4.25	9.50	13.00	375	—
1918D	47,830,000	1.20	1.45	2.65	5.50	15.50	34.00	75.00	3,500	—
1918S	34,680,000	.40	1.00	1.65	3.65	11.00	31.00	66.00	7,950	—
1919	392,021,000	.30	.40	.50	.80	1.60	5.25	8.00	115	—
1919D	57,154,000	1.10	1.35	1.85	4.85	12.75	35.00	57.50	2,650	—
1919S	139,760,000	.40	.60	1.80	2.65	5.75	17.50	42.00	3,950	—
1920	310,165,000	.30	.35	.75	1.25	2.80	7.50	15.00	235	—
1920D	49,280,000	1.15	1.65	2.90	6.85	18.50	37.00	68.50	2,650	—
1920S	46,220,000	.75	.80	1.50	2.75	13.00	34.50	100.00	8,250	—
1921	39,157,000	.60	.80	1.15	2.80	10.50	21.00	41.50	365	—
1921S	15,274,000	1.65	2.10	3.50	6.25	34.50	68.00	100.00	6,150	—
1922D	7,160,000	20.00	21.00	23.00	25.00	37.50	75.00	100.00	2,350	—
1922D Weak Rev	Inc. above	18.00	18.50	19.50	21.00	34.00	65.00	90.00	1,850	—
1922D Weak D	Inc. above	30.00	44.00	60.00	100.00	185	285	550	—	—
1922 No D Die 2 Strong Rev	Inc. above	725	790	1,050	1,375	2,800	5,900	10,500	160,000	—
1922 No D Die 3 Weak Rev	Inc. above	300	400	685	885	1,750	3,500	8,500	—	—
1923	74,723,000	.50	.70	.95	1.25	5.75	10.50	13.50	435	—
1923S	8,700,000	4.00	5.25	7.00	10.00	38.00	88.00	185	14,850	—
1924	75,178,000	.35	.45	.60	1.00	5.25	11.00	17.50	385	—
1924D	2,520,000	36.00	44.00	49.00	60.00	118	170	255	12,500	—
1924S	11,696,000	1.45	1.65	2.75	5.35	32.50	68.00	105	10,000	—
1925	139,949,000	.30	.35	.50	.70	2.75	6.50	9.00	100.00	—
1925D	22,580,000	1.25	1.65	3.10	5.85	15.50	30.00	60.00	4,650	—
1925S	26,380,000	.95	1.25	1.85	2.75	11.50	31.00	83.00	9,850	—
1926	157,088,000	.25	.35	.50	.60	1.65	5.25	7.00	62.00	—
1926D	28,020,000	1.50	1.70	3.40	5.25	15.50	34.00	80.00	3,950	—
1926S	4,550,000	9.00	10.00	11.50	16.00	35.00	70.00	135	110,000	—
1927	144,440,000	.20	.25	.35	.60	1.60	5.25	7.00	92.00	—
1927D	27,170,000	1.35	1.70	2.25	3.35	7.50	25.00	58.50	2,100	—
1927S	14,276,000	1.50	1.85	2.65	5.25	14.50	40.00	62.50	6,350	—
1928	134,116,000	.20	.25	.35	.60	1.25	4.00	7.50	84.00	—
1928D	31,170,000	1.10	1.40	2.15	3.65	6.75	19.00	34.00	985	—

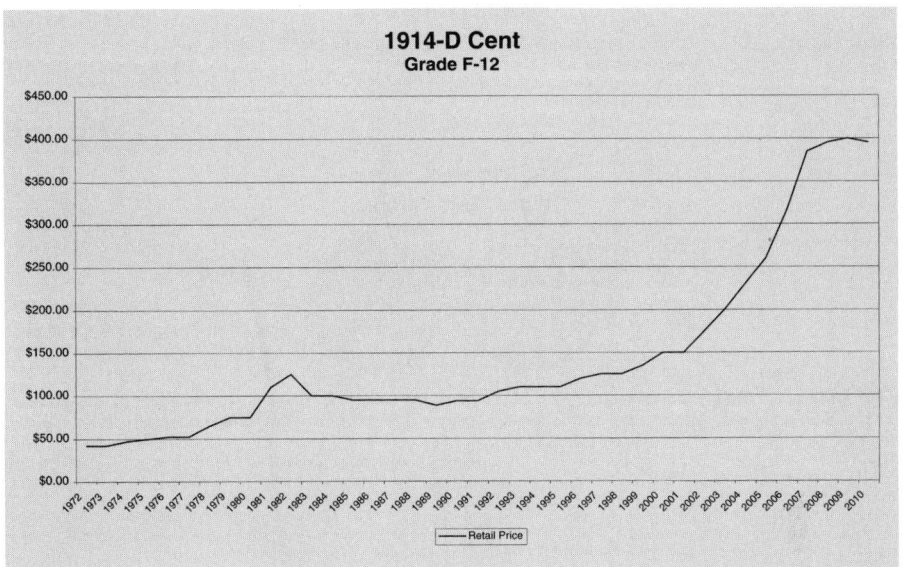

1914-D Cent
Grade F-12

Date	Mintage	G-4	VG-8	F-12	VF-20	XF-40	AU-50	MS-60	MS-65	Prf-65
1928S Small S	17,266,000	1.20	1.65	2.60	4.00	9.50	31.00	71.50	5,450	—
1928S Large S	Inc. above	2.00	2.85	4.25	7.50	16.50	55.00	135	6,850	—
1929	185,262,000	.20	.25	.35	.55	2.75	5.25	6.25	85.00	—
1929D	41,730,000	.60	1.10	1.40	2.75	5.85	13.50	24.00	590	—
1929S	50,148,000	.70	1.15	1.85	2.80	7.00	14.75	19.00	525	—
1930	157,415,000	.20	.25	.35	.60	1.25	2.75	3.75	31.50	—
1930D	40,100,000	.30	.40	.55	.90	2.00	5.50	9.75	92.00	—
1930S	24,286,000	.30	.40	.58	.80	1.50	6.50	9.50	47.50	—
1931	19,396,000	.65	.75	1.10	2.00	4.00	9.50	18.50	130	—
1931D	4,480,000	4.85	5.85	6.50	7.50	12.75	33.50	48.50	925	—
1931S	866,000	112	118	125	132	138	145	163	685	—
1932	9,062,000	1.50	1.95	2.85	3.50	6.75	13.00	17.50	82.00	—
1932D	10,500,000	1.40	1.90	2.50	2.85	4.15	11.00	18.50	110	—
1933	14,360,000	1.40	1.80	2.65	2.85	6.50	11.50	15.50	82.00	—
1933D	6,200,000	3.50	4.25	5.65	7.50	13.50	19.00	23.00	100.00	—
1934	219,080,000	.20	.25	.40	.60	1.25	4.00	8.00	30.00	—
1934D	28,446,000	.35	.50	.80	1.50	3.00	9.00	20.00	52.00	—
1935	245,338,000	.20	.30	.40	.55	.90	1.50	3.50	28.00	—
1935D	47,000,000	.15	.20	.30	.40	.95	2.50	4.50	30.00	—
1935S	38,702,000	.25	.35	.60	1.75	3.00	5.00	12.00	—	—
1936 (Proof in Satin Finish)	309,637,569	.20	.30	.40	.55	.85	1.40	2.00	8.00	1,000
1936 Brilliant Proof	Inc. above	—	—	—	—	—	—	—	—	1,100
1936D	40,620,000	.20	.30	.40	.55	.90	1.50	3.50	22.00	—
1936S	29,130,000	.20	.30	.45	.60	1.00	1.75	3.00	18.00	—
1937	309,179,320	.20	.30	.40	.55	.85	1.40	1.60	20.00	180
1937D	50,430,000	.20	.30	.40	.60	.95	1.00	2.20	24.00	—
1937S	34,500,000	.20	.30	.40	.55	.90	1.25	2.40	23.00	—
1938	156,696,734	.20	.30	.40	.55	.85	1.20	3.00	17.00	90.00
1938D	20,010,000	.20	.30	.45	.60	1.00	1.50	3.50	17.00	—
1938S	15,180,000	.30	.40	.50	.70	1.00	2.00	2.80	26.00	—
1939	316,479,520	.20	.30	.40	.55	.75	.90	1.00	15.00	85.00
1939D	15,160,000	.35	.45	.50	.60	.85	1.90	2.50	20.00	—
1939S	52,070,000	.30	.40	.50	.60	.80	1.10	2.00	19.00	—
1940	586,825,872	.10	.20	.30	.40	.50	.75	1.00	17.00	65.00
1940D	81,390,000	.20	.30	.40	.55	.75	.50	1.20	12.00	—
1940S	112,940,000	.20	.30	.40	.55	.90	1.25	1.40	14.00	—
1941	887,039,100	.10	.20	.30	.40	.50	.70	.85	17.00	80.00
1941 Doubled Die Obv	Inc. above	35.00	50.00	70.00	80.00	95.00	135	200	2,800	—
1941D	128,700,000	.20	.30	.40	.55	.75	1.25	2.25	20.00	—
1941S	92,360,000	.20	.30	.40	.55	.75	1.75	2.75	24.00	—
1942	657,828,600	.10	.20	.30	.40	.50	.70	.85	17.00	115
1942D	206,698,000	.20	.25	.30	.35	.40	.50	.65	22.00	—
1942S	85,590,000	.25	.35	.45	.85	1.25	2.50	4.50	26.00	—

Lincoln Cent
Wheat Ears reverse

KM# 132a • 2.7000 g., **Zinc Coated Steel**, 19 mm. • **Designer:** Victor D. Brenner

Date	Mintage	G-4	VG-8	F-12	VF-20	XF-40	AU-50	MS-60	MS-65	Prf-65
1943	684,628,670	.25	.30	.35	.45	.60	.85	1.25	16.00	—
1943D	217,660,000	.35	.40	.45	.50	.70	1.00	1.25	18.00	—
1943D/D RPM	Inc. above	30.00	38.00	50.00	65.00	90.00	125	200	1,400	—
1943S	191,550,000	.45	.45	.50	.65	.90	1.40	3.00	20.00	—

Lincoln Cent
Wheat Ears reverse

KM# A132 • 3.1100 g., **Copper-Zinc**, 19 mm. • **Designer:** Victor D. Brenner **Notes:** KM#132 design and composition resumed • MS60 prices are for brown coins and MS65 prices are for coins that are at least 90% original red.

Date	Mintage	XF-40	MS-65	Prf-65
1944	1,435,400,000	.40	8.00	—
1944D	430,578,000	.50	12.50	—
1944D/S Type 1	Inc. above	235	3,750	—
1944D/S Type 2	Inc. above	175	1,600	—
1944S	282,760,000	.40	12.00	—
1945	1,040,515,000	.40	15.00	—
1945D	226,268,000	.40	13.50	—
1945S	181,770,000	.40	12.00	—
1946	991,655,000	.30	13.00	—
1946D	315,690,000	.30	6.00	—
1946S	198,100,000	.30	5.50	—
1946S/D	—	70.00	600	—
1947	190,555,000	.45	16.00	—
1947D	194,750,000	.40	10.00	—
1947S	99,000,000	.35	12.00	—
1948	317,570,000	.40	14.00	—
1948D	172,637,000	.40	6.80	—
1948S	81,735,000	.40	6.50	—
1949	217,775,000	.40	15.00	—
1949D	153,132,000	.40	12.00	—
1949S	64,290,000	.50	10.00	—
1950	272,686,386	.40	13.50	70.00
1950D	334,950,000	.35	9.00	—
1950S	118,505,000	.40	8.00	—
1951	295,633,500	.40	14.00	70.00
1951D	625,355,000	.30	8.00	—
1951S	136,010,000	.40	10.00	—
1952	186,856,980	.40	16.00	42.00
1952D	746,130,000	.30	8.00	—
1952S	137,800,004	.60	9.00	—
1953	256,883,800	.30	18.00	30.00
1953D	700,515,000	.30	11.00	—
1953S	181,835,000	.40	11.50	—
1954	71,873,350	.25	17.50	17.00
1954D	251,552,500	.25	10.00	—
1954S	96,190,000	.25	12.00	—
1955	330,958,000	.25	15.00	16.00
1955 Doubled Die	Inc. above	1,600	43,500	—

Note: The 1955 "doubled die" has distinct doubling of the date and lettering on the obverse.

1955D	563,257,500	.20	12.00	—
1955S	44,610,000	.35	7.50	—
1956	421,414,384	.20	16.00	10.00
1956D	1,098,201,100	.20	8.00	—
1957	283,787,952	.20	9.00	6.00
1957D	1,051,342,000	.20	8.00	—
1958	253,400,652	.20	9.00	6.50
1958D	800,953,300	.20	8.00	—

Lincoln Cent
Lincoln Memorial reverse

Small date   Large date

Small date   Large date

KM# 201 • 3.1100 g., **Copper-Zinc** • **Rev. Designer:** Frank Gasparro **Notes:** MS60 prices are for brown coins and MS65 prices are for coins that are at least 90% original red. The dates were modified in 1960, 1970 and 1982, resulting in large-date and small-date varieties for those years. The 1972 "doubled die" shows doubling of IN GOD WE TRUST. The 1979-S and 1981-S Type II proofs have a clearer mint mark than the Type I proofs of those years. Some 1982 cents have the predominantly copper composition; others have the predominantly zinc composition. They can be distinguished by weight.

Date	Mintage	XF-40	MS-65	Prf-65
1959	610,864,291	—	18.00	1.50
1959D	1,279,760,000	—	16.00	—
1960 small date, low 9	588,096,602	2.10	12.00	16.00
1960 large date, high 9	Inc. above	—	10.00	1.25
1960D small date, low 9	1,580,884,000	—	10.00	—
1960D large date, high 9	Inc. above	—	11.00	—
1960D/D small over large date	Inc. above	—	300	—
1961	756,373,244	—	6.50	1.00
1961D	1,753,266,700	—	15.00	—
1962	609,263,019	—	8.00	1.00
1962D	1,793,148,400	—	14.00	—
1963	757,185,645	—	10.00	1.00
1963D	1,774,020,400	—	12.00	—
1964	2,652,525,762	—	6.50	1.00
1964D	3,799,071,500	—	7.00	—
1965	1,497,224,900	—	10.00	—
1965 SMS	Inc. above	—	7.50	—
1966	2,188,147,783	—	10.00	—
1966 SMS	Inc. above	—	8.00	—
1967	3,048,667,100	—	10.00	—
1967 SMS	Inc. above	—	8.00	—
1968	1,707,880,970	—	12.00	—
1968D	2,886,269,600	—	12.00	—
1968S	261,311,510	—	8.00	1.00
1969	1,136,910,000	—	6.50	—
1969D	4,002,832,200	—	10.00	—
1969S	547,309,631	—	8.00	1.10
1969S Doubled Die Obverse	Inc. above	—	—	—
1970	1,898,315,000	—	8.00	—
1970D	2,891,438,900	—	6.00	—
1970S	693,192,814	—	—	1.20
1970S small date, level 7	Inc. above	—	75.00	60.00
1970S large date, low 7	Inc. above	—	16.00	—
1970S Doubled Die Obverse	Inc. above	—	—	—
1971	1,919,490,000	—	25.00	—
1971D	2,911,045,600	—	5.50	—
1971S	528,354,192	—	6.00	1.20
1971S Doubled Die Obverse	Inc. above	—	—	—
1972	2,933,255,000	—	6.00	—
1972 Doubled Die Obverse	Inc. above	240	775	—
1972D	2,665,071,400	—	10.00	—
1972S	380,200,104	—	30.00	1.15
1973	3,728,245,000	—	8.00	—
1973D	3,549,576,588	—	11.00	—
1973S	319,937,634	—	8.00	0.80
1974	4,232,140,523	—	12.00	—
1974D	4,235,098,000	—	12.00	—
1974S	412,039,228	—	10.00	0.75
1975	5,451,476,142	—	8.00	—
1975D	4,505,245,300	—	13.50	—
1975S	2,845,450	—	—	5.50
1976	4,674,292,426	—	18.00	—
1976D	4,221,592,455	—	20.00	—

Date	Mintage	XF-40	MS-65	Prf-65
1976S	4,149,730	—	—	5.00
1977	4,469,930,000	—	14.00	—
1977D	4,149,062,300	—	14.00	—
1977S	3,251,152	—	—	3.00
1978	5,558,605,000	—	14.00	—
1978D	4,280,233,400	—	12.00	—
1978S	3,127,781	—	—	3.50
1979	6,018,515,000	—	12.00	—
1979D	4,139,357,254	—	8.00	—
1979S type I, proof	3,677,175	—	—	4.00
1979S type II, proof	Inc. above	—	—	4.25
1980	7,414,705,000	—	6.50	—
1980D	5,140,098,660	—	10.00	—
1980S	3,554,806	—	—	2.25
1981	7,491,750,000	—	7.50	—
1981D	5,373,235,677	—	9.00	—
1981S type I, proof	4,063,083	—	—	3.50
1981S type II, proof	Inc. above	—	—	60.00
1982 large date	10,712,525,000	—	6.00	—
1982 small date	Inc. above	—	8.00	—
1982D large date	6,012,979,368	—	6.00	—
1982S	3,857,479	—	—	—

Lincoln Cent
Lincoln Memorial reverse

KM# 201a • 2.5000 g., **Copper Plated Zinc**, 19 mm. • **Notes:** MS60 prices are for brown coins and MS65 prices are for coins that are at least 90% original red.

Date	Mintage	XF-40	MS-65	Prf-65
1982 large date	—	—	6.00	—
1982 small date	—	—	9.00	—
1982D large date	—	—	8.00	—
1982D small date	—	—	6.00	—

Lincoln Cent
Lincoln Memorial reverse

KM# 201b • **Copper Plated Zinc**, 19 mm. • **Notes:** MS60 prices are for brown coins and MS65 prices are for coins that are at least 90% original red.

Date	Mintage	XF-40	MS-65	Prf-65
1982S	3,857,479	—	—	3.00
1983	7,752,355,000	—	7.00	—
1983 Doubled Die	Inc. above	—	400	—
1983D	6,467,199,428	—	5.50	—
1983S	3,279,126	—	—	4.00
1984	8,151,079,000	—	7.50	—
1984 Doubled Die	Inc. above	—	275	—
1984D	5,569,238,906	—	5.50	—
1984S	3,065,110	—	—	4.50
1985	5,648,489,887	—	4.50	—
1985D	5,287,399,926	—	4.50	—
1985S	3,362,821	—	—	6.00
1986	4,491,395,493	—	5.00	—
1986D	4,442,866,698	—	8.00	—
1986S	3,010,497	—	—	7.50
1987	4,682,466,931	—	8.50	—
1987D	4,879,389,514	—	6.00	—
1987S	4,227,728	—	—	5.00
1988	6,092,810,000	—	8.50	—
1988D	5,253,740,443	—	5.50	—
1988S	3,262,948	—	—	4.00
1989	7,261,535,000	—	5.00	—
1989D	5,345,467,111	—	5.00	—
1989S	3,220,194	—	—	6.00
1990	6,851,765,000	—	5.00	—
1990D	4,922,894,533	—	5.00	—
1990S	3,299,559	—	—	5.00
1990 no S, Proof only	Inc. above	—	—	2,750
1991	5,165,940,000	—	6.00	—

Date	Mintage	XF-40	MS-65	Prf-65
1991D	4,158,442,076	—	5.00	—
1991S	2,867,787	—	—	5.00
1992	4,648,905,000	—	5.50	—
1992D	4,448,673,300	—	5.50	—
1992D Close AM, Proof Reverse Die	Inc. above	—	—	—
1992S	4,176,560	—	—	5.00
1993	5,684,705,000	—	5.50	—
1993D	6,426,650,571	—	5.50	—
1993S	3,394,792	—	—	7.00
1994	6,500,850,000	—	10.00	—
1994D	7,131,765,000	—	5.50	—
1994S	3,269,923	—	—	4.00
1995	6,411,440,000	—	4.50	—
1995 Doubled Die Obverse	Inc. above	20.00	50.00	—
1995D	7,128,560,000	—	5.00	—
1995S	2,707,481	—	—	9.50
1996	6,612,465,000	—	5.00	—
1996D	6,510,795,000	—	5.00	—
1996S	2,915,212	—	—	6.50
1997	4,622,800,000	—	5.00	—
1997D	4,576,555,000	—	5.00	—
1997S	2,796,678	—	—	11.50
1998	5,032,155,000	—	5.00	—
1998 Wide AM, reverse from proof die	Inc. above	—	—	—
1998D	5,255,353,500	—	5.00	—
1998S	2,957,286	—	—	9.50
1999	5,237,600,000	—	5.00	—
1999 Wide AM, reverse from proof die	Inc. above	—	—	—
1999D	6,360,065,000	—	5.00	—
1999S	3,362,462	—	—	5.00
2000	5,503,200,000	—	4.00	—
2000 Wide AM, reverse from proof die	Inc. above	—	—	—
2000D	8,774,220,000	—	4.00	—
2000S	4,063,361	—	—	4.00
2001	4,959,600,000	—	4.00	—
2001D	5,374,990,000	—	4.00	—
2001S	3,099,096	—	—	4.00
2002	3,260,800,000	—	4.00	—
2002D	4,028,055,000	—	4.00	—
2002S	3,157,739	—	—	4.00
2003	3,300,000,000	—	3.50	—
2003D	3,548,000,000	—	3.50	—
2003S	3,116,590	—	—	4.00
2004	3,379,600,000	—	3.50	—
2004D	3,456,400,000	—	3.50	—
2004S	2,992,069	—	—	4.00
2005	3,935,600,000	—	3.50	—
2005D	3,764,450,000	—	3.50	—
2005S	3,273,000	—	—	4.00
2006	4,290,000,000	—	2.00	—
2006D	3,944,000,000	—	2.50	—
2006S	2,923,105	—	—	4.00
2007	—	—	1.50	—
2007D	—	—	1.50	—
2007S	—	—	—	4.00
2008	—	—	1.50	—
2008D	—	—	1.50	—
2008S	—	—	—	4.00

Lincoln Bicentennial
Log cabin reverse

KM# 441 • 2.5000 g., **Copper Plated Zinc**, 19 mm. • **Rev. Designer:** Richard Masters and Jim Licaretz

Date	Mintage	XF-40	MS-65	Prf-65
2009P	284,400,000	—	1.50	—
2009D	350,400,000	—	1.50	—
2009S	—	—	—	4.00

Lincoln seated on log reverse

KM# 442 • 2.5000 g., **Copper Plated Zinc**, 19 mm. • **Rev. Designer:** Charles Vickers

Date	Mintage	XF-40	MS-65	Prf-65
2009P	376,000,000	—	1.50	—
2009D	363,600,000	—	1.50	—
2009S	—	—	—	4.00

Lincoln standing before Illinois Statehouse reverse

KM# 443 • 2.5000 g., **Copper Plated Zinc**, 19 mm. • **Rev. Designer:** Joel Ishowitz and Don Everhart

Date	Mintage	XF-40	MS-65	Prf-65
2009P	316,000,000	—	1.50	—
2009D	336,000,000	—	1.50	—
2009S	—	—	—	4.00

Capitol Building reverse

KM# 444 • 2.5000 g., **Copper Plated Zinc** • **Rev. Designer:** Susan Gamble and Joseph Menna

Date	Mintage	XF-40	MS-65	Prf-65
2009P	129,600,000	—	1.50	—
2009D	198,000,000	—	1.50	—
2009S	—	—	—	4.00

Lincoln bust right obverse   Shield reverse

KM# 469 • **Copper Plated Zinc** • **Obv. Designer:** Victor D. Brenner

Date	Mintage	XF-40	MS-65	Prf-65
2010P	—	—	1.50	—
2010D	—	—	1.50	—
2010S	—	—	—	4.00

2 CENTS
Shield in front of crossed arrows, banner above, date below obverse
Value within wheat wreath reverse

Small motto   Large motto

KM# 94 • 6.2200 g., **Copper-Tin-Zinc**, 23 mm. • **Rev. Legend:** UNITED STATES OF AMERICA **Designer:** James B. Longacre **Notes:** The motto IN GOD WE TRUST was modified in 1864, resulting in small-motto and large-motto varieties for that year.

Date	Mintage	G-4	VG-8	F-12	VF-20	XF-40	AU-50	MS-60	MS-65	Prf-65
1864 small motto	19,847,500	140	210	285	425	650	725	1,125	7,500	75,000
1864 large motto	Inc. above	16.50	18.50	20.00	27.50	42.50	70.00	84.00	1,650	3,950
1865 fancy 5	13,640,000	16.50	18.50	20.00	27.50	42.50	70.00	84.00	1,650	850
1865 plain 5	Inc. above	16.50	18.50	21.00	29.00	45.00	75.00	90.00	1,750	2,950
1866	3,177,000	17.00	20.00	21.50	29.00	46.00	75.00	94.00	2,550	2,850
1867	2,938,750	18.00	21.00	36.00	46.00	60.00	96.00	125	2,900	2,900
1867 double die obverse	Inc. above	—	65.00	135	200	275	440	575	12,500	—
1868	2,803,750	18.00	22.00	37.50	47.50	65.00	105	135	2,900	2,850
1869	1,546,000	20.00	23.00	40.00	50.00	79.00	125	165	2,400	2,850
1869 repunched 18	Inc. above	35.00	45.00	75.00	150	325	550	—	—	—
1869/8 die crack	Inc. above	150	185	375	435	650	900	—	—	—
1870	861,250	31.00	42.00	60.00	82.00	135	190	295	8,250	2,850
1871	721,250	43.00	49.00	70.00	110	155	215	285	3,850	2,850
1872	65,000	325	395	550	740	925	1,050	1,500	8,850	2,950
1873 closed 3 proof only	Est. 600	1,250	1,375	1,500	1,625	1,750	2,000	—	—	4,250
1873 open 3 proof only	Est. 500	1,275	1,400	1,575	1,700	1,875	2,150	—	—	5,500

SILVER 3 CENTS

Silver 3 Cents - Type 1
Shield within star, no outlines in star obverse
Roman numeral in designed C, within circle of stars reverse

KM# 75 • 0.8000 g., 0.7500 **Silver**, 0.0193 oz. ASW, 14 mm. • **Obv. Legend** UNITED STATES OF AMERICA **Designer:** James B. Longacre

Date	Mintage	G-4	VG-8	F-12	VF-20	XF-40	AU-50	MS-60	MS-65	Prf-65
1851	5,447,400	25.00	41.50	42.50	45.00	65.00	155	185	975	—
1851O	720,000	38.50	47.50	55.00	100.00	160	250	340	2,600	—
1852	18,663,500	25.00	41.50	42.50	45.00	65.00	155	180	975	—
1853	11,400,000	25.00	41.50	42.50	45.00	65.00	155	180	975	—

Silver 3 Cents - Type 2
Shield within star, three outlines in star obverse
Roman numeral in designed C, within circle of stars reverse

KM# 80 • 0.7500 g., 0.9000 **Silver**, 0.0217 oz. ASW, 14 mm. • **Obv. Legend** UNITED STATES OF AMERICA **Designer:** James B. Longacre

Date	Mintage	G-4	VG-8	F-12	VF-20	XF-40	AU-50	MS-60	MS-65	Prf-65
1854	671,000	26.00	42.50	44.00	50.00	105	230	350	3,450	33,500
1855	139,000	44.00	57.50	75.00	125	205	340	550	8,500	15,000
1856	1,458,000	30.00	45.00	46.00	65.00	125	205	275	4,500	15,500
1857	1,042,000	28.50	42.50	45.00	62.50	130	240	300	3,300	13,500
1858	1,604,000	27.50	42.50	44.00	55.00	110	200	240	3,300	6,400

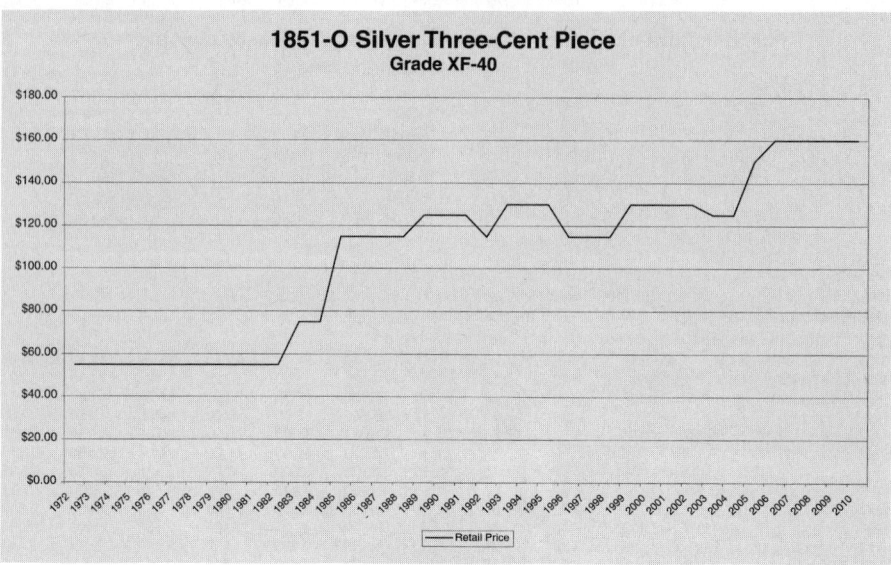

1851-O Silver Three-Cent Piece
Grade XF-40

Silver 3 Cents - Type 2
Shield within star, three outlines in star obverse
Roman numeral in designed C, within circle of stars reverse

KM# 80 • 0.7500 g., 0.9000 **Silver**, 0.0217 oz. ASW, 14 mm. • **Obv. Legend** UNITED STATES OF
AMERICA **Designer:** James B. Longacre

Date	Mintage	G-4	VG-8	F-12	VF-20	XF-40	AU-50	MS-60	MS-65	Prf-65
1854	671,000	26.00	42.50	44.00	50.00	105	230	350	3,450	33,500
1855	139,000	44.00	57.50	75.00	125	205	340	550	8,500	15,000
1856	1,458,000	30.00	45.00	46.00	65.00	125	205	275	4,500	15,500
1857	1,042,000	28.50	42.50	45.00	62.50	130	240	300	3,300	13,500
1858	1,604,000	27.50	42.50	44.00	55.00	110	200	240	3,300	6,400

Silver 3 Cents - Type 3
Shield within star, two outlines in star obverse
Roman numeral in designed C, within circle of stars reverse

KM# 88 • 0.7500 g., 0.9000 **Silver**, 0.0217 oz. ASW, 14 mm. • **Obv. Legend** UNITED STATES OF
AMERICA **Designer:** James B. Longacre

Date	Mintage	G-4	VG-8	F-12	VF-20	XF-40	AU-50	MS-60	MS-65	Prf-65
1859	365,000	30.00	44.00	50.00	62.50	82.50	170	195	975	2,150
1860	287,000	30.00	44.00	45.00	60.00	80.00	170	195	975	4,000
1861	498,000	30.00	44.00	45.00	60.00	80.00	170	195	975	1,800
1862	343,550	38.50	51.00	50.00	70.00	82.50	195	230	975	1,400
1863	21,460	340	375	400	445	480	625	780	2,250	1,350
1863/62 proof only; Rare	Inc. above	—	—	—	—	—	—	—	—	5,400
1864	12,470	340	375	400	445	480	625	780	1,700	1,350
1865	8,500	400	440	475	520	550	600	750	1,700	1,350
1866	22,725	340	375	400	445	495	550	650	1,900	1,325
1867	4,625	400	440	475	520	550	600	720	2,750	1,300
1868	4,100	400	445	480	520	575	625	740	5,750	1,400
1869	5,100	400	445	480	520	575	625	720	2,350	1,400

Date	Mintage	G-4	VG-8	F-12	VF-20	XF-40	AU-50	MS-60	MS-65	Prf-65
1869/68 proof only; Rare	Inc. above	—	—	—	—	—	—	—	—	—
1870	4,000	420	450	495	550	595	670	900	5,500	1,350
1871	4,360	400	440	480	520	575	625	750	1,700	1,450
1872	1,950	420	450	495	550	595	675	795	5,500	1,350
1873 proof only	600	650	685	730	800	890	980	—	—	2,500

NICKEL 3 CENTS

Coronet head left, date below obverse
Roman numeral value within wreath reverse

KM# 95 • 1.9400 g., **Copper-Nickel**, 17.9 mm. • **Obv. Legend** UNITED STATES OF AMERICA
Designer: James B. Longacre

Date	Mintage	G-4	VG-8	F-12	VF-20	XF-40	AU-50	MS-60	MS-65	Prf-65
1865	11,382,000	15.50	16.50	17.50	22.50	37.50	60.00	100.00	650	6,500
1866	4,801,000	15.50	16.50	17.50	22.50	37.50	60.00	100.00	650	1,725
1867	3,915,000	15.50	16.50	17.50	22.50	37.50	60.00	100.00	770	1,575
1868	3,252,000	15.50	16.50	17.50	22.50	37.50	60.00	100.00	650	1,450
1869	1,604,000	16.50	17.50	19.50	25.50	40.50	61.00	120	795	1,050
1870	1,335,000	17.50	18.50	20.50	26.50	41.50	62.00	135	795	2,250
1871	604,000	17.50	19.00	22.50	27.50	42.50	64.00	155	800	1,200
1872	862,000	19.00	22.50	24.50	28.50	43.50	68.00	175	1,075	910
1873	1,173,000	16.50	18.50	22.50	25.50	40.50	62.00	145	1,375	1,125
1874	790,000	17.50	20.50	22.50	27.50	42.50	66.00	160	1,050	950
1875	228,000	19.00	22.50	27.50	30.50	45.50	80.00	190	850	1,500
1876	162,000	20.50	23.50	26.50	34.50	49.50	95.00	225	1,550	1,025
1877 proof	Est. 900	1,100	1,150	1,175	1,250	1,300	1,350	—	—	3,750
1878 proof	2,350	615	645	720	770	795	830	—	—	1,200
1879	41,200	65.00	75.00	96.00	110	115	180	320	850	690
1880	24,955	100.00	115	130	165	185	235	375	800	700
1881	1,080,575	15.50	16.50	19.00	23.50	39.50	60.00	100.00	670	680
1882	25,300	130	150	180	225	300	325	425	1,100	700
1883	10,609	200	225	260	305	375	425	480	4,850	690
1884	5,642	400	445	550	600	645	730	800	6,250	700
1885	4,790	470	520	645	700	745	775	900	2,300	720
1886 proof	4,290	320	330	345	385	385	420	—	—	715
1887/6 proof	7,961	350	390	415	450	460	515	—	—	940
1887	Inc. above	305	355	395	440	455	500	540	1,350	1,125
1888	41,083	54.00	63.00	70.00	80.00	100.00	170	315	725	690
1889	21,561	90.00	115	140	180	220	255	320	800	690

HALF DIME

Flowing Hair Half Dime

KM# 15 • 1.3500 g., 0.8920 **Silver**, 0.0387 oz. ASW, 16.5 mm. • **Designer:** Robert Scot

Date	Mintage	G-4	VG-8	F-12	VF-20	XF-40	MS-60
1794	86,416	1,325	1,625	2,150	3,125	7,325	19,850
1795	Inc. above	1,050	1,350	1,875	2,850	5,750	13,850

Draped Bust Half Dime
Small eagle reverse

KM# 23 • 1.3500 g., 0.8920 **Silver**, 0.0387 oz. ASW, 16.5 mm. • **Designer:** Robert Scot

Date	Mintage	G-4	VG-8	F-12	VF-20	XF-40	MS-60
1796	10,230	1,435	1,550	3,000	4,700	8,700	19,550
1796 LIKERTY	Inc. above	1,485	1,600	3,050	4,750	8,750	19,600
Note: In 1796 Liberty was spelled Likerty on a die.							
1796/5	Inc. above	1,555	1,700	3,150	4,850	8,850	19,700
1797 13 stars	44,527	2,100	2,650	4,100	5,800	9,800	32,750
1797 15 stars	Inc. above	1,385	1,500	2,950	4,650	8,650	19,500
1797 16 stars	Inc. above	1,535	1,750	3,200	4,900	8,900	19,750

Draped Bust Half Dime
Draped bust right, flanked by stars, date at angle below obverse
Heraldic eagle reverse

KM# 34 • 1.3500 g., 0.8920 **Silver**, 0.0387 oz. ASW, 16.5 mm. • **Obv. Legend** LIBERTY **Rev. Legend:** UNITED STATES OF AMERICA **Designer:** Robert Scot

Date	Mintage	G-4	VG-8	F-12	VF-20	XF-40	MS-60
1800	24,000	1,000	1,250	1,875	2,350	6,750	13,850
1800 LIBEKTY	Inc. above	1,000	1,250	1,875	2,350	7,250	15,400
1801	33,910	1,225	1,500	2,125	2,600	7,000	18,100
1802	3,060	44,500	65,000	95,000	135,000	300,000	—
1803 Large 8	37,850	1,100	1,375	2,000	2,475	6,875	13,975
1803 Small 8	Inc. above	1,325	1,625	2,250	2,725	7,125	16,200
1805	15,600	1,225	1,525	2,350	2,825	10,150	31,350

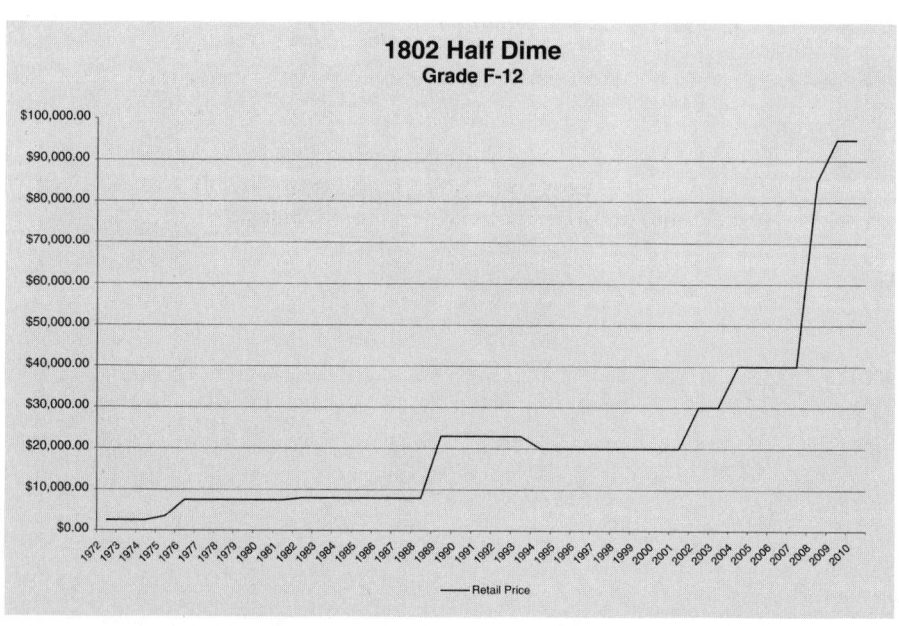

1802 Half Dime
Grade F-12

Liberty Cap Half Dime
Classic head left, flanked by stars, date below obverse
Eagle with arrows in talons, banner above reverse

KM# 47 • 1.3500 g., 0.8920 **Silver**, 0.0387 oz. ASW, 15.5 mm. • **Rev. Legend:** UNITED STATES OF AMERICA **Designer:** William Kneass

Date	Mintage	G-4	VG-8	F-12	VF-20	XF-40	AU-50	MS-60	MS-65
1829	1,230,000	55.00	60.00	72.00	125	185	275	365	3,300
1830	1,240,000	47.50	52.50	62.00	95.00	155	215	350	3,150
1831	1,242,700	47.50	52.50	62.00	95.00	155	215	350	3,150
1832	965,000	47.50	52.50	62.00	95.00	155	215	350	3,150
1833	1,370,000	47.50	52.50	62.00	95.00	155	215	350	3,150
1834	1,480,000	47.50	52.50	62.00	95.00	155	215	350	3,150
1835 large date and 5C.	2,760,000	47.50	60.00	74.00	110	170	235	350	3,150
1835 large date, small 5C.	Inc. above	47.50	52.50	62.00	95.00	155	215	410	4,350
1835 small date, large 5C.	Inc. above	47.50	52.50	62.00	95.00	155	215	375	4,050
1835 small date and 5C.	Inc. above	47.50	52.50	62.00	95.00	155	215	350	3,150
1836 large 5C.	1,900,000	47.50	52.50	62.00	95.00	155	215	350	3,150
1836 small 5C.	Inc. above	49.50	52.50	66.00	105	167	227	362	3,650
1837 large 5C.	2,276,000	47.50	52.50	70.00	113	170	235	395	4,350
1837 small 5C.	Inc. above	54.50	62.50	77.00	125	235	465	950	11,000

Seated Liberty Half Dime
Seated Liberty, no stars around border, date below obverse
Value within wreath reverse

KM# 60 • 1.3400 g., 0.9000 **Silver**, 0.0388 oz. ASW, 15.5 mm. • **Rev. Legend:** UNITED STATES OF AMERICA **Designer:** Christian Gobrecht **Notes:** A design modification in 1837 resulted in small-date and large-date varieties for that year.

Date	Mintage	G-4	VG-8	F-12	VF-20	XF-40	AU-50	MS-60	MS-65
1837 small date	Inc. above	35.00	46.50	75.00	135	220	485	770	4,450
1837 large date	Inc. above	39.00	49.50	82.00	150	235	435	640	3,650
1838O	70,000	110	130	250	475	975	1,450	2,500	29,500

Seated Liberty Half Dime
Seated Liberty, stars around top 1/2 of border, date below obverse
Value within wreath reverse

KM# 62.1 • 1.3400 g., 0.9000 **Silver**, 0.0388 oz. ASW, 15.5 mm. • **Rev. Legend:** UNITED STATES OF AMERICA **Designer:** Christian Gobrecht **Notes:** The two varieties of 1838 are distinguished by the size of the stars on the obverse. The 1839-O with reverse of 1838-O was struck from rusted reverse dies. The result is a bumpy surface on this variety's reverse.

Date	Mintage	G-4	VG-8	F-12	VF-20	XF-40	AU-50	MS-60	MS-65
1838 large stars	2,255,000	21.50	25.50	29.00	36.00	88.00	173	280	2,475
1838 small stars	Inc. above	25.50	31.50	46.00	115	189	274	610	3,950
1839	1,069,150	22.50	26.50	30.00	37.00	93.00	178	280	2,400
1839O	1,034,039	26.50	30.50	34.00	41.00	88.00	173	730	6,850
1839O reverse 1838O	Inc. above	500	700	1,200	1,750	3,000	—	—	—
1840	1,344,085	23.50	27.50	31.00	38.00	80.00	165	270	2,275
1840O	935,000	28.50	32.50	38.00	48.00	138	343	1,250	—

HALF DIME

Seated Liberty Half Dime
Seated Liberty, stars around top 1/2 of border, date below obverse

KM# 62.2 • 1.3400 g., 0.9000 **Silver**, 0.0388 oz. ASW, 15.5 mm. • **Rev. Legend:** UNITED STATES OF
AMERICA **Designer:** Christian Gobrecht **Notes:** In 1840 drapery was added to Liberty's left elbow. Varieties
for the 1848 Philadelphia strikes are distinguished by the size of the numerals in the date.

Date	Mintage	G-4	VG-8	F-12	VF-20	XF-40	AU-50	MS-60	MS-65
1840	Inc. above	20.00	18.00	75.00	135	210	350	490	3,850
1840O	Inc. above	51.00	60.00	115	225	650	1,350	6,500	—
1841	1,150,000	17.00	21.50	23.50	31.00	58.00	125	180	1,325
1841O	815,000	20.00	24.50	30.00	50.00	125	300	650	6,750
1842	815,000	16.00	21.50	23.50	28.00	55.00	125	175	1,850
1842O	350,000	38.00	45.00	75.00	225	550	1,050	2,250	16,500
1843	1,165,000	16.00	21.50	23.50	28.00	55.00	120	175	1,365
1844	430,000	19.00	24.50	26.50	34.00	58.00	125	180	1,250
1844O	220,000	80.00	110	210	600	1,300	2,650	5,400	27,500
1845	1,564,000	16.00	21.50	23.50	35.00	58.00	120	175	1,250
1845/1845	Inc. above	19.00	24.50	26.50	38.00	85.00	130	190	1,300
1846	27,000	410	550	850	1,250	2,475	3,600	11,500	—
1847	1,274,000	16.00	21.50	23.50	28.00	55.00	125	175	1,250
1848 medium date	668,000	19.00	24.50	26.50	34.00	65.00	135	215	3,150
1848 large date	Inc. above	22.50	28.00	48.00	65.00	145	275	635	4,250
1848O	600,000	20.00	25.50	33.00	62.00	135	265	450	2,450
1849/8	1,309,000	28.50	35.00	47.50	67.50	140	250	785	2,950
1849/6	Inc. above	24.00	26.00	30.00	56.50	110	200	425	2,900
1849	Inc. above	19.00	18.50	27.50	52.50	65.00	135	190	1,925
1849O	140,000	29.00	40.00	95.00	225	540	1,100	2,350	—
1850	955,000	19.00	24.50	26.50	34.00	60.00	125	190	1,400
1850O	690,000	20.00	24.50	35.00	65.00	125	280	685	4,450
1851	781,000	16.00	21.50	23.50	28.00	57.00	120	175	1,450
1851O	860,000	19.00	24.50	26.50	41.50	110	220	500	4,350
1852	1,000,500	16.00	21.50	23.50	28.00	57.00	120	175	1,250
1852O	260,000	25.00	44.50	79.00	135	275	475	885	11,500
1853	135,000	40.00	60.00	90.00	175	300	525	850	2,850
1853O	160,000	285	325	450	850	1,800	3,500	6,450	27,500

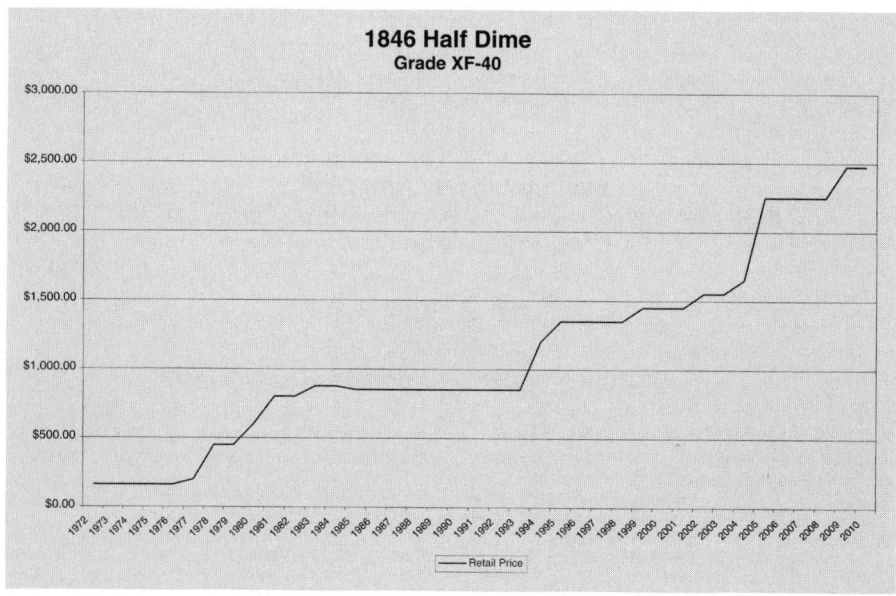

1846 Half Dime
Grade XF-40

Seated Liberty Half Dime
Seated Liberty, stars around top 1/2 of border, arrows at date obverse
Value within wreath reverse

KM# 76 • 1.2400 g., 0.9000 **Silver**, 0.0359 oz. ASW • **Rev. Legend:** UNITED STATES OF AMERICA
Designer: Christian Gobrecht

Date	Mintage	G-4	VG-8	F-12	VF-20	XF-40	AU-50	MS-60	MS-65	Prf-65
1853	13,210,020	16.00	19.00	22.50	28.00	58.00	135	200	2,100	—
1853O	2,200,000	19.00	27.00	30.50	36.00	66.00	143	315	3,950	—
1854	5,740,000	16.00	19.00	24.50	30.00	60.00	137	210	2,100	15,000
1854O	1,560,000	17.00	20.00	32.50	38.00	88.00	165	240	4,250	—
1855	1,750,000	17.00	20.00	24.50	30.00	60.00	137	205	2,500	15,000
1855O	600,000	21.00	25.00	38.50	54.00	140	220	545	4,950	—

Seated Liberty Half Dime
Seated Liberty, stars around top 1/2 of border, date below obverse
Value within wreath reverse

KM# A62.2 • 1.2400 g., 0.9000 **Silver**, 0.0359 oz. ASW • **Rev. Legend:** UNITED STATES OF AMERICA
Designer: Christian Gobrecht **Notes:** On the 1858/inverted date variety, the date was engraved into the die upside down and then re-engraved right side up. Another 1858 variety has the date doubled.

Date	Mintage	G-4	VG-8	F-12	VF-20	XF-40	AU-50	MS-60	MS-65	Prf-65
1856	4,880,000	16.00	21.00	23.00	27.00	52.50	115	175	1,400	15,000
1856O	1,100,000	17.00	22.00	26.00	28.00	97.50	260	470	2,350	—
1857	7,280,000	16.00	21.00	23.00	27.00	52.50	115	175	1,250	5,600
1857O	1,380,000	17.00	22.00	24.00	28.00	62.50	185	320	1,950	—
1858	3,500,000	16.00	21.00	23.00	27.00	52.50	115	175	1,350	5,500
1858 inverted date	Inc. above	30.00	43.50	62.50	100.00	225	300	675	3,950	—
1858 double date	Inc. above	45.00	60.00	90.00	175	285	425	800	—	—
1858O	1,660,000	17.00	22.00	24.00	28.00	71.50	137	245	1,850	—
1859	340,000	18.00	23.00	25.00	29.00	54.50	117	225	1,550	4,000
1859O	560,000	19.00	24.00	26.00	42.00	128.5	200	285	2,050	—

Seated Liberty Half Dime
Seated Liberty, date below obverse   Value within wreath reverse

KM# 91 • 1.2400 g., 0.9000 **Silver**, 0.0359 oz. ASW • **Obv. Legend** UNITED STATES OF AMERICA
Designer: Christian Gobrecht

Date	Mintage	G-4	VG-8	F-12	VF-20	XF-40	AU-50	MS-60	MS-65	Prf-65
1860	799,000	16.00	20.00	23.00	26.00	47.00	77.00	145	1,025	1,550
1860O	1,060,000	16.00	20.00	23.00	29.00	49.00	79.00	170	1,375	—
1861	3,361,000	16.00	20.00	22.00	25.00	45.00	75.00	145	1,025	1,600
1861/0	Inc. above	25.00	32.50	59.00	125	260	435	560	3,650	—
1862	1,492,550	20.00	25.00	34.00	44.00	64.00	94.00	154	1,025	1,550
1863	18,460	200	250	300	400	485	550	800	1,575	1,550
1863S	100,000	35.00	45.00	70.00	95.00	165	300	750	3,450	—
1864	48,470	375	475	575	750	950	1,100	1,375	2,350	1,600
1864S	90,000	60.00	75.00	115	175	250	450	785	3,750	—
1865	13,500	375	475	575	750	950	1,100	1,350	1,950	1,550
1865S	120,000	29.00	40.00	60.00	85.00	145	375	975	5,450	—
1866	10,725	350	475	550	700	875	1,000	1,225	2,575	1,550

Date	Mintage	G-4	VG-8	F-12	VF-20	XF-40	AU-50	MS-60	MS-65	Prf-65
1866S	120,000	29.00	40.00	60.00	85.00	145	285	485	5,000	—
1867	8,625	550	650	775	900	1,100	1,200	1,375	2,350	1,550
1867S	120,000	29.00	40.00	60.00	85.00	150	325	850	3,850	—
1868	89,200	60.00	90.00	190	225	300	425	625	2,400	1,550
1868S	280,000	20.00	25.00	35.00	42.00	59.00	125	325	3,250	—
1869	208,600	20.00	25.00	35.00	42.00	59.00	135	200	1,375	1,560
1869S	230,000	18.00	24.00	30.00	35.00	55.00	125	310	4,150	—
1870	536,600	18.00	24.00	30.00	35.00	55.00	125	185	975	1,550
1870S unique	—	—	—	—	—	—	—	—	—	—
Note: 1870S, Superior Galleries, July 1986, brilliant uncirculated, $253,000.										
1871	1,873,960	16.00	20.00	22.00	25.00	45.00	75.00	135	975	1,550
1871S	161,000	25.00	30.00	45.00	60.00	90.00	175	320	2,425	—
1872	2,947,950	16.00	20.00	22.00	25.00	45.00	75.00	135	975	1,550
1872S mint mark in wreath	837,000	16.00	20.00	22.00	25.00	45.00	75.00	135	975	—
1872S mint mark below wreath	Inc. above	17.00	21.00	24.00	27.00	47.00	80.00	135	975	—
1873	712,600	16.00	20.00	22.00	25.00	45.00	75.00	135	1,375	1,550
1873S	324,000	20.00	25.00	30.00	42.00	62.00	90.00	150	975	—

5 CENTS

Shield Nickel
Draped garland above shield, date below obverse
Value within center of rays between stars reverse

KM# 96 • 5.0000 g., **Copper-Nickel**, 20.5 mm. • **Obv. Legend** IN GOD WE TRUST **Rev. Legend:** UNITED STATES OF AMERICA **Designer:** James B. Longacre

Date	Mintage	G-4	VG-8	F-12	VF-20	XF-40	AU-50	MS-60	MS-65	Prf-65
1866	14,742,500	27.50	38.50	50.00	75.00	155	235	260	2,700	3,850
1867	2,019,000	37.50	50.00	67.50	100.00	200	295	350	4,150	75,000

Shield Nickel
Draped garland above shield, date below obverse
Value within circle of stars reverse

KM# 97 • 5.0000 g., **Copper-Nickel** • **Obv. Legend** IN GOD WE TRUST **Rev. Legend:** UNITED STATES OF AMERICA

Date	Mintage	G-4	VG-8	F-12	VF-20	XF-40	AU-50	MS-60	MS-65	Prf-65
1867	28,890,500	18.00	21.00	28.00	37.50	60.00	120	160	900	3,450
1868	28,817,000	18.00	21.00	28.00	37.50	60.00	120	160	975	1,500
1869	16,395,000	18.00	21.00	28.00	37.50	60.00	120	160	775	1,000
1870	4,806,000	27.00	34.00	52.00	65.00	90.00	145	200	1,700	1,250
1871	561,000	70.00	90.00	125	170	265	325	375	2,100	1,100
1872	6,036,000	35.00	42.00	70.00	80.00	115	150	235	1,350	820
1873 Open 3	4,550,000	28.00	36.00	52.00	65.00	80.00	135	200	2,400	840
1873 Closed 3	Inc. above	34.00	42.00	65.00	90.00	150	220	350	3,250	—
1874	3,538,000	29.00	39.00	70.00	82.00	105	140	225	1,500	1,000
1875	2,097,000	40.00	55.00	80.00	110	145	190	250	2,000	1,650
1876	2,530,000	38.00	50.00	74.00	100.00	135	175	230	1,900	900
1877 proof	Est. 900	1,500	1,650	1,750	2,000	2,150	2,300	—	—	4,300
1878 proof	2,350	800	875	900	1,100	1,300	1,450	—	—	2,150
1879	29,100	415	520	625	675	750	825	970	2,000	840
1879/8	Inc. above	—	—	—	—	—	—	—	—	850
1880	19,995	560	620	775	950	1,300	1,750	3,450	47,500	700
1881	72,375	270	340	445	500	600	730	800	1,900	660
1882	11,476,600	18.00	20.00	27.00	36.00	58.00	115	150	750	660
1883	1,456,919	18.00	21.00	32.00	37.50	60.00	118	160	750	660
1883/2	Inc. above	210	285	425	650	850	1,000	1,400	4,000	—

Liberty Nickel
Liberty head left, within circle of stars, date below obverse
Roman numeral value within wreath, without CENTS below reverse

KM# 111 • 5.0000 g., **Copper-Nickel**, 21.2 mm. • **Rev. Legend:** UNITED STATES OF AMERICA
Designer: Charles E. Barber

Date	Mintage	G-4	VG-8	F-12	VF-20	XF-40	AU-50	MS-60	MS-65	Prf-65
1883	5,479,519	6.50	7.75	8.25	8.75	9.00	12.00	25.00	260	1,075

Liberty Nickel
Liberty head left, within circle of stars, date below obverse
Roman numeral value within wreath, CENTS below reverse

KM# 112 • 5.0000 g., **Copper-Nickel** • **Rev. Legend:** UNITED STATES OF AMERICA

Date	Mintage	G-4	VG-8	F-12	VF-20	XF-40	AU-50	MS-60	MS-65	Prf-65
1883	16,032,983	18.00	28.50	39.50	57.50	88.00	125	160	695	725
1884	11,273,942	21.00	33.00	39.50	60.00	93.50	135	200	1,675	725
1885	1,476,490	600	635	875	1,050	1,350	1,700	2,050	8,250	3,150
1886	3,330,290	290	335	410	510	715	875	1,050	8,450	1,950
1887	15,263,652	14.50	23.00	32.50	45.00	80.00	115	150	1,100	700
1888	10,720,483	30.00	44.00	68.00	130	185	250	295	1,950	700
1889	15,881,361	13.50	18.50	31.00	55.00	80.00	125	160	875	700
1890	16,259,272	10.50	20.00	26.00	39.50	68.50	115	170	1,650	700
1891	16,834,350	6.00	11.00	22.00	38.50	62.50	125	160	1,075	700
1892	11,699,642	6.50	11.00	23.00	41.50	66.00	125	165	1,350	700
1893	13,370,195	5.50	11.00	25.00	38.50	62.50	125	155	1,100	700
1894	5,413,132	16.50	50.00	100.00	165	240	305	365	1,550	700
1895	9,979,884	5.75	7.75	25.00	46.00	70.00	125	150	2,550	700
1896	8,842,920	9.50	20.00	41.50	68.50	100.00	160	215	2,250	700
1897	20,428,735	3.25	4.50	12.50	27.50	45.00	68.50	95.50	1,000	700
1898	12,532,087	2.15	4.25	11.00	23.50	41.50	70.50	110	1,100	700
1899	26,029,031	1.65	2.00	8.00	15.50	34.00	66.50	92.00	615	700
1900	27,255,995	1.65	2.10	8.00	14.50	34.00	66.50	87.00	640	700
1901	26,480,213	1.65	2.10	7.00	14.00	34.00	54.00	108	565	700
1902	31,480,579	1.65	2.10	4.00	14.00	31.00	54.00	105	565	700
1903	28,006,725	1.65	2.10	4.50	14.00	31.00	54.00	83.00	565	700
1904	21,404,984	1.65	2.10	4.50	11.50	30.00	54.00	100.00	565	700
1905	29,827,276	1.65	2.10	4.00	11.50	30.00	54.00	98.00	565	700
1906	38,613,725	1.65	2.10	4.00	11.50	30.00	54.00	98.00	845	700
1907	39,214,800	1.65	1.85	4.00	11.50	30.00	54.00	98.00	1,000	700
1908	22,686,177	1.65	1.85	4.00	11.50	30.00	54.00	104	1,250	700
1909	11,590,526	2.00	2.10	4.00	12.50	33.00	70.00	115	1,225	700
1910	30,169,353	1.65	1.85	4.00	10.00	30.00	40.00	68.00	565	700
1911	39,559,372	1.65	1.85	4.00	10.00	30.00	40.00	68.00	565	700
1912	26,236,714	1.65	1.85	4.00	10.00	30.00	40.00	68.00	585	700
1912D	8,474,000	2.50	3.60	11.50	38.00	74.00	175	290	2,600	—
1912S	238,000	175	245	280	500	850	1,350	1,550	7,500	—
1913 6 known	—	—	—	—	—	—	—	—	—	—

Note: 1913, Superior Sale, March 2001, Proof, $1,840,000.

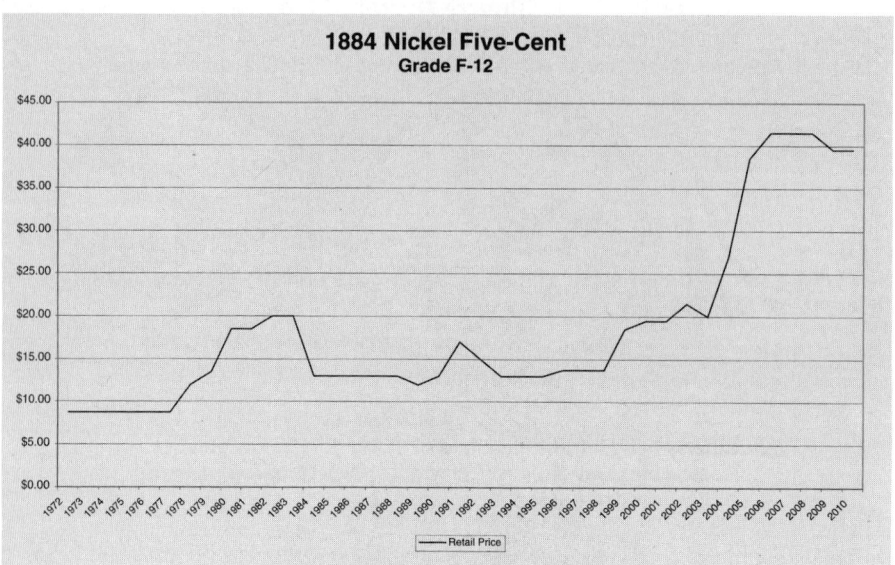

1884 Nickel Five-Cent
Grade F-12

Buffalo Nickel
American Bison standing on a mound reverse

KM# 133 • 5.0000 g., **Copper-Nickel**, 21.2 mm. • **Designer:** James Earle Fraser

Date	Mintage	G-4	VG-8	F-12	VF-20	XF-40	AU-50	MS-60	MS-65	Prf-65
1913	30,993,520	8.00	14.50	15.00	16.00	19.00	25.00	32.50	190	3,150
1913D	5,337,000	16.00	19.50	21.00	25.00	35.00	57.00	62.50	310	—
1913S	2,105,000	43.00	47.00	50.00	60.00	75.00	100.00	125	690	—

Buffalo Nickel
American Bison standing on a line reverse

  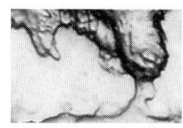 

1937D 3-legged

1918/17D

KM# 134 • 5.0000 g., **Copper-Nickel**, 21.2 mm. • **Designer:** James Earle Fraser **Notes:** In 1913 the reverse design was modified so the ground under the buffalo was represented as a line rather than a mound. On the 1937D 3-legged variety, the buffalo's right front leg is missing, the result of a damaged die.

Date	Mintage	G-4	VG-8	F-12	VF-20	XF-40	AU-50	MS-60	MS-65	Prf-65
1913	29,858,700	8.00	12.00	13.00	14.00	19.00	25.00	34.00	355	2,500
1913D	4,156,000	125	155	180	190	265	240	285	1,450	—
1913S	1,209,000	350	400	420	435	575	675	885	3,850	—
1914	20,665,738	18.00	21.00	22.00	23.00	27.50	37.50	47.00	420	2,250
1914/3	Inc. above	150	300	425	525	700	1,050	2,850	30,000	—
1914D	3,912,000	90.00	132	165	200	335	390	475	1,600	—
1914/3D	Inc. above	115	225	335	450	625	900	3,500	—	—
1914S	3,470,000	26.00	37.50	45.00	62.50	90.00	145	165	22,350	—

Date	Mintage	G-4	VG-8	F-12	VF-20	XF-40	AU-50	MS-60	MS-65	Prf-65
1914/3S	Inc. above	250	500	750	1,000	1,450	2,260	4,300	—	—
1915	20,987,270	6.25	7.00	7.75	11.00	21.50	38.50	50.00	325	2,100
1915D	7,569,500	21.50	31.00	41.50	66.00	115	150	235	2,250	—
1915S	1,505,000	47.00	74.00	105	185	326	490	625	3,150	—
1916	63,498,066	5.50	6.40	7.00	8.00	13.50	24.00	43.50	315	3,250
1916/16	Inc. above	1,800	3,650	7,150	10,850	16,500	34,500	49,500	375,000	—
1916D	13,333,000	15.00	26.50	29.00	38.50	82.50	110	165	2,250	—
1916S	11,860,000	11.00	13.50	26.00	35.00	75.00	125	185	2,300	—
1917	51,424,029	7.50	8.00	8.75	10.00	16.00	32.50	59.00	535	—
1917D	9,910,800	26.00	31.00	55.00	80.00	135	255	345	3,250	—
1917S	4,193,000	23.00	42.00	80.00	110	180	285	395	4,850	—
1918	32,086,314	5.25	6.75	8.00	15.00	31.00	48.50	105	1,550	—
1918/17D	8,362,314	1,075	1,475	2,750	5,450	8,650	10,750	27,500	350,000	—
1918D	Inc. above	22.50	39.00	66.00	135	226	330	430	4,650	—
1918S	4,882,000	14.00	27.50	55.00	100.00	175	300	495	25,500	—
1919	60,868,000	2.60	3.50	3.90	7.00	16.00	32.00	58.00	535	—
1919D	8,006,000	15.50	31.00	66.00	115	235	335	570	6,850	—
1919S	7,521,000	8.00	26.00	50.00	110	225	360	540	24,000	—
1920	63,093,000	1.50	2.75	3.25	8.00	16.00	30.00	59.00	700	—
1920D	9,418,000	8.50	19.00	35.00	125	275	340	575	6,850	—
1920S	9,689,000	4.50	12.75	30.00	100.00	260	300	525	25,500	—
1921	10,663,000	4.00	6.25	8.50	25.00	53.50	73.00	125	800	—
1921S	1,557,000	64.00	110	192	465	825	1,150	1,575	7,350	—
1923	35,715,000	1.70	3.25	4.25	7.00	14.00	37.50	59.00	575	—
1923S	6,142,000	8.00	11.00	27.00	125	275	335	625	11,500	—
1924	21,620,000	1.25	2.40	4.50	10.00	19.00	41.00	73.50	850	—
1924D	5,258,000	8.00	12.00	30.00	90.00	215	315	375	4,950	—
1924S	1,437,000	16.50	32.00	96.00	455	1,100	1,700	2,300	12,850	—
1925	35,565,100	2.50	3.00	3.75	8.50	16.50	32.00	42.00	490	—
1925D	4,450,000	10.00	26.00	38.00	80.00	160	240	375	5,650	—
1925S	6,256,000	4.50	9.00	17.50	77.50	170	250	425	28,500	—
1926	44,693,000	1.50	2.00	2.80	5.40	11.50	26.00	31.50	235	—
1926D	5,638,000	10.00	17.50	28.50	100.00	170	295	335	5,850	—
1926S	970,000	20.00	42.00	100.00	375	875	2,450	4,950	125,000	—
1927	37,981,000	1.40	1.75	2.50	4.50	12.50	26.00	35.00	290	—
1927D	5,730,000	3.00	6.00	7.00	27.50	75.00	115	155	7,950	—
1927S	3,430,000	2.00	3.00	6.00	31.00	80.00	160	490	18,500	—
1928	23,411,000	1.40	1.75	2.50	4.50	12.50	25.00	32.50	310	—
1928D	6,436,000	1.90	2.50	3.75	16.00	40.00	46.50	53.00	685	—
1928S	6,936,000	1.75	2.35	3.00	12.00	27.50	105	225	4,750	—
1929	36,446,000	1.40	1.75	2.50	4.50	13.00	21.00	35.00	325	—
1929D	8,370,000	1.50	1.85	3.00	6.75	32.50	42.50	60.00	1,850	—
1929S	7,754,000	1.50	1.85	2.25	4.00	12.50	25.00	49.50	485	—
1930	22,849,000	1.40	1.75	2.50	4.50	12.00	21.00	32.50	235	—
1930S	5,435,000	1.50	2.00	3.00	4.50	16.00	37.50	65.00	480	—
1931S	1,200,000	15.00	16.00	17.00	19.00	31.00	46.00	59.00	300	—
1934	20,213,003	1.40	1.75	2.50	4.50	11.00	19.00	47.50	355	—
1934D	7,480,000	2.00	3.00	4.75	9.60	22.00	50.00	79.50	800	—
1935	58,264,000	1.25	1.60	2.25	3.00	4.00	11.00	20.00	145	—
1935 Double Die Rev.	Inc. above	50.00	75.00	125	250	675	1,800	4,000	75,000	—
1935D	12,092,000	1.60	2.50	3.00	9.00	26.00	48.00	72.00	415	—
1935S	10,300,000	1.35	1.75	2.50	3.50	4.50	17.50	48.50	250	—
1936	119,001,420	1.25	1.60	2.25	3.00	4.00	6.75	14.50	105	1,650
1936 Brilliant	Inc. above	—	—	—	—	—	—	—	—	2,450
1936D	24,814,000	1.35	1.75	2.75	4.00	5.35	11.50	33.50	118	—
1936D 3-1/2 leg	Inc. above	750	1,250	2,000	3,500	6,000	10,500	17,500	—	—
1935D/S	Inc. above	1.35	—	10.00	16.00	25.00	—	—	—	—
1936S	14,930,000	1.35	1.75	2.50	3.50	4.50	11.00	33.50	115	—
1937	79,485,769	1.25	1.60	2.25	3.00	4.00	6.75	14.50	69.00	2,100
1937D	17,826,000	1.35	1.75	2.50	3.50	4.50	9.00	29.00	73.00	—
1937D 3-legged	Inc. above	535	595	850	1,050	1,250	1,450	2,375	37,000	—
1937S	5,635,000	1.35	1.75	2.50	3.50	4.50	10.00	27.50	72.00	—
1938D	7,020,000	3.50	3.75	3.90	4.00	4.50	8.00	26.00	66.00	—
1938D/D	Inc. above	4.00	4.50	6.00	8.00	10.00	17.00	32.00	125	—
1938D/S	Inc. above	4.50	6.75	9.00	12.50	19.00	32.50	50.00	185	—

5 CENTS

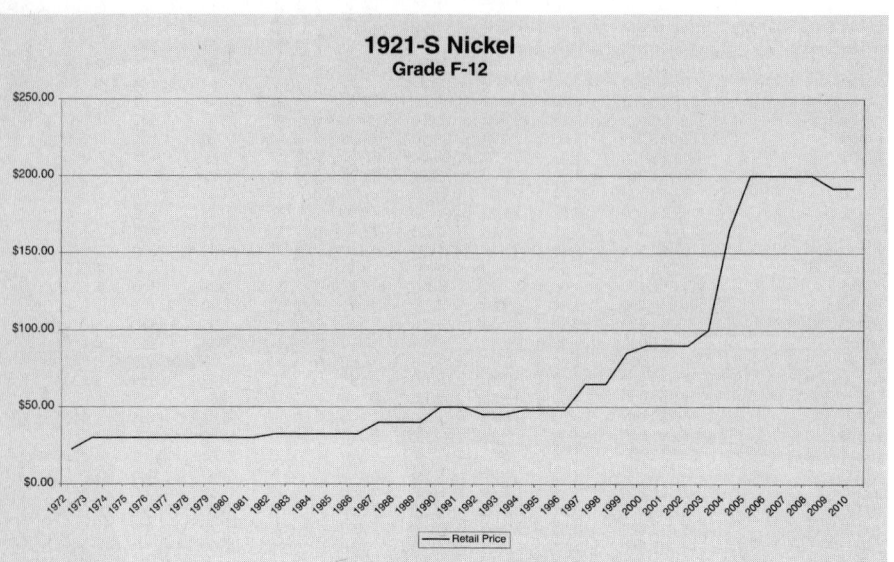

Jefferson Nickel
Monticello, mintmark to right side reverse

KM# 192 • 5.0000 g., **Copper-Nickel**, 21.2 mm. • **Designer:** Felix Schlag **Notes:** Some 1939 strikes have doubling of the word MONTICELLO on the reverse.

Date	Mintage	VG-8	F-12	VF-20	XF-40	MS-60	MS-65	-65FS	Prf-65
1938	19,515,365	.50	.75	1.00	2.00	6.00	12.00	125	130
1938D	5,376,000	1.00	1.25	1.50	2.00	10.00	20.00	95.00	—
1938S	4,105,000	1.75	2.00	2.50	3.00	5.25	12.00	165	—
1939 T I, wavy steps, Rev. of 1939	Inc. below	—	—	—	—	—	—	300	70.00
1939 T II, even steps, Rev. of 1940	120,627,535	—	.20	.25	.30	1.75	3.50	40.00	130
1939 doubled MONTICELLO T II	Inc. above	40.00	60.00	90.00	165	300	1,250	2,000	—
1939D T IT I, wavy steps, Rev. of 1939	Inc. below	—	—	—	—	—	—	275	—
1939D T IIT II, even steps, Rev. of 1940	3,514,000	4.00	5.00	8.00	14.00	44.00	125	250	—
1939S T IT I, wavy steps, Rev. of 1939	Inc. below	—	—	—	—	—	—	250	—
1939S T IIT II, even steps, Rev. of 1940	6,630,000	.45	.60	1.50	4.00	17.00	45.00	275	—
1940	176,499,158	—	—	—	.25	1.00	3.00	35.00	135
1940D	43,540,000	—	.20	.30	.40	1.50	2.75	25.00	—
1940S	39,690,000	—	.20	.25	.50	2.50	6.00	45.00	—
1941	203,283,720	—	—	—	.20	.75	2.50	40.00	130
1941D	53,432,000	—	.20	.30	.50	2.50	6.00	25.00	—
1941S	43,445,000	—	.20	.30	.50	3.75	6.75	60.00	—
1942	49,818,600	—	—	—	.40	5.00	8.50	75.00	115
1942D	13,938,000	1.00	1.50	3.00	5.00	32.00	60.00	70.00	—
1942D D over horizontal D	Inc. above	35.00	60.00	100.00	165	750	10,000	25,000	—

Note: Fully Struck Full Step nickels command higher prices. Bright, Fully Struck coins command even higher prices. 1938 thru 1989 - 5 Full Steps. 1990 to date - 6 Full Steps. Without bag marks or nicks on steps.

Jefferson Nickel
Monticello, mint mark above reverse

  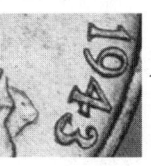

1943/2P

KM# 192a • 0.3500 **Copper-Silver-Manganese**, 21.2 mm. • **Designer:** Felix Schlag **Notes:** War-time composition nickels have the mint mark above MONTICELLO on the reverse.

Date	Mintage	VG-8	F-12	VF-20	XF-40	MS-60	MS-65	-65FS	Prf-65
1942P	57,900,600	1.20	1.30	1.50	2.00	8.00	22.50	70.00	205
1942S	32,900,000	1.20	1.30	1.50	2.50	14.00	20.00	125	—
1943P	271,165,000	1.20	1.30	1.50	2.00	4.00	15.00	35.00	—
1943/2P	Inc. above	35.00	50.00	75.00	110	250	650	1,000	—
1943D	15,294,000	1.50	1.50	1.70	2.10	5.00	13.00	30.00	—
1943S	104,060,000	1.20	1.30	1.50	2.00	6.00	13.00	55.00	—
1944P	119,150,000	1.20	1.30	1.50	2.00	10.00	22.50	100.00	—
1944D	32,309,000	1.30	1.30	1.50	2.30	10.00	17.50	30.00	—
1944S	21,640,000	1.30	1.30	1.50	2.10	7.00	14.00	185	—
1945P	119,408,100	1.20	1.30	1.50	2.00	6.00	13.50	125	—
1945D	37,158,000	1.30	1.40	1.60	2.20	5.50	13.00	40.00	—
1945S	58,939,000	1.20	1.30	1.50	2.00	5.00	14.00	250	—

Note: Fully Struck Full Step nickels command higher prices. Bright, Fully Struck coins command even higher prices. 1938 thru 1989 - 5 Full Steps. 1990 to date - 6 Full Steps. Without bag marks or nicks on steps.

Jefferson Nickel
Pre-war design resumed reverse

KM# A192 • 5.0000 g., **Copper-Nickel**, 21.2 mm. • **Designer:** Felix Schlag **Edge Desc:** Plain

Date	Mintage	VG-8	F-12	VF-20	XF-40	MS-60	MS-65	-65FS	Prf-65
1946	161,116,000	—	—	.20	.25	.80	3.50	40.00	—
1946D	45,292,200	—	—	.25	.35	.95	3.50	30.00	—
1946S	13,560,000	—	—	.30	.40	.50	2.00	45.00	—
1947	95,000,000	—	—	.20	.25	.75	2.00	30.00	—
1947D	37,822,000	—	—	.20	.30	.90	2.50	55.00	—
1947S	24,720,000	—	—	.20	.25	1.00	2.25	60.00	—
1948	89,348,000	—	—	.20	.25	.50	2.50	30.00	—
1948D	44,734,000	—	—	.25	.35	1.20	4.50	45.00	—
1948S	11,300,000	—	—	.25	.50	1.20	3.50	200	—
1949	60,652,000	—	—	.25	.30	2.25	6.00	200	—
1949D	36,498,000	—	—	.30	.40	1.25	5.00	75.00	—
1949D/S	Inc. above	—	35.00	40.00	65.00	170	325	1,750	—
1949S	9,716,000	.25	.35	.45	.90	1.50	3.50	145	—
1950	9,847,386	.20	.30	.35	.75	1.50	4.75	150	70.00
1950D	2,630,030	12.00	12.50	13.00	14.00	16.00	30.00	45.00	—
1951	28,609,500	—	—	.40	.50	1.50	9.00	90.00	70.00
1951D	20,460,000	.25	.30	.40	.50	3.00	10.00	45.00	—
1951S	7,776,000	.30	.40	.50	1.10	1.75	5.00	150	—
1952	64,069,980	—	—	.20	.25	.85	4.50	125	37.50
1952D	30,638,000	—	—	.30	.45	2.00	7.00	65.00	—
1952S	20,572,000	—	—	.20	.25	.75	3.50	195	—
1953	46,772,800	—	—	.20	.25	.40	1.50	200	37.50
1953D	59,878,600	—	—	.20	.25	.40	1.50	100.00	—
1953S	19,210,900	—	—	.20	.25	.60	2.50	1,750	—
1954	47,917,350	—	—	—	.20	.60	2.00	95.00	20.00
1954D	117,136,560	—	—	—	.20	.35	2.00	175	—
1954S	29,384,000	—	—	—	.25	1.00	3.00	1,000	—
1954S/D	Inc. above	—	9.00	14.00	30.00	50.00	500	—	—
1955	8,266,200	.25	.35	.40	.50	.75	2.00	85.00	13.50
1955D	74,464,100	—	—	—	.15	.20	1.00	150	—
1955D/S	Inc. above	—	10.00	16.00	40.00	65.00	135	185	—
1956	35,885,384	—	—	—	.20	.30	.70	35.00	2.50
1956D	67,222,940	—	—	—	.15	.25	.60	90.00	—
1957	39,655,952	—	—	—	.15	.25	.60	40.00	1.50
1957D	136,828,900	—	—	—	.15	.25	.60	55.00	—

Date	Mintage	VG-8	F-12	VF-20	XF-40	MS-60	MS-65	-65FS	Prf-65
1958	17,963,652	—	—	.15	.25	.30	.65	80.00	7.00
1958D	168,249,120	—	—	—	.15	.25	.60	30.00	—

Note: Fully Struck Full Step nickels command higher prices. Bright, Fully Struck coins command even higher prices. 1938 thru 1989 - 5 Full Steps. 1990 to date - 6 Full Steps. Without bag marks or nicks on steps.

Date	Mintage	VG-8	F-12	VF-20	XF-40	MS-60	MS-65	-65FS	Prf-65
1959	28,397,291	—	—	—	—	.30	.65	30.00	1.25
1959D	160,738,240	—	—	—	—	.25	.55	45.00	—
1960	57,107,602	—	—	—	—	.25	2.00	60.00	1.00
1960D	192,582,180	—	—	—	—	.25	.55	650	—
1961	76,668,244	—	—	—	—	.25	.55	100.00	1.00
1961D	229,342,760	—	—	—	—	.25	.55	800	—
1962	100,602,019	—	—	—	—	.25	1.50	75.00	1.00
1962D	280,195,720	—	—	—	—	.25	.55	60.00	—
1963	178,851,645	—	—	—	—	.25	.55	45.00	1.00
1963D	276,829,460	—	—	—	—	.25	.55	650	—
1964	1,028,622,762	—	—	—	—	.25	.55	55.00	1.00
1964D	1,787,297,160	—	—	—	—	.25	.50	500	—
1965	136,131,380	—	—	—	—	.25	.50	225	—
1966	156,208,283	—	—	—	—	.25	.50	350	—
1967	107,325,800	—	—	—	—	.25	.50	275	—
1968 none minted	—	—	—	—	—	—	—	—	—
1968D	91,227,880	—	—	—	—	.25	.50	750	—
1968S	103,437,510	—	—	—	—	.25	.50	300	0.75
1969 none minted	—	—	—	—	—	—	—	—	—
1969D	202,807,500	—	—	—	—	.25	.50	—	—
1969S	123,099,631	—	—	—	—	.25	.50	450	0.75
1970 none minted	—	—	—	—	—	—	—	—	—
1970D	515,485,380	—	—	—	—	.25	.50	500	—
1970S	241,464,814	—	—	—	—	.25	.50	125	0.75
1971	106,884,000	—	—	—	—	.85	2.00	35.00	—
1971D	316,144,800	—	—	—	—	.25	.50	25.00	—
1971S	3,220,733	—	—	—	—	—	—	—	2.00
1972	202,036,000	—	—	—	—	.25	.50	35.00	—
1972D	351,694,600	—	—	—	—	.25	.50	25.00	—
1972S	3,260,996	—	—	—	—	—	—	—	2.00
1973	384,396,000	—	—	—	—	—	.50	20.00	—
1973D	261,405,000	—	—	—	—	—	.50	20.00	—
1973S	2,760,339	—	—	—	—	—	—	—	1.75
1974	601,752,000	—	—	—	—	—	.50	75.00	—
1974D	277,373,000	—	—	—	—	—	.50	50.00	—
1974S	2,612,568	—	—	—	—	—	—	—	2.00
1975	181,772,000	—	—	—	—	—	.75	65.00	—
1975D	401,875,300	—	—	—	—	—	.50	60.00	—
1975S	2,845,450	—	—	—	—	—	—	—	2.25
1976	367,124,000	—	—	—	—	—	.75	150	—
1976D	563,964,147	—	—	—	—	—	.60	55.00	—
1976S	4,149,730	—	—	—	—	—	—	—	2.00
1977	585,376,000	—	—	—	—	—	.40	65.00	—
1977D	297,313,460	—	—	—	—	—	.55	35.00	—
1977S	3,251,152	—	—	—	—	—	—	—	1.75
1978	391,308,000	—	—	—	—	—	.40	40.00	—
1978D	313,092,780	—	—	—	—	—	.40	35.00	—
1978S	3,127,781	—	—	—	—	—	—	—	1.75
1979	463,188,000	—	—	—	—	—	.40	95.00	—
1979D	325,867,672	—	—	—	—	—	.40	35.00	—
1979S type I, proof	3,677,175	—	—	—	—	—	—	—	1.50
1979S type II, proof	Inc. above	—	—	—	—	—	—	—	1.75
1980P	593,004,000	—	—	—	—	—	.40	30.00	—
1980D	502,323,448	—	—	—	—	.25	.40	25.00	—
1980S	3,554,806	—	—	—	—	—	—	—	1.50
1981P	657,504,000	—	—	—	—	.25	.40	70.00	—
1981D	364,801,843	—	—	—	—	.25	.40	40.00	—
1981S type I, proof	4,063,083	—	—	—	—	—	—	—	2.00
1981S type II, proof	Inc. above	—	—	—	—	—	—	—	2.50
1982P	292,355,000	—	—	—	—	2.00	12.50	80.00	—
1982D	373,726,544	—	—	—	—	1.50	3.50	45.00	—
1982S	3,857,479	—	—	—	—	—	—	—	3.50
1983P	561,615,000	—	—	—	—	1.50	4.00	45.00	—
1983D	536,726,276	—	—	—	—	.75	2.50	35.00	—
1983S	3,279,126	—	—	—	—	—	—	—	4.00
1984P	746,769,000	—	—	—	—	1.25	3.00	65.00	—
1984D	517,675,146	—	—	—	—	.30	.85	30.00	—
1984S	3,065,110	—	—	—	—	—	—	—	5.00
1985P	647,114,962	—	—	—	—	.35	.75	60.00	—
1985D	459,747,446	—	—	—	—	.35	.75	35.00	—
1985S	3,362,821	—	—	—	—	—	—	—	4.00
1986P	536,883,483	—	—	—	—	.40	1.00	70.00	—
1986D	361,819,140	—	—	—	—	1.00	2.00	60.00	—
1986S	3,010,497	—	—	—	—	—	—	—	7.00
1987P	371,499,481	—	—	—	—	.25	.75	30.00	—

Date	Mintage	VG-8	F-12	VF-20	XF-40	MS-60	MS-65	-65FS	Prf-65
1987D	410,590,604	—	—	—	—	.25	.75	25.00	—
1987S	4,227,728	—	—	—	—	—	—	—	3.50
1988P	771,360,000	—	—	—	—	.25	.75	30.00	—
1988D	663,771,652	—	—	—	—	—	.75	25.00	—
1988S	3,262,948	—	—	—	—	—	—	—	6.50
1989P	898,812,000	—	—	—	—	.25	.75	75.00	—
1989D	570,842,474	—	—	—	—	.25	.75	25.00	—
1989S	3,220,194	—	—	—	—	—	—	—	5.50
1990P	661,636,000	—	—	—	—	.25	.75	25.00	—
1990D	663,938,503	—	—	—	—	.25	.75	25.00	—
1990S	3,299,559	—	—	—	—	—	—	—	5.50
1991P	614,104,000	—	—	—	—	.25	.75	25.00	—
1991D	436,496,678	—	—	—	—	.25	.75	25.00	—
1991S	2,867,787	—	—	—	—	—	—	—	5.00
1992P	399,552,000	—	—	—	—	.65	2.00	25.00	—
1992D	450,565,113	—	—	—	—	.25	.75	25.00	—
1992S	4,176,560	—	—	—	—	—	—	—	4.00
1993P	412,076,000	—	—	—	—	.25	.75	25.00	—
1993D	406,084,135	—	—	—	—	.25	.75	25.00	—
1993S	3,394,792	—	—	—	—	—	—	—	4.50
1994P	722,160,000	—	—	—	—	.25	.75	25.00	—
1994P matte proof	167,703	—	—	—	—	—	—	—	75.00
1994D	715,762,110	—	—	—	—	.25	.75	25.00	—
1994S	3,269,923	—	—	—	—	—	—	—	4.00
1995P	774,156,000	—	—	—	—	.25	.75	25.00	—
1995D	888,112,000	—	—	—	—	.35	.85	25.00	—
1995S	2,707,481	—	—	—	—	—	—	—	4.00
1996P	829,332,000	—	—	—	—	.25	.75	25.00	—
1996D	817,736,000	—	—	—	—	.25	.75	25.00	—
1996S	2,915,212	—	—	—	—	—	—	—	4.00
1997P	470,972,000	—	—	—	—	.25	.75	25.00	—
1997P matte proof	25,000	—	—	—	—	—	—	—	200
1997D	466,640,000	—	—	—	—	.30	2.00	25.00	—
1997S	1,975,000	—	—	—	—	.25	—	—	5.00
1998P	688,272,000	—	—	—	—	.25	.80	25.00	—
1998D	635,360,000	—	—	—	—	.25	.80	25.00	—
1998S	2,957,286	—	—	—	—	—	—	—	4.50
1999P	1,212,000,000	—	—	—	—	.25	.80	20.00	—
1999D	1,066,720,000	—	—	—	—	.25	.80	20.00	—
1999S	3,362,462	—	—	—	—	—	—	—	3.50
2000P	846,240,000	—	—	—	—	.25	.80	20.00	—
2000D	1,509,520,000	—	—	—	—	.25	.80	20.00	—
2000S	4,063,361	—	—	—	—	—	—	—	2.00
2001P	675,704,000	—	—	—	—	.25	.50	20.00	—
2001D	627,680,000	—	—	—	—	.25	.50	20.00	—
2001S	3,099,096	—	—	—	—	—	—	—	2.00
2002P	539,280,000	—	—	—	—	.25	.50	—	—
2002D	691,200,000	—	—	—	—	.25	.50	—	—
2002S	3,157,739	—	—	—	—	—	—	—	2.00
2003P	441,840,000	—	—	—	—	.25	.50	—	—
2003D	383,040,000	—	—	—	—	.25	.50	—	—
2003S	3,116,590	—	—	—	—	—	—	—	2.00

Jefferson - Westward Expansion - Lewis & Clark Bicentennial

Jefferson era peace medal design: two clasped hands, pipe and hatchet reverse

Lewis and Clark's Keelboat reverse

KM# 360 • 5.0000 g., **Copper-Nickel**, 21.2 mm. •
Obv. Designer: Felix Schlag **Rev. Designer:**
Norman E. Nemeth

Date	Mintage	MS-65	Prf-65
2004P	361,440,000	1.00	—
2004D	372,000,000	1.00	—
2004S	—	—	13.00

KM# 361 • 5.0000 g., **Copper-Nickel**, 21.2 mm. •
Obv. Designer: Felix Schlag **Rev. Designer:** Al
Maletsky

Date	Mintage	MS-65	Prf-65
2004P	366,720,000	1.00	—
2004D	344,880,000	1.00	—
2004S	—	—	13.00

Thomas Jefferson
large profile right obverse
American Bison right reverse

KM# 368 • 5.0000 g., **Copper-Nickel**, 21.2 mm. • **Obv. Designer:** Joe Fitzgerald and Don Everhart II **Rev. Designer:** Jamie Franki and Norman E. Nemeth

Date	Mintage	MS-65	Prf-65
2005P	448,320,000	1.00	—
2005D	487,680,000	1.00	—
2005S	—	—	7.50

Jefferson, large profile obverse
Pacific coastline reverse

KM# 369 • 5.0000 g., **Copper-Nickel**, 21.2 mm. • **Obv. Designer:** Joe Fitzgerald and Don Everhart **Rev. Designer:** Joe Fitzgerald and Donna Weaver

Date	Mintage	MS-65	Prf-65
2005P	394,080,000	1.00	—
2005D	411,120,000	1.00	—
2005S	—	—	6.50

Jefferson large facing portrait -
Enhanced Monticello Reverse
Jefferson head facing obverse
Monticello, enhanced design reverse

KM# 381 • 5.0000 g., **Copper-Nickel**, 21.2 mm. • **Obv. Designer:** Jamie N. Franki and Donna Weaver **Rev. Designer:** Felix Schlag and John Mercanti

Date	Mintage	MS-65	Prf-65
2006P	693,120,000	1.00	—
2006D	809,280,000	1.00	—
2006S	—	—	4.00
2007P	—	1.00	—
2007D	—	1.00	—
2007S	—	—	4.00
2008P	—	1.00	—
2008D	—	1.00	—
2008S	—	—	4.00
2009P	—	1.00	—
2009D	—	1.00	—
2009S	—	—	4.00

DIME

Draped Bust Dime
Small eagle reverse

KM# 24 • 2.7000 g., 0.8920 **Silver**, 0.0774 oz. ASW, 19 mm. • **Designer:** Robert Scot

Date	Mintage	G-4	VG-8	F-12	VF-20	XF-40	MS-60
1796	22,135	2,850	3,465	5,350	7,350	12,350	24,500
1797 13 stars	25,261	3,000	3,615	5,600	7,750	13,150	25,100
1797 16 stars	Inc. above	2,850	3,490	5,425	7,500	12,650	25,100

Draped Bust Dime
Draped bust right, date at angle below obverse   Heraldic eagle reverse

KM# 31 • 2.7000 g., 0.8920 **Silver**, 0.0774 oz. ASW, 19 mm. • **Obv. Legend** LIBERTY **Rev. Legend:** UNITED STATES OF AMERICA **Designer:** Robert Scot **Notes:** The 1805 strikes have either 4 or 5 berries on the olive branch held by the eagle.

Date	Mintage	G-4	VG-8	F-12	VF-20	XF-40	MS-60
1798 large 8	27,550	725	1,250	1,550	1,850	3,375	8,850

Date	Mintage	G-4	VG-8	F-12	VF-20	XF-40	MS-60
1798 small 8	Inc. above	975	1,450	1,750	2,150	4,350	53,500
1798/97 13 stars	Inc. above	2,150	3,850	5,650	8,850	14,750	59,000
1798/97 16 stars	Inc. above	775	1,125	1,800	2,650	4,350	10,500
Note: The 1798 overdates have either 13 or 16 stars on the obverse; Varieties of the regular 1798 strikes are distinguished by the size of the 8 in the date							
1800	21,760	700	1,075	1,400	2,550	4,100	34,500
1801	34,640	750	1,150	1,650	2,750	7,250	47,500
1802	10,975	1,750	2,650	3,500	4,750	11,000	36,500
1803	33,040	675	1,150	1,900	2,750	5,900	49,500
1804 13 stars	8,265	2,650	4,450	10,500	19,000	41,500	—
1804 14 stars	Inc. above	4,850	6,500	12,500	24,500	46,500	—
1805 5 berries	Inc. above	625	1,000	1,400	1,950	3,450	9,100
1805 4 berries	120,780	575	900	1,200	1,500	2,700	6,850
1807	165,000	575	900	1,200	1,500	2,700	6,850

Liberty Cap Dime
Draped bust left, flanked by stars, date below obverse
Eagle with arrows in talons, banner above, value below reverse

KM# 42 • 2.7000 g., 0.8920 **Silver**, 0.0774 oz. ASW, 18.8 mm. • **Rev. Legend:** UNITED STATES OF AMERICA **Designer:** John Reich **Notes:** The 1820 varieties are distinguished by the size of the 0 in the date. The 1823 overdates have either large E's or small E's in UNITED STATES OF AMERICA on the reverse.

Date	Mintage	G-4	VG-8	F-12	VF-20	XF-40	AU-50	MS-60	MS-65
1809	51,065	140	220	450	700	1,500	2,850	4,500	24,500

1809 Dime
Grade F-12

A line chart titled "1809 Dime, Grade F-12" with a vertical axis labeled from $0.00 to $500.00 in $50.00 increments, and a horizontal axis showing years from 1972 to 2010. The "Retail Price" line begins near $90 in 1972, rises to about $160 around 1982, dips to $100 around 1984, peaks near $240 around 1987, drops to $150, rises to $300 by 1990, rises to $375 around 1995, and reaches $450 by 2005 where it stays through 2010.

Date	Mintage	G-4	VG-8	F-12	VF-20	XF-40	AU-50	MS-60	MS-65
1811/9	65,180	110	175	275	650	1,350	2,000	4,000	33,500
1814 small date	421,500	60.00	80.00	145	300	650	1,250	2,000	19,500
1814 large date	Inc. above	43.00	52.00	75.00	135	435	670	1,175	15,000
1814 STATESOF	Inc. above	70.00	88.00	160	335	750	1,400	2,350	24,500
1820 large O	942,587	42.00	50.00	71.00	122	430	665	1,160	12,750
1820 small O	Inc. above	43.00	52.00	75.00	137	450	750	1,425	15,250
1820 STATESOF	Inc. above	43.00	52.00	75.00	135	435	670	1,175	14,500
1821 large date	1,186,512	42.00	50.00	71.00	122	430	665	1,160	12,750
1821 small date	Inc. above	43.00	52.00	75.00	137	450	750	1,425	17,000
1822	100,000	1,000	1,850	3,250	4,500	6,250	7,850	13,500	70,000
1823/22 large E's	440,000	42.00	50.00	71.00	130	450	685	1,210	14,850
1823/22 small E's	Inc. above	42.00	50.00	71.00	130	450	685	1,210	13,600

Date	Mintage	G-4	VG-8	F-12	VF-20	XF-40	AU-50	MS-60	MS-65
1824/22	—	50.00	80.00	145	300	650	1,250	2,000	19,500
1825	510,000	39.00	46.00	65.00	112	410	625	1,100	12,850
1827	1,215,000	39.00	46.00	65.00	112	410	625	1,100	12,500
1827/7	Inc. above	250	—	—	750	1,100	1,500	—	—
1828 large date	125,000	70.00	110	175	375	750	1,250	2,850	6,850

Liberty Cap Dime
Draped bust left, flanked by stars, date below obverse
Eagle with arrows in talons, banner above, value below reverse

KM# 48 • **Silver,** 18.5 mm. • **Rev. Legend:** UNITED STATES OF AMERICA **Designer:** John Reich
Notes: The three varieties of 1829 strikes and two varieties of 1830 strikes are distinguished by the size of "10C." on the reverse. On the 1833 "high 3" variety, the last 3 in the date is higher thatn the first 3. The two varieties of the 1834 strikes are distinguished by the size of the 4 in the date.

Date	Mintage	G-4	VG-8	F-12	VF-20	XF-40	AU-50	MS-60	MS-65
1828 small date	Inc. above	40.00	48.00	80.00	155	425	625	1,250	12,500
1829 very large 10C.	770,000	60.00	75.00	120	235	550	800	1,500	—
1829 large 10C.	Inc. above	54.00	65.00	110	200	400	600	1,150	9,250
1829 medium 10C.	Inc. above	36.00	42.00	54.00	85.00	255	375	775	6,850
1829 small 10C.	Inc. above	36.00	42.00	56.00	90.00	270	395	795	7,050
1829 curl base 2	Inc. above	7,750	10,500	16,500	27,500	38,500	44,000	—	—
1830 large 10C.	510,000	36.00	42.00	56.00	85.00	255	375	775	6,850
1830 small 10C.	Inc. above	36.00	42.00	54.00	90.00	270	400	825	8,850
1830/29	Inc. above	52.00	75.00	120	220	430	750	1,500	—
1831	771,350	36.00	42.00	54.00	85.00	255	375	775	6,850
1832	522,500	36.00	42.00	54.00	85.00	255	375	775	6,850
1833	485,000	36.00	42.00	54.00	85.00	260	390	790	6,850
1833 last 3 high	Inc. above	36.00	42.00	54.00	85.00	260	390	820	9,350
1834 small 4	635,000	36.00	42.00	54.00	85.00	255	375	775	7,000
1834 large 4	Inc. above	36.00	42.00	54.00	85.00	255	375	775	6,850
1835	1,410,000	36.00	42.00	54.00	85.00	255	375	775	6,850
1836	1,190,000	36.00	42.00	54.00	85.00	255	375	775	6,850
1837	1,042,000	36.00	42.00	56.00	90.00	270	395	795	7,000

Seated Liberty Dime
Seated Liberty, date below obverse   Value within wreath reverse

KM# 61 • 2.6700 g., 0.9000 **Silver,** 0.0773 oz. ASW, 17.9 mm. • **Rev. Legend:** UNITED STATES OF AMERICA **Designer:** Christian Gobrecht

Date	Mintage	G-4	VG-8	F-12	VF-20	XF-40	AU-50	MS-60	MS-65
1837 flat top	Inc. above	40.00	50.00	85.00	290	550	750	1,100	6,500
1837 curly top	Inc. above	40.00	50.00	85.00	290	550	750	1,100	6,500
1838O	406,034	40.00	60.00	110	375	725	1,250	3,500	21,000

Seated Liberty Dime
Seated Liberty, stars around top 1/2 of border, date below obverse
Value within wreath reverse

No drapery at elbow

KM# 63.1 • 2.6700 g., 0.9000 **Silver,** 0.0773 oz. ASW, 17.9 mm. • **Obv. Designer:** Christian Gobrecht **Rev. Legend:** UNITED STATES OF AMERICA **Notes:** The 1839-O with reverse of 1838-O variety was struck from rusted dies, it has a bumpy reverse surface.

Date	Mintage	G-4	VG-8	F-12	VF-20	XF-40	AU-50	MS-60	MS-65
1838 small stars	1,992,500	25.00	30.00	50.00	80.00	165	350	600	—
1838 large stars	Inc. above	17.50	20.00	30.00	37.50	110	215	280	8,500
1838 partial drapery	Inc. above	35.00	50.00	85.00	150	225	350	550	—
1839	1,053,115	16.00	18.50	25.00	35.00	105	195	280	3,000
1839O	1,323,000	18.50	22.50	35.00	60.00	150	365	1,250	6,000
1839O reverse 1838O	Inc. above	165	225	375	550	1,150	—	—	—
1840	1,358,580	16.00	18.50	25.00	35.00	105	195	300	4,000
1840O	1,175,000	18.50	22.50	40.00	70.00	165	365	975	6,500

Seated Liberty Dime
Seated Liberty, stars around top 1/2 of border, date below obverse
Value within wreath reverse

Drapery at elbow

KM# 63.2 • 2.6700 g., 0.9000 **Silver**, 0.0773 oz. ASW, 17.9 mm. • **Rev. Legend:** UNITED STATES OF AMERICA **Designer:** Christian Gobrecht **Notes:** Drapery added to Liberty's left elbow

Date	Mintage	G-4	VG-8	F-12	VF-20	XF-40	AU-50	MS-60	MS-65
1840	Inc. above	35.00	50.00	95.00	185	350	1,250	—	—
1841	1,622,500	16.00	18.50	21.50	27.50	50.00	175	260	2,700
1841O	2,007,500	18.50	22.50	28.50	45.00	75.00	250	1,500	5,000
1841O large O	Inc. above	600	900	1,200	2,500	—	—	—	—
1842	1,887,500	15.00	17.50	21.50	26.00	45.00	175	260	2,700
1842O	2,020,000	18.50	23.50	30.00	75.00	225	1,350	2,900	—
1843	1,370,000	15.00	17.50	21.50	26.00	45.00	175	260	3,000
1843/1843	Inc. above	16.00	18.50	22.50	30.00	75.00	200	295	—
1843O	150,000	50.00	80.00	135	325	1,100	2,250	—	—
1844	72,500	275	350	550	800	1,450	2,200	3,000	—
1845	1,755,000	16.00	18.50	21.50	27.50	45.00	120	260	2,600
1845/1845	Inc. above	17.00	20.00	35.00	55.00	100.00	175	—	—
1845O	230,000	25.00	35.00	95.00	250	750	1,750	—	—
1846	31,300	250	350	500	950	1,750	2,750	5,500	—
1847	245,000	19.00	25.00	40.00	85.00	150	350	950	9,000
1848	451,500	18.50	21.50	25.00	50.00	95.00	250	750	7,000
1849	839,000	17.50	19.50	23.50	33.50	60.00	140	500	4,000
1849O	300,000	21.50	30.00	50.00	135	275	750	2,200	—
1850	1,931,500	17.50	19.50	23.50	32.50	55.00	120	260	5,900
1850O	510,000	21.50	25.00	40.00	90.00	175	475	1,250	—
1851	1,026,500	17.50	20.00	22.50	30.00	60.00	120	325	5,000
1851O	400,000	21.50	25.00	40.00	90.00	175	500	1,850	—
1852	1,535,500	15.00	16.00	18.50	23.50	50.00	120	290	2,550
1852O	430,000	22.50	30.00	45.00	125	235	550	1,800	—
1853	95,000	95.00	125	200	295	425	575	800	—

Seated Liberty Dime
Seated Liberty, stars around top 1/2 of border, arrows at date obverse
Value within wreath reverse

KM# 77 • 2.4900 g., 0.9000 **Silver**, 0.0720 oz. ASW • **Rev. Legend:** UNITED STATES OF AMERICA
Designer: Christian Gobrecht

Date	Mintage	G-4	VG-8	F-12	VF-20	XF-40	AU-50	MS-60	MS-65	Prf-65
1853	12,078,010	8.00	9.00	10.00	14.00	45.00	125	330	2,500	31,500
1853O	1,100,000	11.00	14.00	20.00	45.00	145	400	900	—	—
1854	4,470,000	8.75	9.25	10.00	15.00	45.00	125	330	2,500	31,500
1854O	1,770,000	10.00	11.00	14.00	25.00	75.00	175	600	—	—
1855	2,075,000	8.75	9.25	14.00	20.00	55.00	150	350	3,800	31,500

Seated Liberty Dime

Seated Liberty, stars around top 1/2 of border, date below obverse
Value within wreath reverse

KM# A63.2 • 2.4900 g., 0.9000 **Silver**, 0.0720 oz. ASW • **Rev. Legend:** UNITED STATES OF AMERICA
Designer: Christian Gobrecht

Date	Mintage	G-4	VG-8	F-12	VF-20	XF-40	AU-50	MS-60	MS-65	Prf-65
1856 small date	5,780,000	14.00	15.00	18.00	22.00	37.50	115	250	7,050	38,000
1856 large date	Inc. above	16.00	18.50	19.50	25.00	65.00	175	475	—	—
1856O	1,180,000	16.00	18.50	19.50	35.00	85.00	215	625	5,250	—
1856S	70,000	160	225	375	550	1,200	1,750	—	—	—
1857	5,580,000	14.00	15.50	16.50	22.50	37.50	110	260	2,600	3,400
1857O	1,540,000	14.00	16.00	18.50	27.50	70.00	200	375	2,600	—
1858	1,540,000	14.00	15.50	16.50	22.50	55.00	145	260	2,600	3,400
1858O	290,000	19.00	25.00	40.00	85.00	165	280	800	5,000	—
1858S	60,000	150	200	325	475	1,000	1,500	—	—	—
1859	430,000	16.00	20.00	25.00	45.00	70.00	140	350	—	3,400
1859O	480,000	16.00	20.00	25.00	45.00	80.00	225	550	—	—
1859S	60,000	160	225	375	550	1,350	3,000	—	—	—
1860S	140,000	40.00	55.00	75.00	145	325	800	—	—	—

Seated Liberty Dime

UNITED STATES OF AMERICA replaced stars obverse
Value within wreath reverse

KM# 92 • 2.4900 g., 0.9000 **Silver**, 0.0720 oz. ASW • **Obv. Legend** UNITED STATES OF AMERICA **Obv.
Designer:** Christian Gobrecht **Notes:** The 1873 "closed-3" and "open-3" varieties are distinguished by the
amount of space between the upper left and lower left serifs of the 3 in the date.

Date	Mintage	G-4	VG-8	F-12	VF-20	XF-40	AU-50	MS-60	MS-65	Prf-65
1860	607,000	15.00	22.00	29.00	31.00	55.00	125	275	1,350	1,400
1860O	40,000	450	600	1,000	1,950	3,500	5,500	8,500	—	—
1861	1,884,000	15.00	17.00	20.00	23.00	34.00	85.00	150	1,250	1,400
1861S	172,500	55.00	90.00	165	275	400	900	1,400	—	—
1862	847,550	16.00	17.50	19.50	25.00	45.00	77.50	165	1,250	1,400
1862S	180,750	45.00	65.00	95.00	185	375	775	1,000	—	—
1863	14,460	425	500	650	900	950	1,100	1,300	—	1,400
1863S	157,500	40.00	55.00	80.00	145	275	650	1,200	—	—
1864	11,470	425	500	650	750	900	1,000	1,200	—	1,400
1864S	230,000	35.00	45.00	75.00	110	225	425	1,200	—	—
1865	10,500	475	575	700	875	1,000	1,200	1,350	—	1,400
1865S	175,000	45.00	55.00	85.00	145	325	850	—	—	—
1866	8,725	500	600	775	950	1,100	1,200	1,800	—	1,750
1866S	135,000	50.00	65.00	100.00	150	325	700	1,900	—	—
1867	6,625	600	700	950	1,100	1,450	1,600	1,800	—	1,750
1867S	140,000	50.00	60.00	90.00	150	325	700	1,200	—	—
1868	464,000	18.00	22.00	29.00	39.00	85.00	175	300	—	1,400
1868S	260,000	30.00	35.00	50.00	85.00	165	300	600	—	—
1869	256,600	25.00	35.00	45.00	80.00	135	250	600	—	1,400
1869S	450,000	25.00	30.00	40.00	55.00	85.00	175	400	—	—
1870	471,000	18.00	22.00	30.00	40.00	50.00	80.00	150	—	1,400
1870S	50,000	300	375	500	650	850	1,200	2,000	—	—
1871	907,710	16.00	20.00	25.00	33.00	55.00	175	300	—	1,400
1871CC	20,100	2,500	3,500	4,500	6,500	10,000	—	—	—	—
1871S	320,000	35.00	55.00	75.00	130	195	350	900	—	—
1872	2,396,450	12.00	15.00	17.00	20.00	31.00	95.00	175	—	1,400
1872CC	35,480	950	1,250	1,850	3,000	6,500	—	—	—	—
1872S	190,000	40.00	65.00	85.00	150	250	450	1,100	—	—
1873 closed 3	1,568,600	12.50	15.00	18.00	22.00	50.00	100.00	200	—	1,400
1873 open 3	Inc. above	28.00	35.00	50.00	75.00	125	250	650	—	—
1873CC	12,400	—	—	—	—	—	—	—	—	—

Note: 1873-CC, Heritage Sale, April 1999, MS-64, $632,500.

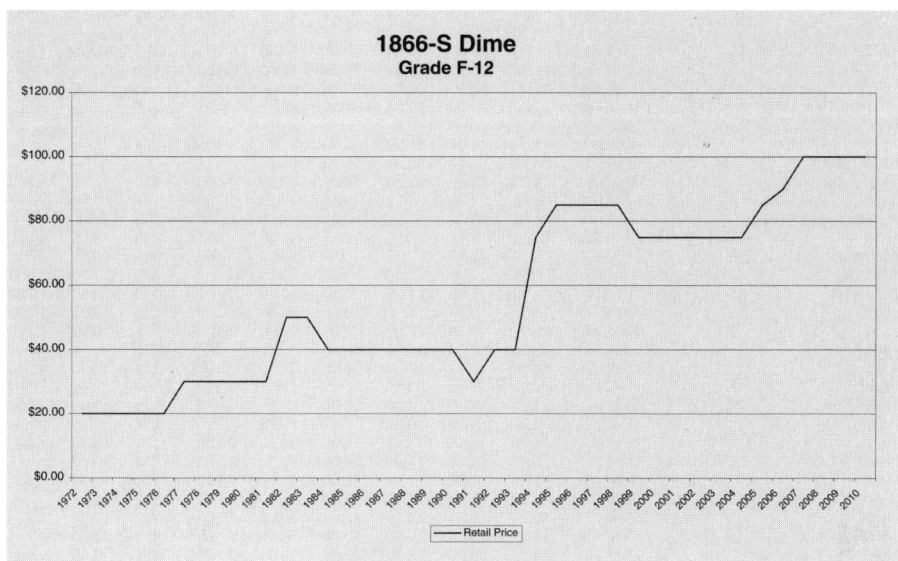

1866-S Dime
Grade F-12

Seated Liberty Dime
Seated Liberty, arrows at date obverse   Value within wreath reverse

KM# 105 • 2.5000 g., 0.9000 **Silver**, 0.0723 oz. ASW • **Obv. Legend** UNITED STATES OF AMERICA
Designer: Christian Gobrecht

Date	Mintage	G-4	VG-8	F-12	VF-20	XF-40	AU-50	MS-60	MS-65	Prf-65
1873	2,378,500	15.00	18.50	25.00	55.00	150	350	500	4,500	4,500
1873CC	18,791	2,350	3,250	4,250	6,500	10,000	—	—	—	—
1873S	455,000	20.00	30.00	40.00	70.00	190	400	1,500	—	—
1874	2,940,700	13.50	17.50	22.50	50.00	150	315	500	4,500	4,500
1874CC	10,817	5,000	6,500	8,000	12,500	25,000	—	—	—	—
1874S	240,000	60.00	75.00	100.00	160	250	450	1,500	—	—

Seated Liberty Dime
Seated Liberty, date below obverse   Value within wreath reverse

KM# A92 • 2.5000 g., 0.9000 **Silver**, 0.0723 oz. ASW • **Obv. Legend** UNITED STATES OF AMERICA
Designer: Christian Gobrecht **Notes:** On the 1876-CC doubled-obverse variety, doubling appears in the words OF AMERICA in the legend.

Date	Mintage	G-4	VG-8	F-12	VF-20	XF-40	AU-50	MS-60	MS-65	Prf-65
1875	10,350,700	14.00	16.00	17.50	20.00	30.00	75.00	125	2,250	4,600
1875CC mint mark in wreath	4,645,000	15.00	19.00	22.50	35.00	47.50	90.00	190	2,700	—
1875CC mint mark under wreath	Inc. above	15.00	19.00	27.50	45.00	75.00	165	235	3,000	—
1875S mint mark in wreath	9,070,000	20.00	25.00	30.00	43.00	65.00	125	225	3,100	—
1875S mint mark under wreath	Inc. above	12.50	15.50	17.50	20.00	27.50	72.50	125	1,100	—
1876 Type 1 rev	11,461,150	14.00	16.00	17.50	20.00	30.00	75.00	125	1,100	1,200
1876 Type 2 rev	Inc. above	20.00	25.00	30.00	40.00	60.00	120	200	—	—
1876CC Type 1 rev	8,270,000	20.00	25.00	30.00	40.00	65.00	125	225	—	—
1876CC Type 2 rev	Inc. above	25.00	35.00	48.00	65.00	90.00	175	300	—	—
1876CC doubled die obverse	Inc. above	20.00	26.00	44.00	100.00	185	340	600	—	—
1876S Type 1 rev	10,420,000	14.00	16.00	17.50	20.00	30.00	75.00	125	1,750	—

Date	Mintage	G-4	VG-8	F-12	VF-20	XF-40	AU-50	MS-60	MS-65	Prf-65
1876S Type 2 rev	Inc. above	18.00	20.00	24.00	30.00	40.00	90.00	150	—	—
1877 Type 1 rev	7,310,510	14.00	16.00	17.50	20.00	30.00	75.00	125	1,100	1,200
1877 Type 2 rev	Inc. above	18.00	20.00	24.00	30.00	40.00	90.00	150	—	—
1877CC Type 1 rev	7,700,000	25.00	35.00	48.00	65.00	90.00	175	300	1,100	—
1877CC Type 2 rev	Inc. above	20.00	25.00	30.00	40.00	65.00	125	225	—	—
1877S Type 1 rev	2,340,000	—	—	—	—	—	—	—	—	—
1877S Type 2 rev	Inc. above	14.00	18.00	20.00	30.00	50.00	105	225	—	—
1878 Type 1 rev	1,678,800	28.00	35.00	50.00	65.00	100.00	175	—	—	—
1878 Type 2 rev	Inc. above	14.00	16.00	20.00	30.00	36.00	72.50	125	1,500	1,200
1878CC Type 1 rev	200,000	100.00	135	175	285	450	700	—	—	—
1878CC Type 2 rev	Inc. above	65.00	90.00	125	225	370	500	900	3,500	—
1879	15,100	275	310	375	425	500	575	675	1,750	1,500
1880	37,335	250	275	315	350	400	450	550	1,750	1,500
1881	24,975	265	300	350	400	475	550	650	2,500	1,600
1882	3,911,100	14.00	16.00	17.50	20.00	30.00	75.00	125	1,100	1,200
1883	7,675,712	14.00	16.00	17.50	20.00	30.00	75.00	125	1,100	1,200
1884	3,366,380	14.00	16.00	17.50	20.00	30.00	75.00	125	1,100	1,200
1884S	564,969	30.00	35.00	45.00	55.00	125	280	650	—	—
1885	2,533,427	14.00	16.00	17.50	20.00	30.00	75.00	125	1,100	1,200
1885S	43,690	450	650	950	1,750	2,400	3,600	5,000	—	—
1886	6,377,570	12.50	15.00	17.00	20.00	27.50	72.50	125	1,100	1,200
1886S	206,524	50.00	70.00	80.00	125	175	280	600	—	—
1887	11,283,939	14.00	16.00	17.50	20.00	30.00	75.00	125	1,100	1,200
1887S	4,454,450	12.50	15.00	17.00	20.00	38.00	80.00	125	1,100	—
1888	5,496,487	14.00	16.00	17.50	20.00	30.00	75.00	125	1,100	1,200
1888S	1,720,000	12.50	15.00	17.00	25.00	40.00	95.00	200	—	—
1889	7,380,711	14.00	16.00	17.50	20.00	30.00	75.00	125	1,100	1,200
1889S	972,678	14.00	18.00	25.00	45.00	70.00	150	475	4,500	—
1890	9,911,541	14.00	16.00	17.50	20.00	30.00	75.00	125	1,100	1,200
1890S	1,423,076	14.00	15.00	22.50	50.00	85.00	155	400	4,900	—
1891	15,310,600	14.00	16.00	17.50	20.00	30.00	75.00	125	1,100	1,200
1891O	4,540,000	12.50	15.00	17.00	20.00	27.50	72.50	175	1,750	—
1891O /horizontal O	Inc. above	65.00	95.00	125	175	225	400	—	—	—
1891S	3,196,116	13.50	15.00	17.50	20.00	30.00	75.00	225	1,650	—
1891S/S	Inc. above	25.00	30.00	40.00	85.00	135	250	—	—	—

Barber Dime

Laureate head right, date at angle below obverse   Value within wreath reverse

KM# 113 • 2.5000 g., 0.9000 **Silver**, 0.0723 oz. ASW, 17.9 mm. • **Obv. Legend** UNITED STATES OF AMERICA **Designer:** Charles E. Barber

Date	Mintage	G-4	VG-8	F-12	VF-20	XF-40	AU-50	MS-60	MS-65	Prf-65
1892	12,121,245	6.75	7.50	16.00	25.00	27.50	63.00	110	705	1,485
1892O	3,841,700	11.00	15.00	32.50	56.00	75.00	96.00	140	1,275	—
1892S	990,710	66.00	115	210	245	285	340	425	3,500	—
1893/2	3,340,792	135	155	175	225	300	325	450	4,850	—
1893	Inc. above	8.25	12.50	20.00	30.00	46.00	80.00	165	1,000	1,485
1893O	1,760,000	31.00	45.00	135	168	190	250	315	2,950	—
1893S	2,491,401	14.00	25.00	39.00	50.00	85.00	155	360	3,750	—
1894	1,330,972	25.00	45.00	122	165	190	235	310	1,150	1,485
1894O	720,000	70.00	105	215	280	425	650	1,550	15,500	—
1894S	24	—	—	—	—	—	—	— 1,900,000	—
Note: 1894S, Eliasberg Sale, May 1996, Prf-64, $451,000.										
1895	690,880	85.00	180	355	480	565	650	750	2,650	1,485
1895O	440,000	385	575	900	1,285	2,500	3,650	6,000	19,500	—
1895S	1,120,000	43.50	60.00	135	190	240	320	500	7,500	—
1896	2,000,762	11.50	23.00	56.00	82.00	100.00	120	150	1,450	1,485
1896O	610,000	80.00	155	305	375	465	700	975	9,500	—
1896S	575,056	85.00	160	310	335	385	525	770	4,650	—
1897	10,869,264	2.50	3.00	8.00	15.00	31.50	73.00	130	705	1,485
1897O	666,000	69.50	115	290	385	480	600	975	4,450	—
1897S	1,342,844	21.00	45.00	98.00	125	185	265	435	3,950	—
1898	16,320,735	2.50	3.00	7.50	15.00	28.00	68.00	130	705	1,485
1898O	2,130,000	13.50	27.50	88.00	145	200	285	450	3,850	—
1898S	1,702,507	8.50	15.00	33.00	48.00	78.00	160	370	3,750	—
1899	19,580,846	2.50	3.00	7.50	12.00	26.00	68.00	115	705	1,485
1899O	2,650,000	10.00	19.50	72.00	110	150	230	415	4,450	—
1899S	1,867,493	9.00	16.00	34.00	37.00	46.00	105	300	4,350	—
1900	17,600,912	4.00	5.00	7.00	11.00	26.00	63.00	110	735	1,485
1900O	2,010,000	19.50	38.50	115	165	225	355	595	5,750	—

Date	Mintage	G-4	VG-8	F-12	VF-20	XF-40	AU-50	MS-60	MS-65	Prf-65
1900S	5,168,270	5.00	6.25	12.50	19.50	31.50	75.00	155	1,850	—
1901	18,860,478	4.00	5.00	6.50	10.00	27.50	63.00	110	750	1,485
1901O	5,620,000	4.00	5.50	16.00	27.50	67.50	175	450	4,350	—
1901S	593,022	80.00	150	360	475	520	675	985	5,350	—

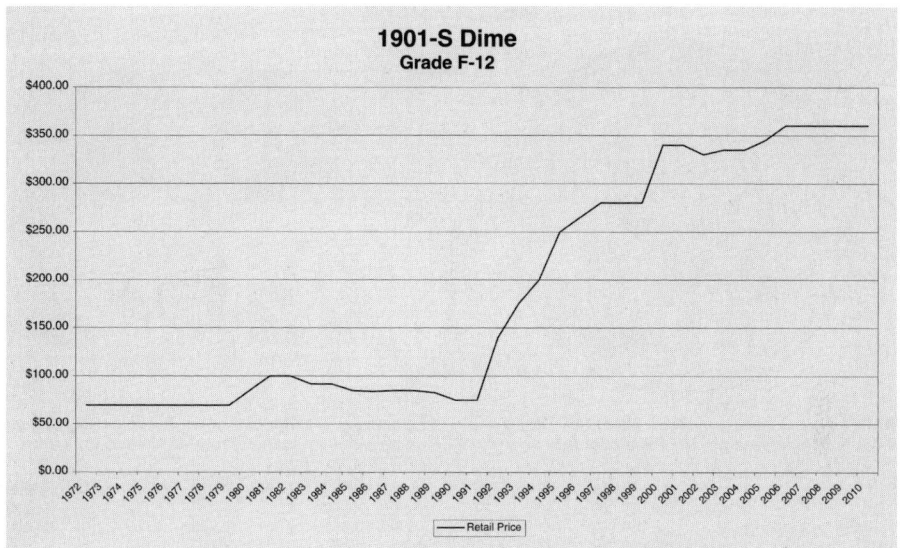

1901-S Dime
Grade F-12

Date	Mintage	G-4	VG-8	F-12	VF-20	XF-40	AU-50	MS-60	MS-65	Prf-65
1902	21,380,777	4.00	5.00	5.50	8.00	23.00	63.00	110	750	1,485
1902O	4,500,000	4.00	5.50	15.00	32.50	62.50	145	350	4,500	—
1902S	2,070,000	8.00	21.00	58.00	90.00	135	195	375	3,950	—
1903	19,500,755	4.00	5.00	5.50	8.00	25.00	63.00	110	1,100	1,485
1903O	8,180,000	4.00	5.50	13.50	23.50	50.00	110	250	4,850	—
1903S	613,300	84.00	130	350	490	750	840	1,100	3,150	—
1904	14,601,027	4.00	5.00	6.25	9.75	25.00	63.00	110	1,850	1,485
1904S	800,000	45.00	75.00	165	245	335	465	725	4,500	—
1905	14,552,350	3.25	4.50	6.00	9.75	25.00	63.00	110	730	1,485
1905O	3,400,000	4.25	10.50	36.50	57.50	92.00	155	285	1,650	—
1905O micro O	Inc. above	35.00	50.00	75.00	140	235	375	1,750	12,500	—
1905S	6,855,199	3.50	4.25	9.00	18.50	43.50	96.00	210	775	—
1906	19,958,406	2.25	3.75	3.75	7.25	22.00	58.00	105	730	1,485
1906D	4,060,000	2.75	4.10	7.00	15.00	35.00	78.00	175	1,650	—
1906O	2,610,000	5.50	13.00	50.00	78.00	100.00	135	195	1,150	—
1906S	3,136,640	3.25	5.50	12.50	22.50	44.00	110	240	1,350	—
1907	22,220,575	2.25	2.75	3.50	7.25	22.00	58.00	105	695	1,485
1907D	4,080,000	2.75	4.25	8.75	17.50	43.50	115	275	3,950	—
1907O	5,058,000	3.25	6.75	33.50	50.00	62.50	110	210	1,350	—
1907S	3,178,470	3.25	5.50	16.00	27.50	67.50	150	410	2,450	—
1908	10,600,545	2.25	2.75	3.50	7.25	22.00	58.00	105	695	1,485
1908D	7,490,000	2.25	2.75	5.00	9.75	29.00	63.00	125	990	—
1908O	1,789,000	5.25	11.00	44.50	64.00	92.00	150	290	1,350	—
1908S	3,220,000	3.50	5.50	11.50	22.00	46.00	175	310	2,350	—
1909	10,240,650	2.25	2.75	3.50	7.25	22.00	58.00	105	695	1,485
1909D	954,000	7.25	18.50	60.00	100.00	135	225	485	3,150	—
1909O	2,287,000	4.00	7.25	12.50	22.00	50.00	92.50	185	1,650	—
1909S	1,000,000	8.75	19.50	88.00	130	182	315	525	3,150	—
1910	11,520,551	2.25	2.75	3.25	9.75	22.00	58.00	105	695	1,485
1910D	3,490,000	2.50	4.00	8.50	19.00	47.50	100.00	210	1,650	—
1910S	1,240,000	5.25	9.00	50.00	74.00	110	195	425	2,450	—
1911	18,870,543	2.25	2.75	3.25	7.00	22.00	58.00	105	695	1,485
1911D	11,209,000	2.25	2.75	3.25	7.00	22.00	58.00	105	695	—
1911S	3,520,000	3.00	4.00	8.50	18.50	39.50	105	195	1,050	—
1912	19,350,700	2.25	2.75	3.25	7.00	22.00	58.00	105	695	1,485
1912D	11,760,000	2.25	2.75	3.25	7.00	22.00	58.00	105	695	—
1912S	3,420,000	2.50	3.75	5.60	12.50	34.00	92.50	155	775	—
1913	19,760,622	2.25	2.75	3.25	7.00	22.00	58.00	105	695	1,485
1913S	510,000	35.00	50.00	120	190	240	325	480	1,375	—
1914	17,360,655	2.25	2.75	3.25	7.00	22.00	58.00	105	695	1,485
1914D	11,908,000	2.25	2.75	3.25	7.00	22.00	58.00	105	695	—

Date	Mintage	G-4	VG-8	F-12	VF-20	XF-40	AU-50	MS-60	MS-65	Prf-65
1914S	2,100,000	2.50	3.75	8.00	17.50	39.50	78.00	150	1,250	—
1915	5,620,450	2.25	2.75	3.25	7.00	22.00	58.00	105	695	1,485
1915S	960,000	7.50	11.50	34.50	49.50	66.50	135	250	1,550	—
1916	18,490,000	2.25	2.75	3.25	8.00	22.00	58.00	105	695	—
1916S	5,820,000	2.50	3.75	4.25	8.50	25.50	63.00	110	790	—

Mercury Dime

Full split bands

Mint mark

1942/41

KM# 140 • 2.5000 g., 0.9000 **Silver**, 0.0723 oz. ASW, 17.8 mm. • **Designer:** Adolph A. Weinman **Notes:** All specimens listed as -65FSB are for fully struck MS-65 coins with fully split and rounded horizontal bands on the fasces.

Date	Mintage	G-4	VG-8	F-12	VF-20	XF-40	MS-60	MS-65	Prf-65	-65FSB
1916	22,180,080	3.50	4.75	6.00	7.00	12.00	30.00	110	—	165
1916D	264,000	1,000	1,650	2,700	3,850	6,200	13,750	26,500	—	48,500
1916S	10,450,000	4.00	5.00	9.25	15.00	25.00	46.00	210	—	800
1917	55,230,000	1.80	2.20	2.50	5.50	8.00	28.00	155	—	375
1917D	9,402,000	4.30	6.00	12.50	26.00	52.50	120	1,100	—	5,650
1917S	27,330,000	1.90	2.40	3.50	7.50	15.00	64.00	470	—	1,265
1918	26,680,000	2.40	3.70	5.75	12.00	34.00	70.00	420	—	1,325
1918D	22,674,800	2.70	3.25	6.50	13.00	32.00	105	600	—	27,500
1918S	19,300,000	2.30	3.00	3.85	11.00	24.00	96.00	660	—	7,450
1919	35,740,000	1.90	2.40	3.00	5.50	12.00	37.00	315	—	685
1919D	9,939,000	3.50	6.00	13.50	31.00	46.00	180	2,100	—	38,500
1919S	8,850,000	2.90	3.25	10.50	20.00	42.00	180	1,250	—	14,350
1920	59,030,000	1.60	2.20	2.50	4.00	8.50	28.00	235	—	540
1920D	19,171,000	2.50	2.85	4.75	9.00	24.00	110	750	—	4,750
1920S	13,820,000	2.40	2.75	7.00	9.00	21.00	110	1,300	—	8,250
1921	1,230,000	60.00	72.00	115	260	525	1,175	3,100	—	4,350
1921D	1,080,000	78.00	120	200	380	660	1,325	3,250	—	5,200
1923	50,130,000	1.60	1.80	2.10	3.50	7.00	28.00	115	—	340
1923S	6,440,000	2.60	3.00	8.25	19.00	75.00	160	1,150	—	7,450
1924	24,010,000	1.60	1.90	2.70	4.50	13.50	42.00	175	—	500
1924D	6,810,000	3.00	4.25	9.00	23.50	63.00	175	1,050	—	1,365
1924S	7,120,000	2.90	3.60	4.25	12.00	59.00	170	1,100	—	16,750
1925	25,610,000	1.60	1.90	2.40	4.00	11.00	28.00	210	—	990
1925D	5,117,000	3.90	4.40	12.75	46.50	135	350	1,750	—	3,500
1925S	5,850,000	2.50	2.85	7.75	18.50	85.00	185	1,400	—	4,650
1926	32,160,000	1.60	1.80	2.10	2.70	5.75	25.00	240	—	525
1926D	6,828,000	2.90	4.00	5.00	12.00	32.00	125	550	—	2,500
1926S	1,520,000	11.75	13.50	29.00	67.50	275	900	3,000	—	6,750
1927	28,080,000	1.60	1.80	2.10	3.50	6.00	26.00	138	—	350
1927D	4,812,000	3.00	5.00	7.75	25.50	88.00	175	1,285	—	8,500
1927S	4,770,000	2.30	3.75	5.50	11.00	30.00	285	1,400	—	7,600
1928	19,480,000	1.60	1.80	2.10	3.70	4.75	27.50	120	—	345
1928D	4,161,000	3.70	4.00	11.50	25.50	62.50	175	875	—	2,750
1928S Large S	7,400,000	2.80	3.25	5.00	12.00	40.00	225	750	—	6,500
1928S Small S	Inc. above	2.00	2.25	3.25	6.50	19.00	125	425	—	2,000
1929	25,970,000	1.60	1.80	2.10	3.00	4.50	21.00	60.00	—	175
1929D	5,034,000	2.00	3.00	3.75	8.00	15.00	27.00	75.00	—	225
1929S	4,730,000	1.80	2.00	2.25	5.00	7.50	32.50	90.00	—	560
1929S Doubled Die Obv	Inc. above	5.00	9.00	16.00	25.00	40.00	90.00	275	—	1,150
1930	6,770,000	1.80	2.00	2.20	3.80	7.00	26.00	120	—	575
1930S	1,843,000	2.50	3.50	4.80	6.50	19.00	82.00	200	—	685
1931	3,150,000	2.30	3.00	3.35	4.70	12.50	33.00	135	—	800
1931D	1,260,000	8.50	10.00	15.00	19.50	48.00	100.00	285	—	375
1931 Doubled Die Obv & Rev	Inc. above	—	—	—	50.00	70.00	135	485	—	650
1931S	1,800,000	4.00	5.00	5.50	11.00	23.50	96.00	275	—	2,500
1931S Doubled Die Obv	Inc. above	7.50	10.00	13.00	25.00	35.00	140	425	—	3,850
1934	24,080,000	—	1.45	1.75	3.00	6.50	29.00	42.00	—	130

Date	Mintage	G-4	VG-8	F-12	VF-20	XF-40	MS-60	MS-65	Prf-65	-65FSB
1934D	6,772,000	1.90	2.14	3.25	7.50	14.00	50.00	78.00	—	320
1935	58,830,000	—	1.35	1.50	2.20	4.25	10.00	30.00	—	68.00
1935D	10,477,000	1.80	1.90	2.85	6.50	13.00	37.00	84.00	—	500
1935S	15,840,000	1.60	1.65	2.00	3.00	5.50	24.00	37.00	—	360
1936	87,504,130	—	—	1.50	2.50	3.50	9.00	26.50	1,950	84.00
1936 Doubled Die Obv	Inc. above	—	—	8.00	15.00	25.00	50.00	165	—	—
1936D	16,132,000	1.60	1.65	2.10	4.30	8.50	28.00	53.00	—	290
1936S	9,210,000	—	1.50	1.90	3.00	6.00	20.00	33.00	—	88.00
1937	56,865,756	1.30	—	1.50	2.00	3.75	8.00	24.00	800	52.00
1937 Doubled Die Obv	Inc. above	—	—	—	6.00	9.00	20.00	60.00	—	175
1937D	14,146,000	1.40	1.44	1.49	3.00	6.00	22.00	43.00	—	105
1937S	9,740,000	—	1.50	2.00	3.00	5.50	22.00	36.00	—	190
1937S Doubled Die Obv	Inc. above	—	—	—	5.00	8.00	28.00	80.00	—	275
1938	22,198,728	1.30	—	1.50	2.30	3.75	13.00	25.00	480	80.00
1938D	5,537,000	1.80	2.25	3.25	5.00	6.00	18.00	34.00	—	62.00
1938S	8,090,000	1.50	2.00	2.75	3.30	5.00	21.00	37.00	—	160
1939	67,749,321	1.30	—	1.50	2.00	3.25	9.00	25.00	425	170
1939 Doubled Die Obv	Inc. above	—	—	—	4.00	6.00	14.00	35.00	—	450
1939D	24,394,000	—	1.25	1.50	2.00	3.50	7.50	26.00	—	49.00
1939S	10,540,000	1.50	1.75	2.25	3.50	6.75	25.00	50.00	—	765
1940	65,361,827	1.20	1.24	1.29	1.50	2.20	6.50	30.00	325	48.00
1940D	21,198,000	—	—	—	1.60	3.30	8.00	32.00	—	48.00
1940S	21,560,000	—	—	—	1.60	3.30	8.50	32.00	—	95.00
1941	175,106,557	1.20	1.24	1.29	1.50	1.90	6.00	30.00	325	46.00
1941 Doubled Die Obv	Inc. above	—	—	—	10.00	16.00	55.00	140	—	295
1941D	45,634,000	—	—	—	1.60	2.30	8.00	23.00	—	46.00
1941D Doubled Die Obv	Inc. above	—	—	—	9.00	14.00	30.00	90.00	—	250
1941S Small S	43,090,000	—	—	—	1.60	2.30	7.00	30.00	—	46.00
1941S Large S	Inc. above	2.50	4.00	8.00	15.00	25.00	110	250	—	425
1941S Doubled Die Rev	Inc. above	1.80	2.50	3.00	4.00	5.00	18.00	50.00	—	85.00
1942	205,432,329	1.20	1.24	1.29	1.50	1.90	6.00	24.00	325	46.00
1942/41	Inc. above	525	545	610	640	750	2,250	15,500	—	35,000
1942D	60,740,000	—	—	—	1.60	2.30	8.00	27.50	—	46.00
1942/41D	Inc. above	475	540	600	650	825	2,650	9,650	—	26,500
1942S	49,300,000	—	—	—	1.60	2.30	9.50	24.00	—	145
1943	191,710,000	1.20	1.24	1.29	1.50	1.90	6.00	31.00	—	50.00
1943D	71,949,000	—	—	—	1.60	2.30	7.75	30.00	—	47.00
1943S	60,400,000	—	—	—	1.60	2.30	9.00	26.50	—	66.00
1944	231,410,000	1.20	1.24	1.29	1.50	1.90	6.00	23.00	—	75.00
1944D	62,224,000	—	—	—	1.60	2.30	7.50	23.00	—	46.00
1944S	49,490,000	—	—	—	1.60	2.30	7.50	30.00	—	50.00
1945	159,130,000	1.20	1.24	1.29	1.50	1.90	6.00	23.00	—	9,750
1945D	40,245,000	—	—	—	1.60	2.30	6.50	24.00	—	4,650
1945S	41,920,000	—	—	—	1.60	2.30	7.00	24.00	—	105
1945S micro S	Inc. above	3.00	4.00	6.00	9.00	13.00	28.00	115	—	685

DIME

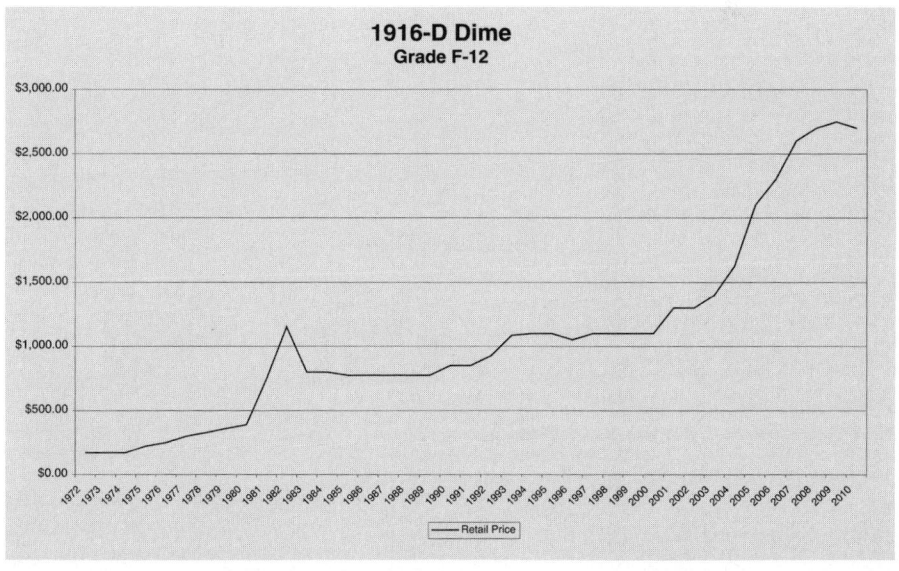

1916-D Dime
Grade F-12

Roosevelt Dime

Mint mark 1946-64

KM# 195 • 2.5000 g., 0.9000 **Silver**, 0.0723 oz. ASW, 17.9 mm. • **Designer:** John R. Sinnock

Date	Mintage	G-4	VG-8	F-12	VF-20	XF-40	AU-50	MS-60	MS-65	Prf-65
1946	225,250,000	—	—	—	—	1.60	1.90	2.00	14.00	—
1946D	61,043,500	—	—	—	—	1.60	2.10	2.30	15.00	—
1946S	27,900,000	—	—	—	—	1.60	2.10	2.40	17.00	—
1947	121,520,000	—	—	—	—	1.60	2.00	4.00	15.00	—
1947D	46,835,000	—	—	—	—	1.80	2.30	5.00	17.00	—
1947S	34,840,000	—	—	—	—	1.60	2.00	5.00	16.00	—
1948	74,950,000	—	—	—	—	1.70	2.00	4.50	15.00	—
1948D	52,841,000	—	—	—	—	2.00	2.50	6.00	17.00	—
1948S	35,520,000	—	—	—	—	1.90	2.30	5.00	14.00	—
1949	30,940,000	—	—	1.50	2.00	3.00	8.00	16.00	45.00	—
1949D	26,034,000	—	—	1.35	1.75	2.25	5.00	9.00	22.00	—
1949S	13,510,000	—	1.60	2.00	3.50	7.50	14.00	40.00	65.00	—
1950	50,181,500	—	—	—	1.75	2.25	3.50	10.00	25.00	55.00
1950D	46,803,000	—	—	—	—	—	2.50	5.00	12.00	—
1950S	20,440,000	—	1.20	1.80	1.95	3.75	9.00	32.00	60.00	—
1951	102,937,602	—	—	—	—	—	2.00	2.50	10.00	60.00
1951D	56,529,000	—	—	—	—	—	1.90	2.50	8.00	—
1951S	31,630,000	—	—	—	1.70	2.00	4.00	10.00	26.00	—
1952	99,122,073	—	—	—	—	—	1.80	2.50	9.00	35.00
1952D	122,100,000	—	—	—	—	—	1.80	2.50	10.00	—
1952S	44,419,500	—	—	—	1.75	2.00	2.80	5.50	15.00	—
1953	53,618,920	—	—	—	—	—	1.80	2.30	8.00	42.00
1953D	136,433,000	—	—	—	—	—	1.80	2.40	8.00	—
1953S	39,180,000	—	—	—	—	—	2.20	3.00	15.00	—
1954	114,243,503	—	—	—	—	—	1.80	2.00	7.00	18.00
1954D	106,397,000	—	—	—	—	—	1.80	2.00	7.00	—
1954S	22,860,000	—	—	—	—	—	1.80	2.10	10.00	—
1955	12,828,381	—	—	—	1.75	1.90	2.20	2.80	8.50	17.00
1955D	13,959,000	—	—	—	1.75	1.90	2.30	2.80	8.50	—
1955S	18,510,000	—	—	—	1.75	1.90	2.20	2.30	8.00	—
1956	109,309,384	—	—	—	—	—	1.80	2.00	9.00	8.00
1956D	108,015,100	—	—	—	—	—	1.80	2.10	10.00	—
1957	161,407,952	—	—	—	—	—	1.80	2.00	8.00	5.00
1957D	113,354,330	—	—	—	—	—	1.80	2.00	8.00	—
1958	32,785,652	—	—	—	—	—	1.80	2.00	8.50	6.00
1958D	136,564,600	—	—	—	—	—	1.80	2.00	9.00	—
1959	86,929,291	—	—	—	—	—	1.80	2.00	8.00	4.50
1959D	164,919,790	—	—	—	—	—	1.80	2.00	8.00	—
1960	72,081,602	—	—	—	—	—	1.80	2.00	7.50	4.50
1960D	200,160,400	—	—	—	—	—	1.80	2.00	7.50	—
1961	96,758,244	—	—	—	—	—	1.80	2.00	6.50	4.00
1961D	209,146,550	—	—	—	—	—	1.80	2.00	6.50	—
1962	75,668,019	—	—	—	—	—	1.80	2.00	7.00	4.00
1962D	334,948,380	—	—	—	—	—	1.80	2.00	7.00	—
1963	126,725,645	—	—	—	—	—	1.80	2.00	6.50	3.75
1963D	421,476,530	—	—	—	—	—	1.80	2.00	6.50	—
1964	933,310,762	—	—	—	—	—	1.80	2.00	6.00	3.75
1964D	1,357,517,180	—	—	—	—	—	1.80	2.00	6.00	—

Roosevelt Dime

Mint mark 1968- present   1982 No mint mark

KM# 195a • 2.2700 g., **Copper-Nickel Clad Copper**, 17.9 mm. • **Designer:** John R. Sinnock **Notes:** The 1979-S and 1981-S Type II proofs have clearer mint marks than the Type I proofs of those years. On the 1982 no-mint-mark variety, the mint mark was inadvertently left off.

Date	Mintage	MS-65	Prf-65	Date	Mintage	MS-65	Prf-65
1965	1,652,140,570	1.00	—	1968D	480,748,280	1.00	—
1966	1,382,734,540	1.00	—	1968S	3,041,506	—	1.00
1967	2,244,007,320	1.50	—	1969	145,790,000	3.00	—
1968	424,470,000	1.00	—	1969D	563,323,870	1.00	—

Date	Mintage	MS-65	Prf-65	Date	Mintage	MS-65	Prf-65
1969S	2,934,631	—	0.80	1989D	896,535,597	1.00	—
1970	345,570,000	1.00	—	1989S	3,220,194	—	4.00
1970S No S	—	—	1,300	1990P	1,034,340,000	1.00	—
1970D	754,942,100	1.00	—	1990D	839,995,824	1.00	—
1970S	2,632,810	—	1.00	1990S	3,299,559	—	2.00
1971	162,690,000	2.00	—	1991P	927,220,000	1.00	—
1971D	377,914,240	1.00	—	1991D	601,241,114	1.00	—
1971S	3,220,733	—	1.00	1991S	2,867,787	—	3.00
1972	431,540,000	1.00	—	1992P	593,500,000	1.00	—
1972D	330,290,000	1.00	—	1992D	616,273,932	1.00	—
1972S	3,260,996	—	1.00	1992S	2,858,981	—	4.00
1973	315,670,000	1.00	—	1993P	766,180,000	1.00	—
1973D	455,032,426	1.00	—	1993D	750,110,166	1.50	—
1973S	2,760,339	—	1.00	1993S	2,633,439	—	7.00
1974	470,248,000	1.00	—	1994P	1,189,000,000	1.00	—
1974D	571,083,000	1.00	—	1994D	1,303,268,110	1.00	—
1974S	2,612,568	—	1.00	1994S	2,484,594	—	5.00
1975	585,673,900	1.00	—	1995P	1,125,500,000	1.50	—
1975D	313,705,300	1.00	—	1995D	1,274,890,000	2.00	—
1975S	2,845,450	—	2.00	1995S	2,010,384	—	20.00
1976	568,760,000	1.50	—	1996P	1,421,163,000	1.00	—
1976D	695,222,774	1.00	—	1996D	1,400,300,000	1.00	—
1976S	4,149,730	—	1.00	1996W	1,457,949	25.00	—
1977	796,930,000	1.00	—	1996S	2,085,191	—	2.50
1977D	376,607,228	1.00	—	1997P	991,640,000	2.00	—
1977S	3,251,152	—	2.00	1997D	979,810,000	1.00	—
1978	663,980,000	1.00	—	1997S	1,975,000	—	11.00
1978D	282,847,540	1.00	—	1998D	1,163,000,000	1.00	—
1978S	3,127,781	—	1.00	1998D	1,172,250,000	1.25	—
1979	315,440,000	1.00	—	1998S	2,078,494	—	4.00
1979D	390,921,184	1.00	—	1999P	2,164,000,000	1.00	—
1979 type I	—	—	1.00	1999D	1,397,750,000	1.00	—
1979S type I	3,677,175	—	1.00	1999S	2,557,897	—	4.00
1979S type II	Inc. above	—	2.00	2000P	1,842,500,000	1.00	—
1980P	735,170,000	1.00	—	2000D	1,818,700,000	1.00	—
1980D	719,354,321	.70	—	2000S	3,097,440	—	1.00
1980S	3,554,806	—	1.00	2001P	1,369,590,000	1.00	—
1981P	676,650,000	1.00	—	2001D	1,412,800,000	1.00	—
1981D	712,284,143	1.00	—	2001S	2,249,496	—	1.00
1981S type I	—	—	1.00	2002P	1,187,500,000	1.00	—
1981S type II	—	—	2.00	2002D	1,379,500,000	1.00	—
1982P	519,475,000	8.50	—	2002S	2,268,913	—	2.00
1982 no mint mark	Inc. above	300	—	2003P	1,085,500,000	1.00	—
1982D	542,713,584	3.00	—	2003D	986,500,000	1.00	—
1982S	3,857,479	—	2.00	2003S	2,076,165	—	2.00
1983P	647,025,000	7.00	—	2004P	1,328,000,000	1.00	—
1983D	730,129,224	2.50	—	2004D	1,159,500,000	1.00	—
1983S	3,279,126	—	2.00	2004S	1,804,396	—	4.75
1984P	856,669,000	1.00	—	2005P	1,412,000,000	1.00	—
1984D	704,803,976	2.00	—	2005D	1,423,500,000	1.00	—
1984S	3,065,110	—	2.00	2005S	—	—	2.25
1985P	705,200,962	1.00	—	2006P	1,381,000,000	1.00	—
1985D	587,979,970	1.00	—	2006D	1,447,000,000	1.00	—
1985S	3,362,821	—	1.00	2006S	—	—	2.25
1986P	682,649,693	2.00	—	2007P	—	1.00	—
1986D	473,326,970	2.00	—	2007D	—	1.00	—
1986S	3,010,497	—	2.75	2007S	—	—	2.25
1987P	762,709,481	1.00	—	2008P	—	1.00	—
1987D	653,203,402	1.00	—	2008D	—	1.00	—
1987S	4,227,728	—	1.00	2008S	—	—	2.25
1988P	1,030,550,000	1.00	—	2009P	—	1.00	—
1988D	962,385,488	1.00	—	2009D	—	1.00	—
1988S	3,262,948	—	3.00	2009S	—	—	2.25
1989P	1,298,400,000	1.00	—				

Roosevelt Dime

KM# 195b • 2.5000 g., 0.9000 **Silver**, 0.0723 oz. ASW, 17.9 mm. • **Designer:** John R. Sinnock

Date	Mintage	Prf-65	Date	Mintage	Prf-65
1992S	1,317,579	5.00	2002S	888,826	5.00
1993S	761,353	9.00	2003S	1,090,425	4.00
1994S	785,329	9.00	2004S	—	4.50
1995S	838,953	25.00	2005S	—	3.50
1996S	830,021	9.00	2006S	—	3.50
1997S	821,678	25.00	2007S	—	3.50
1998S	878,792	9.00	2008S	—	3.50
1999S	804,565	6.50	2009S	—	3.50
2000S	965,921	4.00			
2001S	849,600	5.00			

DIME

20 CENTS
Seated Liberty within circle of stars, date below obverse
Eagle with arrows in talons, value below reverse

KM# 109 • 5.0000 g., 0.9000 **Silver**, 0.1447 oz. ASW, 22 mm. • **Rev. Legend:** UNITED STATES OF AMERICA **Designer:** William Barber

Date	Mintage	G-4	VG-8	F-12	VF-20	XF-40	AU-50	MS-60	MS-65	Prf-65
1875	39,700	165	210	270	325	415	550	835	5,500	9,500
1875S	1,155,000	100.00	110	120	175	210	320	500	4,900	—
Note: 1875-S exists as a branch mint proof										
1875S Clear S	Inc. above	110	120	135	200	235	350	600	5,500	—
1875S over horizontal S	Inc. above	100.00	110	120	175	210	320	500	4,900	—
Note: Also known as filled S										
1875S as $	Inc. above	—	120	130	150	225	260	375	1,300	—
1875CC	133,290	335	385	475	600	775	1,150	1,650	10,000	—
1876	15,900	185	225	285	350	410	535	800	5,600	9,400
1876CC	10,000	20,000	25,000	30,000	35,000	50,000	60,000	—	—	175,000
Note: 1876CC, Eliasberg Sale, April 1997, MS-65, $148,500. Heritage 1999 ANA, MS-63, $86,500.										
1877 proof only	510	—	—	2,700	2,900	3,300	3,500	—	—	10,000
1878 proof only	600	—	—	2,000	2,300	2,400	2,800	—	—	9,500

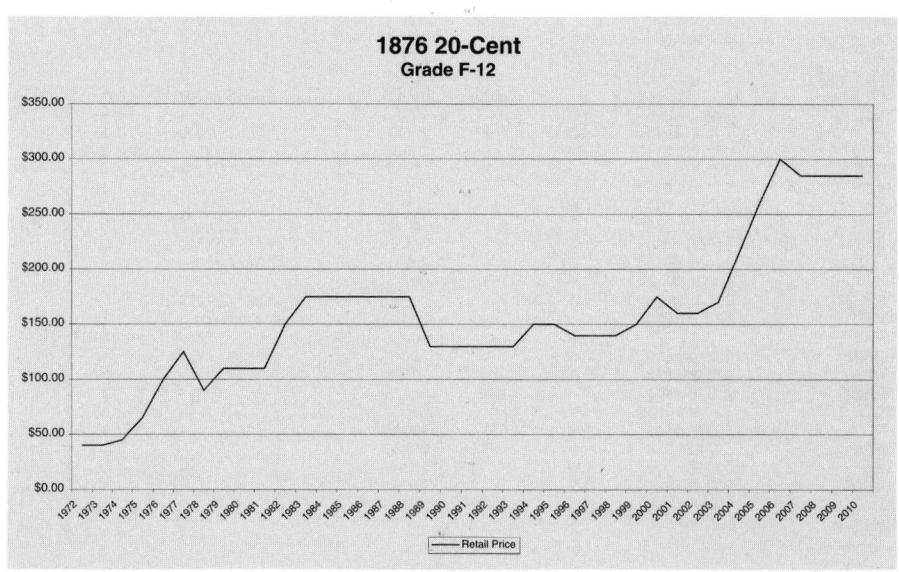

1876 20-Cent
Grade F-12

QUARTER

Draped Bust Quarter
Small eagle reverse

KM# 25 • 6.7400 g., 0.8920 **Silver**, 0.1933 oz. ASW, 27.5 mm. • **Designer:** Robert Scot

Date	Mintage	G-4	VG-8	F-12	VF-20	XF-40	AU-50	MS-60	MS-65
1796	6,146	11,000	16,500	30,000	39,500	42,500	68,000	82,500	235,000

Draped Bust Quarter
Draped bust right, flanked by stars, date at angle below obverse   Heraldic eagle reverse

KM# 36 • 6.7400 g., 0.8920 **Silver**, 0.1933 oz. ASW, 27.5 mm. • **Obv. Legend** LIBERTY **Rev. Legend:** UNITED STATES OF AMERICA **Designer:** Robert Scot

Date	Mintage	G-4	VG-8	F-12	VF-20	XF-40	AU-50	MS-60	MS-65
1804	6,738	5,500	6,750	9,000	14,500	46,500	54,500	88,500	335,000
1805	121,394	230	285	520	960	2,500	4,450	6,600	62,000
1806/5	206,124	250	375	650	1,400	2,850	5,000	7,150	72,000
1806	Inc. above	220	275	500	900	2,350	4,250	6,300	56,000
1807	220,643	220	275	500	925	2,350	4,250	6,300	58,000

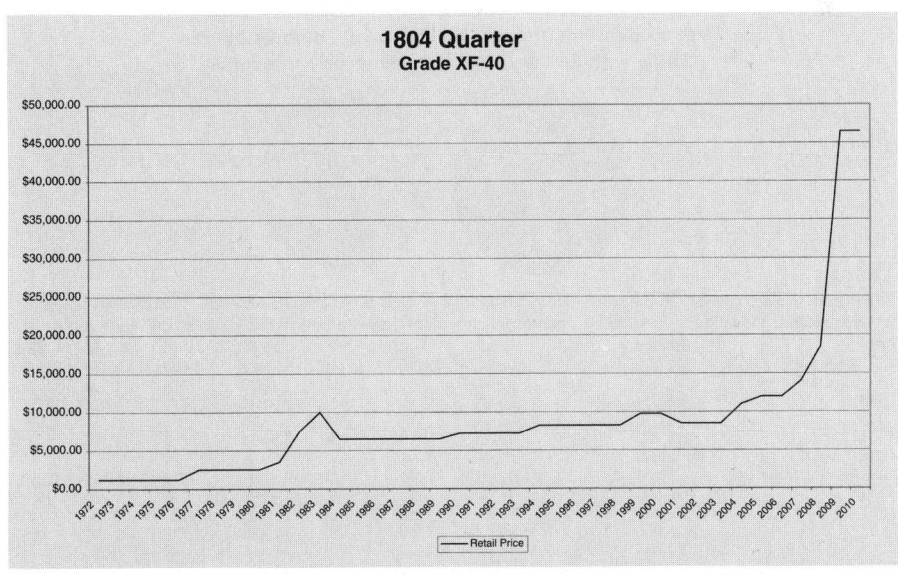

1804 Quarter
Grade XF-40

QUARTER

Liberty Cap Quarter
Draped bust left, flanked by stars, date below obverse
Eagle with arrows in talons, banner above, value below reverse

KM# 44 • 6.7400 g., 0.8920 **Silver**, 0.1933 oz. ASW, 27 mm. • **Rev. Legend:** UNITED STATES OF AMERICA **Designer:** John Reich **Notes:** Varieties of the 1819 strikes are distinguished by the size of the 9 in the date. Varieties of the 1820 strikes are distinguished by the size of the 0 in the date. One 1822 variety and one 1828 variety have "25" engraved over "50" in the denomination. The 1827 restrikes were produced privately using dies sold as scrap by the U.S. Mint.

Date	Mintage	G-4	VG-8	F-12	VF-20	XF-40	AU-50	MS-60	MS-65
1815	89,235	100.00	135	200	425	1,375	1,750	3,250	30,000
1818/15	361,174	100.00	130	190	450	1,350	1,850	3,200	28,500
1818	Inc. above	95.00	125	180	410	1,200	1,600	2,850	19,500
1819 small 9	144,000	95.00	125	180	410	1,225	1,659	2,900	23,500
1819 large 9	Inc. above	95.00	130	185	435	1,300	1,750	3,100	25,000
1820 small 0	127,444	95.00	125	180	420	1,300	1,700	3,100	34,500
1820 large 0	Inc. above	95.00	125	180	415	1,225	1,600	2,900	32,500
1821	216,851	100.00	130	185	420	1,275	1,650	2,875	20,000
1822	64,080	110	135	200	440	1,225	2,750	4,200	—
1822 25/50C.	Inc. above	1,650	3,350	4,350	6,800	12,500	20,000	33,000	125,000
1823/22	17,800	30,000	35,000	48,500	58,500	68,000	100,000	175,000	—
Note: 1823/22, Superior, Aug. 1990, Proof, $62,500.									
1824/2	—	275	425	600	1,650	4,200	7,000	14,500	—
1825/22	168,000	125	175	260	500	1,550	2,100	3,000	—
1825/23	Inc. above	115	150	235	450	1,400	1,850	3,400	25,000
1825/24	Inc. above	100.00	135	210	420	1,325	1,700	3,150	22,000
1827 original curl base 2	4,000	—	—	—	70,000	75,000	80,000	—	—
Note: Eliasberg, April 1997, VF-20, $39,600.									
1827 restrike, square base 2	Inc. above	—	—	—	—	—	—	—	—
Note: 1827 restrike, Eliasberg, April 1997, Prf-65, $77,000.									
1828	102,000	90.00	120	180	400	1,100	1,650	3,000	26,000
1828 25/50C.	Inc. above	165	320	550	1,250	2,650	4,250	9,500	—

Liberty Cap Quarter
Draped bust left, flanked by stars, date below obverse
Eagle with arrows in talons, value below reverse

KM# 55 • 0.8920 **Silver**, 24.3 mm. • **Rev. Legend:** UNITED STATES OF AMERICA **Designer:** William Kneass **Notes:** Varieties of the 1831 strikes are distinguished by the size of the lettering on the reverse.

Date	Mintage	G-4	VG-8	F-12	VF-20	XF-40	AU-50	MS-60	MS-65
1831 small letter rev.	398,000	70.00	95.00	115	160	400	850	1,175	19,500
1831 large letter rev.	Inc. above	70.00	90.00	110	150	385	775	1,100	17,000
1832	320,000	70.00	90.00	110	150	385	775	1,075	22,750
1833	156,000	75.00	100.00	115	170	420	855	1,400	20,500
1834	286,000	70.00	90.00	110	150	385	775	1,100	17,000
1834 0 over O	Inc. above	—	—	—	—	—	—	—	—
1835	1,952,000	70.00	90.00	110	150	385	775	1,100	23,750
1836	472,000	70.00	90.00	110	150	385	775	1,100	18,850
1837	252,400	70.00	90.00	110	150	385	775	1,100	17,000
1838	832,000	70.00	90.00	110	150	385	775	1,100	19,500

Seated Liberty Quarter
Seated Liberty, stars around top 1/2 of border, date below obverse
Eagle with arrows in talons, value below reverse

KM# 64.1 • 6.6800 g., 0.9000 **Silver**, 0.1933 oz. ASW, 24.3 mm. • **Rev. Legend:** UNITED STATES OF AMERICA **Designer:** Christian Gobrecht

Date	Mintage	G-4	VG-8	F-12	VF-20	XF-40	AU-50	MS-60	MS-65
1838	Inc. above	42.00	50.00	60.00	110	360	550	1,250	30,000
1839	491,146	36.00	44.00	52.00	85.00	350	550	1,250	34,000
1840O	425,200	46.00	54.00	75.00	135	375	575	1,350	38,500

Seated Liberty Quarter
Drapery added to Liberty's left elbow, stars around top 1/2 of border obverse
Eagle with arrows in talons, value below reverse

KM# 64.2 • 6.6800 g., 0.9000 **Silver**, 0.1933 oz. ASW, 24.3 mm. • **Rev. Legend:** UNITED STATES OF AMERICA **Designer:** Christian Gobrecht

Date	Mintage	G-4	VG-8	F-12	VF-20	XF-40	AU-50	MS-60	MS-65
1840	188,127	27.00	52.00	75.00	125	225	350	950	12,000
1840O	Inc. above	29.00	39.00	70.00	115	250	450	1,000	—
1841	120,000	65.00	90.00	115	170	275	385	750	11,000
1841O	452,000	21.50	27.50	50.00	85.00	165	350	700	10,000
1842 small date	88,000	—	—	—	—	—	—	—	—
Note: 1842 small date, Eliasberg, April 1997, Prf-63, $66,000.									
1842 large date	Inc. above	100.00	125	190	275	375	850	1,850	—
1842O small date	769,000	425	650	1,200	1,950	4,000	—	—	—
1842O large date	Inc. above	28.00	42.00	55.00	70.00	135	300	900	—
1843	645,600	22.00	26.00	34.00	45.00	75.00	175	400	6,750
1843O	968,000	25.00	31.50	55.00	125	250	750	2,000	11,000
1844	421,200	20.00	25.00	31.50	50.00	80.00	160	450	5,500
1844O	740,000	25.00	28.50	40.00	75.00	140	280	1,000	6,000
1845	922,000	20.00	25.00	31.50	45.00	70.00	150	465	5,000
1846	510,000	20.00	25.00	36.50	55.00	85.00	175	475	6,000
1847	734,000	20.00	25.00	31.50	50.00	70.00	150	450	5,000
1847O	368,000	30.00	45.00	70.00	135	300	750	1,900	—
1848	146,000	40.00	60.00	110	185	225	375	1,000	10,000
1849	340,000	20.00	30.00	45.00	65.00	125	275	750	9,000
1849O	—	550	750	1,150	1,850	3,250	5,750	—	—
1850	190,800	40.00	50.00	80.00	125	175	275	800	—
1850O	412,000	20.00	30.00	60.00	110	175	450	1,300	—
1851	160,000	60.00	75.00	125	225	285	400	850	8,500
1851O	88,000	185	275	425	700	1,250	2,250	4,000	—
1852	177,060	50.00	60.00	100.00	185	225	350	500	4,800
1852O	96,000	195	275	475	800	1,350	3,500	8,000	—
1853 recut date	44,200	450	650	900	1,100	1,350	1,800	2,600	9,000

Seated Liberty Quarter
Seated Liberty, arrows at date obverse   Rays around eagle reverse

KM# 78 • 6.2200 g., 0.9000 **Silver**, 0.1800 oz. ASW, 24.3 mm. • **Rev. Legend:** UNITED STATES OF AMERICA **Designer:** Christian Gobrecht

Date	Mintage	G-4	VG-8	F-12	VF-20	XF-40	AU-50	MS-60	MS-65	Prf-65
1853	15,210,020	20.00	23.00	32.00	46.00	150	275	950	16,500	100,000
1853/4	Inc. above	40.00	65.00	100.00	200	275	750	1,750	—	—
1853O	1,332,000	18.00	35.00	50.00	100.00	275	1,100	2,750	—	—

Seated Liberty Quarter
Seated Liberty, arrows at date obverse   Eagle with arrows in talons, value below reverse

KM# 81 • 6.6800 g., 0.9000 **Silver**, 0.1933 oz. ASW, 24.3 mm. • **Rev. Legend:** UNITED STATES OF AMERICA **Designer:** Christian Gobrecht

Date	Mintage	G-4	VG-8	F-12	VF-20	XF-40	AU-50	MS-60	MS-65	Prf-65
1854	12,380,000	15.00	20.00	27.50	35.00	75.00	225	440	7,500	17,500
1854O	1,484,000	17.00	24.00	35.00	60.00	125	300	1,750	—	—
1854O huge O	Inc. above	800	1,350	2,850	4,750	7,500	12,500	17,000	—	—
1855	2,857,000	15.00	20.00	27.50	35.00	75.00	225	440	8,500	18,500
1855O	176,000	50.00	75.00	110	240	475	950	2,750	—	—
1855S	396,400	40.00	60.00	80.00	225	500	1,250	2,000	—	—

Seated Liberty Quarter
Seated Liberty, date below obverse   Eagle with arrows in talons, value below reverse

KM# A64.2 • 6.2200 g., 0.9000 **Silver**, 0.1800 oz. ASW, 24.3 mm. • **Rev. Legend:** UNITED STATES OF AMERICA **Designer:** Christian Gobrecht

Date	Mintage	G-4	VG-8	F-12	VF-20	XF-40	AU-50	MS-60	MS-65	Prf-65
1856	7,264,000	15.00	20.00	27.50	35.00	60.00	145	290	4,250	15,000
1856O	968,000	20.00	30.00	40.00	60.00	110	250	1,000	8,500	—
1856S	286,000	45.00	65.00	110	250	450	900	2,200	—	—
1856S/S	Inc. above	150	275	500	1,250	2,000	—	—	—	—
1857	9,644,000	15.00	20.00	27.50	35.00	60.00	145	290	4,000	9,500
1857O	1,180,000	15.00	20.00	29.00	40.00	80.00	275	975	—	—
1857S	82,000	125	175	275	450	700	950	2,750	—	—
1858	7,368,000	15.00	20.00	27.50	35.00	60.00	160	300	4,000	6,500
1858O	520,000	25.00	30.00	45.00	70.00	135	360	1,350	—	—
1858S	121,000	70.00	110	175	300	750	1,250	—	—	—
1859	1,344,000	17.00	24.00	30.00	40.00	75.00	175	375	6,000	7,000
1859O	260,000	25.00	30.00	50.00	80.00	150	400	1,000	15,000	—
1859S	80,000	125	150	250	500	1,500	2,500	—	—	—
1860	805,400	18.00	22.00	28.00	33.00	60.00	160	500	—	5,250
1860O	388,000	20.00	30.00	40.00	55.00	100.00	275	1,200	—	—
1860S	56,000	200	350	600	975	4,000	6,000	—	—	—
1861	4,854,600	16.00	19.00	27.00	32.00	55.00	150	290	4,200	5,500

Date	Mintage	G-4	VG-8	F-12	VF-20	XF-40	AU-50	MS-60	MS-65	Prf-65
1861S	96,000	90.00	145	235	400	1,250	2,750	—	—	—
1862	932,550	18.00	22.00	33.00	40.00	65.00	165	300	4,350	5,350
1862S	67,000	80.00	125	200	325	700	1,600	2,750	—	—
1863	192,060	30.00	45.00	60.00	120	185	300	650	4,350	5,500
1864	94,070	90.00	120	160	245	345	400	650	5,000	5,500
1864S	20,000	400	600	900	1,350	2,350	3,750	7,000	—	—
1865	59,300	85.00	115	150	235	325	375	875	9,500	5,500
1865S	41,000	125	175	250	425	750	1,250	2,350	11,500	—
1866 unique	—	—	—	—	—	—	—	—	—	—

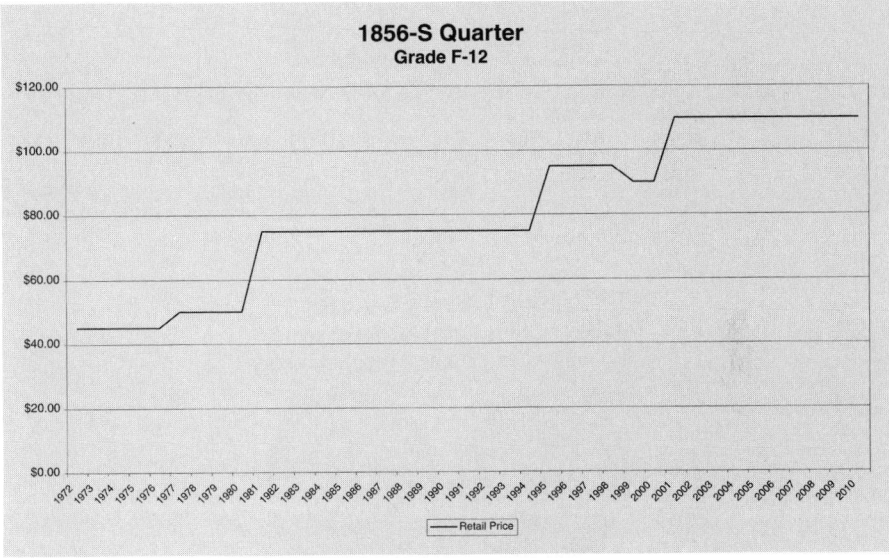

1856-S Quarter
Grade F-12

— Retail Price

Seated Liberty Quarter
Seated Liberty, date below obverse IN GOD WE TRUST above eagle reverse

KM# 98 • 6.2200 g., 0.9000 **Silver**, 0.1800 oz. ASW, 24.3 mm. • **Rev. Legend:** UNITED STATES OF AMERICA **Designer:** Christian Gobrecht **Notes:** The 1873 closed-3 and open-3 varieties are distinguished by the amount of space between the upper left and lower left serifs in the 3.

Date	Mintage	G-4	VG-8	F-12	VF-20	XF-40	AU-50	MS-60	MS-65	Prf-65
1866	17,525	475	600	750	1,000	1,200	1,500	2,250	7,500	3,000
1866S	28,000	325	375	675	1,050	1,450	2,000	3,000	—	—
1867	20,625	250	325	500	675	850	975	1,200	—	2,450
1867S	48,000	275	385	600	900	1,350	1,700	—	—	—
1868	30,000	200	250	325	400	500	650	900	7,000	3,450
1868S	96,000	95.00	110	195	300	625	1,350	2,000	—	—
1869	16,600	350	450	600	800	900	1,000	1,275	—	2,500
1869S	76,000	110	135	225	375	700	1,400	2,400	16,000	—
1870	87,400	55.00	80.00	145	245	295	425	850	6,000	2,750
1870CC	8,340	4,500	6,500	9,500	15,000	—	—	—	—	—
1871	119,160	40.00	65.00	75.00	150	195	350	650	6,000	2,500
1871CC	10,890	3,500	4,500	7,500	12,500	18,000	—	—	—	—
1871S	30,900	375	500	700	950	1,200	1,850	3,000	10,000	—
1872	182,950	30.00	40.00	80.00	110	155	300	600	6,500	2,500
1872CC	22,850	1,100	1,500	2,250	3,750	6,500	7,500	14,000	—	—
1872S	83,000	900	1,250	1,750	2,400	3,500	4,500	7,500	—	—
1873 closed 3	212,600	250	350	475	800	1,200	1,800	2,800	—	2,600
1873 open 3	Inc. above	30.00	42.50	80.00	120	175	250	450	5,000	—
1873CC 6 known	4,000	—	75,000	—	—	—	—	—	—	—

Note: 1873CC, Heritage, April 1999, MS-62, $106,375.

Seated Liberty Quarter
Seated Liberty, arrows at date obverse
"In God We Trust" above eagle reverse

KM# 106 • 6.2500 g., 0.9000 **Silver**, 0.1808 oz. ASW, 24.3 mm. • **Rev. Legend:** UNITED STATES OF AMERICA **Designer:** Christian Gobrecht

Date	Mintage	G-4	VG-8	F-12	VF-20	XF-40	AU-50	MS-60	MS-65	Prf-65
1873	1,271,700	16.00	23.00	30.00	60.00	200	400	775	4,250	8,000
1873CC	12,462	3,500	4,500	8,000	11,000	17,000	—	—	—	—
1873S	156,000	25.00	40.00	85.00	140	275	550	1,200	8,000	—
1874	471,900	20.00	26.00	40.00	70.00	220	420	850	4,000	6,750
1874S	392,000	23.00	30.00	50.00	110	240	425	900	4,500	—

Seated Liberty Quarter
Seated Liberty, date below obverse
"In God We Trust" above eagle reverse

KM# A98 • 6.2500 g., 0.9000 **Silver**, 0.1808 oz. ASW, 24.3 mm. • **Rev. Legend:** UNITED STATES OF AMERICA **Designer:** Christian Gobrecht **Notes:** The 1876-CC fine-reeding variety has a more finely reeded edge.

Date	Mintage	G-4	VG-8	F-12	VF-20	XF-40	AU-50	MS-60	MS-65	Prf-65
1875	4,293,500	14.00	17.00	25.00	30.00	50.00	135	225	1,600	2,300
1875CC	140,000	75.00	110	225	350	550	850	1,600	15,000	—
1875S	680,000	25.00	36.00	67.00	110	175	275	575	3,200	—
1876	17,817,150	14.00	17.00	25.00	30.00	50.00	135	225	1,600	2,250
1876CC	4,944,000	30.00	40.00	50.00	65.00	90.00	150	325	3,600	—
1876CC fine reeding	Inc. above	30.00	40.00	50.00	65.00	90.00	150	325	3,600	—
1876S	8,596,000	16.00	19.00	25.00	30.00	50.00	135	225	2,000	—
1877	10,911,710	14.00	17.00	25.00	30.00	50.00	135	225	1,600	2,250
1877CC	4,192,000	30.00	40.00	50.00	65.00	90.00	150	325	2,000	—
1877S	8,996,000	14.00	17.00	25.00	30.00	50.00	135	225	1,600	—
1877S over horizontal S	Inc. above	45.00	60.00	95.00	175	250	375	650	—	—
1878	2,260,800	16.00	18.00	28.00	34.00	55.00	145	250	2,750	2,300
1878CC	996,000	35.00	45.00	55.00	80.00	110	150	450	3,500	—
1878S	140,000	165	200	300	400	650	875	1,450	—	—
1879	14,700	190	235	285	325	400	485	575	1,700	2,250
1880	14,955	190	235	285	325	400	485	575	1,600	2,250
1881	12,975	200	250	300	350	425	500	600	1,650	2,200
1882	16,300	200	250	300	350	425	500	600	1,850	2,200
1883	15,439	210	265	315	365	435	525	625	2,450	2,200
1884	8,875	375	450	550	650	750	750	850	1,900	2,200
1885	14,530	210	265	315	365	435	525	625	2,600	2,200
1886	5,886	500	600	700	800	900	1,000	1,250	2,600	2,400
1887	10,710	300	350	450	550	650	750	850	2,350	2,200
1888	10,833	275	325	425	500	600	700	800	2,000	2,350
1888S	1,216,000	15.00	20.00	27.50	30.00	60.00	160	245	2,450	—
1889	12,711	250	300	375	425	500	575	675	1,750	2,350
1890	80,590	65.00	85.00	100.00	125	200	300	425	—	2,350
1891	3,920,600	15.00	20.00	27.50	30.00	60.00	160	245	1,750	2,350
1891O	68,000	150	225	325	550	950	1,250	3,000	14,500	—
1891S	2,216,000	16.00	22.00	29.00	65.00	52.50	185	275	2,400	—

Barber Quarter
Laureate head right, flanked by stars, date below obverse   Heraldic eagle reverse

KM# 114 • 6.2500 g., 0.9000 **Silver**, 0.1808 oz. ASW, 24.3 mm. • **Obv. Legend** IN GOD WE TRUST **Rev. Legend:** UNITED STATES OF AMERICA **Designer:** Charles E. Barber

Date	Mintage	G-4	VG-8	F-12	VF-20	XF-40	AU-50	MS-60	MS-65	Prf-65
1892	8,237,245	10.00	14.50	35.00	65.00	100.00	150	285	—	2,450
1892 Type 2 Rev	Inc. above	7.50	8.50	26.00	46.00	75.00	115	210	1,550	2,450
1892O	2,640,000	22.00	30.00	55.00	90.00	155	235	400	—	—
1892O Type 2 Rev	Inc. above	15.00	21.50	43.50	63.50	100.00	150	290	2,000	—
1892S	964,079	50.00	75.00	135	200	300	465	650	—	—
1892S Type 2 Rev	Inc. above	35.00	57.50	95.00	145	195	300	450	4,650	—
1893	5,484,838	6.50	9.00	27.50	41.50	70.00	115	210	1,650	2,450
1893O	3,396,000	13.50	22.00	44.00	75.00	165	285	390	—	—
1893O MM far right	Inc. above	9.00	15.00	31.00	57.50	115	170	265	2,100	—
1893S	1,454,535	26.00	47.50	82.00	158	255	390	635	—	—
1893S MM far right	Inc. above	21.00	38.00	67.50	125	195	310	450	7,950	—
1894	3,432,972	5.50	9.50	34.00	50.00	93.50	140	235	1,550	2,450
1894O	2,852,000	12.50	24.00	50.00	95.00	165	285	415	—	—
1894O MM far right	Inc. above	10.00	18.50	43.00	80.00	142	220	325	2,650	—
1894S	2,648,821	11.00	17.00	50.00	100.00	180	265	410	—	—
1894S MM far right	Inc. above	8.25	13.50	38.00	68.50	128	195	295	2,750	—
1895	4,440,880	6.50	10.50	31.50	41.50	78.00	130	225	1,850	2,450
1895O	2,816,000	17.50	27.50	60.00	92.00	175	290	525	—	—
1895O MM far right	Inc. above	12.50	19.50	46.00	75.00	145	225	390	2,850	—
1895S	1,764,681	28.00	40.00	85.00	165	235	375	560	—	—
1895S MM far right	Inc. above	22.00	30.00	68.50	120	175	290	425	4,450	—
1896	3,874,762	5.00	7.00	25.00	41.50	80.00	130	225	1,550	2,450
1896O	1,484,000	32.00	53.50	122	250	435	725	815	9,850	—
1896S	188,039	900	1,650	2,350	3,350	4,650	6,250	9,750	56,000	—

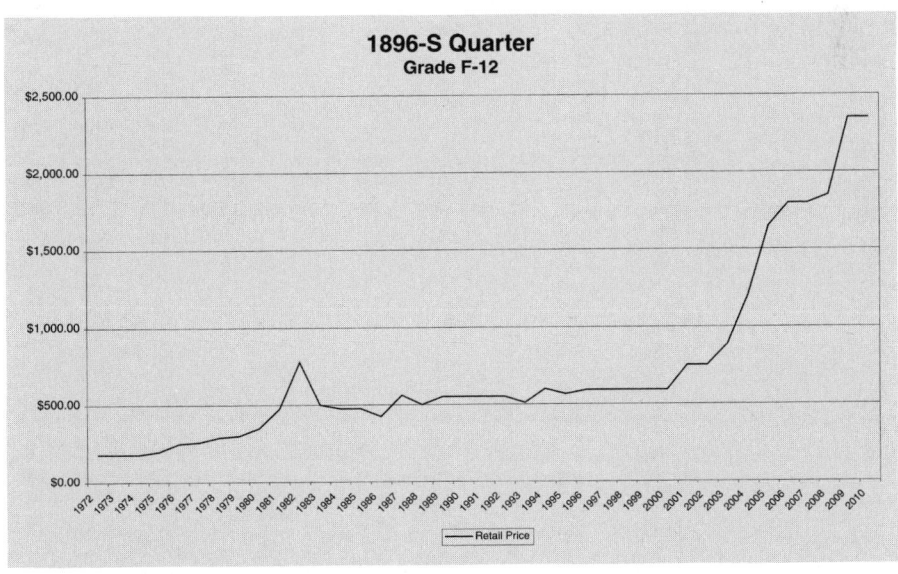

1896-S Quarter
Grade F-12

Date	Mintage	G-4	VG-8	F-12	VF-20	XF-40	AU-50	MS-60	MS-65	Prf-65
1897	8,140,731	5.00	6.25	21.50	33.50	72.00	115	210	1,550	2,450
1897O	1,414,800	19.50	40.00	130	255	400	625	900	3,950	—
1897S	542,229	75.00	115	235	290	440	665	900	7,000	—
1898	11,100,735	5.00	6.25	22.50	35.00	75.00	115	210	1,550	2,450
1898O	1,868,000	16.00	28.50	75.00	160	300	430	665	10,000	—
1898S	1,020,592	12.50	19.00	50.00	70.00	100.00	210	385	6,950	—
1899	12,624,846	5.00	6.25	22.50	35.00	75.00	115	210	1,550	2,450
1899O	2,644,000	14.00	21.00	38.50	72.00	145	290	415	3,750	—
1899S	708,000	18.00	28.50	70.00	92.50	145	275	410	3,650	—
1900	10,016,912	6.00	8.00	23.50	36.00	71.50	130	210	1,550	2,450
1900O	3,416,000	16.00	29.00	69.50	118	170	320	575	3,750	—
1900S	1,858,585	8.00	15.00	38.00	55.00	80.00	135	375	4,950	—
1901	8,892,813	11.00	13.00	25.00	41.50	80.00	135	215	1,850	2,450
1901O	1,612,000	42.50	60.00	145	275	455	665	885	5,850	—
1901S	72,664	6,250	14,000	17,500	25,500	30,000	35,000	40,000	82,500	—
1902	12,197,744	6.00	8.50	19.50	32.50	65.00	120	210	1,400	2,450
1902O	4,748,000	8.50	16.00	52.50	89.00	150	245	485	5,000	—
1902S	1,524,612	14.50	22.00	55.00	95.00	170	260	525	3,750	—
1903	9,670,064	6.75	8.50	19.50	32.50	62.00	112	210	2,600	2,450
1903O	3,500,000	8.00	13.50	41.50	65.00	125	260	435	6,250	—
1903S	1,036,000	15.50	26.00	46.00	88.00	145	285	435	2,900	—
1904	9,588,813	8.00	9.75	20.00	34.50	69.00	120	220	1,500	2,450
1904O	2,456,000	11.50	21.50	62.50	120	225	460	850	3,250	—
1905	4,968,250	13.50	15.00	27.50	39.50	72.00	120	210	1,650	2,450
1905O	1,230,000	18.50	33.50	82.50	170	265	365	500	6,600	—
1905S	1,884,000	12.75	15.00	43.50	66.00	110	220	335	3,650	—
1906	3,656,435	6.75	8.50	18.50	32.50	65.00	112	205	1,400	2,450
1906D	3,280,000	7.00	8.50	25.00	42.50	69.00	155	220	2,250	—
1906O	2,056,000	7.00	13.50	41.50	60.00	110	200	290	1,700	—
1907	7,192,575	5.50	8.00	16.50	32.50	62.00	112	205	1,400	2,450
1907D	2,484,000	6.00	9.00	29.00	52.50	78.00	175	240	2,750	—
1907O	4,560,000	5.50	13.50	19.00	38.50	66.00	135	205	2,600	—
1907S	1,360,000	10.00	18.50	47.50	75.00	135	275	465	4,250	—
1908	4,232,545	5.00	6.25	18.50	33.50	66.00	112	205	1,400	2,450
1908D	5,788,000	5.00	6.25	17.50	35.00	66.00	116	240	1,750	—
1908O	6,244,000	5.00	8.50	17.50	38.50	72.00	120	205	1,400	—
1908S	784,000	18.50	40.00	90.00	165	295	500	775	4,950	—
1909	9,268,650	5.00	6.25	17.50	33.50	66.00	108	205	1,400	2,450
1909D	5,114,000	6.25	8.00	22.00	41.50	88.00	160	205	2,350	—
1909O	712,000	19.50	45.00	95.00	200	375	600	800	8,500	—
1909S	1,348,000	8.00	13.50	37.50	57.50	96.00	200	300	2,500	—
1910	2,244,551	7.75	10.00	30.00	46.00	80.00	140	205	1,400	2,450
1910D	1,500,000	8.00	11.00	47.50	75.00	130	260	375	2,250	—
1911	3,720,543	6.25	8.50	19.50	33.50	72.50	125	215	1,400	2,450
1911D	933,600	9.00	19.50	95.00	215	330	500	700	6,250	—
1911S	988,000	7.00	13.00	51.50	90.00	180	300	400	1,600	—
1912	4,400,700	5.75	8.00	17.50	33.50	70.00	108	205	1,400	2,485
1912S	708,000	9.00	13.00	46.00	84.00	130	230	390	2,750	—
1913	484,613	16.00	26.00	75.00	190	390	535	960	5,000	2,485
1913D	1,450,800	12.50	14.50	38.50	58.50	94.00	185	275	1,400	—
1913S	40,000	1,850	2,450	5,000	7,750	10,500	12,850	15,000	37,500	—
1914	6,244,610	4.50	5.75	17.00	28.00	55.00	108	205	1,400	2,550
1914D	3,046,000	4.50	5.75	17.00	28.00	55.00	108	205	1,400	—
1914S	264,000	82.00	120	235	425	620	775	1,000	3,450	—
1915	3,480,450	4.50	5.75	17.00	28.00	55.00	108	205	1,400	2,485
1915D	3,694,000	4.50	5.75	17.00	28.00	55.00	108	205	1,400	—
1915S	704,000	9.00	13.00	35.00	57.50	110	220	285	1,500	—
1916	1,788,000	4.50	5.75	17.00	28.00	55.00	108	205	1,400	—
1916D	6,540,800	4.50	5.75	17.00	28.00	55.00	108	205	1,400	—
1916D/D	Inc. above	10.00	14.00	24.00	45.00	95.00	150	400	—	—

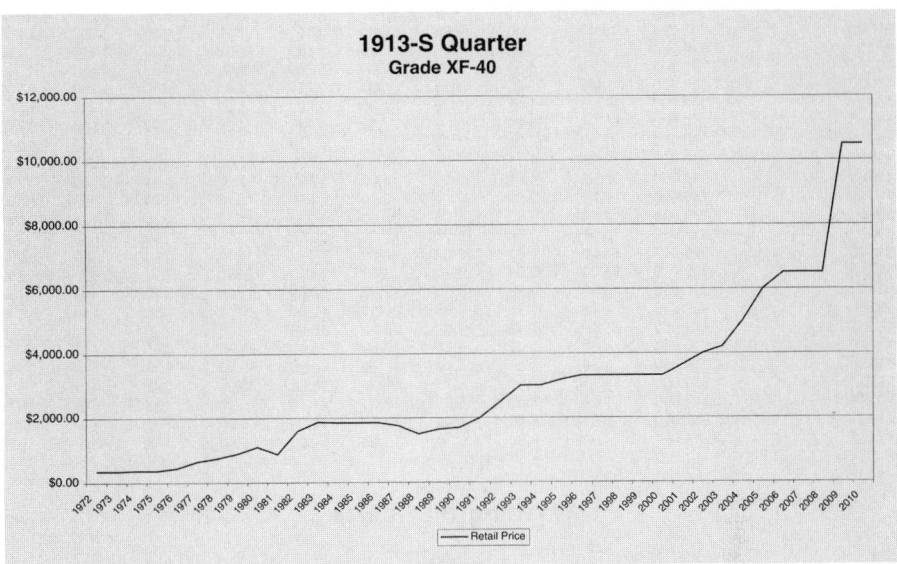

1913-S Quarter
Grade XF-40

Standing Liberty Quarter
Right breast exposed; Type 1 obverse

Right breast exposed

KM# 141 • 6.2500 g., 0.9000 **Silver**, 0.1808 oz. ASW, 24.3 mm. • **Designer:** Hermon A. MacNeil

Date	Mintage	G-4	VG-8	F-12	VF-20	XF-40	AU-50	MS-60	MS-65	-65FH
1916	52,000	3,500	6,350	9,500	13,000	14,500	16,500	18,500	30,000	37,500
1917	8,792,000	24.00	40.00	52.00	70.00	95.00	175	200	750	1,500
1917D	1,509,200	28.00	42.00	55.00	85.00	125	195	235	950	2,550
1917S	1,952,000	30.00	44.00	60.00	90.00	160	210	240	1,200	4,100

Standing Liberty Quarter
Right breast covered; Type 2 obverse   Three stars below eagle reverse

Right breast covered   Mint mark

KM# 145 • 6.2500 g., 0.9000 **Silver**, 0.1808 oz. ASW, 24.3 mm. • **Designer:** Hermon A. MacNeil

Date	Mintage	G-4	VG-8	F-12	VF-20	XF-40	AU-50	MS-60	MS-65	-65FH
1917	13,880,000	22.00	33.00	42.50	54.00	75.00	105	165	575	950
1917D	6,224,400	40.00	45.00	65.00	78.00	110	160	225	1,325	3,500
1917S	5,522,000	40.00	45.00	63.00	75.00	108	155	215	1,100	3,650
1918	14,240,000	17.00	21.00	29.00	35.00	46.00	80.00	135	560	1,750
1918D	7,380,000	26.00	36.00	66.00	78.00	122	195	250	1,485	4,850
1918S	11,072,000	17.00	21.00	32.00	35.00	48.00	95.00	185	1,250	13,500
1918/17S	Inc. above	1,550	2,250	3,850	5,200	7,500	13,500	17,850	110,000	320,000
1919	11,324,000	33.00	44.00	55.00	74.00	80.00	118	175	600	1,650
1919D	1,944,000	85.00	110	195	345	565	695	825	2,950	28,500
1919S	1,836,000	80.00	105	185	285	510	585	750	4,200	30,000
1920	27,860,000	15.00	18.00	25.00	37.00	51.00	90.00	165	600	2,100
1920D	3,586,400	48.00	65.00	88.00	120	160	215	325	2,250	7,200

Date	Mintage	G-4	VG-8	F-12	VF-20	XF-40	AU-50	MS-60	MS-65	-65FH
1920S	6,380,000	19.00	25.00	30.00	37.00	57.00	110	235	2,650	24,000
1921	1,916,000	185	220	450	625	750	1,100	1,500	3,850	5,500
1923	9,716,000	15.00	18.00	35.00	37.00	55.00	95.00	155	620	4,000
1923S	1,360,000	300	425	675	985	1,250	1,650	2,300	4,750	6,500
1924	10,920,000	15.00	18.00	25.00	34.00	45.00	90.00	170	585	1,650
1924D	3,112,000	56.00	68.00	108	135	185	220	300	610	5,750
1924S	2,860,000	27.00	32.00	43.00	57.00	105	220	315	1,850	6,500
1925	12,280,000	4.00	4.75	7.00	18.50	44.00	90.00	150	575	950
1926	11,316,000	3.50	4.00	6.00	14.00	37.00	80.00	140	585	2,250
1926D	1,716,000	6.50	10.00	20.00	40.00	75.00	118	170	545	22,500
1926S	2,700,000	4.50	5.40	11.00	30.00	110	225	325	2,175	28,000
1927	11,912,000	3.50	4.00	6.00	12.00	32.00	70.00	105	550	1,300
1927D	976,400	14.00	19.00	32.00	70.00	140	210	250	600	2,650
1927S	396,000	35.00	48.00	110	285	1,000	2,650	4,750	12,000	165,000
1928	6,336,000	3.50	4.75	6.00	12.00	32.00	65.00	100.00	540	2,150
1928D	1,627,600	4.75	6.00	7.50	20.00	42.50	90.00	135	540	5,650
1928S Large S	2,644,000	6.00	7.50	10.00	25.00	65.00	115	200	—	—
1928S Small S	Inc. above	4.50	5.50	6.50	16.50	38.00	79.00	125	560	900
1929	11,140,000	3.50	4.75	6.00	12.00	32.00	65.00	100.00	540	900
1929D	1,358,000	4.25	5.50	6.75	16.00	38.50	79.00	135	540	5,850
1929S	1,764,000	4.00	5.50	6.50	15.00	34.00	75.00	120	540	875
1930	5,632,000	3.50	4.00	6.00	12.00	32.00	65.00	100.00	540	875
1930S	1,556,000	4.00	5.50	6.50	15.00	34.00	70.00	115	550	925

Washington Quarter

Mint mark 1932-64

KM# 164 • 6.2500 g., 0.9000 **Silver**, 0.1808 oz. ASW, 24.3 mm. • **Designer:** John Flanagan

Date	Mintage	G-4	VG-8	F-12	VF-20	XF-40	AU-50	MS-60	MS-65	Prf-65
1932	5,404,000	4.00	5.20	6.00	7.50	9.75	15.00	25.00	350	—
1932D	436,800	162	168	190	225	310	460	925	14,000	—
1932S	408,000	165	170	195	210	265	285	465	4,650	—

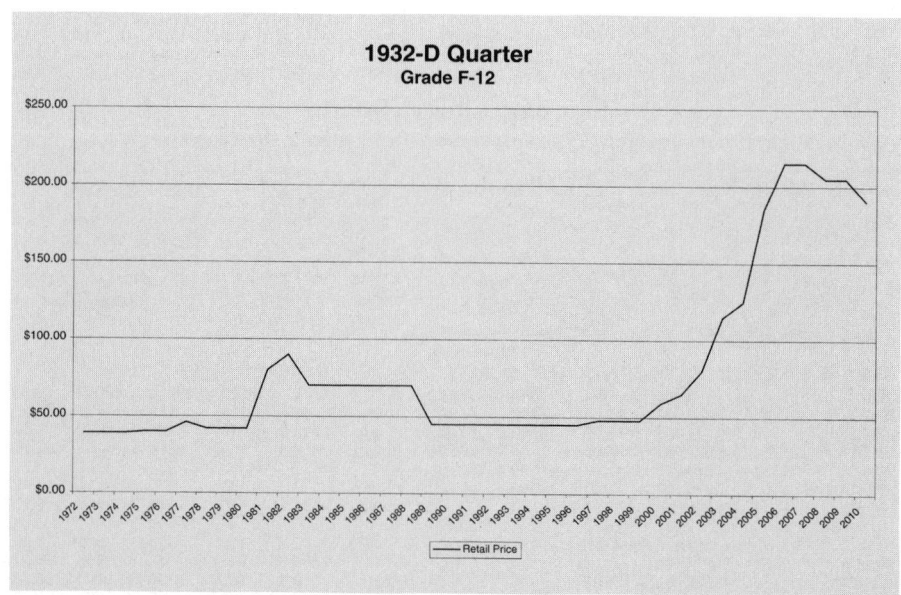

1932-D Quarter
Grade F-12

QUARTER

Date	Mintage	G-4	VG-8	F-12	VF-20	XF-40	AU-50	MS-60	MS-65	Prf-65
1934 Medium Motto	31,912,052	3.80	3.90	4.10	4.40	5.80	10.50	26.00	100.00	—
1934 Heavy Motto	Inc. above	5.50	7.00	9.00	12.50	18.00	30.00	50.00	265	—
1934 Light motto	Inc. above	4.40	5.25	6.00	10.00	15.00	26.00	45.00	400	—
1934 Doubled Die Obverse	Inc. above	75.00	100.00	165	200	320	450	800	8,000	—
1934D Medium Motto	3,527,200	5.00	6.00	8.50	16.50	29.00	90.00	235	1,150	—
1934D Heavy Motto	Inc. above	6.50	8.00	11.00	20.00	37.00	110	295	1,750	—
1935	32,484,000	3.90	4.00	4.10	4.20	4.30	10.00	21.00	100.00	—
1935D	5,780,000	4.10	3.40	7.50	14.00	30.00	125	250	675	—
1935S	5,660,000	4.10	4.20	5.00	7.50	15.00	36.50	95.00	290	—
1936	41,303,837	3.90	4.00	4.10	4.20	4.30	9.50	26.00	105	1,950
1936D	5,374,000	5.00	6.50	8.50	24.00	50.00	265	625	1,175	—
1936S	3,828,000	4.10	4.20	4.30	7.50	14.50	50.00	110	350	—
1937	19,701,542	3.90	4.00	4.10	4.20	4.30	16.50	22.00	87.00	665
1937 Double Die Obverse	Inc. above	—	100.00	235	340	450	850	1,850	11,500	—
1937D	7,189,600	4.10	4.20	5.00	7.25	17.00	32.00	64.00	135	—
1937S	1,652,000	4.30	5.00	7.00	20.00	34.00	95.00	160	360	—
1938	9,480,045	4.10	4.40	4.70	7.50	18.00	46.00	92.00	215	405
1938S	2,832,000	4.75	5.25	6.00	9.75	22.50	55.00	108	235	—
1939	33,548,795	3.90	4.00	4.10	4.20	4.30	7.00	16.00	48.00	345
1939D	7,092,000	4.00	4.10	4.30	5.25	12.00	20.00	42.00	110	—
1939S	2,628,000	4.30	4.40	5.25	10.50	24.00	60.00	110	310	—
1940	35,715,246	3.90	4.00	4.10	4.20	4.30	5.50	17.50	53.50	250
1940D	2,797,600	4.20	4.30	7.00	12.50	26.00	66.00	130	275	—
1940S	8,244,000	4.10	4.20	5.00	6.50	9.00	17.00	28.00	56.00	—
1941	79,047,287	—	—	—	—	3.00	5.00	9.50	37.00	205
1941D	16,714,800	—	—	—	3.70	7.50	15.00	33.00	68.00	—
1941S	16,080,000	—	—	—	3.90	6.50	12.50	30.00	67.00	—
1942	102,117,123	—	—	—	—	3.00	3.20	5.50	29.00	190
1942D Double Die Obv.	—	—	115	250	440	650	1,350	2,150	5,000	—
1942D Double Die Rev.	—	—	22.00	40.00	60.00	75.00	150	350	1,850	—
1942D	17,487,200	—	—	—	3.70	6.00	11.00	18.00	39.00	—
1942S	19,384,000	—	—	—	3.80	11.00	22.50	72.00	145	—
1943	99,700,000	—	—	—	—	3.20	4.50	5.25	40.00	—
1943D	16,095,600	—	—	—	3.90	8.00	16.50	29.00	51.00	—
1943S	21,700,000	—	—	3.60	5.00	7.50	15.00	27.00	52.50	—
1943S Double Die Obv.	Inc. above	40.00	75.00	125	175	225	275	500	3,500	—
1944	104,956,000	—	—	—	—	3.00	3.20	5.00	29.00	—
1944D	14,600,800	—	—	—	3.60	5.50	11.00	19.00	38.50	—
1944S	12,560,000	—	—	—	3.60	5.00	9.50	14.50	32.00	—
1945	74,372,000	—	—	—	—	3.00	3.20	5.00	37.50	—
1945D	12,341,600	—	—	—	3.70	6.50	11.00	18.00	42.50	—
1945S	17,004,001	—	—	—	3.60	4.10	6.00	8.50	32.50	—
1946	53,436,000	—	—	—	—	3.00	4.10	5.00	39.00	—
1946D	9,072,800	—	—	—	3.60	4.20	5.50	9.50	41.00	—
1946S	4,204,000	—	—	—	3.60	4.20	5.00	7.75	34.50	—
1947	22,556,000	—	—	—	—	4.20	5.00	11.50	40.00	—
1947D	15,338,400	—	—	—	3.60	4.10	4.30	11.00	40.00	—
1947S	5,532,000	—	—	—	3.60	4.10	4.30	9.25	28.50	—
1948	35,196,000	—	—	—	3.60	4.10	4.30	5.50	30.00	—
1948D	16,766,800	—	—	—	3.60	4.20	7.00	13.50	52.50	—
1948S	15,960,000	—	—	—	3.60	4.20	5.00	7.50	41.00	—
1949	9,312,000	—	—	—	3.70	6.50	15.00	36.00	53.00	—
1949D	10,068,400	—	—	—	3.50	5.00	10.00	17.00	48.00	—
1950	24,971,512	—	—	—	—	3.00	3.80	5.50	25.00	65.00
1950D	21,075,600	—	—	—	—	3.00	3.70	5.00	34.00	—
1950D/S	Inc. above	30.00	33.00	40.00	60.00	140	215	275	3,400	—
1950S	10,284,004	—	—	—	—	3.50	4.50	9.00	32.00	—
1950S/D	Inc. above	32.00	36.00	44.00	70.00	180	315	400	850	—
1950S/S	Inc. above	4.00	5.00	6.00	8.00	12.50	17.50	22.00	100.00	—
1951	43,505,602	—	—	—	—	3.00	3.20	6.00	32.00	65.00
1951D	35,354,800	—	—	—	—	3.00	3.80	7.00	38.00	—
1951S	9,048,000	—	—	3.00	4.50	6.00	9.00	24.00	52.00	—
1952	38,862,073	—	—	—	—	3.00	3.20	5.50	36.00	46.00
1952D	49,795,200	—	—	—	—	3.00	3.20	5.00	32.00	—
1952S	13,707,800	—	—	—	4.00	7.50	12.50	22.00	47.00	—
1953	18,664,920	—	—	—	—	3.00	3.20	5.50	42.00	46.00
1953D	56,112,400	—	—	—	—	3.00	3.20	4.45	29.00	—
1953S	14,016,000	—	—	—	—	3.00	3.80	5.00	38.00	—
1954	54,645,503	—	—	—	—	3.00	3.20	5.00	30.00	21.00
1954D	42,305,500	—	—	—	—	3.00	3.20	4.75	30.00	—
1954S	11,834,722	—	—	—	—	3.00	3.20	4.45	26.00	—
1955	18,558,381	—	—	—	—	3.00	3.20	4.00	25.00	24.00
1955D	3,182,400	—	—	—	—	4.00	4.10	5.00	42.00	—
1956	44,813,384	—	—	—	—	3.00	3.20	4.00	26.00	23.00
1956 Double Bar 5	Inc. above	—	4.00	4.50	5.00	6.50	9.00	20.00	125	—
1956 Type B rev, proof rev die	Inc. above	—	—	8.00	12.00	20.00	30.00	40.00	100.00	—
1956D	32,334,500	—	—	—	—	3.00	3.20	3.95	23.00	—
1957	47,779,952	—	—	—	—	3.00	3.20	3.95	20.00	10.00
1957 Type B rev, proof rev die	Inc. above	—	—	—	6.50	10.00	16.00	30.00	110	—

Date	Mintage	G-4	VG-8	F-12	VF-20	XF-40	AU-50	MS-60	MS-65	Prf-65
1957D	77,924,160	—	—	—	—	3.00	3.20	3.95	20.00	—
1958	7,235,652	—	—	—	—	3.00	3.20	3.95	16.00	11.00
1958 Type B rev, proof rev die	Inc. above	—	—	—	6.50	10.00	16.00	24.00	90.00	—
1958D	78,124,900	—	—	—	—	3.00	3.20	3.95	16.00	—
1959	25,533,291	—	—	—	—	3.00	3.20	3.95	18.00	10.00
1959 Type B rev, proof rev die	Inc. above	—	—	—	5.00	10.00	14.00	20.00	70.00	—
1959D	62,054,232	—	—	—	—	3.00	3.20	3.95	22.00	—
1960	30,855,602	—	—	—	—	3.00	3.20	3.95	26.00	8.00
1960 Type B rev, proof rev die	Inc. above	—	—	—	6.50	10.00	16.00	24.00	90.00	—
1960D	63,000,324	—	—	—	—	3.00	3.20	3.95	15.00	—
1961	40,064,244	—	—	—	—	3.00	3.20	3.95	20.00	8.00
1961 Type B rev, proof rev die	Inc. above	—	—	—	5.00	10.00	14.00	20.00	70.00	—
1961D	83,656,928	—	—	—	—	3.00	3.20	3.95	36.00	—
1962	39,374,019	—	—	—	—	3.00	3.20	3.95	18.00	6.00
1962 Type B rev, proof rev die	Inc. above	—	—	—	10.00	15.00	25.00	60.00	175	—
1962D	127,554,756	—	—	—	—	3.00	3.20	3.95	45.00	—
1963	77,391,645	—	—	—	—	3.00	3.20	3.95	20.00	6.00
1963 Type B rev, proof rev die	Inc. above	—	—	—	5.00	6.00	8.00	15.00	50.00	—
1963D	135,288,184	—	—	—	—	3.00	3.20	3.95	22.00	—
1964	564,341,347	—	—	—	—	3.00	3.20	3.95	14.00	6.00
1964 Type B rev, proof rev die	Inc. above	—	—	—	5.00	10.00	14.00	20.00	70.00	—
1964 SMS	Inc. above	—	—	—	—	—	250	750	1,400	—
1964D	704,135,528	—	—	—	—	3.00	3.20	3.95	15.00	—
1964D Type C rev, clad rev die	Inc. above	—	—	—	40.00	55.00	75.00	125	450	—

Washington Quarter

KM# 164a • 5.6700 g., **Copper-Nickel Clad Copper**, 24.3 mm. • **Designer:** John Flanagan

Date	Mintage	MS-65	Prf-65
1965	1,819,717,540	9.00	—
1965 SMS	—	7.50	—
1966	821,101,500	7.50	—
1966 SMS	—	9.00	—
1967 SMS	—	10.00	—
1967	1,524,031,848	8.00	—
1968	220,731,500	7.50	—
1968D	101,534,000	9.00	—
1968S	3,041,506	—	6.50
1969	176,212,000	14.00	—
1969D	114,372,000	12.00	—
1969S	2,934,631	—	7.00
1970	136,420,000	12.00	—
1970D	417,341,364	9.50	—
1970S	2,632,810	—	7.00
1971	109,284,000	9.00	—
1971D	258,634,428	8.00	—
1971S	3,220,733	—	4.00
1972	215,048,000	7.50	—
1972D	311,067,732	10.00	—
1972S	3,260,996	—	3.50
1973	346,924,000	10.00	—
1973D	232,977,400	12.50	—
1973S	2,760,339	—	3.00
1974	801,456,000	12.00	—
1974D	353,160,300	18.00	—
1974S	2,612,568	—	6.50
1975 none minted	—	—	—
1975D none minted	—	—	—
1975S none minted	—	—	—

Washington Quarter
Bicentennial design, drummer boy reverse

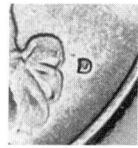

Mint mark
1968-present

KM# 204 • 5.6700 g., **Copper-Nickel Clad Copper**, 24.3 mm. • **Rev. Designer:** Jack L. Ahr

Date	Mintage	MS-60	MS-65	Prf-65
1976	809,784,016	.60	10.00	—
1976D	860,118,839	.60	10.00	—
1976S	4,149,730	—	—	3.25

Washington Quarter
Bicentennial design, drummer boy reverse

KM# 204a • 5.7500 g., **Silver Clad**, 24.3 mm. • **Rev. Designer:** Jack L. Ahr

Date	Mintage	MS-60	MS-65	Prf-65
1976S	4,908,319	2.00	4.00	—
1976S	3,998,621	—	—	5.00

Washington Quarter
Regular design resumed reverse

KM# A164a • 5.6700 g., **Copper-Nickel Clad Copper**, 24.3 mm. • **Edge Desc:** Reeded **Notes:** KM#164 design and composition resumed. The 1979-S and 1981 Type II proofs have clearer mint marks than the Type I proofs for those years.

Date	Mintage	MS-65	Prf-65
1977	468,556,000	10.00	—
1977D	256,524,978	9.00	—
1977S	3,251,152	—	5.00
1978	521,452,000	10.00	—
1978D	287,373,152	11.00	—
1978S	3,127,781	—	5.00
1979	515,708,000	10.00	—
1979D	489,789,780	9.00	—
1979S T-I	—	—	4.00
1979S T-II	—	—	8.00
1980P	635,832,000	11.00	—
1980D	518,327,487	8.50	—
1980S	3,554,806	—	5.00
1981P	601,716,000	10.00	—
1981D	575,722,833	9.00	—
1981S T-I	—	—	5.00
1981S T-II	—	—	7.50
1982P	500,931,000	32.50	—
1982D	480,042,788	22.00	—
1982S	3,857,479	—	7.00
1983P	673,535,000	45.00	—
1983D	617,806,446	40.00	—
1983S	3,279,126	—	5.00
1984P	676,545,000	16.00	—
1984D	546,483,064	12.50	—
1984S	3,065,110	—	4.50
1985P	775,818,962	32.00	—
1985D	519,962,888	10.00	—
1985S	3,362,821	5.00	6.00
1986P	551,199,333	12.00	—
1986D	504,298,660	15.00	—
1986S	3,010,497	—	5.00
1987P	582,499,481	10.50	—
1987D	655,594,696	10.00	—
1987S	4,227,728	—	5.00
1988P	562,052,000	16.00	—
1988D	596,810,688	14.00	—
1988S	3,262,948	—	6.50
1989P	512,868,000	18.00	—
1989D	896,535,597	5.50	—
1989S	3,220,194	—	5.00
1990P	613,792,000	17.00	—
1990D	927,638,181	7.00	—
1990S	3,299,559	—	6.00
1991P	570,968,000	15.00	—
1991D	630,966,693	14.00	—
1991S	2,867,787	—	5.00
1992P	384,764,000	20.00	—
1992D	389,777,107	27.50	—
1992S	2,858,981	—	4.50
1993P	639,276,000	11.00	—
1993D	645,476,128	14.00	—
1993S	2,633,439	—	5.00
1994P	825,600,000	18.00	—
1994D	880,034,110	8.00	—
1994S	2,484,594	—	13.50
1995P	1,004,336,000	22.00	—
1995D	1,103,216,000	20.00	—
1995S	2,010,384	—	12.50
1996P	925,040,000	15.00	—
1996D	906,868,000	14.00	—
1996S	—	—	4.50
1997P	595,740,000	12.50	—
1997D	599,680,000	16.00	—
1997S	1,975,000	—	10.00
1998P	896,268,000	13.50	—
1998D	821,000,000	13.50	—
1998S	—	—	10.00

Washington Quarter

KM# A164b • 6.2000 g., 0.9000 **Silver**, 0.1794 oz. ASW •

Date	Mintage	Prf-65
1992S	1,317,579	5.00
1993S	761,353	6.50
1994S	785,329	13.50
1995S	838,953	18.00
1996S	—	16.00
1997S	—	17.00
1998S	—	10.00

50 State Quarters

Connecticut

KM# 297 • 5.6700 g., **Copper-Nickel Clad Copper** •

Date	Mintage	MS-63	MS-65	Prf-65
1999P	688,744,000	1.00	10.00	—
1999D	657,480,000	1.00	9.00	—
1999S	3,713,359	—	—	12.00

KM# 297a • 6.2500 g., 0.9000 **Silver**, 0.1808 oz. ASW •

Date	Mintage	MS-63	MS-65	Prf-65
1999S	804,565	—	—	65.00

Delaware

KM# 293 • 5.6700 g., **Copper-Nickel Clad Copper**, 24.3 mm. •

Date	Mintage	MS-63	MS-65	Prf-65
1999P	373,400,000	1.40	8.00	—
1999D	401,424,000	1.25	20.00	—
1999S	3,713,359	—	—	12.00

KM# 293a • 6.2500 g., 0.9000 **Silver**, 0.1808 oz. ASW •

Date	Mintage	MS-63	MS-65	Prf-65
1999S	804,565	—	—	65.00

Georgia

KM# 296 • 5.6700 g., **Copper-Nickel Clad Copper** •

Date	Mintage	MS-63	MS-65	Prf-65
1999P	451,188,000	1.20	14.00	—
1999D	488,744,000	1.20	14.00	—
1999S	3,713,359	—	—	12.00

KM# 296a • 6.2500 g., 0.9000 **Silver**, 0.1808 oz. ASW •

Date	Mintage	MS-63	MS-65	Prf-65
1999S	804,565	—	—	65.00

New Jersey

KM# 295 • 5.6700 g., **Copper-Nickel Clad Copper** •

Date	Mintage	MS-63	MS-65	Prf-65
1999P	363,200,000	1.00	10.00	—
1999D	299,028,000	1.00	9.00	—
1999S	3,713,359	—	—	12.00

KM# 295a • 6.2500 g., 0.9000 **Silver**, 0.1808 oz. ASW •

Date	Mintage	MS-63	MS-65	Prf-65
1999S	804,565	—	—	65.00

Pennsylvania

KM# 294 • 5.6700 g., **Copper-Nickel Clad Copper**, 24.3 mm. •

Date	Mintage	MS-63	MS-65	Prf-65
1999P	349,000,000	1.00	15.00	—
1999D	358,332,000	1.00	20.00	—
1999S	3,713,359	—	—	12.00

KM# 294a • 6.2500 g., 0.9000 **Silver**, 0.1808 oz. ASW •

Date	Mintage	MS-63	MS-65	Prf-65
1999S	804,565	—	—	65.00

Maryland

KM# 306 • 5.6700 g., **Copper-Nickel Clad Copper** •

Date	Mintage	MS-63	MS-65	Prf-65
2000P	678,200,000	1.00	11.00	—
2000D	556,526,000	1.00	11.00	—
2000S	4,078,747	—	—	3.50

KM# 306a • 6.2500 g., 0.9000 **Silver**, 0.1808 oz. ASW •

Date	Mintage	MS-63	MS-65	Prf-65
2000S	965,921	—	—	5.50

Massachusetts

KM# 305 • 5.6700 g., **Copper-Nickel Clad Copper** •

Date	Mintage	MS-63	MS-65	Prf-65
2000P	629,800,000	1.00	10.00	—
2000D	535,184,000	1.00	12.00	—
2000S	4,078,747	—	—	3.50

KM# 305a • 6.2500 g., 0.9000 **Silver**, 0.1808 oz. ASW •

Date	Mintage	MS-63	MS-65	Prf-65
2000S	965,921	—	—	5.50

New Hampshire

KM# 308 • 5.6700 g., **Copper-Nickel Clad Copper** •

Date	Mintage	MS-63	MS-65	Prf-65
2000P	673,040,000	1.00	12.50	—
2000D	495,976,000	1.00	10.00	—
2000S	4,078,747	—	—	3.50

KM# 308a • 6.2500 g., 0.9000 **Silver**, 0.1808 oz. ASW •

Date	Mintage	MS-63	MS-65	Prf-65
2000S	965,921	—	—	5.50

South Carolina

KM# 307 • 5.6700 g., **Copper-Nickel Clad Copper** •

Date	Mintage	MS-63	MS-65	Prf-65
2000P	742,756,000	1.40	9.00	—
2000D	566,208,000	1.40	12.00	—
2000S	4,078,747	—	—	3.50

KM# 307a • 6.2500 g., 0.9000 **Silver**, 0.1808 oz. ASW •

Date	Mintage	MS-63	MS-65	Prf-65
2000S	965,921	—	—	5.50

Virginia

KM# 309 • 5.6700 g., **Copper-Nickel Clad Copper** •

Date	Mintage	MS-63	MS-65	Prf-65
2000P	943,000,000	1.00	8.00	—
2000D	651,616,000	1.00	8.00	—
2000S	4,078,747	—	—	3.35

KM# 309a • 6.2500 g., 0.9000 **Silver**, 0.1808 oz. ASW •

Date	Mintage	MS-63	MS-65	Prf-65
2000S	965,921	—	—	5.50

Kentucky

KM# 322 • 5.6700 g., **Copper-Nickel Clad Copper** •

Date	Mintage	MS-63	MS-65	Prf-65
2001P	353,000,000	1.20	7.00	—
2001D	370,564,000	1.00	8.00	—
2001S	3,094,140	—	—	11.00

KM# 322a • 6.2500 g., 0.9000 **Silver**, 0.1808 oz. ASW •

Date	Mintage	MS-63	MS-65	Prf-65
2001S	889,697	—	—	21.00

New York

KM# 318 • 5.6700 g., **Copper-Nickel Clad Copper** •

Date	Mintage	MS-63	MS-65	Prf-65
2001P	655,400,000	1.00	8.50	—
2001D	619,640,000	1.00	8.50	—
2001S	3,094,140	—	—	11.00

KM# 318a • 6.2500 g., 0.9000 **Silver**, 0.1808 oz. ASW •

Date	Mintage	MS-63	MS-65	Prf-65
2001S	889,697	—	—	24.00

North Carolina

KM# 319 • 5.6700 g., **Copper-Nickel Clad Copper** •

Date	Mintage	MS-63	MS-65	Prf-65
2001P	627,600,000	1.00	7.50	—
2001D	427,876,000	1.00	8.50	—
2001S	3,094,140	—	—	11.00

KM# 319a • 6.2500 g., 0.9000 **Silver**, 0.1808 oz. ASW •

Date	Mintage	MS-63	MS-65	Prf-65
2001S	889,697	—	—	22.00

Rhode Island

KM# 320 • 5.6700 g., **Copper-Nickel Clad Copper** •

Date	Mintage	MS-63	MS-65	Prf-65
2001P	423,000,000	1.00	6.50	—
2001D	447,100,000	1.00	8.00	—
2001S	3,094,140	—	—	11.00

KM# 320a • 6.2500 g., 0.9000 **Silver**, 0.1808 oz. ASW •

Date	Mintage	MS-63	MS-65	Prf-65
2001S	889,697	—	—	19.00

Vermont

KM# 321 • 5.6700 g., **Copper-Nickel Clad Copper** •

Date	Mintage	MS-63	MS-65	Prf-65
2001P	423,400,000	1.20	7.00	—
2001D	459,404,000	1.00	7.00	—
2001S	3,094,140	—	—	11.00

KM# 321a • 6.2500 g., 0.9000 **Silver**, 0.1808 oz. ASW •

Date	Mintage	MS-63	MS-65	Prf-65
2001S	889,697	—	—	19.00

Indiana

KM# 334 • 5.6700 g., **Copper-Nickel Clad Copper** •

Date	Mintage	MS-63	MS-65	Prf-65
2002P	362,600,000	1.00	6.00	—
2002D	327,200,000	1.00	6.50	—
2002S	3,084,245	—	—	4.00

KM# 334a • 6.2500 g., 0.9000 **Silver**, 0.1808 oz. ASW •

Date	Mintage	MS-63	MS-65	Prf-65
2002S	892,229	—	—	9.00

Louisiana

KM# 333 • 5.6700 g., **Copper-Nickel Clad Copper** •

Date	Mintage	MS-63	MS-65	Prf-65
2002P	362,000,000	1.00	6.50	—
2002D	402,204,000	1.00	7.00	—
2002S	3,084,245	—	—	4.00

KM# 333a • 6.2500 g., 0.9000 **Silver**, 0.1808 oz. ASW •

Date	Mintage	MS-63	MS-65	Prf-65
2002S	892,229	—	—	9.00

Mississippi

KM# 335 • 5.6700 g., **Copper-Nickel Clad Copper** •

Date	Mintage	MS-63	MS-65	Prf-65
2002P	290,000,000	1.00	5.00	—
2002D	289,600,000	1.00	6.00	—
2002S	3,084,245	—	—	4.00

KM# 335a • 6.2500 g., 0.9000 **Silver**, 0.1808 oz. ASW •

Date	Mintage	MS-63	MS-65	Prf-65
2002S	892,229	—	—	9.00

Ohio

KM# 332 • 5.6700 g., **Copper-Nickel Clad Copper** •

Date	Mintage	MS-63	MS-65	Prf-65
2002P	217,200,000	1.00	6.50	—
2002D	414,832,000	1.00	7.00	—
2002S	3,084,245	—	—	4.00

KM# 332a • 6.2500 g., 0.9000 **Silver**, 0.1808 oz. ASW •

Date	Mintage	MS-63	MS-65	Prf-65
2002S	892,229	—	—	9.00

Tennessee

KM# 331 • 5.6700 g., **Copper-Nickel Clad Copper** •

Date	Mintage	MS-63	MS-65	Prf-65
2002P	361,600,000	1.40	6.50	—
2002D	286,468,000	1.40	7.00	—
2002S	3,084,245	—	—	4.00

KM# 331a • 6.2500 g., 0.9000 **Silver**, 0.1808 oz. ASW •

Date	Mintage	MS-63	MS-65	Prf-65
2002S	892,229	—	—	9.00

QUARTER

Alabama

KM# 344 • 5.6700 g., **Copper-Nickel Clad Copper** •

Date	Mintage	MS-63	MS-65	Prf-65
2003P	225,000,000	1.00	7.00	—
2003D	232,400,000	1.00	7.00	—
2003S	3,408,516	—	—	3.50

KM# 344a • 6.2500 g., 0.9000 **Silver**, 0.1808 oz. ASW •

Date	Mintage	MS-63	MS-65	Prf-65
2003S	1,257,555	—	—	5.25

Arkansas

KM# 347 • 5.6700 g., **Copper-Nickel Clad Copper** •

Date	Mintage	MS-63	MS-65	Prf-65
2003P	228,000,000	1.00	7.00	—
2003D	229,800,000	1.00	7.00	—
2003S	3,408,516	—	—	3.50

KM# 347a • 6.2500 g., 0.9000 **Silver**, 0.1808 oz. ASW •

Date	Mintage	MS-63	MS-65	Prf-65
2003S	1,257,555	—	—	5.25

Illinois

KM# 343 • 5.6700 g., **Copper-Nickel Clad Copper** •

Date	Mintage	MS-63	MS-65	Prf-65
2003P	225,800,000	1.10	7.00	—
2003D	237,400,000	1.10	6.00	—
2003S	3,408,516	—	—	3.50

KM# 343a • 6.2500 g., 0.9000 **Silver**, 0.1808 oz. ASW •

Date	Mintage	MS-63	MS-65	Prf-65
2003S	1,257,555	—	—	5.25

Maine

KM# 345 • 5.6700 g., **Copper-Nickel Clad Copper** •

Date	Mintage	MS-63	MS-65	Prf-65
2003P	217,400,000	1.00	6.50	—
2003D	213,400,000	1.00	8.00	—
2003S	3,408,516	—	—	3.50

KM# 345a • 6.2500 g., 0.9000 **Silver**, 0.1808 oz. ASW •

Date	Mintage	MS-63	MS-65	Prf-65
2003S	1,257,555	—	—	5.25

Missouri

KM# 346 • **Copper-Nickel Clad Copper** •

Date	Mintage	MS-63	MS-65	Prf-65
2003P	225,000,000	1.00	7.00	—
2003D	228,200,000	1.00	7.00	—
2003S	3,408,516	—	—	3.50

KM# 346a • 6.2500 g., 0.9000 **Silver**, 0.1808 oz. ASW •

Date	Mintage	MS-63	MS-65	Prf-65
2003S	1,257,555	—	—	5.25

Florida

KM# 356 • 5.6700 g., **Copper-Nickel Clad Copper** •

Date	Mintage	MS-63	MS-65	Prf-65
2004P	240,200,000	.75	6.50	—
2004D	241,600,000	.75	7.00	—
2004S	2,740,684	—	—	5.00

KM# 356a • 6.2500 g., 0.9000 **Silver**, 0.1808 oz. ASW •

Date	Mintage	MS-63	MS-65	Prf-65
2004S	1,775,370	—	—	6.00

QUARTER

Iowa

KM# 358 • 5.6700 g., Copper-Nickel Clad Copper •

Date	Mintage	MS-63	MS-65	Prf-65
2004P	213,800,000	.75	6.50	—
2004D	251,800,000	.75	7.00	—
2004S	2,740,684	—	—	5.00

KM# 358a • 6.2500 g., 0.9000 Silver, 0.1808 oz. ASW •

Date	Mintage	MS-63	MS-65	Prf-65
2004S	—	—	—	6.00

Michigan

KM# 355 • 5.6700 g., Copper-Nickel Clad Copper •

Date	Mintage	MS-63	MS-65	Prf-65
2004P	233,800,000	.75	6.50	—
2004D	225,800,000	.75	6.50	—
2004S	2,740,684	—	—	5.00

KM# 355a • 6.2500 g., 0.9000 Silver, 0.1808 oz. ASW •

Date	Mintage	MS-63	MS-65	Prf-65
2004S	1,775,370	—	—	6.00

Texas

KM# 357 • 5.6700 g., Copper-Nickel Clad Copper •

Date	Mintage	MS-63	MS-65	Prf-65
2004P	278,800,000	.75	7.00	—
2004D	263,000,000	.75	7.00	—
2004S	2,740,684	—	—	5.00

KM# 357a • 6.2500 g., 0.9000 Silver, 0.1808 oz. ASW •

Date	Mintage	MS-63	MS-65	Prf-65
2004S	1,775,370	—	—	6.00

Wisconsin

KM# 359 • 5.6700 g., Copper-Nickel Clad Copper •

Date	Mintage	MS-63	MS-65	Prf-65
2004P	226,400,000	1.00	8.00	—
2004D	226,800,000	1.00	10.00	—
2004D Extra Leaf Low	Est. 9,000	300	600	—
2004D Extra Leaf High	Est. 3,000	400	900	—
2004S	—	—	—	5.00

KM# 359a • 6.2500 g., 0.9000 Silver, 0.1808 oz. ASW •

Date	Mintage	MS-63	MS-65	Prf-65
2004S	1,775,370	—	—	6.00

California

KM# 370 • 5.6700 g., Copper-Nickel Clad Copper •

Date	Mintage	MS-63	MS-65	Prf-65
2005P	257,200,000	.75	5.00	—
2005P Satin Finish	Inc. above	3.50	6.00	—
2005D	263,200,000	.75	5.00	—
2005D Satin Finish	Inc. above	3.50	6.00	—
2005S	3,262,960	—	—	3.00

KM# 370a • 6.2500 g., 0.9000 Silver, 0.1808 oz. ASW •

Date	Mintage	MS-63	MS-65	Prf-65
2005S	1,679,600	—	—	5.50

Kansas

KM# 373 • 5.6700 g., Copper-Nickel Clad Copper •

Date	Mintage	MS-63	MS-65	Prf-65
2005P	263,400,000	.75	5.00	—
2005P Satin Finish	Inc. above	3.50	6.00	—
2005D	300,000,000	.75	5.00	—
2005D Satin Finish	Inc. above	3.50	6.00	—
2005S	3,262,960	—	—	3.00

KM# 373a • 6.2500 g., 0.9000 Silver, 0.1808 oz. ASW •

Date	Mintage	MS-63	MS-65	Prf-65
2005S	1,679,600	—	—	5.50

Minnesota

KM# 371 • 5.6700 g., **Copper-Nickel Clad Copper** •

Date	Mintage	MS-63	MS-65	Prf-65
2005P	226,400,000	.75	5.00	—
2005P Satin Finish	Inc. above	3.50	6.00	—
2005D	226,800,000	.75	5.00	—
2005D Satin Finish	Inc. above	3.50	6.00	—
2005S	3,262,960	—	—	3.00

KM# 371a • 6.2500 g., 0.9000 **Silver**, 0.1808 oz. ASW •

Date	Mintage	MS-63	MS-65	Prf-65
2005S	1,679,600	—	—	5.50

Oregon

KM# 372 • 5.6700 g., **Copper-Nickel Clad Copper** •

Date	Mintage	MS-63	MS-65	Prf-65
2005P	316,200,000	.75	5.00	—
2005P Satin Finish	Inc. above	3.50	6.00	—
2005D	404,000,000	.75	5.00	—
2005D Satin Finish	Inc. above	3.50	6.00	—
2005S	3,262,960	—	—	3.00

KM# 372a • 6.2500 g., 0.9000 **Silver**, 0.1808 oz. ASW •

Date	Mintage	MS-63	MS-65	Prf-65
2005S	1,679,600	—	—	5.50

West Virginia

KM# 374 • 5.6700 g., **Copper-Nickel Clad Copper** •

Date	Mintage	MS-63	MS-65	Prf-65
2005P	365,400,000	.75	5.00	—
2005P Satin Finish	Inc. above	3.50	6.00	—
2005D	356,200,000	.75	5.00	—
2005D Satin Finish	Inc. above	3.50	6.00	—
2005S	3,262,960	—	—	3.00

KM# 374a • 6.2500 g., 0.9000 **Silver**, 0.1808 oz. ASW •

Date	Mintage	MS-63	MS-65	Prf-65
2005S	1,679,600	—	—	5.50

Colorado

KM# 384 • 5.7100 g., **Copper-Nickel Clad Copper**, 24.2 mm. •

Date	Mintage	MS-63	MS-65	Prf-65
2006P	274,800,000	.75	5.00	—
2006P Satin Finish	Inc. above	3.00	5.00	—
2006D	294,200,000	.75	5.00	—
2006D Satin Finish	Inc. above	3.00	5.00	—
2006S	2,862,078	—	—	5.00

KM# 384a • 6.2500 g., 0.9000 **Silver**, 0.1808 oz. ASW •

Date	Mintage	MS-63	MS-65	Prf-65
2006S	1,571,839	—	—	5.75

Nebraska

KM# 383 • 5.6700 g., **Copper-Nickel Clad Copper** •

Date	Mintage	MS-63	MS-65	Prf-65
2006P	318,000,000	.75	6.00	—
2006P Satin Finish	Inc. above	3.00	5.00	—
2006D	273,000,000	.75	6.00	—
2006D Satin Finish	Inc. above	3.00	5.00	—
2006S	2,862,078	—	—	5.00

KM# 383a • 6.2500 g., 0.9000 **Silver**, 0.1808 oz. ASW •

Date	Mintage	MS-63	MS-65	Prf-65
2006S	1,571,839	—	—	5.75

Nevada

KM# 382 • 5.6700 g., **Copper-Nickel Clad Copper** •

Date	Mintage	MS-63	MS-65	Prf-65
2006P	277,000,000	.75	6.00	—
2006P Satin Finish	Inc. above	3.00	5.00	—
2006D	312,800,000	.75	6.00	—
2006D Satin Finish	Inc. above	3.00	5.00	—
2006S	2,862,078	—	—	5.00

KM# 382a • 6.2500 g., 0.9000 **Silver**, 0.1808 oz. ASW •

Date	Mintage	MS-63	MS-65	Prf-65
2006S	1,571,839	—	—	5.75

QUARTER

North Dakota

KM# 385 • 5.7200 g., **Copper-Nickel Clad Copper**, 24.2 mm. •

Date	Mintage	MS-63	MS-65	Prf-65
2006P	305,800,000	.75	5.00	—
2006P Satin Finish	Inc. above	3.00	5.00	—
2006D	359,000,000	.75	5.00	—
2006D Satin Finish	Inc. above	3.00	5.00	—
2006S	2,862,078	—	—	5.00

KM# 385a • 6.2500 g., 0.9000 **Silver**, 0.1808 oz. ASW •

Date	Mintage	MS-63	MS-65	Prf-65
2006S	1,571,839	—	—	5.75

South Dakota

KM# 386 • 5.6500 g., **Copper-Nickel Clad Copper**, 24.3 mm. •

Date	Mintage	MS-63	MS-65	Prf-65
2006P	245,000,000	.75	5.00	—
2006P Satin Finish	Inc. above	3.00	5.00	—
2006D	265,800,000	.75	5.00	—
2006D Satin Finish	Inc. above	3.00	5.00	—
2006S	2,862,078	—	—	5.00

KM# 386a • 6.2500 g., 0.9000 **Silver**, 0.1808 oz. ASW •

Date	Mintage	MS-63	MS-65	Prf-65
2006S	1,571,839	—	—	5.75

Idaho

KM# 398 • 5.6700 g., **Copper-Nickel Clad Copper** •

Date	Mintage	MS-63	MS-65	Prf-65
2007P	294,600,000	.75	8.00	—
2007D	286,800,000	.75	8.00	—
2007S	2,374,778	—	—	4.00

KM# 398a • 6.2500 g., 0.9000 **Silver**, 0.1808 oz. ASW •

Date	Mintage	MS-63	MS-65	Prf-65
2007S	1,299,878	—	—	6.50

Montana

KM# 396 • 5.6700 g., **Copper-Nickel Clad Copper** •

Date	Mintage	MS-63	MS-65	Prf-65
2007P	257,000,000	.75	8.00	—
2007D	256,240,000	.75	5.00	—
2007S	2,374,778	—	—	4.00

KM# 396a • 6.2500 g., 0.9000 **Silver**, 0.1808 oz. ASW •

Date	Mintage	MS-63	MS-65	Prf-65
2007S	1,299,878	—	—	6.50

Utah

KM# 400 • **Copper-Nickel Clad Copper** •

Date	Mintage	MS-63	MS-65	Prf-65
2007P	255,000,000	.75	8.00	—
2007D	253,200,000	.75	8.00	—
2007S	2,374,778	—	—	4.00

KM# 400a • 6.2500 g., 0.9000 **Silver**, 0.1808 oz. ASW •

Date	Mintage	MS-63	MS-65	Prf-65
2007S	1,299,878	—	—	6.50

Washington

KM# 397 • 5.6700 g., **Copper-Nickel Clad Copper** •

Date	Mintage	MS-63	MS-65	Prf-65
2007P	265,200,000	.75	8.00	—
2007D	280,000,000	.75	8.00	—
2007S	2,374,778	—	—	4.00

KM# 397a • 6.2500 g., 0.9000 **Silver**, 0.1808 oz. ASW •

Date	Mintage	MS-63	MS-65	Prf-65
2007S	1,299,878	—	—	6.50

QUARTER

Wyoming

KM# 399 • 5.6700 g., **Copper-Nickel Clad Copper** •

Date	Mintage	MS-63	MS-65	Prf-65
2007P	243,600,000	.75	8.00	—
2007D	320,800,000	.75	8.00	—
2007S	2,374,778	—	—	4.00

KM# 399a • 6.2500 g., 0.9000 **Silver**, 0.1808 oz. ASW •

Date	Mintage	MS-63	MS-65	Prf-65
2007S	1,299,878	—	—	6.50

Hawaii

KM# 425 • 5.6700 g., **Copper-Nickel Clad Copper** •

Date	Mintage	MS-63	MS-65	Prf-65
2008P	254,000,000	.75	8.00	—
2008D	263,600,000	.75	8.00	—
2008S	2,100,000	—	—	4.50

KM# 425a • 6.2500 g., 0.9000 **Silver**, 0.1808 oz. ASW •

Date	Mintage	MS-63	MS-65	Prf-65
2008S	1,200,000	—	—	6.50

Alaska

KM# 424 • 5.6700 g., **Copper-Nickel Clad Copper** •

Date	Mintage	MS-63	MS-65	Prf-65
2008P	251,800,000	.75	8.00	—
2008D	254,000,000	.75	8.00	—
2008S	2,100,000	—	—	4.00

KM# 424a • 6.2500 g., 0.9000 **Silver**, 0.1808 oz. ASW •

Date	Mintage	MS-63	MS-65	Prf-65
2008S	1,200,000	—	—	6.50

New Mexico

KM# 422 • 5.6700 g., **Copper-Nickel Clad Copper** •

Date	Mintage	MS-63	MS-65	Prf-65
2008P	244,200,000	.75	8.00	—
2008D	244,400,000	.75	8.00	—
2008S	2,100,000	—	—	4.00

KM# 422a • 6.2500 g., 0.9000 **Silver**, 0.1808 oz. ASW •

Date	Mintage	MS-63	MS-65	Prf-65
2008S	1,200,000	—	—	6.50

Arizona

KM# 423 • 5.6700 g., **Copper-Nickel Clad Copper** •

Date	Mintage	MS-63	MS-65	Prf-65
2008P	244,600,000	.75	8.00	—
2008D	265,000,000	.75	8.00	—
2008S	2,100,000	—	—	4.00

KM# 423a • 6.2500 g., 0.9000 **Silver**, 0.1808 oz. ASW •

Date	Mintage	MS-63	MS-65	Prf-65
2008S	1,200,000	—	—	6.50

Oklahoma

KM# 421 • 5.6700 g., **Copper-Nickel Clad Copper** •

Date	Mintage	MS-63	MS-65	Prf-65
2008P	222,000,000	.75	8.00	—
2008D	194,600,000	.75	8.00	—
2008S	2,100,000	—	—	4.00

KM# 421a • 6.2500 g., 0.9000 **Silver**, 0.1808 oz. ASW •

Date	Mintage	MS-63	MS-65	Prf-65
2008S	1,200,000	—	—	6.50

QUARTER

DC and Territories

American Samoa

KM# 448 • 5.6700 g., **Copper-Nickel Clad Copper,** 24 mm. •

Date	Mintage	MS-63	MS-65	Prf-65
2009P	42,600,000	.75	8.00	—
2009D	39,600,000	.75	8.00	—
2009S	—	—	—	4.00

KM# 448a • 6.2500 g., 0.9000 **Silver,** 0.1808 oz. ASW, 24 mm. •

Date	Mintage	MS-63	MS-65	Prf-65
2009S	—	—	—	6.50

District of Columbia

KM# 445 • 5.6700 g., **Copper-Nickel Clad Copper,** 24 mm. •

Date	Mintage	MS-63	MS-65	Prf-65
2009P	83,600,000	.75	8.00	—
2009D	88,800,000	.75	8.00	—
2009S	—	—	—	4.00

KM# 445a • 6.2500 g., 0.9000 **Silver,** 0.1808 oz. ASW, 24 mm. •

Date	Mintage	MS-63	MS-65	Prf-65
2009S	—	—	—	6.50

Guam

KM# 447 • 5.6700 g., **Copper-Nickel Clad Copper,** 24 mm. •

Date	Mintage	MS-63	MS-65	Prf-65
2009P	45,000,000	.75	8.00	—
2009D	42,600,000	.75	8.00	—
2009S	—	—	—	4.00

KM# 447a • 6.2500 g., 0.9000 **Silver,** 0.1808 oz. ASW, 24 mm. •

Date	Mintage	MS-63	MS-65	Prf-65
2009S	—	—	—	6.50

Northern Mariana Islands

KM# 466 • 5.6700 g., **Copper-Nickel Clad Copper** •

Date	Mintage	MS-63	MS-65	Prf-65
2009P	35,200,000	.75	8.00	—
2009D	37,600,000	.75	8.00	—
2009S	—	—	—	4.00

KM# 466a • 6.2500 g., 0.9000 **Silver,** 0.1808 oz. ASW •

Date	Mintage	MS-63	MS-65	Prf-65
2009S	—	—	—	6.50

Puerto Rico

KM# 446 • 5.6700 g., **Copper-Nickel Clad Copper,** 24 mm. •

Date	Mintage	MS-63	MS-65	Prf-65
2009P	53,200,000	.75	8.00	—
2009D	86,000,000	.75	8.00	—
2009S	—	—	—	4.00

KM# 446a • 6.2500 g., 0.9000 **Silver,** 0.1808 oz. ASW, 24 mm. •

Date	Mintage	MS-63	MS-65	Prf-65
2009S	—	—	—	6.50

US Virgin Islands

KM# 449 • 0.6250 g., 0.9000 **Copper-Nickel Clad Copper,** 0.0181 oz., 24 mm. •

Date	Mintage	MS-63	MS-65	Prf-65
2009P	41,000,000	.75	8.00	—
2009D	41,000,000	.75	8.00	—
2009S	—	—	—	4.00

KM# 449a • 6.2500 g., 0.9000 **Silver,** 0.1808 oz. ASW, 24 mm. •

Date	Mintage	MS-63	MS-65	Prf-65
2009S	—	—	—	6.50

National Parks and Historic Sites

Hot Springs, Ark.

KM# 468 • **Copper-Nickel Clad Copper** •

Date	Mintage	MS-63	MS-65	Prf-65
2010P	—	—	—	—
2010D	—	—	—	—
2010S	—	—	—	—

Yellowstone

KM# 470 • **Copper-Nickel Clad Copper** •

Date	Mintage	MS-63	MS-65	Prf-65
2010P	—	—	—	—
2010D	—	—	—	—
2010S	—	—	—	—

Yosemite

KM# 471 • **Copper-Nickel Clad Copper** •

Date	Mintage	MS-63	MS-65	Prf-65
2010P	—	—	—	—
2010D	—	—	—	—
2010S	—	—	—	—

Grand Canyon

KM# 472 • **Copper-Nickel Clad Copper** •

Date	Mintage	MS-63	MS-65	Prf-65
2010P	—	—	—	—
2010D	—	—	—	—
2010S	—	—	—	—

Mount Hood

KM# 473 • **Copper-Nickel Clad Copper** •

Date	Mintage	MS-63	MS-65	Prf-65
2010P	—	—	—	—
2010D	—	—	—	—
2010S	—	—	—	—

QUARTER

HALF DOLLAR
Flowing Hair Half Dollar

KM# 16 • 13.4800 g., 0.8920 **Silver**, 0.3866 oz. ASW, 32.5 mm. • **Designer:** Robert Scot **Notes:** The 1795 "recut date" variety had the date cut into the dies twice, so both sets of numbers are visible on the coin. The 1795 "3 leaves" variety has three leaves under each of the eagle's wings on the reverse.

Date	Mintage	G-4	VG-8	F-12	VF-20	XF-40	MS-60
1794	23,464	2,850	5,750	8,850	19,500	37,500	225,000
1795	299,680	1,025	1,450	2,850	4,850	13,850	46,500
1795 recut date	Inc. above	1,040	1,470	2,895	5,200	14,250	46,500
1795 3 leaves	Inc. above	2,600	3,150	5,350	8,350	17,500	59,500

Draped Bust Half Dollar
Small eagle reverse

KM# 26 • 13.4800 g., 0.8920 **Silver**, 0.3866 oz. ASW, 32.5 mm. • **Designer:** Robert Scot

Date	Mintage	G-4	VG-8	F-12	VF-20	XF-40	MS-60
1796 15 obverse stars	3,918	36,500	46,000	62,000	73,500	118,000	300,000
1796 16 obverse stars	Inc. above	39,500	50,000	67,000	79,500	128,000	320,000
1797	Inc. above	36,700	46,300	62,500	74,300	121,000	310,000

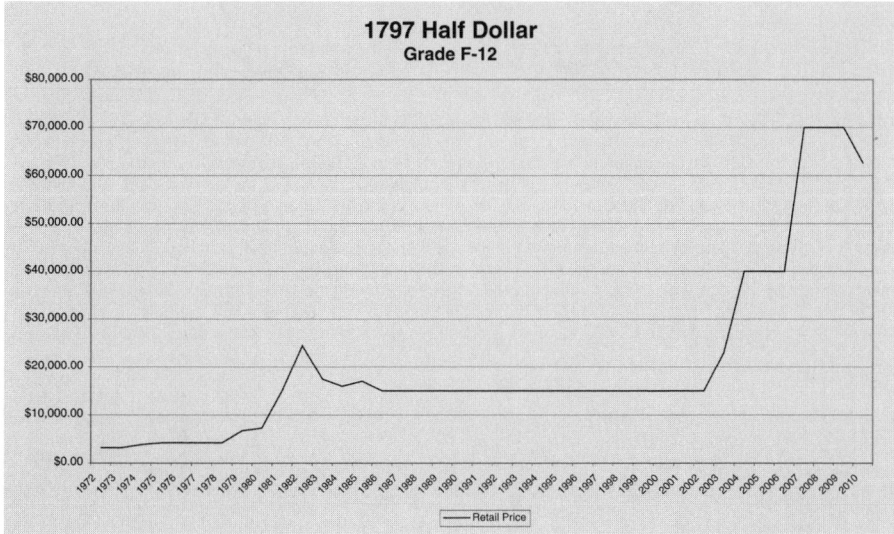

1797 Half Dollar
Grade F-12

Draped Bust Half Dollar

Draped bust right, flanked by stars, date at angle below obverse   Heraldic eagle reverse

KM# 35 • 13.4800 g., 0.8920 **Silver**, 0.3866 oz. ASW, 32.5 mm. • **Obv. Legend** LIBERTY **Rev. Legend:** UNITED STATES OF AMERICA **Designer:** Robert Scot **Notes:** The two varieties of the 1803 strikes are distinguished by the size of the 3 in the date. The several varieties of the 1806 strikes are distinguished by the style of 6 in the date, size of the stars on the obverse, and whether the stem of the olive branch held by the reverse eagle extends through the claw.

Date	Mintage	G-4	VG-8	F-12	VF-20	XF-40	MS-60
1801	30,289	850	1,250	2,550	4,250	10,500	50,000
1802	29,890	900	1,350	2,750	4,500	11,000	52,000
1803 small 3	188,234	255	325	425	825	2,325	17,250
1803 large 3	Inc. above	195	235	295	715	1,925	14,750
1805	211,722	195	235	295	685	1,865	10,750
1805/4	Inc. above	270	385	570	1,515	3,325	30,000
1806 knobbed 6, large stars	839,576	195	235	295	665	1,825	—
1806 knobbed 6, small stars	Inc. above	195	235	295	680	2,025	13,500
1806 knobbed 6, stem not through claw	Inc. above	20,000	35,000	42,000	57,500	95,000	—
1806 pointed-top 6, stem not through claw	Inc. above	195	235	295	665	1,825	15,250
1806 pointed-top 6, stem through claw	Inc. above	195	235	295	665	1,825	9,750
1806/5	Inc. above	215	270	355	775	2,050	10,075
1806 /inverted 6	Inc. above	255	355	845	1,615	4,375	28,500
1807	301,076	195	235	295	665	1,825	9,750

Capped Bust

Draped bust left, flanked by stars, date at angle below obverse   "50 C." below eagle reverse

KM# 37 • 13.4800 g., 0.8920 **Silver**, 0.3866 oz. ASW, 32.5 mm. • **Rev. Legend:** UNITED STATES OF AMERICA **Designer:** John Reich **Notes:** There are three varieties of the 1807 strikes. Two are distinguished by the size of the stars on the obverse. The third was struck from a reverse die that had a 5 cut over a 2 in the "50C" denomination. Two varieties of the 1811 are distinguished by the size of the 8 in the date. A third has a period between the 8 and second 1 in the date. One variety of the 1817 has a period between the 1 and 7 in the date. Two varieties of the 1820 are distinguished by the size of the date. On the 1823 varieties, the "broken 3" appears to be almost separated in the middle of the 3 in the date; the "patched 3" has the error reparied; the "ugly 3" has portions of its detail missing. The 1827 "curled-2" and "square-2" varieties are distinguished by the numeral's base -- either curled or square. Among the 1828 varieties, "knobbed 2" and "no knob" refers to whether the upper left serif of the digit is rounded. The 1830 varieties are distinguished by the size of the 0 in the date. The four 1834 varieties are distinguished by the sizes of the stars, date and letters in the inscriptions. The 1836 "50/00" variety was struck from a reverse die that has "50" recut over "00" in the denomination.

Date	Mintage	G-4	VG-8	F-12	VF-20	XF-40	AU-50	MS-60	MS-65
1807 small stars	750,500	125	175	350	750	1,900	6,500	9,850	54,000
1807 large stars	Inc. above	115	165	300	660	1,750	5,650	8,900	—
1807 50/20 C.	Inc. above	85.00	125	195	450	1,500	3,150	6,500	30,000
1807 bearded goddess	—	450	775	1,500	3,350	6,850	22,500	—	—
1808	1,368,600	67.00	84.00	93.00	145	350	550	1,800	20,000
1808/7	Inc. above	90.00	110	135	240	440	1,850	5,400	32,500

Date	Mintage	G-4	VG-8	F-12	VF-20	XF-40	AU-50	MS-60	MS-65
1809 Normal edge	1,405,810	65.00	82.00	90.00	140	375	750	1,500	14,000
1809 XXXX edge	Inc. above	80.00	105	135	185	550	950	4,450	—
1809 IIIIIII edge	Inc. above	85.00	110	140	210	450	850	4,000	—
1810	1,276,276	64.00	81.00	87.00	135	265	650	1,950	19,500
1811 small 8	1,203,644	70.00	80.00	84.00	125	350	800	2,350	28,500
1811 large 8	Inc. above	80.00	107	115	175	425	1,000	2,400	28,500
1811 dated 18.11	Inc. above	78.00	100.00	110	165	650	1,250	3,500	28,500
1812	1,628,059	64.00	81.00	84.00	110	254	405	1,350	14,800
1812/1 small 8	Inc. above	80.00	97.00	115	200	500	1,350	2,500	—
1812/1 large 8	Inc. above	1,650	2,450	4,500	6,750	12,000	21,000	—	—
1812 Single leaf below wing	Inc. above	750	950	1,250	2,400	4,000	6,800	12,500	—
1813	1,241,903	64.00	81.00	84.00	110	184	445	1,400	14,000
1813 50/UNI reverse	1,241,903	74.00	101	120	175	650	1,350	3,650	27,500
1814	1,039,075	64.00	81.00	84.00	120	285	650	1,650	12,800
1814/3	Inc. above	100.00	165	245	300	850	1,650	3,250	—
1814 E/A in States	Inc. above	85.00	110	150	225	385	950	3,950	—
1814 Single leaf below wing	Inc. above	75.00	97.00	120	190	575	1,350	2,250	—
1815/2	47,150	1,100	1,550	2,250	3,650	5,500	7,950	14,500	85,000
1817	1,215,567	67.00	84.00	87.00	115	189	415	1,300	13,000
1817/3	Inc. above	115	175	280	525	1,150	2,350	4,850	—
1817/4	—	60,000	80,000	150,000	200,000	240,000	—	—	—
1817 dated 181.7	Inc. above	100.00	87.00	90.00	100.00	575	1,350	3,950	27,500
1817 Single leaf below wing	Inc. above	75.00	98.00	120	205	550	2,100	2,750	—
1818	1,960,322	64.00	81.00	84.00	115	225	405	1,350	12,600
1818/7 Large 8	Inc. above	100.00	115	145	190	325	950	1,850	17,500
1818/7 Small 8	Inc. above	98.00	110	130	150	250	850	1,650	16,500
1819	2,208,000	64.00	81.00	84.00	115	175	395	1,350	15,000
1819/8 small 9	Inc. above	75.00	92.00	105	180	290	650	1,900	13,000
1819/8 large 9	Inc. above	85.00	105	150	275	385	850	2,000	27,000
1820 Curl Base 2, small date	751,122	70.00	85.00	92.00	120	285	950	2,250	13,000
1820 Square Base 2 with knob, large date	Inc. above	72.00	90.00	100.00	135	400	800	2,400	14,500
1820 Square Base 2 without know, large date	Inc. above	72.00	90.00	100.00	150	475	1,100	2,500	26,500
1820 E's without Serifs	Inc. above	260	450	900	2,150	3,500	5,500	—	—
1820/19 Square Base 2	Inc. above	110	130	165	240	775	1,650	3,250	25,000
1820/19 Curled Base 2	Inc. above	95.00	115	140	200	650	1,450	2,900	24,500
1821	1,305,797	58.00	76.00	85.00	97.00	185	575	1,350	12,600
1822	1,559,573	58.00	76.00	85.00	97.00	180	450	1,250	12,300
1822/1	Inc. above	83.00	100.00	125	275	385	800	1,900	—
1823	1,694,200	58.00	76.00	85.00	97.00	175	425	1,150	12,500
1823 broken 3	Inc. above	68.00	88.00	100.00	135	500	1,500	3,200	—
1823 patched 3	Inc. above	73.00	94.00	115	155	550	950	2,000	16,500
1823 ugly 3	Inc. above	78.00	99.00	125	180	750	1,750	4,200	—
1824	3,504,954	58.00	76.00	85.00	97.00	175	360	1,075	11,500
1824/21	Inc. above	63.00	82.00	95.00	122	275	650	2,000	17,000
1824/4	Inc. above	61.00	80.00	87.00	110	225	500	1,350	—
1824 1824/various dates	Inc. above	60.00	79.00	87.00	100.00	300	875	2,000	16,500
1825	2,943,166	58.00	76.00	85.00	97.00	175	350	1,050	11,500
1826	4,004,180	58.00	76.00	85.00	97.00	175	350	1,050	11,500
1827 curled 2	5,493,400	61.00	81.00	95.00	130	185	450	1,400	14,000
1827 square 2	Inc. above	58.00	76.00	85.00	97.00	175	350	1,050	11,500
1827/6	Inc. above	85.00	95.00	120	155	265	650	1,450	13,000
1828 curled-base 2, no knob	3,075,200	58.00	76.00	85.00	97.00	175	350	1,150	12,500
1828 curled-base 2, knobbed 2	Inc. above	78.00	99.00	125	180	245	460	1,300	—
1828 small 8s, square-base 2, large letters	Inc. above	60.00	80.00	95.00	120	175	350	1,050	14,000
1828 small 8s, square-base 2, small letters	Inc. above	58.00	76.00	85.00	102	250	750	1,900	—
1828 large 8s, square-base 2	Inc. above	58.00	76.00	85.00	97.00	175	350	1,050	12,500
1829	3,712,156	55.00	72.00	75.00	85.00	159	315	1,000	11,500
1829 Large letters	Inc. above	59.00	79.00	85.00	100.00	180	420	1,250	14,000
1829/7	Inc. above	78.00	99.00	125	170	200	475	1,250	14,000
1830 Small O rev	4,764,800	55.00	72.00	75.00	85.00	159	315	1,000	11,500
1830 Large O	Inc. above	60.00	78.00	84.00	105	189	550	2,000	14,500
1830 Large letter rev	Inc. above	1,500	2,250	3,000	3,750	4,800	9,800	—	—
1831	5,873,660	55.00	72.00	75.00	85.00	159	315	1,000	11,500
1832 small letters	4,797,000	55.00	72.00	75.00	85.00	159	315	1,000	11,500
1832 large letters	Inc. above	58.00	75.00	81.00	95.00	175	375	1,350	14,000
1833	5,206,000	55.00	72.00	75.00	85.00	159	325	1,000	11,750
1834 small date, large stars, small letters	6,412,004	55.00	74.00	77.00	87.00	163	325	1,025	11,750
1834 small date, small stars, small letters	Inc. above	55.00	74.00	77.00	87.00	163	325	1,025	11,750
1834 large date, small letters	Inc. above	55.00	74.00	77.00	87.00	163	325	1,025	11,750
1834 large date, large letters	Inc. above	55.00	72.00	75.00	85.00	159	315	1,000	11,500
1835	5,352,006	55.00	72.00	75.00	85.00	159	315	1,000	11,500
1836	6,545,000	55.00	72.00	75.00	85.00	159	315	1,000	11,500
1836	Inc. above	80.00	95.00	120	265	450	1,000	2,500	—
1836 50/00	Inc. above	93.00	112	125	165	300	800	1,750	19,500

HALF DOLLAR

Bust Half Dollar
Draped bust left, flanked by stars, date at angle below obverse
"50 Cents" below eagle reverse

KM# 58 • 13.3600 g., 0.9000 **Silver**, 0.3866 oz. ASW, 30 mm. • **Rev. Legend:** UNITED STATES OF
AMERICA **Designer:** Christian Gobrecht **Edge Desc:** Reeded.

Date	Mintage	G-4	VG-8	F-12	VF-20	XF-40	AU-50	MS-60	MS-65
1836	1,200	850	1,075	1,600	2,000	3,350	4,400	8,850	66,500
1837	3,629,820	58.00	73.00	80.00	115	200	345	1,100	24,500

Bust Half Dollar
Draped bust left, flanked by stars, date below obverse   HALF DOL. below eagle reverse

KM# 65 • 13.3600 g., 0.9000 **Silver**, 0.3866 oz. ASW, 30 mm. • **Rev. Legend:** UNITED STATES OF
AMERICA **Designer:** Christian Gobrecht

Date	Mintage	G-4	VG-8	F-12	VF-20	XF-40	AU-50	MS-60	MS-65
1838	3,546,000	58.00	70.00	82.00	120	205	360	1,125	21,500
1838O proof only	Est. 20	—	—	—	—	250,000	300,000	—	—
1839	1,392,976	60.00	76.00	92.00	130	245	410	1,350	39,500
1839O	178,976	240	325	425	650	1,350	2,350	4,500	46,500

Seated Liberty Half Dollar
Seated Liberty, date below obverse   "Half Dol." below eagle reverse

KM# 68 • 13.3600 g., 0.9000 **Silver**, 0.3866 oz. ASW, 30.6 mm. • **Rev. Legend:** UNITED STATES OF
AMERICA **Designer:** Christian Gobrecht

Date	Mintage	G-4	VG-8	F-12	VF-20	XF-40	AU-50	MS-60	MS-65
1839 no drapery from elbow	Inc. above	45.00	80.00	150	340	800	1,850	6,000	178,000
1839 drapery	Inc. above	38.00	50.00	59.00	86.00	165	265	1,000	25,000
1840 small letters	1,435,008	36.00	46.00	60.00	84.00	150	325	600	7,500
1840 reverse 1838	Inc. above	150	200	275	350	650	1,350	3,400	30,000
1840O	855,100	36.00	48.00	57.00	90.00	140	275	450	—
1841	310,000	50.00	65.00	100.00	150	235	325	1,200	6,850
1841O	401,000	30.00	44.00	56.00	82.00	180	230	600	7,000
1842 small date	2,012,764	38.00	55.00	75.00	120	175	325	1,300	13,500
1842 medium date	Inc. above	30.00	41.00	51.00	64.00	115	220	750	8,800
1842O small date	957,000	650	850	1,400	2,450	4,650	7,750	16,500	—

Date	Mintage	G-4	VG-8	F-12	VF-20	XF-40	AU-50	MS-60	MS-65
1842O medium date	Inc. above	35.00	42.00	55.00	90.00	185	500	1,250	10,500
1843	3,844,000	28.00	39.00	51.00	65.00	110	225	500	4,500
1843O	2,268,000	30.00	41.00	51.00	65.00	120	240	550	—
1844	1,766,000	30.00	41.00	51.00	65.00	110	210	440	4,500
1844O	2,005,000	30.00	41.00	51.00	70.00	110	225	550	—
1844/1844O	Inc. above	500	775	1,000	1,300	2,500	5,750	10,000	—
1845	589,000	35.00	45.00	65.00	125	210	325	850	12,000
1845O	2,094,000	30.00	41.00	51.00	70.00	135	240	550	9,400
1845O no drapery	Inc. above	35.00	47.00	70.00	115	185	375	750	—
1846 medium date	2,210,000	30.00	41.00	51.00	70.00	110	200	500	9,000
1846 tall date	Inc. above	35.00	47.00	70.00	85.00	145	250	650	12,000
1846 /horizontal 6	Inc. above	175	250	325	450	625	1,000	2,500	—
1846O medium date	2,304,000	30.00	41.00	51.00	65.00	110	225	550	12,000
1846O tall date	Inc. above	165	285	365	620	1,050	2,000	6,650	—
1847/1846	1,156,000	2,000	2,750	3,750	5,250	7,700	12,500	21,000	—
1847	Inc. above	35.00	45.00	54.00	67.00	105	250	480	9,000
1847O	2,584,000	30.00	41.00	51.00	65.00	120	275	640	7,000
1848	580,000	45.00	65.00	95.00	185	265	485	1,000	9,000
1848O	3,180,000	30.00	41.00	51.00	70.00	110	285	750	9,000
1849	1,252,000	35.00	45.00	54.00	67.00	108	365	1,250	15,000
1849O	2,310,000	30.00	41.00	51.00	70.00	110	250	650	9,000
1850	227,000	275	325	400	550	675	1,000	1,500	—
1850O	2,456,000	35.00	28.00	45.00	80.00	135	275	650	9,000
1851	200,750	335	450	550	850	950	1,200	2,250	—
1851O	402,000	40.00	55.00	95.00	120	185	300	700	9,000
1852	77,130	425	500	700	925	1,100	1,350	1,700	—
1852O	144,000	75.00	125	200	350	600	1,250	3,850	26,000
1853O mintage unrecorded	—	—	250,000	—	—	450,000	—	—	—

Note: 1853O, Eliasberg Sale, 1997, VG-8, $154,000.

Seated Liberty Half Dollar
Seated Liberty, arrows at date obverse   Rays around eagle reverse

KM# 79 • 12.4400 g., 0.9000 **Silver**, 0.3599 oz. ASW • **Rev. Legend:** UNITED STATES OF AMERICA
Designer: Christian Gobrecht

Date	Mintage	G-4	VG-8	F-12	VF-20	XF-40	AU-50	MS-60	MS-65	Prf-65
1853	3,532,708	31.00	36.50	50.00	88.00	250	590	1,500	21,500	175,000
1853O	1,328,000	38.00	48.00	57.00	125	310	750	2,350	27,500	—

Seated Liberty Half Dollar
Seated Liberty, arrows at date obverse   HALF DOL. below eagle reverse

KM# 82 • 12.4400 g., 0.9000 **Silver**, 0.3599 oz. ASW • **Rev. Legend:** UNITED STATES OF AMERICA
Designer: Christian Gobrecht

Date	Mintage	G-4	VG-8	F-12	VF-20	XF-40	AU-50	MS-60	MS-65	Prf-65
1854	2,982,000	28.00	38.00	47.00	60.00	100.00	270	675	8,000	37,500
1854O	5,240,000	28.00	38.00	47.00	60.00	100.00	270	600	8,000	—
1855	759,500	30.00	40.00	49.00	63.00	120	325	700	9,000	39,500
1855/4	Inc. above	65.00	84.00	160	250	375	600	2,000	17,500	37,000
1855O	3,688,000	28.00	38.00	47.00	60.00	100.00	270	650	8,000	—
1855S	129,950	350	475	800	1,500	3,150	6,850	19,500	—	—

HALF DOLLAR

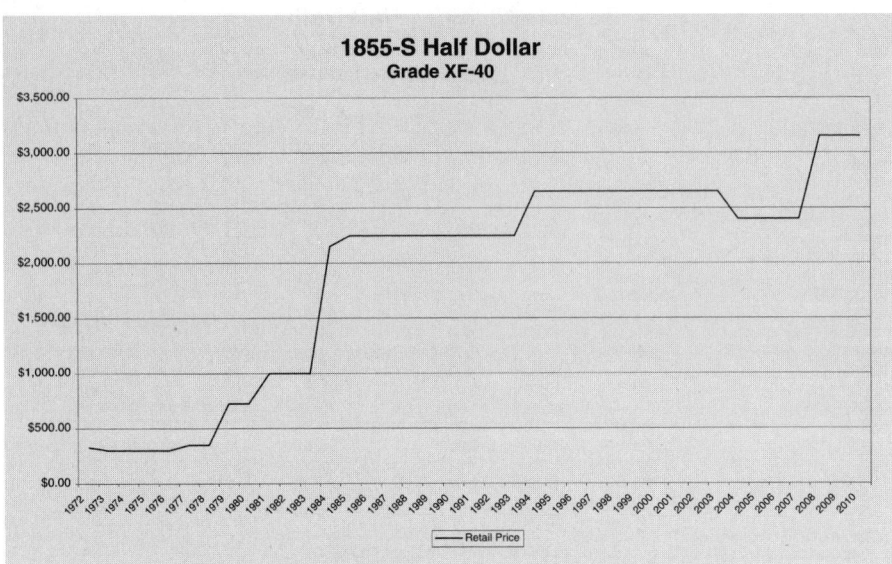

1855-S Half Dollar
Grade XF-40

Seated Liberty Half Dollar
Seated Liberty, date below obverse   HALF DOL. below eagle reverse

KM# A68 • 12.4400 g., 0.9000 **Silver**, 0.3599 oz. ASW • **Rev. Legend:** UNITED STATES OF AMERICA
Designer: Christian Gobrecht

Date	Mintage	G-4	VG-8	F-12	VF-20	XF-40	AU-50	MS-60	MS-65	Prf-65
1856	938,000	32.00	38.00	50.00	70.00	110	195	425	6,500	12,500
1856O	2,658,000	28.00	38.00	52.00	60.00	100.00	190	385	12,500	—
1856S	211,000	85.00	120	160	260	500	1,250	3,500	19,000	—
1857	1,988,000	28.00	38.00	50.00	60.00	100.00	190	385	5,150	12,500
1857O	818,000	33.00	40.00	52.00	85.00	135	275	885	12,500	—
1857S	158,000	100.00	120	145	285	575	975	3,500	19,000	—
1858	4,226,000	28.00	38.00	47.00	60.00	90.00	190	385	6,500	12,500
1858O	7,294,000	28.00	38.00	47.00	60.00	90.00	190	385	12,500	—
1858S	476,000	38.00	48.00	62.00	110	215	400	950	12,500	—
1859	748,000	30.00	41.00	51.00	70.00	120	200	650	6,600	5,500
1859O	2,834,000	28.00	38.00	47.00	60.00	100.00	190	450	6,500	—
1859S	566,000	38.00	44.00	59.00	100.00	215	375	750	12,500	—
1860	303,700	38.00	42.00	51.00	100.00	150	350	1,000	6,500	5,500
1860O	1,290,000	30.00	41.00	52.00	70.00	100.00	190	450	5,150	—
1860S	472,000	38.00	40.00	51.00	85.00	135	245	850	12,500	—
1861	2,888,400	30.00	40.00	49.00	65.00	100.00	190	440	5,150	5,500
1861O	2,532,633	30.00	41.00	53.00	86.00	125	235	450	5,150	—
1861S	939,500	35.00	44.00	53.00	70.00	120	195	975	9,500	—
1862	253,550	38.00	51.00	57.00	120	200	295	750	5,150	5,500
1862S	1,352,000	30.00	41.00	52.00	75.00	120	195	460	9,000	—
1863	503,660	35.00	48.00	57.00	85.00	135	250	750	5,150	5,500
1863S	916,000	33.00	45.00	52.00	70.00	120	195	460	9,000	—
1864	379,570	30.00	48.00	57.00	120	195	250	750	5,150	5,500
1864S	658,000	33.00	45.00	51.00	70.00	125	215	675	9,000	—
1865	511,900	28.00	47.00	55.00	90.00	150	275	750	5,150	5,500
1865S	675,000	35.00	45.00	52.00	70.00	120	235	500	9,000	—
1866 proof, unique	—	—	—	—	—	—	—	—	—	—
1866S	60,000	460	575	850	1,250	2,550	3,350	5,400	68,000	—

Seated Liberty Half Dollar
Seated Liberty, date below obverse
IN GOD WE TRUST above eagle reverse

KM# 99 • 12.4400 g., 0.9000 **Silver**, 0.3599 oz. ASW • **Rev. Legend:** UNITED STATES OF AMERICA
Designer: Christian Gobrecht

Date	Mintage	G-4	VG-8	F-12	VF-20	XF-40	AU-50	MS-60	MS-65	Prf-65
1866	745,625	35.00	45.00	53.00	80.00	120	225	350	4,800	3,750
1866S	994,000	33.00	43.00	51.00	70.00	110	275	650	5,000	—
1867	449,925	38.00	48.00	59.00	110	165	250	350	4,800	3,750
1867S	1,196,000	32.00	42.00	51.00	70.00	110	250	350	7,000	—
1868	418,200	48.00	55.00	95.00	185	225	300	525	7,100	3,750
1868S	1,160,000	32.00	42.00	51.00	70.00	110	250	350	7,000	—
1869	795,900	35.00	45.00	49.00	70.00	110	190	385	4,600	3,750
1869S	656,000	35.00	47.00	51.00	70.00	120	265	600	7,000	—
1870	634,900	35.00	45.00	50.00	80.00	125	250	475	7,000	3,750
1870CC	54,617	900	1,500	1,900	3,900	12,500	30,000	100,000	—	—
1870S	1,004,000	31.00	43.00	53.00	85.00	150	275	575	7,000	—
1871	1,204,560	32.00	42.00	52.00	75.00	120	165	350	7,000	3,750
1871CC	153,950	225	325	600	1,200	1,950	10,000	15,000	—	—
1871S	2,178,000	30.00	41.00	49.00	70.00	110	215	400	7,000	—
1872	881,550	32.00	40.00	49.00	75.00	120	195	430	2,850	3,750
1872CC	272,000	85.00	125	275	400	1,500	4,000	8,000	50,000	—
1872S	580,000	31.00	47.00	67.00	135	225	375	975	7,000	—
1873 closed 3	801,800	35.00	46.00	64.00	98.00	135	250	545	4,500	3,750
1873 open 3	Inc. above	2,650	3,400	4,350	5,500	7,900	13,500	30,000	—	—
1873CC	122,500	225	320	425	950	1,900	6,500	12,000	80,000	—
1873S no arrows	5,000	—	—	—	—	—	—	—	—	—

Note: 1873S no arrows, no specimens known to survive.

Seated Liberty Half Dollar
Seated Liberty, arrows at date obverse
IN GOD WE TRUST above eagle reverse

KM# 107 • 12.5000 g., 0.9000 **Silver**, 0.3617 oz. ASW • **Rev. Legend:** UNITED STATES OF AMERICA
Designer: Christian Gobrecht

Date	Mintage	G-4	VG-8	F-12	VF-20	XF-40	AU-50	MS-60	MS-65	Prf-65
1873	1,815,700	32.00	49.00	60.00	90.00	230	400	850	17,500	9,000
1873CC	214,560	150	275	375	850	2,000	2,400	5,700	42,000	—
1873S	233,000	55.00	78.00	130	245	425	675	2,200	40,000	—
1874	2,360,300	32.00	42.00	56.00	85.00	210	400	850	12,750	9,000
1874CC	59,000	400	575	1,000	1,750	3,600	5,600	10,500	—	—
1874S	394,000	43.00	65.00	85.00	185	365	685	1,850	20,000	—

Seated Liberty Half Dollar
Seated Liberty, date below obverse   IN GOD WE TRUST above eagle reverse

KM# A99 • 12.5000 g., 0.9000 **Silver**, 0.3617 oz. ASW • **Rev. Legend:** UNITED STATES OF AMERICA
Designer: Christian Gobrecht

Date	Mintage	G-4	VG-8	F-12	VF-20	XF-40	AU-50	MS-60	MS-65	Prf-65
1875	6,027,500	28.00	38.00	47.00	56.00	88.00	180	420	3,500	3,375
1875CC	1,008,000	50.00	56.00	75.00	125	200	325	650	8,350	—
1875S	3,200,000	28.00	38.00	47.00	63.00	100.00	165	360	2,700	—
1876	8,419,150	28.00	38.00	47.00	56.00	88.00	165	360	5,300	3,775
1876CC	1,956,000	50.00	56.00	75.00	115	180	275	560	4,200	—
1876S	4,528,000	28.00	38.00	47.00	56.00	88.00	165	360	2,700	—
1877	8,304,510	28.00	38.00	47.00	56.00	88.00	165	360	2,700	3,825
1877CC	1,420,000	50.00	56.00	75.00	115	180	275	630	3,250	—
1877S	5,356,000	28.00	38.00	47.00	56.00	88.00	165	360	2,700	—
1878	1,378,400	35.00	46.00	67.00	80.00	120	165	425	3,650	3,900
1878CC	62,000	450	600	1,000	1,500	3,150	4,850	7,000	43,500	—
1878S	12,000	23,500	37,500	45,000	47,500	52,000	60,000	70,000	175,000	—
1879	5,900	275	310	360	400	465	575	700	3,650	3,150
1880	9,755	260	280	315	355	410	535	700	3,750	3,150
1881	10,975	270	300	335	385	455	565	700	4,000	3,150
1882	5,500	340	365	385	450	525	600	750	3,850	3,150
1883	9,039	325	340	365	435	500	575	775	3,950	3,150
1884	5,275	385	375	415	500	560	635	800	3,850	3,150
1885	6,130	390	425	475	550	625	700	825	3,850	3,150
1886	5,886	400	500	600	700	775	875	1,000	3,900	3,150
1887	5,710	500	525	650	775	875	950	1,100	3,900	3,150
1888	12,833	280	300	365	400	485	550	800	3,900	3,150
1889	12,711	275	315	350	400	485	550	800	3,900	3,150
1890	12,590	285	310	365	415	500	550	800	3,850	3,150
1891	200,600	55.00	60.00	94.00	122	155	260	480	3,850	3,150

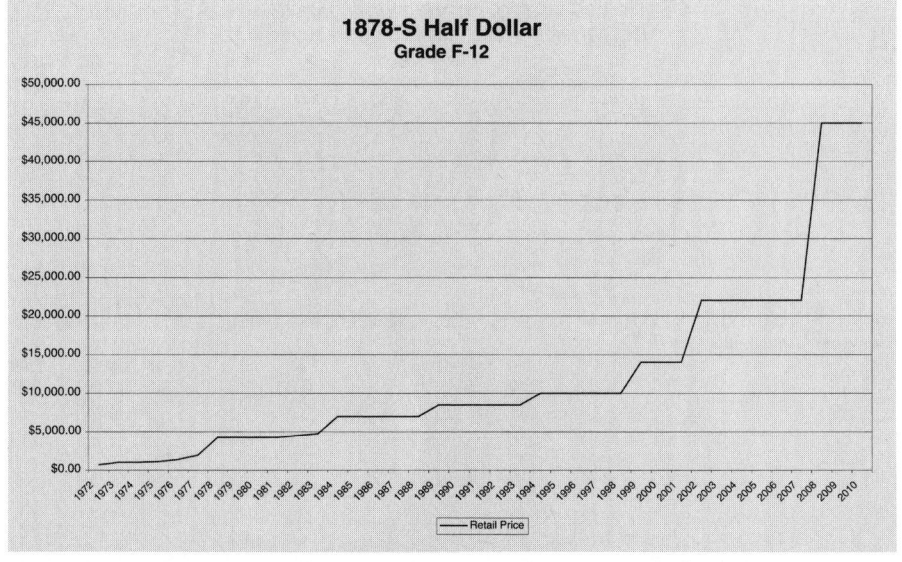

1878-S Half Dollar
Grade F-12

Barber Half Dollar

Laureate head right, flanked by stars, date below obverse **Heraldic eagle reverse**

Mint mark

KM# 116 • 12.5000 g., 0.9000 **Silver**, 0.3617 oz. ASW, 30.6 mm. • **Obv. Legend** IN GOD WE TRUST
Rev. Legend: UNITED STATES OF AMERICA **Designer:** Charles E. Barber

Date	Mintage	G-4	VG-8	F-12	VF-20	XF-40	AU-50	MS-60	MS-65	Prf-65
1892	935,245	28.50	40.00	65.00	120	195	345	475	3,620	4,650
1892O	390,000	310	420	515	575	630	690	850	4,350	—
1892O micro O	Inc. above	2,000	3,750	4,500	7,000	10,000	17,500	24,000	64,000	—
1892S	1,029,028	250	330	425	530	600	700	940	4,850	—
1893	1,826,792	20.00	36.00	75.00	135	205	335	520	3,800	4,650
1893O	1,389,000	36.00	64.50	130	220	360	435	625	9,650	—
1893S	740,000	165	225	300	500	595	725	1,275	25,000	—
1894	1,148,972	32.50	50.00	115	200	280	355	500	3,850	4,650
1894O	2,138,000	22.00	34.00	90.00	170	290	365	525	6,250	—
1894S	4,048,690	18.00	28.00	67.00	125	230	345	490	9,850	—
1895	1,835,218	18.00	25.00	72.00	150	225	345	595	3,900	4,650
1895O	1,766,000	23.00	43.00	110	195	285	385	620	6,950	—
1895S	1,108,086	30.00	54.00	130	235	310	410	580	8,250	—
1896	950,762	21.50	28.00	88.00	160	265	355	565	5,450	4,650
1896O	924,000	42.00	56.00	185	290	475	775	1,750	14,750	—
1896S	1,140,948	115	145	210	350	495	750	1,450	10,500	—
1897	2,480,731	14.10	16.00	47.50	100.00	180	345	485	3,620	4,650
1897O	632,000	170	230	485	835	1,100	1,350	1,800	9,500	—
1897S	933,900	155	225	385	535	840	1,050	1,500	7,350	—
1898	2,956,735	14.10	16.00	38.50	94.00	180	335	485	3,650	4,650
1898O	874,000	37.50	75.00	225	355	525	625	1,250	9,450	—
1898S	2,358,550	27.50	52.50	87.50	175	340	440	950	10,250	—
1899	5,538,846	14.60	16.00	39.50	98.00	180	365	475	3,620	4,650
1899O	1,724,000	26.00	37.50	80.00	170	300	400	675	8,150	—
1899S	1,686,411	23.00	42.50	88.00	135	205	355	660	6,900	—
1900	4,762,912	14.60	16.00	36.50	90.00	180	335	475	3,750	4,650
1900O	2,744,000	17.50	22.50	62.00	165	285	335	860	15,500	—
1900S	2,560,322	15.00	18.50	46.50	98.00	200	335	640	10,000	—
1901	4,268,813	14.60	16.50	38.50	94.00	180	335	510	4,250	4,650
1901O	1,124,000	16.50	26.50	80.00	205	350	475	1,350	14,850	—
1901S	847,044	34.00	55.00	160	355	610	1,050	1,850	19,500	—
1902	4,922,777	13.10	14.50	32.50	86.00	180	335	475	4,600	4,650
1902O	2,526,000	13.50	17.00	52.50	105	225	355	725	11,500	—
1902S	1,460,670	16.00	19.00	62.50	150	260	420	750	7,750	—
1903	2,278,755	14.60	16.00	47.50	100.00	200	335	500	9,250	4,650
1903O	2,100,000	14.10	17.00	53.00	115	210	335	665	9,500	—
1903S	1,920,772	15.00	18.00	55.00	125	220	380	610	5,750	—
1904	2,992,670	13.10	14.50	33.00	85.00	180	345	475	6,450	4,650
1904O	1,117,600	20.00	30.00	80.00	220	385	590	1,100	12,500	—
1904S	553,038	38.50	75.00	260	555	1,075	1,775	9,000	41,500	—
1905	662,727	22.50	32.50	95.00	180	270	370	565	7,500	4,650
1905O	505,000	30.00	44.50	125	235	340	440	760	4,850	—
1905S	2,494,000	15.50	18.00	50.00	125	230	350	615	9,750	—
1906	2,638,675	13.10	14.50	32.00	83.00	180	335	465	3,800	4,650
1906D	4,028,000	13.10	14.50	33.00	89.00	180	335	465	4,500	—
1906O	2,446,000	13.10	14.50	44.00	98.00	190	350	600	6,350	—
1906S	1,740,154	14.60	16.50	57.50	110	215	380	590	5,950	—
1907	2,598,575	13.10	14.50	30.00	83.00	180	335	465	3,600	4,650
1907D	3,856,000	13.10	14.50	30.00	75.00	180	335	465	3,600	—
1907O	3,946,000	13.10	14.50	32.00	89.00	180	33.00	575	3,700	—
1907S	1,250,000	17.40	20.00	80.00	165	315	650	1,275	12,500	—
1908	1,354,545	13.10	14.50	30.00	80.00	180	335	465	4,350	4,650
1908D	3,280,000	13.10	14.50	30.00	80.00	180	335	485	4,250	—
1908O	5,360,000	13.10	14.50	30.00	89.00	180	345	540	3,600	—
1908S	1,644,828	18.50	25.00	72.00	160	285	435	850	6,350	—
1909	2,368,650	14.10	16.00	32.00	83.00	180	335	465	3,600	4,650
1909O	925,400	17.40	23.50	56.00	140	300	510	775	4,850	—
1909S	1,764,000	13.40	14.50	37.00	100.00	180	335	600	4,450	—
1910	418,551	20.00	28.50	90.00	170	330	445	610	3,900	4,650
1910S	1,948,000	16.60	16.50	36.00	100.00	180	355	625	6,650	—

Date	Mintage	G-4	VG-8	F-12	VF-20	XF-40	AU-50	MS-60	MS-65	Prf-65
1911	1,406,543	13.10	14.50	30.00	83.00	180	335	465	3,600	4,650
1911D	695,080	14.10	16.00	40.00	91.00	180	345	565	3,700	—
1911S	1,272,000	14.60	16.50	42.00	98.00	180	345	580	5,950	—
1912	1,550,700	13.10	14.50	30.00	83.00	180	335	465	4,100	4,650
1912D	2,300,800	13.10	14.50	30.00	81.00	180	335	465	3,600	—
1912S	1,370,000	16.40	19.50	41.50	100.00	180	335	535	5,850	—
1913	188,627	77.00	88.00	235	420	600	875	1,150	5,250	4,800
1913D	534,000	17.00	19.50	44.00	100.00	200	335	485	5,450	—
1913S	604,000	20.00	25.00	53.50	110	225	385	725	4,650	—
1914	124,610	155	175	325	550	775	1,025	1,400	11,500	5,000
1914S	992,000	16.40	19.00	41.00	98.00	190	355	575	4,950	—
1915	138,450	112	168	285	380	575	920	1,350	6,650	5,000
1915D	1,170,400	13.10	14.50	30.00	75.00	180	335	465	3,600	—
1915S	1,604,000	16.90	19.50	41.50	94.00	195	350	480	3,600	—

Walking Liberty Half Dollar
Liberty walking left wearing U.S. flag gown, sunrise at left obverse
Eagle advancing left reverse

Obverse mint mark
1916-1917

Reverse mint mark
1917-1947

KM# 142 • 12.5000 g., 0.9000 **Silver**, 0.3617 oz. ASW, 30.6 mm. • **Designer:** Adolph A. Weinman **Notes:**
The mint mark appears on the obverse below the word "Trust" on 1916 and some 1917 issues. Starting with
some 1917 issues and continuing through the remainder of the series, the mint mark was changed to the
reverse, at about the 8 o'clock position near the rim.

Date	Mintage	G-4	VG-8	F-12	VF-20	XF-40	AU-50	MS-60	MS-65	Prf-65
1916	608,000	47.00	55.00	95.00	170	240	275	345	1,950	—
1916D	1,014,400	48.50	55.00	80.00	135	220	255	360	2,500	—
1916S	508,000	108	129	280	440	600	725	1,050	6,250	—
1917D obv. mint mark	765,400	23.50	33.00	80.00	155	235	335	625	7,900	—
1917S obv. mint mark	952,000	27.00	44.00	135	365	700	1,200	2,300	22,500	—
1917	12,292,000	9.00	9.10	10.50	19.50	42.00	72.00	130	1,050	—
1917D rev. mint mark	1,940,000	10.00	16.00	45.00	135	275	555	940	18,500	—
1917S rev. mint mark	5,554,000	9.70	10.00	16.50	32.00	65.00	155	330	13,850	—
1918	6,634,000	9.70	10.00	15.50	64.00	150	265	565	3,800	—
1918D	3,853,040	10.10	12.50	35.00	90.00	225	500	1,300	24,500	—
1918S	10,282,000	9.70	10.00	16.00	34.00	60.00	190	485	17,750	—
1919	962,000	26.00	32.50	78.50	265	535	885	1,325	7,750	—
1919D	1,165,000	25.00	38.50	95.00	320	765	1,750	5,950	130,000	—
1919S	1,552,000	17.50	28.50	72.00	310	825	1,750	3,300	20,000	—
1920	6,372,000	9.70	10.00	15.50	42.00	75.00	155	330	5,250	—
1920D	1,551,000	10.40	17.50	65.00	240	460	920	1,485	17,500	—
1920S	4,624,000	9.70	10.00	19.00	78.00	235	510	850	14,500	—
1921	246,000	165	210	350	750	1,575	2,650	4,500	19,500	—
1921D	208,000	310	370	550	950	2,200	3,150	5,650	29,500	—
1921S	548,000	45.00	65.00	210	750	4,850	7,950	12,850	130,000	—
1923S	2,178,000	10.10	11.50	27.50	110	295	650	1,375	16,500	—
1927S	2,392,000	9.70	11.00	16.50	46.00	165	425	990	9,750	—
1928S Large S	1,940,000	10.00	13.50	28.00	110	325	600	1,650	—	—
1928S Small S	Inc. above	9.70	11.00	18.50	66.00	195	450	985	10,750	—
1929D	1,001,200	10.10	11.00	17.50	32.00	98.00	195	390	3,350	—
1929S	1,902,000	9.70	11.00	14.50	28.50	115	220	400	3,750	—
1933S	1,786,000	10.10	11.50	13.50	20.00	58.00	240	590	4,500	—
1934	6,964,000	7.40	7.80	7.90	8.50	11.00	25.00	85.00	565	—
1934D	2,361,400	737	8.20	11.60	17.50	36.00	88.00	150	1,625	—
1934S	3,652,000	7.40	8.00	8.50	10.70	30.00	100.00	385	4,800	—
1935	9,162,000	7.40	7.80	7.90	8.50	11.90	21.50	45.00	365	—
1935D	3,003,800	7.40	8.00	8.50	14.00	33.00	66.00	140	2,450	—
1935S	3,854,000	7.40	8.00	8.30	13.50	32.00	95.00	285	2,850	—
1936	12,617,901	7.40	7.80	7.90	8.50	11.90	21.00	37.50	265	6,600
1936D	4,252,400	7.40	8.00	8.30	12.50	20.00	52.00	78.00	665	—
1936S	3,884,000	7.40	8.00	8.30	12.50	21.50	58.00	132	1,000	—
1937	9,527,728	7.40	7.80	7.90	8.50	11.90	22.00	38.00	285	1,700
1937D	1,676,000	7.40	9.80	9.90	15.00	33.50	105	220	965	—
1937S	2,090,000	7.40	8.00	8.50	8.50	25.50	62.00	168	785	—
1938	4,118,152	7.40	8.00	8.30	8.50	13.40	38.00	66.00	460	1,275

Date	Mintage	G-4	VG-8	F-12	VF-20	XF-40	AU-50	MS-60	MS-65	Prf-65
1938D	491,600	70.00	75.00	100.00	125	185	250	475	1,750	—
1939	6,820,808	7.40	7.50	6.50	8.50	11.90	22.00	41.00	210	1,150
1939D	4,267,800	7.40	7.20	7.90	9.50	12.70	26.00	45.00	225	—
1939S	2,552,000	7.40	8.00	8.30	9.00	25.00	76.00	145	375	—
1940	9,167,279	7.40	7.50	7.00	7.50	11.40	13.00	31.00	185	1,000
1940S	4,550,000	7.40	7.80	7.90	8.50	12.00	21.00	50.00	315	—
1941	24,207,412	7.40	7.50	7.00	8.04	10.20	13.00	30.00	160	850
1941D	11,248,400	7.40	7.80	7.90	8.50	10.00	18.00	37.50	180	—
1941S	8,098,000	7.40	7.80	7.90	8.50	12.00	27.50	70.00	1,025	—
1942	47,839,120	7.40	7.50	7.00	8.04	10.20	13.00	30.00	160	850
1942D	10,973,800	7.40	7.80	7.90	8.50	10.00	19.00	37.00	325	—
1942S	12,708,000	7.40	7.80	7.90	8.50	10.00	17.50	37.00	610	—
1943	53,190,000	7.40	7.50	7.00	8.04	10.20	13.00	30.00	150	—
1943D	11,346,000	7.40	7.80	7.90	8.50	10.00	25.00	42.00	295	—
1943D Double Die Obverse	—	7.60	7.50	9.00	12.00	15.00	30.00	55.00	450	—
1943S	13,450,000	7.40	7.80	7.90	8.50	10.00	18.50	42.00	460	—
1944	28,206,000	7.40	7.50	7.00	8.04	10.20	13.00	30.00	180	—
1944D	9,769,000	7.40	7.80	7.90	8.50	10.00	20.00	37.00	210	—
1944S	8,904,000	7.40	7.80	7.90	8.50	10.00	18.00	36.00	575	—
1945	31,502,000	7.40	7.50	7.00	8.04	10.20	13.00	30.00	165	—
1945D	9,966,800	7.40	7.80	7.90	8.50	10.00	19.00	36.00	145	—
1945S	10,156,000	7.40	7.80	7.90	8.50	10.00	17.50	36.00	180	—
1946	12,118,000	7.40	7.50	7.00	8.04	10.20	13.00	30.00	200	—
1946 Double Die Reverse	Inc. above	16.00	24.00	35.00	50.00	85.00	175	325	2,750	—
1946D	2,151,000	7.40	8.00	7.90	8.50	25.50	38.50	47.50	150	—
1946S	3,724,000	7.40	7.80	7.90	8.50	12.00	19.00	43.50	175	—
1947	4,094,000	7.40	7.25	7.50	8.50	11.00	22.00	50.00	275	—
1947D	3,900,600	7.40	8.00	7.90	8.50	14.00	31.50	52.50	165	—

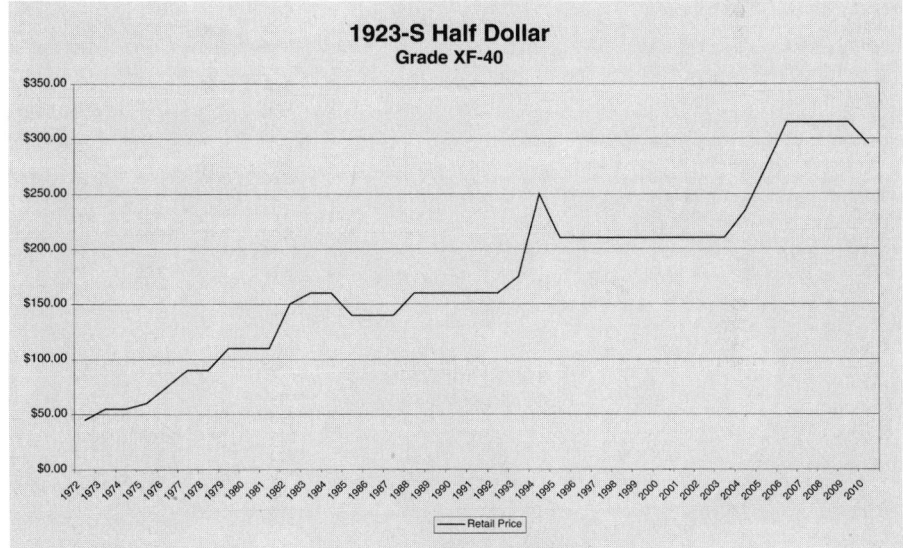

1923-S Half Dollar
Grade XF-40

— Retail Price

Franklin Half Dollar

Franklin bust right obverse   Liberty Bell, small eagle at right reverse

Mint mark

KM# 199 • 12.5000 g., 0.9000 **Silver**, 0.3617 oz. ASW, 30.6 mm. • **Designer:** John R. Sinnock

Date	Mintage	G-4	VG-8	F-12	VF-20	XF-40	AU-50	MS-60	MS-65	-65FBL	-65CAM
1948	3,006,814	—	7.60	7.70	8.30	8.50	11.50	16.00	75.00	190	—

HALF DOLLAR

HALF DOLLAR

Date	Mintage	G-4	VG-8	F-12	VF-20	XF-40	AU-50	MS-60	MS-65	-65FBL	-65CAM
1948D	4,028,600	—	7.60	7.70	8.30	8.00	11.00	15.00	125	260	—
1949	5,614,000	—	—	—	—	9.40	12.00	38.50	120	250	—
1949D	4,120,600	—	—	—	8.00	10.40	25.00	43.50	900	1,750	—
1949S	3,744,000	—	—	—	8.30	11.00	30.00	62.50	160	700	—
1950	7,793,509	—	—	—	—	7.60	10.00	26.00	110	285	2,000
1950D	8,031,600	—	—	—	—	8.60	11.50	22.00	425	900	—
1951	16,859,602	—	—	—	—	7.40	10.40	11.00	75.00	340	1,450
1951D	9,475,200	—	—	—	—	11.60	17.50	26.00	170	540	—
1951S	13,696,000	—	—	—	7.60	8.40	15.00	23.50	125	750	—
1952	21,274,073	—	—	—	—	7.60	10.40	10.80	70.00	210	775
1952D	25,395,600	—	—	—	—	7.60	10.40	10.80	130	450	—
1952S	5,526,000	—	—	7.70	10.30	16.00	32.00	52.00	140	1,500	—
1953	2,796,920	—	—	7.70	7.80	10.00	16.00	25.00	140	1,000	475
1953D	20,900,400	—	—	—	—	7.90	9.60	12.00	150	400	—
1953S	4,148,000	—	—	—	7.60	8.40	15.00	25.00	65.00	16,000	—
1954	13,421,503	—	—	—	—	7.40	10.40	11.60	75.00	225	175
1954D	25,445,580	—	—	—	—	7.40	10.40	11.40	110	235	—
1954S	4,993,400	—	—	—	—	7.70	10.80	13.50	42.00	440	—
1955	2,876,381	—	15.50	16.00	17.50	18.00	18.50	20.00	70.00	140	120
1955 Bugs Bunny	Inc. above	—	20.00	22.00	23.00	25.00	26.00	28.00	120	750	—
1956 Type 1 rev.	4,701,384	—	7.30	7.30	7.50	7.70	9.60	13.50	55.00	125	300
1956 Type 2 rev.	Inc. above	—	—	—	—	—	—	—	—	—	40.00
1957 Type 1 rev.	6,361,952	—	—	—	—	7.40	8.60	9.50	63.00	95.00	55.00
1957 Type 2 rev.	Inc. above	—	—	—	—	—	—	—	—	—	—
1957D	19,966,850	—	—	—	—	7.40	8.60	9.30	60.00	100.00	—
1958 Type 1 rev.	4,917,652	—	—	—	—	7.40	8.60	9.30	55.00	110	60.00
1958 Type 2 rev.	Inc. above	—	—	—	—	12.00	20.00	26.00	—	—	—
1958D	23,962,412	—	—	—	—	7.40	8.60	9.30	55.00	80.00	—
1959 Type 1 rev.	7,349,291	—	—	—	—	7.40	8.60	9.30	110	250	75.00
1959 Type 2 rev.	Inc. above	—	—	—	—	12.00	16.00	30.00	115	—	—
1959D	13,053,750	—	—	—	—	7.40	8.60	9.30	125	215	—
1960 Type 1 rev.	7,715,602	—	—	—	—	7.40	8.60	9.30	110	340	45.00
1960 Type 2 rev.	Inc. above	—	—	—	—	—	—	—	—	—	—
1960D	18,215,812	—	—	—	—	7.40	8.60	9.30	400	1,350	—
1961 Type 1 rev.	11,318,244	—	—	—	—	7.40	8.60	9.30	125	1,300	40.00
1961 Type 2 rev.	Inc. above	—	—	—	—	—	—	—	—	—	—
1961 Double die rev.	Inc. above	—	—	—	—	—	—	—	—	—	3,500
1961D	20,276,442	—	—	—	—	7.40	8.60	9.30	155	875	—
1962 Type 1 rev.	12,932,019	—	—	—	—	7.40	8.60	9.30	145	1,850	35.00
1962 Type 2 rev.	Inc. above	—	—	—	—	—	—	—	—	—	—
1962D	35,473,281	—	—	—	—	7.40	8.60	9.30	175	800	—
1963 Type 1 rev.	25,239,645	—	—	—	—	7.40	8.60	9.30	55.00	1,200	35.00
1963 Type 2 rev.	Inc. above	—	—	—	—	—	—	—	—	—	—
1963D	67,069,292	—	—	—	—	7.40	8.60	9.30	75.00	165	—

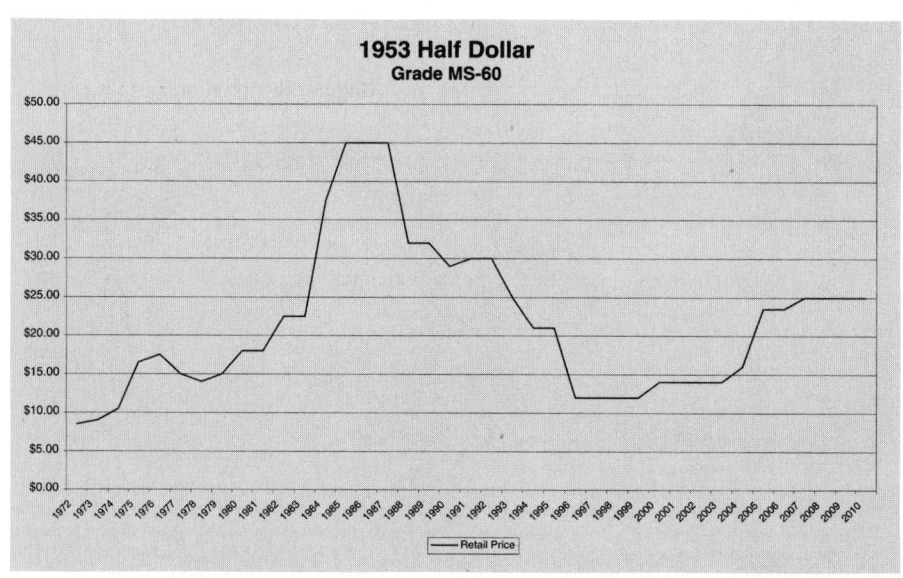

Kennedy Half Dollar

Mint mark 1964

KM# 202 • 12.5000 g., 0.9000 **Silver**, 0.3617 oz. ASW, 30.6 mm. • **Obv. Designer:** Gilroy Roberts **Rev. Designer:** Frank Gasparro **Edge Desc:** Reeded

Date	Mintage	XF-40	MS-60	MS-65	Prf-65
1964	277,254,766	7.00	7.20	20.00	12.00
1964 Accented Hair	Inc. above	—	—	—	40.00
1964D	156,205,446	7.10	7.40	24.00	—

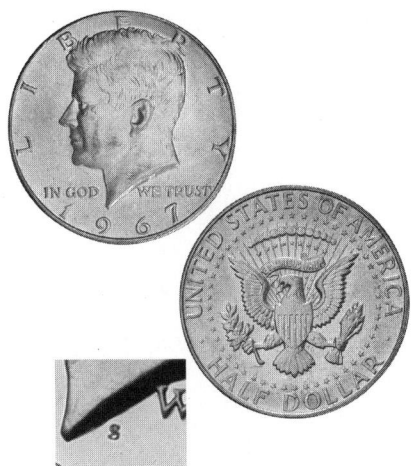

Mint mark 1968 - present

KM# 202a • 11.5000 g., 0.4000 **Silver**, 0.1479 oz. ASW, 30.6 mm. • **Obv. Designer:** Gilroy Roberts **Rev. Designer:** Frank Gasparro **Edge Desc:** Reeded

Date	Mintage	MS-60	MS-65	Prf-65
1965	65,879,366	3.40	18.00	—
1965 SMS	2,360,000	—	15.00	—
1966	108,984,932	3.40	14.00	—
1966 SMS	2,261,583	—	17.00	—
1967	295,046,978	3.40	22.00	—
1967 SMS	1,863,344	—	18.00	—
1968D	246,951,930	3.40	18.00	—
1968S	3,041,506	—	—	7.00
1969D	129,881,800	3.40	20.00	—
1969S	2,934,631	—	—	7.50
1970D	2,150,000	13.00	50.00	—
1970S	2,632,810	—	—	20.00

KM# 202b • 11.3400 g., **Copper-Nickel Clad Copper**, 30.6 mm. • **Obv. Designer:** Gilroy Roberts **Rev. Designer:** Frank Gasparro

Date	Mintage	XF-40	MS-60	MS-65	Prf-65
1971	155,640,000	—	1.00	15.00	—
1971D	302,097,424	—	1.00	15.00	—
1971S	3,244,183	—	—	—	8.00
1972	153,180,000	—	1.00	20.00	—
1972D	141,890,000	—	1.00	14.00	—
1972S	3,267,667	—	—	—	7.00
1973	64,964,000	—	1.00	14.00	—
1973D	83,171,400	—	—	12.00	—
1973S	2,769,624	—	—	—	7.00
1974	201,596,000	—	1.00	18.00	—
1974D	79,066,300	—	1.00	20.00	—
1974D DDO	Inc. above	24.00	32.00	165	—
1974S	2,617,350	—	—	—	—
1975 none minted	—	—	—	—	—
1975D none minted	—	—	—	—	—
1975S none minted	—	—	—	—	—

Bicentennial design, Independence Hall reverse

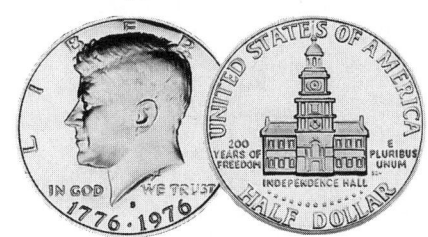

KM# 205 • 11.2000 g., **Copper-Nickel**, 30.5 mm. • **Rev. Designer:** Seth Huntington

Date	Mintage	MS-60	MS-65	Prf-65
1976	234,308,000	1.00	22.00	—
1976D	287,565,248	1.00	9.00	—
1976S	7,059,099	—	—	5.00

KM# 205a • 11.5000 g., 0.4000 **Silver**, 0.1479 oz. ASW • **Rev. Designer:** Seth Huntington

Date	Mintage	MS-60	MS-65	Prf-65
1976S	4,908,319	—	12.00	—
1976S	3,998,621	—	—	6.00

Regular design resumed reverse

KM# A202b • 11.1000 g., **Copper-Nickel Clad Copper**, 30.4 mm. • **Edge Desc:** Reeded **Notes:** KM#202b design and composition resumed. The 1979-S and 1981-S Type II proofs have clearer mint marks than the Type I proofs of those years.

Date	Mintage	MS-65	Prf-65
1977	43,598,000	18.00	—
1977D	31,449,106	20.00	—
1977S	3,251,152	—	4.50
1978	14,350,000	12.00	—
1978D	13,765,799	10.00	—
1978S	3,127,788	—	6.00

Date	Mintage	MS-65	Prf-65
1979	68,312,000	11.00	—
1979D	15,815,422	9.00	—
1979S Type I	3,677,175	—	6.00
1979S Type II	Inc. above	—	20.00
1980P	44,134,000	9.00	—
1980D	33,456,449	6.50	—
1980S	3,547,030	—	6.00
1981P	29,544,000	8.00	—
1981D	27,839,533	8.50	—
1981S Type I	4,063,083	—	5.00
1981S Type II	Inc. above	—	17.50
1982P	10,819,000	10.00	—
1982P no initials FG	Inc. above	40.00	—
1982D	13,140,102	9.00	—
1982S	38,957,479	—	6.50
1983P	34,139,000	20.00	—
1983D	32,472,244	10.00	—
1983S	3,279,126	—	6.50
1984P	26,029,000	13.00	—
1984D	26,262,158	18.00	—
1984S	3,065,110	—	7.00
1985P	18,706,962	10.00	—
1985D	19,814,034	12.00	—
1985S	3,962,138	—	6.00
1986P	13,107,633	25.00	—
1986D	15,336,145	17.00	—
1986S	2,411,180	—	8.00
1987P	2,890,758	14.00	—
1987D	2,890,758	10.00	—
1987S	4,407,728	—	6.50
1988P	13,626,000	16.00	—
1988D	12,000,096	12.00	—
1988S	3,262,948	—	6.00
1989P	24,542,000	18.00	—
1989D	23,000,216	14.00	—
1989S	3,220,194	—	8.00
1990P	22,780,000	18.00	—
1990D	20,096,242	15.00	—
1990S	3,299,559	—	7.00
1991P	14,874,000	15.00	—
1991D	15,054,678	16.00	—
1991S	2,867,787	—	13.00
1992P	17,628,000	12.00	—
1992D	17,000,106	8.00	—
1992S	2,858,981	—	8.00
1993P	15,510,000	15.00	—
1993D	15,000,006	14.00	—
1993S	2,633,439	—	14.00
1994P	23,718,000	8.00	—
1994D	23,828,110	8.00	—
1994S	2,484,594	—	11.00
1995P	26,496,000	9.00	—
1995D	26,288,000	8.00	—
1995S	2,010,384	—	35.00
1996P	24,442,000	10.00	—
1996D	24,744,000	8.00	—
1996S	2,085,191	—	16.00
1997P	20,882,000	14.00	—
1997D	19,876,000	10.00	—
1997S	1,975,000	—	34.00
1998P	15,646,000	12.50	—
1998D	15,064,000	12.50	—
1998S	2,078,494	—	22.00
1999P	8,900,000	9.00	—
1999D	10,682,000	9.00	—
1999S	2,557,897	—	18.00
2000P	22,600,000	9.00	—
2000D	19,466,000	7.00	—
2000S	3,082,944	—	8.00
2001P	21,200,000	9.00	—
2001D	19,504,000	9.00	—
2001S	2,235,000	—	8.00
2002P	3,100,000	10.00	—
2002D	2,500,000	10.00	—
2002S	2,268,913	—	8.00
2003P	2,500,000	14.00	—
2003D	2,500,000	14.00	—
2003S	2,076,165	—	6.00
2004P	2,900,000	7.00	—

Date	Mintage	MS-65	Prf-65
2004D	2,900,000	7.00	—
2004S	1,789,488	—	13.00
2005P	3,800,000	9.00	—
2005P Satin finish	1,160,000	8.00	—
2005D	3,500,000	9.00	—
2005D Satin finish	1,160,000	10.00	—
2005S	2,275,000	—	7.00
2006P	2,400,000	12.00	—
2006P Satin finish	847,361	12.00	—
2006D	2,000,000	20.00	—
2006D Satin finish	847,361	14.00	—
2006S	1,934,965	—	10.00
2007P	—	7.00	—
2007P Satin finish	—	8.00	—
2007D	—	7.00	—
2007D Satin finish	—	8.00	—
2007S	—	—	10.00
2008P	—	7.00	—
2008P Satin finish	—	8.50	—
2008D	—	7.00	—
2008D Satin finish	—	8.50	—
2008S	—	—	12.00
2009P	—	7.00	—
2009P Satin finish	—	8.50	—
2009D	—	7.00	—
2009D Satin finish	—	8.50	—
2009S	—	—	6.00

KM# A202c • 12.5000 g., 0.9000 Silver, 0.3617 oz. ASW, 30.6 mm. • Designer: Gilroy Roberts

Date	Mintage	Prf-65
1992S	1,317,579	12.00
1993S	761,353	32.00
1994S	785,329	36.00
1995S	838,953	92.00
1996S	830,021	40.00
1997S	821,678	75.00
1998S	878,792	25.00
1998S Matte Proof	62,350	285
1999S	804,565	40.00
2000S	965,921	11.00
2001S	849,600	20.00
2002S	888,816	14.00
2003S	1,040,425	15.00
2004S	1,175,935	14.00
2005S	1,069,679	10.00
2006S	988,140	11.00
2007S	1,384,797	12.00
2008S	620,684	12.00
2009S	—	20.00

DOLLAR

Flowing Hair Dollar

KM# 17 • 26.9600 g., 0.8920 **Silver**, 0.7731 oz. ASW, 39-40 mm. • **Designer:** Robert Scot **Notes:** The two
1795 varieties have either two or three leaves under each of the eagle's wings on the reverse.

Date	Mintage	F-12	VF-20	XF-40	AU-50	MS-60	MS-63
1794	1,758	120,000	170,000	245,000	365,000	575,000	950,000
1795 2 leaves	203,033	4,450	7,800	16,150	25,500	80,500	196,500
1795 3 leaves	Inc. above	4,200	7,250	14,500	22,500	69,500	182,500
1795 Silver plug	Inc. above	9,850	13,950	28,500	48,500	115,000	235,000

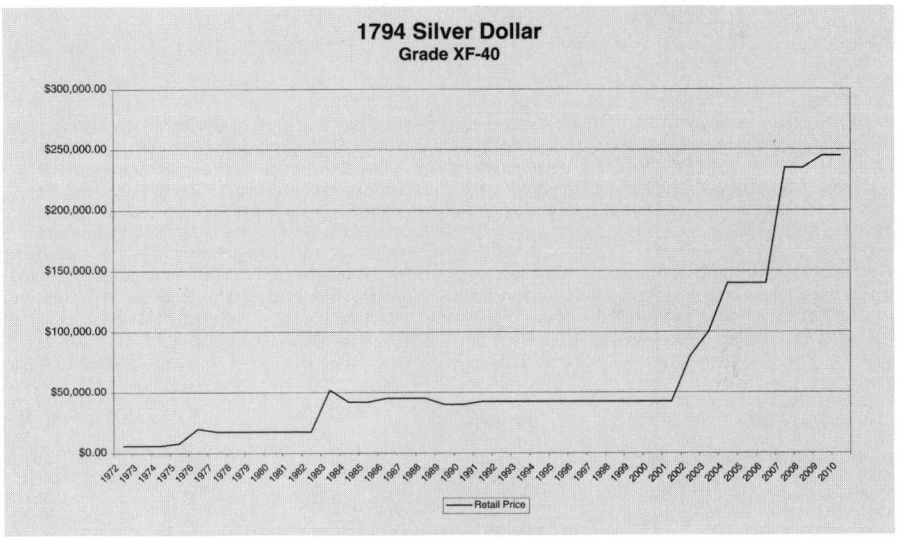

1794 Silver Dollar
Grade XF-40

Draped Bust Dollar
Small eagle reverse

KM# 18 • 26.9600 g., 0.8920 **Silver**, 0.7731 oz. ASW, 39-40 mm. • **Designer:** Robert Scot

Date	Mintage	F-12	VF-20	XF-40	AU-50	MS-60	MS-63
1795 Off-center bust	Inc. above	3,850	5,850	12,500	17,000	52,000	126,000
1795 Centered bust	—	3,900	5,950	12,700	17,250	52,500	126,000
1796 small date, small letters	72,920	4,100	6,300	13,750	18,500	70,000	—
1796 small date, large letters	Inc. above	3,875	6,400	13,700	19,400	—	—
1796 large date, small letters	Inc. above	4,250	6,750	14,350	19,200	57,000	136,000
1797 9 stars left, 7 stars right, small letters	7,776	5,200	9,000	18,850	36,500	—	—
1797 9 stars left, 7 stars right, large letters	Inc. above	4,250	6,850	13,950	20,300	55,500	—
1797 10 stars left, 6 stars right	Inc. above	4,050	6,350	13,600	18,500	53,500	125,000
1798 13 stars	327,536	4,150	6,300	13,750	21,000	85,000	—
1798 15 stars	—	4,700	7,450	16,150	25,500	95,000	—

Draped Bust Dollar

Draped bust right, flanked by stars, date below obverse   Heraldic eagle reverse

KM# 32 • 26.9600 g., 0.8920 **Silver**, 0.7731 oz. ASW, 39-40 mm. • **Obv. Legend** LIBERTY **Rev. Legend:** UNITED STATES OF AMERICA **Designer:** Robert Scot **Notes:** The 1798 "knob 9" variety has a serif on the lower left of the 9 in the date. The 1798 varieties are distinguished by the number of arrows held by the eagle on the reverse and the number of berries on the olive branch. On the 1798 "high-8" variety, the 8 in the date is higher than the other numerals. The 1799 varieties are distinguished by the number and positioning of the stars on the obverse and by the size of the berries in the olive branch on the reverse. On the 1700 "irregular date" variety, the first 9 in the date is smaller than the other numerals. Some varieties of the 1800 strikes had letters in the legend cut twice into the dies; as between the numerals in the date are wider than other varieties and the 8 is lower than the other numerals. The 1800 "small berries" variety refers to the size of the berries in the olive branch on the reverse. The 1800 "12 arrows" and "10 arrows" varieties refer to the number of arrows held by the eagle. The 1800 "Americai" variety appears to have the faint outline of an "I" after "America" in the reverse legend. The "close" and "wide" varieties of the 1802 refer to the amount of space between the numerals in the date. The 1800 large-3 and small-3 varieties are distinguished by the size of the 3 in the date.

Date	Mintage	F-12	VF-20	XF-40	AU-50	MS-60	MS-63
1798 knob 9, 4 stripes	423,515	1,785	2,735	5,550	9,850	21,750	95,000
1798 knob 9, 10 arrows	Inc. above	1,785	2,735	5,550	9,850	21,750	87,000
1798 knob 9, 5 stripes	Inc. above	—	—	—	—	—	124,500
1798 pointed 9, 4 berries	Inc. above	1,785	2,735	5,550	9,850	21,750	43,500
1798 5 berries, 12 arrows	Inc. above	1,785	2,735	5,550	9,850	21,750	43,500
1798 high 8	Inc. above	1,785	2,735	5,550	9,850	21,750	43,500
1798 13 arrows	Inc. above	1,785	2,735	5,550	9,850	21,750	45,000
1799/98 13-star reverse	Inc. above	2,000	2,950	4,300	8,600	23,500	45,000
1799/98 15-star reverse	Inc. above	1,875	2,850	4,000	8,300	24,500	47,500
1799 irregular date, 13-star reverse	Inc. above	1,825	3,000	3,900	8,200	23,500	45,000
1799 irregular date, 15-star reverse	Inc. above	1,825	3,200	5,550	9,850	21,500	42,500
1799 perfect date, 7- and 6-star obverse, no berries	Inc. above	1,750	2,700	3,850	8,150	18,500	42,500
1799 perfect date, 7- and 6-star obverse, small berries	Inc. above	1,750	2,700	3,850	8,150	18,500	42,500
1799 perfect date, 7- and 6-star obverse, medium large berries	Inc. above	1,750	2,700	3,850	8,150	18,500	42,500
1799 perfect date, 7- and 6-star obverse, extra large berries	Inc. above	1,750	2,700	3,850	8,150	18,500	51,500
1799 8 stars left, 5 stars right on obverse	Inc. above	1,825	2,800	3,900	8,200	24,000	45,000
1800 "R" in "Liberty" double cut	220,920	1,825	2,775	5,550	9,850	21,500	45,000
1800 first "T" in "States" double cut	Inc. above	1,800	2,750	5,550	9,850	21,500	45,000
1800 both letters double cut	Inc. above	1,800	2,750	5,550	9,850	21,500	45,000
1800 "T" in "United" double cut	Inc. above	1,800	2,750	5,550	9,850	21,500	45,000
1800 very wide date, low 8	Inc. above	1,800	2,750	5,550	9,850	21,500	—
1800 small berries	Inc. above	1,850	2,800	3,900	8,200	22,000	48,500
1800 dot date	Inc. above	2,000	3,000	4,300	8,600	21,500	45,000
1800 12 arrows	Inc. above	1,825	3,200	5,550	9,850	31,000	—
1800 10 arrows	Inc. above	1,825	3,200	5,550	9,850	—	—
1800 "Americai"	Inc. above	2,000	3,300	4,300	8,600	21,500	49,000
1801	54,454	2,050	3,200	4,000	8,300	25,000	—
1801 proof restrike	—	—	—	—	—	—	—

Date	Mintage	F-12	VF-20	XF-40	AU-50	MS-60	MS-63
1802/1 close	Inc. above	2,000	3,300	4,300	8,600	20,500	—
1802/1 wide	Inc. above	2,000	3,300	4,300	8,600	20,500	—
1802 close, perfect date	Inc. above	1,850	2,800	3,900	8,200	20,500	—
1802 wide, perfect date	Inc. above	1,825	2,775	3,950	8,250	21,500	—
1802 proof restrike, mintage unrecorded	—	—	—	—	—	—	—
1803 large 3	85,634	1,875	3,000	4,000	8,300	20,500	47,500
1803 small 3	Inc. above	2,000	3,300	4,300	8,600	21,500	48,500
1803 proof restrike, mintage unrecorded	—	—	—	—	—	—	—
1804 15 known	—	—	—	—	3,000,000	—	—

Note: 1804, Childs Sale, Aug. 1999, Prf-68, $4,140,000.

Gobrecht Dollar
"C Gobrecht F." in base obverse
Eagle flying left amid stars reverse

KM# 59.1 • 26.7300 g., 0.9000 **Silver**, 0.7734 oz. ASW, 38.1 mm. • **Obv. Designer:** Christian Gobrecht **Rev. Legend:** UNITED STATES OF AMERICA **Edge Desc:** Plain.

Date	Mintage	VF-20	XF-40	AU-50	Prf-60
1836	1,000	11,500	14,850	—	25,500

"C. Gobrecht F." in base obverse
Eagle flying in plain field reverse

KM# 59.2 • 26.7300 g., 0.9000 **Silver**, 0.7734 oz. ASW, 38.1 mm. • **Obv. Designer:** Christian Gobrecht. **Edge Desc:** Plain.

Date	Mintage	VF-20	XF-40	AU-50	Prf-60
1836 Restrike	—	—	—	—	24,000

"C. Gobrecht F." in base obverse

KM# 59a.1 • 26.7300 g., 0.9000 **Silver**, 0.7734 oz. ASW, 38.1 mm. • **Obv. Legend** Eagle flying left amid stars. **Edge Desc:** Plain.

Date	Mintage	VF-20	XF-40	AU-50	Prf-60
1836	600	—	—	—	—

"C. Gobrecht F." in base obverse
Eagle flying left amid stars reverse

KM# 59a.2 • 26.7300 g., 0.9000 **Silver**, 0.7734 oz. ASW, 38.1 mm. • **Edge Desc:** Reeded.

Date	Mintage	VF-20	XF-40	AU-50	Prf-60
1836 Restrike	—	—	—	—	—

Designer's name omitted in base obverse Eagle in plain field reverse

KM# 59a.3 • 26.7300 g., 0.9000 **Silver**, 0.7734 oz. ASW, 38.1 mm. • **Edge Desc:** Reeded.

Date	Mintage	VF-20	XF-40	AU-50	Prf-60
1839	300	—	—	—	38,000

Designer's name omitted in base obverse
Eagle in plain field reverse

KM# 59a.4 • 26.7300 g., 0.9000 **Silver**, 0.7734 oz. ASW, 38.1 mm. •

Date	Mintage	VF-20	XF-40	AU-50	Prf-60
1839 Restrike	—	—	—	—	36,500

Note: All other combinations are restrikes of the late 1850's.

Seated Liberty Dollar
Seated Liberty, date below obverse
No motto above eagle reverse

KM# 71 • 26.7300 g., 0.9000 **Silver**, 0.7734 oz. ASW, 38.1 mm. • **Rev. Legend:** UNITED STATES OF AMERICA **Designer:** Christian Gobrecht

Date	Mintage	G-4	VG-8	F-12	VF-20	XF-40	AU-50	MS-60	MS-63	MS-65	Prf-65
1840	61,005	260	300	330	400	500	925	3,950	21,500	—	—
1841	173,000	250	290	315	375	465	800	2,900	5,600	95,000	—
1842	184,618	250	290	315	375	465	800	2,450	5,100	—	—
1843	165,100	250	290	315	375	465	800	2,700	10,000	—	—
1844	20,000	265	308	360	435	785	1,250	6,400	15,000	100,000	—
1845	24,500	285	330	360	435	540	1,750	10,500	26,500	—	—
1846	110,600	260	308	345	470	650	1,100	2,700	5,950	98,000	120,000
1846O	59,000	270	325	370	460	650	1,325	8,750	20,000	—	—
1847	140,750	250	290	315	375	465	800	2,900	7,500	95,000	—
1848	15,000	310	380	475	775	1,200	1,635	4,050	9,500	65,000	—
1849	62,600	260	300	330	400	500	850	3,150	7,750	95,000	155,000
1850	7,500	450	540	645	775	1,750	2,650	7,850	15,000	—	80,000
1850O	40,000	335	400	500	750	1,550	3,950	12,850	34,500	—	—
1851	1,300	4,000	4,850	5,750	7,750	18,000	27,000	43,500	68,500	150,000	225,000
1851 Restrike	—	—	—	—	—	—	—	—	—	—	90,000
1852	1,100	3,500	4,150	5,200	7,000	15,000	26,000	38,500	60,000	150,000	200,000
1852 Restrike	—	—	—	—	—	—	—	—	—	—	70,000
1853 Restrike	—	400	550	660	1,100	1,425	4,000	7,950	100,000		
1853	46,110	335	400	550	650	875	1,275	3,300	7,350	—	90,000
1854	33,140	1,000	1,450	2,000	2,850	4,500	5,750	8,500	13,500	95,000	80,000
1855	26,000	900	1,150	1,450	2,150	3,750	4,950	8,850	22,500	—	55,000
1856	63,500	400	450	650	775	1,650	2,850	4,350	11,500	—	39,500
1857	94,000	450	525	675	800	1,500	1,850	3,500	9,000	92,000	39,500
1858 proof only	Est. 800	3,200	3,600	4,000	4,800	7,250	8,850	—	—	—	42,500
Note: Later restrike.											
1859	256,500	270	330	390	495	635	1,000	2,800	6,600	92,000	17,500
1859O	360,000	250	290	315	375	465	800	2,200	4,600	56,000	—
1859S	20,000	315	390	510	750	1,550	3,500	15,000	36,500	—	—
1860	218,930	260	300	330	400	500	900	2,500	5,600	85,000	15,700
1860O	515,000	250	290	315	375	465	800	2,200	4,600	56,000	—
1861	78,500	600	760	900	985	1,500	1,975	2,950	5,650	90,000	15,700
1862	12,090	440	600	850	945	1,350	1,650	3,250	5,750	90,000	15,700
1863	27,660	375	525	575	660	975	1,400	3,250	6,000	90,000	18,000
1864	31,170	350	410	500	565	900	1,375	3,350	6,250	90,000	15,700
1865	47,000	300	350	420	550	900	1,350	3,250	6,250	90,000	15,700
1866 2 known without motto	—	—	—	—	—	—	—	—	—	—	—

Seated Liberty Dollar
Seated Liberty, date below obverse   IN GOD WE TRUST above eagle reverse

KM# 100 • 26.7300 g., 0.9000 **Silver**, 0.7734 oz. ASW, 38.1 mm. • **Rev. Legend:** UNITED STATES OF AMERICA **Designer:** Christian Gobrecht **Notes:** In 1866 the motto IN GOD WE TRUST was added to the reverse above the eagle.

Date	Mintage	G-4	VG-8	F-12	VF-20	XF-40	AU-50	MS-60	MS-63	MS-65	Prf-65
1866	49,625	310	345	390	470	555	900	2,350	5,100	69,500	14,500
1867	47,525	305	340	385	465	550	895	2,385	5,150	71,500	14,500
1868	162,700	280	315	370	450	535	920	3,500	7,100	71,500	14,500
1869	424,300	315	350	395	475	560	885	2,350	5,100	69,500	14,500
1870	416,000	260	295	330	410	495	820	2,250	4,950	66,500	14,500
1870CC	12,462	465	600	765	1,350	2,250	6,850	23,500	42,500	—	—
1870S 12-15 known	—	150,000	235,000	350,000	475,000	625,000	1,200,000	1,750,000	2,500,000	—	—

Note: 1870S, Eliasberg Sale, April 1997, EF-45 to AU-50, $264,000.

Date	Mintage	G-4	VG-8	F-12	VF-20	XF-40	AU-50	MS-60	MS-63	MS-65	Prf-65
1871	1,074,760	260	295	330	410	495	820	2,250	4,950	66,500	14,500
1871CC	1,376	2,000	2,750	4,400	6,950	14,000	24,500	68,500	175,000	—	—
1872	1,106,450	260	295	330	410	495	820	2,250	4,950	68,500	14,500
1872CC	3,150	900	1,350	2,650	4,200	7,250	12,500	28,500	120,000	385,000	—
1872S	9,000	310	365	550	700	2,000	4,500	11,000	26,000	—	—
1873	293,600	265	305	340	420	510	840	2,300	5,000	66,500	14,500
1873CC	2,300	6,000	7,250	11,500	18,500	32,500	48,500	85,000	225,000	625,000	—
1873S none known	700	—	—	—	—	—	—	—	—	—	—

Trade Dollar
Seated Liberty, IN GOD WE TRUST in base above date obverse
TRADE DOLLAR below eagle reverse

KM# 108 • 27.2200 g., 0.9000 **Silver**, 0.7876 oz. ASW, 38.1 mm. • **Rev. Legend:** UNITED STATES OF AMERICA. **Designer:** William Barber

Date	Mintage	G-4	VG-8	F-12	VF-20	XF-40	AU-50	MS-60	MS-65	Prf-65
1873	397,500	100.00	125	144	200	250	360	1,050	12,500	11,000
1873CC	124,500	230	275	330	450	700	1,475	8,850	122,000	—
1873S	703,000	115	135	155	210	265	385	1,450	15,500	—
1874	987,800	100.00	130	150	185	250	365	1,150	13,850	10,800
1874CC	1,373,200	235	265	310	375	600	775	3,250	26,500	—
1874S	2,549,000	90.00	135	140	150	175	270	975	11,000	—
1875	218,900	160	185	375	460	590	850	2,450	13,000	10,700
1875CC	1,573,700	200	255	285	335	510	675	2,150	40,000	—
1875S	4,487,000	80.00	125	130	140	165	260	960	11,000	—
1875S/CC	Inc. above	220	285	375	560	925	1,450	4,650	65,000	—
1876	456,150	90.00	135	140	150	175	270	950	7,500	10,500
1876CC	509,000	235	265	300	365	525	720	6,000	78,500	—
1876S	5,227,000	80.00	125	130	140	165	260	940	11,000	—

Date	Mintage	G-4	VG-8	F-12	VF-20	XF-40	AU-50	MS-60	MS-65	Prf-65
1877	3,039,710	90.00	135	140	150	175	270	950	16,000	10,500
1877CC	534,000	235	275	320	410	700	800	2,450	60,000	—
1877S	9,519,000	80.00	125	130	140	165	260	940	11,000	—
1878 proof only	900	—	—	—	1,200	1,300	1,500	—	—	13,500
1878CC	97,000	425	525	710	1,050	2,400	4,200	12,000	112,000	—
1878S	4,162,000	80.00	125	130	140	165	260	940	11,000	—
1879 proof only	1,541	—	—	—	1,175	1,275	1,400	—	—	10,500
1880 proof only	1,987	—	—	—	1,150	1,250	1,350	—	—	10,500
1881 proof only	960	—	—	—	1,200	1,300	1,400	—	—	10,500
1882 proof only	1,097	—	—	—	1,175	1,275	1,375	—	—	10,500
1883 proof only	979	—	—	—	1,200	1,300	1,400	—	—	10,500
1884 proof only	10	—	—	—	—	—	100,000	—	—	—

Note: 1884, Eliasberg Sale, April 1997, Prf-66, $396,000.

| 1885 proof only | 5 | — | — | — | — | — | — | — | — | — |

Note: 1885, Eliasberg Sale, April 1997, Prf-65, $907,500.

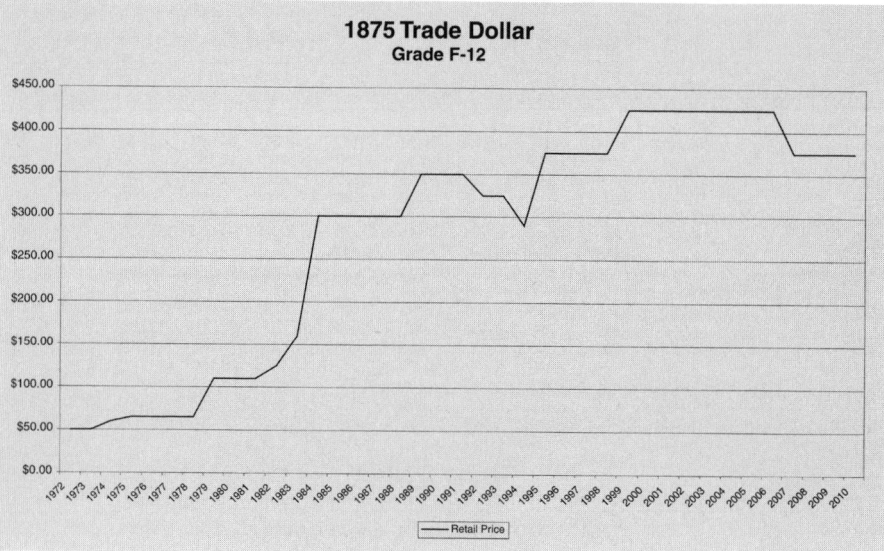

Morgan Dollar

Laureate head left, date below flanked by stars obverse   Eagle within 1/2 wreath reverse

8 Tail feathers   7 Tail feathers   7/8 Tail feathers

KM# 110 • 26.7300 g., 0.9000 **Silver**, 0.7734 oz. ASW, 38.1 mm. • **Obv. Legend** E.PLURIBUS.UNUM
Rev. Legend: UNITED STATES OF AMERICA **Designer:** George T. Morgan **Notes:** "65DMPL" values are
for coins grading MS-65 deep-mirror prooflike. The 1878 "8 tail feathers" and "7 tail feathers" varieties are
distinguished by the number of feathers in the eagle's tail. On the "reverse of 1878" varieties, the top of the
top feather in the arrows held by the eagle is straight across and the eagle's breast is concave. On the

"reverse of 1879 varieties," the top feather in the arrows held by the eagle is slanted and the eagle's breast is convex. The 1890-CC "tail-bar" variety has a bar extending from the arrow feathers to the wreath on the reverse, the result of a die gouge. The Pittman Act of 1918 authorized the melting of 270 Million pieces of various dates. They were not indivudually recorded.

Date	Mintage	VG-8	F-12	VF-20	XF-40	AU-50	MS-60	MS-63	MS-64	MS-65	65DMPL	Prf-65
1878 8 tail feathers	750,000	29.50	32.00	37.50	46.00	74.00	128	175	385	1,500	23,500	8,350
1878 7 over 8 tail feathers	9,759,550	21.00	24.50	27.50	41.50	75.00	145	260	465	2,350	17,000	—
1878 7 tail feathers, reverse of 1878	Inc. above	20.50	22.00	23.00	25.00	40.00	74.00	98.00	225	1,215	11,650	11,500
1878 7 tail feathers, reverse of 1879	Inc. above	21.00	23.00	25.00	27.00	43.50	80.00	175	500	2,650	24,500	185,000
1878CC	2,212,000	85.00	92.00	100.00	125	150	210	310	485	1,825	10,800	—
1878S	9,744,000	20.50	21.50	22.50	27.00	37.50	60.00	63.50	110	265	10.50	—
1879	14,807,100	16.70	18.60	20.10	21.80	27.10	34.80	60.00	129	895	17,250	7,550
1879CC	756,000	150	170	285	735	1,825	3,850	6,350	8,900	29,850	49,000	—
1879CC capped CC	Inc. above	145	165	270	700	1,700	3,750	5,775	9,650	46,500	63,500	—
1879O	2,887,000	16.70	18.60	20.10	26.50	33.60	75.00	185	525	3,650	28,500	—
1879S reverse of 1878	9,110,000	22.50	23.50	25.00	30.00	47.50	125	380	1,150	7,000	24,000	—
1879S reverse of 1879	9,110,000	16.70	18.60	20.10	21.80	27.10	36.80	47.50	55.00	148	1,300	—
1880	12,601,335	16.70	18.60	20.10	22.00	27.60	34.80	51.50	128	790	6,350	7,350
1880CC reverse of 1878	591,000	175	210	245	300	355	575	660	1,100	2,300	21,500	—
1880CC 80/79 reverse of 1878	Inc. above	190	230	270	335	410	640	850	1,700	4,000	—	—
1880CC 8/7 reverse of 1878	Inc. above	170	200	235	290	360	600	700	1,300	2,950	—	—
1880CC reverse of 1879	Inc. above	170	200	240	285	345	510	560	635	1,500	9,850	—
1880CC 8/7 high 7 reverse of 1879	Inc. above	175	205	245	290	355	525	610	765	1,800	—	—
1880CC 8/7 low 7 reverse of 1879	Inc. above	175	205	245	290	355	525	610	765	1,800	—	—
1880O	5,305,000	17.00	18.60	20.10	22.80	27.60	66.00	345	1,825	28,500	70,000	—
1880S	8,900,000	16.70	18.60	20.10	21.80	17.10	34.80	44.50	55.00	148	725	—
1880S 8/7 crossbar	—	20.70	23.60	27.10	45.00	75.00	90.00	265	335	450	—	—
1881	9,163,975	16.70	18.60	20.10	21.80	25.10	34.80	63.00	150	825	21,750	7,650
1881CC	296,000	375	385	410	425	460	500	510	585	1,060	3,050	—
1881O	5,708,000	16.70	18.60	20.10	21.80	25.10	39.50	47.50	195	1,450	35,000	—
1881S	12,760,000	16.70	18.60	20.10	21.80	27.10	34.80	44.50	55.00	148	850	—
1882	11,101,100	16.70	18.60	20.10	21.80	25.10	33.80	47.50	76.00	550	6,800	7,350
1882CC	1,133,000	92.00	100.00	110	130	155	192	225	260	520	1,950	—
1882O	6,090,000	17.00	18.60	20.10	22.80	27.10	39.00	52.00	100.00	1,275	4,950	—
1882O/S	Inc. above	30.00	40.00	48.00	72.00	115	255	1,150	2,600	61,500	65,000	—
1882S	9,250,000	16.70	18.60	20.10	21.80	27.10	35.80	47.50	60.00	150	4,000	—
1883	12,291,039	16.70	18.60	20.10	21.80	25.10	34.80	44.50	58.00	200	1,650	7,500
1883CC	1,204,000	92.00	100.00	110	125	148	184	210	255	505	1,450	—
1883O	8,725,000	16.70	18.60	20.10	21.80	25.10	31.80	44.50	55.00	195	1,400	—
1883S	6,250,000	16.70	19.60	23.60	33.50	145	635	2,700	5,250	46,500	94,500	—
1884	14,070,875	16.70	18.60	20.10	21.80	25.10	34.80	47.50	65.50	330	4,350	7,350
1884CC	1,136,000	125	135	140	145	160	182	210	255	475	1,450	—
1884O	9,730,000	16.70	18.60	20.10	21.80	25.10	32.80	44.50	55.00	180	1,000	—
1884S	3,200,000	16.70	19.10	22.10	43.00	310	6,150	30,500	110,000	235,000	220,000	—
1885	17,787,767	16.70	18.60	20.10	21.80	25.10	31.80	47.50	55.00	182	845	7,350
1885CC	228,000	550	565	580	595	610	630	645	695	1,275	2,400	—
1885O	9,185,000	16.70	18.60	20.10	21.80	25.10	31.80	44.50	55.00	148	1,000	—
1885S	1,497,000	21.00	28.00	40.00	64.00	125	220	305	700	1,950	42,500	—
1886	19,963,886	16.70	18.60	20.10	21.80	25.10	31.80	44.50	55.00	148	1,275	7,350
1886O	10,710,000	16.70	18.60	20.60	29.80	78.00	685	3,550	10,500	190,000	300,000	—
1886S	750,000	47.50	62.50	85.00	90.00	180	320	465	800	3,250	30,000	—
1887	20,290,710	16.70	18.60	20.10	21.80	25.10	31.80	44.50	55.00	148	1,200	7,350
1887/6	Inc. above	23.00	26.00	34.00	55.00	165	425	585	875	2,300	44,750	—
1887O	11,550,000	16.70	18.60	22.10	24.80	25.00	52.00	110	360	2,300	12,000	—
1887/6O	—	24.00	30.00	39.00	65.00	190	450	2,050	6,350	29,500	—	—
1887S	1,771,000	17.20	19.10	23.60	28.80	44.00	110	250	700	3,050	29,500	—
1888	19,183,833	16.70	18.60	20.10	21.80	25.10	34.80	44.50	55.00	186	3,000	7,500
1888O	12,150,000	16.70	18.60	20.10	22.80	26.60	34.40	48.50	68.00	715	2,850	—
1888O Hot Lips	Inc. above	55.00	125	250	600	3,000	—	—	—	—		

Date	Mintage	VG-8	F-12	VF-20	XF-40	AU-50	MS-60	MS-63	MS-64	MS-65	65DMPL	Prf-65
1888S	657,000	115	190	210	225	235	300	465	935	3,050	16,500	—
1889	21,726,811	16.70	18.60	20.10	21.80	25.10	33.80	44.50	58.00	340	4,050	7,350
1889CC	350,000	610	935	1,265	2,700	5,500	23,000	42,000	58,500	320,000	—	—
1889O	11,875,000	17.00	18.60	22.10	24.00	31.50	130	365	825	7,000	14,500	—
1889S	700,000	37.50	60.00	65.00	82.00	125	195	325	610	2,000	38,500	—

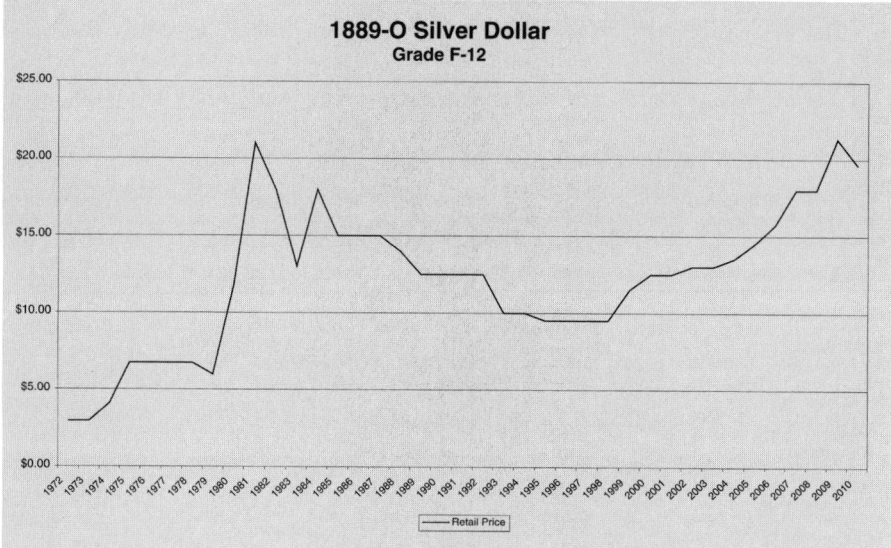

1889-O Silver Dollar
Grade F-12

Date	Mintage	VG-8	F-12	VF-20	XF-40	AU-50	MS-60	MS-63	MS-64	MS-65	65DMPL	Prf-65
1890	16,802,590	16.70	18.60	20.10	21.80	25.10	34.80	44.50	138	2,850	19,750	7,350
1890CC	2,309,041	85.00	95.00	105	140	235	450	785	1,435	5,750	15,500	—
1890CC tail bar	Inc. above	155	175	225	400	700	1,450	3,600	5,500	—	—	—
1890O	10,701,000	17.20	19.10	22.10	23.00	35.00	63.00	98.00	275	2,025	10,000	—
1890S	8,230,373	17.00	18.90	20.60	23.80	28.00	56.00	98.00	280	1,125	10,500	—
1891	8,694,206	17.20	19.60	21.10	23.80	26.00	55.00	160	885	8,250	27,500	7,350
1891CC	1,618,000	85.00	95.00	105	135	215	350	685	1,165	4,650	34,500	—
1891CC Spitting Eagle	Inc. above	105	115	135	185	260	425	900	1,600	6,000	—	—
1891O	7,954,529	17.20	19.00	20.60	23.80	35.00	128	320	775	9,850	37,500	—
1891S	5,296,000	17.20	19.10	21.10	23.80	32.60	56.00	125	280	1,475	21,500	—
1892	1,037,245	20.20	22.60	26.10	35.00	75.00	155	400	1,050	4,850	20,500	7,500
1892CC	1,352,000	190	210	290	485	725	1,485	1,800	2,550	8,950	39,500	—
1892O	2,744,000	20.20	22.60	26.10	35.00	67.50	145	285	825	7,750	52,500	—
1892S	1,200,000	26.00	32.00	136	335	1,750	34,500	63,500	115,000	205,000	225,000	—
1893	378,792	245	250	260	300	400	700	990	2,100	7,000	66,000	7,500
1893CC	677,000	265	345	725	1,850	2,350	3,450	5,250	9,150	70,000	90,000	—
1893O	300,000	205	250	380	620	850	2,250	6,350	16,750	210,000	215,000	—
1893S	100,000	3,300	4,100	5,550	8,400	23,500	90,000	205,000	350,000	715,000	735,000	—
1894	110,972	1,425	1,485	1,550	1,650	1,825	3,650	5,975	10,600	49,000	78,000	7,500
1894O	1,723,000	55.00	57.00	59.00	92.00	310	580	3,450	11,750	63,500	61,500	—
1894S	1,260,000	62.00	65.00	110	150	510	695	1,050	1,825	5,650	26,000	—
1895 proof only	12,880	21,500	29,500	36,500	38,500	40,500	—	—	—	—	—	80,000
1895O	450,000	315	350	480	585	1,225	15,500	57,500	85,000	165,000	—	—
1895S	400,000	450	510	775	1,175	1,875	3,850	6,650	7,000	27,500	42,500	—
1896	9,967,762	16.70	18.60	20.10	21.80	25.10	34.80	45.50	58.00	185	1,450	7,350
1896O	4,900,000	17.20	19.60	21.10	29.30	155	1,450	8,350	46,000	180,000	180,000	—
1896S	5,000,000	20.20	35.00	60.00	235	895	1,775	3,450	4,850	19,500	110,000	—
1897	2,822,731	16.70	18.60	20.10	21.80	25.10	34.80	45.50	62.00	345	3,950	7,350
1897O	4,004,000	17.20	19.60	22.10	37.80	110	735	4,850	15,900	70,000	72,500	—
1897S	5,825,000	17.20	19.60	21.10	23.80	30.60	58.00	118	155	575	3,250	—
1898	5,884,735	16.70	18.60	20.10	22.30	25.10	34.80	45.50	58.00	225	1,440	7,350
1898O	4,440,000	16.70	18.60	20.10	22.30	25.10	35.30	45.50	56.00	153	1,000	—
1898S	4,102,000	18.70	25.00	35.00	55.00	105	260	450	660	2,600	18,000	—
1899	330,846	170	185	215	220	248	295	310	380	990	2,850	7,350
1899O	12,290,000	16.70	18.60	20.10	21.80	25.10	34.80	44.50	62.00	190	1,550	—
1899S	2,562,000	19.20	26.00	37.50	62.50	125	320	460	775	2,075	26,000	—
1900	8,880,938	16.70	18.60	20.10	21.80	25.10	34.80	44.50	62.00	195	42,500	7,350
1900O	12,590,000	16.70	18.60	20.10	21.80	25.10	34.80	44.50	62.00	180	6,250	—
1900O/CC	Inc. above	37.50	47.50	62.50	100.00	190	285	780	990	1,900	19,000	—
1900S	3,540,000	18.70	21.00	25.00	44.00	85.00	325	420	615	1,525	38,500	—
1901	6,962,813	27.50	36.00	57.50	110	350	2,350	17,250	55,000	375,000	—	7,850

Date	Mintage	VG-8	F-12	VF-20	XF-40	AU-50	MS-60	MS-63	MS-64	MS-65	65DMPL	Prf-65
1901 doubled die reverse	Inc. above	275	450	900	2,000	3,850	—	—	—	—	—	—
1901O	13,320,000	16.70	18.60	20.10	21.80	28.10	34.80	44.50	58.00	185	10,000	—
1901S	2,284,000	17.20	21.10	31.50	48.00	220	470	715	1,050	3,400	24,500	—
1902	7,994,777	17.20	19.60	21.10	23.80	25.00	44.00	100.00	145	460	19,500	7,350
1902O	8,636,000	16.70	18.60	20.10	21.80	25.10	33.80	44.50	56.00	182	16,000	—
1902S	1,530,000	77.00	93.00	160	220	315	425	625	975	2,800	15,000	—
1903	4,652,755	48.00	50.00	52.00	58.00	60.00	75.00	85.00	100.00	285	36,850	7,350
1903O	4,450,000	325	350	375	395	400	412	455	465	685	5,950	—
1903S	1,241,000	95.00	130	215	425	1,750	3,950	6,500	7,150	11,500	40,000	—
1903S Micro S	Inc. above	135	225	450	1,150	3,000	—	—	—	—	—	—
1904	2,788,650	21.00	23.00	25.00	27.00	32.00	78.00	250	575	3,500	86,500	7,350
1904O	3,720,000	21.00	23.00	25.00	27.00	29.00	37.00	44.50	55.00	166	1,175	—
1904S	2,304,000	35.00	47.50	87.00	230	570	1,200	2,750	5,000	10,500	19,000	—
1921	44,690,000	15.00	17.30	18.80	19.60	20.60	22.30	35.00	44.00	145	11,500	—
1921D	20,345,000	15.10	17.50	19.00	19.80	20.90	43.00	57.50	155	375	10,000	—
1921S	21,695,000	15.10	17.50	19.00	19.80	20.60	43.00	69.00	135	1,350	31,000	—

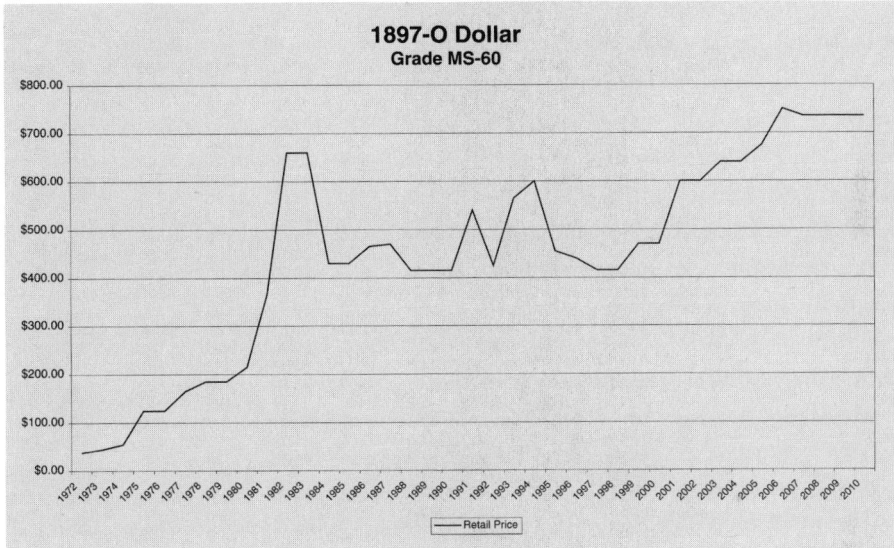

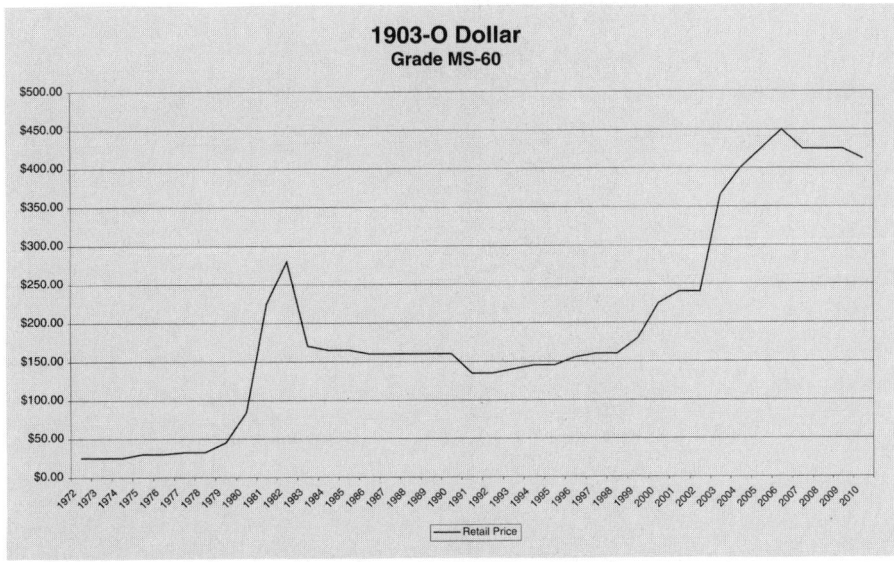

DOLLAR

Peace Dollar

Liberty Head left obverse Eagle facing right perched on rock reverse

Mint mark

KM# 150 • 26.7300 g., 0.9000 **Silver**, 0.7734 oz. ASW, 38.1 mm. • **Designer:** Anthony DeFrancisci

Date	Mintage	G-4	VG-8	F-12	VF-20	XF-40	AU-50	MS-60	MS-63	MS-64	MS-65
1921	1,006,473	100.00	125	135	140	150	170	260	440	715	1,925
1922	51,737,000	15.10	15.90	17.60	17.90	18.60	20.10	25.10	32.00	44.00	153
1922D	15,063,000	15.10	16.20	17.80	18.20	18.80	21.00	26.50	53.00	105	550
1922S	17,475,000	15.10	16.20	17.80	18.20	18.80	21.00	26.50	69.00	245	2,700
1923	30,800,000	15.10	15.90	17.60	17.90	18.60	20.10	25.10	32.00	44.00	148
1923D	6,811,000	15.10	16.20	17.80	18.20	18.80	22.00	48.50	135	280	1,250
1923S	19,020,000	15.10	16.20	17.80	18.20	18.80	21.00	28.50	74.00	355	8,500
1924	11,811,000	15.10	15.90	17.80	17.90	18.60	20.10	25.10	32.00	44.00	171
1924S	1,728,000	25.00	29.00	30.00	33.00	44.00	66.50	180	525	1,375	10,500
1925	10,198,000	15.10	15.90	17.60	17.90	18.60	20.10	23.00	32.00	44.00	160
1925S	1,610,000	16.00	19.50	21.00	25.00	29.00	46.00	75.00	205	825	27,500
1926	1,939,000	16.00	16.80	18.70	19.20	20.10	22.50	43.00	72.00	112	475
1926D	2,348,700	16.00	16.80	18.50	19.00	22.00	32.50	66.00	190	310	910
1926S	6,980,000	15.70	16.50	18.20	18.50	19.20	23.10	44.00	98.00	235	1,065
1927	848,000	25.00	29.00	32.00	33.00	38.00	50.00	70.00	185	535	3,350
1927D	1,268,900	24.00	28.00	29.50	31.00	34.00	80.00	148	345	865	5,450
1927S	866,000	24.00	28.00	29.50	32.00	35.00	80.00	148	420	1,125	10,850
1928	360,649	345	385	390	395	400	415	495	865	1,150	4,850
1928S Large S	1,632,000	30.00	36.00	40.00	46.00	54.00	90.00	220	800	2,100	29,500
1928S Small S	Inc. above	28.00	30.00	31.00	36.00	43.50	66.00	145	470	885	24,850
1934	954,057	18.20	21.50	23.50	25.50	29.00	43.50	120	215	395	725
1934D Large D	1,569,500	17.00	20.00	23.50	23.00	42.00	65.00	165	600	925	3,000
1934D Small D	Inc. above	16.00	16.80	20.50	23.50	34.50	46.00	135	385	585	1,800
1934S	1,011,000	26.00	34.50	52.00	80.00	172	475	1,800	3,850	4,850	7,750
1935	1,576,000	17.60	18.40	20.60	20.90	24.10	30.00	55.00	105	205	765
1935S 3 Rays	1,964,000	17.60	18.40	20.60	20.90	24.10	92.00	235	350	550	1,125
1935S 4 Rays	—	17.90	18.90	21.10	20.90	26.10	100.00	245	425	625	1,350

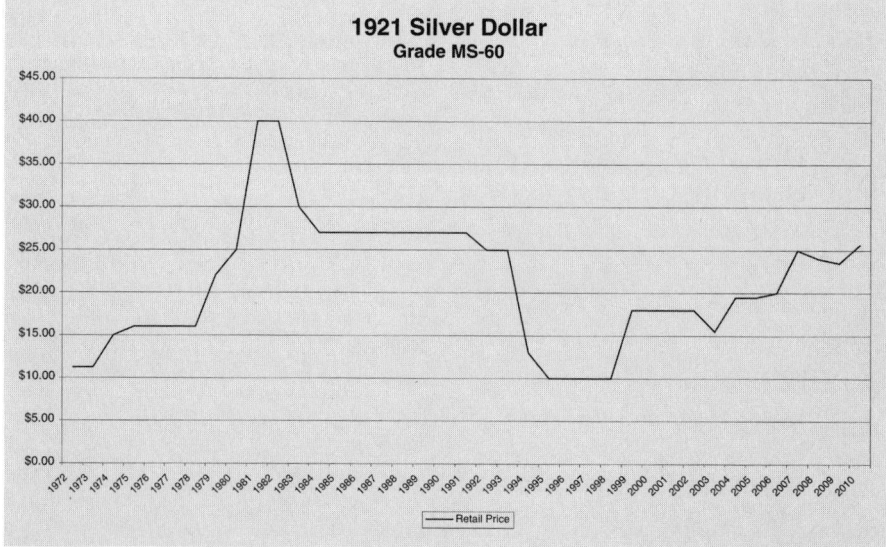

1921 Silver Dollar
Grade MS-60

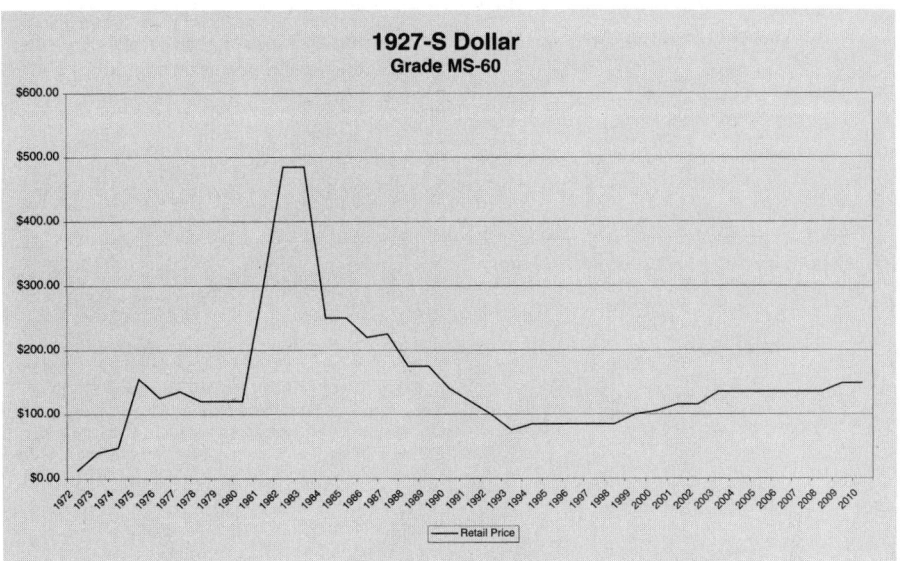

1927-S Dollar
Grade MS-60

Eisenhower Dollar

KM# 203 • 22.8000 g., **Copper-Nickel Clad Copper**, 38 mm. • **Designer:** Frank Gasparro

Date	Mintage	Proof	MS-63	Prf-65
1971	47,799,000	—	10.00	—
1971D	68,587,424	—	8.00	—
1972 Low Relief	75,890,000	—	6.50	—
1972 High Relief	Inc. above	—	175	—
1972 Modified High Relief	Inc. above	—	40.00	—
1972D	92,548,511	—	5.50	—
1973	2,000,056	—	14.00	—
1973D	2,000,000	—	15.00	—
1973S	—	(2,769,624)	—	12.00
1974	27,366,000	—	5.50	—
1974D	35,466,000	—	7.00	—
1974S	—	(2,617,350)	—	11.00

KM# 203a • 24.5900 g., 0.4000 **Silver**, 0.3162 oz. ASW, 38.1 mm. • **Designer:** Frank Gasparro

Date	Mintage	Proof	MS-63	Prf-65
1971S	—	(4,265,234)	—	11.00
1971S	6,868,530	—	7.50	—
1971S Peg Leg "R" Variety	Inc. above	—	—	17.00
1971S Partial Peg Leg "R" Variety	Inc. above	—	—	18.00
1972S	2,193,056	—	7.50	—
1972S	—	(1,811,631)	—	14.00
1973S	1,833,140	—	8.50	—
1973S	—	(1,005,617)	—	35.00
1974S	1,720,000	—	7.50	—
1974S	—	(1,306,579)	—	14.00

**Bicentennial design, moon behind
Liberty Bell reverse**

Type I	Type II
Squared "T"	Slant-top "T"

KM# 206 • 22.6800 g., **Copper-Nickel Clad
Copper**, 38.1 mm. • **Rev. Designer:** Dennis R.
Williams **Notes:** In 1976 the lettering on the reverse
was changed to thinner letters, resulting in the Type
II variety for that year. The Type I variety was
minted 1975 and dated 1976.

Date	Mintage	Proof	MS-63	Prf-65
1976 type I	117,337,000	—	9.00	—
1976 type II	Inc. above	—	5.00	—
1976D type I	103,228,274	—	6.00	—
1976D type II	Inc. above	—	5.00	—
1976S type I	— (2,909,369)	—		13.00
1976S type II	— (4,149,730)	—		9.00

**Bicentennial design, moon behind
Liberty Bell reverse**

KM# 206a • 24.5900 g., 0.4000 **Silver**, 0.3162 oz.
ASW • **Rev. Designer:** Dennis R. Williams

Date	Mintage	Proof	MS-63	Prf-65
1976S	4,908,319	—	12.50	—
1976S	— (3,998,621)	—		20.00

Regular design resumed reverse

KM# A203 • **Copper-Nickel Clad Copper**,
38.1 mm. •

Date	Mintage	Proof	MS-63	Prf-65
1977	12,596,000	—	7.00	—
1977D	32,983,006	—	7.00	—
1977S	— (3,251,152)	—		10.00
1978	25,702,000	—	5.00	—
1978D	33,012,890	—	5.00	—
1978S	— (3,127,788)	—		12.00

Susan B. Anthony Dollar

**Susan B. Anthony bust right obverse
Eagle landing on moon, symbolic of
Apollo manned moon landing reverse**

KM# 207 • 8.1000 g., **Copper-Nickel Clad
Copper**, 26.5 mm. • **Designer:** Frank Gasparro
Edge Desc: Reeded **Notes:** The 1979-S and 1981-
S Type II coins have a clearer mint mark than the
Type I varieties for those years.

Date	Mintage	MS-63	Prf-65
1979P Near date	360,222,000	70.00	—
1979P	Inc. above	2.50	—
1979D	288,015,744	3.00	—
1979S Proof, Type I	3,677,175	—	8.00
1979S Proof, Type II	Inc. above	—	110
1979S	109,576,000	3.00	—
1980P	27,610,000	3.00	—
1980D	41,628,708	3.00	—
1980S	20,422,000	3.50	—
1980S Proof	3,547,030	—	8.00
1981P	3,000,000	7.50	—
1981D	3,250,000	7.50	—
1981S	3,492,000	7.50	—
1981S Proof, Type I	4,063,083	—	8.00
1981S Proof, Type II	Inc. above	—	230
1999P	29,592,000	4.00	—
1999P Proof	Est. 750,000	—	25.00
1999D	11,776,000	4.00	—

Sacagawea Dollar

**Sacagawea bust right, with baby on back
obverse   Eagle in flight left reverse**

KM# 310 • 8.0700 g., **Copper-Zinc-Manganese-
Nickel Clad Copper**, 26.4 mm. •

Date	Mintage	MS-63	Prf-65
2000P	767,140,000	2.00	—
2000D	518,916,000	2.00	—
2000S	4,048,000	—	10.00
2001P	62,468,000	2.00	—
2001D	70,939,500	2.00	—
2001S	3,190,000	—	100.00
2002P	3,865,610	2.00	—
2002D	3,732,000	2.00	—
2002S	3,210,000	—	28.50
2003P	3,080,000	3.00	—
2003D	3,080,000	3.00	—
2003S	3,300,000	—	20.00
2004P	2,660,000	2.50	—
2004D	2,660,000	2.50	—
2004S	2,965,000	—	22.50
2005P	2,520,000	2.50	—
2005D	2,520,000	2.50	—

DOLLAR

Date	Mintage	MS-63	Prf-65
2005S	3,273,000	—	22.50
2006P	4,900,000	2.50	—
2006D	2,800,000	5.00	—
2006S	3,028,828	—	22.50
2007P	3,640,000	2.50	—
2007D	3,920,000	2.50	—
2007S	2,563,563	—	22.50
2008P	9,800,000	2.50	—
2008D	14,840,000	2.50	—
2008S	—	—	22.50

Sacagawea bust right with baby on back obverse   Native American female planting corn, beans and squash reverse

KM# 467 • Copper-Zinc-Manganese-Nickel Clad Copper •

Date	Mintage	MS-63	Prf-65
2009P	37380000	—	—
2009D	33880000	—	—
2009S	—	—	22.50

Sacagawea bust right with baby on back obverse   Hiawatha belt and bundle of five arrows reverse

KM# 474 • 8.0700 g., Copper-Zinc-Manganese-Nickel Clad Copper, 26.4 mm. •

Date	Mintage	XF-40	MS-65	Prf-65
2010P	—	—	—	—
2010D	—	—	—	—
2010S	—	—	—	—

Presidents

George Washington

KM# 401 • 8.0700 g., Copper-Zinc-Manganese-Nickel Clad Copper, 26.4 mm. • Edge Lettering:IN GOD WE TRUST date, mint mark E PLURIBUS UNUM **Notes:** Date and mint mark incuse on edge.

Date	Mintage	MS-63	MS-65	Prf-65
2007P	176,680,000	2.00	5.00	—
(2007) Plain edge error	Inc. above	75.00	—	—
2007D	163,680,000	2.00	5.00	—
2007S	3,883,103	—	—	8.00

John Adams

KM# 402 • 8.0700 g., Copper-Zinc-Manganese-Nickel Clad Copper, 26.4 mm. • Edge Lettering:IN GOD WE TRUST date, mint mark E PLURIBUS UNUM **Notes:** Date and mint mark incuse on edge.

Date	Mintage	MS-63	MS-65	Prf-65
2007P	112,420,000	2.00	5.00	—
2007P Double edge lettering	Inc. above	250	—	—
2007D	112,140,000	2.00	5.00	—
2007S	3,877,409	—	—	8.00

James Madison

KM# 404 • 8.0700 g., Copper-Zinc-Manganese-Nickel Clad Copper, 26.4 mm. • Edge Lettering:IN GOD WE TRUST date, mint mark E PLURIBUS UNUM **Notes:** Date and mint mark incuse on edge.

Date	Mintage	MS-63	MS-65	Prf-65
2007P	84,560,000	2.00	5.00	—
2007D	87,780,000	2.00	5.00	—
2007S	3,876,829	—	—	8.00

Thomas Jefferson

KM# 403 • 8.0700 g., Copper-Zinc-Manganese-Nickel Clad Copper, 26.4 mm. • Edge Lettering:IN GOD WE TRUST date, mint mark E PLURIBUS UNUM **Notes:** Date and mint mark incuse on edge.

Date	Mintage	MS-63	MS-65	Prf-65
2007P	100,800,000	2.00	5.00	—
2007D	102,810,000	2.00	5.00	—
2007S	3,877,573	—	—	8.00

Andrew Jackson

KM# 428 • 8.0700 g., **Copper-Zinc-Manganese-Nickel Clad Copper**, 26.4 mm. • **Edge Lettering:**IN GOD WE TRUST date, mint mark E PLURIBUS UNUM **Notes:** Date and mint mark incuse on edge.

Date	Mintage	MS-63	MS-65	Prf-65
2008P	61,180,000	2.00	5.00	—
2008D	61,070,000	2.00	5.00	—
2008S	3,000,000	—	—	8.00

James Monroe

KM# 426 • 8.0700 g., **Copper-Zinc-Manganese-Nickel Clad Copper**, Date and mint mark incuse on edge., 26.4 mm. • **Edge Lettering:**IN GOD WE TRUST date, mint mark E PLURIBUS UNUM

Date	Mintage	MS-63	MS-65	Prf-65
2008P	64,260,000	2.00	5.00	—
2008D	60,230,000	2.00	5.00	—
2008S	3,000,000	—	—	8.00

John Quincy Adams

KM# 427 • 8.0700 g., **Copper-Zinc-Manganese-Nickel Clad Copper**, 26.4 mm. • **Edge Lettering:**IN GOD WE TRUST date, mint mark E PLURIBUS UNUM **Notes:** Date and mint mark incuse on edge.

Date	Mintage	MS-63	MS-65	Prf-65
2008P	57,540,000	2.00	5.00	—
2008D	57,720,000	2.00	5.00	—
2008S	3,000,000	—	—	8.00

Martin van Buren

KM# 429 • 8.0700 g., **Copper-Zinc-Manganese-Nickel Clad Copper**, 26.4 mm. • **Edge Lettering:**IN GOD WE TRUST date, mint mark E PLURIBUS UNUM **Notes:** Date and mint mark incuse on edge.

Date	Mintage	MS-63	MS-65	Prf-65
2008P	51,520,000	2.00	5.00	—
2008D	50,960,000	2.00	5.00	—
2008S	3,000,000	—	—	8.00

James K. Polk

KM# 452 • 8.0700 g., **Copper-Zinc-Manganese-Nickel Clad Copper**, 26.4 mm. •

Date	Mintage	MS-63	MS-65	Prf-65
2009P	46,620,000	2.00	5.00	—
2009D	41,720,000	2.00	5.00	—
2009S	—	—	—	8.00

John Tyler

KM# 451 • 8.0700 g., **Copper-Zinc-Manganese-Nickel Clad Copper**, 26.4 mm. •

Date	Mintage	MS-63	MS-65	Prf-65
2009P	43,540,000	2.00	5.00	—
2009D	43,540,000	2.00	5.00	—
2009S	—	—	—	8.00

William Henry Harrison

KM# 450 • 8.0700 g., **Copper-Zinc-Manganese-Nickel Clad Copper**, 26.4 mm. • **Edge Lettering:**IN GOD WE TRUST date, mint mark E PLURIBUS UNUM **Notes:** Date and mint mark on edge

Date	Mintage	MS-63	MS-65	Prf-65
2009P	43,260,000	2.00	5.00	—
2009D	55,160,000	2.00	5.00	—
2009S	—	—	—	8.00

Zachary Taylor

KM# 453 • 8.0700 g., **Copper-Zinc-Manganese-Nickel Clad Copper**, 26.4 mm. •

Date	Mintage	MS-63	MS-65	Prf-65
2009P	41,580,000	2.00	5.00	—
2009D	36,680,000	2.00	5.00	—
2009S	—	—	—	8.00

Abraham Lincoln

KM# 478 • 8.0700 g., **Copper-Zinc-Manganese-Nickel Clad Copper** •

Date	Mintage	MS-63	MS-65	Prf-65
2010P	—	—	—	—
2010D	—	—	—	—
2010S	—	—	—	—

DOLLAR

Franklin Pierce

KM# 476 • 8.0700 g., **Copper-Zinc-Manganese-Nickel Clad Copper** •

Date	Mintage	MS-63	MS-65	Prf-65
2010P	—	—	—	—
2010D	—	—	—	—
2010S	—	—	—	—

Millard Filmore

KM# 475 • 8.0700 g., **Copper-Zinc-Manganese-Nickel Clad Copper** •

Date	Mintage	MS-63	MS-65	Prf-65
2010P	—	—	—	—
2010D	—	—	—	—
2010S	—	—	—	—

James Buchanan

KM# 477 • 8.0700 g., **Copper-Zinc-Manganese-Nickel Clad Copper** •

Date	Mintage	MS-63	MS-65	Prf-65
2010P	—	—	—	—
2010D	—	—	—	—
2010S	—	—	—	—

GOLD

Liberty Head - Type 1
Liberty head left within circle of stars obverse
Value, date within 3/4 wreath reverse

KM# 73 • 1.6720 g., 0.9000 **Gold**, 0.0484 oz. AGW, 13 mm. • **Rev. Legend:** UNITED STATES OF AMERICA **Designer:** James B. Longacre **Notes:** On the "closed wreath" varieties of 1849, the wreath on the reverse extends closer to the numeral 1.

Date	Mintage	F-12	VF-20	XF-40	AU-50	MS-60
1849 open wreath	688,567	120	175	220	300	650
1849 small head, no L	—	—	—	—	—	—
1849 closed wreath	Inc. above	120	160	200	215	260
1849C closed wreath	11,634	800	950	1,450	2,400	8,850
1849C open wreath	Inc. above	135,000	240,000	320,000	475,000	600,000
1849D open wreath	21,588	1,050	1,300	1,875	2,600	6,000
1849O open wreath	215,000	140	185	265	335	800
1850	481,953	120	160	200	295	260
1850C	6,966	900	1,150	1,600	2,350	9,000
1850D	8,382	1,050	1,250	1,725	2,950	12,500
1850O	14,000	200	275	390	775	3,300
1851	3,317,671	120	160	200	215	260
1851C	41,267	840	1,150	1,500	1,700	3,150
1851D	9,882	1,000	1,250	1,675	2,500	5,650
1851O	290,000	160	195	240	265	775
1852	2,045,351	120	160	200	215	260
1852C	9,434	845	1,040	1,400	1,700	5,100
1852D	6,360	1,025	1,250	1,675	2,300	10,000
1852O	140,000	130	175	260	385	1,400
1853	4,076,051	120	160	200	215	260
1853C	11,515	900	1,100	1,400	2,000	5,600
1853D	6,583	1,040	1,250	1,700	2,650	9,700
1853O	290,000	135	160	235	270	665
1854	736,709	120	160	200	215	260
1854D	2,935	1,050	1,400	2,350	6,000	13,000
1854S	14,632	260	360	525	775	2,450

Indian Head - Type 2
Indian head with headdress left obverse   Value, date within wreath reverse

KM# 83 • 1.6720 g., 0.9000 **Gold**, 0.0484 oz. AGW, 15 mm. • **Obv. Legend** UNITED STATES OF AMERICA **Designer:** James B. Longacre

Date	Mintage	F-12	VF-20	XF-40	AU-50	MS-60
1854	902,736	225	310	440	575	2,350
1855	758,269	225	310	440	575	2,350
1855C	9,803	975	1,450	3,750	11,500	33,000
1855D	1,811	3,250	4,750	9,800	22,000	48,000
1855O	55,000	345	440	600	1,500	7,800
1856S	24,600	525	820	1,325	2,500	8,650

Indian Head - Type 3
Indian head with headdress left obverse   Value, date within wreath reverse

KM# 86 • 1.6720 g., 0.9000 **Gold**, 0.0484 oz. AGW, 15 mm. • **Obv. Legend** UNITED STATES OF AMERICA **Designer:** James B. Longacre **Notes:** The 1856 varieties are distinguished by whether the 5 in the date is slanted or upright. The 1873 varieties are distinguished by the amount of space between the upper left and lower left serifs in the 3.

Date	Mintage	F-12	VF-20	XF-40	AU-50	MS-60	Prf-65
1856 upright 5	1,762,936	140	170	225	250	460	—
1856 slanted 5	Inc. above	135	160	200	215	310	55,000
1856D	1,460	2,350	3,650	5,800	8,000	32,000	—
1857	774,789	125	155	200	215	310	32,000
1857C	13,280	900	1,150	1,750	3,750	13,250	—
1857D	3,533	1,000	1,300	2,300	4,400	11,000	—
1857S	10,000	260	520	650	1,300	6,200	—
1858	117,995	125	155	200	215	310	28,500
1858D	3,477	1,025	1,250	1,600	2,850	10,000	—
1858S	10,000	300	400	575	1,450	5,350	—
1859	168,244	125	155	200	215	310	17,000
1859C	5,235	885	1,050	1,700	4,250	9,850	—
1859D	4,952	1,050	1,500	2,100	3,250	10,500	—
1859S	15,000	210	265	525	1,250	5,500	—
1860	36,668	125	155	200	215	310	16,500
1860D	1,566	2,150	2,500	4,200	7,000	13,500	—
1860S	13,000	300	380	500	750	1,650	—
1861	527,499	125	155	200	215	310	14,850
1861D mintage unrecorded	—	4,950	7,000	11,000	21,000	41,500	—
1862	1,361,390	125	155	200	215	310	15,000
1863	6,250	370	500	925	2,100	3,900	18,000
1864	5,950	290	370	475	825	1,050	18,000
1865	3,725	290	370	590	750	1,600	18,000
1866	7,130	300	385	470	685	1,025	18,000
1867	5,250	325	420	525	675	1,160	17,500
1868	10,525	265	290	415	500	1,025	19,000
1869	5,925	315	460	530	725	1,150	17,000
1870	6,335	255	290	410	500	875	16,000
1870S	3,000	300	475	785	1,250	2,650	—
1871	3,930	260	290	390	480	750	18,000
1872	3,530	260	295	400	480	975	18,500
1873 closed 3	125,125	325	425	825	950	1,650	—
1873 open 3	Inc. above	125	155	200	215	310	—
1874	198,820	125	155	200	215	310	30,000
1875	420	1,650	2,350	4,650	5,200	10,000	32,500
1876	3,245	240	300	360	475	725	16,750
1877	3,920	150	210	340	460	725	18,000
1878	3,020	195	250	365	480	675	15,500
1879	3,030	170	225	285	3,300	525	14,000
1880	1,636	150	180	215	245	425	14,000
1881	7,707	150	180	215	245	410	11,500
1882	5,125	160	185	215	245	410	10,500
1883	11,007	150	175	215	245	410	11,000
1884	6,236	150	175	215	245	410	10,000
1885	12,261	150	175	215	245	410	10,000
1886	6,016	150	175	215	245	410	10,000
1887	8,543	150	175	215	245	410	10,000
1888	16,580	150	175	215	245	410	10,000
1889	30,729	150	175	215	245	340	10,000

$2.50 (QUARTER EAGLE)

GOLD

Liberty Cap
Liberty cap on head, right, flanked by stars obverse
Heraldic eagle reverse

KM# 27 • 4.3700 g., 0.9160 **Gold**, 0.1287 oz. AGW, 20 mm. • **Obv. Legend** LIBERTY **Rev. Legend:** UNITED STATES OF AMERICA **Designer:** Robert Scot **Notes:** The 1796 "no stars" variety does not have stars on the obverse. The 1804 varieties are distinguished by the number of stars on the obverse.

Date	Mintage	F-12	VF-20	XF-40	MS-60
1796 no stars	963	55,000	71,500	100,000	245,000
1796 stars	432	26,500	32,500	65,000	185,000
1797	427	20,000	25,000	45,000	125,000
1798 close date	1,094	6,250	8,650	16,500	60,000
1798 wide date	Inc. above	5,250	7,650	15,500	57,500
1802/1	3,035	4,250	6,650	14,500	34,500
1804 13-star reverse	3,327	45,000	65,000	125,000	—
1804 14-star reverse	Inc. above	4,550	7,150	15,500	46,500
1805	1,781	4,250	6,650	14,500	37,000
1806/4	1,616	4,250	6,650	15,000	38,000
1806/5	Inc. above	6,250	8,650	21,500	95,000
1807	6,812	4,250	6,650	14,500	34,500

Turban Head
Turban on head left flanked by stars obverse
Banner above eagle reverse

KM# 40 • 4.3700 g., 0.9160 **Gold**, 0.1287 oz. AGW, 20 mm. • **Rev. Legend:** UNITED STATES OF AMERICA **Designer:** John Reich

Date	Mintage	F-12	VF-20	XF-40	MS-60
1808	2,710	26,500	36,500	54,500	175,000

Turban Head
Turban on head left within circle of stars obverse
Banner above eagle reverse

KM# 46 • 4.3700 g., 0.9160 **Gold**, 0.1287 oz. AGW, 18.5 mm. • **Rev. Legend:** UNITED STATES OF AMERICA **Designer:** John Reich

Date	Mintage	F-12	VF-20	XF-40	MS-60
1821	6,448	5,950	7,150	10,350	30,000
1824/21	2,600	5,950	7,150	10,250	29,500
1825	4,434	5,950	7,150	10,250	27,500
1826/25	760	6,450	7,900	11,000	100,000
1827	2,800	6,050	7,350	10,750	29,500

Turban Head
Turban on head left within circle of stars obverse
Banner above eagle reverse

KM# 49 • 4.3700 g., 0.9160 **Gold**, 0.1287 oz. AGW, 18.2 mm. • **Rev. Legend:** UNITED STATES OF AMERICA **Designer:** John Reich

Date	Mintage	F-12	VF-20	XF-40	MS-60
1829	3,403	5,400	6,250	7,950	18,500
1830	4,540	5,400	6,250	7,950	18,500
1831	4,520	5,400	6,250	7,950	19,000
1832	4,400	5,400	6,250	7,950	18,500
1833	4,160	5,400	6,250	7,950	19,000
1834	4,000	8,900	11,750	15,450	48,500

Classic Head
Classic head left within circle of stars obverse
No motto above eagle reverse

KM# 56 • 4.1800 g., 0.8990 **Gold**, 0.1208 oz. AGW, 18.2 mm. • **Rev. Legend:** UNITED STATES OF AMERICA **Designer:** William Kneass

Date	Mintage	VF-20	XF-40	AU-50	MS-60	MS-65
1834	112,234	475	675	965	3,300	27,000
1835	131,402	475	675	950	3,200	32,000
1836	547,986	475	675	940	3,100	29,000
1837	45,080	500	800	1,500	4,000	35,000
1838	47,030	500	625	1,100	3,200	30,000
1838C	7,880	1,700	3,000	8,000	27,000	55,000
1839	27,021	500	900	1,900	5,500	—
1839C	18,140	1,500	2,650	4,500	26,500	—
1839/8	Inc. above	—	—	—	—	—
1839D	13,674	1,750	3,450	8,000	24,000	—
1839O	17,781	700	1,100	2,500	7,250	—

Coronet Head
Coronet head left within circle of stars obverse　　No motto above eagle reverse

1848 "Cal." reverse

KM# 72 • 4.1800 g., 0.9000 **Gold**, 0.1209 oz. AGW, 18 mm. • **Rev. Legend:** UNITED STATES OF AMERICA **Designer:** Christian Gobrecht

Date	Mintage	F-12	VF-20	XF-40	AU-50	MS-60	Prf-65
1840	18,859	160	190	900	2,950	6,000	—
1840C	12,822	975	1,400	1,600	6,000	13,000	—
1840D	3,532	2,000	3,200	8,700	15,500	35,000	—
1840O	33,580	250	400	825	2,100	11,000	—
1841	—	—	48,000	85,000	96,000	—	—
1841C	10,281	750	1,500	2,000	3,500	18,500	—
1841D	4,164	950	2,100	4,750	11,000	25,000	—
1842	2,823	500	900	2,600	6,500	20,000	140,000
1842C	6,729	700	1,700	3,500	8,000	27,000	—
1842D	4,643	900	2,100	4,000	11,750	38,000	—
1842O	19,800	240	370	1,200	2,500	14,000	—
1843	100,546	160	180	450	915	3,000	140,000
1843C small date, Crosslet 4	26,064	1,500	2,400	5,500	9,000	29,000	—

Date	Mintage	F-12	VF-20	XF-40	AU-50	MS-60	Prf-65
1843C large date, Plain 4	Inc. above	800	1,600	2,200	3,500	8,800	—
1843D small date, Crosslet 4	36,209	920	1,800	2,350	3,250	10,500	—
1843O small date, Crosslet 4	288,002	165	190	250	350	1,700	—
1843O large date, Plain 4	76,000	210	260	465	1,600	8,000	—
1844	6,784	225	365	850	2,000	7,500	140,000
1844C	11,622	700	1,600	2,600	7,000	20,000	—
1844D	17,332	785	1,650	2,200	3,200	7,800	—
1845	91,051	190	250	350	600	1,275	140,000
1845D	19,460	950	1,900	2,600	3,900	15,000	—
1845O	4,000	550	1,050	2,300	9,000	20,000	—
1846	21,598	200	275	500	950	6,000	140,000
1846C	4,808	725	1,575	3,500	8,950	18,750	—
1846D	19,303	800	1,400	2,000	3,000	12,000	—
1846O	66,000	170	280	400	1,150	6,500	—
1847	29,814	140	220	360	825	3,800	—
1847C	23,226	900	1,800	2,300	3,500	7,250	—
1847D	15,784	800	1,650	2,250	3,250	10,500	—
1847O	124,000	160	240	400	1,000	4,000	—
1848	7,497	315	500	850	2,400	7,000	125,000
1848 "CAL."	1,389	8,000	15,000	26,000	36,000	50,000	—
1848C	16,788	800	1,600	2,100	3,800	13,750	—
1848D	13,771	1,000	2,000	2,500	4,500	12,000	—
1849	23,294	180	275	475	1,000	2,600	—
1849C	10,220	800	1,475	2,150	5,150	23,500	—
1849D	10,945	950	2,000	2,500	4,500	18,000	—
1850	252,923	160	180	275	350	1,100	—
1850C	9,148	800	1,500	2,100	3,400	17,500	—
1850D	12,148	950	1,800	2,500	4,000	15,000	—
1850O	84,000	170	225	450	1,200	4,900	—
1851	1,372,748	145	180	200	225	325	—
1851C	14,923	900	1,750	2,300	4,800	13,000	—
1851D	11,264	950	1,700	2,600	4,200	13,000	—
1851O	148,000	160	200	220	1,000	4,650	—
1852	1,159,681	150	175	200	250	325	—
1852C	9,772	675	1,500	2,100	4,250	18,000	—
1852D	4,078	840	1,600	2,800	7,250	17,000	—
1852O	140,000	160	190	300	950	5,000	—
1853	1,404,668	150	180	200	225	350	—
1853D	3,178	950	2,100	3,400	4,900	18,000	—
1854	596,258	150	180	215	240	350	—
1854C	7,295	800	1,500	2,400	5,000	14,750	—
1854D	1,760	1,750	2,900	6,950	12,000	27,500	—
1854O	153,000	150	185	240	425	1,600	—
1854S	246	32,500	70,000	115,000	215,000	300,000	—
1855	235,480	145	180	225	250	360	—
1855C	3,677	800	1,675	3,300	6,500	25,000	—
1855D	1,123	1,750	3,250	7,500	24,000	46,000	—
1856	384,240	145	175	210	250	390	75,000
1856C	7,913	650	1,150	2,200	4,400	15,500	—
1856D	874	3,500	6,700	12,500	30,000	72,500	—
1856O	21,100	180	240	750	1,500	8,000	—
1856S	71,120	160	250	375	950	4,500	—
1857	214,130	150	190	205	230	380	75,000
1857D	2,364	875	1,750	2,900	3,850	13,000	—
1857O	34,000	155	210	350	1,100	4,600	—
1857S	69,200	160	210	340	900	5,500	—
1858	47,377	150	200	250	360	1,350	59,000
1858C	9,056	825	1,500	2,100	3,350	9,250	—
1859	39,444	150	185	265	400	1,250	61,000
1859D	2,244	1,000	1,900	3,300	4,900	20,000	—
1859S	15,200	200	350	1,000	2,800	7,000	—
1860	22,675	150	200	265	470	1,300	58,000
1860C	7,469	815	1,550	2,200	3,950	21,000	—
1860S	35,600	170	250	675	1,200	4,000	—
1861	1,283,878	150	180	210	230	325	31,500
1861S	24,000	200	400	1,000	3,700	7,400	—
1862	98,543	160	200	300	520	1,375	32,500
1862/1	Inc. above	450	950	2,000	4,000	8,000	—
1862S	8,000	500	1,000	2,100	4,500	17,000	—
1863	30	—	—	—	—	—	95,000
1863S	10,800	250	500	1,500	3,200	13,500	—
1864	2,874	2,500	5,500	8,800	21,500	37,500	27,000
1865	1,545	2,400	6,000	8,000	19,000	38,000	30,000
1865S	23,376	160	225	650	1,650	5,000	—
1866	3,110	650	1,300	3,500	6,000	11,500	25,000
1866S	38,960	180	300	650	1,600	6,250	—
1867	3,250	190	385	900	1,250	4,800	27,000
1867S	28,000	170	250	625	1,750	4,000	—
1868	3,625	170	235	400	675	1,600	27,000

$2.50 GOLD

Date	Mintage	F-12	VF-20	XF-40	AU-50	MS-60	Prf-65
1868S	34,000	150	200	300	1,100	4,000	—
1869	4,345	170	250	450	715	3,000	24,500
1869S	29,500	160	240	440	775	5,000	—
1870	4,555	290	375	550	900	4,150	33,500
1870S	16,000	270	345	465	1,000	4,900	—
1871	5,350	295	360	385	850	3,100	36,500
1871S	22,000	270	345	415	550	2,350	—
1872	3,030	305	450	800	1,250	4,650	33,500
1872S	18,000	275	340	485	1,150	4,350	—
1873 closed 3	178,025	270	330	375	395	435	42,500
1873 open 3	Inc. above	270	325	355	375	405	—
1873S	27,000	280	345	395	900	2,800	—
1874	3,940	285	345	425	850	2,250	42,500
1875	420	1,950	3,500	5,500	11,000	24,000	70,000
1875S	11,600	270	330	375	850	3,950	—
1876	4,221	285	345	675	1,250	3,350	27,500
1876S	5,000	285	345	625	1,150	2,850	—
1877	1,652	310	395	875	1,250	3,250	35,000
1877S	35,400	265	325	355	415	750	—
1878	286,260	265	320	345	370	410	35,000
1878S	178,000	265	320	345	375	415	—
1879	88,990	270	325	355	385	435	26,000
1879S	43,500	270	340	365	765	2,500	—
1880	2,996	275	345	385	750	1,400	26,000
1881	691	950	2,150	3,150	5,250	9,850	26,500
1882	4,067	270	330	375	550	1,050	23,500
1883	2,002	280	395	750	1,350	3,350	23,500
1884	2,023	275	375	440	750	1,600	23,500
1885	887	400	750	1,850	2,650	4,850	22,500
1886	4,088	275	340	375	650	1,150	23,500
1887	6,282	275	340	365	500	850	17,500
1888	16,098	270	335	365	450	520	18,000
1889	17,648	270	335	365	450	535	20,500
1890	8,813	275	340	365	500	600	18,500
1891	11,040	—	—	—	—	—	17,500
1891 DDR	Inc. above	275	335	365	475	585	—
1892	2,545	275	330	365	500	950	15,500
1893	30,106	270	330	355	375	400	15,500
1894	4,122	275	330	365	440	800	18,000
1895	6,199	265	325	355	400	525	16,750
1896	19,202	265	325	350	370	400	16,750
1897	29,904	270	325	350	370	400	16,750
1898	24,165	265	325	345	365	385	15,000
1899	27,350	265	325	345	365	385	15,000
1900	67,205	265	325	345	365	385	15,000
1901	91,322	265	325	345	365	385	15,000
1902	133,733	265	320	345	365	385	15,000
1903	201,257	265	320	345	365	385	15,000
1904	160,960	265	320	345	365	385	15,000
1905	217,944	265	320	345	365	385	15,000
1906	176,490	265	320	345	365	385	15,000
1907	336,448	265	320	345	365	385	15,000

Indian Head

KM# 128 • 4.1800 g., 0.9000 **Gold**, 0.1209 oz. AGW, 18 mm. • **Designer:** Bela Lyon Pratt

Date	Mintage	VF-20	XF-40	AU-50	MS-60	MS-63	MS-65	Prf-65
1908	565,057	225	255	285	350	1,090	4,075	25,000
1909	441,899	225	255	285	360	1,650	6,540	53,000
1910	492,682	225	255	285	350	1,550	7,500	35,000
1911	704,191	225	255	285	350	1,105	8,500	25,000
1911D D strong D	55,680	3,150	3,950	4,950	9,250	19,500	77,500	—
1911 1D weak D	Inc. above	1,150	1,950	2,850	4,950	—	—	—
1912	616,197	225	255	290	375	1,750	11,850	25,000
1913	722,165	225	255	285	350	1,030	7,500	25,000
1914	240,117	230	270	310	535	4,950	34,500	30,000
1914D	448,000	225	255	295	365	1,500	36,500	—
1915	606,100	225	255	280	350	1,065	6,500	32,500
1925D	578,000	225	255	280	340	815	3,475	—
1926	446,000	225	255	280	340	815	3,475	—
1927	388,000	225	255	280	340	815	3,475	—

Date	Mintage	VF-20	XF-40	AU-50	MS-60	MS-63	MS-65	Prf-65
1928	416,000	225	255	280	340	815	3,475	—
1929	532,000	230	265	295	370	905	7,000	—

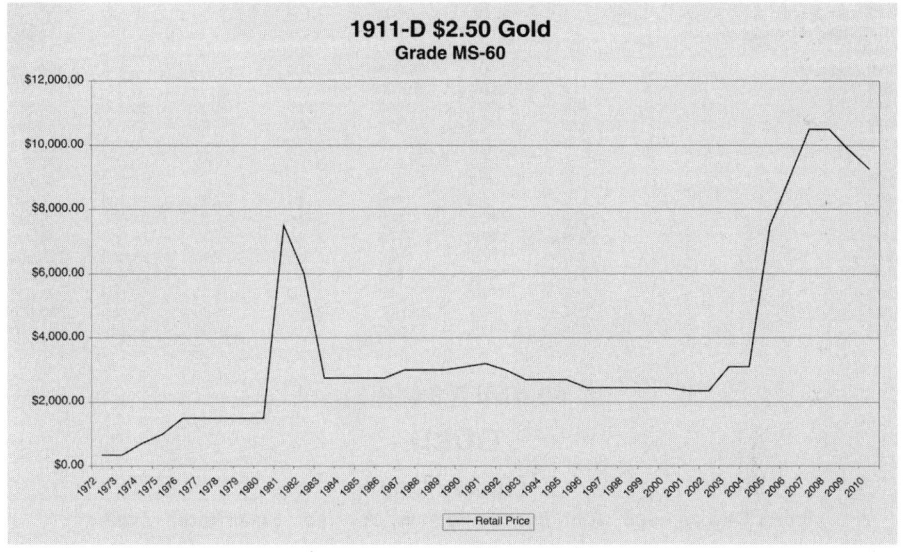

1911-D $2.50 Gold
Grade MS-60

$3

GOLD

Indian head with headdress, left obverse   Value, date within wreath reverse

KM# 84 • 5.0150 g., 0.9000 **Gold**, 0.1451 oz. AGW, 20.5 mm. • **Obv. Legend** UNITED STATES OF AMERICA **Designer:** James B. Longacre **Notes:** The 1873 "closed-3" and "open-3" varieties are distinguished by the amount of space between the upper left and lower left serifs of the 3 in the date.

Date	Mintage	VF-20	XF-40	AU-50	MS-60	MS-65	Prf-65
1854	138,618	850	1,100	2,000	3,400	18,000	125,000
1854D	1,120	8,300	15,000	29,000	65,000	—	—
1854O	24,000	1,000	2,000	4,000	20,000	—	—
1855	50,555	900	1,100	2,000	3,300	32,000	120,000
1855S	6,600	1,025	2,150	5,700	25,000	—	—
1856	26,010	880	1,100	2,150	3,500	27,000	—
1856S	34,500	900	1,500	2,350	10,000	—	—
1857	20,891	900	1,100	2,100	3,500	—	62,500
1857S	14,000	950	2,200	5,500	18,000	—	—
1858	2,133	950	1,800	3,000	9,000	—	62,500
1859	15,638	900	1,800	1,800	3,000	—	60,000
1860	7,155	900	1,600	2,000	3,600	21,000	46,000
1860S	7,000	950	2,000	7,000	17,000	—	—
1861	6,072	925	1,500	2,200	3,600	27,000	46,000
1862	5,785	925	1,850	2,200	3,600	28,000	46,500
1863	5,039	900	1,450	2,200	3,600	20,000	43,000
1864	2,680	950	1,500	2,300	3,600	29,000	42,000
1865	1,165	1,350	2,500	6,000	10,000	39,000	40,000
1866	4,030	970	1,100	2,000	3,600	27,500	42,000
1867	2,650	950	1,100	2,400	4,000	28,000	41,500
1868	4,875	740	1,100	2,100	3,000	22,000	42,000
1869	2,525	1,150	2,200	2,600	4,000	—	46,000
1870	3,535	1,000	1,500	2,400	5,000	—	47,000
1870S unique	—	—	—	—	—	—	—

Date	Mintage	VF-20	XF-40	AU-50	MS-60	MS-65	Prf-65
Note: H. W. Bass Collection. AU50, cleaned. Est. value, $1,250,000.							
1871	1,330	1,000	1,500	2,000	4,000	27,500	47,000
1872	2,030	900	1,800	2,250	3,600	—	33,000
1873 open 3, proof only	25	3,300	5,000	8,700	—	—	—
1873 closed 3, mintage unknown	—	4,000	6,000	10,000	—	—	42,000
1874	41,820	800	1,300	1,900	3,000	16,000	42,000
1875 proof only	20	20,000	28,000	47,500	—	—	175,000
1876	45	6,000	10,000	16,500	—	—	60,000
1877	1,488	1,200	2,900	5,200	12,000	60,000	43,500
1878	82,324	800	1,300	1,900	3,000	16,000	43,000
1879	3,030	850	1,300	2,000	2,650	19,000	32,000
1880	1,036	850	1,700	3,000	4,000	20,000	29,500
1881	554	1,400	2,750	5,500	8,000	24,000	25,000
1882	1,576	925	1,400	2,000	3,500	22,000	25,000
1883	989	1,000	1,600	3,500	3,600	24,000	25,000
1884	1,106	1,250	1,700	2,200	3,600	24,000	24,000
1885	910	1,300	1,800	2,850	3,900	24,000	25,000
1886	1,142	1,250	1,800	3,000	4,000	20,000	24,000
1887	6,160	900	1,300	2,000	3,000	18,000	21,000
1888	5,291	950	1,500	2,000	3,300	20,000	23,000
1889	2,429	925	1,300	1,700	3,100	18,000	22,000

$5 (HALF EAGLE)

GOLD

Liberty Cap
Liberty Cap on head, right, flanked by stars obverse   Small eagle reverse

KM# 19 • 8.7500 g., 0.9160 **Gold**, 0.2577 oz. AGW •

Date	Mintage	F-12	VF-20	XF-40	MS-60
1795	8,707	19,500	25,000	31,000	79,500
1796/95	6,196	20,500	25,350	32,750	84,500
1797 15 obverse stars	Inc. above	23,000	27,500	42,250	—
1797 16 obverse stars	Inc. above	21,000	25,850	41,000	210,000
1798	—	112,000	185,000	350,000	—

Liberty Cap
Liberty cap on head, right, flanked by stars obverse
Large Heraldic eagle reverse

KM# 28 • 8.7500 g., 0.9160 **Gold**, 0.2577 oz. AGW, 25 mm. • **Obv. Legend** LIBERTY **Rev. Legend:** UNITED STATES OF AMERICA **Designer:** Robert Scot

Date	Mintage	F-12	VF-20	XF-40	MS-60
1795	Inc. above	10,000	16,500	22,500	85,000
1797/95	3,609	10,850	17,500	24,000	155,000
1797 15 star obv.; Unique	—	—	—	—	—
Note: Smithsonian collection					
1797 16 star obv.; Unique	—	—	—	—	—
Note: Smithsonian collection					
1798 small 8	24,867	4,850	6,650	10,100	—
1798 large 8, 13-star reverse	Inc. above	4,050	5,050	8,350	33,500
1798 large 8, 14-star reverse	Inc. above	5,050	6,650	10,950	—

Date	Mintage	F-12	VF-20	XF-40	MS-60
1799 small reverse stars	7,451	3,850	4,900	11,100	21,500
1799 large reverse stars	Inc. above	3,950	4,750	14,200	31,700
1800	37,628	3,850	4,650	7,100	15,850
1802/1	53,176	3,850	4,650	7,100	15,850
1803/2	33,506	3,850	4,650	7,100	15,850
1804 small 8	30,475	3,850	4,650	7,100	15,850
1804 small 8 over large 8	Inc. above	3,950	4,850	7,600	17,850
1805	33,183	3,850	4,650	7,100	15,850
1806 pointed 6	64,093	3,850	4,650	7,100	17,750
1806 round 6	Inc. above	3,850	4,650	7,100	15,850
1807	32,488	3,850	4,650	7,100	15,850

Turban Head
Capped draped bust, left, flanked by stars obverse
Heraldic eagle reverse

KM# 38 • 8.7500 g., 0.9160 **Gold**, 0.2577 oz. AGW, 25 mm. • **Rev. Legend:** UNITED STATES OF AMERICA **Designer:** John Reich

Date	Mintage	F-12	VF-20	XF-40	MS-60
1807	51,605	3,100	3,850	5,100	13,850
1808	55,578	3,600	4,500	5,950	18,850
1808/7	Inc. above	3,100	3,850	5,100	13,850
1809/8	33,875	3,100	3,850	5,100	13,850
1810 small date, small 5	100,287	17,500	32,500	48,500	125,000
1810 small date, large 5	Inc. above	3,100	3,850	5,100	16,250
1810 large date, small 5	Inc. above	17,500	37,500	60,000	135,000
1810 large date, large 5	Inc. above	3,100	3,850	5,100	13,850
1811 small 5	99,581	3,100	3,850	5,100	13,850
1811 tall 5	Inc. above	3,100	3,850	5,100	13,850
1812	58,087	3,100	3,850	5,100	13,850

Turban Head
Capped head, left, within circle of stars obverse   Heraldic eagle reverse

KM# 43 • 8.7500 g., 0.9160 **Gold**, 0.2577 oz. AGW, 25 mm. • **Rev. Legend:** UNITED STATES OF AMERICA **Designer:** John Reich

Date	Mintage	F-12	VF-20	XF-40	MS-60
1813	95,428	3,000	3,650	5,350	11,650
1814/13	15,454	4,550	5,200	3,500	10,000
1815	635	33,500	56,500	95,000	200,000
Note: 1815, private sale, Jan. 1994, MS-61, $150,000					
1818	48,588	3,250	3,100	4,000	8,250
1818 5D over 50 Inc. Above	—	4,250	—	—	—
1818 STATES OF Inc. Above	—	3,250	3,900	5,600	—
1819 5D over 50 Inc. Above	—	—	—	—	—
1819	51,723	9,600	16,500	275,000	62,000
1820 curved-base 2, small letters	263,806	3,750	4,400	6,100	11,000
1820 curved-base 2, large letters	Inc. above	3,750	4,400	6,350	20,000
1820 square-base 2	Inc. above	3,750	4,400	6,100	14,000
1821	34,641	7,000	15,000	23,000	70,000
1822 3 known	—	2,500,000	—	5,000,000	—
Note: 1822, private sale, 1993, VF-30, $1,000,000.					
1823	14,485	2,500	3,400	5,000	16,000
1824	17,340	5,000	10,000	16,000	38,000
1825/21	29,060	5,150	9,500	12,000	38,000

Date	Mintage	F-12	VF-20	XF-40	MS-60
1825/24	Inc. above	—	—	250,000	350,000
Note: 1825/4, Bowers & Merena, March 1989, XF, $148,500.					
1826	18,069	4,000	7,500	9,300	32,000
1827	24,913	6,000	10,000	12,250	34,000
1828/7	28,029	15,000	27,500	41,000	125,000
Note: 1828/7, Bowers & Merena, June 1989, XF, $20,900.					
1828	Inc. above	6,000	13,000	21,000	7,000
1829 large planchet	57,442	15,000	27,500	50,000	135,000
Note: 1829 large planchet, Superior, July 1985, MS-65, $104,500.					
1829 small planchet	Inc. above	37,500	50,000	82,500	140,000
Note: 1829 small planchet, private sale, 1992 (XF-45), $89,000.					
1830 small "5D."	126,351	16,500	17,500	21,000	40,000
1830 large "5D."	Inc. above	16,500	17,500	21,000	40,000
1831	140,594	14,500	17,500	21,000	42,500
1832 curved-base 2, 12 stars	157,487	50,000	80,000	135,000	—
1832 square-base 2, 13 stars	Inc. above	16,500	27,500	44,650	70,000
1833	193,630	16,500	27,500	44,650	70,000
1834 plain 4	50,141	16,500	27,500	44,650	70,000
1834 crosslet 4	Inc. above	17,500	30,000	53,250	88,500

Classic Head
Classic head, left, within circle of stars obverse   No motto above eagle reverse

KM# 57 • 8.3600 g., 0.8990 **Gold**, 0.2416 oz. AGW, 22.5 mm. • **Rev. Legend:** UNITED STATES OF AMERICA **Designer:** William Kneass

Date	Mintage	VF-20	XF-40	AU-50	MS-60	MS-65
1834 plain 4	658,028	550	825	1,650	3,000	48,000
1834 crosslet 4	Inc. above	1,650	2,900	6,000	20,000	—
1835	371,534	550	825	1,700	3,150	—
1836	553,147	550	825	1,700	2,950	70,000
1837	207,121	550	825	1,900	3,500	75,000
1838	286,588	550	925	1,700	3,700	58,000
1838C	17,179	2,550	5,500	13,000	42,500	—
1838D	20,583	2,100	4,650	9,750	31,000	—

Coronet Head
Coronet head, left, within circle of stars obverse   No motto above eagle reverse

KM# 69 • 8.3590 g., 0.9000 **Gold**, 0.2419 oz. AGW, 21.6 mm. • **Rev. Legend:** UNITED STATES OF AMERICA **Designer:** Christian Gobrecht **Notes:** Varieties for 1843 are distinguished by the size of the numerals in the date. One 1848 variety has "Cal." incsribed on the reverse, indicating it was made from California gold. The 1873 "closed-3" and "open-3" varieties are distinguished by the amount of space between the upper left and lower left serifs in the 3 in the date.

Date	Mintage	F-12	VF-20	XF-40	MS-60	Prf-65
1839	118,143	250	275	480	4,000	—
1839/8 curved date	Inc. above	275	325	700	2,250	—
1839C	17,205	1,250	2,300	2,900	24,000	—
1839D	18,939	1,125	2,200	3,200	22,000	—
1840	137,382	295	315	360	3,700	—
1840C	18,992	1,200	2,200	3,000	26,000	—
1840D	22,896	1,200	2,200	3,000	16,000	—
1840O	40,120	305	365	875	11,000	—
1841	15,833	305	400	875	5,500	—
1841C	21,467	1,200	1,850	2,400	20,000	—
1841D	30,495	1,400	1,800	2,350	15,000	—
1841O 2 known	50	—	—	—	—	—
1842 small letters	27,578	200	345	1,100	—	—
1842 large letters	Inc. above	350	750	2,000	11,000	—

Date	Mintage	F-12	VF-20	XF-40	MS-60	Prf-65
1842C small date	28,184	4,500	10,000	23,000	110,000	—
1842C large date	Inc. above	900	1,800	2,200	18,000	—
1842D small date	59,608	1,000	2,000	2,300	15,000	—
1842D large date	Inc. above	1,400	2,350	6,500	48,000	—
1842O	16,400	550	1,000	3,400	22,000	—
1843	611,205	295	315	356	1,850	—
1843C	44,201	1,250	1,850	2,500	14,000	—
1843D	98,452	1,250	1,950	2,600	13,000	—
1843O small letters	19,075	300	660	1,700	26,000	—
1843O large letters	82,000	305	349	1,175	12,000	—
1844	340,330	295	315	356	2,000	—
1844C	23,631	1,300	1,900	3,000	24,000	—
1844D	88,982	1,500	1,950	2,400	12,000	—
1844O	364,600	329	349	375	4,700	—
1845	417,099	295	315	260	2,000	—
1845D	90,629	1,300	1,900	2,400	12,500	—
1845O	41,000	329	415	800	9,900	—
1846	395,942	295	315	330	2,400	—
1846C	12,995	1,350	1,900	3,000	24,000	—
1846D	80,294	1,250	1,800	2,400	13,000	—
1846O	58,000	329	375	1,000	11,500	—
1847	915,981	295	315	356	2,200	—
1847C	84,151	1,350	1,800	2,400	13,000	—
1847D	64,405	1,400	2,000	2,000	10,000	—
1847O	12,000	550	2,200	6,750	28,000	—
1848	260,775	295	315	275	1,500	—
1848C	64,472	1,400	1,900	2,250	19,250	—
1848D	47,465	1,450	2,000	2,350	14,500	—
1849	133,070	295	315	280	2,800	—
1849C	64,823	1,500	1,900	2,400	14,000	—
1849D	39,036	1,550	2,000	2,600	16,500	—
1850	64,491	295	300	625	4,250	—
1850C	63,591	1,350	1,850	2,300	14,000	—
1850D	43,984	1,450	1,950	2,500	33,000	—
1851	377,505	295	315	250	2,800	—
1851C	49,176	1,300	1,900	2,350	17,500	—
1851D	62,710	1,400	1,950	2,400	15,000	—
1851O	41,000	280	590	1,500	13,000	—
1852	573,901	295	315	260	1,400	—
1852C	72,574	1,350	1,900	2,450	7,750	—
1852D	91,584	1,450	2,000	2,450	13,000	—
1853	305,770	295	315	250	1,400	—
1853C	65,571	1,500	1,950	2,350	8,500	—
1853D	89,678	1,550	2,000	2,500	11,000	—
1854	160,675	295	315	260	2,000	—
1854C	39,283	1,400	1,900	2,300	14,000	—
1854D	56,413	1,400	1,875	2,200	11,500	—
1854O	46,000	325	300	525	8,250	—
1854S	268	—	—	—	—	—
Note: 1854S, Bowers & Merena, Oct. 1982, AU-55, $170,000.						
1855	117,098	295	315	250	1,800	—
1855C	39,788	1,400	1,900	2,300	16,000	—
1855D	22,432	1,500	1,950	2,400	19,000	—
1855O	11,100	315	675	2,100	20,000	—
1855S	61,000	325	390	1,000	15,500	—
1856	197,990	295	315	356	2,850	—
1856C	28,457	1,450	1,875	2,400	20,000	—
1856D	19,786	1,475	1,950	2,600	15,000	—
1856O	10,000	370	650	1,600	14,000	—
1856S	105,100	305	300	700	6,750	—
1857	98,188	295	315	260	1,600	123,500
1857C	31,360	1,400	1,900	2,500	9,500	—
1857D	17,046	1,500	2,000	2,650	14,500	—
1857O	13,000	340	640	1,400	15,000	—
1857S	87,000	305	300	700	11,000	—
1858	15,136	305	240	550	3,850	190,000
1858C	38,856	1,400	1,900	2,350	11,000	—
1858D	15,362	1,500	2,000	2,450	12,500	—
1858S	18,600	400	825	2,350	31,000	—
1859	16,814	305	325	625	7,000	—
1859C	31,847	1,400	1,900	2,450	16,000	—
1859D	10,366	1,600	2,150	2,600	16,000	—
1859S	13,220	615	1,800	4,150	30,000	—
1860	19,825	200	280	575	3,650	100,000
1860C	14,813	1,500	2,100	3,000	15,000	—
1860D	14,635	1,500	1,900	2,600	15,000	—
1860S	21,200	500	1,100	2,100	27,000	—
1861	688,150	295	315	356	1,850	100,000
1861C	6,879	1,500	2,400	3,900	25,000	—

$5 GOLD

Date	Mintage	F-12	VF-20	XF-40	MS-60	Prf-65
1861D	1,597	3,000	4,700	7,000	50,000	—
1861S	18,000	500	1,100	4,500	36,500	—
1862	4,465	400	800	1,850	20,000	96,000
1862S	9,500	1,500	3,000	6,000	62,000	—
1863	2,472	450	1,200	3,750	27,500	90,000
1863S	17,000	600	1,450	4,100	35,500	—
1864	4,220	350	650	1,850	15,000	72,000
1864S	3,888	2,300	4,750	16,000	55,000	—
1865	1,295	500	1,450	4,100	20,000	82,500
1865S	27,612	475	1,400	2,400	20,000	—
1866S	9,000	750	1,750	4,000	40,000	—

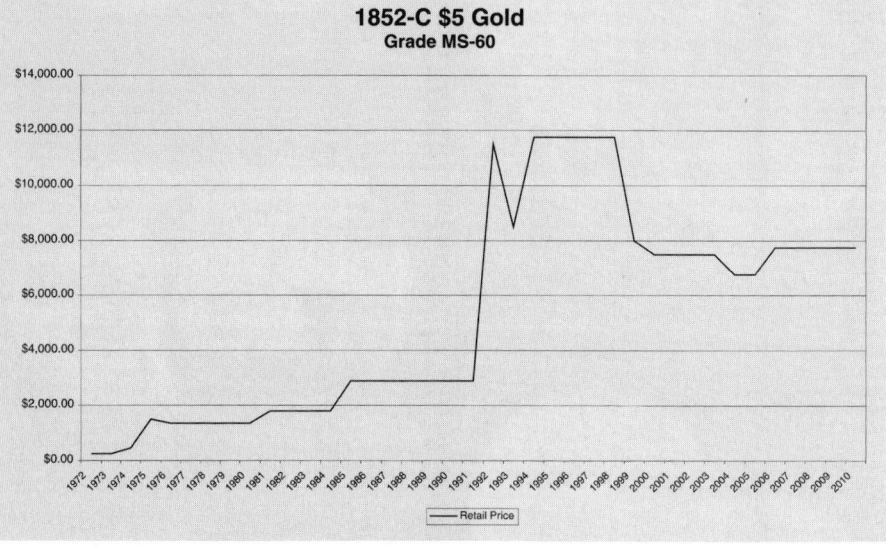

1852-C $5 Gold
Grade MS-60

Coronet Head
Coronet head, left, within circle of stars obverse
IN GOD WE TRUST above eagle reverse

KM# 101 • 8.3590 g., 0.9000 **Gold**, 0.2419 oz. AGW, 21.6 mm. • **Rev. Legend:** UNITED STATES OF AMERICA **Designer:** Christian Gobrecht

Date	Mintage	VF-20	XF-40	AU-50	MS-60	MS-63	MS-65	Prf-65
1866	6,730	750	1,650	3,500	16,500	—	—	70,000
1866S	34,920	900	2,600	8,800	25,000	—	—	—
1867	6,920	500	1,500	3,300	11,500	—	—	70,000
1867S	29,000	1,400	2,900	8,000	34,500	—	—	—
1868	5,725	650	1,000	3,500	11,500	—	—	70,000
1868S	52,000	400	1,550	4,000	20,000	—	—	—
1869	1,785	925	2,400	3,500	17,500	34,000	—	65,000
1869S	31,000	500	1,750	4,000	26,000	—	—	—
1870	4,035	800	2,000	2,850	18,000	—	—	75,000
1870CC	7,675	5,250	15,000	30,000	110,000	137,500	200,000	—
1870S	17,000	950	2,600	8,250	29,000	—	—	—
1871	3,230	900	1,700	3,300	12,500	—	—	70,000
1871CC	20,770	1,250	3,000	12,000	60,000	—	—	—
1871S	25,000	500	950	2,950	13,000	—	—	—
1872	1,690	850	1,925	3,000	15,000	18,000	—	60,000
1872CC	16,980	1,250	5,000	20,000	60,000	—	—	—
1872S	36,400	460	800	3,400	13,500	—	—	—
1873 closed 3	49,305	372	384	440	1,200	6,500	24,000	70,000
1873 open 3	63,200	367	375	350	850	3,650	—	—

Date	Mintage	VF-20	XF-40	AU-50	MS-60	MS-63	MS-65	Prf-65
1873CC	7,416	2,600	12,500	27,500	60,000	—	—	—
1873S	31,000	525	1,400	3,250	21,000	—	—	—
1874	3,508	660	1,675	2,500	13,000	26,000	—	66,000
1874CC	21,198	850	1,700	9,500	36,000	—	—	—
1874S	16,000	640	2,100	4,800	22,500	—	—	—
1875	220	34,000	45,000	60,000	190,000	—	—	185,000
1875CC	11,828	1,400	4,500	11,500	52,000	—	—	—
1875S	9,000	715	2,250	5,000	16,500	32,500	—	—
1876	1,477	1,100	2,500	4,125	11,000	14,500	55,000	60,000
1876CC	6,887	1,450	5,000	14,000	46,500	82,500	165,000	—
1876S	4,000	2,000	3,600	9,500	30,000	—	—	—
1877	1,152	900	2,750	4,000	13,750	29,000	—	75,000
1877CC	8,680	1,000	3,300	11,000	52,500	—	—	—
1877S	26,700	400	650	1,400	9,200	—	—	—
1878	131,740	369	378	422	515	2,000	—	50,000
1878CC	9,054	3,100	7,200	20,000	60,000	—	—	—
1878S	144,700	367	373	3,000	675	4,250	—	—
1879	301,950	367	373	383	485	2,000	12,000	55,000
1879CC	17,281	575	1,500	3,150	22,000	—	—	—
1879S	426,200	369	378	422	950	3,300	—	—
1880	3,166,436	362	368	378	465	840	7,500	54,000
1880CC	51,017	425	815	1,375	9,900	—	—	—
1880S	1,348,900	362	368	378	235	800	5,750	—
1881	5,708,802	362	368	378	465	775	4,800	54,000
1881/80	Inc. above	330	600	750	1,500	4,500	—	—
1881CC	13,886	550	1,500	7,000	22,500	60,000	—	—
1881S	969,000	362	368	378	465	775	7,150	—
1882	2,514,568	362	368	378	465	800	6,150	54,000
1882CC	82,817	415	625	900	7,500	40,000	—	—
1882S	969,000	362	368	378	475	800	4,500	—
1883	233,461	379	385	395	495	1,200	—	40,000
1883CC	12,958	460	1,100	3,200	18,000	—	—	—
1883S	83,200	379	240	315	1,000	2,950	—	—
1884	191,078	379	385	395	650	2,250	—	35,000
1884CC	16,402	550	975	3,000	17,000	—	—	—
1884S	177,000	379	385	395	345	2,000	—	—
1885	601,506	362	368	378	260	825	4,800	35,000
1885S	1,211,500	362	368	378	475	790	4,000	—
1886	388,432	362	368	378	475	1,125	5,600	44,000
1886S	3,268,000	362	368	378	475	815	4,500	—
1887	87	—	14,500	20,000	—	—	—	120,000
1887S	1,912,000	362	368	378	475	800	4,800	—
1888	18,296	377	383	300	550	1,500	—	29,000
1888S	293,900	367	373	320	1,200	4,000	—	—
1889	7,565	350	440	515	1,150	2,400	—	30,000
1890	4,328	400	475	550	2,200	6,500	—	27,000
1890CC	53,800	330	460	615	1,600	7,500	55,000	—
1891	61,413	369	378	422	605	2,000	5,400	29,000
1891CC	208,000	461	415	525	750	3,250	31,500	—
1892	753,572	362	368	378	495	1,350	7,000	30,000
1892CC	82,968	476	400	575	1,500	6,500	33,500	—
1892O	10,000	515	1,000	1,375	3,300	15,000	—	—
1892S	298,400	362	368	383	525	2,850	—	—
1893	1,528,197	362	368	378	475	1,150	3,900	34,000
1893CC	60,000	496	465	770	1,400	6,350	—	—
1893O	110,000	377	479	480	950	5,950	—	—
1893S	224,000	362	368	383	475	1,220	9,000	—
1894	957,955	362	368	378	465	1,085	2,600	35,000
1894O	16,600	379	360	570	1,300	5,500	—	—
1894S	55,900	389	375	575	2,900	10,000	—	—
1895	1,345,936	362	368	378	460	1,085	4,500	29,000
1895S	112,000	367	368	400	3,150	6,500	26,000	—
1896	59,063	362	368	383	475	1,650	4,500	30,000
1896S	155,400	369	378	422	1,150	6,000	24,500	—
1897	867,883	362	368	378	460	1,085	4,500	35,000
1897S	354,000	362	368	383	865	5,150	—	—
1898	633,495	362	368	378	465	1,085	6,000	30,000
1898S	1,397,400	362	368	378	460	1,490	—	—
1899	1,710,729	362	368	378	460	1,070	3,600	30,000
1899S	1,545,000	362	368	378	460	1,440	9,600	—
1900	1,405,730	362	368	378	460	1,070	3,600	30,000
1900S	329,000	362	368	378	465	1,440	14,000	—
1901	616,040	362	368	378	460	1,070	3,650	27,000
1901S	3,648,000	362	368	378	460	1,070	3,600	—
1902	172,562	362	368	378	460	1,070	4,400	27,000
1902S	939,000	362	368	378	460	1,070	3,600	—
1903	227,024	362	368	378	465	1,085	4,000	27,000
1903S	1,855,000	362	368	378	460	1,070	3,600	—
1904	392,136	362	368	378	460	1,070	3,600	27,000

Date	Mintage	VF-20	XF-40	AU-50	MS-60	MS-63	MS-65	Prf-65
1904S	97,000	369	378	422	885	4,000	9,600	—
1905	302,308	362	368	378	465	1,085	4,000	27,000
1905S	880,700	362	368	378	460	3,350	9,600	—
1906	348,820	362	368	378	460	1,070	3,600	26,000
1906D	320,000	362	368	378	460	1,085	3,200	—
1906S	598,000	362	368	378	465	1,370	4,400	—
1907	626,192	362	368	378	460	1,070	3,400	23,000
1907D	888,000	362	368	378	460	1,070	3,400	—
1908	421,874	362	368	383	475	1,085	3,400	—

Indian Head

KM# 129 • 8.3590 g., 0.9000 **Gold**, 0.2419 oz. AGW, 21.6 mm. • **Designer:** Bela Lyon Pratt

Date	Mintage	VF-20	XF-40	AU-50	MS-60	MS-63	MS-65	Prf-65
1908	578,012	370	382	390	515	2,400	16,000	25,500
1908D	148,000	370	382	390	515	2,400	36,500	—
1908S	82,000	445	457	485	1,275	6,000	16,750	—
1909	627,138	370	382	390	495	2,400	16,000	36,000
1909D	3,423,560	370	382	390	495	1,850	16,000	—
1909O	34,200	2,150	3,350	7,250	27,500	64,500	475,000	—
1909S	297,200	400	422	450	1,350	11,000	45,000	—
1910	604,250	370	382	390	495	2,450	16,000	37,000
1910D	193,600	370	382	390	515	4,150	39,500	—
1910S	770,200	410	437	460	975	65,000	44,000	—
1911	915,139	370	382	390	495	1,850	16,000	28,500
1911D	72,500	575	700	1,100	4,650	38,500	255,000	—
1911S	1,416,000	380	417	445	600	5,850	41,500	—
1912	790,144	370	382	390	495	1,850	16,000	28,500
1912S	392,000	415	447	535	1,675	13,500	105,000	—
1913	916,099	370	382	390	495	2,400	16,750	28,000
1913S	408,000	410	442	575	1,450	11,500	125,000	—
1914	247,125	370	382	390	515	2,550	17,000	28,500
1914D	247,000	370	382	390	515	2,450	16,000	—
1914S	263,000	415	437	485	1,375	12,850	105,000	—
1915	588,075	370	382	390	495	2,450	16,000	39,000
1915S	164,000	425	457	570	1,950	17,000	110,000	—
1916S	240,000	395	417	470	710	5,750	28,500	—
1929	662,000	7,500	10,750	11,800	14,500	31,000	50,000	—

$10 (EAGLE)

GOLD

Liberty Cap
Small eagle reverse

KM# 21 • 17.5000 g., 0.9160 **Gold**, 0.5154 oz. AGW, 33 mm. • **Designer:** Robert Scot

Date	Mintage	F-12	VF-20	XF-40	MS-60
1795 13 leaves	5,583	28,500	33,850	48,500	122,500
1795 9 leaves	Inc. above	30,000	45,000	73,500	250,000
1796	4,146	27,500	36,000	50,000	135,000
1797 small eagle	3,615	31,500	40,000	55,000	200,000

Liberty Cap
Liberty cap on head, right, flanked by stars obverse
Heraldic eagle reverse

KM# 30 • 17.5000 g., 0.9160 **Gold**, 0.5154 oz. AGW, 33 mm. • **Obv. Legend** LIBERTY **Rev. Legend:** UNITED STATES OF AMERICA **Designer:** Robert Scot

Date	Mintage	F-12	VF-20	XF-40	MS-60
1797 large eagle	10,940	9,800	12,850	21,400	58,500
1798/97CC 9 stars left, 4 right	900	13,500	19,000	34,500	127,500
1798/97 7 stars left, 6 right	842	28,500	38,500	87,500	235,000
1799 large star obv	37,449	9,350	10,750	18,200	37,500
1799 small star obv	Inc. above	9,350	10,750	18,200	37,500
1800	5,999	9,500	10,750	18,350	39,500
1801	44,344	9,250	10,900	17,400	37,500
1803 extra star	15,017	9,600	11,850	19,550	67,500
1803 large stars rev	Inc. above	9,250	11,400	17,800	37,500
1804 crosslet 4	3,757	16,500	22,750	31,500	92,500
1804 plain 4	—	—	—	—	400,000

Coronet Head
Old-style head, left, within circle of stars obverse   No motto above eagle reverse

KM# 66.1 • 16.7180 g., 0.9000 **Gold**, 0.4837 oz. AGW, 27 mm. • **Rev. Legend:** UNITED STATES OF AMERICA **Designer:** Christian Gobrecht

Date	Mintage	F-12	VF-20	XF-40	MS-60	Prf-65
1838	7,200	1,750	2,650	6,850	43,500	1,500,000
1839/8 Type of 1838	25,801	1,100	1,450	5,850	28,500	1,500,000
1839 large letters	Inc. above	800	1,150	2,150	32,000	—

Coronet Head
New-style head, left, within circle of stars obverse   No motto above eagle reverse

KM# 66.2 • 16.7180 g., 0.9000 **Gold**, 0.4837 oz. AGW, 27 mm. • **Rev. Legend:** UNITED STATES OF AMERICA **Designer:** Christian Gobrecht

Date	Mintage	F-12	VF-20	XF-40	MS-60	Prf-65
1839 small letters	12,447	975	1,550	6,850	75,000	—
1840	47,338	588	603	853	11,500	—
1841	63,131	568	593	753	9,000	—
1841O	2,500	1,750	3,450	6,950	—	—
1842 small date	81,507	568	593	678	15,000	—

Date	Mintage	F-12	VF-20	XF-40	MS-60	Prf-65
1842 large date	Inc. above	568	593	668	9,500	—
1842O	27,400	568	603	983	22,500	—
1843	75,462	568	593	783	16,750	—
1843O	175,162	568	603	738	12,000	—
1844	6,361	800	1,350	3,200	16,750	—
1844O	118,700	568	603	923	15,000	—
1845	26,153	603	763	863	17,500	—
1845O	47,500	588	603	875	16,500	—
1845O repunched	Inc. above	663	963	3,850	—	—
1846	20,095	613	833	1,250	—	—
1846O	81,780	568	603	1,150	—	—
1846/5	Inc. above	663	963	1,135	—	—
1847	862,258	568	593	613	3,250	—
1847O	571,500	568	593	613	6,500	—
1848	145,484	568	593	678	5,000	—
1848O	38,850	643	783	1,850	17,750	—
1849	653,618	568	593	613	3,400	—
1849O	23,900	643	783	2,450	27,500	—
1850 large date	291,451	568	593	613	4,500	—
1850 small date	Inc. above	643	783	1,150	8,500	—
1850O	57,500	588	618	1,275	19,500	—
1851	176,328	568	593	613	5,150	—
1851O	263,000	568	603	668	6,650	—
1852	263,106	568	593	613	5,250	—
1852O	18,000	643	763	1,650	27,500	—
1853	201,253	588	603	613	3,600	—
1853/2	Inc. above	588	618	948	14,950	—
1853O	51,000	568	618	678	14,500	—

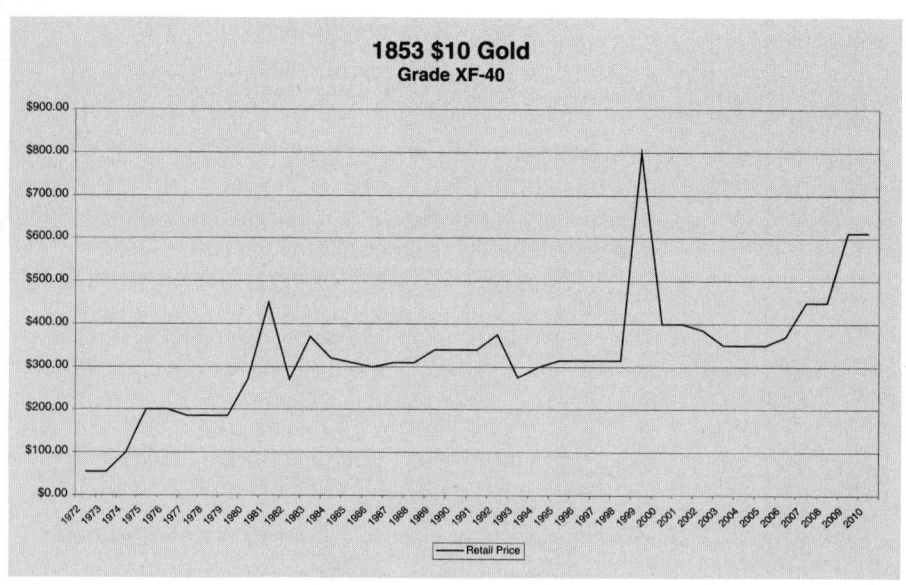

1853 $10 Gold
Grade XF-40

Date	Mintage	F-12	VF-20	XF-40	MS-60	Prf-65
1854	54,250	568	593	638	6,250	—
1854O small date	52,500	588	618	918	11,000	—
1854O large date	Inc. above	643	758	925	9,450	—
1854S	123,826	568	593	638	10,500	—
1855	121,701	568	593	613	4,750	—
1855O	18,000	588	618	2,100	28,000	—
1856	60,490	568	593	613	4,250	—
1856O	14,500	643	918	2,150	18,500	—
1856S	68,000	568	593	688	9,000	—
1857	16,606	588	618	1,050	13,500	—
1857O	5,500	743	1,800	3,650	—	—
1857S	26,000	588	603	1,050	11,500	—
1858	2,521	3,000	5,200	8,250	35,000	—
1858O	20,000	568	593	938	10,000	—
1858S	11,800	900	1,600	3,950	—	—
1859	16,093	588	618	798	10,500	—
1859O	2,300	2,000	4,250	10,500	—	—

Date	Mintage	F-12	VF-20	XF-40	MS-60	Prf-65
1859S	7,000	1,450	2,600	5,250	—	—
1860	15,105	613	658	848	8,450	175,000
1860O	11,100	633	758	1,850	13,750	—
1860S	5,000	1,400	2,950	6,400	—	—
1861	113,233	568	593	613	6,250	170,000
1861S	15,500	690	1,600	3,750	—	—
1862	10,995	643	748	1,200	—	170,000
1862S	12,500	700	2,000	3,450	—	—
1863	1,248	2,400	4,000	10,000	52,500	165,000
1863S	10,000	700	1,600	3,750	29,500	—
1864	3,580	775	1,800	4,950	18,000	165,000
1864S	2,500	2,600	5,100	17,500	—	—
1865	4,005	900	1,950	4,850	34,500	165,000
1865S	16,700	1,700	4,850	12,500	—	—
1865S over inverted 186	Inc. above	1,300	3,450	8,750	50,000	—
1866S	8,500	1,000	2,650	5,950	—	—

Coronet Head
New-style head, left, within circle of stars obverse
IN GOD WE TRUST above eagle reverse

KM# 102 • 16.7180 g., 0.9000 **Gold**, 0.4837 oz. AGW, 27 mm. • **Rev. Legend:** UNITED STATES OF
AMERICA **Designer:** Christian Gobrecht

Date	Mintage	VF-20	XF-40	AU-50	MS-60	MS-63	MS-65	Prf-65
1866	3,780	850	2,450	5,000	—	—	—	110,000
1866S	11,500	1,550	3,850	8,000	—	—	—	—
1867	3,140	1,500	2,600	5,000	33,000	—	—	—
1867S	9,000	2,350	6,650	9,850	—	—	—	—
1868	10,655	550	1,100	2,250	19,000	—	—	110,000
1868S	13,500	1,350	2,400	3,900	—	—	—	—
1869	1,855	1,550	3,000	5,650	36,000	—	—	—
1869S	6,430	1,500	2,700	6,250	25,000	—	—	—
1870	4,025	985	1,650	3,950	—	—	—	—
1870CC	5,908	13,000	30,000	52,500	—	—	—	—
1870S	8,000	1,150	2,850	7,400	33,500	—	—	—
1871	1,820	1,500	3,000	5,000	20,000	—	—	110,000
1871CC	8,085	2,600	6,400	22,500	65,000	—	—	—
1871S	16,500	1,300	2,200	6,000	30,000	—	—	—
1872	1,650	2,400	5,500	8,700	15,000	34,000	—	90,000
1872CC	4,600	2,850	9,850	24,500	—	—	—	—
1872S	17,300	675	1,175	1,900	—	—	—	—
1873 closed 3	825	4,500	9,750	17,500	55,000	—	—	—
1873CC	4,543	6,000	13,500	31,000	—	—	—	—
1873S	12,000	1,150	2,850	5,100	27,500	—	—	—
1874	53,160	559	589	599	2,100	7,250	42,500	110,000
1874CC	16,767	1,150	3,650	11,000	52,500	75,000	—	—
1874S	10,000	1,275	3,400	7,250	—	—	—	—
1875	120	40,000	67,500	80,000	—	—	—	—

Note: 1875, Akers, Aug. 1990, Proof, $115,000.

1875CC	7,715	4,250	9,850	25,000	71,500	—	—	—
1876	732	3,000	8,500	18,500	—	—	—	—
1876CC	4,696	3,600	7,750	21,500	—	—	—	—
1876S	5,000	1,300	2,950	7,500	—	—	—	—
1877	817	3,350	6,350	9,850	37,500	—	—	—
1877CC	3,332	2,400	6,750	15,000	—	—	—	—
1877S	17,000	550	1,250	2,450	33,500	—	—	—
1878	73,800	549	589	599	975	6,750	29,000	—
1878CC	3,244	3,850	10,000	19,000	—	—	—	—
1878S	26,100	589	775	2,150	16,500	29,500	—	—
1879	384,770	552	589	599	746	5,000	15,750	83,000
1879/78	Inc. above	559	601	884	1,250	2,850	—	—
1879CC	1,762	6,650	12,500	26,000	—	—	—	—
1879O	1,500	2,150	5,450	10,250	—	—	—	—
1879S	224,000	552	589	599	1,150	6,500	49,500	—
1880	1,644,876	534	551	561	601	3,650	—	—
1880CC	11,190	625	1,000	1,950	15,500	—	—	—

$10 GOLD

$10 GOLD

Date	Mintage	VF-20	XF-40	AU-50	MS-60	MS-63	MS-65	Prf-65
1880O	9,200	654	1,450	1,850	20,000	—	—	—
1880S	506,250	534	551	561	621	4,850	25,000	—
1881	3,877,260	534	551	561	601	1,015	16,500	63,000
1881CC	24,015	680	825	1,800	6,850	36,500	—	—
1881O	8,350	634	865	1,500	6,950	—	—	—
1881S	970,000	534	551	561	611	1,015	—	—
1882	2,324,480	534	551	561	601	1,015	19,500	63,000
1882CC	6,764	985	1,750	3,250	—	—	—	—
1882O	10,820	562	738	1,250	6,350	18,500	—	—
1882S	132,000	562	589	599	683	3,650	—	—
1883	208,740	534	551	561	611	3,100	—	63,000
1883CC	12,000	734	1,250	2,600	22,500	—	—	—
1883O	800	3,000	7,950	10,500	—	—	—	—
1883S	38,000	562	589	599	1,275	10,500	23,500	—
1884	76,905	562	589	599	781	5,100	15,000	53,000
1884CC	9,925	754	1,450	2,350	12,850	55,000	—	—
1884S	124,250	534	551	561	696	6,500	—	—
1885	253,527	534	551	561	601	4,850	—	53,000
1885S	228,000	534	551	561	601	4,400	—	—
1886	236,160	534	551	561	601	5,100	—	53,000
1886S	826,000	534	551	561	611	1,500	—	—
1887	53,680	562	589	599	800	4,750	—	53,000
1887S	817,000	534	551	561	611	3,500	—	—
1888	132,996	562	589	599	841	6,600	—	—
1888O	21,335	562	589	599	781	5,750	—	—
1888S	648,700	534	551	561	601	2,700	—	—
1889	4,485	592	778	1,100	2,700	—	—	53,000
1889S	425,400	534	551	561	611	1,500	18,500	—
1890	58,043	572	609	619	825	5,500	16,000	46,000
1890CC	17,500	674	771	935	3,850	18,500	—	—
1891	91,868	592	629	639	679	5,000	—	48,000
1891CC	103,732	674	731	840	1,300	7,150	—	—
1892	797,552	534	551	561	601	1,015	9,100	48,000
1892CC	40,000	674	731	825	3,800	22,500	—	—
1892O	28,688	592	589	599	659	11,000	—	—
1892S	115,500	562	613	623	663	4,500	—	—
1893	1,840,895	534	551	561	601	1,015	16,500	46,000
1893CC	14,000	674	771	1,800	8,500	—	—	—
1893O	17,000	562	589	641	881	5,300	—	—
1893S	141,350	562	589	599	639	5,250	19,500	—
1894	2,470,778	534	551	561	601	1,140	—	46,000
1894O	107,500	562	589	591	1,000	6,350	—	—
1894S	25,000	562	613	925	3,950	—	—	—
1895	567,826	534	551	561	601	1,015	17,500	43,500
1895O	98,000	562	589	611	751	8,000	—	—
1895S	49,000	562	601	675	2,400	9,500	—	—
1896	76,348	534	551	561	611	2,550	30,000	43,500
1896S	123,750	562	584	621	2,500	12,000	28,500	—
1897	1,000,159	534	551	561	601	1,140	10,000	—
1897O	42,500	562	589	599	800	5,850	27,500	—
1897S	234,750	562	584	594	870	5,750	22,500	—
1898	812,197	534	551	561	601	1,140	9,000	43,500
1898S	473,600	562	584	594	671	5,100	18,500	—
1899	1,262,305	534	551	561	601	1,015	5,950	43,500
1899O	37,047	562	589	601	781	8,450	—	—
1899S	841,000	534	551	561	611	3,650	12,850	—
1900	293,960	534	551	561	611	1,015	9,500	43,500
1900S	81,000	562	589	599	950	6,750	—	—
1901	1,718,825	534	551	561	601	1,015	5,950	43,500
1901O	72,041	562	589	599	721	3,750	12,500	—
1901S	2,812,750	534	551	561	601	1,015	6,250	—
1902	82,513	534	551	561	611	2,800	11,750	43,500
1902S	469,500	534	551	561	601	1,015	6,250	—
1903	125,926	534	551	561	611	2,450	13,500	43,500
1903O	112,771	562	589	599	711	3,250	18,000	—
1903S	538,000	534	551	561	611	1,040	5,950	—
1904	162,038	534	551	561	611	2,000	9,500	46,000
1904O	108,950	562	589	599	711	3,700	16,500	—
1905	201,078	534	551	561	601	1,450	8,500	43,500
1905S	369,250	562	584	626	1,100	5,600	22,500	—
1906	165,497	534	551	561	611	2,450	10,000	43,500
1906D	981,000	534	551	561	601	1,015	7,000	—
1906O	86,895	562	589	599	751	4,900	14,500	—
1906S	457,000	562	584	599	761	5,000	15,500	—
1907	1,203,973	534	551	561	601	1,015	5,950	43,500
1907D	1,030,000	534	551	561	611	2,250	—	—
1907S	210,500	562	584	621	801	5,450	17,000	—

Indian Head
No motto next to eagle reverse

KM# 125 • 16.7180 g., 0.9000 **Gold**, 0.4837 oz. AGW, 27 mm. • **Designer:** Augustus Saint-Gaudens
Notes: 1907 varieties are distinguished by whether the edge is rolled or wired, and whether the legend E PLURIBUS UNUM has periods between each word.

Date	Mintage	VF-20	XF-40	AU-50	MS-60	MS-63	MS-65	Prf-65
1907 wire edge, periods before and after legend	500	11,000	16,850	19,500	26,500	43,500	83,500	—
1907 same, without stars on edge, unique	—	—	—	—	—	—	—	—
1907 rolled edge, periods	42	26,000	38,500	49,000	66,500	98,500	250,000	—
1907 without periods	239,406	700	720	745	890	3,400	10,000	—
1908 without motto	33,500	685	705	730	875	4,650	14,500	—
1908D without motto	210,000	685	705	730	915	6,350	37,500	—

Indian Head
IN GOD WE TRUST left of eagle reverse

KM# 130 • 16.7180 g., 0.9000 **Gold**, 0.4837 oz. AGW, 27 mm. • **Designer:** Augustus Saint-Gaudens

Date	Mintage	VF-20	XF-40	AU-50	MS-60	MS-63	MS-65	Prf-65
1908	341,486	690	705	720	865	2,750	10,400	52,500
1908D	836,500	695	725	725	885	6,750	29,000	—
1908S	59,850	705	760	775	2,950	8,650	25,500	—
1909	184,863	690	705	720	845	3,550	16,500	54,500
1909D	121,540	695	710	725	910	6,100	34,500	—
1909S	292,350	695	710	725	910	6,350	17,500	—
1910	318,704	690	705	720	835	1,875	11,000	54,500
1910D	2,356,640	685	700	720	835	1,775	8,400	—
1910S	811,000	695	725	725	895	8,850	51,000	—
1911	505,595	685	700	715	850	1,650	9,250	52,500
1911D	30,100	755	975	1,450	5,850	25,000	122,500	—
1911S	51,000	725	730	765	1,050	9,000	17,000	—
1912	405,083	690	705	720	835	1,850	11,000	52,500
1912S	300,000	695	720	725	910	7,250	38,500	—
1913	442,071	690	705	720	835	1,700	11,500	52,500
1913S	66,000	740	745	825	4,000	28,500	100,000	—
1914	151,050	690	705	720	845	2,250	11,500	52,500
1914D	343,500	690	705	720	835	2,650	15,500	—
1914S	208,000	700	715	730	980	7,750	32,500	—
1915	351,075	690	705	720	835	2,000	12,750	55,000
1915S	59,000	740	770	775	3,150	15,250	58,500	—
1916S	138,500	725	740	755	900	6,350	20,000	—
1920S	126,500	9,800	16,500	20,000	36,500	86,000	245,000	—
1926	1,014,000	685	700	715	830	1,575	7,450	—
1932	4,463,000	685	700	715	830	1,375	7,500	—
1933	312,500	110,000	135,000	145,000	165,000	230,000	575,000	—

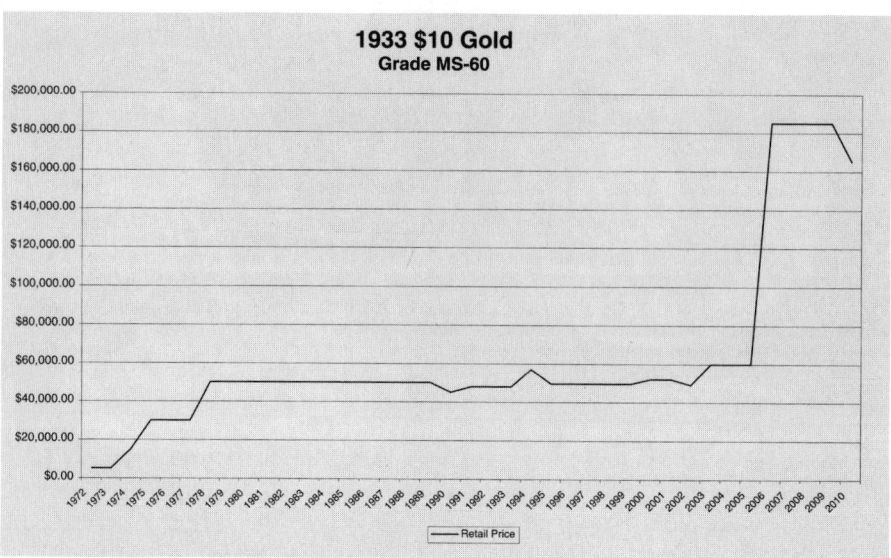

1933 $10 Gold
Grade MS-60

$20 (DOUBLE EAGLE)

GOLD

Liberty Head
Coronet head, left, within circle of stars obverse
TWENTY D. below eagle, no motto above eagle reverse

KM# 74.1 • 33.4360 g., 0.9000 **Gold**, 0.9675 oz. AGW, 34 mm. • **Rev. Legend:** UNITED STATES OF AMERICA **Designer:** James B. Longacre

Date	Mintage	VF-20	XF-40	AU-50	MS-60	MS-63	MS-65	Prf-65
1849 unique, in Smithsonian collection	1	—	—	—	—	—	—	—
1850	1,170,261	1,355	1,425	3,000	8,500	43,500	175,000	—
1850O	141,000	1,250	3,500	9,800	45,000	—	—	—
1851	2,087,155	1,395	1,555	1,805	3,850	19,500	—	—
1851O	315,000	1,470	2,255	4,250	23,000	58,500	—	—
1852	2,053,026	1,395	1,555	1,705	3,950	17,500	—	—
1852O	190,000	1,250	2,650	3,800	22,500	—	—	—
1853	1,261,326	1,395	1,555	1,555	5,000	27,500	—	—
1853/2	Inc. above	1,475	2,250	6,850	33,500	—	—	—
1853O	71,000	1,485	3,650	4,850	32,500	65,000	—	—
1854	757,899	1,395	1,555	1,855	9,250	26,500	—	—
1854	Inc. above	1,635	2,350	6,000	—	—	—	—
1854O	3,250	95,000	225,000	365,000	—	—	—	—
1854S	141,468	1,475	1,325	3,000	6,000	15,500	52,500	—
1855	364,666	1,395	1,555	1,605	8,850	66,500	—	—
1855O	8,000	3,650	19,500	24,500	110,000	—	—	—
1855S	879,675	1,375	1,555	1,805	7,200	19,500	—	—
1856	329,878	1,395	1,555	1,605	8,400	24,500	—	—

Date	Mintage	VF-20	XF-40	AU-50	MS-60	MS-63	MS-65	Prf-65
1856O	2,250	97,500	165,000	300,000	525,000	750,000	—	—
1856S	1,189,750	1,375	1,555	1,605	5,900	15,000	30,000	—
1857	439,375	1,395	1,555	1,705	3,400	26,500	—	—
1857O	30,000	1,300	2,950	6,400	31,000	115,000	—	—
1857S	970,500	1,375	1,555	1,705	4,500	7,250	12,850	—
1858	211,714	450	1,100	1,605	5,500	34,500	—	—
1858O	35,250	1,950	3,850	7,500	42,000	—	—	—
1858S	846,710	1,375	1,575	1,895	8,500	—	—	—
1859	43,597	1,450	2,450	4,400	28,000	—	—	280,000
1859O	9,100	6,400	16,500	44,000	110,000	—	—	—
1859S	636,445	1,375	1,555	1,855	5,000	35,000	—	—
1860	577,670	1,375	1,555	1,705	4,650	18,000	63,500	—
1860O	6,600	3,650	14,500	24,000	100,000	—	—	—
1860S	544,950	1,395	1,845	1,895	7,350	18,500	48,000	—
1861	2,976,453	1,375	1,555	1,680	2,900	12,850	41,500	275,000
1861O	17,741	5,650	17,500	24,000	88,000	—	—	—
1861S	768,000	1,395	1,655	2,250	10,500	31,500	—	—

Liberty
Coronet head, left, within circle of stars obverse
Paquet design, TWENTY D. below eagle reverse

KM# 93 • 33.4360 g., 0.9000 **Gold**, 0.9675 oz. AGW • **Rev. Legend:** UNITED STATES OF AMERICA
Notes: In 1861 the reverse was redesigned by Anthony C. Paquet, but it was withdrawn soon after its release. The letters in the inscriptions on the Paquet-reverse variety are taller than on the regular reverse.

Date	Mintage	VF-20	XF-40	AU-50	MS-60	MS-63	MS-65	Prf-65
1861 2 Known		—	—	—	—	—	—	—

Note: 1861 Paquet reverse, Bowers & Merena, Nov. 1988, MS-67, $660,000.

1861S	—	19,500	52,500	92,500	275,000	—	—	—

Note: Included in mintage of 1861S, KM#74.1

Liberty
Longacre design resumed reverse

KM# A74.1 • 33.4360 g., 0.9000 **Gold**, 0.9675 oz. AGW •

Date	Mintage	VF-20	XF-40	AU-50	MS-60	MS-63	MS-65	Prf-65
1862	92,133	1,375	2,250	4,900	16,500	34,000	—	250,000
1862S	854,173	1,360	1,350	2,100	12,400	36,000	—	—
1863	142,790	1,375	1,900	3,950	19,500	39,500	—	250,000
1863S	966,570	1,360	1,510	1,850	7,350	32,500	—	—
1864	204,285	1,375	1,150	2,450	14,500	40,000	—	250,000
1864S	793,660	1,360	1,490	1,950	8,600	32,000	—	—
1865	351,200	1,375	1,510	1,645	6,200	26,000	—	250,000
1865S	1,042,500	1,360	1,510	1,560	4,200	9,000	19,500	—
1866S	Inc. below	3,400	13,500	44,500	—	—	—	—

Liberty
Coronet head, left, within circle of stars obverse
TWENTY D. below eagle. IN GOD WE TRUST above eagle reverse

KM# 74.2 • 33.4360 g., 0.9000 **Gold**, 0.9675 oz. AGW, 34 mm. • **Rev. Legend:** UNITED STATES OF AMERICA **Designer:** James B. Longacre

Date	Mintage	VF-20	XF-40	AU-50	MS-60	MS-63	MS-65	Prf-65
1866	698,775	1,340	1,493	1,750	6,950	28,500	—	200,000
1866S	842,250	1,340	1,503	2,100	15,500	—	—	—
1867	251,065	1,340	1,513	1,200	3,250	30,000	—	200,000
1867S	920,750	1,340	1,503	1,900	15,000	—	—	—
1868	98,600	1,380	1,603	2,250	11,500	50,000	—	200,000
1868S	837,500	1,340	1,473	1,650	10,000	—	—	—
1869	175,155	1,350	1,463	1,600	6,800	22,750	—	210,000
1869S	686,750	1,340	1,493	1,493	7,000	45,000	—	—
1870	155,185	1,360	1,493	1,925	9,250	50,000	—	215,000
1870CC	3,789	125,000	195,000	360,000	—	—	—	—
1870S	982,000	1,340	1,448	1,495	5,450	34,000	—	—
1871	80,150	1,350	1,448	1,800	4,500	24,500	—	—
1871CC	17,387	9,500	19,500	40,000	97,500	300,000	650,000	—
1871S	928,000	1,340	1,463	1,535	4,750	22,000	—	—
1872	251,880	1,340	1,493	1,565	3,750	24,500	—	—
1872CC	26,900	2,450	5,450	8,950	38,500	—	—	—
1872S	780,000	1,340	1,493	1,540	3,250	23,500	—	—
1873 closed 3	Est. 208,925	1,340	1,553	1,600	3,350	—	—	200,000
1873 open 3	Est. 1,500,900	1,340	1,493	1,550	1,988	12,000	85,000	—
1873CC	22,410	2,900	4,750	11,750	37,500	115,000	—	—
1873S closed 3	1,040,600	1,340	1,463	1,543	2,150	20,000	—	—
1873S open 3	Inc. above	1,340	1,493	1,500	5,900	29,500	—	—
1874	366,800	1,340	1,493	1,540	1,978	19,500	—	—
1874CC	115,085	1,400	1,950	3,000	11,500	—	—	—
1874S	1,214,000	1,340	1,463	1,543	1,870	24,000	—	—
1875	295,740	1,340	1,493	1,540	1,900	13,500	—	—
1875CC	111,151	1,300	1,550	1,950	4,250	26,500	—	—
1875S	1,230,000	1,340	1,463	1,543	2,009	16,850	—	—
1876	583,905	1,340	1,483	1,543	1,275	13,500	78,500	—
1876CC	138,441	1,300	1,500	1,950	6,750	—	—	—
1876S	1,597,000	1,340	1,463	1,543	1,988	12,400	90,000	—

Liberty
Coronet head, left, within circle of stars obverse
TWENTY DOLLARS below eagle reverse

KM# 74.3 • 33.4360 g., 0.9000 **Gold**, 0.9675 oz. AGW • **Rev. Legend:** UNITED STATES OF AMERICA

Date	Mintage	VF-20	XF-40	AU-50	MS-60	MS-63	MS-65	Prf-65
1877	397,670	1,230	1,370	1,413	1,545	11,500	—	—
1877CC	42,565	1,500	1,900	3,350	19,500	—	—	—
1877S	1,735,000	1,220	1,270	1,343	1,510	15,500	—	—

Date	Mintage	VF-20	XF-40	AU-50	MS-60	MS-63	MS-65	Prf-65
1878	543,645	1,240	1,370	1,423	1,630	12,500	—	—
1878CC	13,180	2,450	3,950	8,400	30,000	—	—	—
1878S	1,739,000	1,220	1,245	1,268	1,510	20,500	—	—
1879	207,630	1,300	1,370	1,373	1,510	16,500	—	—
1879CC	10,708	3,000	4,850	8,850	34,000	77,500	—	—
1879O	2,325	12,500	21,500	32,000	75,000	127,500	—	—
1879S	1,223,800	1,220	1,245	1,268	1,750	30,000	—	—
1880	51,456	1,330	1,400	1,448	3,150	25,000	—	110,000
1880S	836,000	1,220	1,245	1,278	1,950	17,500	—	—
1881	2,260	6,800	12,500	21,500	79,000	—	—	110,000
1881S	727,000	1,220	1,245	1,278	1,610	20,000	—	—
1882	630	11,500	29,500	50,000	110,000	185,000	—	130,000
1882CC	39,140	1,350	1,750	2,200	7,950	65,000	—	—
1882S	1,125,000	1,220	1,245	1,258	1,580	18,500	—	—
1883 proof only	92	—	—	14,000	—	—	—	195,000
1883CC	59,962	1,350	1,600	2,000	5,850	30,000	—	—
1883S	1,189,000	1,220	1,245	1,268	1,510	8,500	—	—
1884 proof only	71	—	—	15,000	—	—	—	225,000
1884CC	81,139	1,250	1,550	1,900	4,250	25,000	—	—
1884S	916,000	1,220	1,245	1,268	1,450	6,150	46,500	—
1885	828	8,800	13,850	18,500	48,500	100,000	—	115,000
1885CC	9,450	2,500	3,850	6,200	21,500	48,500	—	—
1885S	683,500	1,220	1,245	1,278	1,450	5,700	29,500	—
1886	1,106	12,500	29,500	42,500	73,500	140,000	—	105,000
1887	121	—	—	26,500	—	—	—	142,500
1887S	283,000	1,220	1,245	1,268	1,510	15,000	36,500	—
1888	226,266	1,220	1,245	1,288	1,560	7,900	36,500	93,500
1888S	859,600	1,220	1,245	1,268	1,450	4,650	—	—
1889	44,111	1,380	1,500	1,613	1,900	13,500	36,500	105,000
1889CC	30,945	1,500	1,750	2,350	6,650	25,500	—	—
1889S	774,700	1,220	1,245	1,268	1,460	5,400	—	—
1890	75,995	1,220	1,270	1,343	1,510	10,000	—	100,000
1890CC	91,209	1,250	1,450	1,850	4,750	32,500	—	—
1890S	802,750	1,220	1,245	1,268	1,450	6,350	30,000	—
1891	1,442	3,500	5,750	9,500	52,000	98,500	—	108,000
1891CC	5,000	4,800	9,000	9,850	26,500	71,500	—	—
1891S	1,288,125	1,220	1,245	1,268	1,450	3,000	—	—
1892	4,523	1,350	2,250	2,650	7,400	19,500	—	90,000
1892CC	27,265	1,350	1,750	2,350	6,950	36,500	—	—
1892S	930,150	1,220	1,245	1,323	1,440	2,950	24,500	—
1893	344,339	1,220	1,265	1,333	1,480	2,100	—	95,000
1893CC	18,402	1,550	1,900	2,500	5,950	29,500	—	—
1893S	996,175	1,180	1,200	1,218	1,285	2,850	28,500	—
1894	1,368,990	1,180	1,200	1,218	1,285	1,800	26,500	85,000
1894S	1,048,550	1,180	1,200	1,218	1,285	2,450	27,500	—
1895	1,114,656	1,180	1,200	1,218	1,285	1,650	17,500	82,500
1895S	1,143,500	1,180	1,200	1,218	1,285	2,200	15,500	—
1896	792,663	1,180	1,200	1,218	1,285	1,850	19,500	200,000
1896S	1,403,925	1,180	1,200	1,218	1,285	1,975	23,500	—
1897	1,383,261	1,180	1,200	1,218	1,285	2,285	18,500	200,000
1897S	1,470,250	1,180	1,200	1,218	1,285	1,450	21,500	—
1898	170,470	1,185	1,230	1,318	1,585	4,500	—	200,000
1898S	2,575,175	1,185	1,200	1,218	1,285	1,650	7,950	—
1899	1,669,384	1,180	1,200	1,218	1,285	1,625	12,500	200,000
1899S	2,010,300	1,180	1,200	1,218	1,285	1,750	21,500	—
1900	1,874,584	1,180	1,200	1,218	1,285	2,220	7,100	200,000
1900S	2,459,500	1,180	1,200	1,218	1,285	2,100	23,000	—
1901	111,526	1,180	1,200	1,218	1,285	2,220	5,850	200,000
1901S	1,596,000	1,180	1,200	1,218	1,285	3,850	21,500	—
1902	31,254	1,180	1,395	1,478	1,695	11,750	37,500	200,000
1902S	1,753,625	1,180	1,200	1,218	1,285	2,900	23,500	—
1903	287,428	1,180	1,200	1,218	1,285	2,220	5,500	200,000
1903S	954,000	1,180	1,200	1,218	1,285	2,250	13,500	—
1904	6,256,797	1,180	1,200	1,218	1,285	2,185	5,600	200,000
1904S	5,134,175	1,180	1,200	1,218	1,285	2,185	5,400	—
1905	59,011	1,185	1,220	1,253	1,585	14,500	—	200,000
1905S	1,813,000	1,180	1,200	1,218	1,285	3,250	20,500	—
1906	69,690	1,185	1,205	1,273	1,465	6,850	26,500	200,000
1906D	620,250	1,180	1,200	1,218	1,285	3,450	22,500	—
1906S	2,065,750	1,180	1,200	1,218	1,285	2,350	19,500	—
1907	1,451,864	1,180	1,200	1,218	1,285	2,185	8,200	200,000
1907D	842,250	1,180	1,200	1,218	1,285	2,650	7,350	—
1907S	2,165,800	1,180	1,200	1,218	1,285	2,650	27,000	—

$20 GOLD

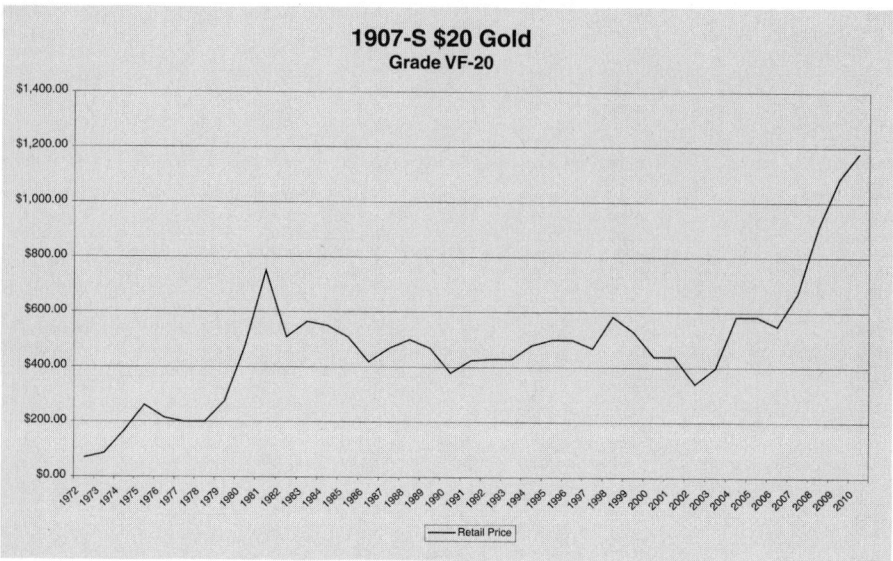

Saint-Gaudens
Roman numerals in date obverse
No motto below eagle reverse

KM# 126 • 33.4360 g., 0.9000 **Gold**, 0.9675 oz. AGW, 34 mm. • **Designer:** Augustus Saint-Gaudens
Edge Desc: Plain.

Date	Mintage	VF-20	XF-40	AU-50	MS-60	MS-63	MS-65	Prf-65
MCMVII (1907) high relief, unique, AU-55, $150,000	—	—	—	—	—	—	—	—
MCMVII (1907) high relief, wire rim	11,250	7,650	8,750	10,350	14,000	25,500	48,500	—
MCMVII (1907) high relief, flat rim	Inc. above	7,900	9,250	11,350	15,250	27,000	50,000	—

Saint-Gaudens
Arabic numerals in date obverse
No motto below eagle reverse

KM# 127 • 33.4360 g., 0.9000 **Gold**, 0.9675 oz. AGW, 34 mm. • **Designer:** Augustus Saint-Gaudens
Edge Desc: Lettered; large letters.

Date	Mintage	VF-20	XF-40	AU-50	MS-60	MS-63	MS-65	Prf-65
1907 large letters on edge, unique	—	—	—	—	—	—	—	—
1907 small letters on edge	361,667	1,423	1,443	1,476	1,510	1,860	4,600	—
1908	4,271,551	1,413	1,433	1,456	1,470	1,650	2,250	—
1908D	663,750	1,423	1,443	1,466	1,495	1,760	11,800	—

Saint-Gaudens
Roman numerals in date obverse
No motto below eagle reverse

KM# Pn1874 • 33.4360 g., 0.9000 **Gold**, 0.9675 oz. AGW, 34 mm. • **Designer:** Augustus Saint-Gaudens **Edge Desc:** Plain. **Notes:** The "Roman numerals" varieties for 1907 use Roman numerals for the date instead of Arabic numerals. The lettered-edge varieties have "E Pluribus Unum" on the edge, with stars between the words.

Date	Mintage	VF-20	XF-40	AU-50	MS-60	MS-63	MS-65	Prf-65
1907 extremely high relief, unique	—	—	—	—	—	—	—	—
1907 extremely high relief, lettered edge	—	—	—	—	—	—	—	—

Note: 1907 extremely high relief, lettered edge, Prf-68, private sale, 1990, $1,500,000.

Saint-Gaudens
IN GOD WE TRUST below eagle reverse

KM# 131 • 33.4360 g., 0.9000 **Gold**, 0.9675 oz. AGW, 34 mm. • **Designer:** Augustus Saint-Gaudens

Date	Mintage	VF-20	XF-40	AU-50	MS-60	MS-63	MS-65	Prf-65
1908	156,359	1,418	1,438	1,466	1,520	2,300	28,000	76,500
1908 Roman finish; Prf64 Rare	—							
Note: Rare								
1908D	349,500	1,423	1,443	1,476	1,510	1,780	7,000	—
1908S	22,000	2,450	3,150	4,850	10,650	24,500	52,500	—
1909/8	161,282	1,423	1,443	1,516	1,850	6,250	52,000	—
1909	Inc. above	1,433	1,463	1,486	1,570	3,150	46,000	92,500
1909D	52,500	1,463	1,483	1,611	3,100	8,950	57,500	—
1909S	2,774,925	1,423	1,443	1,476	1,490	1,735	7,000	—
1910	482,167	1,418	1,438	1,466	1,520	1,750	9,000	84,500
1910D	429,000	1,418	1,438	1,466	1,495	1,720	3,450	—
1910S	2,128,250	1,423	1,443	1,481	1,500	1,785	11,350	—
1911	197,350	1,423	1,443	1,486	1,510	2,900	23,500	76,500
1911D	846,500	1,418	1,438	1,466	1,495	1,720	2,950	—
1911S	775,750	1,418	1,438	1,466	1,500	1,720	6,850	—
1912	149,824	1,423	1,443	1,481	1,535	2,050	31,000	76,500
1913	168,838	1,423	1,443	1,481	1,540	3,250	53,500	82,500
1913D	393,500	1,418	1,438	1,466	1,495	1,800	7,850	—
1913S	34,000	1,473	1,493	1,516	2,000	4,350	36,500	—
1914	95,320	1,433	1,453	1,516	1,275	3,900	25,000	81,500
1914D	453,000	1,418	1,438	1,466	1,495	1,730	3,450	—
1914S	1,498,000	1,418	1,438	1,466	1,495	1,720	3,150	—
1915	152,050	1,423	1,443	1,476	1,500	2,650	28,000	125,000
1915S	567,500	1,418	1,438	1,466	1,495	1,720	3,000	—
1916S	796,000	1,423	1,443	1,476	1,535	1,750	3,250	—
1920	228,250	1,413	1,433	1,456	1,495	2,450	118,000	—
1920S	558,000	14,500	18,500	28,500	53,000	105,000	355,000	—
1921	528,500	35,000	43,500	56,500	125,000	300,000	975,000	—
1922	1,375,500	1,413	1,433	1,456	1,470	1,670	6,850	—
1922S	2,658,000	1,533	1,150	1,300	2,450	5,650	63,500	—
1923	566,000	1,413	1,433	1,456	1,470	1,670	8,000	—
1923D	1,702,250	1,423	1,443	1,466	1,480	1,670	2,360	—
1924	4,323,500	1,413	1,433	1,456	1,470	1,650	2,250	—
1924D	3,049,500	1,636	1,656	2,100	3,950	11,200	115,000	—
1924S	2,927,500	1,665	1,750	2,200	3,800	12,250	180,000	—

Date	Mintage	VF-20	XF-40	AU-50	MS-60	MS-63	MS-65	Prf-65
1925	2,831,750	1,413	1,433	1,456	1,470	1,650	2,250	—
1925D	2,938,500	1,588	2,100	2,375	4,450	11,500	148,000	—
1925S	3,776,500	1,900	2,850	4,850	9,850	23,500	210,000	—
1926	816,750	1,413	1,433	1,456	1,470	1,650	2,250	—
1926D	481,000	10,000	15,500	19,350	27,500	35,000	235,000	—
1926S	2,041,500	1,616	1,550	1,725	3,050	5,650	37,500	—
1927	2,946,750	1,413	1,433	1,456	1,470	1,650	2,250	—
1927D	180,000	155,000	200,000	245,000	325,000	1,500,000	1,950,000	—
1927S	3,107,000	6,850	8,850	13,250	26,750	54,000	160,000	—
1928	8,816,000	1,413	1,433	1,456	1,470	1,650	2,250	—
1929	1,779,750	10,000	13,500	15,500	19,300	38,500	112,000	—
1930S	74,000	35,000	41,000	49,500	72,500	105,000	235,000	—
1931	2,938,250	10,500	13,500	20,500	31,500	63,500	120,000	—
1931D	106,500	8,850	11,500	21,500	42,500	83,500	140,000	—
1932	1,101,750	12,500	14,500	17,850	26,500	73,500	110,000	—
1933	445,500	—	—	—	—	—	9,000,000	—

Note: Sotheby/Stack's Sale, July 2002. Thirteen known, only one currently available.

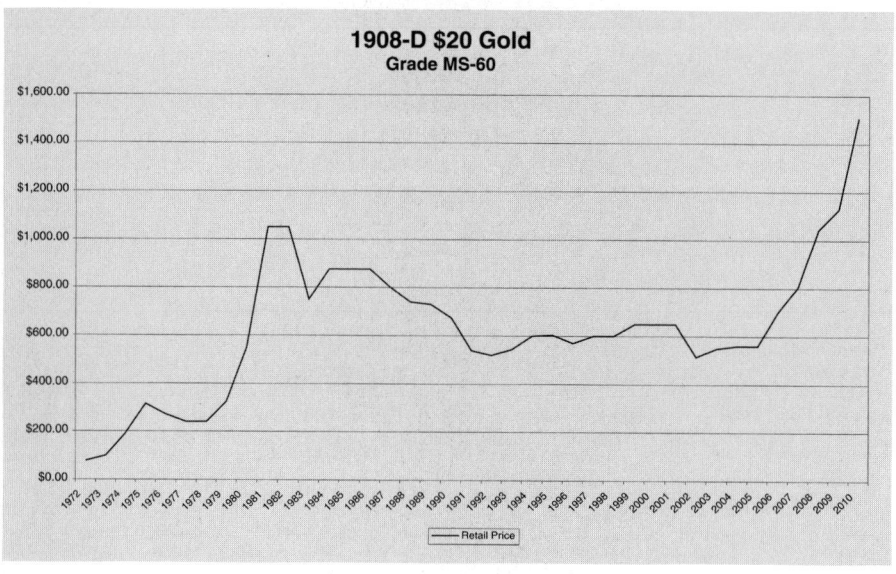

MINT SETS

Mint, or uncirculated, sets contain one uncirculated coin of each denomination from each mint produced for circulation that year. Values listed here are only for those sets sold by the U.S. Mint. Sets were not offered in years not listed. In years when the Mint did not offer the sets, some private companies compiled and marketed uncirculated sets. Mint sets from 1947 through 1958 contained two examples of each coin mounted in cardboard holders, which caused the coins to tarnish. Beginning in 1959, the sets have been packaged in sealed Pliofilm packets and include only one specimen of each coin struck for that year (both P & D mints). Listings for 1965, 1966 and 1967 are for "special mint sets," which were of higher quality than regular mint sets and were prooflike. They were packaged in plastic cases. The 1970 large-date and small-date varieties are distinguished by the size of the date on the coin. The 1976 three-piece set contains the quarter, half dollar and dollar with the Bicentennial design. The 1971 and 1972 sets do not include a dollar coin; the 1979 set does not include an S-mint-marked dollar. Mint sets issued prior to 1959 were double sets (containing two of each coin) packaged in cardboard with a paper overlay. Origional sets will always be toned and can bring large premiums if nicely preserved with good color.

Date	Sets Sold	Issue Price	Value	Date	Sets Sold	Issue Price	Value
1947 Est. 5,000	—	4.87	1,350	1977	2,006,869	7.00	7.50
1948 Est. 6,000	—	4.92	750	1978	2,162,609	7.00	6.50
1949 Est. 5,200	—	5.45	935	1979 Type I	2,526,000	8.00	4.75
1950 None issued	—	—	—	1980	2,815,066	9.00	6.50
1951	8,654	6.75	900	1981 Type I	2,908,145	11.00	12.85
1952	11,499	6.14	825	1982 & 1983 None issued	—	—	—
1953	15,538	6.14	565	1984	1,832,857	7.00	3.65
1954	25,599	6.19	265	1985	1,710,571	7.00	4.40
1955 flat pack	49,656	3.57	168	1986	1,153,536	7.00	8.75
1956	45,475	3.34	165	1987	2,890,758	7.00	5.00
1957	32,324	24.50	275	1988	1,646,204	7.00	4.50
1958	50,314	4.43	150	1989	1,987,915	7.00	4.00
1959	187,000	2.40	46.50	1990	1,809,184	7.00	4.25
1960 large date	260,485	2.40	29.50	1991	1,352,101	7.00	5.50
1961	223,704	2.40	42.00	1992	1,500,143	7.00	5.00
1962	385,285	2.40	25.00	1993	1,297,094	8.00	6.15
1963	606,612	2.40	25.00	1994	1,234,813	8.00	5.00
1964	1,008,108	2.40	27.50	1995	1,038,787	8.00	7.25
1965 Special Mint Set	2,360,000	4.00	6.25	1996	1,457,949	8.00	15.00
1966 Special Mint Set	2,261,583	4.00	5.90	1997	950,473	8.00	12.50
1967 Special Mint Set	1,863,344	4.00	9.60	1998	1,187,325	8.00	4.50
1968	2,105,128	2.50	3.85	1999 9 piece	1,421,625	14.95	11.50
1969	1,817,392	2.50	4.75	2000	1,490,160	14.95	12.75
1970 large date	2,038,134	2.50	15.00	2001	1,066,900	14.95	15.85
1970 small date	Inc. above	2.50	70.00	2002	1,139,388	14.95	21.00
1971	2,193,396	3.50	3.10	2003	1,002,555	14.95	16.75
1972	2,750,000	3.50	3.25	2004	844,484	16.95	29.00
1973	1,767,691	6.00	14.50	2005	—	16.95	9.75
1974	1,975,981	6.75	7.25	2006	—	16.95	14.00
1975	1,921,488	6.00	8.10	2007	—	—	24.50
1976 3 coins	4,908,319	9.00	16.50	2008	—	—	59.00
1976	1,892,513	6.00	6.75				

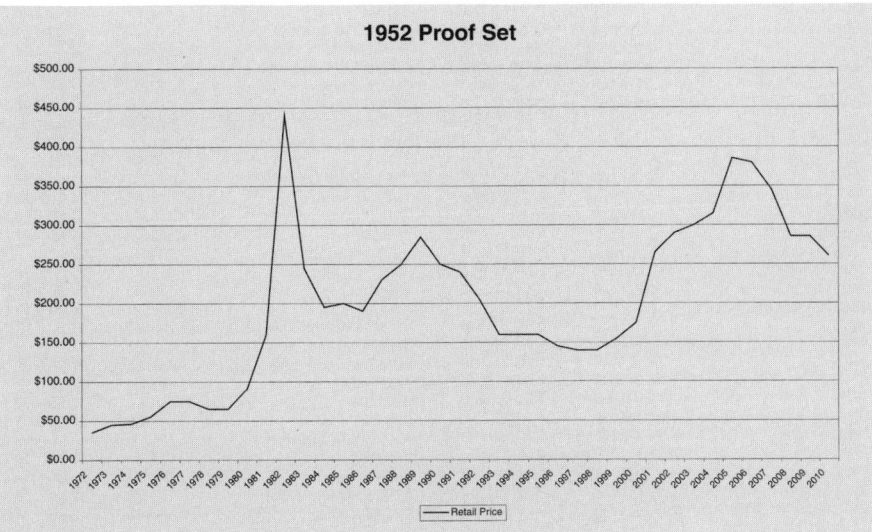

1952 Proof Set

PROOF SETS

Proof coins are produced through a special process involving specially selected, highly polished planchets and dies. They usually receive two strikings from the coin press at increased pressure. The result is a coin with mirrorlike surfaces and, in recent years, a cameo effect on its raised design surfaces. Proof sets have been sold off and on by the U.S. Mint since 1858. Listings here are for sets from what is commonly called the modern era, since 1936. Values for earlier proofs are included in regular date listings. Sets were not offered in years not listed. Since 1968, proof coins have been produced at the San Francisco Mint; before that they were produced at the Philadelphia Mint. In 1942 the five-cent coin was struck in two compositions. Some proof sets for that year contain only one type (five-coin set); others contain both types. Two types of packaging were used in 1955 -- a box and a flat, plastic holder. The 1960 large-date and small-date sets are distinguished by the size of the date on the cent. Some 1968 sets are missing the mint mark on the dime, the result of an error in the preparation of an obverse die. The 1970 large-date and small-date sets are distinguished by the size of the date on the cent. Some 1970 sets are missing the mint mark on the dime, the result of an error in the preparation of an obverse die. Some 1971 sets are missing the mint mark on the five-cent piece, the result of an error in the preparation of an obverse die. The 1976 three-piece set contains the quarter, half dollar and dollar with the Bicentennial designs. The 1979 and 1981 Type II sets have clearer mint marks than the Type I sets for those years. Some 1983 sets are missing the mint mark on the dime, the result of an error in the preparation of an obverse die. Prestige sets contain the five regular-issue coins plus a commemorative silver dollar from that year. Sets issued prior to 1956 came in transparent envelopes stapled together in a small square box. In mid 1955 sets were changed to a flat clear cellophane envelope. In 1968 sets were changed to a clear hard plastic case as they still are currently issued.

Date	Sets Sold	Issue Price	Value
1795 (2006) XPn1-XPn3	—	—	—
1836 (2006) XPn4, 10-11	—	—	—
1863 (2006) XPn12-14	—	—	—
1871 (2006) XPn15-17	—	—	—
1879 (2006) XPn18-20	—	—	—
1879 (2006) XPn21-23	—	—	—
1936	3,837	1.89	7,500
1937	5,542	1.89	4,350
1938	8,045	1.89	1,900
1939	8,795	—	1,800
1940	11,246	—	1,385
1941	15,287	—	1,450
1942 6 coins	21,120	1.89	1,475
1942 5 coins	Inc. above	1.89	1,250
1950	51,386	2.10	690
1951	57,500	2.10	625
1952	81,980	2.10	260
1953	128,800	2.10	235
1954	233,300	2.10	110
1955 box	378,200	2.10	110
1955 flat pack	Inc. above	2.10	155
1956	669,384	2.10	53.00
1957	1,247,952	2.10	24.50
1958	875,652	2.10	42.50
1959	1,149,291	2.10	23.00
1960 large date	1,691,602	2.10	20.50
1960 small date	Inc. above	2.10	33.50
1961	3,028,244	2.10	14.75
1962	3,218,019	2.10	14.75
1963	3,075,645	2.10	15.50
1964	3,950,762	2.10	14.75
1965 Special Mint Set	—	—	—
1966 Special Mint Set	—	—	—
1967 Special mint set	—	—	—
1968S	3,041,509	5.00	5.00
1968S no mint mark dime	Inc. above	5.00	16,500
1969S	2,934,631	5.00	6.00
1970S large date	2,632,810	5.00	7.25
1970S small date	Inc. above	5.00	100.00
1970S no mint mark dime	Inc. above	5.00	1,050
1971S	3,224,138	3.10	5.60
1971S no mint mark nickel Est. 1,655	1,655	5.00	1,650
1972S	3,267,667	5.50	5.50
1973S	2,769,624	7.00	6.50
1974S	2,617,350	7.00	7.25
1975S	2,909,369	7.00	8.00
1975S no mint mark dime	Inc. above	7.00	46,500
1976S 3 coins	3,998,621	13.00	16.50
1976S	4,149,730	7.00	6.65
1977S	3,251,152	9.00	5.85
1978S	3,127,788	9.00	7.50
1979S Type I	3,677,175	9.00	6.65

Date	Sets Sold	Issue Price	Value
1979S Type II	Inc. above	9.00	80.00
1980S	3,547,030	10.00	5.70
1981S Type I	4,063,083	11.00	6.15
1981S Type II	Inc. above	11.00	335
1982S	3,857,479	11.00	3.25
1983S	3,138,765	11.00	5.00
1983S Prestige Set	140,361	59.00	63.00
1983S no mint mark dime	Inc. above	11.00	950
1984S	2,748,430	11.00	5.60
1984S Prestige Set	316,680	59.00	23.50
1985S	3,362,821	11.00	4.45
1986S	2,411,180	11.00	4.95
1986S Prestige Set	599,317	48.50	23.50
1987S	3,972,233	11.00	3.75
1987S Prestige Set	435,495	45.00	21.50
1988S	3,031,287	11.00	5.00
1988S Prestige Set	231,661	45.00	25.50
1989S	3,009,107	11.00	6.65
1989S Prestige Set	211,087	45.00	34.50
1990S	2,793,433	11.00	5.25
1990S no S 1¢	3,555	11.00	5,750
1990S Prestige Set	506,126	45.00	24.50
1990S Prestige Set, no S 1¢	Inc. above	45.00	5,800
1991S	2,610,833	11.00	9.25
1991S Prestige Set	256,954	59.00	52.00
1992S	2,675,618	12.00	4.50
1992S Prestige Set	183,285	59.00	51.00
1992S Silver	1,009,585	21.00	14.50
1992S Silver premier	308,055	37.00	16.00
1993S	2,337,819	12.50	8.60
1993S Prestige Set	224,045	57.00	29.00
1993S Silver	570,213	21.00	23.50
1993S Silver premier	191,140	37.00	23.50
1994S	2,308,701	13.00	8.25
1994S Prestige Set	175,893	57.00	38.50
1994S Silver	636,009	21.00	26.50
1994S Silver premier	149,320	37.50	26.50
1995S	2,010,384	12.50	21.00
1995S Prestige Set	107,112	57.00	110
1995S Silver	549,878	21.00	72.00
1995S Silver premier	130,107	37.50	79.50
1996S	2,085,191	16.00	13.65
1996S Prestige Set	55,000	57.00	335
1996S Silver	623,655	21.00	32.50
1996S Silver premier	151,366	37.50	33.50
1997S	1,975,000	12.50	19.50
1997S Prestige Set	80,000	57.00	110
1997S Silver	605,473	21.00	53.50
1997S Silver premier	136,205	—	63.00
1998S	2,078,494	12.50	10.75
1998S Silver	638,134	21.00	20.00
1998S Silver premier	240,658	37.50	20.00
1999S 9 piece	2,557,899	19.95	36.50

Date	Sets Sold	Issue Price	Value	Date	Sets Sold	Issue Price	Value
1999S 5 quarter set	1,169,958	13.95	33.00	2005S 5 quarter set	—	15.95	8.75
1999S Silver	804,565	31.95	250	2005S Silver 11 piece	—	37.95	30.50
2000S 10 piece	3,097,442	19.95	9.85	2005S Silver 5 quarter set	—	23.95	16.00
2000S 5 quarter set	995,803	13.95	6.00	2005S American Legacy	—	—	98.00
2000S Silver	965,421	31.95	30.00	2006S 10 piece clad	—	22.95	28.50
2001S 10 piece	2,249,498	19.95	63.50	2006S 5 quarter set	—	15.95	19.00
2001S 5 quarter set	774,800	13.95	39.50	2006S Silver 10 piece	—	37.95	31.00
2001S Silver	849,600	31.95	105	2006S Silver 5 quarter set	—	23.95	19.25
2002S 10 piece	2,319,766	19.95	24.50	2007S 5 quarter set	—	13.95	15.25
2002S 5 quarter set	764,419	13.95	16.50	2007S Silver 5 quarter set	—	22.95	19.75
2002S Silver	892,229	31.95	72.00	2007S 14 piece clad	—	—	38.50
2003 X#207, 208, 209.2	—	44.00	28.75	2007S Silver 14 piece	—	—	51.00
2003S 10 piece	2,175,684	16.75	16.75	2007S Presidental $ set	—	—	20.00
2003S 5 quarter set	1,225,507	13.95	9.75	2007S American Legacy	—	—	210
2003S Silver	1,142,858	31.95	30.50	2008 14 pieces clad	—	—	92.00
2004S 11 piece	1,804,396	22.95	28.00	2008S Silver 14 piece	—	—	68.50
2004S 5 quarter set	987,960	23.95	19.25	2008S Presidental $ set	—	—	22.50
2004S Silver 11 piece	1,187,673	37.95	25.00	2008S American Legacy	—	—	145
2004S Silver 5 quarter set	594,137	—	19.25	2008S 5 quarter set	—	22.95	48.50
2005S American Legacy	—	—	88.00	2008S Silver 5 quarter set	—	—	24.50
2005S 11 piece	—	22.95	12.50				

UNCIRCULATED ROLLS

Listings are for rolls containing uncirculated coins. Large date and small date varieties for 1960 and 1970 apply to the one cent coins.

Date	Cents	Nickels	Dimes	Quarters	Halves
1934	585	3,500	2,350	1,650	2,350
1934D	2,650	4,350	2,950	9,000	—
1934S	—	—	—	—	—
1935	885	1,700	1,450	1,725	1,250
1935D	750	3,150	2,950	8,850	4,000
1935S	2,500	1,725	1,950	4,650	6,500
1936	285	1,450	885	1,300	1,750
1936D	400	1,450	1,700	—	2,750
1936S	885	1,800	1,675	6,250	3,500
1937	250	1,100	710	1,250	1,150
1937D	250	1,200	1,550	3,450	5,000
1937S	335	1,285	1,650	4,850	3,450
1938	665	535	1,100	3,100	1,850
1938D	710	485	1,000	—	—
1938S	440	355	1,350	3,250	—
1938D Buffalo	—	1,065	—	—	—
1939	180	160	630	1,040	1,250
1939D	535	3,850	610	1,875	1,975
1939S	265	2,750	1,900	3,200	2,350
1940	225	145	535	1,850	975
1940D	265	120	780	5,350	—
1940S	300	265	675	1,275	1,200
1941	170	215	430	475	750
1941D	335	330	710	2,750	1,200
1941S	360	295	535	2,450	3,000
1942	140	315	465	450	690
1942P	—	600	—	—	—
1942D	140	2,550	740	1,060	1,350
1942S	585	525	1,050	5,350	1,475
1943	60.00	275	470	365	725
1943D	170	210	610	2,000	1,775
1943S	310	325	650	2,100	1,365
1944	30.00	720	460	280	715
1944D	38.00	680	635	725	1,250
1944S	120	565	660	950	1,300
1945	125	375	410	325	730
1945D	110	315	500	1,000	1,000
1945S	80.00	270	525	575	950
1946	39.00	80.00	88.00	365	1,025
1946D	36.50	75.00	92.00	380	900
1946S	115	50.00	105	275	900
1947	220	58.00	215	735	1,000
1947D	46.50	72.00	275	385	1,000
1947S	39.00	72.00	210	415	—
1948	72.50	55.00	188	450	—
1948D	175	155	325	645	425
1948S	165	80.00	255	475	—
1949	180	330	1,200	2,350	1,300
1949D	125	215	550	1,285	1,475
1949S	140	138	2,350	—	2,250

Date	Cents	Nickels	Dimes	Quarters	Halves
1950	115	120	525	395	750
1950D	42.00	410	200	440	875
1950S	78.00	—	1,575	850	—
1951	165	230	120	435	390
1951D	26.50	285	84.00	325	800
1951S	60.00	265	690	1,350	750
1952	165	145	110	535	385
1952D	26.50	260	110	300	230
1952S	300	42.00	290	1,000	1,585
1953	42.00	24.50	120	635	490
1953D	22.50	17.00	85.00	165	260
1953S	35.00	39.00	85.00	245	850
1954	39.00	57.50	82.00	160	185
1954D	22.50	24.00	82.00	160	220
1954S	22.50	39.50	82.00	160	410
1955	24.50	19.00	83.00	170	300
1955D	19.00	7.00	82.00	185	—
1955S	27.50	—	80.00	—	—
1956	10.50	7.50	80.00	160	222
1956D	12.50	9.25	80.00	158	—
1957	10.00	12.50	80.00	156	172
1957D	9.50	4.75	85.00	158	172
1958	10.50	6.50	80.00	156	172
1958D	9.75	5.50	80.00	156	166
1959	2.50	5.00	80.00	156	168
1959D	2.10	5.25	80.00	156	210
1960 large date	1.60	4.40	80.00	195	168
1960 small date	220	—	—	—	—
1960D large date	1.60	5.00	80.00	156	175
1960D small date	2.85	—	—	—	—
1961	1.60	4.25	80.00	156	166
1961D	1.90	4.50	80.00	156	166
1962	1.65	5.25	80.00	156	170
1962D	1.65	5.50	80.00	156	165
1963	1.50	4.25	80.00	156	158
1963D	1.65	4.75	80.00	156	158
1964	1.50	3.50	80.00	156	156
1964D	1.60	3.50	80.00	156	156
1965	2.25	8.75	8.00	25.00	65.00
1966	3.75	6.00	10.00	53.00	68.00
1967	4.50	9.75	8.50	25.00	70.00
1968	1.75	—	8.50	25.00	—
1968D	1.70	6.00	9.50	33.00	68.00
1968S	1.90	6.25	—	—	—
1969	7.75	—	44.00	100.00	—
1969D	2.00	6.25	21.50	82.00	68.00
1969S	3.75	6.75	—	—	—
1970	2.10	—	8.00	26.00	—
1970D	2.10	4.00	7.75	16.00	235
1970S	3.00	4.50	—	—	—
1970S small date	2,650	—	—	—	—
1971	17.00	26.50	16.00	50.00	26.00
1971D	3.00	7.50	9.50	19.50	15.50
1971S	4.00	—	—	—	—
1972	2.00	6.50	11.00	23.00	32.00
1972D	6.00	5.75	10.00	21.50	23.00
1972S	4.75	—	—	—	—
1973	1.75	6.25	10.50	22.00	25.50
1973D	1.75	6.25	9.00	23.00	18.00
1973S	3.00	—	—	—	—
1974	1.75	4.50	7.50	18.50	15.00
1974D	1.75	5.75	7.75	17.50	21.00
1974S	3.50	—	—	—	—
1975	3.75	12.50	8.75	—	—
1975D	1.75	5.25	15.50	—	—
1976	1.75	13.50	21.00	17.50	18.00
1976D	2.50	11.00	18.00	17.50	15.50
1977	1.75	6.25	9.75	16.50	21.50
1977D	2.85	5.75	8.50	17.50	24.00
1978	3.00	4.50	7.25	16.00	32.00
1978D	10.00	5.00	8.00	16.50	46.50
1979	1.75	4.75	8.75	17.00	22.50
1979D	3.00	5.75	8.00	22.50	22.50
1980	1.75	4.25	8.00	16.50	20.50
1980D	2.50	4.50	7.50	16.50	20.50
1981	1.75	4.25	7.50	16.50	16.50
1981D	1.85	4.25	8.00	16.50	19.00
1982	25.00	325	270	250	98.00
1982D	4.00	54.00	66.00	165	80.00

Date	Cents	Nickels	Dimes	Quarters	Halves
1982 Large date	2.50	—	—	—	—
1982 Copper plated Zinc	8.00	—	—	—	—
1982 Small date, copper plated zinc	3.00	—	—	—	—
1982D Large date, copper plated zinc	35.00	—	—	—	—
1982D Small date, copper plated zinc	2.50	—	—	—	—
1983	7.50	90.00	235	945	80.00
1983D	17.50	39.00	39.00	410	120
1984	5.50	22.00	8.50	17.00	26.00
1984D	14.50	6.50	21.00	29.00	37.00
1985	4.25	10.00	9.75	31.00	76.00
1985D	9.75	8.00	9.25	22.00	44.00
1986	20.00	8.75	25.00	85.00	75.00
1986D	31.50	24.50	22.50	210	90.00
1987	6.50	6.00	7.75	15.50	52.00
1987D	13.50	4.50	8.75	15.50	52.00
1988	6.25	5.50	9.75	39.00	75.00
1988D	12.50	9.00	9.25	22.50	45.00
1989	3.25	5.50	12.00	19.50	42.00
1989D	3.50	8.75	12.50	17.00	25.00
1990	4.00	11.50	14.50	20.00	39.00
1990D	5.85	13.75	10.00	25.00	52.00
1991	2.60	12.00	10.00	29.00	37.50
1991D	11.50	12.00	11.00	31.00	33.00
1992	3.00	46.00	8.00	42.00	21.00
1992D	5.00	9.00	8.00	27.50	50.00
1993	3.25	13.50	9.50	39.00	64.00
1993D	7.50	17.50	13.00	36.00	17.00
1994	2.00	7.75	12.00	42.00	15.00
1994D	2.00	8.00	12.00	47.50	20.00
1995	1.85	10.50	16.50	45.00	17.00
1995D	2.00	20.00	19.50	53.00	40.00
1996	2.25	8.75	11.00	19.00	17.00
1996D	2.85	8.25	11.50	27.50	19.00
1997	2.75	14.50	29.00	22.50	20.00
1997D	3.35	60.00	11.00	39.00	16.50
1998	2.00	13.75	9.75	17.00	20.00
1998D	1.85	14.00	12.00	18.00	16.50
1999P	2.35	5.50	8.50	—	20.00
1999D	2.25	6.25	8.50	—	19.00
2000P	2.50	6.25	7.75	—	15.00
2000D	1.75	4.75	7.00	—	17.00
2001P	3.75	4.75	7.75	—	16.50
2001D	2.00	6.50	7.25	—	16.00
2002P	2.00	4.00	7.25	—	20.00
2002D	3.25	4.10	7.25	—	20.00
2003P	3.35	7.50	7.00	—	22.50
2003D	2.00	3.50	7.00	—	19.50
2004P Peace Medal Nickel	1.75	6.75	7.00	—	30.00
2004D Peace Medal Nickel	2.50	7.00	7.00	—	30.00
2004P Keelboat Nickel	—	4.00	—	—	—
2004D Keelboat Nickel	—	3.50	—	—	—
2005P Bison Nickel	1.75	3.25	7.00	—	21.00
2005D Bison Nickel	2.75	3.25	7.00	—	21.00
2005P Ocean in view Nickel	—	3.25	—	—	—
2005D Ocean in view Nickel	—	3.25	—	—	—
2006P	2.75	3.25	8.50	—	29.00
2006D	1.75	3.25	8.50	—	29.00
2007P	1.75	3.50	8.00	—	21.00
2007D	1.75	3.50	7.75	—	21.00
2008P	1.75	3.75	8.00	—	24.50
2008D	1.75	3.75	7.50	—	25.50
2009P Log Cabin	2.00	23.00	13.50	—	18.50
2009D Log Cabin	2.15	13.50	13.50	—	18.50
2009P Log Splitter	1.75	—	—	—	—
2009D Log Splitter	1.75	—	—	—	—
2009P Professional	—	1.75	—	—	—
2009D Professional	1.75	—	—	—	—
2009P President	2.00	—	—	—	—
2009D President	2.00	—	—	—	—
2009 DC	18.00	15.50	—	—	—
2009 Puerto Rico	15.00	15.50	—	—	—
2009 Guam	15.00	16.50	—	—	—
2009 American Samoa	15.00	15.00	—	—	—
2009 Virgin Islands	15.00	15.00	—	—	—
2009 Marianna Islands	15.00	15.00	—	—	—

50 STATE QUARTERS
UNCIRCULATED ROLLS

Listings are for rolls containing uncirculated coins.

State	Philadelphia	Denver	State	Philadelphia	Denver
1999 Delaware	19.75	19.75	2004 Florida	15.25	15.25
1999 New Jersey	17.50	17.00	2004 Texas	14.50	15.50
1999 Georgia	57.50	57.50	2004 Iowa	15.25	15.25
1999 Connecticut	33.50	33.50	2004 Wisconsin	17.00	17.75
2000 Massachusetts	16.00	16.00	2005 California	22.00	22.00
2000 Maryland	16.00	16.50	2005 Minnesota	17.75	18.00
2000 South Carolina	17.50	18.00	2005 Oregon	14.50	14.50
2000 New Hampshire	14.75	15.00	2005 Kansas	15.00	15.00
2000 Virginia	15.00	15.00	2005 West Virginia	15.00	14.00
2001 New York	14.50	14.50	2006 Nevada	15.00	15.00
2001 North Carolina	16.50	15.50	2006 Nebraska	14.50	14.50
2001 Rhode Island	16.00	16.00	2006 Colorado	15.75	14.75
2001 Vermont	17.00	15.00	2006 North Dakota	14.00	14.75
2001 Kentucky	19.25	19.50	2006 South Dakota	15.00	14.50
2002 Mississippi	16.50	16.50	2007 Montana	17.75	17.75
2002 Tennessee	47.50	47.50	2007 Washington	21.00	21.00
2002 Ohio	22.50	22.00	2007 Idaho	16.00	16.25
2002 Louisiana	15.00	15.50	2007 Wyoming	15.75	16.00
2002 Indiana	16.50	16.00	2007 Utah	15.75	15.00
2003 Illinois	57.50	57.50	2008 Oklahoma	16.25	16.50
2003 Alabama	21.00	21.00	2008 New Mexico	17.00	14.25
2003 Maine	17.00	16.25	2008 Arizona	17.00	15.25
2003 Missouri	15.00	15.50	2008 Alaska	14.50	15.25
2003 Arkansas	15.75	16.75	2008 Hawaii	15.00	15.00
2004 Michigan	15.00	15.00			

TRUST TERRITORY QUARTERS
UNCIRCULATED ROLLS

Listings are for rolls containing uncirculated coins.

State	Philadelphia	Denver
2009 Washington D.C.	18.00	15.50
2009 Puerto Rico	15.00	15.50
2009 Guam	15.00	16.50
2009 American Samoa	15.00	15.00
2009 U.S. Virgin Islands	15.00	15.00
2009 Northern Mariana Islands	15.00	15.00

COMMEMORATIVE COINAGE
1892-1954

All commemorative half dollars of 1892-1954 have the following specifications: diameter — 30.6 millimeters; weight — 12.5000 grams; composition — 0.9000 silver, 0.3617 ounces actual silver weight. Values for PDS sets contain one example each from the Philadelphia, Denver and San Francisco mints. Type coin prices are the most inexpensive single coin available from the date and mint mark combinations listed.

QUARTER

KM# 115 COLUMBIAN EXPOSITION
Weight: 6.2500 g. **Composition:** 0.9000 Silver, 0.1808 oz. ASW **Diameter:** 24.3mm. **Obv:** Queen Isabella bust left **Rev:** Female kneeling with distaff adn spindle

Date	Mintage	AU-50	MS-60	MS-63	MS-64	MS-65
1893	24,214	590	665	875	1,400	4,200

HALF DOLLAR

KM# 117 COLUMBIAN EXPOSITION
Obv: Christopher Columbus bust right
Obv. Designer: Charles E. Barber **Rev:** Santa Maria sailing left, two globes below **Rev. Designer:** George T. Morgan

Date	Mintage	AU-50	MS-60	MS-63	MS-64	MS-65
1892	950,000	18.50	28.00	85.00	180	650
1893	1,550,405	15.50	28.00	80.00	195	875

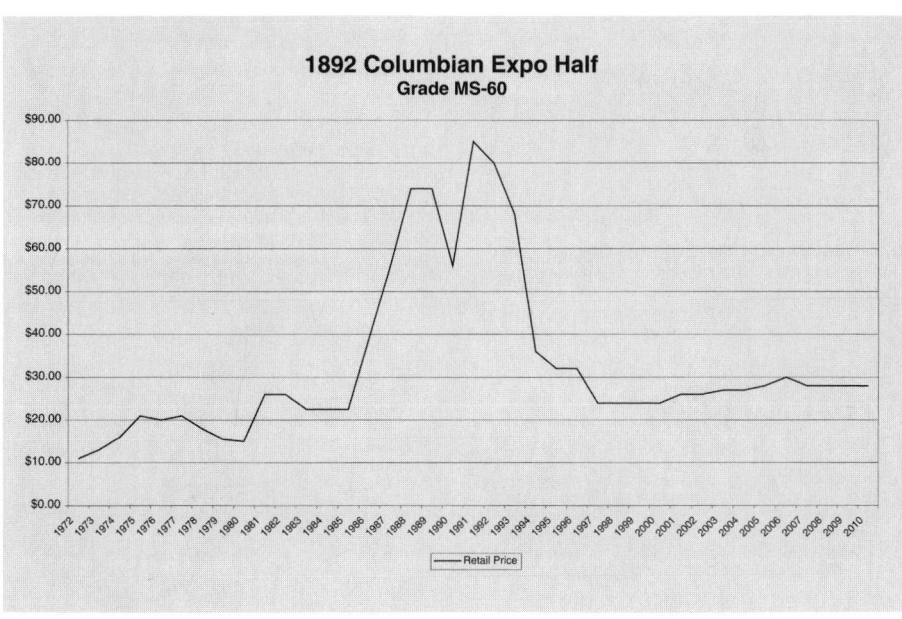

1892 Columbian Expo Half
Grade MS-60

KM# 135 PANAMA-PACIFIC EXPOSITION
Obv: Columbia standing, sunset in background
Rev: Eagle standing on shield **Designer:** Charles
E. Barber

Date	Mintage	AU-50	MS-60	MS-63	MS-64	MS-65
1915S	27,134	465	550	825	1,550	2,650

KM# 143 ILLINOIS CENTENNIAL-LINCOLN
Obv: Abraham Lincon bust right **Obv. Designer:**
George T. Morgan **Rev:** Eagle standing left **Rev.**
Designer: John R. Sinnock

Date	Mintage	AU-50	MS-60	MS-63	MS-64	MS-65
1918	100,058	135	155	170	250	525

KM# 146 MAINE CENTENNIAL   **Obv:** Arms of
the State of Maine **Rev:** Legend within wreath
Designer: Anthony de Francisci

Date	Mintage	AU-50	MS-60	MS-63	MS-64	MS-65
1920	50,028	135	165	195	310	585

KM# 147.1 PILGRIM TERCENTENARY
Obv: William bradford half-length left **Rev:**
Mayflower sailing left **Designer:** Cyrus E. Dallin

Date	Mintage	AU-50	MS-60	MS-63	MS-64	MS-65
1920	152,112	85.00	110	122	160	465

KM# 147.2 PILGRIM TERCENTENARY
Obv: William Bradford half-length left, 1921 added
at left **Rev:** Mayflower sailing left **Designer:**
Cyrus E. Dallin

Date	Mintage	AU-50	MS-60	MS-63	MS-64	MS-65
1921	20,053	175	200	225	285	600

2x2

KM# 148.1 ALABAMA CENTENNIAL
Obv: William W. Bibb and T.E. Kilby conjoint busts
left. "2x2" at right above stars **Rev:** Ealge left on
shield **Designer:** Laura G. Fraser **Notes:** "Fake
2x2" counterstamps exist.

Date	Mintage	AU-50	MS-60	MS-63	MS-64	MS-65
1921	6,006	315	330	600	950	1,975

KM# 148.2 ALABAMA CENTENNIAL
Obv: William W. Bibb and T.E. Kilby conjoint busts
left **Obv. Designer:** Laura G. Fraser **Rev:** Eagle
standing left on shield

Date	Mintage	AU-50	MS-60	MS-63	MS-64	MS-65
1921	59,038	190	215	525	685	1,800

KM# 149.1 MISSOURI CENTENNIAL
Obv: Frontiersman in coonskin cap left
Rev: Frontiersman and Native American standing
left **Designer:** Robert Aitken

Date	Mintage	AU-50	MS-60	MS-63	MS-64	MS-65
1921	15,428	410	725	925	1,775	5,000

2x4

KM# 149.2 MISSOURI CENTENNIAL
Obv: Frontiersman in coonskin cap left, 2(star)4 in
field at left **Rev:** Frontiersman and Native American
standing left **Designer:** Robert Aitken **Notes:** "Fake
"2*4" counterstamps exist.

Date	Mintage	AU-50	MS-60	MS-63	MS-64	MS-65
1921	5,000	650	800	1,100	1,900	5,000

KM# 151.1 GRANT MEMORIAL
Obv: Grant bust right **Rev:** Birthplace in Point
Pleasant, Ohio **Designer:** Laura G. Fraser

Date	Mintage	AU-50	MS-60	MS-63	MS-64	MS-65
1922	67,405	115	125	160	290	800

KM# 151.2 GRANT MEMORIAL **Obv:** Grant bust
left, star above the word GRANT **Rev:** Birthplace in
Point Pleasant, Ohio **Designer:** Laura G. Fraser
Notes: "Fake star" counterstamps exist.

Date	Mintage	AU-50	MS-60	MS-63	MS-64	MS-65
1922	4,256	950	1,300	2,100	2,850	7,250

KM# 153 MONROE DOCTRINE CENTENNIAL
Obv: James Monroe and John Quincy Adams conjoint
busts left **Rev:** Western Hemisphere portraied by two
female figures **Designer:** Chester Beach

Date	Mintage	AU-50	MS-60	MS-63	MS-64	MS-65
1923S	274,077	58.00	75.00	145	525	2,950

KM# 154 HUGUENOT-WALLOON
TERCENTENARY **Obv:** Huguenot leader
Gaspard de Coligny and William I of Orange
conjoint busts right **Rev:** Nieuw Nederland sailing
left **Designer:** George T. Morgan

Date	Mintage	AU-50	MS-60	MS-63	MS-64	MS-65
1924	142,080	135	155	175	250	550

KM# 155 CALIFORNIA DIAMOND JUBILEE
Obv: Fourty-Niner kneeling panning for gold
Rev: Grizzly bear walking left **Designer:** Jo Mora

Date	Mintage	AU-50	MS-60	MS-63	MS-64	MS-65
1925S	86,594	215	240	280	520	1,125

KM# 156 LEXINGTON-CONCORD
SESQUICENTENNIAL Obv: Concord's Minute
Man statue **Rev:** Old Belfry at Lexington
Designer: Chester Beach

Date	Mintage	AU-50	MS-60	MS-63	MS-64	MS-65
1925	162,013	96.00	110	120	185	485

KM# 157 STONE MOUNTAIN MEMORIAL
Obv: Generals Robert E. Lee and Thomas
"Stonewall" Jackson mounted left. **Rev:** Eagle on
rock at right **Designer:** Gutzon Borglum

Date	Mintage	AU-50	MS-60	MS-63	MS-64	MS-65
1925	1,314,709	70.00	77.00	85.00	90.00	285

KM# 158 FORT VANCOUVER CENTENNIAL
Obv: John McLoughlin bust left **Rev:** Frontiersmen
standing with musket, Ft. Vancouver in background
Designer: Laura G. Fraser

Date	Mintage	AU-50	MS-60	MS-63	MS-64	MS-65
1925	14,994	335	415	475	600	1,450

KM# 159 OREGON TRAIL MEMORIAL
Obv: Native American standing in full headdress
and holding bow, US Map in background
Rev: Conestoga wagon pulled by oxen left towards
sunset **Designer:** James E. and Laura G. Fraser

Date	Mintage	AU-50	MS-60	MS-63	MS-64	MS-65
1926	47,955	140	170	190	210	335
1926S	83,055	140	170	185	205	335
Type coin	—	150	180	190	210	320
1928	6,028	220	245	280	290	390
1933D	5,008	375	400	410	420	540
1934D	7,006	205	220	230	240	365
1936	10,006	150	190	200	210	325
1936S	5,006	170	190	210	220	360
1937D	12,008	180	205	210	215	325
1938	6,006	160	175	210	215	335
1938D	6,005	160	175	215	235	335
1938S	6,006	160	175	210	220	335
1939	3,004	525	620	630	655	720
1939D	3,004	525	620	640	675	735
1939S	3,005	525	620	630	655	725

KM# 160 U.S. SESQUICENTENNIAL
Obv: George Washington and Calvin Coolidge
conjoint busts right **Rev:** Liberty Bell
Designer: John R. Sinnock

Date	Mintage	AU-50	MS-60	MS-63	MS-64	MS-65
1926	141,120	88.00	115	150	600	4,400

KM# 162 VERMONT SESQUICENTENNIAL
Obv: Ira Allen bust right **Obv. Designer:** Charles
Keck **Rev:** Catamount advancing left

Date	Mintage	AU-50	MS-60	MS-63	MS-64	MS-65
1927	28,142	255	290	305	350	990

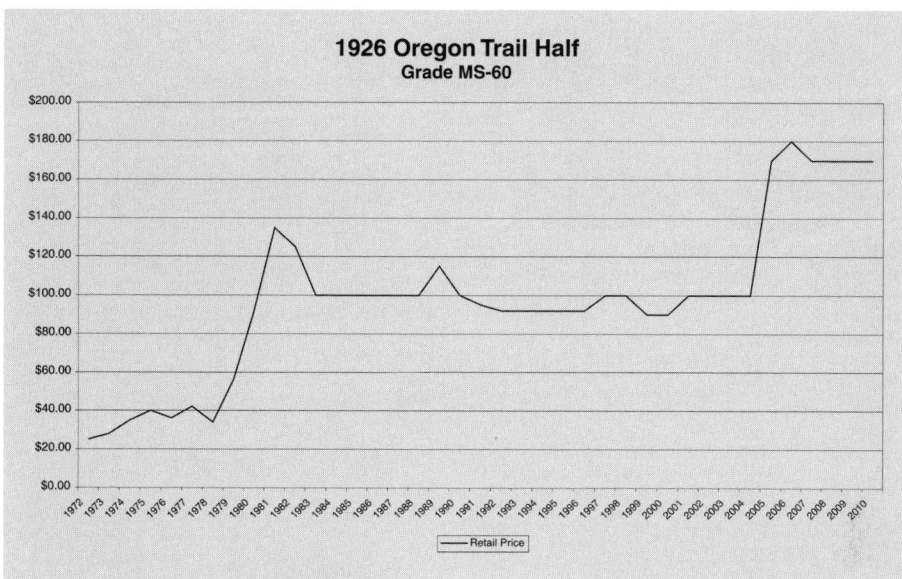

1926 Oregon Trail Half
Grade MS-60

Date	Mintage	AU-50	MS-60	MS-63	MS-64	MS-65
1937	5,505	105	115	128	135	340
1937D	5,505	105	115	128	135	330
1937S	5,506	105	115	128	135	380
1938	3,156	165	190	210	210	620
1938D	3,155	165	190	195	210	610
1938S	3,156	165	190	195	210	675
1939	2,104	330	390	400	410	1,000
1939D	2,104	330	390	400	410	980
1939S	2,105	330	390	400	410	965

KM# 163 HAWAIIAN SESQUICENTENNIAL
Obv: Captain James Cook bust left **Rev:** Native Hawaiian standing over view of Diamond Head **Designer:** Juliette May Fraser and Chester Beach **Notes:** Counterfeits exist.

Date	Mintage	AU-50	MS-60	MS-63	MS-64	MS-65
1928	10,008	1,750	2,650	3,500	4,500	6,850

KM# 168 ARKANSAS CENTENNIAL
Obv: Liberty and Indian Chief's conjoint heads left **Rev:** Eagle with outstreatched wings and Flag of Arkansas in background **Designer:** Edward E. Burr

Date	Mintage	AU-50	MS-60	MS-63	MS-64	MS-65
1935	13,012	100.00	110	120	125	215
Type coin	—	110	115	125	130	210
1935D	5,505	105	115	125	130	300
1935S	5,506	105	115	125	130	300
1936	9,660	100.00	110	120	125	230
1936D	9,660	100.00	110	120	125	230
1936S	9,662	100.00	110	120	125	230

KM# 165.2 DANIEL BOONE BICENTENNIAL
Obv: Daniel Boone bust left **Rev:** Daniel Boone and Native American standing, "1934" added above the word "PIONEER." **Designer:** Augustus Lukeman

Date	Mintage	AU-50	MS-60	MS-63	MS-64	MS-65
Type coin	—	130	135	145	150	240
1935	10,008	118	120	125	130	275
1935D	2,003	375	415	430	485	860
1935S	2,004	375	415	430	450	890
1936	12,012	118	120	125	130	275
1936D	5,005	133	140	145	152	325
1936S	5,006	133	140	145	152	325
1937	9,810	125	130	135	980	285
1937D	2,506	285	385	390	385	560
1937S	2,506	285	385	390	415	590
1938	2,100	360	395	410	415	555
1938D	2,100	360	395	410	430	545
1938S	2,100	360	395	410	415	595

COMMEMORATIVES

KM# 167 TEXAS CENTENNIAL Obv: Eagle standing left, large star in background Rev: Winged Victory kneeling beside Alamo Mission, small busts of Sam Houston and Stephen Austin at sides Designer: Pompeo Coppini

Date	Mintage	AU-50	MS-60	MS-63	MS-64	MS-65
1934	61,463	140	145	155	160	290
Type coin	—	145	158	163	165	260
1935	9,994	140	145	155	160	290
1935D	10,007	140	145	155	160	290
1935S	10,008	140	145	155	160	290
1936	8,911	140	145	155	160	290
1936D	9,039	140	145	155	160	290
1936S	9,055	140	145	155	160	290
1937	6,571	142	148	160	165	295
1937D	6,605	142	148	160	165	295
1937S	6,637	142	148	160	165	295
1938	3,780	240	265	275	300	500
1938D	3,775	240	265	275	300	485
1938S	3,814	240	265	275	300	485

KM# 165.1 DANIEL BOONE BICENTENNIAL
Obv: Daniel Boone bust left Rev: Daniel Boone and Native American standing Designer: Augustus Lukeman

Date	Mintage	AU-50	MS-60	MS-63	MS-64	MS-65
1934	10,007	125	135	140	150	275
1935	10,010	118	120	125	130	275
1935D	5,005	133	140	145	152	325
1935S	5,005	133	140	145	152	325

KM# 166 MARYLAND TERCENTENARY
Obv: Lord Baltimore, Cecil Calvert bust right Rev: Maryland state arms Designer: Hans Schuler

Date	Mintage	AU-50	MS-60	MS-63	MS-64	MS-65
1934	25,015	160	180	195	215	350

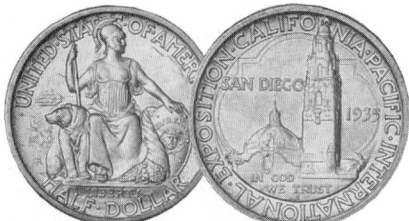

KM# 171 SAN DIEGO-PACIFIC INTERNATIONAL EXPOSITION Obv: Seated female with bear at her side Rev: State of California exposition building Designer: Robert Aitken

Date	Mintage	AU-50	MS-60	MS-63	MS-64	MS-65
1935S	70,132	105	130	145	150	170
1936D	30,092	105	135	150	160	170

KM# 169 CONNECTICUT TERCENTENARY
Obv: Eagle standing left Rev: Charter oak tree Designer: Henry Kreiss

Date	Mintage	AU-50	MS-60	MS-63	MS-64	MS-65
1935	25,018	255	290	310	380	540

KM# 170 HUDSON, N.Y., SESQUICENTENNIAL
Obv: Hudson's ship, the Half Moon sailing right Rev: Seal of the City of Hudson Designer: Chester Beach

Date	Mintage	AU-50	MS-60	MS-63	MS-64	MS-65
1935	10,008	750	925	1,250	1,675	2,250

KM# 172 OLD SPANISH TRAIL Obv: Long-horn cow's head facing Rev: The 1535 route of Cabeza de Vaca's expedition and a yucca tree Designer: L.W. Hoffecker Notes: Counterfeits exist.

Date	Mintage	AU-50	MS-60	MS-63	MS-64	MS-65
1935	10,008	1,250	1,375	1,700	1,900	2,250

KM# 173 ALBANY, N.Y., CHARTER ANNIVERSARY Obv: Beaver knawing on maple branch Rev: Standing figures of Thomas Dongan,

Peter Schyuyler and Robert Livingston **Designer:** Gertrude K. Lathrop

Date	Mintage	AU-50	MS-60	MS-63	MS-64	MS-65
1936	17,671	320	330	380	385	470

KM# 174 SAN FRANCISCO-OAKLAND BAY BRIDGE Obv: Grizzly bear facing **Rev:** Oakland Bay Bridge **Designer:** Jacques Schnier

Date	Mintage	AU-50	MS-60	MS-63	MS-64	MS-65
1936	71,424	170	180	220	225	375

KM# 175 BRIDGEPORT, CONN., CENTENNIAL Obv: P.T. Barnum bust left **Rev:** Eagle standing right **Designer:** Henry Kreiss

Date	Mintage	AU-50	MS-60	MS-63	MS-64	MS-65
1936	25,015	140	150	190	200	315

KM# 176 CINCINNATI MUSIC CENTER Obv: Stephen Foster bust right **Rev:** Kneeling female with lyre **Designer:** Constance Ortmayer

Date	Mintage	AU-50	MS-60	MS-63	MS-64	MS-65
Type coin	—	335	345	375	560	700
1936	5,005	315	330	360	540	925
1936D	5,005	315	330	360	540	750
1936S	5,006	315	330	360	540	750

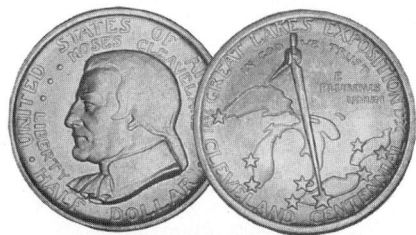

KM# 177 CLEVELAND-GREAT LAKES EXPOSITION Obv: Moses Cleaveland bust left

Rev: Dividers and map of the Great Lakes **Designer:** Brenda Putnam

Date	Mintage	AU-50	MS-60	MS-63	MS-64	MS-65
1936	50,030	135	140	150	160	245

KM# 178 COLUMBIA, S.C., SESQUICENTENNIAL Obv: Figure of Justice between capitols of 1786 and 1936 **Rev:** Palmetto tree **Designer:** A. Wolfe Davidson

Date	Mintage	AU-50	MS-60	MS-63	MS-64	MS-65
1936	9,007	275	280	300	310	415
Type coin	—	280	290	330	335	385
1936D	8,009	275	280	300	310	415
1936S	8,007	275	280	300	310	415

KM# 179 DELAWARE TERCENTENARY Obv: Old Swedes Church in Wilmington **Rev:** Kalmar Nyckel sailing left **Designer:** Carl L. Schmitz

Date	Mintage	AU-50	MS-60	MS-63	MS-64	MS-65
1936	20,993	310	325	365	385	490

KM# 180 ELGIN, ILL., CENTENNIAL Obv: Pioneer head left **Rev:** Statue group **Designer:** Trygve Rovelstad

Date	Mintage	AU-50	MS-60	MS-63	MS-64	MS-65
1936	20,015	245	265	280	295	355

COMMEMORATIVES

KM# 181 BATTLE OF GETTYSBURG 75TH
ANNIVERSARY   **Obv:** Union and Confederate veteran conjoint busts right **Rev:** Double blased fasces seperating two shields **Designer:** Frank Vittor

Date	Mintage	AU-50	MS-60	MS-63	MS-64	MS-65
1936	26,928	435	475	500	525	765

KM# 182 LONG ISLAND TERCENTENARY
Obv: Dutch settler and Native American conjoint head right **Rev:** Dutch sailing vessel **Designer:** Howard K. Weinman

Date	Mintage	AU-50	MS-60	MS-63	MS-64	MS-65
1936	81,826	88.00	98.00	110	130	420

KM# 183 LYNCHBURG, VA.,
SESQUICENTENNIAL   **Obv:** Sen. Carter Glass bust left **Rev:** Liberty standing, old Lynchburg courthouse at right **Designer:** Charles Keck

Date	Mintage	AU-50	MS-60	MS-63	MS-64	MS-65
1936	20,013	235	265	280	295	365

KM# 184 NORFOLK, VA., BICENTENNIAL
Obv: Seal of the City of Norfolk **Rev:** Royal Mace of Norfolk **Designer:** William M. and Marjorie E. Simpson

Date	Mintage	AU-50	MS-60	MS-63	MS-64	MS-65
1936	16,936	535	565	590	610	650

KM# 185 RHODE ISLAND TERCENTENARY
Obv: Roger Williams in canoe hailing Native American **Rev:** Shield with anchor **Designer:** Arthur G. Carey and John H. Benson

Date	Mintage	AU-50	MS-60	MS-63	MS-64	MS-65
1936	20,013	100.00	110	120	130	260
Type coin	—	105	110	125	128	290
1936D	15,010	100.00	110	120	130	275
1936S	15,011	100.00	110	120	130	290

KM# 186 ROANOKE ISLAND, N.C.
Obv: Sir Walter Raleigh bust left **Rev:** Ellinor Dare holding baby Virginia, two small ships flanking **Designer:** William M. Simpson

Date	Mintage	AU-50	MS-60	MS-63	MS-64	MS-65
1937	29,030	255	285	310	330	340

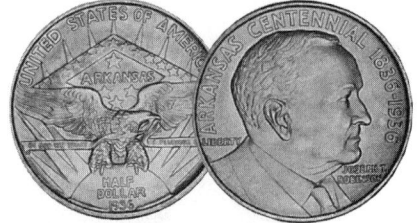

KM# 187 ARKANSAS CENTENNIAL
Obv: Eagle with wings outstreatched, Arkansas flag in backgorund **Obv. Designer:** Henry Kreiss **Rev:** Sen. Joseph T. Robinson bust right **Rev. Designer:** Edward E. Burr

Date	Mintage	AU-50	MS-60	MS-63	MS-64	MS-65
1936	25,265	145	150	165	180	420

KM# 188 WISCONSIN TERRITORIAL
CENTENNIAL   **Obv:** Badger from the Territorial

seal **Rev:** Pick axe and mound of lead ore
Designer: David Parsons

Date	Mintage	AU-50	MS-60	MS-63	MS-64	MS-65
1936	25,015	230	255	275	315	400

**KM# 189 YORK COUNTY, MAINE,
TERCENTENARY Obv:** Stockade **Rev:** York
County seal **Designer:** Walter H. Rich

Date	Mintage	AU-50	MS-60	MS-63	MS-64	MS-65
1936	25,015	135	170	195	300	590

**KM# 190 BATTLE OF ANTIETAM 75TH
ANNIVERSARY Obv:** Generals Robert E. Lee
and George McClellan conjoint busts left **Rev:**
Burnside Bridge **Designer:** William M. Simpson

Date	Mintage	AU-50	MS-60	MS-63	MS-64	MS-65
1937	18,028	725	760	790	850	985

KM# 191 NEW ROCHELLE, N.Y. Obv: John Pell
and a calf **Rev:** Fleur-de-lis from the seal of the city
Designer: Gertrude K. Lathrop

Date	Mintage	AU-50	MS-60	MS-63	MS-64	MS-65
1938	15,266	420	445	460	470	610

**KM# 198 BOOKER T. WASHINGTON
Obv:** Booker T. Washington bust right **Rev:** Cabin
and NYU's Hall of Fame **Designer:** Isaac S.

Hathaway **Notes:** Actual mintages are higher, but
unsold issues were melted to produce Washington
Carver issues.

Date	Mintage	AU-50	MS-60	MS-63	MS-64	MS-65
1946	1,000,546	14.00	18.00	19.50	21.00	50.00
Type coin	—	15.00	16.00	17.50	18.50	56.00
1946D	200,113	16.00	20.00	21.00	30.00	64.00
1946S	500,729	14.00	18.00	19.50	21.00	50.00
1947	100,017	25.00	35.00	55.00	65.00	95.00
1947D	100,017	25.00	35.00	55.00	70.00	115
1947S	100,017	25.00	35.00	55.00	65.00	90.00
1948	8,005	38.00	58.00	85.00	86.00	100.00
1948D	8,005	38.00	58.00	85.00	86.00	94.00
1948S	8,005	38.00	58.00	85.00	95.00	98.00
1949	6,004	67.00	83.00	92.00	98.00	120
1949D	6,004	67.00	83.00	92.00	98.00	120
1949S	6,004	67.00	83.00	95.00	104	110
1950	6,004	45.00	65.00	78.00	88.00	98.00
1950D	6,004	45.00	65.00	75.00	88.00	96.00
1950S	512,091	15.00	20.00	24.00	28.00	52.00
1951	51,082	15.00	20.00	24.00	28.00	50.00
1951D	7,004	45.00	65.00	78.00	90.00	95.00
1951S	7,004	45.00	65.00	78.00	90.00	95.00

**KM# 197 IOWA STATEHOOD CENTENNIAL
Obv:** First Capitol building at Iowa City **Rev:** Iowa
state seal **Designer:** Adam Pietz

Date	Mintage	AU-50	MS-60	MS-63	MS-64	MS-65
1946	100,057	115	120	125	130	260

**KM# 200 BOOKER T. WASHINGTON AND
GEORGE WASHINGTON CARVER Obv:** Booker
T. Washington and George Washington Carver
conjoint busts right **Rev:** Map of the United States
Designer: Isaac S. Hathaway

Date	Mintage	AU-50	MS-60	MS-63	MS-64	MS-65
1951	110,018	26.00	34.00	53.00	54.00	290
Type coin	—	14.00	16.00	18.50	20.00	52.50
1951D	10,004	35.00	43.00	60.00	58.00	140
1951S	10,004	35.00	43.00	60.00	58.00	140
1952	2,006,292	15.00	18.00	26.50	44.00	48.00
1952D	8,006	40.00	50.00	70.00	70.00	200
1952S	8,006	40.00	50.00	80.00	70.00	160
1953	8,003	35.00	47.00	75.00	85.00	260
1953D	8,003	35.00	47.00	75.00	85.00	175
1953S	108,020	26.00	33.00	50.00	55.00	120
1954	12,006	36.00	42.00	60.00	65.00	150
1954D	12,006	36.00	42.00	60.00	65.00	200
1954S	122,024	24.00	32.00	38.00	48.00	65.00

DOLLAR

KM# 118 LA FAYETTE Weight: 26.7300 g.
Composition: 0.9000 Silver, 0.7734 oz. ASW
Diameter: 38.1mm. **Obv:** George Washington and
Marquis de La Fayette conjoint busts right
Rev: La Fayette on horseback left
Designer: Charles E. Barber

Date	Mintage	AU-50	MS-60	MS-63	MS-64	MS-65
1900	36,026	675	1,025	2,150	3,700	10,850

**KM# 119 LOUISIANA PURCHASE EXPOSITION
- JEFFERSON Weight:** 1.6720 g. **Composition:**
0.9000 Gold, 0.0484 oz. AGW **Diameter:** 15mm.
Obv: Jefferson bust left **Rev:** Legend and laurel
branch **Designer:** Charles E. Barber

Date	Mintage	AU-50	MS-60	MS-63	MS-64	MS-65
1903	17,500	700	765	1,160	1,900	3,100

**KM# 120 LOUISIANA PURCHASE EXPOSITION
- MCKINLEY Weight:** 1.6720 g. **Composition:**
0.9000 Gold, 0.0484 oz. AGW **Diameter:** 15mm.
Obv: William McKinley bust left **Obv. Designer:**
Charles E. Barber **Rev:** Legend and laurel branch

Date	Mintage	AU-50	MS-60	MS-63	MS-64	MS-65
1903	17,500	715	765	1,080	2,150	3,300

**KM# 121 LEWIS AND CLARK EXPOSITION
Weight:** 1.6720 g. **Composition:** 0.9000 Gold,
0.0484 oz. AGW **Diameter:** 15mm. **Obv:** Lewis
bust left **Obv. Designer:** Charles E. Barber
Rev: Clark bust left

Date	Mintage	AU-50	MS-60	MS-63	MS-64	MS-65
1904	10,025	1,050	1,350	2,550	5,900	12,250
1905	10,041	1,300	1,625	3,300	7,000	18,500

**KM# 136 PANAMA-PACIFIC EXPOSITION
Weight:** 1.6720 g. **Composition:** 0.9000 Gold,
0.0484 oz. AGW **Diameter:** 15mm. **Obv:** Canal
laborer bust left **Obv. Designer:** Charles Keck
Rev: Value within two dolphins

Date	Mintage	AU-50	MS-60	MS-63	MS-64	MS-65
1915S	15,000	650	750	950	1,500	2,450

**KM# 144 MCKINLEY MEMORIAL
Weight:** 1.6720 g. **Composition:** 0.9000 Gold,
0.0484 oz. AGW **Diameter:** 15mm. **Obv:** William
McKinley head left **Obv. Designer:** Charles E.
Barber **Rev:** Memorial building at Niles, Ohio
Rev. Designer: George T. Morgan

Date	Mintage	AU-50	MS-60	MS-63	MS-64	MS-65
1916	9,977	625	685	800	1,550	2,350
1917	10,000	785	800	1,325	2,200	3,800

KM# 152.1 GRANT MEMORIAL Weight: 1.6720
g. **Composition:** 0.9000 Gold, 0.0484 oz. AGW
Diameter: 15mm. **Obv:** U.S. Grant bust right
Obv. Designer: Laura G. Fraser **Rev:** Birthplace
Notes: Without an incuse "star" above the word
GRANT on the obverse.

Date	Mintage	AU-50	MS-60	MS-63	MS-64	MS-65
1922	5,000	1,875	1,900	2,350	3,650	4,900

   Star

KM# 152.2 GRANT MEMORIAL Weight: 1.6720
g. **Composition:** 0.9000 Gold, 0.0484 oz. AGW
Diameter: 15mm. **Obv:** U.S. Grant bust right
Obv. Designer: Laura G. Fraser **Rev:** Birthplace
Notes: Variety with an incuse "star" above the word
GRANT on the obverse.

Date	Mintage	AU-50	MS-60	MS-63	MS-64	MS-65
1922	5,016	1,800	1,950	2,400	3,700	4,400

$2.50 (QUARTER EAGLE)

**KM# 137 PANAMA-PACIFIC EXPOSITION
Weight:** 4.1800 g. **Composition:** 0.9000 Gold,

0.1209 oz. AGW **Diameter:** 18mm. **Obv:** Columbia
holding cadueus while seated on a hippocamp
Obv. Designer: Charles E. Barber **Rev:** Eagle
standing left **Rev. Designer:** George T. Morgan

Date	Mintage	AU-50	MS-60	MS-63	MS-64	MS-65
1915S	6,749	1,750	2,100	4,350	6,300	8,000

KM# 161 U.S. SESQUICENTENNIAL
Weight: 4.1800 g. **Composition:** 0.9000 Gold,
0.1209 oz. AGW **Diameter:** 18mm. **Obv:** Liberty
standing holding torch and scroll **Obv. Designer:**
John R. Sinnock **Rev:** Independence Hall

Date	Mintage	AU-50	MS-60	MS-63	MS-64	MS-65
1926	46,019	525	565	850	1,700	4,200

$50

KM# 138 PANAMA-PACIFIC EXPOSITION
ROUND **Weight:** 83.5900 g. **Composition:**
0.9000 Gold, 2.4186 oz. AGW **Diameter:** 44mm.
Obv: Minerva bust helmeted left **Obv. Designer:**
Robert Aitken **Rev:** Owl pearched on California pin
branch

Date	Mintage	AU-50	MS-60	MS-63	MS-64	MS-65
1915S	483	54,000	60,000	82,500	105,000	145,000

KM# 139 PANAMA-PACIFIC EXPOSITION
OCTAGONAL **Weight:** 83.5900 g. **Composition:**
0.9000 Gold, 2.4186 oz. AGW **Diameter:** 44mm.
Obv: Minerva bust helmeted left **Obv. Designer:**
Robert Aitken **Rev:** Owl pearched on California
pine branch

Date	Mintage	AU-50	MS-60	MS-63	MS-64	MS-65
1915S	645	52,500	55,000	80,000	99,500	148,000

COMMEMORATIVE COINAGE 1982-PRESENT

All commemorative silver dollar coins of 1982-present have the following specifications: diameter — 38.1 millimeters; weight — 26.7300 grams; composition — 0.9000 silver, 0.7736 ounces actual silver weight. All commemorative $5 coins of 1982-present have the following specificiations: diameter — 21.6 millimeters; weight — 8.3590 grams; composition: 0.9000 gold, 0.242 ounces actual gold weight.

Note: In 1982, after a hiatus of nearly 20 years, coinage of commemorative half dollars resumed. Those designated with a 'W' were struck at the West Point Mint. Some issues were struck in copper-nickel. Those struck in silver have the same size, weight and composition as the prior commemorative half-dollar series.

HALF DOLLAR

KM# 208 GEORGE WASHINGTON, 250TH BIRTH ANNIVERSARY Weight: 12.5000 g.
Composition: 0.9000 Silver, 0.3617 oz. ASW **Diameter:** 30.6mm. **Obv:** George Washington on horseback facing **Obv. Designer:** Elizabeth Jones **Rev:** Mount Vernon

Date	UNC Mintage	Proof Mintage	MS-65	Prf-65
1982D	2,210,458	—	7.75	—
1982S	—	4,894,044	—	7.75

KM# 212 STATUE OF LIBERTY CENTENNIAL
Weight: 11.3400 g. **Composition:** Copper-Nickel Clad Copper, 0 oz. **Obv:** State of Liberty and sunrise **Obv. Designer:** Edgar Z. Steever **Rev:** Emigrant family looking toward mainland **Rev. Designer:** Sherl Joseph Winter

Date	UNC Mintage	Proof Mintage	MS-65	Prf-65
1986D	928,008	—	5.25	—
1986S	—	6,925,627	—	4.95

KM# 224 CONGRESS BICENTENNIAL
Weight: 11.3400 g. **Composition:** Copper-Nickel

Clad Copper, 0 oz. **Obv:** Statue of Freedom head **Obv. Designer:** Patricia L. Verani **Rev:** Capitol building **Rev. Designer:** William Woodward and Edgar Z. Steever

Date	UNC Mintage	Proof Mintage	MS-65	Prf-65
1989D	163,753	—	7.50	—
1989S	762,198	—	—	7.25

KM# 228 MOUNT RUSHMORE 50TH ANNIVERSARY Weight: 11.3400 g. Composition:
Copper-Nickel Clad Copper, 0 oz. **Obv. Designer:** Marcel Jovine **Rev:** Mount Rushmore portraits **Rev. Designer:** T. James Ferrell

Date	UNC Mintage	Proof Mintage	MS-65	Prf-65
1991D	172,754	—	19.50	—
1991S	753,257	—	—	18.50

KM# 233 1992 OLYMPICS Weight: 11.3400 g.
Composition: Copper-Nickel Clad Copper, 0 oz. **Obv:** Torch and laurel **Obv. Designer:** William Cousins **Rev:** Female gymnast and large flag **Rev. Designer:** Steven M. Bieda

Date	UNC Mintage	Proof Mintage	MS-65	Prf-65
1992P	161,607	—	8.50	—
1992S	—	519,645	—	9.00

KM# 237 COLUMBUS VOYAGE - 500TH ANNIVERSARY
Weight: 11.3400 g. **Composition:** Copper-Nickel Clad Copper, 0 oz. **Obv:** Columbus standing on shore **Rev:** Nina, Pinta and Santa Maria sailing right **Designer:** T. James Ferrell

Date	UNC Mintage	Proof Mintage	MS-65	Prf-65
1992D	135,702	—	11.50	—
1992S	—	390,154	—	10.50

KM# 240 JAMES MADISON - BILL OF RIGHTS
Weight: 12.5000 g. **Composition:** 0.9000 Silver, 0.3617 oz. ASW **Obv:** James Madison writing, Montpelier in background **Obv. Designer:** T. James Ferrell **Rev:** Statue of Liberty torch **Rev. Designer:** Dean McMullen

Date	UNC Mintage	Proof Mintage	MS-65	Prf-65
1993W	193,346	—	18.50	—
1993S	586,315	—	—	15.00

KM# 243 WORLD WAR II 50TH ANNIVERSARY
Weight: 11.3400 g. **Composition:** Copper-Nickel Clad Copper, 0 oz. **Obv:** Three portraits, plane above, large V in backgound **Obv. Designer:** George Klauba **Rev:** Pacific island battle scene **Rev. Designer:** William J. Leftwich

Date	UNC Mintage	Proof Mintage	MS-65	Prf-65
(1993)P	197,072	—	24.50	—
(1993)P	317,396	—	—	23.50

KM# 246 1994 WORLD CUP SOCCER
Weight: 11.3400 g. **Composition:** Copper-Nickel Clad Copper, 0 oz. **Obv:** Soccer player with ball **Obv. Designer:** Richard T. LaRoche **Rev:** World Cup 94 logo **Rev. Designer:** Dean McMullen

Date	UNC Mintage	Proof Mintage	MS-65	Prf-65
1994D	168,208	—	9.00	—
1994P	—	609,354	—	8.00

KM# 254 CIVIL WAR BATTLEFIELD PRESERVATION
Weight: 11.3400 g. **Composition:** Copper-Nickel Clad Copper, 0 oz. **Obv:** Drummer and fenceline **Obv. Designer:** Don Troiani **Rev:** Canon overlooking battlefield **Rev. Designer:** T. James Ferrell

Date	UNC Mintage	Proof Mintage	MS-65	Prf-65
1995S	119,510	—	39.50	—
1995S	—	330,099	—	38.50

KM# 257 1996 ATLANTA OLYMPICS - BASKETBALL
Weight: 11.3400 g. **Composition:** Copper-Nickel Clad Copper, 0 oz. **Obv:** Three players, one jumping for a shot **Rev:** Hemisphere and Atlanta Olympics logo

Date	UNC Mintage	Proof Mintage	MS-65	Prf-65
1995S	—	169,655	—	16.00
1995S	171,001	—	19.00	—

COMMEMORATIVES

KM# 262 1996 ATLANTA OLYMPICS -
BASEBALL   **Weight:** 11.3400 g. **Composition:**
Copper-Nickel Clad Copper, 0 oz. **Obv:** Baseball
batter at plate, catcher and umpire **Obv. Designer:**
Edgar Z. Steever **Rev:** Hemisphere and Atlanta
Olympics logo

Date	UNC Mintage	Proof Mintage	MS-65	Prf-65
1995S	164,605	—	20.50	—
1995S	—	118,087	—	18.00

KM# 271 1996 ATLANTA OLYMPICS - SOCCER
Weight: 11.3400 g. **Composition:** Copper-Nickel
Clad Copper, 0 oz. **Obv:** Two female soccer
players **Rev:** Atlanta Olympics logo

Date	UNC Mintage	Proof Mintage	MS-65	Prf-65
1996S	52,836	—	138	—
1996S	—	122,412	—	100.00

KM# 267 1996 ATLANTA OLYMPICS -
SWIMMING   **Weight:** 11.3400 g. **Composition:**
Copper-Nickel Clad Copper, 0 oz. **Obv:** Swimmer
right in butterfly stroke **Rev:** Atlanta Olympics logo

Date	UNC Mintage	Proof Mintage	MS-65	Prf-65
1996S	49,533	—	150	—
1996S	—	114,315	—	34.50

KM# 323 U. S. CAPITOL VISITOR CENTER
Weight: 11.3400 g. **Composition:** Copper-Nickel
Clad Copper, 0 oz. **Obv:** Capitol sillouete, 1800
structure in detail **Obv. Designer:** Dean McMullen
Rev: Legend within circle of stars **Rev. Designer:**
Alex Shagin and Marcel Jovine

Date	UNC Mintage	Proof Mintage	MS-65	Prf-65
2001P	99,157	—	13.50	—
2001P	—	77,962	—	15.50

KM# 348 FIRST FLIGHT CENTENNIAL   **Weight:**
11.3400 g. **Composition:** Copper-Nickel Clad
Copper, 0 oz. **Obv:** Wright Monument at Kitty Hawk
Obv. Designer: John Mercanti **Rev:** Wright Flyer in
flight **Rev. Designer:** Donna Weaver

Date	UNC Mintage	Proof Mintage	MS-65	Prf-65
2003P	57,726	—	15.00	—
2003P	109,710	—	—	16.00

KM# 438 AMERICAN BALD EAGLE   **Weight:**
11.3400 g. **Composition:** Copper-Nickel Clad
Copper, 0 oz. **Diameter:** 30.6mm. **Obv:** Two
eaglets in nest with egg **Rev:** Eagle Challenger
facing right, American Flag in background

Date	UNC Mintage	Proof Mintage	MS-65	Prf-65
2008P	120,000	—	10.00	—
2008P	175,000	—	—	15.00

DOLLAR

KM# 209 1984 LOS ANGELES OLYMPICS - DISCUS
Obv: Trippled discus thrower and five star logo **Obv. Designer:** Elizabeth Jones **Rev:** Eagle bust left

Date	UNC Mintage	Proof Mintage	MS-65	Prf-65
1983P	294,543	—	17.50	—
1983D	174,014	—	18.50	—
1983S	174,014	—	18.50	—
1983S	—	1,577,025	—	18.00

KM# 214 STATUE OF LIBERTY CENTENNIAL
Obv: Statue of Liberty and Ellis Island great hall **Obv. Designer:** John Mercanti **Rev:** Statue of Liberty torch **Rev. Designer:** John Mercanti and Matthew Peloso

Date	UNC Mintage	Proof Mintage	MS-65	Prf-65
1986P	723,635	—	17.80	—
1986S	—	6,414,638	—	18.50

KM# 210 1984 LOS ANGELES OLYMPICS - STADIUM STATUES
Obv: Statues at exterior of Los Angeles Memorial Coliseum **Obv. Designer:** Robert Graham **Rev:** Eagle standing on rock

Date	UNC Mintage	Proof Mintage	MS-65	Prf-65
1984P	217,954	—	17.50	—
1984D	116,675	—	18.50	—
1984S	116,675	—	18.50	—
1984S	—	1,801,210	—	18.50

KM# 220 CONSTITUTION BICENTENNIAL
Obv: Feather pen and document **Obv. Designer:** Patricia L. Verani **Rev:** Group of people

Date	UNC Mintage	Proof Mintage	MS-65	Prf-65
1987P	451,629	—	17.80	—
1987S	—	2,747,116	—	18.50

COMMEMORATIVES

KM# 222 1988 OLYMPICS Obv: Olympic torch and Statue of Liberty torch within laurel wreath **Obv. Designer:** Patricia L. Verani **Rev:** Olympic rings within olive wreath **Rev. Designer:** Sherl Joseph Winter

Date	UNC Mintage	Proof Mintage	MS-65	Prf-65
1988D	191,368	—	17.80	—
1988S	—	1,359,366	—	18.50

KM# 225 CONGRESS BICENTENNIAL Obv: Statue of Freedom in clouds and sunburst **Rev:** Mace from the House of Represenatives **Designer:** William Woodward and Chester Y. Martin

Date	UNC Mintage	Proof Mintage	MS-65	Prf-65
1989D	135,203	—	21.50	—
1989S	—	762,198	—	20.50

KM# 227 EISENHOWER CENTENNIAL Obv: Two Eisenhower profiles, as general, left, as President, right **Obv. Designer:** John Mercanti **Rev:** Eisenhower home at Gettysburg **Rev. Designer:** Marcel Jovine and John Mercanti

Date	UNC Mintage	Proof Mintage	MS-65	Prf-65
1990W	241,669	—	17.80	—
1990P	1,144,461	—	—	17.80

KM# 229 MOUNT RUSHMORE 50TH ANNIVERSARY Obv: Mount Rushmore portraits, wreath below **Obv. Designer:** Marika Somogyi **Rev:** Great seal in rays, United States map in background **Rev. Designer:** Frank Gasparro

Date	UNC Mintage	Proof Mintage	MS-65	Prf-65
1991P	133,139	—	28.50	—
1991S	—	738,419	—	23.50

KM# 231 KOREAN WAR - 38TH ANNIVERSARY
Obv: Solder advancing right up a hill; planes above, ships below **Obv. Designer:** John Mercanti **Rev:** Map of Korean pensiluar, eagle's head **Rev. Designer:** T. James Ferrell

Date	UNC Mintage	Proof Mintage	MS-65	Prf-65
1991D	213,049	—	19.50	—
1991P	—	618,488	—	20.00

KM# 234 1992 OLYMPICS - BASEBALL   Obv:
Baseball pitcher, Nolan Ryan as depicted on card **Obv. Designer:** John R. Deecken and Chester Y. Martin **Rev:** Shield flanked by stylized wreath, olympic rings above **Rev. Designer:** Marcel Jovine

Date	UNC Mintage	Proof Mintage	MS-65	Prf-65
1992D	187,552	—	22.50	—
1992S	—	504,505	—	24.50

KM# 232 USO 50TH ANNIVERSARY   Obv: USO
banner **Obv. Designer:** Robert Lamb **Rev:** Eagle pearched right atop globe **Rev. Designer:** John Mercanti

Date	UNC Mintage	Proof Mintage	MS-65	Prf-65
1991D	124,958	—	18.00	—
1991S	—	321,275	—	18.50

KM# 236 WHITE HOUSE BICENTENNIAL   Obv:
White House's north portico **Obv. Designer:** Edgar Z. Steever **Rev:** John Hoban bust left, main entrance doorway **Rev. Designer:** Chester Y. Martin

Date	UNC Mintage	Proof Mintage	MS-65	Prf-65
1992D	123,803	—	26.00	—
1992W	—	375,851	—	28.00

KM# 238 COLUMBUS DISCOVERY - 500TH ANNIVERSARY
Obv: Columbus standing with banner, three ships in background **Obv. Designer:** John Mercanti **Rev:** Half view of Santa Maria on left, Space Shuttle Discovery on right **Rev. Designer:** Thomas D. Rogers, Sr.

Date	UNC Mintage	Proof Mintage	MS-65	Prf-65
1992D	106,949	—	26.00	—
1992P	—	385,241	—	29.00

KM# 244 WORLD WAR II 50TH ANNIVERSARY
Obv: Soldier on Normandy beach **Rev:** Insignia of the Supreme Headquarters of the AEF above Eisenhower quote **Designer:** Thomas D. Rogers, Sr.

Date	UNC Mintage	Proof Mintage	MS-65	Prf-65
1993D	94,708	—	29.50	—
1993W	342,041	—	—	37.50

KM# 241 JAMES MADISON - BILL OF RIGHTS
Obv: James Madison bust right, at left **Obv. Designer:** William Krawczewicz and Thomas D. Rogers, Sr. **Rev:** Montpelier home **Rev. Designer:** Dean McMullen and Thomas D. Rogers, Sr.

Date	UNC Mintage	Proof Mintage	MS-65	Prf-65
1993D	98,383	—	18.50	—
1993S	—	534,001	—	20.50

KM# 247 1994 WORLD CUP SOCCER
Obv: Two players with ball **Obv. Designer:** Dean McMullen and T. James Ferrell **Rev:** World Cup 94 logo **Rev. Designer:** Dean McMullen

Date	UNC Mintage	Proof Mintage	MS-65	Prf-65
1994D	81,698	—	22.50	—
1994S	—	576,978	—	23.50

KM# 249 THOMAS JEFFERSON 250TH BIRTH ANNIVERSARY Obv: Jefferson's head left Rev: Monticello home Designer: T. James Ferrell

Date	UNC Mintage	Proof Mintage	MS-65	Prf-65
1993P	266,927	—	18.50	—
1993S	—	332,891	—	19.50

KM# 251 NATIONAL PRISONER OF WAR MUSEUM Obv: Eagle in flight left within circle of barbed wire Obv. Designer: Thomas Nielson and Alfred Maletsky Rev: National Prisioner of War Museum Rev. Designer: Edgar Z. Steever

Date	UNC Mintage	Proof Mintage	MS-65	Prf-65
1994W	54,790	—	85.00	—
1994P	—	220,100	—	42.00

KM# 250 VIETNAM VETERANS MEMORIAL Obv: Outstretched hand touching names on the Wall, Washington Monument in background Obv. Designer: John Mercanti Rev: Service Medals Rev. Designer: Thomas D. Rogers, Sr.

Date	UNC Mintage	Proof Mintage	MS-65	Prf-65
1994W	57,317	—	79.00	—
1994P	—	226,262	—	65.00

KM# 252 WOMEN IN MILITARY SERVICE MEMORIAL Obv: Five uniformed women left Obv. Designer: T. James Ferrell Rev: Memorial at Arlington National Cemetery Rev. Designer: Thomas D. Rogers, Sr.

Date	UNC Mintage	Proof Mintage	MS-65	Prf-65
1994W	53,054	—	36.50	—
1994P	—	213,201	—	30.00

COMMEMORATIVES

KM# 253 U.S. CAPITOL BICENTENNIAL   Obv:
Capitol dome, Statue fo Freedom surrounded by
stars **Rev:** Eagle on shield, flags flanking

Date	UNC Mintage	Proof Mintage	MS-65	Prf-65
1994D	68,352	—	18.00	—
1994S	—	279,416	—	22.50

**KM# 259 1996 ATLANTA PARALYMPICS -
BLIND RUNNER   Obv:** Blind runner **Rev:** Two
clasped hands, Atlanta Olympic logo above

Date	UNC Mintage	Proof Mintage	MS-65	Prf-65
1995D	28,649	—	82.00	—
1995P	—	138,337	—	54.00

KM# 255 CIVIL WAR   Obv: Soldier giving water
to wounded soldier **Obv. Designer:** Don Troiani
and Edgar Z. Steever **Rev:** Chamberlain quote and
battlefield monument **Rev. Designer:** John
Mercanti

Date	UNC Mintage	Proof Mintage	MS-65	Prf-65
1995P	45,866	—	69.00	—
1995S	—	437,114	—	69.00

**KM# 260 1996 ATLANTA OLYMPICS -
GYMNASTICS   Obv:** Two gymnasts, female on
floor exercise and male on rings **Rev:** Two clasped
hands, Atlanta Olympic logo above

Date	UNC Mintage	Proof Mintage	MS-65	Prf-65
1995D	42,497	—	67.50	—
1995P	—	182,676	—	50.00

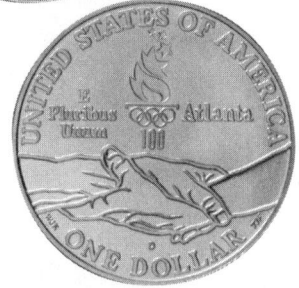

KM# 263 1996 ATLANTA OLYMPICS - CYCLING
Obv: Three cyclists approaching **Obv. Designer:**
John Mercanti **Rev:** Two clasped hands, Atlanta
Olympic logo above

Date	UNC Mintage	Proof Mintage	MS-65	Prf-65
1995D	19,662	—	142	—
1995P	—	118,795	—	46.00

KM# 266 SPECIAL OLYMPICS WORLD GAMES
Obv: Eunice Schriver head left; founder of the
Special Olympics **Obv. Designer:** Jamie Wyeth
and T. James Ferrell **Rev:** Special Olympics Logo
on an award medal, rose, quote from Schriver **Rev.
Designer:** Thomas D. Rogers, Sr.

Date	UNC Mintage	Proof Mintage	MS-65	Prf-65
1995W	89,301	—	29.50	—
1995P	—	351,764	—	26.50

KM# 264 1996 ATLANTA OLYMPICS - TRACK
AND FIELD Obv: Two runners on a track, one
crossing finish line **Obv. Designer:** John Mercanti
Rev: Two clasped hands, Atlanta Olympic logo above

Date	UNC Mintage	Proof Mintage	MS-65	Prf-65
1995D	24,796	—	92.00	—
1995P	—	136,935	—	49.00

KM# 268 1996 ATLANTA PARALYMPICS -
WHEELCHAIR RACER Obv: Wheelchair racer
approaching with uplifted arms **Rev:** Atlanta Olympics
logo **Rev. Designer:** Thomas D. Rogers, Sr.

Date	UNC Mintage	Proof Mintage	MS-65	Prf-65
1996D	14,497	—	365	—
1996P	—	84,280	—	82.00

COMMEMORATIVES

KM# 269 1996 ATLANTA OLYMPICS - TENNIS
Obv: Female tennis player **Rev:** Atlanta Olympics
logo **Rev. Designer:** Thomas D. Rogers, Sr.

Date	UNC Mintage	Proof Mintage	MS-65	Prf-65
1996D	15,983	—	315	—
1996P	—	92,016	—	85.00

KM# 272 1996 ATLANTA OLYMPICS - ROWING
Obv: Four man crew rowing left **Rev:** Atlanta Olympic
logo **Rev. Designer:** Thomas D. Rogers, Sr.

Date	UNC Mintage	Proof Mintage	MS-65	Prf-65
1996D	16,258	—	345	—
1996P	—	151,890	—	70.00

**KM# A272 1996 ATLANTA OLYMPICS - HIGH
JUMP Obv:** High jumper **Rev. Designer:** Thomas
D. Rogers, Sr.

Date	UNC Mintage	Proof Mintage	MS-65	Prf-65
1996D	15,697	—	380	—
1996P	—	124,502	—	58.00

KM# 275 NATIONAL COMMUNITY SERVICE
Obv: Female standing with lamp and shield **Obv.
Designer:** Thomas D. Rogers, Sr. **Rev:** Legend
within wreath **Rev. Designer:** William C. Cousins

Date	UNC Mintage	Proof Mintage	MS-65	Prf-65
1996S	23,500	—	220	—
1996S	—	101,543	—	76.00

KM# 276 SMITHSONIAN INSTITUTION 150TH ANNIVERSARY Obv: Original Smithsonian building, the "Castle" designed by James Renwick **Obv. Designer:** Thomas D. Rogers, Sr. **Rev:** Female seated with torch and scroll on globe **Rev. Designer:** John Mercanti

Date	UNC Mintage	Proof Mintage	MS-65	Prf-65
1996D	31,230	—	135	—
1996P	—	129,152	—	57.50

KM# 279 JACKIE ROBINSON Obv: Jackie Robinson sliding into base **Obv. Designer:** Alfred Maletsky **Rev:** Anniversary logo **Rev. Designer:** T. James Ferrell

Date	UNC Mintage	Proof Mintage	MS-65	Prf-65
1997S	30,007	—	98.00	—
1997S	—	110,495	—	118

KM# 278 U.S. BOTANIC GARDENS 175TH ANNIVERSARY Obv: National Botanic Gardens Conservatory building **Rev:** Rose **Designer:** Edgar Z. Steever

Date	UNC Mintage	Proof Mintage	MS-65	Prf-65
1997P	57,272	—	39.50	—
1997P	—	264,528	—	38.00

KM# 281 NATIONAL LAW ENFORCEMENT OFFICERS MEMORIAL Obv: Male and female officer admiring name on monument **Rev:** Rose on a plain shield **Designer:** Alfred Maletsky

Date	UNC Mintage	Proof Mintage	MS-65	Prf-65
1997P	—	110,428	—	105
1997P	28,575	—	160	—

COMMEMORATIVES

KM# 287 ROBERT F. KENNEDY Obv: Kennedy bust facing **Obv. Designer:** Thomas D. Rogers, Sr. **Rev:** Eagle on sheild, Senate Seal **Rev. Designer:** James M. Peed and Thomas D. Rogers, Sr.

Date	UNC Mintage	Proof Mintage	MS-65	Prf-65
1998S	106,422	—	31.50	—
1998S	—	99,020	—	42.50

KM# 298 DOLLEY MADISON Obv: Madison bust right, at left **Rev:** Montpelier home **Designer:** Tiffany & Co.

Date	UNC Mintage	Proof Mintage	MS-65	Prf-65
1999P	89,104	—	42.00	—
1999P	224,403	—	—	34.50

KM# 288 BLACK REVOLUTIONARY WAR PATRIOTS Obv: Crispus Attucks bust right **Obv. Designer:** John Mercanti **Rev:** Family standing **Rev. Designer:** Ed Dwight

Date	UNC Mintage	Proof Mintage	MS-65	Prf-65
1998S	37,210	—	160	—
1998S	—	75,070	—	96.00

KM# 299 YELLOWSTONE Obv: Old Faithful gyser erupting **Obv. Designer:** Edgar Z. Steever **Rev:** Bison and vista as on National Parks shield **Rev. Designer:** William C. Cousins

Date	UNC Mintage	Proof Mintage	MS-65	Prf-65
1999P	23,614	—	49.50	—
1999P	—	128,646	—	45.00

**KM# 311 LIBRARY OF CONGRESS
BICENTENNIAL Obv:** Open and closed book,
torch in background **Obv. Designer:** Thomas D.
Rogers, Sr. **Rev:** Skylight dome above the main
reading room **Rev. Designer:** John Mercanti

Date	UNC Mintage	Proof Mintage	MS-65	Prf-65
2000P	52,771	—	38.00	—
2000P	—	196,900	—	33.00

KM# 324 CAPITOL VISITOR CENTER Obv:
Original and current Capital facades **Obv.
Designer:** Marika Somogyi **Rev:** Eagle with sheild
and ribbon **Rev. Designer:** John Mercanti

Date	UNC Mintage	Proof Mintage	MS-65	Prf-65
2001P	35,400	—	30.00	—
2001P	143,793	—	—	39.00

KM# 313 LEIF ERICSON Obv: Ericson bust
helmeted right **Obv. Designer:** John Mercanti **Rev:**
Viking ship sailing left **Rev. Designer:** T. James
Ferrell

Date	UNC Mintage	Proof Mintage	MS-65	Prf-65
2000P	28,150	—	87.00	—
2000 Iceland	15,947	—	—	25.00
2000P	144,748	—	—	70.00

KM# 325 NATIVE AMERICAN - BISON Obv:
Native American bust right **Rev:** Bison standing left
Designer: James E. Fraser

Date	UNC Mintage	Proof Mintage	MS-65	Prf-65
2001D	227,100	—	175	—
2001P	272,869	—	—	180

COMMEMORATIVES

KM# 336 2002 WINTER OLYMPICS - SALT LAKE CITY   Obv: Salt Lake City Olympic logo **Obv. Designer:** John Mercanti **Rev:** Stylized skyline with mountains in background **Rev. Designer:** Donna Weaver

Date	UNC Mintage	Proof Mintage	MS-65	Prf-65
2002P	40,257	—	30.00	—
2002P	166,864	—	—	38.00

KM# 349 FIRST FLIGHT CENTENNIAL   Obv: Orville and Wilbur Wright busts left **Obv. Designer:** T. James Ferrell **Rev:** Wright Flyer over dunes **Rev. Designer:** Norman E. Nemeth

Date	UNC Mintage	Proof Mintage	MS-65	Prf-65
2003P	53,761	—	33.50	—
2003P	—	193,086	—	28.50

KM# 338 U.S. MILITARY ACADEMY AT WEST POINT -BICENTENNIAL   Obv: Cadet Review flagbearers, Academy buildings in background **Obv. Designer:** T. James Ferrell **Rev:** Academy emblems - Corinthian helmet and sword **Rev. Designer:** John Mercanti

Date	UNC Mintage	Proof Mintage	MS-65	Prf-65
2002W	103,201	—	18.50	—
2002W	—	288,293	—	18.50

KM# 362 THOMAS A. EDISON - ELECTRIC LIGHT 125TH ANNIVERSARY   Obv: Edison half-length figure facing holding light bulb **Obv. Designer:** Donna Weaver **Rev:** Light bulb and rays **Rev. Designer:** John Mercanti

Date	UNC Mintage	Proof Mintage	MS-65	Prf-65
2004P	68,031	—	34.00	—
2004P	—	213,409	—	34.50

KM# 363 LEWIS AND CLARK CORPS OF DISCOVERY BICENTENNIAL   Obv: Lewis and Clark standing **Rev:** Jefferson era clasped hands peace medal

Date	UNC Mintage	Proof Mintage	MS-65	Prf-65
2004P	90,323	—	31.00	—
2004P	—	288,492	—	27.50

KM# 376 U.S. MARINE CORPS, 230TH ANNIVERSARY   Obv: Flag Raising at Mt. Suribachi on Iwo Jima **Rev:** Marine Corps emblem

Date	UNC Mintage	Proof Mintage	MS-65	Prf-65
2005P	49,671	—	37.00	—
2005P	548,810	—	—	39.00

KM# 375 JOHN MARSHALL, 250TH BIRTH ANNIVERSARY   Obv: Marshall bust left **Obv. Designer:** John Mercanti **Rev:** Marshall era Supreme Court Chamber **Rev. Designer:** Donna Weaver

Date	UNC Mintage	Proof Mintage	MS-65	Prf-65
2005P	67,096	—	32.00	—
2005P	196,753	—	—	35.00

KM# 387 BENJAMIN FRANKLIN, 300TH BIRTH ANNIVERSARY   Obv: Youthful Franklin flying kite **Obv. Designer:** Norman E. Nemeth **Rev:** Revolutionary era "JOIN, or DIE" snake cartoon illustration

Date	UNC Mintage	Proof Mintage	MS-65	Prf-65
2006P	61,856	—	32.00	—
2006P	137,808	—	—	45.00

KM# 388 BENJAMIN FRANKLIN, 300TH BIRTH ANNIVERSARY
Obv: Bust 3/4 right, signature in oval below **Rev:** Continental Dollar of 1776 in center

Date	UNC Mintage	Proof Mintage	MS-65	Prf-65
2006P	64,014	—	33.00	—
2006P	137,808	—	—	44.00

KM# 405 JAMESTOWN - 400TH ANNIVERSARY
Obv: Two settlers and Native American **Obv. Designer:** Donna Weaver **Rev:** Three ships **Rev. Designer:** Don Everhart II

Date	UNC Mintage	Proof Mintage	MS-65	Prf-65
2007P	79,801	—	36.50	—
2007P	258,802	—	—	35.00

KM# 394 SAN FRANCISCO MINT MUSEUM
Obv: 3/4 view of building **Obv. Designer:** Sherl J. Winter **Rev:** Reverse of 1880s Morgan silver dollar

Date	UNC Mintage	Proof Mintage	MS-65	Prf-65
2006S	65,609	—	41.00	—
2006S	255,700	—	—	42.00

KM# 418 CENTRAL HIGH SCHOOL DESEGREGATION
Obv: Children's feet walking left with adult feet in military boots **Rev:** Little Rock's Central High School **Rev. Designer:** Don Everhart II

Date	UNC Mintage	Proof Mintage	MS-65	Prf-65
2007P	66,093	—	50.00	—
2007P	124,618	—	—	50.00

COMMEMORATIVES

KM# 439 AMERICAN BALD EAGLE Obv: Eagle
with flight, mountain in background at right Rev:
Great Seal of the United States

Date	UNC Mintage	Proof Mintage	MS-65	Prf-65
2008P	110,073	—	39.50	—
2008P	243,558	—	—	38.50

KM# 454 LINCOLN BICENTENNIAL Obv: 3/4
portrait facing right Obv. Designer: Justin Kunz and
Don Everhart II Rev: Part of Gettysburg Address
within wreath Rev. Designer: Phebe Hemphill

Date	UNC Mintage	Proof Mintage	MS-65	Prf-65
2009P	125,000	—	41.00	—
2009P	375,000	—	—	38.50

KM# 455 LOUIS BRAILLE BIRTH
BICENTENNIAL Obv: Louis Braille bust facing
Obv. Designer: Joel Iskowitz and Phebe Hemphill
Rev: School child reading book in Braille, BRL in
Braille code above Rev. Designer: Susan Gamble
and Joseph Menna

Date	UNC Mintage	Proof Mintage	MS-65	Prf-65
2009P	82,639	—	32.50	—
2009P	135,235	—	—	42.50

KM# 479 AMERICAN VETERANS DISABLED
FOR LIFE Obv: Soldier's feet, crutches Rev:
Legend within wreath

Date	UNC Mintage	Proof Mintage	MS-65	Prf-65
2010W	—	—	41.00	—
2010W	—	—	—	42.50

KM# 480 BOY SCOUTS OF AMERICA, 100TH
ANNIVERSARY Obv: Cub Scout, Boy Scout and
Venturer saluting Obv. Designer: Donna Weaver
Rev: Boy Scouts of America logo Rev. Designer:
Jim Licaretz

Date	UNC Mintage	Proof Mintage	MS-65	Prf-65
2010P	—	—	35.00	—
2010P	—	—	—	45.00

$5 (HALF EAGLE)

KM# 215 STATUE OF LIBERTY CENTENNIAL
Obv: Statue of Liberty head right Rev: Eagle in
flight left Designer: Elizabeth Jones

Date	UNC Mintage	Proof Mintage	MS-65	Prf-65
1986W	95,248	—	330	—
1986W	—	404,013	—	330

KM# 221 CONSTITUTION BICENTENNIAL
Obv: Eagle left with quill pen in talon Rev: Upright
quill pen Designer: Marcel Jovine

Date	UNC Mintage	Proof Mintage	MS-65	Prf-65
1987W	214,225	—	330	—
1987W	—	651,659	—	330

KM# 223 1988 OLYMPICS Obv: Nike head
wearing olive wreath Obv. Designer: Elizabeth
Jones Rev: Stylized olympic couldron Rev.
Designer: Marcel Jovine

Date	UNC Mintage	Proof Mintage	MS-65	Prf-65
1988W	62,913	—	330	—
1988W	—	281,456	—	330

KM# 226 CONGRESS BICENTENNIAL Obv:
Capitol dome Obv. Designer: John Mercanti Rev:
Eagle atop of the canopy from the Old Senate
Chamber

Date	UNC Mintage	Proof Mintage	MS-65	Prf-65
1989W	46,899	—	330	—
1989W	—	164,690	—	330

COMMEMORATIVES

COMMEMORATIVES

KM# 230 MOUNT RUSHMORE 50TH ANNIVERSARY Obv: Eagle in flight towards Mount Rushmore Obv. Designer: John Mercanti Rev: Legend at center Rev. Designer: Robert Lamb and William C. Cousins

Date	UNC Mintage	Proof Mintage	MS-65	Prf-65
1991W	31,959	—	395	—
1991W	—	111,991	—	345

KM# 235 1992 OLYMPICS Obv: Sprinter, U.S. Flag in background Obv. Designer: James C. Sharpe and T. James Ferrell Rev: Heraldic eagle, olympic rings above Rev. Designer: James M. Peed

Date	UNC Mintage	Proof Mintage	MS-65	Prf-65
1992W	27,732	—	395	—
1992W	—	77,313	—	345

KM# 239 COLUMBUS QUINCENTENARY Obv: Columbus' profile left, at right, map of Western Hemisphere at left Obv. Designer: T. James Ferrell Rev: Arms of Spain, and parchment map Rev. Designer: Thomas D. Rogers, Sr.

Date	UNC Mintage	Proof Mintage	MS-65	Prf-65
1992W	—	79,730	—	345
1992W	24,329	—	395	—

KM# 242 JAMES MADISON - BILL OF RIGHTS Obv: Madison at left holding document Obv. Designer: Scott R. Blazek Rev: Eagle above legend, torch and laurel at sides Rev. Designer: Joseph D. Peña

Date	UNC Mintage	Proof Mintage	MS-65	Prf-65
1993W	—	78,651	—	345
1993W	23,266	—	435	—

KM# 245 WORLD WAR II 50TH ANNIVERSARY Obv: Soldier with expression of victory Obv. Designer: Charles J. Madsen Rev: Morse code dot-dot-dot-dash for V, large in background; V for Victory Rev. Designer: Edward S. Fisher

Date	UNC Mintage	Proof Mintage	MS-65	Prf-65
1993W	—	65,461	—	385
1993W	23,089	—	465	—

KM# 248 1994 WORLD CUP SOCCER Obv: World Cup trophy Obv. Designer: William J. Krawczewicz Rev: World Cup 94 logo Rev. Designer: Dean McMullen

Date	UNC Mintage	Proof Mintage	MS-65	Prf-65
1994W	22,464	—	375	—
1994W	—	89,619	—	385

KM# 256 CIVIL WAR Obv: Bugler on horseback right Obv. Designer: Don Troiani Rev: Eagle on shield Rev. Designer: Alfred Maletsky

Date	UNC Mintage	Proof Mintage	MS-65	Prf-65
1995W	12,735	—	925	—
1995W	—	55,246	—	395

KM# 261 1996 OLYMPICS - TORCH RUNNER Obv: Torch runner, Atlanta skyline and logo in background Rev: Eagle advancing right

Date	UNC Mintage	Proof Mintage	MS-65	Prf-65
1995W	—	57,442	—	375
1995W	14,675	—	900	—

KM# 265 1996 OLYMPICS - STADIUM Obv:
Atlanta Stadium and logo **Rev:** Eagle advancing right

Date	UNC Mintage	Proof Mintage	MS-65	Prf-65
1995W	—	43,124	—	575
1995W	10,579	—	2,400	—

KM# 270 1996 OLYMPICS - CAULDRON Obv:
Torch bearer lighting cauldron **Rev:** Atlanta
Olympics logo flanked by laurel

Date	UNC Mintage	Proof Mintage	MS-65	Prf-65
1996W	—	38,555	—	575
1996W	9,210	—	2,650	—

KM# 274 1996 OLYMPICS - FLAG BEARER
Obv: Flag bearer advancing **Rev:** Atlanta Olympic
logo flanked by laurel

Date	UNC Mintage	Proof Mintage	MS-65	Prf-65
1996W	—	32,886	—	635
1996W	9,174	—	2,650	—

KM# 277 SMITHSONIAN INSTITUTION 150TH
ANNIVERSARY **Obv:** Smithson bust left **Obv.
Designer:** Alfred Maletsky **Rev:** Sunburst museum
logo **Rev. Designer:** T. James Ferrell

Date	UNC Mintage	Proof Mintage	MS-65	Prf-65
1996W	9,068	—	900	—
1996W	21,840	—	—	495

KM# 280 JACKIE ROBINSON Obv: Robinson
head right **Obv. Designer:** William C. Cousins **Rev:**
Legend on baseball **Rev. Designer:** James M. Peed

Date	UNC Mintage	Proof Mintage	MS-65	Prf-65
1997W	5,202	—	3,900	—
1997W	24,072	—	—	575

KM# 282 FRANKLIN DELANO ROOSEVELT
Obv: Roosevelt bust right **Obv. Designer:** T.
James Ferrell **Rev:** Eagle shield **Rev. Designer:**
James M. Peed and Thomas D. Rogers, Sr.

Date	UNC Mintage	Proof Mintage	MS-65	Prf-65
1997W	11,894	—	1,600	—
1997W	29,233	—	—	395

KM# 300 GEORGE WASHINGTON DEATH
BICENTENNIAL **Obv:** Washington's head right
Rev: Eagle with wings outstretched **Designer:**
Laura G. Fraser

Date	UNC Mintage	Proof Mintage	MS-65	Prf-65
1999W	22,511	—	395	—
1999W	—	41,693	—	375

KM# 326 CAPITOL VISITOR CENTER Obv:
Column at right **Rev:** First Capital building
Designer: Elizabeth Jones

Date	UNC Mintage	Proof Mintage	MS-65	Prf-65
2001W	6,761	—	1,750	—
2001W	—	27,652	—	420

KM# 337 2002 WINTER OLYMPICS Obv: Salt
Lake City Olympics logo **Rev:** Stylized cauldron
Designer: Donna Weaver

Date	UNC Mintage	Proof Mintage	MS-65	Prf-65
2002W	10,585	—	440	—
2002W	—	32,877	—	365

KM# 395 SAN FRANCISCO MINT MUSEUM
Obv: Front entrance façade **Rev:** Eagle as on 1860's $5. Gold

Date	UNC Mintage	Proof Mintage	MS-65	Prf-65
2006S	16,230	—	285	—
2006S	41,517	—	—	295

KM# 406 JAMESTOWN - 400TH ANNIVERSARY
Obv: Settler and Native American **Rev:** Jamestown Memorial Church ruins

Date	UNC Mintage	Proof Mintage	MS-65	Prf-65
2007W	18,843	—	345	—
2007W	47,050	—	—	345

KM# 440 AMERICAN BALD EAGLE **Obv:** Two
eagles on branch **Rev:** Eagle with shield

Date	UNC Mintage	Proof Mintage	MS-65	Prf-65
2008W	13,467	—	285	—
2008W	59,269	—	—	300

$10 (EAGLE)

KM# 211 1984 OLYMPICS **Weight:** 16.7180 g.
Composition: 0.9000 Gold, 0.4837 oz. AGW **Diameter:** 27mm. **Obv:** Male and female runner with torch **Obv. Designer:** James M. Peed and John Mercanti **Rev:** Heraldic eagle **Rev. Designer:** John Mercanti

Date	UNC Mintage	Proof Mintage	MS-65	Prf-65
1984W	75,886	—	610	—
1984P	—	33,309	—	650
1984D	—	34,533	—	650
1984S	—	48,551	—	650
1984W	—	381,085	—	650

KM# 312 LIBRARY OF CONGRESS **Weight:**
16.2590 g. **Composition:** Bi-Metallic, 0 oz. **Obv:** Torch and partial facade **Obv. Designer:** John Mercanti **Rev:** Stylized eagle within laurel wreath **Rev. Designer:** Thomas D. Rogers, Sr.

Date	UNC Mintage	Proof Mintage	MS-65	Prf-65
2000W	6,683	—	5,950	—
2000W	—	27,167	—	1,075

KM# 350 FIRST FLIGHT CENTENNIAL **Weight:**
16.7180 g. **Composition:** 0.9000 Gold, 0.4837 oz. AGW **Obv:** Orvile and Wilbur Wright busts facing **Rev:** Wright flyer and eagle **Designer:** Donna Weaver

Date	UNC Mintage	Proof Mintage	MS-65	Prf-65
2003P	10,129	—	650	—
2003P	—	21,846	—	650

$20 (DOUBLE EAGLE)

KM# 464   **Composition:** 0.9990 Gold, 0 oz.
AGW **Diameter:** 27mm. **Obv:** Liberty holding torch, walking forward **Rev:** Eagle in flight left, sunrise in background **Designer:** Augustus Saint-Gaudens **Notes:** Ultra high relief

Date	UNC Mintage	Proof Mintage	MS-65	Prf-65
2009	115,178	—	—	1,275

MODERN COMMEMORATIVE COIN SETS

Olympic, 1983-1984

Date	Price
1983 & 1984 3 coin set: 1983 and one 1984 uncirculated dollar and 1984W uncirculated gold $10; KM209, 210, 211.	684
1983S & 1984S 3 coin set: proof 1983 and 1984 dollar and 1984W gold $10; KM209, 210, 211.	677
1983 & 1984 6 coin set: 1983S and 1984S uncirculated and proof dollars, 1984W uncirculated and proof gold $10; KM209, 210, 211.	1,361
1983S & 1984S 2 coin set: proof dollars.	37.70
1983 collectors 3 coin set: 1983 PDS uncirculated dollars; KM209.	57.10
1984 collectors 3 coin set: 1984 PDS uncirculated dollars; KM210.	57.60

Statue of Liberty

Date	Price
1986 2 coin set: uncirculated silver dollar and clad half dollar; KM212, 214.	24.10
1986 2 coin set: proof silver dollar and clad half dollar; KM212, 214.	23.80
1986 3 coin set: uncirculated silver dollar, clad half dollar and gold $5; KM212, 214, 215.	354
1986 3 coin set: proof silver dollar, clad half dollar and gold $5; KM212, 214, 215.	353
1986 6 coin set: 1 each of the proof and uncirculated issues; KM212, 214, 215.	707

Constitution

Date	Price
1987 2 coin set: uncirculated silver dollar and gold $5; KM220, 221.	348
1987 2 coin set: proof silver dollar and gold $5; KM220, 221.	348
1987 4 coin set: silver dollar and $5 gold proof and uncirculated issues; KM220, 221.	697

Olympic, 1988

Date	Price
1988 2 coin set: uncirculated silver dollar and gold $5; KM222, 223.	348
1988 2 coin set: proof silver dollar and gold $5; KM222, 223.	348
1988 4 coin set: silver dollar and $5 gold proof and uncirculated issues; KM222, 223.	697

Congress

Date	Price
1989 2 coin set: uncirculated silver dollar and clad half dollar; KM224, 225.	33.00
1989 2 coin set: proof silver dollar and clad half dollar; KM224, 225.	33.00
1989 3 coin set: uncirculated silver dollar, clad half and gold $5; KM224, 225, 226.	363
1989 3 coin set: proof silver dollar, clad half and gold $5; KM224, 225, 226.	362
1989 6 coin set: 1 each of the proof and uncirculated issues; KM224, 225, 226.	725

Mt. Rushmore

Date	Price
1991 2 coin set: uncirculated half dollar and silver dollar; KM228, 229.	47.00
1991 2 coin set: proof half dollar and silver dollar; KM228, 229.	43.00
1991 3 coin set: uncirculated half dollar, silver dollar and gold $5; KM228, 229, 230.	442
1991 3 coin set: proof half dollar, silver dollar and gold $5; KM228, 229, 230.	388
1991 6 coin set: 1 each of proof and uncirculated issues; KM228, 229, 230.	830

Olympic, 1992

Date	Price
1992 2 coin set: uncirculated half dollar and silver dollar; KM233, 234.	31.00
1992 2 coin set: proof half dollar and silver dollar; KM233, 234.	32.50
1992 3 coin set: uncirculated half dollar, silver dollar and gold $5; KM233, 234, 235.	426
1992 3 coin set: proof half dollar, silver dollar and gold $5; KM233, 234, 235.	377
1992 6 coin set: 1 each of proof and uncirculated issues; KM233, 234, 235.	803

Columbus Quincentenary

Date	Price
1992 2 coin set: uncirculated half dollar and silver dollar; KM237, 238.	37.00
1992 2 coin set: proof half dollar and silver dollar; KM237, 238.	37.00
1992 3 coin set: uncirculated half dollar, silver dollar and gold $5; KM237, 238, 239.	382
1992 3 coin set: proof half dollar, silver dollar and gold $5; KM237, 238, 239.	265
1992 6 coin set: 1 each of proof and uncirculated issues; KM237, 238, 239.	814

Jefferson

Date	Price
1993 Jefferson: dollar, 1994 matte proof nickel and $2 note; KM249, 192.	53.50

Madison / Bill of Rights

Date	Price
1993 2 coin set: uncirculated half dollar and silver dollar; KM240, 241.	37.00
1993 2 coin set: proof half dollar and silver dollar; KM240, 241.	35.00
1993 3 coin set: uncirculated half dollar, silver dollar and gold $5; KM240, 241, 242.	379
1993 3 coin set: proof half dollar, silver dollar and gold $5; KM240, 241, 242.	250
1993 6 coin set: 1 each of proof and uncirculated issues; KM240, 241, 242.	852

World War II

Date	Price
1993 2 coin set: uncirculated half dollar and silver dollar; KM243, 244.	54.00
1993 2 coin set: proof half dollar and silver dollar; KM243, 244.	61.00
1993 3 coin set: uncirculated half dollar, silver dollar and gold $5; KM243, 244, 245.	519
1993 3 coin set: proof half dollar, silver dollar and gold $5; KM243, 244, 245.	446
1993 6 coin set: 1 each of proof and uncirculated issues; KM243, 244, 245.	965

World Cup

Date	Price
1994 2 coin set: uncirculated half dollar and silver dollar; KM246, 247.	31.50
1994 2 coin set: proof half dollar and silver dollar; KM246, 247.	32.50
1994 3 coin set: uncirculated half dollar, silver dollar and gold $5; KM246, 247, 248.	407
1994 3 coin set: proof half dollar, silver dollar and gold $5; KM246, 247, 248.	417
1994 6 coin set: 1 each of proof and uncirculated issues; KM246, 247, 248.	824

U.S. Veterans

Date	Price
1994 3 coin set: uncirculated POW, Vietnam, Women dollars; KM250, 251, 252.	199
1994 3 coin set: proof POW, Vietnam, Women dollars; KM250, 251, 252.	135

Olympic, 1995-96

Date	Price
1995 4 coin set: uncirculated basketball half, $1 gymnast & blind runner, $5 torch runner; KM257, 259, 260, 261.	1,061
1995 4 coin set: proof basketball half, $1 gymnast & blind runner, $5 torch runner; KM257, 259, 260, 261.	491
1995P 2 coin set: proof $1 gymnast & blind runner; KM259, 260.	100.00
1995P 2 coin set: proof $1 track & field, cycling; KM263, 264.	94.00
1995-96 4 coin set: proof halves, basketball, baseball, swimming, soccer; KM257, 262, 267, 271.	169
1995 & 96 8 coins in cherry wood case: proof silver dollars: blind runner, gymnast, cycling, track & field, wheelchair, tennis, rowing, high jump; KM259, 260, 263, 264, 268, 269, 272, 272A.	481
1995 & 96 16 coins in cherry wood case: bu and proof silver dollars: blind runner, gymnast, cycling, track & field, wheelchair, tennis, rowing, high jump; KM259, 260, 263, 264, 268, 269, 272, 272A.	2,200
1995 & 96 16 coins in cherry wood case: proof half dollars: basketball, baseball, swimming, soccer, KM257, 262, 267, 271. Proof silver dollars: blind runner, gymnast, cycling, track & field, wheelchair, tennis, rowing, high jump, KM259, 260, 263, 264, 268, 269, 272, 272A. Proof $5 gold: torch runner, stadium, cauldron, flag bearer, KM 261, 265, 270, 274.	2,641
1995 & 96 32 coins in cherry wood case: bu & proof half dollars: basketball, baseball, swimming, soccer, KM257, 262, 267, 271. BU & proof silver dollars: blind runner, gymnast, cycling, track & field, wheelchair, tennis, rowing, high jump, KM259, 260, 263, 264, 268, 269, 272, 272A. BU & proof $5 gold: torch runner, stadium, cauldron, flag bearer, KM261, 265, 270, 274.	13,455
1996P 2 coin set: proof $1 wheelchair & tennis; KM268, 269.	163
1996P 2 coin set: proof $1 rowing & high jump; KM272, 272A.	68.00

Civil War

Date	Price
1995 2 coin set: uncirculated half and dollar; KM254, 255.	109
1995 2 coin set: proof half and dollar; KM254, 255.	108
1995 3 coin set: uncirculated half, dollar and gold $5; KM254, 255, 256.	1,034
1995 3 coin set: proof half, dollar and gold $5; KM254, 255, 256.	502
1995 6 coin set: 1 each of proof and uncirculated issues; KM254, 255, 256.	1,536

Smithsonian

Date	Price
1996 2 coin set: proof dollar and $5 gold; KM276, 277.	548
1996 4 coin set: proof and B.U. ; KM276, 277.	1,573

Jackie Robinson

Date	Price
1997 2 coin set: proof dollar & $5 gold; KM279, 280.	691
1997 4 coin set: proof & BU; KM279, 280.	4,683
1997 legacy set.	950

Botanic Garden

Date	Price
1997 2 coin set: dollar, Jefferson nickel and $1 note; KM278, 192.	165

Franklin Delano Roosevelt

Date	Price
1997W 2 coin set: uncirculated and proof; KM282.	2,660

Kennedy

Date	Price
1998 2 coin set: proof; KM287.	82.50
1998 2 coin collectors set: Robert Kennedy dollar and John Kennedy half dollar; KM287, 202b. Matte finished.	235

Black Patriots

Date	Price
1998S 2 coin set: uncirculated and proof; KM288.	239

George Washington

Date	Price
1999 2 coin set: proof and uncirculated gold $5; KM300.	769

Dolley Madison

Date	Price
1999 2 coin set: proof and uncirculated silver dollars; KM298.	77.00

Yellowstone National Park

Date	Price
1999 2 coin set: proof and uncirculated silver dollars; KM299.	88.00

Millennium Coin & Currency

Date	Price
2000 2 coin set: uncirculated Sacagewea $1, silver Eagle & $1 note.	72.00

Leif Ericson

Date	Price
2000 2 coin set: proof and uncirculated silver dollars; KM313.	150

Capitol Visitor Center

Date	Price
2001 3 coin set: proof half, silver dollar, gold $5; KM323, 324, 326.	475

American Buffalo

Date	Price
2001 2 coin set: 90% silver unc. & proof $1.; KM325.	335
2001 coin & currency set 90% unc. dollar & replicas of 1899 $5 silver cert.; KM325.	180

Winter Olympics - Salt Lake City

Date	Price
2002 2 coin set: proof 90% silver dollar KM336 & $5.00 Gold KM337.	413
2002 4 coin set: 90% silver unc. & proof $1, KM336 & unc. & proof gold $5, KM337.	837

COMMEMORATIVE SETS

First Flight Centennial

Date	Price
2003 3 coin set: proof gold ten dollar KM350, proof silver dollar KM349 & proof clad half dollar KM348.	683

Lewis and Clark Bicentennial

Date	Price
2004 Coin and pouch set.	100.00
2004 coin and currency set: Uncirculated silver dollar, two 2005 nickels, replica 1901 $10 Bison note, silver plated peace medal, three stamps & two booklets.	85.00
2004 Westward Journey Nickel series coin and medal set: Proof Sacagawea dollar, two 2005 proof nickels and silver plated peace medal.	35.00

Thomas Alva Edison

Date	Price
2004 Uncirculated silver dollar and light bulb.	60.00

U.S. Marine Corps.

Date	Price
2005 Uncirculated silver dollar and stamp set.	80.00
2005 American Legacy: Proof Marine Corps dollar, Proof John Marshall dollar and 10 piece proof set.	180

Chief Justice John Marshall

Date	Price
2005 Coin and Chronicles set: Uncirculated silver dollar, booklet and BEP intaglio portrait.	60.00
2005 American Legacy: Proof Marine Corps dollar, Proof John Marshall dollar and 10 piece proof set.	180

Benjamin Franklin Tercentennary

Date	Price
2006 Coin and Chronicles set: Uncirculated "Scientist" silver dollar, four stamps, Poor Richards Almanac and intaglio print.	65.00

AMERICAN EAGLE BULLION COINS

SILVER DOLLAR

KM# 273 • 31.1050 g., 0.9993 **Silver**, 0.9993 oz., 40.6mm. • **Obv. Desc:** Liberty walking left **Rev. Desc:** Eagle with shield **Obv. Designer:** Adolph A. Weinman **Rev. Designer:** John Mercanti

Date	Mintage	Unc	Prf.
1986	5,393,005	24.00	—
1986S	1,446,778	—	55.00
1987	11,442,335	23.30	—
1987S	904,732	—	55.00
1988	5,004,646	23.30	—
1988S	557,370	—	57.00
1989	5,203,327	20.50	—
1989S	617,694	—	57.00
1990	5,840,110	24.30	—
1990S	695,510	—	55.00
1991	7,191,066	23.30	—
1991S	511,924	—	55.00
1992	5,540,068	23.30	—
1992S	498,543	—	57.00
1993	6,763,762	23.30	—
1993P	405,913	—	136
1994	4,227,319	24.30	—
1994P	372,168	—	215
1995	4,672,051	25.80	—
1995P	407,822	—	127
1995W 10th Anniversary	30,102	—	3,150
1996	3,603,386	47.00	—
1996P	498,293	—	85.00
1997	4,295,004	23.30	—
1997P	440,315	—	132
1998	4,847,547	24.30	—
1998P	450,728	—	44.00
1999	7,408,640	24.30	—
1999P	549,330	—	47.00
2000P	600,743	—	55.00
2000	9,239,132	23.30	—
2001	9,001,711	20.50	—

Date	Mintage	Unc	Prf.
2001W	746,398	—	55.00
2002	10,539,026	20.50	—
2002W	647,342	—	55.00
2003	8,495,008	20.50	—
2003W	747,831	—	55.00
2004	8,882,754	20.50	—
2004W	801,602	—	55.00
2005	8,891,025	20.50	—
2005W	816,663	—	55.00
2006	10,676,522	22.80	—
2006W	1,093,600	—	55.00
2006P Reverse Proof	—	—	175
2006W Burnished Unc.	468,000	75.00	—
2006 20th Aniv. 3 pc. set	—	—	320
2007	9,028,036	20.80	—
2007W	821,759	—	55.00
2007W Burnished Unc.	690,891	20.00	—
2008	20,583,000	20.50	—
2008W Reverse of '07	—	410	—
2008	—	—	79.00
2008W Burnished Unc.	—	30.50	—
2009	—	20.50	—
2010	—	22.00	—

GOLD $5

KM# 216 • 3.3930 g., 0.9167 **Gold**, 0.1000 oz., 16.5mm. • **Obv. Designer:** Augustus Saint-Gaudens **Rev. Designer:** Miley Busiek

Date	Mintage	Unc	Prf.
MCMLXXXVI (1986)	912,609	151	—
MCMLXXXVII (1987)	580,266	143	—
MCMLXXXVIII (1988)	159,500	200	—
MCMLXXXVIII (1988)P	143,881	—	185
MCMLXXXIX (1989)	264,790	143	—
MCMLXXXIX (1989)P	84,647	—	190
MCMXC (1990)	210,210	143	—
MCMXC (1990)P	99,349	—	190
MCMXCI (1991)	165,200	151	—
MCMXCI (1991)P	70,334	—	185
1992	209,300	141	—
1992P	64,874	—	185
1993	210,709	143	—
1993P	45,960	—	185
1994	206,380	143	—
1994W	62,849	—	185
1995	223,025	141	—
1995W	62,667	—	185
1996	401,964	141	—
1996W	57,047	—	185
1997	528,515	141	—
1997W	34,977	—	185
1998	1,344,520	141	—
1998W	39,395	—	185
1999	2,750,338	141	—
1999W	48,428	—	165
1999W Die error	—	575	—
2000	569,153	180	—
2000W	49,971	—	185
2001	269,147	141	—
2001W	37,530	—	185
2002	230,027	141	—
2002W	40,864	—	185
2003	245,029	141	—
2003W	40,027	—	185
2004	250,016	141	—

Date	Mintage	Unc	Prf.
2004W	35,131	—	185
2005	300,043	141	—
2005W	49,265	—	185
2006	285,006	141	—
2006W	47,277	—	185
2006W Burnished Unc.	20,643	140	—
2007	190,010	141	—
2007W	58,553	—	200
2007W Burnished Unc.	22,501	135	—
2008	305,000	151	—
2008W	—	—	200
2008W	—	215	—
2009	27,000	145	—

Date	Mintage	Unc	Prf.
2008W Burnished Unc.	—	950	—
2009	27,500	321	—

GOLD $25

KM# 218 • 16.9660 g., 0.9167 **Gold**, 0.5000 oz., 27mm. • **Obv. Designer:** Augustus Saint-Gaudens **Rev. Designer:** Miley Busiek

Date	Mintage	Unc	Prf.
MCMLXXXVI (1986)	599,566	627	—
MCMLXXXVII (1987)	131,255	635	—
MCMLXXXVII (1987)P	143,398	—	885
MCMLXXXVIII (1988)	45,000	875	—
MCMLXXXVIII (1988)P	76,528	—	885
MCMLXXXIX (1989)	44,829	990	—
MCMLXXXIX (1989)P	44,798	—	885
MCMXC (1990)	31,000	1,250	—
MCMXC (1990)P	51,636	—	885
MCMXCI (1991)	24,100	1,800	—
MCMXCI (1991)P	53,125	—	885
1992	54,404	780	—
1992P	40,976	—	885
1993	73,324	665	—
1993P	31,130	—	885
1994	62,400	620	—
1994W	44,584	—	885
1995	53,474	645	—
1995W	45,388	—	885
1996	39,287	795	—
1996W	35,058	—	885
1997	79,605	620	—
1997W	26,344	—	885
1998	169,029	620	—
1998W	25,374	—	885
1999	263,013	620	—
1999W	30,427	—	885
2000	79,287	620	—
2000W	32,028	—	885
2001	48,047	750	—
2001W	23,240	—	885
2002	70,027	620	—
2002W	26,646	—	885
2003	79,029	620	—
2003W	28,270	—	885
2004	98,040	620	—
2004W	27,330	—	885
2005	80,023	620	—
2005W	34,311	—	885
2006	66,004	623	—
2006W	34,322	—	885
2006W Burnished Unc.	15,164	900	—
2007	47,002	623	—
2007W	44,025	—	885
2007W Burnished Unc.	11,458	845	—
2008	61,000	623	—
2008W	27,800	—	885
2008W Burnished Unc.	—	1,650	—
2009	55,000	623	—

GOLD $10

KM# 217 • 8.4830 g., 0.9167 **Gold**, 0.2500 oz., 22mm. • **Obv. Designer:** Augustus Saint-Gaudens **Rev. Designer:** Miley Busiek

Date	Mintage	Unc	Prf.
MCMLXXXVI (1986)	726,031	321	—
MCMLXXXVII (1987)	269,255	335	—
MCMLXXXVIII (1988)	49,000	321	—
MCMLXXXVIII (1988)P	98,028	—	433
MCMLXXXIX (1989)	81,789	321	—
MCMLXXXIX (1989)P	54,170	—	433
MCMXC (1990)	41,000	321	—
MCMXC (1990)P	62,674	—	433
MCMXCI (1991)	36,100	375	—
MCMXCI (1991)P	50,839	—	433
1992	59,546	321	—
1992P	46,269	—	433
1993	71,864	321	—
1993P	33,775	—	433
1994	72,650	321	—
1994W	47,172	—	433
1995	83,752	321	—
1995W	47,526	—	433
1996	60,318	321	—
1996W	38,219	—	433
1997	108,805	321	—
1997W	29,805	—	433
1998	309,829	321	—
1998W	29,503	—	433
1999	564,232	321	—
1999W	34,417	—	433
1999W Die error	—	1,050	—
2000	128,964	321	—
2000W	36,036	—	433
2001	71,280	321	—
2001W	25,613	—	433
2002	62,027	321	—
2002W	29,242	—	433
2003	74,029	321	—
2003W	30,292	—	433
2004	72,014	321	—
2004W	28,839	—	433
2005	72,015	321	—
2005W	37,207	—	433
2006	60,004	321	—
2006W	36,127	—	433
2006W Burnished Unc.	15,188	335	—
2007	34,004	321	—
2007W	46,189	—	448
2007W Burnished Unc.	12,786	420	—
2008	—	321	—
2008W	28,000	—	448

GOLD $50

KM# 219 • 33.9310 g., 0.9167 **Gold**, 100000 oz., 32.7mm. • **Obv. Designer:** Augustus Saint-Gaudens **Rev. Designer:** Miley Busiek

Date	Mintage	Unc	Prf.
MCMLXXXVI (1986)	1,362,650	1,184	—
MCMLXXXVI (1986)W	446,290	—	1,710
MCMLXXXVII (1987)	1,045,500	1,184	—
MCMLXXXVII (1987)W	147,498	—	1,710
MCMLXXXVIII (1988)	465,000	1,184	—
MCMLXXXVIII (1988)W	87,133	—	1,710
MCMLXXXIX (1989)	415,790	1,184	—
MCMLXXXIX (1989)W	54,570	—	1,710
MCMXC (1990)	373,219	1,184	—
MCMXC (1990)W	62,401	—	1,710
MCMXCI (1991)	243,100	1,184	—
MCMXCI (1991)W	50,411	—	1,710
1992	275,000	1,184	—
1992W	44,826	—	1,710
1993	480,192	1,184	—
1993W	34,369	—	1,710
1994	221,663	1,184	—
1994W	46,674	—	1,710
1995	200,636	1,184	—
1995W	46,368	—	1,710
1996	189,148	1,184	—
1996W	36,153	—	1,710
1997	664,508	1,184	—
1997W	28,034	—	1,710
1998	1,468,530	1,184	—
1998W	25,886	—	1,720
1999	1,505,026	1,184	—
1999W	31,427	—	1,710
1999 Die error	—	1,800	—
2000	433,319	1,184	—
2000W	33,007	—	1,710
2001	143,605	1,184	—
2001W	24,555	—	1,710
2002	222,029	1,184	—
2002W	27,499	—	1,710
2003	416,032	1,184	—
2003W	28,344	—	1,710
2004	417,149	1,184	—
2004W	28,215	—	1,710
2005	356,555	1,184	—
2005W	35,246	—	1,710
2006	237,510	1,184	—
2006W	47,000	—	1,710
2006W Reverse Proof	10,000	—	2,200
2006W Burnished Unc.	45,912	1,125	—
2007	140,016	1,196	—
2007W	51,810	—	1,710
2007W Burnished Unc.	18,609	1,125	—
2008	710,000	1,184	—
2008W	29,000	—	1,710
2008W Burnished Unc.	—	1,550	—
2009	122,000	1,184	—
2010	—	—	—

PLATINUM $10

KM# 283 • 3.1100 g., 0.9995 **Platinum**, 0.0999 oz., 17mm. • **Rev. Desc:** Eagle flying right over sunrise **Obv. Designer:** John Mercanti **Rev. Designer:** Thomas D. Rogers Sr

Date	Mintage	Unc	Prf.
1997	70,250	300	—
1997W	36,996	—	250
1998	39,525	209	—
1999	55,955	209	—
2000	34,027	209	—
2001	52,017	209	—
2002	23,005	209	—
2003	22,007	209	—
2004	15,010	209	—
2005	14,013	209	—
2006	11,001	209	—
2006W Burnished Unc.	—	425	—
2007	13,003	280	—
2007W Burnished Unc.	—	210	—
2008	17,000	206	—
2008 Burnished Unc.	—	210	—
2009	—	180	—

KM# 289 • 3.1100 g., 0.9995 **Platinum**, 0.0999 oz. • **Rev. Desc:** Eagle in flight over New England costal lighthouse **Obv. Designer:** John Mercanti

Date	Mintage	Unc	Prf.
1998W	19,847	—	250

KM# 301 • 3.1100 g., 0.9995 **Platinum**, 0.0999 oz. • **Rev. Desc:** Eagle in flight over Southeastern Wetlands **Obv. Designer:** John Mercanti

Date	Mintage	Unc	Prf.
1999W	19,133	—	250

KM# 314 • 3.1100 g., 0.9995 **Platinum**, 0.0999 oz. • **Rev. Desc:** Eagle in flight over Heartland **Obv. Designer:** John Mercanti

Date	Mintage	Unc	Prf.
2000W	15,651	—	250

KM# 327 • 3.1100 g., 0.9995 **Platinum**, 0.0999 oz., 17mm. • **Rev. Desc:** Eagle in flight over Southwestern cactus desert **Obv. Designer:** John Mercanti

Date	Mintage	Unc	Prf.
2001W	12,174	—	250

KM# 339 • 3.1100 g., 0.9995 **Platinum**, 0.0999 oz., 17mm. • **Rev. Desc:** Eagle fishing in America's Northwest **Obv. Designer:** John Mercanti

Date	Mintage	Unc	Prf.
2002W	12,365	—	250

KM# 351 • 3.1100 g., 0.9995 **Platinum**, 0.0999 oz., 17mm. • **Rev. Desc:** Eagle pearched on a Rocky Mountain Pine branch against a flag backdrop **Obv. Designer:** John Mercanti **Rev. Designer:** Al Maletsky

Date	Mintage	Unc	Prf.
2003W	9,534	—	255

KM# 364 • 3.1100 g., 0.9995 **Platinum**, 0.0999 oz., 17mm. • **Rev. Desc:** Chester French, 1907. The sculpture is outside the N.Y. Customs House, now part of the Smithsonian's Museum of the American Indian **Obv. Designer:** John Mercanti

Date	Mintage	Unc	Prf.
2004W	7,161	—	595

KM# 377 • 3.1100 g., 0.9995 **Platinum**, 0.0999 oz., 17mm. • **Rev. Desc:** Eagle with cornucopiae **Obv. Designer:** John Mercanti **Rev. Designer:** Donna Weaver

Date	Mintage	Unc	Prf.
2005W	8,104	—	218

KM# 389 • 3.1100 g., 0.9995 **Platinum**, 0.0999 oz., 17mm. • **Event:** Legislative **Rev. Desc:** Liberty seated writing between two columns **Obv. Designer:** John Mercanti

Date	Mintage	Unc	Prf.
2006W	10,205	—	190

KM# 414 • 3.1100 g., 0.9995 **Platinum**, 0.0999 oz., 17mm. • **Event:** Executive **Obv. Designer:** John Mercanti

Date	Mintage	Unc	Prf.
2007W	8,176	—	250

KM# 434 • 3.1100 g., 0.9995 **Platinum**, 0.0999 oz., 17mm. • **Obv. Designer:** John Mercanti

Date	Mintage	Unc	Prf.
2008W	8,176	—	405

KM# 460 • 3.1100 g., 0.9995 **Platinum**, 0.0999 oz., 17mm. • **Event:** Judicial **Obv. Designer:** John Mercanti

Date	Mintage	Unc	Prf.
2009W	5,600	—	245

KM# 485 • 3.1100 g., 0.9990 **Platinum**, 0.0999 oz. • **Obv. Designer:** John Mercanti

Date	Mintage	Unc	Prf.
2010W	—	—	—

PLATINUM $25

KM# 284 • 7.7857 g., 0.9995 **Platinum**, 0.2502 oz., 22mm. • **Rev. Desc:** Eagle in flight over sunrise **Obv. Designer:** John Mercanti **Rev. Designer:** Thomas D. Rogers Sr

Date	Mintage	Unc	Prf.
1997	27,100	490	—
1997W	18,628	—	500
1998	38,887	490	—
1999	39,734	490	—
2000	20,054	490	—
2001	21,815	490	—
2002	27,405	490	—
2003	25,207	490	—
2004	18,010	490	—
2005	12,013	490	—
2006	12,001	490	—
2006W Burnished Unc.	—	585	—
2007	8,402	490	—
2007W Burnished Unc.	—	495	—
2008	22,800	665	—
2008 Burnished Unc.	—	490	—
2009	—	490	—

KM# 290 • 7.7857 g., 0.9995 **Platinum**, 0.2502 oz. •
Rev. Desc: Eagle in flight over New England costal
lighthouse **Obv. Designer:** John Mercanti

Date	Mintage	Unc	Prf.
1998W	14,873	—	500

KM# 302 • 7.7857 g., 0.9995 **Platinum**, 0.2502 oz. •
Rev. Desc: Eagle in flight over Southeastern
Wetlands **Obv. Designer:** John Mercanti

Date	Mintage	Unc	Prf.
1999W	13,507	—	500

KM# 315 • 7.7857 g., 0.9995 **Platinum**,
0.2502 oz. • **Rev. Desc:** Eagle in flight over
Heartland **Obv. Designer:** John Mercanti

Date	Mintage	Unc	Prf.
2000W	11,995	—	500

KM# 328 • 7.7857 g., 0.9995 **Platinum**, 0.2502 oz.,
22mm. • **Rev. Desc:** Eagle in flight over
Southwestern cactus desert **Obv. Designer:**
John Mercanti

Date	Mintage	Unc	Prf.
2001W	8,847	—	500

KM# 340 • 7.7857 g., 0.9995 **Platinum**, 0.2502 oz.,
22mm. • **Rev. Desc:** Eagle fishing in America's
Northwest **Obv. Designer:** John Mercanti

Date	Mintage	Unc	Prf.
2002W	9,282	—	500

KM# 352 • 7.7857 g., 0.9995 **Platinum**, 0.2502 oz.,
22mm. • **Rev. Desc:** Eagle pearched on a Rocky
Mountain Pine branch against a flag backdrop.
Obv. Designer: John Mercanti **Rev. Designer:**
Al Maletsky

Date	Mintage	Unc	Prf.
2003W	7,044	—	500

KM# 365 • 7.7857 g., 0.9995 **Platinum**, 0.2502 oz.,
22mm. • **Rev. Desc:** Chester French, 1907. The
sculpture is outside the N.Y. Customs House, now
part of the Smithsonian's Museum of the American
Indian **Obv. Designer:** John Mercanti

Date	Mintage	Unc	Prf.
2004W	5,193	—	1,150

KM# 378 • 7.7857 g., 0.9995 **Platinum**, 0.2502 oz.,
22mm. • **Rev. Desc:** Eagle with cornucopiae
Obv. Designer: John Mercanti **Rev. Designer:**
Donna Weaver

Date	Mintage	Unc	Prf.
2005W	6,592	—	525

KM# 390 • 7.7857 g., 0.9995 **Platinum**, 0.2502 oz.,
22mm. • **Event:** Legislative **Rev. Desc:** Liberty
seated writing between two columns
Obv. Designer: John Mercanti

Date	Mintage	Unc	Prf.
2006W	7,813	—	445

KM# 415 • 7.7857 g., 0.9995 **Platinum**, 0.2502 oz.,
22mm. • **Event:** Executive **Obv. Designer:**
John Mercanti

Date	Mintage	Unc	Prf.
2007W	6,017	—	440

KM# 435 • 7.7857 g., 0.9995 **Platinum**, 0.2502 oz.,
22mm. • **Obv. Designer:** John Mercanti

Date	Mintage	Unc	Prf.
2008W	6,017	—	690

KM# 461 • 7.7857 g., 0.9995 **Platinum**, 0.2502 oz.,
22mm. • **Event:** Judicial **Obv. Designer:**
John Mercanti

Date	Mintage	Unc	Prf.
2009W	3,800	—	600

KM# 486 • 7.7857 g., 0.9990 **Platinum**, 0.2501 oz. •
Obv. Designer: John Mercanti

Date	Mintage	Unc	Prf.
2010W	—	—	—

PLATINUM $50

KM# 285 • 15.5520 g., 0.9995 **Platinum**, 0.4997 oz., 27mm. • **Rev. Desc:** Eagle flying right over sunrise **Obv. Designer:** John Mercanti **Rev. Designer:** Thomas D. Rogers Sr

Date	Mintage	Unc	Prf.
1997	20,500	996	—
1997W	15,432	—	1,008
1998	32,419	996	—
1999	32,309	996	—
2000	18,892	996	—
2001	12,815	996	—
2002	24,005	996	—
2003	17,409	996	—
2004	13,236	996	—
2005	9,013	996	—
2006	9,602	996	—
2006W Burnished Unc.	—	1,012	—
2007	7,001	996	—
2007W Burnished Unc.	—	1,012	—
2008	14,000	996	—
2008W Burnished Unc.	—	1,200	—
2009	—	996	—

KM# 291 • 15.5520 g., 0.9995 **Platinum**, 0.4997 oz. • **Rev. Desc:** Eagle in flight over New England costal lighthouse **Obv. Designer:** John Mercanti

Date	Mintage	Unc	Prf.
1998W	13,836	—	999

KM# 303 • 15.5520 g., 0.9995 **Platinum**, 0.4997 oz. • **Rev. Desc:** Eagle in flight over Southeastern Wetlands **Obv. Designer:** John Mercanti

Date	Mintage	Unc	Prf.
1999W	11,103	—	999

KM# 316 • 15.5520 g., 0.9995 **Platinum**, 0.4997 oz. • **Rev. Desc:** Eagle in flight over Heartland **Obv. Designer:** John Mercanti

Date	Mintage	Unc	Prf.
2000W	11,049	—	999

KM# 329 • 15.5520 g., 0.9995 **Platinum**, 0.4997 oz., 27mm. • **Rev. Desc:** Eagle in flight over Southwestern cactus desert **Obv. Designer:** John Mercanti

Date	Mintage	Unc	Prf.
2001W	8,254	—	999

KM# 341 • 15.5520 g., 0.9995 **Platinum**, 0.4997 oz., 27mm. • **Rev. Desc:** Eagle fishing in America's Northwest **Obv. Designer:** John Mercanti

Date	Mintage	Unc	Prf.
2002W	8,772	—	999

KM# 353 • 15.5520 g., 0.9995 **Platinum**, 0.4997 oz., 27mm. • **Rev. Desc:** Eagle pearched on a Rocky Mountain Pine branch against a flag backdrop. **Obv. Designer:** John Mercanti **Rev. Designer:** Al Maletsky

Date	Mintage	Unc	Prf.
2003W	7,131	—	999

KM# 366 • 15.5520 g., 0.9995 **Platinum**, 0.4997 oz., 27mm. • **Rev. Desc:** Chester French, 1907. The sculpture is outside the N.Y. Customs House, now part of the Smithsonian's Museum of the American Indian **Obv. Designer:** John Mercanti

Date	Mintage	Unc	Prf.
2004W	5,063	—	1,700

KM# 379 • 15.5520 g., 0.9995 **Platinum**, 0.4997 oz., 27mm. • **Rev. Desc:** Eagle with cornucopiae **Obv. Designer:** John Mercanti **Rev. Designer:** Donna Weaver

Date	Mintage	Unc	Prf.
2005W	5,942	—	980

KM# 391 • 15.5520 g., 0.9995 **Platinum**, 0.4997 oz., 27mm. • **Event:** Legislative **Rev. Desc:** Liberty seated writing between two columns **Obv. Designer:** John Mercanti

Date	Mintage	Unc	Prf.
2006W	7,649	—	865

KM# 416 • 15.5520 g., 0.9995 **Platinum**, 0.4997 oz., 27mm. • **Event:** Executive **Obv. Designer:** John Mercanti

Date	Mintage	Unc	Prf.
2007W	22,873	—	875
2007W Reverse Proof	16,937	—	950

KM# 436 • 15.5520 g., 0.9995 **Platinum**, 0.4997 oz., 27mm. • **Obv. Designer:** John Mercanti

Date	Mintage	Unc	Prf.
2008W	22,873	—	1,185

KM# 462 • 15.5520 g., 0.9995 **Platinum**, 0.4997 oz., 27mm. • **Event:** Judicial **Obv. Designer:** John Mercanti

Date	Mintage	Unc	Prf.
2009	3,600	—	—

KM# 487 • 15.5520 g., 0.9990 **Platinum**, 0.4995 oz. • **Obv. Designer:** John Mercanti

Date	Mintage	Unc	Prf.
2010W	—	—	—

PLATINUM $100

KM# 286 • 31.1050 g., 0.9995 **Platinum**, 0.9995 oz., 33mm. • **Rev. Desc:** Eagle in flight over sun rise **Obv. Designer:** John Mercanti **Rev. Designer:** Thomas D. Rogers Sr

Date	Mintage	Unc	Prf.
1997	56,000	1,916	—
1997W	15,885	—	2,017
1998	133,002	1,916	—
1999	56,707	1,916	—
2000	10,003	1,916	—
2001	14,070	1,916	—
2002	11,502	1,916	—
2003	8,007	1,916	—
2004	7,009	1,916	—
2005	6,310	1,916	—
2006	6,000	1,916	—
2006W Burnished Unc.	—	1,913	—
2007	7,202	1,916	—
2007W Burnished Unc.	—	1,913	—
2008	21,800	1,916	—
2008W Burnished Unc.	—	1,913	—
2009	—	1,680	—

KM# 292 • 31.1050 g., 0.9995 **Platinum**, 0.9995 oz. • **Rev. Desc:** Eagle in flight over New England costal lighthouse **Obv. Designer:** John Mercanti

Date	Mintage	Unc	Prf.
1998W	14,912	—	1,998

KM# 304 • 31.1050 g., 0.9995 **Platinum**, 0.9995 oz. • **Rev. Desc:** Eagle in flight over Southeastern Wetlands **Obv. Designer:** John Mercanti

Date	Mintage	Unc	Prf.
1999W	12,363	—	1,998

KM# 317 • 31.1050 g., 0.9995 **Platinum**, 0.9995 oz. • **Rev. Desc:** Eagle in flight over Heartland **Obv. Designer:** John Mercanti

Date	Mintage	Unc	Prf.
2000W	12,453	—	1,998

KM# 330 • 31.1050 g., 0.9995 **Platinum**, 0.9995 oz., 33mm. • **Rev. Desc:** Eagle in flight over Southwestern cactus desert **Obv. Designer:** John Mercanti

Date	Mintage	Unc	Prf.
2001W	8,969	—	1,998

KM# 342 • 31.1050 g., 0.9995 **Platinum**, 0.9995 oz., 33mm. • **Rev. Desc:** Eagle fishing in America's Northwest **Obv. Designer:** John Mercanti

Date	Mintage	Unc	Prf.
2002W	9,834	—	1,998

KM# 354 • 31.1050 g., 0.9995 **Platinum**, 0.9995 oz., 33mm. • **Rev. Desc:** Eagle pearched on a Rocky Mountain Pine branch against a flag backdrop **Obv. Designer:** John Mercanti **Rev. Designer:** Al Maletsky

Date	Mintage	Unc	Prf.
2003W	8,246	—	2,017

KM# 367 • 31.1050 g., 0.9995 **Platinum**, 0.9995 oz., 33mm. • **Rev. Desc:** Inspired by the sculpture "America" by Daniel Chester French, 1907. The

sculpture is outside the N.Y. Customs House, now part of the Smithsonian's Museum of the American Indian **Obv. Designer:** John Mercanti **Rev. Designer:** Donna Weaver

Date	Mintage	Unc	Prf.
2004W	6,007	—	2,150

KM# 380 • 31.1050 g., 0.9995 **Platinum**, 0.9995 oz., 33mm. • **Rev. Desc:** Eagle with cornucopiae **Obv. Designer:** John Mercanti **Rev. Designer:** Donna Weaver

Date	Mintage	Unc	Prf.
2005W	6,602	—	2,017

KM# 392 • 31.1050 g., 0.9995 **Platinum**, 0.9995 oz., 33mm. • **Event:** Legislaive **Rev. Desc:** Liberty seated writing between two columns **Obv. Designer:** John Mercanti

Date	Mintage	Unc	Prf.
2006W	9,152	—	1,998

KM# 417 • 31.1050 g., 0.9995 **Platinum**, 0.9995 oz., 33mm. • **Event:** Executive **Obv. Designer:** John Mercanti

Date	Mintage	Unc	Prf.
2007W	8,363	—	1,998

KM# 437 • 31.1050 g., 0.9995 **Platinum**, 0.9995 oz., 33mm. • **Obv. Designer:** John Mercanti

Date	Mintage	Unc	Prf.
2008W	8,363	—	2,250

KM# 463 • 31.1020 g., 0.9995 **Platinum**, 0.9994 oz., 33mm. • **Event:** Judicial **Obv. Designer:** John Mercanti

Date	Mintage	Unc	Prf.
2009W	4,900	—	—

KM# 488 • 31.1050 g., 0.9990 **Platinum**, 0.9990 oz. • **Obv. Designer:** John Mercanti

Date	Mintage	Unc	Prf.
2010W	—	—	—

BISON BULLION COINAGE

GOLD $5

KM# 411 • 3.1100 g., 0.9999 **Gold**, 0.1000 oz. •
Obv. Desc: Indian Head right **Rev. Desc:** Bison

Date	Mintage	Unc	Prf.
2008W	19,300	—	675
2008W	19,000	575	—
2009W	—	575	—
2009W	—	—	675

GOLD $10

KM# 412 • 7.7857 g., 0.9999 **Gold**, 0.2503 oz. •
Obv. Desc: Indian Head right **Rev. Desc:** Bison

Date	Mintage	Unc	Prf.
2008W	13,900	—	1,525
2008W	10,500	1,275	—
2009W	—	1,275	—
2009W	—	—	1,525

GOLD $25

KM# 413 • 15.5520 g., 0.9990 **Gold**, 0.4995 oz. •
Obv. Desc: Indian Head right **Rev. Desc:** Bison

Date	Mintage	Unc	Prf.
2008W	12,500	—	1,550
2008W	17,000	1,385	—
2009W	—	1,385	—
2009W	—	—	1,550

GOLD $50

KM# 393 • 31.1050 g., 0.9999 **Gold**, 0.9999 oz.,
32mm. • **Obv. Desc:** Indian head right
Rev. Desc: Bison standing left on mound
Designer: James E. Fraser

Date	Mintage	Unc	Prf.
2006W	246,267	—	1,392
2006W	337,012	1,307	—
2007W	136,503	1,307	—
2007W	58,998	—	1,397
2008W	189,500	1,397	—
2008W	19,500	—	2,925
2008W Moy Family Chop	—	3,965	—
2009W	—	1,347	—
2009W	—	—	1,525

FIRST SPOUSE GOLD COINAGE

GOLD $10

KM# 407 • 15.5520 g., 0.9999 **Gold**, 0.4999 oz. •
Subject: Martha Washington **Obv. Desc:** Bust 3/4
facing **Rev. Desc:** Martha Washington seated sewing

Date	Mintage	Unc	Prf.
2007W	20,000	640	—
2007W	20,000	—	650

KM# 408 • 15.5520 g., 0.9999 **Gold**, 0.4999 oz. •
Subject: Abigail Adams **Obv. Desc:** Bust 3/4
facing **Rev. Desc:** Abigail Adams seated at desk
writing to John during the Revolutionary War

Date	Mintage	Unc	Prf.
2007W	20,000	640	—
2007W	20,000	—	650

KM# 409 • 15.5520 g., 0.9999 **Gold**, 0.4999 oz. •
Subject: Jefferson - Bust coinage design
Obv. Desc: Bust design from coinage **Rev. Desc:**
Jefferson's tombstone

Date	Mintage	Unc	Prf.
2007W	20,000	640	—
2007W	20,000	—	650

KM# 410 • 15.5520 g., 0.9999 **Gold**, 0.4999 oz. •
Subject: Dolley Madison **Obv. Desc:** Bust 3/4
facing **Rev. Desc:** Dolley standing before painting of
Washington, which she saved from the White House

Date	Mintage	Unc	Prf.
2007W	12,500	640	—
2007W	18,300	—	650

KM# 430 • 15.5520 g., 0.9990 **Gold**, 0.4995 oz. • **Subject:** Elizabeth Monroe **Obv. Desc:** Bust 3/4 facing right **Rev. Desc:** Elizabeth standing before mirror

Date	Mintage	Unc	Prf.
2008W	4,500	640	—
2008W	7,900	—	650

KM# 431 • 15.5520 g., 0.9990 **Gold**, 0.4995 oz. • **Subject:** Lousia Adams **Obv. Desc:** Bust 3/4 facing right **Rev. Desc:** Lousia and son Charles before entrance

Date	Mintage	Unc	Prf.
2008W	4,200	640	—
2008W	7,400	—	650

KM# 432 • 15.5520 g., 0.9990 **Gold**, 0.4995 oz. • **Subject:** Jackson's Liberty **Obv. Desc:** Capped and draped bust left **Rev. Desc:** Andrew Jackson on horseback right

Date	Mintage	Unc	Prf.
2008W	4,800	640	—
2008W	7,800	—	650

KM# 433 • 15.5520 g., 0.9990 **Gold**, 0.4995 oz. • **Subject:** van Buren's Liberty **Obv. Desc:** Seated Liberty with shiled **Rev. Desc:** Youthful van Buren seated under tree, family tavern in distance

Date	Mintage	Unc	Prf.
2008W	40,000	640	—
2008W	Inc. above	—	650

KM# 456 • 15.5520 g., 0.9990 **Gold**, 0.4995 oz. • **Subject:** Anna Harrison **Obv. Desc:** Bust 3/4 left **Rev. Desc:** Anna reading to her three children

Date	Mintage	Unc	Prf.
2009W	40,000	640	—
2009W	Inc. above	—	650

KM# 457 • 15.5520 g., 0.9990 **Gold**, 0.4995 oz. • **Subject:** Lettia Tyler **Obv. Desc:** Bust facing **Rev. Desc:** Letitia and two children playing outside of Cedar Grove Plantation

Date	Mintage	Unc	Prf.
2009W	40,000	640	—
2009W	Inc. above	—	650

KM# 458 • 15.5520 g., 0.9990 **Gold**, 0.4995 oz. • **Subject:** Julia Tyler **Obv. Desc:** Bust facing **Rev. Desc:** Julia and John Tyler dancing

Date	Mintage	Unc	Prf.
2009W	40,000	640	—
2009W	Inc. above	—	650

KM# 459 • 15.5520 g., 0.9990 **Gold**, 0.4995 oz. • **Subject:** Sarah Polk **Obv. Desc:** Bust 3/4 right **Rev. Desc:** Sarah seated at desk as personal secretary to James Polk

Date	Mintage	Unc	Prf.
2009W	40,000	640	—
2009W	Inc. above	—	650

KM# 465 • 15.5520 g., 0.9990 **Gold**, 0.4995 oz. •
Subject: Margaret Taylor **Obv. Desc:** Bust 3/4 left
Rev. Desc: Margaret Taylor nurses wounded
soldier during the Seminole War

Date	Mintage	Unc	Prf.
2009W	40,000	640	—
2009W	Inc. above	—	650

KM# 481 • 15.5200 g., 0.9990 **Gold**, 0.4985 oz. •
Subject: Abigail Filmore **Rev. Desc:** Mrs. Filmore
placing books on library shelf

Date	Mintage	Unc	Prf.
2010W	—	640	—
2010W	—	—	650

KM# 482 • 15.5200 g., 0.9990 **Gold**, 0.4985 oz. •
Subject: Jane Pierce **Rev. Desc:** Mrs. Pierce
seated on porch

Date	Mintage	Unc	Prf.
2010W	—	640	—
2010W	—	—	650

KM# 483 • 15.5200 g., 0.9990 **Gold**, 0.4985 oz. •
Subject: Buchanan's Liberty **Rev. Desc:** Buchanan
as clerk

Date	Mintage	Unc	Prf.
2010W	—	640	—
2010W	—	—	650

KM# 484 • 15.5200 g., 0.9990 **Gold**, 0.4985 oz. •
Subject: Mary Todd Lincoln **Rev. Desc:** Mary
Lincoln visiting soldiers at hospital

Date	Mintage	Unc	Prf.
2010	—	640	—
2010	—	—	650

CANADA
CONFEDERATION

CIRCULATION COINAGE

CENT

KM# 1 Obv: Laureate head left **Obv. Legend:** VICTORIA DEI GRATIA REGINA. CANADA **Rev:** Denomination and date within beaded circle, chain of leaves surrounds **Rev. Legend:** ONE CENT **Edge:** plain **Weight:** 4.5400 g. **Composition:** Bronze

Date	Mintage	VG-8	F-12	VF-20	XF-40	MS-60	MS-63	Proof
1858	421,000	75.00	100.00	150	200	500	2,000	—
1859/8 Wide 9	Inc. above	30.00	45.00	60.00	90.00	300	1,800	—
1859 Narrow 9	9,579,000	2.25	3.00	5.00	7.00	45.00	250	—
1859 Double punched narrow 9 type I	Inc. above	175	250	350	540	1,150	4,750	—
1859 Double punched narrow 9 type II	Inc. above	55.00	70.00	95.00	150	500	2,800	—

KM# 7 Obv: Crowned head left within beaded circle **Obv. Legend:** VICTORIA DEI GRATIA REGINA. CANADA **Obv. Designer:** Leonard C. Wyon **Rev:** Denomination and date within beaded circle, chain of leaves surrounds **Edge:** Plain **Weight:** 5.7000 g. **Composition:** Bronze **Size:** 25.5 mm.

Date	Mintage	VG-8	F-12	VF-20	XF-40	MS-60	MS-63	Proof
1876H	4,000,000	3.00	4.00	6.00	9.50	45.00	250	—
1881H	2,000,000	4.00	5.50	11.50	18.00	75.00	300	—
1882H	4,000,000	3.00	3.50	4.00	7.50	40.00	250	—
1884	2,500,000	3.00	4.00	6.50	11.00	60.00	300	—
1886	1,500,000	3.75	7.00	13.00	20.00	90.00	450	—
1887	1,500,000	3.50	5.00	8.00	14.00	70.00	215	—
1888	4,000,000	3.00	4.00	5.00	7.50	35.00	160	—
1890H	1,000,000	8.00	12.00	19.00	30.00	125	425	—
1891 Large date	1,452,000	8.00	11.00	17.50	35.00	140	450	—
1891 S.D.L.L.	Inc. above	65.00	125	200	300	1,000	3,000	—
1891 S.D.S.L.	Inc. above	60.00	125	200	300	1,000	3,500	—
1892	1,200,000	5.50	8.00	12.00	13.50	55.00	220	—
1893	2,000,000	3.00	4.00	5.00	9.50	45.00	200	—
1894	1,000,000	10.50	15.00	20.00	40.00	125	300	—
1895	1,200,000	5.00	9.50	13.00	16.00	55.00	225	—
1896	2,000,000	3.00	5.00	6.50	7.50	40.00	150	—
1897	1,500,000	3.00	5.00	6.50	9.00	45.00	165	—
1898H	1,000,000	9.00	13.00	17.00	35.00	100.00	275	—
1899	2,400,000	3.00	3.50	5.00	7.00	45.00	150	—
1900	1,000,000	9.00	13.50	20.00	30.00	85.00	500	—
1900H	2,600,000	3.00	3.50	5.00	7.50	30.00	95.00	—
1901	4,100,000	2.25	3.00	4.50	8.50	35.00	85.00	—

KM# 8 Obv: Kings bust right within beaded circle **Obv. Designer:** G. W. DeSaulles **Rev:** Denomination above date within circle, chain of leaves surrounds **Edge:** Plain **Weight:** 5.6000 g. **Composition:** Bronze **Size:** 25.5 mm.

Date	Mintage	VG-8	F-12	VF-20	XF-40	MS-60	MS-63	Proof
1902	3,000,000	1.75	2.25	3.50	6.00	25.00	75.00	—
1903	4,000,000	1.75	2.25	3.00	6.00	30.00	80.00	—
1904	2,500,000	2.00	3.50	5.00	8.00	35.00	85.00	—
1905	2,000,000	3.50	6.00	7.50	12.00	45.00	150	—
1906	4,100,000	1.75	2.25	3.00	6.00	35.00	175	—
1907	2,400,000	2.00	3.50	4.50	9.00	35.00	200	—
1907H	800,000	12.00	23.00	30.00	50.00	175	550	—
1908	2,401,506	3.00	3.50	5.00	8.00	30.00	90.00	150
1909	3,973,339	1.75	2.50	3.00	6.00	30.00	100.00	—
1910	5,146,487	1.75	2.50	3.00	5.00	26.00	70.00	—

KM# 15 Obv: King's bust left **Obv. Designer:** E. B. MacKennal **Rev:** Denomination above date within beaded circle, chain of leaves surrounds **Edge:** Plain **Weight:** 4.5400 g. **Composition:** Bronze **Size:** 25.5 mm.

Date	Mintage	VG-8	F-12	VF-20	XF-40	MS-60	MS-63	Proof
1911	4,663,486	0.80	1.30	1.75	3.50	25.00	75.00	250

KM# 21 Obv: King's bust left **Obv. Designer:** E. B. MacKennal **Rev:** Denomination above date within beaded circle, chain of leaves surrounds **Edge:** Plain **Weight:** 5.6200 g. **Composition:** Bronze **Size:** 25.5 mm.

Date	Mintage	VG-8	F-12	VF-20	XF-40	MS-60	MS-63	Proof
1912	5,107,642	0.75	1.50	2.25	3.50	25.00	80.00	—
1913	5,735,405	0.75	1.50	2.25	4.00	23.00	80.00	—
1914	3,405,958	1.00	1.50	2.50	4.00	35.00	125	—
1915	4,932,134	0.75	2.00	3.00	4.00	30.00	100.00	—
1916	11,022,367	0.50	0.65	1.25	3.00	16.00	50.00	—
1917	11,899,254	0.50	0.65	0.90	2.25	13.00	45.00	—
1918	12,970,798	0.50	0.65	0.90	2.25	12.00	45.00	—
1919	11,279,634	0.50	0.65	0.90	2.25	12.00	45.00	—
1920	6,762,247	0.60	0.75	1.00	2.25	20.00	100.00	—

Dot below date

KM# 28 Obv: King's bust left **Obv. Designer:** E. B. MacKennal **Rev:** Denomination above date, leaves flank **Rev. Designer:** Fred Lewis **Edge:** Plain **Weight:** 3.2400 g. **Composition:** Bronze **Size:** 19.10 mm.

Date	Mintage	VG-8	F-12	VF-20	XF-40	MS-60	MS-63	Proof
1920	15,483,923	0.20	0.45	0.95	1.75	15.00	50.00	—
1921	7,601,627	0.45	0.75	1.75	5.00	35.00	200	—
1922	1,243,635	13.00	16.00	21.00	35.00	200	1,200	—

Date	Mintage	VG-8	F-12	VF-20	XF-40	MS-60	MS-63	Proof
1923	1,019,002	29.00	35.00	40.00	50.00	300	2,000	—
1924	1,593,195	5.00	6.50	8.50	15.00	125	850	—
1925	1,000,622	18.00	21.00	27.00	40.00	200	1,450	—
1926	2,143,372	3.50	4.50	7.00	11.00	100.00	650	—
1927	3,553,928	1.25	1.75	3.50	6.00	40.00	225	—
1928	9,144,860	0.15	0.30	0.65	1.50	20.00	90.00	—
1929	12,159,840	0.15	0.30	0.65	1.50	20.00	80.00	—
1930	2,538,613	2.00	2.50	4.50	8.50	50.00	225	—
1931	3,842,776	0.65	1.00	2.50	5.50	40.00	200	—
1932	21,316,190	0.15	0.20	0.50	1.50	14.00	45.00	—
1933	12,079,310	0.15	0.30	0.50	1.50	15.00	55.00	—
1934	7,042,358	0.20	0.30	0.75	1.50	14.00	45.00	—
1935	7,526,400	0.20	0.30	0.75	1.50	14.00	45.00	—
1936	8,768,769	0.15	0.30	0.75	1.50	14.00	45.00	—
1936 dot below date; Rare	678,823	—	—	—	—	—	250,000	—

Note: Only one possible business strike is known to exist. No other examples (or possible business strikes) have ever surfaced.

1936 dot below date, specimen, 3 known   —   —   —   —   —   —   —

Note: At the David Akers auction of the John Jay Pittman collection (Part 1, 10-97), a gem specimen realized $121,000. At the David Akers auction of the John Jay Pittman collection (Part 3, 10-99), a near choice specimen realized $115,000.

Maple leaf

KM# 32 Obv: Head left **Obv. Designer:** T. H. Paget **Rev:** Maple leaf divides date and denomination **Rev. Designer:** George E. Kruger-Gray **Edge:** Plain **Weight:** 3.2400 g. **Composition:** Bronze **Size:** 19.10 mm.

Date	Mintage	VG-8	F-12	VF-20	XF-40	MS-60	MS-63	Proof
1937	10,040,231	0.35	0.45	0.70	0.95	2.50	9.00	—
1938	18,365,608	0.15	0.20	0.30	0.75	2.50	13.00	—
1939	21,600,319	0.10	0.20	0.30	0.70	1.75	5.00	—
1940	85,740,532	0.10	0.10	0.25	0.50	2.25	5.50	—
1941	56,336,011	0.10	0.10	0.25	0.50	8.00	60.00	—
1942	76,113,708	0.10	0.10	0.25	0.50	8.00	60.00	—
1943	89,111,969	0.10	0.10	0.25	0.45	3.50	25.00	—
1944	44,131,216	0.10	0.10	0.30	0.60	12.00	95.00	—
1945	77,268,591	0.10	0.10	0.20	0.35	2.50	22.00	—
1946	56,662,071	0.10	0.10	0.20	0.35	2.50	7.50	—
1947	31,093,901	0.10	0.10	0.20	0.35	2.50	7.50	—
1947 maple leaf	47,855,448	0.10	0.10	0.20	0.35	2.50	8.50	—

KM# 41 Obv: Modified legend **Obv. Designer:** T. H. Paget **Rev. Designer:** George E. Kruger-Gray **Edge:** Plain **Weight:** 3.2400 g. **Composition:** Bronze **Size:** 19.10 mm.

Date	Mintage	VG-8	F-12	VF-20	XF-40	MS-60	MS-63	Proof
1948	25,767,779	—	0.15	0.25	0.70	4.00	35.00	—
1949	33,128,933	—	0.10	0.15	0.35	2.50	9.00	—
1950	60,444,992	—	0.10	0.15	0.25	1.75	9.00	—
1951	80,430,379	—	0.10	0.15	0.20	1.75	13.00	—
1952	67,631,736	—	0.10	0.15	0.20	1.25	7.00	—

   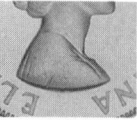

No strap   With strap

KM# 49 Obv: Laureate bust right **Obv. Designer:** Mary Gillick **Rev:** Maple leaf divides date and denomination **Rev. Designer:** George E. Kruger-Gray **Weight:** 3.2400 g. **Composition:** Bronze **Size:** 19.10 mm.

Date	Mintage	VG-8	F-12	VF-20	XF-40	MS-60	MS-63	Proof
1953	67,806,016	0.10	0.10	0.10	0.25	0.65	1.50	—
Note: Without strap								
1953	Inc. above	0.50	1.00	1.50	2.50	12.00	55.00	—
Note: With strap								
1954	22,181,760	0.10	0.10	0.10	0.40	1.75	6.00	—
Note: With strap								
1954 Prooflike only	Inc. above	—	—	—	—	450	600	—
Note: Without strap								
1955	56,403,193	—	0.10	0.10	0.15	0.55	2.50	—
Note: With strap								
1955	Inc. above	85.00	125	150	250	600	1,800	—
Note: Without strap								
1956	78,658,535	—	—	—	0.15	0.30	1.75	—
1957	100,601,792	—	—	—	0.10	0.10	1.00	—
1958	59,385,679	—	—	—	0.10	0.10	1.00	—
1959	83,615,343	—	—	—	0.10	0.10	0.50	—
1960	75,772,775	—	—	—	0.10	0.10	0.50	—
1961	139,598,404	—	—	—	—	0.10	0.50	—
1962	227,244,069	—	—	—	—	0.10	0.30	—

Date	Mintage	VG-8	F-12	VF-20	XF-40	MS-60	MS-63	Proof
1963	279,076,334	—	—	—	—	0.10	0.30	—
1964	484,655,322	—	—	—	—	0.10	0.30	—

KM# 59.1 Obv: Queens bust right **Obv. Designer:** Arnold Machin **Rev:** Maple leaf divides date and denomination **Rev. Designer:** George E. Kruger-Gray **Edge:** Plain **Weight:** 3.2400 g. **Composition:** Bronze **Size:** 19.10 mm.

Date	Mintage	VG-8	F-12	VF-20	XF-40	MS-60	MS-63	Proof
1965	304,441,082	—	—	—	0.40	1.00	4.00	—
Note: Small beads, pointed 5								
1965	Inc. above	—	—	—	—	0.10	0.35	—
Note: Small beads, blunt 5								
1965	Inc. above	1.75	3.00	4.50	7.50	18.00	35.00	—
Note: Large beads, pointed 5								
1965	Inc. above	—	—	—	0.10	0.10	0.35	—
Note: Large beads, blunt 5								
1966	184,151,087	—	—	—	—	0.10	0.35	—
1968	329,695,772	—	—	—	—	0.10	0.35	—
1969	335,240,929	—	—	—	—	0.10	0.35	—
1970	311,145,010	—	—	—	—	0.10	0.35	—
1971	298,228,936	—	—	—	—	0.10	0.35	—
1972	451,304,591	—	—	—	—	0.10	0.35	—
1973	457,059,852	—	—	—	—	0.10	0.30	—
1974	692,058,489	—	—	—	—	0.10	0.35	—
1975	642,318,000	—	—	—	—	0.10	0.35	—
1976	701,122,890	—	—	—	—	0.10	0.35	—
1977	453,762,670	—	—	—	—	0.10	0.35	—

KM# 65 Subject: Confederation Centennial **Obv:** Queen's bust right **Obv. Designer:** Arnold Machin **Rev:** Dove with wings spread, denomination above, two dates below **Rev. Designer:** Alex Coville **Composition:** Bronze **Size:** 19.10 mm.

Date	Mintage	VG-8	F-12	VF-20	XF-40	MS-60	MS-63	Proof
ND(1967)	345,140,645	—	—	—	—	0.10	0.30	1.00

KM# 59.2 Obv: Queen's bust right **Obv. Designer:** Arnold Machin **Rev:** Maple leaves **Rev. Designer:** George E. Kruger-Gray **Edge:** Plain **Weight:** 3.2400 g. **Composition:** Bronze **Size:** 19.10 mm. **Note:** Thin planchet.

Date	Mintage	VG-8	F-12	VF-20	XF-40	MS-60	MS-63	Proof
1978	911,170,647	—	—	—	—	0.10	0.30	—
1979	754,394,064	—	—	—	—	0.10	0.30	—

KM# 127 Obv: Queen's bust right **Obv. Designer:** Arnold Machin **Rev. Designer:** George E. Kruger-Gray **Edge:** Plain **Weight:** 2.8000 g. **Composition:** Bronze **Size:** 19.10 mm. **Note:** Reduced weight.

Date	Mintage	VG-8	F-12	VF-20	XF-40	MS-60	MS-63	Proof
1980	912,052,318	—	—	—	—	0.10	0.30	—
1981	1,209,468,500	—	—	—	—	0.10	0.30	—
1981 Proof	199,000	—	—	—	—	—	—	1.50

KM# 132 Obv: Queen's bust right **Obv. Designer:** Arnold Machin **Rev:** Maple leaf divides date and denomination **Rev. Designer:** George E. Kruger-Gray **Edge:** Plain **Weight:** 2.5000 g. **Composition:** Bronze **Size:** 19.10 mm. **Note:** Reduced weight.

Date	Mintage	VG-8	F-12	VF-20	XF-40	MS-60	MS-63	Proof
1982	911,001,000	—	—	—	—	0.10	0.30	—
1982 Proof	180,908	—	—	—	—	—	—	1.50
1983	975,510,000	—	—	—	—	0.10	0.30	—
1983 Proof	168,000	—	—	—	—	—	—	1.50
1984	838,225,000	—	—	—	—	0.10	0.30	—
1984 Proof	161,602	—	—	—	—	—	—	1.50
1985	771,772,500	0.95	1.75	2.50	3.50	10.00	19.00	—

CENT

Date	Mintage	VG-8	F-12	VF-20	XF-40	MS-60	MS-63	Proof
Note: Pointed 5								
1985	Inc. above	—	—	—	—	0.10	0.30	—
Note: Blunt 5								
1985 Proof	157,037	—	—	—	—	—	—	1.50
Note: Blunt 5								
1986	740,335,000	—	—	—	—	0.10	0.30	—
1986 Proof	175,745	—	—	—	—	—	—	1.50
1987	774,549,000	—	—	—	—	0.10	0.30	—
1987 Proof	179,004	—	—	—	—	—	—	1.50
1988	482,676,752	—	—	—	—	0.10	0.30	—
1988 Proof	175,259	—	—	—	—	—	—	1.50
1989	1,077,347,200	—	—	—	—	0.10	0.30	—
1989 Proof	170,928	—	—	—	—	—	—	1.50

KM# 181   Obv: Crowned Queen's head right
Obv. Designer: Dora dePedery-Hunt **Rev:** Maple leaf divides date and denomination **Rev. Designer:** George E. Kruger-Gray **Edge:** Plain **Weight:** 2.5000 g. **Composition:** Bronze **Size:** 19.10 mm.

Date	Mintage	MS-63	Proof
1990	218,035,000	0.30	—
1990 Proof	140,649	—	2.50
1991	831,001,000	0.30	—
1991 Proof	131,888	—	3.50
1993	752,034,000	0.30	—
1993 Proof	145,065	—	2.00
1994	639,516,000	0.30	—
1994 Proof	146,424	—	2.50
1995	624,983,000	0.30	—
1995 Proof	—	—	2.50
1996	445,746,000	0.30	—
1996 Proof	—	—	2.50

KM# 204   Subject: Confederation 125 **Obv:** Crowned Queen's head right **Obv. Designer:** Dora dePedery-Hunt **Rev:** Maple leaf divides date and denomination **Rev. Designer:** George E. Kruger-Gray **Composition:** Bronze **Size:** 19.10 mm.

Date	Mintage	MS-63	Proof
ND(1992)	673,512,000	0.30	—
ND(1992) Proof	147,061	—	2.50

KM# 289   Obv: Crowned head right
Obv. Designer: Dora dePédery-Hunt **Rev:** Maple twig design **Rev. Designer:** George E. Kruger-Gray **Edge:** Round and plain **Composition:** Copper Plated Steel **Size:** 19.1 mm.

Date	Mintage	MS-63	Proof
1997	549,868,000	0.30	—
1997 Proof	—	—	2.75
1998	999,578,000	0.30	—
1998 Proof	—	—	3.00
1998W	—	1.75	—
1999P	—	6.00	—
1999	1,089,625,000	0.30	—
1999W	—	—	—
1999 Proof	—	—	4.00
2000	771,908,206	0.30	—
2000 Proof	—	—	4.00
2000W	—	1.75	—

Date	Mintage	MS-63	Proof
2001	919,358,000	0.30	—
2001P Proof	—	—	5.00
2003	92,219,775	0.30	—
2003P Proof	—	—	5.00
2003P	235,936,799	1.50	—

KM# 289a   Composition: Bronze **Size:** 19.10 mm.

Date	Mintage	MS-63	Proof
1998	—	0.75	—
Note: In Specimen sets only			

KM# 309   Subject: 90th Anniversary Royal Canadian Mint - 1908-1998 **Obv. Designer:** Dora dePedery-Hunt **Rev. Designer:** G. W. DeSaulles **Weight:** 5.6700 g. **Composition:** 0.9250 Copper Plated Silver 0.1686 oz.

Date	Mintage	MS-63	Proof
ND(1998)	25,000	16.00	—
Note: Antique finish			
ND(1998) Proof	—	—	—

KM# 332   Subject: 90th Anniversary Royal Canadian Mint - 1908-1998 **Obv:** Crowned Queen's head right, with "Canada" added to head **Obv. Designer:** Dora dePedery-Hunt **Rev:** Denomination above dates withn beaded circle, chain of leaves surrounds **Rev. Designer:** G. W. DeSaulles **Weight:** 5.6700 g. **Composition:** 0.9250 Silver 0.1686 oz. ASW

Date	Mintage	MS-63	P/L	Proof
ND(2000) Proof	25,000	—	—	16.00
Note: Mirror finish				

KM# 445   Subject: Elizabeth II Golden Jubilee **Obv:** Crowned head right, Jubilee commemorative dates 1952-2002 **Obv. Designer:** Dora dePédery-Hunt **Rev:** Denomination above maple leaves **Rev. Designer:** George E. Kruger-Gray **Edge:** Plain **Composition:** Copper Plated Steel **Size:** 19.1 mm.

Date	Mintage	MS-63	Proof
ND(2002)	716,366,000	0.75	—
ND(2002)P	114,212,000	1.00	—
ND(2002)P Proof	32,642	—	5.00

KM# 445a Subject: Elizabeth II Golden Jubilee **Obv:** Crowned head right, Jubilee commemorative dates 1952-2002 **Obv. Designer:** Dora dePédery-Hunt **Rev:** Denomination above maple leaves **Rev. Designer:** George E. Kruger-Gray **Composition:** 0.9250 Silver

Date	Mintage	MS-63	Proof
ND(2002)	21,537	—	3.00

Note: In sets only

KM# 490 Obv: New effigy of Queen Elizabeth II right **Obv. Designer:** Susanna Blunt **Rev:** Two maple leaves **Edge:** Plain **Weight:** 2.3500 g. **Composition:** Copper Plated Zinc **Size:** 19.1 mm.

Date	Mintage	MS-63	Proof
2003	56,877,144	0.25	—
2004	653,317,000	0.25	—
2004 Proof	—	—	2.50
2005	759,658,000	0.25	—
2005 Proof	—	—	2.50
2006	886,275,000	0.25	—
2006 Proof	—	—	2.50

KM# 490a Obv: Bust right **Obv. Designer:** Susanna Blunt **Rev:** Two maple leaves **Rev. Designer:** G. E. Kruger-Gray **Weight:** 2.2500 g. **Composition:** Copper Plated Steel **Size:** 19.5 mm.

Date	Mintage	MS-63	Proof
2003P	591,257,000	0.25	—
2003 WP	Inc. above	0.25	—
2004P	134,906,000	0.25	—
2005P	30,525,000	0.25	—
2006P	137,733,000	0.25	—
2006(ml)	Inc. above	0.25	—
2007(ml)	938,270,000	0.25	—
2007(ml) Proof	—	—	2.50
2008(ml)	—	0.25	—

Date	Mintage	MS-63	Proof
2008(ml) Proof	—	—	2.50
2009(ml)	—	0.25	—
2009(ml) Proof	—	—	2.50

KM# 468 Subject: 50th Anniversary of the Coronation of Elizabeth II **Obv:** 1953 effigy of the Queen, Jubilee commemorative dates 1952-2002 **Obv. Designer:** Mary Gillick **Composition:** Copper

Date	Mintage	MS-63	Proof
ND(2002) Proof	—	—	2.50

KM# 490b Obv: Head right **Rev:** Maple leaf, selectively gold plated **Composition:** Copper Plated Zinc **Note:** Bound into Annual Report.

Date	Mintage	MS-63	Proof
2004 Proof	7,746	—	—

3 CENTS

KM# 410 Subject: 1st Canadian Postage Stamp **Obv:** Crowned head right **Obv. Designer:** Dora dePédery-Hunt **Rev:** Partial stamp design **Rev. Designer:** Sandford Fleming **Edge:** Plain **Weight:** 3.1100 g. **Composition:** 0.9250 Silver Gilt 0.0925 oz. ASW **Size:** 21.3 mm.

Date	Mintage	MS-63	Proof
2001 Proof	59,573	—	12.50

5 CENTS

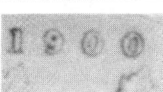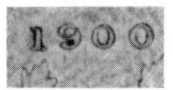

Oval O's   Round O's

KM# 2 Obv: Head left **Obv. Legend:** VICTORIA DEI GRATIA REGINA. CANADA **Rev:** Denomination and date within wreath, crown above **Designer:** Leonard C. Wyon **Weight:** 1.1620 g. **Composition:** 0.9250 Silver 0.0346 oz. ASW

Date	Mintage	VG-8	F-12	VF-20	XF-40	MS-60	MS-63	Proof
1858 Small date	1,500,000	19.00	30.00	45.00	80.00	250	525	—
1858 Large date over small date	Inc. above	130	210	325	550	1,350	3,000	—
1870	2,800,000	13.50	22.50	40.00	60.00	250	850	—
Note: Flat rim								
1870	Inc. above	16.00	24.00	35.00	80.00	225	525	—
Note: Wire rim								
1871	1,400,000	13.50	22.50	40.00	70.00	275	800	—
1872H	2,000,000	13.00	20.00	35.00	80.00	250	1,250	—
1874H Plain 4	800,000	22.00	35.00	75.00	120	400	950	—
1874H Crosslet 4	Inc. above	14.00	30.00	60.00	120	450	1,100	—
1875H Large date	1,000,000	300	500	800	1,400	4,000	15,000	—
1875H Small date	Inc. above	125	225	500	700	1,900	5,000	—
1880H	3,000,000	6.00	12.00	27.00	65.00	250	800	—
1881H	1,500,000	9.00	15.00	30.00	70.00	265	800	—
1882H	1,000,000	12.00	18.00	27.00	80.00	275	800	—
1883H	600,000	23.00	35.00	70.00	150	750	3,000	—
1884	200,000	100.00	165	275	650	2,850	7,250	—
1885 Small 5	1,000,000	16.00	24.00	40.00	125	750	2,900	—
1885 Large 5	Inc. above	11.50	22.50	45.00	150	850	3,000	—
1885 Large 5 over small 5	Inc. above	65.00	125	200	500	4,000	—	—
1886 Small 6	1,700,000	7.00	15.00	25.00	50.00	300	1,300	—
1886 Large 6	Inc. above	9.00	16.00	28.00	60.00	350	1,500	—
1887	500,000	50.00	60.00	75.00	175	500	1,000	—
1888	1,000,000	6.00	9.00	18.00	50.00	165	425	—
1889	1,200,000	20.00	40.00	90.00	150	600	1,600	—
1890H	1,000,000	6.00	12.00	22.00	50.00	200	450	—
1891	1,800,000	6.00	9.00	15.00	30.00	150	385	—
1892	860,000	6.00	10.00	20.00	50.00	250	675	—
1893	1,700,000	6.00	9.00	14.00	30.00	175	500	—

Date	Mintage	VG-8	F-12	VF-20	XF-40	MS-60	MS-63	Proof
1894	500,000	19.00	27.00	75.00	100.00	450	1,400	—
1896	1,500,000	6.00	9.00	14.00	35.00	175	450	—
1897	1,319,283	4.50	6.50	20.00	45.00	150	450	—
1898	580,717	10.00	20.00	35.00	70.00	350	950	—
1899	3,000,000	4.50	6.50	12.00	25.00	115	300	—
1900 Oval 0's	1,800,000	4.50	6.50	12.00	25.00	115	325	—
1900 Round 0's	Inc. above	17.50	37.50	55.00	120	450	800	—
1901	2,000,000	4.50	6.50	12.00	35.00	150	400	—

KM# 9 Obv. Designer: G. W. DeSaulles **Rev. Designer:** Leonard C. Wyon **Weight:** 3.3200 g. **Composition:** 0.9250 Silver 0.0987 oz. ASW **Size:** 20.1 mm.

Date	Mintage	VG-8	F-12	VF-20	XF-40	MS-60	MS-63	Proof
1902	2,120,000	2.25	3.00	4.00	7.00	35.00	55.00	—
1902	2,200,000	2.25	3.25	5.50	11.00	35.00	60.00	—
Note: Large broad H								
1902	Inc. above	7.50	13.00	24.00	40.00	100.00	175	—
Note: Small narrow H								

KM# 13 Obv: King's bust right **Rev:** Denomination and date within wreath, crown at top **Weight:** 1.1500 g. **Composition:** 0.9250 Silver 0.0342 oz. ASW **Size:** 15.5 mm.

Date	Mintage	VG-8	F-12	VF-20	XF-40	MS-60	MS-63	Proof
1903	1,000,000	4.00	7.00	17.00	35.00	150	350	—
Note: 22 leaves								
1903H	2,640,000	1.75	3.00	7.00	16.00	100.00	300	—
Note: 21 leaves								
1904	2,400,000	2.75	4.50	7.00	23.00	175	500	—
1905	2,600,000	1.75	3.00	9.00	16.00	100.00	225	—
1906	3,100,000	2.25	3.00	6.00	13.00	85.00	225	—
1907	5,200,000	2.25	3.00	4.00	10.00	55.00	150	—
1908	1,220,524	6.00	10.00	23.00	35.00	100.00	175	—
1909	1,983,725	3.00	6.50	10.00	30.00	175	500	—
Note: Round leaves								
1909	Inc. above	12.00	18.00	35.00	95.00	550	1,300	—
Note: Pointed leaves								
1910	3,850,325	2.25	2.75	5.00	11.00	50.00	95.00	—
Note: Pointed leaves								
1910	Inc. above	15.00	17.00	30.00	85.00	400	1,300	—
Note: Round leaves								

KM# 16 Obv: King's bust left **Obv. Designer:** E. B. MacKennal **Rev:** Denomination and date within wreath, crown above **Rev. Designer:** Leonard C. Wyon **Weight:** 1.1620 g. **Composition:** 0.9250 Silver 0.0346 oz. ASW

Date	Mintage	VG-8	F-12	VF-20	XF-40	MS-60	MS-63	Proof
1911	3,692,350	2.00	3.00	6.00	9.00	60.00	100.00	—

KM# 22 Obv: King's bust left **Obv. Designer:** E. B. MacKennal **Rev:** Denomination and date within wreath, crown above **Rev. Designer:** Leonard C. Wyon **Weight:** 1.1300 g. **Composition:** 0.9250 Silver 0.0336 oz. ASW **Size:** 15.5 mm.

Date	Mintage	VG-8	F-12	VF-20	XF-40	MS-60	MS-63	Proof
1912	5,863,170	2.00	3.00	5.00	9.00	50.00	150	—
1913	5,488,048	2.00	2.75	4.25	7.50	26.00	50.00	—
1914	4,202,179	2.00	3.00	5.00	9.00	50.00	125	—
1915	1,172,258	11.00	15.00	26.00	50.00	325	600	—
1916	2,481,675	2.75	7.50	13.00	22.00	100.00	250	—
1917	5,521,373	1.75	2.50	3.00	7.00	30.00	80.00	—
1918	6,052,298	1.75	2.50	3.00	6.50	30.00	65.00	—
1919	7,835,400	1.75	2.50	3.00	6.50	30.00	65.00	—

KM# 22a **Obv. Designer:** E. B. MacKennal **Rev. Designer:** Leonard C. Wyon **Weight:** 1.1664 g.
Composition: 0.8000 Silver 0.0300 oz. ASW **Size:** 15.48 mm.

Date	Mintage	VG-8	F-12	VF-20	XF-40	MS-60	MS-63	Proof
1920	10,649,851	1.75	2.50	3.00	6.50	26.00	50.00	—
1921	2,582,495	2,700	3,000	4,500	7,000	10,000	17,500	—

Note: Approximately 460 known; balance remelted. Stack's A.G. Carter Jr. Sale (12-89) choice BU, finest known, realized $57,200

Near 6   Far 6

KM# 29 **Obv:** King's bust left **Obv. Designer:** E. B. MacKennal **Rev:** Maple leaves divide denomination and
date **Rev. Designer:** W. H. J. Blakemore **Weight:** 4.6000 g. **Composition:** Nickel **Size:** 21.2 mm.

Date	Mintage	VG-8	F-12	VF-20	XF-40	MS-60	MS-63	Proof
1922	4,794,119	0.30	0.95	1.75	7.00	45.00	95.00	—
1923	2,502,279	0.40	1.25	5.50	16.00	100.00	275	—
1924	3,105,839	0.30	1.00	3.75	10.00	85.00	200	—
1925	201,921	55.00	70.00	100.00	200	1,200	3,600	—
1926 Near 6	938,162	3.00	7.00	16.00	60.00	375	1,300	—
1926 Far 6	Inc. above	100.00	150	300	600	1,500	4,300	—
1927	5,285,627	0.30	0.65	2.75	14.50	60.00	125	—
1928	4,577,712	0.30	0.65	2.75	14.50	55.00	100.00	—
1929	5,611,911	0.30	0.65	2.75	14.50	60.00	150	—
1930	3,704,673	0.30	1.25	2.75	15.00	90.00	200	—
1931	5,100,830	0.30	1.25	3.25	18.00	175	475	—
1932	3,198,566	0.30	1.00	3.25	16.00	150	350	—
1933	2,597,867	0.40	1.50	6.00	18.00	175	650	—
1934	3,827,304	0.30	1.00	3.00	16.00	150	375	—
1935	3,900,000	0.30	1.00	2.75	11.00	95.00	250	—
1936	4,400,450	0.30	0.65	1.75	9.00	50.00	100.00	—

KM# 33 **Obv:** Head left **Obv. Designer:** T. H. Paget **Rev:** Beaver on rock divides denomination and date
Rev. Designer: George E. Kruger-Gray **Weight:** 4.5000 g. **Composition:** Nickel **Size:** 21.2 mm.

Date	Mintage	VG-8	F-12	VF-20	XF-40	MS-60	MS-63	Proof
1937 Dot	4,593,263	0.20	0.30	1.25	2.50	9.00	22.00	—
1938	3,898,974	0.30	0.90	2.00	7.00	75.00	150	—
1939	5,661,123	0.20	0.35	1.25	3.00	45.00	80.00	—
1940	13,920,197	0.20	0.30	0.75	2.25	18.00	55.00	—
1941	8,681,785	0.20	0.30	0.75	2.25	23.00	70.00	—
1942 Round	6,847,544	0.20	0.30	0.75	1.75	18.00	35.00	—

KM# 39 **Obv:** Head left **Obv. Designer:** T. H. Paget **Rev:** Beaver on rock divides denomination and date
Rev. Designer: George E. Kruger-Gray **Composition:** Tombac **Shape:** 12-sided **Size:** 21.2 mm.

Date	Mintage	VG-8	F-12	VF-20	XF-40	MS-60	MS-63	Proof
1942	3,396,234	0.40	0.65	1.25	1.75	3.00	14.00	—

KM# 40a Obv: Head left **Rev:** Torch on "V" divides date **Weight:** 4.4000 g. **Composition:** Chrome Plated Steel **Size:** 21.2 mm.

Date	Mintage	VG-8	F-12	VF-20	XF-40	MS-60	MS-63	Proof
1944	11,532,784	0.10	0.20	0.50	0.90	2.00	6.50	—
1945	18,893,216	0.10	0.20	0.40	0.80	2.00	6.50	—

  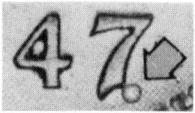 

Dot   Maple leaf

KM# 39a Obv: Head left **Obv. Designer:** T. H. Paget **Rev:** Beaver on rock divides denomination and date **Rev. Designer:** George E. Kruger-Gray **Weight:** 4.5000 g. **Composition:** Nickel **Size:** 21.2 mm.

Date	Mintage	VG-8	F-12	VF-20	XF-40	MS-60	MS-63	Proof
1946	6,952,684	0.10	0.25	0.50	2.00	14.00	32.00	—
1947	7,603,724	0.20	0.25	0.50	1.25	10.00	25.00	—
1947 Dot	Inc. above	12.00	20.00	27.00	60.00	175	300	—
1947 Maple leaf	9,595,124	0.20	0.30	0.45	1.25	10.00	25.00	—

KM# 42 Obv: Head left, modified legend **Obv. Designer:** T. H. Paget **Rev:** Beaver on rock divides date and denomination **Rev. Designer:** George E. Kruger-Gray **Weight:** 4.5400 g. **Composition:** Nickel **Size:** 21.2 mm.

Date	Mintage	VG-8	F-12	VF-20	XF-40	MS-60	MS-63	Proof
1948	1,810,789	0.40	0.50	1.00	3.00	18.00	35.00	—
1949	13,037,090	0.15	0.25	0.45	0.75	6.00	12.00	—
1950	11,970,521	0.15	0.25	0.45	0.75	6.00	12.00	—

KM# 42a Obv: Head left **Obv. Designer:** T. H. Paget **Rev:** Beaver on rock divides date and denomination **Rev. Designer:** George E. Kruger-Gray **Composition:** Chromium And Nickel-Plated Steel **Size:** 21.2 mm.

Date	Mintage	VG-8	F-12	VF-20	XF-40	MS-60	MS-63	Proof
1951	4,313,410	0.10	0.20	0.50	0.80	3.50	11.00	—
Note: Low relief; Second "A" in GRATIA points between denticles								
1951	Inc. above	350	525	700	1,000	1,900	3,100	—
Note: High relief; Second "A" in GRATIA points to a denticle								
1952	10,891,148	0.10	0.20	0.45	0.80	3.00	7.50	—

KM# 48 Subject: Nickel Bicentennial **Obv:** Head left **Obv. Designer:** T. H. Paget **Rev:** Buildings with center tower divide dates and denomination **Rev. Designer:** Stephen Trenka **Weight:** 4.5500 g. **Composition:** Nickel **Shape:** 12-sided **Size:** 21.2 mm.

Date	Mintage	VG-8	F-12	VF-20	XF-40	MS-60	MS-63	Proof
ND(1951)	9,028,507	0.15	0.25	0.30	0.45	1.75	5.50	—

5 CENTS

KM# 50 Obv: Laureate queen's bust, right **Obv. Designer:** Mary Gillick **Rev:** Beaver on rock divides date and denomination **Rev. Designer:** George E. Kruger-Gray **Composition:** Chromium And Nickel-Plated Steel **Shape:** 12-sided **Size:** 21.2 mm.

Date	Mintage	VG-8	F-12	VF-20	XF-40	MS-60	MS-63	Proof
1953	Inc. above	300	450	700	900	1,300	2,300	—
Note: Without strap, near leaf								
1953	Inc. above	150	225	300	475	1,100	2,300	—
Note: With strap, far leaf								
1953	16,635,552	0.10	0.20	0.40	0.90	3.00	7.00	—
Note: Without strap								
1953	Inc. above	0.10	0.20	0.40	0.90	3.50	7.00	—
Note: With strap								
1954	6,998,662	0.10	0.25	0.50	1.00	4.00	8.00	—

KM# 50a Obv: Laureate queen's bust right **Obv. Designer:** Mary Gillick **Rev:** Beaver on rock divides date and denomination **Rev. Designer:** George E. Kruger-Gray **Weight:** 4.5900 g. **Composition:** Nickel **Size:** 21.2 mm.

Date	Mintage	VG-8	F-12	VF-20	XF-40	MS-60	MS-63	Proof
1955	5,355,028	0.15	0.20	0.40	0.75	3.50	4.50	—
1956	9,399,854	—	0.20	0.30	0.45	2.25	5.00	—
1957	7,387,703	—	—	0.25	0.30	1.25	3.00	—
1958	7,607,521	—	—	0.25	0.30	1.25	3.00	—
1959	11,552,523	—	—	—	0.20	0.45	1.50	—
1960	37,157,433	—	—	—	0.20	0.45	1.50	—
1961	47,889,051	—	—	—	—	0.30	0.80	—
1962	46,307,305	—	—	—	—	0.30	0.80	—

KM# 57 Obv: Laureate queen's bust right **Obv. Designer:** Mary Gillick **Rev:** Beaver on rock divides date and denomination **Rev. Designer:** George E. Kruger-Gray **Composition:** Nickel **Shape:** Round **Size:** 21.2 mm.

Date	Mintage	VG-8	F-12	VF-20	XF-40	MS-60	MS-63	Proof
1963	43,970,320	—	—	—	—	0.20	0.45	—
1964	78,075,068	—	—	—	—	0.20	0.45	—
1964	—	14.00	16.00	18.00	21.00	35.00	100.00	—
Note: Extra water line								

KM# 60.1 Obv: Queen's bust right **Obv. Designer:** Arnold Machin **Rev:** Beaver on rock divides date and denomination **Rev. Designer:** George E. Kruger-Gray **Weight:** 4.5400 g. **Composition:** Nickel **Size:** 21.2 mm.

Date	Mintage	MS-63	Proof
1965	84,876,018	0.30	—
1966	27,976,648	0.30	—
1968	101,930,379	0.30	—
1969	27,830,229	0.30	—
1970	5,726,010	0.75	—
1971	27,312,609	0.30	—
1972	62,417,387	0.30	—
1973	53,507,435	0.30	—
1974	94,704,645	0.30	—
1975	138,882,000	0.30	—
1976	55,140,213	0.30	—
1977	89,120,791	0.30	—
1978	137,079,273	0.30	—

5 CENTS

KM# 66　Subject: Confederation Centennial **Obv:** Queen's bust right **Obv. Designer:** Arnold Machin **Rev:** Snowshoe rabbit bounding left divides dates and denomination **Rev. Designer:** Alex Coville **Composition:** Nickel **Size:** 21.2 mm.

Date	Mintage	MS-63	Proof
ND(1967)	36,876,574	0.40	1.00

KM# 60.2　Obv: Queen's bust right **Obv. Designer:** Arnold Machin **Rev:** Beaver on rock divides date and denomination **Rev. Designer:** George E. Kruger-Gray **Composition:** Nickel **Size:** 21.2 mm.

Date	Mintage	MS-63	Proof
1979	186,295,825	0.30	—
1980	134,878,000	0.30	—
1981	99,107,900	0.30	—
1981 Proof	199,000	—	1.50

KM# 60.2a　Obv: Queen's bust right **Obv. Designer:** Arnold Machin **Rev:** Beaver on rock divides date and denomination **Rev. Designer:** George E. Kruger-Gray **Weight:** 4.6000 g. **Composition:** Copper-Nickel **Size:** 21.2 mm.

Date	Mintage	MS-63	Proof
1982	64,924,400	0.30	—
1982 Proof	180,908	—	1.50
1983	72,596,000	0.30	—
1983 Proof	168,000	—	1.50
1984	84,088,000	0.30	—
1984 Proof	161,602	—	1.50
1985	126,618,000	0.30	—
1985 Proof	157,037	—	1.50
1986	156,104,000	0.30	—
1986 Proof	175,745	—	1.50
1987	106,299,000	0.30	—
1987 Proof	179,004	—	1.50
1988	75,025,000	0.30	—
1988 Proof	175,259	—	1.50
1989	141,570,538	0.30	—
1989 Proof	170,928	—	1.50

KM# 182　Obv: Crowned head right **Obv. Designer:** Dora dePedery-Hunt **Rev:** Beaver on rock divides dates and denomination **Rev. Designer:** George E. Kruger-Gray **Edge:** Plain **Weight:** 4.6000 g. **Composition:** Copper-Nickel **Size:** 19.55 mm.

Date	Mintage	MS-63	Proof
1990	42,537,000	0.30	—
1990 Proof	140,649	—	2.50
1991	10,931,000	0.55	—
1991 Proof	131,888	—	7.00
1993	86,877,000	0.30	—
1993 Proof	143,065	—	2.50
1994	99,352,000	0.30	—
1994 Proof	146,424	—	3.00
1995	78,528,000	0.30	—
1995 Proof	50,000	—	2.50
1996 Far 6	36,686,000	2.25	—
1996 Near 6	Inc. above	2.25	—
1996 Proof	—	—	6.00
1997	27,354,000	0.30	—
1997 Proof	—	—	5.00
1998	156,873,000	0.30	—
1998W	—	1.50	—
1998 Proof	—	—	5.00
1999	124,861,000	0.30	—
1999W	—	—	—
1999 Proof	—	—	5.00
2000	108,514,000	0.30	—
2000W	—	1.50	—
2000 Proof	—	—	5.00

Date	Mintage	MS-63	Proof
2001	30,035,000	12.50	—
2001P Proof	—	—	10.00
2003	—	0.30	—

KM# 205　Subject: Confederation 125 **Obv:** Crowned head right **Obv. Designer:** Dora dePedery-Hunt **Rev:** Beaver on rock divides date and denomination **Rev. Designer:** George E. Kruger-Gray **Weight:** 4.6000 g. **Composition:** Copper-Nickel **Size:** 21.2 mm.

Date	Mintage	MS-63	Proof
ND(1992) Proof	147,061	—	4.00
ND(1992)	53,732,000	0.30	—

KM# 182b　Obv: Crowned head right **Obv. Designer:** Dora dePedery-Hunt **Rev:** Beaver on rock divides date and denomination **Rev. Designer:** George E. Kruger-Gray **Edge:** Plain **Weight:** 3.9000 g. **Composition:** Nickel Plated Steel **Size:** 21.2 mm.

Date	Mintage	MS-63	Proof
1999 P	Est. 20,000	15.00	—
2000 P	Est. 2,300,000	3.50	—
2001 P	136,650,000	0.35	—
2003 P	32,986,921	0.35	—

KM# 182a　Obv: Crowned head right **Obv. Designer:** Dora dePedery-Hunt **Rev:** Beaver on rock divides date and denomination **Rev. Designer:** George E. Kruger-Gray **Weight:** 5.3500 g. **Composition:** 0.9250 Silver 0.1591 oz. ASW **Size:** 21.2 mm.

Date	Mintage	MS-63	Proof
1996 Proof	—	—	5.00
1997 Proof	—	—	5.00
1998 Proof	—	—	5.00
1998O Proof	—	—	5.00
1999 Proof	—	—	5.00
2000 Proof	—	—	5.00
2001 Proof	—	—	5.00
2003 Proof	—	—	5.00

KM# 310　Subject: 90th Anniversary Royal Canadian Mint **Obv:** Crowned head right **Obv. Designer:** Dora dePedery-Hunt **Rev:** Denomination and date within wreath, crown above **Rev. Designer:** W. H. J. Blackmore **Weight:** 1.1670 g. **Composition:** 0.9250 Silver 0.0347 oz. ASW

Date	Mintage	MS-63	Proof
ND(1998) Proof	25,000	—	12.00
ND(1998)	25,000	12.00	—

Date	Mintage	MS-63	Proof
2008(ml) Proof	—	—	2.50
2009(ml)	—	0.45	—
2009(ml) Proof	—	—	2.50

KM# 469 Subject: 50th Anniversary of the Coronation of Elizabeth II **Obv:** Crowned head right, Jubilee commemorative dates 1953-2003 **Obv. Designer:** Mary Gillick **Composition:** 0.9250 Silver **Size:** 21.2 mm.

Date	Mintage	MS-63	Proof
ND(2003) Proof	21,573	—	11.50

KM# 491a Obv: Crowned head right **Obv. Designer:** Susanna Blunt **Rev:** Beaver divides date and denomination **Edge:** Plain **Weight:** 5.3500 g. **Composition:** 0.9250 Silver 0.1591 oz. ASW **Size:** 21.1 mm.

Date	Mintage	MS-63	Proof
2004 Proof	—	—	3.50

KM# 400 Subject: First French-Canadian Regiment **Obv:** Crowned head right **Obv. Designer:** Dora dePedery-Hunt **Rev:** Regimental drums, sash and baton, denomination above, date at right **Rev. Designer:** R. C. M. Staff **Edge:** Plain **Composition:** 0.9250 Silver **Size:** 21.2 mm.

Date	Mintage	MS-63	Proof
2000 Proof	—	—	9.00

KM# 413 Subject: Royal Military College **Obv:** Crowned head right **Rev:** Marching cadets and arch **Rev. Designer:** Gerald T. Locklin **Edge:** Plain **Weight:** 5.3500 g. **Composition:** 0.9250 Silver 0.1591 oz. ASW **Size:** 21.2 mm.

Date	Mintage	MS-63	Proof
2001 Proof	25,834	—	7.00

KM# 446 Subject: Elizabeth II Golden Jubilee **Obv:** Crowned head right, Jubilee commemorative dates 1952-2002 **Obv. Designer:** Dora dePedery-Hunt **Rev. Designer:** George E. Kruger-Gray **Composition:** Nickel Plated Steel **Size:** 21.2 mm. **Note:** Magnetic.

Date	Mintage	MS-63	Proof
ND(2002)P	135,960,000	0.45	—
ND(2002)P Proof	32,642	—	10.00

KM# 446a Subject: Elizabeth II Golden Jubilee **Obv:** Queen, Jubilee commemorative dates 1952-2002 **Composition:** 0.9250 Silver **Size:** 21.2 mm.

Date	Mintage	MS-63	Proof
ND(2002) Proof	21,573	—	11.50

KM# 453 Subject: Vimy Ridge - WWI **Obv:** Crowned head right **Rev:** Vimy Ridge Memorial, allegorical figure and dates 1917-2002 **Rev. Designer:** S. A. Allward **Composition:** 0.9250 Silver **Size:** 21.2 mm.

Date	Mintage	MS-63	Proof
ND(2002) Proof	22,646	—	11.50

KM# 491 Obv: Bare head right **Obv. Designer:** Susanna Blunt **Rev:** Beaver divides date and denomination **Rev. Designer:** George E. Kruger-Gray **Weight:** 3.9300 g. **Composition:** Nickel Plated Steel **Size:** 21.2 mm. **Note:** Magnetic.

Date	Mintage	MS-63	Proof
2003P	61,392,180	0.45	—
2004P	132,097,000	0.45	—
2004P Proof	—	—	2.50
2005P	89,664,000	0.45	—
2005P Proof	—	—	2.50
2006P	139,308,000	0.50	—
2006P Proof	—	—	2.50
2006(ml)	221,472,000	0.45	—
2006(ml) Proof	—	—	2.50
2007(ml)	—	0.45	—
2007(ml) Proof	—	—	2.50
2008(ml)	—	0.45	—

KM# 506 Obv: Bare head right **Rev:** "Victory" design of the KM-40 reverse **Edge:** Plain **Weight:** 5.3500 g. **Composition:** 0.9250 Silver 0.1591 oz. ASW **Shape:** 12-sided **Size:** 21.3 mm.

Date	Mintage	MS-63	Proof
ND(2004) Proof	20,019	—	15.00

KM# 627 Subject: 60th Anniversary, Victory in Europe 1945-2005 **Obv:** Head right **Rev:** Large V **Edge:** Plain **Weight:** 3.9000 g. **Composition:** Nickel **Size:** 21.18 mm.

Date	Mintage	MS-63	Proof
ND2005P	59,269,192	4.50	—

KM# 758 Obv: George VI head left **Rev:** Torch and large V **Weight:** 5.3000 g. **Composition:** 0.9250 Silver 0.1576 oz. ASW

Date	Mintage	MS-63	Proof
ND(1945-2005) Proof	42,792	—	35.00

KM# 758a Obv: George VI head left **Rev:** Torch and large V **Weight:** 5.3000 g. **Composition:** 0.9250 Silver 0.1576 oz. ASW **Note:** Bound into Annual Report

Date	Mintage	MS-63	Proof
ND(1945-2005) Proof	6,065	—	40.00

KM# 491b Obv: Bust right **Rev:** Beaver **Composition:** Copper-Nickel

Date	Mintage	MS-63	Proof
2006	43,008,000	5.00	—

5 CENTS

10 CENTS

KM# 3 Obv: Head left **Obv. Legend:** VICTORIA DEI GRATIA REGINA. CANADA **Rev:** Denomination and date within wreath, crown above **Designer:** Leonard C. Wyon **Edge:** Reeded **Weight:** 2.3240 g. **Composition:** 0.9250 Silver 0.0691 oz. ASW **Size:** 18.03 mm.

Date	Mintage	VG-8	F-12	VF-20	XF-40	MS-60	MS-63	Proof
1858/5		800	1,200	1,600	3,600	9,000	—	—
1858	1,250,000	20.00	35.00	65.00	100.00	325	850	—
1870 Narrow 0	1,600,000	18.00	35.00	75.00	125	375	1,300	—
1870 Wide 0	Inc. above	30.00	65.00	100.00	200	500	2,100	—
1871	800,000	29.00	50.00	90.00	175	500	2,500	—
1871H	1,870,000	30.00	60.00	125	200	550	1,900	—
1872H	1,000,000	125	200	300	550	1,750	3,350	—
1874H	600,000	12.00	22.00	45.00	125	350	1,100	—
1875H	1,000,000	400	800	1,200	2,000	6,700	16,000	—
1880H	1,500,000	18.00	30.00	65.00	125	300	1,200	—
1881H	950,000	18.00	30.00	60.00	150	375	1,300	—
1882H	1,000,000	18.00	30.00	60.00	150	385	1,500	—
1883H	300,000	65.00	125	250	500	1,300	3,000	—
1884	150,000	250	500	950	1,500	5,150	20,000	—
1885	400,000	65.00	125	200	500	1,700	6,700	—
1886 Small 6	800,000	30.00	65.00	125	300	1,500	3,600	—
1886 Large 6	Inc. above	35.00	75.00	150	350	1,400	3,000	—
1887	350,000	65.00	85.00	225	375	1,700	3,500	—
1888	500,000	16.00	24.00	45.00	125	300	1,100	—
1889	600,000	500	900	1,550	3,200	13,000	35,000	—
1890H	450,000	20.00	45.00	80.00	175	425	950	—
1891 21 leaves	800,000	20.00	35.00	85.00	175	450	1,300	—
1891 22 leaves	Inc. above	20.00	35.00	85.00	175	435	1,000	—
1892/1	520,000	175	300	600	1,200	3,800	—	—
1892	Inc. above	20.00	35.00	75.00	145	425	1,200	—
1893 Flat-top 3	500,000	45.00	80.00	125	300	1,000	2,200	—
1893 Round-top 3	Inc. above	550	1,200	2,700	4,900	13,000	33,000	—
1894	500,000	45.00	80.00	150	250	750	1,800	—
1896	650,000	12.00	22.00	40.00	75.00	275	650	—
1898	720,000	12.00	24.00	45.00	80.00	300	700	—
1899 Small 9's	1,200,000	12.00	22.00	35.00	75.00	210	575	—
1899 Large 9's	Inc. above	24.00	35.00	75.00	150	400	1,100	—
1900	1,100,000	8.50	18.00	40.00	85.00	225	650	—
1901	1,200,000	8.50	18.00	40.00	85.00	225	650	—

KM# 10 Obv: Crowned bust right **Obv. Designer:** G. W. DeSaulles **Rev:** Denomination and date within wreath, crown above **Rev. Designer:** Leonard C. Wyon **Edge:** Reeded **Weight:** 2.3240 g. **Composition:** 0.9250 Silver 0.0691 oz. ASW **Size:** 18.03 mm.

Date	Mintage	VG-8	F-12	VF-20	XF-40	MS-60	MS-63	Proof
1902	720,000	8.00	16.00	30.00	80.00	325	1,100	—
1902H	1,100,000	4.00	8.00	18.00	40.00	100.00	250	—
1903	500,000	14.00	30.00	75.00	200	1,000	2,100	—
1903H	1,320,000	7.00	16.00	30.00	65.00	250	550	—
1904	1,000,000	11.00	24.00	45.00	100.00	325	700	—
1905	1,000,000	6.50	24.00	55.00	100.00	475	1,100	—
1906	1,700,000	6.50	12.00	30.00	60.00	275	750	—
1907	2,620,000	4.25	11.00	23.00	40.00	200	425	—
1908	776,666	8.00	24.00	55.00	95.00	200	400	—
1909	1,697,200	6.00	18.00	40.00	95.00	375	1,000	—
Note: "Victorian" leaves, similar to 1902-08 coins								
1909	Inc. above	10.00	27.00	55.00	125	500	1,300	—
Note: Broad leaves, similar to 1910-12 coins								
1910	4,468,331	4.00	8.00	18.00	35.00	125	300	—

KM# 17 Obv: Crowned bust left **Obv. Designer:** E. B. MacKennal **Rev:** Denomination and date within wreath, crown above **Rev. Designer:** Leonard C. Wyon **Edge:** Reeded **Weight:** 3.9000 g. **Composition:** 0.9250 Silver 0.1160 oz. ASW **Size:** 23.5 mm.

Date	Mintage	VG-8	F-12	VF-20	XF-40	MS-60	MS-63	Proof
1911	2,737,584	4.50	11.00	18.00	40.00	100.00	200	—

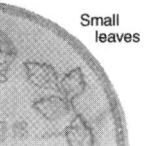
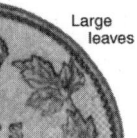

Small leaves

Large leaves

KM# 23 Obv: Crowned bust left **Obv. Designer:** E. B. MacKennal **Rev:** Denomination and date within wreath, crown above **Rev. Designer:** Leonard C. Wyon **Edge:** Reeded **Weight:** 2.3000 g. **Composition:** 0.9250 Silver 0.0684 oz. ASW **Size:** 17.8 mm.

Date	Mintage	VG-8	F-12	VF-20	XF-40	MS-60	MS-63	Proof
1912	3,235,557	1.75	4.25	9.00	30.00	175	500	—
1913	3,613,937	1.50	2.25	8.50	23.00	125	325	—
Note: Small leaves								
1913	Inc. above	95.00	175	350	900	6,000	20,000	—
Note: Large leaves								
1914	2,549,811	1.50	2.50	8.50	25.00	125	375	—
1915	688,057	6.00	15.00	30.00	100.00	325	650	—
1916	4,218,114	1.25	2.25	4.00	17.00	75.00	225	—
1917	5,011,988	1.25	1.50	3.00	10.00	50.00	95.00	—
1918	5,133,602	1.25	1.50	3.00	9.00	45.00	80.00	—
1919	7,877,722	1.25	1.50	3.00	9.00	45.00	80.00	—

KM# 23a Obv: Crowned bust left **Obv. Designer:** E. B. MacKennal **Rev:** Denomination and date within wreath, crown above **Edge:** Reeded **Weight:** 2.2000 g. **Composition:** 0.8000 Silver 0.0566 oz. ASW **Size:** 17.9 mm.

Date	Mintage	VG-8	F-12	VF-20	XF-40	MS-60	MS-63	Proof
1920	6,305,345	1.00	1.50	3.00	12.00	75.00	125	—
1921	2,469,562	1.25	2.00	6.00	20.00	80.00	225	—
1928	2,458,602	1.00	1.75	4.00	12.00	55.00	125	—
1929	3,253,888	1.00	2.00	3.50	12.00	55.00	100.00	—
1930	1,831,043	1.00	2.25	4.50	14.00	60.00	125	—
1931	2,067,421	1.00	1.75	4.00	12.00	55.00	100.00	—
1932	1,154,317	1.50	2.50	9.00	23.00	90.00	225	—
1933	672,368	2.00	4.50	12.00	35.00	175	350	—
1934	409,067	3.00	6.00	22.00	60.00	250	500	—
1935	384,056	3.50	6.00	19.00	60.00	250	500	—
1936	2,460,871	1.00	1.25	3.00	9.00	45.00	80.00	—
1936	—	—	—	—	—	—	—	—

Note: Dot on reverse. Specimen, 4 known; David Akers sale of John Jay Pittman collection, Part 1, 10-97, a gem specimen realized $120,000

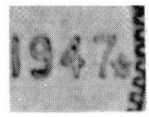

Maple leaf

KM# 34 Obv: Head left **Obv. Designer:** T. H. Paget **Rev:** Bluenose sailing left, date at right, denomination below **Rev. Designer:** Emanuel Hahn **Edge:** Reeded **Weight:** 2.3328 g. **Composition:** 0.8000 Silver 0.0600 oz. ASW **Size:** 18.03 mm.

Date	Mintage	VG-8	F-12	VF-20	XF-40	MS-60	MS-63	Proof
1937	2,500,095	BV	1.25	2.00	3.50	12.00	18.00	—
1938	4,197,323	1.25	1.75	3.25	6.50	40.00	90.00	—
1939	5,501,748	BV	1.25	2.50	5.00	45.00	90.00	—

Date	Mintage	VG-8	F-12	VF-20	XF-40	MS-60	MS-63	Proof
1940	16,526,470	—	BV	1.50	3.00	15.00	30.00	—
1941	8,716,386	BV	1.25	2.50	6.00	35.00	90.00	—
1942	10,214,011	—	BV	1.25	4.00	30.00	50.00	—
1943	21,143,229	—	BV	1.25	4.00	18.00	35.00	—
1944	9,383,582	—	BV	1.50	4.50	25.00	45.00	—
1945	10,979,570	—	BV	1.25	4.00	18.00	27.00	—
1946	6,300,066	BV	1.25	2.00	4.50	30.00	50.00	—
1947	4,431,926	BV	1.25	2.50	6.00	30.00	50.00	—
1947	9,638,793	—	BV	1.50	3.00	10.00	15.00	—

Note: Maple leaf

KM# 43 Obv: Head left, modified legend **Obv. Designer:** T. H. Paget **Rev:** Bluenose sailing left, date at right, denomination below **Rev. Designer:** Emanuel Hahn **Weight:** 2.3328 g. **Composition:** 0.8000 Silver 0.0600 oz. ASW **Size:** 18.03 mm.

Date	Mintage	VG-8	F-12	VF-20	XF-40	MS-60	MS-63	Proof
1948	422,741	2.00	3.50	7.50	13.00	45.00	70.00	—
1949	11,336,172	—	BV	1.25	2.00	9.00	13.00	—
1950	17,823,075	—	—	BV	1.50	8.00	12.00	—
1951	15,079,265	—	—	BV	1.50	6.00	11.00	—
1951	—	—	2.50	4.00	7.00	35.00	60.00	—

Note: Doubled die

| 1952 | 10,474,455 | — | — | BV | 1.50 | 5.00 | 9.00 | — |

KM# 51 Obv: Laureate bust right **Obv. Designer:** Mary Gillick **Rev:** Bluenose sailing left, date at right, denomination below **Rev. Designer:** Emanuel Hahn **Weight:** 2.3100 g. **Composition:** 0.8000 Silver 0.0594 oz. ASW **Size:** 18 mm.

Date	Mintage	VG-8	F-12	VF-20	XF-40	MS-60	MS-63	Proof
1953	Inc. above	—	BV	1.25	1.50	5.00	8.00	—

Note: With straps

| 1953 | 17,706,395 | — | BV | 1.25 | 1.50 | 3.00 | 6.00 | — |

Note: Without straps

1954	4,493,150	—	BV	1.25	2.25	10.00	17.00	—
1955	12,237,294	—	—	BV	1.25	4.50	7.00	—
1956	16,732,844	—	—	BV	1.25	3.00	6.00	—
1956	Inc. above	—	2.25	3.00	4.50	13.00	22.00	—

Note: Dot below date

1957	16,110,229	—	—	—	BV	1.75	3.00	—
1958	10,621,236	—	—	—	BV	1.75	3.00	—
1959	19,691,433	—	—	—	BV	1.75	2.50	—
1960	45,446,835	—	—	—	BV	1.50	2.25	—
1961	26,850,859	—	—	—	BV	1.25	2.25	—
1962	41,864,335	—	—	—	BV	1.25	1.50	—
1963	41,916,208	—	—	—	BV	1.25	1.50	—
1964	49,518,549	—	—	—	BV	1.25	1.50	—

KM# 61 Obv: Young bust right **Obv. Designer:** Arnold Machin **Rev:** Bluenose sailing left, date at right, denomination below **Weight:** 2.3328 g. **Composition:** 0.8000 Silver 0.0600 oz. ASW **Size:** 18.03 mm.

Date	Mintage	VG-8	F-12	VF-20	XF-40	MS-60	MS-63	Proof
1965	56,965,392	—	—	—	BV	1.25	1.50	—
1966	34,567,898	—	—	—	BV	1.25	1.50	—

KM# 67 Subject: Confederation Centennial **Obv:** Bust right **Rev:** Atlantic mackeral left, denomination above, dates below **Rev. Designer:** Alex Colville **Weight:** 2.3328 g. **Composition:** 0.8000 Silver 0.0600 oz. ASW **Size:** 18.03 mm.

Date	Mintage	VG-8	F-12	VF-20	XF-40	MS-60	MS-63	Proof
ND(1967)	62,998,215	—	—	—	BV	1.25	1.50	2.00

KM# 67a Subject: Confederation Centennial **Obv:** Young bust right **Rev:** Fish left, denomination above dates below **Weight:** 2.3328 g. **Composition:** 0.5000 Silver 0.0375 oz. ASW **Size:** 18.03 mm.

Date	Mintage	VG-8	F-12	VF-20	XF-40	MS-60	MS-63	Proof
ND(1967)	Inc. above	—	—	—	BV	0.70	1.50	—

Ottawa

KM# 72 Obv: Young bust right **Obv. Designer:** Arnold Machin **Rev:** Bluenose sailing left, date at right, denomination below **Rev. Designer:** Emanuel Hahn **Weight:** 2.3328 g. **Composition:** 0.5000 Silver 0.0375 oz. ASW **Size:** 18.03 mm. **Note:** Ottawa Mint reeding has pointed deep areas in the edge reeding.

Date	Mintage	VG-8	F-12	VF-20	XF-40	MS-60	MS-63	Proof
1968	70,460,000	—	—	—	BV	0.70	1.25	—

Ottawa

KM# 72a Obv: Young bust right **Obv. Designer:** Arnold Machin **Rev:** Bluenose sailing left, date at right, denomination below **Rev. Designer:** Emanuel Hahn **Composition:** Nickel **Size:** 18.03 mm. **Note:** Ottawa Mint reeding has pointed deep areas in the edge reeding.

Date	Mintage	VG-8	F-12	VF-20	XF-40	MS-60	MS-63	Proof
1968	87,412,930	—	—	—	0.15	0.20	0.35	—

Philadelphia

KM# 73 Obv: Young bust right **Obv. Designer:** Arnold Machin **Rev:** Bluenose sailing left, date at right, denomination below **Rev. Designer:** Emanuel Hahn **Weight:** 2.3300 g. **Composition:** Nickel **Size:** 18.03 mm. **Note:** Philadelphia Mint reeding has pointed deep areas in the edge reeding.

Date	Mintage	VG-8	F-12	VF-20	XF-40	MS-60	MS-63	Proof
1968	85,170,000	—	—	—	0.15	0.25	0.35	—
1969	—	—	6,200	8,400	11,500	19,500	—	—

Note: Large date, large ship, 10-20 known

KM# 77.1 Obv: Young bust right **Obv. Designer:** Arnold Machin **Rev:** Redesigned smaller Bluenose sailing left, date at right, denomination below **Rev. Designer:** Emanuel Hahn **Weight:** 2.0700 g. **Composition:** Nickel **Size:** 18.03 mm.

Date	Mintage	MS-63	Proof
1969	55,833,929	0.35	—
1970	5,249,296	0.90	—
1971	41,016,968	0.35	—
1972	60,169,387	0.35	—
1973	167,715,435	0.35	—
1974	201,566,565	0.35	—
1975	207,680,000	0.35	—
1976	95,018,533	0.35	—
1977	128,452,206	0.35	—
1978	170,366,431	0.35	—

KM# 77.2 Obv: Smaller young bust right **Obv. Designer:** Arnold Machin **Rev:** Redesigned smaller Bluenose sailing left, denomination below, date at right **Rev. Designer:** Emanuel Hahn **Weight:** 2.0700 g. **Composition:** Nickel **Size:** 18.03 mm.

Date	Mintage	MS-63	Proof
1979	237,321,321	0.35	—
1980	170,111,533	0.35	—
1981	123,912,900	0.35	—
1981 Proof	199,000	—	1.50
1982	93,475,000	0.35	—
1982 Proof	180,908	—	1.50
1983	111,065,000	0.35	—
1983 Proof	168,000	—	1.50
1984	121,690,000	0.35	—
1984 Proof	161,602	—	1.50
1985	143,025,000	0.35	—
1985 Proof	157,037	—	1.50
1986	168,620,000	0.35	—

10 CENTS

Date	Mintage	MS-63	Proof
1986 Proof	175,745	—	1.50
1987	147,309,000	0.35	—
1987 Proof	179,004	—	1.50
1988	162,998,558	0.35	—
1988 Proof	175,259	—	1.50
1989	199,104,414	0.35	—
1989 Proof	170,528	—	1.50

KM# 183 Obv: Crowned head right **Obv. Designer:** Dora dePedery-Hunt **Rev:** Bluenose sailing left, date at right, denomination below **Rev. Designer:** Emanuel Hahn **Edge:** Reeded **Weight:** 2.1400 g. **Composition:** Nickel **Size:** 18.03 mm.

Date	Mintage	MS-63	Proof
1990	65,023,000	0.35	—
1990 Proof	140,649	—	2.50
1991	50,397,000	0.45	—
1991 Proof	131,888	—	4.00
1993	135,569,000	0.35	—
1993 Proof	143,065	—	2.00
1994	145,800,000	0.35	—
1994 Proof	146,424	—	2.50
1995	123,875,000	0.35	—
1995 Proof	50,000	—	2.50
1996	51,814,000	0.35	—
1996 Proof	—	—	2.50
1997	43,126,000	0.35	—
1997 Proof	—	—	2.50
1998	203,514,000	0.35	—
1998 Proof	—	—	2.50
1998W	—	1.50	—
1999	258,462,000	0.35	—
1999 Proof	—	—	2.50
2000	159,125,000	0.35	—
2000 Proof	—	—	2.50
2000W	—	1.50	—

KM# 206 Subject: Confederation 125 **Obv:** Crowned head right **Rev:** Bluenose sailing left, date at right, denomination below **Composition:** Nickel **Size:** 18.03 mm.

Date	Mintage	MS-63	Proof
ND(1992)	174,476,000	0.35	—
ND(1992) Proof	147,061	—	3.00

KM# 183a Obv: Crowned head right **Rev:** Bluenose sailing left, date at right, denomination below **Weight:** 2.4000 g. **Composition:** 0.9250 Silver 0.0714 oz. ASW **Size:** 18.03 mm.

Date	Mintage	MS-63	Proof
1996 Proof	—	—	5.50
1997 Proof	—	—	5.50
1998 Proof	—	—	4.00
1998O Proof	—	—	4.00
1999 Proof	—	—	5.00
2000 Proof	—	—	5.00
2001 Proof	—	—	5.00
2002 Proof	—	—	7.50
2003 Proof	—	—	7.50

KM# 299 Subject: John Cabot **Obv:** Crowned head right **Rev:** Ship with full sails divides dates, denomination below **Rev. Designer:** Donald H. Curley **Weight:** 2.4000 g. **Composition:** 0.9250 Silver 0.0714 oz. ASW **Size:** 18.03 mm.

Date	Mintage	MS-63	Proof
ND(1997) Proof	49,848	—	17.50

KM# 311 Subject: 90th Anniversary Royal Canadian Mint **Obv:** Crowned head right **Rev:** Denomination and date within wreath, crown above **Weight:** 2.3200 g. **Composition:** 0.9250 Silver 0.0690 oz. ASW **Size:** 18.03 mm.

Date	Mintage	MS-63	Proof
ND(1998) Proof	25,000	—	10.00
ND(1998) Matte	25,000	—	10.00

KM# 183b Obv: Crowned head right **Obv. Designer:** Dora dePedery-Hunt **Rev:** Bluenose sailing left, date at right, denomination below **Rev. Designer:** Emanuel Hahn **Edge:** Reeded **Composition:** Nickel Plated Steel **Size:** 18.03 mm.

Date	Mintage	MS-63	Proof
1999 P	Est. 20,000	15.00	—
2000 P	Est. 200	1,000	—
2001 P	266,000,000	0.45	—
2003 P	162,398,000	0.20	—

KM# 409 Subject: First Canadian Credit Union **Obv:** Crowned head right **Rev:** Alphonse Desjardins' house (founder of the first credit union in Canada), dates at right, denomination below **Edge:** Reeded **Weight:** 2.4000 g. **Composition:** 0.9250 Silver 0.0714 oz. ASW **Size:** 18.03 mm.

Date	Mintage	MS-63	Proof
ND(2000) Proof	66,336	—	8.00

KM# 412a Subject: Year of the Volunteer **Obv:** Crowned head right **Rev:** 3 portraits left above banner, radiant sun below **Edge:** Reeded **Weight:** 2.4000 g. **Composition:** 0.9250 Silver 0.0714 oz. ASW **Size:** 18 mm.

Date	Mintage	MS-63	Proof
2001P Proof	40,634	—	9.00

KM# 412 Subject: Year of the Volunteer **Obv:** Crowned head right **Rev:** Three portraits left and radiant sun **Edge:** Reeded **Weight:** 1.7700 g. **Composition:** Nickel Plated Steel **Size:** 18 mm.

Date	Mintage	MS-63	Proof
2001P	224,714,000	4.50	—

KM# 447 Subject: Elizabeth II Golden Jubilee **Obv:** Crowned head right, Jubilee commemorative dates 1952-2002 **Weight:** 1.7700 g. **Composition:** Nickel Plated Steel **Size:** 18 mm.

Date	Mintage	MS-63	Proof
ND(2002)P	252,563,000	1.00	—
ND(2002) Proof	32,642	—	2.50

KM# 447a Subject: Elizabeth II Golden Jubilee **Obv:** Crowned head right, Jubilee commemorative dates 1952-2002 **Composition:** 0.9250 Silver **Size:** 18 mm.

Date	Mintage	MS-63	Proof
ND(2002) Proof	21,537	—	12.50

KM# 492 Obv: Head right **Obv. Designer:** Susanna Blunt **Rev:** Bluenose sailing left **Weight:** 1.7700 g. **Composition:** Nickel Plated Steel **Size:** 18 mm.

Date	Mintage	MS-63	Proof
2003P	—	1.25	—
2004P	211,924,000	0.60	—
2004P Proof	—	—	2.50
2005P	212,175,000	0.60	—
2005P Proof	—	—	2.50
2006P	312,122,000	0.60	—
2006P Proof	—	—	2.50
2007(ml) Straight 7	304,110,000	0.60	—
2007(ml) Curved 7	Inc. above	0.60	—
2007(ml) Proof	—	—	2.50
2008(ml)	—	0.60	—
2008(ml) Proof	—	—	2.50
2009(ml)	—	0.60	—
2009(ml) Proof	—	—	2.50

KM# 470 Subject: 50th Anniversary of the Coronation of Elizabeth II **Obv:** Head right **Rev:** Bluenose sailing left **Weight:** 2.3200 g. **Composition:** 0.9250 Silver 0.0690 oz. ASW

Date	Mintage	MS-63	Proof
ND(2003) Proof	21,537	—	12.00

KM# 492a Obv: Bare head right **Obv. Designer:** Susanna Blunt **Rev:** Sailboat **Edge:** Reeded **Weight:** 2.4000 g. **Composition:** 0.9250 Silver 0.0714 oz. ASW **Size:** 18 mm.

Date	Mintage	MS-63	Proof
2004 Proof	—	—	5.00

KM# 524 Subject: Golf, Championship of Canada, Centennial. **Obv:** Head right **Weight:** 2.4000 g. **Composition:** 0.9250 Silver 0.0714 oz. ASW **Size:** 18 mm.

Date	Mintage	MS-63	Proof
2004	39,486	12.50	—

20 CENTS

KM# 4 Obv: Head left **Obv. Legend:** VICTORIA DEI GRATIA REGINA. CANADA **Rev:** Denomination and date within wreath, crown above **Weight:** 4.6480 g. **Composition:** 0.9250 Silver 0.1382 oz. ASW

Date	Mintage	VG-8	F-12	VF-20	XF-40	MS-60	MS-63	Proof
1858	750,000	60.00	100.00	125	225	900	2,500	—

25 CENTS

KM# 5 Obv: Crowned head left **Obv. Legend:** VICTORIA DEI GRATIA REGINA. CANADA **Obv. Designer:** Leonard C. Wyon **Rev:** Denomination and date within wreath, crown above **Weight:** 5.8100 g. **Composition:** 0.9250 Silver 0.1728 oz. ASW **Size:** 23.88 mm.

Date	Mintage	VG-8	F-12	VF-20	XF-40	MS-60	MS-63	Proof
1870	900,000	22.00	45.00	75.00	150	700	2,000	—
1871	400,000	22.00	40.00	125	225	800	2,100	—
1871H	748,000	25.00	50.00	115	250	1,100	2,100	—
1872H	Inc. above	—	—	—	—	2,500	6,000	—
Note: Inverted "A" for "V" in Victoria								
1872H	2,240,000	13.00	20.00	40.00	125	550	1,800	—
1874H	1,600,000	13.00	20.00	40.00	125	375	1,100	—
1875H	1,000,000	350	700	1,700	3,000	20,000	35,000	—
1880H Narrow 0	400,000	60.00	125	300	600	1,700	2,750	—
1880H Wide 0	Inc. above	125	300	600	1,400	4,500	8,000	—
1880H Narrow/wide 0	Inc. above	100.00	225	400	950	2,800	—	—

Date	Mintage	VG-8	F-12	VF-20	XF-40	MS-60	MS-63	Proof
1881H	820,000	30.00	45.00	125	250	1,300	3,600	—
1882H	600,000	30.00	65.00	110	265	1,000	3,000	—
1883H	960,000	20.00	32.00	70.00	175	500	1,700	—
1885	192,000	150	300	450	950	3,500	9,500	—
1886/3	540,000	75.00	125	250	500	2,100	4,300	—
1886	Inc. above	30.00	65.00	110	285	1,600	4,300	—
1887	100,000	125	250	450	1,000	4,250	8,000	—
1888	400,000	26.00	40.00	80.00	185	650	2,200	—
1889	66,324	150	350	650	1,300	4,500	13,000	—
1890H	200,000	25.00	50.00	125	275	950	2,250	—
1891	120,000	70.00	130	320	650	1,600	3,000	—
1892	510,000	20.00	40.00	65.00	175	675	2,300	—
1893	100,000	125	185	375	700	1,750	3,000	—
1894	220,000	30.00	65.00	125	250	700	2,000	—
1899	415,580	11.00	20.00	55.00	150	600	1,350	—
1900	1,320,000	11.00	20.00	45.00	125	525	1,200	—
1901	640,000	12.00	22.00	50.00	150	550	1,200	—

KM# 11 Obv: Crowned bust right **Obv. Designer:** G. W. DeSaulles **Rev:** Denomination and date within wreath, crown above **Weight:** 5.8100 g. **Composition:** 0.9250 Silver 0.1728 oz. ASW **Size:** 23.4 mm.

Date	Mintage	VG-8	F-12	VF-20	XF-40	MS-60	MS-63	Proof
1902	464,000	10.00	27.00	65.00	175	750	1,900	—
1902H	800,000	6.50	16.00	45.00	100.00	250	500	—
1903	846,150	15.00	29.00	75.00	200	800	1,900	—
1904	400,000	20.00	55.00	150	350	1,600	5,000	—
1905	800,000	15.00	30.00	100.00	300	1,400	4,600	—
1906 Large crown	1,237,843	8.00	21.00	55.00	225	750	1,700	—
1906 Small crown, Rare	Inc. above	2,500	3,900	6,000	13,500	17,500	25,000	—
1907	2,088,000	6.50	16.00	55.00	125	425	1,200	—
1908	495,016	15.00	35.00	95.00	200	400	750	—
1909	1,335,929	12.00	26.00	70.00	175	600	1,700	—

KM# 11a Obv: Crowned bust right **Rev:** Denomination and date within wreath, crown above **Weight:** 5.8319 g. **Composition:** 0.9250 Silver 0.1734 oz. ASW

Date	Mintage	VG-8	F-12	VF-20	XF-40	MS-60	MS-63	Proof
1910	3,577,569	5.50	16.00	40.00	85.00	300	600	—

KM# 18 Obv: Crowned bust left **Obv. Legend:** GEORGIVS V REX ET IND IMP **Obv. Designer:** E. B. MacKennal **Rev:** Denomination and date within wreath, crown above **Weight:** 5.8319 g. **Composition:** 0.9250 Silver 0.1734 oz. ASW

Date	Mintage	VG-8	F-12	VF-20	XF-40	MS-60	MS-63	Proof
1911	1,721,341	6.50	18.00	35.00	85.00	250	450	—

KM# 24 Obv: Crowned bust left **Obv. Legend:** GEORGIVS V DEI GRA REX ET IND IMP **Obv. Designer:** E. B. MacKennal **Rev:** Denomination and date within wreath, crown above **Weight:** 5.8319 g. **Composition:** 0.9250 Silver 0.1734 oz. ASW **Size:** 23.5 mm.

Date	Mintage	VG-8	F-12	VF-20	XF-40	MS-60	MS-63	Proof
1912	2,544,199	5.50	9.00	20.00	55.00	350	1,200	—
1913	2,213,595	3.25	8.50	17.00	50.00	300	950	—
1914	1,215,397	5.00	10.00	23.00	60.00	500	1,600	—
1915	242,382	16.00	45.00	150	425	2,200	6,500	—

Date	Mintage	VG-8	F-12	VF-20	XF-40	MS-60	MS-63	Proof
1916	1,462,566	3.00	7.50	18.00	40.00	225	700	—
1917	3,365,644	3.00	6.00	12.00	30.00	125	225	—
1918	4,175,649	3.00	5.00	12.00	26.00	95.00	175	—
1919	5,852,262	3.00	5.00	9.50	25.00	95.00	175	—

Dot below wreath

KM# 24a Obv: Crowned bust left **Obv. Designer:** E. B. MacKennal **Rev:** Denomination and date within wreath, crown below **Weight:** 5.8319 g. **Composition:** 0.8000 Silver 0.1500 oz. ASW

Date	Mintage	VG-8	F-12	VF-20	XF-40	MS-60	MS-63	Proof
1920	1,975,278	3.00	6.00	12.00	30.00	150	400	—
1921	597,337	11.00	24.00	80.00	225	1,100	2,700	—
1927	468,096	27.00	50.00	100.00	225	750	1,600	—
1928	2,114,178	3.00	6.00	13.00	35.00	125	325	—
1929	2,690,562	3.00	6.00	13.00	35.00	125	325	—
1930	968,748	3.00	6.00	18.00	40.00	200	500	—
1931	537,815	3.00	6.00	20.00	50.00	200	500	—
1932	537,994	3.00	6.00	25.00	50.00	200	500	—
1933	421,282	3.00	6.50	28.00	65.00	175	350	—
1934	384,350	3.50	9.00	30.00	70.00	225	500	—
1935	537,772	3.50	7.50	22.00	50.00	150	350	—
1936	972,094	3.00	5.00	12.00	21.00	95.00	175	—
1936 Dot below wreath	153,322	26.00	65.00	150	300	800	1,800	—

Note: David Akers John Jay Pittman sale Part Three, 10-99, nearly Choice Unc. realized $6,900; considered a possible specimen example

Maple leaf after date

KM# 35 Obv: Head left **Obv. Designer:** T. H. Paget **Rev:** Caribou left, denomination above, date at right **Rev. Designer:** Emanuel Hahn **Weight:** 5.7500 g. **Composition:** 0.8000 Silver 0.1479 oz. ASW **Size:** 23.5 mm.

Date	Mintage	VG-8	F-12	VF-20	XF-40	MS-60	MS-63	Proof
1937	2,690,176	3.00	3.50	4.00	6.00	16.00	35.00	—
1938	3,149,245	3.00	3.50	5.00	10.00	65.00	125	—
1939	3,532,495	3.00	3.50	5.00	7.00	50.00	100.00	—
1940	9,583,650	—	BV	3.00	3.50	15.00	30.00	—
1941	6,654,672	—	BV	3.00	3.50	16.00	30.00	—
1942	6,935,871	—	BV	3.00	3.50	17.00	45.00	—
1943	13,559,575	—	BV	3.00	3.50	16.00	30.00	—
1944	7,216,237	—	BV	3.00	3.50	26.00	50.00	—
1945	5,296,495	—	BV	3.00	3.50	16.00	45.00	—
1946	2,210,810	BV	3.00	4.00	8.00	45.00	75.00	—
1947	1,524,554	—	BV	4.00	8.00	50.00	95.00	—
1947 Dot after 7	Inc. above	30.00	45.00	70.00	150	250	500	—
1947 Maple leaf after 7	4,393,938	—	BV	3.00	3.50	16.00	32.00	—

KM# 44 Obv: Head left, modified legend **Obv. Designer:** T. H. Paget **Rev:** Caribou left, denomination above, date at right **Rev. Designer:** Emanuel Hahn **Weight:** 5.8319 g. **Composition:** 0.8000 Silver 0.1500 oz. ASW **Size:** 23.5 mm.

Date	Mintage	VG-8	F-12	VF-20	XF-40	MS-60	MS-63	Proof
1948	2,564,424	BV	3.00	3.50	13.00	55.00	75.00	—
1949	7,988,830	—	BV	3.00	3.50	10.00	20.00	—
1950	9,673,335	—	—	BV	3.00	8.00	15.00	—
1951	8,290,719	—	—	BV	3.00	7.00	12.00	—
1952	8,859,642	—	—	BV	3.00	6.00	11.00	—

KM# 52   Obv: Laureate bust right **Obv. Designer:** Mary Gillick **Rev:** Caribou left, denomination above, date at right **Rev. Designer:** Emanuel Hahn **Weight:** 5.8319 g. **Composition:** 0.8000 Silver 0.1500 oz. ASW **Size:** 23.8 mm.

Date	Mintage	VG-8	F-12	VF-20	XF-40	MS-60	MS-63	Proof
1953 Without strap	10,546,769	—	—	BV	3.00	5.00	10.00	—
1953 With strap	Inc. above	—	—	BV	3.00	6.50	18.00	—
1954	2,318,891	—	BV	3.00	7.00	25.00	40.00	—
1955	9,552,505	—	—	BV	3.00	6.00	15.00	—
1956	11,269,353	—	—	BV	3.00	3.50	6.50	—
1957	12,770,190	—	—	—	BV	3.00	5.00	—
1958	9,336,910	—	—	—	BV	3.00	5.00	—
1959	13,503,461	—	—	—	BV	3.00	3.50	—
1960	22,835,327	—	—	—	BV	3.00	3.50	—
1961	18,164,368	—	—	—	BV	3.00	3.50	—
1962	29,559,266	—	—	—	BV	3.00	3.50	—
1963	21,180,652	—	—	—	BV	3.00	3.50	—
1964	36,479,343	—	—	—	BV	3.00	3.50	—

KM# 62   Obv: Young bust right **Obv. Designer:** Arnold Machin **Rev:** Caribou left, denomination above, date at right **Rev. Designer:** Emanuel Hahn **Weight:** 5.8319 g. **Composition:** 0.8000 Silver 0.1500 oz. ASW **Size:** 23.8 mm.

Date	Mintage	VG-8	F-12	VF-20	XF-40	MS-60	MS-63	Proof
1965	44,708,869	—	—	—	BV	3.00	3.50	—
1966	25,626,315	—	—	—	BV	3.00	3.50	—

KM# 68   Subject: Confederation Centennial **Obv:** Young bust right **Rev:** Lynx striding left divides dates and denomination **Rev. Designer:** Alex Colville **Weight:** 5.8319 g. **Composition:** 0.8000 Silver 0.1500 oz. ASW **Size:** 23.8 mm.

Date	Mintage	VG-8	F-12	VF-20	XF-40	MS-60	MS-63	Proof
ND(1967)	48,855,500	—	—	—	BV	3.00	3.50	—

KM# 68a   Subject: Confederation Centennial **Obv:** Young bust right **Rev:** Lynx striding left divides dates and denomination **Weight:** 5.8319 g. **Composition:** 0.5000 Silver 0.0937 oz. ASW **Size:** 23.8 mm.

Date	Mintage	VG-8	F-12	VF-20	XF-40	MS-60	MS-63	Proof
ND(1967)	Inc. above	—	—	—	BV	2.00	2.50	—

KM# 62a   Obv: Young bust right **Obv. Designer:** Machin **Rev:** Caribou left, denomination above, date at right **Weight:** 5.8319 g. **Composition:** 0.5000 Silver 0.0937 oz. ASW **Size:** 23.8 mm.

Date	Mintage	MS-63	Proof
1968	71,464,000	2.50	—

KM# 62b Obv: Young bust right **Obv. Designer:** Machin **Rev:** Caribou left, denomination above, date at right **Weight:** 5.0600 g. **Composition:** Nickel **Size:** 23.8 mm.

Date	Mintage	MS-63	Proof
1968	88,686,931	0.75	—
1969	133,037,929	0.75	—
1970	10,302,010	2.00	—
1971	48,170,428	0.75	—
1972	43,743,387	0.75	—
1974	192,360,598	0.75	—
1975	141,148,000	0.75	—
1976	86,898,261	0.75	—
1977	99,634,555	0.75	—
1978	176,475,408	0.75	—

KM# 81.1 Subject: Royal Candian Mounted Police Centennial **Obv:** Young bust right **Rev:** Mountie divides dates, denomination above **Rev. Designer:** Paul Cedarberg **Composition:** Nickel **Size:** 23.8 mm. **Note:** 120 beads.

Date	Mintage	MS-63	Proof
ND(1973)	134,958,587	1.00	—

KM# 81.2 Subject: RCMP Centennial **Obv:** Young bust right **Rev:** Mountie divides dates, denomination above **Composition:** Nickel **Size:** 23.8 mm. **Note:** 132 beads.

Date	Mintage	MS-63	Proof
ND(1973)	Inc. above	500	—

KM# 74 Obv: Small young bust right **Obv. Designer:** Machin **Rev. Designer:** Emanuel Hahn **Weight:** 5.0700 g. **Composition:** Nickel **Size:** 23.88 mm.

Date	Mintage	MS-63	Proof
1979	131,042,905	0.75	—
1980	76,178,000	0.75	—
1981	131,580,272	0.75	—
1981 Proof	199,000	—	2.00
1982	171,926,000	0.75	—
1982 Proof	180,908	—	2.00
1983	13,162,000	1.50	—
1983 Proof	168,000	—	3.00
1984	121,668,000	0.75	—
1984 Proof	161,602	—	2.00
1985	158,734,000	0.75	—
1985 Proof	157,037	—	2.00
1986	132,220,000	0.75	—
1986 Proof	175,745	—	2.00
1987	53,408,000	1.25	—
1987 Proof	179,004	—	2.00
1988	80,368,473	0.95	—
1988 Proof	175,259	—	2.00
1989	119,796,307	0.75	—
1989 Proof	170,928	—	2.00

KM# 184 Obv: Crowned head right **Obv. Designer:** Dora dePedery-Hunt **Rev:** Caribou left, denomination above, date at right **Rev. Designer:** Emanuel Hahn **Weight:** 5.0700 g. **Composition:** Nickel **Size:** 23.88 mm.

Date	Mintage	MS-63	Proof
1990	31,258,000	0.90	—
1990 Proof	140,649	—	2.50
1991	459,000	12.00	—
1991 Proof	131,888	—	20.00
1993	73,758,000	0.70	—
1993 Proof	143,065	—	2.00
1994	77,670,000	0.70	—
1994 Proof	146,424	—	3.00
1995	89,210,000	0.70	—
1995 Proof	50,000	—	3.00
1996	28,106,000	0.70	—
1996 Proof	—	—	6.00
1997	—	0.70	—
1997 Proof	—	—	6.00
1998W	—	5.00	—
1999	258,888,000	0.75	—
1999 Proof	—	—	6.00
2000	434,087,000	0.75	—
2000 Proof	—	—	6.00
2000W	—	5.00	—
2001	8,415,000	5.00	—
2001 Proof	—	—	7.50

KM# 184b Obv: Crowned head right **Rev:** Caribou left, denomination above, date at right **Weight:** 4.4000 g. **Composition:** Nickel Plated Steel **Size:** 23.88 mm.

Date	Mintage	MS-63	Proof
1999 P	Est. 20,000	20.00	—
2000 P	—	5,500	—
Note: 3-5 known			
2001 P	55,773,000	0.95	—
2001 P Proof	—	—	5.00
2002 P	156,105,000	2.50	—
2002 P Proof	—	—	5.00
2003 P	87,647,000	2.50	—
2003 P Proof	—	—	5.00

KM# 203 Subject: 125th Anniversary of Confederation, New Brunswick **Obv:** Crowned head right **Rev:** Covered bridge in Newton, denomination below **Rev. Designer:** Ronald Lambert **Weight:** 5.0000 g. **Composition:** Nickel **Size:** 23.9 mm.

Date	Mintage	MS-63	Proof
ND(1992)	12,174,000	0.70	—

KM# 203a Subject: 125th Anniversary of Confederation, New Brunswick **Obv:** Crowned head right **Rev:** Covered bridge in Newton, denomination below **Weight:** 5.8319 g. **Composition:** 0.9250 Silver 0.1734 oz. ASW **Size:** 23.8 mm.

Date	Mintage	MS-63	Proof
ND(1992) Proof	149,579	—	5.50

KM# 207 Subject: Confederation 125 **Obv:** Crowned head right **Obv. Designer:** Dora dePedery-Hunt **Rev:** Caribou left, denomination above, date at right **Rev. Designer:** Emanuel Hahn **Composition:** Nickel **Size:** 23.8 mm.

Date	Mintage	MS-63	Proof
ND(1992)	442,986	12.50	—
ND(1992) Proof	147,061	—	20.00

KM# 212 Subject: 125th Anniversary of Confederation, Northwest Territories **Obv:** Crowned head right **Rev. Designer:** Beth McEachen **Composition:** Nickel **Size:** 23.8 mm.

Date	Mintage	MS-63	Proof
ND(1992)	12,582,000	0.70	—

KM# 212a Subject: 125th Anniversary of Confederation, Northwest Territories **Obv:** Crowned head right **Weight:** 5.8319 g. **Composition:** 0.9250 Silver 0.1734 oz. ASW **Size:** 23.8 mm.

Date	Mintage	MS-63	Proof
ND(1992) Proof	149,579	—	5.50

KM# 213 Subject: 125th Anniversary of Confederation, Newfoundland **Rev:** Fisherman rowing a dory, denomination below **Rev. Designer:** Christopher Newhook **Composition:** Nickel **Size:** 23.8 mm.

Date	Mintage	MS-63	Proof
ND(1992)	11,405,000	0.70	—

KM# 213a Subject: 125th Anniversary of Confederation, Newfoundland **Rev:** Fisherman rowing a dory, denomination below **Weight:** 5.8319 g. **Composition:** 0.9250 Silver 0.1734 oz. ASW **Size:** 23.8 mm.

Date	Mintage	MS-63	Proof
ND(1992) Proof	149,579	—	5.50

KM# 214 Subject: 125th Anniversary of Confederation, Manitoba **Obv:** Crowned head right **Rev. Designer:** Muriel Hope **Composition:** Nickel **Size:** 23.8 mm.

Date	Mintage	MS-63	Proof
ND(1992)	11,349,000	0.70	—

KM# 214a Subject: 125th Anniversary of Confederation, Manitoba **Obv:** Crowned head right **Weight:** 5.8319 g. **Composition:** 0.9250 Silver 0.1734 oz. ASW **Size:** 23.8 mm.

Date	Mintage	MS-63	Proof
ND(1992) Proof	149,579	—	5.50

KM# 220 Subject: 125th Anniversary of Confederation, Yukon **Obv:** Crowned head right **Rev. Designer:** Libby Dulac **Composition:** Nickel **Size:** 23.8 mm.

Date	Mintage	MS-63	Proof
ND(1992)	10,388,000	0.70	—

KM# 220a Subject: 125th Anniversary of Confederation, Yukon **Obv:** Crowned head right **Weight:** 5.8319 g. **Composition:** 0.9250 Silver 0.1734 oz. ASW **Size:** 23.8 mm.

Date	Mintage	MS-63	Proof
ND(1992) Proof	149,579	—	5.50

KM# 221 Subject: 125th Anniversary of Confederation, Alberta **Obv:** Crowned head right

Rev: Rock formations in the badlands near Drumhelter, denomination below **Rev. Designer:** Mel Heath **Composition:** Nickel **Size:** 23.8 mm.

Date	Mintage	MS-63	Proof
ND(1992)	12,133,000	0.70	—

KM# 221a Subject: 125th Anniversary of Confederation, Alberta **Obv:** Crowned head right **Rev:** Rock formations in the badlands near Drumhelter, denomination below **Rev. Designer:** Mel Heath **Weight:** 5.8319 g. **Composition:** 0.9250 Silver 0.1734 oz. ASW **Size:** 23.8 mm.

Date	Mintage	MS-63	Proof
ND(1992) Proof	—	—	5.50

KM# 222 Subject: 125th Anniversary of Confederation, Prince Edward Island **Obv:** Crowned head right **Rev. Designer:** Nigel Roe **Composition:** Nickel **Size:** 23.8 mm.

Date	Mintage	MS-63	Proof
ND(1992)	13,001,000	0.70	—

KM# 222a Subject: 125th Anniversary of Confederation, Prince Edward Island **Obv:** Crowned head right **Rev. Designer:** Nigel Roe **Weight:** 5.8319 g. **Composition:** 0.9250 Silver 0.1734 oz. ASW **Size:** 23.8 mm.

Date	Mintage	MS-63	Proof
ND(1992) Proof	149,579	—	5.50

KM# 223 Subject: 125th Anniversary of Confederation, Ontario **Obv:** Crowned head right **Rev:** Jack pine, denomination below **Rev. Designer:** Greg Salmela **Composition:** Nickel **Size:** 23.8 mm.

Date	Mintage	MS-63	Proof
ND(1992)	14,263,000	0.70	—

KM# 223a Subject: 125th Anniversary of Confederation, Ontario **Obv:** Crowned head right **Rev:** Jack pine, denomination below **Rev. Designer:** Greg Salmela **Weight:** 5.8319 g. **Composition:** 0.9250 Silver 0.1734 oz. ASW **Size:** 23.8 mm.

Date	Mintage	MS-63	Proof
ND(1992) Proof	149,579	—	5.50

KM# 231 Subject: 125th Anniversary of Confederation, Nova Scotia **Obv:** Crowned head right **Rev:** Lighthouse, denomination below **Rev. Designer:** Bruce Wood **Weight:** 5.0300 g. **Composition:** Nickel **Size:** 23.8 mm.

Date	Mintage	MS-63	Proof
ND(1992)	13,600,000	0.70	—

25 CENTS

KM# 231a Subject: 125th Anniversary of Confederation, Nova Scotia **Obv:** Crowned head right **Rev:** Lighthouse, denomination below **Rev. Designer:** Bruce Wood **Weight:** 5.8319 g. **Composition:** 0.9250 Silver 0.1734 oz. ASW **Size:** 23.8 mm.

Date	Mintage	MS-63	Proof
ND(1992) Proof	149,579	—	5.50

KM# 232 Subject: 125th Anniversary of Confederation, British Columbia **Obv:** Crowned head right, dates below **Rev:** Large rock, whales, denomination below **Rev. Designer:** Carla Herrera Egan **Composition:** Nickel **Size:** 23.8 mm.

Date	Mintage	MS-63	Proof
ND(1992)	14,001,000	0.70	—

KM# 232a Subject: 125th Anniversary of Confederation, British Columbia **Obv:** Crowned head right, dates below **Rev:** Large rock, whales, denomination below **Rev. Designer:** Carla Herrera Egan **Weight:** 5.8319 g. **Composition:** 0.9250 Silver 0.1734 oz. ASW **Size:** 23.8 mm.

Date	Mintage	MS-63	Proof
ND(1992) Proof	149,579	—	5.50

KM# 233 Subject: 125th Anniversary of Confederation, Saskatchewan **Obv:** Crowned head right **Rev:** Buildings behind wall, grain stalks on right, denomination below **Rev. Designer:** Brian Cobb **Composition:** Nickel **Size:** 23.8 mm.

Date	Mintage	MS-63	Proof
ND(1992)	14,165,000	0.70	—

KM# 233a Subject: 125th Anniversary of Confederation, Saskatchewan **Obv:** Crowned head right **Rev:** Buildings behind wall, grain stalks on right, denomination below **Rev. Designer:** Brian Cobb **Weight:** 5.8319 g. **Composition:** 0.9250 Silver 0.1734 oz. ASW **Size:** 23.8 mm.

Date	Mintage	MS-63	Proof
ND(1992) Proof	149,579	—	5.50

KM# 234 Subject: 125th Anniversary of Confederation, Quebec **Obv:** Crowned head right **Rev:** Boats on water, large rocks in background, denomination below **Rev. Designer:** Romualdas Bukauskas **Composition:** Nickel **Size:** 23.8 mm.

Date	Mintage	MS-63	Proof
ND(1992)	13,607,000	0.70	—

KM# 234a Subject: 125th Anniversary of Confederation, Quebec **Obv:** Crowned head right **Rev:** Boats on water, large rocks in background, denomination below **Rev. Designer:** Romualdas Bukauskas **Weight:** 5.8319 g. **Composition:** 0.9250 Silver 0.1734 oz. ASW **Size:** 23.8 mm.

Date	Mintage	MS-63	Proof
ND(1992) Proof	149,579	—	5.50

KM# 184a Obv: Crowned head right **Rev:** Caribou left, denomination above, date at right **Weight:** 5.9000 g. **Composition:** 0.9250 Silver 0.1755 oz. ASW **Size:** 23.88 mm.

Date	Mintage	MS-63	Proof
1996 Proof	—	—	6.50
1997 Proof	—	—	6.50
1998 Proof	—	—	5.50
1998O Proof	—	—	5.50
1999 Proof	—	—	5.50
2001 Proof	—	—	6.50
2003 Proof	—	—	6.50

KM# 312 Subject: 90th Anniversary Royal Canadian Mint **Obv:** Crowned head right **Rev:** Denomination and date within wreath, crown above **Size:** 23.8 mm.

Date	Mintage	MS-63	Proof
ND(1998) Matte	25,000	—	15.00
ND(1998) Proof	—	—	15.00

KM# 342 Subject: Millennium, January - A Country Unfolds **Obv:** Crowned head right **Rev:** Totem pole, portraits **Rev. Designer:** P. Ka-Kin Poon **Composition:** Nickel **Size:** 23.8 mm.

Date	Mintage	MS-63	Proof
1999	12,181,200	0.65	—

KM# 342a Subject: Millennium, January **Obv:** Crowned head right **Rev:** Totem pole, portraits **Rev. Designer:** P. Ka-kin Poon **Weight:** 5.8319 g. **Composition:** 0.9250 Silver 0.1734 oz. ASW **Size:** 23.8 mm.

Date	Mintage	MS-63	Proof
1999 Proof	113,645	—	6.50

KM# 343 Subject: Millennium, February - Etched in Stone **Obv:** Crowned head right **Rev:** Native petroglyphs **Rev. Designer:** L. Springer **Weight:** 5.0900 g. **Composition:** Nickel **Size:** 23.8 mm.

Date	Mintage	MS-63	Proof
1999	14,469,250	0.65	—

KM# 343a Subject: Millennium, February **Obv:** Crowned head right **Rev:** Native petroglyphs **Rev. Designer:** L. Springer **Weight:** 5.8319 g. **Composition:** 0.9250 Silver 0.1734 oz. ASW **Size:** 23.8 mm.

Date	Mintage	MS-63	Proof
1999 Proof	113,645	—	6.50

KM# 344 Subject: Millennium, March - The Log Drive **Obv:** Crowned head right **Rev:** Lumberjack **Rev. Designer:** M. Lavoie **Composition:** Nickel **Size:** 23.8 mm.

Date	Mintage	MS-63	Proof
1999	15,033,500	0.65	—

KM# 344a Subject: Millennium, March **Obv:** Crowned head right **Rev:** Lumberjack **Rev. Designer:** M. Lavoie **Weight:** 5.8319 g. **Composition:** 0.9250 Silver 0.1734 oz. ASW **Size:** 23.8 mm.

Date	Mintage	MS-63	Proof
1999 Proof	113,645	—	6.50

KM# 345 Subject: Millennium, April - Our Northern Heritage **Obv:** Crowned head right **Rev:** Owl, polar bear **Rev. Designer:** Ken Ojnak Ashevac **Weight:** 5.0500 g. **Composition:** Nickel **Size:** 23.8 mm.

Date	Mintage	MS-63	Proof
1999	15,446,000	0.65	—

KM# 345a Subject: Millennium, April **Obv:** Crowned head right **Rev:** Owl, polar bear **Rev. Designer:** Ken Ojnak Ashevac **Weight:** 5.8319 g. **Composition:** 0.9250 Silver 0.1734 oz. ASW **Size:** 23.8 mm.

Date	Mintage	MS-63	Proof
1999 Proof	113,645	—	6.50

KM# 346 Subject: Millennium, May - The Voyageures **Obv:** Crowned head right **Rev:** Voyageurs in canoe **Rev. Designer:** S. Mineok **Composition:** Nickel **Size:** 23.8 mm.

Date	Mintage	MS-63	Proof
1999	15,566,100	0.65	—

KM# 346a Subject: Millennium, May **Obv:** Crowned head right **Rev:** Voyageurs in canoe **Rev. Designer:** S. Mineok **Weight:** 5.8319 g. **Composition:** 0.9250 Silver 0.1734 oz. ASW **Size:** 23.8 mm.

Date	Mintage	MS-63	Proof
1999 Proof	113,645	—	6.50

KM# 347 Subject: Millennium, June - From Coast to Coast **Obv:** Crowned head right **Rev:** 19th-century locomotive **Rev. Designer:** G. Ho **Edge:** Reeded **Weight:** 5.0300 g. **Composition:** Nickel **Size:** 23.8 mm.

Date	Mintage	MS-63	Proof
1999	20,432,750	0.65	—

KM# 347a Subject: Millennium, June **Obv:** Crowned head right **Rev:** 19th-century locomotive **Rev. Designer:** G. Ho **Edge:** Reeded **Weight:** 5.8319 g. **Composition:** 0.9250 Silver 0.1734 oz. ASW **Size:** 23.8 mm.

Date	Mintage	MS-63	Proof
1999 Proof	113,645	—	6.50

KM# 348 Subject: Millennium, July - A Nation of People **Obv:** Crowned head right **Rev:** 6 stylized portraits **Rev. Designer:** M. H. Sarkany **Composition:** Nickel **Size:** 23.8 mm.

Date	Mintage	MS-63	Proof
1999	17,321,000	0.65	—

KM# 348a Subject: Millennium, July **Obv:** Crowned head right **Rev:** 6 stylized portraits **Rev. Designer:** M.H. Sarkany **Weight:** 5.8319 g. **Composition:** 0.9250 Silver 0.1734 oz. ASW **Size:** 23.8 mm.

Date	Mintage	MS-63	Proof
1999 Proof	113,645	—	6.50

KM# 349 Subject: Millennium, August - The Pioneer Spirit **Obv:** Crowned head right **Rev:** Hay harvesting **Rev. Designer:** A. Botelho **Weight:** 5.1000 g. **Composition:** Nickel **Size:** 23.8 mm.

Date	Mintage	MS-63	Proof
1999	18,153,700	0.65	—

KM# 349a Subject: Millennium, August **Obv:** Crowned head right **Rev:** Hay harvesting **Rev. Designer:** A. Botelho **Weight:** 5.8319 g. **Composition:** 0.9250 Silver 0.1734 oz. ASW **Size:** 23.8 mm.

Date	Mintage	MS-63	Proof
1999 Proof	113,645	—	6.50

KM# 350 Subject: Millennium, September - Canada Through a Child's Eye **Obv:** Crowned head right **Rev:** Childlike artwork **Rev. Designer:** Claudia Bertrand **Composition:** Nickel **Size:** 23.8 mm.

Date	Mintage	MS-63	Proof
1999	31,539,350	0.65	—

KM# 350a Subject: Millennium, September **Obv:** Crowned head right **Rev:** Childlike artwork **Rev. Designer:** Claudia Bertrand **Weight:** 5.8319 g. **Composition:** 0.9250 Silver 0.1734 oz. ASW **Size:** 23.8 mm.

Date	Mintage	MS-63	Proof
1999 Proof	113,645	—	6.50

KM# 351 Subject: Millennium, October - Tribute to the First Nations **Obv:** Crowned head right **Rev:** Aboriginal artwork **Rev. Designer:** J. E. Read **Weight:** 5.1000 g. **Composition:** Nickel **Size:** 23.8 mm.

Date	Mintage	MS-63	Proof
1999	32,136,650	0.65	—

KM# 351a Subject: Millennium, October **Obv:** Crowned head right **Rev:** Aboriginal artwork **Rev. Designer:** J.E. Read **Weight:** 5.8319 g. **Composition:** 0.9250 Silver 0.1734 oz. ASW **Size:** 23.8 mm.

Date	Mintage	MS-63	Proof
1999 Proof	113,645	—	6.50

KM# 352 Subject: Millennium, November - The Airplane Opens the North **Obv:** Crowned head right **Rev:** Bush plane with landing skis **Rev. Designer:** B. R. Brown **Composition:** Nickel **Size:** 23.8 mm.

Date	Mintage	MS-63	Proof
1999	27,162,800	0.65	—

KM# 352a Subject: Millennium, November **Obv:** Crowned head right **Rev:** Bush plane with landing skis **Rev. Designer:** B.R. Brown **Weight:** 5.8319 g. **Composition:** 0.9250 Silver 0.1734 oz. ASW **Size:** 23.8 mm.

Date	Mintage	MS-63	Proof
1999 Proof	113,645	—	6.50

KM# 353 Subject: Millennium, December - This is Canada **Obv:** Crowned head right **Rev:** Eclectic geometric design **Rev. Designer:** J. L. P. Provencher **Weight:** 5.0900 g. **Composition:** Nickel **Size:** 23.8 mm.

Date	Mintage	MS-63	Proof
1999	43,339,200	0.70	—

KM# 353a Subject: Millennium, December **Obv:** Crowned head right **Rev:** Eclectic geometric design **Rev. Designer:** J.L.P. Provencher **Weight:** 5.1000 g. **Composition:** 0.9250 Silver 0.1517 oz. ASW **Size:** 23.8 mm.

Date	Mintage	MS-63	Proof
1999 Proof	113,645	—	6.50

KM# 373 Subject: Health **Obv:** Crowned head right, denomination below **Rev:** Ribbon and caduceus, date above **Rev. Designer:** Anny Wassef **Composition:** Nickel **Size:** 23.8 mm.

Date	Mintage	MS-63	Proof
2000	35,470,900	0.65	—

25 CENTS

KM# 373a Subject: Health **Obv:** Crowned head right, denomination below **Rev:** Ribbon and caduceus, date above **Rev. Designer:** Anny Wassef **Composition:** 0.9250 Silver **Size:** 23.8 mm.

Date	Mintage	MS-63	Proof
2000 Proof	76,956	—	6.50

KM# 374 Subject: Freedom **Obv:** Crowned head right, denomination below **Rev:** 2 children on maple leaf and rising sun, date above **Rev. Designer:** Kathy Vinish **Weight:** 5.1000 g. **Composition:** Nickel **Size:** 23.85 mm.

Date	Mintage	MS-63	Proof
2000	35,188,900	0.65	—

KM# 374a Subject: Freedom **Obv:** Crowned head right, denomination below **Rev:** 2 children on maple leaf and rising sun, date above **Rev. Designer:** Kathy Vinish **Composition:** 0.9250 Silver **Size:** 23.8 mm.

Date	Mintage	MS-63	Proof
2000 Proof	76,956	—	6.00

KM# 375 Subject: Family **Obv:** Crowned head right, denomination below **Rev:** Wreath of native carvings, date above **Rev. Designer:** Wade Stephen Baker **Composition:** Nickel **Size:** 23.8 mm.

Date	Mintage	MS-63	Proof
2000	35,107,700	0.65	—

KM# 375a Subject: Family **Obv:** Crowned head right, denomination below **Rev:** Wreath of native carvings, date above **Rev. Designer:** Wade Stephen Baker **Composition:** 0.9250 Silver **Size:** 23.8 mm.

Date	Mintage	MS-63	Proof
2000 Proof	76,956	—	6.00

KM# 376 Subject: Community **Obv:** Crowned head right, denomination below **Rev:** Map on globe, symbols surround, date above **Rev. Designer:** Michelle Thibodeau **Weight:** 5.0800 g. **Composition:** Nickel **Size:** 23.8 mm.

Date	Mintage	MS-63	Proof
2000	35,155,400	0.65	—

KM# 376a Subject: Community **Obv:** Crowned head right, denomination below **Rev:** Map on globe, symbols surround, date above **Rev. Designer:** Michelle Thibodeau **Composition:** 0.9250 Silver **Size:** 23.8 mm.

Date	Mintage	MS-63	Proof
2000 Proof	76,956	—	6.00

KM# 377 Subject: Harmony **Obv:** Crowned head right, denomination below **Rev:** Maple leaf, date above **Rev. Designer:** Haver Demirer **Composition:** Nickel **Size:** 23.8 mm.

Date	Mintage	MS-63	Proof
2000	35,184,200	0.65	—

KM# 377a Subject: Harmony **Obv:** Crowned head right, denomination below **Rev:** Maple leaf **Rev. Designer:** Haver Demirer **Composition:** 0.9250 Silver **Size:** 23.8 mm.

Date	Mintage	MS-63	Proof
2000 Proof	76,956	—	6.00

KM# 378 Subject: Wisdom **Obv:** Crowned head right, denomination below **Rev:** Man with young child, date above **Rev. Designer:** Cezar Serbanescu **Composition:** Nickel **Size:** 23.8 mm.

Date	Mintage	MS-63	Proof
2000	35,123,950	0.65	—

KM# 378a Subject: Wisdom **Obv:** Crowned head right, denomination below **Rev:** Man with young child **Rev. Designer:** Cezar Serbanescu **Composition:** 0.9250 Silver **Size:** 23.8 mm.

Date	Mintage	MS-63	Proof
2000 Proof	76,956	—	6.00

KM# 379 Subject: Creativity **Obv:** Crowned head right, denomination below **Rev:** Canoe full of children, date above **Rev. Designer:** Kong Tat Hui **Composition:** Nickel **Size:** 23.8 mm.

Date	Mintage	MS-63	Proof
2000	35,316,770	0.65	—

KM# 379a Subject: Creativity **Obv:** Crowned head right, denomination below **Rev:** Canoe full of children **Rev. Designer:** Kong Tat Hui **Composition:** 0.9250 Silver **Size:** 23.8 mm.

Date	Mintage	MS-63	Proof
2000 Proof	76,956	—	6.00

KM# 380 Subject: Ingenuity **Obv:** Crowned head right, denomination below **Rev:** Crescent-shaped city views, date above **Rev. Designer:** John Jaciw **Composition:** Nickel **Size:** 23.8 mm.

Date	Mintage	MS-63	Proof
2000	36,078,360	0.65	—

KM# 380a Subject: Ingenuity **Obv:** Crowned head right, denomination below **Rev:** Crescent-shaped city views **Rev. Designer:** John Jaciw **Composition:** 0.9250 Silver **Size:** 23.8 mm.

Date	Mintage	MS-63	Proof
2000 Proof	76,956	—	6.00

KM# 381 Subject: Achievement **Obv:** Crowned head right, denomination below **Rev:** Rocket above jagged design, date above **Rev. Designer:** Daryl Dorosz **Composition:** Nickel **Size:** 23.8 mm.

Date	Mintage	MS-63	Proof
2000	35,312,750	0.65	—

KM# 381a Subject: Achievement **Obv:** Crowned head right, denomination below **Rev:** Rocket above jagged design **Rev. Designer:** Daryl Dorosz **Composition:** 0.9250 Silver **Size:** 23.8 mm.

Date	Mintage	MS-63	Proof
2000 Proof	76,956	—	6.00

KM# 382 Subject: Natural legacy **Obv:** Crowned head right, denomination below **Rev:** Environmental elements, date above **Rev. Designer:** Randy Trantau **Composition:** Nickel **Size:** 23.8 mm.

Date	Mintage	MS-63	Proof
2000	36,236,900	0.65	—

KM# 382a Subject: Natural legacy **Obv:** Crowned head right, denomination below **Rev:** Environmental elements **Rev. Designer:** Randy Trantau **Composition:** 0.9250 Silver **Size:** 23.8 mm.

Date	Mintage	MS-63	Proof
2000 Proof	76,956	—	6.00

KM# 383 Subject: Celebration **Obv:** Crowned head right, denomination below **Rev:** Fireworks, children behind flag, date above **Rev. Designer:** Laura Paxton **Composition:** Nickel **Size:** 23.8 mm.

Date	Mintage	MS-63	Proof
2000	35,144,100	0.65	—

KM# 383a Subject: Celebration **Obv:** Crowned head right, denomination below **Rev:** Fireworks, children behind flag **Rev. Designer:** Laura Paxton **Composition:** 0.9250 Silver **Size:** 23.8 mm.

Date	Mintage	MS-63	Proof
2000 Proof	76,956	—	6.00

KM# 384.1 Subject: Pride **Obv:** Crowned head right, denomination below **Rev:** Large ribbon 2 in red with 3 small red maple leaves on large maple leaf, date above **Rev. Designer:** Donald F. Warkentin **Edge:** Reeded **Composition:** Nickel **Size:** 23.8 mm. **Note:** Colorized version.

Date	Mintage	MS-63	Proof
2000	49,399	6.50	—

KM# 384.2 Subject: Pride **Obv:** Crowned head right, denomination below **Rev:** Large ribbon 2 with three small maple leaves on large maple leaf, date above **Rev. Designer:** Donald F. Warkentin **Composition:** Nickel **Size:** 23.8 mm.

Date	Mintage	MS-63	Proof
2000	50,666,800	0.65	—

KM# 384.2a Subject: Pride **Obv:** Crowned head right, denomination below **Rev:** Ribbon 2 with 3 small maple leaves on large maple leaf **Rev. Designer:** Donald F. Warkentin **Composition:** 0.9250 Silver **Size:** 23.8 mm.

Date	Mintage	MS-63	Proof
2000 Proof	76,956	—	6.00

KM# 419 Subject: Canada Day **Obv:** Crowned head right **Rev:** Maple leaf at center, children holding hands below **Rev. Designer:** Silke Ware **Edge:** Reeded **Weight:** 4.4000 g. **Composition:** Nickel Plated Steel **Size:** 23.9 mm.

Date	Mintage	MS-63	Proof
2001	96,352	7.00	—

KM# 448 Subject: Elizabeth II Golden Jubilee **Obv:** Crowned head right **Rev:** Caribou left **Weight:** 4.4000 g. **Composition:** Nickel Plated Steel **Size:** 23.9 mm.

Date	Mintage	MS-63	Proof
ND(2002)P	152,485,000	2.00	—
ND(2002)P Proof	32,642	—	6.00

KM# 448a Subject: Elizabeth II Golden Jubilee **Obv:** Crowned head right, Jubilee commemorative dates 1952-2002 **Composition:** 0.9250 Silver **Size:** 23.9 mm.

Date	Mintage	MS-63	Proof
ND(2002) Proof	100,000	—	12.50

KM# 451 Rev: Small Human figures supporting large maple leaf **Weight:** 4.4000 g. **Composition:** Nickel Plated Steel **Size:** 23.9 mm.

Date	Mintage	MS-63	Proof
ND(1952-2002)P	30,627,000	5.00	—

KM# 451a Subject: Canada Day **Obv:** Crowned head right **Rev:** Human figures supporting large red maple leaf **Edge:** Reeded **Weight:** 4.4000 g. **Composition:** Nickel Plated Steel **Size:** 23.9 mm.

Date	Mintage	MS-63	Proof
ND(1952-2002)P	49,903	6.00	—

KM# 471 Subject: 50th Anniversary of the Coronation of Elizabeth II **Obv:** 1953 effigy of the Queen, Jubilee commemorative dates 1952-2002 **Obv. Designer:** Mary Gillick **Weight:** 5.9000 g. **Composition:** 0.9250 Silver 0.1755 oz. ASW **Size:** 23.9 mm.

Date	Mintage	MS-63	Proof
ND(2002) Proof	21,537	—	12.50

KM# 493 Obv: Bare head right **Obv. Designer:** Susanna Blunt **Weight:** 4.4500 g. **Composition:** Nickel Plated Steel **Size:** 23.9 mm.

Date	Mintage	MS-63	Proof
2003P	66,861,633	2.00	—
2003P W	—	—	—
2004P	177,466,000	2.50	—
2004P Proof	—	—	5.00
2005P	206,346,000	2.50	—
2005P Proof	—	—	5.00
2006P	423,189,000	2.50	—
2006P Proof	—	—	5.00
2007(ml)	274,763,000	2.50	—
2007(ml) Proof	—	—	5.00
2008(ml)	—	2.50	—
2008(ml) Proof	—	—	5.00
2009(ml)	—	2.50	—
2009(ml) Proof	—	—	5.00

KM# 474 Subject: Canada Day **Obv:** Queens head right **Rev:** Polar bear and red colored maple leaves **Weight:** 4.4000 g. **Composition:** 0.9250 Silver 0.1308 oz. ASW **Size:** 23.9 mm.

Date	Mintage	MS-63	Proof
2003 Proof	—	—	12.00

KM# 493a Obv: Bare head right **Obv. Designer:** Suanne Blunt **Rev:** Caribou **Edge:** Reeded **Weight:** 5.9000 g. **Composition:** 0.9250 Silver 0.1755 oz. ASW **Size:** 23.9 mm.

Date	Mintage	MS-63	Proof
2004 Proof	—	—	6.50

KM# 510 Obv: Bare head right **Rev:** Red Poppy in center of maple leaf **Edge:** Reeded **Weight:** 4.4000 g. **Composition:** Nickel Plated Steel **Size:** 23.9 mm.

Date	Mintage	MS-63	Proof
2004	28,500,000	5.00	—

KM# 510a Obv: Bare head right **Rev:** Poppy at center of maple leaf, selectively gold plated **Edge:** Reeded **Weight:** 5.9000 g. **Composition:** 0.9250 Silver 0.1755 oz. ASW **Size:** 23.9 mm. **Note:** Housed in Annual Report.

Date	Mintage	MS-63	Proof
2004 Proof	12,677	—	20.00

KM# 525 Obv: Bare head right **Rev:** Maple leaf, colorized **Weight:** 4.4000 g. **Composition:** Nickel Plated Steel **Size:** 23.9 mm.

Date	Mintage	MS-63	Proof
2004	16,028	8.00	—

KM# 628 Subject: First Settlement, Ile Ste Croix 1604-2004 **Obv:** Bare head right **Rev:** Sailing ship Bonne-Renommee **Weight:** 4.4600 g. **Composition:** Nickel Plated Steel **Size:** 23.9 mm.

Date	Mintage	MS-63	Proof
ND2004P	15,400,000	5.00	—

KM# 698 Rev: Santa, colorized **Weight:** 4.4000 g. **Composition:** Nickel Plated Steel

Date	Mintage	MS-63	Proof
2004	62,777	5.00	—

KM# 699 Subject: Canada Day, **Rev:** Moose head, humorous **Weight:** 4.4000 g. **Composition:** Nickel Plated Steel **Size:** 23.9 mm.

Date	Mintage	MS-63	Proof
2004	44,752	5.00	—

KM# 529 Subject: WWII, 60th Anniversary **Obv:** Head right **Rev:** Three soldiers and flag **Weight:** 4.4300 g. **Composition:** Nickel Plated Steel **Size:** 23.9 mm.

Date	Mintage	MS-63	Proof
2005	3,500	20.00	—

KM# 530 Subject: Alberta **Obv:** Head right **Weight:** 4.4300 g. **Composition:** Nickel Plated Steel **Size:** 23.9 mm.

Date	Mintage	MS-63	Proof
2005P	20,640,000	7.00	—

KM# 531 Subject: Canada Day **Obv:** Head right **Rev:** Beaver, colorized **Weight:** 4.4300 g. **Composition:** Nickel Plated Steel **Size:** 23.9 mm.

Date	Mintage	MS-63	Proof
2005P	58,370	8.50	—

KM# 532 Subject: Saskatchewan **Obv:** Head right **Weight:** 4.4300 g. **Composition:** Nickel Plated Steel **Size:** 23.9 mm.

Date	Mintage	MS-63	Proof
2005P	19,290,000	7.00	—

KM# 533 Obv: Head right **Rev:** Stuffed bear in Christmas stocking, colorized **Weight:** 4.4300 g. **Composition:** Nickel Plated Steel **Size:** 23.9 mm.

Date	Mintage	MS-63	Proof
2005P	72,831	10.00	—

KM# 535 Subject: Year of the Veteran **Obv:** Head right **Rev:** Conjoined busts of young and veteran left **Edge:** Reeded **Weight:** 4.4300 g. **Composition:** Nickel Plated Steel **Size:** 23.9 mm.

Date	Mintage	MS-63	Proof
2005P	29,390,000	7.00	—

KM# 576 Subject: Quebec Winter Carnival **Obv:** Head right **Rev:** Snowman, colorized **Weight:** 4.4300 g. **Composition:** Nickel Plated Steel **Size:** 23.9 mm.

Date	Mintage	MS-63	Proof
2006	8,200	10.00	—

KM# 534 Subject: Toronto Maple Leafs **Obv:** Head right **Rev:** Colorized team logo **Weight:** 4.4300 g. **Composition:** Nickel Plated Steel **Size:** 23.9 mm.

Date	Mintage	MS-63	Proof
2006P	—	12.50	—

KM# 575 Subject: Montreal Canadiens **Obv:** Head right **Rev:** Colorized logo **Weight:** 4.4300 g. **Composition:** Nickel Plated Steel **Size:** 23.9 mm.

Date	Mintage	MS-63	Proof
2006P	—	12.50	—

KM# 629 Obv: Head right **Rev:** Medal of Bravery **Edge:** Reeded **Weight:** 4.4300 g. **Composition:** Nickel Plated Steel **Size:** 23.9 mm.

Date	Mintage	MS-63	Proof
2006(ml)	20,040,000	2.50	—

KM# 632 Subject: Queen Elizabeth II 80th Birthday **Rev:** Crown, colorized **Weight:** 12.6100 g. **Composition:** Nickel Plated Steel **Size:** 35 mm.

Date	Mintage	MS-63	Proof
2006 Specimen	24,977	—	25.00

KM# 633 Subject: Canada Day **Obv:** Crowned head right **Rev:** Boy marching with flag, colorized **Weight:** 4.4300 g. **Composition:** Nickel Plated Steel **Size:** 23.9 mm.

Date	Mintage	MS-63	Proof
2006P	29,760	6.00	—

KM# 634 Subject: Breast Cancer **Rev:** Four ribbons, all colorized **Weight:** 4.4300 g. **Composition:** Nickel Plated Steel **Note:** Sold housed in a bookmark.

Date	Mintage	MS-63	Proof
2006P	40,911	10.00	—

KM# 637 Subject: Wedding **Rev:** Colorized bouquet of flowers **Weight:** 4.4300 g. **Composition:** Nickel Plated Steel

Date	Mintage	MS-63	Proof
2007(ml)	10,318	5.00	—

KM# 642 Subject: Ottawa Senators **Obv:** Head right **Rev:** Logo **Weight:** 4.4300 g. **Composition:** Nickel Plated Steel

Date	Mintage	MS-63	Proof
2006P	—	12.50	—

KM# 644 Subject: Calgary Flames **Obv:** Head right **Rev:** Logo **Weight:** 4.4300 g. **Composition:** Nickel Plated Steel

Date	Mintage	MS-63	Proof
2007(ml)	832	12.50	—

KM# 645 Subject: Edmonton Oilers **Obv:** Head right **Rev:** Logo **Weight:** 4.4300 g. **Composition:** Nickel Plated Steel

Date	Mintage	MS-63	Proof
2007(ml)	2,213	12.50	—

KM# 647 Subject: Santa and Rudolph **Rev:** Colorized Santa in sled, lead by Rudolph **Weight:** 4.4300 g. **Composition:** Nickel Plated Steel

Date	Mintage	MS-63	Proof
2006P	99,258	5.00	—

KM# 711 Subject: 60th Wedding Anniversary **Obv:** Bust right **Rev:** Carriage, multicolor **Weight:** 12.6100 g. **Composition:** Nickel Plated Steel **Size:** 35 mm.

Date	Mintage	MS-63	Proof
ND(2007)	16,264	19.50	—

KM# 638 Subject: Birthday **Rev:** Colorized balloons **Weight:** 4.4300 g. **Composition:** Nickel Plated Steel

Date	Mintage	MS-63	Proof
2007(ml)	24,531	5.00	—

KM# 639 Subject: Baby birth **Rev:** Colorized baby rattle **Edge:** Reeded **Weight:** 4.4300 g. **Composition:** Nickel Plated Steel

Date	Mintage	MS-63	Proof
2007(ml)	29,964	5.00	—

KM# 640 Subject: Oh Canada **Obv:** Head right **Rev:** Maple leaf, colorized **Weight:** 4.4300 g. **Composition:** Nickel Plated Steel

Date	Mintage	MS-63	Proof
2006(ml)	23,582	8.50	—

KM# 641 Subject: Congratulations **Obv:** Head right **Rev:** Fireworks, colorized **Weight:** 4.4300 g. **Composition:** Nickel Plated Steel

Date	Mintage	MS-63	Proof
2006(ml)	8,910	8.00	—

KM# 643 Subject: Vancouver Canucks **Obv:** Head right **Rev:** Logo **Weight:** 4.4300 g. **Composition:** Nickel Plated Steel

Date	Mintage	MS-63	Proof
2007(ml)	1,264	12.50	—

KM# 682 Subject: Curling **Obv:** Head right **Weight:** 4.4300 g. **Composition:** Nickel Plated Steel

Date	Mintage	MS-63	Proof
2007	22,400,000	7.50	—

KM# 683 Subject: Ice Hockey **Obv:** Head right **Weight:** 4.4300 g. **Composition:** Nickel Plated Steel

Date	Mintage	MS-63	Proof
2007	22,400,000	7.50	—

KM# 684 Subject: Paraolympic Winter Games **Obv:** Head right **Rev:** Wheelchair curling **Weight:** 4.4300 g. **Composition:** Nickel Plated Steel

Date	Mintage	MS-63	Proof
2007	22,400,000	7.50	—

KM# 685 Subject: Biathlon **Obv:** Head right **Weight:** 4.4300 g. **Composition:** Nickel Plated Steel

Date	Mintage	MS-63	Proof
2007	22,400,000	7.50	—

KM# 686 Subject: Alpine Skiing **Obv:** Head right **Weight:** 4.4300 g. **Composition:** Nickel Plated Steel

Date	Mintage	MS-63	Proof
2007	22,400,000	7.50	—

KM# 695 Rev: Curling **Weight:** 4.4300 g. **Composition:** Nickel Plated Steel **Note:** Mule obverse 2008, reverse 2007

Date	Mintage	MS-63	Proof
2007 Proof	—	—	20.00

KM# 696 Rev: Ice Hockey **Weight:** 4.4300 g. **Composition:** Nickel Plated Steel **Note:** Mule obverse 2008, reverse 2007

Date	Mintage	MS-63	Proof
2007 Proof	—	—	20.00

KM# 697 Rev: Wheelchair curling **Weight:** 4.4300 g. **Composition:** Nickel Plated Steel **Note:** Mule obverse 2008, reverse 2007

Date	Mintage	MS-63	Proof
2007 Proof	—	—	20.00

KM# 701 Subject: Birthday **Rev:** Party hat, multicolor **Weight:** 4.4300 g. **Composition:** Nickel Plated Steel

Date	Mintage	MS-63	Proof
2007	—	8.00	—

KM# 702 Subject: Congratulations **Rev:** Trophy, multicolor **Weight:** 4.4300 g. **Composition:** Nickel Plated Steel

Date	Mintage	MS-63	Proof
2007	—	8.00	—

KM# 703 Subject: Wedding **Rev:** Cake, multicolor **Weight:** 4.4300 g. **Composition:** Nickel Plated Steel

Date	Mintage	MS-63	Proof
2007	—	8.00	—

KM# 704 Subject: Canada Day **Rev:** Mountie, colorized **Weight:** 4.4300 g. **Composition:** Nickel Plated Steel

Date	Mintage	MS-63	Proof
2007(ml)	27,743	8.00	—

KM# 705 Subject: Christmas **Rev:** Multicolor tree **Weight:** 4.4300 g. **Composition:** Nickel Plated Steel

Date	Mintage	MS-63	Proof
2007	—	8.00	—

KM# 706 Subject: Red-breasted Nuthatch **Obv:** Head right **Obv. Legend:** ELIZABETH II - D • G • REGINA **Obv. Designer:** Susanna Blunt **Rev:** Nuthatch perched on pine branch multicolor **Rev. Legend:** CANADA **Rev. Designer:** Arnold Nogy **Edge:** Plain **Weight:** 12.6100 g. **Composition:** Nickel Plated Steel **Size:** 35.0 mm.

Date	Mintage	MS-63	Proof
2007(ml) Specimen	10,581	25.00	—

KM# 707 Obv: Elizabeth II **Rev:** Multicolor Ruby-throated Hummingbird and flower **Edge:** Plain **Weight:** 12.6100 g, **Composition:** Nickel Plated Steel **Size:** 35 mm.

Date	Mintage	MS-63	Proof
2007 Specimen	16,256	—	25.00

KM# 708 Subject: Queen's 60th Wedding Anniversary **Rev:** Royal carriage **Weight:** 5.9000 g. **Composition:** 0.9250 Silver 0.1755 oz. ASW

Date	Mintage	MS-63	Proof
2007 Specimen	16,264	—	24.00

KM# 713 Rev: Toronto Maple Leaf logo, colorized **Weight:** 4.4000 g. **Composition:** Nickel Plated Steel

Date	Mintage	MS-63	Proof
2007(ml)	—	5.00	—

KM# 714 Rev: Ottawa Senators logo, colorized **Weight:** 4.4000 g. **Composition:** Nickel Plated Steel

Date	Mintage	MS-63	Proof
2007(ml)	—	5.00	—

KM# 723 Rev: Montreal Canadians logo, colorized **Weight:** 4.4000 g. **Composition:** Nickel Plated Steel

Date	Mintage	MS-63	Proof
2007(ml)	—	5.00	—

KM# 693 Rev: Alpine skiing **Weight:** 4.4300 g. **Composition:** Nickel Plated Steel **Note:** Mule obverse of 2008 quarter, reverse 2007

Date	Mintage	MS-63	Proof
2008	—	—	—

KM# 694 Rev: Biathlon **Weight:** 4.4300 g. **Composition:** Nickel Plated Steel **Note:** Mule obverse of 2008, reverse 2007

Date	Mintage	MS-63	Proof
2008	—	8.00	—

KM# 760 Subject: Baby **Rev:** Multicolor blue teddy bear **Weight:** 4.4300 g. **Composition:** Nickel Plated Steel

Date	Mintage	MS-63	Proof
2008	—	8.00	—

KM# 761 Subject: Birthday **Rev:** Multicolor party hat **Weight:** 4.4300 g. **Composition:** Nickel Plated Steel

Date	Mintage	MS-63	Proof
2008	—	8.00	—

KM# 762 Subject: Congratulations **Rev:** Multicolor trophy **Weight:** 4.4300 g. **Composition:** Nickel Plated Steel

Date	Mintage	MS-63	Proof
2008	—	8.00	—

KM# 763 Subject: Wedding **Rev:** Multicolor wedding cake **Weight:** 4.4300 g. **Composition:** Nickel Plated Steel

Date	Mintage	MS-63	Proof
2008	—	8.00	—

KM# 764 Subject: Santa Claus **Rev:** Multicolor Santa **Weight:** 4.4300 g. **Composition:** Nickel Plated Steel

Date	Mintage	MS-63	Proof
2008	—	8.00	—

KM# 765 Subject: Vancouver Olympics **Rev:** Freestyle skiing **Weight:** 4.4300 g. **Composition:** Nickel Plated Steel **Size:** 23.9 mm.

Date	Mintage	MS-63	Proof
2008	—	2.00	—

KM# 766 Subject: Vancouver Olympics **Rev:** Figure skating **Weight:** 4.4300 g. **Composition:** Nickel Plated Steel

Date	Mintage	MS-63	Proof
2008	—	2.00	—

KM# 768 Subject: Vancouver Olympics **Rev:** Snow boarding **Weight:** 4.4300 g. **Composition:** Nickel Plated Steel

Date	Mintage	MS-63	Proof
2008	—	2.00	—

KM# 769 Subject: Vancouver Olympics **Rev:** Olympic mascott - Miga **Weight:** 4.4300 g. **Composition:** Nickel Plated Steel

Date	Mintage	MS-63	Proof
2008	—	3.00	—

KM# 770 Subject: Vancouver Olympics **Rev:** Olympic mascott - Quatchi **Weight:** 4.4300 g. **Composition:** Nickel Plated Steel

Date	Mintage	MS-63	Proof
2008	—	3.00	—

KM# 771 Subject: Vancouver Olympics **Rev:** Olympic mascott - Sumi **Weight:** 4.4300 g. **Composition:** Nickel Plated Steel

Date	Mintage	MS-63	Proof
2008	—	3.00	—

KM# 772 Subject: Oh Canada **Rev:** Multicolor red flag **Weight:** 4.4300 g. **Composition:** Nickel Plated Steel

Date	Mintage	MS-63	Proof
2008	—	8.00	—

KM# 773 Obv: Bust right **Obv. Designer:** Susanna Blunt **Rev:** Downy Woodpecker in tree, multicolor **Rev. Designer:** Arnold Nogy **Edge:** Plain **Weight:** 12.6000 g. **Composition:** Nickel Plated Steel **Size:** 35 mm. **Note:** Prev. KM#717.

Date	Mintage	MS-63	Proof
2008(ml)	25,000	24.00	—

KM# 774 Obv: Bust right **Obv. Designer:** Susanna Blunt **Rev:** Northern Cardinal perched on branch - multicolor **Rev. Designer:** Arnold Nogy **Edge:** Plain **Weight:** 12.6100 g. **Composition:** Nickel Plated Steel **Size:** 35 mm. **Note:** Prev. KM#718.

Date	Mintage	MS-63	Proof
2008(ml)	25,000	25.00	—

KM# 775 Subject: End of WWI, 90th Anniversary **Rev:** Multicolor poppy **Weight:** 4.4300 g. **Composition:** Nickel Plated Steel

Date	Mintage	MS-63	Proof
2008	—	8.00	—

KM# 776 Subject: Anne of Green Gables **Rev:** Image of young girl, multicolor **Rev. Designer:** Ben Stahl **Weight:** 12.6000 g. **Composition:** Nickel Plated Steel **Size:** 35 mm.

Date	Mintage	MS-63	Proof
2008	25,000	17.50	—

KM# 915 Subject: Surprise birthday **Obv:** Bust right **Obv. Designer:** Susanna Blunt **Rev:** Colorized **Weight:** 4.4300 g. **Composition:** Nickel Plated Steel **Size:** 23.9 mm.

Date	Mintage	MS-63	Proof
2009	—	18.50	—

KM# 916 Subject: Share the excitement **Obv:** Bust right **Obv. Designer:** Susanna Blunt **Rev:**

Colorized **Weight:** 4.4300 g. **Composition:** Nickel Plated Steel **Size:** 23.9 mm.

Date	Mintage	MS-63	Proof
2009	—	18.50	—

KM# 917 **Subject:** Share the love **Obv:** Bust right **Obv. Designer:** Susanna Blunt **Rev:** Colorized **Weight:** 4.4300 g. **Composition:** Nickel Plated Steel **Size:** 23.9 mm.

Date	Mintage	MS-63	Proof
2009	—	18.50	—

KM# 918 **Subject:** Thank you **Obv:** Bust right **Obv. Designer:** Susanna Blunt **Rev:** Colorized **Weight:** 4.4300 g. **Composition:** Nickel Plated Steel **Size:** 23.9 mm.

Date	Mintage	MS-63	Proof
2009	—	18.50	—

KM# 840 **Subject:** Edmonton Olympics **Rev:** Cross Country Skiing **Weight:** 4.4300 g. **Composition:** Nickel Plated Steel **Size:** 23.9 mm.

Date	Mintage	MS-63	Proof
2009	—	3.00	—

KM# 841 **Subject:** Vancouver Olympics **Rev:** Bobleigh **Weight:** 4.4300 g. **Composition:** Nickel Plated Steel

Date	Mintage	MS-63	Proof
2009	—	3.00	—

KM# 842 **Subject:** Edmonton Olympics **Rev:** Speed skating **Weight:** 4.4300 g. **Composition:** Nickel Plated Steel **Size:** 23.9 mm.

Date	Mintage	MS-63	Proof
2009	—	3.00	—

KM# 885 **Subject:** Canada Day **Rev:** Animals in boat with flag **Rev. Legend:** Canada 25 cents **Weight:** 4.4000 g. **Composition:** Nickel Plated Steel **Size:** 35 mm.

Date	Mintage	MS-63	Proof
2009	—	5.00	—

KM# 886 **Subject:** Notre-Dame-Du-Saguenay **Obv:** Bust right **Obv. Legend:** Elizabeth II DG Regina **Obv. Designer:** Susanna Blunt **Rev:** Color photo of fjord and statue **Rev. Legend:** Canada 25 cents **Weight:** 12.5000 g. **Composition:** Nickel Plated Steel **Size:** 35 mm.

Date	Mintage	MS-63	Proof
2009 Specimen	—	—	25.00

KM# 880 **Subject:** Miga Mascot Vancouver Olympics **Rev:** Mica Mascot - color **Rev. Legend:** Vancouver 2010 25 cents **Weight:** 4.4000 g. **Composition:** Nickel Plated Steel **Size:** 23.88 mm.

Date	Mintage	MS-63	Proof
2010	—	3.00	—

KM# 881 **Subject:** Quatchi Mascot - Vancouver Olympics **Obv:** Bust right **Rev:** Quatchi Mascot color **Rev. Legend:** Vancouver 2010 25 cents **Weight:** 4.4000 g. **Composition:** Nickel Plated Steel **Size:** 23.88 mm.

Date	Mintage	MS-63	Proof
2010	—	3.00	—

KM# 882 **Subject:** Sumi Mascot **Rev:** Sumi Mascot color **Rev. Legend:** Vancouver 2010 25 cents **Weight:** 4.4000 g. **Composition:** Nickel Plated Steel **Size:** 23.88 mm.

Date	Mintage	MS-63	Proof
2010	—	3.00	—

50 CENTS

KM# 6 **Obv:** VICTORIA DEI GRATIA REGINA. CANADA **Obv. Designer:** Leonard C. Wyon **Rev:** Denomination and date within wreath, crown above **Weight:** 11.6200 g. **Composition:** 0.9250 Silver 0.3456 oz. ASW

Date	Mintage	VG-8	F-12	VF-20	XF-40	MS-60	MS-63	Proof
1870	450,000	800	1,300	2,000	4,500	25,000	38,500	—
1870 LCW	Inc. above	45.00	75.00	165	375	3,500	10,000	—
1871	200,000	65.00	120	350	650	7,000	15,000	—
1871H	45,000	150	225	450	1,100	8,500	22,000	—
1872H	80,000	55.00	95.00	175	400	3,800	10,250	—
1872H Inverted A for V in Victoria	Inc. above	500	700	1,900	5,000	25,000	—	—
1881H	150,000	60.00	100.00	200	550	5,500	16,000	—
1888	60,000	225	350	750	1,400	9,500	22,000	—
1890H	20,000	1,000	1,900	3,200	6,000	28,000	65,000	—
1892	151,000	70.00	125	320	650	9,000	21,000	—
1894	29,036	500	900	1,500	2,500	14,000	35,000	—
1898	100,000	75.00	120	350	750	9,000	26,000	—
1899	50,000	150	300	700	1,600	14,000	35,000	—

Date	Mintage	VG-8	F-12	VF-20	XF-40	MS-60	MS-63	Proof
1900	118,000	55.00	100.00	200	500	5,000	10,500	—
1901	80,000	55.00	150	225	550	6,000	15,000	—

Victorian leaves

KM# 12 Obv: Crowned bust right **Obv. Designer:** G. W. DeSaulles **Rev:** Denomination and date within wreath, crown above **Weight:** 11.6200 g. **Composition:** 0.9250 Silver 0.3456 oz. ASW

Date	Mintage	VG-8	F-12	VF-20	XF-40	MS-60	MS-63	Proof
1902	120,000	15.00	35.00	100.00	250	1,300	3,500	—
1903H	140,000	22.00	45.00	175	450	1,500	4,000	—
1904	60,000	150	200	600	1,000	3,300	9,500	—
1905	40,000	150	300	600	1,400	6,000	15,000	—
1906	350,000	12.00	35.00	95.00	250	1,300	3,500	—
1907	300,000	12.00	35.00	95.00	250	1,400	4,000	—
1908	128,119	21.00	65.00	175	400	1,000	2,000	—
1909	302,118	17.00	60.00	175	500	2,400	8,000	—
1910 Victoria leaves	649,521	22.00	45.00	175	400	1,600	6,000	—

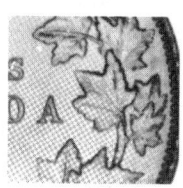

Edwardian leaves

KM# 12a Obv: Crowned bust right **Obv. Designer:** G. W. DeSaulles **Rev:** Denomination and date within wreath **Weight:** 11.6638 g. **Composition:** 0.9250 Silver 0.3469 oz. ASW

Date	Mintage	VG-8	F-12	VF-20	XF-40	MS-60	MS-63	Proof
1910 Edwardian leaves	Inc. above	8.00	29.00	85.00	250	1,200	3,500	—

KM# 19 Obv: Crowned bust left **Obv. Designer:** E. B. MacKennal **Rev:** Denomination and date within wreath, crown above **Weight:** 9.0000 g. **Composition:** 0.9250 Silver 0.2676 oz. ASW **Size:** 28.1 mm.

Date	Mintage	VG-8	F-12	VF-20	XF-40	MS-60	MS-63	Proof
1911	209,972	18.00	70.00	250	550	1,400	3,500	—

KM# 25 Obv: Crowned bust left, modified legend **Obv. Designer:** E. B. MacKennal **Rev:** Denomination and date within wreath, crown above **Weight:** 11.6638 g. **Composition:** 0.9250 Silver 0.3469 oz. ASW

Date	Mintage	VG-8	F-12	VF-20	XF-40	MS-60	MS-63	Proof
1912	285,867	9.00	24.00	100.00	225	1,100	2,900	—
1913	265,889	9.00	24.00	150	300	1,400	5,000	—
1914	160,128	22.00	55.00	225	550	2,800	8,000	—
1916	459,070	7.00	14.00	55.00	175	650	2,100	—
1917	752,213	6.50	11.00	40.00	100.00	500	1,100	—
1918	754,989	6.50	10.00	30.00	90.00	400	1,000	—
1919	1,113,429	6.50	10.00	30.00	90.00	400	1,200	—

KM# 25a **Obv:** Crowned bust left **Obv. Designer:** E. B. MacKennal **Rev:** Denomination and date within wreath, crown below **Weight:** 11.6638 g. **Composition:** 0.8000 Silver 0.3000 oz. ASW

Date	Mintage	VG-8	F-12	VF-20	XF-40	MS-60	MS-63	Proof
1920	584,691	6.00	13.00	35.00	125	500	1,800	—
1921	—	22,000	24,000	28,000	35,000	50,000	90,000	—
Note: 75 to 100 known; David Akers John Jay Pittman sale, Part Three, 10-99, Gem Unc. realized $63,250								
1929	228,328	6.00	13.00	35.00	100.00	500	1,100	—
1931	57,581	11.00	29.00	80.00	225	800	1,800	—
1932	19,213	150	200	400	800	4,000	8,500	—
1934	39,539	15.00	30.00	100.00	225	650	1,300	—
1936	38,550	15.00	29.00	100.00	175	500	1,000	—

KM# 36 **Obv:** Head left **Obv. Designer:** T. H. Paget **Rev:** Crowned arms with supporters, denomination above, date below **Rev. Designer:** George E. Kruger-Gray **Weight:** 11.6000 g. **Composition:** 0.8000 Silver 0.2983 oz. ASW **Size:** 30 mm.

Date	Mintage	VG-8	F-12	VF-20	XF-40	MS-60	MS-63	Proof
1937	192,016	BV	6.00	7.00	10.00	30.00	85.00	—
1938	192,018	BV	6.50	10.00	25.00	95.00	400	—
1939	287,976	BV	6.00	8.00	17.00	60.00	250	—
1940	1,996,566	—	—	BV	6.00	27.00	60.00	—
1941	1,714,874	—	—	BV	6.00	27.00	60.00	—
1942	1,974,164	—	—	BV	6.00	27.00	60.00	—
1943	3,109,583	—	—	BV	6.00	27.00	60.00	—
1944	2,460,205	—	—	BV	6.00	27.00	60.00	—
1945	1,959,528	—	—	BV	6.00	30.00	90.00	—
1946	950,235	—	BV	6.00	8.00	60.00	175	—
1946 hoof in 6	Inc. above	15.00	28.00	45.00	150	1,100	2,800	—
1947 straight 7	424,885	—	6.00	8.00	12.00	65.00	175	—
1947 curved 7	Inc. above	—	6.00	9.00	22.00	100.00	300	—
1947 maple leaf, straight 7	38,433	18.00	23.00	45.00	70.00	160	300	—
1947 maple leaf, curved 7	Inc. above	1,000	1,300	1,700	2,200	4,000	7,000	—

KM# 45 **Obv:** Head left, modified legend **Obv. Designer:** T. H. Paget **Rev:** Crowned arms with supporters, denomination above, date below **Rev. Designer:** George E. Kruger-Gray **Weight:** 11.6638 g. **Composition:** 0.8000 Silver 0.3000 oz. ASW

Date	Mintage	VG-8	F-12	VF-20	XF-40	MS-60	MS-63	Proof
1948	37,784	65.00	85.00	100.00	150	250	350	—
1949	858,991	—	—	BV	7.00	35.00	150	—
1949 hoof over 9	Inc. above	10.00	18.00	35.00	60.00	350	750	—
1950 no lines in 0	2,384,179	6.00	10.00	11.00	35.00	125	225	—
1950 lines in 0	Inc. above	—	—	BV	6.00	9.00	30.00	—
1951	2,421,730	—	—	—	BV	9.00	26.00	—
1952	2,596,465	—	—	—	BV	7.00	18.00	—

KM# 53 Obv: Laureate bust right **Obv. Designer:** Mary Gillick **Rev:** Crowned arms with supporters, denomination above, date below **Weight:** 11.6638 g. **Composition:** 0.8000 Silver 0.3000 oz. ASW

Date	Mintage	VG-8	F-12	VF-20	XF-40	MS-60	MS-63	Proof
1953	1,630,429	—	—	—	BV	7.00	15.00	—
Note: small date								
1953	Inc. above	—	—	BV	6.00	22.00	35.00	—
Note: large date, straps								
1953	Inc. above	—	6.00	7.50	14.00	75.00	150	—
Note: large date without straps								
1954	506,305	—	BV	6.00	7.00	18.00	35.00	—
1955	753,511	—	—	BV	6.00	15.00	30.00	—
1956	1,379,499	—	—	—	BV	7.00	14.00	—
1957	2,171,689	—	—	—	BV	6.00	10.00	—
1958	2,957,266	—	—	—	BV	6.00	8.50	—

KM# 56 Obv: Luareate bust right **Obv. Designer:** Mary Gillick **Rev:** Crown divides date above arms with supporters, denomination at right **Rev. Designer:** Thomas Shingles **Weight:** 11.6638 g. **Composition:** 0.8000 Silver 0.3000 oz. ASW **Size:** 30 mm.

Date	Mintage	VG-8	F-12	VF-20	XF-40	MS-60	MS-63	Proof
1959	3,095,535	—	—	—	BV	6.50	7.50	—
Note: horizontal shading								
1960	3,488,897	—	—	—	BV	6.00	7.00	—
1961	3,584,417	—	—	—	BV	6.00	7.00	—
1962	5,208,030	—	—	—	BV	6.00	7.00	—
1963	8,348,871	—	—	—	BV	6.00	7.00	—
1964	9,377,676	—	—	—	BV	6.00	7.00	—

KM# 63 Obv: Young bust right **Obv. Designer:** Arnold Machin **Rev:** Crown divides date above arms with supporters, denomination at right **Rev. Designer:** Thomas Shingles **Weight:** 11.6638 g. **Composition:** 0.8000 Silver 0.3000 oz. ASW

Date	Mintage	VG-8	F-12	VF-20	XF-40	MS-60	MS-63	Proof
1965	12,629,974	—	—	—	BV	6.00	7.00	—
1966	7,920,496	—	—	—	BV	6.00	7.00	—

50 CENTS

KM# 69 Subject: Confederation Centennial **Obv:** Young bust right **Rev:** Seated wolf howling divides denomination at top, dates at bottom **Rev. Designer:** Alex Colville **Weight:** 11.6638 g. **Composition:** 0.8000 Silver 0.3000 oz. ASW **Size:** 29.5 mm.

Date	Mintage	VG-8	F-12	VF-20	XF-40	MS-60	MS-63	Proof
ND(1967)	4,211,392	—	—	—	BV	6.00	7.00	9.00

KM# 75.1 Obv: Young bust right **Obv. Designer:** Arnold Machin **Rev:** Crown divides date above arms with supporters, denomination at right **Rev. Designer:** Thomas Shingles **Weight:** 8.0600 g. **Composition:** Nickel **Size:** 27.1 mm.

Date	Mintage	VG-8	F-12	VF-20	XF-40	MS-60	MS-63	Proof
1968	3,966,932	—	—	—	0.50	0.65	1.00	—
1969	7,113,929	—	—	—	0.50	0.65	1.00	—
1970	2,429,526	—	—	—	0.50	0.65	1.00	—
1971	2,166,444	—	—	—	0.50	0.65	1.00	—
1972	2,515,632	—	—	—	0.50	0.65	1.00	—
1973	2,546,096	—	—	—	0.50	0.65	1.00	—
1974	3,436,650	—	—	—	0.50	0.65	1.00	—
1975	3,710,000	—	—	—	0.50	0.65	1.00	—
1976	2,940,719	—	—	—	0.50	0.65	1.00	—

KM# 75.2 Obv: Small young bust right **Obv. Designer:** Arnold Machin **Rev:** Crown divides date above arms with supporters, denomination at right **Rev. Designer:** Thomas Shingles **Weight:** 8.1000 g. **Composition:** Nickel **Size:** 27 mm.

Date	Mintage	VG-8	F-12	VF-20	XF-40	MS-60	MS-63	Proof
1977	709,839	—	—	0.50	0.75	1.25	2.00	—

KM# 75.3 Obv: Young bust right **Obv. Designer:** Arnold Machin **Rev:** Crown divides date above arms with supporters, denomination at right, redesigned arms **Rev. Designer:** Thomas Shingles **Weight:** 8.1000 g. **Composition:** Nickel **Size:** 27 mm.

Date	Mintage	VG-8	F-12	VF-20	XF-40	MS-60	MS-63	Proof
1978	3,341,892	—	—	—	0.50	0.65	1.00	—
Note: square jewels								
1978	Inc. above	—	—	1.00	2.50	4.50	6.00	—
Note: round jewels								
1979	3,425,000	—	—	—	0.50	0.65	1.00	—
1980	1,574,000	—	—	—	0.50	0.65	1.00	—
1981	2,690,272	—	—	—	0.50	0.65	1.00	—
1981 Proof	199,000	—	—	—	—	—	—	3.00
1982	2,236,674	—	—	—	30.00	65.00	95.00	—
Note: small beads								
1982 Proof	180,908	—	—	—	—	—	—	3.00
Note: small beads								
1982	Inc. above	—	—	—	0.50	0.65	1.00	—
Note: large beads								
1983	1,177,000	—	—	—	0.50	0.65	1.00	—

Date	Mintage	VG-8	F-12	VF-20	XF-40	MS-60	MS-63	Proof
1983 Proof	168,000	—	—	—	—	—	—	3.00
1984	1,502,989	—	—	—	0.50	0.65	1.00	—
1984 Proof	161,602	—	—	—	—	—	—	3.00
1985	2,188,374	—	—	—	0.50	0.65	1.00	—
1985 Proof	157,037	—	—	—	—	—	—	3.00
1986	781,400	—	—	—	0.50	0.80	1.00	—
1986 Proof	175,745	—	—	—	—	—	—	3.00
1987	373,000	—	—	—	0.50	0.80	1.00	—
1987 Proof	179,004	—	—	—	—	—	—	3.50
1988	220,000	—	—	—	0.50	0.80	1.00	—
1988 Proof	175,259	—	—	—	—	—	—	3.00
1989	266,419	—	—	—	0.50	0.80	1.00	—
1989 Proof	170,928	—	—	—	—	—	—	3.00

KM# 185 Obv: Crowned head right **Obv. Designer:** Dora dePedery-Hunt **Rev:** Crown divides date above arms with supporters, denomination at right **Rev. Designer:** Thomas Shingles **Weight:** 8.2000 g. **Composition:** Nickel **Size:** 27.1 mm.

Date	Mintage	VG-8	F-12	VF-20	XF-40	MS-60	MS-63	Proof
1990	207,000	—	—	—	0.50	0.80	1.00	—
1990 Proof	140,649	—	—	—	—	—	—	5.00
1991	490,000	—	—	—	0.50	0.85	1.00	—
1991 Proof	131,888	—	—	—	—	—	—	7.00
1993	393,000	—	—	—	0.50	0.85	1.00	—
1993 Proof	143,065	—	—	—	—	—	—	3.00
1994	987,000	—	—	—	0.50	0.75	1.00	—
1994 Proof	146,424	—	—	—	—	—	—	4.00
1995	626,000	—	—	—	0.50	0.75	1.00	—
1995 Proof	50,000	—	—	—	—	—	—	4.00
1996	458,000	—	—	—	0.50	0.65	1.00	—
1996 Proof	—	—	—	—	—	—	—	4.00

KM# 208 Subject: Confederation 125 **Obv:** Crowned head right **Obv. Designer:** Dora dePedery-Hunt **Rev:** Crown divides date above arms with supporters, denomination at right **Rev. Designer:** Thomas Shingles **Composition:** Nickel **Size:** 27 mm.

Date	Mintage	MS-63	Proof
ND(1992)	445,000	1.00	—
ND(1992) Proof	147,061	—	5.00

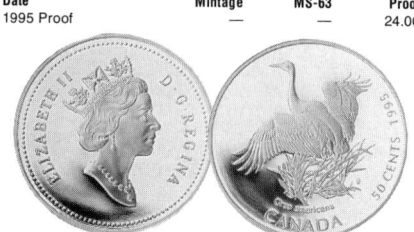

Sheldon Beveridge **Weight:** 11.6638 g. **Composition:** 0.9250 Silver 0.3469 oz. ASW

Date	Mintage	MS-63	Proof
1995 Proof	—	—	24.00

KM# 262 Obv: Crowned head right **Rev:** Whooping crane left, denomination and date at right **Rev. Designer:** Stan Witten **Weight:** 11.6638 g. **Composition:** 0.9250 Silver 0.3469 oz. ASW

Date	Mintage	MS-63	Proof
1995 Proof	—	—	24.00

KM# 261 Obv: Crowned head right **Rev:** Atlantic Puffin, denomination and date at right **Rev. Designer:**

KM# 263 Obv: Crowned head right **Rev:** Gray Jays, denomination and date at right **Rev. Designer:**

Sheldon Beveridge **Weight:** 11.6638 g.
Composition: 0.9250 Silver 0.3469 oz. ASW

Date	Mintage	MS-63	Proof
1995 Proof	—	—	24.00

KM# 264 Obv: Crowned head right **Rev:** White-tailed ptarmigans, date and denomination at right
Rev. Designer: Cosme Saffioti **Weight:** 11.6638 g.
Composition: 0.9250 Silver 0.3469 oz. ASW

Date	Mintage	MS-63	Proof
1995 Proof	—	—	22.00

KM# 283 Obv: Crowned head right **Rev:** Moose calf left, denomination and date at right
Rev. Designer: Ago Aarand **Weight:** 11.6638 g.
Composition: 0.9250 Silver 0.3469 oz. ASW
Size: 27 mm.

Date	Mintage	MS-63	Proof
1996 Proof	—	—	20.00

KM# 284 Obv: Crowned head right **Rev:** Wood ducklings, date and denomination at right
Rev. Designer: Sheldon Beveridge **Weight:** 11.6638 g. **Composition:** 0.9250 Silver 0.3469 oz. ASW **Size:** 27 mm.

Date	Mintage	MS-63	Proof
1996 Proof	—	—	20.00

KM# 285 Obv: Crowned head right **Rev:** Cougar kittens, date and denomination at right
Rev. Designer: Stan Witten **Weight:** 11.6638 g.
Composition: 0.9250 Silver 0.3469 oz. ASW
Size: 27 mm.

Date	Mintage	MS-63	Proof
1996 Proof	—	—	20.00

KM# 286 Obv: Crowned head right **Rev:** Bear cubs standing, date and denomination at right
Rev. Designer: Sheldon Beveridge **Weight:** 11.6638 g. **Composition:** 0.9250 Silver 0.3469 oz. ASW **Size:** 27 mm.

Date	Mintage	MS-63	Proof
1996 Proof	—	—	20.00

KM# 185a Obv: Crowned head right
Obv. Designer: Dora dePedery-Hunt **Rev:** Crown divides date above arms with supporters, denomination at right **Rev. Designer:** Thomas Shingles **Weight:** 11.6380 g. **Composition:** 0.9250 Silver 0.3461 oz. ASW

Date	Mintage	MS-63	Proof
1996 Proof	—	—	9.00

KM# 290 Obv: Crowned head right
Obv. Designer: Dora dePedery-Hunt **Rev:** Redesigned arms **Rev. Designer:** Cathy Bursey-Sabourin **Weight:** 6.9000 g. **Composition:** Nickel **Size:** 27.13 mm.

Date	Mintage	MS-63	Proof
1997	387,000	1.00	—
1997 Proof	—	—	5.00
1998	308,000	1.00	—
1998 Proof	—	—	—
1998W	—	2.00	—
1999	496,000	1.00	—
1999 Proof	—	—	5.00
2000	559,000	1.00	—
2000 Proof	—	—	5.00
2000W	—	1.50	—
2001P	—	1.50	—
2001P Proof	—	—	5.00
2003P	—	1.50	—
2003P Proof	—	—	5.00

KM# 290a Obv: Crowned head right
Obv. Designer: Dora dePedery-Hunt **Rev:** Redesigned arms **Rev. Designer:** Cathy Bursey-Sabourin **Weight:** 11.6380 g. **Composition:** 0.9250 Silver 0.3461 oz. ASW **Size:** 27.13 mm.

Date	Mintage	MS-63	Proof
1997 Proof	—	—	10.00
1998 Proof	—	—	10.00
1999 Proof	—	—	10.00
2000 Proof	—	—	10.00
2001 Proof	—	—	10.00
2003 Proof	—	—	10.00

KM# 290b Obv: Crowned head right
Obv. Designer: Dora dePedery-Hunt **Rev:** Redesigned arms **Rev. Designer:** Cathy Bursey-Sabourin **Weight:** 6.9000 g. **Composition:** Nickel Plated Steel **Size:** 27.13 mm.

Date	Mintage	MS-63	Proof
1999 P	Est. 20,000	15.00	—
2000 P	Est. 50	3,500	—
Note: Available only in RCM presentation coin clocks			
2001 P	389,000	1.50	—
2003 P	—	5.00	—

KM# 292 Obv: Crowned head right **Rev:** Duck Toling Retriever, date and denomination at right **Rev. Designer:** Stan Witten **Weight:** 11.6638 g. **Composition:** 0.9250 Silver 0.3469 oz. ASW **Size:** 27 mm.

Date	Mintage	MS-63	Proof
1997 Proof	—	—	17.00

KM# 293 Obv: Crowned head right **Rev:** Labrador leaping left, date and denomination at right **Rev. Designer:** Sheldon Beveridge **Weight:** 11.6638 g. **Composition:** 0.9250 Silver 0.3469 oz. ASW

Date	Mintage	MS-63	Proof
1997 Proof	—	—	17.00

KM# 294 Obv: Crowned head right **Rev:** Newfoundland right, date and denomination at right **Rev. Designer:** William Woodruff **Weight:** 11.6638 g. **Composition:** 0.9250 Silver 0.3469 oz. ASW

Date	Mintage	MS-63	Proof
1997 Proof	—	—	17.00

KM# 295 Obv: Crowned head right **Rev:** Eskimo dog leaping forward, date and denomination at right **Rev. Designer:** Cosme Saffioti **Weight:** 11.6638 g. **Composition:** 0.9250 Silver 0.3469 oz. ASW **Size:** 27 mm.

Date	Mintage	MS-63	Proof
1997 Proof	—	—	17.00

KM# 313 Subject: 90th Anniversary Royal Canadian Mint **Obv:** Crowned head right **Rev:** Denomination and date within wreath, crown above **Rev. Designer:** W. H. J. Blakemore **Weight:** 11.6638 g. **Comp.:** 0.9250 Silver 0.3469 oz. ASW

Date	Mintage	MS-63	Proof
ND(1998) Matte	25,000	—	15.00
ND(1998) Proof	25,000	—	15.00

KM# 314 Subject: 110 Years Canadian Speed and Figure Skating **Obv:** Crowned head right **Rev:** Speed skaters, dates below, denomination above **Rev. Designer:** Sheldon Beveridge **Weight:** 11.6638 g. **Composition:** 0.9250 Silver 0.3469 oz. ASW

Date	Mintage	MS-63	Proof
ND(1998) Proof	—	—	10.00

KM# 315 Subject: 100 Years Canadian Ski Racing **Obv:** Crowned head right **Rev:** Skiers, dates below, denomination upper left **Rev. Designer:** Ago Aarand **Weight:** 11.6638 g. **Composition:** 0.9250 Silver 0.3469 oz. ASW

Date	Mintage	MS-63	Proof
ND(1998) Proof	—	—	10.00

KM# 318 Obv: Crowned head right **Rev:** Killer Whales, date and denomination at right **Rev. Designer:** William Woodruff **Weight:** 11.6638 g. **Composition:** 0.9250 Silver 0.3469 oz. ASW

Date	Mintage	MS-63	Proof
1998 Proof	—	—	17.00

KM# 319 Obv: Crowned head right **Rev:** Humpback whale, date and denomination at right **Rev. Designer:** Sheldon Beveridge **Weight:** 11.6638 g. **Composition:** 0.9250 Silver 0.3469 oz. ASW **Size:** 27 mm.

Date	Mintage	MS-63	Proof
1998 Proof	—	—	17.00

KM# 320 Obv: Crowned head right **Rev:** Beluga whales, date and denomination at right **Rev. Designer:** Cosme Saffioti **Weight:** 11.6638 g. **Composition:** 0.9250 Silver 0.3469 oz. ASW

Date	Mintage	MS-63	Proof
1998 Proof	—	—	17.00

KM# 321 Obv: Crowned head right **Rev:** Blue whale, date and denomination at right **Rev. Designer:** Stan Witten **Weight:** 11.6638 g. **Composition:** 0.9250 Silver 0.3469 oz. ASW **Size:** 27 mm.

Date	Mintage	MS-63	Proof
1998 Proof	—	—	17.00

KM# 327 Subject: 110 Years Canadian Soccer **Obv:** Crowned head right **Rev:** Soccer players, dates above, denomination at right **Rev. Designer:** Stan Witten **Weight:** 11.6638 g. **Composition:** 0.9250 Silver 0.3469 oz. ASW

Date	Mintage	MS-63	Proof
ND(1998) Proof	—	—	10.00

KM# 328 Subject: 20 Years Canadian Auto Racing **Obv:** Crowned head right **Rev:** Race car divides date and denomination **Rev. Designer:** Cosme Saffioti **Weight:** 11.6638 g. **Composition:** 0.9250 Silver 0.3469 oz. ASW

Date	Mintage	MS-63	Proof
ND(1998) Proof	—	—	10.00

KM# 333 Subject: 1904 Canadian Open **Obv:** Crowned head right **Rev:** Golfers, date at right, denomination below **Rev. Designer:** William Woodruff **Weight:** 11.6638 g. **Composition:** 0.9250 Silver 0.3469 oz. ASW

Date	Mintage	MS-63	Proof
ND(1999) Proof	—	—	13.50

KM# 334 Subject: First U.S.-Canadian Yacht Race **Obv:** Crowned head right **Rev:** Yachts, dates at left, denomination below **Rev. Designer:** Stan Witten **Weight:** 11.6638 g. **Composition:** 0.9250 Silver 0.3469 oz. ASW

Date	Mintage	MS-63	Proof
ND(1999) Proof	—	—	10.00

KM#335 Subject: Canadian Cats, **Obv:** Crowned head right **Rev:** Cymric cat, date below, denomination at bottom **Rev. Designer:** Susan Taylor **Weight:** 11.6638 g. **Composition:** 0.9250 Silver 0.3469 oz. ASW

Date	Mintage	MS-63	Proof
1999 Proof	—	—	0.35

50 CENTS

KM#336 Subject: Canadian Cats, **Obv:** Crowned head right **Rev:** Tonkinese cat, date below, denomination at bottom **Rev. Designer:** Susan Taylor **Weight:** 11.6638 g. **Composition:** 0.9250 Silver 0.3469 oz. ASW

Date	Mintage	MS-63	Proof
1999 Proof	—	—	35.00

KM# 337 Subject: Canadian Cats, **Obv:** Crowned head right **Rev:** Cougar, date and denomination below **Rev. Designer:** Susan Taylor **Weight:** 11.6638 g. **Composition:** 0.9250 Silver 0.3469 oz. ASW

Date	Mintage	MS-63	Proof
1999 Proof	—	—	35.00

KM#338 Subject: Canadian Cats, **Obv:** Crowned head right **Rev:** Lynx, date and denomination below **Rev. Designer:** Susan Taylor **Weight:** 11.6638 g. **Composition:** 0.9250 Silver 0.3469 oz. ASW

Date	Mintage	MS-63	Proof
1999 Proof	—	—	35.00

KM#371 Subject: Basketball **Obv:** Crowned head right **Rev:** Basketball players **Rev. Designer:** Sheldon Beveridge **Edge:** Reeded **Weight:** 9.3600 g. **Composition:** 0.9250 Silver 0.2783 oz. ASW **Size:** 27.1 mm.

Date	Mintage	MS-63	Proof
ND(1999) Proof	—	—	9.00

KM# 372 Obv: Crowned head right **Rev:** Football players **Rev. Designer:** Cosme Saffioti **Edge:** Reeded **Weight:** 9.3600 g. **Composition:** 0.9250 Silver 0.2783 oz. ASW **Size:** 27.1 mm.

Date	Mintage	MS-63	Proof
ND(1999) Proof	—	—	10.00

KM# 385 Subject: Ice Hockey **Obv:** Crowned head right **Rev:** 4 hockey players **Rev. Designer:** Stanley Witten **Composition:** 0.9250 Silver

Date	Mintage	MS-63	Proof
ND(2000) Proof	—	—	12.00

KM# 386 Subject: Curling **Obv:** Crowned head right **Rev:** Motion study of curlers, dates and denomination below **Rev. Designer:** Cosme Saffioti **Composition:** 0.9250 Silver

Date	Mintage	MS-63	Proof
ND(2000) Proof	—	—	10.00

KM# 389 Obv: Crowned head right **Rev:** Great horned owl, facing, date and denomination at right **Rev. Designer:** Susan Taylor **Weight:** 9.3500 g. **Composition:** 0.9250 Silver 0.2781 oz. ASW

Date	Mintage	MS-63	Proof
2000 Proof	—	—	20.00

KM# 390 Obv: Crowned head right **Rev:** Red-tailed hawk, dates and denomination at right **Weight:** 9.3500 g. **Composition:** 0.9250 Silver 0.2781 oz. ASW

Date	Mintage	MS-63	Proof
2000 Proof	—	—	20.00

KM# 391 Obv: Crowned head right **Rev:** Osprey, dates and denomination at right **Rev. Designer:** Susan Taylor **Weight:** 9.3500 g. **Composition:** 0.9250 Silver 0.2781 oz. ASW

Date	Mintage	MS-63	Proof
2000 Proof	—	—	20.00

KM# 392 Obv: Crowned head right **Rev:** Bald eagle, dates and denomination at right
Rev. Designer: William Woodruff **Weight:** 9.3500 g.
Composition: 0.9250 Silver 0.2781 oz. ASW

Date	Mintage	MS-63	Proof
2000 Proof	—	—	20.00

KM# 393 Subject: Steeplechase **Obv:** Crowned head right **Rev:** Steeplechase, dates and denomination below **Rev. Designer:** Susan Taylor
Composition: 0.9250 Silver

Date	Mintage	MS-63	Proof
2000 Proof	—	—	10.00

KM# 394 Subject: Bowling **Obv:** Crowned head right **Rev. Designer:** William Woodruff
Composition: 0.9250 Silver

Date	Mintage	MS-63	Proof
2000 Proof	—	—	10.00

KM# 420 Subject: Festivals - Quebec, **Obv:** Crowned head right **Rev:** Snowman and Chateau Frontenac **Rev. Designer:** Sylvie Daigneault **Edge:** Reeded **Weight:** 9.3000 g. **Composition:** 0.9250 Silver 0.2766 oz. ASW **Size:** 27.13 mm.

Date	Mintage	MS-63	Proof
2001 Proof	58,123	—	8.50

KM# 422 Subject: Festivals - Newfoundland, **Obv:** Crowned head right **Rev:** Sailor and musical people **Rev. Designer:** David Craig **Edge:** Reeded **Weight:** 9.3000 g. **Composition:** 0.9250 Silver 0.2766 oz. ASW **Size:** 27.13 mm.

Date	Mintage	MS-63	Proof
2001 Proof	58,123	—	8.50

KM# 423 Subject: Festivals - Prince Edward Island, **Obv:** Crowned head right **Rev:** Family, juggler and building **Rev. Designer:** Brenda Whiteway **Edge:** Reeded **Weight:** 9.3000 g. **Composition:** 0.9250 Silver 0.2766 oz. ASW **Size:** 27.13 mm.

Date	Mintage	MS-63	Proof
2001 Proof	58,123	—	8.50

KM# 424 Subject: Folklore - The Sled, **Obv:** Crowned head right **Rev:** Family scene **Rev. Designer:** Valentina Hotz-Entin **Edge:** Reeded **Weight:** 9.3000 g. **Composition:** 0.9250 Silver 0.2766 oz. ASW **Size:** 27.13 mm.

Date	Mintage	MS-63	Proof
2001 Proof	28,979	—	9.00

KM# 421 Subject: Festivals - Nunavut, **Obv:** Crowned head right **Rev:** Dancer, dog sled and snowmobiles **Rev. Designer:** John Mardon **Edge:** Reeded **Weight:** 9.3000 g. **Composition:** 0.9250 Silver 0.2766 oz. ASW **Size:** 27.13 mm.

Date	Mintage	MS-63	Proof
2001 Proof	58,123	—	8.50

KM# 425 Subject: Folklore - The Maiden's Cave, **Obv:** Crowned head right **Rev:** Woman shouting **Rev. Designer:** Peter Kiss **Edge:** Reeded **Weight:** 9.3000 g. **Composition:** 0.9250 Silver 0.2766 oz. ASW **Size:** 27.13 mm.

Date	Mintage	MS-63	Proof
2001 Proof	28,979	—	9.00

KM# 426 Subject: Folklore - The Small Jumpers,
Obv: Crowned head right **Rev:** Jumping children on
seashore **Rev. Designer:** Miynki Tanobe **Edge:**
Reeded **Weight:** 9.3000 g. **Composition:** 0.9250
Silver 0.2766 oz. ASW **Size:** 27.13 mm.

Date	Mintage	MS-63	Proof
2001 Proof	28,979	—	9.00

KM# 509 Obv: Crowned head right **Rev:** National
arms **Edge:** Reeded **Weight:** 6.9000 g.
Composition: Nickel Plated Steel **Size:** 27.13 mm.

Date	Mintage	MS-63	Proof
ND(2001) P	—	1.50	—

KM# 444 Subject: Queen's Golden Jubilee **Obv:**
Coronation crowned head right and monogram **Rev:**
Canadian arms **Rev. Designer:** Bursey Sabourin
Edge: Reeded **Weight:** 6.9000 g. **Composition:**
Nickel Plated Steel **Size:** 27.13 mm.

Date	Mintage	MS-63	Proof
ND(2002)P	14,440,000	2.50	—

KM# 444a Subject: Elizabeth II Golden Jubilee
Obv: Crowned head right, Jubilee commemorative
dates 1952-2002 **Weight:** 9.3000 g. **Composition:**
0.9250 Silver 0.2766 oz. ASW **Size:** 27.13 mm.

Date	Mintage	MS-63	Proof
ND(2002) Proof	100,000	—	17.50

KM# 444b Subject: Queen's Golden Jubilee **Obv:**
Crowned head right and monogram **Rev:** Canadian
arms **Edge:** Reeded **Weight:** 9.3000 g.
Composition: 0.9250 Silver Gilt 0.2766 oz. ASW
Size: 27.13 mm. **Note:** Special 24 karat gold plated
issue of KM#444.

Date	Mintage	MS-63	Proof
ND(2002) Proof	32,642	—	35.00

KM# 454 Subject: Nova Scotia Annapolis Valley
Apple Blossom Festival **Obv:** Crowned head right
Rev. Designer: Bonnie Ross **Weight:** 9.3000 g.
Composition: 0.9250 Silver 0.2766 oz. ASW **Size:**
27.13 mm.

Date	Mintage	MS-63	Proof
2002 Proof	59,998	—	8.50

KM# 455 Subject: Stratford Festival **Obv:**
Crowned head right **Rev:** Couple with building in
background **Rev. Designer:** Laurie McGaw
Weight: 9.3000 g. **Composition:** 0.9250 Silver
0.2766 oz. ASW **Size:** 27.13 mm.

Date	Mintage	MS-63	Proof
2002 Proof	59,998	—	8.50

KM# 456 Subject: Folklorama **Obv:** Crowned
head right **Rev. Designer:** William Woodruff
Weight: 9.3000 g. **Composition:** 0.9250 Silver
0.2766 oz. ASW **Size:** 27.13 mm.

Date	Mintage	MS-63	Proof
2002 Proof	59,998	—	8.50

KM# 457 Subject: Calgary Stampede **Obv:**
Crowned head right **Rev. Designer:** Stan Witten
Weight: 9.3000 g. **Composition:** 0.9250 Silver
0.2766 oz. ASW **Size:** 27.13 mm.

Date	Mintage	MS-63	Proof
2002 Proof	59,998	—	8.50

KM# 458 Subject: Squamish Days Logger Sports
Obv: Crowned head right **Rev. Designer:** Jose
Osio **Weight:** 9.3000 g. **Composition:** 0.9250
Silver 0.2766 oz. ASW **Size:** 27.13 mm.

Date	Mintage	MS-63	Proof
2002 Proof	59,998	—	8.50

KM# 459 Subject: Folklore and Legends,   **Obv:**
Crowned head right **Rev:** The Shoemaker in
Heaven **Rev. Designer:** Francine Gravel **Weight:**
9.3000 g. **Composition:** 0.9250 Silver 0.2766 oz.
ASW **Size:** 27.13 mm.

Date	Mintage	MS-63	Proof
2002 Proof	19,267	—	9.50

KM# 460 Subject: Folklore and Legends, The
Ghost Ship **Obv:** Crowned head right
Rev. Designer: Colette Boivin **Weight:** 9.3000 g.
Composition: 0.9250 Silver 0.2766 oz. ASW **Size:**
27.13 mm.

Date	Mintage	MS-63	Proof
2002 Proof	19,267	—	9.50

KM# 461 Subject: Folklore and Legends, The Pig
That Wouldn't Get Over the Stile **Obv:** Crowned
head right **Rev. Designer:** Laura Jolicoeur **Weight:**
9.3000 g. **Composition:** 0.9250 Silver 0.2766 oz.
ASW **Size:** 27.13 mm.

Date	Mintage	MS-63	Proof
2002 Proof	19,267	—	9.50

KM# 494 Obv: Crowned head right
Obv. Designer: Susanna Blunt **Rev. Designer:**
Cathy Bursey-Sabourin **Weight:** 6.9000 g.
Composition: Nickel Plated Steel **Size:** 27.13 mm.

Date	Mintage	MS-63	Proof
2003P W	—	5.00	—
2003P W Proof	—	—	7.50
2004P	—	5.00	—
2004P Proof	—	—	7.50
2005P	—	1.50	—
2005P Proof	—	—	5.00
2006P	—	1.50	—
2006P Proof	—	—	5.00
2007(ml)	—	1.50	—
2007(ml) Proof	—	—	5.00
2008(ml)	—	1.50	—
2008(ml) Proof	—	—	5.00
2009(ml)	—	1.50	—
2009(ml) Proof	—	—	5.00

KM# 472 Subject: 50th Anniversary of the
Coronation of Elizabeth II **Obv:** Crowned head
right, Jubilee commemorative dates 1952-2002
Obv. Designer: Mary Gillick **Weight:** 11.6200 g.
Composition: 0.9250 Silver 0.3456 oz. ASW
Size: 27.13 mm.

Date	Mintage	MS-63	Proof
ND(2003) Proof	30,000	—	15.00

KM# 475 Obv: Crowned head right **Obv. Designer:**
Dora dePédery-Hunt **Rev:** Golden daffodil
Rev. Designer: Christie Paquet, Stan Witten
Composition: 0.9250 Silver **Size:** 27.13 mm.

Date	Mintage	MS-63	Proof
2003 Proof	36,293	—	25.00

KM# 476 Subject: Yukon International Storytelling
Festival **Obv:** Crowned head right **Obv. Designer:**
Dora dePédery-Hunt **Rev. Designer:** Ken Anderson,
Jose Oslo **Weight:** 9.3000 g. **Composition:** 0.9250
Silver 0.2766 oz. ASW **Size:** 27.13 mm.

Date	Mintage	MS-63	Proof
2003 Proof	—	—	11.00

KM# 477 Subject: Festival Acadien de Caraquet
Obv: Crowned head right **Obv. Designer:** Dora
dePédery-Hunt **Rev:** Sailboat and couple
Rev. Designer: Susan Taylor, Hudson Design
Group **Weight:** 9.3000 g. **Composition:** 0.9250
Silver 0.2766 oz. ASW **Size:** 27.13 mm.

Date	Mintage	MS-63	Proof
2003 Proof	—	—	11.00

KM#478 Subject: Back to Batoche **Obv:** Crowned
head right **Obv. Designer:** Dora dePédery-Hunt
Rev. Designer: David Hannan, Stan Witten
Weight: 9.3000 g. **Composition:** 0.9250 Silver
0.2766 oz. ASW **Size:** 27.13 mm.

Date	Mintage	MS-63	Proof
2003 Proof	—	—	11.00

KM# 479 Subject: Great Northern Arts Festival
Obv: Crowned head right **Obv. Designer:** Dora
dePédery-Hunt **Rev. Designer:** Dawn Oman,
Susan Taylor **Weight:** 9.3000 g. **Composition:**
0.9250 Silver 0.2766 oz. ASW **Size:** 27.13 mm.

Date	Mintage	MS-63	Proof
2003 Proof	—	—	11.00

KM# 494a Obv: Crowned head right
Obv. Designer: Susanna Blunt **Rev:** Canadian
coat of arms **Edge:** Reeded **Weight:** 9.3000 g.
Composition: 0.9250 Silver 0.2766 oz. ASW **Size:**
27.13 mm.

Date	Mintage	MS-63	Proof
2004 Proof	—	—	7.50

KM# 526 Subject: Moose **Obv:** Head right **Rev:**
Moose head facing right **Weight:** 1.2700 g.
Composition: 0.9999 Gold 0.0408 oz. AGW **Size:**
14 mm.

Date	Mintage	MS-63	Proof
2004 Proof	—	—	85.00

KM# 606 Obv: Head right **Obv. Designer:**
Susanna Blunt **Rev:** Clouded Sulphur Butterfly,
hologram **Rev. Designer:** Susan Taylor **Weight:**
9.3000 g. **Composition:** 0.9250 Silver 0.2766 oz.
ASW **Size:** 27.13 mm.

Date	Mintage	MS-63	Proof
2004 Proof	15,281	—	30.00

KM# 712 Rev: Hologram of Tiger Swallowtail
Butterfly **Weight:** 9.3000 g. **Composition:** 0.9250
Silver 0.2766 oz. ASW **Size:** 27.13 mm.

Date	Mintage	MS-63	Proof
2004 Proof	20,462	—	30.00

KM# 536 Subject: Golden rose **Obv:** Head right
Obv. Designer: Susanna Blunt **Rev. Designer:**
Christie Paquet **Weight:** 9.3000 g. **Composition:**
0.9250 Silver 0.2766 oz. ASW **Size:** 27.13 mm.

Date	Mintage	MS-63	Proof
2005 Proof	17,418	—	19.00

KM# 537 Subject: Great Spangled Fritillary
butterfly, hologram **Obv:** Head right
Obv. Designer: Susanna Blunt **Rev. Designer:**
Jianping Yan **Weight:** 9.3000 g. **Composition:**
0.9250 Silver 0.2766 oz. ASW **Size:** 27.13 mm.

Date	Mintage	MS-63	Proof
2005 Proof	20,000	—	35.00

KM# 538 Subject: Toronto Maple Leafs **Obv:**
Head right **Obv. Designer:** Susanna Blunt **Rev:**
Darryl Sittler **Weight:** 9.3000 g. **Composition:**
0.9250 Silver 0.2766 oz. ASW **Size:** 27.13 mm.

Date	Mintage	MS-63	Proof
2005 Specimen	25,000	—	16.00

KM# 539 Subject: Toronto Maple Leafs **Obv:**
Head right **Obv. Designer:** Susanna Blunt **Rev:**
Dave Keon **Weight:** 9.3000 g. **Composition:**
0.9250 Silver 0.2766 oz. ASW **Size:** 27.13 mm.

Date	Mintage	MS-63	Proof
2005 Specimen	25,000	—	16.00

KM# 540 Subject: Toronto Maple Leafs **Obv:**
Head right **Obv. Designer:** Susanna Blunt **Rev:**
Jonny Bover **Weight:** 9.3000 g. **Composition:**
0.9250 Silver 0.2766 oz. ASW **Size:** 27.13 mm.

Date	Mintage	MS-63	Proof
2005 Specimen	25,000	—	16.00

KM# 541 Subject: Toronto Maple Leafs **Obv:**
Head right **Obv. Designer:** Susanna Blunt **Rev:**
Tim Horton **Weight:** 9.3000 g. **Composition:**
0.9250 Silver 0.2766 oz. ASW **Size:** 27.13 mm.

Date	Mintage	MS-63	Proof
2005 Specimen	25,000	—	16.00

KM# 542 Subject: Voyageurs **Obv:** Head right
Weight: 1.2700 g. **Composition:** 0.9999 Gold
0.0408 oz. AGW

Date	Mintage	MS-63	Proof
2005 Proof	—	—	65.00

KM# 543 Subject: WWII - Battle of Britain **Obv:**
Head right **Rev:** Fighter plane in sky **Composition:**
Silver

Date	Mintage	MS-63	Proof
2005 Specimen	20,000	—	22.50

KM# 544 Subject: WWII - Battle of Scheldt **Obv:**
Head right **Obv. Designer:** Susanna Blunt **Rev:**
Four soldiers walking down road **Rev. Designer:**
Peter Mossman **Weight:** 9.3000 g. **Composition:**
0.9250 Silver 0.2766 oz. ASW **Size:** 27.13 mm.

Date	Mintage	MS-63	Proof
2005 Specimen	20,000	—	19.00

KM# 545 Subject: WWII - Battle of the Atlantic
Obv: Head right **Obv. Designer:** Susanna Blunt
Rev: Merchant ship sinking **Rev. Designer:** Peter
Mossman **Weight:** 9.3000 g. **Composition:** 0.9250
Silver 0.2766 oz. ASW **Size:** 27.13 mm.

Date	Mintage	MS-63	Proof
2005 Specimen	20,000	—	19.00

KM# 546 Subject: WWII - Conquest of Sicily **Obv:** Head right **Obv. Designer:** Susanna Blunt **Rev:** Tank among town ruins **Rev. Designer:** Peter Mossman **Weight:** 9.3000 g. **Composition:** 0.9250 Silver 0.2766 oz. ASW **Size:** 27.13 mm.

Date	Mintage	MS-63	Proof
2005 Specimen	20,000	—	19.00

KM# 547 Subject: WWII - Liberation of the Netherlands **Obv:** Head right **Obv. Designer:** Susanna Blunt **Rev:** Soldiers in parade, one holding flag **Rev. Designer:** Peter Mossman **Weight:** 9.3000 g. **Composition:** 0.9250 Silver 0.2766 oz. ASW **Size:** 27.13 mm.

Date	Mintage	MS-63	Proof
2005 Specimen	20,000	—	19.00

KM# 548 Subject: WWII - Raid of Dieppe **Obv:** Head right **Obv. Designer:** Susanna Blunt **Rev:** Three soldiers exiting landing craft **Rev. Designer:** Peter Mossman **Weight:** 9.3000 g. **Composition:** 0.9250 Silver 0.2766 oz. ASW **Size:** 27.13 mm.

Date	Mintage	MS-63	Proof
2005 Specimen	20,000	—	19.00

KM# 577 Subject: Montreal Canadiens **Obv:** Head right **Obv. Designer:** Susanna Blunt **Rev:** Guy LaFleur **Weight:** 9.3000 g. **Composition:** 0.9250 Silver 0.2766 oz. ASW **Size:** 27.13 mm.

Date	Mintage	MS-63	Proof
2005 Specimen	25,000	—	17.50

KM# 578 Subject: Montreal Canadiens **Obv:** Head right **Obv. Designer:** Susanna Blunt **Rev:** Jaque Plante **Weight:** 9.3000 g. **Composition:** 0.9250 Silver 0.2766 oz. ASW **Size:** 27.13 mm.

Date	Mintage	MS-63	Proof
2005 Specimen	25,000	—	17.50

KM# 579 Subject: Montreal Canadiens **Obv:** Head right **Obv. Designer:** Susanna Blunt **Rev:** Jean Beliveau **Weight:** 9.3000 g. **Composition:** 0.9250 Silver 0.2766 oz. ASW **Size:** 27.13 mm.

Date	Mintage	MS-63	Proof
2005 Specimen	25,000	—	17.50

KM# 580 Subject: Montreal Canadiens **Obv:** Head right **Obv. Designer:** Susanna Blunt **Rev:** Maurice Richard **Weight:** 9.3000 g. **Composition:** 0.9250 Silver 0.2766 oz. ASW **Size:** 27.13 mm.

Date	Mintage	MS-63	Proof
2005 Specimen	25,000	—	17.50

KM# 599 Subject: Monarch Butterfly, colorized **Obv:** Head right **Obv. Designer:** Susanna Blunt **Rev. Designer:** Susan Taylor **Weight:** 9.3000 g. **Composition:** 0.9250 Silver 0.2766 oz. ASW **Size:** 27.13 mm.

Date	Mintage	MS-63	Proof
2005 Proof	20,000	—	35.00

KM# 648 Subject: Golden Daisy **Obv:** Head right **Weight:** 9.3000 g. **Composition:** 0.9250 Silver 0.2766 oz. ASW

Date	Mintage	MS-63	Proof
2006	18,190	22.00	—

KM# 649 Subject: Short tailed swallotail **Obv:** Head right **Rev:** Colorized butterfly **Weight:** 9.3000 g. **Composition:** 0.9250 Silver 0.2766 oz. ASW

Date	Mintage	MS-63	Proof
2006	20,000	25.00	—

KM# 650 Subject: Butterfly hologram **Obv:** Head right **Rev:** Silvery blue hologram **Weight:** 9.3000 g. **Composition:** 0.9250 Silver 0.2766 oz. ASW

Date	Mintage	MS-63	Proof
2006	16,000	25.00	—

KM#651 Subject: Cowboy **Obv:** Head right **Weight:** 9.3000 g. **Comp.:** 0.9250 Silver 0.2766 oz. ASW

Date	Mintage	MS-63	Proof
2006	—	17.50	—

KM#716 Rev: Multicolor holiday ornaments **Weight:** 9.3000 g. **Comp.:** 0.9250 Silver 0.2766 oz. ASW

Date	Mintage	MS-63	Proof
2006	16,989	17.50	—

KM# 717 Rev: Wolf **Weight:** 1.2400 g. **Composition:** 0.9990 Gold 0.0398 oz. AGW

Date	Mintage	MS-63	Proof
2006	—	60.00	—

KM# 715 Rev: Forget-me-not flower **Weight:** 9.3000 g. **Composition:** 0.9250 Silver 0.2766 oz. ASW **Size:** 27.12 mm.

Date	Mintage	MS-63	Proof
2007 Proof	22,882	—	29.00

KM# 777 Subject: DeHavilland beaver **Weight:** 7.7700 g. **Composition:** Gold

Date	Mintage	MS-63	Proof
2008	20,000	320	—

KM# 778 Subject: Milk delivery **Obv:** Bust right **Rev:** Cow head and milk can **Weight:** 20.0000 g. **Composition:** 0.9250 Silver 0.5948 oz. ASW **Shape:** Triangle **Size:** 34.06 mm.

Date	Mintage	MS-63	Proof
2008 Proof	25,000	—	35.00

KM# 779 Rev: Multicolor snowman **Weight:** 9.3000 g. **Comp.:** 0.9250 Silver 0.2766 oz. ASW

Date	Mintage	MS-63	Proof
2008	—	17.50	—

KM# 780 Subject: Ottawa Mint Centennial 1908-2008 **Weight:** 9.3000 g. **Composition:** 9.2500 Silver 2.7657 oz. ASW

Date	Mintage	MS-63	Proof
2008	—	20.00	—

KM# 845 Rev: Calgary Flames lenticular design, old and new logos **Weight:** 9.3000 g. **Comp.:** 0.9250 Silver 0.2766 oz. ASW **Size:** 27.13 mm.

Date	Mintage	MS-63	Proof
2009	—	15.00	—

KM# 846 Rev: Edmonton Oiler's lenticular design, old and new logos **Weight:** 9.3000 g. **Comp.:** 0.9250 Silver 0.2766 oz. ASW **Size:** 27.13 mm.

Date	Mintage	MS-63	Proof
2009	—	15.00	—

KM#847 Rev: Montreal Canadians lenticular design, old and new logos **Weight:** 9.3000 g. **Comp.:** 0.9250 Silver 0.2766 oz. ASW **Size:** 27.13 mm.

Date	Mintage	MS-63	Proof
2009	—	15.00	—

KM# 848 Rev: Ottawa Senators lenticular design, old and new logos **Weight:** 9.3000 g. **Comp.:** 0.9250 Silver 0.2766 oz. ASW **Size:** 27.13 mm.

Date	Mintage	MS-63	Proof
2009	—	15.00	—

KM# 849 Rev: Toronto Maple Leafs lenticular design, old and new logos **Weight:** 9.3000 g. **Comp.:** 0.9250 Silver 0.2766 oz. ASW **Size:** 27.13 mm.

Date	Mintage	MS-63	Proof
2009	—	15.00	—

KM#850 Rev: Vancouver Canucks lenticular design, old and new logos **Weight:** 9.3000 g. **Comp.:** 0.9250 Silver 0.2766 oz. ASW **Size:** 27.13 mm.

Date	Mintage	MS-63	Proof
2009	—	15.00	—

KM# 887 Subject: Six-string national guitar **Obv:** Bust right **Obv. Legend:** Elizabeth II DG Regina **Obv. Designer:** Susanna Blunt **Rev:** Hologram with 6 "strings" **Rev. Legend:** 50 cents Canada **Weight:** 19.1000 g. **Composition:** Copper-Nickel **Shape:** Triangle **Size:** 34.06 mm.

Date	Mintage	MS-63	Proof
2009 Proof	30,000	—	50.00

DOLLAR

KM# 30 Subject: Silver Jubilee **Obv:** Bust left **Obv. Designer:** Percy Metcalfe **Rev:** Voyager, date and denomination below **Rev. Designer:** Emanuel Hahn **Weight:** 23.3276 g. **Composition:** 0.8000 Silver 0.6000 oz. ASW

Date	Mintage	F-12	VF-20	XF-40	AU-50	MS-60	MS-63	Proof
1935	428,707	13.00	18.00	28.00	30.00	35.00	60.00	4,500

KM# 31 Obv: Crowned bust left **Obv. Designer:** E. B. MacKennal **Rev:** Voyageur, date and denomination below **Rev. Designer:** Emanuel Hahn **Weight:** 23.3276 g. **Composition:** 0.8000 Silver 0.6000 oz. ASW

Date	Mintage	F-12	VF-20	XF-40	AU-50	MS-60	MS-63	Proof
1936	339,600	13.00	15.00	26.00	30.00	35.00	75.00	5,000

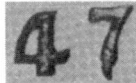 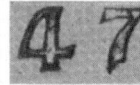

Pointed 7   Blunt 7

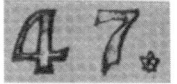

Maple leaf

KM# 37 Obv: Head left **Obv. Designer:** T. H. Paget **Rev:** Voyageur, date and denomination below **Rev. Designer:** Emanuel Hahn **Weight:** 23.3276 g. **Composition:** 0.8000 Silver 0.6000 oz. ASW

Date	Mintage	F-12	VF-20	XF-40	AU-50	MS-60	MS-63	Proof
1937	207,406	—	BV	19.00	22.00	25.00	100.00	—
1937 Mirror Proof	1,295	—	—	—	—	—	—	650
1937 Matte Proof	Inc. above	—	—	—	—	—	—	250
1938	90,304	25.00	35.00	65.00	80.00	100.00	175	6,000
1945	38,391	75.00	150	175	225	300	500	2,000
1946	93,055	15.00	25.00	35.00	45.00	95.00	300	1,800
1947 Pointed 7		60.00	80.00	125	150	300	1,400	3,500
1947 Blunt 7	65,595	45.00	60.00	80.00	95.00	125	250	4,500
1947 Maple leaf	21,135	125	150	175	200	250	500	1,800

KM# 38 Subject: Royal Visit **Obv:** Head left **Obv. Designer:** T. H. Paget **Rev:** Tower at center of building, date and denomination below **Rev. Designer:** Emanuel Hahn **Weight:** 23.3276 g. **Composition:** 0.8000 Silver 0.6000 oz. ASW

Date	Mintage	F-12	VF-20	XF-40	AU-50	MS-60	MS-63	Proof
1939	1,363,816	—	—	BV	12.00	15.00	30.00	—
1939	—	—	—	—	—	—	—	475
Note: Matte specimen								
1939 Proof	—	—	—	—	—	—	—	750
Note: Mirror specimen								

Small beads   Medium beads

Large beads

KM# 46 Obv: Head left, modified left legend **Obv. Designer:** T. H. Paget **Rev:** Voyageur, date and denomination below **Rev. Designer:** Emanuel Hahn **Weight:** 23.3276 g. **Composition:** 0.8000 Silver 0.6000 oz. ASW

Date	Mintage	F-12	VF-20	XF-40	AU-50	MS-60	MS-63	Proof
1948	18,780	500	600	1,000	1,100	1,300	2,000	3,000
1950	261,002	—	BV	12.00	14.00	20.00	50.00	800
Note: With 3 water lines								
1950 Matte Proof	—	—	—	—	—	—	—	—
Note: With 4 water lines, 1 known								
1950	Inc. above	12.00	14.00	21.00	28.00	40.00	90.00	1,500
Note: Arnprior with 2-1/2 water lines								
1951	416,395	—	BV	12.00	14.00	17.00	23.00	650
Note: With 3 water lines								
1951	Inc. above	35.00	50.00	60.00	100.00	175	400	2,000
Note: Arnprior with 1-1/2 water lines								
1952	406,148	—	BV	12.00	14.00	17.00	25.00	1,000
Note: With 3 water lines								
1952	Inc. above	12.00	14.00	22.00	30.00	40.00	100.00	1,250
Note: Arnprior type								
1952	Inc. above	—	BV	12.00	14.00	20.00	45.00	—
Note: Without water lines								

KM# 47 Subject: Newfoundland **Obv:** Head left **Obv. Designer:** T. H. Paget **Rev:** The "Matthew", John Cabot's ship, date and denomination below **Rev. Designer:** Thomas Shingles **Weight:** 23.3276 g. **Composition:** 0.8000 Silver 0.6000 oz. ASW

Date	Mintage	F-12	VF-20	XF-40	AU-50	MS-60	MS-63	Proof
1949	672,218	12.00	14.00	16.50	18.50	23.00	28.00	—
1949 Specimen proof	—	—	—	—	—	—	—	1,200

KM# 54 Obv: Laureate bust right **Obv. Designer:** Mary Gillick **Rev:** Voyageur, date and denomination below **Rev. Designer:** Emanuel Hahn **Weight:** 23.3276 g. **Composition:** 0.8000 Silver 0.6000 oz. ASW **Note:** All genuine circulation strike 1955 Arnprior dollars have a die break running along the top of TI in the word GRATIA on the obverse.

Date	Mintage	F-12	VF-20	XF-40	AU-50	MS-60	MS-63	Proof
1953	1,074,578	—	—	BV	11.50	14.00	25.00	400
Note: Without strap, wire rim
1953	Inc. above	—	—	BV	11.50	14.00	25.00	—
Note: With strap, flat rim
1954	246,606	BV	12.00	13.00	16.00	20.00	35.00	—
1955	268,105	BV	11.50	12.50	15.00	18.00	30.00	—
Note: With 3 water lines
1955	Inc. above	45.00	65.00	90.00	100.00	125	175	—
Note: Arnprior with 1-1/2 water lines* and die break
1956	209,092	BV	12.00	13.00	16.00	20.00	50.00	—
1957	496,389	—	—	—	BV	12.00	16.00	—
Note: With 3 water lines
1957	Inc. above	—	BV	11.50	13.00	15.00	35.00	—
Note: With 1 water line
1959	1,443,502	—	—	—	—	BV	12.00	—
1960	1,420,486	—	—	—	—	BV	12.00	—
1961	1,262,231	—	—	—	—	BV	12.00	—
1962	1,884,789	—	—	—	—	BV	12.00	—
1963	4,179,981	—	—	—	—	BV	11.50	—

KM# 55 Subject: British Columbia **Obv:** Laureate bust right **Obv. Designer:** Mary Gillick **Rev:** Totem Pole, dates at left, denomination below **Rev. Designer:** Stephan Trenka **Weight:** 23.3276 g. **Composition:** 0.8000 Silver 0.6000 oz. ASW

Date	Mintage	F-12	VF-20	XF-40	AU-50	MS-60	MS-63	Proof
ND(1958)	3,039,630	—	—	—	BV	11.50	15.00	—

KM# 58   Subject: Charlottetown **Obv:** Laureate bust right **Rev:** Design at center, dates at outer edges, denomination below **Rev. Designer:** Dinko Voldanovic **Weight:** 23.3276 g. **Composition:** 0.8000 Silver 0.6000 oz. ASW **Size:** 36 mm.

Date	Mintage	F-12	VF-20	XF-40	AU-50	MS-60	MS-63	Proof
ND(1964)	7,296,832	—	—	—	—	BV	11.50	—
ND(1964) Specimen proof	Inc. above	—	—	—	—	—	—	250

KM# 64.1   Obv: Young bust right **Obv. Designer:** Arnold Machin **Rev:** Voyageur, date and denomination below **Rev. Designer:** Emanual Hahn **Weight:** 23.3276 g. **Comp.:** 0.8000 Silver 0.6000 oz. ASW **Size:** 36 mm.

Date	Mintage	F-12	VF-20	XF-40	AU-50	MS-60	MS-63	Proof
1965	10,768,569	—	—	—	—	BV	11.50	—
Note: Small beads, pointed 5								
1965	Inc. above	—	—	—	—	BV	11.50	—
Note: Small beads, blunt 5								
1965	Inc. above	—	—	—	—	BV	11.50	—
Note: Large beads, blunt 5								
1965	Inc. above	—	—	—	—	BV	12.00	—
Note: Large beads, pointed 5								
1965	Inc. above	—	BV	11.50	13.00	15.00	35.00	—
Note: Medium beads, pointed 5								
1966	9,912,178	—	—	—	—	BV	11.50	—
Note: Large beads								
1966	485	—	—	1,200	1,500	1,800	3,500	—
Note: Small beads								

KM# 70   Subject: Confederation Centennial **Obv:** Young bust right **Obv. Designer:** Arnold Machin **Rev:** Goose left, dates below, denomination above **Rev. Designer:** Alex Colville **Weight:** 23.6000 g. **Composition:** 0.8000 Silver 0.6070 oz. ASW **Size:** 36 mm.

Date	Mintage	MS-63	Proof
ND(1967)	6,767,496	12.00	13.00

KM# 76.1 Obv: Young bust right **Obv. Designer:** Arnold Machin **Rev:** Voyageur, date and denomination below **Rev. Designer:** Emanuel Hahn **Weight:** 15.6400 g. **Composition:** Nickel **Size:** 32 mm.

Date	Mintage	MS-63	P/L	Proof
1968	1,408,143	—	2.00	—
1968 Small island	—	8.50	—	—
1968 No Island	—	—	4.00	—
1968	—	—	25.00	—
Note: Doubled die; exhibits extra water lines				
1968	5,579,714	2.00	—	—
1969	4,809,313	2.00	—	—
1969	594,258	—	2.00	—
1972	2,676,041	2.25	—	—
1972	405,865	—	2.50	—

KM# 78 Subject: Manitoba **Obv:** Young bust right **Rev:** Pasque flower divides dates and denomination **Rev. Designer:** Raymond Taylor **Weight:** 15.6000 g. **Composition:** Nickel **Size:** 32 mm.

Date	Mintage	MS-63	P/L	Proof
1970	4,140,058	2.00	—	—
1970	645,869	—	2.50	—

KM# 79 Subject: British Columbia **Obv:** Young bust right **Rev:** Shield divides dates, denomination below, flowers above **Rev. Designer:** Thomas Shingles **Weight:** 15.7000 g. **Composition:** Nickel **Size:** 32.1 mm.

Date	Mintage	MS-63	P/L	Proof
1971	4,260,781	2.00	—	—
1971	468,729	—	2.25	—

KM# 80 Subject: British Columbia **Obv:** Young bust right **Rev:** Crowned arms with supporters divide dates, maple at top divides denomination, crowned lion atop crown on shield **Rev. Designer:** Patrick Brindley **Weight:** 23.3276 g. **Composition:** 0.5000 Silver 0.3750 oz. ASW **Size:** 36 mm.

Date	Mintage	MS-63	P/L	Proof
1971 Specimen	585,674	—	—	—

KM# 64.2a Obv: Smaller young bust right **Obv. Designer:** Arnold Machin **Rev:** Voyageur **Rev. Designer:** Emanuel Hahn **Weight:** 23.3276 g. **Composition:** 0.5000 Silver 0.3750 oz. ASW **Size:** 36 mm.

Date	Mintage	MS-63	P/L	Proof
1972	341,598	—	—	8.50

KM# 82 Subject: Prince Edward Island **Obv:** Young bust right **Rev:** Building, inscription below divides dates, denomination above **Rev. Designer:** Terry Manning **Composition:** Nickel **Size:** 32 mm.

Date	Mintage	MS-63	P/L	Proof
1973	3,196,452	2.00	—	—
1973 (c)	466,881	—	2.50	—

KM# 83 Obv: Young bust right **Rev:** Mountie left, dates below, denomination at right **Rev. Designer:** Paul Cedarberg **Weight:** 23.3276 g. **Composition:** 0.5000 Silver 0.3750 oz. ASW **Size:** 36 mm.

Date	Mintage	MS-63	P/L	Proof
1973 Specimen	1,031,271	—	—	—
1973 Specimen	—	—	—	—

Note: Dollar housed in special blue case with RCMP crest.

KM# 88 Subject: Winnipeg Centennial **Obv:** Young bust right **Rev:** Zeros frame pictures, dates below, denomination at bottom **Rev. Designer:** Paul Pederson and Patrick Brindley **Composition:** Nickel **Size:** 32 mm.

Date	Mintage	MS-63	P/L	Proof
1974	2,799,363	2.00	—	—
1974 (c)	363,786	—	2.50	—

KM# 88a Subject: Winnipeg Centennial **Obv:** Young bust right **Rev:** Zeros frame pictures, dates below, denomination at bottom **Rev. Designer:** Paul Pederson and Patrick Brindley **Composition:** 0.5000 Silver **Size:** 36 mm.

Date	Mintage	MS-63	P/L	Proof
1974 Specimen	728,947	—	—	—

KM# 76.2 Obv: Smaller young bust right **Obv. Designer:** Arnold Machin **Rev:** Voyageur **Rev. Designer:** Emanuel Hahn **Weight:** 15.6200 g. **Composition:** Nickel **Size:** 32 mm.

Date	Mintage	MS-63	P/L	Proof
1975	3,256,000	1.50	—	—
1975	322,325	—	2.50	—
1976	2,498,204	1.50	—	—
1976	274,106	—	2.50	—

KM# 97 Subject: Calgary **Obv:** Youmg bust right **Rev:** Figure on bucking horse, dates divided below, denomination above **Rev. Designer:** Donald D. Paterson **Weight:** 23.3276 g. **Composition:** 0.5000 Silver 0.3750 oz. ASW **Size:** 36 mm.

Date	Mintage	MS-63	P/L	Proof
1975 Specimen	930,956	—	—	—

KM# 76.3 Obv: Young bust right **Obv. Designer:** Arnold Machin **Rev:** Voyageur **Rev. Designer:** Emanuel Hahn **Composition:** Nickel **Size:** 32 mm. **Note:** Only known in prooflike sets with 1976 obverse slightly modified.

Date	Mintage	MS-63	P/L	Proof
1975	Inc. above	—	3.00	—

Note: mule with 1976 obv.

KM# 106 Subject: Parliament Library **Obv:** Young bust right **Rev:** Library building, dates below, denomination above **Rev. Designer:** Walter Ott and Patrick Brindley **Weight:** 23.3276 g. **Composition:** 0.5000 Silver 0.3750 oz. ASW **Size:** 36 mm.

Date	Mintage	MS-63	P/L	Proof
1976 Specimen	578,708	—	—	—
1976 Proof	Inc. above	—	—	23.00

Note: Blue case VIP

KM# 117 Obv: Young bust right **Obv. Designer:** Arnold Machin **Rev:** Voyageur modified **Rev. Designer:** Emanuel Hahn **Composition:** Nickel **Size:** 32 mm.

Date	Mintage	MS-63	P/L	Proof
1977	1,393,745	3.50	—	—
1977	—	—	4.00	—

KM# 118 Subject: Silver Jubilee **Obv:** Young bust right, dates below **Rev:** Throne, denomination below **Rev. Designer:** Raymond Lee **Weight:** 23.3276 g. **Composition:** 0.5000 Silver 0.3750 oz. ASW **Size:** 36 mm.

Date	Mintage	MS-63	P/L	Proof
1977 Specimen	744,848	—	—	—
1977 Specimen	Inc. above	—	—	—

Note: red case VIP

KM# 120.1 Obv: Young bust right **Obv. Designer:** Arnold Machin **Rev:** Voyageur, date and denomination below **Rev. Designer:** Emanuel Hahn **Weight:** 15.5000 g. **Composition:** Nickel **Size:** 32.1 mm. **Note:** Modified design.

Date	Mintage	MS-63	Proof
1978	2,948,488	1.50	—
1979	2,954,842	1.50	—
1980	3,291,221	1.50	—
1981	2,778,900	1.50	—
1981 Proof	—	—	5.25
1982	1,098,500	1.50	—
1982 Proof	180,908	—	5.25
1983	2,267,525	1.50	—

Date	Mintage	MS-63	Proof
1983 Proof	166,779	—	5.25
1984	1,223,486	1.50	—
1984 Proof	161,602	—	6.00
1985	3,104,092	1.50	—
1985 Proof	153,950	—	7.00
1986	3,089,225	2.00	—
1986 Proof	176,224	—	7.50
1987	287,330	3.50	—
1987 Proof	175,686	—	7.50

KM# 121 Subject: XI Commonwealth Games **Obv:** Young bust right **Rev:** Commonwealth games, logo at center **Rev. Designer:** Raymond Taylor **Weight:** 23.3276 g. **Composition:** 0.5000 Silver 0.3750 oz. ASW **Size:** 36 mm.

Date	Mintage	MS-63	P/L	Proof
1978 Specimen	709,602	—	—	—

KM# 124 Subject: Griffon **Obv:** Young bust right **Rev:** Ship, dates below, denomination above **Rev. Designer:** Walter Schluep **Weight:** 23.3276 g. **Composition:** 0.5000 Silver 0.3750 oz. ASW **Size:** 36 mm.

Date	Mintage	MS-63	P/L	Proof
1979 Specimen	826,695	—	—	—

KM# 128 Subject: Arctic Territories **Obv:** Young bust right **Rev:** Bear right, date below, denomination above **Rev. Designer:** Donald D. Paterson **Weight:** 23.3276 g. **Composition:** 0.5000 Silver 0.3750 oz. ASW **Size:** 36 mm.

Date	Mintage	MS-63	P/L	Proof
1980 Specimen	539,617	—	—	—

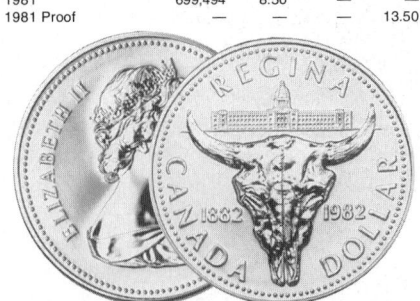

KM# 130 Subject: Transcontinental Railroad **Obv:** Young bust right **Rev:** Train engine and map, date below, denomination above **Rev. Designer:** Christopher Gorey **Weight:** 23.3276 g. **Composition:** 0.5000 Silver 0.3750 oz. ASW **Size:** 36 mm.

Date	Mintage	MS-63	P/L	Proof
1981	699,494	8.50	—	—
1981 Proof	—	—	—	13.50

KM# 133 Subject: Regina **Obv:** Young bust right **Rev:** Cattle skull divides dates and denomination below **Rev. Designer:** Huntley Brown **Weight:** 23.3276 g. **Composition:** 0.5000 Silver 0.3750 oz. ASW **Size:** 36 mm.

Date	Mintage	MS-63	Proof
1982	144,930	8.50	—
1982 Proof	758,958	—	8.50

KM# 134 Subject: Constitution **Obv:** Young bust right **Rev:** Meeting of Government **Rev. Designer:** Ago Aarand **Weight:** 15.4200 g. **Composition:** Nickel **Size:** 32 mm.

Date	Mintage	MS-63	P/L	Proof
1982	9,709,422	3.00	6.00	—

KM# 138 Subject: Edmonton University Games **Obv:** Young bust right **Rev:** Athlete within game logo, date and denomination below **Rev. Designer:** Carola Tietz **Weight:** 23.3276 g. **Composition:** 0.5000 Silver 0.3750 oz. ASW **Size:** 36 mm.

Date	Mintage	MS-63	Proof
1983	159,450	8.50	—
1983 Proof	506,847	—	8.50

KM# 140 Subject: Toronto Sesquicentennial **Obv:** Young bust right **Rev. Designer:** D. J. Craig **Weight:** 23.3276 g. **Composition:** 0.5000 Silver 0.3750 oz. ASW **Size:** 36 mm.

Date	Mintage	MS-63	Proof
1984	133,610	8.50	—
1984 Proof	732,542	—	8.50

KM# 141 Subject: Jacques Cartier **Obv:** Young bust right **Rev:** Cross with shield above figures **Rev. Designer:** Hector Greville **Weight:** 15.5000 g. **Composition:** Nickel **Size:** 32 mm.

Date	Mintage	MS-63	Proof
1984	7,009,323	3.50	—
1984 Proof	87,760	—	6.00

KM# 157 Obv: Young bust right **Obv. Designer:** Arnold Machin **Rev:** Loon right, date and denomination below **Rev. Designer:** Robert R. Carmichael **Weight:** 7.0000 g. **Composition:** Aureate-Bronze Plated Nickel **Shape:** 11-sided **Size:** 26.5 mm.

Date	Mintage	MS-63	Proof
1987	205,405,000	2.25	—
1987 Proof	178,120	—	8.00
1988	138,893,539	2.25	—
1988 Proof	175,259	—	6.75
1989	184,773,902	3.00	—
1989 Proof	170,928	—	6.75

KM# 143 Subject: National Parks **Obv:** Young bust right **Rev:** Moose right, dates above, denomination below **Rev. Designer:** Karel Rohlicek **Weight:** 23.3276 g. **Composition:** 0.5000 Silver 0.3750 oz. ASW **Size:** 36 mm.

Date	Mintage	MS-63	Proof
1985	163,314	8.50	—
1985 Proof	733,354	—	10.00

KM# 120.2 Obv: Young bust right **Rev:** Voyageur **Composition:** Nickel **Size:** 32.13 mm. **Note:** Mule with New Zealand 50 cent, KM-37 obverse.

Date	Mintage	MS-63	Proof
1985	—	3,000	—

KM# 154 Subject: John Davis **Obv:** Young bust right **Rev:** Ship "John Davis" with masts, rock in background, dates below, denomination at bottom **Rev. Designer:** Christopher Gorey **Weight:** 23.3276 g. **Composition:** 0.5000 Silver 0.3750 oz. ASW **Size:** 36 mm.

Date	Mintage	MS-63	Proof
1987	118,722	8.50	—
1987 Proof	602,374	—	9.00

KM# 149 Subject: Vancouver **Obv:** Young bust right **Rev:** Train left, dates divided below, denomination above **Rev. Designer:** Elliot John Morrison **Weight:** 23.3276 g. **Composition:** 0.5000 Silver 0.3750 oz. ASW **Size:** 36 mm.

Date	Mintage	MS-63	Proof
1986	125,949	8.50	—
1986 Proof	680,004	—	8.50

KM# 161 Subject: Ironworks **Obv:** Young bust right **Rev:** Ironworkers, date and denomination below **Rev. Designer:** Robert R. Carmichael **Weight:** 23.3276 g. **Composition:** 0.5000 Silver 0.3750 oz. ASW **Size:** 36 mm.

Date	Mintage	MS-63	Proof
1988	106,872	8.50	—
1988 Proof	255,013	—	16.00

DOLLAR

KM# 168   Subject: MacKenzie River **Obv:** Young
bust right **Rev:** People in canoe, date above,
denomination below **Rev. Designer:** John Mardon
Weight: 23.3276 g. **Composition:** 0.5000 Silver
0.3750 oz. ASW **Size:** 36 mm.

Date	Mintage	MS-63	Proof
1989	99,774	12.50	—
1989 Proof	244,062	—	16.00

KM# 186   Obv: Crowned head right
Obv. Designer: Dora dePedery-Hunt **Rev:** Loon
right, date and denomination **Rev. Designer:**
Robert R. Carmichael **Weight:** 7.0000 g.
Composition: Aureate-Bronze Plated Nickel
Shape: 11-sided **Size:** 26.5 mm.

Date	Mintage	MS-63	Proof
1990	68,402,000	1.75	—
1990 Proof	140,649	—	7.00
1991	23,156,000	1.75	—
1991 Proof	131,888	—	13.00
1993	33,662,000	2.00	—
1993 Proof	143,065	—	6.00
1994	16,232,530	2.00	—
1994 Proof	104,485	—	7.00
1995	27,492,630	2.25	—
1995 Proof	101,560	—	7.00
1996	17,101,000	2.00	—
1996 Proof	112,835	—	7.50
1997	—	5.00	—
1997 Proof	113,647	—	8.00
1998	—	2.50	—
1998 Proof	93,632	—	10.00
1998W	—	—	—
1999	—	2.00	—
1999 Proof	95,113	—	8.00
2000	—	2.00	—
2000 Proof	90,921	—	8.00
2000W	—	—	—
2001	—	2.50	—
2001 Proof	74,194	—	8.00
2002	—	4.50	—
2002 Proof	65,315	—	7.50
2003	5,101,000	5.50	—
2003 Proof	62,507	—	12.00

KM# 170   Subject: Henry Kelsey **Obv:** Crowned
head right **Rev:** Kelsey with natives, dates below,
denomination above **Rev. Designer:** D. J. Craig
Weight: 23.3276 g. **Composition:** 0.5000 Silver
0.3750 oz. ASW **Size:** 36 mm.

Date	Mintage	MS-63	Proof
1990	99,455	8.50	—
1990 Proof	254,959	—	18.00

KM# 179   Subject: S.S. Frontenac **Obv:** Crowned
head right **Rev:** Ship,"Frontenac", date and
denomination below **Rev. Designer:** D. J. Craig
Weight: 23.3276 g. **Composition:** 0.5000 Silver
0.3750 oz. ASW **Size:** 36 mm.

Date	Mintage	MS-63	Proof
1991	73,843	8.50	—
1991 Proof	195,424	—	24.00

KM# 210   Subject: Stagecoach service **Obv:**
Crowned head right **Rev:** Stagecoach, date and
denomination below **Rev. Designer:** Karsten Smith
Weight: 25.1750 g. **Composition:** 0.9250 Silver
0.7487 oz. ASW **Size:** 36 mm.

Date	Mintage	MS-63	Proof
1992	78,160	16.50	—
1992 Proof	187,612	—	16.50

KM# 209 Subject: Loon right, dates and denomination **Obv:** Crowned head right **Rev. Designer:** Robert R. Carmichael **Composition:** Aureate **Size:** 26.5 mm.

Date	Mintage	MS-63	Proof
ND(1992)	4,242,085	2.00	—
ND(1992) Proof	147,061	—	8.00

KM# 218 Subject: Parliament **Obv:** Crowned head right, dates below **Rev:** Backs of three seated figures in front of building, denomination below **Rev. Designer:** Rita Swanson **Composition:** Aureate **Size:** 26 mm.

Date	Mintage	MS-63	Proof
ND(1992)	23,915,000	2.25	—
ND(1992) Proof	24,227	—	9.00

KM# 235 Subject: Stanley Cup hockey **Obv:** Crowned head right **Rev:** Hockey players between cups, dates below, denomination above **Rev. Designer:** Stewart Sherwood **Weight:** 25.1750 g. **Composition:** 0.9250 Silver 0.7487 oz. ASW **Size:** 36 mm.

Date	Mintage	MS-63	Proof
1993	88,150	16.50	—
1993 Proof	294,314	—	16.50

KM# 248 Subject: War Memorial **Obv:** Crowned head right, date below **Rev:** Memorial, denomination at right **Rev. Designer:** R. C. M. Staff **Composition:** Aureate **Size:** 26 mm.

Date	Mintage	MS-63	Proof
1994	20,004,830	2.25	—
1994 Proof	54,524	—	7.50

KM# 251 Subject: Last RCMP sled-dog patrol **Obv:** Crowned head right **Rev:** Dogsled, denomination divides dates below **Rev. Designer:** Ian Sparks **Weight:** 25.1750 g. **Composition:** 0.9250 Silver 0.7487 oz. ASW **Size:** 36 mm.

Date	Mintage	MS-63	Proof
1994	61,561	16.50	—
1994 Proof	170,374	—	25.00

KM# 258 Subject: Peacekeeping Monument in Ottawa **Obv:** Crowned head right, date below **Rev:** Monument, denomination above right **Rev. Designer:** J. K. Harmon, R. G. Henriquez and C. H. Oberlander **Weight:** 7.0000 g. **Composition:** Aureate **Size:** 26 mm. **Note:** Mintage included with KM#186.

Date	Mintage	MS-63	Proof
1995	18,502,750	2.25	—
1995 Proof	43,293	—	7.50

DOLLAR

KM#259 **Subject:** Hudson Bay Co. **Obv:** Crowned head right **Rev:** Explorers and ship, date and denomination below **Rev. Designer:** Vincent McIndoe **Weight:** 25.1750 g. **Composition:** 0.9250 Silver 0.7487 oz. ASW **Size:** 36 mm.

Date	Mintage	MS-63	Proof
1995	61,819	16.50	—
1995 Proof	166,259	—	30.00

KM#274 **Subject:** McIntosh Apple **Obv:** Crowned head right **Rev:** Apple, dates and denomination below **Rev. Designer:** Roger Hill **Weight:** 25.1750 g. **Composition:** 0.9250 Silver 0.7487 oz. ASW **Size:** 36 mm.

Date	Mintage	MS-63	Proof
1996	58,834	16.50	—
1996 Proof	133,779	—	24.00

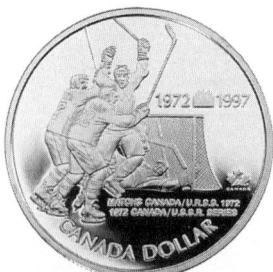

KM# 282 **Subject:** 25th Anniversary Hockey Victory **Obv:** Crowned head right **Rev:** The winning goal by Paul Aenderson. Based on a painting by Andre l'Archeveque, dates at right, denomination at bottom **Rev. Designer:** Walter Burden **Weight:** 25.1750 g. **Composition:** 0.9250 Silver 0.7487 oz. ASW **Size:** 36 mm.

Date	Mintage	MS-63	Proof
ND(1997)	155,252	16.50	—
ND(1997) Proof	184,965	—	24.00

KM# 291 **Subject:** Loon Dollar 10th Anniversary **Obv:** Crowned head right **Rev:** Loon in flight left, dates above, denomination below **Rev. Designer:** Jean-Luc Grondin **Composition:** Aureate **Size:** 26 mm.

Date	Mintage	MS-63	P/L	Proof
1997	—	—	22.00	—

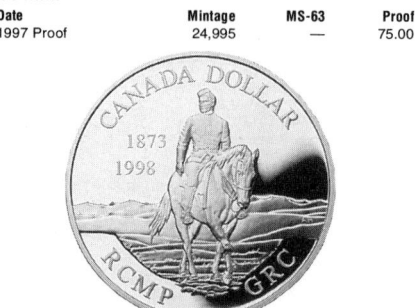

KM# 296 **Subject:** Loon Dollar 10th Anniversary **Obv:** Crowned head right **Rev:** Loon in flight left, dates above, denomination below **Rev. Designer:** Jean-Luc Grondin **Weight:** 25.1750 g. **Composition:** 0.9250 Silver 0.7487 oz. ASW **Size:** 36 mm.

Date	Mintage	MS-63	Proof
1997 Proof	24,995	—	75.00

KM# 306 **Subject:** 120th Anniversary Royal Canadian Mounted Police **Obv:** Crowned head right **Rev:** Mountie on horseback, dates at left, denomination above **Rev. Designer:** Adeline Halvorson **Weight:** 25.1750 g. **Composition:** 0.9250 Silver 0.7487 oz. ASW **Size:** 36 mm. **Note:** Individually cased prooflikes, proofs or specimens are from broken-up prooflike or specimen sets.

Date	Mintage	MS-63	P/L	Proof
1998	79,777	—	16.50	—
1998 Proof	120,172	—	—	20.00

KM# 355 Subject: International Year of Old Persons **Obv:** Crowned head right **Rev:** Figures amid trees, date and denomination below **Rev. Designer:** S. Armstrong-Hodgson **Weight:** 25.1750 g. **Composition:** 0.9250 Silver 0.7487 oz. ASW **Size:** 36 mm.

Date	Mintage	MS-63	Proof
1999 Proof	24,976	—	40.00

KM# 414 Subject: National Ballet **Obv:** Crowned head right **Rev:** Ballet dancers **Rev. Designer:** Scott McKowen **Edge:** Reeded **Weight:** 25.1750 g. **Composition:** 0.9250 Silver 0.7487 oz. ASW **Size:** 36 mm.

Date	Mintage	MS-63	Proof
2001	65,000	14.00	—
2001 Proof	225,000	—	21.50

KM# 356 Subject: Discovery of Queen Charlotte Isle **Obv:** Crowned head right **Rev:** Ship and three boats, dates at right, denomination below **Rev. Designer:** D. J. Craig **Weight:** 25.1750 g. **Composition:** 0.9250 Silver 0.7487 oz. ASW **Size:** 36 mm.

Date	Mintage	MS-63	P/L	Proof
ND(1999)	67,655	—	16.50	—
ND(1999) Proof	126,435	—	—	22.50

KM# 434 Obv: Crowned head right **Rev:** Recycled 1911 pattern dollar design: denomination, country name and dates in crowned wreath **Edge:** Reeded **Weight:** 25.1750 g. **Composition:** 0.9250 Silver 0.7487 oz. ASW **Size:** 36 mm.

Date	Mintage	MS-63	Proof
ND(2001) Proof	24,996	—	55.00

KM# 186a Subject: Olympic Win **Composition:** Gilt **Size:** 26.5 mm.

Date	Mintage	MS-63	Proof
2002 Proof	—	—	40.00

KM# 401 Subject: Voyage of Discovery **Obv:** Crowned head right **Rev:** Human and space shuttle, date above, denomination below **Rev. Designer:** D. F. Warkentine **Weight:** 25.1750 g. **Composition:** 0.9250 Silver 0.7487 oz. ASW **Size:** 36 mm.

Date	Mintage	MS-63	P/L	Proof
2000	60,100	—	16.50	—
2000 Proof	114,130	—	—	22.50

KM# 443 Subject: Queen's Golden Jubilee **Obv:** Crowned head right, with anniversary date at left **Obv. Designer:** Dora dePédery-Hunt **Rev:** Queen in her coach and a view of the coach, denomination below **Edge:** Reeded **Weight:** 25.1750 g. **Composition:** 0.9250 Silver 0.7487 oz. ASW **Size:** 36 mm.

Date	Mintage	MS-63	Proof
ND(2002)	65,140	21.00	—
ND(2002) Proof	29,688	—	40.00

KM# 443a Subject: Queen's Golden Jubilee **Obv:** Crowned head right with anniversary date **Rev:** Queen in her coach and a view of the coach **Edge:** Reeded **Weight:** 25.1800 g. **Composition:** 0.9250 Silver Gilt 0.7488 oz. ASW **Size:** 36 mm. **Note:** Special 24 karat gold plated issue of KM#443.

Date	Mintage	MS-63	Proof
ND(2002) Proof	32,642	—	45.00

KM# 462 Obv: Commemorative dates 1952-2002 **Obv. Designer:** Dora dePédery-Hunt **Rev:** Family of Loons **Weight:** 7.0000 g. **Composition:** Aureate-Bronze Plated Nickel

Date	Mintage	MS-63	Proof
ND(2002) Specimen	67,672	—	—

KM# 467 Subject: Elizabeth II Golden Jubilee **Obv:** Crowned head right, Jubilee commemorative dates 1952-2002 **Obv. Designer:** Dora dePédery-Hunt **Weight:** 7.0000 g. **Composition:** Aureate-Bronze Plated Nickel

Date	Mintage	MS-63	Proof
ND(2002)	2,302,000	2.50	—
ND(2002) Proof	—	—	8.00

KM# 467a Subject: 50th Anniversary, Accession to the Throne **Obv:** Crowned head right **Composition:** Gold **Note:** Sold on the internet.

Date	Mintage	MS-63	Proof
ND(2002)	1	—	55,500

KM# 503 Subject: Queen Mother **Obv:** Crowned head right **Obv. Designer:** Dora de Pedery-Hunt **Rev:** Queen Mother facing **Weight:** 25.1750 g. **Composition:** 0.9250 Silver 0.7487 oz. ASW **Size:** 36 mm.

Date	Mintage	MS-63	Proof
2002 Proof	9,994	—	250

KM# 450 Subject: Cobalt Mining Centennial **Obv:** Queens portrait right **Obv. Designer:** Dora dePédery-Hunt **Rev:** Mine tower and fox **Edge:** Reeded **Weight:** 25.1750 g. **Composition:** 0.9999 Silver 0.8093 oz. ASW **Size:** 36 mm.

Date	Mintage	MS-63	Proof
ND(2003)	51,130	20.00	—
ND(2003) Proof	88,536	—	28.00

KM# 495 Obv: Bare head right **Obv. Designer:** Susanna Blunt **Rev. Designer:** Robert R. Carmichael **Weight:** 7.0000 g. **Composition:** Aureate-Bronze Plated Nickel **Size:** 26.5 mm.

Date	Mintage	MS-63	Proof
2003	5,102,000	5.50	—
2003 Proof	—	—	7.50
2003W	—	7.50	—
2004 Proof	—	—	12.00
2004	3,409,000	1.75	—
2005	—	3.00	—
2005 Proof	—	—	7.50
2006	—	3.00	—
2006 Proof	—	—	7.50
2006(ml)	—	3.00	—
2006(ml) Proof	—	—	7.50
2007(ml)	—	3.00	—
2007(ml) Proof	—	—	7.50
2008(ml)	—	3.00	—

Date	Mintage	MS-63	Proof
2008(ml) Proof	—	—	7.50
2009(ml)	—	3.00	—
2009(ml) Proof	—	—	7.50

KM# 473 Subject: 50th Anniversary of the Coronation of Elizabeth II **Obv:** 1953 effigy of the Queen, Jubilee Commemorative dates 1953-2003 **Obv. Designer:** Mary Gillick **Rev:** Voyageur, date and denomination below **Weight:** 25.1750 g. **Composition:** 0.9999 Silver 0.8093 oz. ASW

Date	Mintage	MS-63	Proof
ND(2003) Proof	29,586	—	35.00

KM# 473a Subject: 50th Anniversary of Coronation **Obv. Designer:** Mary Gilick **Rev:** Voyageur **Composition:** Gold **Note:** Sold on the internet.

Date	Mintage	MS-63	Proof
2003	1	—	62,750

KM# 480 Subject: Coronation of Queen Elizabeth II **Obv:** Head right **Rev:** Voyaguers **Rev. Designer:** Emanuel Hahn **Weight:** 25.1750 g. **Composition:** 0.9999 Silver 0.8093 oz. ASW

Date	Mintage	MS-63	Proof
ND2003 Proof	21,400	—	38.00

KM# 507 Obv: Bare head right, date below **Obv. Designer:** Susanna Blunt **Rev:** Loon **Edge:** Plain **Weight:** 7.0000 g. **Composition:** Aureate-Bronze Plated Nickel **Shape:** 11-sided **Size:** 26.5 mm.

Date	Mintage	MS-63	Proof
2004 Proof	12,550	—	12.50

KM# 512 Subject: First French Settlement in America **Obv:** Crowned head right **Rev:** Sailing ship **Edge:** Reeded **Weight:** 25.1750 g. **Composition:** 0.9999 Silver 0.8093 oz. ASW **Size:** 36 mm.

Date	Mintage	MS-63	Proof
2004	42,582	21.00	—
2004 Fleur-dis-lis	8,315	50.00	—
2004 Proof	106,974	—	35.00

KM# 513 Subject: Olympics **Obv:** Bare head right **Rev:** Maple leaf, Olympic flame and rings above loon **Edge:** Plain **Weight:** 7.0000 g. **Composition:** Aureate-Bronze Plated Nickel **Shape:** 11-sided **Size:** 26.5 mm.

Date	Mintage	MS-63	Proof
2004	6,526,000	8.00	—

KM# 513a Subject: Olympics **Obv:** Bare head right **Rev:** Multicolor maple leaf, Olympic flame and rings above loon **Edge:** Plain **Weight:** 9.3100 g. **Composition:** 0.9250 Silver 0.2769 oz. ASW **Shape:** 11-sided **Size:** 26.5 mm.

Date	Mintage	MS-63	Proof
2004 Proof	19,994	—	50.00

KM# 549 Subject: 40th Anniversary of National Flag **Obv:** Head right **Obv. Designer:** Susanna Blunt **Rev. Designer:** William Woodruff **Weight:** 25.1750 g. **Composition:** 0.9250 Silver 0.7487 oz. ASW

Date	Mintage	MS-63	Proof
2005	50,948	23.00	—
2005 Proof	95,431	—	35.00

KM# 549a Subject: 40th Anniversary of National Flag **Obv:** Head right **Weight:** 7.0000 g. **Composition:** 0.9250 Silver 0.2082 oz. ASW

Date	Mintage	MS-63	Proof
2005	62,483	65.00	—

KM# 549b Subject: 40th Anniversary National Flag **Rev:** National flag, colorized **Weight:** 25.1800 g. **Composition:** 0.9250 Silver 0.7488 oz. ASW **Size:** 36.07 mm.

Date	Mintage	MS-63	Proof
ND(1965-2005)	4,898	—	—

KM# 552 Subject: Terry Fox **Obv:** Head right **Weight:** 7.0000 g. **Composition:** Aureate-Bronze Plated Nickel

Date	Mintage	MS-63	Proof
2005	1,290,900	3.50	—

KM# 553 Subject: Tuffed Puffin **Obv:** Head right **Obv. Designer:** Susanna Blunt **Weight:** 7.0000 g. **Composition:** Aureate-Bronze Plated Nickel

Date	Mintage	MS-63	Proof
2005 Specimen	40,000	—	30.00

KM# 581 Subject: Lullabies Loonie **Obv:** Head right **Obv. Designer:** Susanna Blunt **Rev:** Loon and moon, teddy bear in stars **Weight:** 7.0000 g. **Composition:** 0.9250 Silver 0.2082 oz. ASW

Date	Mintage	MS-63	Proof
2006	18,103	4.50	—

KM# 582 Subject: Snowy owl **Obv:** Head right **Obv. Designer:** Susanna Blunt **Rev:** Snowy owl with year above **Weight:** 7.0000 g. **Composition:** Aureate-Bronze Plated Nickel

Date	Mintage	MS-63	Proof
2006 Specimen	40,000	—	30.00

KM# 583 Subject: Victoria Cross **Obv:** Head right **Weight:** 25.1750 g. **Composition:** 0.9250 Silver 0.7487 oz. ASW

Date	Mintage	MS-63	Proof
2006	27,254	24.00	—
2006 Proof	54,835	—	35.00

KM# 583a Subject: Victoria Cross **Obv:** Head right **Weight:** 25.1750 g. **Composition:** 0.9250 Silver 0.7487 oz. ASW

Date	Mintage	MS-63	Proof
2006 Proof	—	—	60.00

KM#630 Subject: Olympic Games **Obv:** Crowned head right **Rev:** Loon in flight, colored olympic logo above **Weight:** 7.0000 g. **Composition:** 0.9250 Silver 0.2082 oz. ASW

Date	Mintage	MS-63	Proof
2006	19,956	30.00	—

KM# 653 Subject: Thayendanegea **Obv:** Head right **Rev:** Bust **Weight:** 25.1750 g. **Composition:** 0.9250 Silver 0.7487 oz. ASW **Size:** 36.07 mm.

Date	Mintage	MS-63	Proof
2006(ml)	16,378	30.00	—
2006(ml) Proof	65,000	—	40.00

KM# 653a Subject: Thayendanega **Obv:** Bust right **Rev:** Bust, partially gilt **Weight:** 25.1750 g. **Composition:** 0.9250 Silver 0.7487 oz. ASW **Size:** 36.07 mm.

Date	Mintage	MS-63	P/L	Proof
2006	60,000	—	—	50.00

KM# 654 Obv: Head right **Rev:** Snowflake, colorized **Weight:** 7.0000 g. **Composition:** 0.9250 Silver 0.2082 oz. ASW **Note:** Sold in a CD package.

Date	Mintage	MS-63	Proof
2006(ml)	34,014	30.00	—

KM# 655 Subject: Baby Rattle **Obv:** Head right **Rev:** Baby rattle **Weight:** 7.0000 g. **Composition:** 0.9250 Silver 0.2082 oz. ASW

Date	Mintage	MS-63	Proof
2006	3,207	20.00	—

KM# 656 Subject: Medal of Bravery **Obv:** Head right **Weight:** 28.1750 g. **Composition:** 0.9250 Silver 0.8379 oz. ASW

Date	Mintage	MS-63	Proof
2006	7,846	20.00	—

KM# 656a Subject: Medal of Bravery **Obv:** Head right **Rev:** Maple leaf within wreath. Colorized. **Weight:** 28.1750 g. **Composition:** 0.9250 Silver 0.8379 oz. ASW

Date	Mintage	MS-63	Proof
2006	4,951	35.00	—

DOLLAR

KM# 687   Subject: Joseph Brant **Obv:** Head right **Weight:** 28.1750 g. **Composition:** 0.9250 Silver 0.8379 oz. ASW

Date	Mintage	MS-63	Proof
2007	—	20.00	—

KM# 688   Subject: Trumpeter Swan **Obv:** Head right **Rev:** Loon **Weight:** 7.0000 g. **Composition:** Aureate-Bronze Plated Nickel

Date	Mintage	MS-63	Proof
2007(ml)	40,000	20.00	—

KM# 655a   Obv: Bust right **Rev:** Baby Rattle, partially gilt **Weight:** 7.0000 g. **Composition:** 0.9250 Silver 0.2082 oz. ASW

Date	Mintage	MS-63	Proof
2007	1,911	15.00	—

KM# 700   Rev: Alphabet Letter Blocks **Weight:** 7.0000 g. **Composition:** 0.9250 Silver 0.2082 oz. ASW

Date	Mintage	MS-63	Proof
2007	3,229	—	25.00

KM# 719   Subject: Celebration of the Arts **Rev:** Book, TV set, musical instruments, film montage **Rev. Designer:** Friedrich Peter **Edge:** Reeded **Weight:** 25.1800 g. **Composition:** 0.9250 Silver 0.7488 oz. ASW **Size:** 36.07 mm.

Date	Mintage	MS-63	Proof
2007	6,466	—	50.00

KM# 781   Subject: Ottawa Mint Centennial 1908-2008 **Rev:** Maple leaf transforming into a common loon **Rev. Designer:** Jason Bowman **Weight:** 25.1800 g. **Composition:** 0.9250 Silver 0.7488 oz. ASW **Size:** 36.07 mm.

Date	Mintage	MS-63	Proof
2008 Proof	25,000	—	50.00

KM# 784   Rev: Common elder **Weight:** 7.0000 g. **Composition:** Nickel-Bronze **Size:** 26.5 mm.

Date	Mintage	MS-63	Proof
2008 Specimen	40,000	—	50.00

KM# 785   Subject: Founding of Quebec 400th Anniversary **Rev:** Samuel de Champlain, ship and town view **Rev. Designer:** Susanna Duranceau **Weight:** 25.1800 g. **Composition:** 0.9250 Silver 0.7488 oz. ASW **Size:** 36.07 mm.

Date	Mintage	MS-63	Proof
2008 Proof	65,000	—	30.00

KM# 785a   Subject: Founding of Quebec 400th Anniversary **Rev:** Samuel de Champlain selectively gold plated, ship, town view **Rev. Designer:** Susanne Duranceau **Weight:** 25.1800 g. **Composition:** 0.9250 Silver 0.7488 oz. ASW **Size:** 36.07 mm.

Date	Mintage	MS-63	Proof
2008	—	27.00	—

KM# 787a   Rev: Loon splashing with Olympic logo and maple leaf in color above **Rev. Designer:** Steve Hepurn **Weight:** 7.0000 g. **Composition:** 0.9250 Silver 0.2082 oz. ASW **Size:** 26.5 mm.

Date	Mintage	MS-63	Proof
2008 Proof	—	—	25.00

KM# 787   Subject: Lucky Loonie **Rev:** Loon splashing and Olympic logo at right **Rev. Designer:** Steve Hepurn **Weight:** 7.0000 g. **Composition:** Nickel-Brass **Size:** 26.5 mm.

Date	Mintage	MS-63	Proof
2008	—	20.00	—

KM# 791   Rev: Edmonton Oilers **Composition:** 0.9990 Silver

Date	Mintage	MS-63	Proof
2008	—	25.00	—

KM# 792   Rev: Montreal Canadians **Composition:** 0.9990 Silver

Date	Mintage	MS-63	Proof
2008	—	25.00	—

KM# 793   Rev: Ottawa Senators **Composition:** 0.9990 Silver

Date	Mintage	MS-63	Proof
2008	—	25.00	—

KM# 794   Rev: Toronto Maple Leafs **Composition:** 0.9990 Silver

Date	Mintage	MS-63	Proof
2008	—	25.00	—

KM# 795   Rev: Vancouver Canucks **Composition:** 0.9990 Silver

Date	Mintage	MS-63	Proof
2008	—	25.00	—

KM# 889   Subject: 100th Anniversary of flight in Canada **Obv:** Bust right **Obv. Legend:** Elizabeth II DG Regina **Obv. Designer:** Susanna Blunt **Rev:** Silhouette with arms spread, 3 planes, plane cutout **Rev. Legend:** Canada Dollar 1909-2009 **Rev. Designer:** Jason Bouwman **Weight:** 25.1800 g. **Composition:** 0.9250 Silver 0.7488 oz. ASW **Size:** 36.07 mm.

Date	Mintage	MS-63	Proof
2009	50,000	35.00	—
2009 Proof	50,000	—	55.00

KM# 914   Obv: Bust right **Obv. Designer:** Susanna Blunt **Rev:** Blue heron in flight **Weight:** 7.0000 g. **Composition:** Aureate-Bronze Plated Nickel **Size:** 26.5 mm.

Date	Mintage	MS-63	Proof
2009 Specimen	40,000	50.00	—

KM# 921   Subject: Montreal Canadians 100th Anniversary **Obv:** Bust right **Obv. Designer:** Susanna Blunt **Rev:** Montreal Canadians logo partially gilt **Weight:** 25.1700 g. **Composition:** 0.9250 Silver 0.7485 oz. ASW **Size:** 36.07 mm.

Date	Mintage	MS-63	Proof
2009 Proof	1,500	—	150

KM# 855 Rev: Toronto Maple Leafs Jersey
Weight: 33.6500 g. **Composition:** Nickel **Size:**
26.5 mm.

Date	Mintage	MS-63	Proof
2009	—	25.00	—

KM# 889a Obv: Bust right **Rev:** Silouette with arms
spread, 3 planes, plane shadow partially gilt
Weight: 25.1800 g. **Composition:** 0.9250 Silver
0.7488 oz. ASW **Size:** 36.07 mm.

Date	Mintage	MS-63	Proof
2009(ml) Proof	—	—	50.00

KM# 883 Subject: Lucky Loonie **Obv:** Bust right
Obv. Legend: Elizabeth II DG Regina **Rev:**
Canadian Olympic Team logo **Rev. Legend:**
Canada Dollar **Weight:** 7.0000 g. **Composition:**
Bronze-Nickel **Size:** 26.5 mm.

Date	Mintage	MS-63	Proof
2010	12,000	—	—

KM# 883a Subject: Lucky Loonie **Obv:** Bust right
Obv. Legend: Elizabeth II DG Regina **Rev:**
Canadian Olympic Team logo in color
Rev. Legend: Vancouver 2010 Canada Dollar
Weight: 7.0000 g. **Composition:** 0.9250 Silver
0.2082 oz. ASW **Shape:** 11-sided **Size:** 26.5 mm.

Date	Mintage	MS-63	Proof
2010 Proof	4,000	—	—

KM# 727 Rev: Vancouver Olympics "stone man"
logo **Weight:** 7.0000 g. **Composition:** Aureate
Bonded Bronze **Shape:** 11-sided **Size:** 26.5 mm.

Date	Mintage	MS-63	Proof
2010	—	5.00	—

Note: Issued in 2007.

DOLLAR (Louis)

KM# 652 Subject: Gold Louis **Obv:** Bust right
Obv. Designer: Susanna Blunt **Rev:** Crowned
double L monogram within wreath **Weight:**
1.5000 g. **Composition:** 0.9990 Gold 0.0482 oz.
AGW **Size:** 14.1 mm.

Date	Mintage	MS-63	Proof
2006 Proof	5,648	—	100

KM# 756 Obv: Bust right **Obv. Designer:**
Susanna Blunt **Rev:** Crown above two oval shields
Weight: 1.5550 g. **Composition:** 0.9990 Gold
0.0499 oz. AGW **Size:** 14.1 mm.

Date	Mintage	MS-63	Proof
2007 Proof	3,457	—	100

KM# 834 Obv: Bust right **Obv. Designer:**
Susanna Blunt **Weight:** 1.5550 g. **Composition:**
0.9990 Gold 0.0499 oz. AGW **Size:** 14 mm.

Date	Mintage	MS-63	Proof
2008 Proof	—	—	125

2 DOLLARS

KM# 270 Obv: Crowned head right within circle,
date below **Obv. Designer:** Dora dePedery-Hunt
Rev: Polar bear right within circle, denomination
below **Rev. Designer:** Brent Townsend **Weight:**
7.3000 g. **Composition:** Bi-Metallic **Size:** 28 mm.

Date	Mintage	MS-63	P/L	Proof
1996	375,483,000	3.25	5.00	—
1996 Proof	—	—	—	10.00
1997	16,942,000	3.25	—	—
1998	4,926,000	3.25	—	—
1998W	Inc. above	3.25	—	—
1999	25,130,000	3.25	—	—
2000	29,847,000	3.25	—	—
2000W	Inc. above	3.25	—	—
2001	27,008,000	5.00	—	—
2001 Proof	74,944	—	—	12.50
2002	11,910,000	5.00	—	—
2002 Proof	65,315	—	—	12.50
2003	7,123,667	5.00	—	—
2003 Proof	62,007	—	—	12.50

KM# 270b Obv: Crowned head right within circle,
date below **Rev:** Polar bear right within circle,
denomination below **Edge:** 4.5mm thick **Weight:**
25.0000 g. **Composition:** 0.9250 Bi-Metallic
0.7435 oz. **Size:** 28 mm.

Date	Mintage	MS-63	Proof
1996 Proof	10,000	—	55.00
1998 Proof	—	—	—

KM# 270c Obv: Crowned head right within circle,
date below **Rev:** Polar bear right within circle,
denomination below **Weight:** 8.8300 g.
Composition: 0.9250 Silver 0.2626 oz. ASW **Size:**
28 mm. **Note:** 1.9mm thick.

Date	Mintage	MS-63	Proof
1996 Proof	10,000	—	12.00
1997 Proof	—	—	10.00
1998O Proof	—	—	12.00
1999 Proof	—	—	12.00
2000 Proof	—	—	12.00
2001 Proof	—	—	12.00

KM# 270a Obv: Crowned head right within circle,
date below **Rev:** Polar bear right within circle,
denomination below **Weight:** 10.8414 g.
Composition: Bi-Metallic **Size:** 28 mm.

Date	Mintage	MS-63	Proof
1996 Proof	5,000	—	165

KM# 357 Subject: Nunavut **Obv:** Crowned head
right **Rev:** Inuit person with drum, denomination
below **Rev. Designer:** G. Arnaktavyok **Edge:**
Segmented reeding **Weight:** 7.3000 g.
Composition: Bi-Metallic **Size:** 28 mm.

Date	Mintage	MS-63	Proof
1999	—	4.00	—

KM# 357a Subject: Nunavut **Obv:** Crowned head
right **Rev:** Drum dancer **Edge:** Interrupted reeding
Weight: 8.5200 g. **Composition:** 0.9250 Silver
0.2534 oz. ASW **Size:** 28 mm.

Date	Mintage	MS-63	Proof
1999 Proof	39,873	—	15.00

KM# 357b Subject: Nunavut **Obv:** Crowned head
right **Rev:** Drum dancer **Composition:** Gold

Date	Mintage	MS-63	Proof
1999 Proof	4,298	—	200

2 DOLLARS

KM# 399 Subject: Knowledge **Obv:** Crowned head right within circle, denomination below **Rev:** Polar bear and 2 cubs right within circle, date above **Rev. Designer:** Tony Bianco **Edge:** Reeded and plain sections **Weight:** 7.3000 g. **Composition:** Bi-Metallic **Size:** 28 mm.

Date	Mintage	MS-63	Proof
2000	—	3.50	—

KM# 399a Subject: Knowledge **Obv:** Crowned head right within circle, denomination below **Rev:** Polar bear and 2 cubs within circle, date above **Weight:** 8.5200 g. **Composition:** 0.9250 Silver 0.2534 oz. ASW

Date	Mintage	MS-63	Proof
2000 Proof	39,768	—	15.00

KM# 399b Subject: Knowledge **Obv:** Crowned head right within circle, denomination below **Rev:** Polar bear and two cubs right within circle, date above **Weight:** 6.3100 g. **Composition:** 0.9160 Gold 0.1858 oz. AGW

Date	Mintage	MS-63	Proof
2000 Proof	5,881	—	200

KM# 449 Subject: Elizabeth II Golden Jubilee **Obv:** Crowned head right, jubilee commemorative dates 1952-2002 **Weight:** 7.3000 g. **Composition:** Bi-Metallic

Date	Mintage	MS-63	Proof
ND(2002)	27,020,00 0	4.00	—

KM# 449a Subject: Elizabeth II Golden Jubilee **Obv:** Crowned head right, jubilee commemorative dates 1952-2002 **Weight:** 8.8300 g. **Composition:** 0.9250 Silver 0.2626 oz. ASW

Date	Mintage	MS-63	Proof
ND(2002) Proof	100,000	—	14.00

KM# 496 Obv: Head right **Obv. Designer:** Susanna Blunt **Rev. Designer:** Brent Townsend **Weight:** 7.3000 g. **Composition:** Bi-Metallic

Date	Mintage	MS-63	Proof
2003	4,120,104	5.00	—
2003W	71,142	25.00	—
2004	12,907,000	5.00	—
2004 Proof	—	—	12.50
2005	38,318,000	5.00	—
2005 Proof	—	—	12.50
2006(ml)	25,274,000	5.00	—
2006(ml) Proof	—	—	12.50
2007(ml)	—	5.00	—
2007(ml) Proof	—	—	12.50
2008(ml)	—	5.00	—
2008(ml) Proof	—	—	12.50
2009(ml)	—	5.00	—
2009(ml) Proof	—	—	12.50

KM# 270d Subject: 100th Anniversary of the Cobalt Silver Strike **Obv:** Crowned head right, within circle, date below **Rev:** Polar bear right, within circle, denomination below **Weight:** 8.8300 g. **Composition:** 0.9250 Silver 0.2626 oz. ASW

Date	Mintage	MS-63	Proof
2003 Proof	100,000	—	25.00

KM# 496a Obv: Head right **Obv. Designer:** Suanne Blunt **Rev:** Polar Bear **Edge:** Segmented reeding **Weight:** 10.8414 g. **Composition:** 0.9250 Bi-Metallic 0.3224 oz. **Size:** 28 mm.

Date	Mintage	MS-63	Proof
2004 Proof	—	—	25.00

KM# 835 Rev: Proud Polar Bear advancing right **Weight:** 8.8000 g. **Composition:** 0.9250 Silver 0.2617 oz. ASW **Size:** 27.95 mm.

Date	Mintage	MS-63	Proof
2004 Proof	12,607	—	40.00

KM# 836 Subject: 10th Anniversary, 2 dollar coin **Rev:** "Churchill" Polar Bear, northern lights **Composition:** Bi-Metallic

Date	Mintage	MS-63	Proof
ND(1996-2006)(ml)	—	7.50	—

KM# 837 Obv: Bust left, date at top **Rev:** Polar Bear advancing right **Composition:** Bi-Metallic

Date	Mintage	MS-63	Proof
2006(ml)	—	7.50	—
2007(ml)	38,957,00 0	7.50	—

KM# 631 Subject: 10th Anniversary of $2 coin **Obv:** Crowned head right **Composition:** Bi-Metallic

Date	Mintage	MS-63	Proof
ND(2006)(ml)	5,005,000	25.00	—
ND(2006)(ml) Proof	—	—	40.00

KM# 631a Subject: 10th Anniversary of $2 coin **Obv:** Crowned head right **Rev:** Polar bear **Composition:** Bi-Metallic

Date	Mintage	MS-63	Proof
ND(2006) Proof	2,068	—	400

KM# 796 Rev: Bear, gold plated center **Weight:** 8.8300 g. **Composition:** 0.9250 Silver 0.2626 oz. ASW **Size:** 28.07 mm.

Date	Mintage	MS-63	Proof
2008	—	25.00	—

3 DOLLARS

KM# 657 Rev: Beaver within wreath **Composition:** 0.9250 Silver Gilt **Shape:** Square **Size:** 27x27 mm.

Date	Mintage	MS-63	Proof
2006 Proof	19,963	—	200

4 DOLLARS

KM# 728 Subject: Dinosaur fossil **Obv:** Bust right **Rev:** Parasaurolophus, selective enameling **Weight:** 15.8700 g. **Composition:** 0.9250 Silver 0.4719 oz. ASW **Size:** 34 mm.

Date	Mintage	MS-63	Proof
2007	13,010	50.00	—

KM# 797 Subject: Dinosaur fossil **Obv:** Bust right **Rev:** Triceratops, enameled **Rev. Designer:** Kerri Burnett **Weight:** 15.8700 g. **Composition:** 0.9990 Silver 0.5097 oz. ASW **Size:** 34 mm.

Date	Mintage	MS-63	Proof
2008	20,000	25.00	—

KM# 890 Subject: Tyrannosaurus Rex **Obv:** Bust right **Obv. Legend:** Elizabeth II DG Regina **Obv. Designer:** Susanna Blunt **Rev:** T-Rex skeleton in selective aging **Rev. Legend:** Canada 4 Dollars **Rev. Designer:** Kerri Burnette **Weight:** 15.8700 g. **Composition:** 0.9990 Silver 0.5097 oz. ASW **Size:** 34 mm.

Date	Mintage	MS-63	Proof
2009 Proof	20,000	25.00	—

SOVEREIGN

KM# 14 Rev: St. George slaying dragon, mint mark below horse's rear hooves **Weight:** 7.9881 g. **Composition:** 0.9170 Gold 0.2355 oz. AGW

Date	Mintage	F-12	VF-20	XF-40	AU-50	MS-60	MS-63
1908C	636	1,300	1,900	2,400	2,600	2,900	4,000
1909C	16,273	275	300	325	350	350	1,600
1910C	28,012	—	BV	275	300	500	3,000

KM# 20 Rev: St. George slaying dragon, mint mark below horse's rear hooves **Weight:** 7.9881 g. **Composition:** 0.9170 Gold 0.2355 oz. AGW

Date	Mintage	F-12	VF-20	XF-40	AU-50	MS-60	MS-63
1911C	256,946	—	—	—	BV	275	300
1911C Specimen	—	—	—	—	—	—	—
1913C	3,715	550	700	950	1,200	1,500	3,000
1914C	14,871	275	300	350	450	600	950
1916C About 20 known	—	8,000	13,000	16,000	18,000	20,000	30,000
Note: Stacks' A.G. Carter Jr. Sale 12-89 Gem BU realized $82,500							
1917C	58,845	—	—	—	BV	275	700
1918C	106,514	—	—	—	BV	275	700
1919C	135,889	—	—	—	BV	275	700

5 DOLLARS

KM# 26 Obv: Crowned bust left **Obv. Designer:** E. B. MacKennal **Rev:** Arms within wreath, date and denomination below **Rev. Designer:** W. H. J. Blakemore **Weight:** 8.3592 g. **Composition:** 0.9000 Gold 0.2419 oz. AGW

Date	Mintage	F-12	VF-20	XF-40	AU-50	MS-60	MS-63
1912	165,680	BV	300	350	400	450	450
1913	98,832	BV	300	350	400	450	450
1914	31,122	300	450	450	500	550	3,000

KM# 89 Subject: 1976 Montreal Olympics **Obv:** Young bust right, small maple leaf below, date at right **Rev:** Olympic rings, denomination below **Rev. Designer:** Anthony Mann **Weight:** 24.3000 g. **Composition:** 0.9250 Silver 0.7226 oz. ASW **Size:** 38 mm. **Note:** Series II.

Date	Mintage	MS-63	Proof
1974	—	14.50	—
1974 Proof	97,431	—	14.50

KM# 84 Subject: 1976 Montreal Olympics **Obv:** Young bust right, small maple below, date at right **Rev:** Sailboat "Kingston", date at left, denomination below **Rev. Designer:** Georges Huel **Weight:** 24.3000 g. **Composition:** 0.9250 Silver 0.7226 oz. ASW **Size:** 38 mm. **Note:** Series I.

Date	Mintage	MS-63	Proof
1973	—	14.50	—
1973 Proof	165,203	—	14.50

KM# 90 Subject: 1976 Montreal Olympics **Obv:** Young bust right, small maple leaf below, date at right **Rev:** Athlete with torch, denomination below **Rev. Designer:** Anthony Mann **Weight:** 24.3000 g. **Composition:** 0.9250 Silver 0.7226 oz. ASW **Size:** 38 mm. **Note:** Series II.

Date	Mintage	MS-63	Proof
1974	—	14.50	—
1974 Proof	97,431	—	14.50

KM# 85 Subject: 1976 Montreal Olympics **Obv:** Young bust right, small maple leaf below, date at right **Rev:** North American map, denominaton below **Rev. Designer:** Georges Huel **Weight:** 24.3000 g. **Composition:** 0.9250 Silver 0.7226 oz. ASW **Size:** 38 mm. **Note:** Series I.

Date	Mintage	MS-63	Proof
1973	—	14.50	—
1973 Proof	165,203	—	14.50

KM# 91 Subject: 1976 Montreal Olympics **Obv:** Young bust right, small maple leaf below, date at right **Rev:** Rower, denomination below **Rev. Designer:** Ken Danby **Weight:** 24.3000 g. **Composition:** 0.9250 Silver 0.7226 oz. ASW **Size:** 38 mm. **Note:** Series III.

Date	Mintage	MS-63	Proof
1974	—	14.50	—
1974 Proof	104,684	—	14.50

KM# 92 Subject: 1976 Montreal Olympics **Obv:**
Young bust right, small maple leaf below, date at
right **Rev:** Canoeing, denomination below
Rev. Designer: Ken Danby **Weight:** 24.3000 g.
Composition: 0.9250 Silver 0.7226 oz. ASW **Size:**
38 mm. **Note:** Series III.

Date	Mintage	MS-63	Proof
1974	—	14.50	—
1974 Proof	104,684	—	14.50

KM# 98 Subject: 1976 Montreal Olympics **Obv:**
Young bust right, small maple leaf below, date at
right **Rev:** Marathon, denomination below
Rev. Designer: Leo Yerxa **Weight:** 24.3000 g.
Composition: 0.9250 Silver 0.7226 oz. ASW **Size:**
38 mm. **Note:** Series IV.

Date	Mintage	MS-63	Proof
1975	—	14.50	—
1975 Proof	89,155	—	14.50

KM# 99 Subject: Montreal 1976 - 21st Summer
Olympic Games **Obv:** Young bust right, small maple
leaf below, date at right **Rev:** Women's javelin event,
denomination below **Rev. Designer:** Leo Yerxa
Weight: 24.3000 g. **Composition:** 0.9250 Silver
0.7226 oz. ASW **Size:** 38 mm. **Note:** Series IV.

Date	Mintage	MS-63	Proof
1975	—	14.50	—
1975 Proof	89,155	—	14.50

KM# 100 Subject: 1976 Montreal Olympics **Obv:**
Young bust right, small maple leaf below, date at
right **Rev:** Swimmer, denomination below
Rev. Designer: Lynda Cooper **Weight:** 24.3000 g.
Composition: 0.9250 Silver 0.7226 oz. ASW **Size:**
38 mm. **Note:** Series V.

Date	Mintage	MS-63	Proof
1975	—	14.50	—
1975 Proof	89,155	—	14.50

KM# 101 Subject: Montreal 1976 - 21st Summer
Olympic Games **Obv:** Young bust right, small maple
leaf below, date at right **Rev:** Platform Diver,
denomination below **Rev. Designer:** Lynda Cooper
Weight: 24.3000 g. **Composition:** 0.9250 Silver
0.7226 oz. ASW **Size:** 38 mm. **Note:** Series V.

Date	Mintage	MS-63	Proof
1975	—	14.50	—
1975 Proof	89,155	—	14.50

KM# 107 Subject: 1976 Montreal Olympics **Obv:**
Young bust right, small maple leaf below, date at
right **Rev:** Fencing, denomination below
Rev. Designer: Shigeo Fukada **Weight:**
24.3000 g. **Composition:** 0.9250 Silver 0.7226 oz.
ASW **Size:** 38 mm. **Note:** Series VI.

Date	Mintage	MS-63	Proof
1976	—	14.50	—
1976 Proof	82,302	—	14.50

5 DOLLARS

KM# 108 Subject: 1976 Montreal Olympics **Obv:**
Young bust right, small maple leaf below, date at right
Obv. Legend: Boxing **Rev:** Boxers, denomination
below **Rev. Designer:** Shigeo Fukada **Weight:**
24.3000 g. **Composition:** 0.9250 Silver 0.7226 oz.
ASW **Size:** 38 mm. **Note:** Series VI.

Date	Mintage	MS-63	Proof
1976	—	14.50	—
1976 Proof	82,302	—	14.50

KM# 109 Subject: 1976 Montreal Olympics **Obv:**
Young bust right, small maple leaf below, date at
right **Rev:** Olympic village, denomination below
Rev. Designer: Elliot John Morrison **Weight:**
24.3000 g. **Composition:** 0.9250 Silver 0.7226 oz.
ASW **Size:** 38 mm. **Note:** Series VII.

Date	Mintage	MS-63	Proof
1976	—	14.50	—
1976 Proof	76,908	—	14.50

KM# 110 Subject: 1976 Montreal Olympics **Obv:**
Young bust right, maple leaf below, date at right
Rev: Olympic flame, denomination below
Rev. Designer: Elliot John Morrison **Weight:**
24.3000 g. **Composition:** 0.9250 Silver 0.7226 oz.
ASW **Size:** 38 mm. **Note:** Series VII.

Date	Mintage	MS-63	Proof
1976 Proof	79,102	—	14.50
1976	—	14.50	—

KM# 316 Subject: Dr. Norman Bethune **Obv:**
Young bust right **Rev:** Bethune and party, date at
upper right **Rev. Designer:** Harvey Chan **Weight:**
31.3900 g. **Composition:** 0.9999 Silver
1.0091 oz. ASW

Date	Mintage	MS-63	Proof
1998 Proof	61,000	—	30.00

KM# 398 Obv: Young bust right **Rev:** Viking ship
under sail **Rev. Designer:** Donald Curley
Composition: Copper-Zinc-Nickel **Note:** Sold in
sets with Norway 20 kroner, KM#465.

Date	Mintage	MS-63	Proof
1999 Proof	—	—	18.50

KM# 435 Subject: Guglielmo Marconi **Obv:**
Crowned head right **Rev:** Gold-plated cameo
portrait of Marconi **Rev. Designer:** Cosme Saffioti
Edge: Reeded **Weight:** 16.8600 g. **Composition:**
0.9250 Silver 0.5014 oz. ASW **Size:** 28.4 mm.
Note: Only issued in two coin set with British 2
pounds KM#1014a.

Date	Mintage	MS-63	Proof
ND(2001) Proof	15,011	—	22.00

KM# 519 Obv: Crowned head right **Rev:** National
arms **Edge:** Reeded **Weight:** 8.3600 g.
Composition: 0.9000 Gold 0.2419 oz. AGW **Size:**
21.6 mm.

Date	Mintage	MS-63	Proof
ND (2002) Proof	2,002	—	325

KM# 518 Subject: F.I.F.A. World Cup Soccer ,
Germany 2006 **Obv:** Crowned head right,
denomination **Rev:** Goalie on knees **Edge:** Reeded
Weight: 31.1200 g. **Composition:** 0.9999 Silver
1.0004 oz. ASW **Size:** 38 mm.

Date	Mintage	MS-63	Proof
2003 Proof	21,542	—	29.00

KM# 514 **Obv:** Crowned head right **Rev:** Moose **Edge:** Reeded **Weight:** 31.1200 g. **Composition:** 0.9999 Silver 1.0004 oz. ASW **Size:** 38 mm.

Date	Mintage	MS-63	Proof
2004 Proof	12,822	—	125

KM# 527 **Subject:** Golf, Championship of Canada, Centennial **Obv:** Head right **Weight:** 31.1200 g. **Composition:** 0.9999 Silver 1.0004 oz. ASW

Date	Mintage	MS-63	Proof
2004 Proof	18,750	—	25.00

KM# 554 **Subject:** Alberta **Obv. Designer:** Head right **Rev. Designer:** Michelle Grant **Weight:** 31.1200 g. **Composition:** 0.9999 Silver 1.0004 oz. ASW

Date	Mintage	MS-63	Proof
2005 Proof	20,000	—	35.00

KM# 555 **Subject:** Saskatchewan **Obv:** Head right **Obv. Designer:** Susanna Blunt **Rev. Designer:** Paulett Sapergia **Weight:** 31.1200 g. **Composition:** 0.9999 Silver 1.0004 oz. ASW

Date	Mintage	MS-63	Proof
2005 Proof	20,000	—	35.00

KM# 556.1 **Subject:** 60th Anniversay Victory WWII - Veterans **Obv:** Bust right **Rev:** Large V and heads of sailor, soldier and aviator on large maple leaf **Edge:** Reeded **Weight:** 31.1200 g. **Composition:** 0.9990 Silver 0.9995 oz. ASW **Size:** 38.02 mm.

Date	Mintage	MS-63	Proof
2005	25,000	30.00	—

KM# 556.2 **Subject:** 60th Anniversary Victory WW II - Veterans **Obv:** Bust right **Rev:** Large V and heads of sailor, soldier and aviator on maple leaf

with small maple leaf added at left and right **Edge:** Reeded **Weight:** 31.1200 g. **Composition:** 0.9999 Silver 1.0004 oz. ASW **Size:** 38.02 mm.

Date	Mintage	MS-63	Proof
2005	10,000	100.00	—

KM# 557 **Subject:** Walrus and calf **Obv:** Head right **Obv. Designer:** Susanna Blunt **Rev:** Two walrusus and calf **Rev. Designer:** Pierre Leduc **Weight:** 31.1200 g. **Composition:** 0.9999 Silver 1.0004 oz. ASW **Size:** 36 mm.

Date	Mintage	MS-63	Proof
2005 Proof	5,519	—	35.00

KM# 558 **Subject:** White tailed deer **Obv:** Head right **Obv. Designer:** Susanna Blunt **Rev:** Two deer standing **Rev. Designer:** Xerxes Irani **Weight:** 31.1200 g. **Composition:** 0.9999 Silver 1.0004 oz. ASW **Size:** 36 mm.

Date	Mintage	MS-63	Proof
2005 Proof	6,439	—	35.00

KM# 585 **Obv:** Head right **Obv. Designer:** Susanna Blunt **Rev:** Peregrine Falcon feeding young ones **Rev. Designer:** Dwayne Harty **Weight:** 31.1200 g. **Composition:** 0.9999 Silver 1.0004 oz. ASW **Size:** 36 mm.

Date	Mintage	MS-63	Proof
2006 Proof	6,145	—	40.00

KM# 586 **Subject:** Sable Island horses **Obv:** Head right **Obv. Designer:** Susanna Blunt **Rev:** Horse and foal standing **Rev. Designer:** Christie Paquet **Weight:** 31.1200 g. **Composition:** 0.9999 Silver 1.0004 oz. ASW **Size:** 36 mm.

Date	Mintage	MS-63	Proof
2006 Proof	7,589	—	40.00

KM# 658 **Subject:** Breast Cancer Awareness **Rev:** Colorized pink ribbon **Weight:** 31.1200 g. **Composition:** 0.9999 Silver 1.0004 oz. ASW **Size:** 36.07 mm.

Date	Mintage	MS-63	Proof
2006 Proof	11,048	—	50.00

KM# 659 **Subject:** C.A.F. Snowbirds Acrobatic Jet Flying Team **Rev:** Image of fighter jets and piolt **Weight:** 31.1200 g. **Composition:** 0.9999 Silver 1.0004 oz. ASW

Date	Mintage	MS-63	Proof
2006 Proof	7,896	—	50.00

KM# A799 **Subject:** Breast Cancer Awareness **Rev:** Pink ribbon and groups of people **Weight:** 25.1750 g. **Composition:** 0.9959 Silver 0.8060 oz. ASW **Size:** 36.07 mm.

Date	Mintage	MS-63	Proof
2006 Proof	11,048	—	60.00

KM# 799 **Subject:** Breast Cancer Awareness **Rev:** Multicolor, green maple leaf and pink ribbon **Weight:** 31.1050 g. **Composition:** 0.9990 Silver 0.9990 oz. ASW **Size:** 38 mm.

Date	Mintage	MS-63	Proof
2008	—	85.00	—

8 DOLLARS

KM# 515   Obv: Head right **Obv. Designer:**
Susanna Blunt **Rev:** Grizzly bear walking left **Edge:**
Reeded **Weight:** 28.8000 g. **Composition:** 0.9250
Silver 0.8565 oz. **ASW Size:** 39 mm.

Date	Mintage	MS-63	Proof
2004 Proof	12,942	—	60.00

KM# 597   Subject: Canadian Pacific Railway,
120th Anniversary **Obv:** Head right **Obv. Designer:**
Susanna Blunt **Rev:** Railway bridge **Weight:**
32.1500 g. **Composition:** 0.9999 Silver 1.0335 oz.
ASW

Date	Mintage	MS-63	Proof
2005 Proof	9,892	—	45.00

KM# 598   Subject: Canadian Pacific Railway,
120th Anniversary **Obv:** Head right **Rev:** Railway
memorial to the Chinese workers **Weight:**
32.1500 g. **Composition:** 0.9999 Silver 1.0335 oz.
ASW

Date	Mintage	MS-63	Proof
2005 Proof	9,892	—	45.00

KM# 730   Obv: Queens's head at top in circle, three
Chinese characters **Rev:** Dragon and other
creatures **Weight:** 25.1800 g. **Composition:**
0.9999 Silver 0.8094 oz. ASW **Size:** 36.1 mm.

Date	Mintage	MS-63	Proof
2007 Proof	19,954	—	55.00

10 DOLLARS

KM# 86.1   Subject: 1976 Montreal Olympics **Obv:**
Young bust right, maple leaf below, date at right
Rev: World map, denomination below
Rev. Designer: Georges Huel **Weight:** 48.6000 g.
Composition: 0.9250 Silver 1.4453 oz. ASW **Size:**
45 mm. **Note:** Series I.

Date	Mintage	MS-63	Proof
1973	103,426	28.00	—
1973 Proof	165,203	—	28.00

KM# 27   Obv: Crowned bust left **Obv. Designer:**
E. B. MacKennal **Rev:** Arms within wreath, date and
denomination below **Rev. Designer:** W. H. J.
Blakemore **Weight:** 16.7185 g. **Composition:**
0.9000 Gold 0.4837 oz. AGW **Size:** 26.92 mm.

Date	Mintage	F-12	VF-20	XF-40	AU-50	MS-60	MS-63
1912	74,759	—	BV	600	650	800	2,900
1913	149,232	—	BV	600	650	800	3,000
1914	140,068	BV	600	650	700	1,000	3,500

KM# 87   Subject: 1976 Montreal Olympics **Obv:**
Young bust right, small maple leaf below, date at
right **Rev:** Montreal skyline, denomination below
Rev. Designer: Georges Huel **Weight:** 48.6000 g.
Composition: 0.9250 Silver 1.4453 oz. ASW **Size:**
45 mm. **Note:** Series I.

Date	Mintage	MS-63	Proof
1973	—	28.00	—
1973 Proof	165,203	—	28.00

8 DOLLARS

KM# 86.2 Subject: 1976 Montreal Olympics **Obv:** Young bust right, small maple leaf below, date at right **Rev:** World map **Rev. Designer:** Georges Huel **Weight:** 48.6000 g. **Composition:** 0.9250 Silver 1.4453 oz. ASW **Size:** 45 mm. **Note:** Series I.

Date	Mintage	MS-63	Proof
1974	320	285	—

Note: Error: mule

KM# 93 Subject: 1976 Montreal Olympics **Obv:** Young bust right, small maple leaf below, date at right **Rev:** Head of Zeus, denomination below **Rev. Designer:** Anthony Mann **Weight:** 48.6000 g. **Composition:** 0.9250 Silver 1.4453 oz. ASW **Size:** 45 mm. **Note:** Series II.

Date	Mintage	MS-63	Proof
1974 Proof	104,684	—	28.00
1974	—	28.00	—

KM# 94 Subject: 1976 Montreal Olympics **Obv:** Young bust right, small maple leaf below, date at right **Rev:** Temple of Zeus, denomination below **Rev. Designer:** Anthony Mann **Weight:** 48.6000 g. **Composition:** 0.9250 Silver 1.4453 oz. ASW **Size:** 45 mm. **Note:** Series II.

Date	Mintage	MS-63	Proof
1974	—	28.00	—
1974 Proof	104,684	—	28.00

KM# 95 Subject: 1976 Montreal Olympics **Obv:** Young bust right, small maple leaf below, date at right **Rev:** Cycling, denomination below **Rev. Designer:** Ken Danby **Weight:** 48.6000 g. **Composition:** 0.9250 Silver 1.4453 oz. ASW **Size:** 45 mm. **Note:** Series III.

Date	Mintage	MS-63	Proof
1974	—	28.00	—
1974 Proof	97,431	—	28.00

KM# 96 Subject: 1976 Montreal Olympics **Obv:** Young bust right, small maple leaf below, date at right **Rev:** Lacrosse, denomination below **Rev. Designer:** Ken Danby **Weight:** 48.6000 g. **Composition:** 0.9250 Silver 1.4453 oz. ASW **Size:** 45 mm. **Note:** Series III.

Date	Mintage	MS-63	Proof
1974	—	28.00	—
1974 Proof	97,431	—	28.00

KM# 102 Subject: 1976 Montreal Olympics **Obv:** Young bust right, small maple leaf below, date at

right **Rev:** Men's hurdles, denomination below
Rev. Designer: Leo Yerxa **Weight:** 48.6000 g.
Composition: 0.9250 Silver 1.4453 oz. ASW **Size:**
45 mm. **Note:** Series IV.

Date	Mintage	MS-63	Proof
1975	—	28.00	—
1975 Proof	82,302	—	28.00

KM# 105 Subject: 1976 Montreal Olympics **Obv:**
Young bust right, small maple leaf below, date at
right **Rev:** Canoeing, denomination below
Rev. Designer: Lynda Cooper **Weight:** 48.6000 g.
Composition: 0.9250 Silver 1.4453 oz. ASW **Size:**
45 mm. **Note:** Series V.

Date	Mintage	MS-63	Proof
1975	—	28.00	—
1975 Proof	89,155	—	28.00

KM# 103 Subject: Montreal 1976 - 21st Summer
Olympic Games **Obv:** Young bust right, small maple
leaf below, date at right **Rev:** Women's shot put,
denomination below **Rev. Designer:** Leo Yerxa
Weight: 48.6000 g. **Composition:** 0.9250 Silver
1.4453 oz. ASW **Size:** 45 mm. **Note:** Series IV.

Date	Mintage	MS-63	Proof
1975	—	28.00	—
1975 Proof	82,302	—	28.00

KM# 111 Subject: 1976 Montreal Olympics **Obv:**
Young bust right, small maple leaf below, date at
right **Rev:** Football, denomination below
Rev. Designer: Shigeo Fukada **Weight:**
48.6000 g. **Composition:** 0.9250 Silver 1.4453 oz.
ASW **Size:** 45 mm. **Note:** Series VI.

Date	Mintage	MS-63	Proof
1976 Proof	76,908	—	28.00
1976	—	28.00	—

KM# 104 Subject: 1976 Montreal Olympics **Obv:**
Young bust right, small maple leaf below, date at
right **Rev:** Sailing, denomination below
Rev. Designer: Lynda Cooper **Weight:** 48.6000 g.
Composition: 0.9250 Silver 1.4453 oz. ASW **Size:**
45 mm. **Note:** Series V.

Date	Mintage	MS-63	Proof
1975 Proof	89,155	—	28.00
1975	—	28.00	—

KM# 112 Subject: 1976 Montreal Olympics **Obv:**
Young bust right, small maple leaf below, date at right
Rev: Field hockey **Rev. Designer:** Shigeo Fukada

Weight: 48.6000 g. **Composition:** 0.9250 Silver
1.4453 oz. ASW **Size:** 45 mm. **Note:** Series VI.

Date	Mintage	MS-63	Proof
1976	—	28.00	—
1976 Proof	76,908	—	28.00

KM# 113 Subject: 1976 Montreal Olympics **Obv:**
Young bust right, small maple leaf below, date at
right **Rev:** Olympic Stadium, denomination below
Rev. Designer: Elliot John Morrison **Weight:**
48.6000 g. **Composition:** 0.9250 Silver 1.4453 oz.
ASW **Size:** 45 mm. **Note:** Series VII.

Date	Mintage	MS-63	Proof
1976 Proof	79,102	—	28.00
1976	—	28.00	—

KM# 114 Subject: 1976 Montreal Olympics **Obv:**
Young bust right, small maple leaf below, date at
right **Rev:** Olympic Velodrome, denomination below
Rev. Designer: Elliot John Morrison **Weight:**
48.6000 g. **Composition:** 0.9250 Silver 1.4453 oz.
ASW **Size:** 45 mm. **Note:** Series VII.

Date	Mintage	MS-63	Proof
1976	—	28.00	—
1976 Proof	79,102	—	28.00

KM# 520 Obv: Crowned head right **Rev:** National
arms **Edge:** Reeded **Weight:** 16.7200 g.
Composition: 0.9000 Gold 0.4838 oz. AGW **Size:**
26.92 mm.

Date	Mintage	MS-63	Proof
ND (2002) Proof	2,002	—	650

KM# 559 Subject: Pope John Paul II **Obv:** Head
right **Weight:** 25.1750 g. **Composition:** 0.9999
Silver 0.8093 oz. ASW

Date	Mintage	MS-63	Proof
2005 Proof	24,716	—	35.00

KM# 757 Subject: Year of the Veteran **Rev:** Profile
left of young and old veteran **Weight:** 25.1750 g.
Composition: 0.9999 Silver 0.8093 oz. ASW

Date	Mintage	MS-63	Proof
2005 Proof	6,549	—	45.00

KM# 661 Subject: National Historic Sites **Obv:**
Head right **Rev:** Fortress of Louisbourg **Weight:**
25.1750 g. **Composition:** 0.9999 Silver 0.8093 oz.
ASW

Date	Mintage	MS-63	Proof
2006 Proof	5,544	—	35.00

15 DOLLARS

KM# 215 Subject: 1992 Olympics **Obv:** Crowned
head right, date at left, denomination below **Rev:**
Coaching track **Rev. Designer:** Stewart Sherwood
Weight: 33.6300 g. **Composition:** 0.9250 Silver
1.0000 oz. ASW **Size:** 39 mm.

Date	Mintage	MS-63	Proof
1992 Proof	275,000	—	28.00

KM# 216 Subject: 1992 Olympics **Obv:** Crowned head right, date at left, denomination below **Rev:** High jump, rings, speed skating **Rev. Designer:** David Craig **Weight:** 33.6300 g. **Composition:** 0.9250 Silver 1.0000 oz. ASW

Date	Mintage	MS-63	Proof
1992 Proof	275,000	—	28.00

KM#304 Subject: Year of the Tiger **Obv:** Crowned head right **Rev:** Tiger within octagon at center, animal figures surround **Rev. Designer:** Harvey Chan **Composition:** Bi-Metallic **Size:** 40 mm.

Date	Mintage	MS-63	Proof
1998 Proof	68,888	—	275

KM# 331 Subject: Year of the Rabbitt **Obv:** Crowned head right **Rev:** Rabbit within octagon at center, animal figures surround **Rev. Designer:** Harvey Chan **Composition:** Bi-Metallic

Date	Mintage	MS-63	Proof
1999 Proof	77,791	—	100

KM# 387 Subject: Year of the Dragon **Obv:** Crowned head right **Rev. Designer:** Harvey Chan **Composition:** Bi-Metallic

Date	Mintage	MS-63	Proof
2000 Proof	88,634	—	125

KM# 415 Subject: Year of the Snake **Obv:** Crowned head right **Rev:** Snake within circle of lunar calendar signs **Rev. Designer:** Harvey Chain **Edge:** Reeded **Weight:** 33.6300 g. **Composition:** 0.9250 Silver 1.0000 oz. ASW **Size:** 40 mm.

Date	Mintage	MS-63	Proof
2001 Proof	60,754	—	45.00

KM# 463 Subject: Year of the Horse **Obv. Designer:** Dora dePédery-Hunt **Rev:** Horse in center with Chinese Lunar calendar around **Rev. Designer:** Harvey Chain **Weight:** 33.6300 g. **Composition:** 0.9250 Silver 1.0000 oz. ASW

Date	Mintage	MS-63	Proof
2002 Proof	59,395	—	65.00

KM# 481 Subject: Year of the Sheep **Obv:** Crowned head right **Rev:** Sheep in center with Chinese Lunar calendar around **Rev. Designer:** Harvey Chain **Weight:** 33.6300 g. **Composition:** 0.9250 Silver 1.0000 oz. ASW **Size:** 40 mm.

Date	Mintage	MS-63	Proof
2003 Proof	53,714	—	60.00

KM# 610 Subject: Year of the Monkey **Obv:** Crowned head right **Rev:** Monkey in center with Chinese Lunar calendar around **Weight:** 33.6300 g. **Composition:** 0.9250 Silver 1.0000 oz. ASW

Date	Mintage	MS-63	Proof
2004 Proof	46,175	—	150

KM# 560 Subject: Year of the Rooster **Obv:** Crowned head right **Rev:** Rooster in center with Chinese Lunar calendar around **Weight:** 33.6300 g. **Composition:** 0.9250 Silver 1.0000 oz. ASW

Date	Mintage	MS-63	Proof
2005 Proof	44,690	—	75.00

KM# 587 Subject: Year of the Dog **Obv:** Crowned head left **Rev:** Dog in center with Chinese Lunar calendar around **Weight:** 33.6300 g. **Composition:** 0.9250 Silver 1.0000 oz. ASW

Date	Mintage	MS-63	Proof
2006 Proof	41,617	—	65.00

KM# 662 Subject: Year of the Pig **Obv:** Crowned head right **Rev:** Pig in center with Chinese Lunar calendar around **Weight:** 33.6300 g. **Composition:** 0.9250 Silver 1.0000 oz. ASW

Date	Mintage	MS-63	Proof
2006 Proof	48,888	—	80.00

KM# 732 Subject: Year of the Pig **Rev:** Octagonal gold insert **Weight:** 34.0000 g. **Composition:** 0.9250 Silver 1.0111 oz. ASW **Size:** 40 mm.

Date	Mintage	MS-63	Proof
2007 Proof	48,888	—	80.00

KM# 801 Subject: Year of the Rat **Rev:** Rat, gold octagonal insert at center **Weight:** 34.0000 g. **Composition:** 0.9250 Silver 1.0111 oz. ASW **Size:** 40 mm.

Date	Mintage	MS-63	Proof
2008 Proof	—	—	75.00

KM# 919 Obv: Bust right **Obv. Designer:** Susanna Blunt **Rev:** Ten of spades, multicolor **Weight:** 31.5600 g. **Composition:** 0.9250 Silver 0.9385 oz. ASW **Shape:** rectangle **Size:** 49.8 x 28.6 mm.

Date	Mintage	MS-63	Proof
2009 Proof	25,000	—	100

KM# 920 Obv: Bust right **Obv. Designer:** Susanna Blunt **Rev:** King of hearts, multicolor **Weight:** 31.5600 g. **Composition:** 0.9250 Silver 0.9385 oz. ASW **Shape:** Rectangle **Size:** 49.8 x 28.6 mm.

Date	Mintage	MS-63	Proof
2009 Proof	25,000	—	100

KM# 866 Subject: Year of the Ox **Rev:** Ox, octagon gold insert **Weight:** 34.0000 g. **Composition:** 0.9250 Silver 1.0111 oz. ASW **Size:** 40 mm.

Date	Mintage	MS-63	Proof
2009 Proof	—	—	80.00

KM# 922 Obv: Bust right **Obv. Designer:** Susanna Blunt **Rev:** Pages portrait of George VI **Weight:** 30.0000 g. **Composition:** 0.9250 Silver 0.8921 oz. ASW **Size:** 36.15 mm.

Date	Mintage	MS-63	P/L	Proof
2009(ml) Prooflike	10,000	—	100.00	—

KM# 923 Obv: Bust right **Obv. Designer:** Susanna Blunt **Rev:** Glick portrait of Queen Elizabeth II **Weight:** 30.0000 g. **Composition:** 0.9250 Silver 0.8921 oz. ASW **Size:** 36.15 mm.

Date	Mintage	MS-63	Proof
2009(ml) Prooflike	10,000	—	—

20 DOLLARS

KM# 71 Subject: Centennial **Obv:** Crowned head right **Rev:** Crowned and supported arms **Edge:** Reeded **Weight:** 18.2733 g. **Composition:** 0.9000 Gold 0.5287 oz. AGW **Size:** 27.05 mm.

Date	Mintage	MS-63	Proof
1967 Proof	337,688	—	650

KM# 145 Subject: 1988 Calgary Olympics **Obv:**
Young bust right, maple leaf below, date at right
Rev: Downhill skier, denomination below
Rev. Designer: Ian Stewart **Edge:** Lettered
Weight: 33.6300 g. **Composition:** 0.9250 Silver
1.0000 oz. ASW **Size:** 40 mm.

Date	Mintage	MS-63	Proof
1985 Proof	406,360	—	22.00
1985 Proof	Inc. above	—	175

Note: Plain edge

KM# 146 Subject: 1988 Calgary Olympics **Obv:**
Young bust right, small maple leaf below, date at
right **Rev:** Speed skater, denomination below
Rev. Designer: Friedrich Peter **Edge:** Lettered
Weight: 33.6300 g. **Composition:** 0.9250 Silver
1.0000 oz. ASW **Size:** 40 mm.

Date	Mintage	MS-63	Proof
1985 Proof	354,222	—	22.00
1985 Proof	Inc. above	—	175

Note: Plain edge

KM# 150 Subject: Calgary 1988 - 15th Winter
Olympic Games **Obv:** Young bust right, small maple
leaf below, date at right **Rev:** Cross-country skier,
denomination below **Rev. Designer:** Ian Stewart
Edge: Lettered **Weight:** 33.6300 g. **Composition:**
0.9250 Silver 1.0000 oz. ASW **Size:** 40 mm.

Date	Mintage	MS-63	Proof
1986 Proof	303,199	—	22.00

KM# 147 Subject: 1988 Calgary Olympics **Obv:**
Young bust right, small maple leaf below, date at
right **Rev:** Biathlon, denomination below
Rev. Designer: John Mardon **Edge:** Lettered
Weight: 33.6300 g. **Composition:** 0.9250 Silver
1.0000 oz. ASW **Size:** 40 mm.

Date	Mintage	MS-63	Proof
1986 Proof	308,086	—	22.00
1986 Proof	Inc. above	—	175

Note: Plain edge

KM# 148 Subject: 1988 Calgary Olympics **Obv:**
Young bust right, small maple leaf below, date at
right **Rev:** Hockey, denomination below
Rev. Designer: Ian Stewart **Edge:** Lettered
Weight: 33.6300 g. **Composition:** 0.9250 Silver
1.0000 oz. ASW **Size:** 40 mm.

Date	Mintage	MS-63	Proof
1986 Proof	396,602	—	22.00
1986 Proof	Inc. above	—	175

Note: Plain edge

KM# 151 Subject: 1988 Calgary Olympics **Obv:** Young bust right, small maple leaf below, date at right **Rev:** Free-style skier, denomination below **Rev. Designer:** Walter Ott **Edge:** Lettered **Weight:** 33.6300 g. **Composition:** 0.9250 Silver 1.0000 oz. ASW **Size:** 40 mm.

Date	Mintage	MS-63	Proof
1986 Proof	294,322	—	22.00
1986 Proof	Inc. above	—	175

Note: Plain edge

KM# 155 Subject: Calgary 1988 - 15th Winter Olympic Games **Obv:** Young bust right, small maple leaf below, date at right **Rev:** Figure skating pairs event, denomination below **Rev. Designer:** Raymond Taylor **Edge:** Lettered **Weight:** 34.1070 g. **Composition:** 0.9250 Silver 1.0143 oz. ASW **Size:** 40 mm.

Date	Mintage	MS-63	Proof
1987 Proof	334,875	—	22.00

KM# 156 Subject: 1988 Calgary Olympics **Obv:** Young bust right, small maple leaf below, date at

right **Rev:** Curling, denomination below **Rev. Designer:** Ian Stewart **Edge:** Lettered **Weight:** 34.1070 g. **Composition:** 0.9250 Silver 1.0143 oz. ASW **Size:** 40 mm.

Date	Mintage	MS-63	Proof
1987 Proof	286,457	—	22.00

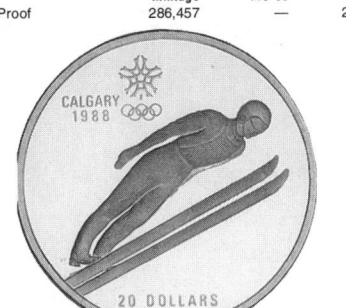

KM# 159 Subject: 1988 Calgary Olympics **Obv:** Young bust right, small maple leaf below, date at right **Rev:** Ski jumper, denomination below **Rev. Designer:** Raymond Taylor **Edge:** Lettered **Weight:** 34.1070 g. **Composition:** 0.9250 Silver 1.0143 oz. ASW **Size:** 40 mm.

Date	Mintage	MS-63	Proof
1987 Proof	290,954	—	22.00

KM# 160 Subject: 1988 Calgary Olympics **Obv:** Young bust right, maple leaf below, date at right **Rev:** Bobsled, denomination below **Rev. Designer:** John Mardon **Edge:** Lettered **Weight:** 34.1070 g. **Composition:** 0.9250 Silver 1.0143 oz. ASW **Size:** 40 mm.

Date	Mintage	MS-63	Proof
1987 Proof	274,326	—	22.00

KM# 172 Subject: Aviation **Obv:** Crowned head right, date below **Rev:** Lancaster, Fauquier in cameo, denomination below **Rev. Designer:**

Robert R. Carmichael **Weight:** 31.1030 g.
Composition: 0.9250 Silver 0.9249 oz. ASW
Size: 38 mm.

Date	Mintage	MS-63	Proof
1990 Proof	43,596	—	100

KM# 173   Subject: Aviation **Obv:** Crowned head
right, date below **Rev:** Anson and Harvard, Air
Marshal Robert Leckie in cameo, denomination
below **Rev. Designer:** Geoff Bennett **Weight:**
31.1030 g. **Composition:** 0.9250 Silver 0.9249 oz.
ASW **Size:** 38 mm.

Date	Mintage	MS-63	Proof
1990 Proof	41,844	—	35.00

KM# 196   Subject: Aviation **Obv:** Crowned head
right, date below **Rev:** Silver Dart, John A. D.
McCurdy and F. W. "Casey" Baldwin in cameo,
denomination below **Rev. Designer:** George
Velinger **Weight:** 31.1030 g. **Composition:** 0.9250
Silver 0.9249 oz. ASW **Size:** 38 mm.

Date	Mintage	MS-63	Proof
1991 Proof	28,791	—	30.00

KM# 197   Subject: Aviation **Obv:** Crowned head
right, date below **Rev:** de Haviland Beaver, Philip
C. Garratt in cameo, denomination below
Rev. Designer: Peter Massman **Weight:**
31.1030 g. **Composition:** 0.9250 Silver 0.9249 oz.
ASW **Size:** 38 mm.

Date	Mintage	MS-63	Proof
1991 Proof	29,399	—	30.00

KM# 224   Subject: Aviation **Obv:** Crowned head
right, date below **Rev:** Curtiss JN-4 Canick
("Jenny"), Sir Frank W. Baillie in cameo,
denomination below **Rev. Designer:** George
Velinger **Weight:** 31.1030 g. **Composition:** 0.9250
Silver 0.9249 oz. ASW **Size:** 38 mm.

Date	Mintage	MS-63	Proof
1992 Proof	33,105	—	30.00

KM# 225   Subject: Aviation **Obv:** Crowned head
right, date below **Rev:** de Haviland Gypsy Moth,
Murton A. Seymour in cameo, denomination below
Rev. Designer: John Mardon **Weight:** 31.1030 g.
Composition: 0.9250 Silver 0.9249 oz. ASW
Size: 38 mm.

Date	Mintage	MS-63	Proof
1992 Proof	32,537	—	30.00

KM# 236   Subject: Aviation **Obv:** Crowned head
right, date below **Rev:** Fairchild 71C float plane,
James A. Richardson, Sr. in cameo, denomination
below **Rev. Designer:** Robert R. Carmichael
Weight: 31.1030 g. **Composition:** 0.9250 Silver
0.9249 oz. ASW **Size:** 38 mm.

Date	Mintage	MS-63	Proof
1993 Proof	32,199	—	30.00

KM# 237 Subject: Aviation **Obv:** Crowned head right, date below **Rev:** Lockheed 14, Zebulon Lewis Leigh in cameo, denomination below
Rev. Designer: Robert R. Carmichael **Weight:** 31.1030 g. **Composition:** 0.9250 Silver 0.9249 oz. ASW **Size:** 38 mm.

Date	Mintage	MS-63	Proof
1993 Proof	32,550	—	30.00

KM# 246 Subject: Aviation **Obv:** Crowned head right, date below **Rev:** Curtiss HS-2L seaplane, Stewart Graham in cameo, denomination below
Rev. Designer: John Mardon **Weight:** 31.1030 g. **Composition:** 0.9250 Silver 0.9249 oz. ASW **Size:** 38 mm.

Date	Mintage	MS-63	Proof
1994 Proof	31,242	—	30.00

KM# 247 Subject: Aviation **Obv:** Crowned head right, date below **Rev:** Vickers Vedette, Wilfred T. Reid in cameo, denomination below
Rev. Designer: Robert R. Carmichael **Weight:** 31.1030 g. **Composition:** 0.9250 Silver 0.9249 oz. ASW **Size:** 38 mm.

Date	Mintage	MS-63	Proof
1994 Proof	30,880	—	30.00

KM# 271 Subject: Aviation **Obv:** Crowned head right, date below **Rev:** C-FEA1 Fleet Cannuck, denomination below **Rev. Designer:** Robert Bradford **Weight:** 31.1030 g. **Composition:** 0.9250 Silver 0.9249 oz. ASW **Size:** 38 mm.

Date	Mintage	MS-63	Proof
1995 Proof	17,438	—	30.00

KM# 272 Subject: Aviation **Obv:** Crowned head right, date below **Rev:** DHC-1 Chipmunk, denomination below **Rev. Designer:** Robert Bradford **Weight:** 31.1030 g. **Composition:** 0.9250 Silver 0.9249 oz. ASW **Size:** 38 mm.

Date	Mintage	MS-63	Proof
1995 Proof	17,722	—	30.00

KM# 276 Subject: Aviation **Obv:** Crowned head right, date below **Rev:** CF-100 Cannuck, denomination below **Rev. Designer:** Jim Bruce **Weight:** 31.1030 g. **Composition:** 0.9250 Silver 0.9249 oz. ASW **Size:** 38 mm.

Date	Mintage	MS-63	Proof
1996 Proof	18,508	—	35.00

20 DOLLARS

KM# 277 Subject: Aviation **Obv:** Crowned head right, date below **Obv. Legend:** CF-105 Arrow, denomination below **Rev. Designer:** Jim Bruce **Weight:** 31.1030 g. **Composition:** 0.9250 Silver 0.9249 oz. ASW **Size:** 38 mm.

Date	Mintage	MS-63	Proof
1996 Proof	27,163	—	65.00

KM# 297 Subject: Aviation **Obv:** Crowned head right, date below **Rev:** Canadair F-86 Sabre, denomination below **Rev. Designer:** Ross Buckland **Weight:** 31.1030 g. **Composition:** 0.9250 Silver 0.9249 oz. ASW **Size:** 38 mm.

Date	Mintage	MS-63	Proof
1997 Proof	14,389	—	30.00

KM# 298 Subject: Aviation **Obv:** Crowned head right, date below **Rev:** Canadair CT-114 Tutor, denomination below **Rev. Designer:** Ross Buckland **Weight:** 31.1030 g. **Composition:** 0.9250 Silver 0.9249 oz. ASW **Size:** 38 mm.

Date	Mintage	MS-63	Proof
1997 Proof	15,669	—	30.00

KM# 329 Subject: Aviation **Obv:** Crowned head, right, date below **Rev:** CP-107 Argus, denomination below **Weight:** 31.1030 g. **Composition:** 0.9250 Silver 0.9249 oz. ASW **Size:** 38 mm.

Date	Mintage	MS-63	Proof
1998 Proof	Est. 50,000	—	40.00

KM# 330 Subject: Aviation **Obv:** Crowned head right, date below **Rev:** CP-215 Waterbomber, denomination below **Rev. Designer:** Peter Mossman **Weight:** 31.1030 g. **Composition:** 0.9250 Silver 0.9249 oz. ASW **Size:** 38 mm.

Date	Mintage	MS-63	Proof
1998 Proof	Est. 50,000	—	60.00

KM# 339 Subject: Aviation **Obv:** Crowned head right, date below **Rev:** DHC-6 Twin Otter, denomination below **Rev. Designer:** Neil Aird **Weight:** 31.1030 g. **Composition:** 0.9250 Silver 0.9249 oz. ASW **Size:** 38 mm.

Date	Mintage	MS-63	Proof
1999 Proof	Est. 50,000	—	65.00

KM# 340 Subject: Aviation **Obv:** Crowned head right, date below **Rev:** DHC-8 Dash 8, denomination below **Weight:** 31.1030 g. **Composition:** 0.9250 Silver 0.9249 oz. ASW **Size:** 38 mm.

Date	Mintage	MS-63	Proof
1999 Proof	50,000	—	75.00

KM# 397 Subject: Bluenose sailboat **Obv:** Crowned head right, date below **Rev:** Bluenose sailing left below multicolored cameo, denomination below **Composition:** 0.9250 Silver **Size:** 38 mm.

Date	Mintage	MS-63	Proof
2000 Proof	—	—	100

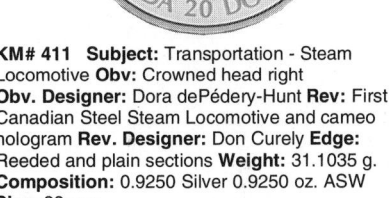

KM# 395 Subject: First Canadian locomotive **Obv:** Crowned head right, date below **Rev:** Locomotive below multicolored cameo, denomination below **Composition:** 0.9250 Silver **Size:** 38 mm.

Date	Mintage	MS-63	Proof
2000 Proof	—	—	40.00

KM# 411 Subject: Transportation - Steam Locomotive **Obv:** Crowned head right **Obv. Designer:** Dora dePédery-Hunt **Rev:** First Canadian Steel Steam Locomotive and cameo hologram **Rev. Designer:** Don Curely **Edge:** Reeded and plain sections **Weight:** 31.1035 g. **Composition:** 0.9250 Silver 0.9250 oz. ASW **Size:** 38 mm.

Date	Mintage	MS-63	Proof
2001 Proof	15,000	—	35.00

KM# 396 Subject: First Canadian self-propelled car **Obv:** Crowned head right, date below **Rev:** Car below multicolored cameo, denomination below **Composition:** 0.9250 Silver **Size:** 38 mm.

Date	Mintage	MS-63	Proof
2000 Proof	—	—	40.00

KM# 427 Subject: Transportation - The Marco Polo, **Obv:** Crowned head right **Rev:** Sailship with hologram cameo **Rev. Designer:** J. Franklin Wright **Edge:** Reeded and plain sections **Weight:** 31.1030 g. **Composition:** 0.9250 Silver 0.9249 oz. ASW **Size:** 38 mm.

Date	Mintage	MS-63	Proof
2001 Proof	15,000	—	35.00

KM# 428 Subject: Transportation - Russell Touring Car, **Obv:** Crowned head right **Rev:** Russell touring car with hologram cameo **Rev. Designer:** John Mardon **Edge:** Reeded and plain sections **Weight:** 31.1030 g. **Composition:** 0.9250 Silver 0.9249 oz. ASW **Size:** 38 mm.

Date	Mintage	MS-63	Proof
2001 Proof	15,000	—	35.00

KM# 464 Obv: Crowned head right **Obv. Designer:** Dora dePédery-Hunt **Rev:** Gray-Dort Model 25-SM with cameo hologram **Rev. Designer:** John Mardon **Weight:** 31.1030 g. **Composition:** 0.9250 Silver 0.9249 oz. ASW

Date	Mintage	MS-63	Proof
2002 Proof	15,000	—	40.00

KM# 465 Obv: Crowned head right **Obv. Designer:** Dora dePédery-Hunt **Rev:** Sailing ship William D. Lawrence **Rev. Designer:** Bonnie Ross **Weight:** 31.1030 g. **Composition:** 0.9250 Silver 0.9249 oz. ASW

Date	Mintage	MS-63	Proof
2002 Proof	15,000	—	40.00

KM# 482 Obv: Crowned head right **Obv. Designer:** Dora dePédery-Hunt **Rev:** Niagara Falls hologram **Rev. Designer:** Gary Corcoran **Weight:** 31.3900 g. **Composition:** 0.9999 Silver 1.0091 oz. ASW

Date	Mintage	MS-63	Proof
2003 Proof	29,967	—	65.00

KM# 483 Subject: The HMCS Bras d'or (FHE-400) **Obv:** Crowned head right **Obv. Designer:** Dora dePédery-Hunt **Rev:** Ship in water **Rev. Designer:** Donald Curley, Stan Witten **Weight:** 31.1030 g. **Composition:** 0.9250 Silver 0.9249 oz. ASW

Date	Mintage	MS-63	Proof
2003 Proof	15,000	—	40.00

KM# 523 Subject: Canadian Rockies, colorized **Obv:** Crowned head right **Obv. Designer:** Dora dePédery-Hunt **Rev:** Canadian Rockies **Weight:** 31.3900 g. **Composition:** 0.9990 Silver 1.0082 oz. ASW

Date	Mintage	MS-63	Proof
2003 Proof	29,967	—	50.00

KM# 484 Subject: Canadian National FA-1 diesel-electric locomotive **Obv:** Crowned head right **Obv. Designer:** Dora dePédery-Hunt **Rev. Designer:** John Mardon, William Woodruff **Weight:** 31.1030 g. **Composition:** 0.9250 Silver 0.9249 oz. ASW

Date	Mintage	MS-63	Proof
2003 Proof	15,000	—	40.00

KM# 485 Obv: Crowned head right **Obv. Designer:** Dora dePédery-Hunt **Rev:** The Bricklin SV-1 **Rev. Designer:** Brian Hughes, José Oslo **Weight:** 31.1030 g. **Composition:** 0.9250 Silver 0.9249 oz. ASW

Date	Mintage	MS-63	Proof
2003 Proof	15,000	—	45.00

KM# 611 Obv: Head right **Obv. Designer:** Susanna Blunt **Rev:** Iceberg, hologram **Weight:** 31.3900 g. **Composition:** 0.9999 Silver 1.0091 oz. ASW

Date	Mintage	MS-63	Proof
2004 Proof	24,879	—	45.00

KM# 838 Rev: Hopewell Rocks **Weight:** 31.3900 g. **Composition:** 0.9999 Silver 1.0091 oz. ASW

Date	Mintage	MS-63	Proof
2004 Proof	16,918	—	45.00

KM# 561 Subject: Three-masted sailing ship, hologram **Obv:** Head right **Obv. Designer:** Susanna Blunt **Rev. Designer:** Bonnie Ross **Weight:** 31.3900 g. **Composition:** 0.9999 Silver 1.0091 oz. ASW

Date	Mintage	MS-63	Proof
2005 Proof	18,276	—	55.00

KM# 562 Subject: Northwest Territories Diamonds **Obv:** Head right **Obv. Designer:** Susanna Blunt **Rev:** Multicolor diamond hologram on landscape **Rev. Designer:** José Oslo **Edge:** Reeded **Weight:** 31.3900 g. **Composition:** 0.9999 Silver 1.0091 oz. ASW **Size:** 38 mm.

Date	Mintage	MS-63	Proof
2005 Proof	35,000	—	45.00

KM# 563 Subject: Mingan Archepelago **Obv:** Head right **Obv. Designer:** Susanna Blunt **Rev:** Cliffs with whale tail out of water **Rev. Designer:** Pierre Leduc **Weight:** 31.3900 g. **Composition:** 0.9999 Silver 1.0091 oz. ASW

Date	Mintage	MS-63	Proof
2005 Proof	—	—	45.00

KM# 564 Subject: Rainforests of the Pacific Northwest **Obv:** Head right **Rev:** Open winged bird **Designer:** Susanna Blunt **Weight:** 31.3900 g. **Composition:** 0.9999 Silver 1.0091 oz. ASW

Date	Mintage	MS-63	Proof
2005 Proof	—	—	45.00

KM# 565 Subject: Toronto Island National Park **Obv:** Head right **Rev:** Toronto Island Lighthouse **Weight:** 31.3900 g. **Composition:** 0.9999 Silver 1.0091 oz. ASW

Date	Mintage	MS-63	Proof
2005 Proof	—	—	45.00

KM# 588 Subject: Georgian Bay National Park **Obv:** Head right **Rev:** Canoe and small trees on island **Weight:** 31.3900 g. **Composition:** 0.9999 Silver 1.0091 oz. ASW

Date	Mintage	MS-63	Proof
2006 Proof	—	—	60.00

KM# 589 Subject: Notre Dame Basilica, Montreal, as a hologram **Obv:** Head right **Weight:** 31.1000 g. **Composition:** 0.9999 Silver 0.9997 oz. ASW

Date	Mintage	MS-63	Proof
2006 Proof	15,000	—	50.00

KM# 663 Subject: Nahanni National Park **Obv:** Head right **Rev:** Bear walking along sream, cliff in background **Weight:** 31.3900 g. **Composition:** 0.9999 Silver 1.0091 oz. ASW

Date	Mintage	MS-63	Proof
2006 Proof	—	—	60.00

KM# 664 Subject: Jasper National Park **Obv:** Head right **Rev:** Cowboy on horseback in majestic scene **Weight:** 31.3900 g. **Composition:** 0.9999 Silver 1.0091 oz. ASW

Date	Mintage	MS-63	Proof
2006 Proof	—	—	60.00

KM# 665 Subject: CN Tower, Toronto **Obv:** Head right **Rev:** Holographic rendering of CN Tower **Weight:** 31.1000 g. **Composition:** 0.9999 Silver 0.9997 oz. ASW

Date	Mintage	MS-63	Proof
2006 Proof	15,000	—	60.00

KM# 666 Subject: Pengrowth (Calgary Saddledome) **Obv:** Head right **Rev:** Holographic view of Saddledome **Weight:** 31.1000 g. **Composition:** 0.9999 Silver 0.9997 oz. ASW

Date	Mintage	MS-63	Proof
2006 Proof	15,000	—	55.00

KM# 667 Subject: Tall Ship **Obv:** Head right **Rev:** Ketch and holographic image **Weight:** 31.3900 g. **Composition:** 0.9999 Silver 1.0091 oz. ASW

Date	Mintage	MS-63	Proof
2006 Proof	10,299	—	60.00

KM# 734 Rev: Holiday sleigh ride **Weight:** 31.1000 g. **Composition:** 0.9990 Silver 0.9988 oz. ASW **Size:** 38 mm.

Date	Mintage	MS-63	Proof
2007 Proof	6,041	—	50.00

KM# 735 Rev: Snowflake, blue crystal **Weight:** 31.1000 g. **Composition:** 0.9990 Silver 0.9988 oz. ASW

Date	Mintage	MS-63	Proof
2007 Proof	1,433	—	175

KM# 737 Subject: International Polar Year **Weight:** 31.1000 g. **Composition:** 0.9990 Silver 0.9988 oz. ASW **Size:** 38 mm.

Date	Mintage	MS-63	Proof
2007 Proof	8,352	—	50.00

KM# 737a Subject: International Polar Year **Rev:** Blue plasma coating **Weight:** 31.1000 g. **Composition:** 0.9990 Silver 0.9988 oz. ASW **Size:** 38 mm.

Date	Mintage	MS-63	Proof
2007 Proof	3,005	—	150

KM# 738 Subject: Tall ships **Rev:** Brigantine in harbor, hologram **Weight:** 31.3900 g. **Composition:** 0.9999 Silver 1.0091 oz. ASW **Size:** 38 mm.

Date	Mintage	MS-63	Proof
2007 Proof	16,000	—	60.00

KM# 839 Rev: Northern lights in hologram **Weight:** 31.3900 g. **Composition:** 0.9999 Silver 1.0091 oz. ASW

Date	Mintage	MS-63	Proof
2007	—	35.00	—

KM# 808 Subject: Agriculture trade **Weight:** 31.5000 g. **Composition:** 0.9250 Silver 0.9368 oz. ASW **Size:** 40 mm.

Date	Mintage	MS-63	Proof
2008 Proof	10,000	—	50.00

KM# 809 Rev: Royal Hudson Steam locomotive **Weight:** 31.1050 g. **Composition:** 0.9990 Silver 0.9990 oz. ASW **Size:** 38 mm.

Date	Mintage	MS-63	Proof
2008 Proof	—	—	50.00

KM# 810 Rev: Green leaf and crystal raindrop **Rev. Designer:** Stanley Witten **Weight:** 31.3900 g. **Composition:** 0.9990 Silver 1.0082 oz. ASW **Size:** 38 mm.

Date	Mintage	MS-63	Proof
2008 Proof	—	—	65.00

KM# 811 Rev: Snowflake, amethyst crystal **Weight:** 31.1050 g. **Composition:** 0.9990 Silver 0.9990 oz. ASW

Date	Mintage	MS-63	Proof
2008 Proof	—	—	90.00

KM# 813 Rev: Carolers around tree **Weight:** 31.1050 g. **Composition:** 0.9990 Silver 0.9990 oz. ASW **Size:** 38 mm.

Date	Mintage	MS-63	Proof
2008	—	50.00	—

KM# 872 Rev: Snowflake, sapphire crystal **Weight:** 31.1050 g. **Composition:** 0.9990 Silver 0.9990 oz. ASW **Size:** 38 mm.

Date	Mintage	MS-63	Proof
2008 Proof	—	—	85.00

20 DOLLARS

KM# 893 Subject: Coal mining trade **Obv:** Bust right **Obv. Legend:** Elizabeth II DG Regina **Obv. Designer:** Susanna Blunt **Rev:** Miner pushing cart with coal **Rev. Legend:** Canada 20 Dollars **Rev. Designer:** John Marder **Weight:** 31.3900 g. **Composition:** 0.9990 Silver 1.0082 oz. ASW **Size:** 38 mm.

Date	Mintage	MS-63	Proof
2009 Proof	10,000	—	—

KM# 891 Subject: Great Canadian Locomotives - Jubilee **Obv:** Bust right **Obv. Legend:** Elizabeth II DG Regina **Obv. Designer:** Susanna Blunt **Rev:** Jubilee locomotive side view **Rev. Legend:** Canada 20 Dollars **Edge Lettering:** Jubilee **Weight:** 31.3900 g. **Composition:** 0.9990 Silver 1.0082 oz. ASW **Size:** 38 mm.

Date	Mintage	MS-63	Proof
2009 Proof	10,000	—	—

KM# 892 Subject: Crystal raindrop **Obv:** Bust right **Obv. Legend:** Elizabeth II DG Regina **Obv. Designer:** Susanna Blunt **Rev:** Colored maple leaves with crystal raindrop **Rev. Legend:** Canada 20 Dollars **Rev. Designer:** Celia Godkin **Weight:** 31.3900 g. **Composition:** 0.9990 Silver 1.0082 oz. ASW **Size:** 38 mm.

Date	Mintage	MS-63	Proof
2009 Proof	10,000	—	—

KM# 876 Rev: Summer moon mask **Weight:** 31.5000 g. **Composition:** 0.9250 Silver 0.9368 oz. ASW **Size:** 40 mm.

Date	Mintage	MS-63	Proof
2009 Proof	—	—	75.00

25 DOLLARS

KM# 742 Subject: Vancouver Olympics **Rev:** Alpine skiing, hologram **Weight:** 27.7800 g. **Composition:** 0.9250 Silver 0.8261 oz. ASW **Size:** 40 mm.

Date	Mintage	MS-63	Proof
2007 Proof	45,000	—	50.00

KM# 743 Subject: Vancouver Olympics **Rev:** Athletics pride hologram **Weight:** 27.7800 g. **Composition:** 0.9250 Silver 0.8261 oz. ASW **Size:** 40 mm.

Date	Mintage	MS-63	Proof
2007 Proof	45,000	—	50.00

KM# 744 Subject: Vancouver Olympics **Rev:** Biathleon hologram **Weight:** 27.7500 g. **Composition:** 0.9250 Silver 0.8252 oz. ASW **Size:** 40 mm.

Date	Mintage	MS-63	Proof
2007 Proof	54,000	—	50.00

KM# 745 Subject: Vancouver Olympics **Rev:** Curling hologram **Weight:** 27.7800 g. **Composition:** 0.9250 Silver 0.8261 oz. ASW **Size:** 40 mm.

Date	Mintage	MS-63	Proof
2007 Proof	—	—	50.00

KM# 746 Subject: Vancouver Olympics **Rev:** Hockey, hologram **Weight:** 27.7800 g. **Composition:** 0.9250 Silver 0.8261 oz. ASW **Size:** 40 mm.

Date	Mintage	MS-63	Proof
2007 Proof	45,000	—	50.00

KM# 814 Subject: Vancouver Olympics **Rev:** Bobsleigh, hologram **Weight:** 27.7800 g. **Composition:** 0.9250 Silver 0.8261 oz. ASW **Size:** 40 mm.

Date	Mintage	MS-63	Proof
2008 Proof	45,000	—	50.00

KM# 815 Subject: Vancouver Olympics **Rev:** Figure skating, hologram **Weight:** 27.7800 g. **Composition:** 0.9250 Silver 0.8261 oz. ASW **Size:** 40 mm.

Date	Mintage	MS-63	Proof
2008 Proof	45,000	—	50.00

KM# 816 Subject: Vancouver Olympics **Rev:** Freestyle skating, hologram **Weight:** 27.7800 g. **Composition:** 0.9250 Silver 0.8261 oz. ASW **Size:** 40 mm.

Date	Mintage	MS-63	Proof
2008 Proof	45,000	—	50.00

KM# 817 Subject: Vancouver Olympics **Rev:** Snowboarding, hologram **Weight:** 27.7800 g. **Composition:** 0.9250 Silver 0.8261 oz. ASW **Size:** 40 mm.

Date	Mintage	MS-63	Proof
2008 Proof	45,000	—	50.00

KM# 818 Subject: Vancouver Olympics **Rev:** Home of the 2010 Olympics **Weight:** 27.7800 g. **Composition:** 0.9250 Silver 0.8261 oz. ASW **Size:** 40 mm.

Date	Mintage	MS-63	Proof
2008 Proof	45,000	—	50.00

KM# 903 Subject: 2010 Vancouver Olympics **Obv:** Bust right **Obv. Designer:** Susanna Blunt

Rev: Cross Country Skiing and hologram at left
Weight: 27.7800 g. **Composition:** 0.9250 Silver
0.8261 oz. ASW **Size:** 40 mm.

Date	Mintage	MS-63	Proof
2009 Proof	45,000	—	50.00

KM# 904 Subject: 2010 Vancouver Olympics
Obv: Bust right **Obv. Designer:** Susanna Blunt
Rev: Olympians holding torch, hologram at left
Weight: 27.7800 g. **Composition:** 0.9250 Silver
0.8261 oz. ASW **Size:** 40 mm.

Date	Mintage	MS-63	Proof
2009 Proof	45,000	—	50.00

KM# 905 Subject: 2010 Vancouver Olympics
Obv: Bust right **Obv. Designer:** Susanna Blunt
Rev: Sled, hologram at left **Weight:** 27.7800 g.
Composition: 0.9250 Silver 0.8261 oz. ASW
Size: 40 mm.

Date	Mintage	MS-63	Proof
2009 Proof	45,000	—	50.00

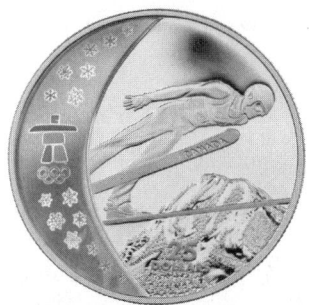

KM# 906 Subject: 2010 Vancouver Olympics
Obv: Bust right **Obv. Designer:** Susanna Blunt
Rev: Ski Jumper, hologram at left **Weight:**
27.7800 g. **Composition:** 0.9250 Silver 0.8261 oz.
ASW **Size:** 40 mm.

Date	Mintage	MS-63	Proof
2009 Proof	45,000	—	50.00

KM# 907 Subject: 2010 Vancouver Olympics
Obv: Bust right **Obv. Designer:** Susanna Blunt
Rev: Speed Skaters, hologram at left **Weight:**
27.7800 g. **Composition:** 0.9250 Silver 0.8261 oz.
ASW **Size:** 40 mm.

Date	Mintage	MS-63	Proof
2009 Proof	45,000	—	50.00

30 DOLLARS

KM# 590 Subject: Pacific Northwest Wood
Carvings **Obv:** Head right **Rev:** Welcome figure
totem pole **Weight:** 31.5000 g. **Composition:**
0.9250 Silver 0.9368 oz. ASW

Date	Mintage	MS-63	Proof
2006 Proof	9,904	—	55.00

KM# 668 Subject: Canadarm and Col. C. Hadfield
Obv: Head right **Rev:** Hologram of Canadarm
Weight: 31.5000 g. **Composition:** 0.9250 Silver
0.9368 oz. ASW

Date	Mintage	MS-63	Proof
2006 Proof	9,357	—	60.00

KM# 669   Subject: National War Memorial **Obv:** Head right **Rev:** Statue of three soldiers **Weight:** 31.5000 g. **Composition:** 0.9250 Silver 0.9368 oz. ASW

Date	Mintage	MS-63	Proof
2006 Proof	8,876	—	80.00

KM# 670   Subject: Beaumont Hamel Newfoundland **Obv:** Head right **Rev:** Caribou statue on rock outcrop **Weight:** 31.5000 g. **Composition:** 0.9250 Silver 0.9368 oz. ASW

Date	Mintage	MS-63	Proof
2006 Proof	15,325	—	75.00

KM# 671   Subject: Dog Sled Team **Obv:** Head right **Rev:** Colorized **Weight:** 31.5000 g. **Composition:** 0.9250 Silver 0.9368 oz. ASW

Date	Mintage	MS-63	Proof
2006 Proof	7,384	—	80.00

KM# 739   Rev: Niagra Falls panoramic hologram **Weight:** 31.5000 g. **Composition:** 0.9250 Silver 0.9368 oz. ASW **Size:** 40 mm.

Date	Mintage	MS-63	Proof
2007 Proof	5,181	—	50.00

KM# 741   Rev: War Memorial, Vimy Ridge **Weight:** 31.5000 g. **Composition:** 0.9250 Silver 0.9368 oz. ASW **Size:** 40 mm.

Date	Mintage	MS-63	Proof
2007 Proof	5,190	—	75.00

KM# 819   Rev: IMAX **Weight:** 31.5000 g. **Composition:** 0.9250 Silver 0.9368 oz. ASW **Size:** 40 mm.

Date	Mintage	MS-63	Proof
2008 Proof	—	—	70.00

KM# 895   Subject: International year of astronomy **Obv:** Bust right **Obv. Legend:** Elizabeth II 30 Dollars DG Regina **Obv. Designer:** Susanna Blunt **Rev:** Observatory with planets and colored sky **Rev. Legend:** Canada **Rev. Designer:** Colin Mayne **Weight:** 33.7500 g. **Composition:** 0.9250 Silver 1.0037 oz. ASW **Size:** 40 mm.

Date	Mintage	MS-63	Proof
2009 Proof	10,000	—	75.00

50 DOLLARS

KM# 566   Subject: WWII **Obv:** Head right **Rev:** Large V and three portraits **Weight:** 12.0000 g. **Composition:** 0.5833 Gold 0.2250 oz. AGW **Size:** 27 mm.

Date	Mintage	MS-63	Proof
2005 Specimen	4,000	—	300

KM# 672   Subject: Constellation in Spring sky position **Rev:** Large Bear at top **Weight:** 31.1600 g. **Composition:** 0.9995 Palladium 1.0013 oz.

Date	Mintage	MS-63	Proof
2006 Proof	297	—	1,200

KM# 673   Subject: Constellation in Summer sky position **Rev:** Large Bear at left **Weight:** 31.1600 g. **Composition:** 0.9995 Palladium 1.0013 oz.

Date	Mintage	MS-63	Proof
2006 Proof	296	—	1,200

KM# 674   Subject: Constellation in Autumn sky position **Rev:** Large Bear towards bottom **Weight:** 31.1600 g. **Composition:** 0.9995 Palladium 1.0013 oz.

Date	Mintage	MS-63	Proof
2006 Proof	296	—	1,200

KM# 675 Subject: Constellation in Winter sky position **Rev:** Large Bear towards right **Weight:** 31.1600 g. **Composition:** 0.9995 Palladium 1.0013 oz.

Date	Mintage	MS-63	Proof
2006 Proof	293	—	1,200

KM# 709 Subject: Queen's 60th Wedding Anniversary **Rev:** Coat of Arms and Mascots of Elizabeth and Philip **Weight:** 155.5000 g. **Composition:** 0.9999 Silver 4.9987 oz. ASW

Date	Mintage	MS-63	Proof
2007	4,000	300	—

KM# 783 Subject: Ottawa Mint Centennial 1908-2008 **Rev:** Mint building facade **Weight:** 156.7700 g. **Composition:** 0.9990 Silver 5.0350 oz. ASW **Size:** 65 mm.

Date	Mintage	MS-63	Proof
2008	4,000	400	—

KM# 896 Subject: 150 Anniversary of the start of construction of the parliament buildings **Obv:** Bust right **Obv. Legend:** Elizabeth II Canada DG Regina **Obv. Designer:** Susanna Blunt **Rev:** Incomplete west block, original architecture **Rev. Legend:** 50 Dollars 1859-2009 **Weight:** 156.7700 g. **Composition:** 0.9990 Silver 5.0350 oz. ASW **Size:** 65.25 mm.

Date	Mintage	MS-63	Proof
2009 Proof	2,000	—	200

75 DOLLARS

KM# 567 Subject: Pope John Paul II **Obv:** Head right **Rev:** Pope giving blessing **Weight:** 31.4400 g. **Composition:** 0.4166 Gold 0.4211 oz. AGW

Date	Mintage	MS-63	Proof
2005 Proof	1,870	—	550

KM# 747 Subject: Vancouver Olympics **Rev:** Athletics Pride, multicolor flag **Weight:** 12.0000 g. **Composition:** 0.5830 Gold 0.2249 oz. AGW **Size:** 27 mm.

Date	Mintage	MS-63	Proof
2007 Proof	8,000	—	300

KM# 748 Obv: Bust right **Obv. Designer:** SUsanna Blunt **Rev:** Canada geese in flight left, multicolor **Weight:** 12.0000 g. **Composition:** 0.5830 Gold 0.2249 oz. AGW **Size:** 27 mm.

Date	Mintage	MS-63	Proof
2007 Proof	8,000	—	300

KM# 749 Rev: Mountie, multicolor **Weight:** 12.0000 g. **Composition:** 0.5830 Gold 0.2249 oz. AGW **Size:** 27 mm.

Date	Mintage	MS-63	Proof
2007 Proof	8,000	—	300

KM# 821 Subject: Host Nations of the 2010 Olympics **Obv:** Bust right **Rev:** Four masks **Weight:** 12.0000 g. **Composition:** 0.5830 Gold 0.2249 oz. AGW **Size:** 27 mm.

Date	Mintage	MS-63	Proof
2008 Proof	8,000	—	300

KM# 822 Rev: Four Host Nations emblem, colored **Rev. Designer:** Jody Broomfield **Weight:** 12.0000 g. **Composition:** 0.5830 Gold 0.2249 oz. AGW **Size:** 27 mm.

Date	Mintage	MS-63	Proof
2008 Proof	—	—	300

KM# 908 Subject: 2010 Vancouver Olympics **Obv:** Bust right **Obv. Designer:** Susana Blunt **Rev:** Multicolor moose **Weight:** 12.0000 g. **Composition:** 0.5830 Gold 0.2249 oz. AGW **Size:** 27 mm.

Date	Mintage	MS-63	Proof
2009 Proof	800	—	300

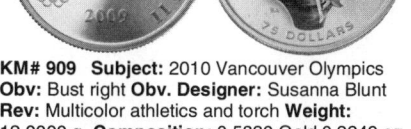

KM# 909 Subject: 2010 Vancouver Olympics **Obv:** Bust right **Obv. Designer:** Susanna Blunt **Rev:** Multicolor athletics and torch **Weight:** 12.0000 g. **Composition:** 0.5830 Gold 0.2249 oz. AGW **Size:** 27 mm.

Date	Mintage	MS-63	Proof
2009 Proof	800	—	300

KM# 910 Subject: 2010 Vancouver Olympics **Obv:** Bust right **Obv. Designer:** Susanna Blunt **Rev:** Wolf, multicolor **Weight:** 12.0000 g. **Composition:** 0.5830 Gold 0.2249 oz. AGW **Size:** 27 mm.

Date	Mintage	MS-63	Proof
2009 Proof	800	—	300

100 DOLLARS

KM# 115 Subject: 1976 Montreal Olympics
Obv: Young bust right, maple leaf below, date at right, beaded borders **Rev:** Past and present Olympic figures, denomination at right
Rev. Designer: Dora dePedery-Hunt
Weight: 13.3375 g. **Composition:** 0.5830 Gold 0.2500 oz. AGW **Size:** 27 mm.

Date	Mintage	MS-63	Proof
1976	650,000	310	—

KM# 116 Subject: 1976 Montreal Olympics
Obv: Young bust right, maple leaf below, date at right, plain borders **Rev:** Past and present Olympic figures, denomination at right **Rev. Designer:** Dora dePedery-Hunt **Weight:** 16.9655 g.
Composition: 0.9170 Gold 0.5002 oz. AGW **Size:** 25 mm.

Date	Mintage	MS-63	Proof
1976 Proof	337,342	—	620

KM# 119 Subject: Queen's silver jubilee
Obv: Young bust right **Rev:** Bouquet of provincial flowers, denomination below **Rev. Designer:** Raymond Lee **Weight:** 16.9655 g. **Composition:** 0.9170 Gold 0.5002 oz. AGW

Date	Mintage	MS-63	Proof
ND(1977) Proof	180,396	—	620

KM# 122 Subject: Canadian unification **Obv:** Young bust right, denomination at left, date upper right **Rev:** Geese (representing the provinces) in flight formation **Rev. Designer:** Roger Savage **Weight:** 16.9655 g. **Composition:** 0.9170 Gold 0.5002 oz. AGW

Date	Mintage	MS-63	Proof
1978 Proof	200,000	—	620

KM# 126 Subject: International Year of the Child **Obv:** Young bust right **Rev:** Children with hands joined divide denomination and date
Rev. Designer: Carola Tietz **Weight:** 16.9655 g. **Composition:** 0.9170 Gold 0.5002 oz. AGW

Date	Mintage	MS-63	Proof
1979 Proof	250,000	—	620

KM# 129 Subject: Arctic Territories **Obv:** Young bust right, denomination at left, date above right **Rev:** Kayaker **Rev. Designer:** Arnaldo Marchetti **Weight:** 16.9655 g. **Composition:** 0.9170 Gold 0.5002 oz. AGW

Date	Mintage	MS-63	Proof
1980 Proof	300,000	—	620

KM# 131 Subject: National anthem **Obv:** Young bust right, denomination at left, date above right **Rev:** Music score on map **Rev. Designer:** Roger Savage **Weight:** 16.9655 g. **Composition:** 0.9170 Gold 0.5002 oz. AGW

Date	Mintage	MS-63	Proof
1981 Proof	102,000	—	620

KM# 137 Subject: New Constitution **Obv:** Young bust right, denomination at left **Rev:** Open book, maple leaf on right page, date below

Rev. Designer: Friedrich Peter **Weight:** 16.9655 g. **Composition:** 0.9170 Gold 0.5002 oz. AGW

Date	Mintage	MS-63	Proof
1982 Proof	121,708	—	620

KM# 139 Subject: 400th Anniversary of St. John's, Newfoundland **Obv:** Young bust right **Rev:** Anchor divides building and ship, denomination below, dates above **Rev. Designer:** John Jaciw **Weight:** 16.9655 g. **Composition:** 0.9170 Gold 0.5002 oz. AGW

Date	Mintage	MS-63	Proof
ND(1983) Proof	83,128	—	620

KM# 142 Subject: Jacques Cartier **Obv:** Young bust right **Rev:** Cartier head on right facing left, ship on left, date lower right, denomination above **Rev. Designer:** Carola Tietz **Weight:** 16.9655 g. **Composition:** 0.9170 Gold 0.5002 oz. AGW

Date	Mintage	MS-63	Proof
ND(1984) Proof	67,662	—	620

KM# 144 Subject: National Parks **Obv:** Young bust right **Rev:** Bighorn sheep, denomination divides dates below **Rev. Designer:** Hector Greville **Weight:** 16.9655 g. **Composition:** 0.9170 Gold 0.5002 oz. AGW

Date	Mintage	MS-63	Proof
ND(1985) Proof	61,332	—	620

KM# 152 Subject: Peace **Obv:** Young bust right **Rev:** Maple leaves and letters intertwined, date at right, denomination below **Rev. Designer:** Dora

dePedery-Hunt **Weight:** 16.9655 g. **Composition:** 0.9170 Gold 0.5002 oz. AGW

Date	Mintage	MS-63	Proof
1986 Proof	76,409	—	620

KM# 158 Subject: 1988 Calgary Olympics **Obv:** Young bust right, maple leaf below, date at right **Rev:** Torch and logo, denomination below **Rev. Designer:** Friedrich Peter **Edge Lettering:** In English and French **Weight:** 13.3375 g. **Composition:** 0.5830 Gold 0.2500 oz. AGW

Date	Mintage	MS-63	Proof
1987 Proof, letter edge	142,750	—	310
1987 Proof, plain edge	Inc. above	—	350

KM# 162 Subject: Bowhead Whales, balaera mysticetus **Rev:** Whales left, date below, within circle, denomination below **Rev. Designer:** Robert R. Carmichael **Weight:** 13.3375 g. **Composition:** 0.5830 Gold 0.2500 oz. AGW

Date	Mintage	MS-63	Proof
1988 Proof	52,594	—	310

KM# 169 Subject: Sainte-Marie **Obv:** Young bust right **Rev:** Huron Indian, Missionary and Mission building, denomination below, dates above **Rev. Designer:** D. J. Craig **Weight:** 13.3375 g. **Composition:** 0.5830 Gold 0.2500 oz. AGW

Date	Mintage	MS-63	Proof
ND(1989) Proof	59,657	—	310

KM# 171 Subject: International Literacy Year **Obv:** Crowned head right, date below **Rev:** Woman

with children, denomination below **Rev. Designer:**
John Mardon **Weight:** 13.3375 g. **Composition:**
0.5830 Gold 0.2500 oz. AGW

Date	Mintage	MS-63	Proof
1990 Proof	49,940	—	310

KM# 180   Subject: S.S. Empress of India **Obv:**
Crowned head right, date below **Rev:** Ship, "SS
Empress", denomination below **Rev. Designer:**
Karsten Smith **Weight:** 13.3375 g. **Composition:**
0.5830 Gold 0.2500 oz. AGW

Date	Mintage	MS-63	Proof
1991 Proof	33,966	—	310

KM# 211   Subject: Montreal **Obv:** Crowned head
right, date below **Rev:** Half figure in foreground with
paper, buildings in back, denomination below
Rev. Designer: Stewart Sherwood
Weight: 13.3375 g. **Composition:** 0.5830 Gold
0.2500 oz. AGW

Date	Mintage	MS-63	Proof
1992 Proof	28,162	—	310

KM# 245   Subject: Antique Automobiles
Obv: Crowned head right, date below **Rev:** German
Bene Victoria; Simmonds Steam Carriage; French
Panhard-Levassor's Daimler; American Duryea;
Canadian Featherston Haugh in center,
denomination below **Rev. Designer:** John Mardon
Weight: 13.3375 g. **Composition:** 0.5830 Gold
0.2500 oz. AGW

Date	Mintage	MS-63	Proof
1993 Proof	25,971	—	310

KM# 249   Subject: World War II Home Front
Obv: Crowned head right, date below **Rev:** Kneeling
figure working on plane, denomination below
Rev. Designer: Paraskeva Clark
Weight: 13.3375 g. **Composition:** 0.5830 Gold
0.2500 oz. AGW

Date	Mintage	MS-63	Proof
1994 Proof	16,201	—	310

KM# 260   Subject: Louisbourg **Obv:** Crowned
head right, date below **Rev:** Ship and buildings,
dates and denomination above **Rev. Designer:**
Lewis Parker **Weight:** 13.3375 g. **Composition:**
0.5830 Gold 0.2500 oz. AGW

Date	Mintage	MS-63	Proof
1995 Proof	16,916	—	310

KM# 273   Subject: Klondike Gold Rush Centennial
Obv: Crowned head right, date below **Rev:** Scene
of Kate Carmack panning for gold, dates above,
denomination lower left **Rev. Designer:** John
Mantha **Weight:** 13.3375 g. **Composition:** 0.5830
Gold 0.2500 oz. AGW

Date	Mintage	MS-63	Proof
ND(1996) Proof	17,973	—	310

KM# 287   Subject: Alexander Graham Bell **Obv:**
Crowned head right, date below **Rev:** A. G. Bell head
right, globe and telephone, denomination upper right
Rev. Designer: Donald H. Carley **Weight:** 13.3375 g.
Composition: 0.5830 Gold 0.2500 oz. AGW

Date	Mintage	MS-63	Proof
1997 Proof	14,775	—	310

KM# 307 Subject: Discovery of Insulin **Obv:** Crowned head right, date below **Rev:** Nobel prize award figurine, dates at left, denomination at right **Rev. Designer:** Robert R. Carmichael **Weight:** 13.3375 g. **Comp:** 0.5830 Gold 0.2500 oz. AGW

Date	Mintage	MS-63	Proof
1998 Proof	11,220	—	310

KM# 341 Subject: 50th Anniversary Newfoundland Unity With Canada **Obv:** Crowned head right, date below **Rev:** Two designs at front, mountains in back, denomination below **Rev. Designer:** Jackie Gale-Vaillancourt **Weight:** 13.3375 g. **Composition:** 0.5830 Gold 0.2500 oz. AGW

Date	Mintage	MS-63	Proof
1999 Proof	10,242	—	310

KM# 402 Subject: McClure's Arctic expedition **Obv:** Crowned head right, date below **Rev:** Six men pulling supply sled to an icebound ship, denomination below **Rev. Designer:** John Mardon **Edge:** Reeded **Weight:** 13.3375 g. **Composition:** 0.5830 Gold 0.2500 oz. AGW **Size:** 27 mm.

Date	Mintage	MS-63	Proof
2000 Proof	9,767	—	310

KM# 416 Subject: Library of Parliament **Obv:** Crowned head right **Obv. Designer:** Dora dePedery-Hunt **Rev:** Statue in domed building **Rev. Designer:** Robert R. Carmichael **Edge:** Reeded **Weight:** 13.3375 g. **Composition:** 0.5830 Gold 0.2500 oz. AGW **Size:** 27 mm.

Date	Mintage	MS-63	Proof
2001 Proof	8,080	—	320

KM# 452 Subject: Discovery of Oil in Alberta **Obv:** Crowned head right **Rev:** Oil well with black oil spill on ground **Rev. Designer:** John Marden **Edge:** Reeded **Weight:** 13.3375 g. **Composition:** 0.5830 Gold 0.2500 oz. AGW **Size:** 27 mm.

Date	Mintage	MS-63	Proof
2002 Proof	9,994	—	325

KM# 486 Subject: 100th Anniversary of the Discovery of Marquis Wheat **Obv:** Head right **Weight:** 13.3375 g. **Composition:** 0.5830 Gold 0.2500 oz. AGW

Date	Mintage	MS-63	Proof
2003 Proof	9,993	—	325

KM# 528 Subject: St. Lawrence Seaway, 50th Anniversary **Obv:** Head right **Weight:** 12.0000 g. **Composition:** 0.5830 Gold 0.2249 oz. AGW

Date	Mintage	MS-63	Proof
2004 Proof	7,454	—	300

KM# 616 Subject: Supreme Court **Obv:** Head right **Rev:** Draped figure with sword **Weight:** 12.0000 g. **Composition:** 0.5833 Gold 0.2250 oz. AGW

Date	Mintage	MS-63	Proof
2005 Proof	5,092	—	300

KM# 591 Subject: 75th Anniversary, Hockey Classic between Royal Military College and U.S. Military Academy **Obv:** Head right **Weight:** 12.0000 g. **Composition:** 0.5833 Gold 0.2250 oz. AGW

Date	Mintage	MS-63	Proof
2006 Proof	5,439	—	300

KM# 593 Subject: 130th Anniversary, Supreme Court **Obv:** Head right **Weight:** 12.0000 g. **Composition:** 0.5833 Gold 0.2250 oz. AGW

Date	Mintage	MS-63	Proof
2006 Proof	5,092	—	420

KM# 689 Subject: 140th Anniversary Dominion **Obv:** Head right **Weight:** 12.0000 g. **Composition:** 0.5833 Gold 0.2250 oz. AGW **Size:** 27 mm.

Date	Mintage	MS-63	Proof
2007 Proof	4,453	—	300

KM# 823 Rev: Fraser River **Weight:** 12.0000 g. **Composition:** 0.5830 Gold 0.2249 oz. AGW **Size:** 27 mm.

Date	Mintage	MS-63	Proof
2008 Proof	5,000	—	350

100 DOLLARS

KM# 898 Subject: 10th Anniversary of Nunavut **Obv:** Bust right **Obv. Legend:** Elizabeth II DG Regina **Obv. Designer:** Susanna Blunt **Rev:** Inuit dancer with 3 faces behind **Rev. Legend:** Canada 100 Dollars 1999-2009 **Weight:** 12.0000 g. **Composition:** 0.5830 Gold 0.2249 oz. AGW **Size:** 27 mm.

Date	Mintage	MS-63	Proof
2009 Proof	5,000	—	500

150 DOLLARS

KM# 388 Subject: Year of the Dragon **Obv:** Crowned head right **Rev. Designer:** Harvey Chan **Weight:** 13.6100 g. **Composition:** 0.7500 Gold 0.3282 oz. AGW

Date	Mintage	MS-63	Proof
2000 Proof	8,851	—	650

KM# 417 Subject: Year of the Snake **Obv:** Crowned head right **Obv. Designer:** Dora dePedery-Hunt **Rev:** Multicolor snake hologram **Edge:** Reeded **Weight:** 13.6100 g. **Composition:** 0.7500 Gold 0.3282 oz. AGW **Size:** 28 mm.

Date	Mintage	MS-63	Proof
2001 Proof	6,571	—	425

KM# 604 Obv: Head right **Rev:** Stylized horse left **Weight:** 13.6100 g. **Composition:** 0.7500 Gold 0.3282 oz. AGW

Date	Mintage	MS-63	Proof
2002 Proof	6,843	—	425

KM# 487 Subject: Year of the Ram **Obv:** Crowned head right **Rev:** Stylized ram left, hologram **Rev. Designer:** Harvey Chan **Weight:** 13.6100 g. **Composition:** 0.7500 Gold 0.3282 oz. AGW

Date	Mintage	MS-63	Proof
2003 Proof	3,927	—	425

KM# 614 Obv: Head right **Rev:** Year of the Monkey, hologram **Weight:** 13.6100 g. **Composition:** 0.7500 Gold 0.3282 oz. AGW

Date	Mintage	MS-63	Proof
2004 Proof	3,392	—	425

KM# 568 Subject: Year of the Rooster **Obv:** Head right **Rev:** Rooster left, hologram **Weight:** 13.6100 g. **Composition:** 0.7500 Gold 0.3282 oz. AGW

Date	Mintage	MS-63	Proof
2005 Proof	3,731	—	425

KM# 592 Subject: Year of the Dog, hologram **Obv:** Head right **Rev:** Stylized dog left **Weight:** 13.6100 g. **Composition:** 0.7500 Gold 0.3282 oz. AGW

Date	Mintage	MS-63	Proof
2006 Proof	2,604	—	425

KM# 733 Subject: Year of the Pig **Obv:** Head right **Rev:** Pig in center with Chinese lunar calendar around, hologram **Weight:** 11.8400 g. **Composition:** 0.7500 Gold 0.2855 oz. AGW **Size:** 28 mm.

Date	Mintage	MS-63	Proof
2007 Proof	4,888	—	450

KM# 802 Subject: Year of the Rat **Rev:** Rat, hologram **Weight:** 11.8400 g. **Composition:** 0.7500 Gold 0.2855 oz. AGW **Size:** 28 mm.

Date	Mintage	MS-63	Proof
2008 Proof	4,888	—	450

KM# 899 Subject: Blessings of wealth **Obv:** Bust right **Obv. Legend:** Elizabeth II, DG Regina, Fine Gold 99999 or PUR **Obv. Designer:** Susanna Blunt **Rev:** Three goldfish surround peony, clouds **Rev. Legend:** Canada 150 Dollars (Chinese symbols of good fortune) **Rev. Designer:** Harvey Chan **Edge:** Scalloped **Weight:** 10.4000 g. **Composition:** 0.9990 Gold 0.3340 oz. AGW **Size:** 22.5 mm.

Date	Mintage	MS-63	Proof
2009 Proof	50,000	—	650

KM# 867 Subject: Year of the Ox **Rev:** Ox, hologram **Weight:** 11.8400 g. **Composition:** 0.7500 Gold 0.2855 oz. AGW **Size:** 28 mm.

Date	Mintage	MS-63	Proof
2009 Proof	—	—	450

175 DOLLARS

KM# 217 Subject: 1992 Olympics **Obv:** Crowned head right, date at left, denomination below **Rev:** Passing the torch **Rev. Designer:** Stewart Sherwood **Edge:** Lettered **Weight:** 16.9700 g. **Composition:** 0.9170 Gold 0.5003 oz. AGW

Date	Mintage	MS-63	Proof
1992 Proof	22,092	—	620

200 DOLLARS

KM# 178 Subject: Canadian flag silver jubilee **Obv:** Crowned head right, date below **Rev:** People with flag, denomination above **Rev. Designer:**

Stewart Sherwood **Weight:** 17.1350 g.
Composition: 0.9166 Gold 0.5049 oz. AGW
Size: 29 mm.

Date	Mintage	MS-63	Proof
1990 Proof	20,980	—	625

KM# 202 Subject: Hockey **Obv:** Crowned head
right **Rev:** Hockey players, denomination above
Rev. Designer: Stewart Sherwood **Weight:**
17.1350 g. **Composition:** 0.9166 Gold 0.5049 oz.
AGW **Size:** 29 mm.

Date	Mintage	MS-63	Proof
1991 Proof	10,215	—	625

KM# 230 Subject: Niagara Falls **Obv:** Crowned
head right **Rev:** Niagara Falls, denomination above
Rev. Designer: John Mardon **Weight:** 17.1350 g.
Composition: 0.9166 Gold 0.5049 oz. AGW
Size: 29 mm.

Date	Mintage	MS-63	Proof
1992 Proof	9,465	—	625

KM# 244 Subject: Mounted police **Obv:** Crowned
head right, date below **Rev:** Mountie with children,
denomination above **Rev. Designer:** Stewart
Sherwood **Weight:** 17.1350 g. **Composition:**
0.9166 Gold 0.5049 oz. AGW **Size:** 29 mm.

Date	Mintage	MS-63	Proof
1993 Proof	10,807	—	625

KM# 250 Subject: Interpretation of 1908 novel by
Lucy Maud Montgomery, 1874-1942, Anne of Green

Gables **Obv:** Crowned head right **Rev:** Figure sitting
in window, denomination above **Rev. Designer:**
Phoebe Gilman **Weight:** 17.1350 g. **Composition:**
0.9166 Gold 0.5049 oz. AGW **Size:** 29 mm.

Date	Mintage	MS-63	Proof
1994 Proof	10,655	—	625

KM# 265 Subject: Maple-syrup production **Obv:**
Crowned head right, date below **Rev:** Maple syrup
making, denomination at right **Rev. Designer:** J. D.
Mantha **Weight:** 17.1350 g. **Composition:** 0.9166
Gold 0.5049 oz. AGW **Size:** 29 mm.

Date	Mintage	MS-63	Proof
1995 Proof	6,579	—	625

KM# 275 Subject: Transcontinental Canadian
Railway **Obv:** Crowned head right, date below **Rev:**
Train going through mountains, denomination below
Rev. Designer: Suzanne Duranceau **Weight:**
17.1350 g. **Composition:** 0.9166 Gold 0.5049 oz.
AGW **Size:** 29 mm.

Date	Mintage	MS-63	Proof
1996 Proof	8,047	—	625

KM# 288 Subject: Haida mask **Obv:** Crowned
head right, date below **Rev:** Haida mask
Rev. Designer: Robert Davidson **Weight:**
17.1350 g. **Composition:** 0.9166 Gold 0.5049 oz.
AGW **Size:** 29 mm.

Date	Mintage	MS-63	Proof
1997 Proof	11,610	—	625

200 DOLLARS

KM# 317 Subject: Legendary white buffalo
Obv: Crowned head right, date below **Rev:** Buffalo
Rev. Designer: Alex Janvler **Weight:** 17.1350 g.
Composition: 0.9166 Gold 0.5049 oz. AGW
Size: 29 mm.

Date	Mintage	MS-63	Proof
1998 Proof	7,149	—	625

KM# 358 Subject: Mikmaq butterfly
Obv: Crowned head right **Rev:** Butterfly within
design **Rev. Designer:** Alan Syliboy **Weight:**
17.1350 g. **Composition:** 0.9166 Gold 0.5049 oz.
AGW **Size:** 29 mm.

Date	Mintage	MS-63	Proof
1999 Proof	6,510	—	625

KM# 403 Subject: Motherhood **Obv:** Crowned
head right, date above, denomination at right
Rev: Inuit mother with infant **Rev. Designer:**
Germaine Arnaktauyak **Edge:** Reeded **Weight:**
17.1350 g. **Composition:** 0.9166 Gold 0.5049 oz.
AGW **Size:** 29 mm.

Date	Mintage	MS-63	Proof
2000 Proof	6,284	—	625

KM# 418 Subject: Cornelius D. Krieghoff's "The
Habitant farm" **Obv:** Queens head right **Edge:**

Reeded **Weight:** 17.1350 g. **Composition:** 0.9166
Gold 0.5049 oz. AGW **Size:** 29 mm.

Date	Mintage	MS-63	Proof
2001 Proof	5,406	—	675

KM# 466 Subject: Thomas Thompson "The Jack
Pine" (1916-17) **Obv:** Crowned head right **Weight:**
17.1350 g. **Composition:** 0.9166 Gold 0.5049 oz.
AGW **Size:** 29 mm.

Date	Mintage	MS-63	Proof
2002 Proof	5,264	—	675

KM# 488 Subject: Fitzgerald's "Houses" (1929)
Obv: Crowned head right **Rev:** House with trees
Weight: 17.1350 g. **Composition:** 0.9166 Gold
0.5049 oz. AGW

Date	Mintage	MS-63	Proof
2003 Proof	4,118	—	675

KM# 516 Subject: "Fragments" **Obv:** Crowned
head right **Rev:** Fragmented face **Edge:** Reeded
Weight: 16.0000 g. **Composition:** 0.9166 Gold
0.4715 oz. AGW **Size:** 29 mm.

Date	Mintage	MS-63	Proof
2004 Proof	3,917	—	625

KM# 569 Subject: Fur traders **Obv:** Head right
Rev: Men in canoe riding wave **Weight:** 16.0000 g.
Composition: 0.9166 Gold 0.4715 oz. AGW

Date	Mintage	MS-63	Proof
2005 Proof	3,669	—	625

KM# 594 Subject: Timber trade **Obv:** Head right
Rev: Lumberjacks felling tree **Weight:** 16.0000 g.
Composition: 0.9166 Gold 0.4715 oz. AGW

Date	Mintage	MS-63	Proof
2006 Proof	3,185	—	625

KM# 691 Subject: Fishing Trade **Obv:** Head right
Weight: 16.0000 g. **Composition:** 0.9166 Gold
0.4715 oz. AGW

Date	Mintage	MS-63	Proof
2007 Proof	4,000	—	625

KM# 750 Rev: Three maple leaves **Weight:**
31.1500 g. **Composition:** 1.0000 Gold 1.0014 oz.
AGW **Size:** 30 mm.

Date	Mintage	MS-63	Proof
2007 Proof	500	—	1,275

KM# 824 Subject: Commerce **Rev:** Horse drawn
plow **Weight:** 16.0000 g. **Composition:** 0.9170
Gold 0.4717 oz. AGW **Size:** 29 mm.

Date	Mintage	MS-63	Proof
2008 Proof	4,000	—	625

KM# 894 Subject: Coal mining trade **Obv:** Bust right **Obv. Legend:** Elizabeth II DG Regina **Obv. Designer:** Susanna Blunt **Rev:** Miner pushing cart with black coal **Rev. Legend:** Canada 200 Dollars **Rev. Designer:** John Marder **Weight:** 16.0000 g. **Composition:** 0.9160 Gold 0.4712 oz. AGW **Size:** 29 mm.

Date	Mintage	MS-63	Proof
2009 Proof	4,000	—	750

250 DOLLARS

KM# 677 Subject: Dog Sled Team **Weight:** 45.0000 g. **Composition:** 0.5833 Gold 0.8439 oz. AGW

Date	Mintage	MS-63	Proof
2006 Proof	953	—	1,100

KM# 751 Subject: Vancouver Olympics, 2010 **Rev:** Early Canada motif **Weight:** 1000.0000 g. **Composition:** 0.9999 Silver 32.146 oz. ASW **Size:** 101.6 mm. **Note:** Illustration reduced.

Date	Mintage	MS-63	Proof
2007 Proof	2,500	—	1,250

KM# 833 Subject: Vancouver Olympics 2010 **Rev:** Towards confederation **Weight:** 1000.0000 g. **Composition:** 0.9990 Silver 32.117 oz. ASW **Size:** 101.6 mm. **Note:** Illustration reduced.

Date	Mintage	MS-63	Proof
2008 Proof	2,500	—	1,200

KM# 913 Obv: Bust right **Obv. Designer:** Susanna Blunt **Rev:** Mask with fish - Surviving the flood **Weight:** 1000.0000 g. **Composition:** 0.9999 Silver 32.146 oz. ASW **Note:** Illustration reduced.

Date	Mintage	MS-63	Proof
2009 Proof	—	—	5,000

KM# 878 Subject: Vancouver Olympics, 2010 **Rev:** Surviving the flood **Weight:** 1000.0000 g. **Composition:** 0.9990 Silver 32.117 oz. ASW **Size:** 101.6 mm. **Note:** Illustration reduced.

Date	Mintage	MS-63	Proof
2009 Proof	2,500	—	1,200

300 DOLLARS

KM# 501 Obv: Triple cameo portraits of Queen Elizabeth II by Gillick, Machin and de Pedery-Hunt, each in 14K gold, rose in center **Rev:** Dates "1952-2002" and denomination in legend, rose in center **Weight:** 60.0000 g. **Composition:** 0.5833 Gold 1.1252 oz. AGW **Size:** 50 mm. **Note:** Housed in anodized gold-colored aluminum box with cherrywood stained siding

Date	Mintage	MS-63	Proof
ND(2002) Proof	999	—	1,500

KM# 517 Obv: Four coinage portraits of Elizabeth II **Rev:** Canadian arms above value **Edge:** Plain **Weight:** 60.0000 g. **Composition:** 0.5833 Gold 1.1252 oz. AGW **Size:** 50 mm.

Date	Mintage	MS-63	Proof
2004 Proof	998	—	1,500

KM# 570.1 Subject: Standard Time - 4 AM Pacific **Obv:** Head right **Rev:** Roman numeral clock with world inside **Weight:** 60.0000 g. **Composition:** 0.5833 Gold 1.1252 oz. AGW

Date	Mintage	MS-63	Proof
2005 Proof	200	—	1,500

KM# 596 Subject: Shinplaster **Obv:** Head right **Rev:** Britannia bust, spear over shoulder **Weight:** 60.0000 g. **Composition:** 0.5833 Gold 1.1252 oz. AGW

Date	Mintage	MS-63	Proof
2005 Proof	994	—	1,500

KM# 600 Subject: Welcome Figure Totem Pole **Obv:** Head right **Rev:** Men with totem pole **Weight:** 60.0000 g. **Composition:** 0.5833 Gold 1.1252 oz. AGW

Date	Mintage	MS-63	Proof
2005 Proof	947	—	1,500

KM# 570.2 Subject: Standard Time - Mountian 5 AM **Obv:** Head right **Rev:** Roman numeral clock with world inside. **Weight:** 60.0000 g. **Composition:** 0.5830 Gold 1.1246 oz. AGW

Date	Mintage	MS-63	Proof
2005 Proof	200	—	1,500

KM# 570.3 Subject: Standard Time - Central 6 PM **Obv:** Head right **Rev:** Roman numeral clock with world inside **Weight:** 60.0000 g. **Composition:** 0.5830 Gold 1.1246 oz. AGW

Date	Mintage	MS-63	Proof
2005 Proof	200	—	1,500

KM# 570.4 Subject: Standard Time - Eastern 7 AM **Obv:** Head right **Rev:** Roman numeral clock with world inside **Weight:** 60.0000 g. **Composition:** 0.5830 Gold 1.1246 oz. AGW

Date	Mintage	MS-63	Proof
2005 Proof	200	—	1,500

KM# 570.5 Subject: Standard Time - Atlantic 8 AM **Obv:** Head right **Rev:** Roman numeral clock with world inside **Weight:** 60.0000 g. **Composition:** 0.5830 Gold 1.1246 oz. AGW

Date	Mintage	MS-63	Proof
2005 Proof	200	—	1,500

KM# 570.6 Subject: Standard Time - Newfoundland 8:30 **Obv:** Head right **Rev:** Roman numeral clock with world inside **Weight:** 60.0000 g. **Composition:** 0.5830 Gold 1.1246 oz. AGW

Date	Mintage	MS-63	Proof
2005 Proof	200	—	1,500

KM# 595 Subject: Shinplaster **Obv:** Head right **Rev:** Seated Britannia with shield **Weight:** 60.0000 g. **Composition:** 0.5833 Gold 1.1252 oz. AGW

Date	Mintage	MS-63	Proof
2006 Proof	940	—	1,500

KM# 678 Subject: Canadam and Col. C. Hadfield **Rev:** Hologram of Canadarm **Weight:** 45.0000 g. **Composition:** 0.5833 Gold 0.8439 oz. AGW

Date	Mintage	MS-63	Proof
2006 Proof	581	—	1,100

KM# 679 Subject: Queen Elizabeth's 80th Birthday **Rev:** State Crown, colorized **Weight:** 60.0000 g. **Composition:** 0.5833 Gold 1.1252 oz. AGW

Date	Mintage	MS-63	Proof
2006 Proof	996	—	1,500

KM# 680 Subject: Crystal Snowflake **Weight:** 60.0000 g. **Composition:** 0.5833 Gold 1.1252 oz. AGW

Date	Mintage	MS-63	Proof
2006 Proof	998	—	1,500

KM# 692 Subject: Shinplaster **Rev:** 1923 25 cent bank note **Weight:** 60.0000 g. **Composition:** 0.5833 Gold 1.1252 oz. AGW

Date	Mintage	MS-63	Proof
2007 Proof	778	—	1,500

KM# 740 Rev: Canadian Rockies panoramic hologram **Weight:** 45.0000 g. **Composition:** 0.5830 Gold 0.8434 oz. AGW **Size:** 40 mm.

Date	Mintage	MS-63	Proof
2007 Proof	511	—	1,100

KM# 752 Subject: Vancouver Olympics **Rev:** Olympic ideals, classic figures and torch **Weight:** 60.0000 g. **Composition:** 0.5830 Gold 1.1246 oz. AGW **Size:** 50 mm.

Date	Mintage	MS-63	Proof
2007 Proof	2,500	—	1,500

KM# 825 Rev: Alberta Coat of Arms **Weight:** 45.0000 g. **Composition:** 0.5830 Gold 0.8434 oz. AGW **Size:** 40 mm.

Date	Mintage	MS-63	Proof
2008 Proof	—	—	1,100

KM# 826 Rev: Newfoundland and Labrador Coat of Arms **Weight:** 45.0000 g. **Composition:** 0.5830 Gold 0.8434 oz. AGW **Size:** 40 mm.

Date	Mintage	MS-63	Proof
2008 Proof	1,000	—	1,250

KM# 827 Subject: Canadian achievements **Rev:** IMAX **Weight:** 45.0000 g. **Composition:** 0.5830 Gold 0.8434 oz. AGW **Size:** 40 mm.

Date	Mintage	MS-63	Proof
2008 Proof	—	—	1,100

KM# 828 Rev: Four seasons moon mask **Weight:** 45.0000 g. **Composition:** 0.5830 Gold 0.8434 oz. AGW **Size:** 40 mm.

Date	Mintage	MS-63	Proof
2008 Proof	1,200	—	1,100

KM# 829 Rev: Cedar Summer Moon mask carved by Judy Broomfield **Weight:** 60.0000 g. **Composition:** 0.5830 Gold 1.1246 oz. AGW **Size:** 50 mm.

Date	Mintage	MS-63	Proof
2008 Proof	—	—	1,100

KM# 830 Subject: Vancouver Olympics **Rev:** Olympic competition, athletics and torch **Weight:** 60.0000 g. **Composition:** 0.5830 Gold 1.1246 oz. AGW **Size:** 50 mm.

Date	Mintage	MS-63	Proof
2008 Proof	—	—	1,500

KM# 900 Subject: Yukon Coat of Arms **Obv:** Bust right **Obv. Legend:** Elizabeth II DG Regina **Obv. Designer:** Susanna Blunt **Rev:** Yukon Coat of Arms **Rev. Legend:** Canada 300 Dollars **Weight:** 60.0000 g. **Composition:** 0.5830 Gold 1.1246 oz. AGW **Size:** 50 mm.

Date	Mintage	MS-63	Proof
2009 Proof	1,000	—	1,650

KM# 404 Obv: Crowned head right **Rev:** Three Pacific Dogwood flowers **Rev. Designer:** Caren Heine **Edge:** Reeded **Weight:** 38.0500 g. **Composition:** 0.9999 Gold 1.2232 oz. AGW **Size:** 34 mm.

Date	Mintage	MS-63	Proof
2000 Proof	1,506	—	1,550

KM# 911 Subject: 2010 Vancouver Olympics **Obv:** Bust right **Obv. Designer:** Susanna Blunt **Rev:** Athletics with torch - Olympic firendship **Weight:** 60.0000 g. **Composition:** 0.5830 Gold 1.1246 oz. AGW **Size:** 50 mm.

Date	Mintage	MS-63	Proof
2009 Proof	—	—	1,500

KM# 877 Rev: Summer moon mask, enameled **Weight:** 45.0000 g. **Composition:** 0.5830 Gold 0.8434 oz. AGW **Size:** 40 mm.

Date	Mintage	MS-63	Proof
2009 Proof	—	—	1,100

350 DOLLARS

KM# 433 Subject: The Mayflower Flower

Obv: Crowned head right **Rev:** Two flowers **Rev. Designer:** Bonnie Ross **Edge:** Reeded **Weight:** 38.0500 g. **Composition:** 0.9999 Gold 1.2232 oz. AGW **Size:** 34 mm.

Date	Mintage	MS-63	Proof
2001 Proof	1,988	—	1,600

KM# 502 Subject: The Wild Rose **Obv:** Crowned head right **Obv. Designer:** Dora de Pedery-Hunt **Rev:** Wild rose plant **Rev. Designer:** Dr. Andreas Kare Hellum **Weight:** 38.0500 g. **Composition:** 0.9999 Gold 1.2232 oz. AGW **Size:** 34 mm.

Date	Mintage	MS-63	Proof
2002 Proof	2,001	—	1,600

KM# 308 Subject: Flowers of Canada's Coat of Arms **Obv:** Crowned head right, date behind, denomination at bottom **Rev:** Flowers **Rev. Designer:** Pierre Leduc **Weight:** 38.0500 g. **Composition:** 0.9999 Gold 1.2232 oz. AGW

Date	Mintage	MS-63	Proof
1998 Proof	664	—	1,550

KM# 370 Rev: Lady's slipper **Rev. Designer:** Henry Purdy **Weight:** 38.0500 g. **Composition:** 0.9999 Gold 1.2232 oz. AGW

Date	Mintage	MS-63	Proof
1999 Proof	1,990	—	1,550

KM# 504 Subject: The White Trillium **Obv:** Crowned head right **Obv. Designer:** Dora de Pedery-Hunt **Rev:** White Trillium **Weight:** 38.0500 g. **Composition:** 0.9999 Gold 1.2232 oz. AGW **Size:** 34 mm.

Date	Mintage	MS-63	Proof
2003 Proof	1,865	—	1,600

KM# 601 Subject: Western Red Lilly **Obv:** Head right **Rev:** Western Red Lilies **Weight:** 38.0500 g. **Composition:** 0.9999 Gold 1.2232 oz. AGW

Date	Mintage	MS-63	Proof
2005 Proof	1,634	—	1,600

KM# 626 Subject: Iris Vericolor **Obv:** Crowned head right **Rev:** Iris **Weight:** 38.0500 g. **Composition:** 0.9999 Gold 1.2232 oz. AGW **Size:** 34 mm.

Date	Mintage	MS-63	Proof
2006 Proof	1,995	—	1,600

KM# 754 Rev: Purple violet **Weight:** 35.0000 g. **Composition:** 0.9999 Gold 1.1251 oz. AGW **Size:** 34 mm.

Date	Mintage	MS-63	Proof
2007 Proof	1,171	—	1,500

KM# 832 Rev: Purple saxifrage **Weight:** 35.0000 g. **Composition:** 0.9999 Gold 1.1251 oz. AGW **Size:** 34 mm.

Date	Mintage	MS-63	Proof
2008 Proof	1,400	—	1,500

KM# 901 Subject: Pitcher plant **Obv:** Bust right **Obv. Legend:** Elizabeth II Canada DG Regina Fine Gold 350 Dollars or PUR 99999 **Obv. Designer:** Susana Blunt **Rev:** Cluster of pitcher flowers **Rev. Legend:** Julie Wilson **Weight:** 35.0000 g. **Composition:** 0.9990 Gold 1.1241 oz. AGW **Size:** 34 mm.

Date	Mintage	MS-63	Proof
2009 Proof	1,400	—	2,000

500 DOLLARS

KM# 710 Subject: Queen's 60th Wedding **Rev:** Coat of Arms and Mascots of Elizabeth and Philip **Weight:** 155.5000 g. **Composition:** 0.9999 Gold 4.9987 oz. AGW **Size:** 60 mm.

Date	Mintage	MS-63	Proof
2007	198	8,500	—

KM# 782 Subject: Ottawa Mint Centennial 1908-2008 **Rev:** Mint building facade **Weight:** 155.7600 g. **Composition:** 0.9990 Gold 5.0026 oz. AGW **Size:** 60 mm.

Date	Mintage	MS-63	Proof
2008	250	8,500	—

KM# 897 Subject: 150th Anniversary of the start of construction of the Parliament Buildings **Obv:** Bust right **Rev:** Incomplete west block, original architecture **Rev. Legend:** 500 Dollars 1859-2009 **Weight:** 156.0500 g. **Composition:** 0.9990 Gold 5.0119 oz. AGW **Size:** 60.15 mm.

Date	Mintage	MS-63	Proof
2009 Proof	200	—	9,500

2500 DOLLARS

KM# 902 Subject: History and Culture Collection, Modern Canada **Obv:** Bust right **Obv. Legend:** Vancouver 2010, 2500 Dollars, Elizabeth II **Obv. Designer:** Susanna Blunt **Rev:** Canadian landscape with modern elements **Weight:** 1000.0000 g. **Composition:** 0.9990 Silver 32.117 oz. ASW **Size:** 101.6 mm.

Date	Mintage	MS-63	Proof
2009 Proof	2,500	—	750

KM# 902a Subject: History and Culture Collection, Modern Canada **Obv:** Bust right **Obv. Legend:** Vancouver 2010, 2500 Dollars, Elizabeth II **Obv. Designer:** Susana Blunt **Rev:** Canadian landscape with modern elements **Weight:** 1000.0000 g. **Composition:** 0.9990 Gold 32.117 oz. AGW **Size:** 101.6 mm.

Date	Mintage	MS-63	Proof
2009 Proof	50	—	45,000

KM# 912 Obv: Bust right **Obv. Designer:** Susanna Blunt **Rev:** Mask with fish - Surviving the flood **Weight:** 1000.0000 g. **Composition:** 0.9999 Gold 32.146 oz. AGW **Size:** 101 mm. **Note:** Illustration reduced.

Date	Mintage	MS-63	Proof
2009 Proof	—	—	46,000

SILVER BULLION COINAGE

DOLLAR

KM# 617 Obv: Crowned head right **Rev:** Holographic Maple leaf **Edge:** Reeded **Weight:** 1.5550 g. **Composition:** 0.9999 Silver 0.0500 oz. ASW **Size:** 16 mm.

Date	Mintage	MS-63	Proof
2003 Proof	—	—	4.50

KM# 621 Obv: Crowned head right **Rev:** Maple leaf **Edge:** Reeded **Weight:** 1.5550 g. **Composition:** 0.9999 Silver 0.0500 oz. ASW **Size:** 17 mm.

Date	Mintage	MS-63	Proof
2004 Mint logo privy mark Proof	13,859	—	4.50

2 DOLLARS

KM# 618 Obv: Crowned head right **Rev:** Holographic Maple leaf **Edge:** Reeded **Weight:** 3.1100 g. **Composition:** 0.9999 Silver 0.1000 oz. ASW **Size:** 20.1 mm.

Date	Mintage	MS-63	Proof
2003 Proof	—	—	7.50

KM# 622 Obv: Crowned head right **Rev:** Maple leaf **Edge:** Reeded **Weight:** 3.1100 g. **Composition:** 0.9999 Silver 0.1000 oz. ASW **Size:** 21 mm.

Date	Mintage	MS-63	Proof
2004 Mint logo privy mark Proof	13,859	—	7.50

KM# 571 Obv: Head right **Rev:** Lynx **Weight:** 3.1050 g. **Composition:** 0.9999 Silver 0.0998 oz. ASW

Date	Mintage	MS-63	Proof
2005 Proof	—	—	7.50

3 DOLLARS

KM# 619 Obv: Crowned head right **Rev:** Holographic Maple leaf **Edge:** Reeded **Weight:** 7.7760 g. **Composition:** 0.9999 Silver 0.2500 oz. ASW **Size:** 26.9 mm.

Date	Mintage	MS-63	Proof
2003 Proof	—	—	15.00

KM# 623 Obv: Crowned head right **Rev:** Maple leaf **Edge:** Reeded **Weight:** 7.7760 g. **Composition:** 0.9999 Silver 0.2500 oz. ASW **Size:** 27 mm.

Date	Mintage	MS-63	Proof
2004 Mint logo privy mark Proof	13,859	—	12.50

KM# 572 Obv: Head right **Rev:** Lynx **Weight:** 7.7760 g. **Composition:** 0.9999 Silver 0.2500 oz. ASW

Date	Mintage	MS-63	Proof
2005 Proof	—	—	12.50

4 DOLLARS

KM# 620 Obv: Crowned head right **Rev:** Holographic Maple leaf **Edge:** Reeded **Weight:** 15.5500 g. **Composition:** 0.9999 Silver 0.4999 oz. ASW **Size:** 33.9 mm.

Date	Mintage	MS-63	Proof
2003 Proof	—	—	30.00

KM# 624 Obv: Crowned head right **Rev:** Maple leaf **Edge:** Reeded **Weight:** 15.5500 g. **Composition:** 0.9999 Silver 0.4999 oz. ASW **Size:** 34 mm.

Date	Mintage	MS-63	Proof
2004 Mint logo privy mark Proof	13,859	—	25.00

KM# 573 Obv: Head right **Rev:** Lynx **Weight:** 15.5500 g. **Composition:** 0.9999 Silver 0.4999 oz. ASW

Date	Mintage	MS-63	Proof
2005 Proof	—	—	22.50

5 DOLLARS

Date	Mintage	MS-63	Proof
1993	889,946	20.00	—
1994	1,133,900	20.00	—
1995	326,244	20.00	—
1996	250,445	32.50	—
1997	100,970	22.00	—
1998 Tiger privy mark	25,000	22.00	—
1998	591,359	20.00	—
1998 Titanic privy mark	26,000	75.00	—
1998 R.C.M.P. privy mark	25,000	32.50	—
1998 90th Anniversary R.C.M. privy mark	13,025	20.00	—
1999	1,229,442	20.00	—
1999 Rabbit privy mark	25,000	22.50	—
1999 "Y2K" privy mark	9,999	27.50	—
2000 Dragon privy mark	25,000	25.00	—
2000 Expo Hanover privy mark	—	35.00	—
2000	403,652	20.00	—
2001	398,563	20.00	—
2001 Snake privy mark	25,000	25.00	—
2002	576,196	20.00	—
2002 Horse privy mark	25,000	25.00	—
2003	—	20.00	—
2003 Sheep privy mark	25,000	22.00	—

KM# 163 Obv: Young bust right, denomination and date below **Obv. Designer:** Arnold Machin **Rev:** Maple leaf flanked by 9999 **Weight:** 31.1000 g. **Composition:** 0.9999 Silver 0.9997 oz. ASW

Date	Mintage	MS-63	Proof
1988	1,155,931	20.00	—
1989	3,332,200	20.00	—
1989 Proof	29,999	—	30.00

KM# 187 Obv: Crowned head right, date and denomination below **Obv. Designer:** Dora de Pedery-Hunt **Rev:** Maple leaf flanked by 9999 **Weight:** 31.1000 g. **Composition:** 0.9999 Silver 0.9997 oz. ASW

Date	Mintage	MS-63	Proof
1990	1,708,800	20.00	—
1991	644,300	20.00	—
1992	343,800	20.00	—

KM# 363 Obv: Crowned head right, date and denomination below **Rev:** Maple leaf flanked by 9999 **Weight:** 31.1000 g. **Composition:** 0.9999 Silver 0.9997 oz. ASW

Date	Mintage	MS-63	Proof
1999/2000 Fireworks privy mark	298,775	22.00	—

KM# 437 Obv: Crowned head right, date and denomination below **Rev:** Radiant maple leaf hologram **Edge:** Reeded **Weight:** 31.1035 g. **Composition:** 0.9999 Silver 0.9999 oz. ASW **Size:** 38 mm.

Date	Mintage	MS-63	Proof
2001 Good fortune privy mark	29,906	75.00	—

KM# 436 Obv: Crowned head right, date and denomination below **Rev:** Three maple leaves in autumn colors, 9999 flanks **Rev. Designer:** Debbie Adams **Edge:** Reeded **Weight:** 31.1035 g. **Comp:** 0.9999 Silver 0.9999 oz. ASW **Size:** 38 mm.

Date	Mintage	MS-63	Proof
2001 Proof	49,709	—	32.50

KM# 505 Obv: Crowned head right, date and denomination below **Rev:** Two maple leaves in spring color (green) **Edge:** Reeded **Weight:** 31.1035 g. **Composition:** 0.9999 Silver 0.9999 oz. ASW **Size:** 38 mm.

Date	Mintage	MS-63	Proof
2002	29,509	35.00	—

KM# 603 Obv: Head right **Rev:** Loon splashing in the water, hologram **Weight:** 31.1050 g. **Composition:** 0.9999 Silver 0.9999 oz. ASW

Date	Mintage	MS-63	Proof
2002 Satin Proof	30,000	—	45.00

KM# 521 Obv: Head right **Rev:** Maple leaf, summer colors **Rev. Designer:** Stan Witten **Weight:** 31.1035 g. **Composition:** 0.9999 Silver 0.9999 oz. ASW

Date	Mintage	MS-63	Proof
2003	29,416	30.00	—

KM# 508 Obv: Crowned head right, date and denomination below **Obv. Designer:** Dora de

Pedery-Hunt **Rev:** Holographic Maple leaf flanked by 9999 **Edge:** Reeded **Weight:** 31.1035 g. **Comp:** 0.9999 Silver 0.9999 oz. ASW **Size:** 38 mm.

Date	Mintage	MS-63	Proof
2003 Proof	—	—	35.00

KM# 607 Obv: Head right **Rev:** Maple leaf, winter colors **Weight:** 31.1200 g. **Composition:** 0.9999 Silver 1.0004 oz. ASW

Date	Mintage	MS-63	Proof
2004	—	35.00	—

KM# 625 Obv: Bust right **Obv. Designer:** Susanna Blunt **Rev:** Maple leaf **Edge:** Reeded **Weight:** 31.1035 g. **Composition:** 0.9999 Silver 0.9999 oz. ASW **Size:** 38 mm.

Date	Mintage	MS-63	Proof
2004 Mint logo privy mark Specimen	13,859	—	35.00
2004 Monkey privy mark Specimen	25,000	—	35.00
2004 D-Day privy mark Specimen	11,698	—	35.00
2004 Desjardins privy mark	15,000	35.00	—
2004 Capricorn privy Mark Reverse proof	5,000	—	35.00
2004 Aquarius privy mark Reverse proof	5,000	—	35.00
2004 Pisces privy mark Reverse proof	5,000	—	35.00
2004 Aries privy mark Reverse proof	5,000	—	35.00
2004 Taurus privy mark Reverse proof	5,000	—	35.00
2004 Gemini privy mark Reverse proof	5,000	—	35.00
2004 Cancer privy mark Reverse proof	5,000	—	35.00
2004 Leo privy mark Reverse proof	5,000	—	35.00
2004 Virgo privy mark Reverse proof	5,000	—	35.00
2004 Libra privy mark Reverse proof	5,000	—	35.00
2004 Scorpio privy mark Reverse proof	5,000	—	35.00
2004 Sagittarius privy mark Reverse proof	5,000	—	35.00

KM# 522 Obv: Head right **Rev:** Maple leaf, winter color **Rev. Designer:** Stan Witten **Weight:** 31.1050 g. **Composition:** 0.9999 Silver 0.9999 oz. ASW

Date	Mintage	MS-63	Proof
2004	26,763	32.50	—

KM# 574 Obv: Head right **Rev:** Lynx **Weight:** 1.1035 g. **Comp:** 0.9999 Silver 0.0355 oz. ASW

Date	Mintage	MS-63	Proof
2005 Proof	—	—	35.00

KM# 550 Obv: Head right **Rev:** Big Leaf Maple, colorized **Rev. Designer:** Stan Witten **Weight:** 31.1035 g. **Comp:** 0.9999 Silver 0.9999 oz. ASW

Date	Mintage	MS-63	Proof
2005	21,233	30.00	—

KM# 660 Obv: Bust right **Obv. Designer:** Susanna Blunt **Rev:** Silver maple, colorized **Rev. Designer:** Stan Witten **Weight:** 31.1035 g. **Composition:** 0.9990 Silver 0.9990 oz. ASW

Date	Mintage	MS-63	Proof
2006	14,157	35.00	—

KM# 729 Obv: Bust right **Rev:** Maple leaf orange multicolor **Weight:** 31.1050 g. **Composition:** 0.9990 Silver 0.9990 oz. ASW **Size:** 38 mm.

Date	Mintage	MS-63	Proof
2007 Proof	—	—	45.00

KM# 925 Obv: Bust right **Obv. Designer:** Susanna Blunt **Rev:** Sugar maple, colorized **Rev. Designer:** Stan Witten **Weight:** 31.1050 g. **Composition:** 0.9990 Silver 0.9990 oz. ASW

Date	Mintage	MS-63	Proof
2007	11,495	35.00	—

KM# 800 Subject: Vancouver Olympics **Obv:** Bust right **Obv. Designer:** Susanna Blunt **Rev:** Maple leaf, Olympic logo at left **Weight:** 31.1050 g. **Comp:** 0.9990 Silver 0.9990 oz. ASW **Size:** 38 mm.

Date	Mintage	MS-63	Proof
2008	—	28.00	—
2009	—	28.00	—
2010	—	28.00	—

KM# 798 Subject: Maple Leaf 20th Anniversary **Rev:** Maple Leaf, selective gold plating **Weight:** 31.1050 g. **Composition:** 0.9990 Silver 0.9990 oz. ASW **Size:** 38 mm.

Date	Mintage	MS-63	Proof
2008 Proof	10,000	—	28.00

8 DOLLARS

KM# 731 Rev: Maple leaf, long life hologram **Composition:** 0.9990 Silver

Date	Mintage	MS-63	Proof
2007	—	35.00	—

50 DOLLARS

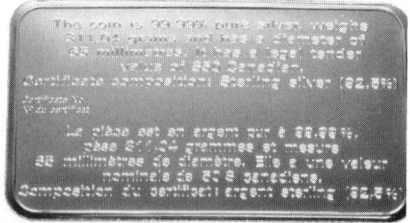

KM# 326 Subject: 10th Anniversary Silver Maple Leaf **Obv:** Crowned head right **Rev:** Maple leaf flanked by 9999 **Edge:** 10th ANNIVERSARY 10e ANNIVERSAIRE **Weight:** 311.0350 g. **Composition:** 0.9999 Silver 9.9986 oz. ASW

Date	Mintage	MS-63	Proof
1998 Proof	25,000	—	200

250 DOLLARS

KM# 676 Subject: Kilo **Weight:** 1000.0000 g. **Composition:** 0.9999 Silver 32.146 oz. ASW

Date	Mintage	MS-63	Proof
2006	—	650	—

GOLD BULLION COINAGE

50 CENTS

KM# 888 Subject: Red maple **Obv:** Bust right **Obv. Legend:** Elizabeth II 50 cents **Obv. Designer:** Susanna Blunt **Rev:** Two maple leaves **Rev. Legend:** Canada, Fine gold 1/25 oz or PUR 9999 **Weight:** 1.2700 g. **Composition:** 0.9990 Gold 0.0408 oz. AGW **Size:** 13.92 mm.

Date	Mintage	MS-63	Proof
2009 Proof	150,000	—	60.00

DOLLAR

KM# 238 Obv: Crowned head right, denomination and date below **Rev:** Maple leaf flanked by 9999 **Weight:** 1.5551 g. **Composition:** 0.9999 Gold 0.0500 oz. AGW

Date	Mintage	MS-63	Proof
1993	37,080	BV+37%	—
1994	78,860	BV+37%	—
1995	85,920	BV+37%	—
1996	56,520	BV+37%	—
1997	59,720	BV+37%	—
1998	44,260	BV+37%	—
1999 oval "20 YEARS ANS" privy mark	—	BV+46%	—
2000 oval "2000" privy mark	—	BV+46%	—

KM# 365 Obv: Crowned head right **Rev:** Maple leaf hologram **Weight:** 1.5551 g. **Composition:** 0.9999 Gold 0.0500 oz. AGW

Date	Mintage	MS-63	Proof
1999	500	90.00	—

2 DOLLARS

KM# 256 Obv: Crowned head right, denomination and date below **Rev:** Maple leaf flanked by 9999 **Weight:** 2.0735 g. **Composition:** 0.9999 Gold 0.0667 oz. AGW

Date	Mintage	MS-63	Proof
1994	5,493	85.00	—

5 DOLLARS

KM# 135 Obv: Young bust right, date and denomination below **Obv. Designer:** Arnold

Machin **Rev:** Maple leaf flanked by 9999 **Weight:** 3.1200 g. **Comp:** 0.9999 Gold 0.1003 oz. AGW

Date	Mintage	MS-63	Proof
1982	246,000	BV+14%	—
1983	304,000	BV+14%	—
1984	262,000	BV+14%	—
1985	398,000	BV+14%	—
1986	529,516	BV+14%	—
1987	459,000	BV+14%	—
1988	506,500	BV+14%	—
1989	539,000	BV+14%	—
1989 Proof	16,992	—	180

KM# 188 Obv: Elizabeth II effigy **Obv. Designer:** Dora dePedery-Hunt **Rev:** Maple leaf **Weight:** 3.1200 g. **Comp:** 0.9999 Gold 0.1003 oz. AGW

Date	Mintage	MS-63	Proof
1990	476,000	BV+14%	—
1991	322,000	BV+14%	—
1992	384,000	BV+14%	—
1993	248,630	BV+14%	—
1994	313,150	BV+14%	—
1995	294,890	BV+14%	—
1996	179,220	BV+14%	—
1997	188,540	BV+14%	—
1998	301,940	BV+14%	—
1999 oval "20 Years ANS" privy mark	—	BV+19%	—
2000 oval "2000" privy mark	—	BV+19%	—

KM# 366 Rev: Maple leaf hologram **Weight:** 3.1200 g. **Comp:** 0.9999 Gold 0.1003 oz. AGW

Date	Mintage	MS-63	Proof
1999	500	160	—

KM# 439 Subject: Holographic Maple Leaves **Obv:** Crowned head right **Rev:** Three maple leaves multicolor hologram **Edge:** Reeded **Weight:** 3.1310 g. **Composition:** 0.9999 Gold 0.1006 oz. AGW **Size:** 16 mm.

Date	Mintage	MS-63	Proof
2001	600	150	—

10 DOLLARS

KM# 136 Obv: Young bust right, date and denomination below **Obv. Designer:** Arnold Machin **Rev:** Maple leaf flanked by 9999 **Weight:** 7.7850 g. **Comp:** 0.9999 Gold 0.2503 oz. AGW

Date	Mintage	MS-63	Proof
1982	184,000	BV+10%	—
1983	308,800	BV+10%	—
1984	242,400	BV+10%	—
1985	620,000	BV+10%	—
1986	915,200	BV+10%	—
1987	376,000	BV+10%	—
1988	436,000	BV+10%	—
1989	328,800	BV+10%	—
1989 Proof	6,998	—	265

KM# 189 Obv: Crowned head right, date and denomination below **Obv. Designer:** Dora dePedery-Hunt **Rev:** Maple leaf flanked by 9999 **Weight:** 7.7850 g. **Composition:** 0.9999 Gold 0.2503 oz. AGW

Date	Mintage	MS-63	Proof
1990	253,600	BV+10%	—
1991	166,400	BV+10%	—
1992	179,600	BV+10%	—
1993	158,452	BV+10%	—
1994	148,792	BV+10%	—
1995	127,596	BV+10%	—
1996	89,148	BV+10%	—
1997	98,104	BV+10%	—
1998	85,472	BV+10%	—
1999 oval "20 Years ANS" privy mark	—	BV+15%	—
2000 oval "2000" privy mark	—	BV+15%	—

KM# 367 Rev: Maple leaf hologram **Weight:** 7.7850 g. **Comp:** 0.9999 Gold 0.2503 oz. AGW

Date	Mintage	MS-63	Proof
1999	—	325	—

KM# 440 Subject: Holographic Maples Leaves **Obv:** Crowned head right **Rev:** Three maple leaves multicolor hologram **Edge:** Reeded **Weight:** 7.7970 g. **Composition:** 0.9999 Gold 0.2506 oz. AGW **Size:** 20 mm.

Date	Mintage	MS-63	Proof
2001	15,000	325	—

20 DOLLARS

KM# 153 Obv: Young bust right, date and denomination below **Obv. Designer:** Arnold Machin **Rev:** Maple leaf flanked by 9999 **Weight:** 15.5515 g. **Composition:** 0.9999 Gold 0.4999 oz. AGW **Size:** 32 mm.

Date	Mintage	MS-63	Proof
1986	529,200	BV+7%	—
1987	332,800	BV+7%	—
1988	538,400	BV+7%	—
1989	259,200	BV+7%	—
1989 Proof	6,998	—	525

KM# 190 Obv: Crowned head right, date and denomination below **Obv. Designer:** Dora dePedery-Hunt **Rev:** Maple leaf flanked by 9999 **Weight:** 15.5515 g. **Composition:** 0.9999 Gold 0.4999 oz. AGW

Date	Mintage	MS-63	Proof
1990	174,400	BV+7%	—
1991	96,200	BV+7%	—
1992	108,000	BV+7%	—
1993	99,492	BV+7%	—

Date	Mintage	MS-63	Proof
1994	104,766	BV+7%	—
1995	103,162	BV+7%	—
1996	66,246	BV+7%	—
1997	63,354	BV+7%	—
1998	65,366	BV+7%	—
1999 oval "20 Years ANS" privy mark	—	BV+12%	—
2000 oval "2000" privy mark	—	BV+12%	—

KM# 368 Rev: Maple leaf hologram **Weight:** 15.5515 g. **Comp:** 0.9999 Gold 0.4999 oz. AGW

Date	Mintage	MS-63	Proof
1999	500	700	—

KM# 441 Subject: Holographic Maples Leaves **Obv:** Crowned head right **Rev:** Three maple leaves multicolor hologram **Edge:** Reeded **Weight:** 15.5840 g. **Composition:** 0.9999 Gold 0.5010 oz. AGW **Size:** 25 mm.

Date	Mintage	MS-63	Proof
2001	600	675	—

50 DOLLARS

KM# 125.1 Obv: Young bust right, denomination and date below **Rev:** Maple leaf flanked by .999 **Weight:** 31.1030 g. **Composition:** 0.9990 Gold 0.9989 oz. AGW

Date	Mintage	MS-63	Proof
1979	1,000,000	BV+4%	—
1980	1,251,500	BV+4%	—
1981	863,000	BV+4%	—
1982	883,000	BV+4%	—

KM# 125.2 Obv: Young bust right, date and denomination below **Rev:** Maple leaf flanked by .9999 **Weight:** 31.1030 g. **Composition:** 0.9999 Gold 0.9998 oz. AGW

Date	Mintage	MS-63	Proof
1983	843,000	BV+4%	—
1984	1,067,500	BV+4%	—
1985	1,908,000	BV+4%	—
1986	779,115	BV+4%	—
1987	978,000	BV+4%	—
1988	826,500	BV+4%	—
1989	856,000	BV+4%	—
1989 Proof	17,781	—	1,000

KM# 191 Obv: Crowned head right, date and denomination below **Obv. Designer:** Dora dePedery-Hunt **Rev:** Maple leaf flanked by .9999 **Weight:** 31.1030 g. **Composition:** 0.9999 Gold 0.9998 oz. AGW

Date	Mintage	MS-63	Proof
1990	815,000	BV+4%	—
1991	290,000	BV+4%	—
1992	368,900	BV+4%	—
1993	321,413	BV+4%	—
1994	180,357	BV+4%	—
1995	208,729	BV+4%	—
1996	143,682	BV+4%	—
1997	478,211	BV+4%	—
1998	593,704	BV+4%	—
1999 oval "20 Years ANS" privy mark	—	BV+7%	—
2000 oval "2000" privy mark	—	BV+7%	—
2000 oval fireworks privy mark	—	BV+7%	—

KM# 305 Obv: Crowned head denomination below, within circle, dates below **Rev:** Mountie at gallop right, within circle **Rev. Designer:** Ago Aarand **Weight:** 31.1030 g. **Composition:** 0.9999 Gold 0.9998 oz. AGW **Shape:** 10-sided

Date	Mintage	MS-63	Proof
1997	12,913	1,000	—

KM# 369 Obv: Crowned head right, date and denomination below **Rev:** Maple leaf hologram flanked by 9999, with fireworks privy mark **Weight:** 31.1030 g. **Comp:** 0.9999 Gold 0.9998 oz. AGW

Date	Mintage	MS-63	Proof
2000	500	1,400	—

KM# 442 Subject: Holographic Maples Leaves **Obv:** Crowned head right **Rev:** Three maple leaves multicolor hologram **Edge:** Reeded **Weight:** 31.1500 g. **Composition:** 0.9999 Gold 1.0014 oz. AGW **Size:** 30 mm.

Date	Mintage	MS-63	Proof
2001	600	1,350	—

2500 DOLLARS

KM# 681 Subject: Kilo **Rev:** Common Characters, Early Canada **Weight:** 1000.0000 g. **Composition:** 0.9999 Gold 32.146 oz. AGW **Size:** 101.6 mm. **Note:** Illustration reduced.

Date	Mintage	MS-63	Proof
2007	20	42,500	—

1000000 DOLLARS

KM# 755 Rev: Maple leaf **Weight:** 100000.0000 g. **Comp:** 0.9999 Gold 3214.6 oz. AGW **Note:** Cast

Date	Mintage	MS-63	Proof
2007	10	4,250,000	—

PLATINUM BULLION COINAGE

DOLLAR

KM# 239 Obv: Crowned head right, date and denomination below **Rev:** Maple leaf flanked by 9995 **Weight:** 1.5552 g. **Composition:** 0.9995 Platinum 0.0500 oz. APW

Date	Mintage	MS-63	Proof
1993	2,120	BV+35%	—
1994	4,260	BV+35%	—
1995	460	135	—
1996	1,640	BV+35%	—
1997	1,340	BV+35%	—
1998	2,000	BV+35%	—
1999	2,000	BV+35%	—

2 DOLLARS

KM# 257 Obv: Crowned head right, date and denomination below **Rev:** Maple leaf flanked by 9995 **Weight:** 2.0735 g. **Composition:** 0.9995 Platinum 0.0666 oz. APW

Date	Mintage	MS-63	Proof
1994	1,470	235	—

5 DOLLARS

KM# 164 Obv: Young bust right, date and denomination below **Obv. Designer:** Arnold Machin **Rev:** Maple leaf flanked by 9995 **Weight:** 3.1203 g. **Composition:** 0.9995 Platinum 0.1003 oz. APW

Date	Mintage	MS-63	Proof
1988	74,000	BV+18%	—

Date	Mintage	MS-63	Proof
1989	18,000	BV+18%	—
1989 Proof	11,999	—	250

KM# 192 Obv. Designer: dePedery-Hunt **Rev:** Maple leaf **Weight:** 3.1203 g. **Composition:** 0.9995 Platinum 0.1003 oz. APW

Date	Mintage	MS-63	Proof
1990	9,000	BV+18%	—
1991	13,000	BV+18%	—
1992	16,000	BV+18%	—
1993	14,020	BV+18%	—
1994	19,190	BV+18%	—
1995	8,940	BV+18%	—
1996	8,820	BV+18%	—
1997	7,050	BV+18%	—
1998	5,710	BV+18%	—
1999	2,000	BV+18%	—

10 DOLLARS

KM# 165 Obv: Young bust right, date and denomination below **Obv. Designer:** Machin **Rev:** Maple leaf flanked by 9995 **Weight:** 7.7857 g. **Composition:** 0.9995 Platinum 0.2502 oz. APW

Date	Mintage	MS-63	Proof
1988	93,600	BV+13%	—
1989	3,200	BV+13%	—
1989 Proof	1,999	—	500

KM# 193 Obv. Designer: dePedery-Hunt **Rev:** Maple leaf **Weight:** 7.7857 g. **Composition:** 0.9995 Platinum 0.2502 oz. APW

Date	Mintage	MS-63	Proof
1990	1,600	BV+13%	—
1991	7,200	BV+13%	—
1992	11,600	BV+13%	—
1993	8,048	BV+13%	—
1994	9,456	BV+13%	—
1995	6,524	BV+13%	—
1996	6,160	BV+13%	—
1997	4,552	BV+13%	—
1998	3,816	BV+13%	—
1999	2,000	BV+13%	—

20 DOLLARS

KM# 166 Obv: Young bust right, denomination and date below **Obv. Designer:** Machin **Rev:** Maple leaf flanked by 9995 **Weight:** 15.5519 g. **Composition:** 0.9995 Platinum 0.4997 oz. APW

Date	Mintage	MS-63	Proof
1988	23,600	BV+9%	—
1989	4,800	BV+9%	—
1989 Proof	1,999	—	900

KM# 194 Obv. Designer: dePedery-Hunt **Rev:** Maple leaf **Weight:** 15.5519 g. **Composition:** 0.9995 Platinum 0.4997 oz. APW

Date	Mintage	MS-63	Proof
1990	2,600	BV+9%	—
1991	5,600	BV+9%	—
1992	12,800	BV+9%	—

Date	Mintage	MS-63	Proof
1993	6,022	BV+9%	—
1994	6,710	BV+9%	—
1995	6,308	BV+9%	—
1996	5,490	BV+9%	—
1997	3,990	BV+9%	—
1998	5,486	BV+9%	—
1999	500	BV+15%	—

30 DOLLARS

KM# 174 Obv: Crowned head right **Rev:** Polar bear swimming, denomination below
Rev. Designer: Robert Bateman **Weight:** 3.1100 g. **Comp:** 0.9990 Platinum 0.0999 oz. APW

Date	Mintage	MS-63	Proof
1990 Proof	2,629	—	200

KM# 198 Obv: Crowned head right **Rev:** Snowy owl, denomination below **Rev. Designer:** Glen Loates **Weight:** 3.1100 g. **Composition:** 0.9990 Platinum 0.0999 oz. APW

Date	Mintage	MS-63	Proof
1991 Proof	3,500	—	200

KM# 226 Obv: Crowned head right **Rev:** Cougar head and shoulders, denomination below
Rev. Designer: George McLean **Weight:** 3.1100 g. **Composition:** 0.9990 Platinum 0.0999 oz. APW

Date	Mintage	MS-63	Proof
1992 Proof	3,500	—	200

KM# 240 Obv: Crowned head right **Rev:** Arctic fox, denomination below **Rev. Designer:** Claude D'Angelo **Weight:** 3.1100 g. **Composition:** 0.9990 Platinum 0.0999 oz. APW

Date	Mintage	MS-63	Proof
1993 Proof	3,500	—	200

KM# 252 Obv: Crowned head right, date below
Rev: Sea otter, denomination below
Rev. Designer: Ron S. Parker **Weight:** 3.1100 g. **Composition:** 0.9990 Platinum 0.0999 oz. APW

Date	Mintage	MS-63	Proof
1994 Proof	1,500	—	200

KM# 266 Obv: Crowned head right, date below
Rev: Canadian lynx, denomination below
Rev. Designer: Michael Dumas **Weight:** 3.1100 g.
Composition: 0.9990 Platinum 0.0999 oz. APW

Date	Mintage	MS-63	Proof
1995 Proof	620	—	200

KM# 278 Obv: Crowned head right, date below
Rev: Falcon portrait, denomination below
Rev. Designer: Dwayne Harty **Weight:** 3.1100 g.
Composition: 0.9990 Platinum 0.0999 oz. APW

Date	Mintage	MS-63	Proof
1996 Proof	489	—	200

KM# 300 Obv: Crowned head right, date below
Rev: Bison head, denomination below
Rev. Designer: Chris Bacon **Weight:** 3.1100 g.
Composition: 0.9995 Platinum 0.0999 oz. APW

Date	Mintage	MS-63	Proof
1997 Proof	5,000	—	200

KM# 322 Obv: Crowned head right, date below
Rev: Grey wolf **Rev. Designer:** Kerr Burnett
Weight: 3.1100 g. **Composition:** 0.9990 Platinum 0.0999 oz. APW

Date	Mintage	MS-63	Proof
1998 Proof	2,000	—	200

KM# 359 Obv: Crowned head right, date below
Rev: Musk ox **Rev. Designer:** Mark Hobson
Weight: 3.1100 g. **Composition:** 0.9995 Platinum 0.0999 oz. APW

Date	Mintage	MS-63	Proof
1999 Proof	1,500	—	200

KM# 405 Obv: Crowned head right, date below
Rev: Pronghorn antelope head, denomination below **Rev. Designer:** Mark Hobson **Edge:** Reeded
Weight: 3.1100 g. **Composition:** 0.9995 Platinum 0.0999 oz. APW **Size:** 16 mm.

Date	Mintage	MS-63	Proof
2000 Proof	600	—	200

KM# 429 Obv: Crowned head right **Rev:** Harlequin duck's head **Rev. Designer:** Cosme Saffioti and Susan Taylor **Edge:** Reeded **Weight:** 3.1100 g.

Composition: 0.9995 Platinum 0.0999 oz. APW
Size: 16 mm.

Date	Mintage	MS-63	Proof
2001 Proof	448	—	175

50 DOLLARS

KM# 167 Obv: Young bust right, denomination and date below **Obv. Designer:** Machin **Rev:** Maple leaf flanked by 9995 **Weight:** 31.1030 g. **Composition:** 0.9995 Platinum 0.9994 oz. APW

Date	Mintage	MS-63	Proof
1988	37,500	BV+4%	—
1989	10,000	BV+4%	—
1989 Proof	5,965	—	1,750

KM# 195 Obv. Designer: dePedery-Hunt **Rev:** Maple leaf **Weight:** 31.1030 g. **Composition:** 0.9995 Platinum 0.9994 oz. APW

Date	Mintage	MS-63	Proof
1990	15,100	BV+4%	—
1991	31,900	BV+4%	—
1992	40,500	BV+4%	—
1993	17,666	BV+4%	—
1994	36,245	BV+4%	—
1995	25,829	BV+4%	—
1996	62,273	BV+4%	—
1997	25,480	BV+4%	—
1998	10,403	BV+4%	—
1999	1,300	BV+10%	—

75 DOLLARS

KM# 175 Obv: Crowned head right **Rev:** Polar bear resting, denomination below **Rev. Designer:** Robert Bateman **Weight:** 7.7760 g. **Composition:** 0.9990 Platinum 0.2497 oz. APW

Date	Mintage	MS-63	Proof
1990 Proof	2,629	—	500

KM# 199 Obv: Crowned head right **Rev:** Snowy owls perched on branch, denomination below **Rev. Designer:** Glen Loates **Weight:** 7.7760 g. **Composition:** 0.9990 Platinum 0.2497 oz. APW

Date	Mintage	MS-63	Proof
1991 Proof	3,500	—	500

KM# 227 Obv: Crowned head right **Rev:** Cougar prowling, denomination below **Rev. Designer:** George McLean **Weight:** 7.7760 g. **Composition:** 0.9990 Platinum 0.2497 oz. APW

Date	Mintage	MS-63	Proof
1992 Proof	3,500	—	500

KM# 241 Obv: Crowned head right **Rev:** Two Arctic foxes, denomination below **Rev. Designer:** Claude D'Angelo **Weight:** 7.7760 g. **Composition:** 0.9990 Platinum 0.2497 oz. APW

Date	Mintage	MS-63	Proof
1993 Proof	3,500	—	500

KM# 253 Obv: Crowned head right, date below **Rev:** Sea otter eating urchin, denomination below **Rev. Designer:** Ron S. Parker **Weight:** 7.7760 g. **Composition:** 0.9990 Platinum 0.2497 oz. APW

Date	Mintage	MS-63	Proof
1994 Proof	1,500	—	500

KM# 267 Obv: Crowned head right, date below **Rev:** Two lynx kittens, denomination below **Rev. Designer:** Michael Dumas **Weight:** 7.7760 g. **Composition:** 0.9990 Platinum 0.2497 oz. APW

Date	Mintage	MS-63	Proof
1995 Proof	1,500	—	500

KM# 279 Obv: Crowned head right, date below **Rev:** Peregrine falcon, denomination below **Rev. Designer:** Dwayne Harty **Weight:** 7.7760 g. **Composition:** 0.9990 Platinum 0.2497 oz. APW

Date	Mintage	MS-63	Proof
1996 Proof	1,500	—	500

KM# 301 Obv: Crowned head right, date below
Rev: Two bison calves, denomination below
Rev. Designer: Chris Bacon **Weight:** 7.7760 g.
Composition: 0.9990 Platinum 0.2497 oz. APW

Date	Mintage	MS-63	Proof
1997 Proof	1,500	—	500

KM# 323 Obv: Crowned head right, date below
Rev: Gray wolf **Rev. Designer:** Kerr Burnett
Weight: 7.7760 g. **Composition:** 0.9990 Platinum
0.2497 oz. APW

Date	Mintage	MS-63	Proof
1998 Proof	1,000	—	500

KM# 360 Obv: Crowned head right, date below
Rev: Musk ox **Rev. Designer:** Mark Hobson
Weight: 7.7760 g. **Composition:** 0.9990 Platinum
0.2497 oz. APW

Date	Mintage	MS-63	Proof
1999 Proof	500	—	500

KM# 406 Obv: Crowned head right **Rev:** Standing
pronghorn antelope, denomination below
Rev. Designer: Mark Hobson **Edge:** Reeded
Weight: 7.7760 g. **Composition:** 0.9990 Platinum
0.2497 oz. APW **Size:** 20 mm.

Date	Mintage	MS-63	Proof
2000 Proof	600	—	500

KM# 430 Obv: Crowned head right **Rev:** Harlequin
duck in flight **Rev. Designer:** Cosme Saffioti and
Susan Taylor **Edge:** Reeded **Weight:** 7.7760 g.
Composition: 0.9995 Platinum 0.2499 oz. APW
Size: 20 mm.

Date	Mintage	MS-63	Proof
2001 Proof	448	—	500

150 DOLLARS

KM# 176 Obv: Crowned head right **Rev:** Polar
bear walking, denomination below **Rev. Designer:**
Robert Bateman **Weight:** 15.5520 g.
Composition: 0.9990 Platinum 0.4995 oz. APW

Date	Mintage	MS-63	Proof
1990 Proof	2,629	—	900

KM# 200 Obv: Crowned head right **Rev:** Snowy
owl flying, denomination below **Rev. Designer:**
Glen Loates **Weight:** 15.5520 g. **Composition:**
0.9990 Platinum 0.4995 oz. APW

Date	Mintage	MS-63	Proof
1991 Proof	3,500	—	900

KM# 228 Obv: Crowned head right **Rev:** Cougar
mother and cub, denomination below
Rev. Designer: George McLean **Weight:**
15.5520 g. **Composition:** 0.9990 Platinum
0.4995 oz. APW

Date	Mintage	MS-63	Proof
1992 Proof	3,500	—	900

KM# 242 Obv: Crowned head right **Rev:** Arctic fox
by lake, denomination below **Rev. Designer:**
Claude D'Angelo **Weight:** 15.5520 g.
Composition: 0.9990 Platinum 0.4995 oz. APW

Date	Mintage	MS-63	Proof
1993 Proof	3,500	—	900

KM# 254 Obv: Crowned head right, date below
Rev: Sea otter mother carrying pup, denomination
below **Rev. Designer:** Ron S. Parker **Weight:**
15.5520 g. **Composition:** 0.9990 Platinum
0.4995 oz. APW

Date	Mintage	MS-63	Proof
1994 Proof	—	—	900

KM# 268 Obv: Crowned head right, date below **Rev:** Prowling lynx, denomination below **Rev. Designer:** Michael Dumas **Weight:** 15.5520 g. **Composition:** 0.9990 Platinum 0.4995 oz. APW

Date	Mintage	MS-63	Proof
1995 Proof	226	—	900

KM# 280 Obv: Crowned head right, date below **Rev:** Peregrine falcon on branch, denomination below **Rev. Designer:** Dwayne Harty **Weight:** 15.5520 g. **Composition:** 0.9990 Platinum 0.4995 oz. APW

Date	Mintage	MS-63	Proof
1996 Proof	100	—	900

KM# 302 Obv: Crowned head right, date below **Rev:** Bison bull, denomination below **Rev. Designer:** Chris Bacon **Weight:** 15.5520 g. **Composition:** 0.9990 Platinum 0.4995 oz. APW

Date	Mintage	MS-63	Proof
1997 Proof	4,000	—	900

KM# 324 Obv: Crowned head right, date below **Rev:** Two gray wolf cubs, denomination below **Rev. Designer:** Kerr Burnett **Weight:** 15.5520 g. **Composition:** 0.9990 Platinum 0.4995 oz. APW

Date	Mintage	MS-63	Proof
1998 Proof	2,000	—	900

KM# 361 Obv: Crowned head right **Rev:** Musk ox, denomination below **Rev. Designer:** Mark Hobson **Weight:** 15.5520 g. **Composition:** 0.9990 Platinum 0.4995 oz. APW

Date	Mintage	MS-63	Proof
1999 Proof	500	—	900

KM# 407 Obv: Crowned head right **Rev:** Two pronghorn antelope, denomination below **Rev. Designer:** Mark Hobson **Edge:** Reeded **Weight:** 15.5500 g. **Composition:** 0.9990 Platinum 0.4994 oz. APW **Size:** 25 mm.

Date	Mintage	MS-63	Proof
2000 Proof	600	—	900

KM# 431 Obv: Crowned head right **Rev:** Two harlequin ducks **Rev. Designer:** Cosme Saffioti and Susan Taylor **Edge:** Reeded **Weight:** 15.5500 g. **Composition:** 0.9995 Platinum 0.4997 oz. APW **Size:** 25 mm.

Date	Mintage	MS-63	Proof
2001 Proof	448	—	900

300 DOLLARS

KM# 177 Obv: Crowned head right **Rev:** Polar bear mother and cub, denomination below **Rev. Designer:** Robert Bateman **Weight:** 31.1035 g. **Composition:** 0.9990 Platinum 0.9990 oz. APW

Date	Mintage	MS-63	Proof
1990 Proof	2,629	—	1,800

PLATINUM BULLION

KM# 201 Obv: Crowned head right **Rev:** Snowy owl with chicks, denomination below
Rev. Designer: Glen Loates **Weight:** 31.1035 g.
Composition: 0.9990 Platinum 0.9990 oz. APW

Date	Mintage	MS-63	Proof
1991 Proof	3,500	—	1,800

KM# 229 Obv: Crowned head right **Rev:** Cougar resting in tree, denomination below **Rev. Designer:** George McLean **Weight:** 31.1035 g. **Composition:** 0.9990 Platinum 0.9990 oz. APW

Date	Mintage	MS-63	Proof
1992 Proof	3,500	—	1,800

KM# 243 Obv: Crowned head right **Rev:** Mother fox and three kits, denomination below
Rev. Designer: Claude D'Angelo **Weight:** 31.1035 g. **Composition:** 0.9990 Platinum 0.9990 oz. APW

Date	Mintage	MS-63	Proof
1993 Proof	3,500	—	1,800

KM# 255 Obv: Crowned head right, date below
Rev: Two otters swimming, denomination below
Rev. Designer: Ron S. Parker **Weight:** 31.1035 g.
Composition: 0.9990 Platinum 0.9990 oz. APW

Date	Mintage	MS-63	Proof
1994 Proof	—	—	1,800

KM# 269 Obv: Crowned head right, date below
Rev: Female lynx and three kittens, denomination below **Rev. Designer:** Michael Dumas **Weight:** 31.1035 g. **Composition:** 0.9990 Platinum 0.9990 oz. APW

Date	Mintage	MS-63	Proof
1995 Proof	1,500	—	1,800

KM# 281 Obv: Crowned head right, date below
Rev: Peregrine falcon feeding nestlings, denomination below **Rev. Designer:** Dwayne Harty **Weight:** 31.1035 g. **Composition:** 0.9990 Platinum 0.9990 oz. APW

Date	Mintage	MS-63	Proof
1996 Proof	1,500	—	1,800

KM# 303 Obv: Crowned head right, date below
Rev: Bison family, denomination below
Rev. Designer: Chris Bacon **Weight:** 31.1035 g.
Composition: 0.9990 Platinum 0.9990 oz. APW

Date	Mintage	MS-63	Proof
1997 Proof	1,500	—	1,800

KM# 325 Obv: Crowned head right, date below
Rev: Gray wolf and two cubs, denomination below
Rev. Designer: Kerr Burnett **Weight:** 31.1035 g.
Composition: 0.9990 Platinum 0.9990 oz. APW

Date	Mintage	MS-63	Proof
1998 Proof	—	—	1,800

KM# 362 Obv: Crowned head right, date below
Rev: Musk ox **Rev. Designer:** Mark Hobson
Weight: 31.1035 g. **Composition:** 0.9990
Platinum 0.9990 oz. APW

Date	Mintage	MS-63	Proof
1999 Proof	500	—	1,800

KM# 408 Obv: Crowned head right, date below
Rev: Four pronghorn antelope, denomination below
Rev. Designer: Mark Hobson **Edge:** Reeded
Weight: 31.1035 g. **Composition:** 0.9990
Platinum 0.9990 oz. APW **Size:** 30 mm.

Date	Mintage	MS-63	Proof
2000 Proof	600	—	1,800

KM# 432 Obv: Crowned head right **Rev:** Two
standing harlequin ducks **Rev. Designer:** Cosme
Saffioti and Susan Taylor **Edge:** Reeded **Weight:**
31.1035 g. **Composition:** 0.9995 Platinum
0.9995 oz. APW **Size:** 30 mm.

Date	Mintage	MS-63	Proof
2001 Proof	448	—	1,800

KM# 753 Rev: Wooly mammoth **Weight:**
31.1050 g. **Composition:** 0.9999 Platinum
0.9999 oz. APW **Size:** 50 mm.

Date	Mintage	MS-63	Proof
2007 Proof	—	—	1,700

KM# 831 Rev: Scimitar cat **Weight:** 31.1050 g.
Composition: 0.9990 Platinum 0.9990 oz. APW

Date	Mintage	MS-63	Proof
2008 Proof	—	—	1,700

PLATINUM BULLION

SETS

Custom Proof-Like Sets (CPL)

KM#	Date	Mintage	Identification	Issue Price	Mkt. Value
CPL1	1971 (7)	33,517	KM59.1 (2 pcs.), 60.1, 62b, 75.1, 77.1 ,79	6.50	5.00
CPL2	1971 (6)	38,198	KM59.1 (2 pcs.), 60.1, 62b, 75.1, 77.1	6.50	5.00
CPL3	1973 (6)	35,676	KM59.1 (2 pcs.), 60.1, 75.1, 77.1, 81.1 obv. 120 beads, 82	6.50	6.50
CPL4	1973 (6)	Inc. above	KM59.1 (2 pcs.), 60.1, 75.1, 77.1, 81.1 obv. 132 beads, 82	6.50	200
CPL5	1974 (5)	44,296	KM59.1 (2 pcs.), 60.1, 62b-75.1, 88	8.00	5.00
CPL6	1975 (6)	36,851	KM59.1 (2 pcs.), 60.1, 62b-75.1, 76.2, 77.1	8.00	5.00
CPL7	1976 (6)	28,162	KM59.1 (2 pcs.), 60.1, 62b-75.1, 76.2, 77.1	8.00	5.50
CPL8	1977 (6)	44,198	KM59.1 (2 pcs.), 60.1, 62b-75.2, 77.1, 117	8.15	5.00
CPL9	1978 (6)	41,000	KM59.1 (2 pcs.), 60.1, 62b-75.3, 77.1, 120.1	—	5.00
CPL10	1979 (6)	31,174	KM59.2 (2 pcs.), 60.2, 74, 75.3, 77.2, 120.1	10.75	5.00
CPL11	1980 (7)	41,447	KM60.2, 74, 75.3, 77.2, 120.1, 127 (2 pcs.)	10.75	6.00

Mint Sets

KM#	Date	Mintage	Identification	Issue Price	Mkt. Value
MS1	1973 (4)	Inc. above	KM84, 85, 86.1, 87; Olympic Commemoratives, Series I	45.00	85.00
MS2	1974 (4)	Inc. above	KM89, 90, 93, 94; Olympic Commemoratives, Series II	48.00	85.00
MS3	1974 (4)	Inc. above	KM91-92, 95-96; Olympic Commemorative, Series III	48.00	85.00
MS4	1975 (4)	Inc. above	KM98, 99, 102, 103; Olympic Commemoratives, Series IV	48.00	85.00
MS5	1975 (4)	Inc. above	KM100, 101, 104, 105; Olympic Commemoratives, Series V	60.00	85.00
MS6	1976 (4)	Inc. above	KM107, 108, 111, 112; Olympic Commemoratives, Series VI	60.00	85.00
MS7	1976 (4)	Inc. above	KM109, 110, 113, 114; Olympic Commemoratives, Series VII	60.00	85.00
MS8	2001 (5)	600	KM438-442	1,996	2,600
MS10	2002 (7)	—	KM#444-449, 467, Oh! Canada! 135th Birthday Gift set.	17.00	16.00
MS11	2002 (7)	—	KM#444-449, 467, Tiny Treasures Uncirculated Gift Set	17.00	16.00
MS12	2003 (7)	135,000	KM#289, 182b, 183b, 184b, 290, 186, 270	12.00	16.00
MS13	2003 (7)	75,000	KM490-496	13.25	20.00
MS14	2003 (7)	—	KM289, 182-184, 290, 186, 270, Oh! Canada!	17.75	16.00
MS15	2003 (7)	—	KM289, 182-184, 290, 186, 270, Tiny Treasures Uncirculated Gift Set	17.75	16.00

Olympic Commemoratives (OCP)

KM#	Date	Mintage	Identification	Issue Price	Mkt. Value
OCP1	1973 (4)	Inc. above	KM84-87, Series I	78.50	85.00
OCP2	1974 (4)	Inc. above	KM89-90, 93-94, Series II	88.50	85.00
OCP3	1974 (4)	Inc. above	KM91-92, 95-96, Series III	88.50	85.00
OCP4	1975 (4)	Inc. above	KM98-99, 102-103, Series IV	88.50	85.00
OCP5	1975 (4)	Inc. above	KM100-101, 104-105, Series V	88.50	85.00
OCP6	1976 (4)	Inc. above	KM107-108, 111-112, Series VI	88.50	85.00
OCP7	1976 (4)	Inc. above	KM109-110, 113-114, Series VII	88.50	85.00

Proof Sets

KM#	Date	Mintage	Identification	Issue Price	Mkt. Value
XPS1	1952 (6)	—	X#MB41-MB46	—	—
XPS2	1979 (5)	100	X#Tn1a-Tn5a	—	40.00
XPS3	1980 (6)	1,500	X#MB51-MB56	—	110
PS1	1981 (7)	199,000	KM60.2, 74, 75.3, 77.2, 120.1, 127, 130	36.00	30.00
PS2	1982 (7)	180,908	KM60.2a, 74, 75.3, 77.2, 120.1, 132-133	36.00	30.00
PS3	1983 (7)	166,779	KM60.2a, 74, 75.3, 77.2, 120.1, 132, 138	36.00	25.00
PS4	1984 (7)	161,602	KM60.2a, 74, 75.3, 77.2, 120.1, 132, 140	30.00	24.00
PS5	1985 (7)	157,037	KM60.2a, 74, 75.3, 77.2, 120.1, 132, 143	30.00	27.50
PS6	1986 (7)	175,745	KM60.2a, 74, 75.3, 77.2, 120.1, 132, 149	30.00	26.00
PS7	1987 (7)	179,004	KM60.2a, 74, 75.3, 77.2, 120.1, 132, 154	34.00	27.50
PS8	1988 (7)	175,259	KM60.2a, 74, 75.3, 77.2, 132, 157, 161	37.50	33.00
PS10	1989 (4)	6,823	KM125.2, 135-136, 153	1,190	2,000
PS11	1989 (4)	1,995	KM164-167	1,700	3,400
PS12	1989 (3)	2,550	KM125.2, 163, 167	1,530	2,800
PS13	1989 (3)	9,979	KM135, 163, 164	165	460
PS9	1989 (7)	170,928	KM60.2a, 74, 75.3, 77.2, 132, 157, 168	40.00	33.00
PS14	1990 (7)	158,068	KM170, 181, 182, 183, 184, 185, 186	41.00	40.00
PS15	1990 (4)	2,629	KM174-177	1,720	3,400
PS16	1991 (7)	14,629	KM179, 181, 182, 183, 184, 185, 186	—	80.00
PS17	1991 (4)	873	KM198-201	1,760	3,400
PS18	1992 (11)	84,397	KM203a, 212a-214a, 218, 220a-223a, 231a-234a	—	75.00
PS19	1992 (7)	147,061	KM204-210	42.75	60.00
PS20	1992 (4)	3,500	KM226-229	1,680	3,400
PS21	1993 (7)	143,065	KM181, 182, 183, 184, 185, 186, 235	42.75	34.00
PS22	1993 (4)	3,500	KM240-243	1,329	3,400
PS23	1994 (7)	47,303	KM181-186, 248	47.50	30.00
PS24	1994 (7)	99,121	KM181-186, 251	43.00	4,700
PS25	1994 (4)	1,500	KM252-255	915	3,400
PS26	1995 (7)	Inc. above	KM181-186, 259	37.45	52.00
PS27	1995 (7)	50,000	KM181-185, 258, 259	49.45	52.00

KM#	Date	Mintage	Identification	Issue Price	Mkt. Value
PS28	1995 (4)	Inc. above	KM261-264	42.00	95.00
PS29	1995 (4)	682	KM266-269	1,555	3,400
PS30	1995 (2)	Inc. above	KM261-262	22.00	48.00
PS31	1995 (2)	Inc. above	KM263-264	22.00	46.00
PS32	1996 (4)	423	KM278-281	1,555	3,400
PS33	1996 (7)	Inc. above	KM181, 182a, 183a, 184a, 185a, 186, 274	49.00	60.00
PS34	1996 (4)	Inc. above	KM283-286	44.45	80.00
PS35	1997 (7)	Inc. above	KM182a, 183a, 184a, 270c, 282, 289, 290	60.00	67.00
PS36	1997 (4)	Inc. above	KM292-295	44.45	68.00
PS37	1997 (4)	Inc. above	KM300-303	1,530	3,400
PS38	1998 (8)	Inc. above	KM182a, 183a, 184a, 186, 270b, 289, 290a, 306	59.45	60.00
PS39	1998 (5)	25,000	KM309-313	73.50	55.00
PS40	1998 (2)	61,000	KM316 w/China Y-727	72.50	40.00
PS41	1998 (4)	Inc. above	KM318-321	44.45	68.00
PS42	1998 (4)	1,000	KM322-325	1,552	3,400
PS43	1998 (5)	25,000	KM310-313, 332	73.50	68.00
PS44	1999 (7)	Inc. above	KM182a-184a, 186, 270c, 289, 290a,	59.45	50.00
PS45	1999 (4)	Inc. above	KM335-338	39.95	105
PS46	1999 (12)	Inc. above	KM342a-353a	99.45	80.00
PS47	1999 (4)	Inc. above	KM359-362	1,425	3,400
PS48	2000 (12)	—	KM373a-383a, 384.2a	101	75.00
PS49	2000 (4)	—	KM389-392	44.00	80.00
PS50	2000 (4)	600	KM405-408	1,416	3,400
PS51	2001 (4)	—	KM429, 430, 431, 432	—	3,400
PS54	2002 (2)	—	KM#519, 520	750	1,000
PS57	2004 (8)	—	KM#490, 491a-494a, 495, 496a, 512	—	105
PS58	2004 (5)	25,000	KM#621-625	—	100.00

Proof-Like Dollars

KM#	Date	Mintage	Identification	Issue Price	Mkt. Value
D1.1	1951 (1)	—	KM46, Canoe	—	250
D1.2	1951 (1)	—	KM46, Arnprior	—	700
D2.1	1952 (1)	—	KM46, water lines	—	1,100
D2.2	1952 (1)	—	KM46, without water lines	—	350
D3	1953 (1)	1,200	KM54, Canoe w/shoulder fold	—	325
D4	1954 (1)	5,300	KM54, Canoe	1.25	150
D5	1955 (1)	7,950	KM54, Canoe	1.25	125
D5a	1955 (1)	Inc. above	KM54, Arnprior	1.25	175
D6	1956 (0)	10,212	KM54, Canoe	1.25	70.00
D7	1957 (1)	16,241	KM54, Canoe	1.25	40.00
D8	1958 (1)	33,237	KM55, British Columbia	1.25	25.00
D9	1959 (1)	45,160	KM54, Canoe	1.25	15.00
D10	1960 (1)	82,728	KM54, Canoe	1.25	12.00
D11	1961 (1)	120,928	KM54, Canoe	1.25	12.00
D12	1962 (1)	248,901	KM54, Canoe	1.25	12.00
D13	1963 (1)	963,525	KM54, Canoe	1.25	12.00
D14	1964 (1)	2,862,441	KM58, Charlottetown	1.25	12.00
D15	1965 (1)	2,904,352	KM64.1, Canoe	—	12.00
D16	1966 (1)	672,514	KM64.1, Canoe	—	12.00
D17	1967 (1)	1,036,176	KM70, Confederation	—	12.00

Proof-Like Sets (PL)

KM#	Date	Mintage	Identification	Issue Price	Mkt. Value
PL1	1953 (6)	1,200	KM49 w/o shoulder fold, 50-54	2.20	1,250
PL3	1954 (6)	3,000	KM49-54	2.50	450
PL4	1954 (6)	Inc. above	KM49 w/o shoulder fold, 50-54	2.50	1,100
PL5	1955 (6)	6,300	KM49, 50a, 51-54	2.50	375
PL6	1955 (6)	Inc. above	KM49, 50a, 51-54, Arnprior	2.50	500
PL7	1956 (6)	6,500	KM49, 50a, 51-54	2.50	225
PL8	1957 (6)	11,862	KM49, 50a, 51-54	2.50	150
PL9	1958 (6)	18,259	KM49, 50a, 51-53, 55	2.50	100.00
PL10	1959 (6)	31,577	KM49, 50a, 51, 52, 54, 56	2.50	45.00
PL11	1960 (6)	64,097	KM49, 50a, 51, 52, 54, 56	3.00	35.00
PL12	1961 (6)	98,373	KM49, 50a, 51, 52, 54, 56	3.00	30.00
PL13	1962 (6)	200,950	KM49, 50a, 51, 52, 54, 56	3.00	17.50
PL14	1963 (6)	673,006	KM49, 51, 52, 54, 56, 57	3.00	17.00
PL15	1964 (5)	1,653,162	KM49, 51, 52, 56-58	3.00	17.00
PL16	1965 (4)	2,904,352	KM59.1-60.1, 61-63, 64.1	4.00	17.00
PL17	1966 (5)	672,514	KM59.1-60.1, 61-63, 64.1	4.00	17.00
PL18	1967 (6)	961,887	KM65-70 (pliofilm flat pack)	4.00	17.00
PL18A	1967 (6)	70,583	KM65-70 and Silver Medal (red box)	12.00	29.00
PL18B	1967 (7)	337,688	KM65-71 (black box)	40.00	475
PL19	1968 (6)	521,641	KM59.1-60.1, 62b, 72a, 75.1-76.1	4.00	2.25
PL20	1969 (6)	326,203	KM59.1-60.1, 62b, 75.1-77.1	4.00	2.75
PL21	1970 (6)	349,120	KM59.1-60.1, 62b, 75.1, 77.1, 78	4.00	3.25
PL22	1971 (6)	253,311	KM59.1-60.1, 62b, 75.1, 77.1, 79	4.00	2.75
PL23	1972 (6)	224,275	KM59.1-60.1, 62b-77.1	4.00	2.75
PL24	1973 (6)	243,695	KM59.1-60.1, 62b-75.1 obv. 120 beads, 77.1, 81.1, 82	4.00	4.00
PL25	1973 (3)	Inc. above	KM59.1-60.1, 62b-75.1 obv. 132 beads, 77.1, 81.2, 82	4.00	250
PL26	1974 (6)	213,589	KM59.1-60.1, 62b-75.1, 77.1, 88	5.00	3.00
PL27.1	1975 (4)	197,372	KM59.1, 60.1, 62b-75.1, 76.2, 77.1	5.00	3.50

KM#	Date	Mintage	Identification	Issue Price	Mkt. Value
PL27.2	1975 (6)	Inc. above	KM59.1, 60.1, 62b-75.1, 76.3, 77.1	5.00	5.00
PL28	1976 (6)	171,737	KM59.1, 60.1, 62b-75.1, 76.2, 77.1	5.15	2.75
PL29	1977 (6)	225,307	KM59.1, 60.1, 62b, 75.2, 77.1, 117.1	5.15	2.75
PL30	1978 (6)	260,000	KM59.1-60.1, 62b, 75.3, 77.1, 120.1	5.25	2.75
PL31	1979 (6)	187,624	KM59.2-60.2, 74, 75.3, 77.2, 120.1	6.25	2.75
PL32	1980 (6)	410,842	KM60.2, 74, 75.3, 77.2, 120.1, 127	6.50	4.50
PL33	1981 (6)	186,250	KM60.2, 74, 75.3, 77.2, 120.1, 123	5.00	3.25
PL34	1982 (5)	203,287	KM60.2, 74, 75.3, 77.2, 120.1, 123	6.00	3.50
PL36	1983 (6)	190,838	KM60.2a, 74, 75.3, 77.2, 120.1, 132	5.00	5.00
PL36.1	1983 (6)	Inc. above	KM60.2a, 74, 75.3, 77.2, 120.1, 132; set in folder packaged by British Royal Mint Coin Club	—	—
PL37	1984 (6)	181,249	KM60.2a, 74, 75.3, 77.2, 120.1, 132	5.25	5.00
PL38	1985 (6)	173,924	KM60.2a, 74, 75.3, 77.2, 120.1, 132	5.25	6.00
PL39	1986 (6)	167,338	KM60.2a, 74, 75.3, 77.2, 120.1, 132	5.25	6.50
PL40	1987 (6)	212,136	KM60.2a, 74, 75.3, 77.2, 120.1, 132	5.25	5.00
PL41	1988 (6)	182,048	KM60.2a, 74, 75.3, 77.2, 132, 157	6.05	5.00
PL42	1989 (6)	173,622	KM60.2a, 74, 75.3, 77.2, 132, 157	6.60	8.00
PL43	1990 (6)	170,791	KM181-186	7.40	8.00
PL44	1991 (6)	147,814	KM181-186	7.40	25.00
PL45	1992 (6)	217,597	KM204-209	8.25	11.00
PL46	1993 (6)	171,680	KM181-186	8.25	4.00
PL47	1994 (6)	141,676	KM181-185, 258	8.50	5.50
PL48	1994 (6)	18,794	KM181-185, 258 (Oh Canada holder)	—	8.50
PL49	1995 (6)	143,892	KM181-186	6.95	5.50
PL50	1995 (6)	50,927	KM181-186 (Oh Canada holder)	14.65	8.50
PL51	1995 (6)	36,443	KM181-186 (Baby Gift holder)	—	9.00
PL52	1996 (4)	116,736	KM181-186	—	27.00
PL53	1996 (6)	29,747	KM181-186 (Baby Gift holder)	—	14.00
PL54	1996 (6)	Inc. above	KM181a-185a, 186	8.95	16.00
PL55	1996 (6)	Inc. above	KM181a-185a, 186 (Oh Canada holder)	14.65	12.00
PL56	1996 (6)	Inc. above	KM181a-185a, 186 (Baby Gift holder)	—	12.00
PL57	1997 (7)	Inc. above	KM182a-184a, 209, 270, 289-290	10.45	8.00
PL58	1997 (7)	Inc. above	KM182a-184a, 270, 289-291 (Oh Canada holder)	16.45	30.00
PL59	1997 (7)	Inc. above	KM182a-184a, 209, 270, 289-290 (Baby Gift holder)	18.50	9.50
PL60	1998 (7)	Inc. above	KM182-184, 186, 270, 289-290	10.45	15.00
PL61	1998 (7)	Inc. above	KM182-184, 186, 270, 289-290 (Oh Canada holder)	16.45	17.00
PL62	1998 (7)	Inc. above	KM182-184, 186, 270, 289-290 (Tiny Treasures holder)	16.45	17.00
PL63	1999 (12)	Inc. above	KM342-353	16.95	10.00
PL64	2000 (12)	—	KM373-384	16.95	10.00

Specimen Sets (SS)

KM#	Date	Mintage	Identification	Issue Price	Mkt. Value
SS1	1858 (4)	Inc. above	KM1-4, Reeded edge	—	12,000
SS2	1858 (4)	Inc. above	KM1-4, Plain edge	—	10,000
SS3	1858 (4)	Inc. above	KM1-4; Double Set	—	20,000
SS4	1858 (1)	Inc. above	KM1 (overdate), 2-4; Double Set	—	20,000
SS5	1870 (1)	100	KM2, 3, 5, 6 (reeded edges)	—	40,000
SS6	1870 (1)	Inc. above	KM2, 3, 5, 6; Double Set (plain edges)	—	80,000
SS7	1872 (4)	Inc. above	KM2, 3, 5, 6	—	12,500
SS8	1875 (2)	Inc. above	KM2 (Large date), 3, 5	—	100,000
SS9	1880 (2)	Inc. above	KM2, 3, 5 (Narrow 0)	—	55,000
SS10	1881 (5)	Inc. above	KM7, 2, 3, 5, 6	—	35,000
SS11	1892 (2)	Inc. above	KM3, 5	—	10,000
SS12	1902 (5)	100	KM8-12	—	25,000
SS13	1902 (3)	Inc. above	KM9 (Large H), 10, 11	—	6,500
SS14	1903 (3)	Inc. above	KM10, 12, 13	—	7,000
SS15	1908 (5)	1,000	KM8, 10-13	—	5,000
SS16	1911 (5)	1,000	KM15-19	—	6,000
SS17	1911/12 (0)	5	KM15-20, 26-27	—	52,250
SS18	1921 (5)	Inc. above	KM22a-25a, 28	—	120,000
SS19	1922 (2)	Inc. above	KM28, 29	—	2,500
SS20	1923 (2)	Inc. above	KM28, 29	—	5,000
SS21	1924 (2)	Inc. above	KM28, 29	—	4,000
SS22	1925 (2)	Inc. above	KM28, 29	—	7,000
SS23	1926 (2)	Inc. above	KM28, 29 (Near 6)	—	5,000
SS24	1927 (3)	Inc. above	KM24a, 28, 29	—	8,000
SS25	1928 (4)	Inc. above	KM23a, 24a, 28, 29	—	12,000
SS26	1929 (5)	Inc. above	KM23a,-25a, 28, 29	—	22,500
SS27	1930 (4)	Inc. above	KM23a, 24a. 28, 29	—	16,000
SS28	1931 (5)	Inc. above	KM23a-25a, 28, 29	—	26,500
SS29	1932 (5)	Inc. above	KM23a-25a, 28, 29	—	20,000
SS30	1934 (5)	Inc. above	KM23-25, 28, 29	—	23,000
SS31	1936 (5)	Inc. above	KM23a-25a, 28, 29	—	12,000
SS32	1936 (5)	Inc. above	KM23a(dot), 24a(dot), 25a, 28(dot), 29, 30	—	400,000
SS33	1937 (6)	1,025	KM32-37, Matte Finish	—	750
SS34	1937 (4)	Inc. above	KM32-35, Mirror Fields	—	1,350
SS35	1937 (6)	75	KM32-37, Mirror Fields	—	3,900
SS36	1938 (6)	Inc. above	KM32-37	—	18,250
SS-A36	1939 (5)	Inc. above	KM32-35, 38, Matte Finish	—	—
SS-B36	1939 (5)	Inc. above	KM32-35, 38, Mirror Fields	—	—
SS-C36	1942 (2)	Inc. above	KM32, 33	—	1,000
SS-D36	1943 (2)	Inc. above	KM32, 40	—	1,000
SS-A37	1944 (2)	Inc. above	KM32, 40a	—	1,000

SETS

KM#	Date	Mintage	Identification	Issue Price	Mkt. Value
SS37	1944 (5)	3	KM32, 34-37, 40a	—	11,300
SS-A38	1945 (2)	Inc. above	KM32, 40a	—	1,000
SS38	1945 (6)	6	KM32, 34-37, 40a	—	4,650
SS39	1946 (6)	15	KM32, 34-37, 39a	—	4,000
SS40	1947 (6)	Inc. above	KM32, 34-37(7 curved), 37(7 pointed),	—	8,500
SS41	1947 (6)	Inc. above	KM32, 34-36(7 curved), 37(blunt 7), 39a	—	6,200
SS42	1947 (6)	Inc. above	KM32, 34-36(7 curved right), 37, 39a	—	4,250
SS43	1948 (6)	30	KM41-46	—	6,000
SS44	1949 (6)	20	KM41-45, 47	—	6,400
SS44A	1949 (2)	Inc. above	KM47	—	1,550
SS45	1950 (6)	12	KM41-46	—	1,650
SS46	1950 (6)	Inc. above	KM41-45, 46 (Arnprior)	—	3,175
SS47	1951 (7)	12	KM41, 48, 42a, 43-46 (w/water lines)	—	2,725
SS48	1952 (6)	2,317	KM41, 42a, 43-46 (water lines)	—	3,175
SS48A	1952 (6)	Inc. above	KM41, 42a, 43-46 (w/o water lines)	—	3,175
SS49	1953 (6)	28	KM49 w/o straps, 50-54	—	1,850
SS50	1953 (6)	Inc. above	KM49 w/ straps, 50-54	—	875
SS51	1964 (6)	Inc. above	KM49, 51, 52, 56-58	—	850
SS52	1965 (6)	Inc. above	KM59.1-60.1, 61-63, 64.1	—	850
SS56	1971 (6)	66,860	KM59.1-60.1, 62b-75.1, 77.1, 79 (2 pcs.); Double Dollar Prestige Sets	12.00	14.50
SS57	1972 (5)	36,349	KM59.1,-60.1, 62b-75.1, 76.1 (2 pcs.)	12.00	18.00
SS58	1973 (6)	119,819	KM59.1-60.1, 75.1, 77.1, 81.1, 82, 83	12.00	16.00
SS59	1973 (6)	Inc. above	KM59.1-60.1, 75.1, 77.1, 81.2, 82, 83	—	225
SS60	1974 (5)	85,230	KM59.1-60.1, 62b-75.1, 77.1, 88, 88a	15.00	10.00
SS61	1975 (5)	97,263	KM59.1-60.1, 62b-75.1, 76.2, 77.1, 97	15.00	10.00
SS62	1976 (5)	87,744	KM59.1-60.1, 62b-75.1, 76.2, 77.1, 106	16.00	10.00
SS63	1977 (5)	142,577	KM59.1-60.1, 62b, 75.2, 77.1, 117.1, 118	16.50	10.00
SS64	1978 (6)	147,000	KM59.1-60.1, 62b, 75.3, 77.1, 120.1, 121	16.50	10.00
SS65	1979 (6)	155,698	KM59.2-60.2, 74, 75.3, 77.2, 120, 124	18.50	11.50
SS66	1980 (6)	162,875	KM60.2, 74-75.3, 77.2, 120, 127, 128	30.50	22.50
SS67	1981 (6)	71,300	KM60.2, 74, 75.3, 77.2, 120.1, 127; Regular Specimen Sets	10.00	5.50
SS68	1982 (10)	62,298	KM60.2a, 74, 75.3, 77.2, 120.1, 132	11.50	5.50
SS69	1983 (6)	60,329	KM60.2a, 74, 75.3, 77.2, 120.1, 132	12.75	5.50
SS70	1984 (2)	60,400	KM60.2a, 74, 75.3, 77.2, 120.1, 132	10.00	5.50
SS71	1985 (6)	61,553	KM60.2a, 74, 75.3, 77.2, 120.1, 132	10.00	6.00
SS72	1986 (6)	67,152	KM60.2a, 74, 75.3, 77.2, 120.1, 132	10.00	9.00
SS72A	1987 (6)	75,194	KM60.2a, 74, 75.3, 77.2, 120.1, 132	11.00	7.50
SS73	1988 (6)	70,205	KM60.2a, 74, 75.3, 77.2, 132, 157	12.30	7.50
SS74	1989 (6)	75,306	KM60.2a, 74, 75.3, 77.2, 132, 157	14.50	8.50
SS75	1990 (6)	76,611	KM181-186	15.50	8.50
SS76	1991 (6)	68,552	KM181-186	15.50	17.50
SS77	1992 (6)	78,328	KM204-209	16.25	17.50
SS78	1993 (6)	77,351	KM181-186; Regular Specimen Sets Resumed	16.25	13.00
SS79	1994 (6)	77,349	KM181-186	16.50	9.50
SS80	1995 (6)	Inc. above	KM181-186	13.95	9.50
SS82	1996 (4)	Inc. above	KM181a-185a, 186	18.95	35.00
SS83	1997 (7)	Inc. above	KM182a-184a, 270, 289-291	19.95	40.00
SS84	1998 (7)	Inc. above	KM182-184, 186, 270, 289, 290	19.95	18.00
SS85	1999 (7)	Inc. above	KM182-184, 186, 270, 289a, 290	19.95	20.00
SS91	2003 (3)	75,000	KM#(uncertain), 270, 289, 290	30.00	50.00

V.I.P. Specimen Sets (VS)

KM#	Date	Mintage	Identification	Issue Price	Mkt. Value
VS1	1969 (0)	4		—	2,000
VS2	1970 (0)	100	KM59.1-60.1, 74.1-75.1, 77.1, 78	—	525
VS3	1971 (0)	69	KM59.1-60.1, 74.1-75.1, 77.1, 79(2 pcs.)	—	525
VS4	1972 (0)	25	KM59.1-60.1, 74.1-75.1, 76.1, (2 pcs.), 77.1	—	650
VS5	1973 (0)	26	KM59.1-60.1, 75.1, 77.1, 81.1, 82, 83	—	650
VS6	1974 (0)	72	KM59.1-60.1, 74.1-75.1, 77.1, 88, 88a	—	525
VS7	1975 (0)	94	KM59.1-60.1, 74.1-75.1, 76.2, 77.1, 97	—	525
VS8	1976 (0)	Inc. above	KM59.1-60.1, 74.1-75.1, 76.2, 77.1, 106	—	525

NEW BRUNSWICK
PROVINCE

STERLING COINAGE

HALFPENNY TOKEN

KM# 1   Obv: Crowned head left **Obv. Legend:** VICTORIA DEI GRATIA REGINA **Rev:** Three masted ship **Rev. Legend:** NEW BRUNSWICK **Composition:** Copper

Date	Mintage	VG-8	F-12	VF-20	XF-40	MS-60	MS-63	Proof
1843	480,000	4.00	7.50	15.00	45.00	300	400	—
1843 Proof	—	—	—	—	—	—	—	750

KM# 3   Obv: Head left **Obv. Legend:** VICTORIA DEI GRATIA REGINA **Rev:** Three masted ship **Rev. Legend:** NEW BRUNSWICK **Composition:** Copper

Date	Mintage	VG-8	F-12	VF-20	XF-40	MS-60	MS-63	Proof
1854	864,000	4.00	7.50	15.00	45.00	300	400	—

KM# 3a   Obv: Head left **Obv. Legend:** VICTORIA DEI GRATIA REGINA **Rev:** Three masted ship **Rev. Legend:** NEW BRUNSWICK **Composition:** Bronze

Date	Mintage	VG-8	F-12	VF-20	XF-40	MS-60	MS-63	Proof
1854 Proof	—	—	—	—	—	—	—	400

1 PENNY TOKEN

KM# 2   Obv: Crowned head left **Obv. Legend:** VICTORIA DEI GRATIA REGINA **Rev:** Three masted ship **Rev. Legend:** NEW BRUNSWICK **Composition:** Copper

Date	Mintage	VG-8	F-12	VF-20	XF-40	MS-60	MS-63	Proof
1843	480,000	5.00	9.50	23.00	65.00	250	350	—
1843 Proof	—	—	—	—	—	—	—	800

KM# 4 Obv: Head left **Obv. Legend:** VICTORIA DEI GRATIA REGINA **Rev:** Three masted ship **Rev. Legend:** NEW BRUNSWICK **Composition:** Copper

Date	Mintage	VG-8	F-12	VF-20	XF-40	MS-60	MS-63	Proof
1854	432,000	3.75	7.50	22.00	65.00	300	400	—

DECIMAL COINAGE

HALF CENT

KM# 5 Obv: Laureate bust left **Obv. Legend:** VICTORIA D:G:

BRITT: REG: F:D: **Rev:** Crown and date within beaded circle, wreath surrounds **Composition:** Bronze

Date	Mintage	VG-8	F-12	VF-20	XF-40	MS-60	MS-63	Proof
1861	222,800	125	175	225	350	650	1,500	—
1861 Proof	—	—	—	—	—	—	—	2,200

CENT

KM# 6 Obv: Laureate bust left **Obv. Legend:** VICTORIA D:G:

BRITT: REG: F:D: **Rev:** Crown and date within beaded circle, wreath surrounds **Rev. Legend:** NEW BRUNSWICK **Composition:** Bronze

Date	Mintage	VG-8	F-12	VF-20	XF-40	MS-60	MS-63	Proof
1861	1,000,000	3.50	6.00	9.00	14.00	100.00	450	—
1861 Proof	—	—	—	—	—	—	—	450
1864 short 6	1,000,000	3.50	6.00	9.00	20.00	125	550	—
1864 long 6	Inc. above	4.00	6.50	13.00	24.00	175	650	—

5 CENTS

KM# 7 Obv: Laureate head left **Obv. Legend:** VICTORIA D: G: REG: / NEW BRUNSWICK **Rev:** Denomination and date within wreath, crown above **Weight:** 1.1620 g. **Composition:** 0.9250 Silver 0.0346 oz. ASW

Date	Mintage	VG-8	F-12	VF-20	XF-40	MS-60	MS-63	Proof
1862	100,000	65.00	100.00	225	500	1,700	3,200	—
1862 Proof	—	—	—	—	—	—	—	3,500
1864 small 6	100,000	65.00	100.00	225	1,000	2,200	4,900	—
1864 large 6	Inc. above	75.00	125	300	600	2,500	5,000	—

10 CENTS

KM# 8   Obv: Laureate head left **Obv. Legend:** VICTORIA D: G: REG: /
NEW BRUNSWICK **Rev:** Denomination and date within wreath, crown above **Weight:** 2.3240 g. **Composition:** 0.9250 Silver 0.0691 oz. ASW

Date	Mintage	VG-8	F-12	VF-20	XF-40	MS-60	MS-63	Proof
1862	150,000	65.00	100.00	225	450	1,600	3,000	—
1862 recut 2	Inc. above	95.00	175	350	750	2,900	6,700	—
1862 Proof	—	—	—	—	—	—	—	2,850
1864	100,000	65.00	100.00	225	450	2,700	6,300	—

20 CENTS

KM# 9   Obv: Laureate head left **Obv. Legend:** VICTORIA D: G: REG: / NEW BRUNSWICK **Rev:** Denomination and date within wreath, crown above **Weight:** 4.6480 g. **Composition:** 0.9250 Silver 0.1382 oz. ASW

Date	Mintage	VG-8	F-12	VF-20	XF-40	MS-60	MS-63	Proof
1862	150,000	29.00	50.00	100.00	225	1,050	4,400	—
1862 Proof	—	—	—	—	—	—	—	2,850
1864	150,000	29.00	50.00	100.00	225	1,600	4,600	—

NEWFOUNDLAND
PROVINCE

CIRCULATION COINAGE

LARGE CENT

KM# 1   Obv: Laureate bust left **Obv. Legend:** VICTORIA D:G: BRITT: REG:F:D: **Rev:** Crown and date within circle, florals surround **Rev. Legend:** NEWFOUNDLAND **Composition:** Bronze

Date	Mintage	VG-8	F-12	VF-20	XF-40	MS-60	MS-63	Proof
1865	240,000	3.50	5.50	12.00	30.00	175	900	—
1872H	200,000	2.50	4.00	7.00	17.00	70.00	250	—
1872H Proof	—	—	—	—	—	—	—	800
1873	200,025	4.00	6.50	20.00	40.00	300	1,600	—
1873 Proof	—	—	—	—	—	—	—	3,000
1876H	200,000	3.50	7.00	15.00	60.00	300	1,600	—

Date	Mintage	VG-8	F-12	VF-20	XF-40	MS-60	MS-63	Proof
1876H Proof, reported not confirmed	—	—	—	—	—	—	—	—
1880 round 0, even date	400,000	3.00	3.50	7.00	20.00	125	500	—
1880 round and low 0	Inc. above	4.50	12.00	20.00	50.00	400	2,600	—
1880 oval 0	Inc. above	200	300	500	950	2,000	6,000	—
1880 oval 0 Proof	—	—	—	—	—	—	—	2,500
1885	40,000	27.50	50.00	75.00	125	500	2,400	—
1885 Proof	—	—	—	—	—	—	—	2,500
1888	50,000	30.00	55.00	80.00	175	750	4,800	—
1890	200,000	3.00	6.00	15.00	45.00	300	1,200	—
1894	200,000	3.00	5.00	10.00	25.00	140	1,200	—
1894 Proof	—	—	—	—	—	—	—	1,500
1896	200,000	3.00	3.50	7.00	27.00	120	500	—
1896 Proof	—	—	—	—	—	—	—	1,500

KM# 9 Obv: Crowned bust right **Obv. Designer:** G.W. DeSaulles **Rev:** Crown and date within center circle, wreath surrounds, denomination above **Rev. Designer:** Horace Morehen **Composition:** Bronze

Date	Mintage	VG-8	F-12	VF-20	XF-40	MS-60	MS-63	Proof
1904H	100,000	7.00	14.00	20.00	55.00	300	700	—
1904H Proof	—	—	—	—	—	—	—	4,000
1907	200,000	2.00	4.00	8.00	30.00	220	650	—
1909	200,000	2.00	4.00	7.00	19.00	100.00	150	—
1909 Proof	—	—	—	—	—	—	—	400

KM# 16 Obv: Crowned bust left **Obv. Designer:** E.B. MacKennal **Rev:** Crown and date within center circle, wreath surrounds, denomination above **Rev. Designer:** Horace Morehen **Composition:** Bronze

Date	Mintage	VG-8	F-12	VF-20	XF-40	MS-60	MS-63	Proof
1913	400,000	1.00	1.50	3.00	7.00	40.00	75.00	—
1917C	702,350	1.00	1.50	3.00	6.00	75.00	200	—
1917C Proof	—	—	—	—	—	—	—	800
1919C	300,000	1.00	2.00	3.00	10.00	175	300	—
1919C Proof	—	—	—	—	—	—	—	1,000
1920C	302,184	1.00	2.00	5.00	18.00	300	1,000	—
1929	300,000	1.00	1.50	3.00	6.00	55.00	100.00	—
1929C Proof	—	—	—	—	—	—	—	1,000
1936	300,000	1.00	1.25	1.75	4.00	28.00	75.00	—

SMALL CENT

KM# 18 Obv: Crowned head left **Obv. Designer:** Percy Metcalfe **Rev:** Pitcher plant divides date, denomination below **Rev. Designer:** Walter J. Newman **Weight:** 3.2000 g. **Composition:** Bronze **Size:** 19 mm.

Date	Mintage	VG-8	F-12	VF-20	XF-40	MS-60	MS-63	Proof
1938	500,000	0.50	0.75	1.50	2.50	16.00	40.00	—
1938 Proof	—	—	—	—	—	—	—	1,000
1940	300,000	1.25	2.00	3.00	10.00	75.00	250	—
1940 Re-engraved date	Inc. above	30.00	40.00	125	70.00	500	900	—
1940 Proof	—	—	—	—	—	—	—	1,000
1941C	827,662	0.35	0.45	0.70	2.00	20.00	120	—
1941C Re-engraved date	Inc. above	9.00	13.00	30.00	65.00	250	700	—
1942	1,996,889	0.35	0.45	0.70	2.00	30.00	125	—
1943C	1,239,732	0.35	0.45	0.70	2.00	13.50	70.00	—
1944C	1,328,776	1.00	2.00	10.00	30.00	250	550	—
1947C	313,772	0.90	1.65	5.00	12.00	80.00	200	—
1947C Proof	—	—	—	—	—	—	—	2,000

5 CENTS

KM# 2 Obv: Laureate head left **Obv. Legend:** VICTORIA D: G: REG:

NEWFOUNDLAND **Rev:** Denomination and date within ornamental circle **Edge:** Reeded **Weight:** 1.1782 g. **Composition:** 0.9250 Silver 0.0350 oz. ASW

Date	Mintage	VG-8	F-12	VF-20	XF-40	MS-60	MS-63	Proof
1865	80,000	35.00	50.00	150	300	1,200	3,000	—
1865 Proof	—	—	—	—	—	—	—	4,000
1870	40,000	65.00	125	225	500	1,900	3,000	—
1870 Proof	—	—	—	—	—	—	—	4,000
1872H	40,000	40.00	70.00	125	175	600	2,400	—

Date	Mintage	VG-8	F-12	VF-20	XF-40	MS-60	MS-63	Proof
1873	44,260	125	200	450	1,100	4,600	—	—
1873H	Inc. above	950	1,400	2,000	3,700	12,500	22,000	—
1873 Proof	—	—	—	—	—	—	—	10,000
1876H	20,000	125	200	350	650	1,200	2,750	—
1880	40,000	45.00	65.00	150	300	1,600	2,400	—
1880 Proof	—	—	—	—	—	—	—	5,000
1881	40,000	45.00	65.00	150	300	1,900	2,500	—
1881 Proof	—	—	—	—	—	—	—	5,000
1882H	60,000	23.00	45.00	90.00	200	800	2,000	—
1882H Proof	—	—	—	—	—	—	—	2,000
1885	16,000	130	210	335	750	2,400	4,500	—
1885 Proof	—	—	—	—	—	—	—	7,500
1888	40,000	40.00	75.00	225	375	1,900	4,900	—
1888 Proof	—	—	—	—	—	—	—	7,500
1890	160,000	11.00	21.00	45.00	125	800	2,000	—
1890 Proof	—	—	—	—	—	—	—	5,000
1894	160,000	10.00	19.00	30.00	100.00	800	2,500	—
1894 Proof	—	—	—	—	—	—	—	5,000
1896	400,000	4.00	8.00	20.00	50.00	700	2,700	—
1896 Proof	—	—	—	—	—	—	—	5,000

KM# 7 Obv: Crowned bust right **Rev:** Denomination and date within circle **Designer:** G.W. DeSaulles
Weight: 1.1782 g. **Composition:** 0.9250 Silver 0.0350 oz. ASW

Date	Mintage	VG-8	F-12	VF-20	XF-40	MS-60	MS-63	Proof
1903	100,000	4.00	9.00	18.00	45.00	435	1,350	—
1903 Proof	—	—	—	—	—	—	—	2,000
1904H	100,000	3.00	5.00	14.00	35.00	160	285	—
1904H Proof	—	—	—	—	—	—	—	1,200
1908	400,000	3.00	6.00	11.50	30.00	260	750	—

KM# 13 Obv: Crowned bust left **Obv. Designer:** E.B. MacKennal **Rev:** Denomination and date within circle
Rev. Designer: G.W. DeSaulles **Weight:** 1.1782 g. **Composition:** 0.9250 Silver 0.0350 oz. ASW

Date	Mintage	VG-8	F-12	VF-20	XF-40	MS-60	MS-63	Proof
1912	300,000	1.50	2.00	5.00	20.00	125	275	—
1912 Proof	—	—	—	—	—	—	—	2,000
1917C	300,319	1.50	3.00	7.00	25.00	250	650	—
1917C Proof	—	—	—	—	—	—	—	2,000
1919C	100,844	5.00	9.00	25.00	100.00	950	2,800	—
1919C Proof	—	—	—	—	—	—	—	2,000
1929	300,000	1.50	2.50	3.25	12.00	165	350	—

KM# 19 Obv: Crowned head left **Obv. Designer:** Percy Metcalfe **Rev:** Denomination and date within circle
Rev. Designer: G.W. DeSaulles **Weight:** 1.1782 g. **Composition:** 0.9250 Silver 0.0350 oz. ASW

Date	Mintage	VG-8	F-12	VF-20	XF-40	MS-60	MS-63	Proof
1938	100,000	0.85	1.50	2.00	7.00	70.00	225	—
1938 Proof	—	—	—	—	—	—	—	1,000
1940C	200,000	0.85	1.50	2.00	7.00	85.00	300	—
1940C Proof	—	—	—	—	—	—	—	2,000
1941C	621,641	0.65	1.50	2.00	4.00	15.00	35.00	—
1942C	298,348	0.85	1.50	2.00	4.00	17.50	40.00	—
1943C	351,666	0.65	1.00	2.00	4.00	15.00	30.00	—

KM# 19a Obv: Crowned head left **Obv. Designer:** Percy Metcalfe **Rev:** Denomination and date within circle
Rev. Designer: G.W. DeSaulles **Edge:** Reeded **Weight:** 1.1664 g. **Composition:** 0.8000 Silver 0.0300 oz.
ASW **Size:** 15.67 mm.

Date	Mintage	VG-8	F-12	VF-20	XF-40	MS-60	MS-63	Proof
1944C	286,504	1.25	1.75	3.00	7.00	50.00	120	—
1945C	203,828	0.65	1.00	2.00	4.00	14.00	32.00	—
1946C	2,041	200	300	350	400	1,200	1,900	—
1946C Prooflike	—	—	—	—	—	—	2,500	—
1947C	38,400	2.00	3.00	5.00	17.00	65.00	200	—
1947C Prooflike	—	—	—	—	—	—	375	—

10 CENTS

KM# 3 Obv: Laureate head left **Obv. Legend:** VICTORIA D: G: REG: NEWFOUNDLAND **Rev:** Denomination and date within ornamental circle **Weight:** 2.3564 g. **Composition:** 0.9250 Silver 0.0701 oz. ASW

Date	Mintage	VG-8	F-12	VF-20	XF-40	MS-60	MS-63	Proof
1865	80,000	27.00	45.00	75.00	250	1,100	2,250	—
1865 Proof, plain edge	—	—	—	—	—	—	—	5,500
1870	30,000	150	250	450	725	2,350	5,000	—
1870 Proof	—	—	—	—	—	—	—	10,000
1872H	40,000	22.00	35.00	80.00	200	800	1,700	—
1873 flat 3	23,614	55.00	70.00	250	650	4,000	5,000	—
1873 round 3	Inc. above	55.00	70.00	250	650	4,000	5,000	—
1873 Proof	—	—	—	—	—	—	—	12,000
1876H	10,000	55.00	70.00	225	350	1,400	2,500	—
1880/70	10,000	55.00	100.00	250	400	1,800	2,950	—
1880 Proof	—	—	—	—	—	—	—	7,500
1882H	20,000	30.00	55.00	150	475	2,200	6,700	—
1882H Proof	—	—	—	—	—	—	—	3,000
1885	8,000	70.00	130	300	800	2,200	4,250	—
1885 Proof	—	—	—	—	—	—	—	8,000
1888	30,000	35.00	70.00	200	700	4,000	5,000	—
1888 Proof	—	—	—	—	—	—	—	8,000
1890	100,000	9.00	19.00	35.00	150	1,100	3,200	—
1890 Proof	—	—	—	—	—	—	—	5,000
1894	100,000	8.50	12.00	25.00	125	1,200	3,000	—
1894 Proof	—	—	—	—	—	—	—	5,000
1896	230,000	5.00	10.00	25.00	90.00	1,200	3,200	—
1896 Proof	—	—	—	—	—	—	—	5,000

KM# 8 Obv: Crowned bust right **Rev:** Denomination and date within circle **Designer:** G.W. DeSaulles **Weight:** 2.3564 g. **Composition:** 0.9250 Silver 0.0701 oz. ASW

Date	Mintage	VG-8	F-12	VF-20	XF-40	MS-60	MS-63	Proof
1903	100,000	8.00	25.00	70.00	200	1,200	4,400	—
1903 Proof	—	—	—	—	—	—	—	2,500
1904H	100,000	4.00	10.00	30.00	90.00	200	350	—
1904H Proof	—	—	—	—	—	—	—	1,500

KM# 14 Obv: Crowned bust left **Obv. Designer:** E.B. MacKennal **Rev. Designer:** G.W. DeSaulles **Weight:** 2.3564 g. **Composition:** 0.9250 Silver 0.0701 oz. ASW

Date	Mintage	VG-8	F-12	VF-20	XF-40	MS-60	MS-63	Proof
1912	150,000	1.20	3.00	10.00	40.00	165	300	—
1917C	250,805	1.20	3.00	11.00	40.00	400	1,500	—
1919C	54,342	2.00	6.00	18.00	55.00	175	350	—

KM# 20 Obv: Crowned head left **Obv. Designer:** Percy Metcalfe **Rev:** Denomination and date within circle **Rev. Designer:** G.W. DeSaulles **Weight:** 2.3564 g. **Composition:** 0.9250 Silver 0.0701 oz. ASW

Date	Mintage	VG-8	F-12	VF-20	XF-40	MS-60	MS-63	Proof
1938	100,000	1.10	1.75	3.00	11.00	80.00	300	—
1938 Proof	—	—	—	—	—	—	—	2,000
1940	100,000	1.10	1.50	3.00	10.00	80.00	300	—
1940 Proof	—	—	—	—	—	—	—	2,500
1941C	483,630	1.10	1.50	2.20	5.00	40.00	125	—
1942C	293,736	1.10	1.50	2.20	5.00	50.00	130	—
1943C	104,706	1.10	1.50	2.50	6.00	60.00	200	—
1944C	151,471	2.50	3.50	10.00	20.00	200	800	—

KM# 20a Obv: Crowned head left **Obv. Designer:** Percy Metcalfe **Rev. Designer:** G.W. DeSaulles **Weight:** 2.3328 g. **Composition:** 0.8000 Silver 0.0600 oz. ASW

Date	Mintage	VG-8	F-12	VF-20	XF-40	MS-60	MS-63	Proof
1945C	175,833	1.00	1.35	2.25	4.50	45.00	225	—
1946C	38,400	2.00	4.00	10.00	25.00	100.00	275	—
1946C Proof	—	—	—	—	—	—	—	750
1947C	61,988	1.50	3.00	4.50	14.00	65.00	275	—

20 CENTS

KM# 4 Obv: Laureate head left **Rev:** Denomination and date within ornamental circle **Weight:** 4.7127 g. **Composition:** 0.9250 Silver 0.1401 oz. ASW **Size:** 23.19 mm.

Date	Mintage	VG-8	F-12	VF-20	XF-40	MS-60	MS-63	Proof
1865	100,000	16.00	30.00	60.00	225	950	2,600	—
1865 Proof, plain edge	—	—	—	—	—	—	—	6,500
1865 Proof, reeded edge	—	—	—	—	—	—	—	10,000
1870	50,000	21.00	45.00	100.00	250	1,250	2,600	—
1870 Proof, plain edge	—	—	—	—	—	—	—	6,500
1870 Proof, reeded edge	—	—	—	—	—	—	—	6,500
1872H	90,000	12.00	25.00	60.00	140	750	1,800	—
1873	45,797	21.00	65.00	175	550	5,400	8,000	—
1873 Proof	—	—	—	—	—	—	—	12,000
1876H	50,000	25.00	50.00	80.00	300	1,350	2,700	—
1880/70	30,000	27.00	55.00	100.00	350	2,000	3,000	—
1880 Proof	—	—	—	—	—	—	—	8,000
1881	60,000	12.00	25.00	80.00	300	1,200	2,900	—
1881 Proof	—	—	—	—	—	—	—	8,000
1882H	100,000	9.00	19.00	50.00	140	1,000	3,400	—
1882H Proof	—	—	—	—	—	—	—	3,500
1885	40,000	14.00	30.00	80.00	300	2,900	4,500	—
1885 Proof	—	—	—	—	—	—	—	10,000
1888	75,000	12.00	25.00	70.00	225	1,400	4,200	—
1888 Proof	—	—	—	—	—	—	—	10,000
1890	100,000	9.00	15.00	45.00	225	1,400	3,500	—
1890 Proof	—	—	—	—	—	—	—	6,500
1894	100,000	12.00	24.00	50.00	175	1,200	—	—
1894 Proof	—	—	—	—	—	—	—	6,500
1896 small 96	125,000	6.00	12.00	35.00	150	1,400	3,600	—
1896 large 96	Inc. above	7.00	15.00	50.00	200	1,700	4,500	—
1896 large 96, Proof	—	—	—	—	—	—	—	6,500
1899 hook 99	125,000	27.00	50.00	125	350	1,800	4,900	—
1899 large 99	Inc. above	5.00	12.00	30.00	125	1,400	3,600	—
1900	125,000	5.00	8.00	25.00	80.00	1,100	3,400	—
1900 Proof	—	—	—	—	—	—	—	6,500

KM# 10 Obv: Crowned bust right **Obv. Designer:** G.W. DeSaulles **Rev:** Denomination and date within circle
Rev. Designer: W.H.J. Blakemore **Weight:** 4.7127 g. **Composition:** 0.9250 Silver 0.1401 oz. ASW

Date	Mintage	VG-8	F-12	VF-20	XF-40	MS-60	MS-63	Proof
1904H	75,000	10.00	30.00	55.00	275	2,500	6,000	—
1904H Proof	—	—	—	—	—	—	—	1,850

KM# 15 Obv: Crowned bust left **Obv. Designer:** E.B. MacKennal **Rev:** Denomination and date within circle
Rev. Designer: W.H.J. Blakemore **Weight:** 4.7127 g. **Composition:** 0.9250 Silver 0.1401 oz. ASW

Date	Mintage	VG-8	F-12	VF-20	XF-40	MS-60	MS-63	Proof
1912	350,000	2.50	5.00	14.00	55.00	325	850	—
1912 Proof	—	—	—	—	—	—	—	2,500

25 CENTS

KM# 17 Obv: Crowned bust left **Obv. Designer:** E.B. MacKennal **Rev:** Denomination and date within circle
Rev. Designer: W.H.J. Blakemore **Weight:** 5.8319 g. **Composition:** 0.9250 Silver 0.1734 oz. ASW

Date	Mintage	VG-8	F-12	VF-20	XF-40	MS-60	MS-63	Proof
1917C	464,779	3.00	4.00	7.00	17.00	145	300	—
1917C Proof	—	—	—	—	—	—	—	2,500
1919C	163,939	3.00	5.00	14.00	25.00	350	1,250	—
1919C Proof	—	—	—	—	—	—	—	2,500

50 CENTS

KM# 6 Obv: Laureate head left **Obv. Legend:** VICTORIA DEI GRATIA REGINA NEWFOUNDLAND
Rev: Denomination and date within ornamental circle **Weight:** 11.7818 g. **Composition:** 0.9250 Silver
0.3504 oz. ASW **Size:** 29.85 mm.

Date	Mintage	VG-8	F-12	VF-20	XF-40	MS-60	MS-63	Proof
1870	50,000	26.00	50.00	150	600	3,500	8,500	—
1870 Proof, plain edge	—	—	—	—	—	—	—	25,000
1870 Proof, reeded edge	—	—	—	—	—	—	—	25,000
1872H	48,000	18.00	35.00	90.00	400	1,600	3,600	—
1873	37,675	40.00	75.00	200	650	9,600	11,000	—
1873 Proof	—	—	—	—	—	—	—	40,000

Date	Mintage	VG-8	F-12	VF-20	XF-40	MS-60	MS-63	Proof
1874	80,000	25.00	45.00	125	550	8,900	10,000	—
1874 Proof	—	—	—	—	—	—	—	40,000
1876H	28,000	35.00	85.00	150	450	2,250	5,250	—
1880	24,000	45.00	95.00	250	900	6,500	16,000	—
1880 Proof	—	—	—	—	—	—	—	40,000
1881	50,000	20.00	35.00	135	400	3,300	9,300	—
1881 Proof	—	—	—	—	—	—	—	40,000
1882H	100,000	12.00	30.00	95.00	350	1,600	5,400	—
1882H Proof	—	—	—	—	—	—	—	8,000
1885	40,000	30.00	60.00	175	650	2,800	7,100	—
1885 Proof	—	—	—	—	—	—	—	40,000
1888	20,000	50.00	90.00	250	925	11,000	13,000	—
1888 Proof	—	—	—	—	—	—	—	40,000
1894	40,000	12.00	28.00	75.00	300	3,700	9,700	—
1896	60,000	8.50	16.00	65.00	300	3,000	8,100	—
1896 Proof	—	—	—	—	—	—	—	25,000
1898	76,607	8.50	13.00	60.00	200	3,100	8,100	—
1899 wide 9's	150,000	8.50	13.00	60.00	200	2,800	7,200	—
1899 narrow 9's	Inc. above	8.50	13.00	45.00	150	2,600	7,700	—
1900	150,000	8.50	13.00	45.00	175	2,600	7,200	—

KM# 11   Obv: Crowned bust right **Obv. Designer:** G.W. DeSaulles **Rev. Designer:** W.H.J. Blakemore
Weight: 11.7800 g. **Composition:** 0.9250 Silver 0.3503 oz. ASW **Size:** 30 mm.

Date	Mintage	VG-8	F-12	VF-20	XF-40	MS-60	MS-63	Proof
1904H	140,000	5.00	6.00	14.00	55.00	275	850	—
1904H Proof	—	—	—	—	—	—	—	5,000
1907	100,000	5.00	6.00	22.00	65.00	350	1,000	—
1908	160,000	5.00	6.00	13.50	50.00	225	700	—
1909	200,000	5.00	12.00	21.00	55.00	300	800	—

KM# 12   Obv: Crowned bust left **Obv. Designer:** E.B. MacKennal **Rev:** Denomination and date within circle
Rev. Designer: W.H.J. Blakemore **Weight:** 11.7800 g. **Composition:** 0.9250 Silver 0.3503 oz. ASW
Size: 30 mm.

Date	Mintage	VG-8	F-12	VF-20	XF-40	MS-60	MS-63	Proof
1911	200,000	5.00	6.00	11.00	35.00	200	550	—
1917C	375,560	5.00	6.00	11.00	28.00	145	350	—
1917C Proof	—	—	—	—	—	—	—	2,500
1918C	294,824	5.00	6.00	11.00	28.00	145	350	—
1919C	306,267	5.00	6.00	11.00	30.00	325	1,150	—
1919C Proof	—	—	—	—	—	—	—	2,500

2 DOLLARS

KM# 5   Obv: Laureate head left **Obv. Legend:** VICTORIA D: G: REG: NEWFOUNDLAND **Rev:** Denomination
and date within circle **Weight:** 3.3284 g. **Composition:** 0.9170 Gold 0.0981 oz. AGW

Date	Mintage	F-12	VF-20	XF-40	AU-50	MS-60	MS-63
1865	10,000	150	225	300	375	1,100	8,500
1865 plain edge, Specimen-63, $15,000.	Est. 10	—	—	—	—	—	—
1870	10,000	150	225	300	450	1,500	7,500
1870 reeded edge, Specimen-63 $20,000.	Est. 5	—	—	—	—	—	—
1872	6,050	220	400	500	900	2,200	8,800
1872 Specimen-63 $12,500.	Est. 10	—	—	—	—	—	—
1880	2,500	800	1,000	1,200	2,300	4,650	14,250
1880/70	—	—	—	—	—	—	—
Note: Specimen. Bowers and Merena Norweb sale 11-96, specimen 64 realized $70,400.							
1881	10,000	150	200	250	325	1,600	2,500
1881 Specimen; Rare	—	—	—	—	—	—	—
1882H	25,000	150	200	250	300	700	2,200
1882H Specimen $4,250.	—	—	—	—	—	—	—
1885	10,000	150	200	250	300	850	2,750
1885 Specimen	—	—	—	—	—	—	—
Note: Bowers and Merena Norweb sale 11-96, specimen 66 realized $44,000							
1888	25,000	150	175	200	250	600	2,000
1888 Specimen; Rare	—	—	—	—	—	—	—

NOVA SCOTIA
PROVINCE

DECIMAL COINAGE

HALF CENT

KM# 7 Obv: Laureate bust left **Obv. Legend:** VICTORIA D:G: BRITT: REG:F:D: **Rev:** Crown and date within beaded circle, wreath of roses surrounds **Rev. Legend:** NOVA SCOTIA **Composition:** Bronze

Date	Mintage	VG-8	F-12	VF-20	XF-40	MS-60	MS-63	Proof
1861	400,000	5.00	7.00	8.00	13.00	60.00	300	—
1864	400,000	5.00	7.00	8.00	13.00	55.00	250	—
1864 Proof	—	—	—	—	—	—	—	300

CENT

KM# 8.2 Obv: Laureate bust left **Obv. Legend:** VICTORIA D:G: BRITT: REG:F:D: **Rev:** Crown and date within beaded circle, wreath of roses surrounds **Rev. Legend:** NOVA SCOTIA **Composition:** Bronze
Note: Prev. KM#8. Small rosebud right of SCOTIA. The Royal Mint report records mintage of 1 million for 1862, which is considered incorrect.

Date	Mintage	VG-8	F-12	VF-20	XF-40	MS-60	MS-63	Proof
1861	800,000	3.00	4.50	5.00	11.00	125	400	—
1862	Est. 1,000,000	45.00	75.00	150	300	1,300	—	—
1864	800,000	3.00	4.50	5.00	16.00	150	450	—

STERLING COINAGE

HALFPENNY TOKEN

KM# 1a   Obv: Laureate head left, draped collar **Obv. Legend:** PROVINCE OF NOVA SCOTIA **Rev:** Thistle
Composition: Copper

Date	Mintage	VG-8	F-12	VF-20	XF-40	MS-60	MS-63	Proof
1382 1382 (error)	—	500	700	1,650	—	—	—	—
1832/1382	—	10.00	15.00	50.00	150	—	—	—
1832 (imitation)	—	3.00	9.00	27.00	75.00	125	200	—

KM# 1   Obv: Laureate head left **Obv. Legend:** PROVINCE OF NOVA SCOTIA **Rev:** Thistle
Composition: Copper

Date	Mintage	VG-8	F-12	VF-20	XF-40	MS-60	MS-63	Proof
1823	400,000	3.00	6.00	13.00	60.00	275	—	—
1823 without hyphen	Inc. above	5.00	10.00	35.00	125	325	—	—
1824	118,636	6.00	12.00	27.00	65.00	450	—	—
1832	800,000	3.00	5.00	13.50	40.00	225	—	—

KM# 3   Obv: Head left **Obv. Legend:** PROVINCE OF NOVA SCOTIA **Rev:** Thistle **Composition:** Copper

Date	Mintage	VG-8	F-12	VF-20	XF-40	MS-60	MS-63	Proof
1840 small 0	300,000	3.50	10.00	25.00	60.00	175	—	—
1840 medium 0	Inc. above	3.50	9.00	25.00	60.00	175	—	—
1840 large 0	Inc. above	4.00	10.00	40.00	125	225	—	—
1843	300,000	3.00	6.00	24.00	60.00	175	—	—

KM# 5   Composition: Copper

Date	Mintage	VG-8	F-12	VF-20	XF-40	MS-60	MS-63	Proof
1856 without LCW	720,000	3.00	4.00	7.50	23.00	175	—	—
1856 without LCW, Proof	—	—	—	—	—	—	—	600
1856 without LCW, inverted A for V in PROVINCE, Proof	—	—	—	—	—	—	—	600

KM# 5a   Composition: Bronze

Date	Mintage	VG-8	F-12	VF-20	XF-40	MS-60	MS-63	Proof
1856 with LCW, Proof	—	—	—	—	—	—	—	600

1 PENNY TOKEN

KM# 2   Obv: Laureate head left **Obv. Legend:** PROVINCE OF NOVA SCOTIA **Rev:** Thistle
Composition: Copper

Date	Mintage	VG-8	F-12	VF-20	XF-40	MS-60	MS-63	Proof
1824	217,776	4.00	10.00	26.00	85.00	400	—	—
1832	200,000	4.00	8.00	15.00	55.00	350	—	—

KM# 2a Obv: Laureate head left **Obv. Legend:** PROVINCE OF NOVA SCOTIA **Rev:** Thistle
Composition: Copper

Date	Mintage	VG-8	F-12	VF-20	XF-40	MS-60	MS-63	Proof
1832 (imitation)	—	3.75	7.50	22.50	85.00	—	—	—

KM# 4 Obv: Head left **Obv. Legend:** PROVINCE OF NOVA SCOTIA **Rev:** Thistle **Composition:** Copper
Size: 32 mm.

Date	Mintage	VG-8	F-12	VF-20	XF-40	MS-60	MS-63	Proof
1840	150,000	3.50	9.00	23.00	60.00	450	—	—
1843/0	150,000	45.00	75.00	250	—	—	—	—
1843	Inc. above	4.00	12.00	24.00	60.00	450	—	—

KM# 6 Obv: Crowned head left **Obv. Legend:** VICTORIA D: G: BRITANNIA R: REG: F: D: **Rev:** Plant
Rev. Legend: PROVINCE OF NOVA SCOTIA **Composition:** Copper

Date	Mintage	VG-8	F-12	VF-20	XF-40	MS-60	MS-63	Proof
1856 without LCW	360,000	4.00	7.50	13.00	35.00	300	—	—
1856 with LCW	Inc. above	2.50	5.00	12.00	35.00	350	—	—

KM# 6a Obv: Crowned head left **Obv. Legend:** VICTORIA D: G: BRITANNIA R: REG: F: D: **Rev:** Plant
Rev. Legend: PROVINCE OF NOVA SCOTIA **Composition:** Bronze

Date	Mintage	VG-8	F-12	VF-20	XF-40	MS-60	MS-63	Proof
1856 Proof	—	—	—	—	—	—	—	400

PRINCE EDWARD ISLAND
PROVINCE

CUT & COUNTERMARKED COINAGE
ca. 1813

SHILLING

KM# 1 Composition: Silver **Note:** Countermark on center plug of Spanish or Spanish Colonial 8 Reales.

Date	Mintage	VG-8	F-12	VF-20	XF-40	MS-60	MS-63	Proof
ND	1,000	2,000	3,000	5,000	—	—	—	—

5 SHILLING

KM# 3 Composition: Silver **Note:** Countermark on holed Lima 8 Reales, KM#106.2.

Date	Mintage	VG-8	F-12	VF-20	XF-40	MS-60	MS-63	Proof
ND1809-11	1,000	2,000	3,000	5,000	—	—	—	—

KM# 2.1 Composition: Silver **Note:** Countermark on holed Mexico City 8 Reales, KM#109.

Date	Mintage	VG-8	F-12	VF-20	XF-40	MS-60	MS-63	Proof
1791-1808	—	1,400	1,800	2,250	—	—	—	—

KM# 2.2 Composition: Silver **Note:** Countermark on holed Mexico City 8 Reales, KM#110.

Date	Mintage	VG-8	F-12	VF-20	XF-40	MS-60	MS-63	Proof
ND1808-11	—	1,400	1,800	2,250	—	—	—	—

DECIMAL COINAGE

CENT

KM# 4 Obv: Crowned head left within beaded circle **Obv. Legend:** VICTORIA QUEEN **Rev:** Trees within beaded circle **Rev. Legend:** PRINCE EDWARD ISLAND **Composition:** Bronze

Date	Mintage	VG-8	F-12	VF-20	XF-40	MS-60	MS-63	Proof
1871	2,000,000	2.50	4.00	6.50	20.00	100.00	185	—
1871 Proof	—	—	—	—	—	—	—	2,000

MEXICO

The United States of Mexico, located immediately south of the United States has an area of 759,529 sq. mi. (1,967,183 sq. km.) and an estimated population of 100 million. Capital: Mexico City. The economy is based on agriculture, manufacturing and mining. Oil, cotton, silver, coffee, and shrimp are exported.

Mexico was the site of highly advanced Indian civilizations 1,500 years before conquistador Hernando Cortes conquered the wealthy Aztec empire of Montezuma, 1519-21, and founded a Spanish colony, which lasted for nearly 300 years. During the Spanish period, Mexico, then called New Spain, stretched from Guatemala to the present states of Wyoming and California, its present northern boundary having been established by the secession of Texas during 1836 and the war of 1846-48 with the United States.

Independence from Spain was declared by Father Miguel Hidalgo on Sept. 16, 1810, (Mexican Independence Day) and was achieved by General Agustin de Iturbide in1821. Iturbide became emperor in 1822 but was deposed when a republic was established a year later. For more than fifty years following the birth of the republic, the political scene of Mexico was characterized by turmoil, which saw two emperors (including the unfortunate Maximilian), several dictators and an average of one new government every nine months passing swiftly from obscurity to oblivion. The land, social, economic and labor reforms promulgated by the Reform Constitution of Feb. 5, 1917 established the basis for sustained economic development and participative democracy that have made Mexico one of the most politically stable countries of modern Latin America.

SPANISH COLONY

COB COINAGE

KM# 24   1/2 REAL
1.6900 g., 0.9310 Silver 0.0506 oz. ASW   **Ruler:** Philip V **Obv:** Legend around crowned PHILIPVS monogram **Rev:** Legend around cross, lions and castles **Mint:** Mexico City **Note:** Mint mark M, Mo.

Date	Mintage	Good	VG	F	VF	XF
ND(1701-28)	—	—	25.00	40.00	65.00	—
Date off flan						
1701 L	—	—	100	125	225	—
1702 L	—	—	100	125	225	—
1703 L	—	—	100	125	225	—
1704 L	—	—	100	125	225	—
1705 L	—	—	100	125	225	—
1706 J	—	—	100	125	225	—
1707 J	—	—	100	125	225	—
1708 J	—	—	100	125	175	—
1709 J	—	—	100	125	175	—
1710 J	—	—	100	125	175	—
1711 J	—	—	100	125	175	—
1712 J	—	—	100	125	175	—
1713 J	—	—	100	125	175	—
1714 J	—	—	100	125	175	—
1715 J	—	—	100	125	175	—
1716 J	—	—	100	125	175	—
1717 J	—	—	100	125	175	—
1718 J	—	—	100	125	175	—
1719 J	—	—	100	125	175	—
1720 J	—	—	100	125	175	—
1721 J	—	—	100	125	175	—
1722 J	—	—	100	125	175	—
1723 J	—	—	100	125	175	—
1724 J	—	—	100	125	175	—
1724 D	—	—	100	125	175	—
1725 D	—	—	100	125	175	—
1726 D	—	—	100	125	175	—
1727 D	—	—	100	125	175	—
1728 D	—	—	100	125	175	—

KM# 24a   1/2 REAL
1.6900 g., 0.9160 Silver 0.0498 oz. ASW   **Ruler:** Philip V **Obv:** Legend around crowned PHILIPVS monogram **Rev:** Legend around cross, lions and castles **Mint:** Mexico City **Note:** Mint mark M, Mo.

Date	Mintage	Good	VG	F	VF	XF
ND(1729-33)	—	—	25.00	40.00	65.00	—
Date off flan						
1729 R	—	—	90.00	120	150	—
1730 R	—	—	90.00	120	150	—
1731 F	—	—	90.00	120	150	—
1732/1 F	—	—	90.00	120	150	—
1732 F	—	—	90.00	120	150	—
1733/2 F	—	—	90.00	120	150	—
1733 F	—	—	90.00	120	150	—

KM# 30   REAL
3.3800 g., 0.9310 Silver 0.1012 oz. ASW   **Ruler:** Philip V **Obv:** Legend and date around crowned arms **Obv. Legend:** PHILIPVS V DEI G **Rev:** Lions and castles in angles of cross **Mint:** Mexico City **Note:** Mint mark M, Mo.

Date	Mintage	Good	VG	F	VF	XF
ND(1701-28)	—	—	35.00	55.00	75.00	—
Date off flan						
1701 L	—	—	125	175	275	—
1702 L	—	—	125	175	275	—
1703 L	—	—	125	175	275	—
1704 L	—	—	125	175	275	—
1705 L	—	—	125	175	275	—
1706 J	—	—	125	175	275	—
1707 J	—	—	125	175	275	—
1708 J	—	—	125	175	275	—
1709 J	—	—	125	175	275	—
1710 J	—	—	125	175	275	—
1711 J	—	—	125	175	275	—
1712 J	—	—	125	175	275	—
1713 J	—	—	125	175	275	—
1714 J	—	—	125	175	275	—
1715 J	—	—	100	175	275	—
1716 J	—	—	100	175	275	—
1717 J	—	—	100	175	275	—
1718 J	—	—	100	175	275	—
1719 J	—	—	100	175	275	—
1720/19 J	—	—	100	175	275	—

KM# 25   1/2 REAL
1.6900 g., 0.9310 Silver 0.0506 oz. ASW   **Ruler:** Luis I **Obv:** Legend around crowned LVDOVICVS monogram **Rev:** Legend around cross, lions and castles **Note:** Mint mark M, Mo.

Date	Mintage	Good	VG	F	VF	XF
ND(1724-25)	—	—	125	200	250	—
Date off flan						
1724 D	—	—	325	450	550	—
1725 D	—	—	325	450	550	—

Date	Mintage	Good	VG	F	VF	XF
1720 J	—	—	100	175	275	—
1721 J	—	—	100	175	275	—
1722 J	—	—	100	175	275	—
1723 J	—	—	100	175	275	—
1726 D	—	—	100	175	275	—
1727 D	—	—	100	175	275	—
1728 D	—	—	100	175	275	—

KM# A31   REAL
3.3834 g., 0.9310 Silver 0.1013 oz. ASW **Ruler:** Luis I **Mint:** Mexico City **Note:** A significant portion of the legend must be visibile for proper attribution. Mint mark M, Mo.

Date	Mintage	Good	VG	F	VF	XF
1724 D Rare	—	—	—	—	—	—
1725 D Rare	—	—	—	—	—	—

KM# 30a   REAL
3.3800 g., 0.9160 Silver 0.0995 oz. ASW **Ruler:** Philip V **Obv:** Legend and date around crowned arms **Obv. Legend:** PHILIPVS V DEI G **Rev:** Lions and castles in angles of cross **Mint:** Mexico City **Note:** Mint mark M, Mo.

Date	Mintage	Good	VG	F	VF	XF
ND (1729-32) Date off flan	—	—	30.00	50.00	70.00	—
1729 R	—	—	90.00	125	175	—
1730 R	—	—	90.00	125	175	—
1730 F	—	—	90.00	125	175	—
1730 G	—	—	90.00	125	175	—
1731 F	—	—	90.00	125	175	—
1732 F	—	—	90.00	125	175	—

KM# 35   2 REALES
6.7700 g., 0.9310 Silver 0.2026 oz. ASW **Ruler:** Philip V **Obv:** Legend and date around crowned arms **Obv. Legend:** PHILIPVS V DEI G **Rev:** Lions and castles in angles of cross **Mint:** Mexico City **Note:** Mint mark M, Mo.

Date	Mintage	Good	VG	F	VF	XF
ND(1701-28) Date off flan	—	—	45.00	65.00	90.00	—
1701 L	—	—	125	150	250	—
1702 L	—	—	125	150	250	—
1703 L	—	—	125	150	250	—
1704 L	—	—	125	150	250	—
1705 L	—	—	125	150	250	—
1706 J	—	—	125	150	250	—
1707 J	—	—	125	150	250	—
1708 J	—	—	125	150	250	—
1710 J	—	—	125	150	250	—
1711 J	—	—	125	150	250	—
1712 J	—	—	125	150	250	—
1713 J	—	—	125	150	250	—
1714 J	—	—	150	185	300	—
1715 J	—	—	150	185	300	—
1716 J	—	—	150	185	300	—
1717 J	—	—	150	185	300	—
1718 J	—	—	150	185	300	—
1719 J	—	—	150	185	300	—
1720 J	—	—	150	185	300	—
1721 J	—	—	150	185	300	—
1722 J	—	—	150	185	300	—
1723 J	—	—	150	185	300	—
1724 J	—	—	150	185	300	—
1725 D Rare	—	—	—	—	—	—
1726 D	—	—	150	185	300	—
1727 D	—	—	150	185	300	—
1728 D	—	—	150	185	300	—

KM# 35a   2 REALES
6.7700 g., 0.9160 Silver 0.1994 oz. ASW **Ruler:** Philip V **Obv:** Legend and date around crowned arms **Obv. Legend:** PHILIPVS V DEI G **Rev:** Lions and castles in angles of cross **Mint:** Mexico City **Note:** Mint mark M, Mo.

Date	Mintage	Good	VG	F	VF	XF
ND(1729-32) Date off flan	—	—	40.00	60.00	90.00	—
1729 R	—	—	100	125	150	—

Date	Mintage	Good	VG	F	VF	XF
1730 R	—	—	100	125	150	—
1731 F	—	—	100	125	150	—
1731/0 F	—	—	100	125	150	—
1732 F	—	—	100	125	150	—
1733 F Rare	—	—	—	—	—	—

 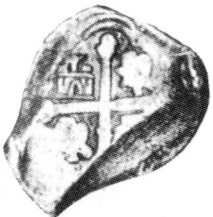

KM# 40   4 REALES
13.5400 g., 0.9310 Silver 0.4053 oz. ASW **Ruler:** Philip V **Obv:** Legend and date around crowned arms **Obv. Legend:** PHILIPVS V DEI G **Rev:** Lions and castles in angles of cross **Mint:** Mexico City **Note:** Mint mark M, Mo.

Date	Mintage	Good	VG	F	VF	XF
ND (1701-28) Date off flan	—	—	50.00	75.00	100	—
1701 L	—	—	175	250	375	—
1702 L	—	—	175	250	375	—
1703 L	—	—	175	250	375	—
1704 L	—	—	175	250	375	—
1705 L	—	—	175	250	375	—
1706 J	—	—	175	250	375	—
1707 J	—	—	175	250	375	—
1708 J	—	—	175	250	375	—
1709 J	—	—	175	250	375	—
1710 J	—	—	175	250	375	—
1711 J	—	—	150	200	300	—
1712 J	—	—	150	200	300	—
1713 J	—	—	150	200	300	—
1714 J	—	—	150	200	300	—
1715 J	—	—	125	225	375	—
1716 J	—	—	200	300	500	—
1717 J	—	—	200	300	500	—
1718 J	—	—	200	300	500	—
1719 J	—	—	200	300	500	—
1720 J	—	—	200	300	500	—
1721 J	—	—	200	300	500	—
1722 J	—	—	200	300	500	—
1723 J	—	—	200	300	500	—
1726 D	—	—	200	300	500	—
1727 D	—	—	200	300	500	—
1728 D	—	—	200	300	500	—

KM# 42   4 REALES
13.5400 g., 0.9310 Silver 0.4053 oz. ASW **Ruler:** Luis I **Obv:** Legend around crowned arms **Obv. Legend:** LVDOVICVS I DEI G **Rev:** Lions and castles in angles of cross, legend around **Mint:** Mexico City **Note:** A significant portion of the legend must be visible for proper attribution. Mint mark M, Mo.

Date	Mintage	Good	VG	F	VF	XF
1724 D Rare	—	—	—	—	—	—
1725 D Rare	—	—	—	—	—	—

KM# 40a 4 REALES
13.5400 g., 0.9160 Silver 0.3987 oz. ASW **Ruler:** Philip V
Obv: Legend and date around crowned arms **Obv. Legend:**
PHILIPVS V DEI G **Rev:** Lions and castles in angles of cross
Mint: Mexico City **Note:** Mint mark M, Mo.

Date	Mintage	Good	VG	F	VF	XF
ND(1729-33) Date off flan	—	—	50.00	75.00	100	—
1729 D	—	—	125	200	275	—
1730 R	—	—	125	200	275	—
1730 G	—	—	125	200	275	—
1731 F	—	—	125	200	275	—
1732/1 F	—	—	125	175	250	—
1732 F	—	—	125	175	250	—
1733/2 F	—	—	125	175	250	—
1733 F	—	—	200	300	400	—

Date	Mintage	Good	VG	F	VF	XF
1702 L	—	—	200	350	500	—
1703 L	—	—	200	350	500	—
1704 L Rare	—	—	—	—	—	—
1705 L	—	—	200	350	600	—
1706 J	—	—	200	350	600	—
1707 J	—	—	200	350	500	—
1708 J	—	—	200	350	500	—
1709 J	—	—	200	350	500	—
1710 J	—	—	200	350	500	—
1711 J	—	—	175	275	400	—
1712 J	—	—	175	275	400	—
1713 J	—	—	175	275	400	—
1714 J	—	—	175	275	400	—
1715 J	—	—	175	300	450	—
1716 J	—	—	375	575	800	—
1717 J	—	—	375	575	800	—
1718/7 J	—	—	375	575	800	—
1718 J	—	—	350	500	800	—
1719 J	—	—	350	500	800	—
1720 J	—	—	350	500	800	—
1721 J	—	—	350	500	800	—
1722 J	—	—	350	500	800	—
1723 J	—	—	350	500	800	—
1724 D	—	—	350	500	800	—
1725 D	—	—	350	500	800	—
1726 D	—	—	350	500	800	—
1727 D	—	—	350	500	800	—
1728 D	—	—	400	600	1,000	—

KM# 41 4 REALES
13.5400 g., 0.9160 Silver 0.3987 oz. ASW **Ruler:** Philip V
Obv: Legend and date around crowned arms **Obv. Legend:**
PHILIPVS V DEI G **Rev:** Lions and castles in angles of cross,
legend around **Mint:** Mexico City **Note:** Klippe. Similar to
KM#40a. Mint mark M, Mo.

Date	Mintage	Good	VG	F	VF	XF
1733 F	—	—	450	600	750	—
1733 MF	—	—	450	600	750	—
1734/3 MF	—	—	450	600	750	—

KM# 46 8 REALES
27.0700 g., 0.9310 Silver 0.8102 oz. ASW **Ruler:** Charles II
Obv: Legend and date around crowned arms **Obv. Legend:**
CAROLVS II DEI G **Rev:** Legend around cross, lions and
castles **Note:** Struck at Mexico City Mint, mint mark M, Mo.

Date	Mintage	Good	VG	F	VF	XF
1701 L	—	—	700	1,000	1,700	—

KM# 49 8 REALES
27.0700 g., 0.9310 Silver 0.8102 oz. ASW **Ruler:** Luis I **Obv:**
Legend and date around crowned arms **Obv. Legend:**
LVDOVICVS I DEI G **Rev:** Lions and castles in angles of cross,
legend around **Rev. Legend:** INDIARVM * REX HISPANIARV
... **Mint:** Mexico City **Note:** A significant portion of the legend
must be visible for proper attribution. Mint mark M, Mo.

Date	Mintage	Good	VG	F	VF	XF
ND(1724-25) Date off flan; Rare	—	—	—	—	—	—
1724 D Rare	—	—	—	—	—	—
1725 D Rare	—	—	—	—	—	—

KM# 47 8 REALES
27.0700 g., 0.9310 Silver 0.8102 oz. ASW **Ruler:** Philip V
Obv: Legend and date around crowned arms **Obv. Legend:**
PHILIPVS V DEI G **Rev:** Lions and castles in angles of cross,
legend around **Mint:** Mexico City **Note:** Mint mark M, Mo.

Date	Mintage	Good	VG	F	VF	XF
1701 L	—	—	200	350	500	—
ND(1701-28) Date off flan	—	—	70.00	90.00	120	—

KM# 47a   8 REALES
27.0700 g., 0.9160 Silver 0.7972 oz. ASW   **Ruler:** Philip V
Obv: Legend and date around crowned arms **Obv. Legend:**
PHILIPVS V DEI G **Rev:** Lions and castles in angles of cross,
legend around **Mint:** Mexico City **Note:** Mint mark M, Mo.

Date	Mintage	Good	VG	F	VF	XF
ND(1729-33)	—	—	70.00	90.00	110	—
Date off flan						
1729 R	—	—	150	225	350	—
1730 G/R	—	—	150	225	350	—
1730 R	—	—	150	225	350	—
1730 G	—	—	150	225	350	—
1730 F	—	—	150	225	350	—
1731/0 F	—	—	150	225	350	—
1731 F	—	—	135	210	325	—
1732/1 F	—	—	135	210	325	—
1732 F	—	—	135	210	350	—
1733/2 F	—	—	200	300	400	—
1733 F	—	—	200	300	400	—

KM# 48   8 REALES
0.9160 g., Silver   **Ruler:** Philip V **Obv:** Legend around

crowned arms **Rev:** Lions and castles in angles of cross,
legend around **Mint:** Mexico City **Note:** Klippe. Similar to
KM#47a. Mint mark M, Mo.

Date	Mintage	Good	VG	F	VF	XF
ND(1733-34)	—	—	200	350	500	—
Date off flan						
1733 F	—	—	550	750	1,150	—
1733 MF	—	—	450	600	750	—
1734/3 MF	—	—	500	750	1,000	—
1734 MF	—	—	500	750	1,000	—

KM# 50   ESCUDO
3.3800 g., 0.9170 Gold 0.0996 oz. AGW   **Ruler:** Charles II
Obv: Legend and date around crowned arms **Obv. Legend:**
CAROLVS II DEI G **Rev:** Lions and castles in angles of cross,
legend around **Mint:** Mexico City

Date	Mintage	VG	F	VF	XF	Unc
1701/0MXo L	—	—	3,000	4,000	5,000	—

KM# 51.1   ESCUDO
3.3800 g., 0.9170 Gold 0.0996 oz. AGW   **Ruler:** Philip V **Obv:**
Legend and date around crowned arms **Obv. Legend:**
PHILIPVS V DEI G **Rev:** Lions and castles in angles of cross,
legend around **Mint:** Mexico City

Date	Mintage	VG	F	VF	XF	Unc
ND(1702-13)	—	—	1,000	1,350	1,500	—
Date off flan						
1702MXo L	—	—	1,500	2,500	3,500	—
1703/2MXo L	—	—	1,500	2,500	3,500	—
1704MXo L	—	—	1,500	2,500	3,500	—
1707MXo J	—	—	1,500	2,500	3,500	—
1708MXo J	—	—	1,500	2,500	3,500	—
1709MXo J	—	—	1,500	2,500	3,500	—
1710MXo J	—	—	1,500	2,500	3,500	—
1711MXo J	—	—	1,500	2,500	3,500	—
1712MXo J	—	—	1,500	2,500	3,500	—
1713MXo J	—	—	1,500	2,500	3,500	—

KM# 51.2   ESCUDO
3.3800 g., 0.9170 Gold 0.0996 oz. AGW   **Ruler:** Philip V **Obv:**
Legend and date around crowned arms **Obv. Legend:**
PHILIPVS V DEI G **Rev:** Lions and castles in angles of cross,
legend around **Mint:** Mexico City

Date	Mintage	VG	F	VF	XF	Unc
1712Mo J	—	—	2,000	3,000	4,000	—
1714Mo J	—	—	1,400	2,000	3,000	—
1714Mo J J's 1's	—	—	—	—	—	—
(J7J4J) Rare						
1715Mo J	—	—	2,000	3,000	4,000	—
1727Mo J Rare	—	—	—	—	—	—
1728Mo J Rare	—	—	—	—	—	—

Note: Die-struck counterfeits of 1731 F exist

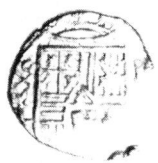 

KM# 52 2 ESCUDOS
6.7700 g., 0.9170 Gold 0.1996 oz. AGW **Ruler:** Philip V **Obv:** Legend and date around crowned arms **Obv. Legend:** CAROLVS II DEI G **Rev:** Legend around cross **Mint:** Mexico City

Date	Mintage	VG	F	VF	XF	Unc
1701MXo L Rare	—	—	—	—	—	—

KM# 53.1 2 ESCUDOS
6.7700 g., 0.9170 Gold 0.1996 oz. AGW **Ruler:** Philip V **Obv:** Legend and date around crowned arms **Obv. Legend:** PHILIPVS V DEI G **Rev:** Legend around cross **Mint:** Mexico City

Date	Mintage	VG	F	VF	XF	Unc
ND(1704-13) Date off flan	—	—	1,500	2,000	2,500	—
1704MXo L	—	—	2,750	3,750	4,750	—
1708MXo J	—	—	2,750	3,750	4,750	—
1710MXo J	—	—	2,750	3,750	4,750	—
1711MXo J	—	—	2,750	3,750	4,750	—
1712MXo J	—	—	2,750	3,750	4,750	—
1713MXo J	—	—	2,750	3,750	4,750	—

KM# 53.2 2 ESCUDOS
6.7700 g., 0.9170 Gold 0.1996 oz. AGW **Ruler:** Philip V **Obv:** Legend and date around crowned arms **Obv. Legend:** PHILIPVS V DEI G **Rev:** Legend around cross **Mint:** Mexico City **Note:** Struck counterfeits exist for 1731.

Date	Mintage	VG	F	VF	XF	Unc
ND(1714-31) Date off flan	—	—	1,500	1,750	2,500	—
1714Mo J	—	—	—	2,500	3,500	—
1715Mo J	—	—	—	3,000	4,000	—
1717Mo J Rare	—	—	—	—	—	—
1722Mo J Rare	—	—	—	—	—	—
1729Mo R Rare	—	—	—	—	—	—
1731Mo F Rare	—	—	—	—	—	—

KM# A54 2 ESCUDOS
6.7700 g., 0.9170 Gold 0.1996 oz. AGW **Ruler:** Luis I **Obv:** Legend and date around crowned arms **Obv. Legend:** LVDOVICVS I DEI G. **Rev:** Legend around cross **Mint:** Mexico City **Note:** A significant portion of the legend must be visible for proper attribution.

Date	Mintage	VG	F	VF	XF	Unc
NDMo D Rare	—	—	—	—	—	—

KM# 55.1 4 ESCUDOS
13.5400 g., 0.9170 Gold 0.3992 oz. AGW **Ruler:** Philip V **Obv:** Legend and date around crowned arms **Obv. Legend:** PHILIPVS V DEI G **Rev:** Legend around cross **Mint:** Mexico City

Date	Mintage	VG	F	VF	XF	Unc
ND(1705-13) Date off flan	—	—	2,500	3,000	4,000	—
1705MXo J	—	—	4,000	5,750	6,750	—
1706MXo L	—	—	4,000	5,750	6,750	—
1711MXo J	—	—	4,000	5,750	6,750	—
1712MXo J	—	—	4,000	5,750	6,750	—
1713MXo J	—	—	4,000	5,750	6,750	—

KM# 55.2 4 ESCUDOS
13.5400 g., 0.9170 Gold 0.3992 oz. AGW **Ruler:** Philip V **Obv:** Legend and date around crowned arms **Obv. Legend:** PHILIPVS V DEI G **Rev:** Legend around cross **Mint:** Mexico City

Date	Mintage	VG	F	VF	XF	Unc
ND(1714-20) Date off flan	—	—	2,500	3,750	5,000	—
1714Mo J	—	—	—	5,750	7,500	—
1715Mo J	—	—	—	5,750	7,500	—
1720Mo J Rare	—	—	—	—	—	—

KM# 57.1 8 ESCUDOS
27.0700 g., 0.9170 Gold 0.7981 oz. AGW **Ruler:** Philip V **Obv:** Legend and date around crowned arms **Obv. Legend:** PHILIPVS V DEI G **Rev:** Legend around cross **Mint:** Mexico City

Date	Mintage	VG	F	VF	XF	Unc
ND(1701-13) Date off flan	—	—	2,000	3,000	4,000	—
1701MXo L	—	—	6,000	7,500	9,000	—

Date	Mintage	VG	F	VF	XF	Unc
1703MXo L	—	—	6,000	7,500	9,000	—
1706MXo J	—	—	6,000	7,500	9,000	—
1708MXo J	—	—	6,000	7,500	9,000	—
1709MXo J	—	—	6,000	7,500	9,000	—
1710MXo J	—	—	6,000	7,500	9,000	—
1711MXo J	—	—	3,500	4,000	5,750	—
1712MXo J	—	—	3,500	4,000	5,750	—
1713MXo J	—	—	3,500	4,000	5,750	—

KM# 57.2   8 ESCUDOS
27.0700 g., 0.9170 Gold 0.7981 oz. AGW **Ruler:** Philip V
Obv: Legend and date around crowned arms **Obv. Legend:**
PHILIPVS V DEI G **Rev:** Legend around cross **Mint:** Mexico
City

Date	Mintage	VG	F	VF	XF	Unc
ND(1714-32)Mo	—	—	2,750	3,750	4,750	—
Date off flan						
1714Mo J	—	—	5,000	6,000	7,500	—
1714Mo Date over	—	—	6,000	7,500	9,000	—
GRAT on obverse						
1715Mo J	—	—	5,000	6,500	8,000	—
1717/6Mo J Rare	—	—	—	—	—	—
1720/19Mo J Rare	—	—	—	—	—	—
1723Mo J Rare	—	—	—	—	—	—
1727/6Mo D Rare	—	—	—	—	—	—
1728/7Mo D Rare	—	—	—	—	—	—
1729Mo R Rare	—	—	—	—	—	—
1730Mo R Rare	—	—	—	—	—	—
1730Mo F Rare	—	—	—	—	—	—
1731Mo F Rare	—	—	—	—	—	—
1732Mo F Rare	—	—	—	—	—	—

KM# 57.3   8 ESCUDOS
27.0700 g., 0.9170 Gold 0.7981 oz. AGW **Ruler:** Philip V **Obv:**
Date around crowned arms **Obv. Legend:** PHILIPVS V DEI G
Rev: Legend and date around cross **Mint:** Mexico City

Date	Mintage	VG	F	VF	XF	Unc
1714Mo J Date	—	—	6,000	7,500	9,000	—
on reverse						

KM# 58   8 ESCUDOS
27.0700 g., 0.9170 Gold 0.7981 oz. AGW **Ruler:** Luis I **Obv:**
Legend and date around crowned arms **Obv. Legend:**
LVDOVICVS I DEI G **Rev:** Legend around cross **Mint:** Mexico
City **Note:** A significant portion of the legend must be visible
for proper attribution.

Date	Mintage	VG	F	VF	XF	Unc
ND(1724-25)Mo	—	—	—	—	—	—
D Rare						

ROYAL COINAGE

Struck on specially prepared round planchets
using well centered dies in excellent condition to
prove the quality of the minting to the Viceroy or
even to the King.

KM# R24   1/2 REAL
1.6917 g., 0.9310 Silver 0.0506 oz. ASW **Ruler:** Philip V
Mint: Mexico City **Note:** Normally found holed. Mint
mark Mo.

Date	Mintage	Good	VG	F	VF	XF
1715Mo J	—	—	250	500	750	—
1719Mo J	—	—	250	500	750	—

Date	Mintage	Good	VG	F	VF	XF
1721Mo J	—	—	250	500	750	—
1722Mo J	—	—	250	500	750	—
1726Mo D	—	—	250	500	750	—
1727Mo D	—	—	250	500	750	—

KM# R25   1/2 REAL
1.6917 g., 0.9310 Silver 0.0506 oz. ASW **Ruler:** Luis I **Obv:**
Legend around crowned LVDOVICVS monogram **Rev:** Lions
and castles in angles of cross, legend around **Mint:** Mexico
City **Note:** Mint mark Mo.

Date	Mintage	Good	VG	F	VF	XF
1724Mo D Rare	—	—	—	—	—	—

KM# R24a   1/2 REAL
1.6917 g., 0.9170 Silver 0.0499 oz. ASW **Ruler:** Philip V
Mint: Mexico City **Note:** Normally found holed. Mint mark Mo.

Date	Mintage	Good	VG	F	VF	XF
1730Mo D	—	—	250	500	750	—

KM# R30   REAL
3.3834 g., 0.9310 Silver 0.1013 oz. ASW **Ruler:** Philip V
Obv. Legend: PHILIPVS V DEI G **Mint:** Mexico City **Note:**
Mint mark Mo.

Date	Mintage	Good	VG	F	VF	XF
1715Mo J Rare	—	—	—	—	—	—
1716Mo J Rare	—	—	—	—	—	—
1718Mo J Rare	—	—	—	—	—	—

KM# R35   2 REALES
6.7668 g., 0.9310 Silver 0.2025 oz. ASW **Ruler:** Philip V
Obv. Legend: PHILIPVS V DEI G **Mint:** Mexico City **Note:**
Mint mark Mo.

Date	Mintage	Good	VG	F	VF	XF
1715Mo J Rare	—	—	—	—	—	—

KM# R35a   2 REALES
6.7668 g., 0.9170 Silver 0.1995 oz. ASW **Ruler:** Philip V
Mint: Mexico City **Note:** Mint mark Mo.

Date	Mintage	Good	VG	F	VF	XF
1730Mo R Rare	—	—	—	—	—	—

KM# R40   4 REALES
13.5337 g., 0.9310 Silver 0.4051 oz. ASW **Ruler:** Philip V
Obv. Legend: PHILIPVS V DEI G **Mint:** Mexico City **Note:**
Mint mark Mo.

Date	Mintage	Good	VG	F	VF	XF
1716Mo J Rare	—	—	—	—	—	—
1719Mo J Rare	—	—	—	—	—	—
1721Mo J Rare	—	—	—	—	—	—
1722Mo J Rare	—	—	—	—	—	—
1723Mo J Rare	—	—	—	—	—	—

KM# R47   8 REALES
27.0674 g., 0.9310 Silver 0.8102 oz. ASW **Ruler:** Philip V
Obv. Legend: PHILIPVS V DEI G **Mint:** Mexico City **Note:**
Struck at Mexico City Mint, mint mark Mo.

Date	Mintage	Good	VG	F	VF	XF
1702Mo L Rare	—	—	—	—	—	—
1703Mo L Rare	—	—	—	—	—	—
1705Mo J Rare	—	—	—	—	—	—
1706Mo J Rare	—	—	—	—	—	—
1709Mo J Rare	—	—	—	—	—	—
1711Mo J Rare	—	—	—	—	—	—
1714Mo J Rare	—	—	—	—	—	—
1715Mo J Rare	—	—	—	—	—	—
1716Mo J Rare	—	—	—	—	—	—
1717Mo J Rare	—	—	—	—	—	—
1719Mo J Rare	—	—	—	—	—	—
1721Mo J Rare	—	—	—	—	—	—
1722Mo J Rare	—	—	—	—	—	—
1723Mo J Rare	—	—	—	—	—	—
1724Mo D Rare	—	—	—	—	—	—
1725Mo D Rare	—	—	—	—	—	—
1726/5Mo D	—	—	—	—	—	—
Rare						
1726Mo D Rare	—	—	—	—	—	—
1727Mo D Rare	—	—	—	—	—	—

KM# R49   8 REALES
27.0674 g., 0.9310 Silver 0.8102 oz. ASW   **Ruler:** Luis I
Note: Mint mark Mo.

Date	Mintage	Good	VG	F	VF	XF
1724 D Rare	—	—	—	—	—	—
1725 D Rare	—	—	—	—	—	—

KM# R47a   8 REALES
27.0674 g., 0.9170 Silver 0.7980 oz. ASW   **Ruler:** Philip V
Mint: Mexico City **Note:** Mint mark Mo.

Date	Mintage	Good	VG	F	VF	XF
1729Mo R Rare	—	—	—	—	—	—
1730Mo R/D Rare	—	—	—	—	—	—
1730Mo G Rare	—	—	—	—	—	—

KM# R51.2   ESCUDO
3.3834 g., 0.9170 Gold 0.0997 oz. AGW   **Ruler:** Philip V
Mint: Mexico City

Date	Mintage	Good	VG	F	VF	XF
1714Mo J Rare	—	—	—	—	—	—
1715Mo J Rare	—	—	—	—	—	—

KM# R53.1   2 ESCUDOS
6.7668 g., 0.9170 Gold 0.1995 oz. AGW   **Ruler:** Philip V
Mint: Mexico City

Date	Mintage	Good	VG	F	VF	XF
1711MXo J Rare	—	—	—	—	—	—
1712MXo J Rare	—	—	—	—	—	—

KM# R55.1   4 ESCUDOS
13.5337 g., 0.9170 Gold 0.3990 oz. AGW   **Ruler:** Philip V
Mint: Mexico City **Note:** Mint mark M, Mo.

Date	Mintage	Good	VG	F	VF	XF
1711 Rare	—	—	—	—	—	—

KM# R55.2   4 ESCUDOS
13.5337 g., 0.9170 Gold 0.3990 oz. AGW   **Ruler:** Philip V
Mint: Mexico City **Note:** Mint mark M, Mo.

Date	Mintage	Good	VG	F	VF	XF
1714 Rare	—	—	—	—	—	—

KM# R57.1   8 ESCUDOS
27.0674 g., 0.9170 Gold 0.7980 oz. AGW   **Ruler:** Philip V
Mint: Mexico City

Date	Mintage	Good	VG	F	VF	XF
1702MXo L Rare	—	—	—	—	—	—
1711MXo J Rare	—	—	—	—	—	—
1712MXo J Rare	—	—	—	—	—	—
1713MXo J Rare	—	—	—	—	—	—

KM# R57.3   8 ESCUDOS
27.0674 g., 0.9170 Gold 0.7980 oz. AGW   **Ruler:** Philip V
Mint: Mexico City

Date	Mintage	Good	VG	F	VF	XF
1714Mo J Rare	—	—	—	—	—	—
1715Mo J Rare	—	—	—	—	—	—
1717Mo J Rare	—	—	—	—	—	—
1718Mo J Rare	—	—	—	—	—	—
1723Mo J Rare	—	—	—	—	—	—

MILLED COINAGE

KM# 59   1/8 PILON (1/16 Real)
Copper **Ruler:** Ferdinand VII **Obv:** Crowned monogram **Rev:**
Castles and lions in wreath **Mint:** Mexico City **Note:** Mint mark
Mo.

Date	Mintage	VG	F	VF	XF	Unc
1814	—	12.00	25.00	55.00	145	—
1815	—	12.00	25.00	55.00	145	—

KM# 63   1/4 TLACO (1/8 Real)
Copper   **Ruler:** Ferdinand VII **Obv:** Crowned monogram
flanked by value and mint mark **Obv. Legend:** FERDIN. VII...
Rev: Arms without shield within wreath **Mint:** Mexico City
Note: Mint mark Mo.

Date	Mintage	VG	F	VF	XF	Unc
1814	—	14.00	30.00	60.00	180	—
1815	—	14.00	30.00	60.00	180	—
1816	—	14.00	30.00	60.00	180	—

KM# 62   1/4 REAL
0.8458 g., 0.8960 Silver 0.0244 oz. ASW   **Ruler:** Charles IV
Obv: Crowned rampant lion, left **Rev:** Castle **Mint:** Mexico
City **Note:** Mint mark Mo.

Date	Mintage	VG	F	VF	XF	Unc
1796	—	15.00	30.00	55.00	90.00	—
1797	—	15.00	30.00	55.00	90.00	—
1798	—	12.50	22.00	50.00	75.00	—
1799/8	—	12.50	22.00	50.00	75.00	—
1799	—	10.00	20.00	40.00	70.00	—
1800	—	10.00	25.00	55.00	90.00	—
1801/0	—	10.00	20.00	40.00	70.00	—
1801	—	10.00	20.00	40.00	70.00	—
1802	—	10.00	20.00	40.00	70.00	—
1803	—	10.00	20.00	40.00	70.00	—
1804	—	10.00	20.00	40.00	75.00	—
1805/4	—	12.50	25.00	55.00	85.00	—
1805	—	10.00	22.00	50.00	75.00	—
1806	—	10.00	22.00	50.00	80.00	—
1807/797	—	15.00	30.00	55.00	85.00	—
1807	—	12.50	25.00	50.00	80.00	—
1808	—	12.50	25.00	50.00	80.00	—
1809/8	—	12.50	25.00	50.00	80.00	—
1809	—	12.50	25.00	50.00	80.00	—
1810	—	12.50	25.00	50.00	75.00	—
1811	—	12.50	25.00	50.00	75.00	—
1812	—	12.50	25.00	50.00	75.00	—
1813	—	10.00	20.00	40.00	70.00	—
1815	—	12.50	22.00	50.00	75.00	—
1816	—	10.00	20.00	40.00	70.00	—

KM# 64   2/4 SENAL (1/4 Real)
Copper   **Ruler:** Ferdinand VII **Obv:** Legend around crowned
monogram flanked by mint mark and value **Obv. Legend:**
FERDIN. VII... **Rev:** Arms without shield within wreath **Mint:**
Mexico City **Note:** Mint mark Mo.

Date	Mintage	VG	F	VF	XF	Unc
1814	—	14.00	30.00	60.00	180	—
1815/4	—	18.00	36.00	70.00	200	—
1815	—	14.00	30.00	60.00	180	—
1816	—	14.00	30.00	60.00	180	—
1821	—	25.00	48.00	90.00	240	—

KM# 65 1/2 REAL
1.6917 g., 0.9170 Silver 0.0499 oz. ASW **Ruler:** Philip V
Obv: Crowned shield flanked by M F, rosettes and small cross
Obv. Legend: PHILIP • V • D • G • HISPAN • ET IND • REX
Rev: Crowned globes flanked by crowned pillars with banner,
date below **Mint:** Mexico City **Note:** Mint mark M, Mo, MX.

Date	Mintage	VG	F	VF	XF	Unc
1732 Rare	—	—	—	—	—	—
1732 F	—	500	800	1,200	2,000	—
1733 MF (MX)	—	400	600	1,000	1,500	—
1733 F	—	200	325	550	800	—
1733/2 MF	—	300	400	600	800	—
1733 MF	—	300	400	600	800	—
1734/3 MF	—	12.00	25.00	45.00	85.00	—
1734 MF	—	12.00	25.00	45.00	85.00	—
1735/4 MF	—	10.00	20.00	45.00	85.00	—
1735 MF	—	10.00	20.00	45.00	85.00	—
1736/5 MF	—	10.00	20.00	45.00	85.00	—
1736 MF	—	10.00	20.00	45.00	85.00	—
1737/6 MF	—	10.00	20.00	45.00	85.00	—
1737 MF	—	10.00	20.00	45.00	85.00	—
1738/7 MF	—	10.00	20.00	45.00	85.00	—
1738 MF	—	10.00	20.00	45.00	85.00	—
1739 MF	—	10.00	20.00	45.00	85.00	—
1740/30 MF	—	8.00	18.00	40.00	75.00	—
1740 MF	—	8.00	18.00	40.00	75.00	—
1741 MF	—	8.00	18.00	40.00	75.00	—

KM# 66 1/2 REAL
1.6900 g., 0.9170 Silver 0.0498 oz. ASW **Ruler:** Philip V
Obv: Crowned shield flanked by stars **Obv. Legend:** PHS •
V • D • G • HISP • ET IND • R **Rev:** Crowned globes flanked
by crowned pillars with banner, date below **Mint:** Mexico City
Note: Mint mark M, Mo.

Date	Mintage	VG	F	VF	XF	Unc
1742 M	—	8.00	18.00	40.00	75.00	—
1743 M	—	8.00	18.00	40.00	75.00	—
1744/3 M	—	8.00	18.00	40.00	75.00	—
1744 M	—	8.00	18.00	40.00	75.00	—
1745 M Rare	—	—	—	—	—	—

Note: Legend variation: PHS. V. D. G. HISP. EST IND. R

1745 M	—	8.00	18.00	40.00	75.00	—
1746/5 M	—	8.00	18.00	40.00	75.00	—
1746 M	—	8.00	18.00	40.00	75.00	—
1747 M	—	8.00	18.00	40.00	75.00	—

KM# 67.1 1/2 REAL
1.6900 g., 0.9170 Silver 0.0498 oz. ASW **Ruler:**
Ferdinand VI **Obv:** Royal crown **Obv. Legend:** FRD • VI • D
• G • HIPS • ET IND • R **Mint:** Mexico City **Note:** Mint mark
M, Mo.

Date	Mintage	VG	F	VF	XF	Unc
1747/6 M	—	—	—	—	—	—
1747 M	—	8.00	18.00	40.00	75.00	—
1748/7 M	—	8.00	18.00	40.00	75.00	—
1748 M	—	8.00	18.00	40.00	75.00	—
1749 M	—	8.00	18.00	40.00	75.00	—
1750 M	—	8.00	18.00	40.00	75.00	—
1751 M	—	10.00	20.00	45.00	85.00	—
1752 M	—	8.00	18.00	40.00	75.00	—
1753 M	—	8.00	18.00	40.00	75.00	—
1754 M	—	12.00	25.00	55.00	100	—
1755/6 M	—	12.00	25.00	55.00	100	—
1755 M	—	8.00	18.00	40.00	75.00	—
1756/5 M	—	8.00	18.00	40.00	75.00	—
1756 M	—	8.00	18.00	40.00	75.00	—
1757/6 M	—	8.00	18.00	40.00	75.00	—
1757 M	—	8.00	18.00	40.00	75.00	—

KM# 67.2 1/2 REAL
1.6917 g., 0.9170 Silver 0.0499 oz. ASW **Ruler:**
Ferdinand VI **Obv:** Different crown **Mint:** Mexico City **Note:**
Mint mark M, Mo.

Date	Mintage	VG	F	VF	XF	Unc
1757 M	—	8.00	18.00	40.00	75.00	—
1758/7 M	—	8.00	18.00	40.00	75.00	—
1758 M	—	8.00	18.00	40.00	75.00	—
1759 M	—	8.00	18.00	40.00	75.00	—
1760/59 M	—	8.00	18.00	40.00	75.00	—
1760 M	—	8.00	18.00	40.00	75.00	—

KM# 68 1/2 REAL
1.6900 g., 0.9170 Silver 0.0498 oz. ASW **Ruler:** Charles III
Obv: Crowned shield flanked by stars **Obv. Legend:** CAR •
III • D • G • HISP • ET IND • R **Rev:** Crowned globes flanked
by crowned pillars with banner, date below **Mint:** Mexico City
Note: Mint mark M, Mo.

Date	Mintage	VG	F	VF	XF	Unc
1760/59 M	—	8.00	18.00	40.00	75.00	—
1760 M	—	8.00	18.00	40.00	75.00	—
1761 M	—	8.00	18.00	40.00	75.00	—
1762 M	—	8.00	18.00	40.00	75.00	—
1763/2 M	—	8.00	18.00	40.00	75.00	—
1763 M	—	8.00	18.00	40.00	75.00	—
1764 M	—	8.00	18.00	40.00	75.00	—
1765/4 M	—	10.00	20.00	42.00	80.00	—
1765 M	—	8.00	18.00	40.00	75.00	—
1766 M	—	8.00	18.00	40.00	75.00	—
1767 M	—	10.00	20.00	45.00	85.00	—
1768/6 M	—	10.00	20.00	42.00	80.00	—
1768 M	—	8.00	18.00	40.00	75.00	—
1769 M	—	10.00	20.00	42.00	80.00	—
1770 M	—	10.00	20.00	42.00	80.00	—
1770 F	—	15.00	30.00	60.00	100	—
1771 F	—	10.00	20.00	42.00	80.00	—

KM# 69.2 1/2 REAL
1.6917 g., 0.9030 Silver 0.0491 oz. ASW **Ruler:** Charles III
Obv: Armored bust of Charles III, right **Obv. Legend:**
CAROLUS • III • DEI • GRATIA **Rev:** Crown above shield
flanked by pillars with banner, normal initials and mint mark
Mint: Mexico City **Note:** Mint mark Mo.

Date	Mintage	VG	F	VF	XF	Unc
1772Mo FF	—	9.00	18.00	35.00	80.00	—
1773Mo FM	—	4.50	10.00	25.00	60.00	—
1773Mo FM CAROLS (error)	—	75.00	150	250	400	—
1774Mo FM	—	4.50	10.00	25.00	55.00	—
1775Mo FM	—	4.50	10.00	25.00	55.00	—
1776Mo FM	—	4.50	10.00	25.00	55.00	—
1777Mo FM	—	10.00	18.00	35.00	75.00	—
1777Mo FF	—	7.00	15.00	30.00	65.00	—
1778Mo FF	—	4.50	10.00	25.00	55.00	—
1779Mo FF	—	4.50	10.00	25.00	55.00	—
1780/79Mo FF	—	6.00	12.50	30.00	75.00	—
1780Mo FF	—	4.50	10.00	25.00	55.00	—
1781Mo FF	—	4.50	10.00	25.00	55.00	—
1782/1Mo FF	—	6.00	12.50	30.00	75.00	—
1782Mo FF	—	4.50	10.00	25.00	55.00	—
1783Mo FF	—	4.50	10.00	25.00	55.00	—
1783Mo FM	—	125	300	450	—	—
1784Mo FF	—	4.50	10.00	25.00	55.00	—
1784Mo FM	—	7.00	15.00	35.00	80.00	—

KM# 69.1   1/2 REAL
1.6900 g., 0.9030 Silver 0.0491 oz. ASW **Ruler:** Charles III
Obv. Legend: CAROLUS • III • DEI • GRATIA **Rev:** Inverted
FM and mint mark **Mint:** Mexico City **Note:** Mint mark Mo.

Date	Mintage	VG	F	VF	XF	Unc
1772Mo FM	—	5.00	12.00	27.00	65.00	—
1773Mo FM	—	4.50	10.00	25.00	55.00	—

KM# 69.2a   1/2 REAL
1.6917 g., 0.8960 Silver 0.0487 oz. ASW **Ruler:** Charles III
Rev: Normal initials and mint mark **Note:** Mint mark M, Mo.

Date	Mintage	VG	F	VF	XF	Unc
1785/4 FM	—	7.00	15.00	35.00	80.00	—
1785 FM	—	5.00	12.00	27.00	60.00	—
1786 FM	—	4.50	10.00	25.00	55.00	—
1787 FM	—	4.50	10.00	25.00	55.00	—
1788 FM	—	4.50	10.00	25.00	55.00	—
1789 FM	—	8.00	16.00	40.00	100	—

KM# 70   1/2 REAL
1.6917 g., 0.8960 Silver 0.0487 oz. ASW **Ruler:** Charles IV
Obv: Armored bust of Charles IV, right **Obv. Legend:**
CAROLUS • IV •... **Rev:** Crown above shield flanked by pillars
with banner **Mint:** Mexico City **Note:** Mint mark M, Mo.

Date	Mintage	VG	F	VF	XF	Unc
1789 FM	—	12.00	25.00	50.00	100	—
1790 FM	—	12.00	25.00	50.00	100	—

KM# 71   1/2 REAL
1.6917 g., 0.8960 Silver 0.0487 oz. ASW **Ruler:** Charles IV
Obv: Armored bust of Charles IIII, right **Obv. Legend:**
CAROLUS • IIII •... **Rev:** Crown above shield flanked by pillars
with banner **Mint:** Mexico City **Note:** Mint mark M, Mo.

Date	Mintage	VG	F	VF	XF	Unc
1790 FM	—	12.00	25.00	50.00	100	—

KM# 72   1/2 REAL
1.6900 g., 0.9030 Silver 0.0491 oz. ASW **Ruler:** Charles IV
Obv: Armored bust of Charles IIII, right **Obv. Legend:**
CAROLUS • IIII • ... **Rev:** Crowned shield flanked by pillars
with banner **Rev. Legend:** IND • R • .... **Mint:** Mexico City
Note: Mint mark Mo.

Date	Mintage	VG	F	VF	XF	Unc
1792 FM	—	6.00	12.00	25.00	50.00	—
1793 FM	—	6.00	12.00	25.00	50.00	—
1794/3 FM	—	7.50	15.00	30.00	75.00	—
1794 FM	—	5.00	10.00	22.00	45.00	—
1795 FM	—	4.00	10.00	22.00	45.00	—
1796 FM	—	4.00	10.00	22.00	45.00	—
1797 FM	—	4.00	10.00	22.00	45.00	—
1798/7 FM	—	5.00	11.50	25.00	55.00	—
1798 FM	—	4.00	10.00	22.00	45.00	—
1799 FM	—	4.00	10.00	22.00	45.00	—
1800/799 FM	—	5.00	11.50	25.00	50.00	—
1800 FM	—	4.00	10.00	22.00	45.00	—
1801 FM	—	8.00	17.00	33.00	85.00	—
1801 FT	—	4.00	11.00	25.00	50.00	—
1802 FT	—	4.00	11.00	25.00	50.00	—
1803 FT	—	6.00	13.00	27.50	55.00	—
1804 TH	—	4.00	11.00	25.00	50.00	—
1805 TH	—	4.00	11.00	25.00	50.00	—
1806 TH	—	4.00	11.00	25.00	50.00	—
1807/6 TH	—	6.00	13.00	27.50	55.00	—

Date	Mintage	VG	F	VF	XF	Unc
1807 TH	—	4.00	11.00	25.00	50.00	—
1808/7 TH	—	6.00	13.00	27.50	55.00	—
1808 TH	—	4.00	11.00	25.00	50.00	—

KM# 73   1/2 REAL
1.6900 g., 0.9030 Silver 0.0491 oz. ASW **Ruler:**
Ferdinand VII **Obv:** Armored laureate bust right **Obv.**
Legend: FERDIN.VII... **Rev:** Crowned shield flanked by
pillars **Rev. Legend:** IND.R.... **Mint:** Mexico City **Note:** Mint
mark Mo.

Date	Mintage	VG	F	VF	XF	Unc
1808 TH	—	4.00	9.00	22.50	40.00	—
1809 TH	—	4.00	9.00	22.50	40.00	—
1810 TH	—	6.00	11.00	25.00	50.00	—
1810 HJ	—	4.00	9.00	22.50	40.00	—
1811 HJ	—	4.00	9.00	22.50	40.00	—
1812/1 HJ	—	8.00	17.00	38.50	85.00	—
1812 JJ	—	13.00	27.50	49.50	105	—
1812 HJ	—	4.00	9.00	22.50	40.00	—
1813/2 JJ	—	13.00	27.50	49.50	105	—
1813 JJ	—	7.00	13.00	27.50	80.00	—
1813 TH	—	4.00	9.00	22.50	40.00	—
1813 HJ	—	8.00	17.00	38.50	95.00	—
1814/3 JJ	—	8.00	17.00	38.50	95.00	—
1814 JJ	—	6.00	11.00	25.00	50.00	—

KM# 74   1/2 REAL
1.6900 g., 0.9030 Silver 0.0491 oz. ASW **Ruler:**
Ferdinand VII **Obv:** Draped laureate bust right **Obv. Legend:**
FERDIN.VII.... **Rev:** Crowned shield flanked by pillars **Rev.**
Legend: IND.R.... **Mint:** Mexico City **Note:** Mint mark Mo.

Date	Mintage	VG	F	VF	XF	Unc
1815 JJ	—	4.00	9.00	22.50	45.00	—
1816 JJ	—	4.00	9.00	22.50	45.00	—
1817/6 JJ	—	13.00	27.50	55.00	125	—
1817 JJ	—	4.00	9.00	30.75	50.00	—
1818/7 JJ	—	4.00	9.00	27.50	55.00	—
1818 JJ	—	4.00	9.00	27.50	55.00	—
1819/8 JJ	—	7.00	13.00	38.50	95.00	—
1819 JJ	—	4.00	9.00	22.50	45.00	—
1820 JJ	—	4.00	9.00	27.50	55.00	—
1821 JJ	—	4.00	9.00	22.50	45.00	—

KM# 75.1   REAL
3.3834 g., 0.9170 Silver 0.0997 oz. ASW **Ruler:** Philip V
Obv: Crowned shield flanked by MF I ** **Obv. Legend:** PHILIP
• V • D • G • HISPAN • ET IND • REX **Rev:** Crowned globes
flanked by crowned pillars with banner, date below **Mint:**
Mexico City **Note:** Mint mark M, Mo, (MX).

Date	Mintage	VG	F	VF	XF	Unc
1732 Rare	—	—	—	—	—	—
1732 F	—	—	—	—	—	—
1733 F (MX)	—	150	350	425	750	—
1733 MF (MX)	—	150	350	425	750	—
1733 F Rare	—	—	—	—	—	—
1733 MF	—	100	200	300	500	—
1734/3 MF	—	15.00	.30.00	65.00	150	—
1734 MF	—	12.00	25.00	60.00	140	—
1735 MF	—	12.00	25.00	60.00	140	—
1736 MF	—	12.00	25.00	60.00	140	—

Date	Mintage	VG	F	VF	XF	Unc
1737 MF	—	12.00	25.00	60.00	140	—
1738 MF	—	12.00	25.00	60.00	140	—
1739 MF	—	12.00	25.00	60.00	140	—
1740 MF	—	12.00	25.00	60.00	140	—
1741 MF	—	12.00	25.00	60.00	140	—

KM# 75.2 REAL
3.3834 g., 0.9170 Silver 0.0997 oz. ASW **Ruler:** Philip V
Obv. Legend: PHS • V • D • G • HISP • ET • IND • R **Note:**
Mint mark M, Mo.

Date	Mintage	VG	F	VF	XF	Unc
1742 M	—	10.00	20.00	50.00	120	—
1743 M	—	10.00	20.00	50.00	120	—
1744/3 M	—	10.00	20.00	50.00	120	—
1744 M	—	10.00	20.00	50.00	120	—
1745 M	—	8.00	18.00	50.00	120	—
1746/5 M	—	12.00	25.00	75.00	200	—
1746 M	—	10.00	20.00	55.00	125	—
1747 M	—	10.00	20.00	55.00	125	—

KM# 76.1 REAL
3.3800 g., 0.9170 Silver 0.0996 oz. ASW **Ruler:**
Ferdinand VI **Obv:** Crowned shield flanked by R I **Obv.
Legend:** FRD • VI • D • G • HISP • ET IND • R **Rev:** Crowned
globes flanked by crowned pillars with banner, date below
Mint: Mexico City **Note:** Mint mark M, Mo.

Date	Mintage	VG	F	VF	XF	Unc
1747 M	—	10.00	20.00	50.00	100	—
1748/7 M	—	10.00	20.00	50.00	100	—
1748 M	—	10.00	20.00	50.00	100	—
1749 M	—	10.00	20.00	50.00	100	—
1750/40 M	—	10.00	20.00	50.00	100	—
1750 M	—	10.00	20.00	50.00	100	—
1751 M	—	10.00	20.00	55.00	110	—
1752 M	—	10.00	20.00	50.00	100	—
1753 M	—	10.00	20.00	50.00	100	—
1754 M	—	10.00	20.00	55.00	110	—
1755/4 M	—	10.00	20.00	50.00	100	—
1755 M	—	10.00	20.00	50.00	100	—
1756 M	—	10.00	20.00	55.00	110	—
1757 M	—	10.00	20.00	55.00	110	—
1758/5 M	—	10.00	20.00	50.00	100	—
1758 M	—	10.00	20.00	50.00	100	—

KM# 76.2 REAL
3.3834 g., 0.9170 Silver 0.0997 oz. ASW **Ruler:**
Ferdinand VI **Obv:** Royal and Imperial crowns **Note:** Mint
mark M, Mo.

Date	Mintage	VG	F	VF	XF	Unc
1757 M	—	10.00	20.00	50.00	100	—
1758/7 M	—	10.00	20.00	50.00	100	—
1758 M	—	10.00	20.00	50.00	100	—
1759 M	—	10.00	20.00	55.00	110	—
1760 M	—	15.00	30.00	70.00	140	—

KM# 77 REAL
3.3800 g., 0.9170 Silver 0.0996 oz. ASW **Ruler:** Charles III
Obv: Crowned shield flanked by R I **Obv. Legend:** CAR • III
• D • G • HISP • ET IND • R **Rev:** Crowned globes flanked by
crowned pillars with banner, date below **Mint:** Mexico City
Note: Mint mark M, Mo.

Date	Mintage	VG	F	VF	XF	Unc
1760 M	—	10.00	20.00	50.00	100	—
1761/0 M	—	10.00	20.00	55.00	125	—
1761 M	—	10.00	20.00	50.00	100	—
1762 M	—	10.00	20.00	50.00	100	—
1763/2 M	—	12.00	25.00	60.00	120	—

Date	Mintage	VG	F	VF	XF	Unc
1763 M	—	10.00	20.00	50.00	100	—
1764 M	—	10.00	20.00	55.00	110	—
1765 M	—	10.00	20.00	55.00	110	—
1766 M	—	10.00	20.00	50.00	100	—
1767 M	—	10.00	20.00	55.00	110	—
1768 M	—	10.00	20.00	50.00	100	—
1769 M	—	10.00	20.00	50.00	100	—
1769/70 M	—	10.00	20.00	55.00	125	—
1770 M	—	10.00	20.00	55.00	125	—
1770 F	—	20.00	40.00	90.00	250	—
1771 F	—	20.00	40.00	90.00	250	—

KM# 78.1 REAL
3.3834 g., 0.9030 Silver 0.0982 oz. ASW **Ruler:** Charles III
Obv. Legend: CAROLUS • III • DEI • GRATIA **Rev:** Inverted
FM and mint mark **Note:** Mint mark M, Mo.

Date	Mintage	VG	F	VF	XF	Unc
1772 FM	—	5.00	10.00	25.00	60.00	—
1773 FM	—	5.00	10.00	25.00	60.00	—

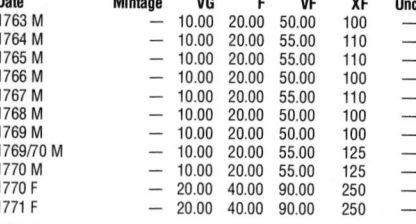

KM# 78.2 REAL
3.3800 g., 0.9030 Silver 0.0981 oz. ASW **Ruler:** Charles III
Obv: Armored bust of Charles III, right **Obv. Legend:**
CAROLUS • III • DEI • GRATIA **Rev. Legend:** Crowned shield
flanked by pillars with banner, normal initials and mint mark
Mint: Mexico City **Note:** Mint mark M, Mo.

Date	Mintage	VG	F	VF	XF	Unc
1774 FM	—	5.00	10.00	25.00	60.00	—
1775/4 FM	—	6.00	12.00	28.00	75.00	—
1775 FM	—	5.00	10.00	25.00	60.00	—
1776 FM	—	5.00	10.00	25.00	60.00	—
1777 FM	—	5.00	10.00	25.00	60.00	—
1778 FF/M	—	6.00	12.00	28.00	75.00	—
1778 FF	—	5.00	10.00	25.00	60.00	—
1779 FF	—	5.00	10.00	25.00	60.00	—
1780 FF	—	5.00	10.00	25.00	60.00	—
1780 F F/M	—	5.00	10.00	25.00	60.00	—
1781 FF	—	5.00	10.00	25.00	60.00	—
1782 FF	—	5.00	10.00	25.00	60.00	—
1783 FF	—	5.00	10.00	25.00	60.00	—
1784 FF	—	5.00	10.00	25.00	60.00	—

KM# 78.2a REAL
3.3834 g., 0.8960 Silver 0.0975 oz. ASW **Ruler:** Charles III
Rev: Normal initials and mint mark **Note:** Mint mark M, Mo.

Date	Mintage	VG	F	VF	XF	Unc
1785 FF	—	6.00	12.00	28.00	75.00	—
1785 FM	—	6.00	12.00	28.00	75.00	—
1786 FM	—	6.00	12.00	28.00	75.00	—
1787 FF	—	15.00	30.00	60.00	125	—
1787 FM	—	12.00	25.00	50.00	100	—
1788 FF	—	50.00	100	200	—	—
1788 FM	—	5.00	10.00	25.00	60.00	—
1789 FM	—	6.00	12.00	28.00	75.00	—

KM# 79 REAL
3.3800 g., 0.9030 Silver 0.0981 oz. ASW **Ruler:** Charles IV
Obv: Armored bust of Charles III, right **Obv. Legend:**
CAROLUS • IV • ... **Rev:** Crown above shield flanked by pillars
with banner **Mint:** Mexico City **Note:** Mint mark M, Mo.

Date	Mintage	VG	F	VF	XF	Unc
1789 FM	—	15.00	30.00	60.00	150	—
1790 FM	—	15.00	30.00	60.00	150	—

KM# 80 REAL
3.3800 g., 0.9030 Silver 0.0981 oz. ASW **Ruler:** Charles IV
Obv: Armored bust of Charles IIII, right **Obv. Legend:**
CAROLUS • IIII • ... **Rev:** Crowned shield flanked by pillars
with banner **Mint:** Mexico City **Note:** Mint mark M, Mo.

Date	Mintage	VG	F	VF	XF	Unc
1790 FM	—	17.00	35.00	70.00	165	—

KM# 81 REAL
3.3834 g., 0.8960 Silver 0.0975 oz. ASW **Ruler:** Charles IV
Obv: Armored bust of Charles IIII, right **Obv. Legend:**
CAROLUS • IIII • ... **Rev:** Crowned shield flanked by pillars
with banner **Rev. Legend:** IND • REX ... **Mint:** Mexico City
Note: Mint mark Mo.

Date	Mintage	VG	F	VF	XF	Unc
1792 FM	—	10.00	20.00	35.00	90.00	—
1793 FM	—	15.00	30.00	60.00	150	—
1794 FM	—	25.00	50.00	100	250	—
1795 FM	—	15.00	30.00	60.00	150	—
1796 FM	—	5.00	10.00	25.00	65.00	—
1797/6 FM	—	8.00	15.00	28.00	80.00	—
1797 FM	—	5.00	10.00	25.00	60.00	—
1798/7 FM	—	5.00	10.00	25.00	65.00	—
1798 FM	—	5.00	10.00	25.00	60.00	—
1799 FM	—	5.00	10.00	25.00	60.00	—
1800 FM	—	5.00	10.00	25.00	60.00	—
1801 FT/M	—	6.00	11.00	27.50	65.00	—
1801 FT	—	6.00	11.00	27.50	65.00	—
1801 FM	—	9.00	17.00	30.75	65.00	—
1802 FM	—	6.00	11.00	27.50	65.00	—
1802 FT	—	6.00	11.00	27.50	65.00	—
1802/1 FT	—	6.00	11.00	27.50	65.00	—
1802 FT/M	—	6.00	11.00	27.50	65.00	—
1803 FT	—	6.00	11.00	27.50	65.00	—
1804 TH	—	6.00	11.00	27.50	65.00	—
1805 TH	—	6.00	11.00	27.50	65.00	—
1806 TH	—	6.00	11.00	27.50	65.00	—
1807/6 TH	—	6.00	11.00	27.50	65.00	—
1807 TH	—	6.00	11.00	27.50	65.00	—
1808/7 TH	—	6.00	11.00	27.50	65.00	—
1808 FM	—	6.00	11.00	27.50	65.00	—

KM# 82 REAL
3.3800 g., 0.9030 Silver 0.0981 oz. ASW **Ruler:**
Ferdinand VII **Obv:** Armored laureate bust right **Obv.
Legend:** FERDIN.VII... **Rev:** Crowned shield flanked by
pillars **Rev. Legend:** IND.REX.... **Mint:** Mexico City **Note:**
Mint mark Mo.

Date	Mintage	VG	F	VF	XF	Unc
1809 TH	—	9.00	17.00	30.75	95.00	—
1810/09 TH	—	9.00	17.00	30.75	95.00	—
1810 TH	—	9.00	17.00	30.75	95.00	—
1811 TH	—	27.50	38.50	65.00	250	—
1811 HJ	—	9.00	17.00	30.75	95.00	—
1812 HJ	—	4.00	10.00	30.75	85.00	—
1812 JJ	—	11.00	22.50	44.00	125	—

Date	Mintage	VG	F	VF	XF	Unc
1813 HJ	—	11.00	22.50	44.00	125	—
1813 JJ	—	55.00	110	165	250	—
1814 HJ	—	17.00	33.00	165	155	—
1814 JJ	—	55.00	110	195	300	—

KM# 83 REAL
3.3800 g., 0.9030 Silver 0.0981 oz. ASW **Ruler:**
Ferdinand VII **Obv:** Draped laureate bust right **Obv. Legend:**
FERDIN.VII... **Rev:** Crowned shield flanked by pillars **Rev.
Legend:** IND.REX... **Mint:** Mexico City **Note:** Mint mark Mo.

Date	Mintage	VG	F	VF	XF	Unc
1814 JJ	—	27.50	55.00	110	350	—
1815 HJ	—	17.00	33.00	65.00	150	—
1815 JJ	—	11.00	22.50	44.00	125	—
1816 JJ	—	6.00	11.00	27.50	75.00	—
1817 JJ	—	6.00	11.00	27.50	75.00	—
1818 JJ	—	33.00	65.00	140	500	—
1819 JJ	—	6.00	11.00	27.50	75.00	—
1820 JJ	—	6.00	11.00	27.50	75.00	—
1821/0 JJ	—	9.00	17.00	33.00	115	—
1821 JJ	—	6.00	11.00	27.50	55.00	—

KM# 84 2 REALES
6.7668 g., 0.9170 Silver 0.1995 oz. ASW **Ruler:** Philip V
Obv: Crowned shield flanked by M F 2 **Obv. Legend:** PHILIP
• V • D • G • HISPAN • ET IND • REX **Rev:** Crowned globes
flanked by crowned pillars with banner, date below **Rev.
Legend:** VTRAQUE VNUM **Mint:** Mexico City **Note:** Mint
mark M, Mo, (MX).

Date	Mintage	VG	F	VF	XF	Unc
1732 Rare	—	—	—	—	—	—
1732 F	—	800	1,300	1,750	2,750	—
1733 F	—	600	800	1,350	2,250	—
1733 MF (MX)	—	350	600	1,000	1,650	—
1733 MF	—	600	900	1,500	2,500	—
1734/3 MF	—	20.00	40.00	85.00	170	—
1734 MF	—	20.00	40.00	85.00	170	—
1735/3 MF	—	15.00	30.00	75.00	150	—
1735/4 MF	—	15.00	30.00	75.00	150	—
1735 MF	—	15.00	30.00	75.00	150	—
1736/3 MF	—	18.00	35.00	80.00	160	—
1736/4 MF	—	18.00	35.00	80.00	160	—
1736/5 MF	—	18.00	35.00	80.00	160	—
1736 MF	—	18.00	35.00	80.00	160	—
1737/3 MF	—	18.00	35.00	80.00	160	—
1737 MF	—	18.00	35.00	80.00	160	—
1738/7 MF	—	18.00	35.00	80.00	160	—
1738 MF	—	18.00	35.00	80.00	160	—
1739 MF	—	18.00	35.00	80.00	160	—
1740/30 MF	—	18.00	35.00	80.00	160	—
1740 MF	—	18.00	35.00	80.00	160	—
1741 MF	—	18.00	35.00	80.00	160	—

KM# 85   2 REALES
6.7700 g., 0.9170 Silver 0.1996 oz. ASW **Ruler:** Philip V
Obv: Crowned shield flanked by R 2 **Obv. Legend:** PHS • V
• D • G • HISP • ET IND • R * **Rev:** Crowned globes flanked
by crowned pillars with banner, date below **Rev. Legend:**
VTRA QUE VNUM **Mint:** Mexico City **Note:** Mint mark M, Mo.

Date	Mintage	F	VF	XF	Unc	BU
1742 M	—	30.00	75.00	125	—	—
1743/2 M	—	30.00	75.00	125	—	—
1743 M	—	30.00	75.00	125	—	—
1744/3 M	—	30.00	75.00	125	—	—
1744 M	—	30.00	75.00	125	—	—
1745/4 M	—	30.00	75.00	125	—	—
1745 M	—	30.00	75.00	125	—	—
1745 M HIP	—	400	—	—	—	—
1746/5 M	—	30.00	75.00	125	—	—
1746 M	—	30.00	75.00	125	—	—
1747 M	—	30.00	75.00	125	—	—
1750 M	—	450	650	1,000	—	—

KM# 86.1   2 REALES
6.7668 g., 0.9170 Silver 0.1995 oz. ASW **Ruler:**
Ferdinand VI **Obv:** Crowned shield flanked by R 2 **Obv.
Legend:** FRD • VI • D • G • HISP • ET IND • R **Rev:** Crowned
globes flanked by crowned pillars with banner, date below
Rev. Legend: VTRA QUE VNUM **Mint:** Mexico City **Note:**
Mint mark M, Mo.

Date	Mintage	VG	F	VF	XF	Unc
1747 M	—	16.00	32.00	78.00	135	—
1748/7 M	—	16.00	32.00	78.00	135	—
1748 M	—	15.00	30.00	75.00	125	—
1749 M	—	15.00	30.00	75.00	125	—
1750 M	—	15.00	30.00	75.00	125	—
1751/41 M	—	18.00	35.00	80.00	150	—
1751 M	—	15.00	30.00	75.00	125	—
1752 M	—	15.00	30.00	75.00	125	—
1753/2 M	—	18.00	35.00	80.00	150	—
1753 M	—	18.00	35.00	80.00	150	—
1754 M	—	18.00	35.00	80.00	150	—
1755/4 M	—	18.00	35.00	80.00	150	—
1755 M	—	18.00	35.00	80.00	150	—
1756/55 M	—	18.00	35.00	80.00	150	—
1756 M	—	18.00	35.00	80.00	140	—
1757/6 M	—	15.00	30.00	75.00	125	—
1757 M	—	18.00	35.00	80.00	150	—

KM# 86.2   2 REALES
6.7668 g., 0.9170 Silver 0.1995 oz. ASW **Ruler:**
Ferdinand VI **Obv:** Royal and Imperial crowns **Note:** Mint
mark M, Mo.

Date	Mintage	VG	F	VF	XF	Unc
1757 M	—	15.00	30.00	75.00	125	—
1758 M	—	15.00	30.00	75.00	125	—
1759/8 M	—	15.00	30.00	75.00	125	—
1759 M	—	20.00	40.00	90.00	175	—
1760 M	—	20.00	40.00	90.00	175	—

KM# 87   2 REALES
6.7700 g., 0.9170 Silver 0.1996 oz. ASW **Ruler:** Charles III
Obv: Crowned shield flanked by R 2 **Obv. Legend:** CAR • III
• D • G • HISP • ET IND • R **Rev:** Crowned globes flanked by
crowned pillars with banner, date below **Rev. Legend:** VTRA
QUE VNUM **Mint:** Mexico City **Note:** Mint mark M, Mo.

Date	Mintage	VG	F	VF	XF	Unc
1760 M	—	15.00	30.00	75.00	125	—
1761 M	—	15.00	30.00	75.00	125	—
1762/1 M	—	15.00	30.00	75.00	125	—
1762 M	—	15.00	30.00	75.00	125	—
1763/2 M	—	15.00	30.00	75.00	125	—
1763 M	—	15.00	30.00	75.00	125	—
1764 M	—	15.00	30.00	75.00	125	—
1765 M	—	15.00	30.00	75.00	125	—
1766 M	—	12.00	35.00	80.00	160	—
1767 M	—	15.00	30.00	75.00	125	—
1768/6 M	—	15.00	30.00	75.00	125	—
1768 M	—	15.00	30.00	75.00	125	—
1769 M	—	15.00	30.00	75.00	125	—
1770 M	—	350	550	—	—	—
1770 F Rare	—	—	—	—	—	—
1771 F	—	15.00	30.00	75.00	125	—

KM# 88.1   2 REALES
6.7668 g., 0.9030 Silver 0.1964 oz. ASW **Ruler:** Charles III
Obv: Armored bust of Charles III, right **Obv. Legend:**
CAROLUS • III • DEI • GRATIA **Rev:** Inverted FM and mint
mark **Note:** Mint mark M, Mo.

Date	Mintage	VG	F	VF	XF	Unc
1772 FM	—	7.00	15.00	30.00	100	—
1773 FM	—	7.00	15.00	30.00	100	—

KM# 88.2   2 REALES
6.7700 g., 0.9030 Silver 0.1965 oz. ASW **Ruler:** Charles III
Obv: Armored bust od Charles III, right **Obv. Legend:**
CAROLUS • III • DEI • GRATIA • **Rev:** Crowned shield flanked
by pillars with banner, normal initials and mint mark **Rev.
Legend:** • HISPAN • ET IND • REX • ... **Mint:** Mexico City
Note: Mint mark M, Mo.

Date	Mintage	VG	F	VF	XF	Unc
1773 FM	—	7.00	15.00	30.00	100	—
1774 FM	—	7.00	15.00	30.00	100	—
1775 FM	—	7.00	15.00	30.00	100	—
1776 FM	—	7.00	15.00	30.00	100	—
1777 FM	—	7.00	15.00	30.00	100	—
1778/7 FF	—	7.00	15.00	30.00	100	—
1778 FF	—	7.00	15.00	30.00	100	—
1778 F F/M	—	7.00	15.00	30.00	100	—
1779/8 FF	—	7.00	15.00	30.00	100	—
1779 FF	—	7.00	15.00	30.00	100	—
1780 FF	—	7.00	15.00	30.00	100	—
1781 FF	—	7.00	15.00	30.00	100	—

Date	Mintage	VG	F	VF	XF	Unc
1782/1 FF	—	7.00	15.00	30.00	100	—
1782 FF	—	7.00	15.00	30.00	100	—
1783 FF	—	7.00	15.00	30.00	100	—
1784 FF	—	7.00	15.00	30.00	100	—
1784 FF DEI GRATIA (error)	—	100	150	250	600	—
1784 FM	—	70.00	120	225	575	—

KM# 88.2a 2 REALES
6.7668 g., 0.8960 Silver 0.1949 oz. ASW **Ruler:** Charles III
Obv: Armored bust of Charles III, right **Rev:** Crowned shield
flanked by pillars with banner **Mint:** Mexico City **Note:** Mint
mark Mo.

Date	Mintage	VG	F	VF	XF	Unc
1785Mo FM	—	7.00	15.00	30.00	100	—
1786Mo FF	—	200	350	550	950	—
1786Mo FM	—	7.00	15.00	30.00	100	—
1787Mo FM	—	7.00	15.00	30.00	100	—
1788/98Mo FM	—	7.00	15.00	30.00	100	—
1788Mo FM	—	7.00	15.00	30.00	100	—
1789Mo FM	—	12.00	25.00	50.00	150	—

KM# 89 2 REALES
6.7700 g., 0.9030 Silver 0.1965 oz. ASW **Ruler:** Charles IV
Obv: Armored bust of Charles IV, right **Obv. Legend:**
CAROLUS • IV • DEI • GRATIA • **Rev:** Crowned shield flanked
by pillars with banner **Rev. Legend:** • HISPAN • ET IND •
REX • ... **Mint:** Mexico City **Note:** Mint mark M, Mo.

Date	Mintage	VG	F	VF	XF	Unc
1789 FM	—	15.00	30.00	75.00	200	—
1790 FM	—	15.00	30.00	75.00	200	—

KM# 90 2 REALES
6.7700 g., 0.9030 Silver 0.1965 oz. ASW **Ruler:** Charles IV
Obv: Armored bust of Charles IIII, right **Obv. Legend:**
CAROLUS • IIII • DEI • GRATIA • **Rev:** Crowned shield flanked
by pillars with banner **Rev. Legend:** • HISPAN • ET IND REX
• ... **Mint:** Mexico City **Note:** Mint mark M, Mo.

Date	Mintage	VG	F	VF	XF	Unc
1790 FM	—	17.00	35.00	80.00	200	—

KM# 91 2 REALES
6.7668 g., 0.8960 Silver 0.1949 oz. ASW **Ruler:** Charles III
Obv: Armored bust of Charles IIII, right **Obv. Legend:**
CAROLUS • IIII • DEI • GRATIA • **Rev:** Crowned shield flanked
by pillars with banner **Rev. Legend:** • HISPAN • ET IND REX
• ... **Mint:** Mexico City **Note:** Mint mark Mo.

Date	Mintage	VG	F	VF	XF	Unc
1792 FM	—	15.00	30.00	60.00	200	—

Date	Mintage	VG	F	VF	XF	Unc
1793 FM	—	15.00	30.00	60.00	200	—
1794/3 FM	—	50.00	100	200	450	—
1794 FM	—	40.00	75.00	150	400	—
1795 FM	—	7.00	15.00	30.00	85.00	—
1796 FM	—	7.00	15.00	30.00	85.00	—
1797 FM	—	7.00	15.00	30.00	85.00	—
1798 FM	—	7.00	15.00	30.00	85.00	—
1799/8 FM	—	7.00	15.00	32.00	90.00	—
1799 FM	—	7.00	15.00	30.00	85.00	—
1800 FM	—	7.00	15.00	30.00	85.00	—
1801 FT/M	—	7.00	15.00	30.00	85.00	—
1801 FT	—	7.00	15.00	30.00	85.00	—
1801 FT	—	20.00	40.00	75.00	250	—
1802 FT	—	7.00	15.00	30.00	85.00	—
1803 FT	—	7.00	15.00	30.00	85.00	—
1804/3 TH	—	7.00	15.00	30.00	85.00	—
1804 TH	—	7.00	15.00	30.00	85.00	—
1805 TH	—	7.00	15.00	30.00	85.00	—
1806/5 TH	—	7.00	15.00	32.00	90.00	—
1806 TH	—	7.00	15.00	30.00	85.00	—
1807/5 TH	—	7.00	15.00	32.00	90.00	—
1807/6 TH	—	15.00	30.00	60.00	200	—
1807 TH	—	7.00	15.00	30.00	85.00	—
1808/7 TH	—	7.00	15.00	32.00	90.00	—
1808 TH	—	7.00	15.00	30.00	85.00	—

KM# 92 2 REALES
6.7700 g., 0.9030 Silver 0.1965 oz. ASW **Ruler:**
Ferdinand VII **Obv:** Armored laureate bust right **Obv.
Legend:** FERDIN.VII... **Rev:** Crowned shield flanked by
pillars **Rev. Legend:** IND.REX... **Mint:** Mexico City **Note:** Mint
mark Mo.

Date	Mintage	VG	F	VF	XF	Unc
1809 TH	—	15.00	30.00	75.00	200	—
181/00 TH	—	15.00	30.00	75.00	200	—
1810 TH	—	15.00	30.00	75.00	200	—
181/00 HJ	—	15.00	30.00	75.00	200	—
181/00 HJ/TH	—	15.00	30.00	75.00	200	—
1810 HJ	—	15.00	30.00	75.00	200	—
1811/0 HJ/TH	—	40.00	80.00	150	300	—
1811 TH	—	150	250	350	750	—
1811 HJ	—	15.00	30.00	75.00	200	—
1811 HJ/TH	—	40.00	80.00	150	300	—

KM# 93 2 REALES
6.7700 g., 0.9030 Silver 0.1965 oz. ASW **Ruler:**
Ferdinand VII **Obv:** Draped laureate bust right **Obv. Legend:**
FERDIN.VII... **Rev:** Crowned shield flanked by pillars **Rev.
Legend:** IND.REX... **Mint:** Mexico City **Note:** Mint mark Mo.

Date	Mintage	VG	F	VF	XF	Unc
1812 TH	—	60.00	125	250	550	—
1812 HJ	—	40.00	100	200	500	—
1812 JJ	—	10.00	20.00	60.00	200	—
1813 JJ	—	15.00	30.00	100	400	—
1813 JJ	—	20.00	60.00	125	350	—
1813 HJ	—	40.00	100	200	500	—
1814/3 JJ	—	15.00	30.00	100	400	—
1814/2 JJ	—	15.00	30.00	100	400	—

Date	Mintage	VG	F	VF	XF	Unc
1814 JJ	—	15.00	30.00	100	400	—
1815 JJ	—	6.00	12.00	28.00	85.00	—
1816 JJ	—	6.00	12.00	28.00	85.00	—
1817 JJ	—	6.00	12.00	28.00	85.00	—
1818 JJ	—	6.00	12.00	28.00	85.00	—
1819/8 JJ	—	5.50	12.00	30.00	85.00	—
1819 JJ	—	6.00	12.00	28.00	85.00	—
1820 JJ	—	175	—	—	—	—
1821/0 JJ	—	7.00	15.00	30.00	90.00	—
1821 JJ	—	6.00	12.00	28.00	85.00	—

KM# 94   4 REALES
13.5337 g., 0.9170 Silver 0.3990 oz. ASW   **Ruler:** Philip V
Obv: Crowned shield flanked by F 4 **Obv. Legend:** PHILLIP
• V • D • G • HISPAN • ET IND • REX **Rev:** Crowned globes
flanked by crowned pillars with banner, date below **Rev.
Legend:** VTRAQUE VNUM **Mint:** Mexico City **Note:** Mint
mark M, Mo, MX.

Date	Mintage	VG	F	VF	XF	Unc
1732 Rare; Specimen	—	—	—	—	—	—
1732 F	—	2,000	3,000	5,000	10,000	—
1733/2 F	—	1,500	2,000	4,000	6,500	—
1733 MF	—	1,100	1,650	2,250	4,250	—
1733 MF (MX)	—	1,500	2,200	3,250	5,500	—
1733 MX/XM	—	1,500	2,200	3,250	5,500	—
1734/3 MF	—	150	300	600	1,200	—
1734 MF	—	150	300	600	1,200	—
1735/4 MF	—	100	175	300	600	—
1735 MF	—	100	175	300	600	—
1736 MF	—	100	175	300	600	—
1737 MF	—	100	175	300	600	—
1738/7 MF	—	100	175	300	600	—
1738 MF	—	100	175	300	600	—
1739 MF	—	100	175	300	600	—
1740/30 MF	—	100	200	325	625	—
1740 MF	—	100	175	300	600	—
1741 MF	—	100	175	300	600	—
1742/1 MF	—	100	175	300	600	—
1742/32 MF	—	100	175	300	600	—
1742 MF	—	100	175	300	600	—
1743 MF	—	100	175	300	600	—
1744/3 MF	—	100	200	325	625	—
1744 MF	—	100	175	300	600	—
1745 MF	—	100	175	300	600	—
1746 MF	—	100	175	300	600	—
1747 MF	—	150	275	400	650	—

KM# 95   4 REALES
13.5400 g., 0.9170 Silver 0.3992 oz. ASW   **Ruler:**
Ferdinand VI **Obv:** Crowned shield flanked by M F 4 **Obv.
Legend:** FERDND • VI • D • G • HISPAN • ET IND • REX
Rev: Crowned globes flanked by crowned pillars with banner,

date below **Rev. Legend:** ...QUE VNUM **Mint:** Mexico City
Note: Struck at Mexico City Mint, mint mark M, Mo.

Date	Mintage	VG	F	VF	XF	Unc
1747 MF	—	100	150	300	550	—
1748/7 MF	—	100	150	300	550	—
1748 MF	—	100	125	250	500	—
1749 MF	—	150	225	350	650	—
1750/40 MF	—	100	125	250	500	—
1751/41 MF	—	100	125	250	500	—
1751 MF	—	100	125	250	500	—
1752 MF	—	100	125	250	500	—
1753 MF	—	100	125	300	550	—
1754 MF	—	250	375	500	850	—
1755 MM	—	100	125	250	500	—
1756 MM	—	100	150	300	550	—
1757 MM	—	100	150	300	550	—
1758 MM	—	100	125	250	500	—
1759 MM	—	100	125	250	500	—
1760/59 MM	—	100	175	350	600	—
1760 MM	—	100	175	350	600	—

KM# 96   4 REALES
13.5400 g., 0.9170 Silver 0.3992 oz. ASW   **Ruler:** Charles III
Obv: Crowned shield flanked by F M 4 **Obv. Legend:**
CAROLVS • III • D • G • HISPAN • ET IND • REX **Rev:** Crowned
globes flanked by crowned pillars with banner, date below
Rev. Legend: ...AQUE VNUM **Mint:** Mexico City **Note:** Mint
mark M, Mo.

Date	Mintage	VG	F	VF	XF	Unc
1760 MM	—	100	150	250	900	—
1761 MM	—	100	150	250	900	—
1761 MM Cross between H and I	—	100	150	250	900	—
1762 MM	—	75.00	125	250	500	—
1763/1 MM	—	100	150	300	600	—
1763 MM	—	100	150	300	600	—
1764 MM	—	400	600	1,000	2,000	—
1764 MF	—	350	500	1,000	2,000	—
1765 MF	—	350	500	1,000	2,000	—
1766 MF	—	250	350	550	1,250	—
1767 MF	—	100	150	300	600	—
1768 MF	—	75.00	125	250	500	—
1769 MF	—	75.00	125	250	500	—
1770 MF	—	75.00	125	250	500	—
1771 MF	—	125	200	325	700	—

KM# 97.1   4 REALES
13.5337 g., 0.9030 Silver 0.3929 oz. ASW   **Ruler:** Charles III
Obv: Armored bust of Charles III, right **Obv. Legend:**
CAROLUS • III • DEI • GRATIA • **Rev:** Crowned shield flanked
by pillars with banner, inverted FM and mint mark **Rev.
Legend:** •HISPAN • ET IND REX • ... **Mint:** Mexico City **Note:**
Mint mark M, Mo.

Date	Mintage	VG	F	VF	XF	Unc
1772 FM	—	90.00	125	250	500	—
1773 FM	—	100	175	300	650	—

KM# 97.2 4 REALES
13.5400 g., 0.9030 Silver 0.3931 oz. ASW **Ruler:** Charles III
Obv: Armored bust of Charles III, right **Obv. Legend:**
CAROLUS • III • DEI • GRATIA • **Rev:** Crowned shield flanked
by pillars with banner, normal initials and mint mark **Rev.**
Legend: • HISPAN • ET IND REX • ... **Mint:** Mexico City **Note:**
Mint mark M, Mo.

Date	Mintage	VG	F	VF	XF	Unc
1774 FM	—	50.00	100	200	500	—
1775 FM	—	50.00	100	200	500	—
1776 FM	—	50.00	100	200	500	—
1777 FM	—	50.00	100	200	500	—
1778 FF	—	50.00	100	200	500	—
1779 FF	—	50.00	100	200	500	—
1780 FF	—	50.00	100	200	500	—
1781 FF	—	50.00	100	200	500	—
1782 FF	—	50.00	100	200	500	—
1783 FF	—	50.00	100	200	500	—
1784 FF	—	50.00	100	200	500	—
1784 FM	—	100	200	350	600	—

KM# 97.2a 4 REALES
13.5337 g., 0.8960 Silver 0.3898 oz. ASW **Ruler:** Charles III
Obv: Armored bust of Charles III, right **Obv. Legend:**
CAROLUS • III • DEI • GRATIA • **Rev:** Crowned shield flanked
by pillars with banner, normal initials and mint mark **Rev.**
Legend: • HISPAN • ET IND REX • ... **Note:** Mint mark M, Mo.

Date	Mintage	VG	F	VF	XF	Unc
1785 FM	—	100	200	350	600	—
1786 FM	—	50.00	100	200	500	—
1787 FM	—	50.00	100	200	500	—
1788 FM	—	50.00	100	200	500	—
1789 FM	—	50.00	100	200	500	—

KM# 98 4 REALES
13.5400 g., 0.9030 Silver 0.3931 oz. ASW **Ruler:** Charles IV
Obv: Armored bust of Charles III, right **Obv. Legend:**
CAROLUS • IV • DEI • GRATIA • **Rev:** Crowned shield flanked
by pillars with banner **Rev. Legend:** • HISPAN • ET IND REX
• ... **Mint:** Mexico City **Note:** Mintint mark M, Mo, using old
bust punch.

Date	Mintage	VG	F	VF	XF	Unc
1789 FM	—	65.00	125	250	550	—
1790 FM	—	50.00	100	200	500	—

KM# 99 4 REALES
13.5400 g., 0.9030 Silver 0.3931 oz. ASW **Ruler:** Charles IV
Obv: Armored bust of Charles III, right **Obv. Legend:**
CAROLUS • IIII • DEI • GRATIA • **Rev:** Crowned shield flanked
by pillars with banner **Rev. Legend:** • HISPAN • ET IND •
REX • ... **Mint:** Mexico City **Note:** Mint mark M, Mo, using old
bust punch.

Date	Mintage	VG	F	VF	XF	Unc
1790 FM	—	65.00	125	250	550	—

KM# 100 4 REALES
13.5337 g., 0.8960 Silver 0.3898 oz. ASW **Ruler:** Charles IV
Obv: Armored bust of Charles IIII, right **Obv. Legend:**
CAROLUS • IIII • DEI • GRATIA • **Rev:** Crowned shield flanked
by pillars with banner **Rev. Legend:** • HISPAN • ET IND •
REX • ... **Mint:** Mexico City **Note:** Mint mark Mo.

Date	Mintage	VG	F	VF	XF	Unc
1792 FM	—	35.00	65.00	150	400	—
1793 FM	—	75.00	125	200	500	—
1794/3 FM	—	35.00	65.00	150	400	—
1794 FM	—	35.00	65.00	150	400	—
1795 FM	—	35.00	65.00	150	400	—
1796 FM	—	150	250	400	800	—
1797 FM	—	60.00	120	200	500	—
1798/7 FM	—	35.00	65.00	150	400	—
1798 FM	—	35.00	65.00	150	400	—
1799 FM	—	35.00	65.00	150	400	—
1800 FM	—	35.00	65.00	150	400	—
1801 FM	—	35.00	65.00	150	425	—
1801 FT	—	60.00	120	200	525	—
1802 FT	—	200	300	500	1,000	—
1803 FT	—	75.00	135	225	575	—
1803 FM	—	200	300	500	1,000	—
1804 TH	—	40.00	75.00	175	475	—
1805 TH	—	35.00	65.00	150	425	—
1806 TH	—	35.00	65.00	150	425	—
1807 TH	—	35.00	65.00	150	425	—
1808/7 TH	—	40.00	75.00	175	475	—
1808 TH	—	40.00	75.00	175	475	—

KM# 101   4 REALES
13.5400 g., 0.9030 Silver 0.3931 oz. ASW   **Ruler:**
Ferdinand VII **Obv:** Armored laureate bust right **Obv.**
Legend: FERDIN.VII... **Rev:** Crowned shield flanked by
pillars **Rev. Legend:** IND.REX... **Mint:** Mexico City **Note:** Mint
mark Mo.

Date	Mintage	VG	F	VF	XF	Unc
1809 HJ	—	75.00	135	250	750	—
1810 HJ	—	75.00	135	250	750	—
1811 HJ	—	75.00	135	250	750	—
1812 HJ	—	400	650	900	1,850	—

KM# 102   4 REALES
13.5400 g., 0.9030 Silver 0.3931 oz. ASW   **Ruler:**
Ferdinand VII **Obv:** Draped laureate bust right **Obv. Legend:**
FERDIN.VII... **Rev:** Crowned shield flanked by pillars **Rev.**
Legend: IND.REX... **Mint:** Mexico City **Note:** Mint mark Mo.

Date	Mintage	VG	F	VF	XF	Unc
1816 JJ	—	150	200	325	700	—
1817 JJ	—	250	400	500	1,000	—
1818/7 JJ	—	250	400	500	1,000	—
1819 JJ	—	175	250	325	700	—
1820 JJ	—	175	250	325	700	—
1821 JJ	—	75.00	135	250	650	—

KM# 103   8 REALES
27.0674 g., 0.9170 Silver 0.7980 oz. ASW   **Ruler:** Philip V
Obv: Crowned shield flanked by M F 8 **Obv. Legend:** PHILIP
• V • D • G • HISPAN • ET IND • REX **Rev:** Crowned globes
flanked by crowned pillars with banner, date below **Rev.**
Legend: ...VNUM **Mint:** Mexico City **Note:** Mint mark M, Mo,
MX.

Date	Mintage	VG	F	VF	XF	Unc
1732 F	—	2,750	4,750	8,000	—	—
1733/2 F (MX)	—	3,000	5,250	9,000	—	—
1733 F	—	2,000	3,000	5,000	9,000	—
1733 MF Large crown; Rare	—	—	—	—	—	—
1733 F (MX) Rare	—	—	—	—	—	—
Note: Bonhams Patterson sale 7-96 VF 1733 F (MX) realized $11,710						
1733 MF (MX) Rare	—	—	—	—	—	—
1733 MF Small crown	—	700	1,500	2,500	4,250	—
1734/3 MF	—	100	150	275	575	—
1734 MF	—	100	150	250	450	—
1735 MF	—	100	150	250	450	—
1736/5 MF	—	100	150	275	575	—
1736 MF Small planchet	—	100	150	250	450	—
1736 MF	—	100	150	250	450	—
1737 MF	—	65.00	100	200	400	—
1738/6 MF	—	65.00	100	200	400	—
1738/7 MF	—	65.00	100	200	400	—
1738 MF	—	65.00	100	200	400	—
1739/6 MF 9 over inverted 6	—	65.00	100	200	400	—
1739 MF	—	65.00	100	200	400	—
1740/30 MF	—	100	150	275	500	—
1740/39 MF	—	100	150	275	500	—
1740 MF	—	65.00	100	200	400	—
1741/31 MF	—	65.00	100	200	400	—
1741 MF	—	65.00	100	200	400	—
1742/32 MF	—	75.00	125	220	500	—
1742/1 MF	—	65.00	100	200	400	—
1742 MF	—	65.00	100	200	400	—
1743/2 MF	—	65.00	100	200	400	—
1743 MF	—	65.00	100	200	400	—
1744/34 MF	—	65.00	100	200	400	—
1744/3 MF	—	65.00	100	200	400	—
1744 MF	—	65.00	100	200	400	—
1745/4 MF	—	65.00	100	200	425	—
1745 MF	—	65.00	100	200	400	—
1746/5 MF	—	100	150	275	575	—
1746 MF	—	65.00	100	200	400	—
1747 MF	—	65.00	100	200	400	—

KM# 104.1 8 REALES
27.0674 g., 0.9170 Silver 0.7980 oz. ASW **Ruler:**
Ferdinand VI **Obv:** Crowned shield flaned by M F 8 **Obv.
Legend:** FERDND • VI • D • G • HISPAN • ET IND • REX
Rev: Crowned globes flanked by crowned pillars with banner,
date below **Rev. Legend:** ...VNUM M **Mint:** Mexico City **Note:**
Mint mark M, Mo.

Date	Mintage	VG	F	VF	XF	Unc
1747 MF	—	55.00	100	175	300	—
1748/7 MF	—	60.00	120	250	450	—
1748 MF	—	50.00	75.00	125	250	—
1749/8 MF	—	50.00	75.00	125	250	—
1749 MF	—	50.00	75.00	125	250	—
1750 MF	—	50.00	75.00	125	250	—
1751/0 MF	—	55.00	100	165	275	—
1751 MF	—	50.00	75.00	125	250	—
1752/1 MF	—	55.00	100	165	275	—
1752 MF	—	50.00	75.00	125	250	—
1753/2 MF	—	50.00	75.00	125	250	—
1753 MF	—	55.00	100	165	275	—
1754/3 MF	—	55.00	100	185	325	—
1754 MF	—	50.00	75.00	125	250	—
1754 MM/MF	—	300	700	1,500	3,500	—
1754 MM	—	300	700	1,500	3,500	—

KM# 104.2 8 REALES
27.0674 g., 0.9170 Silver 0.7980 oz. ASW **Ruler:**
Ferdinand VI **Obv:** Crowned shield flanked by M M 8 **Obv.
Legend:** FERDND • VI • D • G • HISPAN • ET IND • REX
Rev: Imperial crown on left pillar **Rev. Legend:** ...VNUM M
Mint: Mexico City **Note:** Mint mark M, Mo.

Date	Mintage	VG	F	VF	XF	Unc
1754 MM/MF	—	75.00	125	250	500	—
1754 MM	—	60.00	110	200	375	—
1754 MF	—	150	285	550	950	—
1755/4 MM	—	55.00	100	185	325	—
1755 MM	—	50.00	75.00	125	250	—
1756/5 MM	—	55.00	100	165	275	—
1756 MM	—	50.00	75.00	125	250	—
1757/6 MM	—	50.00	75.00	125	250	—
1757 MM	—	55.00	100	185	325	—
1758 MM	—	50.00	75.00	125	250	—
1759 MM	—	50.00	75.00	125	250	—
1760/59 MM	—	55.00	100	165	275	—
1760 MM	—	50.00	75.00	125	250	—

KM# 105 8 REALES
27.0674 g., 0.9170 Silver 0.7980 oz. ASW **Ruler:** Charles III
Obv: Crowned shield flanked by M M 8 **Obv. Legend:**
CAROLUS • III • D • G • HISPAN • ET IND • REX **Rev:** Crowned
globes flanked by crowned pillars with banner, date below
Rev. Legend: ...E VNUM M **Mint:** Mexico City **Note:** Mint
mark M, Mo.

Date	Mintage	VG	F	VF	XF	Unc
1760/59 MM	—	450	700	—	—	—
Note: CAROLUS. III/Ferdin. Vi						
1760 MM	—	60.00	100	150	325	—
Note: CAROLUS. III/FERDIN. VI. recut die						
1760 MM	—	60.00	100	150	300	—
1761/50 MM	—	65.00	110	165	325	—
Note: Tip of cross between I and S in legend						
1761/51 MM	—	65.00	110	165	325	—
Note: Tip of cross between I and S in legend						
1761/0 MM	—	65.00	110	165	325	—
Note: Tip of cross between H and I in legend						
1761 MM	—	60.00	100	150	275	—
Note: Cross under I in legend						
1761 MM	—	60.00	100	150	275	—
Note: Tip of cross between H and I in legend						
1761 MM	—	65.00	110	165	325	—
Note: Tip of cross between I and S in legend						
1762/1 MM	—	70.00	120	175	450	—
Note: Tip of cross between H and I in legend						
1762/1 MM	—	70.00	120	175	450	—
1762 MM	—	60.00	100	150	275	—
Note: Tip of cross between H and I in legend						
1762 MM	—	50.00	75.00	125	250	—
Note: Tip of cross between I and S in legend						
1762 MF	—	500	750	1,250	2,300	—
1763/2 MM	—	300	450	750	1,350	—
1763 MM	—	450	650	1,150	2,250	—
1763/1 MF	—	50.00	75.00	125	250	—
1763/2 MF	—	50.00	75.00	125	250	—
1763 MF	—	50.00	75.00	125	250	—
1764 MF	—	50.00	75.00	125	250	—
Note: CAR/CRA						

Date	Mintage	VG	F	VF	XF	Unc
1764 MF	—	50.00	75.00	125	250	—
1765 MF	—	50.00	75.00	125	250	—
1766/5 MF	—	75.00	150	225	575	—
1766 MF	—	50.00	75.00	125	250	—
1767/6 MF	—	50.00	75.00	125	250	—
1767 MF	—	50.00	75.00	125	250	—
1768/7 MF	—	85.00	165	250	600	—
1768 MF	—	50.00	75.00	125	250	—
1769 MF	—	50.00	75.00	125	250	—
1770/60 MF	—	100	185	300	650	—
1770 MF	—	50.00	75.00	125	250	—
1770/60 FM	—	100	185	300	650	—
1770/69 FM	—	100	185	300	650	—
1770 FM/F	—	50.00	75.00	125	250	—
1770 FM	—	50.00	75.00	125	250	—
1771/0 FM	—	50.00	75.00	125	250	—
1771 FM	—	50.00	75.00	125	250	—

KM# 106.1   8 REALES
27.0674 g., 0.9030 Silver 0.7858 oz. ASW **Ruler:** Charles III
Obv: Armored bust of Charles III, right **Obv. Legend:**
CAROLUS • III • DEI • GRATIA • **Rev:** Crowned shield flanked
by pillars with banner, inverted initials and mint mark **Rev.
Legend:** • HISPAN • ET IND • REX • ... **Mint:** Mexico City
Note: Two varieties exist, one with inverted initials "F.M." (left),
and one with normal presentation (right). Mint mark M, Mo.

Date	Mintage	VG	F	VF	XF	Unc
1772 FM	—	25.00	50.00	120	250	—
1772 FM Inverted	—	150	350	750	1,250	—
1773 FM	—	25.00	50.00	100	175	—

KM# 106.2   8 REALES
27.0674 g., 0.9030 Silver 0.7858 oz. ASW **Ruler:** Charles III
Obv: Armored bust of Charles III, right **Obv. Legend:**
CAROLUS • III • DEI • GRATIA • **Rev:** Crowned shield flanked
by pillars with banner, normal initials and mint mark **Rev.
Legend:** • HISPAN • ET IND • REX • ... **Note:** Mint mark M, Mo.

Date	Mintage	VG	F	VF	XF	Unc
1773 FM	—	25.00	50.00	80.00	160	—
1774 FM	—	25.00	45.00	75.00	150	—
1775 FM	—	25.00	45.00	75.00	150	—
1776 FM	—	25.00	45.00	75.00	150	—
1776 FF	—	35.00	65.00	180	300	—
1777/6 FM	—	35.00	65.00	180	300	—
1777 FM	—	25.00	45.00	75.00	150	—
1777 FF	—	35.00	50.00	100	250	—
1778 FM	—	35.00	50.00	100	250	—
Note: Superior Casterline sale 5-89 VF realized $17,600					
1778/7 FF	—	25.00	45.00	75.00	150	—
1778 FF	—	25.00	45.00	75.00	150	—
1779 FF	—	25.00	45.00	75.00	150	—
1780 FF	—	25.00	45.00	75.00	150	—
1781 FF	—	25.00	45.00	75.00	150	—
1782 FF	—	25.00	45.00	75.00	150	—
1783 FF	—	25.00	45.00	75.00	150	—
1783 FM	—	4,000	6,000	9,000	—	—
1784 FF	—	150	300	500	1,250	—
1784 FM	—	25.00	45.00	75.00	150	—

KM# 106.2a   8 REALES
27.0674 g., 0.8960 Silver 0.7797 oz. ASW **Ruler:** Charles III
Obv: Armored bust of Charles III, right **Obv. Legend:**
CAROLUS • III • DEI • GRATIA • **Rev:** Crowned shield flanked

by pillars with banner, normal initials and mint mark **Rev.
Legend:** • HISPAN • ET IND • REX • ... **Note:** Mint mark M, Mo.

Date	Mintage	VG	F	VF	XF	Unc
1785 FM	—	25.00	45.00	75.00	150	—
1786/5 FM	—	50.00	100	200	400	—
1786 FM	—	25.00	45.00	75.00	150	—
1787/6 FM	—	100	250	450	1,200	—
1787 FM	—	25.00	45.00	75.00	150	—
1788 FM	—	25.00	45.00	75.00	150	—
1789 FM	—	50.00	100	150	225	—

KM# 107 8 REALES
27.0674 g., 0.9030 Silver 0.7858 oz. ASW **Ruler:** Charles IV
Obv: Armored bust of Charles III, right **Obv. Legend:**
CAROLUS • IV • DEI • GRATIA • **Rev:** Crowned shield flanked
by pillars with banner **Rev. Legend:** • HISPAN • ET IND •
REX • ... **Mint:** Mexico City **Note:** Mint mark M, Mo, using old
bust punch.

Date	Mintage	VG	F	VF	XF	Unc
1789 FM	—	40.00	65.00	120	250	—
1790 FM	—	30.00	50.00	100	200	—

KM# 108 8 REALES
27.0674 g., 0.9030 Silver 0.7858 oz. ASW **Ruler:** Charles IV
Obv: Armored bust of Charles III, right **Obv. Legend:**
CAROLUS • IIII • DEI • GRATIA • **Rev:** Crowned shield flanked
by pillars with banner **Rev. Legend:** • HISPAN • ET IND •
REX • ... **Mint:** Mexico City **Note:** Mint mark M, Mo, using old
portait punch.

Date	Mintage	VG	F	VF	XF	Unc
1790 FM	—	30.00	50.00	100	200	—

KM# 109 8 REALES
27.0674 g., 0.8960 Silver 0.7797 oz. ASW **Ruler:** Charles IV
Obv: Armored bust of Charles IIII, right **Obv. Inscription:**
CAROLUS • IIII • DEI • GRATIA • **Rev:** Crowned shield flanked
by pillars with banner **Rev. Legend:** • HISPAN • ET IND •
REX • ... **Mint:** Mexico City **Note:** Mint mark Mo.

Date	Mintage	VG	F	VF	XF	Unc
1791 FM	—	20.00	35.00	50.00	100	—
1792 FM	—	20.00	35.00	50.00	100	—
1793 FM	—	20.00	35.00	50.00	100	—
1794 FM	—	20.00	35.00	50.00	100	—
1795/4 FM	—	20.00	35.00	50.00	100	—
1795 FM	—	20.00	35.00	50.00	100	—
1796 FM	—	20.00	35.00	50.00	100	—
1797 FM	—	20.00	35.00	50.00	100	—
1798 FM	—	20.00	35.00	50.00	100	—
1799 FM	—	20.00	35.00	50.00	100	—
1800/700 FM	—	20.00	35.00	50.00	100	—
1800 FM	—	20.00	35.00	50.00	100	—
1801/0 FT/FM	—	20.00	35.00	50.00	100	—
1801/791 FM	—	38.50	65.00	110	275	—
1801/0 FM	—	38.50	65.00	110	275	—
1801 FM	—	22.50	44.00	110	275	—
1801 FT/M	—	38.50	65.00	110	275	—
1801 FT	—	22.50	38.50	55.00	115	—
1802/1 FT	—	38.50	65.00	110	275	—
1802 FT	—	22.50	38.50	55.00	115	—
1802 FT/M	—	22.50	38.50	55.00	115	—
1803 FT	—	22.50	38.50	55.00	125	—
1803 FT/M	—	22.50	38.50	55.00	115	—
1803 TH	—	85.00	165	275	500	—
1804/3 TH	—	38.50	65.00	110	275	—
1804 TH	—	22.50	38.50	55.00	115	—
Note: CARLUS (error)						
1805/4 TH	—	44.00	90.00	140	300	—
1805 TH	—	22.50	38.50	55.00	115	—
Note: Narrow date						
1805 TH	—	22.50	38.50	55.00	115	—
Note: Wide date						
1806 TH	—	22.50	38.50	55.00	115	—
1807/6 TH	—	165	275	375	775	—
1807 TH	—	22.50	38.50	55.00	115	—
1808/7 TH	—	22.50	38.50	55.00	115	—
1808 TH	—	22.50	38.50	55.00	115	—

KM# 110   8 REALES
27.0674 g., 0.8960 Silver 0.7797 oz. ASW   **Ruler:**
Ferdinand VII **Obv:** Armored laureate bust right **Obv.**
Legend: FERDIN • VII... **Rev:** Crowned shield flanked by
pillars **Rev. Legend:** IND • REX... **Mint:** Mexico City **Note:**
Mint mark Mo.

Date	Mintage	VG	F	VF	XF	Unc
1808 TH	—	27.50	44.00	85.00	165	—
1809/8 TH	—	27.50	44.00	85.00	165	—
1809 TH	—	22.50	38.50	60.00	140	—
1809 HJ	—	27.50	44.00	85.00	165	—
1809 HJ/TH	—	22.50	38.50	60.00	140	—
1810/09 HJ	—	27.50	44.00	85.00	165	—
1810 TH	—	85.00	165	325	675	—
1810 HJ/TH	—	27.50	44.00	85.00	165	—
1810 HJ	—	27.50	44.00	85.00	165	—
1811/0 HJ	—	22.50	38.50	60.00	140	—
1811 HJ	—	22.50	38.50	60.00	140	—
1811 HJ/TH	—	22.50	38.50	55.00	115	—

KM# 111   8 REALES
27.0700 g., 0.9030 Silver 0.7859 oz. ASW   **Ruler:**
Ferdinand VII **Obv:** Draped laureate bust right **Obv. Legend:**
FERDIN • VII... **Rev:** Crowned shield flanked by pillars **Rev.**
Legend: IND • REX... **Mint:** Mexico City **Note:** Mint mark Mo.

Date	Mintage	VG	F	VF	XF	Unc
1811 HJ	—	22.50	44.00	65.00	145	—
1812 HJ	—	55.00	85.00	140	290	—
1812 JJ/HJ	—	22.50	38.50	55.00	115	—
1812 JJ	—	22.50	38.50	55.00	115	—
1813 HJ	—	55.00	85.00	140	290	—
1813 JJ	—	22.50	38.50	55.00	115	—
1814/3 HJ	—	1,300	2,750	5,500	—	—
1814/3 JJ	—	22.50	38.50	55.00	115	—
1814 JJ	—	22.50	38.50	55.00	115	—
1815/4 JJ	—	22.50	38.50	55.00	115	—
1815 JJ	—	22.50	38.50	55.00	115	—
1816/5 JJ	—	22.50	38.50	55.00	105	—
1816 JJ	—	22.50	38.50	55.00	105	—
1817 JJ	—	22.50	38.50	55.00	105	—
1818 JJ	—	22.50	38.50	55.00	105	—
1819 JJ	—	22.50	38.50	55.00	105	—
1820 JJ	—	22.50	38.50	55.00	105	—
1821 JJ	—	22.50	38.50	55.00	105	—

KM# 112   1/2 ESCUDO
1.6917 g., 0.8750 Gold 0.0476 oz. AGW   **Ruler:**
Ferdinand VII **Obv:** Laureate head right **Obv. Legend:** FERD
• VII • D • G • HISP • ET IND **Rev:** Crowned oval shield **Mint:**
Mexico City **Note:** Mint mark Mo.

Date	Mintage	VG	F	VF	XF	Unc
1814 JJ	—	100	150	225	375	525
1815/4 JJ	—	150	200	250	400	875
1815 JJ	—	150	200	250	400	—
1816 JJ	—	100	150	225	375	—
1817 JJ	—	150	200	250	400	—
1818 JJ	—	150	200	250	400	—
1819 JJ	—	150	200	250	400	—
1820 JJ	—	200	300	400	550	—

KM# 113   ESCUDO
3.3834 g., 0.9170 Gold 0.0997 oz. AGW   **Ruler:** Philip V **Obv:**
Armored bust right **Obv. Legend:** PHILIP • V • D • G • HISPAN
• ET IND • REX **Rev:** Crowned shield flanked by M F I **Mint:**
Mexico City

Date	Mintage	VG	F	VF	XF	Unc
1732 F	—	1,000	2,000	3,000	4,000	—
1733/2 F	—	1,000	2,000	3,000	4,000	—
1734/3 MF	—	150	250	400	850	—
1735/4 MF	—	150	250	400	850	—
1735 MF	—	150	250	400	850	—
1736/5 MF	—	150	250	400	850	—
1736 MF	—	150	250	400	850	—
1737 MF	—	200	300	600	1,200	—
1738/7 MF	—	200	300	600	1,200	—
1738 MF	—	200	300	600	1,200	—
1739 MF	—	200	300	600	1,200	—
1740/30 MF	—	200	300	600	1,200	—
1741 MF	—	200	300	600	1,200	—
1742 MF	—	200	300	600	1,200	—
1743/2 MF	—	150	275	450	800	—
1743 MF	—	150	250	400	700	—
1744/3 MF	—	150	250	400	700	—
1744 MF	—	150	250	400	700	—
1745 MF	—	150	250	400	700	—
1746/5 MF	—	150	250	400	700	—
1747 MF Rare	—	—	—	—	—	—

KM# 114   ESCUDO
3.3834 g., 0.9170 Gold 0.0997 oz. AGW **Ruler:** Ferdinand VI
Obv: Armored bust right **Obv. Legend:** FERD • VI • D • G •
HISPAN • ET IND • REX **Rev:** Crowned shield flanked by M
F I **Mint:** Mexico City **Note:** Mint mark M, Mo.

Date	Mintage	VG	F	VF	XF	Unc
1747 MF	—	1,650	3,000	5,000	7,500	—

KM# 115.1   ESCUDO
3.3834 g., 0.9170 Gold 0.0997 oz. AGW **Ruler:** Ferdinand VI
Obv: Short armored bust right **Obv. Legend:** FERD • VI • D
• G • HISPAN • ET IND • REX **Rev:** Crowned shield **Mint:**
Mexico City **Note:** Mint mark M, Mo.

Date	Mintage	VG	F	VF	XF	Unc
1748 MF	—	250	350	550	950	—
1749 MF	—	300	450	700	1,150	—
1750 MF	—	150	250	400	800	—
1751 MF	—	150	250	400	800	—

KM# 115.2   ESCUDO
3.3834 g., 0.9170 Gold 0.0997 oz. AGW **Ruler:** Ferdinand VI
Obv: Short armored bust right **Obv. Legend:** FERD • VI • D
• G • HISPAN • ET IND • REX **Rev:** Without 1 S flanking
crowned shield **Mint:** Mexico City

Date	Mintage	VG	F	VF	XF	Unc
1752 MF	—	125	225	375	750	—
1753/2 MF	—	150	250	400	800	—
1753 MF	—	150	250	400	800	—
1754 MF	—	150	250	400	800	—
1755 MM	—	150	250	400	800	—
1756 MM	—	150	250	400	800	—

KM# A116   ESCUDO
3.3834 g., 0.9170 Gold 0.0997 oz. AGW **Ruler:** Ferdinand VI
Obv: Armored bust right **Obv. Legend:** FERDIND • VI • D • G
• HISPAN • ETIND • REX • **Rev:** Crowned shield **Rev. Legend:**
M • NOMINA MAGNA SEQUOR • M **Mint:** Mexico City

Date	Mintage	VG	F	VF	XF	Unc
1757 MM	—	150	250	400	800	—
1759 MM	—	150	250	400	800	—

KM# 116   ESCUDO
3.3834 g., 0.9170 Gold 0.0997 oz. AGW **Ruler:** Charles III

Obv: Armored bust right **Obv. Legend:** CAROLVS • III • D •
G • HISPAN • ET IND • REX **Rev:** Crowned shield **Rev.
Legend:** M • NOMINA MAGNA SEQUOR • M • **Mint:** Mexico
City **Note:** Mint mark M, Mo.

Date	Mintage	VG	F	VF	XF	Unc
1760 MM	—	400	800	1,500	2,500	—
1761/0 MM	—	400	800	1,500	2,500	—
1761 MM	—	400	800	1,500	2,500	—

KM# 117   ESCUDO
3.3834 g., 0.9170 Gold 0.0997 oz. AGW   **Ruler:** Charles III
Obv: Large armored bust right **Obv. Legend:** CAR • III • D • G
• HISP • ET IND • R **Rev:** Crowned shield **Rev. Legend:** IN •
UTROQ • FELIX • **Mint:** Mexico City **Note:** Mint mark M, Mo.

Date	Mintage	VG	F	VF	XF	Unc
1762 MM	—	250	375	600	1,000	—
1763 MM	—	275	425	700	1,100	—
1764 MM	—	250	375	600	1,000	—
1765 MF	—	250	375	600	1,000	—
1766 MF	—	250	375	600	1,000	—
1767 MF	—	250	375	600	1,000	—
1768 MF	—	250	375	600	1,000	—
1769 MF	—	250	375	600	1,000	—
1770 MF	—	250	375	600	1,000	—
1771 MF	—	250	375	600	1,000	—

KM# 118.1   ESCUDO
3.3834 g., 0.9010 Gold 0.0980 oz. AGW   **Ruler:** Charles III
Obv: Large armored bust right **Obv. Legend:** CAROL • III •
D • G • HISPAN • ET IND • R **Rev:** Crowned shield flanked
by 1 S within order chain **Rev. Legend:** FELIX • A • D • ...
Mint: Mexico City **Note:** Mint mark M, Mo.

Date	Mintage	VG	F	VF	XF	Unc
1772 MF	—	125	150	275	475	—
1772 FM	—	125	150	275	475	—
1773 FM	—	125	150	275	475	—

KM# 118.2   ESCUDO
3.3834 g., 0.9010 Gold 0.0980 oz. AGW   **Ruler:** Charles III
Obv: Large armored bust right **Obv. Legend:** CAROL • III •
D • G • HISPAN • ET IND • R **Rev:** crowned shield in order
chain, initials and mint mark inverted **Rev. Legend:** FELIX •
A • D • ... **Mint:** Mexico City **Note:** Mint mark M, Mo.

Date	Mintage	VG	F	VF	XF	Unc
1773 FM	—	125	150	275	475	—
1774 FM	—	125	150	275	475	—
1775 FM	—	125	150	275	475	—
1776 FM	—	125	150	275	475	—
1777 FM	—	125	150	275	475	—
1778 FF	—	125	150	275	475	—
1779 FF	—	125	150	275	475	—
1780 FF	—	125	150	275	475	—
1781 FF	—	125	150	275	475	—
1782 FF	—	125	150	275	475	—
1783/2 FF	—	125	150	275	475	—
1783 FF	—	125	150	275	475	—
1784/3 FF	—	125	150	275	475	—
1784/3 FM/F	—	125	150	275	475	—

SPANISH COLONIAL - MILLED

KM# 118.2a ESCUDO
3.3800 g., 0.8750 Gold 0.0951 oz. AGW **Ruler:** Charles III **Obv:** Large armored bust right **Obv. Legend:** CAROL • III • D • G • HISPAN • ET IND • R • **Rev:** Crowned shield in order chain, initials and mint mark inverted **Rev. Legend:** FELIX • A • D • ... **Mint:** Mexico City **Note:** Mint mark M, Mo.

Date	Mintage	VG	F	VF	XF	Unc
1785 FM	—	125	150	275	475	—
1786 FM	—	125	150	275	475	—
1787 FM	—	125	150	275	475	—
1788 FM	—	125	150	275	475	—

KM# 118.1a ESCUDO
3.3834 g., 0.8750 Gold 0.0952 oz. AGW **Ruler:** Charles III **Obv:** Large armored bust right **Obv. Legend:** CAROL • III • D • G • HISPAN • ET IND • R **Rev:** Crowned shield in order chain, initial letters and mint mark upright **Rev. Legend:** FELIX • A • D • ... **Mint:** Mexico City **Note:** Mint mark M, Mo.

Date	Mintage	VG	F	VF	XF	Unc
1788 FM	—	125	150	275	475	—

KM# 119 ESCUDO
3.3834 g., 0.8750 Gold 0.0952 oz. AGW **Ruler:** Charles IV **Obv:** Armored bust of Charles III, right **Obv. Legend:** CAROL • IV • D • G • ... **Rev:** Crowned shield in order chain, letters and mint mark upright **Rev. Legend:** FELIX • A • D • ... **Mint:** Mexico City **Note:** Mint mark M, Mo, using old portrait punch.

Date	Mintage	VG	F	VF	XF	Unc
1789 FM	—	300	550	1,000	2,000	—
1790 FM	—	300	550	1,000	2,000	—

KM# 120 ESCUDO
3.3834 g., 0.8750 Gold 0.0952 oz. AGW **Ruler:** Charles IV **Obv:** Armored bust right **Obv. Legend:** CAROL • IIII • D • G • ... **Rev:** Crowned shield in order chain, initial letters and mint mark upright **Rev. Legend:** FELIX • A • D • ... **Mint:** Mexico City **Note:** Mint mark Mo.

Date	Mintage	VG	F	VF	XF	Unc
1792 MF	—	125	165	235	345	—
1793 FM	—	125	165	235	345	—
1794 FM	—	125	165	235	345	—
1795 FM	—	125	165	235	345	—
1796 FM	—	125	165	235	345	—
1797 FM	—	125	165	235	345	—
1798 FM	—	125	165	235	345	—
1799 FM	—	125	165	235	345	—
1800 FM	—	125	165	235	345	—
1801 FM	—	125	165	235	345	—
1801 FT	—	125	165	235	345	650
1802 FT	—	125	165	235	345	—
1803 FT	—	125	165	235	345	—
1804/3 TH	—	125	165	235	345	750
1804 TH	—	125	165	235	345	—
1805 TH	—	125	165	235	345	—
1806/5 TH	—	125	165	235	345	—
1806 TH	—	125	165	235	345	—
1807 TH	—	125	165	235	345	—
1808 TH	—	125	165	235	345	—

KM# 121 ESCUDO
3.3834 g., 0.8750 Gold 0.0952 oz. AGW **Ruler:** Ferdinand VII **Obv:** Armored bust right **Obv. Legend:** FERDIN.VII... **Rev:** Crowned shield divides designed wreath **Rev. Legend:** FELIX. A. D, initial letters and mint mark upright **Mint:** Mexico City **Note:** Mint mark Mo.

Date	Mintage	VG	F	VF	XF	Unc
1809 HJ/TH	—	125	165	235	400	—
1809 HJ	—	125	165	235	400	1,150
1811/0 HJ	—	125	165	235	400	—
1812 HJ	—	150	250	300	500	—

KM# 122 ESCUDO
3.3834 g., 0.8750 Gold 0.0952 oz. AGW **Ruler:** Ferdinand VII **Obv:** Laureate head right **Obv. Legend:** FERDIN • VII • D • G... **Rev:** Crowned shield designed wreath, initial letters and mint mark upright **Rev. Legend:** FELIX • A • D... **Mint:** Mexico City **Note:** Mint mark Mo.

Date	Mintage	VG	F	VF	XF	Unc
1814 HJ	—	150	250	300	500	—
1815 HJ	—	150	250	300	500	—
1815 JJ	—	150	250	300	500	—
1816 JJ	—	175	275	325	550	—
1817 JJ	—	150	250	300	500	—
1818 JJ	—	150	250	300	500	—
1819 JJ	—	150	250	300	500	—
1820 JJ	—	150	250	300	500	—

KM# 124 2 ESCUDOS
6.7660 g., 0.9170 Gold 0.1995 oz. AGW **Ruler:** Philip V **Obv:** Armored bust right **Obv. Legend:** PHILIP • V • D • G • HISPAN • ET IND • REX **Rev:** Crowned shield flanked by M F 2 **Rev. Legend:** INITIUM SAPIENTIAE TIMOR DOMINI **Mint:** Mexico City

Date	Mintage	VG	F	VF	XF	Unc
1732 F	—	1,000	1,500	2,000	3,000	—
1733 F	—	750	1,000	1,500	2,500	—
1734/3 MF	—	400	500	900	1,400	—
1735 MF	—	400	500	900	1,400	—
1736/5 MF	—	400	500	900	1,400	—
1736 MF	—	400	500	900	1,400	—
1737 MF	—	400	500	900	1,400	—
1738/7 MF	—	400	500	900	1,400	—
1739 MF	—	400	500	900	1,400	—
1740/30 MF	—	400	500	900	1,400	—
1741 MF	—	400	500	900	1,400	—
1742 MF	—	400	500	900	1,400	—
1743 MF	—	400	500	900	1,400	—
1744/2 MF	—	400	500	900	1,400	—
1744 MF	—	400	500	900	1,400	—
1745 MF	—	400	500	900	1,400	—
1746/5 MF	—	400	500	900	1,400	—
1747 MF	—	400	500	900	1,400	—

KM# 125 2 ESCUDOS
6.7660 g., 0.9170 Gold 0.1995 oz. AGW **Ruler:** Ferdinand VI
Obv: Large armored bust right **Obv. Legend:** FERD • VI • D
• G • ... **Rev:** Crowned shield flanked by M F 2 **Rev. Legend:**
INITIUM... **Mint:** Mexico City

Date	Mintage	VG	F	VF	XF	Unc
1747 MF	—	3,000	5,500	9,000	15,000	—

KM# 126.1 2 ESCUDOS
6.7660 g., 0.9170 Gold 0.1995 oz. AGW **Ruler:** Ferdinand VI
Obv: Head right **Obv. Legend:** FERD • VI • D • G • ... **Rev:**
Crowned shield **Rev. Legend:** NOMINA MAGNA SEQUOR
Mint: Mexico City **Note:** Mint mark M, Mo.

Date	Mintage	VG	F	VF	XF	Unc
1748 MF	—	450	750	1,500	3,000	—
1749/8 MF	—	450	750	1,500	3,000	—
1750 MF	—	400	700	1,400	2,850	—
1751 MF	—	400	700	1,400	2,850	—

KM# 126.2 2 ESCUDOS
6.7660 g., 0.9170 Gold 0.1995 oz. AGW **Ruler:** Ferdinand VI
Obv: Head right **Obv. Legend:** FERD • VI • D • G • ... **Rev:**
Without 2 S by crowned shield **Rev. Legend:** NOMINA
MAGNA SEQUOR **Mint:** Mexico City **Note:** Mint mark M, Mo.

Date	Mintage	VG	F	VF	XF	Unc
1752 MF	—	400	700	1,400	2,850	—
1753 MF	—	400	700	1,400	2,850	—
1754 MF	—	600	850	1,750	3,500	—
1755 MM	—	400	700	1,400	2,850	—
1756 MM	—	600	850	1,750	3,500	—

KM# 127 2 ESCUDOS
6.7660 g., 0.9170 Gold 0.1995 oz. AGW **Ruler:** Ferdinand VI
Obv: Armored bust right **Obv. Legend:** FERDIND • VI • D •
G • ... **Rev:** Without 2 S by crowned shield **Rev. Legend:**
NOMINA MAGNA SEQUOR **Mint:** Mexico City **Note:** Mint
mark M, Mo.

Date	Mintage	VG	F	VF	XF	Unc
1757 MM	—	450	750	1,500	3,000	—
1759 MM	—	450	750	1,500	3,000	—

KM# 128 2 ESCUDOS
6.7660 g., 0.9170 Gold 0.1995 oz. AGW **Ruler:** Charles III
Obv: Armored bust right **Obv. Legend:** CAROLVS • III • D •
G • ... **Rev:** Without 2 S by crowned shield **Rev. Legend:**
NOMINA MAGNA SEQUOR **Mint:** Mexico City **Note:** Mint
mark M, Mo.

Date	Mintage	VG	F	VF	XF	Unc
1760 MM	—	550	1,000	2,000	4,000	—
1761 MM	—	550	1,000	2,000	4,000	—

KM# 129 2 ESCUDOS
6.7668 g., 0.9170 Gold 0.1995 oz. AGW **Ruler:** Charles III
Obv: Large armored bust right **Obv. Legend:** CAROLUS • III
• D • G • ... **Rev:** Without 2 S by crowned shield **Rev. Legend:**
IN • UTROQ • FELIX • AUSPICE • DEO **Mint:** Mexico City
Note: Mint mark M, Mo.

Date	Mintage	VG	F	VF	XF	Unc
1762 MF	—	500	900	1,850	3,750	—
1763 MF	—	500	900	1,850	3,750	—
1764/3 MF	—	500	900	1,850	3,750	—
1765 MF	—	500	900	1,850	3,750	—
1766 MF	—	500	900	1,850	3,750	—
1767 MF	—	500	900	1,850	3,750	—
1768 MF	—	500	900	1,850	3,750	—
1769 MF	—	500	900	1,850	3,750	—
1770 MF	—	500	900	1,850	3,750	—
1771 MF	—	500	900	1,850	3,750	—

KM# 130.1 2 ESCUDOS
6.7668 g., 0.9010 Gold 0.1960 oz. AGW **Ruler:** Charles III
Obv: Older, armored bust right **Obv. Legend:** CAROLUS •
III • D • G • ... **Rev:** Crowned shield in order chain, initials and
mint mark upright **Rev. Legend:** IN • UTROQ • FELIX •
AUSPICE • DEO **Mint:** Mexico City **Note:** Mint mark M, Mo.

Date	Mintage	VG	F	VF	XF	Unc
1772 FM	—	200	375	550	1,000	—
1773 FM	—	200	375	550	1,000	—

KM# 130.2 2 ESCUDOS
6.7668 g., 0.9010 Gold 0.1960 oz. AGW **Ruler:** Charles III
Obv: Older, armored bust right **Obv. Legend:** CAROLUS •
III • D • G • ... **Rev:** Crowned shield in order chain, initials and
mint mark inverted **Rev. Legend:** IN • UTROQ • FELIX •
AUSPICE • DEO **Mint:** Mexico City **Note:** Mint mark M, Mo.

Date	Mintage	VG	F	VF	XF	Unc
1773 FM	—	200	375	550	1,000	—
1774 FM	—	200	375	550	1,000	—
1775 FM	—	200	375	550	1,000	—
1776 FM	—	200	375	550	1,000	—
1777 FM	—	175	300	450	900	—
1778 FF	—	175	300	450	900	—
1779 FF	—	175	300	450	900	—
1780 FF	—	175	300	450	900	—
1781 FM/M	—	175	300	450	900	—
1781 FF	—	175	300	450	900	—
1782 FF	—	175	300	450	900	—
1783 FF	—	175	300	450	900	—
1784 FF	—	175	300	450	900	—
1784 FM/F	—	175	300	450	900	—

SPANISH COLONIAL - MILLED

KM# 130.2a 2 ESCUDOS
6.7668 g., 0.8750 Gold 0.1904 oz. AGW **Ruler:** Charles III **Obv:** Older, armored bust right **Obv. Legend:** CAROLUS • III • D • G • ... **Rev:** Crowned shield in order chain, initials and mint mark inverted **Rev. Legend:** IN • UTROQ • FELIX • AUSPICE • DEO **Mint:** Mexico City **Note:** Mint mark M, Mo.

Date	Mintage	VG	F	VF	XF	Unc
1785 FM	—	175	300	450	900	—
1786 FM	—	175	300	450	900	—
1787 FM	—	175	300	450	900	—
1788 FM	—	175	300	450	900	—

KM# 130.1a 2 ESCUDOS
6.7668 g., 0.8750 Gold 0.1904 oz. AGW **Ruler:** Charles III **Obv:** Older, armored bust right **Obv. Legend:** CAROLUS • III • D • G • ... **Rev:** Crowned shield in order chain, initials and mint mark upright **Rev. Legend:** IN • UTROQ • FELIX • AUSPICE • DEO **Mint:** Mexico City **Note:** Mint mark M, Mo.

Date	Mintage	VG	F	VF	XF	Unc
1788 FM	—	175	300	450	900	—

KM# 131 2 ESCUDOS
6.7668 g., 0.8750 Gold 0.1904 oz. AGW **Ruler:** Charles IV **Obv:** Armored bust of Charles III, right **Obv. Legend:** CAROL • IV • D • G • ... **Rev:** Crowned shield in order chain, initials and mint mark upright **Rev. Legend:** IN • UTROQ • FELIX • AUSPICE • DEO **Mint:** Mexico City **Note:** Mint mark M, Mo, using old portrait punch.

Date	Mintage	VG	F	VF	XF	Unc
1789 FM	—	650	1,200	2,000	3,500	—
1790 FM	—	650	1,200	2,000	3,500	—

KM# 132 2 ESCUDOS
6.7668 g., 0.8750 Gold 0.1904 oz. AGW **Ruler:** Charles IV **Obv:** Armored bust of Charles IIII, right **Obv. Legend:** CAROL • IIII • D • G • ... **Rev:** Crowned shield flanked by 2 S in order chain **Rev. Legend:** IN • UTROQ • FELIX • AUSPICE • DEO; initials and mint mark upright **Mint:** Mexico City **Note:** Mint mark Mo.

Date	Mintage	VG	F	VF	XF	Unc
1791 FM Mo over inverted Mo	—	300	375	600	950	—
1792 FM	—	185	225	350	575	—
1793 FM	—	185	225	350	575	—
1794 FM	—	185	225	350	575	—
1795 FM	—	185	225	350	575	—
1796 FM	—	185	225	350	575	—
1797 FM	—	185	225	350	575	—
1798 FM	—	185	225	350	575	—
1799 FM	—	185	225	350	575	—
1800 FM	—	185	225	350	575	—
1801 FT	—	185	225	350	575	—
1802 FT	—	185	225	350	575	—
1803 FT	—	185	225	350	575	—
1804 TH	—	185	225	350	575	—
1805 TH	—	185	225	350	575	—
1806/5 TH	—	185	225	350	575	—
1807 TH	—	185	225	350	575	—
1808 TH	—	185	225	350	575	1,500

KM# 134 2 ESCUDOS
6.7668 g., 0.8750 Gold 0.1904 oz. AGW **Ruler:** Ferdinand VII **Obv:** Laureate head right **Obv. Legend:** FERDIN • VII • D • G... **Rev:** Crowned shield divides designed wreath, initials and mint mark upright **Rev. Legend:** IN • UTROQ • FELIX • AUSPICE • DEO **Mint:** Mexico City **Note:** Mint mark Mo.

Date	Mintage	VG	F	VF	XF	Unc
1814Mo HJ	—	250	425	700	1,150	—
1815 JJ	—	250	425	700	1,150	—
1816 JJ	—	250	425	700	1,150	—
1817 JJ	—	250	425	700	1,150	—
1818 JJ	—	250	425	700	1,150	3,750
1819 JJ	—	250	425	700	1,150	—
1820 JJ	—	250	425	700	1,150	—
1821 JJ	—	250	425	700	1,150	—

KM# 135 4 ESCUDOS
13.5337 g., 0.9170 Gold 0.3990 oz. AGW **Ruler:** Philip V **Obv:** Armored bust right **Obv. Legend:** PHILIP • V • D • G • HISPAN • ET IND • REX **Rev:** Crowned shield flanked by F 4 **Rev. Legend:** INITIUM SAPIENTIAE TIMOR DOMINI **Mint:** Mexico City

Date	Mintage	VG	F	VF	XF	Unc
1732 Rare	—	—	—	—	—	—
1732 F Rare	—	—	—	—	—	—
1733 F Rare	—	—	—	—	—	—
1734/3 F	—	1,200	1,800	3,350	5,400	—
1734 MF	—	1,000	1,600	3,000	5,100	—
1735 MF	—	1,000	1,600	3,000	5,400	—
1736 MF	—	1,000	1,600	3,000	5,400	—
1737 MF	—	900	1,500	2,900	4,800	—
1738/7 MF	—	900	1,500	2,900	4,800	—
1738 MF	—	900	1,500	2,900	4,800	—
1739 MF	—	900	1,500	2,900	4,800	—
1740/30 MF	—	900	1,500	2,900	4,800	—
1740 MF	—	900	1,500	2,900	4,800	—
1741 MF	—	900	1,500	2,900	4,800	—
1742/32 MF	—	900	1,500	2,900	4,800	—
1743 MF	—	900	1,500	2,900	4,800	—
1744 MD	—	900	1,500	2,900	4,800	—
1745 MF	—	900	1,500	2,900	4,800	—
1746 MF	—	900	1,500	2,900	4,800	—
1747 MF	—	900	1,500	2,900	4,800	—
1746/5 MF	—	900	1,500	2,900	4,800	—

KM# 136 4 ESCUDOS
13.5337 g., 0.9170 Gold 0.3990 oz. AGW **Ruler:**
Ferdinand VI **Obv:** Large, armored bust right **Obv. Legend:**
FERDND • VI • D • G • ... **Rev:** Crowned shield flanked by F
4 **Rev. Legend:** INITIUM SAPIENTIAE TIMOR DOMINI **Mint:**
Mexico City **Note:** Mint mark M, Mo.

Date	Mintage	VG	F	VF	XF	Unc
1747 MF	—	7,500	13,500	20,000	30,000	—

KM# 137 4 ESCUDOS
13.5337 g., 0.9170 Gold 0.3990 oz. AGW **Ruler:**
Ferdinand VI **Obv:** Armored bust right **Obv. Legend:**
FERDND • VI • D • G • ... **Rev:** Crowned shield flanked by 4
S **Rev. Legend:** NOMINA MAGNA SEQUOR **Mint:** Mexico
City **Note:** Mint mark M, Mo.

Date	Mintage	VG	F	VF	XF	Unc
1748 MF	—	1,500	3,000	5,000	8,000	—
1749 MF	—	1,500	3,000	5,000	8,000	—
1750/48 MF	—	1,500	3,000	5,000	8,000	—
1750 MF	—	1,500	3,000	5,000	8,000	—
1751 MF	—	1,500	3,000	5,000	8,000	—

KM# 138 4 ESCUDOS
13.5337 g., 0.9170 Gold 0.3990 oz. AGW **Ruler:**
Ferdinand VI **Obv:** Small, armored bust right **Obv. Legend:**
FERDND • VI • D • G • ... **Rev:** Crowned shield, without value
Rev. Legend: NOMINA MAGNA... **Mint:** Mexico City **Note:**
Mint mark M, Mo.

Date	Mintage	VG	F	VF	XF	Unc
1752 MF	—	1,000	2,000	3,500	6,000	—
1753 MF	—	1,000	2,000	3,500	6,000	—
1754 MF	—	1,000	2,000	3,500	6,000	—
1755 MM	—	1,000	2,000	3,500	6,000	—
1756 MM	—	1,000	2,000	3,500	6,000	—

KM# 139 4 ESCUDOS
13.5337 g., 0.9170 Gold 0.3990 oz. AGW **Ruler:**
Ferdinand VI **Obv:** Armored bust right **Obv. Legend:**
FERDND • VI • D • G • ... **Rev:** Crowned shield, without value
Rev. Legend: NOMINA MAGNA... **Mint:** Mexico City **Note:**
Mint mark M, Mo.

Date	Mintage	VG	F	VF	XF	Unc
1757 MM	—	1,250	2,500	4,000	6,500	—
1759 MM	—	1,250	2,500	4,000	6,500	—

KM# 140 4 ESCUDOS
13.5337 g., 0.9170 Gold 0.3990 oz. AGW **Ruler:** Charles III
Obv: Armored bust right **Obv. Legend:** CAROLVS • III • D •
G • ... **Rev:** Crowned shield, without value **Rev. Legend:**
NOMINA MAGNA SEQUOR **Mint:** Mexico City **Note:** Mint
mark M, Mo.

Date	Mintage	VG	F	VF	XF	Unc
1760 MM	—	3,500	6,500	10,000	20,000	—
1761 MM	—	3,500	6,500	10,000	20,000	—

KM# 141 4 ESCUDOS
13.5337 g., 0.9170 Gold 0.3990 oz. AGW **Ruler:** Charles III
Obv: Large, armored bust right **Obv. Legend:** CAROLUS •
III • D • G •... **Rev:** Crowned shield in order chain, without
value **Rev. Legend:** IN • UTROQ • FELIX • AUSPICE • DEO
Mint: Mexico City **Note:** Mint mark M, Mo.

Date	Mintage	VG	F	VF	XF	Unc
1762 MF	—	2,500	4,500	7,500	15,000	—
1763 MF	—	2,500	4,500	7,500	15,000	—
1764 MF	—	2,500	4,500	7,500	15,000	—
1765 MF	—	2,500	4,500	7,500	15,000	—
1766/5 MF	—	2,500	4,500	7,500	15,000	—
1767 MF	—	2,500	4,500	7,500	15,000	—
1768 MF	—	2,500	4,500	7,500	15,000	—
1769 MF	—	2,500	4,500	7,500	15,000	—
1770 MF	—	2,500	4,500	7,500	15,000	—
1771 MF	—	2,500	4,500	7,500	15,000	—

KM# 142.1   4 ESCUDOS
13.5337 g., 0.9010 Gold 0.3920 oz. AGW **Ruler:** Charles III
Obv: Large, armored bust right **Obv. Legend:** CAROL • III •
D • G • ... **Rev:** Crowned shield in order chain, initials and mint
mark upright **Rev. Legend:** IN • UTROQ • FELIX • AUSPICE
• DEO **Mint:** Mexico City **Note:** Mint mark M, Mo.

Date	Mintage	VG	F	VF	XF	Unc
1772 FM	—	600	975	1,500	3,000	—
1773 FM	—	600	975	1,500	3,000	—

KM# 142.2   4 ESCUDOS
13.5337 g., 0.9010 Gold 0.3920 oz. AGW **Ruler:** Charles III
Obv: Large, armored bust right **Obv. Legend:** CAROL • III •
D • G • ... **Rev:** Crowned shield flanked by 4 S in order chain,
initials and mint mark inverted **Rev. Legend:** IN • UTROQ •
FELIX • AUSPICE • DEO **Mint:** Mexico City **Note:** Mint mark
M, Mo.

Date	Mintage	VG	F	VF	XF	Unc
1773 FM	—	475	725	1,100	2,200	—
1774 FM	—	475	725	1,100	2,200	—
1775 FM	—	475	725	1,100	2,200	—
1776 FM	—	475	725	1,100	2,200	—
1777 FM	—	475	725	1,100	2,200	—
1778 FF	—	475	725	1,100	2,200	—
1779 FF	—	475	725	1,100	2,200	—
1780 FF	—	475	725	1,100	2,200	—
1781 FF	—	475	725	1,100	2,200	—
1782 FF	—	475	725	1,100	2,200	—
1783 FF	—	475	725	1,100	2,200	—
1784 FF	—	475	725	1,100	2,200	—
1784/3 FM/F	—	475	725	1,100	2,200	—

KM# 142.2a   4 ESCUDOS
13.5337 g., 0.8750 Gold 0.3807 oz. AGW **Ruler:** Charles III
Obv: Large, armored bust right **Obv. Legend:** CAROL • III •
D • G • ... **Rev:** Crowned shield in order chain, initials and mint
mark inverted **Rev. Legend:** IN • UTROQ • FELIX • AUSPICE
• DEO **Mint:** Mexico City **Note:** Mint mark M, Mo.

Date	Mintage	VG	F	VF	XF	Unc
1785 FM	—	475	725	1,100	2,200	—
1786 FM/F	—	475	725	1,100	2,200	—
1786 FM	—	475	725	1,100	2,200	—
1787 FM	—	475	725	1,100	2,200	—
1788 FM	—	475	725	1,100	2,200	—

KM# 142.1a   4 ESCUDOS
13.5337 g., 0.8750 Gold 0.3807 oz. AGW **Ruler:** Charles III
Obv: Large, armored bust right **Obv. Legend:** CAROL • III •
D • G • ... **Rev:** Crowned shield in order chain, initials and mint
mark upright **Rev. Legend:** IN • UTROQ • FELIX • AUSPICE
• DEO **Mint:** Mexico City **Note:** Mint mark M, Mo.

Date	Mintage	VG	F	VF	XF	Unc
1788 FM	—	600	975	1,500	3,000	—

KM# 143.1   4 ESCUDOS
13.5337 g., 0.8750 Gold 0.3807 oz. AGW **Ruler:** Charles IV
Obv: Armored bust of Charles III, right **Obv. Legend:** CAROL
• IV • D • G • ... **Rev:** Crowned shield in order chain, initials
and mint mark upright **Rev. Legend:** IN • UTROQ • FELIX •
AUSPICE • DEO **Mint:** Mexico City **Note:** Mint mark M, Mo,
using old portrait punch.

Date	Mintage	VG	F	VF	XF	Unc
1789 FM	—	500	700	1,100	2,150	—
1790 FM	—	500	700	1,100	2,150	—

KM# 143.2   4 ESCUDOS
13.5337 g., 0.8750 Gold 0.3807 oz. AGW **Ruler:** Charles IV
Obv: Armored bust of Charles III, right **Obv. Legend:** CAROL
• IIII • D • G • ... **Rev:** Crowned shield in order chain, initials
and mint mark upright **Rev. Legend:** IN • UTROQ • FELIX •
AUSPICE • DEO **Mint:** Mexico City **Note:** Mint mark M, Mo,
using old portrait punch.

Date	Mintage	VG	F	VF	XF	Unc
1790 FM	—	600	1,000	1,800	3,000	—

KM# 144   4 ESCUDOS
13.5337 g., 0.8750 Gold 0.3807 oz. AGW **Ruler:** Charles IV
Obv: Armored bust of Charles IIII, right **Obv. Legend:** CAROL
• IIII • D • G • ... **Rev:** Crowned shield flanked by 4 S in order
chain **Rev. Legend:** IN • UTROQ • FELIX • AUSPICE • DEO;
initials and mint mark upright **Mint:** Mexico City **Note:** Mint
mark Mo.

Date	Mintage	VG	F	VF	XF	Unc
1792 FM	—	375	500	750	1,500	—
1793 FM	—	375	500	750	1,500	—
1794/3 FM	—	375	500	750	1,500	—
1795 FM	—	375	500	750	1,500	—
1796 FM	—	375	500	750	1,500	—
1797 FM	—	375	500	750	1,500	—
1798/7 FM	—	375	500	750	1,500	—
1798 FM	—	375	500	750	1,500	—
1799 FM	—	375	500	750	1,500	—
1800 FM	—	375	500	750	1,500	—
1801 FM	—	375	500	750	1,500	—
1801 FT	—	375	500	750	1,500	—
1802 FT	—	375	600	850	1,650	—
1803 FT	—	375	500	750	1,500	—
1804/3 TH	—	375	500	750	1,500	—
1804 TH	—	375	500	750	1,500	—
1805 TH	—	375	500	750	1,500	—
1806/5 TH	—	375	500	750	1,500	—
1807 TH	—	375	600	850	1,650	—
1808/0 TH	—	375	500	750	1,500	—
1808 TH	—	375	500	750	1,500	—

KM# 145   4 ESCUDOS
13.5337 g., 0.8750 Gold 0.3807 oz. AGW   **Ruler:**
Ferdinand VII **Obv:** Armored bust right **Obv. Legend:**
FERDIN • VII D • G... **Rev:** Crowned shield divides designed
wreath, initials and mint mark upright **Rev. Legend:** IN •
UTROQ • FELIX • AUSPICE • DEO **Mint:** Mexico City **Note:**
Mint mark Mo.

Date	Mintage	VG	F	VF	XF	Unc
1810 HJ	—	375	550	1,000	2,300	—
1811 HJ	—	375	550	1,000	2,300	—
1812 HJ	—	375	550	1,000	2,300	—

KM# 146   4 ESCUDOS
13.5337 g., 0.8750 Gold 0.3807 oz. AGW **Ruler:**

Ferdinand VII **Obv:** Laureate head right **Obv. Legend:**
FERDIN. VII D. G... **Rev:** Crowned shield divides designed
wreath **Rev. Legend:** IN. UTROQ. FELIX. AUSPICE. DEO;
initials and mint mark upright **Mint:** Mexico City **Note:** Mint
mark Mo.

Date	Mintage	VG	F	VF	XF	Unc
1814 HJ	—	400	700	1,150	2,500	—
1815 HJ	—	400	700	1,150	2,500	—
1815 JJ	—	400	700	1,150	2,500	—
1816 JJ	—	400	700	1,150	2,500	—
1817 JJ	—	400	700	1,150	2,500	—
1818 JJ	—	400	700	1,150	2,500	—
1819 JJ	—	400	700	1,150	2,500	—
1820 JJ	—	400	700	1,150	2,500	—

KM# 148   8 ESCUDOS
27.0674 g., 0.9170 Gold 0.7980 oz. AGW   **Ruler:** Philip V
Obv: Large, armored bust right **Obv. Legend:** PHILIP • V •
D • G • HISPAN • ET IND • REX **Rev:** Crowned shield flanked
by M F 8 in order chain **Rev. Legend:** INITIUM SAPIENTIAE
TIMOR DOMINI **Mint:** Mexico City **Note:** Mint mark M, Mo.

Date	Mintage	VG	F	VF	XF	Unc
1732 Rare	—	—	—	—	—	—
1732 F Rare	—	—	—	—	—	—
1733 F Rare	—	—	—	—	—	—

Note: Heritage World Coin Auctions #3004, 1-09, MS64
realized $54,625

Date	Mintage	VG	F	VF	XF	Unc
1734 MF/F	—	1,200	2,000	3,300	5,800	—
1734 MF	—	1,200	2,000	3,300	5,800	—
1735 MF	—	1,200	1,800	3,000	5,400	—
1736 MF	—	1,200	1,800	3,000	5,400	—
1737 MF	—	1,200	1,800	3,000	5,400	—
1738/7 MF	—	1,200	1,800	3,000	5,400	—
1738 MF	—	1,200	1,800	3,000	5,400	—
1739 MF	—	1,200	1,800	3,000	5,400	—
1740/30 MF	—	1,200	1,800	3,000	5,400	—
1740 MF	—	1,200	1,800	3,000	5,400	—
1741 MF	—	1,200	1,800	3,000	5,400	—
1742 MF	—	1,200	1,800	3,000	5,400	—
1743 MF	—	1,200	1,800	3,000	5,400	—
1744/3 MF	—	1,200	1,800	3,000	5,400	—
1744 MF	—	1,200	1,800	3,000	5,400	—
1745 MF	—	1,200	1,800	3,000	5,400	—
1745/4 MF	—	1,200	1,800	3,000	5,400	—
1746 MF	—	1,200	1,800	3,000	5,400	—
1746/5 MF	—	1,200	1,800	3,000	5,400	—
1747 MF	—	1,300	2,100	3,400	6,000	—

KM# 149   8 ESCUDOS
27.0674 g., 0.9170 Gold 0.7980 oz. AGW   **Ruler:**
Ferdinand VI **Obv:** Large, armored bust right **Obv. Legend:**
FERDND • VI • D • G • ... **Rev:** Crowned shield flanked by M

F 8 in order chain **Rev. Legend:** INITIUM SAPIENTIAE
TIMOR DOMINI **Mint:** Mexico City **Note:** Mint mark M, Mo.

Date	Mintage	VG	F	VF	XF	Unc
1747 MF	—	9,000	15,000	22,000	35,000	—

KM# 150   8 ESCUDOS
27.0674 g., 0.9170 Gold 0.7980 oz. AGW   **Ruler:**
Ferdinand VI **Obv:** Small, armored bust right **Obv. Legend:**
FERDND • VI • D • G • ... **Rev:** Crowned shield flanked by 8
S in order chain **Rev. Legend:** NOMINA MAGNA SEQUOR
Mint: Mexico City **Note:** Mint mark M, Mo.

Date	Mintage	VG	F	VF	XF	Unc
1748 MF	—	1,450	2,400	4,200	7,200	—
1749/8 MF	—	1,450	2,400	4,200	7,200	—
1749 MF	—	1,450	2,400	4,200	7,200	—
1750 MF	—	1,450	2,400	4,200	7,200	—
1751/0 MF	—	1,800	2,400	4,200	7,200	—
1751 MF	—	1,450	2,400	4,200	7,200	—

KM# 151   8 ESCUDOS
27.0674 g., 0.9170 Gold 0.7980 oz. AGW   **Ruler:**
Ferdinand VI **Obv:** Armored bust right **Obv. Legend:**
FERDND • VI • D • G • ... **Rev:** Crowned shield in order chain
Rev. Legend: NOMINA MAGNA SEQUOR **Mint:** Mexico City
Note: Mint mark M, Mo.

Date	Mintage	VG	F	VF	XF	Unc
1752 MF	—	1,450	2,400	4,200	7,200	—
1753 MF	—	1,450	2,400	4,200	7,200	—
1754 MF	—	1,450	2,400	4,200	7,200	—
1755 MM	—	1,450	2,400	4,200	7,200	—
1756 MM	—	1,450	2,400	4,200	7,200	—

KM# 152   8 ESCUDOS
27.0674 g., 0.9170 Gold 0.7980 oz. AGW   **Ruler:**
Ferdinand VI **Obv:** Armored bust right **Obv. Legend:**
FERDND • VI • D • G • ... **Rev:** Crowned shield in order chain
Rev. Legend: NOMINA MAGNA SEQUOR **Mint:** Mexico City
Note: Mint mark M, Mo.

Date	Mintage	VG	F	VF	XF	Unc
1757 MM	—	1,450	2,400	4,200	7,200	—
1758 MM	—	1,450	2,400	4,200	7,200	—
1759 MM	—	1,450	2,400	4,200	7,200	—

Date	Mintage	VG	F	VF	XF	Unc
1765/4 MM	—	2,200	3,750	6,300	11,500	—
1765 MF	—	2,200	3,750	6,300	11,500	—
1765 MM	—	1,900	3,150	5,000	9,400	—
1766 MF	—	1,900	3,150	5,000	9,400	—
1767/6 MF	—	1,900	3,150	5,000	9,400	—
1767 MF	—	1,900	3,150	5,000	9,400	—
1768/7 MF	—	1,900	3,150	5,000	9,400	—
1768 MF	—	1,900	3,150	5,000	9,400	—
1769 MF	—	1,900	3,150	5,000	9,400	—
1770 MF	—	1,900	3,150	5,000	9,400	—
1771 MF	—	2,200	3,750	6,300	11,500	—

KM# 153 8 ESCUDOS
27.0674 g., 0.9170 Gold 0.7980 oz. AGW **Ruler:** Charles III
Obv: Armored bust right **Obv. Legend:** CAROLVS • III • D •
G • ... **Rev:** Crowned shield in order chain **Rev. Legend:**
NOMINA MAGNA SEQUOR **Mint:** Mexico City **Note:** Mint
mark M, Mo.

Date	Mintage	VG	F	VF	XF	Unc
1760 MM	—	2,100	3,600	6,000	11,000	—
1761/0 MM	—	2,400	4,200	6,600	12,000	—
1761 MM	—	2,400	4,200	6,600	12,000	—

KM# 156.1 8 ESCUDOS
27.0674 g., 0.9010 Gold 0.7841 oz. AGW **Ruler:** Charles III
Obv: Large, armored bust right **Obv. Legend:** CAROL • III •
D • G • ... **Rev:** Crowned shield flanked by 8 S in order chain,
initials and mint mark upright **Rev. Legend:** ... AUSPICE •
DEO • **Mint:** Mexico City **Note:** Mint mark M, Mo.

Date	Mintage	VG	F	VF	XF	Unc
1772 FM	—	775	900	1,450	2,300	—
1773 FM	—	800	1,050	1,550	2,600	—

KM# 154 8 ESCUDOS
27.0674 g., 0.9170 Gold 0.7980 oz. AGW **Ruler:** Charles III
Obv: Armored bust right **Obv. Legend:** CAROLVS • III • D •
G • ... **Rev:** Crowned shield in order chain **Rev. Legend:**
NOMINA MAGNA SEQUOR **Mint:** Mexico City **Note:** Mint
mark M, Mo.

Date	Mintage	VG	F	VF	XF	Unc
1761 MM	—	2,100	3,600	6,300	11,500	—

KM# 156.2 8 ESCUDOS
27.0674 g., 0.9010 Gold 0.7841 oz. AGW **Ruler:** Charles III
Obv: Large, armored bust right **Obv. Legend:** CAROL • III •
D • G • ... **Rev:** Crowned shield flanked by 8 S in order chain,
initials and mint mark inverted **Rev. Legend:** ... AUSPICE •
DEO • **Mint:** Mexico City **Note:** Mint mark M, Mo.

Date	Mintage	VG	F	VF	XF	Unc
1773 FM	—	775	875	1,250	1,900	—
1774 FM	—	775	875	1,250	1,900	—
1775 FM	—	775	875	1,250	1,900	—
1776 FM	—	775	875	1,250	1,900	—
1777/6 FM	—	775	875	1,250	1,900	—
1777 FM	—	775	875	1,250	1,900	—
1778 FF	—	775	875	1,250	1,900	—
1779 FF	—	775	875	1,250	1,900	—
1780 FF	—	775	875	1,250	1,900	—
1781 FF	—	775	875	1,250	1,900	—
1782 FF	—	775	875	1,250	1,900	—
1783 FF	—	775	875	1,250	1,900	—
1784 FF	—	775	875	1,250	1,900	—
1784 FM/F	—	775	875	1,250	1,900	—
1784 FM	—	775	875	1,250	1,900	—
1785 FM	—	775	875	1,250	1,900	—

KM# 155 8 ESCUDOS
27.0674 g., 0.9170 Gold 0.7980 oz. AGW **Ruler:** Charles III
Obv: Large, armored bust right **Obv. Legend:** CAROLUS •
III • D • G • ... **Rev:** Crowned shield in order chain **Rev. Legend:**
IN • UTROQ • FELIX • AUSPICE • DEO • **Mint:** Mexico City
Note: Mint mark M, Mo.

Date	Mintage	VG	F	VF	XF	Unc
1762 MM	—	2,000	3,450	5,600	10,500	—
1763 MM	—	2,000	3,450	5,600	10,500	—
1764 MF	—	2,200	3,750	6,300	11,500	—
1764/2 MF	—	2,200	3,750	6,300	11,500	—
1764 MM	—	2,200	3,750	6,300	11,500	—
1765/4 MF	—	2,200	3,750	6,300	11,500	—

KM# 156.2a 8 ESCUDOS

27.0674 g., 0.8750 Gold 0.7614 oz. AGW **Ruler:** Charles III **Obv:** Large, armored bust right **Obv. Legend:** CAROL • III • D • G • ... **Rev:** Crowned shield flanked by 8 S in order chain, initials and mint mark inverted **Rev. Legend:** ... AUSPICE • DEO • **Mint:** Mexico City **Note:** Mint mark M, Mo.

Date	Mintage	VG	F	VF	XF	Unc
1786 FM	—	775	875	1,250	1,900	—
1787 FM	—	775	875	1,250	1,900	—
1788 FM	—	775	875	1,250	1,900	—

KM# 156.1a 8 ESCUDOS

27.0674 g., 0.8750 Gold 0.7614 oz. AGW **Ruler:** Charles III **Obv:** Large, armored bust right **Obv. Legend:** CAROL • III • D • G • ... **Rev:** Crowned shield flanked by 8 S in order chain, initials and mint mark upright **Rev. Legend:** ... AUSPICE • DEO • **Mint:** Mexico City **Note:** Mint mark M, Mo.

Date	Mintage	VG	F	VF	XF	Unc
1788 FM	—	775	875	1,250	1,900	—

KM# 157 8 ESCUDOS

27.0674 g., 0.8750 Gold 0.7614 oz. AGW **Ruler:** Charles IV **Obv:** Armored bust of Charles III, right **Obv. Legend:** CAROL • IV • D • G • ... **Rev:** Crowned shield flanked by 8 S in order chain **Rev. Legend:** IN • UTROQ • ... **Mint:** Mexico City **Note:** Mint mark M, Mo, using old portrait punch.

Date	Mintage	VG	F	VF	XF	Unc
1789 FM	—	850	950	1,450	2,500	—
1790 FM	—	850	950	1,450	2,500	—

KM# 158 8 ESCUDOS

27.0674 g., 0.8750 Gold 0.7614 oz. AGW **Ruler:** Charles IV **Obv:** Armored bust of Charles III, right **Obv. Legend:** CAROL • IIII • D • G • ... **Rev:** Crowned shield flanked by 8 S in order chain **Rev. Legend:** IN • UTROQ • ... **Mint:** Mexico City **Note:** Mint mark M, Mo, using old portrait punch.

Date	Mintage	VG	F	VF	XF	Unc
1790 FM	—	850	950	1,450	2,500	—

KM# 159 8 ESCUDOS

27.0674 g., 0.8750 Gold 0.7614 oz. AGW **Ruler:** Charles IV **Obv:** Armored bust right **Obv. Legend:** CAROL • IIII • D • G • ... **Rev:** Crowned shield flanked by 8 S in order chain **Rev. Legend:** IN • UTROQ • ... **Mint:** Mexico City **Note:** Mint mark Mo.

Date	Mintage	VG	F	VF	XF	Unc
1791 FM	—	725	750	850	1,500	—
1792 FM	—	725	750	850	1,500	—
1793 FM	—	725	750	850	1,500	—
1794 FM	—	725	750	850	1,500	—
1795 FM	—	725	750	850	1,500	—
1796/5 FM	—	750	750	850	1,750	—
1796 FM	—	725	750	850	1,500	—
1797 FM EPLIX	—	750	750	900	1,750	—
1797 FM	—	725	750	850	1,500	—
1798 FM	—	725	750	850	1,500	—
1799 FM	—	725	750	850	1,500	—
1800 FM	—	725	750	850	1,500	—
1801/0 FT	—	750	750	925	1,750	—
1801 FM	—	750	750	850	1,500	—
1801 FT	—	750	750	850	1,500	—
1802 FT	—	750	750	850	1,500	—
1803 FT	—	750	775	875	1,500	—
1804/3 TH	—	750	775	900	1,750	—
1804 TH	—	750	750	850	1,500	5,300
1805 TH	—	750	750	850	1,500	—
1806 TH	—	750	750	850	1,500	5,300
1807/6 TH	—	750	775	900	1,750	—
1807 TH Mo over inverted Mo	—	750	775	900	1,750	—
1808/7 TH	—	750	750	850	1,900	—
1807 TH	—	750	775	1,050	1,500	—
1808 TH	—	750	775	1,050	1,900	—

KM# 160   8 ESCUDOS
27.0674 g., 0.8750 Gold 0.7614 oz. AGW **Ruler:**
Ferdinand VII **Obv:** Armored bust right **Obv. Legend:**
FERDIN • VII • D • G... **Rev:** Crowned shield divides designed
wreath **Rev. Legend:** IN UTROQ • FELIX **Mint:** Mexico City
Note: Mint mark Mo.

Date	Mintage	VG	F	VF	XF	Unc
1808 TH	—	750	775	1,050	2,150	—
1809 HJ	—	750	775	1,050	2,300	—
1810 HJ	—	750	775	1,000	2,050	—
1811/0 HJ	—	750	775	1,100	2,300	—
1811 HJ H/T	—	750	775	1,100	2,300	—
1811 HJ	—	750	775	1,100	2,300	—
1811 JJ	—	750	775	1,000	2,050	—
1812 JJ	—	750	775	1,000	2,050	—

KM# 161   8 ESCUDOS
27.0674 g., 0.8750 Gold 0.7614 oz. AGW **Ruler:**
Ferdinand VII **Obv:** Laureate head right **Obv. Legend:**
FERDIN • VII • D • G... **Rev:** Crowned shield divides designed
wreath **Rev. Legend:** IN UTROQ • FELIX **Mint:** Mexico City
Note: Mint mark Mo.

Date	Mintage	VG	F	VF	XF	Unc
1814 JJ	—	750	775	1,000	1,700	—
1815/4 JJ	—	750	775	1,050	1,950	—
1815/4 HJ	—	750	775	1,050	1,950	—
1815 JJ	—	750	775	1,000	1,700	—
1815 HJ	—	750	775	1,000	1,700	—
1816 JJ	—	750	775	1,000	1,700	—
1817 JJ	—	750	775	1,000	1,950	—
1818/7 JJ	—	750	775	1,000	1,850	—
1818 JJ	—	750	775	1,000	1,850	—
1819 JJ	—	750	775	1,000	1,850	—
1820 JJ	—	750	775	1,000	1,850	—
1821 JJ	—	750	775	1,050	2,200	—

PROCLAMATION MEDALLIC COINAGE

The Q used in the following listings refer to
Standard Catalog of Mexican Coins, Paper Money,
Stocks, Bonds, and Medals by Krause Publications,
Inc., ©1981.

KM# Q22   1/2 REAL
1.6000 g., Silver **Issuer:** Mexico City **Obv:** Crowned shield
flanked by crowned pillars with banner **Obv. Legend:** A
CARLOS IV REY DE ESPANA Y DE LAS YNDIAS **Rev:**
Legend, date within wreath **Rev. Legend:** PROCLAMADO
EN MEXICO ANO DE 1789

Date	Mintage	F	VF	XF	Unc	BU
1789	—	20.00	28.50	40.00	—	—

KM# Q22a   1/2 REAL
Bronze **Issuer:** Mexico City **Obv:** Crowned shield flanked
by crowned pillars with banner **Obv. Legend:** A CARLOS IV
REY DE ESPANA Y DE LAS YNDIAS **Rev:** Legend, date
within wreath **Rev. Legend:** PROCLAMADO EN MEXICO
ANO DE 1789

Date	Mintage	F	VF	XF	Unc	BU
1789	—	22.50	35.00	50.00	—	—

KM# Q23   1/2 REAL
Silver **Issuer:** Mexico City **Obv:** Crowned arms in double-
lined circle **Obv. Legend:** A CARLOS IV REY DE ESPANA
Y DE LAS YNDIAS **Rev. Legend:** PROCLAMADO EN
MEXICO ANO DE 1789

Date	Mintage	F	VF	XF	Unc	BU
1789	—	20.00	28.50	40.00	—	—

KM# Q23a   1/2 REAL
Bronze **Issuer:** Mexico City **Obv:** Crowned arms in double-
lined circle **Obv. Legend:** A CARLOS IV REY DE ESPANA
Y DE LAS YNDIAS **Rev. Legend:** PROCLAMADO EN
MEXICO ANO DE 1789

Date	Mintage	F	VF	XF	Unc	BU
1789	—	22.50	35.00	50.00	—	—

KM# Q24   REAL
Silver **Issuer:** Mexico City **Obv:** Crowned shield flanked by
crowned pillars with banner **Obv. Legend:** A CARLOS IV REY
DE ESPANA Y DE LAS YNDIAS **Rev:** Legend, date, value
within wreath **Rev. Legend:** PROCLAMADO EN MEXICO
ANO DE 1789

Date	Mintage	F	VF	XF	Unc	BU
1789	—	20.00	28.50	40.00	—	—

KM# Q24a   REAL
Bronze **Issuer:** Mexico City **Obv:** Crowned shield flanked
by crowned pillars with banner **Obv. Legend:** A CARLOS IV
REY DE ESPANA Y DE LAS YNDIAS **Rev:** Legend, date,
value within wreath **Rev. Legend:** PROCLAMADO EN
MEXICO ANO DE 1789

Date	Mintage	F	VF	XF	Unc	BU
1789	—	22.50	35.00	50.00	—	—

KM# Q-A24   REAL
Silver **Issuer:** Mexico City **Obv:** Crowned arms in double-
lined circle **Obv. Legend:** A CARLOS IV REY DE ESPANA
Y DE LAS YNDIAS **Rev. Legend:** PROCLAMADO EN
MEXICO ANO DE 1789

Date	Mintage	F	VF	XF	Unc	BU
1789	—	20.00	28.50	40.00	—	—

KM# Q-A24a   REAL
Copper **Issuer:** Mexico City **Obv:** Crowned arms in double-
lined circle **Obv. Legend:** A CARLOS IV REY DE ESPANA
Y DE LAS YNDIAS **Rev. Legend:** PROCLAMADO EN
MEXICO ANO DE 1789

Date	Mintage	F	VF	XF	Unc	BU
1789	—	22.50	35.00	50.00	—	—

KM# Q8 REAL
Silver **Issuer:** Chiapa **Obv:** Crowned shield flanked by pillars **Obv. Legend:** FERNANDO. VII. REY DE ESPANA. Y DE SUS IND. **Rev:** Legend within wreath **Rev. Legend:** PROCLA/MADO ENCUID•R•DE/ CHIAPA•/•A1808•

Date	Mintage	F	VF	XF	Unc	BU
1808	—	20.00	32.50	55.00	95.00	—

KM# Q25 2 REALES
6.7000 g., Silver **Issuer:** Mexico City **Obv:** Crowned shield flanked by crowned pillars with banner **Obv. Legend:** A CARLOS IV REY DE ESPANA Y DE LAS YNDIAS **Rev:** Legend, date, value within wreath **Rev. Legend:** PROCLAMADO EN MEXICO ANO DE 1789

Date	Mintage	F	VF	XF	Unc	BU
1789	—	35.00	50.00	75.00	—	—

KM# Q25a 2 REALES
6.7000 g., Bronze **Issuer:** Mexico City **Obv:** Crowned shield flanked by crowned pillars with banner **Obv. Legend:** A CARLOS IV REY DE ESPANA Y DE LAS YNDIAS **Rev:** Legend, date, value within wreath **Rev. Legend:** PROCLAMADO EN MEXICO ANO DE 1789

Date	Mintage	F	VF	XF	Unc	BU
1789	—	30.00	45.00	60.00	—	—

KM# Q64 2 REALES
Silver **Issuer:** Queretaro **Obv:** Crowned shield flanked by pillars **Obv. Legend:** FERNANDO VII REY DE ESPANA **Rev:** Legend, date within wreath

Date	Mintage	F	VF	XF	Unc	BU
1808	—	20.00	37.50	75.00	125	—

KM# Q10 2 REALES
Silver **Issuer:** Chiapa **Obv:** Crowned shield flanked by pillars **Obv. Legend:** FERNANDO VII REY DE ESPANA Y DE SUS INDIAS **Rev:** Legend, date within wreath

Date	Mintage	F	VF	XF	Unc	BU
1808	—	37.50	57.50	85.00	145	—

KM# Q27 4 REALES
13.6000 g., Silver **Issuer:** Mexico City **Obv:** Crowned shield flanked by crowned pillars with banner **Obv. Legend:** A CARLOS IV REY DE ESPANA Y DE LAS YNDIAS **Rev:** Legend date, value within wreath **Rev. Legend:** PROCLAMADO EN MEXICO ANO DE 1789

Date	Mintage	F	VF	XF	Unc	BU
1789	—	100	150	225	—	—

KM# Q27a 4 REALES
13.6000 g., Bronze **Issuer:** Mexico City **Obv:** Crowned shield flanked by crowned pillars with banner **Obv. Legend:** A CARLOS IV REY DE ESPANA Y DE LAS YNDIAS **Rev:** Legend, date, value within wreath **Rev. Legend:** PROCLAMADO EN MEXICO ANO DE 1789

Date	Mintage	F	VF	XF	Unc	BU
1789	—	70.00	100	150	—	—

KM# Q-A66 4 REALES
Silver **Issuer:** Queretaro **Obv:** Crowned shield flanked by pillars **Obv. Legend:** FERNANDO VII REY DE ESPANA **Rev:** Legend, date within wreath

Date	Mintage	F	VF	XF	Unc	BU
1808	—	85.00	135	245	400	—

KM# Q28 8 REALES
27.0000 g., Silver **Issuer:** Mexico City **Obv:** Crowned shield flanked by crowned pillars with banner **Obv. Legend:** A CARLOS IV REY DE ESPANA Y DE LAS YNDIAS **Rev:** Legend, date, value within wreath **Rev. Legend:** PROCLAMADO EN MEXICO ANO DE 1789

Date	Mintage	F	VF	XF	Unc	BU
1789	—	200	275	400	—	—

KM# Q28a 8 REALES
27.0000 g., Bronze **Issuer:** Mexico City **Obv:** Crowned shield flanked by crowned pillars with banner **Obv. Legend:** A CARLOS IV REY DE ESPANA Y DE LAS YNDIAS **Rev:** Legend, date, value within wreath **Rev. Legend:** PROCLAMADO EN MEXICO ANO DE 1789

Date	Mintage	F	VF	XF	Unc	BU
1789	—	70.00	100	150	—	—

KM# Q68 8 REALES
Silver **Issuer:** Queretaro **Obv:** Crowned shield flanked by pillars **Obv. Legend:** FERNANDO VII REY DE ESPANA **Rev:** Legend, date within wreath

Date	Mintage	F	VF	XF	Unc	BU
1808	—	185	350	485	800	—

WAR OF INDEPENDENCE

CHIHUAHUA

The Chihuahua Mint was established by a decree of October 8, 1810 as a temporary mint. Their first coins were cast 8 Reales using Mexico City coins as patterns and obliterating/changing the mint mark and moneyer initials. Two c/m were placed on the obverse - on the left, a T designating receipt by the Royal Treasurer, crowned pillars of Hercules on the right with pomegranate beneath, the comptrollers symbol.

In 1814, standard dies were made available, thus machine struck 8 Reales were produced until 1822. Only the one denomination was made at Chihuahua.

Mint mark: CA.

ROYALIST COINAGE

KM# 123 8 REALES
Cast Silver **Ruler:** Ferdinand VII **Countermark:** T at left, pillars at right, pomegranate below **Obv:** Armored bust right **Obv. Legend:** FERDIN• VII • DEI • GRATIA **Rev:** Crowned shield flanked by pillars **Mint:** Chihuahua

Date	Mintage	Good	VG	F	VF	XF
1810CA RP Rare	—	—	—	—	—	—
1811CA RP	—	45.00	70.00	120	200	—
1812CA RP	—	40.00	65.00	90.00	175	—
1813CA RP	—	35.00	50.00	70.00	120	—

KM# 111.1 8 REALES
27.0700 g., 0.9030 Silver 0.7859 oz. ASW **Ruler:** Ferdinand VII **Obv:** Draped bust right **Obv. Legend:** FERDIN • VII • DEI • GRATIA **Rev:** Crowned shield flanked by pillars

Date	Mintage	VG	F	VF	XF	Unc
1815 RP	—	220	300	525	750	—
1816 RP	—	90.00	140	225	425	—
1817 RP	—	110	165	280	425	—

Date	Mintage	VG	F	VF	XF	Unc
1818 RP	—	110	165	280	425	—
1819/8 RP	—	140	195	375	525	—
1819 RP	—	140	195	375	525	—
1820 RP	—	220	300	525	750	—
1821 RP	—	220	300	525	750	—
1822 RP	—	450	650	1,200	1,650	—

Note: KM#111.1 is normally found struck over earlier cast 8 Reales, KM#123 and Monclova (MVA) 1812 cast countermark 8 Reales, KM#202 and Zacatecas 8 Reales, KM#190

DURANGO

The Durango mint was authorized as a temporary mint on the same day as the Chihuahua Mint, October 8, 1810. The mint opened in 1811 and made coins of 6 denominations between 1811 and 1822.

Mint mark: D.

ROYALIST COINAGE

KM# 60 1/8 REAL
Copper **Ruler:** Ferdinand VII **Obv:** Crowned monogram **Rev:** EN DURANGO, value, date **Mint:** Durango

Date	Mintage	VG	F	VF	XF	Unc
1812D	—	40.00	75.00	125	250	—
1813D	—	65.00	135	185	375	—
1814D Rare	—	—	—	—	—	—

KM# 61 1/8 REAL
Copper **Ruler:** Ferdinand VII **Obv:** Crowned monogram **Rev:** Value within spray, date below **Rev. Legend:** ENDURANGO. **Mint:** Durango

Date	Mintage	VG	F	VF	XF	Unc
1814D	—	18.00	32.50	55.00	95.00	—
1815D	—	18.00	35.00	60.00	100	—
1816D	—	18.00	35.00	60.00	100	—
1817D	—	15.00	30.00	50.00	95.00	—
1818D	—	15.00	30.00	50.00	95.00	—
1818D	—	45.00	80.00	125	225	—

Note: OCTAVO DD REAL, error

KM# 74.1 1/2 REAL
1.6900 g., 0.9030 Silver 0.0491 oz. ASW **Ruler:** Ferdinand VII **Obv:** Draped laureate bust right **Rev:** Crowned shield flanked by pillars **Mint:** Durango

Date	Mintage	VG	F	VF	XF	Unc
1813D RM	—	250	450	750	1,850	—
1814D MZ	—	250	450	750	1,850	—
1816D MZ	—	250	450	750	1,850	—

KM# 83.1 REAL
3.3800 g., 0.9030 Silver 0.0981 oz. ASW **Ruler:** Ferdinand VII **Obv:** Draped laureate bust right **Obv. Legend:**

FERDIN • VII... **Rev:** Crowned shield flanked by pillars **Rev.**
Legend: IND • REX... **Mint:** Durango

Date	Mintage	VG	F	VF	XF	Unc
1813D RM	—	250	450	650	1,650	—
1814D MZ	—	250	450	650	1,650	—
1815D MZ	—	250	450	650	1,650	—

KM# 92.2 2 REALES
6.7700 g., 0.9030 Silver 0.1965 oz. ASW **Ruler:**
Ferdinand VII **Obv:** Armored bust right **Rev:** Crowned shield
flanked by pillars **Rev. Legend:** MON PROV DE DURANGO...
Mint: Durango

Date	Mintage	VG	F	VF	XF	Unc
1811D RM	—	575	675	1,300	2,650	—

KM# 92.3 2 REALES
6.7700 g., 0.9030 Silver 0.1965 oz. ASW **Ruler:**
Ferdinand VII **Obv:** Armored bust right **Rev:** Crowned shield
flanked by pillars **Rev. Legend:** HISPAN ET IND REX...

Date	Mintage	VG	F	VF	XF	Unc
1812 RM	—	375	600	1,150	2,500	—

KM# 93.1 2 REALES
6.7700 g., 0.9030 Silver 0.1965 oz. ASW **Ruler:**
Ferdinand VII **Obv:** Draped laureate bust right **Obv. Legend:**
FERDIN • VII... **Rev:** Crowned shield flanked by pillars **Rev.**
Legend: IND • REX... **Mint:** Durango

Date	Mintage	VG	F	VF	XF	Unc
1812D RM	—	350	550	1,050	2,300	—
1813D RM	—	425	850	1,400	3,850	—
1813D MZ	—	425	850	1,400	3,850	—
1814D MZ	—	425	850	1,400	3,850	—
1815D MZ	—	425	850	1,400	3,850	—
1816D MZ	—	425	850	1,400	3,850	—
1817D MZ	—	425	850	1,400	3,850	—

KM# 102.1 4 REALES
13.5400 g., 0.9030 Silver 0.3931 oz. ASW **Ruler:**
Ferdinand VII **Obv:** Draped laureate bust right **Obv. Legend:**
FERDIN • VII... **Rev:** Crowned shield flanked by pillars **Rev.**
Legend: IND • REX... **Mint:** Durango

Date	Mintage	VG	F	VF	XF	Unc
1814D MZ	—	775	1,400	2,300	6,300	—
1816D MZ	—	625	1,250	1,950	5,600	—
1817D MZ	—	625	1,250	1,950	5,600	—

KM# 110.1 8 REALES
27.0700 g., 0.9030 Silver 0.7859 oz. ASW **Ruler:**
Ferdinand VII **Obv:** Armored bust right **Obv. Legend:** FERD
• VII... **Rev:** Crowned shield flanked by pillars **Rev. Legend:**
DURANGO • 8R R • M... **Mint:** Durango

Date	Mintage	VG	F	VF	XF	Unc
1811D RM	—	2,500	5,000	8,000	—	—
1812D RM	—	350	650	1,000	3,500	—
1814D MZ	—	350	650	1,000	3,500	—

KM# 111.2 8 REALES
27.0700 g., 0.9030 Silver 0.7859 oz. ASW **Ruler:**
Ferdinand VII **Obv:** Draped laureate bust right **Obv. Legend:**
FERDIN • VII... **Rev:** Crowned shield flanked by pillars **Rev.**
Legend: IND • REX... **Mint:** Durango

Date	Mintage	VG	F	VF	XF	Unc
1812D RM	—	125	175	275	825	—
1813D RM	—	150	200	325	875	—
1813D MZ	—	125	175	275	775	—
1814/2D MZ	—	150	200	300	775	—
1814D MZ	—	150	200	300	775	—
1815D MZ	—	75.00	125	225	625	—
1816D MZ	—	50.00	75.00	125	350	—
1817D MZ	—	30.00	50.00	90.00	275	—
1818D MZ	—	50.00	75.00	125	375	—
1818D RM	—	50.00	75.00	125	350	—
1818D CG/RM	—	100	125	150	375	—
1818D CG	—	50.00	75.00	125	350	—
1819D CG/RM	—	50.00	100	150	325	—
1819D CG	—	30.00	60.00	100	275	—
1820D CG	—	30.00	60.00	100	275	—
1821D CG	—	30.00	40.00	80.00	225	—
1822D CG	—	30.00	50.00	90.00	265	—

Note: Occasionally these are found struck over cast Chihuahua 8 reales and are very rare in general, specimens
dated prior to 1816 are rather crudely struck

GUADALAJARA

The Guadalajara Mint made its first coins in 1812 and the mint operated until April 30, 1815. It was to reopen in 1818 and continue operations until 1822. It was the only Royalist mint to strike gold coins, both 4 and 8 Escudos. In addition to these it struck the standard 5 denominations in silver.
    Mint mark: GA.

ROYALIST COINAGE

KM# 74.2   1/2 REAL
1.6900 g., 0.9030 Silver 0.0491 oz. ASW **Ruler:**
Ferdinand VII **Obv:** Draped laureate bust right **Obv. Legend:**
FERDIN • VII... **Rev:** Crowned shield flanked by pillars **Rev.**
Legend: IND... **Mint:** Guadalajara

Date	Mintage	VG	F	VF	XF	Unc
1812GA MR Rare	—	—	—	—	—	—
1814GA MR	—	48.00	120	240	350	—
1815GA MR	—	240	425	600	1,200	—

KM# 83.2   REAL
3.3800 g., 0.9030 Silver 0.0981 oz. ASW **Ruler:**
Ferdinand VII **Obv:** Draped laureate bust right **Obv. Legend:**
FERDIN • VII... **Rev:** Crowned shield flanked by pillars **Rev.**
Legend: IND • REX... **Mint:** Guadalajara

Date	Mintage	VG	F	VF	XF	Unc
1813GA MR	—	350	600	950	—	—
1814GA MR	—	180	240	425	775	—
1815GA MR	—	350	600	950	—	—

KM# 93.2   2 REALES
6.7700 g., 0.9030 Silver 0.1965 oz. ASW **Ruler:**
Ferdinand VII **Obv:** Draped laureate bust right **Obv. Legend:**
FERDIN • VII... **Rev:** Crowned shield flanked by pillars **Rev.**
Legend: IND • REX... **Mint:** Guadalajara

Date	Mintage	VG	F	VF	XF	Unc
1812GA MR	—	300	500	800	2,500	—
1814/2GA MR	—	75.00	125	250	650	—
1814GA MR	—	75.00	125	250	650	—
1815/4GA MR	—	425	725	1,100	3,600	—
1815GA MR	—	400	700	1,000	3,500	—
1821GA FS	—	200	250	350	950	—

KM# 102.2   4 REALES
13.5400 g., 0.9030 Silver 0.3931 oz. ASW **Ruler:**
Ferdinand VII **Obv:** Draped laureate bust right **Obv. Legend:**
FERDIN • VII... **Rev:** Crowned shield flanked by pillars **Rev.**
Legend: IND • REX... **Mint:** Guadalajara

Date	Mintage	VG	F	VF	XF	Unc
1814GA MR	—	50.00	80.00	190	325	—
1815GA MR	—	100	190	375	625	—

KM# 102.3   4 REALES
13.5400 g., 0.9030 Silver 0.3931 oz. ASW **Ruler:**
Ferdinand VII **Obv:** Draped laureate bust right **Obv. Legend:**
FERDIN • VII... **Rev:** Crowned shield flanked by pillars **Rev.**
Legend: IND • REX... **Mint:** Guadalajara

Date	Mintage	VG	F	VF	XF	Unc
1814GA MR	—	65.00	125	250	500	—

KM# 102.4   4 REALES
13.5400 g., 0.9030 Silver 0.3931 oz. ASW **Ruler:**
Ferdinand VII **Obv:** Draped laureate bust right **Obv. Legend:**
FERDIN • VII... **Rev:** Crowned shield flanked by pillars **Rev.**
Legend: IND • REX... **Mint:** Guadalajara

Date	Mintage	VG	F	VF	XF	Unc
1814GA MR	—	75.00	150	325	575	—

KM# 111.3 8 REALES
27.0700 g., 0.9030 Silver 0.7859 oz. ASW **Ruler:**
Ferdinand VII **Obv:** Draped laureate bust right **Obv. Legend:**
FERDIN • VII... **Rev:** Crowned shield flanked by pillars **Rev.**
Legend: IND • REX... **Mint:** Guadalajara

Date	Mintage	VG	F	VF	XF	Unc
1812GA MR	—	2,500	4,400	6,300	8,800	—
1813/2GA MR	—	90.00	150	225	600	—
1813GA MR	—	90.00	150	225	600	—
1814GA MR	—	30.00	55.00	90.00	270	—

Note: Several bust varieties exist for the 1814 issue

1815GA MR	—	190	250	450	950	—
1818GA FS	—	45.00	75.00	115	300	—
1821/18GA FS	—	45.00	75.00	115	300	—
1821GA FS	—	37.50	55.00	90.00	250	—
1821/2GA FS	—	45.00	75.00	115	300	—
1822GA FS	—	37.50	65.00	95.00	250	—

Note: Die varieties exist. Early dates are also encountered
struck over other types

1822/1GA FS	—	45.00	75.00	115	300	—

KM# 147 4 ESCUDOS
13.5400 g., 0.8750 Gold 0.3809 oz. AGW **Ruler:**
Ferdinand VII **Obv:** Uniformed bust right **Rev:** Crowned shield
divides designed wreath **Mint:** Guadalajara

Date	Mintage	VG	F	VF	XF	Unc
1812GA MR Rare	—					

KM# 162 8 ESCUDOS
27.0700 g., 0.8750 Gold 0.7615 oz. AGW **Ruler:**
Ferdinand VII **Obv:** Large uniformed bust right **Obv. Legend:**
FERDIN • VII • D • G... **Rev:** Crowned shield divides designed
wreath **Rev. Legend:** UTROQ • FELIX... **Mint:** Guadalajara

Date	Mintage	VG	F	VF	XF	Unc
1812GA MR Rare	—					
1813GA MR	—	6,000	9,000	15,000	25,000	—

Note: Heritage Long Beach sale 5-08, Choice AU realized
$37,500. American Numismatic Rarities Eliasberg sale 4-
05, VF-30 realized $23,000.

KM# 163 8 ESCUDOS
27.0700 g., 0.8750 Gold 0.7615 oz. AGW **Ruler:**
Ferdinand VII **Obv:** Small uniformed bust right **Obv. Legend:**
FERDIN • VII... **Rev:** Crowned shield divides designed wreath
Rev. Legend: UTROQ • FELIX... **Mint:** Guadalajara

Date	Mintage	VG	F	VF	XF	Unc
1813GA MR	—	10,000	16,000	30,000	45,000	—

Note: Spink America Gerber sale 6-96 VF or better realized
$46,200

KM# 161.1 8 ESCUDOS
27.0700 g., 0.8750 Gold 0.7615 oz. AGW **Ruler:**
Ferdinand VII **Obv:** Laureate head right **Obv. Legend:**
FERDIN • VII • D • G... **Rev:** Crowned shield divides designed
wreath **Rev. Legend:** UTROQ • FELIX... **Mint:** Guadalajara

Date	Mintage	VG	F	VF	XF	Unc
1821GA FS	—	2,000	4,000	10,000	17,000	—

Note: American Numismatic Rarities Eliasberg sale 4-05,
AU-55 realized $20,700.

KM# 164 8 ESCUDOS
27.0700 g., 0.8750 Gold 0.7615 oz. AGW **Ruler:**
Ferdinand VII **Obv:** Draped laureate bust right **Rev:** Crowned
shield flanked by pillars **Mint:** Guadalajara

Date	Mintage	VG	F	VF	XF	Unc
1821GA FS	—	5,500	8,000	14,500	23,500	—

GUANAJUATO

The Guanajuato Mint was authorized December 24,
1812 and started production shortly thereafter; closing for
unknown reasons on May 15, 1813. The mint was reopened in
April, 1821 by the insurgents, who struck coins of the old royal
Spanish design to pay their army, even after independence,
well into 1822.
Only the 2 and 8 Reales coins were made.
Mint mark: Go.

ROYALIST COINAGE

KM# 93.3 2 REALES

6.7700 g., 0.9030 Silver 0.1965 oz. ASW **Ruler:**
Ferdinand VII **Obv:** Draped laureate bust right **Obv. Legend:**
FERDIN • VII... **Rev:** Crowned shield flanked bu pillars **Rev.
Legend:** IND • REX... **Mint:** Guanajuato

Date	Mintage	VG	F	VF	XF	Unc
1821Go JM	—	42.00	80.00	120	220	—
1822Go JM	—	36.00	60.00	90.00	175	—

KM# 111.4   8 REALES
27.0700 g., 0.9030 Silver 0.7859 oz. ASW **Ruler:**
Ferdinand VII **Obv:** Draped laureate bust right **Obv. Legend:**
FERDIN • VII... **Rev:** Crowned shield flanked by pillars **Rev.
Legend:** IND • REX... **Mint:** Guanajuato

Date	Mintage	VG	F	VF	XF	Unc
1812Go JJ	—	3,500	6,000	—	—	—
1813Go JJ	—	150	210	325	725	—
1821Go JM	—	30.00	60.00	90.00	240	—
1822Go JM	—	25.00	42.00	70.00	220	—

NUEVA GALICIA

(Later became Jalisco State)

In early colonial times, Nueva Galicia was an extensive
province which substantially combined later provinces of
Zacatecas and Jalisco. These are states of Mexico today
although the name was revived during the War of Independence. The only issue was 2 Reales of rather enigmatic origin.
No decrees or other authorization to strike this coin has yet
been located or reported.

INSURGENT COINAGE

KM# 218   2 REALES
0.9030 Silver **Obv:** N. G. in center, date **Obv. Legend:**
PROVYCIONAL... **Rev:** 2R in center **Rev. Legend:** ... A.
JUNIANA...

Date	Mintage	Good	VG	F	VF	XF
1813	—	1,000	2,500	4,500	—	—

Note: Excellent struck counterfeits exist

NUEVA VISCAYA

(Later became Durango State)

This 8 Reales, intended for the province of Nueva Vis-
caya, was minted in the newly-opened Durango Mint during
February and March of 1811, before the regular coinage of
Durango was started.

ROYALIST COINAGE

KM# 181   8 REALES
27.0700 g., 0.9030 Silver 0.7859 oz. ASW **Ruler:**
Ferdinand VII **Obv:** Crowned shield within sprays **Obv.
Legend:** MON • PROV • DE NUEV • VIZCAYA **Rev:** Crowned
shield flanked by pillars

Date	Mintage	Good	VG	F	VF	XF
1811 RM	—	1,000	2,250	2,850	5,500	—

Note: Several varieties exist.

OAXACA

The city of Oaxaca was in the midst of a coin shortage
when it became apparent the city would be taken by the Insurgents. Royalist forces under Lt. Gen. Saravia had coins made.
They were cast in a blacksmith shop. 1/2, 1, and 8 Reales
were made only briefly in 1812 before the Royalists surren-
dered the city.

ROYALIST COINAGE

KM# 166   1/2 REAL
0.9030 Silver **Ruler:** Ferdinand VII **Obv:** Cross separating
castle, lion, Fo, 7o **Rev:** Legend around shield **Rev. Legend:**
PROV • D • OAXACA

Date	Mintage	Good	VG	F	VF	XF
1812	—	1,000	1,500	2,500	3,500	—

KM# 167   REAL
0.9030 Silver **Ruler:** Ferdinand VII **Obv:** Cross separating

castle, lion, Fo, 7o **Rev:** Legend around shield **Rev. Legend:** PROV • D • OAXACA

Date	Mintage	Good	VG	F	VF	XF
1812	—	350	650	1,200	2,500	—

KM# 168 8 REALES
0.9030 Silver **Obv:** Cross separating castle, lion, Fo, 7o **Obv. Legend:** OAXACA 1812... **Rev:** Shield, authorization mark above **Note:** These issues usually display a second mark 'O' between the crowned pillars on the obverse. Varieties of large and small lion in shield also exist.

Date	Mintage	Good	VG	F	VF	XF
1812 "A"	—	1,300	1,900	3,300	5,500	—
1812 "B"	—	1,300	1,900	3,300	5,500	—
1812 "C"	—	1,300	1,900	3,300	5,500	—
1812 "D"	—	1,300	1,900	3,300	5,500	—
1812 "K"	—	1,300	1,900	3,300	5,500	—
1812 "L"	—	1,300	1,900	3,300	5,500	—
1812 "Mo"	—	1,300	1,900	3,300	5,500	—
1812 "N"	—	1,300	1,900	3,300	5,500	—
1812 "O"	—	1,300	1,900	3,300	5,500	—
1812 "R"	—	1,300	1,900	3,300	5,500	—
1812 "V"	—	1,300	1,900	3,300	5,500	—
1812 "Z"	—	1,300	1,900	3,300	5,500	—

INSURGENT COINAGE

Oaxaca was the hub of Insurgent activity in the south where coinage started in July 1811 and continued until October 1814. The Oaxaca issues represent episodic strikings, usually under dire circumstances by various individuals. Coins were commonly made of copper due to urgency and were intended to be redeemed at face value in gold or silver once silver was available to the Insurgents. Some were later made in silver, but most appear to be of more recent origin, to satisfy collectors.

KM# 219 1/2 REAL
Struck Copper **Issuer:** SUD, Under General Morelos **Obv:** Bow, arrow, SUD **Rev:** Morelos monogram Mo, date

Date	Mintage	Good	VG	F	VF	XF
1811	—	6.75	11.50	20.00	35.00	—
1812	—	6.75	11.50	20.00	35.00	—
1813	—	5.50	9.00	17.50	30.00	—
1814	—	9.00	16.50	25.00	40.00	—

Note: Uniface strikes exist of #219

KM# 220.1 1/2 REAL
Struck Silver **Issuer:** SUD, Under General Morelos **Obv:** Bow, arrow, SUD **Rev:** Morelos monogram Mo, date

Date	Mintage	Good	VG	F	VF	XF
1811	—	—	—	—	—	—
1812	—	—	—	—	—	—
1813	—	—	—	—	—	—

KM# 220.2 1/2 REAL
Struck Silver **Issuer:** SUD, Under General Morelos **Obv:** Bow, arrow, SUD **Rev:** Morelos monogram Mo, date

Date	Mintage	Good	VG	F	VF	XF
1811	—	—	—	—	—	—
1812	—	—	—	—	—	—
1813	—	27.50	55.00	110	165	—

Note: Use caution as silver specimens appear questionable and may be considered spurious

KM# 221 1/2 REAL
Struck Silver **Issuer:** SUD, Under General Morelos **Obv:** Bow, arrow **Obv. Legend:** PROVICIONAL DE OAXACA **Rev:** Lion **Rev. Legend:** AMERICA MORELOS

Date	Mintage	Good	VG	F	VF	XF
1812	—	38.50	65.00	110	165	—
1813	—	38.50	65.00	110	165	—

KM# 221a 1/2 REAL
Struck Copper **Issuer:** SUD, Under General Morelos **Obv:** Bow, arrow **Obv. Legend:** PROVICIONAL DE OAXACA **Rev:** Lion **Rev. Legend:** AMERICA MORELOS

Date	Mintage	Good	VG	F	VF	XF
1812	—	30.25	46.75	75.00	110	—
1813	—	22.50	38.50	65.00	95.00	—

KM# A222 1/2 REAL
Struck Copper **Issuer:** SUD, Under Ge5neral Morelos **Obv:** Similar to KM#220 **Rev:** Similar to KM#221 but with 1/2 at left of lion **Rev. Legend:** AMERICA MORELOS

Date	Mintage	Good	VG	F	VF	XF
1813	—	30.25	46.75	75.00	110	—

KM# 243 1/2 REAL
Struck Copper **Issuer:** Tierra Caliente (Hot Country), Under General Morelos **Obv:** Bow, T.C., SUD **Rev:** Morelos monogram, value, date

Date	Mintage	Good	VG	F	VF	XF
1813	—	41.25	75.00	140	220	—

KM# 222 REAL
Struck Copper **Issuer:** SUD, Under General Morelos **Obv:** Bow, arrow, SUD **Rev:** Morelos monogram, 1 R., date

Date	Mintage	Good	VG	F	VF	XF
1811	—	5.00	10.00	20.00	41.75	—
1812	—	4.00	8.00	15.00	33.00	—
1813	—	4.00	8.00	15.00	33.00	—

KM# 222a REAL
Struck Silver **Issuer:** SUD, Under General Morelos **Obv:** Bow, arrow, SUD **Rev:** Morelos monogram, 1 R., date

Date	Mintage	Good	VG	F	VF	XF
1812	—	—	—	—	—	—
1813	—	—	—	—	—	—

KM# 223 REAL
Cast Silver **Issuer:** SUD, Under General Morelos **Obv:** Bow, arrow, SUD with floral ornaments **Rev:** Morelos monogram, 1 R., date

Date	Mintage	Good	VG	F	VF	XF
1812	—	—	—	—	—	—
1813	—	30.25	65.00	125	175	—

Note: Use caution as many silver specimens appear questionable and may be considered spurious

KM# 224 REAL
Struck Copper **Issuer:** SUD, Under General Morelos **Obv:** Bow, arrow/SUD **Rev:** Lion **Rev. Legend:** AMERICA MORELOS

Date	Mintage	Good	VG	F	VF	XF
1813	—	30.25	46.75	85.00	120	—

KM# 225 REAL
Silver **Issuer:** SUD, Under General Morelos **Obv:** Bow, arrow/SUD **Rev:** Lion **Rev. Legend:** AMERICA MORELOS

Date	Mintage	Good	VG	F	VF	XF
1813 Rare	—	—	—	—	—	—

KM# 244 REAL
Struck Copper **Issuer:** Tierra Caliente (Hot Country), Under General Morelos **Obv:** Bow, T.C., SUD **Rev:** Morelos monogram, value, date

Date	Mintage	Good	VG	F	VF	XF
1813	—	15.00	27.50	55.00	90.00	—

KM# 226.1 2 REALES
Struck Copper **Issuer:** SUD, Under General Morelos **Obv:** Bow, arrow/SUD **Rev:** Morelos monogram, .2.R., date

Date	Mintage	Good	VG	F	VF	XF
1811	—	14.00	27.50	60.00	110	—
1811 inverted 2	—	17.00	33.00	65.00	130	—
1812	—	2.75	4.00	7.00	13.00	—
1813	—	3.00	6.00	9.00	17.00	—
1814	—	15.00	30.75	70.00	130	—

KM# 226.1a 2 REALES
Struck Silver **Issuer:** SUD, Under General Morelos **Obv:** Bow, arrow/SUD **Rev:** Morelos monogram, .2.R., date

Date	Mintage	Good	VG	F	VF	XF
1812	—	195	325	550	825	—

KM# 229 2 REALES
Cast Silver **Issuer:** SUD, Under General Morelos **Obv:** Bow, arrow, SUD **Rev:** Morelos monogram, value, date in center with ornamentation around

Date	Mintage	Good	VG	F	VF	XF
1812 Filled in D in SUD	—	65.00	110	165	250	—

Note: Use caution as many silver specimens appear questionable and may be considered spurious

1812	—	65.00	110	165	250	—

KM# 245 2 REALES
Struck Copper **Issuer:** Tierra Caliente (Hot Country), Under General Morelos **Obv:** Bow, T.C., SUD **Rev:** Morelos monogram, value, date

Date	Mintage	Good	VG	F	VF	XF
1813	—	10.00	25.00	38.50	55.00	—

KM# 227 2 REALES
Struck Silver **Issuer:** SUD, Under General Morelos **Obv:** Bow, arrow **Obv. Legend:** SUD-OXA **Rev:** Morelos monogram, value, date

Date	Mintage	Good	VG	F	VF	XF
1813	—	65.00	110	220	325	—
1814	—	65.00	110	220	325	—

KM# 228 2 REALES
Struck Silver **Issuer:** SUD, Under General Morelos **Obv:** Bow, arrow **Obv. Legend:** SUD. OAXACA **Rev:** Morelos monogram, value, date

Date	Mintage	Good	VG	F	VF	XF
1814	—	65.00	110	220	350	—

KM# 226.2 2 REALES
Struck Silver **Issuer:** SUD, Under General Morelos **Obv:** Three large stars added **Rev:** Morelos monogram, .2.R., date

Date	Mintage	Good	VG	F	VF	XF
1814	—	11.00	22.50	44.00	65.00	—

KM# 246 2 REALES
Struck Copper **Issuer:** Tierra Caliente (Hot Country), Under General Morelos **Obv:** Bow, T.C., SUD **Rev:** Morelos monogram, value, date

Date	Mintage	Good	VG	F	VF	XF
1814	—	27.50	60.00	120	210	—

KM# 234 8 REALES
Copper **Issuer:** SUD, Under General Morelos **Obv:** Bow, arrow, SUD in floral ornamentation **Rev:** Morelos monogram, .8.R., date surrounded by ornate flowery fields

Date	Mintage	Good	VG	F	VF	XF
1811	—	90.00	150	180	270	—
1812	—	8.00	12.00	20.00	40.00	—
1813	—	8.00	12.00	20.00	40.00	—
1814	—	15.00	22.50	37.50	75.00	—

KM# 235 8 REALES
Cast Silver **Issuer:** SUD, Under General Morelos **Obv:** Bow, arrow, SUD in floral ornamentation **Rev:** Morelos monogram, value, date surrounded by ornate flowery fields

Date	Mintage	Good	VG	F	VF	XF
1811	—	—	—	—	—	—
1812	—	90.00	150	240	425	—
1813	—	70.00	120	210	350	—
1814	—	—	—	—	—	—

Note: Most silver specimens available in today's market are considered spurious

KM# 234a 8 REALES
Struck Silver **Issuer:** SUD, under General Morelos **Obv:**

Bow, arrow, SUD in floral ornamentation **Rev:** Morelos monogram, .8.R., date surrounded by ornate flowery fields

Date	Mintage	Good	VG	F	VF	XF
1811	—	—	—	2,500	4,000	—
1812	—	—	—	1,200	2,000	—

KM# 233.5a 8 REALES
Silver **Issuer:** SUD, Under General Morelos **Obv:** 8 dots below bow, SUD, plain fields **Rev:** Morelos monogram, 8.R., date

Date	Mintage	Good	VG	F	VF	XF
1812	—	—	—	1,200	2,000	—

KM# 236 8 REALES
0.9030 Struck Silver **Issuer:** SUD, Under General Morelos **Obv:** M monogram **Obv. Legend:** PROV • D • OAXACA **Rev:** Lion shield with or without bow above

Date	Mintage	Good	VG	F	VF	XF
1812 Rare	—	—	—	—	—	—

KM# 233.1 8 REALES
Copper **Issuer:** SUD, Under General Morelos **Obv:** Bow, arrow, SUD **Rev:** Morelos monogram, 8.R., date, plain fields

Date	Mintage	Good	VG	F	VF	XF
1812	—	22.50	45.00	90.00	135	—

KM# 233.1a 8 REALES
Struck Silver **Issuer:** SUD, Under General Morelos **Obv:** Bow, arrow, SUD **Rev:** Morelos monogram, 8.R., date, plain fields

Date	Mintage	Good	VG	F	VF	XF
1812	—	120	180	300	550	—

KM# 233.2   8 REALES
Copper   **Issuer:** SUD, Under General Morelos **Obv:** Bow,
arrow, SUD **Rev:** Morelos monogram, 8 R, date, plain fields

Date	Mintage	Good	VG	F	VF	XF
1812	—	12.00	16.00	25.00	30.00	—
1813	—	12.00	16.00	25.00	30.00	—
1814	—	20.00	25.00	30.00	40.00	—

Note: Similar to KM#233.4 but lines below bow slant left

KM# 242   8 REALES
Copper   **Issuer:** Huautla, Under General Morelos **Obv:**
Legend around bow, arrow/SUD **Obv. Legend:** MONEDA
PROVI • CIONAL PS • ES • **Rev. Legend:** FABRICADO EN
HUAUTLA

Date	Mintage	Good	VG	F	VF	XF
1812	—	1,000	1,500	2,000	—	—

KM# 248   8 REALES
Struck Copper   **Issuer:** Tierra Caliente (Hot Country), Under
General Morelos **Obv:** Bow, T.C., SUD **Rev:** Morelos
monogram, value, date

Date	Mintage	Good	VG	F	VF	XF
1813	—	14.00	30.00	60.00	115	—

KM# 249   8 REALES
Cast Silver   **Issuer:** Tierra Caliente (Hot Country), Under
General Morelos **Obv:** Bow, T.C., SUD **Rev:** Morelos
monogram, value, date

Date	Mintage	Good	VG	F	VF	XF
1813	—	—	—	—	—	—

Note: Use caution as many silver specimens appear questionable and may be considered spurious

KM# 233.2a   8 REALES
Silver   **Issuer:** SUD, Under General Morelos **Obv:** bow,
arrow, SUD **Rev:** Morelos monogram, 8R, date, plain fields

Date	Mintage	Good	VG	F	VF	XF
1813	—	—	—	1,200	2,000	—

KM# 233.3   8 REALES
Struck Copper   **Issuer:** SUD, Under General Morelos **Obv:**
Bow, arrow, SUD, with left slant lines below bow **Rev:** Morelos
monogram, 8.R., date, plain fields

Date	Mintage	Good	VG	F	VF	XF
1813	—	15.00	27.50	45.00	75.00	—

KM# 233.4   8 REALES
Struck Copper   **Issuer:** SUD, Under General Morelos **Obv:**
Bow, arrow, SUD, with right slant lines below bow **Rev:**
Morelos monogram, 8.R., date, plain fields

Date	Mintage	Good	VG	F	VF	XF
1813	—	15.00	27.50	45.00	75.00	—

KM# 237   8 REALES
0.9250 Silver   **Issuer:** SUD, Under General Morelos **Obv:** M
monogram, without legend **Rev:** Lion shield with or without
bow above

Date	Mintage	Good	VG	F	VF	XF
1813 Rare	—	—	—	—	—	—

KM# 238   8 REALES
0.9030 Struck Silver   **Issuer:** SUD, Under General Morelos
Obv: Bow/M/SUD **Rev:** PROV. DE. ... arms

Date	Mintage	Good	VG	F	VF	XF
1813 Rare	—	—	—	—	—	—

KM# 239   8 REALES
Cast Silver   **Issuer:** SUD, Under General Morelos **Obv:** Bow,
arrow **Obv. Legend:** SUD-OXA **Rev:** Morelos monogram

Date	Mintage	Good	VG	F	VF	XF
1814 Rare	—	—	—	—	—	—

KM# 240 8 REALES
Copper **Issuer:** SUD, Under General Morelos **Obv:** Bow,
arrow **Obv. Legend:** SUD-OXA **Rev:** Morelos monogram,
8.R., date

Date	Mintage	Good	VG	F	VF	XF
1814	—	42.00	85.00	180	300	—

KM# 241 8 REALES
Copper **Issuer:** SUD, Under General Morelos **Obv:** Bow,
arrow **Obv. Legend:** SUD-OAXACA **Rev:** Morelos
monogram, 8.R., date

Date	Mintage	Good	VG	F	VF	XF
1814	—	100	200	350	550	—

PUEBLA

INSURGENT COINAGE

KM# 250 1/2 REAL
Copper **Issuer:** Zacatlan, struck by General Osorno **Obv:**
Osorno monogram, ZACATLAN, date **Rev:** Crossed arrows,
wreath, value

Date	Mintage	Good	VG	F	VF	XF
1813 Rare	—	—	—	—	—	—

KM# 251 REAL
Copper **Issuer:** Zacatlan, struck by General Osorno **Obv:**
Osorno monogram, ZACATLAN, date **Rev:** Crossed arrows,
wreath, value

Date	Mintage	Good	VG	F	VF	XF
1813	—	125	190	280	575	—

KM# 252 2 REALES
Copper **Issuer:** Zacatlan, struck by General Osorno **Obv:**

Osorno monogram, ZACATLAN, date **Rev:** Crossed arrows,
wreath, value

Date	Mintage	Good	VG	F	VF	XF
1813	—	155	220	350	625	—

REAL DEL CATORCE

(City in San Luis Potosi)

Real del Catorce is an important mining center in the
Province of San Luis Potosi. In 1811 an 8 Reales coin was
issued under very primitive conditions while the city was still in
Royalist hands. Few survive.

ROYALIST COINAGE

KM# 169 8 REALES
0.9030 Silver **Ruler:** Ferdinand VII **Obv. Legend:** EL R • D
• CATORC • POR FERNA • VII **Rev. Legend:** MONEDA •
PROVISIONAL • VALE • 8R

Date	Mintage	VG	F	VF	XF	Unc
1811	—	7,000	15,000	35,000	65,000	—

Note: Spink America Gerber Sale 6-96 VF or XF realized
$63,800

SAN FERNANDO DE BEXAR

TOKEN COINAGE

KM# Tn1 1/2 REAL (Jola)
Copper **Ruler:** Ferdinand VII **Note:** Prev. KM#170.

Date	Mintage	Good	VG	F	VF	XF
1818	8,000	—	—	—	25,000	30,000

KM# Tn2 1/2 REAL (Jola)
Copper **Ruler:** Ferdinand VII **Note:** Prev. KM#171.

Date	Mintage	Good	VG	F	VF	XF
1818	Inc. above	—	—	—	22,500	27,500

SAN LUIS POTOSI

Sierra de Pinos

ROYALIST COINAGE

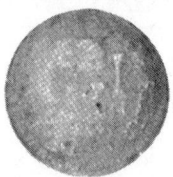 

KM# A172   1/4 REAL
Copper   **Ruler:** Ferdinand VII **Issuer:** Sierra de Pinos, Villa

Date	Mintage	Good	VG	F	VF	XF
1814	—	100	150	250	400	—

KM# A172a   1/4 REAL
Silver   **Ruler:** Ferdinand VII

Date	Mintage	Good	VG	F	VF	XF
1814 Rare	—	—	—	—	—	—

SOMBRERETE

(Under Royalist Vargas)

The Sombrerete Mint opened on October 8, 1810 in an area that boasted some of the richest mines in Mexico. The mint operated only until July 16, 1811, only to reopen in 1812 and finally close for good at the end of the year. Mines Administrator Fernando Vargas, was also in charge of the coining, all coins bear his name.

ROYALIST COINAGE

KM# 172   1/2 REAL
0.9030 Silver   **Ruler:** Ferdinand VII **Obv:** Legend around crowned globes **Obv. Legend:** FERDIN • VII • SOMBRERETE... **Rev:** Legend above lys in oval, sprays, date below **Rev. Legend:** VARGAS

Date	Mintage	Good	VG	F	VF	XF
1811	—	45.00	70.00	150	275	—
1812	—	50.00	90.00	175	300	—

KM# 173   REAL
0.9030 Silver   **Ruler:** Ferdinand VII **Obv:** Legend around crowned globes **Obv. Legend:** FERDIN • VII • SOMBRERETE... **Rev:** Legend above lys in oval with denomination flanking, sprays, date below **Rev. Legend:** VARGAS

Date	Mintage	Good	VG	F	VF	XF
1811	—	45.00	70.00	150	275	—

Note: For 1811, denomination reads as '1R' or 'R1'

1812	—	50.00	90.00	175	300	—

KM# 175   4 REALES
0.9030 Silver   **Ruler:** Ferdinand VII **Obv:** Crowned Royal arms **Obv. Legend:** R • CAXA • DE • SOMBRERETE **Rev:** Large legend **Rev. Legend:** VARGAS / 1812 **Note:** Prev. KM#172.

Date	Mintage	Good	VG	F	VF	XF
1812	—	50.00	100	200	500	—

KM# 176   8 REALES
0.9030 Silver   **Ruler:** Ferdinand VII **Countermark:** VARGAS, date, S **Obv:** Royal arms **Obv. Legend:** R • CAXA • DE SOMBRERETE **Rev:** Several countermarks between crowned pillars

Date	Mintage	Good	VG	F	VF	XF
1810	—	1,000	1,750	2,750	4,500	8,750
1811	—	225	325	450	600	—

KM# 177   8 REALES
0.9030 Silver   **Ruler:** Ferdinand VII **Obv:** Crowned Royal arms **Obv. Legend:** R • CAXA • DE SOMBRETE **Rev. Legend:** VARGAS / date /3, S between crowned pillars

Date	Mintage	Good	VG	F	VF	XF
1811	—	140	200	400	800	—
1812	—	125	185	375	775	—

VALLADOLID MICHOACAN

ROYALIST COINAGE

KM# 178   8 REALES
0.9030 Silver   **Ruler:** Ferdinand VII **Obv:** Royal arms in wreath, value at sides **Rev. Legend:** PROVISIONAL / DE VALLADOLID / 1813

Date	Mintage	Good	VG	F	VF	XF
1813 Rare	—	—	—	—	—	—

KM# 179   8 REALES
0.9030 Silver   **Ruler:** Ferdinand VII **Obv:** Draped laureate bust right **Obv. Legend:** FERDIN • VII •... **Rev:** Crowned shield flanked by pillars, P. D. V. in legend **Rev. Legend:** REX • P • D • V...

Date	Mintage	Good	VG	F	VF	XF
1813 Rare	—	—	—	—	—	—

Note: Spink America Gerber sale 6-96 good realized $23,100

VERACRUZ

In Zongolica, in the province of Veracruz, 2 priests and a lawyer decided to raise an army to fight for independence. Due to isolation from other Insurgent forces, they decided to make their own coins. Records show that they intended to mint coins of 1/2, 1, 2, 4, and 8 Reales, but specimens are extant of only the three higher denominations.

INSURGENT COINAGE

KM# 253   2 REALES
0.9030 Silver   **Issuer:** Zongolica **Obv:** Bow and arrow **Obv. Legend:** VIVA FERNANDO VII Y AMERICA **Rev:** Value, crossed palm branch, sword, date **Rev. Legend:** ZONGOLICA

Date	Mintage	Good	VG	F	VF	XF
1812	—	100	200	350	650	—

KM# 255   8 REALES
0.9030 Silver   **Issuer:** Zongolica **Obv:** Bow and arrow **Obv. Legend:** VIVA FERNANDO VII Y AMERICA **Rev:** Value, crossed palm branch, sword, date **Rev. Legend:** ZONGOLICA **Note:** Similar to 2 Reales, KM#253.

Date	Mintage	Good	VG	F	VF	XF
1812 Rare	—	—	—	—	—	—

Note: Spink America Gerber sale 6-96 VF to XF realized $57,200

INSURGENT COUNTERMARKED COINAGE

Congress of Chilpanzingo

Type A: Hand holding bow and arrow between quiver with arrows, sword and bow.

Type B: Crowned eagle on bridge.

KM# 256.1   1/2 REAL
Silver   **Issuer:** Congress of Chilpanzingo **Countermark:** Type A hand holding bow and arrow between quiver with arrows, sword and bow **Note:** Countermark on cast Mexico City KM#72.

CM Date	Host Date	Good	VG	F	VF	XF
ND	1812	42.50	70.00	90.00	140	—

WAR OF INDEPENDENCE

KM# 256.2　1/2 REAL
Silver　**Issuer:** Congress of Chilpanzingo **Countermark:** Type A hand holding bow and arrow between quiver with arrows, sword and bow **Note:** Countermark on Zacatecas KM#181.

CM Date	Host Date	Good	VG	F	VF	XF
ND	1811	50.00	75.00	100	150	—

KM# A257　REAL
Cast Silver **Issuer:** Congress of Chilpanzingo **Countermark:** Type A hand holding bow and arrow between quiver with arrows, sword and bow **Note:** Countermark on cast Mexico City KM#81.

CM Date	Host Date	Good	VG	F	VF	XF
ND	1803	18.50	30.00	50.00	85.00	—

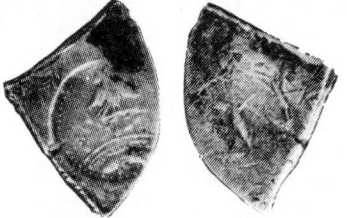

KM# 257.1　2 REALES
Silver　**Issuer:** Congress of Chilpanzingo **Countermark:** Type B crowned eagle on bridge **Note:** Countermark on 1/4 cut of 8 Reales.

CM Date	Host Date	Good	VG	F	VF	XF
	ND Unique	—	—	—	—	—

KM# 257.2　2 REALES
Silver　**Issuer:** Congress of Chilpanzingo **Countermark:** Type B crowned eagle on bridge **Note:** Countermark on Zacatecas KM#186.

CM Date	Host Date	Good	VG	F	VF	XF
ND	1811 Unique	—	—	—	—	—

KM# 258.1　8 REALES
Silver　**Issuer:** Congress of Chilpanzingo **Countermark:**

Type A hand holding bow and arrow between quiver with arrows, sword and bow **Note:** Countermark on cast Mexico City KM#109.

CM Date	Host Date	Good	VG	F	VF	XF
ND	1805	45.00	65.00	85.00	150	—

Note: A countermark appears on coins dated 1805 TH

KM# 258.2　8 REALES
Silver　**Issuer:** Congress of Chilpanzingo **Countermark:** Type A hand holding bow and arrow between quiver with arrows, sword and bow **Note:** Countermark on cast Mexico City KM#110.

CM Date	Host Date	Good	VG	F	VF	XF
ND	1810 HJ	50.00	75.00	100	175	—

KM# 258.3　8 REALES
Silver　**Issuer:** Congress of Chilpanzingo **Countermark:** Type A hand holding bow and arrow between quiver with arrows, sword and bow **Note:** Countermark on cast Mexico City KM#111.

CM Date	Host Date	Good	VG	F	VF	XF
ND	1811 HJ	45.00	65.00	85.00	150	—
ND	1812 HJ	100	125	175	275	—

KM# 259.1　8 REALES
Silver　**Issuer:** Congress of Chilpanzingo **Countermark:** Type B crowned eagle on bridge **Note:** Countermark on Chihuahua KM#111.1.

CM Date	Host Date	Good	VG	F	VF	XF
ND	1816 RP	200	250	300	400	—

KM# 259.2　8 REALES
Silver　**Issuer:** Congress of Chilpanzingo **Countermark:** Type B crowned eagle on bridge **Note:** Countermark on cast Mexico City KM#111.

CM Date	Host Date	Good	VG	F	VF	XF
ND	1811 HJ	130	150	175	250	—

KM# 259.3　8 REALES
Silver　**Issuer:** Congress of Chilpanzingo **Countermark:**

Type B crowned eagle on bridge **Note:** Countermark on Valladolid KM#178.

CM Date	Host Date	Good	VG	F	VF	XF
ND	1813	1,000	2,000	3,000	5,000	—

KM# 259.4 8 REALES
Silver **Issuer:** Congress of Chilpanzingo **Countermark:** Type B crowned eagle on bridge **Note:** Countermark on Zacatecas KM#190.

CM Date	Host Date	Good	VG	F	VF	XF
ND	1810	400	500	600	775	—

Don Jose Maria De Linares

KM# 263.1 8 REALES
Silver **Issuer:** Don Jose Maria De Linares **Countermark:** LINA/RES* **Note:** Countermark on Mexico City KM#110.

CM Date	Host Date	Good	VG	F	VF	XF
ND	1808 TH	250	300	375	550	—

KM# 263.2 8 REALES
Silver **Issuer:** Don Jose Maria De Linares **Countermark:** LINA/RES * **Note:** Countermark on Zacatecas KM#190.

CM Date	Host Date	Good	VG	F	VF	XF
ND	1811	300	375	450	650	—

KM# 263.3 8 REALES
Silver **Issuer:** Don Jose Maria De Linares **Countermark:** LINA/RES* **Note:** Countermark on Zacatecas KM#191.

CM Date	Host Date	Good	VG	F	VF	XF
ND	1812	250	300	375	550	—

General Vicente Guerrero

The countermark of an eagle facing left within a pearled oval has been attributed by some authors as that of General Vicente Guerrero, a leader of the insurgents in the south, 1816-1821.

KM# 276 1/2 REAL
Silver **Issuer:** General Vicente Guerrero **Countermark:** Eagle **Note:** Countermark on Mexico City KM#72.

CM Date	Host Date	Good	VG	F	VF	XF
ND	ND	40.00	60.00	80.00	175	—

KM# 277 REAL
Silver **Issuer:** General Vicente Guerrero **Countermark:** Eagle **Note:** Countermark on Mexico City KM#78.

CM Date	Host Date	Good	VG	F	VF	XF
ND	1772 FM	35.00	50.00	75.00	165	—

KM# 278.1 2 REALES
Silver **Issuer:** General Vicente Guerrero **Countermark:** Eagle **Note:** Countermark on Mexico City KM#88.

CM Date	Host Date	Good	VG	F	VF	XF
ND	1784 FM	40.00	60.00	100	225	—
ND	1798	40.00	60.00	100	225	—

KM# 278.2 2 REALES
Silver **Issuer:** General Vicente Guerrero **Countermark:** Eagle **Note:** Countermark on Mexico KM#91.

CM Date	Host Date	Good	VG	F	VF	XF
ND	1807 PJ	30.00	50.00	80.00	200	—

KM# 279 8 REALES
Silver **Issuer:** General Vicente Guerrero **Countermark:** Eagle **Note:** Countermark on Zacatecas KM#191.

CM Date	Host Date	Good	VG	F	VF	XF
ND	1811	100	150	200	350	—

Ensaie

KM# 260.3 8 REALES
Silver **Issuer:** Ensaie **Countermark:** Eagle over ENSAIE, crude sling below **Note:** Countermark on Zacatecas KM#190.

CM Date	Host Date	Good	VG	F	VF	XF
ND	1810	—	—	—	—	—
ND	1811	100	150	200	325	—

KM# 260.4 8 REALES
Silver **Issuer:** Ensaie **Countermark:** Eagle over ENSAIE,
crude sling below **Note:** Countermark on Zacatecas KM#191.

CM Date	Host Date	Good	VG	F	VF	XF
ND	1810	500	700	900	1,250	—
ND	1811	250	300	375	550	—
ND	1812	200	250	285	450	—

KM# 260.1 8 REALES
Silver **Issuer:** Ensaie **Countermark:** Eagle over ENSAIE,
crude sling below **Note:** Countermark on Mexico City
KM#110.

CM Date	Host Date	Good	VG	F	VF	XF
ND	1811 HJ	150	200	275	375	—

KM# 260.2 8 REALES
Silver **Issuer:** Ensaie **Countermark:** Eagle over ENSAIE,
crude sling below **Note:** Countermark on Zacatecas KM#189.

CM Date	Host Date	Good	VG	F	VF	XF
ND	1811	200	400	600	850	—

Jose Maria Liceaga

J.M.L. with banner on cross,
crossed olive branches.

(J.M.L./V., D.s, S.M., S.Y.S.L., Ve,
A.P., s.r.a., Sea, P.G., S., S.M., El)

KM# A260 1/2 REAL
Silver **Issuer:** Jose Maria Liceaga **Countermark:** JML/SM
with banner on cross, crossed olive branches **Note:**
Countermark on cast Mexico City 1/2 Real.

CM Date	Host Date	Good	VG	F	VF	XF
ND	ND	100	150	200	300	—

KM# 261.6 2 REALES
Silver **Issuer:** Jose Maria Liceaga **Countermark:** J.M.L./V.
with banner on cross, crossed olive branches **Note:**
Countermark on Zacatecas KM#187.

CM Date	Host Date	Good	VG	F	VF	XF
ND	1811	200	225	250	325	—

KM# 261.7 2 REALES
Silver **Issuer:** Jose Maria Liceaga **Countermark:** J.M.L./DS
with banner on cross, crossed olive branches **Note:**
Countermark on Zacatecas KM#187.

CM Date	Host Date	Good	VG	F	VF	XF
ND	1811	200	235	275	350	—

KM# 261.8 2 REALES
Silver **Issuer:** Jose Maria Liceaga **Countermark:** J.M.L./
S.M. with banner on cross, crossed olive branches **Note:**
Countermark on Zacatecas KM#187.

CM Date	Host Date	Good	VG	F	VF	XF
ND	1811	200	235	275	350	—

KM# 261.9 2 REALES
Silver **Issuer:** Jose Maria Liceaga **Countermark:** J.M.L./
S.Y. with banner on cross, crossed olive branches **Note:**
Countermark on Zacatecas KM#187.

CM Date	Host Date	Good	VG	F	VF	XF
ND	1811	200	235	275	350	—

KM# 261.1 2 REALES
Silver **Issuer:** Jose Maria Liceaga **Countermark:** J.M.L./Ve
with banner on cross, crossed olive branches **Note:**
Countermark on 1/4 cut of 8 Reales.

CM Date	Host Date	Good	VG	F	VF	XF
ND	ND	175	225	325	—	—

KM# 261.2 2 REALES
Silver **Issuer:** Jose Maria Liceaga **Countermark:** J.M.L./V
with banner on cross, crossed olive branchs **Note:**
Countermark on Zacatecas KM#186.

CM Date	Host Date	Good	VG	F	VF	XF
ND	1811	200	225	250	325	—

KM# 261.3 2 REALES
Silver **Issuer:** Jose Maria Liceaga **Countermark:** J.M.L./DS
with banner on cross, crossed olive branches **Note:**
Countermark on Zacatecas KM#186.

CM Date	Host Date	Good	VG	F	VF	XF
ND	1811	200	235	275	350	—

KM# 261.4 2 REALES
Silver **Issuer:** Jose Maria Liceaga **Countermark:** J.M.L./
S.M. with banner on cross, crossed olive branches **Note:**
Countermark on Zacatecas KM#186.

CM Date	Host Date	Good	VG	F	VF	XF
ND	1811	200	235	275	350	—

KM# 261.5 2 REALES
Silver **Issuer:** Jose Maria Liceaga **Countermark:** J.M.L./
S.Y. with banner on cross, crossed olive branches **Note:**
Countermark on Zacatecas KM#186.

CM Date	Host Date	Good	VG	F	VF	XF
ND	1811	200	235	275	350	—

KM# 262.1 8 REALES
Silver **Issuer:** Jose Maria Liceaga **Countermark:** J.M.L./ D.S. with banner on cross, crossed olive branches **Note:** Countermark on Zacatecas KM#190.

CM Date	Host Date	Good	VG	F	VF	XF
ND	1811	250	325	425	625	—

KM# 262.4 8 REALES
Silver **Issuer:** Jose Maria Liceaga **Countermark:** J.M.L./ S.F. with banner on cross, crossed olive branches **Note:** Countermark on Zacatecas KM#190.

CM Date	Host Date	Good	VG	F	VF	XF
ND	1811	200	275	375	575	—

KM# 262.2 8 REALES
Silver **Issuer:** Jose Maria Liceaga **Countermark:** J.M.L./E with banner on cross, crossed olive branches **Note:** Countermark on Zacatecas KM#190.

CM Date	Host Date	Good	VG	F	VF	XF
ND	1811	225	300	400	600	—

KM# 262.3 8 REALES
Silver **Issuer:** Jose Maria Liceaga **Countermark:** J.M.L./ P.G. with banner on cross, crossed olive branches **Note:** Countermark on Durango KM#111.2.

CM Date	Host Date	Good	VG	F	VF	XF
ND	1813 RM	200	275	375	575	—

KM# 262.5 8 REALES
Silver **Issuer:** Jose Maria Liceaga **Countermark:** J.M.L./ S.M. with banner on cross, crossed olive branches **Note:** Countermark on Zacatecas KM#190.

CM Date	Host Date	Good	VG	F	VF	XF
ND	1811	200	275	375	550	—

KM# 262.10 8 REALES
Silver **Issuer:** Jose Maria Liceaga, J.M.L. with banner on cross, crossed olive branches. (J.M.L./V. D.s., S.M., S.Y.S.L.,Ve, A.P., s.r.a., Sea, P.G., S., S.M., E.) **Countermark:** J.M.L./S.M. **Note:** Countermark on Zacatecas KM#190.

CM Date	Host Date	Good	VG	F	VF	XF
ND	1811	—	—	—	—	—

KM# 262.6 8 REALES
Silver **Issuer:** Jose Maria Liceaga **Countermark:** J.M.L./ V.E. with banner on cross, cross olive branches **Note:** Countermark on Zacatecas KM#190.

CM Date	Host Date	Good	VG	F	VF	XF
ND	1811	200	275	375	550	—

KM# 262.12 8 REALES
Silver **Issuer:** Jose Maria Liceaga, Banner on cross, crossed olive branches **Countermark:** J.M.L. / P.G. **Note:** Countermark on Guanajuato 8 Reales, KM#111.4.

CM Date	Host Date	Good	VG	F	VF	XF
ND	ND1813	150	250	450	—	—

KM# 262.7 8 REALES
Silver **Issuer:** Jose Maria Liceaga, J.M.L with banner on cross, crossed olive branches. (J.M.L./V., D,s, S.M., S.Y.S.L., Ve, A.P., s.r.a., Sea, P.G., S., S.M., E.) **Countermark:** J.M.L./ D.S. **Note:** Countermark on Zacatecas KM#190.

CM Date	Host Date	Good	VG	F	VF	XF
ND	1811	—	—	—	—	—

KM# 262.9 8 REALES
Silver **Issuer:** Jose Maria Liceaga, J.M.L. with banner on cross, crossed olive branches. (J.M.L./V. D.s., S.M., S.Y.S.L.,Ve, A.P., s.r.a., Sea, P.G., S., S.M., E.) **Countermark:** J.M.L./S.F. **Note:** Countermark on Zacatecas KM#190.

CM Date	Host Date	Good	VG	F	VF	XF
ND	1811	—	—	—	—	—

KM# 262.11 8 REALES
Silver **Issuer:** Jose Maria Liceaga, J.M.L. with banner on cross, crossed olive branches. (J.M.L./V. D.s., S.M., S.Y.S.L.,Ve, A.P., s.r.a., Sea, P.G., S., S.M., E.) **Countermark:** J.M.L./V.E. **Note:** Countermark on Zacatecas KM#190.

CM Date	Host Date	Good	VG	F	VF	XF
ND	1811	—	—	—	—	—

KM# 262.8　8 REALES
Silver　**Issuer:** Jose Maria Liceaga
, J.M.L. with banner on cross, crossed olive branches. (J.M.L./
V. D.s., S.M., S.Y.S.L., Ve, A.P., s.r.a., Sea, P.G., S., S.M.,
E.) **Countermark:** J.M.L./E **Note:** Countermark on Zacatecas
KM#190.

CM Date	Host Date	Good	VG	F	VF	XF
ND	1811	—	—	—	—	—

L.V.S. -
Labor Vincit Semper

Some authorities believe L.V.S. is for
La Villa de Sombrerete.

KM# 264.1　8 REALES
Cast Silver　**Issuer:** Labor Vincit Semper, Some authorities
believe L.V.S. is for "La Villa de Sombrerete" **Countermark:**
L.V.S. **Note:** Countermark on Chihuahua KM#123.

CM Date	Host Date	Good	VG	F	VF	XF
ND	1811 RP	275	350	450	600	—
ND	1812 RP	200	250	300	400	—

KM# 264.2　8 REALES
Silver　**Issuer:** Labor Vincit Semper, Some authorities believe
L.V.S. is for "La Villa de Sombrerete" **Countermark:** L.V.S.
Note: Countermark on Chihuahua KM#111.1 overstruck on
KM#123.

CM Date	Host Date	Good	VG	F	VF	XF
ND	1816 RP	250	300	325	425	—
ND	1817 RP	250	300	325	425	—
ND	1818 RP	250	300	325	425	—
ND	1819 RP	400	450	500	700	—
ND	1820 RP	450	500	550	350	—

KM# 264.3　8 REALES
Silver　**Issuer:** Labor Vincit Semper, Some authorities believe
L.V.S. is for "La Villa de Sombrerete" **Countermark:** L.V.S.
Note: Countermark on Guadalajara KM#111.3.

CM Date	Host Date	Good	VG	F	VF	XF
ND	1817	185	220	250	350	—

KM# 264.4　8 REALES
Silver　**Issuer:** Labor Vincit Semper, Some authorities believe
L.V.S. is for "La Villa de Sombrerete" **Countermark:** L.V.S.
Note: Countermark on Nueva Vizcaya KM#165.

CM Date	Host Date	Good	VG	F	VF	XF
ND	1811 RM	1,150	3,150	5,250	8,250	—

KM# 264.5　8 REALES
Silver　**Issuer:** Labor Vincit Semper, Some authorities believe
L.V.S. is for "La Villa de Sombrerete" **Countermark:** L.V.S.
Note: Countermark on Sombrerete KM#177.

CM Date	Host Date	Good	VG	F	VF	XF
ND	1811	300	350	450	650	—
ND	1812	300	350	450	650	—

KM# 264.6　8 REALES
Silver　**Issuer:** Labor Vincit Semper, Some authorities believe
L.V.S. is for "La Villa de Sombrerete" **Countermark:** L.V.S.
Note: Countermark on Zacatecas KM#190.

CM Date	Host Date	Good	VG	F	VF	XF
ND	1811	350	400	450	650	—

KM# 264.7　8 REALES
Silver　**Issuer:** Labor Vincit Semper, Some authorities believe
L.V.S. is for "La Villa de Sombrerete" **Countermark:** L.V.S.
Note: Countermark on Zacatecas KM#192.

CM Date	Host Date	Good	VG	F	VF	XF
ND	1813	350	400	450	650	—

Morelos

Morelos monogram

Type A: Stars above and
below monogram in circle.

Type B: Dots above and below monogram in oval.

Type C: Monogram in rectangle.

Note: Many specimens of Type C available in
todays market are considered spurious.

KM# A265　2 REALES
Copper　**Issuer:** Morelos **Countermark:** Type A stars above
and below monogram in circle **Note:** Countermark on Oaxaca
Sud, KM#226.1.

CM Date	Host Date	Good	VG	F	VF	XF
ND	1812	—	—	—	—	—

KM# 265.1   8 REALES
Silver **Issuer:** Morelos **Countermark:** Type A star above
and below monogram in circle **Note:** Countermark on Mexico
City KM#109.

CM Date	Host Date	Good	VG	F	VF	XF
ND	1797 FM	45.00	50.00	60.00	95.00	—
ND	1798 FM	45.00	50.00	60.00	95.00	—
ND	1800 FM	45.00	50.00	60.00	95.00	—
ND	1807 TH	45.00	50.00	60.00	95.00	—

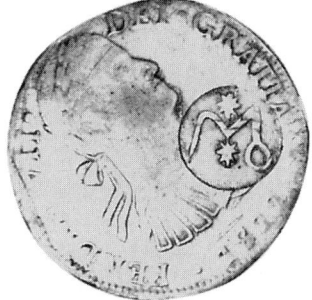

KM# 265.2   8 REALES
Silver **Issuer:** Morelos **Countermark:** Type A stars above
and below monogram in circle **Note:** Countermark on Mexico
City KM#110.

CM Date	Host Date	Good	VG	F	VF	XF
ND	1809 TH	55.00	75.00	120	200	—
ND	1811 HJ	55.00	75.00	120	200	—

KM# 265.3   8 REALES
Silver **Issuer:** Morelos **Countermark:** Type A stars above
and below monogram in circle **Note:** Countermark on Mexico
City KM#111.

CM Date	Host Date	Good	VG	F	VF	XF
ND	1812 JJ	50.00	60.00	75.00	125	—

KM# 265.5   8 REALES
Cast Silver **Issuer:** Morelos **Countermark:** Type A stars

above and below monogram in circle **Note:** Countermark on
Supreme National Congress KM#206.

CM Date	Host Date	Good	VG	F	VF	XF
ND	1811	200	250	375	600	—

KM# 266.1   8 REALES
Silver **Issuer:** Morelos **Countermark:** Type B dots above
and below monogram in oval **Note:** Countermark on
Guatamala 8 Reales, C#67.

CM Date	Host Date	Good	VG	F	VF	XF
ND	1810 M Rare	—	—	—	—	—

KM# 266.2   8 REALES
Silver **Issuer:** Morelos **Countermark:** Type B dots above
and below monogram in oval **Note:** Countermark on Mexico
City KM#110.

CM Date	Host Date	Good	VG	F	VF	XF
ND	1809 TH	45.00	55.00	65.00	100	—

KM# 267.1   8 REALES
Silver **Issuer:** Morelos **Countermark:** Type C monogram in
rectangle **Note:** Countermark on Zacatecas KM#189. Many
specimens of Type C available in today's market are
considered spurious.

CM Date	Host Date	Good	VG	F	VF	XF
ND	1811	300	350	450	750	—

KM# 265.4   8 REALES
Copper **Issuer:** Morelos **Countermark:** Type A stars above
and below monogram in circle **Note:** Countermark on Oaxaca
Sud KM#233.2.

CM Date	Host Date	Good	VG	F	VF	XF
ND	1812	19.00	27.50	37.50	60.00	—
ND	1813	19.00	27.50	37.50	60.00	—
ND	1814	19.00	27.50	37.50	60.00	—

KM# 265.6 8 REALES
Silver **Issuer:** Morelos **Countermark:** Type A stars above
and below monogram in circle **Note:** Countermark on
Zacatecas KM#190.

CM Date	Host Date	Good	VG	F	VF	XF
ND	1811	375	625	900	—	—

KM# 265.7 8 REALES
Silver **Issuer:** Morelos **Countermark:** Type A stars above
and below monogram in circle **Note:** Countermark on
Zacatecas KM#191.

CM Date	Host Date	Good	VG	F	VF	XF
ND	1811	200	250	375	600	—

KM# 267.2 8 REALES
Silver **Issuer:** Morelos **Countermark:** Type C: monogram
in rectangle **Note:** Countermark Type C on Zacatecas
KM#190. Many specimens of Type C available in today's
market are considered spurious.

CM Date	Host Date	Good	VG	F	VF	XF
ND	1811	300	350	450	750	—

Norte

Issued by the Supreme National Congress
and the Army of the North.

Countermark: Eagle on cactus;
star to left; NORTE below.

KM# 268 1/2 REAL
Silver **Issuer:** Supreme National Congress and the Army of
the North **Countermark:** Eagle on cactus; star to left; NORTE
below **Note:** Countermark on Zacatecas KM#180.

CM Date	Host Date	Good	VG	F	VF	XF
ND	1811	250	300	375	500	—

KM# 270.4 8 REALES
Silver **Issuer:** Supreme National Congress and the Army of
the North **Countermark:** Eagle on cactus; star to left; NORTE
below **Note:** Countermark on Zacatecas KM#191.

CM Date	Host Date	Good	VG	F	VF	XF
ND	1811	200	300	400	550	—
ND	1811	200	300	400	550	—
ND	1812	200	300	400	550	—

KM# 270.1 8 REALES
Silver **Issuer:** Supreme National Congress and the Army of
the North **Countermark:** Eagle on cactus; star to left; NORTE
below **Note:** Countermark on Chihuahua KM#111.1.

CM Date	Host Date	Good	VG	F	VF	XF
ND	1813 RP	250	350	450	550	—

KM# 270.2 8 REALES
Silver **Issuer:** Supreme National Congress and the Army of
the North **Countermark:** Eagle on cactus; star to left; NORTE
below **Note:** Countermark on Guanajuato KM#111.4.

CM Date	Host Date	Good	VG	F	VF	XF
ND	1813 JM	400	550	700	850	—

KM# 269 2 REALES
Silver **Issuer:** Supreme National Congress and the Army of
the North **Countermark:** Eagle on cactus; star to left; NORTE
below **Note:** Countermark on Zacatecas KM#187.

CM Date	Host Date	Good	VG	F	VF	XF
ND	1811	225	275	325	450	—

KM# A269 2 REALES
Silver **Issuer:** Supreme National Congress and the Army of
the North **Countermark:** Eagle on cactus; star to left; NORTE
below **Note:** Countermark on Zacatecas KM#188.

CM Date	Host Date	Good	VG	F	VF	XF
ND	1812	—	—	—	—	—

KM# B269 4 REALES
Silver **Issuer:** Supreme National Congress and the Army of
the North **Countermark:** Eagle on cactus; star to left; NORTE
below **Note:** Countermark on Sombrerete KM#175.

CM Date	Host Date	Good	VG	F	VF	XF
ND	1812	100	150	200	300	—

KM# 270.3 8 REALES
Silver **Issuer:** Supreme National Congress and the Army of

the North **Countermark:** Eagle on cactus; star to left; NORTE below **Note:** Countermark on Zacatecas KM#190.

CM Date	Host Date	Good	VG	F	VF	XF
ND	1811	300	400	500	675	—

Osorno

Countermark: Osorno monogram.
(Jose Francisco Osorno)

KM# 271.1   1/2 REAL
Silver **Issuer:** Jose Francisco Osorno **Countermark:** Osorno monogram **Note:** Countermark on Mexico City KM#72.

CM Date	Host Date	Good	VG	F	VF	XF
ND	1798 FM	65.00	100	150	225	—
ND	1802 FT	65.00	100	150	225	—
ND	1806	65.00	100	150	225	—

KM# 271.2   1/2 REAL
Silver **Issuer:** Jose Francisco Osorno **Countermark:** Osorno monogram **Note:** Countermark on Mexico City KM#73.

CM Date	Host Date	Good	VG	F	VF	XF
ND	1809 TH	65.00	100	150	225	—

KM# 272.1   REAL
Silver **Issuer:** Jose Francisco Osorno **Countermark:** Osorno monogram **Note:** Countermark on Mexico City KM#81.

CM Date	Host Date	Good	VG	F	VF	XF
ND	1803 FT	65.00	100	150	250	—

 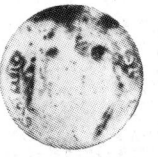

KM# 272.2   REAL
Silver **Issuer:** Jose Francisco Osorno **Countermark:** Osorno monogram **Note:** Countermark on Potosi KM#70.

CM Date	Host Date	Good	VG	F	VF	XF
ND	ND	75.00	115	175	275	—

KM# 272.3   REAL
Silver **Issuer:** Jose Francisco Osorno **Countermark:** Osorno monogram **Note:** Countermark on Guatemala KM#54.

CM Date	Host Date	Good	VG	F	VF	XF
ND	1804	75.00	115	175	275	—

KM# A272.1   2 REALES
Silver **Issuer:** Jose Francisco Osorno **Countermark:** Osorno monogram **Note:** Countermark on Mexico City KM#88.2.

CM Date	Host Date	Good	VG	F	VF	XF
ND	1788 FM	75.00	125	175	275	—

KM# A272.2   2 REALES
Silver **Issuer:** Jose Francisco Osorno **Countermark:** Osorno monogram **Note:** Countermark on Mexico City KM#91.

CM Date	Host Date	Good	VG	F	VF	XF
ND	1808 TH	75.00	125	175	275	—

KM# A272.3   2 REALES
Silver **Issuer:** Jose Francisco Osorno **Countermark:** Osorno monogram **Note:** Countermark on Mexico City KM#92.

CM Date	Host Date	Good	VG	F	VF	XF
ND	1809 TH	75.00	125	175	275	—

KM# A272.4   2 REALES
Silver **Issuer:** Jose Francisco Osorno **Countermark:** Osorno monogram **Note:** Countermark on Zacatlian KM#252.

CM Date	Host Date	Good	VG	F	VF	XF
ND	1813	150	200	350	500	—

KM# 273.1   4 REALES
Silver **Issuer:** Jose Francisco Osorno **Countermark:** Osorno monogram **Note:** Countermark on Mexico City KM#97.2.

CM Date	Host Date	Good	VG	F	VF	XF
ND	1782 FF	85.00	150	200	300	—

KM# 273.2   4 REALES
Silver **Issuer:** Jose Francisco Osorno **Countermark:** Osorno monogram **Note:** Countermark on Mexico City KM#100.

CM Date	Host Date	Good	VG	F	VF	XF
ND	1799 FM	85.00	150	200	300	—

KM# 274.1 8 REALES
Silver **Issuer:** Jose Francisco Osorno **Countermark:** Osorno monogram **Note:** Countermark on Lima 8 Reales, C#101.

CM Date	Host Date	Good	VG	F	VF	XF
ND	1811 JP	200	225	250	350	—

KM# 274.2 8 REALES
Silver **Issuer:** Jose Francisco Osorno **Countermark:** Osorno monogram **Note:** Countermark on Mexico City KM#110.

CM Date	Host Date	Good	VG	F	VF	XF
ND	1809 TH	125	150	225	375	—
ND	1810 HJ	125	150	225	375	—
ND	1811 HJ	125	150	225	375	—

VILLA / GRAN

(Julian Villagran)

KM# 298 2 REALES
Cast Silver , Julian Villagran **Countermark:** VILLA/GRAN **Note:** Countermark on cast Mexico City KM#91.

CM Date	Host Date	Good	VG	F	VF	XF
ND	1799 FM	150	200	250	350	—
ND	1802 FT	150	200	250	350	—

KM# 275 8 REALES
Cast Silver **Issuer:** Julian Villagran **Countermark:** VILLA/GRAN **Note:** Countermark on cast Mexico City KM#109.

CM Date	Host Date	Good	VG	F	VF	XF
ND	1796 FM	200	250	350	500	—
ND	1806 TH	200	250	350	500	—

ZMY

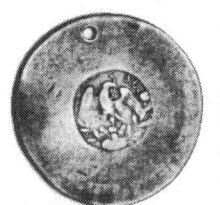

KM# 286 8 REALES
Silver **Issuer:** Unknown, presumed insurgent **Countermark:** ZMY **Note:** Countermark on Zacatecas KM#191.

CM Date	Host Date	Good	VG	F	VF	XF
ND	1812	100	150	200	350	—

MULTIPLE COUNTERMARKED

Many combinations of Royalist and Insurgent countermarks are usually found on the cast copies produced by Chihuahua and Mexico City and on the other crude provisional issues of this period. Struck Mexico City coins were used to make molds for casting necessity issues and countermarked afterwards to show issuing authority. Some were marked again by either both or separate opposing friendly forces to authorize circulation in their areas of occupation. Some countermarks are only obtainable with companion markings.

KM# 289 2 REALES
Silver **Issuer:** C.M.S. and S.C.M. **Countermark:** C.M.S. (Comandancia Militar Suriana) and eagle with S.C.M. (Soberano Congreso Mexicano) **Note:** Countermark on Mexico City KM#91.

CM Date	Host Date	Good	VG	F	VF	XF
ND	ND	—	—	—	—	—

KM# 295 2 REALES
Silver **Issuer:** Militar del Sur and Soberano Congreso Mexicano **Countermark:** M.d.S. and eagle with S.C.M **Note:** Countermark on Mexico City KM#91.

CM Date	Host Date	Good	VG	F	VF	XF
ND	ND	150	250	450	—	—

KM# 296 2 REALES
Silver **Issuer:** Jose Francisco Osorno and Julian Villagran
Countermark: Osorno monogram and VILLA/GRAN **Note:**
Countermark on cast Mexico City KM#110.

CM Date	Host Date	Good	VG	F	VF	XF
ND	1809 TH	—	—	—	—	—

KM# A286 2 REALES
Silver **Issuer:** Jose Maria Liceaga and VTIL **Countermark:**
J.M.L./D.S. AND VTIL **Note:** Countermark on Zacatecas
KM#186.

CM Date	Host Date	Good	VG	F	VF	XF
ND	1811	75.00	125	175	275	—

KM# B286 2 REALES
Silver **Issuer:** Jose Maria Liceaga and VTIL **Countermark:**
J.M.L./V.E. and VTIL **Note:** Countermark on Zacatecas
KM#186.

CM Date	Host Date	Good	VG	F	VF	XF
ND	1810	75.00	125	175	275	—
ND	1811	75.00	125	175	275	—

KM# 285.2 8 REALES
Silver **Issuer:** Chilpanzingo and Morelos **Countermark:**
Chilpanzingo Type A and Morelos monogram Type A **Note:**
Countermark on cast Mexico City KM#110.

CM Date	Host Date	Good	VG	F	VF	XF
ND	1810 HJ	35.00	45.00	60.00	150	—
ND	1811 HJ	35.00	45.00	60.00	150	—

KM# C286 8 REALES
Silver **Issuer:** Chilpanzingo and Morelos and LVS
Countermark: Chilpanzingo Type A, Morelos Type A and
LVS monogram on cast Mexico City KM#110

CM Date	Host Date	Good	VG	F	VF	XF
ND	1809 HJ	50.00	75.00	125	325	—

KM# A298 8 REALES
Silver **Issuer:** S.J.N.G. and VTIL **Countermark:** S.J.N.G
and VTIL on Zacatecas KM#191

CM Date	Host Date	Good	VG	F	VF	XF
ND	ND	35.00	50.00	75.00	200	—

KM# A297 8 REALES
Silver **Issuer:** Chilpanzingo and ENSAIE **Countermark:**
Chilpanzingo Type B and ENSAIE **Note:** Countermark on
Zacatecas KM#189.

CM Date	Host Date	Good	VG	F	VF	XF
ND	ND	175	250	350	—	—

KM# 297 8 REALES
Silver **Issuer:** Chilpanzingo and LVA **Countermark:**
Chilpanzingo Type A and LVA **Note:** Countermark on Mexico
City KM#109.

CM Date	Host Date	Good	VG	F	VF	XF
ND	1805 TH	45.00	75.00	145	300	—

KM# 281 8 REALES
Silver **Issuer:** Chilpanzingo and LVS **Countermark:**

Chilpanzingo Type A and script LVS **Note:** Countermark on
cast Mexico City KM#110.

CM Date	Host Date	Good	VG	F	VF	XF
ND	1809 HJ	45.00	65.00	135	300	—

KM# 288.2   8 REALES
Silver **Issuer:** Chilpanzingo and Suprema Junta Nacional
Gubernativa **Countermark:** Chilpanzingo Type B **Note:**
Countermark on Zacatecas KM#190. Prev. KM#288.

CM Date	Host Date	Good	VG	F	VF	XF
ND	1811	—	—	—	—	—

KM# 290.2   8 REALES
Silver **Issuer:** ENSAIE and VTIL **Countermark:** ENSAIE
and VTIL **Note:** Countermark on Zacatecas KM#190. Prev.
KM#290.

CM Date	Host Date	Good	VG	F	VF	XF
ND	1811	100	175	275	375	—

KM# 291   8 REALES
Silver **Issuer:** Jose Maria Liceaga and VTIL **Countermark:**
J.M.L./D.S. and VTIL **Note:** Countermark on Mexico City
KM#110.

CM Date	Host Date	Good	VG	F	VF	XF
ND	1810 HJ	85.00	150	250	450	—

KM# 282   8 REALES
Silver **Issuer:** La Comandancia Militar and Morelos
Countermark: L.C.M and Morelos monogram Type A **Note:**
Countermark on cast Mexico City KM#109.

CM Date	Host Date	Good	VG	F	VF	XF
ND	1792 FM	—	—	—	—	—

KM# 283   8 REALES
Silver **Issuer:** Morelos and Morelos **Countermark:** Morelos
Type A and C **Note:** Countermark on cast Mexico City
KM#109.

CM Date	Host Date	Good	VG	F	VF	XF
ND	1806 TH	—	—	—	—	—

KM# 284   8 REALES
Silver **Issuer:** Chilpanzingo and Morelos **Countermark:**
Chilpanzingo Type A and Morelos monogram Type A **Note:**
Countermark on cast Mexico City KM#109.

CM Date	Host Date	Good	VG	F	VF	XF
ND	1806 TH	35.00	50.00	100	225	—
ND	1807 TH	35.00	50.00	100	225	—

KM# 285.1   8 REALES
Silver **Issuer:** Chilpanzingo and Morelos **Countermark:**
Chilpanzingo Type A and Morelos monogram Type A **Note:**
Countermark on struck Mexico City KM#110.

CM Date	Host Date	Good	VG	F	VF	XF
ND	1809 TH	45.00	65.00	135	300	—

KM# 285.3   8 REALES
Silver **Issuer:** Chilpanzingo and Morelos **Countermark:**
Chilpanzingo Type A and Morelos monogram Type A **Note:**
Countermark on cast Mexico City KM#111.

CM Date	Host Date	Good	VG	F	VF	XF
ND	1811 HJ	75.00	120	175	350	—

KM# A290 8 REALES
Silver **Issuer:** ENSAIE and Jose Maria Liceaga
Countermark: ENSAIE and J.M.L. **Note:** Countermark on
Zacatecas KM#190.

CM Date	Host Date	Good	VG	F	VF	XF
ND	1811	100	175	275	475	—

KM# 294 8 REALES
Silver **Issuer:** L.V.A. and Morelos **Countermark:** Script LVA
and Morelos monogram Type A **Note:** Countermark on cast
Mexico City KM#110.

CM Date	Host Date	Good	VG	F	VF	XF
ND	ND HJ	45.00	75.00	135	300	—

KM# 288.1 8 REALES
Silver **Issuer:** Chilpanzingo and Suprema Junta Nacional
Gubernativa **Countermark:** Chilpanzingo Type B and
S.J.N.G **Note:** Countermark on Zacatecas KM#189.

CM Date	Host Date	Good	VG	F	VF	XF
ND	1811	—	—	—	—	—

KM# 290.1 8 REALES
Silver **Issuer:** ENSAIE and VTIL **Countermark:** ENSAIE
and VTIL **Note:** Countermark on Zacatecas KM#189.

CM Date	Host Date	Good	VG	F	VF	XF
ND	1811	100	175	275	475	—

KM# 280.1 8 REALES
Silver **Issuer:** Chilpanzingo and Crown and flag
Countermark: Chilpanzingo Type B and Crown and flag
Note: Countermark on Zacatecas KM#189.

CM Date	Host Date	Good	VG	F	VF	XF
ND	1811	—	—	—	—	—

KM# 280.2 8 REALES
Silver **Issuer:** Chilpanzingo and crown and flag
Countermark: Chilpanzingo Type B and crown and flag **Note:**
Countermark on Zacatecas KM#190.

CM Date	Host Date	Good	VG	F	VF	XF
ND	1811	—	—	—	—	—

KM# 287 8 REALES

Silver **Issuer:** Chilpanzingo - Provisional De Valladolid
Countermark: Chilpanzingo Type B and P.D.V **Note:**
Countermark on Valladolid KM#178.

CM Date	Host Date	Good	VG	F	VF	XF
ND	1813	—	—	—	—	—

ZACATECAS

The city of Zacatecas, in a rich mining region has provided silver for the world since mid-1500. On November 14,
1810 a mint began production for the Royalist cause. Zacatecas was the most prolific during the War of Independence.
Four of the 5 standard silver denominations were made here,
4 Reales were not. The first, a local type showing mountains
of silver on the coins were made only in 1810 and 1811. Some
1811 coins were made by the Insurgents who took the city on
April 15, 1811, later retaken by the Royalists on May 21, 1811.
Zacatecas struck the standard Ferdinand VII bust type until
1922.
Mint marks: Z, ZS, Zs.

ROYALIST COINAGE

KM# 180 1/2 REAL
0.9030 Silver **Ruler:** Ferdinand VII **Obv:** Crowned shield
flanked by pillars **Obv. Legend:** FERDIN • VII... **Rev:**
Mountain within beaded circle **Mint:** Zacatecas **Note:** Mint
marks: Z, ZS, Zs.

Date	Mintage	Good	VG	F	VF	XF
1810	—	75.00	125	200	400	—
1811	—	30.00	50.00	90.00	200	—

Note: Date aligned with legend

KM# 181 1/2 REAL
0.9030 Silver **Ruler:** Ferdinand VII **Obv:** Crowned shield
flanked by pillars **Rev:** Mountain within beaded circle **Rev.
Legend:** MONEDA PROVISIONAL DE ZACATECAS **Mint:**
Zacatecas **Note:** Mint marks: Z, ZS, Zs.

Date	Mintage	Good	VG	F	VF	XF
1811	—	30.00	50.00	90.00	200	—

KM# 182 1/2 REAL
0.9030 Silver **Ruler:** Ferdinand VII **Obv:** Provincial bust right
Obv. Legend: FERDIN • VII **Rev:** Crowned shield flanked by
pillars **Rev. Legend:** MONEDA PROVISIONAL DE
ZACATECAS **Mint:** Zacatecas **Note:** Mint marks: Z, ZS, Zs.

Date	Mintage	Good	VG	F	VF	XF
1811	—	30.00	40.00	65.00	140	—
1812	—	25.00	35.00	60.00	125	—

KM# 73.1 1/2 REAL
1.6900 g., 0.9030 Silver 0.0491 oz. ASW **Ruler:**
Ferdinand VII **Obv:** Armored laureate bust right **Obv.
Legend:** FERDIN • VII... **Rev:** Crowned shield flanked by
pillars **Rev. Legend:** IND... **Mint:** Zacatecas **Note:** Mint
marks: Z, ZS, Zs.

Date	Mintage	Good	VG	F	VF	XF
1813 AG	—	20.00	40.00	60.00	110	—
1813 FP	—	25.00	45.00	85.00	185	—
1814 AG	—	15.00	30.00	60.00	110	—
1815 AG	—	12.50	25.00	40.00	70.00	—
1816 AG	—	10.00	15.00	25.00	55.00	—

WAR OF INDEPENDENCE

Date	Mintage	Good	VG	F	VF	XF
1817 AG	—	10.00	15.00	25.00	55.00	—
1818 AG	—	10.00	15.00	25.00	55.00	—
1819 AG	—	10.00	15.00	25.00	55.00	—

KM# 74.3   1/2 REAL
1.6900 g., 0.9030 Silver 0.0491 oz. ASW **Ruler:**
Ferdinand VII **Obv:** Draped laureate bust right **Obv. Legend:**
FERDIN • VII... **Rev:** Crowned shield flanked by pillars **Rev.**
Legend: IND... **Mint:** Zacatecas **Note:** Mint marks: Z, ZS, Zs.

Date	Mintage	VG	F	VF	XF	Unc
1819 AG	—	8.00	12.00	25.00	50.00	—
1820 AG	—	8.00	12.00	25.00	50.00	—
1820 RG	—	5.00	10.00	20.00	45.00	—
1821 AG	—	150	250	450	850	—
1821 RG	—	5.00	10.00	20.00	45.00	—

KM# 183   REAL
0.9030 Silver **Ruler:** Ferdinand VII **Obv:** Crowned shield
flanked by pillars **Rev:** Mountain within beaded circle **Mint:**
Zacatecas **Note:** Mint marks: Z, ZS, Zs.

Date	Mintage	Good	VG	F	VF	XF
1810	—	100	150	300	500	—
1811	—	20.00	40.00	75.00	150	—

Note: Date aligned with legend

KM# 184   REAL
0.9030 Silver **Ruler:** Ferdinand VII **Obv:** Crowned shield
flanked by pillars **Rev:** Mountain within beaded circle **Rev.**
Legend: MONEDA PROVISIONAL DE ZACATECAS **Mint:**
Zacatecas **Note:** Mint marks: Z, ZS, Zs.

Date	Mintage	Good	VG	F	VF	XF
1811	—	15.00	30.00	60.00	135	—

KM# 185   REAL
0.9030 Silver **Ruler:** Ferdinand VII **Obv:** Provincial bust right
Obv. Legend: FERDIN • VII... **Rev:** Crowned shield flanked
by pillars **Rev. Legend:** MONEDA PROVISIONAL DE
ZACATECAS **Mint:** Zacatecas **Note:** Mint marks: Z, ZS, Zs.

Date	Mintage	Good	VG	F	VF	XF
1811	—	50.00	85.00	130	220	—
1812	—	40.00	70.00	110	195	—

KM# 82.1   REAL
3.3800 g., 0.9030 Silver 0.0981 oz. ASW **Ruler:**
Ferdinand VII **Obv:** Armored laureate bust right **Obv.**
Legend: FERDIN • VII... **Rev:** Crowned shield flanked by
pillars **Rev. Legend:** IND • REX... **Mint:** Zacatecas **Note:** Mint
marks: Z, ZS, Zs.

Date	Mintage	Good	VG	F	VF	XF
1813 FP	—	50.00	100	150	250	—
1814 AG	—	20.00	35.00	50.00	85.00	—

Date	Mintage	Good	VG	F	VF	XF
1814 FP	—	20.00	35.00	50.00	85.00	—
1815 AG	—	20.00	35.00	50.00	85.00	—
1816 AG	—	12.00	20.00	30.00	65.00	—
1817 AG	—	8.00	12.50	20.00	45.00	—
1818 AG	—	8.00	12.50	20.00	45.00	—
1819 AG	—	6.00	11.00	18.00	35.00	—

KM# 83.3   REAL
3.3800 g., 0.9030 Silver 0.0981 oz. ASW **Ruler:**
Ferdinand VII **Obv:** Draped laureate bust right **Obv. Legend:**
FERDIN • VII... **Rev:** Crowned shield flanked by pillars **Rev.**
Legend: REX • Z... **Mint:** Zacatecas **Note:** Mint marks: Z, ZS,
Zs.

Date	Mintage	VG	F	VF	XF	Unc
1820 AG	—	6.00	12.00	20.00	60.00	—
1820 RG	—	6.00	12.00	20.00	60.00	—
1821 AG	—	18.00	30.00	45.00	90.00	—
1821 AZ	—	12.00	20.00	40.00	85.00	—
1821 RG	—	7.00	12.50	25.00	65.00	—
1822 AZ	—	7.00	12.50	25.00	65.00	—
1822 RG	—	18.00	30.00	45.00	90.00	—

KM# 186   2 REALES
0.9030 Silver **Ruler:** Ferdinand VII **Obv:** Crowned shield
flanked by pillars **Obv. Legend:** FERDIN • VII... **Rev:**
Mountain within beaded circle **Rev. Legend:** MONEDA •
PROVISION... **Mint:** Zacatecas **Note:** Mint marks: Z, ZS, Zs.

Date	Mintage	Good	VG	F	VF	XF
1810 Rare	—	—	—	—	—	—
1811	—	30.00	48.00	85.00	145	—

Note: Date aligned with legend

KM# 187   2 REALES
0.9030 Silver **Ruler:** Ferdinand VII **Obv:** Crowned shield
flanked by pillars **Rev:** Mountain above L. V. O within beaded
circle **Rev. Legend:** MONEDA PROVISIONAL DE
ZACATECAS **Mint:** Zacatecas **Note:** Mint marks: Z, ZS, Zs.

Date	Mintage	Good	VG	F	VF	XF
1811	—	18.00	36.00	70.00	120	—

KM# 188   2 REALES
0.9030 Silver **Ruler:** Ferdinand VII **Obv:** Armored bust right
Obv. Legend: FERDIN • VII... **Rev:** Crowned shield flanked
by pillars **Rev. Legend:** MONEDA PROVISIONAL DE
ZACATECAS **Mint:** Zacatecas **Note:** Mint marks: Z, ZS, Zs.

Date	Mintage	Good	VG	F	VF	XF
1811	—	38.50	70.00	150	250	—
1812	—	33.00	65.00	140	220	—

KM# 92.1   2 REALES
6.7700 g., 0.9030 Silver 0.1965 oz. ASW **Ruler:**
Ferdinand VII **Obv:** Large armored bust right **Obv. Legend:**
FERDIN • VII **Rev:** Crowned shield flanked by pillars **Rev.**
Inscription: MONEDA • PROVISION... **Mint:** Zacatecas
Note: Mint marks: Z, ZS, Zs.

Date	Mintage	Good	VG	F	VF	XF
1813 FP	—	35.00	50.00	75.00	125	—
1814 FP	—	35.00	50.00	75.00	125	—
1814 AG	—	35.00	50.00	75.00	125	—
1815 AG	—	7.50	15.00	30.00	55.00	—
1816 AG	—	7.50	15.00	30.00	55.00	—
1817 AG	—	7.50	15.00	30.00	55.00	—
1818 AG	—	7.50	15.00	30.00	55.00	—

KM# 93.4   2 REALES
6.7700 g., 0.9030 Silver 0.1965 oz. ASW **Ruler:**
Ferdinand VII **Obv:** Draped laureate bust right **Obv. Legend:**
FERDIN • VII **Rev:** Crowned shield flanked by pillars **Rev.**
Legend: IND • REX... **Mint:** Zacatecas **Note:** Mint marks: Z,
ZS, Zs.

Date	Mintage	VG	F	VF	XF	Unc
1818 AG	—	7.50	15.00	30.00	55.00	—
1819 AG	—	10.00	20.00	40.00	85.00	—
1819 AG	—	10.00	20.00	40.00	85.00	—
Note: Reversed 'S' in HISPAN						
1820 AG	—	10.00	20.00	40.00	85.00	—
1820 RG	—	10.00	20.00	40.00	85.00	—
1821 AG	—	10.00	20.00	40.00	85.00	—
1821 AZ/RG	—	10.00	20.00	40.00	85.00	—
1821 AZ	—	10.00	20.00	40.00	85.00	—
1821 RG	—	10.00	20.00	40.00	85.00	—
1822 AG	—	10.00	20.00	40.00	85.00	—
1822 RG	—	10.00	20.00	40.00	85.00	—

KM# A92   2 REALES
6.7700 g., 0.9030 Silver 0.1965 oz. ASW **Ruler:**
Ferdinand VII **Obv:** Small armored bust right **Obv. Legend:**
FERDIN • VII **Rev:** Crowned shield flanked by pillars **Rev.**
Legend: IND • REX... **Mint:** Zacatecas **Note:** Mint marks: Z,
ZS, Zs.

Date	Mintage	Good	VG	F	VF	XF
1819 AG	—	45.00	100	200	400	—

KM# 189   8 REALES
0.9030 Silver **Ruler:** Ferdinand VII **Obv:** Crowned shield
flanked by pillars **Rev:** Mountain above L.V.O. within beaded
circle **Rev. Legend:** MONEDA.PROVISION... **Mint:**
Zacatecas **Note:** Mint Zacatecas.

Date	Mintage	Good	VG	F	VF	XF
1810	—	300	500	750	1,250	—
1811	—	100	150	225	350	—

Note: Date aligned with legend. Also exists with incomplete
date

KM# 190   8 REALES
0.9030 Silver **Ruler:** Ferdinand VII **Obv:** Crowned shield
flanked by pillars **Obv. Legend:** FERDIN • VII • DEI... **Rev:**
Mountain above L. V. O within beaded circle **Rev. Legend:**
MONEDA PROVISIONAL DE ZACATECAS **Mint:** Zacatecas

Date	Mintage	Good	VG	F	VF	XF
1811	—	65.00	100	135	350	650
Note: Date aligned with legend						
1811 Error	—	—	—	—	3,000	5,000
FERDIN • VI						

KM# 191   8 REALES
0.9030 Silver **Ruler:** Ferdinand VII **Obv:** Armored bust right
Obv. Legend: FERDIN • VII • 8 •R • DEI... **Rev:** Crowned
shield flanked by pillars **Rev. Legend:** MONEDA
PROVISIONAL DE ZACATECAS **Mint:** Zacatecas

Date	Mintage	Good	VG	F	VF	XF
1811	—	45.00	75.00	145	275	—
1812	—	50.00	85.00	160	300	—

KM# 192   8 REALES
0.9030 Silver **Ruler:** Ferdinand VII **Obv:** Draped laureate
bust right **Obv. Legend:** FERDIN • VII • DEI... **Rev:** Crowned
shield flanked by pillars **Rev. Legend:** MONEDA
PROVISIONAL DE ZACATECAS **Mint:** Zacatecas

Date	Mintage	Good	VG	F	VF	XF
1812	—	75.00	150	275	450	—

KM# 111.5   8 REALES
27.0700 g., 0.9030 Silver 0.7859 oz. ASW **Ruler:**
Ferdinand VII **Obv:** Draped laureate bust right **Obv. Legend:**
FERDIN • VII • DEI • GRATIA **Rev:** Crowned shield flanked
by pillars **Rev. Legend:** HISPAN • ET IND • REX **Mint:**
Zacatecas **Note:** Mint mark: Zs. Several bust types exist for
the 1821 issues.

Date	Mintage	VG	F	VF	XF	Unc
1813 FP	—	75.00	125	175	275	—
1814 FP	—	150	250	350	450	—
1814 AG	—	100	150	200	300	—
1814 AG	—	125	175	225	325	—

Note: D over horizontal D in IND

Date	Mintage	VG	F	VF	XF	Unc
1814 AG/FP	—	100	150	200	300	—
1815 AG	—	50.00	100	150	250	—
1816 AG	—	35.00	50.00	65.00	125	—
1817 AG	—	35.00	50.00	65.00	125	—
1818 AG	—	30.00	40.00	50.00	100	—
1819 AG	—	30.00	40.00	50.00	100	—
1819 AG 'GRATIA' error	—	100	200	300	400	—
1820 AG 18/11 error	—	100	200	300	400	—
1820 AG	—	30.00	40.00	50.00	100	500
1820 RG	—	30.00	40.00	50.00	100	—
1821/81 RG	—	75.00	150	225	300	—
1821 RG	—	15.00	25.00	35.00	65.00	—
1821 AZ/RG	—	50.00	100	150	200	—
1821 AZ	—	50.00	100	150	200	—
1822 RG	—	40.00	60.00	100	175	650

KM# 111.6   8 REALES
27.0700 g., 0.9030 Silver 0.7859 oz. ASW **Ruler:**
Ferdinand VII **Obv:** Draped laureate bust right **Obv. Legend:**
FERDIN • VII • DEI • GRATIA **Rev:** Crowned shield flanked
by pillars **Rev. Legend:** HISAV • ET IND • REX **Mint:**
Zacatecas

Date	Mintage	VG	F	VF	XF	Unc
1821Zs	—	160	320	550	750	—

ROYALIST
COUNTERMARKED COINAGE

LCM -
La Comandancia Militar

Crown and Flag

This countermark exists in 15 various sizes.

KM# 193.1   2 REALES
0.9030 Silver **Issuer:** La Comandancia Militar **Countermark:**
LCM **Note:** Countermark on Mexico KM#92.

CM Date	Host Date	Good	VG	F	VF	XF
ND	1809 TH	85.00	165	250	450	—

WAR OF INDEPENDENCE

KM# 193.2   2 REALES
0.9030 Silver   **Issuer:** La Comandancia Militar, (The LCM countermark exists in 15 various sizes) **Countermark:** LCM
Note: Countermark on Mexico KM#186.

CM Date	Host Date	Good	VG	F	VF	XF
ND	1811	85.00	165	250	450	—

KM# 194.1   8 REALES
Cast Silver   **Issuer:** La Comandancia Militar, (The LCM countermark exists in 15 various sizes) **Countermark:** LCM
Note: Countermark on Chihuahua KM#123.

CM Date	Host Date	Good	VG	F	VF	XF
ND	1811 RP	100	200	300	500	—
ND	1812 RP	100	200	300	500	—

KM# 194.2   8 REALES
0.9030 Silver   **Issuer:** La Comandancia Militar, The LCM countermark exists in 15 different sizes **Countermark:** LCM
Note: Countermark on Chihuahua KM#111.1 struck over KM#123.

CM Date	Host Date	Good	VG	F	VF	XF
ND	1815 RP	200	275	400	600	—
ND	1817 RP	125	175	225	350	—
ND	1820 RP	125	175	225	350	—
ND	1821 RP	125	175	225	350	—

KM# 194.3   8 REALES
0.9030 Silver   **Issuer:** La Comandancia Militar, The LCM countermark exists in 15 different sizes **Countermark:** LCM
Note: Countermark on Durango KM#111.2.

CM Date	Host Date	Good	VG	F	VF	XF
ND	1812 RM	70.00	125	200	300	—
ND	1821 CG	70.00	125	200	300	—

KM# 194.4   8 REALES
0.9030 Silver   **Issuer:** La Comandancia Militar, The LCM countermark exists in 15 different sizes **Countermark:** LCM
Note: Countermark on Guadalajara KM#111.3.

CM Date	Host Date	Good	VG	F	VF	XF
ND	1813 MR	150	225	300	500	—

KM# 194.5   8 REALES
0.9030 Silver   **Issuer:** La Comandancia Militar, The LCM countermark exists in 15 different sizes **Countermark:** LCM
Note: Countermark on Guanajuato KM#111.4.

CM Date	Host Date	Good	VG	F	VF	XF
ND	1813 JJ	225	350	475	700	—

KM# 194.6   8 REALES
0.9030 Silver   **Issuer:** La Comandancia Militar, The LCM countermark exists in 15 different sizes **Countermark:** LCM
Note: Countermark on Nueva Viscaya KM#165.

CM Date	Host Date	Good	VG	F	VF	XF
ND	1811 RM Rare	—	—	—	—	—

KM# 194.7   8 REALES
0.9030 Silver   **Issuer:** La Comandancia Militar, The LCM countermark exists in 15 different sizes **Countermark:** LCM
Note: Countermark on Mexico KM#111.

CM Date	Host Date	Good	VG	F	VF	XF
ND	1811 HJ	125	225	350	650	—
ND	1812 JJ	110	135	200	350	—
ND	1817 JJ	50.00	65.00	85.00	175	—
ND	1818 JJ	50.00	65.00	85.00	175	—
ND	1820 JJ	—	—	—	—	—

KM# 194.8   8 REALES
0.9030 Silver   **Issuer:** La Comandancia Militar, The LCM countermark exists in 15 different sizes **Countermark:** LCM
Note: Countermark on Sombrerete KM#176.

CM Date	Host Date	Good	VG	F	VF	XF
ND	1811 Rare	—	—	—	—	—
ND	1812 Rare	—	—	—	—	—

KM# 194.9   8 REALES
0.9030 Silver **Issuer:** La Comandancia Militar, The LCM
countermark exists in 15 different sizes **Countermark:** LCM
Note: Countermark on Zacatecas KM#190.

CM Date	Host Date	Good	VG	F	VF	XF
ND	1811	225	350	500	—	—

KM# 194.10   8 REALES
0.9030 Silver **Issuer:** La Comandancia Militar, The LCM
countermark exists in 15 different sizes **Countermark:** LCM
Note: Countermark on Zacatecas KM#111.5.

CM Date	Host Date	Good	VG	F	VF	XF
ND	1813 FP	—	—	—	—	—
ND	1814 AG	—	—	—	—	—
ND	1822 RG	—	—	—	—	—

LCV -
Las Cajas de Veracruz

The Royal Treasury of the City of Veracruz

KM# 195   7 REALES
Silver **Issuer:** Las Cajas de Veracruz, The Royal Treasury
of the City of Veracruz **Countermark:** LCV **Note:**
Countermark and 7 on underweight 8 Reales.

CM Date	Host Date	Good	VG	F	VF	XF
ND	ND Rare	—	—	—	—	—

Note: Most examples are counterfeit

KM# 196   7-1/4 REALES
Silver **Issuer:** Las Cajas de Veracruz, The Royal Treasury
of the City of Veracruz **Countermark:** LCV **Note:**
Countermark and 7-1/4 on underweight 8 Reales.

CM Date	Host Date	Good	VG	F	VF	XF
ND	ND Rare	—	—	—	—	—

Note: Most examples are counterfeit

KM# 197   7-1/2 REALES
Silver **Issuer:** Las Cajas de Veracruz, The Royal Treasury
of the City of Veracruz **Countermark:** LCV **Note:**
Countermark and 7-1/2 on underweight 8 Reales.

CM Date	Host Date	Good	VG	F	VF	XF
ND	ND Rare	—	—	—	—	—

Note: Most examples are counterfeit

KM# 198   7-3/4 REALES
Silver **Issuer:** Las Cajas de Veracruz, The Royal Treasury
of the City of Veracruz **Countermark:** LCV **Note:**
Countermark and 7-3/4 on underweight 8 Reales.

CM Date	Host Date	Good	VG	F	VF	XF
ND	ND	300	375	450	700	—

Note: Many examples are counterfeit

KM# A198   8 REALES
Cast Silver **Issuer:** Las Cajas de Veracruz, The Royal
Treasury of the City of Veracruz **Countermark:** LCV **Note:**
Countermark on Chihuahua KM#123.

CM Date	Host Date	Good	VG	F	VF	XF
ND	1811 RP	150	250	400	600	—

KM# 199   8 REALES
Silver **Issuer:** Las Cajas de Veracruz, The Royal Treasury
of the City of Veracruz **Countermark:** LCV **Note:**
Countermark on Zacatecas KM#191.

CM Date	Host Date	Good	VG	F	VF	XF
ND	1811	175	225	275	375	—
ND	1812	175	225	275	375	—

MS (Monogram) - Manuel Salcedo

KM# 200 8 REALES
Silver **Issuer:** Manuel Salcedo **Countermark:** MS monogram **Note:** Countermark on Mexico KM#110.

CM Date	Host Date	Good	VG	F	VF	XF
ND	1809 TH	150	250	400	600	—
ND	1810 HJ	150	250	400	600	—
ND	1811 HJ	150	250	400	600	—

MVA - Monclova

KM# 202.3 8 REALES
Silver **Issuer:** Monclova, MVA **Countermark:** MVA/1812 **Note:** Countermark on cast Mexico KM#110.

CM Date	Host Date	Good	VG	F	VF	XF
1812	1809 HJ	100	150	250	375	—
1812	1809 TH	100	150	250	375	—
1812	1810 HJ	100	150	250	375	—

KM# 201 8 REALES
Silver **Issuer:** Monclova, MVA **Countermark:** MVA/1811 **Note:** Countermark on Chihuahua KM#111.1; struck over cast Mexico KM#110.

CM Date	Host Date	Good	VG	F	VF	XF
ND	1809	250	450	700	1,000	—
ND	1816 RP	250	450	700	1,000	—
ND	1821 RP	250	450	700	1,000	—

KM# 202.5 8 REALES
Silver **Issuer:** Monclova, MVA **Countermark:** MVA/1812 **Note:** Countermark on Zacatecas KM#189.

CM Date	Host Date	Good	VG	F	VF	XF
1812	1813	300	350	450	700	—

KM# 202.1 8 REALES
Silver **Issuer:** Monclova, MVA **Countermark:** MVA/1812 **Note:** Countermark on Chihuahua KM#111.1; struck over cast Mexico KM#109.

CM Date	Host Date	Good	VG	F	VF	XF
1812	1810	125	175	250	375	—

KM# 202.2 8 REALES
Silver **Issuer:** Monclova, MVA **Countermark:** MVA/1812 **Note:** Countermark on cast Mexico KM#109.

CM Date	Host Date	Good	VG	F	VF	XF
1812	1798 FM	100	150	250	375	—
1812	1802 FT	100	150	250	375	—

INSURGENT COINAGE

American Congress

KM# 216 REAL
0.9030 Silver **Issuer:** American Congress **Obv:** Eagle on cactus **Obv. Legend:** CONGRESO AMERICANO **Rev:** F. 7 on spread mantle **Rev. Legend:** DEPOSIT D.L. AUCTORI J **Mint:** Mexico City

Date	Mintage	Good	VG	F	VF	XF
ND(1813)	—	35.00	75.00	125	225	—

KM# 217 REAL
0.9030 Silver **Issuer:** American Congress **Obv:** Eagle on cactus **Obv. Legend:** CONGR. AMER. **Rev:** F. 7 on spread mantle **Rev. Legend:** DEPOS. D. L. AUT. D. **Mint:** Mexico City

Date	Mintage	Good	VG	F	VF	XF
ND(1813)	—	35.00	75.00	125	225	—

National Congress

KM# 209 1/2 REAL
Struck Copper **Issuer:** National Congress **Obv:** Eagle on bridge **Obv. Legend:** VICE FERD. VII DEI GRATIA ET **Rev:** Value, bow quiver, etc **Rev. Legend:** S. P. CONG. NAT. IND.

Date	Mintage	Good	VG	F	VF	XF
1811	—	45.00	85.00	150	250	—
1812	—	27.50	60.00	100	175	—
1813	—	27.50	60.00	100	175	—
1814	—	45.00	85.00	150	250	—

KM# 210 1/2 REAL
0.9030 Silver **Issuer:** National Congress **Obv:** Eagle on bridge **Obv. Legend:** VICE FERD. VII DEI GRATIA ET **Rev:** Value, bow quiver, etc **Rev. Legend:** S. P. CONG. NAT. IND.

Date	Mintage	Good	VG	F	VF	XF
1812	—	27.50	60.00	100	175	—
1813	—	45.00	90.00	175	275	—

Note: 1812 exists with the date reading inwards and outwards

KM# 211 REAL
0.9030 Silver **Issuer:** National Congress **Obv:** Eagle on bridge **Obv. Legend:** VICE FERD. VII DEI GRATIA ET **Rev:** Value, bow quiver, etc **Rev. Legend:** S. P. CONG. NAT. IND.

Date	Mintage	Good	VG	F	VF	XF
1812	—	22.50	45.00	80.00	150	—
1813	—	22.50	45.00	80.00	150	—

Note: 1812 exists with the date reading either inward or outward

KM# 212 2 REALES
Struck Copper **Issuer:** National Congress **Obv:** Eagle on bridge **Obv. Legend:** VICE FERD. VII DEI GRATIA ET **Rev:** Value, bow quiver, etc **Rev. Legend:** S. P. CONG. NAT. IND.

Date	Mintage	Good	VG	F	VF	XF
1812	—	100	150	225	350	—
1813	—	23.50	50.00	75.00	150	—
1814	—	32.50	75.00	110	185	—

KM# A213 2 REALES
Struck Silver **Issuer:** National Congress **Obv:** Eagle on bridge **Obv. Legend:** VICE FERD. VII DEI GRATIA ET **Rev:** Value, bow, quiver, etc **Rev. Legend:** S. P. CONG. NAT. IND.

Date	Mintage	Good	VG	F	VF	XF
1813	—	950	1,750	3,000	5,000	—

KM# 213 2 REALES
0.9030 Silver **Issuer:** National Congress **Obv:** Eagle on bridge in shield, denomination at sides **Obv. Legend:** VICE FERD. VII DEI GRATIA ET **Rev:** Canon, quiver, arm, etc

Date	Mintage	Good	VG	F	VF	XF
1813	—	75.00	160	275	400	—

Note: These dies were believed to be intended for the striking of 2 Escudos

KM# 214 4 REALES
0.9030 Silver **Issuer:** National Congress **Obv:** Eagle on bridge **Obv. Legend:** VICE FERD. VII DEI GRATIA ET **Rev:** Value, bow, quiver, etc **Rev. Legend:** S. P. CONG. NAT. IND. **Mint:** Mexico City

Date	Mintage	Good	VG	F	VF	XF
1813	—	600	1,200	2,450	4,750	—

KM# 215.1 8 REALES
0.9030 Silver **Issuer:** National Congress **Obv:** Small

crowned eagle **Obv. Legend:** VICE FERD. VII DEI GRATIA ET **Rev:** Value, bow, quiver, etc **Rev. Legend:** S. P. CONG. NAT. IND. **Mint:** Mexico City

Date	Mintage	Good	VG	F	VF	XF
1812Mo	—	600	1,150	2,350	4,500	—

KM# 215.2 8 REALES
0.9030 Silver **Issuer:** National Congress **Obv:** Large crowned eagle **Obv. Legend:** VICE FERD. VII DEI GRATIA ET **Rev:** Value, bow, quiver, etc **Rev. Legend:** S. P. CONG. NAT. IND. **Mint:** Mexico City

Date	Mintage	Good	VG	F	VF	XF
1813Mo	—	600	1,150	2,350	4,500	—

Supreme National Congress of America

PDV - Provisional de Valladolid

VTIL - Util = useful

(Refer to Multiple countermarks)

KM# 203 1/2 REAL
Struck Copper **Issuer:** Supreme National Congress of America **Obv:** Eagle on bridge **Obv. Legend:** FERDIN. VII DEI GRATIA **Rev:** Value, bow, quiver, etc **Rev. Legend:** S. P. CONG. NAT. IND. GUV.T.

Date	Mintage	Good	VG	F	VF	XF
1811	—	27.50	45.00	65.00	120	—
1812	—	27.50	45.00	65.00	120	—
1813	—	27.50	45.00	65.00	120	—
1814	—	27.50	45.00	65.00	120	—

KM# 204 REAL
Struck Copper **Issuer:** Supreme National Congress of America **Obv:** Eagle on bridge **Obv. Legend:** FERDIN. VII DEI GRATIA **Rev:** Value, bow, quiver, etc **Rev. Legend:** S. P. CONG. NAT. IND. GUV.T.

Date	Mintage	Good	VG	F	VF	XF
1811	—	45.00	75.00	125	200	—

KM# 205 2 REALES
Struck Copper **Issuer:** Supreme National Congress of America **Obv:** Eagle on bridge **Obv. Legend:** FERDIN. VII DEI GRATIA **Rev:** Value, bow, quiver, etc

Date	Mintage	Good	VG	F	VF	XF
1812	—	225	325	475	750	—

KM# 206 8 REALES
Cast Silver **Issuer:** Supreme National Congress of America **Obv:** Eagle on bridge **Obv. Legend:** FERDIN. VII DEI GRATIA **Rev:** Value, bow, quiver, etc

Date	Mintage	Good	VG	F	VF	XF
1811	—	150	250	350	550	—
1812	—	150	250	375	550	—

KM# 207 8 REALES
Struck Silver **Issuer:** Supreme National Congress of America **Obv:** Eagle on bridge **Obv. Legend:** FERDIN. VII DEI GRATIA **Rev:** Value, bow, quiver, etc

Date	Mintage	Good	VG	F	VF	XF
1811	—	—	—	—	—	—

Note: Ira & Larry Goldberg Millennia Sale 5-08, QU-55 realized $55,000.

1812	—	500	1,000	1,500	2,500	—

KM# 208 8 REALES
Struck Copper **Issuer:** Supreme National Congress of America **Obv:** Eagle on bridge **Obv. Legend:** FERDIN. VII... **Rev:** Bow, sword and quiver **Rev. Legend:** PROVICIONAL POR LA SUPREMA JUNTA DE AMERICA

Date	Mintage	Good	VG	F	VF	XF
1811	—	100	150	225	475	—
1812	—	100	150	225	475	—

WAR OF INDEPENDENCE

EMPIRE OF ITURBIDE

RULER
Augustin I Iturbide, 1822-1823
MINT MARK
Mo - Mexico City
ASSAYERS' INITIALS
JA - Jose Garcia Ansaldo, 1812-1833
JM - Joaquin Davila Madrid, 1809-1833

MILLED COINAGE

KM# 299   1/8 REAL
Copper   **Ruler:** Augustin I Iturbide **Obv:** Crowned shield
within sprays **Rev:** Inscription, date **Rev. Inscription:** DE LA
PROVINCIA DE NUEVA VISCAYA **Mint:** Durango

Date	Mintage	Good	VG	F	VF	XF
1821D	—	22.50	50.00	85.00	150	—
1822D	—	7.50	13.50	28.50	60.00	—
1823D	—	9.00	13.50	26.50	55.00	—

KM# 300   1/4 REAL
Copper   **Ruler:** Augustin I Iturbide **Obv:** Crowned shield
within sprays **Rev:** Inscription, date **Rev. Inscription:** DE LA
PROVINCIA DE NUEVA VISCAYA **Mint:** Durango

Date	Mintage	Good	VG	F	VF	XF
1822D	—	160	275	400	550	—

KM# 301   1/2 REAL
0.9030 Silver   **Ruler:** Augustin I Iturbide **Obv:** Head right
Obv. Legend: AUGUSTINUS DEI... **Rev:** Crowned eagle
Rev. Legend: I.M.E.X.I... **Mint:** Mexico City

Date	Mintage	F	VF	XF	Unc	BU
1822Mo JM	—	22.50	55.00	110	375	700
1823Mo JM	—	17.00	42.00	85.00	325	—

KM# 302   REAL
0.9030 Silver   **Ruler:** Augustin I Iturbide **Obv:** Head right
Obv. Legend: AUGUSTINUS DEI... **Rev:** Crowned eagle
Rev. Legend: MEX.I.IMPERATOR... **Mint:** Mexico City

Date	Mintage	VG	F	VF	XF	Unc
1822Mo JM	—	100	175	350	550	1,150

KM# 303   2 REALES
6.7667 g., 0.9030 Silver 0.1964 oz. ASW   **Ruler:**
Augustin I Iturbide **Obv:** Head right **Obv. Legend:**
AUGUSTINUS DEI... **Rev:** Crowned eagle **Rev. Legend:**
MEX • I • IMPERATOR... **Mint:** Mexico City

Date	Mintage	F	VF	XF	Unc	BU
1822Mo JM	—	60.00	120	350	1,000	—
1823Mo JM	—	40.00	80.00	250	850	—

KM# 304   8 REALES
27.0674 g., 0.9030 Silver 0.7858 oz. ASW   **Ruler:**
Augustin I Iturbide **Obv:** Head right **Obv. Legend:**
AUGUST.... **Rev:** Crowned eagle **Rev. Legend:** ...MEX • I •
IMPERATOR... **Mint:** Mexico City

Date	Mintage	F	VF	XF	Unc	BU
1822Mo JM	—	75.00	150	300	1,100	—
1822Mo JM	—	—	—	—	—	—
Proof, 3 known						

  Note: Ponterio & Associates Sale #86, 04-97, choice AU
Proof realized $12,650

KM# 305   8 REALES
0.9030 Silver   **Ruler:** Augustin I Iturbide **Obv:** Bust similar to
8 Escudos, KM#131 **Rev:** Crowned eagle **Mint:** Mexico City

Date	Mintage	F	VF	XF	Unc	BU
1822Mo JM Rare	—	—	—	—	—	—

KM# 306.1   8 REALES
0.9030 Silver   **Ruler:** Augustin I Iturbide **Obv:** Head right
Obv. Legend: AUGUST... **Rev:** Crowned eagle, 8 R.J.M. at

upper left of eagle **Rev. Legend:** MEX • I • IMPERATOR...
Mint: Mexico City **Note:** Type I.

Date	Mintage	F	VF	XF	Unc	BU
1822Mo JM	—	100	200	450	1,500	—

KM# 306.2 8 REALES
0.9030 Silver **Ruler:** Augustin I Iturbide **Obv:** Head right
Rev: Cross on crown **Mint:** Mexico City **Note:** Type I.

Date	Mintage	F	VF	XF	Unc	BU
1822Mo JM	—	650	1,000	—	—	—

KM# 307 8 REALES
0.9030 Silver **Ruler:** Augustin I Iturbide **Obv:** Head right
Rev: Crowned eagle **Mint:** Mexico City **Note:** Type II.

Date	Mintage	F	VF	XF	Unc	BU
1822Mo JM	—	150	350	700	2,500	—

KM# 308 8 REALES
0.9030 Silver **Ruler:** Augustin I Iturbide **Obv:** Head right,
continuous legend with long smooth truncation **Obv. Legend:**
AUGUSTINUS DEI... **Rev:** Crowned eagle **Mint:** Mexico City
Note: Type III.

Date	Mintage	F	VF	XF	Unc	BU
1822Mo JM	—	175	500	950	2,500	—

Note: Variety with long, straight truncation is valued at
$5,000 in uncirculated condition

KM# 309 8 REALES
0.9030 Silver **Ruler:** Augustin I Iturbide **Obv:** Head right
Obv. Legend: AUGUSTINUS DEI... **Rev:** Crowned eagle
Rev. Legend: MEX • I • IMPERATOR... **Mint:** Mexico City
Note: Type IV.

Date	Mintage	F	VF	XF	Unc	BU
1822Mo JM	—	50.00	120	250	850	—

KM# 310 8 REALES
0.9030 Silver **Ruler:** Augustin I Iturbide **Obv:** Head right,
continuous legend with short irregular truncation **Obv.
Legend:** AUGUSTINUS DEI... **Rev:** Crowned eagle, 8 R.J.M.
below eagle **Rev. Legend:** MEX • I • IMPERATOR... **Mint:**
Mexico City **Note:** Type V.

Date	Mintage	F	VF	XF	Unc	BU
1822Mo JM	—	50.00	120	250	1,000	—
1823Mo JM	—	50.00	120	250	1,000	—

KM# 311 8 REALES
0.9030 Silver **Ruler:** Augustin I Iturbide **Obv:** Head
right, long truncation **Rev:** Crowned eagle **Mint:** Mexico City
Note: Type VI.

Date	Mintage	F	VF	XF	Unc	BU
1822Mo JM Rare	—	—	—	—	—	—

KM# 312 4 SCUDOS
13.5334 g., 0.8750 Gold 0.3807 oz. AGW **Ruler:**
Augustin I Iturbide **Obv:** Head right **Obv. Legend:**
AUGUSTINUS DEI... **Rev:** Crowned eagle within ornate shield
Rev. Legend: CONSTITUT.4.S.I.M... **Mint:** Mexico City

Date	Mintage	F	VF	XF	Unc	BU
1823Mo JM	—	1,200	2,500	5,000	10,000	—

KM# 313.1 8 SCUDOS
27.0674 g., 0.8750 Gold 0.7614 oz. AGW **Ruler:**
Augustin I Iturbide **Obv:** Head right **Obv. Legend:**

AUGUSTINUS . DEI... **Rev:** Crowned eagle **Rev. Legend:** CONSTITUT.8.S.I.M... **Mint:** Mexico City

Date	Mintage	F	VF	XF	Unc	BU
1822Mo JM	—	1,500	3,500	6,500	12,000	15,000

Note: American Numismatic Rarities Eliasberg sale 4-05, MS-62 realized $20,700. Superior Casterline sale 5-89 choice AU realized $11,000

KM# 313.2   8 SCUDOS
0.8750 Gold **Ruler:** Augustin I Iturbide **Obv:** Head right, error in legend **Obv. Legend:** AUGSTINUS • DEI... **Rev:** Crowned eagle **Rev. Legend:** CONSTITUT • 8 • S • I • M... **Mint:** Mexico City

Date	Mintage	F	VF	XF	Unc	BU
1822Mo JM	—	1,250	3,650	6,750	12,500	16,000

KM# 314   8 SCUDOS
0.8750 Gold **Ruler:** Augustin I Iturbide **Obv:** Head right **Obv. Legend:** AUGUSTINUS DEI... **Rev:** Crowned eagle within ornate shield **Rev. Legend:** CONSTITUT • 8 • S • I • M... **Mint:** Mexico City

Date	Mintage	F	VF	XF	Unc	BU
1823Mo JM	—	1,200	2,500	6,000	10,000	—

LOCAL COINAGE

Ahualulco

KM# L2   1/8 REAL (Octavo)
Copper **Issuer:** Ahualulco **Obv:** Script AHO, 1/8 below **Note:** Uniface.

Date	Mintage	Good	VG	F	VF	XF
ND	—	10.00	17.50	25.00	40.00	—

KM# L1   1/8 REAL (Octavo)
Copper **Issuer:** Ahualulco **Obv:** AHUALULCO and 1813 arfound 1/8 in circle **Note:** Uniface.

Date	Mintage	Good	VG	F	VF	XF
1813	—	15.00	25.00	35.00	60.00	—

Ameca

KM# L10   1/8 REAL (Octavo)
Copper **Issuer:** Ameca **Obv:** F 1/8 Z within wavy circle **Note:** Octagonal planchet.

Date	Mintage	Good	VG	F	VF	XF
ND	—	16.50	25.00	33.50	57.50	—

KM# L9   1/8 REAL (Octavo)
Copper **Issuer:** Ameca **Obv:** AME/CA 1811 in circle **Note:** Octagonal planchet.

Date	Mintage	Good	VG	F	VF	XF
1811	—	16.50	27.50	38.50	65.00	—

KM# L8   1/8 REAL (Octavo)
Copper **Issuer:** Ameca **Obv:** AME/CA 1811 in circle **Note:** Uniface.

Date	Mintage	Good	VG	F	VF	XF
1811	—	15.00	25.00	35.00	55.00	—

KM# L7   1/8 REAL (Octavo)
Copper **Issuer:** Ameca **Obv:** QTG monogram in toothed circle **Obv. Legend:** TLACO DE AMECA

Date	Mintage	Good	VG	F	VF	XF
ND(1812)	—	10.00	17.50	25.00	40.00	—

KM# L6   1/8 REAL (Octavo)
Copper **Issuer:** Ameca **Obv:** Church flanked by trees **Note:** Uniface.

Date	Mintage	Good	VG	F	VF	XF
1824	—	10.00	17.50	25.00	40.00	—

KM# L11   1/8 REAL (Octavo)
Copper **Issuer:** Ameca **Obv:** T.Z. AMECA 1833 around value **Note:** Octagonal planchet.

Date	Mintage	Good	VG	F	VF	XF
1833	—	10.00	15.00	22.50	35.00	—

KM# L12   1/8 REAL (Octavo)
Copper **Issuer:** Ameca **Obv:** V.F AMECA 1858 below value **Note:** Octagonal planchet.

Date	Mintage	Good	VG	F	VF	XF
1858	—	12.50	17.50	25.00	40.00	—

Amescua

KM# L15   1/8 REAL (Octavo)
Copper **Issuer:** Amescua **Obv:** Mexican eagle

Date	Mintage	Good	VG	F	VF	XF
1828	—	10.00	15.00	25.00	40.00	—

KM# L16 1/8 REAL (Octavo)
Copper **Issuer:** Amescua **Obv:** Darte below eagle

Date	Mintage	Good	VG	F	VF	XF
1838	—	13.50	20.00	30.00	50.00	—

Atencinco

KM# L19 1/8 REAL (Octavo)
Copper **Issuer:** Atencinco **Obv:** ATENCINCO in outer border, 8-leaved rosette above branch in center

Date	Mintage	Good	VG	F	VF	XF
ND	—	13.50	20.00	30.00	50.00	—

Atotonilco

KM# L23 1/4 REAL (Octavo)
Copper **Issuer:** Atotonilco **Obv:** Legend in outer border, 1821 in center **Obv. Legend:** ATOTONILCO ANO DE **Rev:** Legend around outer border **Rev. Legend:** V.F.7.q.D.C...

Date	Mintage	Good	VG	F	VF	XF
1821	—	15.00	25.00	35.00	55.00	—

KM# L22 1/8 REAL (Octavo)
Copper **Issuer:** Atotonilco **Obv:** ATOTONILCO ANO DE 1808 in outer border, L. S. S. / JUSU/ESES in circle

Date	Mintage	Good	VG	F	VF	XF
1808	—	25.00	37.50	55.00	85.00	—

KM# L24 1/8 REAL (Octavo)
Copper **Issuer:** Atotonilco **Obv:** Legend in outer border, 1826 in center **Obv. Legend:** VILL ATOTONILCO **Rev:** Legend in center, stars in outer border **Rev. Legend:** 1/8

Date	Mintage	Good	VG	F	VF	XF
1826	—	15.00	25.00	35.00	55.00	—

Campeche

KM# L27 CENTAVO
Brass **Issuer:** Campeche

Date	Mintage	Good	VG	F	VF	XF
1861	—	7.00	10.00	17.50	27.50	—

Catorce

KM# L30 1/4 REAL
Copper **Issuer:** Catorce **Obv:** Legend around border, 1/4 below flower and raised rectangle **Obv. Legend:** FONDOS PUBLICOS **Rev:** Legend around border, eagle on cactus **Rev. Legend:** DE CATORCE 1822

Date	Mintage	Good	VG	F	VF	XF
1822	—	12.00	18.50	30.00	50.00	—

Celaya

KM# L33 1/8 REAL (Octavo)
Copper **Issuer:** Celaya **Obv. Legend:** EN/CELAYA/DE/ 1803 **Rev:** Branches below legend, flower above **Rev. Legend:** LUIS/VASQUE S

Date	Mintage	Good	VG	F	VF	XF
1803	—	25.00	37.50	55.00	85.00	—

KM# L34 1/8 REAL (Octavo)
Copper **Issuer:** Celaya **Obv. Legend:** VIDERI/QUE/ CELALLA/1808 **Rev:** Branches below legend, flower above **Rev. Legend:** LUIS/VASQUE S **Note:** Uniface.

Date	Mintage	Good	VG	F	VF	XF
1808	—	25.00	37.50	55.00	85.00	—

KM# L35 1/8 REAL (Octavo)
Copper **Issuer:** Celaya **Obv. Legend:** VISCARA/CELAYA/ 1814 with ornament above **Rev:** Branches below legend, flower above **Rev. Legend:** LUIS/VASQUE S **Note:** Uniface.

Date	Mintage	Good	VG	F	VF	XF
1814	—	17.50	25.00	35.00	60.00	—

Chilchota

KM# L38 1/8 REAL (Octavo)
Copper **Issuer:** Chilchota **Obv:** Head to right, date below legend **Obv. Legend:** CHILCHOTA UN OCTAVO **Rev:** Wreath in center **Rev. Legend:** RESPONSAVILIDAD DE MURGVIA

Date	Mintage	Good	VG	F	VF	XF
1858	—	15.00	25.00	35.00	60.00	—

Colima

KM# L41 1/8 REAL (Octavo)
Copper **Issuer:** Colima **Obv:** Legend around border as continuos legend **Obv. Legend:** VILLA DE COLIMA **Rev:** Blank

Date	Mintage	Good	VG	F	VF	XF
1813	—	12.50	17.50	25.00	45.00	—

KM# L42 1/8 REAL (Octavo)
Copper **Issuer:** Colima **Obv:** Legend and date in three lines **Obv. Legend:** VILLA DE COLIMA **Rev:** Blank

Date	Mintage	Good	VG	F	VF	XF
1814	—	12.50	17.50	25.00	42.50	—

KM# L44 1/8 REAL (Octavo)
Copper **Issuer:** Colima **Obv:** Legend and date in three lines **Obv. Legend:** OCT. DE COLI **Rev:** Date

Date	Mintage	Good	VG	F	VF	XF
1819	—	15.00	22.50	30.00	50.00	—

KM# L46 1/8 REAL (Octavo)
Copper **Issuer:** Colima **Obv:** Legend around border, date in center circle **Obv. Legend:** OCTO DE COLIMA **Rev:** Legend within wreath, pellet in center **Rev. Legend:** OCTAVO

Date	Mintage	Good	VG	F	VF	XF
1824	—	13.50	17.50	25.00	45.00	—

KM# L47 1/8 REAL (Octavo)
Copper **Issuer:** Colima **Obv:** Legend in three lines **Obv. Legend:** OCTO DE COLA **Rev:** Legend within wreath, pellet in center **Rev. Legend:** OCTAVO

Date	Mintage	Good	VG	F	VF	XF
1824	—	13.50	17.50	25.00	45.00	—
1828	—	13.50	17.50	25.00	45.00	—

KM# L48   1/8 REAL (Octavo)
Copper **Issuer:** Colima **Obv:** Legend in three lines **Obv. Legend:** OCTO DE COLIMA **Rev:** Legend in three lines **Rev. Legend:** ANO DE 1830

Date	Mintage	Good	VG	F	VF	XF
1830	—	13.50	17.50	25.00	45.00	—

KM# L43   1/4 REAL (Quarto)
Copper **Issuer:** Colima **Obv:** Legend in three lines in wreath **Obv. Legend:** QUART COLIMA 1816 **Rev:** Colima monogram in wreath

Date	Mintage	Good	VG	F	VF	XF
1816	—	10.00	16.50	22.50	42.00	—

KM# L45   1/4 REAL (Quarto)
Copper **Issuer:** Colima **Obv:** Legend around border, date in center circle **Obv. Legend:** QUARTo DE COLIMA **Rev:** Colima monogram in wreath

Date	Mintage	Good	VG	F	VF	XF
1824	—	12.50	16.50	22.50	42.00	—

Cotija

KM# L51   1/4 REAL (Quarto)
Copper **Issuer:** Cotija **Obv:** Seated Liberty with staff and liberty cap **Obv. Legend:** DE. D. JOSE NUNES **Rev:** Value and date in wreath **Rev. Legend:** COMMERCIO. D. COTIJA

Date	Mintage	Good	VG	F	VF	XF
ND	—	12.50	18.50	25.00	45.00	—

Cuido

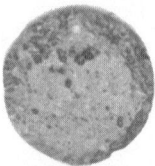 

KM# L52   1/8 REAL (Octavo)
Copper **Issuer:** Cuido **Note:** Uniface. "CUIDO" above "1/8" in spray.

Date	Mintage	Good	VG	F	VF	XF
ND	—	12.50	20.00	28.50	45.00	—

Guadalajara

KM# L57   1/8 REAL (Octavo)
Copper **Issuer:** Guadalajara **Obv:** Eagle with wings spread **Obv. Legend:** GUADALAXARA **Note:** Uniface.

Date	Mintage	Good	VG	F	VF	XF
ND	—	27.50	37.50	55.00	85.00	—

Lagos

KM# L59   1/4 REAL
Bronze **Issuer:** Lagos **Obv:** 2 globes with crown above, wreath and 1/4 below **Rev:** Coat of arms of Lagos

Date	Mintage	Good	VG	F	VF	XF
ND	—	60.00	75.00	120	185	—

KM# L59a   1/4 REAL
Silver **Issuer:** Lagos **Obv:** 2 globes with crown above, wreath and 1/4 below **Rev:** Coat of arms of Lagos

Date	Mintage	Good	VG	F	VF	XF
ND	—	150	200	300	500	—

Merida

KM# L60   1/2 GRANO
Lead **Issuer:** Merida **Obv:** First part of legend in center, second part of legend around border, 1859 below **Obv. Legend:** PART/DE LA SO/CIED • MERIDADE YUCATAN **Rev. Legend:** 1/2/GRANO/DE PESO/FUERTE

Date	Mintage	Good	VG	F	VF	XF
1859	—	10.00	16.00	32.50	55.00	—

Pazcuaro

KM# L63   1/8 REAL (Octavo)
Copper **Issuer:** Pazcuaro **Obv:** Town at base of mountains, lake in foreground, value 1/8 above **Rev:** Woman walking right, carrying bag, fish net and fish

Date	Mintage	Good	VG	F	VF	XF
ND	—	11.00	16.50	22.50	35.00	—

Note: Also in brass and cast in bronze; minor die varieties have been observed

KM# L64   1/8 REAL (Octavo)
Copper **Issuer:** Pazcuaro **Obv:** 1/8 PAZCUARO **Rev:** Crude rendering of Woman walking right, carrying bag, fish net and fish.

Date	Mintage	Good	VG	F	VF	XF
ND	—	12.50	17.50	25.00	45.00	—

Progreso

KM# L66 1/8 REAL (Octavo)
Copper **Issuer:** Progreso **Obv:** Radiant star above open book **Rev:** Value 1/8 in double wreath

Date	Mintage	Good	VG	F	VF	XF
1858	—	15.00	22.50	35.00	60.00	—

KM# L67 CENTAVO
Lead **Issuer:** Progreso **Obv:** Legend and 1873 in center **Obv. Legend:** MUNICIPALIDAD DE PROGRESO UN CENT **Rev:** Flank in oval band

Date	Mintage	Good	VG	F	VF	XF
1873	—	12.50	20.00	30.00	50.00	—

Quitupan

KM# L69 1/8 REAL (Octavo)
Copper **Issuer:** Quitupan **Obv:** Bow and two arrows in center **Obv. Legend:** QUITUPAN ... 1854 **Rev:** 1/8 in center, mongram countermark **Rev. Legend:** YGNACIO BUENROSTRO

Date	Mintage	Good	VG	F	VF	XF
1854	—	15.00	22.50	32.50	55.00	—

Tacambaro

KM# L72 1/8 REAL (Octavo)
Copper **Issuer:** Tacambaro **Obv:** Winged caduceus in sprays **Rev:** Value 1/8 in sprays

Date	Mintage	Good	VG	F	VF	XF
ND	—	12.50	18.50	25.00	45.00	—

Taretan

KM# L75 1/8 REAL (Octavo)
Copper **Issuer:** Taretan **Obv:** Head of man right **Rev:** Tree

Date	Mintage	Good	VG	F	VF	XF
1858	—	15.00	25.00	37.50	65.00	—

Tlazasalca

KM# L78 1/8 REAL (Octavo)
Copper **Issuer:** Tlazasalca **Obv:** Two mountains, date below **Rev:** Value 1/8 in wreath

Date	Mintage	Good	VG	F	VF	XF
1853	—	16.50	25.00	35.00	60.00	—

Xalostotitlan

KM# L54 1/8 REAL (Octavo)
Copper **Issuer:** Xalostotitlan **Obv:** Crown in center **Obv. Legend:** ILVSTRE AYVNTAMIENTO **Rev:** 4 in center **Rev. Legend:** DE XALOS.TOTITAN. 1820

Date	Mintage	Good	VG	F	VF	XF
1820	—	22.50	35.00	55.00	85.00	—

Zamora

KM# L80 1/8 REAL (Octavo)
Copper **Issuer:** Zamora

Date	Mintage	Good	VG	F	VF	XF
1842	—	6.00	12.50	22.50	37.50	—
1848	—	6.00	12.50	22.50	37.50	—
1854	—	6.00	12.50	22.50	37.50	—
1858	—	6.00	12.50	22.50	37.50	—

KM# L81 1/8 REAL (Octavo)
Copper Or Bronze **Issuer:** Zamora **Obv:** Eagle on cactus above sprays **Rev:** Liberty cap, bow and arrows above sprays. With or without various countermarks

Date	Mintage	Good	VG	F	VF	XF
1852	—	6.00	12.50	22.50	37.50	—
1853	—	6.00	12.50	22.50	37.50	—
1854	—	6.00	12.50	22.50	37.50	—
1856	—	6.00	12.50	22.50	37.50	—
1857	—	6.00	12.50	22.50	37.50	—
1858	—	6.00	12.50	22.50	37.50	—

Note: These pieces are also found with various countermarks; "Za" in a dentilated circle is the most common; "1/8" in a circular countermark is also encountered

Zapotlan

KM# L84 1/8 REAL (Octavo)
Copper **Issuer:** Zapotlan **Obv. Legend:** ZAPO/TLAN/1813

Date	Mintage	Good	VG	F	VF	XF
1813	—	17.50	27.50	40.00	65.00	—

REPUBLIC

First

MINT MARKS
A, AS - Alamos
CE - Real de Catorce
CA,CH - Chihuahua
C, Cn, Gn(error) - Culiacan
D, Do - Durango
EoMo - Estado de Mexico
Ga - Guadalajara
GC - Guadalupe y Calvo
G, Go - Guanajuato
H, Ho - Hermosillo
M, Mo - Mexico City
O, OA - Oaxaca
SLP, PI, P, I/P - San Luis Potosi
Z, Zs – Zacatecas
ASSAYERS' INITIALS

ALAMOS MINT

PG	1862-68	Pascual Gaxiola
DL, L	1866-79	Domingo Larraguibel
AM	1872-74	Antonio Moreno
ML, L	1878-95	Manuel Larraguibel

REAL DE CATORCE MINT

ML	1863	Mariano Cristobal Ramirez

CHIHUAHUA MINT

MR	1831-34	Mariano Cristobal Ramirez
AM	1833-39	Jose Antonio Mucharraz
MJ	1832	Jose Mariano Jimenez
RG	1839-56	Rodrigo Garcia
JC	1856-65	Joaquin Campa
BA	1858	Bruno Arriada
FP	1866	Francisco Potts
JC	1866-1868	Jose Maria Gomez del Campo
MM, M	1868-95	Manuel Merino
AV	1873-80	Antonio Valero
EA	1877	Eduardo Avila
JM	1877	Jacobo Mucharraz
GR	1877	Guadalupe Rocha
MG	1880-82	Manuel Gameros

CULIACAN MINT

CE	1846-70	Clemente Espinosa de los Monteros
C	1870	???
PV	1860-61	Pablo Viruega
MP, P	1871-76	Manuel Onofre Parodi
GP	1876	Celso Gaxiola & Manuel Onofre Parodi
CG, G	1876-78	Celso Gaxiola
JD, D	1878-82	Juan Dominguez
AM, M	1882-1899	Antonio Moreno
F	1870	Fernando Ferrari
JQ, Q	1899-1903	Jesus S. Quiroz

DURANGO MINT

RL	1825-1832	???
RM	1830-48	Ramon Mascarenas
OMC	1840	Octavio Martinez de Castro
CM	1848-76	Clemente Moron
JMR	1849-52	Jose Maria Ramirez
CP, P	1853-64, 1867-73	Carlos Leon de la Pena
LT	1864-65	???
JMP, P	1877	Carlos Miguel de la Palma
PE, E	1878	Pedro Espejo
TB, B	1878-80	Trinidad Barrera
JP	1880-94	J. Miguel Palma
MC, C,	1882-90	Manuel M. Canseco or Melchor Calderon
JB	1885	Jocobo Blanco
ND, D	1892-95	Norberto Dominguez

ESTADO DE MEXICO MINT

L	1828-30	Luis Valazquez de la Cadena
F	1828-30	Francisco Parodi

GUADALAJARA MINT

FS	1818-35	Francisco Suarez
JM	1830-32	???
JG	1836-39, 1842-67	Juan de Dios Guzman
MC	1839-46	Manuel Cueras
JM	1867-69	Jesus P. Manzano
IC, C	1869-77	Ignacio Canizo y Soto
MC	1874-75	Manuel Contreras
JA, A	1877-81	Julio Arancivia
FS, S	1880-82	Fernando Sayago
TB, B	1883-84	Trinidad Barrera
AH, H	1884-85	Antonio Hernandez y Prado
JS, S	1885-95	Jose S. Schiafino

GUADALUPE Y CALVO MINT

MP	1844-52	Manuel Onofre Parodi

GUANAJUATO MINT

JJ	1825-26	Jose Mariano Jimenez
MJ, MR, JM, PG, PJ, PF		???
PM	1841-48, 1853-61	Patrick Murphy
YF	1862-68	Yldefonso Flores
YE	1862-63	Ynocencio Espinoza
FR	1870-78	Faustino Ramirez
SB, RR		???
RS	1891-1900	Rosendo Sandoval

HERMOSILLO MINT

PP	1835-36	Pedro Peimbert
FM	1871-76	Florencio Monteverde
MP	1866	Manuel Onofre Parodi
PR	1866-75	Pablo Rubio
R	1874-75	Pablo Rubio
GR	1877	Guadalupe Rocha
AF, F	1876-77	Alejandro Fourcade
JA, A	1877-83	Jesus Acosta
FM, M	1883-86	Fernando Mendez
FG, G	1886-95	Fausto Gaxiola

MEXICO CITY MINT

Because of the great number of assayers for this mint (Mexico City is a much larger mint than any of the others)there is much confusion as to which initial stands for which assayer at any one time. Therefore we feel that it would be of no value to list the assayers.

OAXACA MINT

AE	1859-91	Agustin Endner
E	1889-90	Agustin Endner
FR	1861-64	Francisco de la Rosa
EN	1890	Eduardo Navarro Luna
N	1890	Eduardo Navarro Luna

POTOSI MINT

JS	1827-42	Juan Sanabria
AM	1838, 1843-49	Jose Antonio Mucharraz
PS	1842-43, 1848-49, 1857-61, 1867-70	Pompaso Sanabria
S	1869-70	Pomposo Sanabria
MC	1849-59	Mariano Catano
RO	1859-65	Romualdo Obregon
MH, H	1870-85	Manuel Herrera Razo
O	1870-73	Juan R. Ochoa
CA, G	1867-70	Carlos Aguirre Gomez
BE, E	1879-81	Blas Escontria
LC, C	1885-86	Luis Cuevas
MR, R	1886-93	Mariano Reyes

ZACATECAS MINT

A	1825-29	Adalco
Z	1825-26	Mariano Zaldivar
V	1824-31	Jose Mariano Vela
O	1829-67	Manuel Ochoa
M	1831-67	Manuel Miner
VL	1860-66	Vicente Larranaga
JS	1867-68, 1876-86	J.S. de Santa Ana
YH	1868-74	Ygnacio Hierro
JA	1874-76	Juan H. Acuna
FZ	18861905	Francisco de P. Zarate

PROFILE EAGLE COINAGE

The first coins of the Republic were of the distinctive Profile Eagle style, sometimes called the "Hooked Neck Eagle". They were struck first in Mexico City in 1823 in denominations of eight reales and eight escudos. In 1824, they were produced at the Durango and Guanajuato mints in addition to Mexico City. Denominations included the one half, one, two and eight reales. No gold escudos of this design were struck in 1824. In 1825, only the eight reales were struck briefly at the Guanajuato mint.

NOTE: For a more extensive examination of Profile Eagle Coinage, please refer to Hookneck - El Aguila de Perfil by Clyde Hubbard and David O Harrow.

KM# 369   1/2 REAL
1.6900 g., 0.9030 Silver 0.0491 oz. ASW **Obv:** Full breast Profile eagle **Rev:** Cap and rays **Mint:** Mexico City **Note:** Die varieties exist.

Date	Mintage	F	VF	XF	Unc	BU
1824Mo JM	—	45.00	75.00	150	750	—

KM# 371.1   REAL
3.3800 g., 0.9030 Silver 0.0981 oz. ASW **Obv:** Thin Profile eagle **Rev:** Superscript S reversed **Mint:** Durango

Date	Mintage	F	VF	XF	Unc	BU
1824Do RL	—	5,500	9,500	13,000	—	—

KM# 371.2   REAL
3.3800 g., 0.9030 Silver 0.0981 oz. ASW **Obv:** Thin Profile eagle **Rev:** Superscript S normal **Mint:** Durango

Date	Mintage	F	VF	XF	Unc	BU
1824Do RL 3 known	—	—	—	—	—	—

Mint mark: Do

KM# 373.1   2 REALES
6.7600 g., 0.9030 Silver 0.1962 oz. ASW **Obv:** Profile eagle, snake in beak **Obv. Legend:** REPUBLICA • MEXICANA **Rev:** Radiant cap **Mint:** Durango **Note:** Die varieties exist.

Date	Mintage	F	VF	XF	Unc	BU
1824Do RL	—	50.00	125	850	2,200	—

KM# 373.2   2 REALES
6.7600 g., 0.9030 Silver 0.1962 oz. ASW **Obv:** Profile eagle, snake in beak **Obv. Legend:** Thin profile **Rev:** Radiant cap **Rev. Legend:** Type 1, dot before 2R in legend **Mint:** Durango

Date	Mintage	F	VF	XF	Unc	BU
1824D RL	—	100	200	1,000	3,000	—

KM# 373.3   2 REALES
6.7600 g., 0.9030 Silver 0.1962 oz. ASW **Obv:** Profile eagle, snake in beak **Obv. Legend:** Thin profile **Rev:** Radiant cap **Rev. Legend:** Type II, no dot before 2R in legend **Mint:** Durango

Date	Mintage	F	VF	XF	Unc	BU
1824D RL	—	100	200	1,000	3,000	—

KM# 373.4   2 REALES
Obv: Profile eagle, snake in beak **Obv. Legend:** REPUBLICA • MEXICANA **Rev:** Radiant cap **Mint:** Mexico City **Note:** Varieties exist.

Date	Mintage	F	VF	XF	Unc	BU
1824Mo JM	—	30.00	70.00	450	2,000	—

Note: No coins are known with visible feather details on the eagle's breast

KM# A376.2   8 REALES
27.0700 g., 0.9030 Silver 0.7859 oz. ASW **Obv:** Full breast profile eagle, snake in beak **Obv. Legend:** REPUBLICA MEXICANA **Rev:** Radiant cap **Edge:** Standard or Republic **Mint:** Mexico City

Date	Mintage	F	VF	XF	Unc	BU
1823Mo JM	—	150	300	800	4,500	—
1824Mo JM	—	125	250	700	4,000	—

Typical Submissive
Snake Obverse

KM# A376.1   8 REALES
27.0700 g., 0.9030 Silver 0.7859 oz. ASW **Obv:** Full breast profile eagle, snake in beak **Obv. Legend:** REPUBLICA MEXICANA. **Rev:** Radiant cap **Mint:** Guanajuato

Date	Mintage	F	VF	XF	Unc	BU
1824Go JM	—	250	400	1,100	3,500	—
1825/4Go JJ	—	600	1,200	2,750	7,000	—
1825Go JJ	—	500	750	1,400	5,500	—

KM# A376.3   8 REALES
27.0700 g., 0.9030 Silver 0.7859 oz. ASW **Obv:** Full breast profile eagle, snake in beak **Rev:** Radiant cap **Edge:** Colonial or circle and rectangle **Mint:** Mexico City

Date	Mintage	F	VF	XF	Unc	BU
1823Mo JM	—	—	—	—	—	—
Rare						

The Round-Topped Three

KM# A376.4   8 REALES
27.0700 g., 0.9030 Silver 0.7859 oz. ASW **Obv:** Full breast profile eagle, snake in beak **Rev:** Radiant cap, round topped three **Edge:** Standard or Republic **Mint:** Mexico City

Date	Mintage	F	VF	XF	Unc	BU
1823Mo JM	—	2,000	4,000	6,000	8,000	—

Note: Many die varieties exist; Illustrations of one of the die differences is the size of the snake loop at the eagle's beak; This difference is not apparent except on the 1824 Mo 8 Reales

Typical Folded
Snake Obverse

NOTE: Legible Libertads on the Cap are common on Durango eight reales.

Med. Libertad	**Small Libertad**	**Large Libertad**
Cap Reverse	**Cap Reverse**	**Cap Reverse**

NOTE: The three styles of obverses and the three styles of reverses were combined   to make six distinct varieties of coins.

KM# 376.1   8 REALES
27.0700 g., 0.9030 Silver 0.7859 oz. ASW **Obv:** Thin profile eagle, defiant snake **Rev:** Radiant cap, medium Libertad **Mint:** Durango

Date	Mintage	F	VF	XF	Unc	BU
1824Do RL	—	500	1,200	4,500	7,000	—

Note: Five die varieties are known, all are rare. Ira & Larry Goldberg Millennia Sale 5-08, MS-64 realized $25,000.

KM# A376.5   8 REALES
27.0700 g., 0.9030 Silver 0.7859 oz. ASW **Obv:** Full breast profile eagle, snake in beak, REPULICA (error) **Rev:** Radiant cap **Mint:** Mexico City

Date	Mintage	F	VF	XF	Unc	BU
1824Mo JM	—	6,000	9,000	11,000	—	—

Note: Legible Libertads on the cap are not as prevalent on the Mexico City 8 Reales as on the Durango 8 Reales; They are much more numerous than on the Guanajuato 8 Reales

KM# 376.2 8 REALES
27.0700 g., 0.9030 Silver 0.7859 oz. ASW **Obv:** Thin profile
eagle, defiant snake **Obv. Legend:** REPUBLICA MEXICANA
Rev: Radiant cap, small Libertad **Mint:** Durango

Date	Mintage	F	VF	XF	Unc	BU
1824Do RL	—	300	400	1,600	3,500	—

Note: Eleven die varieties are known, some are rare

KM# 376.3 8 REALES
27.0700 g., 0.9030 Silver 0.7859 oz. ASW **Obv:** Thin profile
eagle, submissive snake **Obv. Legend:** REPUBLICA
MEXICANA **Rev:** Radiant cap, small Libertad **Mint:** Durango

Date	Mintage	F	VF	XF	Unc	BU
1824Do RL	—	200	350	1,250	2,750	—

Note: Seven die varieties are known, some are rare

KM# 376.4 8 REALES
27.0700 g., 0.9030 Silver 0.7859 oz. ASW **Obv:** Thin profile
eagle, submissive snake **Rev:** Radiant cap, large Libertad
Mint: Durango

Date	Mintage	F	VF	XF	Unc	BU
1824Do RL	—	200	350	1,250	2,750	—

Note: Twelve die varieties known, some are rare

KM# 376.5 8 REALES
27.0700 g., 0.9030 Silver 0.7859 oz. ASW **Obv:** Thin profile
eagle, folded snake **Rev:** Radiant cap, small Libertad **Mint:**
Durango

Date	Mintage	F	VF	XF	Unc	BU
1824Do RL	—	200	350	1,200	2,500	—

Note: Only one die variety is known

KM# 376.6 8 REALES
27.0700 g., 0.9030 Silver 0.7859 oz. ASW **Obv:** Thin profile
eagle, folded snake **Rev:** Radiant cap, large Libertad **Mint:**
Durango

Date	Mintage	F	VF	XF	Unc	BU
1824Do RL	—	200	400	1,500	3,000	—

Note: Eleven die varieties known, some are rare

Type I Obverse/Reverse

NOTE: The cap on the reverse of the curved tail Type I
points to the "A" of LIBERTAD.

KM# 382.1 8 ESCUDOS
27.0700 g., 0.8750 Gold 0.7615 oz. AGW **Obv:** Profile eagle,
snake's tail curved **Obv. Legend:** REPUBLICA MEXICANA
Rev: Open book, hand holding stick with cap, cap points to
"A" of LIBERTAD **Rev. Legend:** LIBERTAD EN... **Mint:**
Mexico City

Date	Mintage	F	VF	XF	Unc	BU
1823Mo JM	—	7,000	10,000	20,000	35,000	—

Note: American Numismatic Rarities Eliasberg sale 4-05,
MS-61 realized $55,200.

Type II Obverse/Reverse

NOTE: The cap on the reverse of the looped tail Type II
points to the "T" of LIBERTAD.

KM# 382.2 8 ESCUDOS
27.0700 g., 0.8750 Gold 0.7615 oz. AGW **Obv:** Profile eagle,
snake's tail looped **Obv. Legend:** REPUBLICA MEXICANA
Rev: Open book, hand holding stick with cap, cap points to
"T" of LIBERTAD **Rev. Legend:** LIBERTAD EN... **Mint:**
Mexico City

Date	Mintage	F	VF	XF	Unc	BU
1823Mo JM	—	6,000	9,000	18,000	35,000	—

Note: The quality of the strikes of Type I coins is almost
always superior to that of the Type II; Details of the eagle
feathers, cactus and lettering on the open book are better on
most Type I coins but the Type II coins are scarcer; Type I
coins outnumber Type II coins by about two to one

STATE COINAGE

KM# 316   1/16 REAL (Medio Octavo)
4.7500 g., Copper, 21 mm. **Obv:** Bow, quiver and flag **Obv. Legend:** DEPARTAMENTO DE JALISCO **Rev:** Seated figure, left, cap on pole **Edge:** Oblique reeding **Mint:** Guadalajara

Date	Mintage	Good	VG	F	VF	XF
1860	—	3.00	8.00	17.50	55.00	—

KM# 317   1/16 REAL (Medio Octavo)
4.7500 g., Copper, 21 mm. **Obv. Legend:** ESTADO LIBRE DE JALISCO **Edge:** Oblique reeding **Mint:** Guadalajara

Date	Mintage	Good	VG	F	VF	XF
1861	—	2.50	6.00	13.50	32.50	—

KM# 320   1/8 REAL (Octavo Real)
Copper **Obv:** Facing eagle, snake in beak, value at lower left **Rev:** Radiant Libertad above date within wreath **Rev. Legend:** LIBERTAD **Edge:** Oblique reeding **Mint:** Durango **Note:** Size varies 17-18mm. Weight varies 2.5-4 g. These pieces were frequently struck over 1/8 Real, dated 1821-23 of Nueva Vizcaya. All known examples struck over these coins are believed to be contemporary counterfeits.

Date	Mintage	Good	VG	F	VF	XF
1824D	—	5.00	12.50	35.00	85.00	—
1828D	—	150	250	400	1,000	—

KM# 338   1/8 REAL (Octavo Real)
4.0000 g., Brass, 21 mm. **Obv:** Monument **Obv. Legend:** ESTo LIBe FEDo DE ZACATECAS **Rev:** Floating angel holding radiant cap **Edge:** Oblique reeding **Mint:** Zacatecas

Date	Mintage	Good	VG	F	VF	XF
1825	—	3.00	5.50	12.00	25.00	—
1827	—	3.00	5.50	12.00	25.00	—
1827	—	12.00	20.00	40.00	100	—
Note: Inverted A for V in OCTAVO						
1827	—	15.00	25.00	50.00	120	—
Note: OCTAVA (error)						
1827 Inverted 1	—	12.00	20.00	40.00	100	—
1829 Rare	—	—	—	—	—	—
1830	—	2.75	5.00	8.00	20.00	—
1831	—	4.50	6.75	13.50	27.50	—
1832	—	2.75	5.00	8.00	20.00	—
1833	—	2.75	5.00	8.00	20.00	—
1835	—	3.50	6.00	10.00	25.00	—
1846	—	3.50	6.00	10.00	25.00	—
1851	—	38.00	70.00	115	220	—
1852	—	3.50	6.00	10.00	25.00	—
1858	—	2.75	5.00	8.00	20.00	—
1859	—	2.75	5.00	8.00	20.00	—
1862	—	2.75	5.00	8.00	20.00	—
1863 Reversed 6 in date	—	2.75	5.00	8.00	20.00	—

KM# 321   1/8 REAL (Octavo Real)
3.3000 g., Copper **Obv:** Child holding bow, right, small tree **Rev:** Radiant cap **Rev. Legend:** OCTo. DE. R. DE DO **Edge:** Oblique reeding **Mint:** Durango **Note:** Size varies 18-19mm.

Date	Mintage	Good	VG	F	VF	XF
1828D	—	7.50	18.50	40.00	115	—

KM# 335   1/8 REAL (Octavo Real)
Copper **Obv. Legend:** ESTADO DE OCCIDENTE **Edge:** Oblique reeding **Mint:** Alamos **Note:** Size varies: 17-18mm, weight varies: 2-3 g. The C before date on reverse may be a mint mark standing for Concepcion de Alamos.

Date	Mintage	Good	VG	F	VF	XF
1828 Reverse S	—	35.00	65.00	120	—	—
1829	—	30.00	60.00	110	—	—

KM# 329   1/8 REAL (Octavo Real)
4.8000 g., Copper, 21 mm. **Obv:** Bow, quiver and flag **Obv. Legend:** ESTADO LIBRE DE JALISCO **Rev:** Seated figure, left, cap on pole **Edge:** Oblique reeding **Mint:** Guadalajara

Date	Mintage	Good	VG	F	VF	XF
1828	—	3.00	5.00	8.00	22.50	—
1831	—	62.50	100	185	275	—
1832/28	—	4.50	6.50	11.00	27.50	—
1832	—	4.50	6.00	10.00	25.00	—
1833	—	3.50	5.50	9.00	23.50	—
1834	—	37.50	80.00	150	235	—

KM# 326   1/8 REAL (Octavo Real)
3.5000 g., Copper, 21 mm. **Obv:** Seated figure **Obv. Legend:** ESTADO LIBRE DE GUANAJUATO **Rev:** Cap within center wreath of stylized rays, date below **Edge:** Ornamented with incuse dots **Mint:** Guanajuato

Date	Mintage	Good	VG	F	VF	XF
1829	—	3.00	5.00	10.00	26.50	—
1829	—	4.00	6.50	12.50	28.50	—
Note: Error with GUANJUATO						
1830	—	8.00	13.50	28.50	65.00	—

KM# 336   1/8 REAL (Octavo Real)
Copper, 21 mm. **Obv:** Value above divides wreath, open book within **Obv. Legend:** ESTADO LIBRE DE SAN LUIS POTOSI **Rev:** Seated figure **Edge:** Oblique reeding **Mint:** San Luis Potosi **Note:** Weight varies (1829-31) 4.5-5.5 g; (1859) 4-4.5 g.

Date	Mintage	Good	VG	F	VF	XF
1829	—	6.00	11.00	26.50	62.50	—
1830	—	8.50	15.00	30.00	70.00	—
1831	—	6.00	9.50	18.50	47.50	—
1859	—	5.00	8.00	16.50	45.00	—

Date	Mintage	Good	VG	F	VF	XF
1865/1	—	—	—	—	—	—

Note: Reported, not confirmed

KM# 318   1/8 REAL (Octavo Real)
3.5400 g., Copper, 20 mm. **Obv. Legend:** ESTADO SOBERANO DE CHIHUAHUA **Edge:** Plain **Mint:** Chihuahua

Date	Mintage	Good	VG	F	VF	XF
1833	—	350	750	—	—	—
1834	—	350	750	—	—	—
1835/3	—	350	750	—	—	—

KM# 322   1/8 REAL (Octavo Real)
3.5000 g., Copper, 20 mm. **Obv:** Profile eagle, snake in beak **Obv. Legend:** ESTADO DE DURANGO **Rev:** Value and date within circle and wreath **Mint:** Durango

Date	Mintage	Good	VG	F	VF	XF
1833	—	350	—	—	—	—

KM# 339   1/8 REAL (Octavo Real)
4.0000 g., Copper, 21 mm. **Obv:** Monument **Obv. Legend:** DEPARTAMENTO DE ZACATECAS **Rev:** Floating angel holding radiant cap **Edge:** Oblique reeding **Mint:** Zacatecas

Date	Mintage	Good	VG	F	VF	XF
1836	—	5.00	8.50	17.50	40.00	—
1845	—	7.50	12.50	22.50	50.00	—
1846	—	8.50	10.00	20.00	45.00	—

KM# 323   1/8 REAL (Octavo Real)
3.5000 g., Copper **Obv:** Facing eagle, snake in beak **Obv. Legend:** REPUBLICA MEXICANA **Rev:** Value and date within circle and wreath **Mint:** Durango **Note:** Size varies: 19-23mm.

Date	Mintage	Good	VG	F	VF	XF
1842/33	—	12.50	22.50	42.50	115	—
1842	—	8.50	15.00	32.50	100	—

KM# 324   1/8 REAL (Octavo Real)
Copper, 19 mm. **Obv:** Facing eagle, snake in beak **Obv. Legend:** REPUBLICA MEXICANA **Rev. Legend:** DEPARTAMENTO DE DURANGO **Edge:** Ornamented with arc and dot pattern **Mint:** Durango **Note:** Weight varies: 3.5-3.8 g.

Date	Mintage	Good	VG	F	VF	XF
1845	—	22.50	55.00	115	250	—
1846 Rare	—	—	—	—	—	—
1847	—	3.50	7.50	17.50	37.50	—

KM# 325   1/8 REAL (Octavo Real)
Copper, 19 mm. **Obv:** Facing eagle, snake in beak **Obv. Legend:** REPUBLICA MEXICANA **Rev:** Value within circle **Rev. Legend:** ESTADO DE DURANGO **Edge:** Ornamented with arc and dot pattern **Mint:** Durango **Note:** Weight varies: 3.5-3.8 g.

Date	Mintage	Good	VG	F	VF	XF
1851	—	3.50	8.00	12.50	33.50	—
1852/1	—	3.50	6.50	11.00	33.50	—
1852	—	3.00	5.00	8.00	30.00	—
1854	—	7.00	13.50	28.50	62.50	—

KM# 319   1/8 REAL (Octavo Real)
3.5400 g., Copper, 20 mm. **Obv:** Standing figure facing holding bow and arrow **Obv. Legend:** ESTADO DE CHIHUAHUA **Rev:** Date and value within wreath **Edge:** Plain **Mint:** Chihuahua

Date	Mintage	Good	VG	F	VF	XF
1855	—	5.00	8.50	25.00	75.00	—

KM# 327   1/8 REAL (Octavo Real)
7.2000 g., Brass, 29 mm. **Obv:** Facing eagle, snake in beak **Obv. Legend:** ESTADO LIBRE DE GUANAJUATO **Rev:** Oval arms within sprays below radiant cap **Edge:** Plain **Mint:** Guanajuato

Date	Mintage	Good	VG	F	VF	XF
1856	—	7.50	12.00	20.00	75.00	—

KM# 330   1/8 REAL (Octavo Real)
9.5000 g., Copper, 28 mm. **Obv. Legend:** ESTADO LIBRE DE JALISCO **Rev:** Seated figure, left, cap on pole **Edge:** Oblique reeding **Mint:** Guadalajara

Date	Mintage	Good	VG	F	VF	XF
1856	—	3.00	6.00	9.00	18.50	—
1857	—	3.00	6.00	9.00	18.50	—
1858	—	3.00	6.00	9.00	18.50	—
1861	—	75.00	135	200	300	—
1862/1	—	4.00	7.00	10.00	22.50	—
1862	—	4.00	7.00	10.00	22.50	—

KM# 328   1/8 REAL (Octavo Real)
Brass, 25 mm. **Obv:** Facing eagle, snake in beak **Obv.**
Legend: ESTADO LIBRE DE GUANAJUATO **Rev:** Oval
arms within sprays below radiant cap **Edge:** Plain **Mint:**
Guanajuato **Note:** Weight varies: 7.1-7.2 g.

Date	Mintage	Good	VG	F	VF	XF
1856	—	4.00	7.50	12.50	35.00	—
1857	—	3.50	6.00	10.00	30.00	—

KM# 328a   1/8 REAL (Octavo Real)
Copper, 25 mm. **Obv:** Facing eagle, snake in beak **Obv.**
Legend: ESTADO LIBRE DE GUANAJUATO **Rev:** Oval
arms within sprays below radiant cap **Edge:** Plain **Mint:**
Guanajuato **Note:** Weight varies: 7.1-7.2 g.

Date	Mintage	Good	VG	F	VF	XF
1857	—	7.00	16.50	32.50	55.00	—

KM# 331   1/8 REAL (Octavo Real)
9.5000 g., Copper, 28 mm. **Obv:** Bow, quiver and flag **Obv.**
Legend: DEPARTAMENTO DE JALISCO **Edge:** Oblique
reeding **Mint:** Guadalajara

Date	Mintage	Good	VG	F	VF	XF
1858	—	4.00	7.00	13.50	28.50	—
1859	—	3.00	5.75	8.00	20.00	—
1860/59	—	3.25	6.00	9.00	22.50	—
1860	—	3.25	6.00	9.00	22.50	—
1862	—	4.00	8.00	17.50	37.50	—

KM# 337   1/8 REAL (Octavo Real)
6.7000 g., Copper, 28 mm. **Obv. Legend:** ESTO LIBE Y
SOBO DE SONORA **Edge:** Reeded **Mint:** Hermosillo

Date	Mintage	Good	VG	F	VF	XF
1859 Rare	—	—	—	—	—	—

KM# 366   1/4 REAL (Un Quarto/Una Quartilla)
8.0000 g., Brass **Obv:** Monument **Obv. Legend:** ESTO LIBE
FEDO DE ZACATECAS **Rev:** Floating angel with radiant cap
on tip of arrow **Edge:** Oblique reeding **Mint:** Zacatecas **Note:**
Size varies: 28-29mm.

Date	Mintage	Good	VG	F	VF	XF
1824 Rare	—	—	—	—	—	—
1825	—	2.50	5.00	10.00	20.00	—
1826	—	75.00	130	220	325	—
1827/17	—	2.50	5.00	9.00	20.00	—
1829	—	2.50	5.00	9.00	20.00	—
1830	—	2.50	5.00	8.50	20.00	—
1831	—	40.00	85.00	140	220	—
1832	—	2.50	5.00	9.00	20.00	—
1833	—	2.50	5.00	9.00	20.00	—
1834 Rare	—	—	—	—	—	—
1835	—	2.50	5.00	9.00	20.00	—

Date	Mintage	Good	VG	F	VF	XF
1846	—	2.50	5.00	8.50	20.00	—
1847	—	2.50	5.00	8.50	20.00	—
1852	—	2.50	5.00	8.50	20.00	—
1853	—	2.50	5.00	8.50	20.00	—
1855	—	4.50	10.00	25.00	65.00	—
1858	—	2.50	5.00	8.50	20.00	—
1859	—	2.50	5.00	8.50	20.00	—
1860	—	75.00	125	200	310	—
1862/57	—	2.50	5.00	8.50	20.00	—
1862/59/7	—	8.00	18.00	37.50	75.00	—
1862	—	2.50	5.00	8.00	20.00	—
1863/2	—	2.50	5.00	8.00	20.00	—
1863	—	2.50	5.00	8.00	20.00	—
1864	—	4.00	11.00	25.00	60.00	—

KM# 359   1/4 REAL (Un Quarto/Una Quartilla)
Copper **Obv:** Value above divides wreath, open book within
Obv. Legend: ESTADO LIBRE DE SAN LUIS POTOSI **Rev:**
Seated figure with cap on tip of arrow **Rev. Legend:** MEXICO
LIBRE **Edge:** Oblique reeding **Mint:** San Luis Potosi **Note:**
Size varies: 25-31mm, weight varies: (1828-32) 9-10 g.;
(1859-60) 8-9 g.

Date	Mintage	Good	VG	F	VF	XF
1828	—	2.25	4.00	9.00	19.00	—
1829	—	3.00	5.00	9.00	20.00	—
1830	—	2.25	4.00	8.00	17.00	—
1832	—	4.00	6.00	10.00	22.50	—
1859 Large LIBRE	—	2.75	4.00	8.00	18.00	—
1859 Small LIBRE	—	2.75	4.00	8.00	18.00	—
1860	—	2.75	4.00	8.00	18.00	—

KM# 351   1/4 REAL (Un Quarto/Una Quartilla)
7.0000 g., Copper, 27 mm. **Obv:** Seated figure with head
right **Obv. Legend:** ESTADO LIBRE DE GUANAJUATO **Rev:**
Cap within radiant wreath **Edge:** Ornamented with incuse dots
Mint: Guanajuato

Date	Mintage	Good	VG	F	VF	XF
1828	—	3.75	8.00	18.50	40.00	—
1828	—	4.00	9.00	20.00	42.50	—

Note: Error with GUANJUATO

1829	—	5.50	12.00	22.50	47.50	—

KM# 353   1/4 REAL (Un Quarto/Una Quartilla)
9.3500 g., Copper, 28 mm. **Obv:** Oblique reeding **Obv.**
Legend: ESTADO LIBRE DE JALISCO **Rev:** Seated figure,
left, cap on pole **Mint:** Guadalajara

Date	Mintage	Good	VG	F	VF	XF
1828	—	3.75	7.00	15.00	37.50	—
1829/8	—	3.00	6.00	13.00	33.00	—
1829	—	3.00	6.00	13.00	33.00	—
1830/20	—	3.00	5.00	10.00	28.50	—
1830/29	—	3.00	5.00	10.00	28.50	—
1830	—	3.00	5.00	10.00	28.50	—
1831 Rare	—	—	—	—	—	—
1832/20	—	3.00	5.00	10.00	28.50	—
1832/28	—	3.00	5.00	10.00	28.50	—
1832	—	2.50	5.00	9.00	27.50	—
1833/2	—	3.00	5.00	9.00	27.50	—
1834	—	2.50	5.00	9.00	27.50	—
1835/3	—	3.00	5.00	9.00	27.50	—
1835	—	2.50	5.00	9.00	27.50	—
1836 Rare	—	—	—	—	—	—

KM# 364   1/4 REAL (Un Quarto/Una Quartilla)
Copper **Obv:** Arrow divides quivers **Obv. Legend:** EST. D.
SONORA UNA CUART **Rev:** Stylized radiant cap **Edge:**
Oblique reeding **Mint:** Hermosillo **Note:** Size varies: 21-
22mm. Weight varies: 2.3-5.5 g.

Date	Mintage	Good	VG	F	VF	XF
1831 L.S. Rare	—	—	—	—	—	—
1832 L.S.	—	2.75	5.50	15.00	50.00	—
1833/2 L.S.	—	2.00	4.00	12.50	37.50	—
1833 L.S.	—	2.00	4.00	12.50	37.50	—
1834 L.S.	—	2.00	4.00	12.50	37.50	—
1835/3 L.S.	—	2.50	5.50	15.00	40.00	—
1835 L.S.	—	2.00	4.00	12.50	37.50	—
1836 L.S.	—	2.00	4.00	12.50	37.50	—

KM# 340   1/4 REAL (Un Quarto/Una Quartilla)
Copper, 27 mm. **Obv:** Child facing, holding bow and arrow
Obv. Legend: ESTADO SOBERANO DE CHIHUAHUA **Rev:**
Value and date within palm wreath **Edge:** Herringbone pattern
Mint: Chihuahua

Date	Mintage	Good	VG	F	VF	XF
1833	—	7.50	16.50	37.50	85.00	—
1834	—	6.50	13.50	28.00	55.00	—
1835	—	5.00	10.00	22.00	50.00	—
1835 Plain edge	—	5.00	8.00	12.00	50.00	—

KM# 354   1/4 REAL (Un Quarto/Una Quartilla)
9.3500 g., Copper, 28 mm. **Obv. Legend:**
DEPARTAMENTO DE JALISCO **Edge:** Oblique reeding
Mint: Guadalajara

Date	Mintage	Good	VG	F	VF	XF
1836	—	120	200	350	—	—

KM# 367   1/4 REAL (Un Quarto/Una Quartilla)
8.0000 g., Brass **Obv:** Monument **Obv. Legend:**
DEPARTAMENTO DE ZACATECAS **Rev:** Floating angel with

radiant cap on tip of arrow **Edge:** Oblique reeding **Mint:**
Zacatecas **Note:** Size varies: 28-29mm.

Date	Mintage	Good	VG	F	VF	XF
1836	—	4.00	8.50	13.50	25.00	—
1845 Rare	—	—	—	—	—	—
1846	—	3.50	6.75	9.00	20.00	—

KM# 345   1/4 REAL (Un Quarto/Una Quartilla)
7.0000 g., Copper, 27 mm. **Obv:** Facing eagle, snake in beak
Obv. Legend: REPUBLICA MEXICANA **Rev:** Value and date
within circle, DURANGO above in wreath **Mint:** Durango

Date	Mintage	Good	VG	F	VF	XF
1845 Rare	—	—	—	—	—	—

KM# 341   1/4 REAL (Un Quarto/Una Quartilla)
7.0800 g., Copper, 27 mm. **Obv:** Stylized figure facing,
holding bow and arrow **Obv. Legend:** ESTADO LIBRE DE
CHIHUAHUA **Rev:** Value and date within designed wreath
Edge: Plain **Mint:** Chihuahua

Date	Mintage	Good	VG	F	VF	XF
1846	—	3.50	6.00	12.00	37.50	—
Note: With fraction bar						
1846	—	5.00	8.50	15.00	45.00	—
Note: Without fraction bar						

KM# 363   1/4 REAL (Un Quarto/Una Quartilla)
27.0000 g., Copper, 27 mm. **Obv:** Head left within wreath
Obv. Legend: ESTADO LIBRE Y SOBERANO DE SINALOA
Rev: Value and date within wreath **Edge:** Reeded **Mint:**
Culiacan

Date	Mintage	Good	VG	F	VF	XF
1847	—	3.50	5.50	12.00	23.50	—
1848	—	3.50	5.50	11.00	22.00	—
1859	—	3.00	4.50	7.50	16.50	—
1861	—	1.75	3.00	4.00	10.00	—
1862	—	1.75	3.00	4.00	11.00	—
1863	—	2.50	4.00	5.00	11.00	—
1864/3	—	2.50	4.00	5.00	11.00	—
1864	—	1.75	3.00	4.75	10.00	—
1865	—	3.00	5.50	8.50	18.50	—
1866/5	7,401,000	2.50	3.50	5.00	11.00	—
1866	Inc. above	1.75	3.00	4.00	10.00	—

KM# 363a   1/4 REAL (Un Quarto/Una Quartilla)
7.0000 g., Brass, 27 mm. **Obv:** Head left within wreath **Obv.
Legend:** ESTADO LIBRE Y SOBERANO DE SINALOA **Rev:**
Value and date within wreath **Edge:** Reeded **Mint:** Culiacan

Date	Mintage	Good	VG	F	VF	XF
1847	—	5.00	10.00	18.50	40.00	—

KM# 342   1/4 REAL (Un Quarto/Una Quartilla)
7.0800 g., Copper, 27 mm.   **Obv:** Stylized figure facing,
holding bow and arrow **Obv. Legend:** ESTADO DE
CHIHUAHUA **Rev:** Value and date within designed wreath
Edge: Plain **Mint:** Chihuahua

Date	Mintage	Good	VG	F	VF	XF
1855	—	2.50	5.75	13.50	40.00	—
1856	—	2.50	5.75	13.50	40.00	—

KM# 343   1/4 REAL (Un Quarto/Una Quartilla)
7.0800 g., Copper, 27 mm.   **Obv:** Stylized figure facing,
holding bow and arrow **Obv. Legend:** DEPARTAMENTO DE
CHIHUAHUA **Rev:** Value and date within designed wreath
Edge: Plain **Mint:** Chihuahua

Date	Mintage	Good	VG	F	VF	XF
1855	—	3.00	5.75	14.00	37.50	—
1855 DE (reversed D)	—	4.50	8.50	17.50	40.00	—

KM# 352   1/4 REAL (Un Quarto/Una Quartilla)
14.0000 g., Copper, 32 mm.   **Obv:** Facing eagle, snake in
beak **Obv. Legend:** EST. LIB. DE GUANAXUATO **Rev:** Oval
arms within sprays below radiant cap **Rev. Legend:** OMNIA
VINCIT LABOR **Edge:** Plain **Mint:** Guanajuato

Date	Mintage	Good	VG	F	VF	XF
1856	—	7.50	18.50	37.50	70.00	—
1857	—	6.50	13.50	27.50	50.00	—

KM# 352a   1/4 REAL (Un Quarto/Una Quartilla)
14.0000 g., Brass, 32 mm.   **Obv:** Facing eagle, snake in beak
Obv. Legend: EST. LIB. DE GUANAXUATO **Rev:** Oval arms
within sprays below radiant cap **Rev. Legend:** OMNIA VINCIT
LABOR **Edge:** Plain **Mint:** Guanajuato

Date	Mintage	Good	VG	F	VF	XF
1856	—	3.25	6.75	13.50	30.00	—
1857	—	3.25	6.75	13.50	30.00	—

KM# 346   1/4 REAL (Un Quarto/Una Quartilla)
7.5000 g., Copper, 27 mm.   **Obv:** Facing eagle, snake in beak

Obv. Legend: REPUBLICA MEXICANA **Rev:** Date, value
Rev. Legend: DURANGO **Edge:** Ornamented with arc and
dot pattern **Mint:** Durango

Date	Mintage	Good	VG	F	VF	XF
1858 Rare	—	—	—	—	—	—

KM# 347   1/4 REAL (Un Quarto/Una Quartilla)
7.5000 g., Copper, 27 mm.   **Obv:** Facing eagle, snake in beak
Obv. Legend: ESTADO DE DURANGO **Rev:** Radiant cap
above value and date within stylized sprays **Rev. Legend:**
CONSTITUCION **Edge:** Ornamented with arc and dot pattern
Mint: Durango **Note:** Brass examples have been reported,
but not confirmed.

Date	Mintage	Good	VG	F	VF	XF
1858	—	4.00	8.50	22.00	50.00	—

KM# 355   1/4 REAL (Un Quarto/Una Quartilla)
19.0000 g., Copper, 32 mm.   **Obv:** Bow, quiver and flag **Obv.
Legend:** ESTADO LIBRE DE JALISCO **Rev:** Seated figure,
left, cap on pole **Edge:** Oblique reeding **Mint:** Guadalajara

Date	Mintage	Good	VG	F	VF	XF
1858	—	3.00	6.00	11.00	25.00	—
1861	—	4.00	8.00	17.00	33.00	—
1862	—	3.00	6.00	11.00	25.00	—

KM# 356   1/4 REAL (Un Quarto/Una Quartilla)
19.0000 g., Copper, 32 mm.   **Obv:** Bow, quiver and flag **Obv.
Legend:** DEPARTAMENTO DE JALISCO **Rev:** Seated
figure, left, cap on pole **Edge:** Oblique reeding **Mint:**
Guadalajara

Date	Mintage	Good	VG	F	VF	XF
1858	—	3.00	6.00	9.00	20.00	—
1859/8	—	3.00	6.00	9.00	20.00	—
1859	—	3.00	6.00	9.00	20.00	—
1860	—	3.00	6.00	9.00	20.00	—

KM# 365 1/4 REAL (Un Quarto/Una Quartilla)
14.3000 g., Copper, 32 mm. **Obv:** Facing eagle, snake in beak **Obv. Legend:** ESTO. LIBE. Y SOBO. DE SONORA **Rev:** Seated figure, left, cap on pole **Edge:** Reeded **Mint:** Hermosillo

Date	Mintage	Good	VG	F	VF	XF
1859	—	3.00	8.00	12.00	30.00	—
1861/59	—	4.00	10.00	17.00	37.50	—
1861	—	3.00	8.00	12.00	30.00	—
1862	—	3.00	8.00	12.00	30.00	—
1863/2	—	8.00	19.00	37.50	85.00	—

KM# 344 1/4 REAL (Un Quarto/Una Quartilla)
Copper, 28 mm. **Obv:** Seated figure, right **Obv. Legend:** E. CHIHA LIBERTAD **Rev:** Value and date within wreath **Edge:** Plain **Mint:** Chihuahua **Note:** Weight varies 11-11.5 g.

Date	Mintage	Good	VG	F	VF	XF
1860	—	2.00	4.00	11.00	25.00	—
1861	—	2.00	4.00	11.00	25.00	—
1865/1	—	2.50	5.50	13.50	30.00	—
1865	—	6.00	14.00	28.50	65.00	—
1866/5	—	5.00	9.50	25.00	60.00	—
1866	—	2.00	4.00	11.00	25.00	—

Note: Coin rotation

1866	—	2.00	4.00	11.00	25.00	—

Note: Medal rotation

KM# 348 1/4 REAL (Un Quarto/Una Quartilla)
Copper, 27 mm. **Obv:** Facing eagle, snake in beak **Obv. Legend:** DEPARTAMENTO DE DURANGO **Rev:** Value and date within circular legend and wreath **Rev. Legend:** LIBERTAD EN EL ORDEN **Edge:** Ornamented with arc and dot pattern **Mint:** Durango **Note:** Weight varies: 7-7.5 g.

Date	Mintage	Good	VG	F	VF	XF
1860	—	2.50	7.00	17.00	42.25	—
1866	—	3.00	8.00	18.00	46.75	—

KM# 360 1/4 REAL (Un Quarto/Una Quartilla)
Copper **Obv:** Value above divides wreath, open book within **Obv. Legend:** ESTADO LIBRE DE SAN LUIS POTOSI **Rev:** Seated figure with cap on tip of arrow **Rev. Legend:** REPUBLICA MEXICANA **Edge:** Oblique reeding **Mint:** San Luis Potosi **Note:** Size varies: 25-31mm.

Date	Mintage	Good	VG	F	VF	XF
1862	1,367	2.75	4.00	8.00	17.00	—
1862 LIBR	Inc. above	4.00	6.00	9.00	18.00	—

KM# 349 1/4 REAL (Un Quarto/Una Quartilla)
7.0000 g., Copper **Obv:** Facing eagle, snake in beak **Obv. Legend:** ESTADO DE DURANGO **Rev:** Value and date above sprays **Rev. Legend:** INDEPENDENCIA Y LIBERTAD **Edge:** Ornamented with arc and dot pattern **Mint:** Durango **Note:** Size varies: 26-27mm.

Date	Mintage	Good	VG	F	VF	XF
1866	—	4.00	9.00	25.00	55.00	—

KM# 361 1/4 REAL (Un Quarto/Una Quartilla)
Copper **Obv. Legend:** ESTADO LIBRE Y SOBERANO DE S.L. POTOSI **Rev:** Radiant cap and value within wrath, date below **Rev. Legend:** LIBERTAD Y REFORMA **Edge:** Reeded or plain **Mint:** San Luis Potosi **Note:** Size varies: 27-28mm. Weight varies: 9-10 g.

Date	Mintage	Good	VG	F	VF	XF
1867	3,177,000	2.75	4.00	7.00	17.00	—
1867 AFG	Inc. above	2.75	4.00	7.00	17.00	—

Note: "AFG" are the coin designer/engraver initials

KM# 362 1/4 REAL (Un Quarto/Una Quartilla)
Copper **Obv. Legend:** ESTADO LIBRE Y SOBERANO DE S.L. POTOSI **Rev. Legend:** LIBERTAD Y REFORMA **Edge:** Plain **Mint:** San Luis Potosi

Date	Mintage	Good	VG	F	VF	XF
1867	Inc. above	2.75	4.00	7.00	17.00	—
1867 AFG	Inc. above	2.75	4.00	7.00	17.00	—

Note: "AFG" are the coin designer/engraver initials

KM# 350   1/4 REAL (Un Quarto/Una Quartilla)
7.5000 g., Copper, 27 mm. **Obv:** Facing eagle, snake in beak
Obv. Legend: ESTADO DE DURANGO **Rev:** Date and
circular legend, value within **Rev. Legend:** SUFRAGIO
LIBRE **Edge:** Ornamented with arc and dot pattern **Mint:**
Durango **Note:** Brass examples have been reported, but not
confirmed.

Date	Mintage	Good	VG	F	VF	XF
1872	—	2.25	4.00	9.00	20.00	—

FEDERAL COINAGE

KM# 315   1/16 REAL (Medio Octavo)
1.7500 g., Copper, 17 mm. **Obv. Legend:** REPUBLICA
MEXICANA **Edge:** Ornamented with small incuse rectangles
Mint: Mexico City

Date	Mintage	VG	F	VF	XF	Unc
1831	—	10.00	20.00	50.00	100	—
1832/1	—	12.00	22.00	55.00	125	—
1832	—	10.00	20.00	50.00	100	—
1833	—	10.00	20.00	50.00	100	—

KM# 315a   1/16 REAL (Medio Octavo)
1.7500 g., Brass, 17 mm. **Obv. Legend:** REPUBLICA
MEXICANA **Edge:** Ornamented with small incuse rectangles
Mint: Mexico City

Date	Mintage	VG	F	VF	XF	Unc
1832	—	13.50	22.50	60.00	165	—
1833	—	10.00	17.50	50.00	135	—
1835	—	400	800	1,250	2,500	—

KM# 333   1/8 REAL (Octavo Real)
3.5000 g., Copper, 21 mm. **Obv:** Facing eagle, snake in beak
Obv. Legend: REPUBLICA MEXICANA **Rev:** Value and date
within wreath **Edge:** Ornamented with small incuse rectangles
Mint: Mexico City

Date	Mintage	Good	VG	F	VF	XF
1829	—	7.50	12.00	25.00	55.00	—
1830	—	1.00	2.00	6.00	20.00	—
1831	—	1.50	3.50	7.00	25.00	—
1832	—	1.50	3.50	7.00	25.00	—
1833/2	—	1.50	3.50	7.00	25.00	—
1833	—	1.50	2.75	6.00	20.00	—
1834	—	1.50	2.75	6.00	20.00	—
1835	—	1.50	2.75	6.00	20.00	—
1835/4	—	1.75	3.50	7.00	25.00	—

KM# 332   1/8 REAL (Octavo Real)
7.0000 g., Copper, 27 mm. **Obv. Legend:** REPUBLICA
MEXICANA **Edge:** Ornamented with small incuse rectangles
Mint: Mexico City

Date	Mintage	VG	F	VF	XF	Unc
1829	—	450	900	1,500	2,500	—

KM# 334   1/8 REAL (Octavo Real)
14.0000 g., Copper **Obv:** Seated figure, right **Obv. Legend:**
LIBERTAD **Rev:** Value and date within wreath **Edge:** Lettered
(1841-42); Plain (1850-61) **Edge Lettering:** REPUBLICA
MEXICANA **Mint:** Mexico City **Note:** Size varies: 29-30mm.

Date	Mintage	Good	VG	F	VF	XF
1841	—	6.00	15.00	30.00	75.00	—
1842	—	2.50	5.00	10.00	30.00	—
1850	—	12.50	20.00	30.00	80.00	—
1861	—	5.00	12.00	25.00	70.00	—

KM# 357   1/4 REAL (Un Quarto/Una Quartilla)
14.0000 g., Copper, 33 mm. **Obv:** Facing eagle, snake in
beak **Obv. Legend:** REPUBLICA MEXICANA **Rev:** Value
and date within wreath **Edge:** Ornamented with small incuse
rectangles **Mint:** Mexico City

Date	Mintage	VG	F	VF	XF	Unc
1829	—	10.00	30.00	75.00	250	—

KM# 358   1/4 REAL (Un Quarto/Una Quartilla)
7.0000 g., Copper, 27 mm. **Obv:** Facing eagle, snake in beak
Obv. Legend: REPUBLICA MEXICANA **Rev:** Value and date
within wreath **Edge:** Ornamented with small incuse rectangles
Mint: Mexico City **Note:** Reduced size.

Date	Mintage	VG	F	VF	XF	Unc
1829	—	12.00	25.00	50.00	150	—
1830	—	1.50	2.75	5.00	10.00	—
1831	—	1.50	2.75	5.00	10.00	—
1832	—	5.50	10.00	20.00	35.00	—
1833	—	1.50	2.75	5.00	10.00	—
1834/3	—	1.75	3.00	6.00	12.00	—
1834	—	1.50	2.75	5.00	10.00	—
1835	—	1.50	2.75	5.00	10.00	—
1836/5	—	1.75	3.00	6.00	12.00	—
1836	—	1.50	2.75	5.00	10.00	—
1837	—	6.50	13.50	22.50	45.00	—

KM# 358a.1 1/4 REAL (Un Quarto/Una Quartilla)
7.0000 g., Brass, 27 mm. **Countermark:** JM **Obv. Legend:**
REPUBLICA MEXICANA **Edge:** Ornamented with small
incuse rectangles **Mint:** Mexico City **Note:** Reduced size.

Date	Mintage	VG	F	VF	XF	Unc
1831	—	8.00	13.50	27.50	50.00	—

KM# 358a.2 1/4 REAL (Un Quarto/Una Quartilla)
7.0000 g., Brass, 27 mm. **Obv. Legend:** REPUBLICA
MEXICANA **Edge:** Ornamented with small incuse rectangles
Mint: Mexico City **Note:** Without countermark.

Date	Mintage	VG	F	VF	XF	Unc
1831	—	—	—	—	—	—

KM# 368.2 1/4 REAL (Un Quarto/Una Quartilla)
0.8450 g., 0.9030 Silver 0.0245 oz. ASW **Mint:** Durango
Note: Struck at Durango Mint, mint mark Do.

Date	Mintage	VG	F	VF	XF	Unc
1842Do LR	—	12.00	20.00	40.00	125	—
1843Do	—	20.00	40.00	90.00	200	—

KM# 368 1/4 REAL (Un Quarto/Una Quartilla)
0.8450 g., 0.9030 Silver 0.0245 oz. ASW **Obv:** Head left
Rev: Value **Mint:** Chihuahua **Note:** Mint mark CA.

Date	Mintage	VG	F	VF	XF	Unc
1843CA RG	—	75.00	125	300	500	—

KM# 368.3 1/4 REAL (Un Quarto/Una Quartilla)
0.8450 g., 0.9030 Silver 0.0245 oz. ASW **Mint:** Guadalajara
Note: Mint mark Ga.

Date	Mintage	VG	F	VF	XF	Unc
1842Ga JG	—	2.50	5.50	8.00	20.00	—
1843/2Ga JG	—	—	—	—	—	—
1843Ga JG	—	6.00	9.00	12.50	30.00	—
1843Ga MC	—	4.00	6.50	9.00	25.00	—
1844Ga MC	—	4.00	6.50	9.00	25.00	—
1844Ga LR	—	2.50	5.00	10.00	20.00	—
1845Ga LR	—	8.00	20.00	40.00	75.00	—
1846Ga LR	—	10.00	25.00	40.00	60.00	—
1847Ga LR	—	8.00	20.00	40.00	60.00	—
1848Ga LR Rare	—	—	—	—	—	—
1850Ga LR Rare	—	—	—	—	—	—
1851Ga LR	—	6.00	10.00	20.00	50.00	—
1852Ga LR	—	50.00	100	135	200	—
1854/3Ga LR	—	50.00	100	135	200	—
1854Ga LR	—	10.00	20.00	50.00	100	—
1855Ga LR	—	10.00	20.00	50.00	100	—
1857Ga LR	—	10.00	20.00	50.00	100	—
1862Ga LR	—	10.00	20.00	50.00	100	—

KM# 368.5 1/4 REAL (Un Quarto/Una Quartilla)
0.8450 g., 0.9030 Silver 0.0245 oz. ASW **Mint:** Guanajuato
Note: Mint mark Go.

Date	Mintage	VG	F	VF	XF	Unc
1842Go PM	—	5.00	15.00	35.00	75.00	—
1842Go LR	—	2.00	4.00	8.00	15.00	—
1843/2Go LR	—	4.00	6.00	10.00	20.00	—
1843Go LR	—	2.00	4.00	8.00	15.00	—
1844/3Go LR	—	—	—	—	—	—
1844Go LR	—	10.00	25.00	60.00	125	—
1845Go LR	—	8.00	17.00	40.00	80.00	—
1846/5Go LR	—	—	—	—	—	—
1846Go LR	—	6.00	15.00	30.00	60.00	—
1847Go LR	—	2.00	4.00	8.00	15.00	—
1848/7Go LR	—	2.00	4.00	8.00	15.00	—
1848Go LR	—	2.00	4.00	8.00	15.00	—
1849/7Go LR	—	8.00	15.00	30.00	60.00	—
1849Go LR	—	2.00	4.00	8.00	15.00	—
1850Go LR	—	2.00	4.00	8.00	15.00	—
1851Go LR	—	2.00	4.00	8.00	15.00	—
1852Go LR	—	2.00	4.00	8.00	15.00	—
1853Go LR	—	2.00	4.00	8.00	15.00	—
1855Go LR	—	4.00	8.00	15.00	30.00	—
1856/4Go LR	—	20.00	40.00	60.00	100	—
1856Go LR	—	5.00	10.00	20.00	35.00	—
1862/1Go LR	—	3.00	5.00	10.00	20.00	—
1862Go LR	—	2.00	4.00	8.00	15.00	—
1863Go	—	2.00	4.00	8.00	15.00	—

KM# 368.6 1/4 REAL (Un Quarto/Una Quartilla)
0.8450 g., 0.9030 Silver 0.0245 oz. ASW **Mint:** Mexico City
Note: Mint mark Mo.

Date	Mintage	VG	F	VF	XF	Unc
1842Mo LR	—	2.00	4.00	8.00	15.00	—
1843Mo LR	—	2.00	4.00	8.00	15.00	—
1844/3Mo LR	—	20.00	30.00	75.00	125	—
1844Mo LR	—	4.00	6.00	10.00	20.00	—
1845Mo LR	—	6.00	15.00	35.00	70.00	—
1846Mo LR	—	10.00	20.00	35.00	65.00	—
1850Mo LR Rare	—	—	—	—	—	—
1858Mo LR	—	4.00	8.00	15.00	30.00	—
1859Mo LR	—	4.00	6.00	10.00	20.00	—
1860Mo LR	—	4.00	6.00	10.00	20.00	—
1861Mo LR	—	4.00	6.00	10.00	20.00	—
1862Mo LR	—	4.00	6.00	10.00	20.00	—
1863/53Mo LR	—	4.00	6.00	10.00	20.00	—
1863Mo LR	—	4.00	6.00	10.00	20.00	—

KM# 368.7 1/4 REAL (Un Quarto/Una Quartilla)
0.8450 g., 0.9030 Silver 0.0245 oz. ASW **Mint:** San Luis
Potosi **Note:** Mint mark SLP, PI, P, I/P.

Date	Mintage	VG	F	VF	XF	Unc
1842S.L.Pi	—	2.00	5.00	10.00	20.00	—
1843/2S.L.Pi	—	4.00	6.00	10.00	20.00	—
1843S.L.Pi	—	2.00	4.00	8.00	20.00	—
1844S.L.Pi	—	2.00	4.00	8.00	20.00	—
1845/3S.L.Pi	—	4.00	6.00	10.00	25.00	—
1845/4S.L.Pi	—	4.00	6.00	10.00	25.00	—
1845S.L.Pi	—	2.00	4.00	8.00	20.00	—
1847/5S.L.Pi	—	4.00	9.00	20.00	40.00	—
1847S.L.Pi	—	3.00	6.00	12.00	25.00	—
1851/47S.L.Pi	—	10.00	20.00	35.00	60.00	—
1854S.L.Pi	—	125	200	275	400	—
1856S.L.Pi	—	10.00	20.00	35.00	60.00	—
1857S.L.Pi	—	30.00	60.00	100	175	—
1862/57S.L.Pi	—	10.00	20.00	40.00	85.00	—

KM# 368.1 1/4 REAL (Un Quarto/Una Quartilla)
0.8450 g., 0.9030 Silver 0.0245 oz. ASW **Mint:** Culiacan
Note: Mint mark C.

Date	Mintage	VG	F	VF	XF	Unc
1855C LR	—	50.00	100	225	475	—

KM# 368.4 1/4 REAL (Un Quarto/Una Quartilla)
0.8450 g., 0.9030 Silver 0.0245 oz. ASW **Mint:** Guadalupe
y Calvo **Note:** Mint mark GC.

Date	Mintage	VG	F	VF	XF	Unc
1844GC LR	—	50.00	75.00	200	450	—

KM# 368.8 1/4 REAL (Un Quarto/Una Quartilla)
0.8450 g., 0.9030 Silver 0.0245 oz. ASW **Mint:** Zacatecas
Note: Mint mark Zs.

Date	Mintage	VG	F	VF	XF	Unc
1842/1Zs LR	—	4.00	8.00	15.00	30.00	—
1842Zs LR	—	4.00	8.00	15.00	30.00	—

KM# 370.5 1/2 REAL
1.6900 g., 0.9030 Silver 0.0491 oz. ASW **Obv:** Facing eagle,
snake in beak **Mint:** Guadalajara

Date	Mintage	F	VF	XF	Unc	BU
1825Ga FS	—	25.00	40.00	75.00	200	—
1826Ga FS	—	10.00	15.00	35.00	80.00	—
1828/7Ga FS	—	12.50	20.00	40.00	90.00	—
1829Ga FS	—	7.50	15.00	30.00	70.00	—
1830/29Ga FS	—	40.00	60.00	100	200	—
1831Ga LP	—	350	—	—	—	—
1832Ga FS	—	10.00	20.00	35.00	80.00	—
1834/3Ga FS	—	65.00	100	175	250	—
1834Ga FS	—	10.00	20.00	35.00	80.00	—
1835/4/3Ga FS/LP	—	15.00	25.00	40.00	90.00	—
1837/6Ga JG	—	100	250	500	1,000	—
1838/7Ga JG	—	15.00	25.00	40.00	90.00	—
1839/8Ga JG/FS	—	35.00	75.00	150	250	—
1839Ga MC	—	10.00	20.00	35.00	80.00	—
1840/39Ga MC/JG	—	—	—	—	—	—
1840Ga MC	—	15.00	25.00	40.00	90.00	—
1841Ga MC	—	20.00	35.00	50.00	100	—
1842/1Ga JG	—	15.00	25.00	40.00	90.00	—
1842Ga JG	—	10.00	20.00	35.00	80.00	—
1843/2Ga JG	—	15.00	30.00	50.00	100	—
1843Ga JG	—	10.00	20.00	35.00	80.00	—
1843Ga MC/JG	—	10.00	20.00	35.00	80.00	—
1843Ga MC	—	10.00	20.00	35.00	80.00	—
1844Ga MC	—	10.00	20.00	35.00	80.00	—
1845Ga MC	—	10.00	20.00	35.00	80.00	—
1845Ga JG	—	10.00	20.00	35.00	80.00	—

Date	Mintage	F	VF	XF	Unc	BU
1846Ga MC	—	10.00	20.00	35.00	80.00	—
1846Ga JG	—	10.00	20.00	35.00	80.00	—
1847Ga JG	—	10.00	20.00	35.00	80.00	—
1848/7Ga JG	—	10.00	20.00	35.00	80.00	—
1849Ga JG	—	10.00	20.00	35.00	80.00	—
1850/49Ga JG	—	—	—	—	—	—
1850Ga JG	—	10.00	20.00	35.00	80.00	—
1851/0Ga JG	—	10.00	20.00	35.00	80.00	—
1852Ga JG	—	10.00	20.00	35.00	80.00	—
1853Ga JG	—	10.00	20.00	35.00	80.00	—
1854Ga JG	—	10.00	20.00	35.00	80.00	—
1855/4Ga JG	—	10.00	20.00	35.00	80.00	—
1855Ga JG	—	10.00	20.00	35.00	80.00	—
1856Ga JG	—	10.00	20.00	35.00	80.00	—
1857Ga JG	—	10.00	20.00	35.00	80.00	—
1858/7Ga JG	—	10.00	20.00	35.00	80.00	—
1858Ga JG	—	10.00	20.00	35.00	80.00	—
1859/7Ga JG	—	10.00	20.00	35.00	80.00	—
1860/59Ga JG	—	10.00	20.00	35.00	80.00	—
1861Ga JG	—	5.00	12.50	25.00	60.00	—
1862/1Ga JG	—	15.00	20.00	40.00	90.00	—

KM# 370.6　1/2 REAL
1.6900 g., 0.9030 Silver 0.0491 oz. ASW **Obv:** Facing eagle, snake in beak **Mint:** Guadalupe y Calvo

Date	Mintage	F	VF	XF	Unc	BU
1844GC MP	—	50.00	100	150	375	—
1845GC MP	—	25.00	50.00	100	220	—
1846GC MP	—	25.00	50.00	100	220	—
1847GC MP	—	25.00	50.00	100	325	—
1848GC MP	—	20.00	40.00	75.00	165	—
1849GC MP	—	25.00	50.00	100	220	—
1850GC MP	—	30.00	60.00	125	275	—
1851GC MP	—	25.00	50.00	100	220	—

KM# 370.8　1/2 REAL
1.6900 g., 0.9030 Silver 0.0491 oz. ASW **Obv:** Facing eagle, snake in beak **Mint:** Hermosillo

Date	Mintage	F	VF	XF	Unc	BU
1839Ho PP Unique	—	—	—	—	—	—
1862Ho FM	—	500	650	1,000	—	—
1867Ho PR/FM Inverted 6, and 7/1	—	100	175	250	550	—

KM# 370.9　1/2 REAL
1.6900 g., 0.9030 Silver 0.0491 oz. ASW **Obv:** Facing eagle, snake in beak **Mint:** Mexico City

Date	Mintage	F	VF	XF	Unc	BU
1825Mo JM Short top 5	—	10.00	20.00	40.00	80.00	—
1825Mo JM Long top 5	—	10.00	20.00	40.00	80.00	—
1826/5Mo JM	—	10.00	20.00	40.00	80.00	—
1826Mo JM	—	5.00	10.00	20.00	60.00	—
1827/6Mo JM	—	5.00	10.00	20.00	60.00	—
1827Mo JM	—	5.00	10.00	20.00	60.00	—
1828/7Mo JM	—	7.50	15.00	25.00	85.00	—
1828Mo JM	—	10.00	20.00	40.00	90.00	—
1829Mo JM	—	7.50	15.00	25.00	75.00	—
1830Mo JM	—	5.00	10.00	20.00	60.00	—
1831Mo JM	—	5.00	10.00	20.00	60.00	—
1832Mo JM	—	7.50	12.50	27.50	60.00	—
1833Mo MJ	—	7.50	12.50	27.50	60.00	—
1834Mo ML	—	5.00	10.00	20.00	60.00	—
1835Mo ML	—	5.00	10.00	20.00	60.00	—
1836/5Mo ML/MF	—	7.50	15.00	25.00	65.00	—
1836Mo ML	—	7.50	15.00	25.00	65.00	—
1838Mo ML	—	5.00	10.00	20.00	60.00	—
1839/8Mo ML	—	5.00	10.00	25.00	65.00	—
1839Mo ML	—	5.00	10.00	20.00	50.00	—
1840Mo ML	—	5.00	10.00	20.00	50.00	—
1841Mo ML	—	5.00	10.00	20.00	50.00	—
1842Mo ML	—	15.00	35.00	80.00	200	—
1842Mo MM	—	5.00	10.00	20.00	50.00	—
1843Mo MM	—	10.00	20.00	40.00	80.00	—
1844Mo MF	—	5.00	10.00	20.00	60.00	—
1845/4Mo MF	—	5.00	10.00	25.00	60.00	—
1845Mo MF	—	5.00	10.00	20.00	50.00	—
1846Mo MF	—	5.00	10.00	20.00	50.00	—
1847Mo RC	—	10.00	20.00	40.00	80.00	—
1847Mo RC R/M	—	10.00	20.00	40.00	80.00	—
1848/7Mo GC/RC	—	5.00	10.00	20.00	50.00	—
1849Mo GC	—	5.00	10.00	20.00	50.00	—

Date	Mintage	F	VF	XF	Unc	BU
1850Mo GC	—	5.00	10.00	20.00	50.00	—
1851Mo GC	—	5.00	10.00	20.00	50.00	—
1852Mo GC	—	5.00	10.00	20.00	50.00	—
1853Mo GC	—	5.00	10.00	20.00	50.00	—
1854Mo GC	—	5.00	10.00	20.00	50.00	—
1855Mo GC	—	5.00	10.00	20.00	50.00	—
1855Mo GF/GC	—	7.50	12.50	25.00	65.00	—
1856/5Mo GF	—	7.50	12.50	25.00	65.00	—
1857Mo GF	—	5.00	10.00	20.00	50.00	—
1858Mo FH	—	3.00	5.00	12.50	40.00	—
1858Mo FH F/G	—	5.00	10.00	20.00	50.00	—
1858/9Mo FH	—	5.00	10.00	20.00	50.00	—
1859Mo FH/GC	—	5.00	10.00	20.00	50.00	—
1859Mo FH	—	3.00	6.00	15.00	50.00	—
1860Mo FH/GC	—	5.00	10.00	20.00	50.00	—
1860Mo FH	—	3.00	6.00	15.00	50.00	—
1860Mo TH	—	25.00	50.00	100	200	—
1860/59Mo FH	—	7.50	12.50	25.00	65.00	—
1861Mo CH	—	3.00	6.00	15.00	45.00	—
1862/52Mo CH	—	5.00	10.00	20.00	50.00	—
1862Mo CH	—	3.00	6.00	15.00	45.00	—
1863/55Mo TH/GC	—	5.00	10.00	20.00	50.00	—
1863Mo CH/GC	—	5.00	10.00	20.00	50.00	—
1863Mo CH	—	3.00	6.00	15.00	45.00	—

KM# 370.10　1/2 REAL
1.6900 g., 0.9030 Silver 0.0491 oz. ASW **Obv:** Facing eagle, snake in beak **Mint:** San Luis Potosi

Date	Mintage	F	VF	XF	Unc	BU
1831Pi JS	—	7.50	12.50	25.00	65.00	—
1841/36Pi JS	—	20.00	40.00	75.00	125	—
1842/1Pi PS	—	20.00	40.00	75.00	125	—
1842/1Pi PS P/J	—	60.00	80.00	150	300	—
1842Pi PS/PJ	—	50.00	75.00	125	250	—
1842 PS	—	60.00	80.00	150	300	—
1842Pi JS	—	20.00	40.00	75.00	125	—
1843/2Pi PS	—	17.50	25.00	40.00	80.00	—
1843Pi PS	—	15.00	25.00	35.00	70.00	—
1843Pi AM	—	10.00	15.00	25.00	60.00	—
1844Pi AM	—	10.00	15.00	30.00	65.00	—
1845Pi AM	—	250	375	500	1,500	—
1846/5Pi AM	—	40.00	75.00	125	200	—
1847/6Pi AM	—	15.00	25.00	40.00	80.00	—
1848Pi AM	—	15.00	25.00	40.00	80.00	—
1849Pi MC/AM	—	15.00	25.00	40.00	80.00	—
1849Pi MC	—	12.50	20.00	35.00	70.00	—
1850/49Pi MC	—	—	—	—	—	—
1850Pi MC	—	10.00	15.00	25.00	60.00	—
1850P MC	—	—	—	—	—	—
1851Pi MC	—	10.00	15.00	25.00	60.00	—
1852Pi MC	—	10.00	20.00	30.00	65.00	—
1853Pi MC	—	7.50	12.50	20.00	60.00	—
1854Pi MC	—	7.50	12.50	20.00	60.00	—
1855Pi MC	—	15.00	20.00	35.00	70.00	—
1856Pi MC	—	15.00	25.00	50.00	100	—
1856PI (no I)	—	—	—	—	—	—
1857Pi MC	—	7.50	12.50	20.00	60.00	—
1857Pi PS	—	10.00	15.00	30.00	65.00	—
1858Pi MC	—	12.50	20.00	35.00	70.00	—
1858Pi PS	—	12.50	20.00	35.00	70.00	—
1859Pi MC Rare	—	—	—	—	—	—
1860/59Pi PS	—	125	200	600	—	—
1861Pi RO	—	10.00	15.00	30.00	60.00	—
1862/1Pi RO	—	15.00	25.00	50.00	125	—
1862Pi RO	—	15.00	25.00	50.00	125	—
1863/2Pi RO	—	15.00	25.00	45.00	100	—

KM# 370.2　1/2 REAL
1.6900 g., 0.9030 Silver 0.0491 oz. ASW **Obv:** Facing eagle, snake in beak **Obv. Legend:** REPUBLICA MEXICANA **Rev:** Radiant cap **Mint:** Culiacan **Note:** Mint mark C.

Date	Mintage	F	VF	XF	Unc	BU
1846 CE	—	30.00	50.00	75.00	150	—

Date	Mintage	F	VF	XF	Unc	BU
1848/7 CE	—	15.00	25.00	45.00	90.00	—
1849/8 CE	—	15.00	25.00	45.00	90.00	—
1849 CE	—	—	—	—	—	—
1852 CE	—	12.50	20.00	40.00	80.00	—
1853/1 CE	—	12.50	20.00	40.00	80.00	—
1854 CE	—	20.00	35.00	50.00	100	—
1856 CE	—	12.50	20.00	40.00	80.00	—
1857/6 CE	—	20.00	35.00	50.00	100	—
1857 CE	—	15.00	25.00	45.00	90.00	—
1858 CE Error 1 for 1/2	—	12.50	20.00	40.00	80.00	—
1860/59 PV	—	20.00	35.00	50.00	100	—
1860 PV	—	12.50	20.00	40.00	80.00	—
1861 PV	—	12.50	20.00	40.00	80.00	—
1863 CE Error 1 for 1/2	—	15.00	25.00	45.00	90.00	—
1867 CE	—	12.50	20.00	40.00	80.00	—
1869 6/5 CE Error 1 for 1/2	—	12.50	20.00	40.00	80.00	—

KM# 370.3 1/2 REAL
1.6900 g., 0.9030 Silver 0.0491 oz. ASW **Obv:** Facing eagle, snake in beak **Mint:** Durango **Note:** Mint mark D, Do.

Date	Mintage	F	VF	XF	Unc	BU
1832 RM	—	125	225	350	600	—
1832 RM/L	—	—	—	—	—	—
1833/2 RM/L	—	75.00	100	150	225	—
1833/1 RM/L	—	12.50	20.00	40.00	80.00	—
1833 RM	—	25.00	40.00	75.00	150	—
1834/1 RM	—	25.00	40.00	75.00	150	—
1834 RM	—	12.50	20.00	40.00	80.00	—
1837/1 RM	—	12.50	30.00	60.00	200	—
1837/4 RM	—	12.50	30.00	60.00	200	—
1837/6 RM	—	12.50	30.00	60.00	200	—
1841/33 RM	—	15.00	30.00	60.00	250	—
1842/32 RM	—	12.50	20.00	40.00	80.00	—
1842 RM	—	12.50	20.00	40.00	80.00	—
1842 8R RM Error	—	12.50	20.00	40.00	80.00	—
1842 1/2/8R RM	—	12.50	20.00	40.00	80.00	—
1843/33 RM	—	15.00	25.00	50.00	100	—
1843 RM	—	15.00	25.00	50.00	100	—
1845/31 RM	—	12.50	20.00	40.00	80.00	—
1845/34 RM	—	12.50	20.00	40.00	80.00	—
1845/35 RM	—	12.50	20.00	40.00	80.00	—
1845 RM	—	15.00	25.00	50.00	100	—
1846 RM	—	30.00	50.00	80.00	200	—
1848/5 RM	—	35.00	55.00	110	250	—
1848/36 RM	—	25.00	40.00	75.00	200	—
1849 JMR	—	25.00	40.00	75.00	200	—
1850 RM Rare	—	—	—	—	—	—
1850 JMR	—	25.00	40.00	75.00	200	—
1851 JMR	—	20.00	35.00	50.00	100	—
1852/1 JMR	—	65.00	125	250	600	—
1852 JMR	—	30.00	50.00	80.00	200	—
1853 CP	—	12.50	20.00	40.00	80.00	—
1854 CP	—	25.00	40.00	75.00	200	—
1855 CP	—	25.00	40.00	60.00	150	—
1856/5 CP	—	20.00	35.00	50.00	100	—
1857 CP	—	20.00	35.00	50.00	100	—
1858/7 CP	—	20.00	35.00	50.00	100	—
1859 CP	—	20.00	35.00	50.00	100	—
1860/59 CP	—	40.00	65.00	135	300	—
1861 CP	—	125	250	400	700	—
1862 CP	—	25.00	40.00	60.00	125	—
1864 LT	—	100	300	500	1,000	—
1869 CP	—	40.00	65.00	125	275	—

KM# 370.11 1/2 REAL
1.6900 g., 0.9030 Silver 0.0491 oz. ASW **Obv:** Facing eagle, snake in beak **Mint:** Zacatecas **Note:** Mint mark Z, Zs.

Date	Mintage	F	VF	XF	Unc	BU
1826 AZ	—	5.00	10.00	20.00	60.00	—
1826 AO	—	5.00	10.00	20.00	60.00	—
1827 AO	—	5.00	10.00	20.00	60.00	—
1828/7 AO	—	5.00	10.00	20.00	60.00	—
1829 AO	—	5.00	10.00	20.00	60.00	—
1830 OV	—	5.00	10.00	20.00	60.00	—
1831 OV	—	25.00	50.00	75.00	150	—
1831 OM	—	5.00	10.00	20.00	60.00	—
1832 OM	—	5.00	10.00	20.00	60.00	—
1833 OM	—	5.00	10.00	20.00	60.00	—
1834 OM	—	5.00	10.00	20.00	60.00	—
1835/4 OM	—	5.00	10.00	20.00	60.00	—
1835 OM	—	5.00	10.00	20.00	60.00	—
1836 OM	—	5.00	10.00	20.00	60.00	—
1837 OM	—	10.00	20.00	40.00	80.00	—
1838 OM	—	5.00	10.00	20.00	60.00	—
1839 OM	—	7.50	15.00	30.00	65.00	—
1840 OM	—	10.00	25.00	45.00	90.00	—
1841 OM	—	10.00	25.00	45.00	90.00	—
1842/1 OM	—	5.00	10.00	20.00	60.00	—
1842 OM	—	5.00	10.00	20.00	60.00	—
1843 OM	—	40.00	75.00	115	250	—
1844 OM	—	5.00	10.00	20.00	60.00	—
1845 OM	—	5.00	10.00	20.00	60.00	—
1846 OM	—	7.50	15.00	30.00	65.00	—
1847 OM	—	5.00	10.00	20.00	50.00	—
1848 OM	—	5.00	10.00	20.00	50.00	—
1849 OM	—	5.00	10.00	20.00	50.00	—
1850 OM	—	5.00	10.00	20.00	50.00	—
1851 OM	—	5.00	10.00	20.00	50.00	—
1852 OM	—	5.00	10.00	20.00	50.00	—
1853 OM	—	5.00	10.00	20.00	50.00	—
1854/3 OM	—	5.00	10.00	20.00	50.00	—
1854 OM	—	5.00	10.00	20.00	50.00	—
1855/3 OM	—	7.50	15.00	30.00	65.00	—
1855 OM	—	5.00	10.00	20.00	50.00	—
1856 OM	—	5.00	10.00	20.00	50.00	—
1857 MO	—	5.00	10.00	20.00	50.00	—
1858 MO	—	5.00	10.00	20.00	50.00	—
1859 MO	—	6.00	8.50	17.50	35.00	—
1859 VL	—	6.00	8.50	17.50	40.00	—
1860/50 VL Inverted A for V	—	5.00	10.00	20.00	50.00	—
1860/59 VL Inverted A for V	—	5.00	10.00	20.00	50.00	—
1860 MO	—	5.00	10.00	20.00	50.00	—
1860 VL	—	5.00	10.00	20.00	50.00	—
1861/0 VL Inverted A for V	—	7.50	15.00	30.00	65.00	—
1861 VL Inverted A for V	—	5.00	10.00	20.00	50.00	—
1862 VL Inverted A for V	—	5.00	10.00	20.00	50.00	—
1863 VL Inverted A for V	—	5.00	10.00	20.00	50.00	—
1863/1 VL Inverted A for V	—	7.50	15.00	30.00	65.00	—
1869 YH	—	5.00	10.00	20.00	50.00	—

KM# 370.7 1/2 REAL
1.6900 g., 0.9030 Silver 0.0491 oz. ASW **Obv:** Facing eagle, snake in beak **Mint:** Guanajuato **Note:** Varieties exist.

Date	Mintage	F	VF	XF	Unc	BU
1826Go MJ	—	125	250	400	1,000	—
1827/6Go MJ	—	7.50	15.00	30.00	75.00	—
1828/7Go MJ	—	7.50	15.00	30.00	75.00	—
1828Go MJ	—	—	—	—	—	—
Note: Denomination 2/1						
1828Go JG	—	—	—	—	—	—
1828Go MR	—	50.00	100	150	250	—
1829/8Go MJ	—	5.00	10.00	25.00	50.00	—

Date	Mintage	F	VF	XF	Unc	BU
1829Go MJ	—	5.00	10.00	25.00	50.00	—
1829Go MJ	—	5.00	10.00	25.00	50.00	—
Note: Reversed N in MEXICANA						
1830Go MJ	—	5.00	10.00	25.00	50.00	—
1831/29Go MJ	—	15.00	30.00	60.00	150	—
1831Go MJ	—	10.00	20.00	40.00	80.00	—
1832/1Go MJ	—	7.50	15.00	30.00	75.00	—
1832Go MJ	—	7.50	15.00	30.00	75.00	—
1833Go MJ Round top 3	—	10.00	20.00	40.00	80.00	—
1833Go MJ Flat top 3	—	10.00	20.00	40.00	80.00	—
1834Go PJ	—	5.00	10.00	25.00	50.00	—
1835Go PJ	—	5.00	10.00	25.00	50.00	—
1836/5Go PJ	—	7.50	15.00	30.00	75.00	—
1836Go PJ	—	5.00	10.00	25.00	50.00	—
1837Go PJ	—	5.00	10.00	25.00	50.00	—
1838/7Go PJ	—	5.00	10.00	25.00	50.00	—
1839Go PJ	—	5.00	10.00	25.00	50.00	—
1839Go PJ	—	5.00	10.00	25.00	50.00	—
Note: Error: REPUBLIGA						
1840/39Go PJ	—	7.50	10.00	25.00	75.00	—
1840Go PJ Straight J	—	5.00	10.00	25.00	50.00	—
1840Go PJ Curved J	—	5.00	10.00	25.00	50.00	—
1841/31Go PJ	—	5.00	10.00	25.00	50.00	—
1841Go PJ	—	5.00	10.00	25.00	50.00	—
1842/1Go PJ	—	5.00	10.00	25.00	50.00	—
1842/1Go PM	—	5.00	10.00	25.00	50.00	—
1842Go PM/J	—	5.00	10.00	25.00	50.00	—
1842Go PJ	—	5.00	10.00	25.00	50.00	—
1842Go PM	—	5.00	10.00	25.00	50.00	—
1843/33Go PM 1/2 over 8	—	5.00	10.00	25.00	50.00	—
1843Go PM	—	5.00	10.00	25.00	50.00	—
Note: Convex wings						
1843Go PM	—	5.00	10.00	25.00	50.00	—
Note: Concave wings						
1844/3Go PM	—	5.00	10.00	25.00	50.00	—
1844Go PM	—	10.00	20.00	40.00	90.00	—
1845/4Go PM	—	5.00	10.00	25.00	50.00	—
1845Go PM	—	5.00	10.00	25.00	50.00	—
1846/4Go PM	—	5.00	10.00	25.00	50.00	—
1846/5Go PM	—	5.00	10.00	25.00	50.00	—
1846Go PM	—	5.00	10.00	25.00	50.00	—
1847/6Go PM	—	7.50	15.00	30.00	60.00	—
1847Go PM	—	7.50	15.00	30.00	60.00	—
1848/35Go PM	—	5.00	10.00	25.00	50.00	—
1848Go PM	—	5.00	10.00	25.00	50.00	—
1848Go PF/M	—	5.00	10.00	25.00	50.00	—
1849/39Go PF	—	5.00	10.00	25.00	50.00	—
1849Go PF	—	5.00	10.00	25.00	50.00	—
Note: Error: MEXCANA						
1850Go PF	—	5.00	10.00	25.00	50.00	—
1851Go PF	—	5.00	10.00	25.00	50.00	—
1852/1Go PF	—	5.00	10.00	25.00	50.00	—
1852Go PF	—	2.50	7.50	17.50	40.00	—
1853Go PF/R	—	5.00	10.00	25.00	50.00	—
1853Go PF	—	5.00	10.00	25.00	50.00	—
1854Go PF	—	5.00	10.00	25.00	50.00	—
1855Go PF	—	5.00	10.00	25.00	50.00	—
1856/4Go PF	—	5.00	10.00	25.00	50.00	—
1856/5Go PF	—	5.00	10.00	25.00	50.00	—
1856Go PF	—	5.00	10.00	25.00	50.00	—
1857/6Go PF	—	5.00	10.00	25.00	50.00	—
1857Go PF	—	5.00	10.00	25.00	50.00	—
1858/7Go PF	—	7.50	15.00	30.00	60.00	—
1858Go PF	—	5.00	10.00	25.00	50.00	—
1859Go PF	—	5.00	10.00	25.00	50.00	—
1860Go PF Small 1/2	—	5.00	10.00	25.00	50.00	—
1860Go PF Large 1/2	—	5.00	10.00	25.00	50.00	—
1860/59Go PF	—	5.00	10.00	25.00	50.00	—
1861Go PF Small 1/2	—	5.00	10.00	25.00	50.00	—
1861Go PF Large 1/2	—	5.00	10.00	25.00	50.00	—

Date	Mintage	F	VF	XF	Unc	BU
1862/1Go YE	—	5.00	10.00	25.00	50.00	—
1862Go YE	—	2.50	7.50	17.50	40.00	—
1862Go YF	—	5.00	10.00	25.00	50.00	—
1867Go YF	—	2.50	7.50	17.50	40.00	—
1868Go YF	—	2.50	7.50	17.50	40.00	—

KM# 370.1   1/2 REAL
1.6900 g., 0.9030 Silver 0.0491 oz. ASW **Obv:** Facing eagle **Mint:** Chihuahua

Date	Mintage	F	VF	XF	Unc	BU
1844Ca RG	—	75.00	125	175	300	—
1845Ca RG	—	75.00	125	150	275	—

KM# 370   1/2 REAL
1.6900 g., 0.9030 Silver 0.0491 oz. ASW **Obv:** Hooked-neck eagle **Mint:** Alamos

Date	Mintage	F	VF	XF	Unc	BU
1862A PG Rare	—	—	—	—	—	—

KM# 370.4   1/2 REAL
1.6900 g., 0.9030 Silver 0.0491 oz. ASW **Obv:** Facing eagle, snake in beak **Mint:** Estado de Mexico

Date	Mintage	F	VF	XF	Unc	BU
1829EoMo LF	—	175	300	500	1,500	—

KM# 372   REAL
3.3800 g., 0.9030 Silver 0.0981 oz. ASW **Obv:** Facing eagle, snake in beak **Mint:** Chihuahua

Date	Mintage	F	VF	XF	Unc	BU
1844Ca RG	—	500	1,000	1,500	2,750	—
1845Ca RG	—	500	1,000	1,500	2,750	—
1855Ca RG	—	100	150	225	475	—

KM# 372.1   REAL
3.3800 g., 0.9030 Silver 0.0981 oz. ASW **Obv:** Facing eagle, snake in beak **Mint:** Culiacan

Date	Mintage	F	VF	XF	Unc	BU
1846C CE	—	12.50	25.00	40.00	110	—
1848C CE	—	12.50	25.00	40.00	110	—
1850C CE	—	12.50	25.00	40.00	110	—
1851/0C CE	—	12.50	25.00	40.00	110	—
1852/1C CE	—	7.50	15.00	30.00	100	—
1853/2C CE	—	7.50	15.00	30.00	100	—
1854C CE	—	7.50	15.00	30.00	100	—
1856C CE	—	40.00	65.00	100	225	—
1857/4C CE	—	10.00	20.00	35.00	100	—
1857/6C CE	—	10.00	20.00	35.00	100	—
1858C CE	—	5.00	7.50	15.00	100	—
1859C CE	—	—	—	—	—	—
1860/9C PV/N	—	6.00	10.00	17.50	120	—
1860C PV	—	5.00	7.50	15.00	100	—
1861C PV	—	5.00	7.50	15.00	100	—
1863C CE	—	—	—	1,650	2,250	—
Note: 3 known						
1869C CE	—	—	7.50	15.00	100	—

KM# 372.2   REAL
3.3800 g., 0.9030 Silver 0.0981 oz. ASW **Obv:** Facing eagle, snake in beak **Mint:** Durango

Date	Mintage	F	VF	XF	Unc	BU
1832/1Do RM	—	5.00	10.00	20.00	90.00	—
1832Do RM/RL	—	10.00	15.00	30.00	100	—
1832Do RM	—	5.00	10.00	20.00	100	—
1834/24Do RM/RL	—	15.00	25.00	50.00	150	—
1834/3Do RM/RL	—	15.00	25.00	50.00	150	—
1834Do RM	—	10.00	20.00	40.00	110	—
1836/4Do RM	—	5.00	7.50	15.00	100	—
1836Do RM	—	5.00	7.50	15.00	100	—
1837Do RM 3/2	—	12.50	20.00	40.00	110	—
1837Do RM	—	12.50	20.00	40.00	110	—
1841Do RM	—	7.50	15.00	30.00	100	—
1842/32Do RM	—	10.00	20.00	40.00	110	—
1842Do RM	—	7.50	15.00	30.00	100	—
1843/37Do RM	—	10.00	20.00	40.00	110	—
1843Do RM	—	5.00	7.50	15.00	100	—
1844/34Do RM	—	15.00	25.00	45.00	125	—
1845Do RM	—	5.00	7.50	15.00	100	—
1846Do RM	—	7.50	15.00	30.00	100	—
1847Do RM	—	10.00	15.00	35.00	100	—
1848/31Do RM	—	10.00	15.00	35.00	100	—
1848/33Do RM	—	10.00	15.00	35.00	100	—
1848/5Do RM	—	10.00	15.00	35.00	100	—
1848Do RM	—	7.50	12.50	20.00	100	—
1849/8Do CM	—	10.00	15.00	30.00	100	—
1850Do JMR	—	20.00	40.00	75.00	175	—
1851Do JMR	—	20.00	40.00	75.00	175	—
1852Do JMR	—	20.00	40.00	75.00	175	—

Date	Mintage	F	VF	XF	Unc	BU
1853Do CP	—	12.50	20.00	35.00	100	—
1854/1Do CP	—	10.00	15.00	25.00	100	—
1854Do CP	—	7.50	12.50	20.00	100	—
1855Do CP	—	10.00	15.00	25.00	100	—
1856Do CP	—	12.50	20.00	35.00	100	—
1857Do CP	—	12.50	20.00	35.00	100	—
1858Do CP	—	12.50	20.00	35.00	100	—
1859Do CP	—	7.50	12.50	20.00	100	—
1860/59Do CP	—	10.00	15.00	25.00	100	—
1861Do CP	—	15.00	25.00	40.00	110	—
1862/1Do CP	—	225	300	450	1,250	—
1864Do LT	—	15.00	25.00	40.00	110	—

KM# 372.4 REAL
3.3800 g., 0.9030 Silver 0.0981 oz. ASW **Obv:** Facing eagle, snake in beak **Mint:** Guadalajara

Date	Mintage	F	VF	XF	Unc	BU
1826Ga FS	—	15.00	30.00	50.00	125	—
1828/7Ga FS	—	15.00	30.00	50.00	125	—
1829/8/7Ga FS	—	—	—	—	—	—
1829Ga FS	—	15.00	30.00	50.00	125	—
1830Ga FS	—	250	425	600	—	—
1831Ga LP	—	15.00	30.00	50.00	125	—
1831Ga LP/FS	—	300	450	600	—	—
1832Ga FS	—	250	350	500	—	—
1833/2Ga G FS	—	100	150	275	550	—
1833Ga FS	—	75.00	125	225	500	—
1834/3Ga FS	—	75.00	125	225	500	—
1835Ga FS	—	—	—	—	—	—
1837/6Ga JG/FS	—	12.50	20.00	35.00	100	—
1838/7Ga JG/FS	—	100	200	400	—	—
1839Ga JG	—	250	350	500	—	—
1840Ga JG	—	12.50	20.00	35.00	100	—
1840Ga MC	—	7.50	12.50	25.00	70.00	—
1841Ga MC	—	50.00	75.00	125	250	—
1842/0Ga JG/MC	—	10.00	15.00	30.00	100	—
1842Ga JG	—	7.50	12.50	20.00	100	—
1843Ga JG	—	150	200	300	750	—
1843Ga MC	—	5.00	7.50	15.00	100	—
1844Ga MC	—	7.50	12.50	20.00	100	—
1845Ga MC	—	10.00	15.00	25.00	100	—
1845Ga JG	—	5.00	7.50	20.00	100	—
1846Ga JG	—	12.50	20.00	35.00	100	—
1847/6Ga JG	—	10.00	15.00	25.00	100	—
1847Ga JG	—	10.00	15.00	25.00	100	—
1848Ga JG	—	400	550	700	—	—
1849Ga JG	—	7.50	12.50	25.00	100	—
1850Ga JG	—	175	275	400	—	—
1851Ga JG	—	10.00	15.00	25.00	100	—
1852Ga JG	—	10.00	15.00	25.00	100	—
1853/2Ga JG	—	10.00	15.00	25.00	100	—
1854Ga JG	—	10.00	15.00	25.00	100	—
1855Ga JG	—	15.00	25.00	40.00	100	—
1856Ga JG	—	7.50	12.50	20.00	100	—
1857/6Ga JG	—	12.50	20.00	35.00	100	—
1858/7Ga JG	—	15.00	25.00	40.00	110	—
1859/8Ga JG	—	25.00	50.00	75.00	150	—
1860/59Ga JG	—	30.00	60.00	90.00	225	—
1861/0Ga JG	—	20.00	30.00	50.00	125	—
1861Ga JG	—	25.00	50.00	100	250	—
1862Ga JG	—	7.50	12.50	20.00	100	—

KM# 372.5 REAL
3.3800 g., 0.9030 Silver 0.0981 oz. ASW **Obv:** Facing eagle, snake in beak **Obv. Legend:** REPUBLICA MEXICANA **Rev:** Radiant cap **Mint:** Guadalupe y Calvo

Date	Mintage	F	VF	XF	Unc	BU
1844GC MP	—	40.00	60.00	100	300	—
1845GC MP	—	40.00	60.00	100	300	—
1846GC MP	—	40.00	60.00	100	300	—
1847GC MP	—	40.00	60.00	100	300	—
1848GC MP	—	40.00	60.00	100	300	—
1849/7GC MP	—	40.00	60.00	100	300	—
1849/8GC MP	—	40.00	60.00	100	300	—
1849GC MP	—	40.00	60.00	100	300	—
1850GC MP	—	40.00	60.00	100	300	—
1851GC MP	—	40.00	60.00	100	300	—

KM# 372.6 REAL
3.3800 g., 0.9030 Silver 0.0981 oz. ASW **Obv:** Facing eagle, snake in beak **Mint:** Guanajuato

Date	Mintage	F	VF	XF	Unc	BU
1826/5Go JJ	—	5.00	7.50	15.00	85.00	—
1826Go MJ	—	4.00	6.00	15.00	85.00	—
1827Go MJ	—	4.00	6.00	15.00	65.00	—
1827Go JM	—	10.00	15.00	25.00	75.00	—
1828/7Go MR	—	4.00	6.00	15.00	85.00	—
1828Go MJ	—	4.00	6.00	15.00	85.00	—
Note: Straight J, small 8						
1828Go MJ	—	4.00	6.00	15.00	85.00	—
Note: Full J, large 8						
1828/6G MR/JJ	—	4.00	6.00	15.00	85.00	—
1828G MR/JJ	—	4.00	6.00	15.00	85.00	—
1828Go MR	—	4.00	6.00	15.00	85.00	—
1829/8Go MG Small eagle	—	4.00	6.00	15.00	85.00	—
1829Go MJ Small eagle	—	4.00	6.00	15.00	85.00	—
1829Go MJ Large eagle	—	4.00	6.00	15.00	85.00	—
1830Go MJ Small initials	—	4.00	6.00	15.00	85.00	—
1830Go MJ Medium initials	—	4.00	6.00	15.00	85.00	—
1830Go MJ Large initials	—	4.00	6.00	15.00	85.00	—
1830Go MJ	—	4.00	6.00	15.00	85.00	—
Note: Reversed N in MEXICANA						
1830GC MJ 3/2	—	4.00	6.00	15.00	85.00	—
1831/0Go MJ	—	4.00	6.00	15.00	85.00	—
Note: Reversed N in MEXICANA						
1831Go MJ	—	4.00	6.00	15.00	85.00	—
1832/1Go MJ	—	15.00	30.00	50.00	125	—
1832Go MJ	—	15.00	30.00	50.00	125	—
1833Go MJ Top of 3 round	—	4.00	6.00	15.00	85.00	—
1833Go MJ Top of 3 flat	—	4.00	6.00	15.00	85.00	—
1834Go PJ	—	4.00	6.00	15.00	85.00	—
1835Go PJ	—	7.50	12.50	20.00	85.00	—
1836Go PJ	—	4.00	6.00	15.00	85.00	—
1837Go PJ	—	15.00	30.00	50.00	125	—
1838/7Go PJ	—	10.00	20.00	35.00	85.00	—
1839Go PJ	—	4.00	6.00	15.00	85.00	—
1840/39Go PJ	—	4.00	6.00	15.00	85.00	—
1840Go PJ	—	4.00	6.00	15.00	85.00	—
1841/31Go PJ	—	10.00	20.00	35.00	85.00	—
1841Go PJ	—	4.00	6.00	15.00	85.00	—
1842Go PJ	—	4.00	6.00	15.00	85.00	—
1842Go PM	—	4.00	6.00	15.00	85.00	—
1843Go PM Convex wings	—	4.00	6.00	15.00	85.00	—
1843Go PM Concave wings	—	4.00	6.00	15.00	85.00	—
1844Go PM	—	4.00	6.00	15.00	85.00	—
1845/4Go PM	—	4.00	6.00	15.00	85.00	—
1845Go PM	—	4.00	6.00	15.00	85.00	—
1846/5Go PM	—	7.50	12.50	20.00	85.00	—
1846Go PM	—	4.00	6.00	15.00	85.00	—
1847/6Go PM	—	4.00	6.00	15.00	85.00	—
1847Go PM	—	4.00	6.00	15.00	85.00	—
1848Go PM	—	4.00	6.00	15.00	85.00	—
1849Go PF	—	10.00	20.00	35.00	85.00	—
1850Go PF	—	4.00	6.00	15.00	85.00	—
1851Go PF	—	10.00	20.00	35.00	100	—
1853/2Go PF	—	7.50	12.50	20.00	75.00	—
1853Go PF	—	4.00	6.00	15.00	75.00	—
1853Go PF/M 5/4	—	7.50	12.50	20.00	75.00	—
1854/3Go PF	—	4.00	6.00	15.00	75.00	—
1854Go PF Large eagle	—	4.00	6.00	15.00	75.00	—
1854Go PF Small eagle	—	4.00	6.00	15.00	75.00	—
1855/3Go PF	—	4.00	6.00	15.00	75.00	—

Date	Mintage	F	VF	XF	Unc	BU
1855/4Go PF	—	4.00	6.00	15.00	75.00	—
1855Go PF	—	4.00	6.00	15.00	75.00	—
1856/5Go PF	—	4.00	6.00	15.00	75.00	—
1856Go PF	—	4.00	6.00	15.00	75.00	—
1857/6Go PF	—	4.00	6.00	15.00	75.00	—
1857Go PF	—	4.00	6.00	15.00	75.00	—
1858Go PF	—	4.00	6.00	15.00	75.00	—
1859Go PF	—	4.00	6.00	15.00	75.00	—
1860/50Go PF	—	4.00	6.00	15.00	75.00	—
1860Go PF	—	4.00	6.00	15.00	75.00	—
1861Go PF	—	4.00	6.00	15.00	75.00	—
1862Go YE	—	4.00	6.00	15.00	75.00	—
1862/1Go YF	—	7.50	12.50	20.00	75.00	—
1862Go YF	—	4.00	6.00	15.00	75.00	—
1867Go YF	—	4.00	6.00	15.00	75.00	—
1868/7Go YF	—	4.00	6.00	15.00	75.00	—

KM# 372.7 REAL
3.3800 g., 0.9030 Silver 0.0981 oz. ASW **Obv:** Facing eagle, snake in beak **Mint:** Hermosillo

Date	Mintage	F	VF	XF	Unc	BU
1867Ho PR	—	38.50	75.00	120	250	—
Note: Small 7/1						
1867Ho PR	—	38.50	75.00	120	250	—
Note: Large 7/ small 7						
1868Ho PR	—	38.50	75.00	120	250	—

KM# 372.8 REAL
3.3800 g., 0.9030 Silver 0.0981 oz. ASW **Obv:** Facing eagle, snake in beak **Mint:** Mexico City

Date	Mintage	F	VF	XF	Unc	BU
1825Mo JM	—	10.00	20.00	40.00	125	—
1826Mo JM	—	7.50	15.00	30.00	115	—
1827/6Mo JM	—	7.50	15.00	30.00	85.00	—
1827Mo JM	—	5.00	10.00	20.00	80.00	—
1828Mo JM	—	7.50	15.00	30.00	110	—
1830/29Mo JM	—	5.00	10.00	20.00	110	—
1830Mo JM	—	5.00	12.50	25.00	110	—
1831Mo JM	—	100	200	300	800	—
1832Mo JM	—	5.00	10.00	20.00	110	—
1833/2Mo MJ	—	5.00	10.00	20.00	110	—
1850Mo GC	—	5.00	10.00	20.00	110	—
1852Mo GC	—	275	425	575	—	—
1854Mo GC	—	10.00	20.00	40.00	110	—
1855Mo GF	—	5.00	10.00	20.00	90.00	—
1856Mo GF	—	100	200	400	1,000	—
1857Mo GF	—	5.00	10.00	20.00	90.00	—
1858Mo FH	—	5.00	10.00	20.00	90.00	—
1859Mo FH	—	5.00	10.00	20.00	90.00	—
1861Mo CH	—	5.00	10.00	20.00	90.00	—
1862Mo CH	—	5.00	10.00	20.00	90.00	—
1863/2Mo CH	—	7.50	12.50	25.00	90.00	—

KM# 372.9 REAL
3.3800 g., 0.9030 Silver 0.0981 oz. ASW **Obv:** Facing eagle, snake in beak **Mint:** San Luis Potosi

Date	Mintage	F	VF	XF	Unc	BU
1831Pi JS	—	5.00	10.00	20.00	125	—
1837Pi JS	—	600	750	1,000	—	—
1838/7Pi JS	—	250	300	375	—	—
1838Pi JS	—	20.00	35.00	60.00	125	—
1840/39Pi JS	—	7.50	15.00	30.00	125	—
1840Pi JS	—	7.50	15.00	30.00	125	—
1841Pi JS	—	7.50	15.00	30.00	125	—
1842Pi JS	—	15.00	30.00	55.00	150	—
1842Pi PS	—	5.00	10.00	20.00	125	—
1843Pi PS	—	12.50	20.00	35.00	125	—
1843Pi AM	—	40.00	60.00	80.00	150	—
1844Pi AM	—	40.00	60.00	80.00	150	—
1845Pi AM	—	7.50	15.00	30.00	125	—
1846/5Pi AM	—	7.50	15.00	30.00	125	—
1847/6Pi AM	—	7.50	15.00	30.00	125	—
1847Pi AM	—	7.50	15.00	30.00	125	—
1848/7Pi AM	—	7.50	15.00	30.00	125	—
1849Pi PS	—	7.50	15.00	30.00	125	—
1849/8Pi SP	—	60.00	100	150	—	—
1849Pi SP	—	15.00	25.00	40.00	125	—
1850Pi MC	—	5.00	10.00	20.00	125	—
1851/0Pi MC	—	7.50	15.00	30.00	125	—
1851Pi MC	—	7.50	15.00	30.00	125	—
1852/1/0Pi MC	—	10.00	20.00	35.00	125	—
1852Pi MC	—	7.50	15.00	30.00	125	—
1853/1Pi MC	—	12.50	20.00	35.00	125	—

Date	Mintage	F	VF	XF	Unc	BU
1853Pi MC	—	10.00	20.00	35.00	125	—
1854/2Pi MO	—	30.00	60.00	100	—	—
1854/3Pi MC	—	20.00	40.00	60.00	150	—
1855/4Pi MC	—	20.00	40.00	60.00	150	—
1855Pi MC	—	15.00	25.00	45.00	125	—
1856Pi MC	—	15.00	25.00	45.00	125	—
1857Pi PS	—	20.00	35.00	55.00	135	—
1857Pi MC	—	20.00	40.00	60.00	150	—
1858Pi MC	—	12.50	20.00	35.00	125	—
1859Pi PS	—	10.00	15.00	30.00	125	—
1860/59Pi PS	—	10.00	15.00	30.00	125	—
1861Pi PS	—	7.50	12.50	20.00	125	—
1861Pi RO	—	12.50	20.00	35.00	125	—
1862/1Pi RO	—	12.50	20.00	35.00	90.00	—
1862Pi RO	—	7.50	12.50	20.00	125	—

KM# 372.10 REAL
3.3800 g., 0.9030 Silver 0.0981 oz. ASW **Obv:** Facing eagle, snake in beak **Mint:** Zacatecas

Date	Mintage	F	VF	XF	Unc	BU
1826Zs AZ	—	5.00	12.50	35.00	120	—
1826Zs AO	—	5.00	12.50	35.00	120	—
1827Zs AO	—	5.00	12.50	35.00	120	—
1828/7Zs AO	—	5.00	12.50	35.00	120	—
1828Zs AO	—	5.00	12.50	35.00	120	—
1828Zs AO Inverted V for A	—	5.00	12.50	35.00	120	—
1829Zs AO	—	5.00	12.50	35.00	120	—
1830Zs ZsOV	—	5.00	12.50	35.00	120	—
1830Zs ZOV	—	5.00	12.50	35.00	120	—
1831Zs OV	—	5.00	12.50	35.00	120	—
1831Zs OM	—	5.00	12.50	30.00	120	—
1832Zs OM	—	5.00	12.50	30.00	120	—
1833/2Zs OM	—	5.00	12.50	30.00	120	—
1833/2Zs OM/V	—	5.00	12.50	30.00	120	—
1833Zs OM	—	5.00	12.50	30.00	120	—
1834/3Zs OM	—	5.00	12.50	30.00	120	—
1834Zs OM	—	5.00	12.50	30.00	120	—
1835/4Zs OM	—	20.00	35.00	60.00	150	—
1835Zs OM	—	4.00	8.00	20.00	65.00	—
1836/5Zs OM	—	4.00	8.00	20.00	85.00	—
1836Zs OM	—	4.00	8.00	20.00	85.00	—
1837Zs OM	—	4.00	8.00	20.00	85.00	—
1838Zs OM	—	4.00	8.00	20.00	85.00	—
1839Zs OM	—	4.00	8.00	20.00	85.00	—
1840Zs OM	—	4.00	8.00	20.00	85.00	—
1841Zs OM	—	20.00	40.00	60.00	150	—
1842/1Zs OM	—	4.00	8.00	20.00	85.00	—
1842Zs OM	—	4.00	8.00	20.00	85.00	—
1843Zs OM	—	4.00	8.00	20.00	85.00	—
1844Zs OM	—	4.00	8.00	20.00	85.00	—
1845/4Zs OM	—	5.00	12.50	30.00	100	—
1845Zs OM	—	4.00	8.00	20.00	85.00	—
1846Zs OM	—	4.00	8.00	20.00	85.00	—
Note: Old font and obverse						
1846Zs OM	—	4.00	8.00	20.00	85.00	—
Note: New font and obverse						
1847Zs OM	—	4.00	8.00	20.00	85.00	—
1848Zs OM	—	4.00	8.00	20.00	85.00	—
1849Zs OM	—	10.00	25.00	50.00	125	—
1850Zs OM	—	4.00	6.00	15.00	85.00	—
1851Zs OM	—	4.00	6.00	15.00	85.00	—
1852Zs OM	—	4.00	6.00	15.00	85.00	—
1853Zs OM	—	4.00	6.00	15.00	85.00	—
1854/2Zs OM	—	4.00	6.00	15.00	85.00	—
1854/3Zs OM	—	4.00	6.00	15.00	85.00	—
1854Zs OM	—	4.00	6.00	15.00	85.00	—
1855/4Zs OM	—	4.00	6.00	15.00	85.00	—
1855Zs OM	—	4.00	6.00	15.00	85.00	—
1855Zs MO	—	4.00	6.00	15.00	85.00	—
1856Zs MO	—	4.00	6.00	15.00	85.00	—
1856Zs MO/OM	—	4.00	6.00	15.00	85.00	—
1857Zs MO	—	4.00	6.00	15.00	85.00	—
1858Zs MO	—	4.00	6.00	15.00	85.00	—
1859Zs MO	—	4.00	6.00	15.00	75.00	—
1860 MO	250	—	—	—	—	—
1860Zs VL	—	4.00	6.00	15.00	75.00	—
1860Zs VL Inverted A for V	—	4.00	6.00	15.00	75.00	—
1861Zs VL	—	4.00	6.00	15.00	75.00	—

Date	Mintage	F	VF	XF	Unc	BU
1861Zs VL	—	4.00	6.00	15.00	75.00	—
Inverted A for V						
1862Zs VL	—	5.00	12.50	30.00	100	—
1868Zs JS	—	25.00	45.00	90.00	175	—
1869Zs YH	—	4.00	8.00	20.00	75.00	—

KM# 372.3 REAL
3.3800 g., 0.9030 Silver 0.0981 oz. ASW **Obv:** Facing eagle, snake in beak **Mint:** Estado de Mexico

Date	Mintage	F	VF	XF	Unc	BU
1828EoMo LF	—	200	300	450	1,600	—

KM# 374.2 2 REALES
6.7600 g., 0.9030 Silver 0.1962 oz. ASW **Obv:** Facing eagle, snake in beak **Edge:** Reeded **Mint:** Chihuahua

Date	Mintage	F	VF	XF	Unc	BU
1832Ca MR	—	30.00	60.00	100	200	—
1833Ca MR	—	30.00	60.00	125	500	—
1834Ca MR	—	35.00	75.00	125	500	—
1834Ca AM	—	35.00	75.00	125	500	—
1835Ca AM	—	35.00	75.00	125	500	—
1836Ca AM	—	20.00	40.00	80.00	200	—
1844Ca AM Rare	—	—	—	—	—	—
1844Ca RG Unique	—	—	—	—	—	—
1845Ca RG	—	20.00	40.00	80.00	200	—
1855Ca RG	—	20.00	40.00	80.00	200	—

KM# 374.3 2 REALES
6.7600 g., 0.9030 Silver 0.1962 oz. ASW **Obv:** Facing eagle, snake in beak **Edge:** Reeded **Mint:** Culiacan

Date	Mintage	F	VF	XF	Unc	BU
1846/1146C CE	—	25.00	50.00	100	225	—
1847C CE	—	12.50	20.00	40.00	200	—
1848C CE	—	12.50	20.00	40.00	200	—
1850C CE	—	25.00	50.00	75.00	200	—
1851C CE	—	12.50	20.00	40.00	200	—
1852/1C CE	—	12.50	20.00	40.00	200	—
1853/2C CE	—	12.50	20.00	40.00	200	—
1854C CE	—	15.00	30.00	50.00	200	—
1856C CE	—	20.00	35.00	70.00	200	—
1857C CE	—	12.50	20.00	40.00	200	—
1860C PV	—	12.50	20.00	40.00	200	—
1861C PV	—	12.50	20.00	40.00	200	—
1869C CE	—	12.50	20.00	40.00	200	—

KM# 374.4 2 REALES
6.7600 g., 0.9030 Silver 0.1962 oz. ASW **Obv:** Facing eagle, snake in beak **Edge:** Reeded **Mint:** Durango

Date	Mintage	F	VF	XF	Unc	BU
1826Do RL	—	20.00	40.00	60.00	200	—
1832Do RM	—	20.00	40.00	60.00	200	—
Note: Style of pre-1832						
1832Do RM	—	20.00	40.00	60.00	200	—
Note: Style of post-1832						
1834/2Do RM	—	20.00	40.00	60.00	200	—
1834/3Do RM	—	20.00	40.00	60.00	200	—
1835/4Do RM/RL	—	200	300	500	—	—
1841/31Do RM	—	50.00	75.00	125	250	—
1841Do RM	—	50.00	75.00	125	250	—
1842/32Do RM	—	12.50	20.00	40.00	200	—
1843Do RM/RL	—	12.50	20.00	40.00	200	—
1844Do RM	—	35.00	50.00	80.00	200	—
1845/34Do RM/RL	—	12.50	20.00	40.00	200	—
1846/36Do RM	—	100	150	200	350	—
1848/36Do RM	—	12.50	20.00	40.00	200	—
1848/37Do RM	—	12.50	20.00	40.00	200	—
1848/7Do RM	—	12.50	20.00	40.00	200	—
1848Do RM	—	12.50	20.00	40.00	200	—
1849Do CM/RM	—	12.50	20.00	40.00	200	—
1849Do CM	—	12.50	20.00	40.00	200	—
1851Do JMR/RL	—	12.50	20.00	40.00	200	—
1852Do JMR	—	12.50	20.00	40.00	200	—
1854Do CP/CR	—	30.00	50.00	80.00	200	—
1855Do CP	—	250	350	500	—	—
1856Do CP	—	100	150	250	500	—
1858Do CP	—	12.50	20.00	40.00	200	—
1859/8Do CP	—	12.50	20.00	40.00	200	—
1861Do CP	—	12.50	20.00	40.00	200	—

KM# 374.6 2 REALES
6.7600 g., 0.9030 Silver 0.1962 oz. ASW **Obv:** Facing eagle, snake in beak **Edge:** Reeded **Mint:** Guadalajara

Date	Mintage	F	VF	XF	Unc	BU
1825Ga FS	—	20.00	40.00	80.00	200	—
1826Ga FS	—	20.00	40.00	80.00	200	—

Date	Mintage	F	VF	XF	Unc	BU
1828/7Ga FS	—	100	150	225	400	—
1829Ga FS Rare	—	—	—	—	—	—
1832/0Ga FS/LP	—	100	150	225	350	—
1832Ga FS	—	12.50	20.00	40.00	200	—
1833/2Ga FS/LP	—	12.50	20.00	40.00	200	—
1834/27Ga FS Rare	—	—	—	—	—	—
1834Ga FS	—	12.50	20.00	40.00	200	—
1835Ga FS	—	2,100	—	—	—	—
1837Ga JG	—	12.50	20.00	40.00	200	—
1838Ga JG	—	12.50	20.00	40.00	200	—
1840/30Ga MC	—	12.50	20.00	40.00	200	—
1841Ga MC	—	30.00	50.00	200	500	—
1842/32Ga JG/MC	—	35.00	50.00	100	200	—
1842Ga JG	—	20.00	40.00	80.00	200	—
1843Ga JG	—	12.50	20.00	40.00	200	—
1843Ga MC/JG	—	12.50	20.00	40.00	200	—
1844Ga MC	—	12.50	20.00	40.00	200	—
1845/3Ga MC/JG	—	12.50	20.00	40.00	200	—
1845/4Ga MC/JG	—	12.50	20.00	40.00	200	—
1845Ga JG	—	12.50	20.00	40.00	200	—
1846Ga JG	—	12.50	20.00	40.00	200	—
1847/6Ga JG	—	25.00	40.00	80.00	200	—
1848/7Ga JG	—	12.50	20.00	40.00	200	—
1849Ga JG	—	12.50	20.00	40.00	200	—
1850/40Ga JG	—	12.50	20.00	40.00	200	—
1851Ga JG	—	250	350	500	—	—
1852Ga JG	—	12.50	20.00	40.00	200	—
1853/1Ga JG	—	12.50	20.00	40.00	200	—
1854/3Ga JG	—	250	350	500	—	—
1855Ga JG	—	35.00	50.00	80.00	200	—
1856Ga JG	—	12.50	20.00	40.00	200	—
1857Ga JG	—	250	350	500	—	—
1859/8Ga JG	—	12.50	20.00	40.00	200	—
1859Ga JG	—	12.50	20.00	40.00	200	—
1862/1Ga JG	—	12.50	20.00	40.00	200	—

KM# 374.7 2 REALES
6.7600 g., 0.9030 Silver 0.1962 oz. ASW **Obv:** Facing eagle, snake in beak **Edge:** Reeded **Mint:** Guadalupe y Calvo

Date	Mintage	F	VF	XF	Unc	BU
1844GC MP	—	40.00	60.00	125	275	—
1845GC MP	—	40.00	60.00	125	275	—
1846GC MP	—	50.00	100	150	300	—
1847GC MP	—	35.00	50.00	100	250	—
1848GC MP	—	50.00	100	150	300	—
1849GC MP	—	50.00	100	150	300	—
1850GC MP	—	125	250	—	—	—
1851/0GC MP	—	50.00	100	150	300	—
1851GC MP	—	50.00	100	150	300	—

KM# 374.9 2 REALES
6.7600 g., 0.9030 Silver 0.1962 oz. ASW **Obv:** Facing eagle, snake in beak **Edge:** Reeded **Mint:** Hermosillo

Date	Mintage	F	VF	XF	Unc	BU
1861Ho FM	—	200	300	400	650	—
1862/52Ho FM/C. CE	—	250	350	550	—	—
1867/1Ho PR/FM	—	75.00	150	250	500	—

KM# 374.11 2 REALES
6.7600 g., 0.9030 Silver 0.1962 oz. ASW **Obv:** Facing eagle, snake in beak **Edge:** Reeded **Mint:** San Luis Potosi

Date	Mintage	F	VF	XF	Unc	BU
1829Pi JS	—	10.00	15.00	30.00	200	—
1830/20Pi JS	—	20.00	30.00	60.00	200	—
1837Pi JS	—	10.00	15.00	30.00	200	—
1841Pi JS	—	10.00	15.00	30.00	200	—
1842/1Pi JS	—	10.00	15.00	30.00	200	—
1842Pi JS	—	10.00	15.00	30.00	200	—
1842Pi PS	—	20.00	35.00	60.00	200	—
1843Pi PS	—	12.50	20.00	40.00	200	—
1843Pi AM	—	10.00	15.00	30.00	200	—
1844Pi AM	—	10.00	15.00	30.00	200	—
1845Pi AM	—	10.00	15.00	30.00	200	—
1846Pi AM	—	10.00	15.00	30.00	200	—
1849Pi MC	—	10.00	15.00	30.00	200	—
1850Pi MC	—	10.00	15.00	30.00	200	—
1856Pi MC	—	40.00	60.00	125	250	—
1857Pi MC	—	—	—	—	—	—
1858Pi MC	—	12.50	20.00	40.00	200	—
1859Pi MC	—	50.00	70.00	100	200	—
1861Pi PS	—	10.00	15.00	30.00	200	—
1862Pi RO	—	12.50	20.00	40.00	200	—
1863Pi RO	—	100	250	350	500	—

FIRST REPUBLIC - FEDERAL

Date	Mintage	F	VF	XF	Unc	BU
1868Pi PS	—	10.00	15.00	30.00	200	—
1869/8Pi PS	—	10.00	15.00	30.00	200	—
1869Pi PS	—	10.00	15.00	30.00	200	—

KM# 374.8 2 REALES
6.7600 g., 0.9030 Silver 0.1962 oz. ASW **Obv:** Facing eagle, snake in beak **Edge:** Reeded **Mint:** Guanajuato **Note:** Varieties exist.

Date	Mintage	F	VF	XF	Unc	BU
1825Go JJ	—	7.50	15.00	30.00	150	—
1826/5Go JJ	—	7.50	15.00	30.00	150	—
1826Go JJ	—	7.50	10.00	25.00	150	—
1826Go MJ	—	7.50	10.00	25.00	150	—
1827/6Go MJ	—	7.50	10.00	25.00	150	—
1827Go MJ	—	7.50	10.00	25.00	150	—
1828/7Go MR	—	7.50	15.00	30.00	150	—
1828Go MJ	—	7.50	10.00	20.00	150	—
1828Go JM	—	7.50	10.00	20.00	150	—
1829Go MJ	—	7.50	10.00	20.00	150	—
1831Go MJ	—	7.50	10.00	20.00	150	—
1832Go MJ	—	7.50	10.00	20.00	150	—
1833Go MJ	—	7.50	10.00	20.00	150	—
1834Go PJ	—	7.50	10.00	20.00	150	—
1835/4Go PJ	—	7.50	15.00	30.00	150	—
1835Go PJ	—	7.50	10.00	20.00	150	—
1836Go PJ	—	7.50	10.00	20.00	150	—
1837/6Go PJ	—	7.50	10.00	20.00	150	—
1837Go PJ	—	7.50	10.00	20.00	150	—
1838/7Go PJ	—	7.50	10.00	20.00	150	—
1838Go PJ	—	7.50	10.00	20.00	150	—
1839/8Go PJ	—	7.50	15.00	30.00	150	—
1839Go PJ	—	7.50	10.00	20.00	150	—
1840Go PJ	—	7.50	10.00	20.00	150	—
1841Go PJ	—	7.50	10.00	20.00	150	—
1842Go PJ	—	7.50	10.00	20.00	150	—
1842Go PM/PJ	—	7.50	10.00	20.00	150	—
1842Go PM	—	7.50	10.00	20.00	150	—
1843/2Go PM	—	7.50	10.00	20.00	150	—

Note: Concave wings, thin rays, small letters

| 1843Go PM | — | 7.50 | 10.00 | 20.00 | 150 | — |

Note: Convex wings, thick rays, large letters

1844Go PM	—	7.50	10.00	20.00	150	—
1845/4Go PM	—	7.50	10.00	20.00	150	—
1845Go PM	—	7.50	10.00	20.00	150	—
1846/5Go PM	—	10.00	15.00	35.00	150	—
1846Go PM	—	7.50	10.00	20.00	150	—
1847Go PM	—	7.50	10.00	20.00	150	—
1848/7Go PM	—	7.50	15.00	30.00	150	—
1848Go PM	—	7.50	15.00	30.00	150	—
1848Go PF	—	100	150	250	500	—
1849/8Go PF/PM	—	7.50	10.00	20.00	150	—
1849Go PF	—	7.50	10.00	20.00	150	—
1850/40Go PF	—	7.50	10.00	20.00	150	—
1850Go PF	—	7.50	10.00	20.00	150	—
1851Go PF	—	7.50	10.00	20.00	150	—
1852/1Go PF	—	7.50	10.00	20.00	150	—
1852Go PF	—	7.50	10.00	20.00	150	—
1853Go PF	—	7.50	10.00	20.00	150	—
1854/3Go PF	—	7.50	10.00	20.00	150	—
1854Go PF	—	7.50	10.00	20.00	150	—

Note: Old font and obverse

| 1854Go PF | — | 7.50 | 10.00 | 20.00 | 150 | — |

Note: New font and obverse

| 1855Go PF | — | 7.50 | 10.00 | 20.00 | 150 | — |
| 1855Go PF | — | 7.50 | 10.00 | 20.00 | 150 | — |

Note: Star in G of mint mark

1856/5Go PF	—	10.00	15.00	35.00	150	—
1856Go PF	—	10.00	15.00	25.00	150	—
1857/6Go PF	—	7.50	10.00	20.00	150	—
1857Go PF	—	7.50	10.00	20.00	150	—
1858/7Go PF	—	7.50	10.00	20.00	150	—
1858Go PF	—	7.50	10.00	20.00	150	—
1859/7Go PF	—	7.50	10.00	20.00	150	—
1859Go PF	—	7.50	10.00	20.00	150	—
1860/7Go PF	—	7.50	10.00	20.00	150	—
1860/50Go PF	—	7.50	10.00	20.00	150	—
1860/59Go PF	—	7.50	10.00	20.00	150	—
1860Go PF	—	7.50	10.00	20.00	150	—
1861/51Go PF	—	7.50	10.00	20.00	150	—
1861/57Go PF	—	7.50	10.00	20.00	150	—

Date	Mintage	F	VF	XF	Unc	BU
1861/0Go PF	—	7.50	10.00	20.00	150	—
1861Go PF	—	7.50	10.00	20.00	150	—
1862/1Go YE	—	7.50	10.00	20.00	125	—
1862Go YE	—	7.50	10.00	20.00	125	—
1862/57Go YE	—	7.50	10.00	20.00	125	—
1862Go YE/PF	—	7.50	10.00	20.00	125	—
1862/57Go YF/E	—	7.50	10.00	20.00	125	—
1862/57Go YF	—	7.50	10.00	20.00	125	—
1862Go YF	—	7.50	10.00	20.00	125	—
1863/52Go YF/PE	—	7.50	10.00	20.00	125	—
1863/52Go YF	—	7.50	10.00	20.00	125	—
1863Go YF	—	7.50	10.00	20.00	125	—
1867/57Go YF	—	7.50	10.00	20.00	125	—
1868/57Go YF	—	10.00	15.00	25.00	125	—

KM# 374.10 2 REALES
6.7600 g., 0.9030 Silver 0.1962 oz. ASW **Obv:** Facing eagle, snake in beak **Obv. Legend:** REPUBLICA MEXICANA. **Rev:** Radiant cap **Edge:** Reeded **Mint:** Mexico City **Note:** Varieties exist.

Date	Mintage	F	VF	XF	Unc	BU
1825Mo JM	—	10.00	15.00	30.00	175	—
1826Mo JM	—	10.00	15.00	30.00	175	—
1827Mo JM	—	10.00	15.00	30.00	175	—
1828Mo JM	—	10.00	15.00	30.00	175	—
1829/8Mo JM	—	10.00	15.00	30.00	175	—
1829Mo JM	—	10.00	15.00	30.00	175	—
1830Mo JM	—	40.00	60.00	125	250	—
1831Mo JM	—	10.00	15.00	30.00	175	—
1832Mo JM	—	100	200	400	—	—
1833/2Mo MJ/JM	—	10.00	15.00	30.00	175	—
1834Mo ML	—	50.00	100	200	400	—
1836Mo MF	—	10.00	15.00	30.00	175	—
1837Mo ML	—	10.00	15.00	30.00	175	—
1840/7Mo ML	—	150	225	350	—	—
1840Mo ML	—	150	225	350	—	—
1841Mo ML	—	15.00	40.00	100	250	—
1842 ML Rare	—	—	—	—	—	—
1847Mo RC Narrow date	—	10.00	15.00	30.00	175	—
1847Mo RC Wide date	—	10.00	15.00	30.00	175	—
1848Mo GC	—	10.00	15.00	30.00	175	—
1849Mo GC	—	10.00	15.00	30.00	175	—
1850Mo GC	—	10.00	15.00	30.00	175	—
1851Mo GC	—	40.00	60.00	125	250	—
1852Mo GC	—	10.00	15.00	30.00	175	—
1853Mo GC	—	10.00	15.00	30.00	175	—
1854/44Mo GC	—	10.00	15.00	30.00	175	—
1855Mo GC	—	10.00	15.00	30.00	175	—
1855Mo GF/GC	—	10.00	15.00	30.00	175	—
1855Mo GF	—	10.00	15.00	30.00	175	—
1856/5Mo GF/GC	—	10.00	15.00	30.00	175	—
1857Mo GF	—	10.00	15.00	30.00	175	—
1858Mo FH	—	7.50	12.50	25.00	150	—
1858Mo FH/GF	—	7.50	12.50	25.00	150	—
1859Mo FH	—	7.50	12.50	25.00	150	—
1860Mo FH	—	7.50	12.50	25.00	150	—
1860Mo TH	—	7.50	12.50	25.00	150	—
1861Mo CH	—	7.50	12.50	25.00	150	—
1862Mo CH	—	7.50	12.50	25.00	150	—
1863Mo CH	—	7.50	12.50	25.00	150	—
1863Mo TH	—	7.50	12.50	25.00	150	—
1867Mo CH	—	7.50	12.50	25.00	150	—
1868Mo CH	—	10.00	15.00	30.00	150	—
1868Mo PH	—	7.50	12.50	25.00	150	—

KM# 374.12 2 REALES
6.7600 g., 0.9030 Silver 0.1962 oz. ASW **Obv:** Facing eagle, snake in beak **Edge:** Reeded **Mint:** Zacatecas **Note:** Varieties exist.

Date	Mintage	F	VF	XF	Unc	BU
1825Zs AZ	—	10.00	15.00	30.00	150	—
1826Zs AV	—	7.50	10.00	25.00	150	—
Note: A is inverted V						
1826Zs AZ	—	7.50	10.00	25.00	150	—
Note: A is inverted V						
1826Zs AO	—	10.00	15.00	30.00	150	—
1827Zs AO	—	6.00	8.00	12.00	150	—
Note: A is inverted V						
1827Zs AO	—	6.00	8.00	12.00	150	—
1828/7Zs AO	—	15.00	30.00	60.00	175	—
1828Zs AO	—	7.50	10.00	25.00	100	—
1828Zs AO	—	7.50	10.00	25.00	150	—
Note: A is inverted V						
1829Zs AO	—	7.50	10.00	25.00	150	—
1829Zs OV	—	7.50	10.00	25.00	150	—
1830Zs OV	—	7.50	10.00	25.00	150	—
1831Zs OV	—	7.50	10.00	25.00	150	—
1831Zs OM/OV	—	7.50	10.00	25.00	150	—
1831Zs OM	—	7.50	10.00	25.00	150	—
1832/1Zs OM	—	15.00	30.00	60.00	150	—
1832Zs OM	—	7.50	10.00	25.00	150	—
1833/27Zs OM	—	7.50	10.00	25.00	150	—
1833/2Zs OM	—	7.50	10.00	25.00	150	—
1833Zs OM	—	7.50	10.00	25.00	150	—
1834Zs OM	—	40.00	60.00	125	200	—
1835Zs OM	—	7.50	10.00	25.00	150	—
1836Zs OM	—	7.50	10.00	25.00	150	—
1837Zs OM	—	7.50	10.00	25.00	150	—
1838Zs OM	—	15.00	30.00	60.00	150	—
1839Zs OM	—	7.50	10.00	20.00	150	—
1840Zs OM	—	7.50	10.00	20.00	150	—
1841/0Zs OM	—	7.50	10.00	20.00	150	—
1841Zs OM	—	7.50	10.00	20.00	150	—
1842Zs OM	—	7.50	10.00	20.00	150	—
Narrow date						
1842Zs OM	—	7.50	10.00	20.00	150	—
Wide date						
1843Zs OM	—	7.50	10.00	20.00	150	—
1844Zs OM	—	7.50	10.00	20.00	150	—
1845Zs OM	—	7.50	10.00	20.00	150	—
Note: Small letters with leaves						
1845Zs OM	—	7.50	10.00	20.00	150	—
Note: Large letters with leaves						
1846Zs OM	—	7.50	10.00	20.00	150	—
1847Zs OM	—	7.50	10.00	20.00	150	—
1848Zs OM	—	7.50	10.00	20.00	150	—
1849Zs OM	—	7.50	10.00	20.00	150	—
1850Zs OM	—	7.50	10.00	20.00	150	—
1851Zs OM	—	7.50	10.00	20.00	150	—
1852Zs OM	—	7.50	10.00	20.00	150	—
1853Zs OM	—	7.50	10.00	20.00	150	—
1854/3Zs OM	—	7.50	10.00	20.00	150	—
1854Zs OM	—	7.50	10.00	20.00	150	—
1855/4Zs OM	—	7.50	10.00	20.00	150	—
1855Zs OM	—	7.50	10.00	20.00	150	—
1855Zs MO	—	7.50	10.00	20.00	150	—
1856/5Zs MO	—	7.50	10.00	20.00	150	—
1856Zs MO	—	7.50	10.00	20.00	150	—
1857Zs MO	—	7.50	10.00	20.00	150	—
1858Zs MO	—	7.50	10.00	20.00	150	—
1859Zs MO	—	7.50	10.00	20.00	150	—
1860/59Zs MO	—	7.50	10.00	20.00	150	—
1860Zs MO	—	7.50	10.00	20.00	100	—
1860Zs VL	—	7.50	10.00	20.00	150	—
1861Zs VL	—	7.50	10.00	20.00	150	—
1862Zs VL	—	7.50	10.00	20.00	100	—
1863Zs MO	—	12.50	20.00	40.00	150	—
1863Zs VL	—	7.50	10.00	20.00	150	—
1864Zs MO	—	7.50	10.00	20.00	150	—
1864Zs VL	—	7.50	10.00	20.00	150	—
1865Zs MO	—	7.50	10.00	20.00	150	—
1867Zs JS	—	7.50	10.00	20.00	150	—
1868Zs JS	—	10.00	15.00	35.00	150	—
1868Zs YH	—	7.50	10.00	20.00	150	—
1869Zs YH	—	7.50	10.00	20.00	150	—
1870Zs YH	—	7.50	10.00	20.00	150	—

KM# 374 2 REALES
6.7600 g., 0.9030 Silver 0.1962 oz. ASW **Obv:** Facing eagle, snake in beak **Edge:** Reeded **Mint:** Alamos

Date	Mintage	F	VF	XF	Unc	BU
1872A AM	15,000	60.00	125	250	600	—

KM# 374.1 2 REALES
6.7600 g., 0.9030 Silver 0.1962 oz. ASW **Obv:** Facing eagle, snake in beak **Mint:** Real de Catorce

Date	Mintage	F	VF	XF	Unc	BU
1863Ce ML	—	125	200	325	700	—

KM# 374.5 2 REALES
6.7600 g., 0.9030 Silver 0.1962 oz. ASW **Obv:** Facing eagle, snake in beak **Edge:** Reeded **Mint:** Estado de Mexico

Date	Mintage	F	VF	XF	Unc	BU
1828EoMo LF	—	325	525	900	2,500	—

KM# 375.1 4 REALES
13.5400 g., 0.9030 Silver 0.3931 oz. ASW **Obv:** Facing eagle, snake in beak **Mint:** Culiacan

Date	Mintage	F	VF	XF	Unc	BU
1846C CE	—	400	550	950	—	—
1850C CE	—	75.00	125	250	—	—
1852C CE	—	200	300	500	—	—
1857C CE Rare	—	—	—	—	—	—
1858C CE	—	100	200	350	—	—
1860C PV	—	25.00	50.00	125	—	—

KM# 375.2 4 REALES
13.5400 g., 0.9030 Silver 0.3931 oz. ASW **Obv:** Facing eagle, snake in beak **Mint:** Guadalajara

Date	Mintage	F	VF	XF	Unc	BU
1843Ga MC	—	20.00	40.00	80.00	—	—
1844/3Ga MC	—	30.00	60.00	125	—	—
1844Ga MC	—	20.00	40.00	80.00	—	—
1845Ga MC	—	20.00	40.00	80.00	—	—
1845Ga JG	—	20.00	40.00	80.00	—	—
1846Ga JG	—	20.00	40.00	80.00	—	—
1847Ga JG	—	40.00	80.00	150	—	—
1848/7Ga JG	—	40.00	80.00	150	—	—
1849Ga JG	—	40.00	80.00	150	—	—
1850Ga JG	—	65.00	125	250	—	—
1852Ga JG Rare	—	—	—	—	—	—
1854Ga JG Rare	—	—	—	—	—	—
1855Ga JG	—	100	200	400	—	—
1856Ga JG Rare	—	—	—	—	—	—
1857/6Ga JG	—	65.00	125	250	—	—
1858Ga JG	—	125	250	450	—	—
1859/8Ga JG	—	125	250	450	—	—

Date	Mintage	F	VF	XF	Unc	BU
1860Ga JG	—	850	1,450	—	—	—
1863/2Ga JG	—	150	300	1,250	—	—
1863Ga JG	—	150	300	1,250	—	—

KM# 375.3   4 REALES
13.5400 g., 0.9030 Silver 0.3931 oz. ASW   **Obv:** Facing eagle, snake in beak **Mint:** Guadalupe y Calvo

Date	Mintage	F	VF	XF	Unc	BU
1844GC MP	—	3,000	5,000	—	—	—
1845GC MP	—	6,500	8,000	—	—	—
1846GC MP	—	1,700	2,800	—	—	—
1847GC MP	—	1,500	2,500	—	—	—
1849GC MP	—	3,000	4,000	—	—	—
1850GC MP	—	1,500	2,500	—	—	—

KM# 375.5   4 REALES
13.5400 g., 0.9030 Silver 0.3931 oz. ASW   **Obv:** Facing eagle, snake in beak **Mint:** Hermosillo

Date	Mintage	F	VF	XF	Unc	BU
1861Ho FM	—	200	350	500	—	—
1867/1Ho PR/FM	—	150	275	400	—	—

KM# 375.6   4 REALES
13.5400 g., 0.9030 Silver 0.3931 oz. ASW   **Obv:** Facing eagle, snake in beak **Mint:** Mexico City

Date	Mintage	F	VF	XF	Unc	BU
1827/6Mo JM	—	200	400	800	—	—
1850Mo GC Rare	—	—	—	—	—	—
1852Mo GC Rare	—	—	—	—	—	—
1854Mo GC Rare	—	—	—	—	—	—
1855Mo GF/GC	—	50.00	100	200	—	—
1855Mo GF	—	100	200	350	—	—
1856Mo GF/GC	—	50.00	125	400	—	—
1856Mo GF Rare	—	—	—	—	—	—
1859Mo FH	—	20.00	50.00	150	—	—
1861Mo CH	—	15.00	35.00	125	—	—
1862Mo CH	—	20.00	50.00	150	—	—
1863/2Mo CH	—	20.00	50.00	150	—	—
1863Mo CH	—	75.00	150	300	—	—
1867Mo CH	—	20.00	50.00	150	—	—
1868Mo CH/PH	—	30.00	75.00	150	—	—
1868Mo CH	—	20.00	50.00	150	—	—
1868Mo PH	—	30.00	75.00	200	—	—

KM# 375.8   4 REALES
13.5400 g., 0.9030 Silver 0.3931 oz. ASW   **Obv:** Facing eagle, snake in beak **Mint:** San Luis Potosi

Date	Mintage	F	VF	XF	Unc	BU
1837Pi JS	—	200	350	—	—	—
1838Pi JS	—	150	250	400	—	—
1842Pi PS	—	50.00	100	200	—	—
1843/2Pi PS	—	50.00	100	200	—	—
1843/2Pi PS	—	50.00	100	200	—	—
Note: 3 cut from 8 punch						
1843Pi AM	—	30.00	75.00	150	—	—
1843Pi PS	—	50.00	100	200	—	—
1844Pi AM	—	30.00	75.00	150	—	—
1845/4Pi AM	—	20.00	50.00	100	—	—
1845Pi AM	—	20.00	50.00	100	—	—
1846Pi AM	—	20.00	50.00	100	—	—
1847Pi AM	—	75.00	150	250	—	—
1848Pi AM Rare	—	—	—	—	—	—
1849Pi MC/AM	—	20.00	50.00	100	—	—
1849Pi MC	—	20.00	50.00	100	—	—
1849Pi PS	—	20.00	50.00	100	—	—
1850Pi MC	—	20.00	50.00	100	—	—
1851Pi MC	—	20.00	50.00	100	—	—
1852Pi MC	—	20.00	50.00	100	—	—
1853Pi MC	—	20.00	50.00	100	—	—
1854Pi MC	—	100	200	400	—	—
1855Pi MC	—	175	300	750	—	—

Date	Mintage	F	VF	XF	Unc	BU
1856Pi MC	—	250	400	700	—	—
1857Pi MC Rare	—	—	—	—	—	—
1857Pi PS Rare	—	—	—	—	—	—
1858Pi MC	—	100	200	400	—	—
1859Pi MC	—	2,000	3,000	—	—	—
1860Pi PS	—	300	450	700	—	—
1861/0Pi PS	—	300	600	—	—	—
1861Pi PS	—	150	300	600	—	—
1861Pi RO/PS	—	30.00	75.00	150	—	—
1861Pi RO	—	50.00	100	200	—	—
1862Pi RO	—	30.00	75.00	150	—	—
1863Pi RO	—	30.00	75.00	150	—	—
1864Pi RO	—	2,500	3,500	—	—	—
1868Pi PS	—	30.00	75.00	150	—	—
1869/8Pi PS	—	30.00	75.00	150	—	—
1869Pi PS	—	30.00	75.00	150	—	—

KM# 375.9   4 REALES
13.5400 g., 0.9030 Silver 0.3931 oz. ASW   **Obv:** Facing eagle, snake in beak **Mint:** Zacatecas

Date	Mintage	F	VF	XF	Unc	BU
1830Zs OM	—	20.00	50.00	100	—	—
1831Zs OM	—	15.00	30.00	75.00	—	—
1832/1Zs OM	—	20.00	50.00	100	—	—
1832Zs OM	—	20.00	50.00	100	—	—
1833/2Zs OM	—	20.00	50.00	100	—	—
1833/27Zs OM	—	15.00	30.00	75.00	—	—
1833Zs OM	—	15.00	30.00	75.00	—	—
1834/3Zs OM	—	20.00	50.00	100	—	—
1834Zs OM	—	15.00	30.00	75.00	—	—
1835Zs OM	—	15.00	30.00	75.00	—	—
1836Zs OM	—	15.00	30.00	75.00	—	—
1837/5Zs OM	—	20.00	50.00	100	—	—
1837/6Zs OM	—	20.00	50.00	100	—	—
1837Zs OM	—	20.00	50.00	100	—	—
1838/7Zs OM	—	15.00	30.00	75.00	—	—
1839Zs OM	—	250	375	500	—	—
1840Zs OM	—	500	1,300	—	—	—
1841Zs OM	—	15.00	30.00	75.00	—	—
1842Zs OM Small letters	—	15.00	40.00	85.00	—	—
1842Zs OM Large letters	—	15.00	30.00	75.00	—	—
1843Zs OM	—	15.00	30.00	75.00	—	—
1844Zs OM	—	20.00	50.00	100	—	—
1845Zs OM	—	20.00	50.00	100	—	—
1846/5Zs OM	—	25.00	60.00	125	—	—
1846Zs OM	—	20.00	50.00	100	—	—
1847Zs OM	—	15.00	30.00	75.00	—	—
1848/6Zs OM	—	50.00	75.00	125	—	—
1848Zs OM	—	20.00	50.00	100	—	—
1849Zs OM	—	20.00	50.00	100	—	—
1850Zs OM	—	20.00	50.00	100	—	—
1851Zs OM	—	15.00	30.00	75.00	—	—
1852Zs OM	—	15.00	30.00	75.00	—	—
1853Zs OM	—	20.00	50.00	100	—	—
1854/3Zs OM	—	30.00	75.00	150	—	—
1855/4Zs OM	—	20.00	50.00	100	—	—
1855Zs OM	—	15.00	30.00	75.00	—	—
1856Zs OM	—	15.00	30.00	75.00	—	—
1856Zs MO	—	20.00	50.00	100	—	—
1857/5Zs MO	—	20.00	50.00	100	—	—
1857Zs O/M	—	20.00	50.00	100	—	—
1857Zs MO	—	15.00	30.00	75.00	—	—
1858Zs MO	—	20.00	50.00	100	—	—
1859Zs MO	—	15.00	30.00	75.00	—	—
1860/59Zs MO	—	20.00	50.00	100	—	—
1860Zs MO	—	15.00	30.00	75.00	—	—
1860Zs VL	—	20.00	50.00	100	—	—
1861/0Zs VL	—	20.00	50.00	100	—	—
1861Zs VL	—	15.00	30.00	75.00	—	—
1861Zs VL 6/5	—	20.00	50.00	100	—	—
1862/1Zs VL	—	20.00	50.00	100	—	—
1862Zs VL	—	20.00	50.00	100	—	—
1863Zs VL	—	20.00	50.00	100	—	—
1863Zs MO	—	20.00	50.00	100	—	—
1864Zs VL	—	15.00	30.00	75.00	—	—
1868Zs JS	—	20.00	50.00	100	—	—
1868Zs YH	—	15.00	30.00	75.00	—	—
1869Zs YH	—	15.00	30.00	75.00	—	—
1870Zs YH	—	15.00	30.00	75.00	—	—

KM# 375.4 4 REALES
13.5400 g., 0.9030 Silver 0.3931 oz. ASW **Obv:** Facing
eagle, snake in beak **Obv. Legend:** REPUBLICA MEXICANA
Rev: Radiant cap **Mint:** Guanajuato **Note:** Varieties exist.
Some 1862 dates appear to be 1869 because of weak dies.

Date	Mintage	F	VF	XF	Unc	BU
1835Go PJ	—	12.50	25.00	60.00	—	—
1836/5Go PJ	—	15.00	30.00	75.00	—	—
1836Go PJ	—	15.00	30.00	75.00	—	—
1837Go PJ	—	12.50	25.00	60.00	—	—
1838/7Go PJ	—	15.00	30.00	75.00	—	—
1838Go PJ	—	12.50	30.00	75.00	—	—
1839Go PJ	—	12.50	25.00	60.00	—	—
1840/30Go PJ	—	20.00	50.00	100	—	—
1840 PJ	—	20.00	50.00	100	—	—
1841/30 PJ	—	200	325	600	—	—
1841/31Go PJ	—	150	250	450	—	—
1842Go PJ Rare	—	—	—	—	—	—
1842Go PM	—	15.00	30.00	75.00	—	—
1843/2Go PM	—	12.50	25.00	60.00	—	—

Note: Eagle with convex wings, thick rays

| 1843Go PM | — | 12.50 | 25.00 | 60.00 | — | — |

Note: Eagle with concave wings, thin rays

1844/3Go PM	—	15.00	30.00	75.00	—	—
1844Go PM	—	20.00	50.00	100	—	—
1845/4Go PM	—	20.00	50.00	100	—	—
1845Go PM	—	20.00	50.00	100	—	—
1846/5Go PM	—	15.00	30.00	75.00	—	—
1846Go PM	—	15.00	30.00	75.00	—	—
1847/6Go PM	—	15.00	30.00	75.00	—	—
1847Go PM	—	15.00	30.00	75.00	—	—
1848/7Go PM	—	20.00	50.00	100	—	—
1848Go PM	—	20.00	50.00	100	—	—
1849Go PF	—	20.00	50.00	100	—	—
1850Go PF	—	12.50	25.00	60.00	—	—
1851Go PF	—	12.50	25.00	60.00	—	—
1852Go PF	—	15.00	30.00	75.00	—	—
1852Go PF 5/4	—	20.00	50.00	100	—	—
1853Go PF	—	15.00	30.00	75.00	—	—
1854Go PF	—	15.00	30.00	75.00	—	—

Note: Large eagle

| 1854Go PF | — | 15.00 | 30.00 | 75.00 | — | — |

Note: Small eagle

1855/4Go PF	—	15.00	30.00	75.00	—	—
1855Go PF	—	12.50	25.00	60.00	—	—
1856Go PF	—	12.50	25.00	60.00	—	—
1857Go PF	—	20.00	50.00	100	—	—
1858Go PF	—	20.00	50.00	100	—	—
1859Go PF	—	20.00	50.00	100	—	—
1860/59Go PF	—	15.00	30.00	75.00	—	—
1860Go PF	—	15.00	30.00	75.00	—	—
1861/51Go PF	—	15.00	30.00	75.00	—	—
1861Go PF	—	20.00	50.00	100	—	—
1862/1Go YE	—	15.00	30.00	75.00	—	—
1862/1Go YF	—	15.00	30.00	75.00	—	—
1862Go YE/PF	—	15.00	30.00	75.00	—	—
1862Go YE	—	15.00	30.00	75.00	—	—
1862Go YF	—	15.00	30.00	75.00	—	—
1863/53Go YF	—	15.00	30.00	75.00	—	—
1863Go YF/PF	—	15.00	30.00	75.00	—	—
186/53Go YF	—	15.00	30.00	75.00	—	—
1863Go YF	—	15.00	30.00	75.00	—	—
1867/57Go YF/PF	—	15.00	30.00	75.00	—	—
1868/58Go YF/PF	—	15.00	30.00	75.00	—	—
1870Go FR	—	15.00	30.00	75.00	—	—

KM# 375 4 REALES
13.5400 g., 0.9030 Silver 0.3931 oz. ASW **Obv:** Facing
eagle, snake in beak **Obv. Legend:** REPUBLICA
MEXICANA. **Rev:** Radiant cap **Mint:** Real de Catorce

Date	Mintage	F	VF	XF	Unc	BU
1863Ce ML Large C	—	200	500	850	—	—
1863Ce ML Small C	—	225	650	1,500	—	—

KM# 375.7 4 REALES
13.5400 g., 0.9030 Silver 0.3931 oz. ASW **Obv:** Facing
eagle, snake in beak **Obv. Legend:** REPUBLICA
MEXICANA. **Rev:** Radiant cap **Mint:** Oaxaca

Date	Mintage	F	VF	XF	Unc	BU
1861O FR	—	225	450	750	—	—

Note: Ornamental edge

| 1861O FR | — | 300 | 550 | 850 | — | — |

Note: Herringbone edge

| 1861O FR | — | 200 | 400 | 700 | — | — |

Note: Obliquely reeded edge

KM# 377.5 8 REALES
27.0700 g., 0.9030 Silver 0.7859 oz. ASW **Obv:** Facing
eagle, snake in beak **Rev:** Radiant cap **Mint:** Estado de
Mexico

Date	Mintage	F	VF	XF	Unc	BU
1828EoMo LF/LP	—	350	850	2,150	—	—
1828EoMo LF	—	350	850	2,150	6,000	—
1829EoMo LF	—	300	750	1,850	4,800	—
1830/20EoMo LF	—	1,250	2,750	4,250	—	—
1830EoMo LF	—	1,000	2,000	3,250	6,500	—

KM# 377.7   8 REALES
27.0700 g., 0.9030 Silver 0.7859 oz. ASW **Obv:** Facing
eagle, snake in beak **Obv. Legend:** REPUBLICA
MEXICANA. **Rev:** Radiant cap **Mint:** Guadalupe y Calvo

Date	Mintage	F	VF	XF	Unc	BU
1844GC MP	—	350	500	1,000	2,000	—
1844GC MP	—	400	600	1,200	2,250	—
Note: Error, reversed S in Ds, Gs						
1845GC MP	—	125	200	325	700	—
Note: Eagle's tail square						
1845GC MP	—	175	350	650	1,200	—
Note: Eagle's tail round						
1846GC MP	—	175	350	750	1,650	—
Note: Eagle's tail square						
1846GC MP	—	125	200	350	750	—
Note: Eagle's tail round						
1847GC MP	—	150	250	400	800	—
1848GC MP	—	175	300	500	900	—
1849GC MP	—	175	300	525	1,000	—
1850GC MP	—	175	300	575	1,100	—
1851GC MP	—	300	500	900	1,600	—
1852GC MP	—	350	600	1,250	2,500	—

Date	Mintage	F	VF	XF	Unc	BU
1865 PG	—	500	750	1,000	—	—
1866/5 PG Rare	—	—	—	—	—	—
1866 PG	—	1,250	2,250	—	—	—
1866 DL Rare	—	—	—	—	—	—
1867 DL	—	1,150	2,150	—	—	—
1868 DL	—	50.00	90.00	150	300	—
1869/8 DL	—	50.00	90.00	150	—	—
1869 DL	—	50.00	80.00	120	300	—
1870 DL	—	30.00	60.00	120	300	—
1871 DL	—	20.00	35.00	75.00	200	—
1872 AM/DL	—	25.00	50.00	100	300	—
1872 AM	—	25.00	50.00	100	250	—
1873 AM	509,000	18.00	25.00	50.00	150	—
1874/3As DL	—	25.00	50.00	100	250	—
1874 DL	—	18.00	25.00	50.00	150	—
1875A DL 7/7	—	40.00	80.00	120	300	—
1875A DL	—	18.00	25.00	50.00	150	—
1875As DL	—	30.00	60.00	110	250	—
1876 DL	—	18.00	25.00	50.00	150	—
1877 DL	515,000	18.00	25.00	50.00	150	—
1878 DL	513,000	18.00	25.00	50.00	150	—
1879 DL	—	20.00	35.00	75.00	175	—
1879 ML	—	30.00	60.00	125	350	—
1880 ML	—	16.00	18.00	30.00	140	—
1881 ML	966,000	16.00	18.00	30.00	140	—
1882 ML	480,000	16.00	18.00	30.00	140	—
1883 ML	464,000	16.00	18.00	30.00	140	—
1884 ML	—	16.00	18.00	30.00	140	—
1885 ML	280,000	16.00	18.00	30.00	140	—
1886 ML	857,000	16.00	18.00	25.00	115	—
1886/0As/Cn ML/JD	Inc. above	17.00	20.00	35.00	160	—
1887 ML	650,000	16.00	18.00	25.00	115	—
1888/7 ML	508,000	30.00	60.00	100	400	—
1888 ML	Inc. above	16.00	18.00	25.00	115	—
1889 ML	427,000	16.00	18.00	25.00	115	—
1890 ML	450,000	16.00	18.00	25.00	115	—
1891 ML	533,000	16.00	18.00	25.00	115	—
1892/0 ML	—	20.00	30.00	60.00	160	—
1892 ML	465,000	16.00	18.00	25.00	115	—
1893 ML	734,000	14.00	16.00	22.00	95.00	—
1894 ML	725,000	14.00	16.00	22.00	95.00	—
1895 ML	477,000	14.00	16.00	22.00	95.00	—

KM# 377   8 REALES
27.0700 g., 0.9030 Silver 0.7859 oz. ASW **Obv:** Facing
eagle, snake in beak **Obv. Legend:** REPUBLICA
MEXICANA. **Rev:** Radiant cap **Mint:** Alamos **Note:** Mint mark
A, As. Varieties exist.

Date	Mintage	F	VF	XF	Unc	BU
1864 PG	—	750	1,250	2,000	—	—
1865/4 PG Rare	—	—	—	—	—	—

KM# 377.3   8 REALES
27.0700 g., 0.9030 Silver 0.7859 oz. ASW **Obv:** Facing
eagle, snake in beak **Obv. Legend:** REPUBLICA MEXICANA
Rev: Radiant cap **Mint:** Culiacan **Note:** Mint mark C, Cn.
Varieties exist.

Date	Mintage	F	VF	XF	Unc	BU
1846 CE	—	150	300	800	1,500	—
1846 CE	—	175	385	900	1,650	—
Note: Dot after G						
1846 CE	—	125	265	750	1,450	—
Note: No dot after G						
1847 CE	—	400	700	1,500	—	—

Date	Mintage	F	VF	XF	Unc	BU
1848 CE	—	125	250	450	1,000	—
1849 CE C/G	—	75.00	125	200	400	—
1849 CE	—	75.00	125	200	400	—
1850 CE	—	75.00	125	200	400	—
1851 CE	—	125	250	450	1,000	—
1852/1 CE	—	100	150	250	500	—
1852 CE	—	100	200	300	600	—
1853/0 CE	—	200	350	700	1,300	—
1853/2/0	—	200	400	750	1,400	—
1853 CE	—	100	175	300	600	—
Note: Thick rays						
1853 CE	—	200	350	650	—	—
Note: Error: MEXIGANA						
1854 CE	—	750	1,250	—	—	—
1854 CE	—	175	350	750	1,200	—
Note: Large eagle and hat						
1855/6 CE	—	40.00	60.00	100	200	—
1855 CE	—	25.00	40.00	75.00	150	—
1856 CE	—	50.00	100	175	350	—
1857 CE	—	20.00	35.00	75.00	160	—
1858 CE	—	30.00	40.00	75.00	160	—
1859 CE	—	20.00	35.00	75.00	160	—
1860/9 PV/CV	—	50.00	70.00	100	200	—
1860/9 PV/E	—	50.00	70.00	100	200	—
1860 CE	—	25.00	40.00	75.00	160	—
1860/9 PV	—	40.00	60.00	90.00	175	—
1860 PV	—	40.00	60.00	90.00	175	—
1861/0 CE	—	50.00	80.00	120	250	—
1861 PV/CE	—	75.00	125	200	350	—
1861 CE	—	20.00	35.00	60.00	150	—
1862 CE	—	20.00	35.00	60.00	150	—
1863/2 CE	—	30.00	50.00	75.00	200	—
1863 CE	—	20.00	30.00	60.00	150	—
1864 CE	—	30.00	60.00	100	300	—
1865 CE	—	125	200	325	650	—
1866 CE	—	400	750	1,250	2,250	—
1867 CE	—	125	200	350	700	—
1868/7 CE	—	30.00	40.00	75.00	160	—
1868/8	—	50.00	100	150	300	—
1868 CE	—	30.00	40.00	75.00	160	—
1869 CE	—	30.00	40.00	75.00	175	—
1870 CE	—	50.00	100	150	350	—
1873 MP	—	50.00	100	150	300	—
1874/3 MP	—	30.00	40.00	75.00	160	—
1874C MP	—	20.00	30.00	45.00	125	—
1874CN MP	—	125	200	300	600	—
1875 MP	—	16.00	18.00	22.00	95.00	—
1876 GP	—	16.00	18.00	30.00	100	—
1876 CG	—	16.00	18.00	22.00	95.00	—
1877 CG	339,000	16.00	18.00	22.00	95.00	—
1877Gn CG Error	—	65.00	125	200	400	—
1877 JA	Inc. above	35.00	75.00	125	250	—
1878/7 CG	483,000	35.00	75.00	125	250	—
1878 CG	Inc. above	18.00	25.00	35.00	125	—
1878 JD/CG	—	25.00	35.00	50.00	150	—
1878 JD	Inc. above	18.00	22.00	30.00	125	—
1878 JD	Inc. above	20.00	30.00	40.00	150	—
Note: D over retrograde D						
1879 JD	—	16.00	18.00	30.00	135	—
1880/70 JD	—	18.00	22.00	30.00	100	—
1880 JD	—	16.00	18.00	22.00	120	—
1881/0 JD	1,032,000	18.00	20.00	30.00	100	—
1881C JD	Inc. above	16.00	18.00	22.00	95.00	—
1881Cn JD	Inc. above	40.00	60.00	90.00	150	—
1882 JD	397,000	16.00	18.00	22.00	95.00	—
1882 AM	Inc. above	16.00	18.00	22.00	95.00	—
1883 AM	333,000	16.00	18.00	22.00	125	—
1884 AM	—	16.00	18.00	22.00	95.00	—
1885/6 AM	227,000	20.00	30.00	45.00	125	—
1885C AM	Inc. above	35.00	70.00	150	350	—
1885Cn AM	Inc. above	16.00	18.00	22.00	95.00	—
1885Gn AM Error	Inc. above	25.00	50.00	100	275	—
1886 AM	571,000	16.00	18.00	22.00	95.00	—
1887 AM	732,000	16.00	18.00	22.00	95.00	—
1888 AM	768,000	16.00	18.00	22.00	95.00	—
1889 AM	1,075,000	16.00	18.00	22.00	95.00	500
1890 AM	874,000	14.00	16.00	20.00	90.00	—
1891 AM	777,000	14.00	16.00	20.00	90.00	—
1892 AM	681,000	14.00	16.00	20.00	90.00	—

Date	Mintage	F	VF	XF	Unc	BU
1893 AM	1,144,000	14.00	16.00	20.00	90.00	—
1894 AM	2,118,000	14.00	16.00	20.00	90.00	—
1895 AM	1,834,000	14.00	16.00	20.00	90.00	—
1896 AM	2,134,000	14.00	16.00	20.00	90.00	—
1897 AM	1,580,000	14.00	16.00	20.00	90.00	—

KM# 377.11   8 REALES
27.0700 g., 0.9030 Silver 0.7859 oz. ASW **Obv:** Facing eagle, snake in beak **Rev:** Radiant cap **Mint:** Oaxaca **Note:** Mint mark O, Oa. Varieties exist.

Date	Mintage	F	VF	XF	Unc	BU
1858O AE	—	2,500	4,000	—	—	—
1858Oa AE Unique	—	—	—	—	—	—
1859 AE	—	500	900	1,750	—	—
Note: A in O of mint mark						
1860 AE	—	200	450	800	—	—
Note: A in O of mint mark						
1861O FR	—	125	250	550	1,350	—
1861Oa FR	—	150	350	700	—	—
1862O FR	—	40.00	80.00	200	375	—
1862Oa FR	—	65.00	125	250	450	—
1863O FR	—	30.00	60.00	100	250	—
1863O AE	—	30.00	60.00	100	250	—
1863Oa AE	—	100	150	250	450	—
Note: A in O of mint mark						
1863Oa AE	—	1,000	1,750	2,750	—	—
Note: A above O in mint mark						
1864 FR	—	25.00	50.00	75.00	200	—
1865 AE	—	1,850	3,000	—	—	—
1867 AE	—	40.00	80.00	150	400	—
1868 AE	—	40.00	80.00	150	400	—
1869 AE	—	30.00	60.00	100	250	—
1873 AE	—	200	300	550	1,350	—
1874 AE	142,000	18.00	30.00	50.00	200	—
1875/4 AE	131,000	25.00	50.00	75.00	200	—
1875 AE	Inc. above	18.00	30.00	40.00	135	—
1876 AE	140,000	20.00	35.00	55.00	200	—
1877 AE	139,000	20.00	30.00	50.00	200	—
1878 AE	125,000	18.00	30.00	50.00	200	—
1879 AE	153,000	20.00	30.00	50.00	200	—
1880 AE	143,000	18.00	30.00	45.00	150	—
1881 AE	134,000	20.00	35.00	60.00	150	—
1882 AE	100,000	20.00	35.00	60.00	150	—
1883 AE	122,000	18.00	30.00	45.00	150	—
1884 AE	142,000	18.00	30.00	50.00	150	—
1885 AE	158,000	18.00	25.00	40.00	135	—
1886 AE	120,000	18.00	30.00	45.00	150	—
1887/6 AE	115,000	25.00	50.00	80.00	200	—
1887 AE	Inc. above	18.00	25.00	40.00	135	—
1888 AE	145,000	18.00	25.00	40.00	135	—
1889 AE	150,000	20.00	30.00	60.00	175	—
1890 AE	181,000	20.00	30.00	60.00	175	—
1891 EN	160,000	18.00	25.00	40.00	135	—
1892 EN	120,000	18.00	25.00	40.00	135	—
1893 EN	66,000	45.00	75.00	115	300	—

KM# 377.4   8 REALES
27.0700 g., 0.9030 Silver 0.7859 oz. ASW **Obv:** Facing
eagle, snake in beak **Mint:** Durango **Note:** Varieties exist.

Date	Mintage	F	VF	XF	Unc	BU
1825Do RL	—	30.00	65.00	150	375	—
1826Do RL	—	40.00	85.00	200	475	—
1827/6Do RL	—	35.00	60.00	85.00	200	—
1827/8Do RL	—	150	275	500	—	—
1827Do RL	—	30.00	50.00	90.00	200	—
1828/7Do RL	—	35.00	60.00	90.00	200	—
1828Do RL	—	25.00	50.00	80.00	175	—
1829Do RL	—	25.00	50.00	80.00	175	—
1830Do RM	—	25.00	50.00	90.00	200	—
Note: B on eagle's claw						
1831Do RM	—	20.00	30.00	60.00	150	—
Note: B on eagle's claw						
1832Do RM	—	35.00	60.00	120	300	—
Note: Mexican dies, B on eagle's claw						
1832/1Do RM/RL	—	25.00	35.00	75.00	165	—
Note: French dies, REPUB MEX spaced						
1833/2Do RM/RL	—	20.00	35.00	75.00	165	—
1833Do RM	—	18.00	30.00	60.00	150	—
1834/3/2Do RM/RL	—	20.00	35.00	75.00	165	—
1834Do RM	—	18.00	25.00	50.00	150	—
1835/4Do RM/RL	—	20.00	35.00	65.00	150	—
1835Do RM	—	20.00	35.00	65.00	150	—
Note: Mexican dies, REPUBMEX not spaced						
1836/1Do RM	—	20.00	35.00	65.00	150	—
1836/4Do RM	—	20.00	35.00	65.00	150	—
1836/5/4Do RM/RL	—	75.00	150	250	500	—
1836Do RM	—	20.00	30.00	55.00	150	—
1836Do RM	—	20.00	30.00	55.00	150	—
Note: M on snake						
1837/1Do RM	—	20.00	30.00	55.00	150	—
1837Do RM	—	20.00	30.00	55.00	150	—
1838/1Do RM	—	20.00	30.00	60.00	165	—
1838/7Do RM	—	20.00	30.00	60.00	165	—
1838Do RM	—	20.00	30.00	55.00	150	—
1839/1Do RM/RL	—	20.00	30.00	55.00	150	—
1839/1Do RM	—	20.00	30.00	55.00	150	—
1839Do RM	—	20.00	30.00	55.00	150	—
1840/38/31Do RM	—	20.00	30.00	55.00	150	—
1840/39Do RM	—	20.00	30.00	55.00	150	—
1840Do RM	—	20.00	30.00	55.00	150	—
1841/31Do RM	—	65.00	125	275	450	—
1841/39Do RM/L	—	25.00	50.00	85.00	200	—
1841/39Do RM	—	25.00	50.00	85.00	200	—
1842/31Do RM	—	125	250	400	750	—
Note: B below cactus						
1842/31Do RM	—	40.00	80.00	125	250	—
1842/32Do RM	—	40.00	80.00	125	250	—
1842Do RM	—	20.00	30.00	55.00	150	—
Note: Eagle of 1832-41						
1842Do RM	—	20.00	30.00	55.00	150	—
Note: Pre-1832 eagle resumed						
1842Do RM	—	40.00	80.00	125	250	—

Date	Mintage	F	VF	XF	Unc	BU
1843/33Do RM	—	50.00	90.00	150	250	—
1843Do RM	—	50.00	90.00	150	250	—
1844/34Do RM	—	100	200	300	500	—
1844/35Do RM	—	100	200	300	500	—
1844/43Do RM	—	60.00	120	220	425	—
1845/31Do RM	—	100	200	300	500	—
1845/34Do RM	—	35.00	75.00	125	250	—
1845/35Do RM	—	35.00	75.00	125	250	—
1845Do RM	—	20.00	30.00	55.00	150	—
1846/31Do RM	—	20.00	30.00	55.00	150	—
1846/36Do RM	—	20.00	30.00	55.00	150	—
1846Do RM	—	20.00	30.00	55.00	150	—
1847Do RM	—	25.00	50.00	80.00	185	—
1848/7Do RM	—	125	250	400	750	—
1848/7Do CM/RM	—	100	200	350	700	—
1848Do CM/RM	—	100	200	350	700	—
1848Do RM	—	100	200	300	600	—
1848Do CM	—	50.00	100	200	400	—
1849/39Do CM	—	100	200	350	700	—
1849Do CM	—	65.00	125	250	550	—
1849Do JMR/CM Oval 0	—	200	400	450	800	—
1849Do JMR Oval 0	—	200	325	450	800	—
1849Do JMR Round 0	—	200	400	600	1,000	—
1850Do JMR	—	100	150	250	500	—
1851/0Do JMR	—	65.00	125	225	475	—
1851Do JMR	—	100	150	250	500	—
1852Do CP/JMR	—	450	800	1,500	—	—
1852Do CP	—	750	1,200	2,250	—	—
1852Do JMR	—	175	250	375	650	—
1853Do CP/JMR	—	125	235	350	600	—
1853Do CP	—	200	350	600	1,200	—
1854Do CP	—	25.00	35.00	65.00	300	—
1855Do CP	—	50.00	100	175	350	—
Note: Eagle type of 1854						
1855Do CP	—	50.00	100	175	350	—
Note: Eagle type of 1856						
1856Do CP	—	50.00	100	175	350	—
1857Do CP	—	35.00	65.00	125	250	—
1858/7Do CP	—	25.00	35.00	70.00	165	—
1858Do CP	—	20.00	30.00	60.00	165	—
1859Do CP	—	20.00	30.00	60.00	165	—
1860/59Do CP	—	30.00	50.00	100	200	—
1860Do CP	—	20.00	30.00	60.00	165	—
1861/0Do CP	—	20.00	30.00	60.00	165	—
1861Do CP	—	20.00	30.00	50.00	125	—
1862/1Do CP	—	25.00	35.00	60.00	125	—
1862Do CP	—	20.00	30.00	60.00	175	—
1863/1Do CP	—	30.00	60.00	90.00	200	—
1863/2Do CP	—	25.00	50.00	75.00	175	—
1863/53Do CP	—	30.00	60.00	90.00	200	—
1863Do CP	—	25.00	50.00	75.00	175	—
1864Do CP	—	100	150	250	500	—
1864Do LT	—	25.00	40.00	80.00	175	—
1864Do LT/T	—	25.00	40.00	80.00	175	—
1864Do LT/CP	—	50.00	100	175	350	—
1865Do LT Rare	—	—	—	—	—	—
1866/4Do CM	—	2,750	5,500	—	—	—
1866Do CM	—	1,750	3,250	5,500	8,500	—
1867Do CM	—	3,500	—	—	—	—
1867/6Do CP	—	200	400	600	1,200	—
1867Do CP	—	175	300	500	1,000	—
1867Do CP/CM	—	125	250	400	900	—
1867Do CP/LT	—	200	400	650	1,250	—
1868Do CP	—	25.00	40.00	80.00	175	—
1869Do CP	—	20.00	30.00	50.00	135	—
1870/69Do CP	—	20.00	30.00	50.00	125	—
1870/9Do CP	—	20.00	30.00	50.00	125	—
1870Do CP	—	20.00	30.00	50.00	125	—
1873Do CP	—	125	225	325	600	—
1873Do CM	—	30.00	50.00	100	200	—
1874/3Do CM	—	14.00	18.00	25.00	125	—
1874Do CM	—	14.00	18.00	25.00	125	—
1874Do JH	—	1,150	1,750	2,750	—	—
1875Do CM	—	14.00	18.00	25.00	125	—
1875Do JH	—	80.00	150	250	450	—
1876Do CM	—	14.00	18.00	25.00	125	—
1877Do CM	431,000	1,450	2,500	—	—	—
1877Do CP	Inc. above	14.00	18.00	25.00	125	—

Date	Mintage	F	VF	XF	Unc	BU
1877Do JMP	Inc. above	750	1,250	2,000	—	—
1878Do PE	409,000	18.00	25.00	40.00	125	—
1878Do TB	Inc. above	14.00	18.00	25.00	125	—
1879Do TB	—	14.00	18.00	25.00	125	—
1880/70Do TB	—	60.00	100	175	350	—
1880/70Do TB/JP	—	150	250	375	650	—
1880/70Do JP	—	18.00	25.00	40.00	125	—
1880Do TB	—	150	250	375	650	—
1880Do JP	—	14.00	18.00	25.00	125	—
1881Do JP	928,000	14.00	18.00	25.00	125	—
1882Do JP	414,000	14.00	18.00	25.00	125	—
1882Do MC/JP	Inc. above	30.00	60.00	100	200	—
1882Do MC	Inc. above	25.00	50.00	75.00	150	—
1883/73Do MC	452,000	18.00	25.00	40.00	125	—
1883Do MC	Inc. above	14.00	18.00	25.00	125	—
1884/3Do MC	—	18.00	25.00	40.00	125	—
1884Do MC	—	14.00	18.00	25.00	125	—
1885Do MC M/J	—	18.00	25.00	40.00	125	—
1885Do MC	547,000	14.00	16.00	22.00	125	—
1885Do JB	Inc. above	25.00	35.00	50.00	135	—
1886/5Do MC	—	18.00	25.00	40.00	100	—
1886/3Do MC	955,000	18.00	25.00	40.00	100	—
1886Do MC	Inc. above	14.00	16.00	22.00	90.00	—
1887Do MC	1,004,000	14.00	16.00	22.00	90.00	—
1888/7Do MC	—	65.00	125	250	450	—
1888Do MC	996,000	14.00	16.00	22.00	90.00	—
1889Do MC	874,000	14.00	16.00	22.00	90.00	—
1890Do MC	1,119,000	14.00	16.00	22.00	90.00	—
1890Do JP	Inc. above	14.00	16.00	22.00	90.00	—
1891Do JP	1,487,000	14.00	16.00	22.00	90.00	—
1892Do JP	1,597,000	14.00	16.00	22.00	90.00	—
1892Do ND	Inc. above	25.00	50.00	100	200	—
1893Do ND	1,617,000	14.00	16.00	22.00	90.00	—
1894Do ND	1,537,000	14.00	16.00	22.00	90.00	—
1895/3Do ND	761,000	18.00	25.00	40.00	100	—
1895Do ND	Inc. above	14.00	16.00	22.00	90.00	—
1895Do ND/P	—	18.00	25.00	40.00	100	—

KM# 377.6 8 REALES
27.0700 g., 0.9030 Silver 0.7859 oz. ASW **Obv:** Facing eagle, snake in beak **Obv. Legend:** REPUBLICA MEXICANA. **Rev:** Radiant cap **Mint:** Guadalajara **Note:** Varieties exist.

Date	Mintage	F	VF	XF	Unc	BU
1825Ga FS	—	150	275	475	1,000	—
1826/5Ga FS	—	125	250	450	1,000	—
1826Ga FS	—	125	250	450	1,000	—
1827/87Ga FS	—	125	250	450	1,000	—
1827Ga FS	—	125	250	450	1,000	—
1287Ga FS Error	—	8,500	9,500	—	—	—
1828Ga FS	—	200	375	550	1,200	—
1829/8Ga FS	—	200	375	550	1,200	—
1829Ga FS	—	175	325	475	950	—
1830/29Ga FS	—	100	175	300	600	—

Date	Mintage	F	VF	XF	Unc	BU
1830Ga FS	—	100	175	300	600	—
1830Ga LP/FS	—	800	1,450	—	—	—

Note: The 1830 LP/FS is currently only known with a Philippine countermark

Date	Mintage	F	VF	XF	Unc	BU
1831Ga LP	—	200	400	600	1,200	—
1831Ga FS/LP	—	300	500	750	1,500	—
1831Ga FS	—	125	275	400	—	—
1832/1Ga FS	—	50.00	100	175	300	—
1832/1Ga FS/LP	—	50.00	100	175	300	—
1832Ga FS/LP	—	75.00	150	285	550	—
1832Ga FS	—	25.00	50.00	100	225	—
1833/2/1Ga FS/LP	—	45.00	75.00	125	250	—
1833/2Ga FS	—	25.00	50.00	100	225	—
1834/2Ga FS	—	60.00	125	200	350	—
1834/3Ga FS	—	60.00	125	200	350	—
1834/0Ga FS	—	50.00	100	150	300	—
1834Ga FS	—	50.00	100	150	300	—
1835Ga FS	—	25.00	50.00	100	225	—
1836/5Ga FS	—	175	350	—	—	—
1836/1Ga JG/FS	—	40.00	80.00	125	250	—
1836Ga FS	—	275	450	750	—	—
1836Ga JG/FS	—	25.00	50.00	100	225	—
1836Ga JG	—	25.00	50.00	100	225	—
1837/6Ga JG/FS	—	50.00	100	175	300	—
1837/6Ga JG	—	45.00	90.00	160	285	—
1837Ga JG	—	40.00	80.00	125	250	—
1838/7Ga JG	—	100	175	300	550	—
1838Ga JG	—	100	150	275	500	—
1839Ga MC	—	100	200	350	600	—
1839Ga MC/JG	—	100	200	300	550	—
1839Ga JG	—	60.00	125	200	350	—
1840/30Ga MC	—	50.00	75.00	150	275	—
1840Ga MC	—	30.00	60.00	125	250	—
1841Ga MC	—	30.00	60.00	125	250	—
1842/1Ga JG/MG	—	100	150	250	450	—
1842/1Ga JG/MC	—	100	150	250	450	—
1842Ga JG	—	25.00	50.00	100	225	—
1842Ga JG/MG	—	25.00	50.00	100	225	—
1843/2Ga MC/JG	—	25.00	50.00	100	225	—
1843Ga MC/JG	—	25.00	50.00	100	225	—
1843Ga JG	—	400	600	900	1,800	—
1843Ga MC	—	50.00	100	150	300	—
1844Ga MC	—	50.00	100	150	300	—
1845Ga MC	—	75.00	150	300	700	—
1845Ga JG	—	500	850	1,250	1,850	—
1846Ga JG	—	40.00	80.00	150	300	—
1847Ga JG	—	100	150	225	400	—
1848/7Ga JG	—	55.00	85.00	125	250	—
1848Ga JG	—	50.00	75.00	100	225	—
1849Ga JG	—	90.00	125	175	325	—
1849/39Ga JG	—	250	500	—	—	—
1850Ga JG	—	50.00	100	150	300	—
1851Ga JG	—	125	200	350	650	—
1852Ga JG	—	100	150	250	450	—
1853/2Ga JG	—	125	175	250	475	—
1853Ga JG	—	90.00	125	175	300	—
1854/3Ga JG	—	65.00	90.00	125	250	—
1854Ga JG	—	50.00	75.00	110	225	—
1855/4Ga JG	—	50.00	100	150	275	—
1855Ga JG	—	25.00	50.00	100	225	—
1856/4Ga JG	—	60.00	125	175	300	—
1856/5Ga 56	—	60.00	125	175	300	—
1856Ga JG	—	50.00	100	150	275	—
1857Ga JG	—	50.00	100	225	450	—
1858Ga JG	—	100	150	300	500	—
1859/7Ga JG	—	25.00	50.00	110	225	—
1859/8Ga JG	—	25.00	50.00	100	200	—
1859Ga JG	—	20.00	40.00	80.00	175	—
1860Ga JG Without dot	—	350	750	1,200	2,250	—
1860Ga JG	—	2,000	3,250	4,500	—	—

Note: Dot in loop of snake's tail, base alloy

Date	Mintage	F	VF	XF	Unc	BU
1861Ga JG	—	2,200	5,750	—	—	—
1862Ga JG	—	850	1,350	2,750	4,500	—
1863/52Ga JG	—					—
1863/59Ga JG	—	45.00	50.00	85.00	145	—
1863/2Ga JG	—	30.00	50.00	90.00	175	—
1863/4Ga JG	—	40.00	75.00	150	250	—
1863Ga JG	—	25.00	45.00	75.00	150	—

Date	Mintage	F	VF	XF	Unc	BU
1863Ga FV Rare	—	—	—	—	—	—
1867Ga JM Rare	—	—	—	—	—	—
1868/7Ga JM	—	50.00	75.00	125	200	—
1868Ga JM	—	50.00	75.00	125	200	—
1869Ga JM	—	50.00	75.00	125	200	—
1869Ga IC	—	75.00	125	200	375	—
1870/60Ga IC	—	60.00	90.00	150	275	—
1870Ga IC	—	60.00	90.00	150	275	—
1873Ga IC	—	15.00	25.00	50.00	135	—
1874Ga IC	—	14.00	15.00	22.00	90.00	—
1874Ga MC	—	25.00	50.00	100	200	—
1875Ga IC	—	18.00	30.00	60.00	135	—
1875Ga MC	—	14.00	15.00	22.00	125	—
1876Ga IC	559,000	18.00	30.00	50.00	125	—
1876Ga MC	Inc. above	125	175	250	375	—
1877Ga IC	928,000	14.00	18.00	25.00	125	—
1877/6Ga JA	—	14.00	18.00	25.00	125	—
1877Ga JA	Inc. above	14.00	18.00	25.00	125	—
1878Ga JA	764,000	14.00	18.00	25.00	125	—
1879Ga JA	—	14.00	18.00	25.00	125	—
1880/70Ga FS	—	18.00	25.00	50.00	135	—
1880Ga JA	—	14.00	18.00	25.00	125	—
1880Ga FS	—	14.00	18.00	25.00	125	—
1881Ga FS	1,300,000	14.00	18.00	25.00	125	—
1882/1Ga FS	537,000	18.00	25.00	50.00	135	—
1882Ga FS	Inc. above	14.00	18.00	25.00	125	—
1882Ga TB/FS	Inc. above	50.00	100	175	300	—
1882Ga TB	Inc. above	50.00	100	175	300	—
1883Ga TB	561,000	18.00	25.00	40.00	135	—
1884Ga TB	—	14.00	16.00	22.00	125	—
1884Ga AH	—	14.00	16.00	22.00	125	—
1885Ga AH	443,000	14.00	16.00	22.00	125	—
1885Ga JS	Inc. above	30.00	60.00	100	200	—
1886Ga JS/H	—	14.00	16.00	22.00	125	—
1886Ga JS	1,038,999	14.00	16.00	22.00	125	—
1887Ga JS	878,000	14.00	16.00	22.00	125	—
1888Ga JS	1,159,000	14.00	16.00	22.00	125	—
1889Ga JS	1,583,000	14.00	16.00	22.00	125	—
1890Ga JS	1,658,000	14.00	16.00	22.00	110	—
1891Ga JS	1,507,000	14.00	16.00	22.00	110	—
1892/1Ga JS	1,627,000	18.00	25.00	50.00	125	—
1892Ga JS	Inc. above	14.00	16.00	22.00	110	—
1893Ga JS	1,952,000	14.00	16.00	22.00	110	—
1894Ga JS	2,045,999	14.00	16.00	22.00	110	—
1895/3Ga JS	—	16.00	20.00	35.00	115	—
1895Ga JS	1,146,000	14.00	16.00	22.00	110	—

KM# 377.8   8 REALES
27.0700 g., 0.9030 Silver 0.7859 oz. ASW **Obv:** Facing
eagle, snake in beak **Obv. Legend:** REPUBLICA
MEXICANA. **Rev:** Radiant cap **Mint:** Guanajuato **Note:**
Varieties exist.

Date	Mintage	F	VF	XF	Unc	BU
1825Go JJ	—	40.00	70.00	150	300	—
1825G JJ	—	1,250	1,650	—	—	—

Date	Mintage	F	VF	XF	Unc	BU
Note: Error mint mark G						
1826Go JJ	—	40.00	80.00	175	350	—
Note: Straight J's						
1826Go JJ	—	30.00	60.00	125	250	—
Note: Full J's						
1826Go MJ	—	250	450	850	—	—
1827Go MJ	—	40.00	75.00	125	250	—
1827Go MJ/JJ	—	—	—	—	—	—
1827Go MR	—	100	200	350	600	—
1828Go MJ	—	—	—	—	—	—
Note: Error mint mark Goo						
1828Go MJ	—	30.00	60.00	125	250	—
1828/7Go MR	—	150	300	600	1,200	—
1828Go MR	—	150	300	600	1,200	—
1829Go MJ	—	20.00	35.00	55.00	165	—
1830Go MJ	—	20.00	35.00	55.00	165	—
Note: Oblong beading and narrow J						
1830Go MJ	—	20.00	30.00	55.00	165	—
Note: Regular beading and wide J						
1831Go MJ	—	15.00	20.00	40.00	150	—
Note: Colon after date						
1831Go MJ	—	15.00	20.00	40.00	150	—
Note: 2 stars after date						
1832Go MJ	—	15.00	20.00	40.00	150	—
1832Go MJ	—	20.00	35.00	65.00	175	—
Note: 1 of date over inverted 1						
1833Go MJ/1	—	20.00	35.00	65.00	175	—
1833Go MJ	—	15.00	20.00	40.00	150	—
1833Go JM	—	400	750	1,250	2,500	—
1834Go PJ	—	15.00	20.00	40.00	150	—
1835Go PJ	—	15.00	20.00	40.00	150	—
Note: Star on cap						
1835Go PJ	—	15.00	20.00	40.00	150	—
Note: Dot on cap						
1836Go PJ	—	15.00	20.00	40.00	150	—
1837Go PJ	—	15.00	20.00	40.00	150	—
1838Go PJ	—	15.00	20.00	40.00	150	—
1839Go PJ/JJ	—	15.00	20.00	40.00	150	—
1839Go PJ	—	15.00	20.00	40.00	150	—
1840/30Go PJ	—	20.00	30.00	50.00	150	—
1840Go PJ	—	15.00	20.00	35.00	125	—
1841/31Go PJ	—	15.00	20.00	35.00	125	—
1841Go PJ	—	5.00	20.00	35.00	125	—
1842/1Go PM	—	20.00	30.00	50.00	125	—
1842/31Go PM/ PJ	—	25.00	35.00	60.00	150	—
1842/1Go PJ	—	20.00	30.00	50.00	125	—
1842Go PJ	—	15.00	20.00	35.00	125	—
1842Go PM/PJ	—	15.00	20.00	35.00	125	—
1842Go PM	—	15.00	20.00	35.00	125	—
1843Go PM	—	15.00	20.00	35.00	125	—
Note: Dot after date						
1843Go PM	—	15.00	20.00	35.00	125	—
Note: Triangle of dots after date						
1844Go PM	—	15.00	20.00	35.00	125	—
1845Go PM	—	15.00	20.00	35.00	125	—
1846/5Go PM	—	20.00	30.00	50.00	150	—
Note: Eagle type of 1845						
1846Go PM	—	20.00	30.00	50.00	150	—
Note: Eagle type of 1845						
1846Go PM	—	18.00	25.00	40.00	135	—
Note: Eagle type of 1847						
1847Go PM Narrow date	—	15.00	20.00	35.00	125	—
1847Go PM Wide date	—	15.00	20.00	35.00	125	—
1848/7Go PM	—	15.00	35.00	65.00	150	—
1848Go PM	—	20.00	35.00	65.00	150	—
1848Go PF	—	15.00	20.00	35.00	125	—
1849Go PF	—	15.00	20.00	35.00	125	—
1850Go PF	—	15.00	20.00	35.00	125	—
1851/0Go PF	—	20.00	30.00	50.00	150	—
1851Go PF	—	15.00	20.00	35.00	125	—
1852/1Go PF	—	20.00	30.00	50.00	150	—
1852Go PF	—	15.00	20.00	35.00	125	—
1853/2Go PF	—	20.00	30.00	50.00	150	—
1853Go PF	—	15.00	20.00	35.00	125	—
1854Go PF	—	15.00	20.00	35.00	125	—
1855Go PF Large letters	—	15.00	20.00	35.00	125	—

Date	Mintage	F	VF	XF	Unc	BU
1855Go PF Small letters	—	15.00	20.00	35.00	125	—
1856/5Go PF	—	20.00	30.00	50.00	150	—
1856Go PF	—	15.00	20.00	35.00	125	—
1857/5Go PF	—	20.00	30.00	50.00	150	—
1857/6Go PF	—	20.00	35.00	70.00	200	—
1857Go PF	—	15.00	18.00	22.00	90.00	—
1858/7Go PI Narrow date	—	15.00	20.00	35.00	125	—
1858Go PF Wide date	—	15.00	20.00	35.00	125	—
1859/7Go PF	—	15.00	20.00	35.00	125	—
1859/8Go PF	—	20.00	30.00	50.00	150	—
1859Go PF	—	15.00	20.00	35.00	125	—
1860/50Go PF	—	20.00	30.00	50.00	150	—
1860/59Go PF	—	15.00	18.00	25.00	95.00	—
1860Go PF	—	15.00	18.00	22.00	90.00	—
1861/51Go PF	—	15.00	20.00	30.00	100	—

Note: Narrow and wide dates exist

Date	Mintage	F	VF	XF	Unc	BU
1861/0Go PF	—	15.00	18.00	22.00	90.00	—
1861Go PF	—	15.00	18.00	22.00	90.00	—
186/52Go YE	—	18.00	20.00	30.00	100	—
1862Go YE/PF	—	15.00	18.00	22.00	90.00	—
186/52Go YF	—	18.00	20.00	30.00	100	—
1862Go YE	—	15.00	18.00	22.00	90.00	—
1862Go YF	—	15.00	18.00	22.00	90.00	—
1862Go YF/PF	—	15.00	18.00	22.00	90.00	—
1863/53Go YF	—	15.00	18.00	25.00	90.00	—
1863/54Go YF	—	18.00	20.00	30.00	100	—
1863Go YE Rare	—	—	—	—	—	—
1863Go YF	—	15.00	18.00	22.00	90.00	—
1867/57Go YF	—	18.00	20.00	30.00	100	—
1867Go YF	—	15.00	18.00	22.00	90.00	—
1868/58Go YF	—	18.00	20.00	30.00	100	—
1868/7Go YF	—	18.00	20.00	30.00	100	—
1868Go YF	—	15.00	18.00	2.00	90.00	—
1870/60Go FR	—	20.00	30.00	50.00	150	—
1870Go YF	—	1,800	3,000	5,000	7,500	—
1870Go FR/YF	—	20.00	35.00	70.00	200	—
1870Go FR	—	15.00	18.00	22.00	90.00	—
1873Go FR	—	15.00	18.00	2.00	90.00	—
1874/3Go FR	—	18.00	20.00	30.00	95.00	—
1874Go FR	—	18.00	25.00	35.00	100	—
1875/3Go FR	—	18.00	20.00	30.00	95.00	—
1875/6Go FR	—	18.00	20.00	30.00	95.00	—
1875Go FR	—	15.00	18.00	2.00	90.00	—

Note: Small circle with dot on eagle

Date	Mintage	F	VF	XF	Unc	BU
1876/5Go FR	—	18.00	20.00	30.00	95.00	—
1876Go FR	—	15.00	18.00	22.00	90.00	—
1877Go FR Narrow date	—	15.00	18.00	22.00	90.00	—
1877Go FR Wide date	2,477,000	15.00	18.00	22.00	90.00	—
1878/7Go FR	2,273,000	18.00	20.00	30.00	90.00	—
1878/7Go SM, S/F	—	18.00	20.00	30.00	90.00	—
1878/7Go SM	—	18.00	20.00	30.00	90.00	—
1878Go FR	Inc. above	15.00	18.00	22.00	90.00	—
1878Go SM, S/F	—	18.00	20.00	25.00	90.00	—
1878Go SM	—	15.00	18.00	22.00	90.00	—
1879/7Go SM	—	18.00	20.00	30.00	90.00	—
1879/8Go SM	—	18.00	20.00	30.00	90.00	—
1879/8Go SM/FR	—	18.00	20.00	30.00	90.00	—
1879Go SM	—	15.00	18.00	22.00	90.00	—
1879Go SM/FR	—	18.00	20.00	30.00	90.00	—
1880/70Go SB	—	18.00	20.00	30.00	90.00	—
1880Go SB/SM	—	15.00	18.00	22.00	90.00	—
1880Go SB	—	15.00	18.00	22.00	90.00	—
1881/71Go SB	3,974,000	18.00	20.00	30.00	90.00	—
1881/0Go SB	Inc. above	18.00	20.00	30.00	90.00	—
1881Go SB	Inc. above	15.00	18.00	22.00	90.00	—
1882Go SB	2,015,000	15.00	18.00	22.00	90.00	—
1883Go SB	2,100,000	35.00	75.00	125	250	—
1883Go BR	Inc. above	15.00	18.00	22.00	90.00	—
1883Go BR/SR	—	15.00	18.00	22.00	90.00	—
1883Go BR/SB	Inc. above	15.00	18.00	22.00	90.00	—
1884/73Go BR	—	20.00	30.00	40.00	100	—
1884/74Go BR	—	20.00	30.00	40.00	100	—
1884/3Go BR	—	20.00	30.00	60.00	150	—

Date	Mintage	F	VF	XF	Unc	BU
1884Go BR	—	15.00	18.00	22.00	90.00	—
1884/74Go RR	—	50.00	100	175	350	—
1884Go RR	—	25.00	50.00	100	250	—
1885/75Go RR/BR	—	18.00	20.00	300	90.00	—
1885/75Go RR	2,363,000	18.00	20.00	30.00	90.00	—
1885Go RR	Inc. above	15.00	18.00	22.00	90.00	—
1886/75Go RR/BR	—	18.00	20.00	25.00	90.00	—
1886/75Go RR	4,127,000	18.00	20.00	25.00	90.00	—
1886/76Go RR/BR	—	15.00	18.00	22.00	90.00	—
1886/76Go RR	Inc. above	15.00	18.00	22.00	90.00	—
1886/5Go RR/BR	Inc. above	15.00	18.00	22.00	90.00	—
1886Go RR	Inc. above	15.00	18.00	22.00	90.00	—
1887Go RR	4,205,000	14.00	18.00	22.00	90.00	—
1888Go RR	3,985,000	14.00	18.00	22.00	90.00	—
1889Go RR	3,646,000	14.00	18.00	22.00	90.00	—
1890Go RR	3,615,000	14.00	18.00	22.00	90.00	—
1891Go RS/R	—	14.00	18.00	22.00	90.00	—
1891Go RS	3,197,000	14.00	18.00	22.00	90.00	—
1892/0Go/A RS	—	14.00	18.00	22.00	90.00	—
1892/0Go RS	—	14.00	18.00	22.00	90.00	—
1892Go RS	3,672,000	14.00	18.00	22.00	90.00	—
1892Go/A RS	—	14.00	18.00	22.00	90.00	—
1893Go RS	3,854,000	14.00	18.00	22.00	90.00	—
1894Go RS	4,127,000	14.00	18.00	22.00	90.00	—
1895/1Go RS	3,768,000	18.00	20.00	22.00	90.00	—
1895/3Go RS	Inc. above	18.00	20.00	25.00	90.00	—
1895Go RS	Inc. above	14.00	18.00	22.00	90.00	—
1896/1Go/As RS/ML	5,229,000	18.00	20.00	25.00	90.00	—
1896/1Go RS	Inc. above	15.00	18.00	22.00	90.00	—
1896Go/Ga RS	Inc. above	—	—	—	—	—
1896Go RS	Inc. above	14.00	15.00	20.00	90.00	—
1897Go RS	4,344,000	14.00	15.00	20.00	90.00	—

KM# 377.9 8 REALES
27.0700 g., 0.9030 Silver 0.7859 oz. ASW **Obv:** Facing eagle, snake in beak **Rev:** Radiant cap **Mint:** Hermosillo **Note:** Varieties exist.

Date	Mintage	F	VF	XF	Unc	BU
1835Ho PP Rare	—	—	—	—	—	—
1836Ho PP Rare	—	—	—	—	—	—
1839Ho PR Unique	—	—	—	—	—	—
1861Ho FM	—	4,500	7,500	—	—	—

Note: Reeded edge

| 1862Ho FM Rare | — | — | — | — | — | — |

Note: Plain edge, snakes tail left, long ray over *8R

| 1862Ho FM | — | 1,550 | 2,700 | — | — | — |

Note: Plain edge, snake's tail left

| 1862Ho FM | — | 1,650 | 2,750 | — | — | — |

Note: Reeded edge, snakes tail right

| 1863Ho FM | — | 150 | 300 | 800 | — | — |
| 1864Ho FM | — | 850 | 1,650 | 2,750 | — | — |

Date	Mintage	F	VF	XF	Unc	BU
1864Ho PR/FM	—	1,200	2,200	—	—	—
1864Ho PR	—	650	1,250	2,150	3,350	—
1865Ho FM	—	250	500	950	1,850	—
1866Ho FM	—	1,150	2,150	3,500	5,500	—
1866Ho MP	—	950	1,750	3,000	4,650	—
1867Ho PR	—	100	175	275	500	—
1868Ho PR	—	20.00	35.00	65.00	175	—
1869Ho PR	—	40.00	60.00	125	250	—
1870Ho PR	—	100	175	275	550	—
1871/0Ho PR	—	50.00	75.00	125	250	—
1871Ho PR	—	30.00	50.00	90.00	200	—
1872/1Ho PR	—	35.00	60.00	90.00	200	—
1872Ho PR	—	30.00	50.00	75.00	175	—
1873Ho PR	351,000	30.00	50.00	85.00	150	—
1874Ho PR	—	18.00	22.00	40.00	125	—
1875Ho PR	—	18.00	22.00	40.00	125	—
1876Ho AF	—	18.00	22.00	40.00	125	—
1877Ho AF	410,000	20.00	30.00	50.00	150	—
1877Ho GR	Inc. above	100	150	225	400	—
1877Ho JA	Inc. above	25.00	50.00	85.00	175	—
1878Ho JA	451,000	18.00	22.00	40.00	120	—
1879Ho JA	—	18.00	22.00	40.00	120	—
1880Ho JA	—	18.00	22.00	40.00	120	—
1881Ho JA	586,000	18.00	22.00	40.00	120	—
1882Ho JA	240,000	25.00	40.00	65.00	125	—
Note: O above H						
1882Ho JA	Inc. above	25.00	40.00	65.00	125	—
Note: O after H						
1883/2Ho JA	204,000	200	350	500	1,000	—
1883/2Ho FM/JA	Inc. above	25.00	40.00	75.00	150	—
1883Ho FM/JA	—	27.00	45.00	85.00	165	—
1883Ho FM	Inc. above	20.00	30.00	60.00	125	—
1883Ho JA	Inc. above	275	450	800	1,500	—
1884/3Ho FM	—	20.00	25.00	50.00	125	—
1884Ho FM	—	18.00	22.00	40.00	120	—
1885Ho FM	132,000	18.00	22.00	40.00	120	—
1886Ho FM	225,000	20.00	30.00	45.00	125	—
1886Ho FG	Inc. above	20.00	30.00	45.00	125	—
1887/6Ho FG	—	20.00	35.00	65.00	150	—
1887Ho FG	150,000	20.00	35.00	65.00	150	—
1888Ho FG	364,000	15.00	20.00	30.00	110	—
1889Ho FG	490,000	15.00	20.00	30.00	110	—
1890Ho FG	565,000	15.00	20.00	30.00	110	—
1891Ho FG	738,000	15.00	20.00	30.00	110	—
1892Ho FG	643,000	15.00	20.00	30.00	110	—
1893Ho FG	518,000	15.00	20.00	30.00	110	—
1894Ho FG	504,000	15.00	20.00	30.00	110	—
1895Ho FG	320,000	15.00	20.00	30.00	110	—

Date	Mintage	F	VF	XF	Unc	BU
1827Pi SA	—	6,000	9,000	—	—	—
1828/7Pi JS	—	275	425	650	1,350	—
1828Pi JS	—	225	375	550	1,200	—
1829Pi JS	—	35.00	65.00	125	250	—
1830Pi JS	—	30.00	50.00	100	200	—
Note: Varities with low cap or centered cap						
1831/0Pi JS	—	35.00	75.00	200	350	—
1831Pi JS	—	25.00	35.00	75.00	200	—
1832/22Pi JS	—	25.00	35.00	65.00	165	—
18/032Pi JS	—	40.00	80.00	175	300	—
1832Pi JS	—	25.00	35.00	65.00	165	—
1833/2Pi JS	—	30.00	45.00	80.00	250	—
1833Pi JS Narrow date	—	20.00	30.00	50.00	150	—
Note: Planchet diameter 37.5 mm						
1833Pi JS Wide date	—	20.00	30.00	50.00	150	—
Note: Planchet diameter 38.5 mm						
1834/3Pi JS	—	35.00	65.00	125	300	—
1834Pi JS	—	18.00	25.00	50.00	150	—
Note: Varieties with low cap or centered cap						
1835/4Pi JS	—	60.00	125	250	500	—
1835Pi JS	—	20.00	30.00	65.00	175	—
Note: Denomination as 8R						
1835Pi JS	—	18.00	25.00	50.00	150	—
Note: Denomination as 8Rs						
1836Pi JS	—	20.00	30.00	55.00	150	—
1837Pi JS	—	30.00	50.00	85.00	200	—
1838Pi JS	—	20.00	30.00	55.00	150	—
1839Pi JS	—	20.00	40.00	70.00	150	—
Note: Varieties with small low cap or large high cap						
1840Pi JS	—	20.00	30.00	60.00	150	—
184/31Pi JS	—	25.00	40.00	85.00	200	—
1841Pi JS	—	25.00	40.00	85.00	200	—
1841iP JS Error	—	200	350	550	—	—
1842/1Pi JS	—	40.00	65.00	125	300	—
1842/1Pi JS/PS	—	35.00	50.00	90.00	200	—
1842Pi JS	—	30.00	50.00	80.00	175	—
Note: Eagle type of 1843						
1842Pi PS	—	30.00	50.00	80.00	175	—
1842Pi PS/JS	—	30.00	50.00	80.00	175	—
Note: Eagle type of 1841						
1843/2Pi PS Round-top 3	—	50.00	75.00	150	300	—
1843Pi PS Flat-top 3	—	60.00	100	200	475	—
1843Pi AM Round-top 3	—	20.00	30.00	55.00	150	—
1843Pi AM Flat-top 3	—	20.00	30.00	55.00	150	—
1844Pi AM	—	20.00	30.00	55.00	150	—
1845/4Pi AM	—	35.00	55.00	120	250	—
1845Pi AM	—	25.00	50.00	100	225	—
1846/5Pi AM	—	40.00	65.00	125	300	—
1846Pi AM	—	18.00	25.00	50.00	150	—
1847Pi AM	—	30.00	50.00	85.00	175	—
1848/7Pi AM	—	30.00	60.00	100	200	—
1848Pi AM	—	30.00	50.00	85.00	175	—
1849/8Pi PS/AM	—	950	1,750	—	—	—
1849Pi PS	—	950	1,750	—	—	—
1849Pi MC/PS	—	60.00	125	250	500	—
1849Pi AM	—	1,850	3,250	5,000	—	—
1849Pi MC	—	60.00	125	250	500	—
1850Pi MC	—	40.00	80.00	150	300	—
185/41Pi MC	—	75.00	150	275	550	—
1851Pi MC	—	75.00	150	275	550	—
1852Pi MC	—	75.00	125	200	400	—
1853Pi MC	—	150	275	400	850	—
1854Pi MC	—	100	150	250	500	—
1855Pi MC	—	100	150	250	500	—
1856Pi MC	—	65.00	100	200	400	—
1857Pi MC	—	400	700	1,250	—	—
1857Pi PS/MC	—	150	250	450	1,000	—
1857Pi PS	—	125	200	350	650	—
1858Pi MC/PS	—	250	400	650	1,200	—
1858Pi MC	—	250	400	650	1,200	—
1858Pi PS	—	650	1,150	1,750	—	—
1859/8Pi MC/PS	—	3,650	5,750	—	—	—
1859Pi MC/PS	—	900	1,750	—	—	—
1859Pi MC	—	2,000	3,500	5,000	—	—

KM# 377.12   8 REALES
27.0700 g., 0.9030 Silver 0.7859 oz. ASW **Obv:** Facing eagle, snake in beak **Obv. Legend:** REPUBLICA MEXICANA **Rev:** Radiant cap **Mint:** San Luis Potosi **Note:** Varieties exist.

Date	Mintage	F	VF	XF	Unc	BU
1827Pi JS	—	3,800				

Note: Heritage World Coin Auction #3004, 1-09, MS63 realized $63,250

Date	Mintage	F	VF	XF	Unc	BU
1859Pi PS/MC	—	800	1,500	2,500	—	—
1860Pi FC Rare	—	—	—	—	—	—
1860Pi FE Rare	—	—	—	—	—	—
1860Pi MC	—	1,750	2,750	6,000	—	—
1860Pi PS/FE	—	500	1,000	—	—	—
1860Pi RO Rare	—	—	—	—	—	—

Note: Spink America Gerber sale 6-96 cleaned VF or better realized $33,000

Date	Mintage	F	VF	XF	Unc	BU
1860Pi PS	—	400	600	900	1,750	—
1861Pi PS	—	30.00	60.00	90.00	175	—
1861Pi RO	—	25.00	35.00	55.00	135	—
1862/1Pi RO	—	20.00	25.00	50.00	135	—
1862Pi RO	—	18.00	22.00	45.00	120	—

Note: Round O/M

1862Pi RO	—	18.00	22.00	45.00	120	—

Note: Oval O in RO

1862Pi RO	—	20.00	30.00	50.00	135	—

Note: Round O in RO, 6 is an inverted 9

1863/2Pi RO	—	25.00	35.00	65.00	150	—
1863Pi RO/MO/FC	—	20.00	30.00	50.00	150	—
1863/5Pi RO	—	20.00	25.00	45.00	150	—
1863Pi RO	—	18.00	20.00	40.00	135	—
1863	—	25.00	35.00	55.00	135	—

Note: 6 over inverted 6

1863Pi FC	—	2,750	4,750	—	—	—
1864Pi RO Rare	—	—	—	—	—	—
1867Pi CA	—	300	500	—	—	—
1867Pi LR	—	250	400	650	—	—
1867Pi PS/CA	—	850	—	—	—	—
1867Pi PS	—	30.00	60.00	125	275	—
1868/7Pi PS	—	30.00	60.00	125	250	—
1868Pi PS	—	20.00	30.00	50.00	135	—
1869/8Pi PS	—	20.00	25.00	45.00	135	—
1869Pi PS	—	18.00	22.00	45.00	135	—
1870/69Pi PS	—	750	1,450	3,500	—	—
1870Pi PS	—	650	1,250	2,500	—	—
1873Pi MH	—	18.00	25.00	45.00	150	—
1874/3Pi MH	—	25.00	50.00	120	250	—
1874Pi MH	—	14.00	16.00	22.00	120	—
1875Pi MH	—	14.00	16.00	22.00	110	—
1876/5Pi MH	—	18.00	25.00	45.00	150	—
1876Pi MH	—	14.00	16.00	22.00	110	—
1877/6Pi MH	—	165	325	550	—	—
1877Pi MH	1,018,000	14.00	16.00	22.00	120	—
1878Pi MH	1,046,000	18.00	30.00	100	225	—
1879/8Pi MH	—	18.00	22.00	30.00	125	—
1879Pi MH	—	14.00	12.00	22.00	110	—
1879Pi BE	—	25.00	50.00	75.00	150	—
1879Pi MR	—	30.00	50.00	100	200	—
1880Pi MR	—	250	375	750	—	—
1880/70Pi MH/R	—	14.00	16.00	22.00	110	—
1880Pi MH/R	—	14.00	16.00	22.00	110	—
1880Pi MH	—	14.00	16.00	22.00	110	—
1881/71Pi MH/R	—	14.00	16.00	22.00	110	—
1881Pi MH/R	—	14.00	16.00	22.00	110	—
1881Pi MH	2,100,000	14.00	16.00	22.00	110	—
1882/1Pi MH	1,602,000	18.00	22.00	30.00	125	—
1882Pi MH	Inc. above	14.00	16.00	22.00	110	—
1883/2Pi MH	—	18.00	22.00	30.00	125	—
1883Pi MH	1,545,000	14.00	16.00	22.00	110	—
1884/3Pi MH	—	18.00	22.00	30.00	125	—
1884Pi MH/MM	—	16.00	18.00	22.00	95.00	—
1884Pi MH	—	14.00	16.00	20.00	90.00	—
1885/4Pi MH	1,736,000	18.00	22.00	30.00	125	—
1885/8Pi MH	Inc. above	18.00	22.00	30.00	125	—
1885Pi MH	Inc. above	14.00	16.00	20.00	90.00	—
1885Pi LC	Inc. above	16.00	20.00	25.00	110	—
1886Pi LC	3,347,000	14.00	16.00	20.00	90.00	—
1886Pi MR	Inc. above	14.00	16.00	20.00	90.00	—
1887Pi MR	2,922,000	14.00	16.00	20.00	90.00	—
1888/7Pi MR	—	18.00	22.00	30.00	125	—
1888Pi MR	2,438,000	14.00	16.00	20.00	90.00	—
1889Pi MR	2,103,000	14.00	16.00	20.00	90.00	—
1890Pi MR	1,562,000	14.00	16.00	20.00	90.00	—
1891Pi MR	1,184,000	14.00	16.00	20.00	90.00	—
1892Pi MR	1,336,000	14.00	16.00	20.00	90.00	—
1893Pi MR	530,000	14.00	16.00	20.00	90.00	—

KM# 377.13 8 REALES
27.0700 g., 0.9030 Silver 0.7859 oz. ASW **Obv:** Facing eagle, snake in beak **Obv. Legend:** REPUBLICA MEXICANA. **Rev:** Radiant cap **Mint:** Zacatecas **Note:** Varieties exist.

Date	Mintage	F	VF	XF	Unc	BU
1825Zs AZ	—	25.00	35.00	65.00	175	—
1826/5Zs AZ	—	25.00	45.00	85.00	200	—
1826Zs AZ	—	100	200	400	800	—
1826Zs AV	—	175	350	600	1,500	—
1826/5Zs AO/AZ	—	300	600	1,000	2,000	—
1826Zs AO	—	200	350	750	2,000	—
1827Zs AO/AZ	—	35.00	50.00	125	250	—
1827Zs AO	—	25.00	45.00	85.00	200	—
1828Zs AO	—	18.00	22.00	45.00	165	—

Note: Wide and narrow date varieties exist

1829Zs AO	—	18.00	2.00	45.00	165	—
1829Zs OV	—	50.00	90.00	150	300	—
1830Zs OM	—	—	—	—	—	—
1830Zs OV	—	18.00	22.00	45.00	165	—
1831Zs OV	—	25.00	50.00	90.00	200	—
1831Zs OM	—	18.00	25.00	55.00	165	—
1832/1Zs OM	—	20.00	25.00	45.00	165	—
1832Zs OM	—	18.00	22.00	40.00	150	—
1833/2Zs OM	—	20.00	30.00	45.00	165	—
1833Zs OM/MM	—	18.00	25.00	40.00	150	—
1833Zs OM	—	18.00	22.00	35.00	150	—
1834Zs OM	—	18.00	22.00	35.00	150	—

Note: Known with large, medium and small "34" in date

1835Zs OM	—	18.00	22.00	40.00	150	—
1836/4Zs OM	—	20.00	30.00	50.00	165	—
1836/5Zs OM	—	20.00	30.00	50.00	165	—
1836Zs OM	—	18.00	22.00	35.00	150	—
1837Zs OM	—	18.00	22.00	35.00	150	—
1838/7Zs OM	—	20.00	30.00	45.00	165	—
1838Zs OM	—	18.00	22.00	35.00	150	—
1839Zs OM	—	18.00	22.00	35.00	150	—
1840Zs OM	—	18.00	22.00	35.00	150	—
1841Zs OM	—	18.00	22.00	35.00	150	—
1842Zs OM	—	18.00	22.00	35.00	150	—

Note: Eagle type of 1841

1842Zs OM	—	18.00	22.00	35.00	150	—

Note: Eagle type of 1843

1843Zs OM	—	18.00	22.00	35.00	150	—
1844Zs OM	—	18.00	22.00	35.00	150	—
1845Zs OM	—	18.00	22.00	35.00	150	—
1846Zs OM	—	18.00	22.00	35.00	150	—
1847Zs OM	—	18.00	22.00	35.00	150	—
1848/7Zs OM	—	20.00	30.00	45.00	165	—
1848Zs OM	—	18.00	22.00	35.00	150	—
1849Zs OM	—	18.00	22.00	35.00	150	—
1850Zs OM	—	18.00	22.00	35.00	150	—
1851Zs OM	—	18.00	22.00	35.00	150	—
1852Zs OM	—	18.00	22.00	35.00	150	—
1853Zs OM	—	30.00	45.00	75.00	200	—
1854/3Zs OM	—	20.00	30.00	60.00	175	—
1854Zs OM	—	18.00	25.00	45.00	165	—

Date	Mintage	F	VF	XF	Unc	BU
1855Zs OM	—	20.00	30.00	60.00	175	—
1855Zs MO	—	30.00	60.00	90.00	200	—
1856/5Zs MO	—	20.00	30.00	45.00	165	—
1856Zs MO	—	18.00	22.00	35.00	150	—
1857/5Zs MO	—	20.00	30.00	45.00	165	—
1857Zs MO	—	18.00	22.00	35.00	150	—
1858/7Zs MO	—	18.00	22.00	35.00	150	—
1858Zs MO	—	18.00	22.00	35.00	150	—
1859/8Zs MO	—	18.00	22.00	35.00	150	—
1859Zs MO	—	18.00	22.00	35.00	150	—
1859Zs VL/MO	—	25.00	50.00	75.00	175	—
1859Zs VL	—	20.00	40.00	60.00	165	—
1860/50Zs MO	—	14.00	16.00	22.00	90.00	—
1860/59Zs MO	—	14.00	16.00	22.00	90.00	—
1860Zs MO	—	14.00	16.00	22.00	90.00	—
1860Zs VL/MO	—	14.00	16.00	22.00	90.00	—
1860Zs VL	—	14.00	16.00	22.00	90.00	—
1861/0Zs VL/MO	—	14.00	16.00	22.00	90.00	—
1861Zs VL	—	14.00	16.00	22.00	90.00	—
1861/0Zs VL	—	14.00	16.00	22.00	90.00	—
1862/1Zs VL	—	16.00	22.00	35.00	110	—
1862Zs VL	—	14.00	16.00	22.00	90.00	—
1863Zs VL	—	14.00	16.00	22.00	90.00	—
1863Zs MO	—	14.00	16.00	22.00	90.00	—
1864/3Zs VL	—	16.00	22.00	35.00	110	—
1864Zs VL	—	14.00	16.00	22.00	90.00	—
1864Zs MO	—	16.00	22.00	35.00	110	—
1865/4Zs MO	—	200	450	800	1,550	—
1865Zs MO	—	150	300	600	1,250	—
1866Zs VL	—	—	—	—	—	—
Note: Contemporary counterfeit						
1867Zs JS Rare	—	—	—	—	—	—
1868Zs JS	—	14.00	16.00	22.00	90.00	—
1868Zs YH	—	14.00	16.00	22.00	90.00	—
1869Zs YH	—	14.00	16.00	22.00	90.00	—
1870Zs YH Rare	—	—	—	—	—	—
1873Zs YH	—	14.00	16.00	22.00	90.00	—
1874Zs YH	—	14.00	16.00	22.00	90.00	—
1874Zs JA/YA	—	14.00	16.00	22.00	90.00	—
1874Zs JA	—	14.00	16.00	22.00	90.00	—
1875Zs JA	—	14.00	16.00	22.00	90.00	—
1876Zs JA	—	14.00	16.00	22.00	90.00	—
1876Zs JS	—	14.00	16.00	22.00	90.00	—
1877Zs JS	2,700,000	14.00	16.00	22.00	90.00	—
1878Zs JS	2,310,000	14.00	16.00	2.00	90.00	—
1879/8Zs JS	—	18.00	22.00	35.00	110	—
1879Zs JS	—	14.00	16.00	22.00	90.00	—
1880Zs JS	—	14.00	16.00	22.00	90.00	—
1881Zs JS	5,592,000	14.00	16.00	22.00	90.00	—
1882/1Zs JS	2,485,000	18.00	22.00	35.00	110	—
1882Zs JS Straight J	Inc. above	14.00	16.00	22.00	90.00	—
1882Zs JS Full J	Inc. above	14.00	16.00	22.00	90.00	—
1883/2Zs JS	2,563,000	18.00	22.00	35.00	110	—
1883Zs JS	Inc. above	14.00	16.00	22.00	90.00	—
1884Zs JS	—	14.00	16.00	22.00	90.00	—
1885Zs JS	2,252,000	14.00	16.00	22.00	90.00	—
1886/5Zs JS	5,303,000	18.00	22.00	35.00	110	—
1886/8Zs JS	Inc. above	18.00	22.00	35.00	110	—
1886Zs JS	Inc. above	14.00	16.00	22.00	90.00	—
1886Zs FZ	Inc. above	14.00	16.00	22.00	90.00	—
1887Zs FZ	4,733,000	14.00	16.00	22.00	90.00	—
1887Z FZ	Inc. above	20.00	30.00	50.00	110	—
1888/7Zs FZ	5,132,000	16.00	18.00	25.00	95.00	—
1888Zs FZ	Inc. above	14.00	16.00	22.00	90.00	—
1889Zs FZ	4,344,000	14.00	16.00	22.00	90.00	—
1890Zs FZ	3,887,000	14.00	16.00	22.00	90.00	—
1891Zs FZ	4,114,000	14.00	16.00	22.00	90.00	—
1892/1Zs FZ	4,238,000	16.00	18.00	25.00	95.00	—
1892Zs FZ Narrow date	Inc. above	14.00	16.00	22.00	90.00	—
1892Zs FZ Wide date	—	14.00	16.00	22.00	90.00	—
1893Zs FZ	3,872,000	14.00	16.00	22.00	90.00	—
1894Zs FZ	3,081,000	14.00	16.00	22.00	90.00	—
1895Zs FZ	4,718,000	14.00	16.00	22.00	90.00	—
1896Zs FZ	4,226,000	14.00	16.00	22.00	90.00	—
1897Zs FZ	4,877,000	14.00	16.00	22.00	90.00	—

KM# 377.10   8 REALES
27.0700 g., 0.9030 Silver 0.7859 oz. ASW   **Obv:** Facing
eagle, snake in beak **Obv. Legend:** REPUBLICA
MEXICANA. **Rev:** Radiant cap **Mint:** Mexico City **Note:**
Varieties exist. 1874 CP is a die struck counterfeit.

Date	Mintage	F	VF	XF	Unc	BU
1824Mo JM Round tail	—	75.00	125	250	500	—
1824Mo JM Square tail	—	75.00	125	250	500	—
1825Mo JM	—	25.00	40.00	75.00	200	—
1826/5Mo JM	—	25.00	40.00	75.00	200	—
1826Mo JM	—	20.00	30.00	55.00	165	—
1827Mo JM	—	25.00	35.00	60.00	175	—
Note: Medal alignment						
1827Mo JM	—	25.00	35.00	60.00	175	—
Note: Coin alignment						
1828Mo JM	—	30.00	60.00	100	250	—
1829Mo JM	—	20.00	30.00	90.00	220	—
1830/20Mo JM	—	35.00	5.00	150	300	—
1830Mo JM	—	30.00	50.00	90.00	220	—
1831Mo JM	—	30.00	50.00	100	240	—
1832/1Mo JM	—	25.00	40.00	65.00	180	—
1832Mo JM	—	20.00	30.00	55.00	165	—
1833Mo MJ	—	25.00	40.00	80.00	200	—
1833Mo ML	—	450	650	950	2,000	—
1834/3Mo ML	—	25.00	35.00	60.00	175	—
1834Mo ML	—	20.00	30.00	55.00	165	—
1835Mo ML Narrow date	—	20.00	30.00	55.00	165	—
1835Mo ML Wide date	—	20.00	30.00	55.00	165	—
1836Mo ML	—	50.00	100	150	325	—
1836Mo ML/MF	—	50.00	100	150	325	—
1836Mo MF	—	30.00	50.00	90.00	220	—
1836Mo MF/ML	—	35.00	60.00	100	240	—
1837/6Mo ML	—	30.00	50.00	80.00	200	—
1837/6Mo MM	—	30.00	50.00	80.00	200	—
1837/6Mo MM/ML	—	30.00	50.00	80.00	200	—
1837/6Mo MM/MF	—	30.00	50.00	80.00	200	—
1837Mo ML	—	30.00	50.00	80.00	200	—
1837Mo MM	—	75.00	125	175	325	—
1838Mo MM	—	30.00	50.00	80.00	200	—
1838Mo ML	—	20.00	35.00	60.00	180	—
1838Mo ML/MM	—	20.00	35.00	60.00	180	—
1839Mo ML Narrow date	—	18.00	25.00	50.00	165	—
1839Mo ML Wide date	—	18.00	25.00	50.00	165	—
1840Mo ML	—	18.00	25.00	50.00	165	—
1841Mo ML	—	18.00	25.00	45.00	150	—
1842Mo ML	—	18.00	25.00	45.00	150	—
1842Mo MM	—	18.00	25.00	45.00	150	—
1843Mo MM	—	18.00	25.00	45.00	150	—
1844Mo MF/MM	—	—	—	—	—	—
1844Mo MF	—	18.00	25.00	45.00	150	—
1845/4Mo MF	—	18.00	25.00	45.00	150	—
1845Mo MF	—	18.00	25.00	45.00	150	—

Date	Mintage	F	VF	XF	Unc	BU
1846/5Mo MF	—	18.00	25.00	50.00	165	—
1846Mo MF	—	18.00	25.00	50.00	165	—
1847/6Mo MF	—	2,000	3,550	—	—	—
1847Mo MF	—	1,500	2,750	5,000	7,500	—
1847Mo RC	—	20.00	30.00	55.00	165	—
1847Mo RC/MF	—	18.00	25.00	45.00	150	—
1848Mo GC	—	18.00	25.00	45.00	150	—
1849/8Mo GC	—	20.00	35.00	60.00	180	—
1849Mo GC	—	18.00	25.00	45.00	150	—
1850/40Mo GC	—	25.00	50.00	100	240	—
1850/49Mo GC	—	25.00	50.00	100	240	—
1850Mo GC	—	20.00	40.00	75.00	200	—
1851Mo GC	—	20.00	40.00	60.00	175	—
1852Mo GC	—	20.00	40.00	75.00	200	—
1853Mo GC	—	18.00	25.00	50.00	160	—
1854Mo GC	—	16.00	18.00	30.00	125	—
1855Mo GC	—	20.00	35.00	65.00	180	—
1855Mo GF	—	16.00	18.00	30.00	125	—
1855Mo GF/GC	—	16.00	18.00	30.00	125	—
1856/4Mo GF	—	18.00	25.00	45.00	145	—
1856/5Mo GF	—	18.00	25.00	45.00	145	—
1856Mo GF	—	16.00	18.00	30.00	125	—
1857Mo GF	—	14.00	18.00	30.00	125	—
1858/7Mo FH/GF	—	14.00	18.00	30.00	125	—
1858Mo FH Narrow date	—	14.00	18.00	30.00	125	—
1858Mo FH Wide date	—	14.00	18.00	30.00	125	—
1859Mo FH	—	14.00	18.00	30.00	125	—
1859/8Mo FH	—	25.00	50.00	100	240	—
1860/59Mo FH	—	18.00	20.00	30.00	125	—
1860Mo FH	—	14.00	18.00	30.00	125	—
1860Mo TH	—	16.00	18.00	40.00	145	—
1861Mo TH	—	16.00	18.00	40.00	145	—
1861Mo CH	—	14.00	18.00	22.00	90.00	—
1862Mo CH	—	14.00	18.00	22.00	90.00	—
1863Mo CH	—	14.00	18.00	22.00	90.00	—
1863Mo CH/TH	—	14.00	18.00	22.00	90.00	—
1863Mo TH	—	14.00	18.00	22.00	90.00	—
1867Mo CH	—	14.00	18.00	22.00	90.00	—
1867Mo CH/TH	—	20.00	45.00	70.00	185	—
1868Mo CH	—	14.00	18.00	22.00	90.00	—
1868Mo PH	—	14.00	18.00	22.00	90.00	—
1868Mo CH/PH	—	14.00	18.00	22.00	90.00	—
1868Mo PH Narrow date	—	14.00	18.00	22.00	90.00	—
1868Mo PH Wide date	—	14.00	18.00	22.00	90.00	—
1869Mo CH	—	14.00	18.00	22.00	—	—
1873Mo MH	—	14.00	18.00	22.00	90.00	—
1873Mo MH/HH	—	16.00	18.00	25.00	95.00	—
1874/69Mo MH	—	20.00	45.00	70.00	185	—
1874Mo MH	—	16.00	18.00	25.00	95.00	—
1874Mo BH/MH	—	16.00	18.00	25.00	95.00	—
1874Mo BH	—	16.00	18.00	25.00	95.00	—
1875Mo BH	—	14.00	18.00	22.00	90.00	—
1876/4Mo BH	—	16.00	18.00	25.00	95.00	—
1876/5Mo BH	—	16.00	18.00	25.00	95.00	—
1876Mo BH	—	14.00	18.00	22.00	90.00	—
1877Mo MH	898,000	14.00	18.00	22.00	90.00	—
1877Mo MH/BH	Inc. above	16.00	18.00	25.00	95.00	—
1878Mo MH	2,154,000	14.00	18.00	22.00	90.00	—
1879/8Mo MH	—	14.00	18.00	22.00	95.00	—
1879Mo MH	—	14.00	18.00	22.00	90.00	—
1880/79Mo MH	—	18.00	20.00	30.00	100	—
1880Mo MH	—	14.00	18.00	22.00	90.00	—
1881Mo MH	5,712,000	14.00	18.00	22.00	90.00	—
1882/1Mo MH	2,746,000	16.00	18.00	22.00	90.00	—
1882Mo MH	Inc. above	14.00	18.00	22.00	90.00	—
1883/2Mo MH	2,726,000	16.00	18.00	25.00	95.00	—
1883Mo MH Narrow date	Inc. above	14.00	18.00	22.00	90.00	—
1883Mo MH Wide date	—	14.00	18.00	22.00	90.00	—
1884/3Mo MH	—	18.00	20.00	30.00	100	—
1884Mo MH	—	14.00	18.00	22.00	90.00	—
1885Mo MH	3,649,000	14.00	18.00	22.00	90.00	—
1886Mo MH	7,558,000	14.00	16.00	20.00	90.00	—
1887Mo MH	7,681,000	14.00	16.00	20.00	90.00	—

Date	Mintage	F	VF	XF	Unc	BU
1888Mo MH Narrow date	7,179,000	14.00	16.00	20.00	90.00	—
1888Mo MH Wide date	—	14.00	16.00	20.00	90.00	—
1889Mo MH	7,332,000	14.00	18.00	22.00	90.00	—
1890Mo MH Narrow date	7,412,000	14.00	16.00	20.00	90.00	—
1890Mo AM Wide date	—	14.00	16.00	20.00	90.00	—
1890Mo AM	Inc. above	14.00	16.00	20.00	90.00	—
1891Mo AM	8,076,000	14.00	16.00	20.00	90.00	—
1892Mo AM	9,392,000	14.00	16.00	20.00	90.00	—
1893Mo AM	10,773,000	14.00	16.00	20.00	90.00	—
1894Mo AM	12,394,000	14.00	16.00	20.00	90.00	—
1895Mo AM	10,474,000	14.00	16.00	20.00	90.00	—
1895Mo AB	Inc. above	14.00	16.00	20.00	90.00	—
1896Mo AB	9,327,000	14.00	16.00	20.00	90.00	—
1896Mo AM	Inc. above	14.00	16.00	20.00	90.00	—
1897Mo AM	8,621,000	14.00	16.00	20.00	90.00	—

KM# 377.1   8 REALES
27.0700 g., 0.9030 Silver 0.7859 oz. ASW   **Obv:** Facing eagle, snake in beak **Obv. Legend:** REPUBLICA MEXICANA. **Rev:** Radiant cap **Mint:** Real de Catorce

Date	Mintage	F	VF	XF	Unc	BU
1863Ce ME	—	425	700	1,350	3,000	—
1863Ce /PI ML/MC	—	425	750	1,500	3,250	—

KM# 377.2   8 REALES
27.0700 g., 0.9030 Silver 0.7859 oz. ASW   **Obv:** Facing eagle, snake in beak **Obv. Legend:** REPUBLICA MEXICANA. **Rev:** Radiant cap **Mint:** Chihuahua **Note:** Varieties exist.

Date	Mintage	F	VF	XF	Unc	BU
1831Ca MR	—	1,000	1,750	2,250	3,250	—
1832Ca MR	—	125	200	300	600	—
1833Ca MR	—	250	550	1,000	—	—
1834Ca MR	—	300	600	1,150	—	—
1834Ca AM	—	350	500	700	—	—

Date	Mintage	F	VF	XF	Unc	BU
1835Ca AM	—	150	250	475	900	—
1836Ca AM	—	100	200	300	600	—
1837Ca AM	—	550	1,150	—	—	—
1838Ca AM	—	100	200	300	600	—
1839Ca RG	—	750	1,250	2,500	—	—
1840Ca RG	—	300	500	800	1,500	—
Note: 1 dot after date						
1840Ca RG	—	300	500	800	1,500	—
Note: 3 dots after date						
1841Ca RG	—	50.00	100	150	300	—
1842Ca RG	—	25.00	40.00	75.00	150	—
1843Ca RG	—	40.00	80.00	125	250	—
1844/1Ca RG	—	35.00	70.00	100	200	—
1844Ca RG	—	25.00	40.00	75.00	160	—
1845Ca RG	—	25.00	40.00	75.00	160	—
1846Ca RG	—	30.00	60.00	100	250	—
1847Ca RG	—	40.00	80.00	125	250	—
1848Ca RG	—	35.00	70.00	125	250	—
1849Ca RG	—	30.00	60.00	100	200	—
1850/40Ca RG	—	40.00	80.00	125	250	—
1850Ca RG	—	30.00	60.00	100	200	—
1851/41Ca RG	—	100	200	300	500	—
1851Ca RG	—	150	250	400	750	—
1852/42Ca RG	—	150	250	400	750	—
1852Ca RG	—	150	250	400	750	—
1853/43Ca RG	—	150	250	400	750	—
1853Ca RG	—	150	250	350	700	—
1854/44Ca RG	—	100	200	300	500	—
1854Ca RG	—	50.00	100	150	300	—
1855Ca RG	—	100	200	350	650	—
1855Ca RG	—	50.00	100	150	300	—
1856/Ca RG	—	275	450	750	1,250	—
1856/5Ca RG	—	400	700	1,500	3,500	—
1857Ca JC/RG	—	40.00	80.00	125	250	—
1857Ca JC	—	50.00	100	150	250	—
1858Ca JC	—	35.00	70.00	125	250	—
1858Ca BA	—	2,000	3,500	—	—	—
1859Ca JC	—	40.00	80.00	125	250	—
1860Ca JC	—	20.00	40.00	90.00	175	—
1861Ca JC	—	18.00	25.00	55.00	135	—
1862Ca JC	—	18.00	25.00	55.00	135	—
1863Ca JC	—	20.00	35.00	75.00	150	—
1864Ca JC	—	20.00	35.00	75.00	150	—
1865Ca JC	—	100	200	350	600	—
1865Ca FP	—	1,275	2,150	3,250	—	—
1866Ca JC	—	750	1,150	2,250	—	—
1866Ca FP	—	1,000	2,000	3,250	5,000	—
1866Ca JG	—	850	1,650	2,750	4,250	—
1867Ca JG	—	100	200	350	600	—
1868Ca JG	—	75.00	150	250	400	—
1868Ca MM	—	65.00	125	200	350	—
1869Ca MM	—	20.00	35.00	65.00	145	—
1870Ca MM	—	20.00	35.00	65.00	145	—
1871/0Ca MM	—	18.00	25.00	55.00	135	—
1871Ca MM	—	18.00	25.00	55.00	135	—
1871Ca MM	—	20.00	35.00	65.00	145	—
Note: Known with first M over inverted M and second M over inverted M						
1873/5Ca MM	—	20.00	35.00	65.00	145	—
1873Ca MM	—	20.00	35.00	65.00	145	—
1873Ca MM/T	—	18.00	25.00	55.00	135	—
1874Ca MM	—	16.00	18.00	30.00	110	—
1875Ca MM	—	16.00	18.00	30.00	110	—
1876Ca MM	—	16.00	18.00	30.00	110	—
1877Ca EA E/G	—	20.00	40.00	85.00	200	—
1877Ca EA	472,000	20.00	40.00	85.00	200	—
1877Ca GR	Inc. above	25.00	45.00	65.00	150	—
1877Ca JM	Inc. above	16.00	18.00	30.00	110	—
1877Ca AV	Inc. above	100	200	350	750	—
1878Ca AV	439,000	16.00	18.00	25.00	90.00	—
1879Ca AV	—	16.00	18.00	25.00	90.00	—
1880Ca AV	—	200	350	600	1,250	—
1880Ca PM	—	500	800	1,250	2,500	—
1880Ca MG	—	16.00	18.00	25.00	110	—
Note: Normal initials						
1880Ca MG	—	16.00	18.00	25.00	110	—
Note: Tall initials						
1880Ca MM	—	16.00	18.00	25.00	110	—
1881Ca MG	1,085,000	14.00	16.00	22.00	90.00	—

Date	Mintage	F	VF	XF	Unc	BU
1882Ca MG	779,000	14.00	16.00	22.00	90.00	—
1882Ca MM	Inc. above	14.00	16.00	22.00	90.00	—
1882Ca MM	Inc. above	20.00	45.00	100	175	—
Note: Second M over sideways M						
1883Ca MM	818,000	—	—	—	—	—
Note: Sideways M						
1883/2Ca MM/G	—	16.00	18.00	30.00	95.00	—
1883Ca MM	Inc. above	14.00	16.00	22.00	90.00	—
1884/3Ca MM	—	16.00	18.00	30.00	90.00	—
1884Ca MM	—	14.00	16.00	22.00	90.00	—
1885/4Ca MM	1,345,000	18.00	25.00	55.00	135	—
1885/6Ca MM	Inc. above	18.00	25.00	55.00	135	—
1885Ca MM	Inc. above	14.00	16.00	22.00	90.00	—
1886Ca MM	2,483,000	14.00	16.00	22.00	90.00	—
1887Ca MM	2,625,000	14.00	16.00	22.00	90.00	—
1888/7Ca MM	2,434,000	18.00	25.00	65.00	145	—
1888Ca MM	Inc. above	14.00	16.00	22.00	90.00	—
1889Ca MM	2,681,000	14.00	16.00	22.00	90.00	—
1890/89Ca MM	—	18.00	25.00	55.00	135	—
1890Ca MM	2,137,000	14.00	16.00	22.00	90.00	—
1891/0Ca MM	2,268,000	18.00	25.00	55.00	135	—
1891Ca MM	Inc. above	14.00	16.00	22.00	95.00	—
1892Ca MM	2,527,000	14.00	16.00	22.00	90.00	—
1893Ca MM	2,632,000	14.00	16.00	22.00	90.00	—
1894Ca MM	2,642,000	14.00	16.00	22.00	90.00	—
1895Ca MM	1,112,000	14.00	16.00	22.00	90.00	—

KM# 378.2 1/2 ESCUDO
1.6900 g., 0.8750 Gold 0.0475 oz. AGW **Obv:** Facing eagle, snake in beak **Obv. Legend:** REPUBLICA MEXICANA **Rev:** Hand holding cap on stick, open book **Rev. Legend:** LIBERTAD... **Mint:** Guadalajara

Date	Mintage	VG	F	VF	XF	Unc
1825Ga FS	—	55.00	70.00	120	210	—
1829Ga FS	—	55.00	70.00	120	210	—
1831Ga FS	—	55.00	70.00	120	210	—
1834Ga FS	—	55.00	70.00	120	210	—
1835Ga FS	—	55.00	70.00	120	210	—
1837Ga JG	—	55.00	70.00	120	210	—
1838Ga JG	—	55.00	70.00	120	210	—
1839Ga JG	—	—	—	—	—	—
1840Ga MC Unique	—	—	—	—	—	—
1842Ga JG	—	—	—	—	—	—
1847Ga JG	—	55.00	70.00	120	210	—
1850Ga JG	—	55.00	80.00	150	270	—
1852Ga JG	—	48.00	80.00	90.00	180	—
1859Ga JG	—	55.00	70.00	120	210	—
1861Ga JG	—	48.00	65.00	90.00	180	—

KM# 378.3 1/2 ESCUDO
1.6900 g., 0.8750 Gold 0.0475 oz. AGW **Obv:** Facing eagle, snake in beak **Obv. Legend:** REPUBLICA MEXICANA. **Rev:** Hand holding cap on stick, open book **Rev. Legend:** LIBERTAD... **Mint:** Guadalupe y Calvo

Date	Mintage	VG	F	VF	XF	Unc
1846GC MP	—	60.00	90.00	120	210	—
1847GC MP	—	60.00	90.00	120	210	550
1848/7GC MP	—	60.00	90.00	120	240	775
1850GC MP	—	60.00	90.00	120	210	—
1851GC MP	—	60.00	90.00	120	210	—
Revised eagle						

KM# 378.4 1/2 ESCUDO
1.6900 g., 0.8750 Gold 0.0475 oz. AGW **Obv:** Facing eagle, snake in beak **Rev:** Hand holding cap on stick, open book **Mint:** Guanajuato

Date	Mintage	VG	F	VF	XF	Unc
1845Go PM	—	42.00	55.00	80.00	150	—
1849Go PF	—	42.00	60.00	110	210	750

Date	Mintage	VG	F	VF	XF	Unc
1851/41Go PF	—	42.00	55.00	80.00	150	—
1851Go PF	—	42.00	55.00	80.00	150	—
1852Go PF/FF	—	—	—	—	—	—
1852Go PF	—	42.00	55.00	80.00	150	—
1853Go PF	—	42.00	55.00	80.00	150	—
1855Go PF	—	42.00	60.00	95.00	180	—
1857Go PF	—	42.00	55.00	80.00	150	—
1858/7Go PF	—	42.00	55.00	80.00	150	—
1859Go PF	—	42.00	55.00	80.00	150	—
1860Go PF	—	42.00	55.00	80.00	150	—
1861Go PF	—	42.00	55.00	80.00	150	—
1862/1Go YE	—	42.00	55.00	80.00	150	—
1863Go PF	—	42.00	60.00	95.00	180	—
1863Go YF	—	42.00	55.00	80.00	150	—

KM# 378.5 1/2 ESCUDO
1.6900 g., 0.8750 Gold 0.0475 oz. AGW **Obv:** Facing eagle, snake in beak **Obv. Legend:** REPUBLICA MEXICANA. **Rev:** Hand holding cap on stick, open book **Rev. Legend:** LIBERTAD... **Mint:** Mexico City

Date	Mintage	VG	F	VF	XF	Unc
1825/1Mo JM	—	60.00	90.00	150	240	—
1825/4Mo JM	—	60.00	90.00	150	240	—
1825Mo JM	—	42.00	60.00	95.00	180	425
1827/6Mo JM	—	42.00	60.00	95.00	180	—
1827Mo JM	—	42.00	60.00	95.00	180	425
1829Mo JM	—	42.00	60.00	95.00	180	—
1831/0Mo JM	—	42.00	60.00	95.00	180	—
1831Mo JM	—	42.00	55.00	80.00	150	—
1832Mo	—	42.00	55.00	80.00	150	—
1833Mo MJ	—	42.00	60.00	110	210	550

Note: Olive and oak branches reversed

Date	Mintage	VG	F	VF	XF	Unc
1834Mo ML	—	42.00	55.00	90.00	180	475
1835Mo ML	—	42.00	55.00	95.00	180	—
1838Mo ML	—	42.00	60.00	110	210	—
1839Mo ML	—	42.00	60.00	110	210	—
1840Mo ML	—	42.00	55.00	80.00	150	—
1841Mo ML	—	42.00	55.00	80.00	150	—
1842Mo ML	—	42.00	55.00	95.00	180	—
1842Mo MM	—	42.00	55.00	95.00	180	—
1843Mo MM	—	42.00	55.00	80.00	150	—
1844Mo MF	—	42.00	55.00	80.00	150	300
1845Mo MF	—	42.00	55.00	80.00	150	—
1846/5Mo MF	—	42.00	55.00	80.00	150	—
1846Mo MF	—	42.00	55.00	80.00	150	—
1848Mo GC	—	42.00	60.00	110	210	550
1850Mo GC	—	42.00	55.00	80.00	150	—
1851Mo GC	—	42.00	55.00	80.00	150	—
1852Mo GC	—	42.00	55.00	80.00	150	—
1853Mo GC	—	48.00	70.00	120	240	775
1854Mo GC	—	42.00	55.00	80.00	150	—
1855Mo GF	—	42.00	55.00	90.00	180	425
1856/4Mo GF	—	42.00	55.00	80.00	150	—
1857Mo GF	—	42.00	55.00	80.00	150	—
1858/7Mo FH/GF	—	42.00	60.00	90.00	180	—
1858Mo FH	—	42.00	55.00	80.00	150	—
1859Mo FH	—	42.00	55.00	80.00	150	—
1860/59Mo FH	—	42.00	55.00	80.00	150	300
1861Mo CH/FH	—	42.00	55.00	95.00	180	—
1862Mo CH	—	42.00	55.00	80.00	150	240
1863/57Mo CH/GF	—	42.00	55.00	80.00	150	300
1868/58Mo PH	—	42.00	55.00	95.00	180	—
1869/59Mo CH	—	42.00	55.00	95.00	180	—

KM# 378.6 1/2 ESCUDO
1.6900 g., 0.8750 Gold 0.0475 oz. AGW **Obv:** Facing eagle, snake in beak **Obv. Legend:** REPUBLICA MEXICANA. **Rev:** Hand holding cap on stick, open book **Rev. Legend:** LIBERTAD... **Mint:** Zacatecas

Date	Mintage	VG	F	VF	XF	Unc
1860Zs VL	—	48.00	60.00	90.00	180	—
1862/1Zs VL	—	48.00	60.00	90.00	180	—
1862Zs VL	—	42.00	55.00	80.00	150	—

KM# 378 1/2 ESCUDO
1.6900 g., 0.8750 Gold 0.0475 oz. AGW **Obv:** Facing eagle, snake in beak **Obv. Legend:** REPUBLICA MEXICANA **Rev:** Hand holding cap on stick, open book **Rev. Legend:** LIBERTAD... **Mint:** Culiacan

Date	Mintage	VG	F	VF	XF	Unc
1848C CE	—	48.00	60.00	90.00	180	350
1853C CE	—	48.00	60.00	90.00	180	—
1854C CE	—	48.00	60.00	90.00	180	—

Revised eagle

Note: Dates 1854-1870 of this type display the revised eagle

Date	Mintage	VG	F	VF	XF	Unc
1856C CE	—	60.00	120	180	300	—
1857C CE	—	48.00	60.00	90.00	180	—
1859C CE	—	48.00	60.00	90.00	180	—
1860C CE	—	48.00	60.00	90.00	180	—
1862C CE	—	48.00	60.00	90.00	150	—
1863C CE	—	48.00	60.00	90.00	150	350
1866C CE	—	48.00	60.00	90.00	150	—
1867C CE	—	48.00	60.00	90.00	150	300
1870C CE	—	90.00	180	325	550	—

KM# 378.1 1/2 ESCUDO
1.6900 g., 0.8750 Gold 0.0475 oz. AGW **Obv:** Facing eagle, snake in beak **Rev:** Hand holding cap on stick, open book **Mint:** Durango

Date	Mintage	VG	F	VF	XF	Unc
1833Do RM/RL	—	48.00	60.00	90.00	180	—
1834/1Do RM	—	48.00	60.00	90.00	180	—
1834/3Do RM	—	48.00	60.00	90.00	180	—
1835/2Do RM	—	48.00	60.00	90.00	180	—
1835/3Do RM	—	48.00	60.00	90.00	180	—
1835/4Do RM	—	48.00	60.00	90.00	180	—
1836/5/4Do RM/L	—	55.00	70.00	120	210	550
1836/4Do RM	—	48.00	60.00	90.00	180	—
1837Do RM	—	48.00	60.00	90.00	180	—
1838Do RM	—	55.00	70.00	120	210	—
1843Do RM	—	55.00	70.00	120	210	—
1844/33Do RM	—	55.00	70.00	120	210	—
1844/33Do R./RL	—	80.00	150	325	550	—
1845Do CM	—	55.00	70.00	120	210	—
1846Do RM	—	55.00	70.00	120	210	—
1848Do RM	—	55.00	70.00	120	210	—
1850/33Do JMR	—	55.00	70.00	120	210	575
1851Do JMR	—	55.00	70.00	120	240	—
1852Do JMR	—	55.00	70.00	120	210	—
1853/33Do CP	—	90.00	180	350	600	—
1853Do CP	—	60.00	85.00	180	300	650
1854Do CP	—	48.00	60.00	90.00	180	—
1855Do CP	—	48.00	60.00	90.00	180	—
1859Do CP	—	48.00	60.00	90.00	180	—
1861Do CP	—	48.00	60.00	90.00	180	—
1862Do CP	—	48.00	60.00	90.00	180	—
1864Do LT	—	90.00	150	300	475	—

KM# 379 ESCUDO
3.3800 g., 0.8750 Gold 0.0951 oz. AGW **Obv:** Facing eagle, snake in beak **Rev:** Hand holding cap on stick, open book **Mint:** Culiacan

Date	Mintage	VG	F	VF	XF	Unc
1846C CE	—	100	120	240	425	—
1847C CE	—	80.00	90.00	150	210	—
1848C CE	—	80.00	90.00	150	210	850
1849/8C CE	—	85.00	120	180	270	—

Date	Mintage	VG	F	VF	XF	Unc
1850C CE	—	80.00	90.00	150	210	—
1851C CE	—	85.00	120	180	270	—
1853/1C CE	—	85.00	120	180	270	—
1854C CE	—	80.00	90.00	150	210	—
1856/5/4C CE	—	85.00	120	180	270	—
1856C CE	—	80.00	90.00	150	210	—
1857/1C CE	—	85.00	120	180	270	—
1857C CE	—	80.00	90.00	150	210	—
1861C PV	—	80.00	90.00	150	210	—
1862C CE	—	80.00	90.00	150	210	—
1863C CE	—	80.00	90.00	150	210	—
1866C CE	—	80.00	90.00	150	210	—
1870C CE	—	80.00	90.00	150	210	—

KM# 379.1 ESCUDO
3.3800 g., 0.8750 Gold 0.0951 oz. AGW **Obv:** Facing eagle, snake in beak **Obv. Legend:** REPUBLICA MEXICANA. **Rev:** Hand holding cap on stick, open book **Rev. Legend:** LIBERTAD... **Mint:** Durango

Date	Mintage	VG	F	VF	XF	Unc
1832Do R.L.	—	—	—	—	—	—
1833/2Do RM/R.L.	—	100	150	240	350	—
1834Do RM	—	85.00	120	180	300	—
1835Do RM	—	—	—	—	—	—
1836Do RM/RL	—	85.00	120	180	300	—
1838Do RM	—	85.00	120	180	300	—
1846/38Do RM	—	100	150	240	350	—
1850Do JMR	—	100	150	210	325	—
1851/31Do JMR	—	100	150	240	350	—
1851Do JMR	—	100	150	210	325	—
1853Do CP	—	100	150	210	325	—
1854/34Do CP	—	100	150	210	325	—
1854/44Do CP/RP	—	100	150	210	325	—
1855Do CP	—	100	150	210	325	—
1859Do CP	—	100	150	210	325	—
1861Do CP	—	100	150	210	325	—
1864Do LT/CP Rare	—	—	—	—	—	—

KM# 379.2 ESCUDO
3.3800 g., 0.8750 Gold 0.0951 oz. AGW **Obv:** Facing eagle, snake in beak **Obv. Legend:** REPUBLICA MEXICANA. **Rev:** Hand holding cap on stick, open book **Mint:** Guadalajara

Date	Mintage	VG	F	VF	XF	Unc
1825Ga FS	—	85.00	110	150	240	—
1826Ga FS	—	85.00	110	150	240	—
1829Ga FS	—	—	—	—	—	—
1831Ga FS	—	85.00	110	150	240	—
1834Ga FS	—	85.00	110	150	240	—
1835Ga JG	—	85.00	110	150	240	—
1842Ga JG/MC	—	85.00	110	150	240	—
1843Ga MC	—	85.00	110	150	240	—
1847Ga JG	—	85.00	110	150	240	—
1848/7Ga JG	—	85.00	110	150	240	—
1849Ga JG	—	85.00	110	150	240	—
1850/40Ga JG	—	90.00	150	270	400	—
1850Ga JG	—	85.00	110	150	240	—
1852/1Ga JG	—	85.00	110	150	240	1,100
1856Ga JG	—	85.00	110	150	240	—
1857Ga JG	—	85.00	110	150	240	—
1859/7Ga JG	—	85.00	110	150	240	—
1860/59Ga JG	—	90.00	120	210	325	—
1860Ga	—	85.00	110	150	240	—

KM# 379.3 ESCUDO
3.3800 g., 0.8750 Gold 0.0951 oz. AGW **Obv:** Facing eagle, snake in beak **Obv. Legend:** REPUBLICA MEXICANA. **Rev:** Hand holding cap on stick, open book **Mint:** Guadalupe y Calvo

Date	Mintage	VG	F	VF	XF	Unc
1844GC MP	—	100	120	210	300	—
1845GC MP	—	100	120	210	300	—
1846GC MP	—	100	120	210	300	—
1847GC MP	—	100	120	210	300	—
1848GC MP	—	100	120	210	300	—
1849GC MP	—	100	120	210	300	—
1850GC MP	—	130	180	300	600	2,400
1851GC MP Revised eagle	—	100	120	210	300	—

KM# 379.4 ESCUDO
3.3800 g., 0.8750 Gold 0.0951 oz. AGW **Obv:** Facing eagle, snake in beak **Rev:** Hand holding cap on stick, open book **Mint:** Guanajuato

Date	Mintage	VG	F	VF	XF	Unc
1845Go PM	—	85.00	95.00	150	240	—
1849Go PF	—	85.00	95.00	150	240	—
1851Go PF	—	85.00	95.00	150	240	—
1853Go PF	—	85.00	95.00	150	240	—
1860Go PF	—	100	150	240	350	—
1862Go YE	—	85.00	95.00	150	240	725

KM# 379.5 ESCUDO
3.3800 g., 0.8750 Gold 0.0951 oz. AGW **Obv:** Facing eagle, snake in beak **Obv. Legend:** REPUBLICA MEXICANA. **Rev:** Hand holding cap on stick, open book **Mint:** Mexico City

Date	Mintage	VG	F	VF	XF	Unc
1825Mo JM/FM	—	80.00	85.00	120	180	425
1825Mo JM	—	80.00	85.00	120	180	—
1827/6Mo JM	—	80.00	85.00	120	180	—
1827Mo JM	—	80.00	85.00	120	180	—
1830/29Mo JM	—	80.00	85.00	120	180	—
1831Mo JM	—	80.00	90.00	150	210	650
1832Mo JM	—	80.00	90.00	150	210	—
1833Mo MJ	—	80.00	85.00	120	180	—
1834Mo ML	—	80.00	90.00	150	210	—
1841Mo ML	—	80.00	90.00	150	210	—
1843Mo MM	—	80.00	90.00	150	210	1,050
1845Mo MF	—	80.00	85.00	120	180	—
1846/5Mo MF	—	80.00	85.00	120	180	—
1848Mo GC	—	80.00	90.00	150	210	—
1850Mo GC	—	80.00	90.00	150	210	—
1856/4Mo GF	—	80.00	85.00	120	180	—
1856/5Mo GF	—	80.00	85.00	120	180	—
1856Mo GF	—	80.00	85.00	120	180	—
1858Mo FH	—	80.00	90.00	150	210	—
1859Mo FH	—	80.00	90.00	150	210	900
1860Mo TH	—	80.00	90.00	150	210	—
1861Mo CH	—	80.00	90.00	150	210	1,200
1862Mo CH	—	80.00	90.00	150	210	—
1863Mo TH	—	80.00	85.00	120	180	—
1869Mo CH	—	80.00	90.00	150	210	775

KM# 379.6 ESCUDO
3.3800 g., 0.8750 Gold 0.0951 oz. AGW **Obv:** Facing eagle,

snake in beak **Rev:** Hand holding cap on stick, open book **Mint:** Zacatecas **Note:** Struck at Zacatecas Mint, mint mark Zs.

Date	Mintage	VG	F	VF	XF	Unc
1853Zs OM	—	130	150	240	350	—
1860/59Zs VL V is inverted A	—	100	120	240	425	—
1860Zs VL	—	100	120	180	240	—
1862Zs VL	—	100	120	180	240	—

KM# 380.3   2 ESCUDOS
6.7700 g., 0.8750 Gold 0.1904 oz. AGW **Obv:** Facing eagle, snake in beak **Obv. Legend:** REPUBLICA MEXICANA. **Rev:** Hand holding cap on stick, open book **Rev. Legend:** LIBERTAD... **Mint:** Guadalajara

Date	Mintage	VG	F	VF	XF	Unc
1835Ga FS	—	165	190	270	400	—
1836/5Ga JG	—	190	240	475	600	—
1839/5Ga JG	—	—	—	—	—	—
1839Ga JG	—	165	180	240	350	—
1840Ga MC	—	165	180	240	350	—
1841Ga MC	—	165	200	300	475	—
1847/6Ga JG	—	165	190	270	350	—
1848/7Ga JG	—	165	190	270	350	—
1850/40Ga JG	—	165	180	240	350	—
1851Ga JG	—	165	180	240	350	—
1852Ga JG	—	165	190	270	400	—
1853Ga JG	—	165	180	240	350	—
1854/2Ga JG	—	—	—	—	—	—
1858Ga JG	—	165	180	240	350	—
1859/8Ga JG	—	165	190	270	350	—
1859Ga JG	—	165	190	270	350	—
1860/50Ga JG	—	165	190	270	350	—
1860Ga JG	—	165	190	270	350	900
1861/59Ga JG	—	165	180	240	350	—
1861/0Ga JG	—	165	180	240	350	—
1863/2Ga JG	—	165	190	270	350	950
1863/1Ga JG	—	165	180	240	350	—
1870Ga IC	—	165	180	240	350	—

KM# 380.4   2 ESCUDOS
6.7700 g., 0.8750 Gold 0.1904 oz. AGW **Obv:** Facing eagle, snake in beak **Rev:** Hand holding cap on stick, open book **Mint:** Guadalupe y Calvo

Date	Mintage	VG	F	VF	XF	Unc
1844GC MP	—	300	550	1,200	2,400	—
1845GC MP	—	900	1,500	2,400	3,600	—
1846GC MP	—	900	1,500	2,400	3,600	—
1847GC MP	—	600	1,200	2,400	3,600	—
1848GC MP	—	195	240	475	725	—
1849GC MP	—	900	1,500			—
1850GC MP	—	300	550	1,200	2,400	—

KM# 380.5   2 ESCUDOS
6.7700 g., 0.8750 Gold 0.1904 oz. AGW **Obv:** Facing eagle, snake in beak **Rev:** Hand holding cap on stick, open book **Mint:** Guanajuato

Date	Mintage	VG	F	VF	XF	Unc
1845Go PM	—	165	190	300	475	—
1849Go PF	—	165	190	300	475	—
1853Go PF	—	195	350	775	1,200	—
1856Go PF	—	—	—	—	—	—
1859Go PF	—	195	350	775	1,200	—
1860/59Go PF	—	—	—	—	—	—

Date	Mintage	VG	F	VF	XF	Unc
1860Go PF	—	165	190	300	475	—
1862Go YE	—	165	190	300	475	—

KM# 380   2 ESCUDOS
6.7700 g., 0.8750 Gold 0.1904 oz. AGW **Obv:** Facing eagle, snake in beak **Obv. Legend:** REPUBLICA MEXICANA. **Rev:** Hand holding cap on stick, open book **Mint:** Culiacan

Date	Mintage	VG	F	VF	XF	Unc
1846C CE	—	165	190	270	400	—
1847C CE	—	165	190	270	400	—
1848C CE	—	165	190	270	400	—
1852C CE	—	165	190	270	400	—
1854C CE	—	165	210	300	450	—
1856/4C CE	—	165	210	300	450	—
1857C CE	—	165	190	270	400	—

KM# 380.1   2 ESCUDOS
6.7700 g., 0.8750 Gold 0.1904 oz. AGW **Obv:** Facing eagle, snake in beak **Obv. Legend:** REPUBLICA MEXICANA. **Rev:** Hand holding cap on stick, open book **Rev. Legend:** LIBERTAD... **Mint:** Durango

Date	Mintage	VG	F	VF	XF	Unc
1833Do RM	—	400	550	850	1,450	—
1837/4Do RM	—	—	—	—	—	—
1837Do RM	—	—	—	—	—	—
1844Do RM	—	350	475	725	1,200	—

KM# 380.7   2 ESCUDOS
6.7700 g., 0.8750 Gold 0.1904 oz. AGW **Obv:** Facing eagle, snake in beak **Obv. Legend:** REPUBLICA MEXICANA **Rev:** Hand holding cap on stick, open book **Rev. Legend:** LIBERTAD... **Mint:** Mexico City

Date	Mintage	VG	F	VF	XF	Unc
1825Mo JM	—	165	180	240	350	—
1827/6Mo JM	—	165	180	240	350	—
1827Mo JM	—	165	180	240	350	—
1830/29Mo JM	—	165	180	240	350	—
1831Mo JM	—	165	180	240	350	—
1833Mo ML	—	165	180	240	350	—
1841Mo ML	—	165	180	240	350	—
1844Mo MF	—	165	180	240	350	—
1845Mo MF	—	165	180	240	350	—
1846Mo MF	—	180	240	475	725	—
1848Mo GC	—	165	180	240	350	—
1850Mo GC	—	165	180	240	350	—
1856/5Mo GF	—	165	180	240	350	—
1856Mo GF	—	165	180	240	350	—
1858Mo FH	—	165	180	240	350	—
1859Mo FH	—	165	180	240	350	—
1861Mo TH	—	165	180	240	350	—
1861Mo CH	—	165	180	240	350	—
1862Mo CH	—	165	180	240	350	—
1863Mo TH	—	165	180	240	350	900

Date	Mintage	VG	F	VF	XF	Unc
1868Mo PH	—	165	180	240	350	—
1869Mo CH	—	165	180	240	350	—

KM# 380.8 2 ESCUDOS
6.7700 g., 0.8750 Gold 0.1904 oz. AGW **Obv:** Facing eagle, snake in beak **Obv. Legend:** REPUBLICA MEXICANA. **Rev:** Hand holding cap on stick, open book **Rev. Legend:** LA LIBERTAD... **Mint:** Zacatecas

Date	Mintage	VG	F	VF	XF	Unc
1860Zs VL	—	180	350	725	1,450	—
1862Zs VL	—	325	600	950	1,450	—
1864Zs MO	—	180	350	725	1,450	—

KM# 380.2 2 ESCUDOS
6.7700 g., 0.8750 Gold 0.1904 oz. AGW **Obv:** Facing eagle, snake in beak **Obv. Legend:** REPUBLICA MEXICANA. **Rev:** Hand holding cap on stick, open book **Rev. Legend:** LIBERTAD... **Mint:** Estado de Mexico

Date	Mintage	VG	F	VF	XF	Unc
1828EoMo LF	—	850	1,200	2,100	3,600	—

KM# 380.6 2 ESCUDOS
6.7700 g., 0.8750 Gold 0.1904 oz. AGW **Obv:** Facing eagle, snake in beak **Rev:** Hand holding cap on stick, open book **Mint:** Hermosillo

Date	Mintage	VG	F	VF	XF	Unc
1861Ho FM	—	600	1,200	1,800	2,650	—

KM# 381 4 ESCUDOS
13.5400 g., 0.8750 Gold 0.3809 oz. AGW **Obv:** Facing eagle, snake in beak **Obv. Legend:** REPUBLICA MEXICANA. **Rev:** Hand holding cap on stick, open book **Rev. Legend:** LA LIBERTAD... **Mint:** Culiacan

Date	Mintage	VG	F	VF	XF	Unc
1846C CE	—	1,450	2,050	—	—	—
1847C CE	—	475	775	1,000	1,800	—
1848C CE	—	725	1,100	1,500	2,400	—

KM# 381.1 4 ESCUDOS
13.5400 g., 0.8750 Gold 0.3809 oz. AGW **Obv:** Facing eagle, snake in beak **Obv. Legend:** REPUBLICA MEXICANA. **Rev:**

Hand holding cap on stick, open book **Rev. Legend:** LA LIBERTAD.... **Mint:** Durango

Date	Mintage	VG	F	VF	XF	Unc
1832Do RM/LR Rare	—	—	—	—	—	—
1832Do RM	—	725	1,100	1,500	2,400	—
1833Do RM/RL Rare	—	—	—	—	—	—
1852Do JMR Rare	—	—	—	—	—	—

KM# 381.3 4 ESCUDOS
13.5400 g., 0.8750 Gold 0.3809 oz. AGW **Obv:** Facing eagle, snake in beak **Obv. Legend:** REPUBLICA MEXICANA **Rev:** Hand holding cap on stick, open book **Rev. Legend:** LA LIBERTAD... **Mint:** Guadalupe y Calvo

Date	Mintage	VG	F	VF	XF	Unc
1844GC MP	—	475	775	1,000	1,600	—
1845GC MP	—	425	600	850	1,200	—
1846GC MP	—	475	775	1,000	1,600	—
1848GC MP	—	475	775	1,000	1,600	—
1850GC MP	—	550	825	1,200	1,900	—

KM# 381.4 4 ESCUDOS
13.5400 g., 0.8750 Gold 0.3809 oz. AGW **Obv:** Facing eagle, snake in beak **Obv. Legend:** REPUBLICA MEXICANA. **Rev:** Hand holding cap on stick, open book **Rev. Legend:** LA LIBERTAD... **Mint:** Guanajuato

Date	Mintage	VG	F	VF	XF	Unc
1829/8Go MJ	—	350	425	550	1,000	—
1829Go JM	—	350	425	550	1,000	—
1829Go MJ	—	350	425	550	1,000	—
1831Go MJ	—	350	425	550	1,000	—
1832Go MJ	—	350	425	550	1,000	—
1833Go MJ	—	350	450	600	1,100	—
1834Go PJ	—	375	625	775	1,200	—
1835Go PJ	—	375	625	775	1,200	—
1836Go PJ	—	350	450	600	1,100	—
1837Go PJ	—	350	450	600	1,100	3,300
1838Go PJ	—	350	450	600	1,100	—
1839Go PJ	—	375	625	775	1,200	—
1840Go PJ	—	350	450	650	1,200	—
1841Go PJ	—	375	625	775	1,200	—
1845Go PM	—	350	450	600	1,100	—
1847/5Go YE	—	375	625	775	1,200	—
1847Go PM	—	375	625	775	1,200	—
1849Go PF	—	375	625	775	1,200	—
1851Go PF	—	375	625	775	1,200	—
1852Go PF	—	350	450	600	1,100	—
1855Go PF	—	350	450	600	1,100	—
1857/5Go PF	—	350	450	600	1,100	—
1858/7Go PF	—	375	625	775	1,200	—
1858Go PF	—	350	450	600	1,100	—
1859/7Go PF	—	375	625	775	1,200	—
1860Go PF	—	375	675	900	1,450	—
1862Go YE	—	350	450	600	1,100	—
1863Go YF	—	350	450	600	1,100	—

KM# 381.6 4 ESCUDOS
13.5400 g., 0.8750 Gold 0.3809 oz. AGW **Obv:** Facing eagle, snake in beak **Obv. Legend:** REPUBLICA MEXICANA. **Rev:** Hand holding cap on stick, open book **Rev. Legend:** LA LIBERTAD... **Mint:** Mexico City

Date	Mintage	VG	F	VF	XF	Unc
1825Mo JM	—	350	450	625	1,150	—
1827/6Mo JM	—	350	450	600	1,100	—
1829Mo JM	—	350	500	775	1,200	—
1831Mo JM	—	350	500	775	1,200	—
1832Mo JM	—	375	675	900	1,450	—
1844Mo MF	—	350	500	775	1,200	—
1850Mo GC	—	350	500	775	1,200	—
1856Mo GF	—	350	450	600	1,100	—
1857/6Mo GF	—	350	450	600	1,100	—
1857Mo GF	—	350	450	600	1,100	—
1858Mo FH	—	350	500	775	1,200	—
1859/8Mo FH	—	350	500	775	1,200	—
1861Mo CH	—	550	1,100	1,450	2,100	—
1863Mo CH	—	350	500	775	1,200	2,400
1868Mo PH	—	350	450	600	1,100	—
1869Mo CH	—	350	450	600	1,100	1,800

KM# 381.8 4 ESCUDOS
13.5400 g., 0.8750 Gold 0.3809 oz. AGW **Obv:** Facing eagle, snake in beak **Obv. Legend:** REPUBLICA MEXICANA. **Rev:** Hand holding cap on stick, open book **Rev. Legend:** LA LIBERTAD... **Mint:** Zacatecas

Date	Mintage	VG	F	VF	XF	Unc
1860Zs VL Rare	—	—	—	—	—	—
1862Zs VL	—	900	1,500	2,700	4,500	—

Note: American Numismatic Rarities Eliasberg sale 4-05, MS-64 realized $18,400.

KM# 381.2 4 ESCUDOS
13.5400 g., 0.8750 Gold 0.3809 oz. AGW **Obv:** Facing eagle, snake in beak **Obv. Legend:** REPUBLICA MEXICANA. **Rev:** Hand holding cap on stick, open book **Rev. Legend:** LA LIBERTAD... **Mint:** Guadalajara

Date	Mintage	VG	F	VF	XF	Unc
1844Ga MC	—	600	900	1,200	1,900	—
1844Ga JG	—	475	775	1,000	1,600	—

KM# 381.5 4 ESCUDOS
13.5400 g., 0.8750 Gold 0.3809 oz. AGW **Obv:** Facing eagle, snake in beak **Rev:** Hand holding cap on stick, open book **Mint:** Hermosillo

Date	Mintage	VG	F	VF	XF	Unc
1861Ho FM	—	1,200	1,800	3,000	4,800	—

KM# 381.7 4 ESCUDOS
13.5400 g., 0.8750 Gold 0.3809 oz. AGW **Obv:** Facing eagle, snake in beak **Obv. Legend:** REPUBLICA MEXICANA. **Rev:** Hand holding cap on stick, open book **Rev. Legend:** LA LIBERTAD EN LA LEY... **Mint:** Oaxaca **Note:** Mint mark O, Oa.

Date	Mintage	VG	F	VF	XF	Unc
1861O FR	—	1,800	3,000	4,800	8,400	—

KM# 383 8 ESCUDOS
27.0700 g., 0.8750 Gold 0.7615 oz. AGW **Obv:** Facing eagle, snake in beak **Obv. Legend:** REPUBLICA MEXICANA **Rev:** Hand holding cap on stick, open book **Rev. Legend:** LA LIBERTAD... **Mint:** Alamos

Date	Mintage	F	VF	XF	Unc	BU
1864A PG	—	875	1,550	3,000	—	—
1866A DL	—	—	—	9,000	—	—
1868/7A DL	—	2,500	4,400	6,600	—	—
1869A DL	—	—	5,000	7,200	—	—
1870A DL	—	—	3,150	6,000	—	—
1872A AM Rare	—	—	—	—	—	—

KM# 383.1 8 ESCUDOS
27.0700 g., 0.8750 Gold 0.7615 oz. AGW **Obv:** Facing eagle, snake in beak **Obv. Legend:** REPUBLICA MEXICANA. **Rev:** Hand holding cap on stick, open book **Rev. Legend:** LA LIBERTAD.... **Mint:** Chihuahua

Date	Mintage	F	VF	XF	Unc	BU
1841Ca RG	—	800	1,100	1,550	2,300	—
1842Ca RG	—	725	875	1,250	1,950	—
1843Ca RG	—	725	875	1,250	1,950	—
1844Ca RG	—	725	875	1,250	1,950	—
1845Ca RG	—	725	875	1,250	1,950	—
1846Ca RG	—	950	1,800	1,900	2,600	—

Date	Mintage	F	VF	XF	Unc	BU
1847Ca RG	—	1,450	3,650	—	—	—
1848Ca RG	—	725	875	1,250	1,950	—
1849Ca RG	—	725	875	1,250	1,950	—
1850/40Ca RG	—	725	875	1,250	1,950	—
1851/41Ca RG	—	725	875	1,250	1,950	—
1852/42Ca RG	—	725	875	1,250	1,950	—
1853/43Ca RG	—	725	875	1,250	1,950	—
1854/44Ca RG	—	725	875	1,250	1,950	—
1855/43Ca RG	—	725	875	1,250	1,950	—
1856/46Ca RG	—	750	950	1,550	2,300	—
1857Ca JC/RG	—	725	800	1,000	1,650	—
1858Ca JC	—	725	800	1,000	1,650	—
1858Ca BA/RG	—	725	800	1,000	1,650	—
1859Ca JC/RG	—	725	800	1,000	1,650	—
1860Ca JC/RG	—	725	875	1,250	1,950	—
1861Ca JC	—	725	800	1,000	1,650	—
1862Ca JC	—	725	800	1,000	1,650	—
1863Ca JC	—	875	1,450	2,200	2,950	—
1864Ca JC	—	800	1,100	1,550	2,300	—
1865Ca JC	—	1,100	2,200	3,150	4,550	—
1866Ca JC	—	725	725	1,250	1,950	—
1866Ca FP	—	950	1,800	2,500	3,250	—
1866Ca JG	—	725	875	1,250	1,950	—
1867Ca JG	—	725	800	1,000	1,650	—
1868Ca JG Concave wings	—	725	800	1,000	1,650	—
1869Ca MM Regular eagle	—	725	800	1,000	1,650	—
1870/60Ca MM	—	725	800	950	1,650	—
1871/61Ca MM	—	725	800	950	1,650	—

Date	Mintage	F	VF	XF	Unc	BU
1867C CB Error	—	725	800	950	1,550	—
1867C CE/CB	—	725	800	950	1,550	—
1868C CB Error	—	725	800	950	1,550	—
1869C CE	—	725	800	950	1,550	—
1870C CE	—	725	800	1,000	1,650	—

KM# 383.3   8 ESCUDOS
27.0700 g., 0.8750 Gold 0.7615 oz. AGW **Obv:** Facing eagle, snake in beak **Obv. Legend:** REPUBLICA MEXICANA **Rev:** Hand holding cap on stick, open book **Rev. Legend:** LA LIBERTAD.... **Mint:** Durango

Date	Mintage	F	VF	XF	Unc	BU
1832Do RM	—	725	2,550	2,500	3,900	—
1833Do RM/RL	—	725	800	1,000	1,650	—
1834Do RM	—	725	800	1,000	1,650	—
1835Do RM	—	725	800	1,000	1,650	—
1836Do RM/RL	—	725	800	1,000	1,650	—
1836Do RM	—	725	800	1,000	1,650	—
Note: M on snake						
1837Do RM	—	725	800	1,000	1,650	—
1838/6Do RM	—	725	800	1,000	1,650	—
1838Do RM	—	725	800	1,000	1,650	—
1839Do RM	—	725	800	950	1,650	2,600
1840/30Do RM/RL	—	725	950	1,250	2,300	—
1841/30Do RM	—	800	1,100	1,550	2,600	—
1841/0Do RM	—	725	800	950	1,650	—
1841/31Do RM	—	725	800	1,000	1,650	—
1841/34Do RM	—	725	800	1,000	1,650	—
1841Do RM/RL	—	725	800	1,000	1,650	—
1842/32Do RM	—	725	800	1,000	1,650	—
1843/33Do RM	—	800	1,100	1,550	2,600	—
1843/1Do RM	—	725	800	1,000	1,650	—
1843Do RM	—	725	800	1,000	1,650	—
1844/34Do RM/RL	—	875	1,450	1,900	3,250	—
1844Do RM	—	800	1,150	1,550	2,600	—
1845/36Do RM	—	725	950	1,250	2,300	—
1845Do RM	—	725	950	1,250	2,300	—
1846Do RM	—	725	800	1,000	1,650	—
1847/37Do RM	—	725	800	1,000	1,650	—
1848/37Do RM	—	—	—	—	—	—
1848/38Do CM	—	725	800	1,000	1,650	—
1849/39Do CM	—	725	800	1,000	1,650	—
1849Do J.M.R. Rare	—	—	—	—	—	—
1850Do .JMR.	—	725	1,100	1,550	2,600	—
1851Do JMR	—	725	1,100	1,550	2,600	—
1852/1Do JMR	—	725	1,150	1,550	2,600	—
1852Do CP	—	725	1,150	1,550	2,600	—
1853Do CP	—	725	1,150	1,550	2,600	—
1854Do CP	—	725	950	1,250	2,300	—
1855/4Do CP	—	725	800	1,000	1,650	—
1855Do CP	—	725	800	1,000	1,650	—
1856Do CP	—	725	875	1,150	2,150	—
1857Do CP	—	725	800	1,000	1,650	—
Note: French style eagle, 1832-57						
1857Do CP	—	725	800	1,000	1,650	—
Note: Mexican style eagle						
1858Do CP	—	725	875	1,150	2,150	—
1859Do CP	—	725	800	1,000	1,650	—
1860/59Do CP	—	725	1,100	1,550	2,850	—
1861/0Do CP	—	725	950	1,250	2,300	—
1862/52Do CP	—	725	800	1,000	1,650	—
1862/1Do CP	—	725	800	1,000	1,650	—
1862Do CP	—	725	800	1,000	1,650	—
1863/53Do CP	—	725	800	1,000	1,650	—
1864Do LT	—	725	800	1,000	1,650	2,600
1865/4Do LT	—	875	1,450	2,050	3,600	—

KM# 383.2   8 ESCUDOS
27.0700 g., 0.8750 Gold 0.7615 oz. AGW **Obv:** Facing eagle, snake in beak **Obv. Legend:** REPUBLICA MEXICANA. **Rev:** Hand holding cap on stick, open book **Rev. Legend:** LA LIBERTAD... **Mint:** Culiacan

Date	Mintage	F	VF	XF	Unc	BU
1846C CE	—	725	875	1,250	2,300	—
1847C CE	—	725	800	1,000	1,650	—
1848C CE	—	725	875	1,250	2,300	—
1849C CE	—	725	800	950	1,650	—
1850C CE	—	725	800	950	1,650	—
1851C CE	—	725	800	1,000	1,650	—
1852C CE	—	725	800	1,000	1,650	—
1853/1C CE	—	725	800	950	1,550	—
1854C CE	—	725	800	950	1,550	—
1855/4C CE	—	725	725	1,250	2,300	—
1855C CE	—	725	800	1,000	1,650	—
1856C CE	—	725	800	950	1,550	—
1857C CE	—	725	800	950	1,550	—
1857C CE	—	—	—	—	—	—
Note: Without periods after C's						
1858C CE	—	725	800	950	1,550	—
1859C CE	—	725	800	950	1,550	—
1860/58C CE	—	725	800	1,000	1,650	—
1860C CE	—	725	800	1,000	1,650	—
1860C PV	—	725	800	950	1,550	—
1861C PV	—	725	800	1,000	1,650	—
1861C CE	—	725	800	1,000	1,650	—
1862C CE	—	725	800	1,000	1,650	—
1863C CE	—	725	800	1,000	1,650	—
1864C CE	—	725	800	950	1,650	—
1865C CE	—	725	800	950	1,550	—
1866/5C CE	—	725	800	950	1,550	—
1866C CE	—	725	800	950	1,550	—

Date	Mintage	F	VF	XF	Unc	BU
1866/4Do CM	—	1,800	2,900	3,150	—	—
1866Do CM	—	725	950	1,250	2,300	—
1867/56Do CP	—	725	950	1,250	2,300	—
1867/4Do CP	—	725	800	1,000	1,650	—
1868/4Do CP/LT	—	—	—	—	—	—
1869Do CP	—	950	1,800	2,200	3,600	—
1870Do CP	—	725	950	1,250	2,300	—

KM# 383.4   8 ESCUDOS
27.0700 g., 0.8750 Gold 0.7615 oz. AGW **Obv:** Facing eagle, snake in beak **Obv. Legend:** REPUBLICA MEXICANA **Rev:** Hand holding cap on stick, open book **Rev. Legend:** LA LIBERTAD... **Mint:** Estado de Mexico

Date	Mintage	F	VF	XF	Unc	BU
1828EoMo LF Rare	—	—	—	—	—	—
1829EoMo LF	—	4,400	6,900	10,500	—	—

KM# 383.5   8 ESCUDOS
27.0700 g., 0.8750 Gold 0.7615 oz. AGW **Obv:** Facing eagle, snake in beak **Obv. Legend:** REPUBLICA MEXICANA **Rev:** Hand holding cap on stick, open book **Rev. Legend:** LA LIBERTAD... **Mint:** Guadalajara

Date	Mintage	F	VF	XF	Unc	BU
1825Ga FS	—	875	1,450	1,550	2,300	—
1826Ga FS	—	875	1,450	1,550	2,300	—
1830Ga FS	—	875	1,450	1,550	2,300	—
1836Ga FS	—	1,100	2,200	2,500	3,900	—
1836Ga JG	—	1,450	3,650	4,400	—	—
1837Ga JG	—	1,450	3,650	4,400	—	—
1840Ga MC Rare	—	—	—	—	—	—
1841/31Ga MC	—	1,450	3,650	—	—	—
1841Ga MC	—	1,250	2,400	2,800	—	—
1842Ga JG Rare	—	—	4,350	6,300	—	—
1843Ga MC	—	—	3,650	8,100	—	—
1845Ga MC Rare	—	—	—	—	—	—
1847Ga JG	—	3,250	—	—	—	—
1849Ga JG	—	875	1,450	1,550	2,300	—
1850Ga JG	—	800	1,250	1,400	2,150	—
1851Ga JG	—	1,450	3,650	4,400	—	—
1852/1Ga JG	—	875	1,450	1,550	2,300	—
1855Ga JG	—	1,450	3,650	4,400	—	—
1856Ga JG	—	800	1,250	1,400	2,150	—
1857Ga JG	—	800	1,250	1,400	2,150	—
1861/0Ga JG	—	875	1,450	1,550	2,300	—
1861Ga JG	—	725	1,000	1,500	2,300	—
1863/1Ga JG	—	875	1,450	1,550	2,300	—
1866Ga JG	—	800	1,250	1,400	2,150	—

KM# 383.6   8 ESCUDOS
27.0700 g., 0.8750 Gold 0.7615 oz. AGW **Obv:** Facing eagle, snake in beak **Obv. Legend:** REPUBLICA MEXICANA **Rev:** Hand holding cap on stick, open book **Rev. Legend:** LA LIBERTAD... **Mint:** Guadalupe y Calvo

Date	Mintage	F	VF	XF	Unc	BU
1844GC MP	—	800	1,100	1,550	2,600	—
1845GC MP	—	800	1,100	1,550	2,600	—
Note: Eagle's tail square						
1845GC MP	—	800	1,100	1,550	2,600	—
Note: Eagle's tail round						
1846GC MP	—	725	950	1,250	2,300	—
Note: Eagle's tail square						
1846GC MP	—	725	950	1,250	2,300	—
Note: Eagle's tail round						
1847GC MP	—	725	950	1,250	2,300	—
1848GC MP	—	800	1,100	1,550	2,600	—
1849GC MP	—	800	1,100	1,550	2,600	—
1850GC MP	—	725	950	1,250	2,300	—
1851GC MP	—	725	950	1,250	2,300	—
1852GC MP	—	800	1,100	1,550	2,600	—

KM# 383.7   8 ESCUDOS
27.0700 g., 0.8750 Gold 0.7615 oz. AGW **Obv:** Facing eagle, snake in beak **Obv. Legend:** REPUBLICA MEXICANA **Rev:** Hand holding cap on stick, open book **Rev. Legend:** LA LIBERTAD... **Mint:** Guanajuato

Date	Mintage	F	VF	XF	Unc	BU
1828Go MJ	—	1,100	2,550	2,800	3,900	—
1829Go MJ	—	950	2,200	2,500	3,600	—
1830Go MJ	—	725	800	950	1,300	—
1831Go MJ	—	950	2,200	2,500	3,600	—
1832Go MJ	—	800	1,450	1,900	3,250	—
1833Go MJ	—	725	800	875	1,300	—
1834Go PJ	—	725	800	875	1,300	—
1835Go PJ	—	725	800	875	1,300	—
1836Go PJ	—	725	950	1,150	1,650	—
1837Go PJ	—	725	950	1,150	1,650	—
1838/7Go PJ	—	725	800	875	1,300	—
1838Go PJ	—	725	800	1,000	1,550	—
1839/8Go PJ	—	725	800	875	1,300	—
1839Go PJ	—	725	800	1,000	1,550	—
Note: Regular eagle						
1840Go PJ	—	725	800	875	1,300	—
Note: Concave wings						
1841Go PJ	—	725	800	875	1,300	—
1842Go PJ	—	725	800	750	1,150	—
1842Go PM	—	725	800	875	1,300	—
1843Go PM	—	725	800	875	1,300	—
Note: Small eagle						
1844/3Go PM	—	725	950	1,150	1,650	—

Date	Mintage	F	VF	XF	Unc	BU
1844Go PM	—	725	800	825	1,300	—
1845Go PM	—	725	800	875	1,300	—
1846/5Go PM	—	725	800	1,000	1,550	—
1846Go PM	—	725	800	875	1,300	—
1847Go PM	—	725	950	1,150	1,650	—
1848/7Go PM	—	725	800	875	1,300	—
1848Go PM	—	725	800	875	1,300	—
1848Go PF	—	725	800	875	1,300	—
1849Go PF	—	725	800	750	1,250	—
1850Go PF	—	725	800	750	1,250	—
1851Go PF	—	725	800	875	1,300	—
1852Go PF	—	725	800	825	1,300	—
1853Go PF	—	725	800	825	1,300	—
1854Go PF	—	725	800	875	1,300	—
Note: Eagle of 1853						
1854Go PF	—	725	800	875	1,300	—
Note: Eagle of 1855						
1855/4Go PF	—	725	800	875	1,300	—
1855Go PF	—	725	800	875	1,300	—
1856Go PF	—	725	800	875	1,300	—
1857Go PF	—	725	800	875	1,300	—
1858Go PF	—	725	800	875	1,300	—
1859Go PF	—	725	800	750	1,150	—
1860/50Go PF	—	725	800	750	1,150	—
1860/59Go PF	—	725	800	875	1,450	—
1860Go PF	—	725	800	875	1,450	—
1861/0Go PF	—	725	800	750	1,100	—
1861Go PF	—	725	800	750	1,100	—
1862/1Go YE	—	725	800	875	1,300	—
1862Go YE	—	725	800	825	1,250	—
1862Go YF	—	—	—	—	—	—
1863/53Go YF	—	725	800	875	1,300	3,250
1863Go PF	—	725	800	875	1,300	—
1867/57Go YF/PF	—	725	800	875	1,300	—
1867Go YF	—	725	800	825	1,250	—
1868/58Go YF	—	725	800	875	1,300	2,300
1870Go FR	—	725	800	750	1,150	—

KM# 383.10 8 ESCUDOS
27.0700 g., 0.8750 Gold 0.7615 oz. AGW **Obv:** Facing eagle, snake in beak **Obv. Legend:** REPUBLICA MEXICANA **Rev:** Hand holding cap on stick, open book **Rev. Legend:** LA LIBERTAD... **Mint:** Oaxaca

Date	Mintage	F	VF	XF	Unc	BU
1858Oa AE	—	2,900	4,350	5,000	7,800	—
1859O AE	—	1,450	3,650	4,700	7,200	—
1860O AE	—	1,450	3,650	4,700	7,200	—
1861O FR	—	875	1,250	1,550	3,600	—
1862O FR	—	875	1,250	1,550	3,600	—
1863O FR	—	875	1,250	1,550	3,600	—
1864O FR	—	875	1,250	1,550	3,600	—
1867O AE	—	875	1,250	1,550	3,600	—
1868O AE	—	875	1,250	1,550	3,600	—
1869O AE	—	875	1,250	1,550	3,600	—

KM# 383.8 8 ESCUDOS
27.0700 g., 0.8750 Gold 0.7615 oz. AGW **Obv:** Facing eagle, snake in beak **Obv. Legend:** REPUBLICA MEXICANA. **Rev:** Hand holding cap on stick, open book **Rev. Legend:** LA LIBERTAD... **Mint:** Hermosillo

Date	Mintage	F	VF	XF	Unc	BU
1863Ho FM	—	800	1,000	1,250	2,600	—
1864Ho FM	—	950	1,800	2,200	3,600	—
1864Ho PR/FM	—	800	1,000	1,250	2,600	—
1865Ho FM/PR	—	875	1,150	1,550	3,250	—
1867/57Ho PR	—	800	1,000	1,250	2,600	—
1868Ho PR	—	875	1,150	1,550	3,250	—
1868Ho PR/FM	—	875	1,150	1,550	3,250	—
1869Ho PR/FM	—	800	1,000	1,250	2,600	—
1869Ho PR	—	800	1,000	1,250	2,600	—
1870Ho PR	—	875	1,150	1,550	3,600	7,200
1871/0Ho PR	—	875	1,150	1,550	3,250	—
1871Ho PR	—	875	1,150	1,550	3,250	—
1872/1Ho PR	—	950	1,800	2,200	3,600	—
1873Ho PR	—	800	1,000	1,250	2,600	—

KM# 383.11 8 ESCUDOS
27.0700 g., 0.8750 Gold 0.7615 oz. AGW **Obv:** Facing eagle, snake in beak **Obv. Legend:** REPUBLICA MEXICANA **Rev:** Hand holding cap on stick, open book **Rev. Legend:** LA LIBERTAD... **Mint:** Zacatecas

Date	Mintage	F	VF	XF	Unc	BU
1858Zs MO	—	800	1,100	1,250	2,600	—
1859Zs MO	—	725	800	750	1,300	—
1860/59Zs VL/MO	—	2,900	4,350	5,000	—	—
1860/9Zs MO	—	800	1,100	1,250	2,600	—
1860Zs MO	—	725	800	875	1,450	—
1861/0Zs VL	—	725	800	875	1,450	—
1861Zs VL	—	725	800	875	1,450	3,900
1862Zs VL	—	725	800	875	1,500	—
1863Zs VL	—	725	800	950	1,550	—
1863Zs MO	—	725	800	875	1,450	—
1864Zs MO	—	1,100	1,450	1,900	4,550	—
1865Zs MO	—	1,100	1,450	2,000	4,900	—
1868Zs JS	—	725	875	1,000	1,650	—
1868Zs YH	—	725	875	1,000	1,650	—
1869Zs YH	—	725	875	1,000	1,650	—
1870Zs YH	—	725	875	1,000	1,650	—
1871Zs YH	—	725	875	1,000	1,650	—

KM# 383.9 8 ESCUDOS
27.0700 g., 0.8750 Gold 0.7615 oz. AGW **Obv:** Facing eagle, snake in beak **Obv. Legend:** REPUBLICA MEXICANA **Rev:** Hand holding cap on stick, open book **Rev. Legend:** LA LIBERTAD... **Mint:** Mexico City **Note:** Formerly reported 1825/3 JM is merely a reworked 5.

Date	Mintage	F	VF	XF	Unc	BU
1824Mo JM	—	875	1,450	1,550	2,600	—

Note: Large book reverse

1825Mo JM	—	725	800	875	1,300	2,600

Note: Small book reverse

1826/5Mo JM	—	1,100	2,550	2,800	3,900	—
1827/6Mo JM	—	725	800	875	1,300	—
1827Mo JM	—	725	800	875	1,300	—
1828Mo JM	—	725	800	875	1,300	—
1829Mo JM	—	725	800	875	1,300	—
1830Mo JM	—	725	800	875	1,300	—
1831Mo JM	—	725	800	875	1,300	—
1832/1Mo JM	—	725	800	875	1,300	—
1832Mo JM	—	725	800	875	1,300	—
1833Mo MJ	—	800	1,100	1,250	1,950	—
1833Mo ML	—	725	800	825	1,300	—
1834Mo ML	—	800	1,100	1,250	1,950	—
1835/4Mo ML	—	875	1,450	1,550	2,600	—
1836Mo ML	—	725	800	825	1,300	—
1836Mo MF	—	800	1,100	1,500	2,600	—
1837/6Mo ML	—	725	800	825	1,300	—
1838Mo ML	—	725	800	825	1,300	—
1839Mo ML	—	725	800	825	1,300	—
1840Mo ML	—	725	800	825	1,300	—
1841Mo ML	—	725	800	825	1,300	—
1842/1Mo ML	—	—	—	—	—	—
1842Mo ML	—	725	800	825	1,300	—
1842Mo MM	—	—	—	—	—	—
1843Mo MM	—	725	800	825	1,300	—
1844Mo MF	—	725	800	825	1,300	—
1845Mo MF	—	725	800	825	1,300	—
1846Mo MF	—	875	1,450	1,550	2,600	—
1847Mo MF	—	1,450	3,250	—	—	—
1847Mo RC	—	725	875	1,000	1,650	—
1848Mo GC	—	725	800	825	1,300	—
1849Mo GC	—	725	800	825	1,300	—
1850Mo GC	—	725	800	825	1,300	2,600
1851Mo GC	—	725	800	825	1,300	—
1852Mo GC	—	725	800	825	1,300	—
1853Mo GC	—	725	800	825	1,300	—
1854/44Mo GC	—	725	800	825	1,300	—
1854/3Mo GC	—	725	800	825	1,300	—
1855Mo GF	—	725	800	825	1,300	—
1856/5Mo GF	—	725	800	750	1,250	—
1856Mo GF	—	725	800	750	1,250	—
1857Mo GF	—	725	800	750	1,250	—
1858Mo FH	—	725	800	750	1,250	—
1859Mo FH	—	800	1,100	1,250	1,950	—
1860Mo FH	—	725	800	750	1,250	—
1860Mo TH	—	725	800	750	1,250	—
1861/51Mo CH	—	725	800	750	1,250	—
1862Mo CH	—	725	800	750	1,250	—
1863/53Mo CH	—	725	800	750	1,250	6,200
1863/53Mo TH	—	725	800	750	1,250	—
1867Mo CH	—	725	800	750	1,250	—
1868Mo CH	—	725	800	750	1,250	—
1868Mo PH	—	725	800	750	1,250	—
1869Mo CH	—	725	800	750	1,250	—

EMPIRE OF MAXIMILIAN

RULER
Maximilian, Emperor, 1864-1867
MINT MARKS
Refer To Republic Coinage
MONETARY SYSTEM
100 Centavos = 1 Peso (8 Reales)

MILLED COINAGE

KM# 384 CENTAVO
Copper **Ruler:** Maximilian **Obv:** Crowned facing eagle, snake in beak **Obv. Legend:** IMPERIO MEXICANO **Rev:** Value and date within wreath **Edge:** Coarsely reeded **Mint:** Mexico City

Date	Mintage	F	VF	XF	Unc	BU
1864M	—	50.00	100	250	1,250	1,850

KM# 385 5 CENTAVOS
1.3537 g., 0.9030 Silver 0.0393 oz. ASW **Ruler:** Maximilian **Mint:** Guanajuato

Date	Mintage	F	VF	XF	Unc	BU
1864G	90,000	17.50	35.00	85.00	320	—
1865G	—	20.00	30.00	65.00	300	—
1866G	—	75.00	150	300	2,000	—

KM# 385.1 5 CENTAVOS
1.3537 g., 0.9030 Silver 0.0393 oz. ASW **Ruler:** Maximilian **Mint:** Mexico City

Date	Mintage	F	VF	XF	Unc	BU
1864M	—	12.50	20.00	55.00	300	—
1866/4M	—	25.00	40.00	75.00	425	—
1866M	—	20.00	35.00	65.00	400	—

KM# 385.2 5 CENTAVOS
1.3537 g., 0.9030 Silver 0.0393 oz. ASW **Ruler:** Maximilian **Mint:** San Luis Potosi

Date	Mintage	F	VF	XF	Unc	BU
1864P	—	150	400	1,500	2,500	—

KM# 385.3 5 CENTAVOS
1.3537 g., 0.9030 Silver 0.0393 oz. ASW **Ruler:** Maximilian **Obv:** Crowned facing eagle, snake in beak **Obv. Legend:** IMPERIO MEXICANO **Rev:** Value and date within wreath **Mint:** Zacatecas

Date	Mintage	F	VF	XF	Unc	BU
1865Z	—	25.00	45.00	150	450	—

KM# 386 10 CENTAVOS
2.7073 g., 0.9030 Silver 0.0786 oz. ASW **Ruler:** Maximilian **Obv:** Crowned facing eagle, snake in beak **Obv. Legend:** IMPERIO MEXICANO **Rev:** Value and date within wreath **Mint:** Guanajuato

Date	Mintage	F	VF	XF	Unc	BU
1864G	45,000	20.00	45.00	90.00	325	—
1865G	—	30.00	60.00	110	375	—

KM# 386.1   10 CENTAVOS
2.7073 g., 0.9030 Silver 0.0786 oz. ASW **Ruler:** Maximilian
Obv: Crowned facing eagle, snake in beak **Obv. Legend:**
IMPERIO MEXICANO **Rev:** Value and date within wreath **Mint:**
Mexico City **Note:** Struck at Mexico City Mint, mint mark M.

Date	Mintage	F	VF	XF	Unc	BU
1864M	—	15.00	25.00	55.00	285	—
1866/4M	—	25.00	35.00	70.00	320	—
1866/5M	—	25.00	40.00	85.00	375	—
1866M	—	25.00	35.00	75.00	375	—

KM# 386.2   10 CENTAVOS
2.7073 g., 0.9030 Silver 0.0786 oz. ASW **Ruler:** Maximilian
Mint: San Luis Potosi

Date	Mintage	F	VF	XF	Unc	BU
1864P	—	70.00	150	300	700	—

KM# 386.3   10 CENTAVOS
2.7073 g., 0.9030 Silver 0.0786 oz. ASW **Ruler:** Maximilian
Mint: Zacatecas

Date	Mintage	F	VF	XF	Unc	BU
1865Z	—	22.50	55.00	165	525	750

KM# 387   50 CENTAVOS
13.5365 g., 0.9030 Silver 0.3930 oz. ASW **Ruler:** Maximilian
Obv: Head right, with beard **Obv. Legend:** MAXIMILIANO
EMPERADOR **Rev:** Crowned oval shield **Rev. Legend:**
IMPERIO MEXICANO **Mint:** Mexico City **Designer:** S.
Navalon

Date	Mintage	F	VF	XF	Unc	BU
1866Mo	31,000	40.00	95.00	200	750	2,250

KM# 388   PESO
27.0700 g., 0.9030 Silver 0.7859 oz. ASW **Ruler:** Maximilian
Obv: Head right, with beard **Obv. Legend:** MAXIMILIANO
EMPERADOR **Rev:** Crowned arms with supporters **Rev.**
Legend: IMPERIO MEXICANO **Mint:** Guanajuato **Designer:**
S. Navalon

Date	Mintage	F	VF	XF	Unc	BU
1866Go	—	300	450	950	3,500	—

KM# 388.1   PESO
27.0700 g., 0.9030 Silver 0.7859 oz. ASW **Ruler:** Maximilian
Obv: Head right, with beard **Obv. Legend:** MAXIMILIANO
EMPERADOR **Rev:** Crowned arms with supporters **Rev.**
Legend: IMPERIO MEXICANO **Mint:** Mexico City **Designer:**
S. Navalon

Date	Mintage	F	VF	XF	Unc	BU
1866Mo	2,148,000	30.00	45.00	135	400	—
1867Mo	1,238,000	40.00	65.00	185	450	—

KM# 388.2   PESO
27.0700 g., 0.9030 Silver 0.7859 oz. ASW **Ruler:** Maximilian
Obv: Head right, with beard **Obv. Legend:** MAXIMILIANO
EMPERADOR **Rev:** Crowned arms with supporters **Rev.**
Legend: IMPERIO MEXICANO **Mint:** San Luis Potosi
Designer: S. Navalon

Date	Mintage	F	VF	XF	Unc	BU
1866Pi	—	45.00	90.00	275	775	—

KM# 389   20 PESOS
33.8400 g., 0.8750 Gold 0.9519 oz. AGW **Ruler:** Maximilian
Obv: Head right, with beard **Obv. Legend:** MAXIMILIANO
EMPERADOR **Rev:** Crowned arms with supporters **Rev.**
Legend: IMPERIO MEXICANO **Mint:** Mexico City **Designer:**
S. Navalon

Date	Mintage	F	VF	XF	Unc	BU
1866Mo	8,274	1,100	1,350	2,200	3,500	—

REPUBLIC
Second

DECIMAL COINAGE

100 Centavos = 1 Peso

KM# 390   CENTAVO
Copper, 25 mm. **Obv:** Seated Liberty **Rev:** Thick wreath.
Mint: Mexico City

Date	Mintage	F	VF	XF	Unc	BU
1863Mo	—	13.50	32.50	75.00	500	—

Note: Round-top 3, plain edge

Date	Mintage	F	VF	XF	Unc	BU
1863Mo	—	10.00	30.00	70.00	500	—

Note: Flat-top 3, reeded edge

Date	Mintage	F	VF	XF	Unc	BU
1863Mo	—	13.50	32.50	75.00	500	—

Note: Round-top 3, reeded edge

KM# 390.1 CENTAVO
Copper, 26.5 mm. **Obv:** Seated liberty **Obv. Legend:**
LIBERTAD V REFORMA. **Rev:** Value and date within wreath
Mint: San Luis Potosi

Date	Mintage	F	VF	XF	Unc	BU
1863SLP	1,024,999	15.00	32.50	75.00	425	—

KM# 391 CENTAVO
Copper **Obv:** Facing eagle, snake in beak **Rev:** Value and
date within wreath **Edge:** Reeded. **Mint:** Alamos

Date	Mintage	F	VF	XF	Unc	BU
1875As Rare	—	—	—	—	—	—
1876As	50,000	100	200	300	650	—
1880As	—	25.00	50.00	200	500	—
1881As	—	30.00	60.00	125	350	—

KM# 391.1 CENTAVO
Copper **Obv:** Facing eagle, snake in beak **Obv. Legend:**
REPUBLICA MEXICANA **Rev:** Value and date within wreath
Edge: Plain **Mint:** Culiacan

Date	Mintage	F	VF	XF	Unc	BU
1874Cn	266,000	12.50	17.50	35.00	250	—
1875/4Cn	153,000	15.00	20.00	45.00	250	—
1875Cn	Inc. above	10.00	15.00	25.00	250	—
1876Cn	154,000	5.00	8.00	15.00	200	—
1877/6Cn	993,000	7.50	11.50	17.50	200	—
1877Cn	Inc. above	6.00	9.00	15.00	200	—
1880Cn	142,000	7.50	10.00	12.50	200	—
1881Cn	167,000	7.50	10.00	25.00	200	—
1897Cn	300,000	2.50	5.00	12.00	50.00	—

Note: Large N in mint mark

Date	Mintage	F	VF	XF	Unc	BU
1897Cn	Inc. above	2.50	5.00	9.00	45.00	—

Note: Small N in mint mark

KM# 391.2 CENTAVO
Copper **Obv:** Facing eagle, snake in beak **Rev:** Value and
date within wreath **Mint:** Durango

Date	Mintage	F	VF	XF	Unc	BU
1879Do	110,000	10.00	35.00	60.00	200	—
1880Do	69,000	40.00	90.00	175	500	—
1891Do/Mo	—	8.00	25.00	50.00	200	—
1891Do	—	8.00	25.00	50.00	200	—

KM# 391.3 CENTAVO
Copper **Obv:** Facing eagle, snake in beak **Obv. Legend:**
REPUBLICA MEXICANA **Rev:** Value and date within wreath
Mint: Guadalajara

Date	Mintage	F	VF	XF	Unc	BU
1872Ga	263,000	15.00	30.00	60.00	225	—
1873Ga	333,000	6.00	9.00	25.00	200	—
1874Ga	76,000	15.00	25.00	50.00	200	—
1875Ga	—	10.00	15.00	30.00	200	—
1876Ga	303,000	3.00	6.00	17.50	200	—
1877Ga	108,000	4.00	6.00	20.00	200	—
1878Ga	543,000	4.00	6.00	15.00	200	—
1881/71Ga	975,000	7.00	9.00	20.00	—	—
1881Ga	Inc. above	7.00	9.00	20.00	200	—
1889Ga/Mo	—	3.50	5.00	25.00	200	—
1890Ga	—	4.00	7.50	20.00	200	—

KM# 391.4 CENTAVO
Copper **Obv:** Facing eagle, snake in beak **Rev:** Value and
date within wreath **Mint:** Guanajuato

Date	Mintage	F	VF	XF	Unc	BU
1874Go	—	20.00	40.00	80.00	250	—
1875Go	190,000	11.50	20.00	60.00	200	—
1876Go	—	125	200	350	750	—
1877Go Rare	—	—	—	—	—	—
1878Go	576,000	8.00	11.00	30.00	200	—
1880Go	890,000	6.00	10.00	25.00	200	—

KM# 391.5 CENTAVO
Copper **Obv:** Facing eagle, snake in beak **Obv. Inscription:**
REPUBLICA MEXICANA **Rev:** Value and date within wreath
Mint: Hermosillo

Date	Mintage	F	VF	XF	Unc	BU
1875Ho	3,500	450	—	—	—	—
1876Ho	8,508	50.00	100	225	500	—
1880Ho Short H, round O	102,000	7.50	15.00	50.00	200	—
1880Ho Tall H, oval O	Inc. above	7.50	15.00	50.00	200	—
1881Ho	459,000	5.00	10.00	50.00	200	—

KM# 391.7 CENTAVO
Copper **Obv:** Facing eagle, snake in beak **Obv. Legend:**
REPUBLICA MEXICANA **Rev:** Value and date within wreath
Mint: Oaxaca

Date	Mintage	F	VF	XF	Unc	BU
1872Oa	16,000	300	500	1,200	—	—
1873Oa	11,000	350	600	—	—	—
1874Oa	4,835	450	—	—	—	—
1875Oa	2,860	500	—	—	—	—

KM# 391.8 CENTAVO
Copper **Obv:** Facing eagle, snake in beak **Obv. Legend:**
REPUBLICA MEXICANA **Rev:** Value and date within wreath
Mint: San Luis Potosi

Date	Mintage	F	VF	XF	Unc	BU
1871Pi Rare	—	—	—	—	—	—
1877Pi	249,000	15.00	50.00	200	—	—
1878Pi	751,000	12.50	25.00	50.00	200	—
1878	—	—	—	—	—	—

Note: Pp error mintmark - rare

Date	Mintage	F	VF	XF	Unc	BU
1891Pi/Mo	—	10.00	50.00	150	300	—
1891Pi	—	8.00	25.00	125	250	—

KM# 391.9 CENTAVO
Copper **Obv:** Facing eagle, snake in beak **Rev:** Value and date within wreath **Mint:** Zacatecas **Note:** Struck at Zacatecas Mint, mint mark Zs.

Date	Mintage	F	VF	XF	Unc	BU
1872Zs	55,000	22.50	30.00	100	300	—
1873Zs	1,460,000	4.00	8.00	25.00	150	—
1874/3Zs	685,000	5.50	11.00	30.00	250	—
1874Zs	Inc. above	4.00	8.00	25.00	200	—
1875/4Zs	200,000	8.50	17.00	45.00	250	—
1875Zs	Inc. above	7.00	14.00	35.00	200	—
1876Zs	—	5.00	10.00	25.00	200	—
1877Zs	—	50.00	125	300	750	—
1878Zs	—	4.50	9.00	25.00	200	—
1880Zs	100,000	5.00	10.00	30.00	200	—
1881Zs	1,200,000	4.25	8.00	25.00	150	—

KM# 391.6 CENTAVO
7.4000 g., Copper **Obv:** Facing eagle, snake in beak **Obv. Legend:** REPUBLICA MEXICANA **Rev:** Value and date within wreath **Mint:** Mexico City **Note:** Varieties exist.

Date	Mintage	F	VF	XF	Unc	BU
1869Mo	1,874,000	7.50	25.00	60.00	200	—
1870/69Mo	1,200,000	10.00	25.00	60.00	225	—
1870Mo	Inc. above	8.00	20.00	50.00	200	—
1871Mo	918,000	8.00	15.00	40.00	200	—
1872/1Mo	1,625,000	6.50	10.00	30.00	200	—
1872Mo	Inc. above	6.00	9.00	25.00	200	—
1873Mo	1,605,000	4.00	7.50	20.00	200	—
1874/3Mo	1,700,000	5.00	7.00	15.00	100	—
1874Mo	Inc. above	3.00	5.50	15.00	100	—
1874Mo	Inc. above	5.00	10.00	25.00	200	—
1875Mo	1,495,000	6.00	8.00	30.00	100	—
1876Mo	1,600,000	3.00	5.50	12.50	100	—
1877Mo	1,270,000	3.00	5.50	13.50	100	—
1878/5Mo	1,900,000	7.50	11.00	22.50	125	—
1878/6Mo	Inc. above	7.50	11.00	22.50	125	—
1878/7Mo	Inc. above	7.50	11.00	20.00	125	—
1878Mo	Inc. above	6.00	9.00	13.50	100	—
1879/8Mo	1,505,000	4.50	6.50	13.50	100	—
1879Mo	Inc. above	3.00	5.50	12.50	75.00	—
1880/70Mo	1,130,000	5.50	7.50	15.00	100	—
1880/72Mo	Inc. above	20.00	50.00	100	250	—
1880/79Mo	Inc. above	15.00	35.00	75.00	175	—
1880Mo	Inc. above	4.25	6.00	12.50	75.00	—
1881Mo	1,060,000	4.50	7.00	15.00	75.00	—
1886Mo	12,687,000	1.50	2.00	10.00	40.00	—
1887Mo	7,292,000	1.50	2.00	10.00	35.00	—
1888/78Mo	9,984,000	2.50	3.00	10.00	30.00	—
1888/7Mo	Inc. above	2.50	3.00	10.00	30.00	—
1888Mo	Inc. above	1.50	2.00	10.00	30.00	—
1889Mo	19,970,000	2.00	3.00	10.00	30.00	—
1890/89Mo	18,726,000	2.50	3.00	12.00	40.00	—
1890/990Mo	Inc. above	2.50	3.00	12.00	40.00	—
1890Mo	Inc. above	1.50	2.00	10.00	30.00	—
1891Mo	14,544,000	1.50	2.00	10.00	30.00	—
1892Mo	12,908,000	1.50	2.00	10.00	30.00	—
1893/2Mo	5,078,000	2.50	3.00	12.00	35.00	—
1893Mo	Inc. above	1.50	2.00	10.00	30.00	—
1894/3Mo	1,896,000	3.00	6.00	15.00	50.00	—
1894Mo	Inc. above	2.00	3.00	12.00	35.00	—
1895/3Mo	3,453,000	3.00	4.50	12.50	35.00	—
1895/85Mo	Inc. above	3.00	6.00	15.00	50.00	—

Date	Mintage	F	VF	XF	Unc	BU
1895Mo	Inc. above	2.00	3.00	10.00	30.00	—
1896Mo	3,075,000	2.00	3.00	10.00	30.00	—
1897Mo	4,150,000	1.50	2.00	10.00	30.00	—

KM# 392 CENTAVO
Copper-Nickel **Obv:** Crossed bow and quiver above date **Obv. Legend:** REPUBLICA MEXICANA **Rev:** Value within wreath **Mint:** Mexico City

Date	Mintage	F	VF	XF	Unc	BU
1882Mo	99,955,000	7.50	12.50	17.50	35.00	—
1883Mo	Inc. above	0.50	0.75	1.00	1.50	—

KM# 393 CENTAVO
Copper **Obv:** Facing eagle, snake in beak **Obv. Legend:** REPUBLICA MEXICANA **Rev:** Value and date within wreath **Mint:** Mexico City **Note:** Varieties exist.

Date	Mintage	F	VF	XF	Unc	BU
1898Mo	1,529,000	4.00	6.00	15.00	50.00	—

KM# 394.1 CENTAVO
2.6100 g., Copper **Obv:** Facing eagle, snake in beak **Obv. Legend:** REPUBLICA MEXICANA **Rev:** Value below date within wreath **Mint:** Mexico City **Note:** Reduced size. Varieties exist.

Date	Mintage	F	VF	XF	Unc	BU
1899M	51,000	150	175	300	800	—
1900M Wide date	4,010,000	2.50	4.00	8.00	28.00	—
1900M Narrow date	Inc. above	2.50	4.00	8.00	28.00	—
1901M	1,494,000	3.00	8.00	17.50	50.00	—
1902/899M	2,090,000	30.00	60.00	125	225	—
1902M	Inc. above	2.25	4.00	10.00	40.00	—
1903M	8,400,000	1.50	3.00	7.00	20.00	—
1904/3M	10,250,000	1.50	10.00	20.00	55.00	—
1904M	Inc. above	1.50	3.00	8.00	25.00	—
1905M	3,643,000	2.25	4.00	10.00	40.00	—

KM# 394 CENTAVO
Copper **Obv:** National arms **Rev:** Value below date within wreath **Mint:** Culiacan **Note:** Reduced size. Varieties exist.

Date	Mintage	F	VF	XF	Unc	BU
1901C	220,000	15.00	22.50	35.00	65.00	—
1902C	320,000	15.00	22.50	50.00	90.00	—
1903C	536,000	7.50	12.50	20.00	50.00	—
1904/3C	148,000	35.00	50.00	75.00	125	—
1905C	110,000	100	150	300	600	—

KM# 395 2 CENTAVOS
Copper-Nickel **Obv:** Crossed bow and quiver above date
Obv. Legend: REPUBLICA MEXICANA **Rev:** Value within
wreath **Mint:** Mexico City

Date	Mintage	F	VF	XF	Unc	BU
1882	50,023,000	2.00	3.00	7.50	15.00	—
1883/2	Inc. above	2.00	3.00	7.50	15.00	—
1883	Inc. above	0.50	0.75	1.00	2.50	—

KM# 396.1 5 CENTAVOS
1.3530 g., 0.9030 Silver 0.0393 oz. ASW **Obv:** Facing eagle,
snake in beak **Rev:** Value within wreath **Mint:** San Luis Potosi

Date	Mintage	F	VF	XF	Unc	BU
1863SLP	—	37.50	135	350	1,200	—

KM# 397 5 CENTAVOS
1.3530 g., 0.9030 Silver 0.0393 oz. ASW **Obv:** Facing eagle,
snake in beak **Obv. Legend:** REPUBLICA MEXICANA **Rev:**
Radiant cap **Mint:** Mexico City **Note:** Varieties exist.

Date	Mintage	F	VF	XF	Unc	BU
1867Mo	—	20.00	45.00	110	400	—
1867/3Mo	—	22.50	50.00	125	425	—
1868/7Mo	—	22.50	50.00	150	500	—
1868Mo	—	18.50	42.50	100	400	—

KM# 397.1 5 CENTAVOS
1.3530 g., 0.9030 Silver 0.0393 oz. ASW **Obv:** Facing eagle,
snake in beak **Rev:** Radiant cap **Mint:** San Luis Potosi

Date	Mintage	F	VF	XF	Unc	BU
1868P	Inc. above	20.00	45.00	100	400	—
1868/7P	34,000	25.00	50.00	125	450	—
1869P	14,000	150	300	600	—	—

KM# 396 5 CENTAVOS
1.3530 g., 0.9030 Silver 0.0393 oz. ASW **Obv:** Facing eagle,
snake in beak **Obv. Legend:** REPUBLICA MEXICANA **Rev:**
Value within wreath **Mint:** Chihuahua

Date	Mintage	F	VF	XF	Unc	BU
1868Ca	—	40.00	65.00	125	450	—
1869Ca	30,000	25.00	40.00	100	400	—
1870/69Ca	—	35.00	55.00	120	425	—
1870Ca	35,000	30.00	50.00	100	400	—

KM# 398.7 5 CENTAVOS
1.3530 g., 0.9030 Silver 0.0393 oz. ASW **Obv:** Facing eagle,
snake in beak **Obv. Legend:** REPUBLICA MEXICANA **Rev:**
Value within 1/2 wreath **Mint:** Mexico City **Note:** Mint mark
Mo. Varieties exist.

Date	Mintage	F	VF	XF	Unc	BU
1869/8Mo C	40,000	8.00	15.00	40.00	120	—
1870Mo C	140,000	4.00	7.00	20.00	60.00	—
1871Mo C	103,000	9.00	20.00	40.00	100	—
1871Mo M	Inc. above	7.50	12.50	25.00	60.00	—
1872Mo M	266,000	5.00	8.00	20.00	55.00	—
1873Mo M	20,000	40.00	60.00	100	225	—
1874/69Mo M	—	7.50	15.00	30.00	75.00	—
1874Mo M	—	4.00	7.00	17.50	50.00	—
1874/3Mo B	—	5.00	8.00	22.50	55.00	—
1874Mo B	—	5.00	8.00	22.50	55.00	—

Date	Mintage	F	VF	XF	Unc	BU
1875Mo B	—	4.00	7.00	15.00	50.00	—
1875Mo B/M	—	6.00	9.00	17.50	60.00	—
1876/5Mo B	—	4.00	7.00	15.00	50.00	—
1876Mo B	—	4.00	7.00	12.50	50.00	—
1877/6Mo M	80,000	4.00	7.00	15.00	60.00	—
1877Mo M	Inc. above	4.00	7.00	12.50	60.00	—
1878/7Mo M	100,000	4.00	7.00	15.00	55.00	—
1878Mo M	Inc. above	2.50	5.00	12.50	45.00	—
1879/8Mo M	—	8.00	12.50	22.50	55.00	—
1879Mo M	—	4.50	7.00	15.00	50.00	—
1879Mo M 9/ inverted 9	—	10.00	15.00	25.00	75.00	—
1880/76Mo M/B	—	5.00	7.50	15.00	50.00	—
1880/76Mo M	—	5.00	7.50	15.00	50.00	—
1880Mo M	—	4.00	6.00	12.00	40.00	—
1881/0Mo M	180,000	4.00	6.00	10.00	35.00	—
1881Mo M	Inc. above	3.00	4.50	9.00	35.00	—
1886/0Mo M	398,000	2.00	2.75	7.50	25.00	—
1886/1Mo M	Inc. above	2.00	2.75	7.50	25.00	—
1886Mo M	Inc. above	1.75	2.25	6.00	20.00	—
1887Mo m	720,000	1.75	2.00	5.00	20.00	—
1887Mo M/m	Inc. above	1.75	2.00	6.00	20.00	—
1888/7Mo M	1,360,000	2.25	2.50	6.00	20.00	—
1888Mo M	Inc. above	1.75	2.00	5.00	20.00	—
1889/8Mo M	1,242,000	2.25	2.50	6.00	20.00	—
1889Mo M	Inc. above	1.75	2.00	5.00	20.00	—
1890/00Mo M	1,694,000	1.75	2.75	6.00	20.00	—
1890Mo M	Inc. above	1.50	2.00	5.00	20.00	—
1891Mo M	1,030,000	1.75	2.00	5.00	20.00	—
1892Mo M	1,400,000	1.75	2.00	5.00	20.00	—
1892Mo M 9/ inverted 9	Inc. above	2.00	2.75	7.50	20.00	—
1893Mo M	220,000	1.75	2.00	5.00	15.00	—
1894Mo M	320,000	1.75	2.00	5.00	15.00	—
1895Mo M	78,000	3.00	5.00	8.00	25.00	—
1896Mo B	80,000	1.75	5.00	20.00	—	—
1897Mo B	160,000	1.75	2.00	5.00	15.00	—

KM# 398.1 5 CENTAVOS
1.3530 g., 0.9030 Silver 0.0393 oz. ASW **Obv:** Facing eagle,
snake in beak **Rev:** Value within 1/2 wreath **Mint:** Chihuahua
Note: Mint mark: *Ca or Ch*.

Date	Mintage	F	VF	XF	Unc	BU
1871* M	14,000	20.00	40.00	100	250	—
1873* M Crude date	—	100	150	250	500	—
1874* M Crude date	—	25.00	50.00	75.00	150	—
1886* M	25,000	7.50	15.00	30.00	100	—
1887* M	37,000	7.50	15.00	30.00	100	—
1887* Ca/MoM	Inc. above	10.00	20.00	40.00	125	—
1888* M	145,000	1.50	3.00	6.00	25.00	—
1889* M	44,000	5.00	10.00	20.00	50.00	—
1890* M	102,000	1.50	3.00	6.00	25.00	—
1891* M	164,000	1.50	3.00	6.00	25.00	—
1892* M	85,000	1.50	3.00	6.00	25.00	—
1892* M/U	—	2.00	4.00	7.50	30.00	—
1892* M 9/inverted 9	Inc. above	2.00	4.00	7.50	30.00	—
1893* M	133,000	1.50	3.00	6.00	25.00	—
1894* M	108,000	1.50	3.00	6.00	25.00	—
1895* M	74,000	2.00	4.00	7.50	30.00	—

KM# 398 5 CENTAVOS
1.3530 g., 0.9030 Silver 0.0393 oz. ASW **Obv:** Facing eagle,
snake in beak **Rev:** Value within 1/2 wreath **Mint:** Alamos

Date	Mintage	F	VF	XF	Unc	BU
1874As DL	—	10.00	20.00	40.00	150	—
1875As DL	—	10.00	20.00	40.00	150	—
1876As L	—	22.00	45.00	70.00	160	—
1878As L	—	250	350	650	—	—

Note: Mule, gold peso reverse

1879As L	—	40.00	65.00	120	275	—

Note: Mule, gold peso obverse

1880As L	12,000	55.00	85.00	165	325	—

Note: Mule, gold peso obverse

1886As L	43,000	12.00	25.00	50.00	165	—
1886As L	Inc. above	55.00	85.00	165	300	—

Note: Mule, gold peso obverse

1887As L	20,000	25.00	50.00	75.00	165	—
1888As L	32,000	12.00	25.00	50.00	125	—
1889As L	16,000	50.00	75.00	100	200	—
1890As L	30,000	25.00	50.00	85.00	175	—
1891As L	8,000	65.00	125	200	400	—
1892As L	13,000	20.00	40.00	60.00	125	—

Date	Mintage	F	VF	XF	Unc	BU
1893As L	24,000	10.00	20.00	45.00	90.00	—
1895As L	20,000	10.00	20.00	45.00	90.00	—

KM# 398.2 5 CENTAVOS
1.3530 g., 0.9030 Silver 0.0393 oz. ASW **Obv:** Facing eagle, snake in beak **Rev:** Value within 1/2 wreath **Mint:** Culiacan

Date	Mintage	F	VF	XF	Unc	BU
1871Cn P	—	125	200	350	—	—
1873Cn P	4,992	50.00	100	200	400	—
1874Cn P	—	25.00	50.00	100	200	—
1875Cn P Rare	—	—	—	—	—	—
1876Cn P	—	25.00	50.00	100	200	—
1886Cn M	10,000	25.00	50.00	100	200	—
1887Cn M	10,000	25.00	50.00	100	200	—
1888Cn M	119,000	1.50	3.00	6.00	30.00	—
1889Cn M	66,000	4.00	7.50	15.00	50.00	—
189/80Cn M	—	2.00	4.00	8.00	40.00	—
1890Cn M	180,000	1.50	3.00	6.00	25.00	—
1890/9Cn M	—	2.00	4.00	8.00	40.00	—
1890Cn D Error	Inc. above	125	175	250	—	—
1891Cn M	87,000	2.00	4.00	7.50	25.00	—
1894Cn M	24,000	4.00	7.50	15.00	40.00	—
1896Cn M	16,000	7.50	12.50	25.00	75.00	—
1897Cn M	223,000	1.50	2.50	5.00	20.00	—

KM# 398.3 5 CENTAVOS
1.3530 g., 0.9030 Silver 0.0393 oz. ASW **Obv:** Facing eagle, snake in beak **Rev:** Value within 1/2 wreath **Mint:** Durango

Date	Mintage	F	VF	XF	Unc	BU
1874Do M	—	100	150	225	500	—
1877Do P	4,795	75.00	125	225	450	—
1878/7Do E/P	4,300	200	300	450	—	—
1879Do B	—	125	200	350	—	—
1880Do B Rare	—	—	—	—	—	—
1881Do P	3,020	300	500	800	—	—
1887Do C	42,000	5.00	8.00	17.50	60.00	—
1888/9Do C	91,000	6.00	10.00	20.00	70.00	—
1888Do C	Inc. above	4.00	7.50	15.00	55.00	—
1889Do C	49,000	3.50	6.00	12.50	50.00	—
1890Do C	136,000	4.00	7.50	15.00	55.00	—
1890Do P	Inc. above	5.00	8.00	17.50	60.00	—
1891/0Do P	48,000	3.50	6.00	12.50	50.00	—
1891Do P	Inc. above	3.00	5.00	10.00	45.00	—
1894Do D	38,000	3.50	6.00	12.50	50.00	—

KM# 398.4 5 CENTAVOS
1.3530 g., 0.9030 Silver 0.0393 oz. ASW **Obv:** Facing eagle, snake in beak **Rev:** Value within 1/2 wreath **Mint:** Guadalajara

Date	Mintage	F	VF	XF	Unc	BU
1877Ga A	—	15.00	30.00	60.00	150	—
1881Ga S	156,000	4.00	7.50	15.00	60.00	—
1886Ga S	87,000	2.00	4.00	7.50	25.00	—
1888Ga S Large G	262,000	2.00	4.00	10.00	30.00	—
1888Ga S Small G	Inc. above	2.00	4.00	10.00	30.00	—
1889Ga S	178,000	1.50	3.00	7.50	25.00	—
1890Ga S	68,000	4.00	7.50	12.50	35.00	—
1891Ga S	50,000	4.00	6.50	10.00	35.00	—
1892Ga S	78,000	2.00	4.00	7.50	25.00	—
1893Ga S	44,000	4.00	7.50	15.00	45.00	—

KM# 398.5 5 CENTAVOS
1.3530 g., 0.9030 Silver 0.0393 oz. ASW **Obv:** Facing eagle, snake in beak **Obv. Legend:** REPUBLICA MEXICANA **Rev:** Value within 1/2 wreath **Mint:** Guanajuato

Date	Mintage	F	VF	XF	Unc	BU
1869Go S	80,000	15.00	30.00	75.00	175	—
1871Go S	100,000	5.00	10.00	25.00	75.00	—
1872Go S	30,000	30.00	60.00	125	250	—
1873Go S	40,000	30.00	60.00	125	250	—
1874Go S	—	7.00	12.00	25.00	75.00	—
1875Go S	—	8.00	15.00	30.00	75.00	—
1876Go S	—	8.00	15.00	30.00	75.00	—
1877Go S	—	7.00	12.00	20.00	75.00	—
1878/7Go S	20,000	8.00	15.00	25.00	75.00	—
1879Go S	—	8.00	15.00	25.00	75.00	—
1880Go S	55,000	15.00	30.00	60.00	200	—

Date	Mintage	F	VF	XF	Unc	BU
1881/0Go S	160,000	5.00	8.00	17.50	60.00	—
1881Go S	Inc. above	4.00	6.00	12.00	45.00	—
1886Go R	230,000	1.50	3.00	6.00	30.00	—
1887Go R/S	—	1.50	3.00	6.00	30.00	—
1887Go R	230,000	1.50	2.50	5.00	30.00	—
1888Go R	320,000	1.50	2.50	5.00	20.00	—
1889Go R/S	—	4.00	6.00	12.00	45.00	—
1889Go R	60,000	4.00	6.00	12.00	45.00	—
1890/5Go R/S	—	1.50	3.00	6.00	30.00	—
1890Go R	250,000	1.50	2.50	5.00	20.00	—
1891/0Go R	168,000	1.80	3.00	6.00	30.00	—
1891Go R	Inc. above	1.50	2.50	5.00	20.00	—
1892Go R	138,000	1.50	3.00	6.00	25.00	—
1893Go R	200,000	1.25	2.50	5.00	20.00	—
1894Go R	200,000	1.25	2.50	5.00	20.00	—
1896Go R/S	—	1.50	3.00	6.00	25.00	—
1896Go R	525,000	1.25	2.00	4.00	15.00	—
1897Go R	596,000	1.50	2.00	4.00	15.00	—
1898Go R	—	—	—	—	—	—

KM# 398.6 5 CENTAVOS
1.3530 g., 0.9030 Silver 0.0393 oz. ASW **Obv:** Facing eagle, snake in beak **Rev:** Value within 1/2 wreath **Mint:** Hermosillo

Date	Mintage	F	VF	XF	Unc	BU
1874/69Ho R	—	125	225	350	—	—
1874Ho R	—	100	200	325	—	—
1878/7Ho A Rare	22,000	—	—	—	—	—
1878Ho A	Inc. above	20.00	40.00	80.00	175	—
1878Ho A	Inc. above	40.00	80.00	150	300	—
Note: Mule, gold peso obverse						
1880Ho A	43,000	7.50	15.00	30.00	75.00	—
1886Ho G	44,000	5.00	10.00	20.00	75.00	—
1887Ho G	20,000	5.00	10.00	20.00	75.00	—
1888Ho G	12,000	7.50	15.00	30.00	85.00	—
1889Ho G	67,000	3.00	6.00	12.50	40.00	—
1890Ho G	50,000	3.00	6.00	12.50	40.00	—
1891Ho G	46,000	3.00	6.00	12.50	40.00	—
1893Ho G	84,000	2.50	5.00	10.00	30.00	—
1894Ho G	68,000	2.00	4.00	10.00	30.00	—

KM# 398.9 5 CENTAVOS
1.3530 g., 0.9030 Silver 0.0393 oz. ASW **Obv:** Facing eagle, snake in beak **Rev:** Value within 1/2 wreath **Mint:** San Luis Potosi **Note:** Varieties exist.

Date	Mintage	F	VF	XF	Unc	BU
1869Pi S	—	300	400	500	—	—
1870Pi G/MoC Rare	20,000	150	250	400	—	—
1870Pi O	Inc. above	200	300	450	—	—
1871Pi O Rare	5,400	—	—	—	—	—
1872Pi O	—	75.00	100	175	400	—
1873Pi Rare	5,000	—	—	—	—	—
1874Pi H	—	30.00	50.00	100	225	—
1875Pi H	—	7.50	12.50	30.00	75.00	—
1876Pi H	—	10.00	20.00	45.00	100	—
1877Pi H	—	7.50	12.50	20.00	60.00	—
1878/7Pi H Rare	—	—	—	—	—	—
1878Pi H	—	60.00	90.00	150	300	—
1879 H	—	200	400	—	—	—
1880Pi H Rare	6,200	—	—	—	—	—
1881Pi H Rare	4,500	—	—	—	—	—
1886Pi R	33,000	12.50	25.00	50.00	125	—
1887/0Pi R	169,000	4.00	7.50	15.00	45.00	—
1887Pi R	Inc. above	3.00	5.00	10.00	32.00	—
1888Pi R	210,000	2.00	4.00	9.00	30.00	—
1889/7Pi R	197,000	2.50	5.00	10.00	32.00	—
1889Pi R	Inc. above	2.00	4.00	9.00	30.00	—
1890Pi R	221,000	2.00	3.00	6.00	25.00	—
1891/89Pi R/B	176,000	2.00	4.00	8.00	25.00	—
1891/0Pi R/B	—	2.00	4.00	8.00	25.00	—
1891Pi R	Inc. above	2.00	3.00	6.00	20.00	—
1892/89Pi R	182,000	2.00	4.00	8.00	25.00	—
1892/0Pi R	Inc. above	2.00	4.00	8.00	25.00	—
1892Pi R	Inc. above	2.00	3.00	6.00	20.00	—
1893Pi R	41,000	5.00	10.00	20.00	60.00	—

KM# 398.10 5 CENTAVOS
1.3530 g., 0.9030 Silver 0.0393 oz. ASW **Obv:** Facing eagle, snake in beak **Rev:** Value within 1/2 wreath **Mint:** Zacatecas

Date	Mintage	F	VF	XF	Unc	BU
1870Zs H	40,000	12.50	25.00	50.00	125	—
1871Zs H	40,000	12.50	25.00	50.00	125	—
1872Zs H	40,000	12.50	25.00	50.00	125	—
1873/2Zs H	20,000	35.00	65.00	125	275	—

Date	Mintage	F	VF	XF	Unc	BU
1873Zs H	Inc. above	25.00	50.00	100	250	—
1874Zs H	—	7.50	12.50	25.00	75.00	—
1874Zs A	—	40.00	75.00	150	300	—
1875Zs A	—	7.50	12.50	25.00	75.00	—
1876Zs A	—	50.00	75.00	150	500	—
1876/5Zs S	—	15.00	30.00	60.00	150	—
1876Zs S	—	12.50	25.00	50.00	125	—
1877Zs S	—	3.00	6.00	12.00	40.00	—
1878Zs S	60,000	3.00	6.00	12.00	40.00	—
1879/8Zs S	—	3.00	6.00	15.00	50.00	—
1879Zs S	—	3.00	6.00	12.00	40.00	—
1880/79Zs S	130,000	6.00	10.00	20.00	60.00	—
1880Zs S	Inc. above	5.00	8.00	16.00	45.00	—
1881Zs S	210,000	2.50	5.00	10.00	35.00	—
1886/4Zs S	360,000	6.00	10.00	20.00	60.00	—
1886Zs S	Inc. above	2.00	3.00	6.00	20.00	—
1886Zs Z	Inc. above	5.00	10.00	25.00	65.00	—
1887Zs Z	400,000	2.00	3.00	6.00	25.00	—
1888/7Zs Z	500,000	2.00	3.00	6.00	25.00	—
1888Zs Z	Inc. above	2.00	3.00	6.00	25.00	—
1889Zs Z	520,000	2.00	3.00	6.00	25.00	—
1889Zs Z 9/inverted 9	Inc. above	2.00	3.00	6.00	25.00	—
1889Zs Z/MoM	Inc. above	2.00	3.00	6.00	25.00	—
1890Zs Z	580,000	1.75	2.50	5.00	20.00	—
1890Zs Z/MoM	Inc. above	2.00	3.00	6.00	25.00	—
1890Zs ZsZ 9/8	—	2.00	3.00	6.00	25.00	—
1890Zs ZsZ 0/9 Z/M	—	2.00	3.00	6.00	25.00	—
1891Zs Z	420,000	1.75	2.50	5.00	20.00	—
1892Zs Z	346,000	1.75	2.50	5.00	20.00	—
1893Zs Z	258,000	1.75	2.50	5.00	20.00	—
1894Zs ZoZ Error	Inc. above	2.00	4.00	8.00	30.00	—
1894Zs Z	228,000	1.75	2.50	5.00	20.00	—
1895/4Zs ZsZ	—	2.00	3.00	6.00	25.00	—
1895Zs Z	260,000	1.75	2.50	5.00	20.00	—
1896Zs Z	200,000	1.75	2.50	5.00	20.00	—
1896Zs 6/inverted 6	Inc. above	2.00	3.00	6.00	25.00	—
1897/6Zs Z	200,000	2.00	3.00	6.00	25.00	—
1897Zs Z	Inc. above	1.75	2.50	5.00	20.00	—

KM# 398.8 5 CENTAVOS
1.3530 g., 0.9027 Silver 0.0393 oz. ASW **Obv:** Facing eagle, snake in beak **Obv. Legend:** REPUBLICA MEXICANA **Rev:** Value within 1/2 wreath **Mint:** Oaxaca

Date	Mintage	F	VF	XF	Unc	BU
18900a E Rare	48,000	—	—	—	—	—
18900a N	Inc. above	65.00	125	200	350	—

KM# 399 5 CENTAVOS
Copper-Nickel **Obv:** Crossed bow and quiver above date **Obv. Legend:** REPUBLICA MEXICANA **Rev:** Value within wreath **Mint:** Mexico City

Date	Mintage	F	VF	XF	Unc	BU
1882	Inc. above	0.50	1.00	2.50	7.50	—
1883	Inc. above	25.00	50.00	80.00	250	—

KM# 400.2 5 CENTAVOS
1.3530 g., 0.9027 Silver 0.0393 oz. ASW **Obv:** Facing eagle, snake in beak **Rev:** Value within 1/2 wreath **Mint:** Mexico City

Date	Mintage	F	VF	XF	Unc	BU
1898Mo M	80,000	2.00	4.00	7.00	25.00	—
1899Mo M	168,000	1.75	2.50	4.50	15.00	—
1900/800Mo M	300,000	4.50	6.50	10.00	30.00	—
1900Mo M	Inc. above	1.75	2.50	4.50	15.00	—
1901Mo M	100,000	1.75	2.50	4.50	15.00	17.50
1902Mo M	144,000	1.25	2.00	3.75	12.00	15.00

Date	Mintage	F	VF	XF	Unc	BU
1902/1Mo MoM	—	1.75	3.00	7.00	16.50	18.50
1903Mo M	500,000	1.25	2.00	3.75	12.00	15.00
1904/804Mo M	1,090,000	1.75	3.50	8.50	16.50	18.50
1904/94Mo M	Inc. above	1.75	3.75	9.00	16.50	18.50
1904Mo M	Inc. above	1.75	3.00	6.00	15.00	17.50
1905Mo M	344,000	1.75	3.00	7.00	16.50	18.50

KM# 400.3 5 CENTAVOS
1.3530 g., 0.9027 Silver 0.0393 oz. ASW **Obv:** Facing eagle, snake in beak **Rev:** Value within 1/2 wreath **Mint:** Zacatecas

Date	Mintage	F	VF	XF	Unc	BU
1898Zs Z	100,000	1.75	2.25	4.50	12.50	—
1899Zs Z	50,000	2.00	3.00	7.00	20.00	—
1900Zs Z	55,000	1.75	2.50	5.00	16.50	—
1901Zs Z	40,000	1.75	2.50	5.00	16.50	18.50
1902/1Zs Z	34,000	2.00	4.50	9.00	22.50	25.00
1902Zs Z	Inc. above	1.75	3.75	7.50	18.50	22.00
1903Zs Z	217,000	1.25	2.00	5.00	12.50	16.00
1904Zs Z	191,000	1.75	2.50	5.00	12.50	16.00
1904Zs M	Inc. above	1.75	2.50	6.00	16.50	18.50
1905Zs M	46,000	2.00	4.50	9.00	22.50	25.00
1905Zs M	Inc. above	—	—	—	—	—
Repullica; Rare						

KM# 400 5 CENTAVOS
1.3530 g., 0.9027 Silver 0.0393 oz. ASW, 14 mm. **Obv:** Facing eagle, snake in beak **Obv. Legend:** REPUBLICA MEXICANA **Rev:** Value within 1/2 wreath **Mint:** Culiacan **Note:** Varieties exist.

Date	Mintage	F	VF	XF	Unc	BU
1898Cn M	44,000	1.75	4.00	8.00	20.00	—
1899Cn M	111,000	5.50	8.50	20.00	50.00	—
1899Cn Q	Inc. above	1.75	2.50	4.50	15.00	—
1900/800Cn Q	239,000	3.50	5.00	12.50	30.00	—
1900Cn Q	Inc. above	1.75	3.00	6.00	16.50	—
Note: Round Q, single tail						
1900Cn Q	Inc. above	1.75	3.00	6.00	16.50	—
Note: Narrow Q, oval Q						
1900Cn Q	Inc. above	1.75	3.00	6.00	16.50	—
Note: Wide C, oval Q						
1901Cn Q	148,000	1.75	2.50	4.50	15.00	18.00
1902Cn Q	262,000	1.75	3.00	6.00	16.50	20.00
Note: Narrow C, heavy serifs						
1902Cn Q	Inc. above	1.75	3.00	6.00	16.50	20.00
Note: Wide C, light serifs						
1903/1Cn Q	331,000	2.00	3.00	6.00	16.50	20.00
1903Cn Q	Inc. above	1.75	2.50	4.50	15.00	18.00
1903/1898Cn V	Inc. above	3.50	4.50	9.00	22.50	23.00
1903Cn V	Inc. above	1.75	2.50	4.50	15.00	18.00
1904Cn H 0/9	—	1.75	2.50	5.00	16.50	20.00
1904Cn H	352,000	1.75	2.25	5.00	16.50	20.00
1904Cn H/C	—	1.75	2.50	5.00	16.50	20.00

KM# 400.1 5 CENTAVOS
1.3530 g., 0.9027 Silver 0.0393 oz. ASW **Obv:** Facing eagle, snake in beak **Rev:** Value within 1/2 wreath **Mint:** Guanajuato **Note:** Varieties exist.

Date	Mintage	F	VF	XF	Unc	BU
1898Go R	180,000	7.50	15.00	30.00	75.00	—
Note: Mule, gold peso obverse						
1899Go R	260,000	1.75	2.50	4.50	15.00	—
1900Go R	200,000	1.75	2.50	4.50	15.00	—

KM# 402 10 CENTAVOS
2.7070 g., 0.9030 Silver 0.0786 oz. ASW **Obv:** Facing eagle, snake in beak **Rev:** Radiant cap **Mint:** Mexico City

Date	Mintage	F	VF	XF	Unc	BU
1867/3Mo	—	50.00	100	200	550	—
1867Mo	—	20.00	50.00	150	450	—
1868/7Mo	—	20.00	50.00	175	500	—
1868Mo	—	20.00	55.00	175	500	—

KM# 402.1   10 CENTAVOS
2.7070 g., 0.9030 Silver 0.0786 oz. ASW **Obv:** Facing eagle, snake in beak **Obv. Legend:** REPUBLICA MEXICANA **Rev:** Radiant cap **Mint:** San Luis Potosi

Date	Mintage	F	VF	XF	Unc	BU
1868/7P	38,000	45.00	90.00	175	650	—
1868P	Inc. above	20.00	40.00	100	550	—
1869/7P	4,900	55.00	125	250	800	—

KM# 401.1   10 CENTAVOS
2.7070 g., 0.9030 Silver 0.0786 oz. ASW **Obv:** Facing eagle, snake in beak **Rev:** Value within wreath **Mint:** Chihuahua **Note:** Previous KM#401.

Date	Mintage	F	VF	XF	Unc	BU
1868/7Ca	—	30.00	60.00	150	550	—
1868Ca	—	30.00	60.00	150	550	—
1869Ca	15,000	25.00	50.00	125	600	—
1870Ca	17,000	22.50	45.00	100	550	—

KM# 401.2   10 CENTAVOS
2.7070 g., 0.9030 Silver 0.0786 oz. ASW **Obv:** Facing eagle, snake in beak **Obv. Legend:** REPUBLICA MEXICANA **Rev:** Value and date within wreath **Mint:** San Luis Potosi

Date	Mintage	F	VF	XF	Unc	BU
1863SLP	—	75.00	150	275	900	—

KM# 403   10 CENTAVOS
2.7070 g., 0.9030 Silver 0.0786 oz. ASW **Obv:** Facing eagle, snake in beak **Rev:** Value within 1/2 wreath **Mint:** Alamos **Note:** Varieties exist.

Date	Mintage	F	VF	XF	Unc	BU
1874As DL	—	20.00	40.00	80.00	175	—
1875As L	—	5.00	10.00	25.00	90.00	—
1876As L	—	10.00	18.00	40.00	110	—
1878/7As L	—	10.00	18.00	45.00	120	—
1878As L	—	5.00	10.00	30.00	100	—
1879As L	—	10.00	18.00	40.00	110	—
1880As L	13,000	10.00	18.00	40.00	110	—
1882As L	22,000	10.00	18.00	40.00	110	—
1883As L	8,520	25.00	50.00	100	225	—
1884As L	—	7.50	12.50	35.00	100	—
1885As L	15,000	7.50	12.50	35.00	100	—
1886As L	45,000	7.50	12.50	35.00	100	—
1887As L	15,000	7.50	12.50	35.00	100	—
1888As L	38,000	7.50	12.50	35.00	100	—
1889As L	20,000	7.50	12.50	35.00	100	—
1890As L	40,000	7.50	12.50	35.00	100	—
1891As L	38,000	7.50	12.50	35.00	100	—
1892As L	57,000	5.00	10.00	25.00	90.00	—
1893As L	70,000	10.00	18.00	40.00	110	—

Note: An 1891 As L over 1889 HoG exists which was evidently produced at the Alamos Mint using dies sent from the Hermosillo Mint

KM# 403.4   10 CENTAVOS
2.7070 g., 0.9030 Silver 0.0786 oz. ASW **Obv:** Facing eagle, snake in beak **Rev:** Value within 1/2 wreath **Mint:** Guadalajara **Note:** Varieties exist.

Date	Mintage	F	VF	XF	Unc	BU
1871Ga C	4,734	75.00	125	200	500	—
1873/1Ga C	25,000	10.00	15.00	35.00	150	—
1873Ga C	Inc. above	10.00	15.00	35.00	150	—
1874Ga C	—	10.00	15.00	35.00	150	—
1877Ga A	—	10.00	15.00	30.00	150	—
1881Ga S	115,000	5.00	10.00	25.00	150	—
1883Ga B	90,000	4.00	8.00	15.00	90.00	—
1884Ga H	—	3.00	5.00	10.00	90.00	—
1884Ga B	—	5.00	10.00	20.00	90.00	—
1884Ga B/S	—	6.00	12.50	25.00	90.00	—

Date	Mintage	F	VF	XF	Unc	BU
1885Ga H	93,000	3.00	5.00	10.00	90.00	—
1886Ga S	151,000	2.50	4.00	9.00	90.00	—
1887Ga S	162,000	1.50	3.00	6.00	90.00	—
1888Ga S	225,000	1.50	3.00	6.00	90.00	—
1888Ga GaS/HoG	Inc. above	1.50	3.00	6.00	90.00	—
1889Ga S	310,000	1.50	3.00	6.00	40.00	—
1890Ga S	303,000	1.50	3.00	6.00	40.00	—
1891Ga S	199,000	5.00	10.00	20.00	45.00	—
1892Ga S	329,000	1.50	3.00	6.00	40.00	—
1893Ga S	225,000	1.50	3.00	6.00	40.00	—
1894Ga S	243,000	3.00	6.00	12.00	40.00	—
1895Ga S	80,000	1.50	3.00	6.00	40.00	—

KM# 403.5   10 CENTAVOS
2.7070 g., 0.9030 Silver 0.0786 oz. ASW **Obv:** Facing eagle, snake in beak **Rev:** Value within 1/2 wreath **Mint:** Guanajuato **Note:** Varieties exist.

Date	Mintage	F	VF	XF	Unc	BU
1869Go S	7,000	20.00	40.00	80.00	200	—
1871/0Go S	60,000	15.00	25.00	50.00	125	—
1872Go S	60,000	15.00	25.00	50.00	125	—
1873Go S	50,000	15.00	25.00	50.00	125	—
1874Go S	—	15.00	25.00	50.00	125	—
1875Go S	—	250	350	500	800	—
1876Go S	—	10.00	20.00	40.00	100	—
1877Go S	—	80.00	120	190	400	—
1878/7Go S	10,000	10.00	20.00	45.00	110	—
1878Go S	Inc. above	7.50	12.00	20.00	75.00	—
1879Go S	—	7.50	12.00	20.00	75.00	—
1880Go S	—	100	200	300	450	—
1881/71Go S	100,000	3.00	5.00	10.00	75.00	—
1881/0Go S	Inc. above	3.50	5.00	10.00	75.00	—
1881Go S	Inc. above	3.00	5.00	10.00	75.00	—
1882/1Go S	40,000	3.00	6.00	12.00	75.00	—
1883Go B	—	3.00	5.00	10.00	75.00	—
1884Go B	—	1.50	3.00	6.00	75.00	—
1884Go S	—	6.00	12.50	25.00	90.00	—
1885Go R	100,000	1.50	3.00	6.00	75.00	—
1886Go R	95,000	3.00	5.00	10.00	75.00	—
1887Go R	330,000	2.50	5.00	10.00	75.00	—
1888Go R	270,000	1.50	3.00	6.00	75.00	—
1889Go R	205,000	2.00	4.00	8.00	75.00	—
1889Go GoR/HoG	Inc. above	3.00	5.00	10.00	75.00	—
1890Go R	270,000	1.50	3.00	6.00	35.00	—
1890Go GoR/Cn M	Inc. above	1.50	3.00	6.00	35.00	—
1891Go R/G	—	1.50	3.00	6.00	35.00	—
1891Go R	523,000	1.50	3.00	6.00	35.00	—
1891Go GoR/HoG	Inc. above	1.50	3.00	6.00	35.00	—
1892Go R	440,000	1.50	3.00	6.00	35.00	—
1893/1Go R	389,000	3.00	5.00	10.00	35.00	—
1893Go R	Inc. above	1.50	3.00	6.00	35.00	—
1894Go R	400,000	1.50	2.50	5.00	35.00	—
1895Go R	355,000	1.50	2.50	5.00	35.00	—
1896Go R	190,000	1.50	2.50	5.00	35.00	—
1897Go R	205,000	1.50	2.50	5.00	35.00	—

KM# 403.7   10 CENTAVOS
2.7070 g., 0.9020 Silver 0.0785 oz. ASW **Obv:** Facing eagle, snake in beak **Obv. Legend:** REPUBLICA MEXICANA **Rev:** Value within 1/2 wreath **Mint:** Mexico City **Note:** Varieties exist.

Date	Mintage	F	VF	XF	Unc	BU
1869/8Mo C	30,000	10.00	20.00	40.00	100	—
1869Mo C	Inc. above	8.00	17.50	35.00	90.00	—
1870Mo C	110,000	4.00	7.50	15.00	50.00	—
1871Mo C	84,000	50.00	75.00	125	250	—
1871Mo M	Inc. above	12.00	17.50	45.00	125	—
1872/69Mo M	198,000	10.00	20.00	35.00	100	—
1872Mo M	Inc. above	4.00	7.50	15.00	65.00	—
1873Mo M	40,000	10.00	15.00	30.00	75.00	—
1874Mo M	—	5.00	10.00	20.00	65.00	—
1874Mo M/C	—	5.00	10.00	20.00	65.00	—
1874/64Mo B	—	5.00	10.00	20.00	65.00	—

Date	Mintage	F	VF	XF	Unc	BU
1874Mo B/M	—	20.00	40.00	60.00	125	—
1874Mo B	—	5.00	10.00	15.00	65.00	—
1875Mo B	—	20.00	40.00	60.00	125	—
1876/5Mo B	—	4.00	6.00	10.00	65.00	—
1876/5Mo B/M	—	4.00	6.00	10.00	65.00	—
1877/6Mo M	—	4.00	6.00	10.00	65.00	—
1877/6Mo M/B	—	4.00	6.00	10.00	65.00	—
1877Mo M	—	4.00	6.00	10.00	65.00	—
1878/7Mo M	100,000	4.00	6.00	10.00	65.00	—
1878Mo M	Inc. above	4.00	6.00	10.00	65.00	—
1879/69Mo M	—	4.00	6.00	10.00	65.00	—
1879Mo M/C	—	4.00	6.00	10.00	65.00	—
1880/79Mo M	—	4.00	6.00	10.00	65.00	—
1881/0Mo M	510,000	4.00	6.00	10.00	35.00	—
1881Mo M	Inc. above	4.00	6.00	10.00	35.00	—
1882/1Mo M	550,000	4.00	6.00	10.00	35.00	—
1882Mo M	Inc. above	4.00	6.00	10.00	35.00	—
1883/2Mo M	250,000	4.00	6.00	10.00	35.00	—
1884Mo M	—	4.00	6.00	10.00	35.00	—
1885Mo M	470,000	4.00	6.00	10.00	35.00	—
1886Mo M	603,000	4.00	6.00	10.00	35.00	—
1887/6Mo M	—	4.00	6.00	10.00	35.00	—
1887Mo M	580,000	4.00	6.00	10.00	35.00	—
1888/7Mo MoM	710,000	4.00	6.00	10.00	35.00	—
1888Mo MoM	Inc. above	4.00	6.00	10.00	35.00	—
1888Mo MOM	Inc. above	4.00	6.00	10.00	35.00	—
1889/8Mo M	622,000	4.00	6.00	10.00	35.00	—
1889Mo M	Inc. above	4.00	6.00	10.00	35.00	—
1890/89Mo M	815,000	4.00	6.00	10.00	35.00	—
1890Mo M	Inc. above	4.00	6.00	10.00	35.00	—
1891Mo M	859,000	2.00	4.00	8.00	25.00	—
1892Mo M	1,030,000	2.00	4.00	8.00	25.00	—
1893Mo M	310,000	2.00	4.00	8.00	25.00	—
1893Mo M/C	Inc. above	2.00	4.00	8.00	25.00	—
1893Mo Mo/Ho M/G	—	2.00	4.00	8.00	25.00	—
1894/3Mo M	—	5.00	10.00	20.00	60.00	—
1894Mo M	350,000	5.00	10.00	20.00	60.00	—
1895Mo M	320,000	2.00	4.00	8.00	25.00	—
1896Mo B/G	340,000	2.00	4.00	8.00	25.00	—
1896Mo M	Inc. above	35.00	70.00	100	150	—
1897Mo M	170,000	2.00	4.00	6.00	20.00	—

KM# 403.9 10 CENTAVOS
2.7070 g., 0.9030 Silver 0.0786 oz. ASW **Obv:** Facing eagle, snake in beak **Rev:** Value within 1/2 wreath **Mint:** San Luis Potosi **Note:** Varieties exist.

Date	Mintage	F	VF	XF	Unc	BU
1869/8Pi S Rare	4,000	—	—	—	—	—
1870/69Pi O Rare	18,000	—	—	—	—	—
1870Pi G	Inc. above	125	200	325	600	—
1871Pi O	21,000	50.00	100	150	300	—
1872Pi O	16,000	150	225	350	650	—
1873Pi O Rare	4,750	—	—	—	—	—
1874Pi H	—	25.00	50.00	100	200	—
1875Pi H	—	75.00	125	200	400	—
1876Pi H	—	75.00	125	200	400	—
1877Pi H	—	75.00	125	200	400	—
1878Pi H	—	250	500	750	—	—
1879Pi H	—	—	—	—	—	—
1880Pi H	—	150	250	350	—	—
1881Pi H	7,600	250	350	500	—	—
1882Pi H Rare	4,000	—	—	—	—	—
1883Pi H	—	125	200	300	500	—
1884Pi H	—	25.00	50.00	100	200	—
1885Pi H	51,000	25.00	50.00	100	200	—
1885Pi C Rare	Inc. above	—	—	—	—	—
1886Pi C	52,000	15.00	30.00	60.00	150	—
1886Pi R	Inc. above	5.00	10.00	20.00	65.00	—
1887Pi R	118,000	3.00	6.00	12.00	50.00	—
1888Pi R	136,000	3.00	6.00	12.00	50.00	—
1889/8Pi R/G	—	7.50	12.50	20.00	60.00	—
1889/7Pi R	131,000	7.50	12.50	20.00	60.00	—
1890Pi R/G	—	2.50	5.00	10.00	40.00	—
1890Pi R	204,000	2.00	4.00	8.50	40.00	—
1891/89Pi R	163,000	3.00	6.00	12.00	40.00	—
1891Pi R	Inc. above	2.00	4.50	8.00	30.00	—
1892/0Pi R/G	—	2.50	5.00	10.00	40.00	—
1892/0Pi R	200,000	2.50	3.50	10.00	40.00	—
1892Pi R	Inc. above	2.00	2.50	5.00	40.00	—
1892Pi R/G	—	2.50	5.00	10.00	40.00	—
1893Pi R/G	—	2.00	10.00	17.50	60.00	—
1893Pi R	48,000	7.50	10.00	17.50	60.00	—

KM# 403.2 10 CENTAVOS
2.7070 g., 0.9030 Silver 0.0786 oz. ASW **Obv:** Facing eagle, snake in beak **Rev:** Value within 1/2 wreath **Mint:** Culiacan

Date	Mintage	F	VF	XF	Unc	BU
1871Cn P Rare	—	—	—	—	—	—
1873Cn P	8,732	20.00	50.00	100	225	—
1881Cn D	9,440	75.00	175	325	500	—
1882Cn D	12,000	75.00	125	200	400	—
1885Cn M	18,000	25.00	50.00	100	200	—
Note: Mule, gold 2-1/2 peso obverse						
1886Cn M	13,000	50.00	100	150	300	—
Note: Mule, gold 2-1/2 peso obverse						
1887Cn M	11,000	20.00	40.00	75.00	175	—
1888Cn M	56,000	5.00	10.00	25.00	125	—
1889Cn M	42,000	5.00	10.00	20.00	75.00	—
1890Cn M	132,000	2.50	5.00	9.50	75.00	—
1891Cn M	84,000	5.00	10.00	20.00	75.00	—
1892/1Cn M	37,000	4.00	8.00	15.00	75.00	—
1892Cn M	Inc. above	3.00	6.00	12.00	75.00	—
1894Cn M	43,000	3.00	6.00	12.00	75.00	—
1895Cn M	23,000	3.00	6.00	12.00	60.00	—
1896Cn M	121,000	2.00	3.50	7.00	50.00	—

KM# 403.3 10 CENTAVOS
2.7070 g., 0.9030 Silver 0.0786 oz. ASW **Obv:** Facing eagle, snake in beak **Rev:** Value within 1/2 wreath **Mint:** Durango

Date	Mintage	F	VF	XF	Unc	BU
1878Do E	2,500	100	175	300	600	—
1879Do B Rare	—	—	—	—	—	—
1880/70Do B Rare	—	—	—	—	—	—
1880/79Do B Rare	—	—	—	—	—	—
1884Do C	—	30.00	60.00	100	225	—
1886Do C	13,000	75.00	150	300	500	—
1887Do C	81,000	4.00	8.00	15.00	100	—
1888Do C	31,000	6.00	12.00	30.00	100	—
1889Do C	55,000	4.00	8.00	15.00	100	—
1890Do C	50,000	4.00	8.00	15.00	100	—
1891Do P	139,000	2.00	4.00	8.00	80.00	—
1892Do P	212,000	2.00	4.00	8.00	80.00	—
1892Do D	Inc. above	2.00	4.00	8.00	80.00	—
1893Do D	258,000	2.00	4.00	8.00	80.00	—
1893Do D/C	Inc. above	2.50	5.00	10.00	80.00	—
1894Do D	184,000	1.50	3.00	6.00	80.00	—
1894Do D/C	Inc. above	2.00	4.00	8.00	80.00	—
1895Do D	142,000	1.50	3.00	6.00	80.00	—

KM# 403.6 10 CENTAVOS
2.7070 g., 0.9030 Silver 0.0786 oz. ASW **Obv:** Facing eagle, snake in beak **Rev:** Value within 1/2 wreath **Mint:** Hermosillo

Date	Mintage	F	VF	XF	Unc	BU
1874Ho R	—	30.00	60.00	100	200	—
1876Ho F	3,140	200	300	450	750	—
1878Ho A	—	5.00	10.00	15.00	85.00	—
1879Ho A	—	25.00	50.00	90.00	175	—
1880Ho A	—	3.50	7.00	13.50	85.00	—
1881Ho A	28,000	4.00	8.00	17.00	85.00	—
1882/1Ho A	25,000	5.00	10.00	20.00	85.00	—
1882/1Ho a	Inc. above	6.00	12.50	25.00	85.00	—
1882Ho A	Inc. above	4.00	8.00	17.00	85.00	—
1883Ho	7,000	65.00	100	200	400	—
1884/3Ho M	—	10.00	20.00	40.00	90.00	—
1884Ho A	—	35.00	75.00	150	300	—
1884/3Ho M	—	7.50	15.00	30.00	85.00	—
1884Ho M	—	7.50	15.00	30.00	85.00	—
1885Ho M	21,000	12.50	25.00	50.00	100	—
1886Ho M Rare	10,000	—	—	—	—	—
1886Ho G	Inc. above	7.50	12.50	25.00	85.00	—
1887Ho G	—	25.00	50.00	75.00	150	—
1888Ho G	25,000	6.00	12.50	25.00	85.00	—
1889Ho G	42,000	3.50	7.00	12.00	85.00	—
1890Ho G	48,000	3.50	7.00	12.00	85.00	—
1891/80Ho G	136,000	3.50	7.00	12.00	85.00	—
1891/0Ho G	Inc. above	3.50	7.00	12.00	85.00	—
1891Ho G	Inc. above	3.50	7.00	12.00	85.00	—
1892Ho G	67,000	3.50	7.00	12.00	85.00	—
1893Ho G	67,000	3.50	7.00	12.00	85.00	—

KM# 403.8 10 CENTAVOS

2.7070 g., 0.9030 Silver 0.0786 oz. ASW **Obv:** Facing eagle, snake in beak **Rev:** Value within 1/2 wreath **Mint:** Oaxaca

Date	Mintage	F	VF	XF	Unc	BU
1889Oa E	21,000	200	400	600	—	—
1890Oa E	31,000	100	150	250	500	—
1890Oa N Rare	Inc. above	—	—	—	—	—

KM# 403.10 10 CENTAVOS

2.7070 g., 0.9030 Silver 0.0786 oz. ASW **Obv:** Facing eagle, snake in beak **Obv. Legend:** REPUBLICA MEXICANA **Rev:** Value within 1/2 wreath **Mint:** Zacatecas **Note:** Varieties exist.

Date	Mintage	F	VF	XF	Unc	BU
1870Zs H	20,000	100	150	200	400	—
1871/0Zs H	10,000	—	—	—	—	—
1871Zs H	Inc. above	—	—	—	—	—
1872Zs H	10,000	150	200	275	500	—
1873Zs H	10,000	250	350	600	—	—
1874/3Zs H	—	50.00	75.00	150	300	—
1874Zs A	—	200	300	500	—	—
1875Zs A	—	5.00	10.00	25.00	100	—
1876Zs S	—	100	200	300	500	—
1876Zs A	—	5.00	10.00	25.00	100	—
1877Zs S Small S	—	7.50	12.50	25.00	100	—
1877Zs Regular S over small S	—	7.50	12.50	25.00	100	—
1877Zs S Regular S	—	7.50	12.50	25.00	100	—
1878Zs S	Inc. above	5.00	10.00	20.00	80.00	—
1878/7Zs S	30,000	5.00	10.00	20.00	80.00	—
1879Zs S	—	5.00	10.00	20.00	80.00	—
1880Zs S	—	5.00	10.00	20.00	80.00	—
1881/0Zs S	120,000	3.50	7.00	12.50	50.00	—
1881Zs S	Inc. above	3.50	7.00	12.50	50.00	—
1882Zs S	Inc. above	12.50	25.00	50.00	125	—
1882/1Zs S	64,000	12.50	25.00	50.00	125	—
1883/73Zs S	102,000	2.50	5.00	10.00	50.00	—
1883Zs S	Inc. above	2.50	5.00	10.00	50.00	—
1884/3Zs S	—	2.50	5.00	10.00	50.00	—
1884Zs S	—	2.50	5.00	10.00	50.00	—
1885Zs S	297,000	2.00	3.50	7.00	50.00	—
1885Zs S Small S in mint mark	Inc. above	3.00	5.00	10.00	50.00	—
1885Zs Z	Inc. above	4.00	8.50	17.00	65.00	—

Note: Without assayers initials, error

Date	Mintage	F	VF	XF	Unc	BU
1886Zs Z	Inc. above	12.50	25.00	50.00	125	—
1886Zs S	274,000	2.00	3.50	7.00	30.00	—
1887Zs ZsZ	233,000	2.00	3.50	7.00	30.00	—
1887Zs Z Z Error	Inc. above	4.00	10.00	25.00	100	—
1888Zs Z Z Error	Inc. above	4.00	10.00	25.00	100	—
1888Zs ZsZ	270,000	2.00	3.50	7.00	30.00	—
1889/7Zs Z/S	240,000	4.50	8.00	12.50	40.00	—
1889Zs ZS	Inc. above	2.00	5.00	10.00	30.00	—
1889Zs Z/G	—	2.00	5.00	10.00	30.00	—
1889Zs Z	Inc. above	2.00	3.50	7.00	30.00	—
1890Zs Z Z Error	Inc. above	4.25	10.00	25.00	100	—
1890Zs ZsZ	410,000	2.00	3.50	7.00	30.00	—
1891Zs Z	1,105,000	2.00	3.50	7.00	30.00	—
1891Zs ZsZ Double s	Inc. above	2.50	5.00	9.00	30.00	—
1892Zs Z/G	—	2.50	5.00	9.00	30.00	—
1892Zs Z	1,102,000	2.00	3.50	7.00	30.00	—
1893/2Zs Z	—	2.50	5.00	10.00	40.00	—
1893Zs Z	1,010,999	2.00	3.50	7.00	25.00	—
1894Zs Z	892,000	2.00	3.50	7.00	30.00	—
1895Zs Z	920,000	2.00	3.50	7.00	30.00	—
1895Zs Z 9/5	—	2.50	5.00	10.00	30.00	—
1896/5Z S/O Z/G	—	2.50	5.00	10.00	30.00	—
1896/5Zs Z/G	—	2.00	3.50	7.00	30.00	—
1896Zs Z/G	—	2.00	3.50	7.00	30.00	—
1896/5Zs ZsZ	700,000	2.00	3.50	7.00	30.00	—
1896Zs ZsZ	Inc. above	2.00	3.50	7.00	30.00	—
1896Zs Z Z Error	Inc. above	4.25	10.00	25.00	100	—
1897Zs Z	Inc. above	2.00	3.50	7.00	30.00	—
1897/6Zs ZsZ	900,000	2.50	6.00	10.00	30.00	—
1897/6Zs Z Z Error	Inc. above	4.25	10.00	25.00	100	—

KM# 403.1 10 CENTAVOS

2.7070 g., 0.9030 Silver 0.0786 oz. ASW **Obv:** Facing eagle, snake in beak **Rev:** Value within 1/2 wreath **Mint:** Chihuahua **Note:** Mint mark CH, Ca. Varieties exist.

Date	Mintage	F	VF	XF	Unc	BU
1871 M	8,150	15.00	30.00	60.00	150	—
1873 M Crude date	—	35.00	75.00	125	175	—
1874 M	—	10.00	17.50	35.00	100	—
1880/70 G	7,620	20.00	40.00	60.00	175	—
1880 G/g	Inc. above	15.00	25.00	50.00	125	—
1881 Rare	340	—	—	—	—	—
1883 M	9,000	10.00	20.00	40.00	125	—
1884/73	—	5.00	30.00	60.00	150	—
1884 M	—	10.00	20.00	40.00	125	—
1886 M	45,000	7.50	12.50	30.00	100	—
1887/3 M/G	96,000	5.00	10.00	20.00	75.00	—
1887 M/G	—	2.50	5.00	10.00	75.00	—
1887 M	Inc. above	2.50	5.00	10.00	75.00	—
1888 M/G	—	2.50	5.00	10.00	75.00	—
1888 M	299,000	2.00	4.00	7.00	75.00	—
1888 Ca/Mo	Inc. above	2.00	4.00	7.00	75.00	—
1889 M	Inc. above	2.50	5.00	10.00	75.00	—

Note: Small 89 (5 Centavo font)

Date	Mintage	F	VF	XF	Unc	BU
1889/8 M	115,000	2.50	5.00	10.00	75.00	—
1890 M	Inc. above	2.00	4.00	9.00	75.00	—
1890/80 M	140,000	2.50	5.00	10.00	75.00	—
1890/89 M	Inc. above	2.50	5.00	10.00	75.00	—
1891 M	163,000	2.00	4.00	9.00	75.00	—
1892 M 9/ inverted 9	Inc. above	2.50	5.00	10.00	75.00	—
1892 M	169,000	2.00	4.00	9.00	75.00	—
1893 M	246,000	2.00	4.00	9.00	75.00	—
1894 M	163,000	2.00	4.00	9.00	75.00	—
1895 M	127,000	2.00	4.00	9.00	75.00	—

KM# 404 10 CENTAVOS

2.7070 g., 0.9030 Silver 0.0786 oz. ASW **Obv:** Facing eagle, snake in beak **Obv. Legend:** REPUBLICA MEXICANA **Rev:** Value within 1/2 wreath **Mint:** Culiacan **Note:** Varieties exist.

Date	Mintage	F	VF	XF	Unc	BU
1898Cn M	9,870	50.00	100	200	500	—
1899Cn Q Oval Q, double tail	Inc. above	5.00	7.50	25.00	100	—
1899Cn Q Round Q, single tail	80,000	5.00	7.50	25.00	100	—
1900Cn Q	160,000	1.75	2.50	5.00	20.00	—
1901Cn Q	235,000	1.75	2.50	5.00	18.00	20.00
1902Cn Q	186,000	1.75	2.50	5.00	20.00	22.00
1903Cn V	Inc. above	1.75	2.50	5.00	15.00	22.00
1903Cn Q	256,000	1.75	2.50	6.00	20.00	17.00
1904Cn H	307,000	1.75	2.50	5.00	15.00	17.00

KM# 404.1 10 CENTAVOS

2.7070 g., 0.9030 Silver 0.0786 oz. ASW **Obv:** Facing eagle, snake in beak **Rev:** Value within 1/2 wreath **Mint:** Guanajuato

Date	Mintage	F	VF	XF	Unc	BU
1898Go R	435,000	2.00	3.50	7.00	20.00	—
1899Go R	270,000	2.00	3.50	7.00	25.00	—
1900Go R	130,000	7.50	12.50	25.00	60.00	—

KM# 404.2 10 CENTAVOS

2.7070 g., 0.9030 Silver 0.0786 oz. ASW **Obv:** Facing eagle, snake in beak **Obv. Legend:** REPUBLICA MEXICANA **Rev:** Value within 1/2 wreath **Mint:** Mexico City

Date	Mintage	F	VF	XF	Unc	BU
1898Mo M	130,000	2.00	3.50	6.00	20.00	—
1899Mo M	190,000	2.00	3.50	6.00	20.00	—
1900Mo M	311,000	2.00	3.50	6.00	20.00	—
1901Mo M	80,000	2.50	3.50	7.00	22.50	25.00
1902Mo M	181,000	1.75	2.50	6.00	20.00	22.00
1903Mo M	581,000	1.75	2.50	6.00	20.00	22.00
1904Mo M	1,266,000	1.75	2.25	4.50	18.00	20.00
1904Mo MM (Error)	Inc. above	2.50	5.00	10.00	25.00	28.00
1905Mo M	266,000	2.00	3.75	7.50	20.00	22.00

KM# 404.3 10 CENTAVOS

2.7070 g., 0.9020 Silver 0.0785 oz. ASW **Obv:** Facing eagle, snake in beak **Rev:** Value within 1/2 wreath **Mint:** Zacatecas

Date	Mintage	F	VF	XF	Unc	BU
1898Zs Z	240,000	2.00	3.50	9.50	20.00	—
1899Zs Z	105,000	2.00	3.50	12.00	22.00	—
1900Zs Z	219,000	7.50	10.00	20.00	45.00	—
1901Zs Z	70,000	2.50	5.00	10.00	25.00	28.00
1902Zs Z	120,000	2.50	5.00	10.00	25.00	28.00
1903Zs Z	228,000	1.75	3.00	9.00	18.00	20.00
1904Zs Z	368,000	1.75	3.00	9.00	18.00	20.00
1904Zs M	Inc. above	1.75	3.00	9.00	22.00	25.00
1905Zs M	66,000	7.50	20.00	50.00	200	—

KM# 405 20 CENTAVOS

5.4150 g., 0.9030 Silver 0.1572 oz. ASW **Obv:** Facing eagle, snake in beak **Rev:** Value within 1/2 wreath **Mint:** Culiacan

Date	Mintage	F	VF	XF	Unc	BU
1898Cn M	114,000	5.00	12.50	35.00	140	—
1899Cn M	44,000	12.00	20.00	45.00	225	—
1899Cn Q	Inc. above	20.00	35.00	100	250	—
1900Cn Q	68,000	6.50	12.50	35.00	140	—
1901Cn Q	185,000	5.00	10.00	30.00	120	—
1902/802Cn Q	98,000	6.00	10.00	30.00	120	—
1902Cn Q	Inc. above	4.00	9.00	30.00	120	—
1903Cn Q	93,000	4.00	9.00	30.00	120	—
1904/3Cn H	258,000	—	—	—	—	—
1904Cn H	Inc. above	5.00	10.00	30.00	120	—

KM# 405.1 20 CENTAVOS

5.4150 g., 0.9027 Silver 0.1572 oz. ASW **Obv:** Facing eagle, snake in beak **Obv. Legend:** REPUBLICA MEXICANA **Rev:** Value within 1/2 wreath **Mint:** Guanajuato

Date	Mintage	F	VF	XF	Unc	BU
1898Go R	135,000	5.00	10.00	20.00	100	—
1899Go R	215,000	5.00	10.00	20.00	100	—
1900/800Go R	38,000	10.00	20.00	60.00	250	—

KM# 405.3 20 CENTAVOS

5.4150 g., 0.9027 Silver 0.1572 oz. ASW **Obv:** Facing eagle, snake in beak **Obv. Legend:** REPUBLICA MEXICANA **Rev:** Value within 1/2 wreath **Mint:** Zacatecas

Date	Mintage	F	VF	XF	Unc	BU
1898Zs Z	195,000	6.00	12.00	25.00	100	—
1899Zs Z	210,000	6.00	12.00	25.00	100	—
1900/800Zs Z	97,000	6.00	12.00	45.00	200	—
1901Zs Z	Inc. above	5.00	10.00	20.00	100	—
1901/0Zs Z	130,000	25.00	50.00	100	250	—
1902Zs Z	105,000	5.00	10.00	20.00	100	—
1903Zs Z	143,000	5.00	10.00	20.00	100	—
1904Zs Z	246,000	5.00	10.00	20.00	100	—
1904Zs M	Inc. above	5.00	10.00	50.00	300	—
1905Zs M	59,000	10.00	70.00	50.00	400	—

KM# 405.2 20 CENTAVOS

5.4150 g., 0.9030 Silver 0.1572 oz. ASW **Obv:** Facing eagle, snake in beak **Rev:** Value within 1/2 wreath **Mint:** Mexico City **Note:** Varieties exist.

Date	Mintage	F	VF	XF	Unc	BU
1898Mo M	150,000	5.00	10.00	20.00	125	—
1899Mo M	425,000	5.00	10.00	20.00	125	—
1900/800Mo M	295,000	5.00	10.00	20.00	125	—
1901Mo M	110,000	4.00	8.00	20.00	90.00	—
1902Mo M	120,000	4.00	8.00	20.00	90.00	—
1903Mo M	213,000	4.00	8.00	20.00	90.00	—
1904Mo M	276,000	4.00	8.00	20.00	90.00	—
1905Mo M	117,000	6.50	20.00	50.00	150	—

KM# 406.2 25 CENTAVOS

6.7680 g., 0.9030 Silver 0.1965 oz. ASW **Obv:** Facing eagle, snake in beak **Rev:** Radiant cap above scales **Mint:** Culiacan

Date	Mintage	F	VF	XF	Unc	BU
1871Cn P	—	250	500	750	—	—
1872Cn P	2,780	300	550	800	—	—
1873Cn P	20,000	100	150	250	500	—
1874Cn P	—	20.00	50.00	125	250	—
1875Cn P	—	250	500	750	—	—
1876Cn P Rare	—	—	—	—	—	—
1878/7Cn D/S	—	100	150	250	500	—
1878Cn Cn/Go D/S	—	100	150	250	500	—
1878Cn D	—	100	150	250	500	—
1879Cn D	—	15.00	35.00	70.00	175	—
1880Cn D	—	250	500	750	—	—
1881/0Cn D	18,000	15.00	30.00	60.00	175	—
1882Cn D	—	200	350	600	—	—
1882Cn M Rare	—	—	—	—	—	—
1883Cn M	15,000	50.00	100	150	300	—
1884Cn M	—	20.00	40.00	80.00	175	—
1885/4Cn M	19,000	20.00	40.00	80.00	175	—
1886Cn M	22,000	12.50	20.00	50.00	175	—
1887Cn M	32,000	12.50	20.00	50.00	175	—
1888Cn M Cn/Mo	—	—	—	—	—	—
1888Cn M	86,000	8.00	15.00	30.00	175	—
1889Cn M	50,000	10.00	25.00	50.00	175	—
1890Cn M 9/8	—	9.00	17.50	40.00	175	—
1890Cn M	91,000	9.00	17.50	40.00	175	—
1892/0Cn M	16,000	20.00	40.00	80.00	200	—
1892Cn M	Inc. above	20.00	40.00	80.00	200	—

KM# 406.3 25 CENTAVOS

6.7680 g., 0.9030 Silver 0.1965 oz. ASW **Obv:** Facing eagle, snake in beak **Rev:** Radiant cap above scales **Mint:** Durango

Date	Mintage	F	VF	XF	Unc	BU
1873Do P Rare	892	—	—	—	—	—
1877Do P	—	25.00	50.00	100	200	—
1878/7Do E	—	250	500	750	—	—
1878Do B Rare	—	—	—	—	—	—
1879Do B	—	50.00	75.00	125	250	—
1880Do B Rare	—	—	—	—	—	—
1882Do C	17,000	25.00	50.00	100	225	—
1884/3Do C	—	25.00	50.00	100	200	—
1885Do C/S	—	20.00	40.00	80.00	200	—
1885Do C	15,000	20.00	40.00	80.00	200	—
1886Do C	33,000	15.00	30.00	60.00	200	—
1887Do C	27,000	10.00	20.00	50.00	200	—
1888Do C	25,000	10.00	20.00	50.00	200	—
1889Do C	29,000	10.00	20.00	50.00	200	—
1890Do C	68,000	8.00	15.00	40.00	200	—

KM# 406.4 25 CENTAVOS

6.7680 g., 0.9030 Silver 0.1965 oz. ASW **Obv:** Facing eagle, snake in beak **Rev:** Radiant cap above scales **Mint:** Guadalajara

Date	Mintage	F	VF	XF	Unc	BU
1880Ga A	38,000	25.00	50.00	100	200	—
1881/0Ga S	39,000	25.00	50.00	100	200	—
1881Ga S	Inc. above	25.00	50.00	100	200	—
1882Ga S	18,000	25.00	50.00	100	200	—
1883/2Ga B/S	—	50.00	100	150	300	—
1884Ga B	—	20.00	40.00	80.00	150	—
1889Ga S	30,000	20.00	40.00	80.00	150	—

KM# 406 25 CENTAVOS

6.7680 g., 0.9030 Silver 0.1965 oz. ASW **Obv:** Facing eagle, snake in beak **Rev:** Radiant cap above scales **Mint:** Alamos **Note:** Mint mark A, As.

Date	Mintage	F	VF	XF	Unc	BU
1874 L	—	20.00	40.00	90.00	200	—

Date	Mintage	F	VF	XF	Unc	BU
1875 L	—	15.00	30.00	70.00	200	—
1876 L	—	30.00	50.00	100	200	—
1877 L	11,000	200	300	500	—	—
1877.	Inc. above	10.00	25.00	60.00	200	—
1878 L	25,000	10.00	25.00	60.00	200	—
1879 L	—	10.00	25.00	60.00	200	—
1880 L	—	10.00	25.00	60.00	200	—
1880. L	—	10.00	25.00	60.00	200	—
1881 L	8,800	500	700	—	—	—
1882 L	7,777	15.00	35.00	80.00	200	—
1883 L	28,000	10.00	25.00	60.00	200	—
1884 L	—	10.00	25.00	60.00	200	—
1885 L	—	20.00	40.00	90.00	200	—
1886 L	46,000	15.00	30.00	70.00	200	—
1887 L	12,000	12.50	27.50	65.00	200	—
1888 L	20,000	12.50	27.50	65.00	200	—
1889 L	14,000	12.50	27.50	65.00	200	—
1890 L	23,000	10.00	25.00	60.00	200	—

KM# 406.1 25 CENTAVOS
6.7680 g., 0.9030 Silver 0.1965 oz. ASW **Obv:** Facing eagle, snake in beak **Rev:** Radiant cap above scales **Mint:** Chihuahua **Note:** Mint mark CA, CH, Ca.

Date	Mintage	F	VF	XF	Unc	BU
1871 M	18,000	25.00	50.00	100	200	—
1872 M Very crude date	24,000	50.00	100	150	300	—
1883 M	12,000	10.00	25.00	50.00	175	—
1885/3 M	35,000	10.00	25.00	50.00	175	—
1885 M	Inc. above	10.00	25.00	50.00	175	—
1886 M	22,000	10.00	25.00	50.00	175	—
1887/6 M	26,000	10.00	15.00	30.00	175	—
1887 M	Inc. above	10.00	15.00	30.00	175	—
1888 M	14,000	10.00	25.00	50.00	175	—
1889 M	50,000	10.00	15.00	30.00	175	—

KM# 406.5 25 CENTAVOS
6.7680 g., 0.9030 Silver 0.1965 oz. ASW **Obv:** Facing eagle, snake in beak **Rev:** Radiant cap above scales **Mint:** Guanajuato **Note:** Varieties exist.

Date	Mintage	F	VF	XF	Unc	BU
1870Go S	128,000	10.00	20.00	50.00	125	—
1871Go S	172,000	10.00	20.00	50.00	125	—
1872/1Go S	178,000	10.00	20.00	50.00	125	—
1872Go S	Inc. above	10.00	20.00	50.00	125	—
1873Go S	120,000	10.00	20.00	50.00	125	—
1874Go S	—	15.00	30.00	60.00	150	—
1875/4Go S	—	15.00	30.00	60.00	150	—
1875Go S	—	10.00	20.00	50.00	125	—
1876Go S	—	20.00	40.00	80.00	175	—
1877Go S	124,000	10.00	20.00	50.00	125	—
1878Go S	146,000	10.00	20.00	50.00	125	—
1879Go S	—	10.00	20.00	50.00	125	—
1880Go S	—	20.00	40.00	80.00	175	—
1881Go S	408,000	9.00	17.50	45.00	125	—
1882Go S	204,000	9.00	17.50	45.00	125	—
1883Go B	168,000	9.00	17.50	45.00	125	—
1884/69Go B	—	9.00	17.50	45.00	125	—
1884/3Go B	—	9.00	17.50	45.00	125	—
1884/3Go B/R	—	9.00	17.50	45.00	125	—
1884Go B	—	9.00	17.50	45.00	125	—
1885/65Go R	300,000	9.00	17.50	45.00	125	—
1885/69Go R	Inc. above	9.00	17.50	45.00	125	—
1885Go R	Inc. above	9.00	17.50	45.00	125	—
1886/65Go R	—	9.00	17.50	45.00	125	—
1886/66Go R	322,000	9.00	17.50	45.00	125	—
1886/69Go R/S	Inc. above	9.00	17.50	45.00	125	—
1886/5/69Go R	Inc. above	9.00	15.00	45.00	125	—
1887Go R	254,000	9.00	15.00	45.00	125	—
1887Go/Cn R/D	Inc. above	9.00	15.00	45.00	125	—
1888Go R	312,000	8.00	15.00	45.00	125	—
1889/8Go R RS inverted B	—	—	—	—	—	—
1889/8Go R	304,000	8.00	15.00	45.00	125	—
1889/8Go/Cn R/D	Inc. above	8.00	15.00	45.00	125	—
1889Go R	Inc. above	8.00	15.00	45.00	125	—
1890Go R	236,000	8.00	15.00	45.00	125	—

KM# 406.6 25 CENTAVOS
6.7680 g., 0.9030 Silver 0.1965 oz. ASW **Obv:** Facing eagle, snake in beak **Rev:** Radiant cap above scales **Mint:** Hermosillo **Note:** Varieties exist.

Date	Mintage	F	VF	XF	Unc	BU
1874/64Ho R	Inc. above	10.00	20.00	40.00	125	—
1874/69Ho R	—	10.00	20.00	40.00	125	—
1874Ho R	23,000	10.00	20.00	40.00	125	—
1875Ho R Rare	—	—	—	—	—	—
1876/4Ho F/R	34,000	10.00	20.00	50.00	150	—
1876Ho F/R	Inc. above	10.00	25.00	60.00	150	—
1876Ho F	Inc. above	10.00	25.00	55.00	135	—
1877Ho F	—	10.00	20.00	50.00	125	—
1878Ho A	23,000	10.00	20.00	50.00	125	—
1879Ho A	—	10.00	20.00	50.00	125	—
1880Ho A	—	15.00	30.00	60.00	125	—
1881Ho A	19,000	15.00	30.00	60.00	125	—
1882Ho A	8,120	20.00	40.00	80.00	150	—
1883Ho M	2,000	100	200	300	600	—
1884Ho M	—	12.50	25.00	50.00	150	—
1885Ho M	—	10.00	20.00	50.00	125	—
1886Ho G	6,400	30.00	60.00	125	250	—
1887Ho G	12,000	10.00	20.00	40.00	125	—
1888Ho G	20,000	10.00	20.00	40.00	125	—
1889Ho G	28,000	10.00	20.00	40.00	125	—
1890/80Ho G	18,000	25.00	50.00	100	125	—
1890Ho G	Inc. above	25.00	50.00	100	125	—

KM# 406.7 25 CENTAVOS
6.7680 g., 0.9027 Silver 0.1964 oz. ASW **Obv:** Facing eagle, snake in beak **Obv. Legend:** REPUBLICA MEXICANA **Rev:** Radiant cap above scales **Mint:** Mexico City **Note:** Varieties exist.

Date	Mintage	F	VF	XF	Unc	BU
1869Mo C	76,000	10.00	25.00	50.00	125	—
1870/69Mo C	—	6.50	12.00	30.00	125	—
1870/9Mo C	136,000	6.50	12.00	30.00	125	—
1870Mo C	Inc. above	6.50	12.00	30.00	125	—
1871Mo M	138,000	6.50	12.00	30.00	125	—
1872Mo M	220,000	6.50	12.00	30.00	125	—
1873/1Mo M	48,000	10.00	25.00	50.00	125	—
1873Mo M	Inc. above	10.00	25.00	50.00	125	—
1874/69Mo B/M	—	10.00	25.00	50.00	125	—
1874/3Mo M	—	10.00	25.00	50.00	125	—
1874/3Mo B	—	10.00	25.00	50.00	125	—
1874/3Mo B/M	—	10.00	25.00	50.00	125	—
1874Mo M	—	6.50	12.00	30.00	125	—
1874Mo B/M	—	10.00	25.00	50.00	125	—
1875Mo B	—	6.50	12.00	30.00	125	—
1876/5Mo B	—	8.00	15.00	40.00	125	—
1876Mo B	—	6.50	12.00	30.00	125	—
1877Mo M	56,000	10.00	25.00	50.00	125	—
1878/1Mo M	120,000	10.00	25.00	50.00	125	—
1878/7Mo M	Inc. above	10.00	25.00	50.00	125	—
1878Mo M	Inc. above	6.50	12.00	30.00	125	—
1879Mo M	—	10.00	20.00	40.00	125	—
1880Mo M	—	8.00	15.00	35.00	125	—
1881/0Mo M	300,000	10.00	25.00	50.00	125	—
1881Mo M	Inc. above	10.00	25.00	50.00	125	—
1882Mo M	212,000	8.00	15.00	35.00	125	—
1883Mo M	108,000	8.00	15.00	35.00	125	—
1884/3Mo M	—	10.00	25.00	50.00	125	—
1884Mo M	—	10.00	20.00	40.00	125	—
1885Mo M	216,000	10.00	20.00	40.00	125	—
1886/5Mo M	436,000	8.00	15.00	35.00	125	—
1886Mo M	Inc. above	8.00	15.00	35.00	125	—
1887Mo M	376,000	8.00	15.00	35.00	125	—
1888Mo M	192,000	8.00	15.00	35.00	125	—
1889Mo M	132,000	8.00	15.00	35.00	125	—
1890Mo M	60,000	10.00	20.00	40.00	125	—

KM# 406.8 25 CENTAVOS
6.7680 g., 0.9030 Silver 0.1965 oz. ASW **Obv:** Facing eagle, snake in beak **Rev:** Radiant cap above scales **Mint:** San Luis Potosi **Note:** Varieties exist.

Date	Mintage	F	VF	XF	Unc	BU
1869Pi S	—	25.00	75.00	150	300	—
1870Pi G	50,000	10.00	30.00	75.00	150	—
1870Pi O	Inc. above	15.00	35.00	85.00	175	—
1871Pi O	30,000	10.00	30.00	75.00	150	—
1872Pi O	46,000	10.00	30.00	75.00	150	—
1873Pi O	13,000	15.00	40.00	90.00	175	—
1874Pi H	—	15.00	40.00	90.00	200	—
1875Pi H	—	10.00	20.00	60.00	150	—
1876/5Pi H	—	15.00	30.00	80.00	175	—
1876Pi H	—	10.00	25.00	65.00	150	—
1877Pi H	19,000	10.00	25.00	65.00	150	—
1878Pi H	—	15.00	30.00	60.00	150	—
1879/8Pi H	—	10.00	25.00	60.00	150	—
1879Pi H	—	10.00	25.00	60.00	150	—
1879Pi E	—	100	200	300	600	—
1880Pi H/M	—	20.00	40.00	100	200	—
1880Pi H	—	20.00	40.00	100	200	—
1881Pi H	50,000	20.00	40.00	80.00	175	—
1881Pi E Rare	Inc. above	—	—	—	—	—
1882Pi H	20,000	10.00	20.00	60.00	150	—
1883Pi H	17,000	10.00	25.00	65.00	150	—
1884Pi H	—	10.00	25.00	65.00	150	—
1885/4Pi H	—	10.00	20.00	60.00	150	—
1885Pi H	43,000	10.00	20.00	60.00	150	—
1886Pi C	78,000	10.00	25.00	65.00	150	—
1886Pi R	Inc. above	9.00	20.00	50.00	150	—
1886Pi R 6/ inverted 6	Inc. above	9.00	20.00	50.00	150	—
1887Pi/ZsR	92,000	9.00	20.00	50.00	150	—
1887Pi/ZsB	Inc. above	100	150	300	500	—
1887Pi R	—	9.00	20.00	50.00	150	—
1888Pi R	106,000	9.00	20.00	50.00	150	—
1888Pi/ZsR	Inc. above	10.00	20.00	50.00	150	—
1888Pi R/B	Inc. above	10.00	20.00	50.00	150	—
1889Pi R	115,000	8.00	15.00	40.00	150	—
1889Pi/ZsR	Inc. above	10.00	20.00	50.00	150	—
1889Pi R/B	Inc. above	10.00	20.00	50.00	150	—
1890Pi R	64,000	10.00	20.00	50.00	150	—
1890Pi/ZsR/B	Inc. above	8.00	15.00	40.00	150	—
1890Pi R/B	Inc. above	10.00	20.00	50.00	150	—

KM# 406.9 25 CENTAVOS
6.7680 g., 0.9030 Silver 0.1965 oz. ASW **Obv:** Facing eagle, snake in beak **Rev:** Radiant cap above scales **Mint:** Zacatecas **Note:** Varieties exist.

Date	Mintage	F	VF	XF	Unc	BU
1870Zs H	152,000	8.00	15.00	50.00	125	—
1871Zs H	250,000	8.00	15.00	50.00	125	—
1872Zs H	260,000	8.00	15.00	50.00	125	—
1872Zs/Cn H	—	—	—	—	—	—
1872Zs H	—	—	—	—	—	—
1873Zs H	132,000	8.00	15.00	50.00	125	—
1874Zs H	—	10.00	20.00	60.00	125	—
1874Zs A	—	10.00	20.00	60.00	125	—
1875Zs A	—	9.00	20.00	60.00	125	—
1876Zs A	—	8.00	15.00	50.00	125	—
1876Zs S	—	8.00	15.00	50.00	125	—
1877Zs S	350,000	8.00	15.00	50.00	125	—
1878/7Zs S	—	9.00	20.00	60.00	125	—
1878Zs S	252,000	8.00	15.00	50.00	125	—
1878/1Zs S	—	9.00	20.00	60.00	125	—
1879Zs S	—	8.00	15.00	50.00	125	—
1880Zs S	—	8.00	15.00	50.00	125	—
1881/0Zs S	570,000	8.00	15.00	50.00	125	—
1881Zs S	Inc. above	8.00	15.00	50.00	125	—
1882/1Zs S	300,000	10.00	17.50	55.00	125	—
1882Zs S	Inc. above	8.00	15.00	50.00	125	—
1883/2Zs S	193,000	10.00	17.50	55.00	125	—
1883Zs S	Inc. above	8.00	15.00	50.00	125	—
1884/3Zs S	—	10.00	17.50	55.00	125	—
1884Zs S	—	8.00	15.00	50.00	125	—
1885Zs S	309,000	8.00	15.00	50.00	125	—
1886/2Zs S	—	10.00	17.50	55.00	125	—
1886/5Zs S	613,000	8.00	15.00	50.00	125	—
1886Zs S	Inc. above	8.00	15.00	50.00	125	—
1886Zs Z	Inc. above	8.00	15.00	55.00	125	—
1887Zs Z	389,000	8.00	15.00	50.00	125	—

Date	Mintage	F	VF	XF	Unc	BU
1888Zs Z	408,000	8.00	15.00	50.00	125	—
1889Zs Z	400,000	8.00	15.00	50.00	125	—
1890Zs Z	269,000	8.00	15.00	50.00	125	—

KM# 407.7 50 CENTAVOS
13.5360 g., 0.9030 Silver 0.3930 oz. ASW **Obv:** Facing eagle, snake in beak **Rev:** Radiant cap above scales **Mint:** San Luis Potosi

Date	Mintage	F	VF	XF	Unc	BU
1870Pi G	Inc. above	20.00	40.00	100	450	—
1870/780Pi G	50,000	25.00	45.00	110	500	—
1870Pi O	Inc. above	20.00	40.00	100	450	—
1871Pi O	—	15.00	30.00	80.00	400	—
1871Pi O/G	64,000	15.00	30.00	80.00	400	—
1872Pi O	52,000	15.00	30.00	80.00	400	—
1872Pi O/G	Inc. above	15.00	30.00	80.00	400	—
1873Pi O	32,000	20.00	40.00	100	450	—
1873Pi H	Inc. above	25.00	50.00	125	550	—
1874Pi H/O	—	15.00	30.00	80.00	400	—
1875/3Pi H	—	15.00	30.00	80.00	400	—
1875Pi H	—	15.00	30.00	80.00	400	—
1876Pi H	—	30.00	60.00	150	700	—
1877Pi H	34,000	20.00	40.00	100	450	—
1878Pi H	9,700	20.00	40.00	100	450	—
1879Pi H	—	15.00	35.00	90.00	400	—
1879/7Pi H	—	15.00	35.00	90.00	400	—
1880Pi H	—	20.00	40.00	100	450	—
1881Pi H	28,000	20.00	40.00	100	450	—
1882Pi H	22,000	15.00	30.00	80.00	400	—
1883Pi H 8/8	29,000	50.00	100	200	750	—
1883Pi H	Inc. above	15.00	30.00	80.00	400	—
1884Pi H	—	50.00	100	175	600	—
1885/3Pi H	—	20.00	40.00	100	450	—
1885/0Pi H	45,000	20.00	40.00	100	450	—
1885/4Pi H	Inc. above	20.00	40.00	100	450	—
1885Pi H	Inc. above	25.00	50.00	125	450	—
1885Pi C	Inc. above	15.00	30.00	80.00	400	—
1886/1Pi R	92,000	50.00	100	175	600	—
1886/1Pi C	—	25.00	40.00	100	450	—
1886Pi C	Inc. above	15.00	30.00	80.00	400	—
1886Pi R	Inc. above	15.00	30.00	80.00	400	—
1887Pi R	32,000	15.00	30.00	90.00	450	—

KM# 407 50 CENTAVOS
13.5360 g., 0.9030 Silver 0.3930 oz. ASW **Obv:** Facing eagle, snake in beak **Rev:** Radiant cap above scales **Mint:** Alamos **Note:** Mint mark A, As.

Date	Mintage	F	VF	XF	Unc	BU
1875 L	—	12.00	25.00	70.00	400	—
1876/5 L	—	25.00	50.00	120	450	—
1876 L	—	12.00	25.00	70.00	400	—
1876. L	—	12.00	25.00	70.00	400	—
1877 L	26,000	15.00	30.00	85.00	450	—
1878 L	—	12.00	25.00	70.00	400	—
1879 L	—	25.00	50.00	120	450	—
1880 L	57,000	12.00	25.00	70.00	400	—
1881 L	18,000	15.00	30.00	80.00	450	—
1884 L	6,286	65.00	120	250	650	—
1885As/HoL	21,000	15.00	35.00	90.00	450	—
1888 L	—	4,000	5,000	7,000	—	—

KM# 407.1 50 CENTAVOS
13.5360 g., 0.9030 Silver 0.3930 oz. ASW **Obv:** Facing eagle, snake in beak **Rev:** Radiant cap above scales **Mint:** Chihuahua **Note:** Mint mark Ca, CHa.

Date	Mintage	F	VF	XF	Unc	BU
1883 M	12,000	30.00	60.00	125	500	—
1884 M	—	25.00	50.00	125	500	—
1885 M	13,000	15.00	35.00	90.00	400	—
1886 M	18,000	20.00	40.00	100	450	—
1887 M	26,000	25.00	65.00	150	500	—

KM# 407.4 50 CENTAVOS
13.5360 g., 0.9030 Silver 0.3930 oz. ASW **Obv:** Facing eagle, snake in beak **Rev:** Radiant cap above scales **Mint:** Guanajuato **Note:** Struck at Guanajuato Mint, mitn mark Go. Varieties exist.

Date	Mintage	F	VF	XF	Unc	BU
1869Go S	—	15.00	35.00	75.00	550	—
1870Go S	166,000	12.00	25.00	50.00	450	—
1871Go S	148,000	12.00	25.00	50.00	450	—
1872/1Go S	144,000	15.00	30.00	60.00	500	—
1872Go S	Inc. above	12.00	25.00	50.00	450	—
1873Go S	50,000	12.00	25.00	50.00	450	—
1874Go S	—	12.00	25.00	50.00	450	—

Date	Mintage	F	VF	XF	Unc	BU
1875Go S	—	15.00	35.00	75.00	450	—
1876/5Go S	—	12.00	25.00	50.00	450	—
1877Go S	76,000	12.00	25.00	60.00	450	—
1878Go S	37,000	15.00	30.00	75.00	550	—
1879/8Go S	—	15.00	30.00	60.00	500	—
1879Go S	—	12.00	25.00	50.00	450	—
1880Go S	—	12.00	25.00	50.00	450	—
1881/79Go S	32,000	15.00	30.00	60.00	500	—
1881Go S	Inc. above	12.00	25.00	50.00	450	—
1882Go S	18,000	12.00	25.00	50.00	450	—
1883/2Go B/S	—	15.00	30.00	60.00	500	—
1883Go B	—	12.00	25.00	50.00	450	—
1883Go S Rare	—	—	—	—	—	—
1884Go B/S	—	15.00	30.00	60.00	500	—
1885/4Go R/B	—	15.00	30.00	60.00	500	—
1885Go R	53,000	12.00	25.00	50.00	450	—
1886/5Go R/B	59,000	15.00	30.00	60.00	500	—
1886/5Go R/S	Inc. above	20.00	40.00	75.00	500	—
1886Go R	Inc. above	20.00	40.00	75.00	450	—
1887Go R	18,000	20.00	40.00	75.00	550	—
1888Go R 1 known; Rare	—	—	—	—	—	—

KM# 407.8 50 CENTAVOS
13.5360 g., 0.9030 Silver 0.3930 oz. ASW **Obv:** Facing eagle, snake in beak **Rev:** Radiant cap above scales **Mint:** Zacatecas **Note:** Varieties exist.

Date	Mintage	F	VF	XF	Unc	BU
1870Zs H	86,000	12.00	25.00	60.00	450	—
1871Zs H	146,000	12.00	25.00	50.00	400	—
1872Zs H	132,000	12.00	25.00	50.00	400	—
1873Zs H	56,000	12.00	25.00	50.00	400	—
1874Zs H	—	12.00	25.00	50.00	400	—
1874Zs A Rare	—	—	—	—	—	—
1875Zs A	—	12.00	25.00	50.00	400	—
1876Zs A	—	12.00	25.00	50.00	400	—
1876/5Zs A	—	15.00	30.00	60.00	450	—
1876Zs S	—	100	200	350	750	—
1877Zs S	100,000	12.00	25.00	50.00	400	—
1878Zs S	Inc. above	15.00	30.00	60.00	400	—
1878/7Zs S	254,000	15.00	30.00	60.00	450	—
1879Zs S	—	12.00	25.00	50.00	400	—
1880Zs S	—	12.00	25.00	50.00	400	—
1881Zs S	201,000	12.00	25.00	50.00	400	—
1882Zs S	Inc. above	50.00	100	250	650	—
1882/1Zs S	2,000	50.00	100	250	650	—
1883Zs S	Inc. above	25.00	50.00	100	450	—
1883Zs/Za S	31,000	30.00	60.00	100	450	—
1884Zs S	—	12.00	25.00	50.00	400	—
1884/3Zs S	—	15.00	30.00	60.00	450	—
1885Zs S	Inc. above	25.00	50.00	125	450	—
1885/4Zs S	2,000	25.00	50.00	125	450	—
1886Zs Z	2,000	150	275	400	1,000	—
1887Zs Z	63,000	30.00	60.00	125	450	—

KM# 407.5 50 CENTAVOS
13.5360 g., 0.9030 Silver 0.3930 oz. ASW **Obv:** Facing eagle, snake in beak **Rev:** Radiant cap above scales **Mint:** Hermosillo **Note:** With and without dot after 50 of denomination, in medal and coin alignment.

Date	Mintage	F	VF	XF	Unc	BU
1874Ho R	—	20.00	40.00	100	600	—
1875/4Ho R	—	20.00	50.00	125	600	—
1875Ho R	—	20.00	50.00	125	600	—
1876/5Ho F/R	—	15.00	35.00	100	550	—
1876Ho F	—	15.00	30.00	100	550	—
1877Ho F	—	50.00	75.00	150	650	—
1880/70Ho A	—	15.00	35.00	100	550	—
1880Ho A	—	15.00	35.00	100	550	—

Date	Mintage	F	VF	XF	Unc	BU
1881Ho A	13,000	15.00	35.00	100	550	—
1882Ho A	—	75.00	150	250	750	—
1888Ho G	—	2,000	3,000	6,000	—	—
1894Ho G	59,000	15.00	30.00	100	450	—
1895Ho G	8,000	250	350	700	1,500	—

KM# 407.2 50 CENTAVOS
13.5360 g., 0.9030 Silver 0.3930 oz. ASW **Obv:** Facing eagle, snake in beak **Obv. Legend:** REPUBLICA MEXICANA **Rev:** Radiant cap above scales **Mint:** Culiacan

Date	Mintage	F	VF	XF	Unc	BU
1871Cn P	—	400	550	750	1,500	—
1873Cn P	—	400	550	750	1,500	—
1874Cn P	—	200	300	500	1,000	—
1875/4Cn P	—	20.00	40.00	75.00	450	—
1875Cn P	—	12.00	25.00	50.00	450	—
1876Cn P	—	15.00	30.00	60.00	450	—
1877/6Cn G	—	15.00	30.00	60.00	450	—
1877Cn G	—	12.00	25.00	50.00	450	—
1878Cn G	18,000	20.00	40.00	75.00	450	—
1878Cn/Mo D	Inc. above	30.00	60.00	100	450	—
1878Cn D	Inc. above	15.00	35.00	75.00	450	—
1879Cn D	—	12.00	25.00	50.00	450	—
1879Cn D/G	—	12.00	25.00	50.00	450	—
1880/8Cn D	—	15.00	30.00	60.00	450	—
1880Cn D	—	15.00	30.00	60.00	450	—
1881/0Cn D	188,000	15.00	30.00	60.00	450	—
1881Cn D	Inc. above	15.00	30.00	60.00	450	—
1881Cn G	Inc. above	125	175	275	550	—
1882Cn D	—	175	300	500	2,000	—
1882Gn G	—	100	250	300	1,000	—
1883 D	19,000	25.00	50.00	100	500	—
1885Cn M/M/G	—	30.00	60.00	100	500	—
1885/3Cn M/H	9,254	30.00	60.00	100	500	—
1886Cn M/G	7,030	50.00	100	300	1,500	—
1886Cn M	Inc. above	40.00	80.00	150	800	—
1887Cn M	76,000	20.00	40.00	100	450	—
1888Cn M	—	4,000	6,000	—	—	—
1892Cn M	8,200	40.00	80.00	150	650	—

KM# 407.3 50 CENTAVOS
13.5360 g., 0.9030 Silver 0.3930 oz. ASW **Obv:** Facing eagle, snake in beak **Obv. Legend:** REPUBLICA MEXICANA **Rev:** Radiant cap above scales **Mint:** Durango

Date	Mintage	F	VF	XF	Unc	BU
1871Do P Rare	591	—	—	—	—	—
1873Do P	4,010	150	250	500	1,250	—
1873Do M/P	Inc. above	150	250	500	1,250	—
1874Do M	—	20.00	40.00	175	750	—
1875Do M	—	20.00	40.00	80.00	350	—
1875Do H	—	150	250	450	1,000	—
1876/5Do M	—	35.00	70.00	150	500	—
1876Do M	—	35.00	70.00	150	500	—
1877Do P	2,000	30.00	45.00	150	1,250	—
1878Do B Rare	—	—	—	—	—	—
1879Do B Rare	—	—	—	—	—	—

Date	Mintage	F	VF	XF	Unc	BU
1880Do P	—	30.00	60.00	125	500	—
1881Do P	10,000	40.00	80.00	150	550	—
1882Do C	8,957	30.00	75.00	200	800	—
1884/2Do C	—	20.00	50.00	125	600	—
1884Do C	—	—	—	—	—	—
1885Do B/P	—	15.00	40.00	100	500	—
1885Do B	—	15.00	40.00	100	500	—
1886Do C	16,000	15.00	40.00	100	500	—
1887Do/Mo C	28,000	15.00	40.00	100	500	—
1887Do C	—	15.00	40.00	100	500	—

KM# 407.6   50 CENTAVOS
13.5360 g., 0.9027 Silver 0.3928 oz. ASW **Obv:** Facing eagle, snake in beak **Obv. Legend:** REPUBLICA MEXICANA **Rev:** Radiant cap above scales **Mint:** Mexico City

Date	Mintage	F	VF	XF	Unc	BU
1869Mo C	46,000	15.00	35.00	95.00	600	—
1870Mo C	52,000	15.00	30.00	90.00	550	—
1871Mo M/C	Inc. above	35.00	75.00	150	600	—
1871Mo C	14,000	40.00	75.00	150	650	—
1872/1Mo M	60,000	35.00	75.00	150	550	—
1872Mo M	Inc. above	35.00	75.00	150	550	—
1873Mo M	6,000	35.00	75.00	150	600	—
1874/3Mo M	—	200	400	600	1,250	—
1874/2Mo B	—	15.00	30.00	75.00	500	—
1874/2Mo B/M	—	15.00	30.00	75.00	500	—
1874/3Mo B/M	—	15.00	30.00	75.00	500	—
1874Mo B	—	15.00	30.00	75.00	500	—
1875Mo B	—	15.00	30.00	75.00	550	—
1876/5Mo B	—	15.00	30.00	75.00	500	—
1876Mo B	—	12.00	25.00	75.00	500	—
1877Mo M	—	15.00	30.00	90.00	500	—
1877/2Mo M	—	20.00	40.00	100	550	—
1878/7Mo M	8,000	25.00	50.00	125	600	—
1878Mo M	Inc. above	15.00	35.00	100	550	—
1879Mo M	—	25.00	50.00	125	550	—
1880Mo M	—	100	150	250	750	—
1881/0Mo M	—	30.00	50.00	125	600	—
1881Mo M	16,000	25.00	50.00	125	600	—
1882/1Mo M	2,000	30.00	60.00	150	750	—
1883/2Mo M	4,000	150	225	350	1,000	—
1884Mo M	—	150	225	350	1,000	—
1885Mo M	12,000	30.00	60.00	150	600	—
1886Mo M	Inc. above	12.00	25.00	75.00	450	—
1886/5Mo M	66,000	15.00	35.00	90.00	475	—
1887Mo M	Inc. above	15.00	35.00	75.00	475	—
1887/6Mo M	88,000	15.00	35.00	90.00	475	—
1888Mo M	—	3,000	4,000	6,000	—	—

KM# 408   PESO
27.0730 g., 0.9030 Silver 0.7860 oz. ASW **Obv:** Facing eagle, snake in beak **Rev:** Radiant cap above scales **Mint:** Chihuahua

Date	Mintage	F	VF	XF	Unc	BU
1872CH P/M	747,000	750	1,500	3,500	—	—
1872CH P	Inc. above	350	700	1,500	—	—
1872/1CH M	Inc. above	27.50	45.00	80.00	400	—
1872CH M	Inc. above	20.00	30.00	55.00	250	—
1873CH M	320,000	22.50	35.00	65.00	265	—
1873CH M/P	Inc. above	27.50	45.00	80.00	350	—

KM# 408.1   PESO
27.0730 g., 0.9030 Silver 0.7860 oz. ASW **Obv:** Facing eagle, snake in beak **Rev:** Radiant cap above scales **Mint:** Culiacan

Date	Mintage	F	VF	XF	Unc	BU
1870Cn E	—	40.00	80.00	150	500	—
1871Cn P	Inc. above	20.00	40.00	75.00	300	—
1871/11Cn P	478,000	25.00	45.00	100	450	—
1872/1Cn P	—	20.00	40.00	75.00	300	—

Date	Mintage	F	VF	XF	Unc	BU
1872Cn P	209,000	20.00	40.00	75.00	300	—
1873Cn P Wide date	Inc. above	20.00	40.00	75.00	300	—
1873Cn P Narrow date	527,000	20.00	40.00	75.00	300	—

KM# 408.2   PESO
27.0730 g., 0.9027 Silver 0.7857 oz. ASW **Obv:** Facing eagle, snake in beak **Obv. Legend:** REPUBLICA MEXICANA **Rev:** Radiant cap above scales **Mint:** Durango

Date	Mintage	F	VF	XF	Unc	BU
1870Do P	—	50.00	100	175	450	—
1871Do P	427,000	27.50	52.50	80.00	300	—
1872Do P	296,000	22.50	42.50	80.00	350	—
1872Do PT	Inc. above	100	175	250	850	—
1873Do P	203,000	27.50	47.50	90.00	350	—

KM# 408.3   PESO
27.0730 g., 0.9030 Silver 0.7860 oz. ASW **Obv:** Facing eagle, snake in beak **Obv. Legend:** REPUBLICA MEXICANA **Rev:** Radiant cap above scales **Mint:** Guadalajara

Date	Mintage	F	VF	XF	Unc	BU
1870Ga C	—	650	850	—	—	—
1871Ga C	829,000	27.50	70.00	140	600	—
1872Ga C	485,000	42.50	95.00	180	650	—
1873/2Ga C	277,000	42.50	95.00	180	700	—
1873Ga C	Inc. above	27.50	70.00	140	600	—

KM# 408.4 PESO
27.0730 g., 0.9027 Silver 0.7857 oz. ASW **Obv:** Facing eagle, snake in beak **Obv. Legend:** REPUBLICA MEXICANA **Rev:** Radiant cap above scales **Mint:** Guanajuato

Date	Mintage	F	VF	XF	Unc	BU
1871/0Go S	3,946,000	32.50	55.00	95.00	350	—
1871/3Go S	Inc. above	22.50	40.00	75.00	275	—
1871Go S	Inc. above	15.00	25.00	45.00	220	—
1872Go S	4,067,000	15.00	25.00	45.00	250	—
1873/2Go S	1,560,000	18.00	30.00	55.00	250	—
1873Go S	Inc. above	15.00	25.00	50.00	250	—
1873Go/Mo/S/M	Inc. above	15.00	25.00	50.00	250	—

KM# 408.6 PESO
27.0730 g., 0.9030 Silver 0.7860 oz. ASW **Obv:** Facing eagle, snake in beak **Obv. Legend:** REPUBLICA MEXICANA **Rev:** Radiant cap above scales **Mint:** Oaxaca

Date	Mintage	F	VF	XF	Unc	BU
1869Oa E	—	275	400	600	2,000	—
1870Oa E Small A	Inc. above	17.50	35.00	80.00	400	—
1870OA E Large A	Inc. above	100	150	300	900	—
1871/69Oa E	140,000	32.50	55.00	130	550	—
1871Oa E Small A	Inc. above	18.00	35.00	65.00	300	—
1871Oa E Large A	Inc. above	18.00	35.00	80.00	400	—
1872Oa E Small A	180,000	18.00	35.00	80.00	400	—
1872Oa E Large A	Inc. above	55.00	100	200	450	—
1873Oa E	105,000	18.00	35.00	80.00	350	—

KM# 408.5 PESO
27.0730 g., 0.9030 Silver 0.7860 oz. ASW **Obv:** Facing eagle, snake in beak **Rev:** Radiant cap above scales **Mint:** Mexico City

Date	Mintage	F	VF	XF	Unc	BU
1869Mo C	—	37.50	70.00	140	600	—
1870Mo M/C	Inc. above	20.00	35.00	65.00	275	—
1870/69Mo C	5,115,000	18.00	30.00	60.00	275	—
1870Mo C	Inc. above	15.00	25.00	45.00	250	—
1870Mo M	Inc. above	20.00	35.00	65.00	275	—
1871/0Mo M	6,974,000	18.00	30.00	60.00	275	—
1871Mo M	Inc. above	15.00	25.00	45.00	250	—
1872/1Mo M	—	18.00	30.00	55.00	275	—
1872/1Mo M/C	4,801,000	18.00	30.00	55.00	275	—
1872Mo M	Inc. above	15.00	25.00	45.00	250	—
1873Mo M	1,765,000	15.00	25.00	45.00	250	—

Note: The 1869 C with large LEY on the scroll is a pattern

KM# 409 PESO
27.0730 g., 0.9030 Silver 0.7860 oz. ASW **Obv:** Facing eagle, snake in beak **Rev:** Radiant cap **Mint:** Culiacan

Date	Mintage	F	VF	XF	Unc	BU
1898Cn/MoAM	Inc. above	17.50	32.50	95.00	155	—
1898Cn AM	1,720,000	14.50	17.50	30.00	70.00	—
1899Cn AM	1,722,000	27.50	52.50	95.00	180	—
1899Cn JQ	Inc. above	14.50	17.50	55.00	130	—
1900Cn JQ	1,804,000	14.50	17.50	30.00	80.00	—
1901Cn JQ	1,473,000	15.00	16.50	25.00	75.00	—
1902Cn JQ	1,194,000	15.00	16.50	45.00	125	—
1903Cn JQ	1,514,000	15.00	16.50	30.00	85.00	—
1903Cn FV	Inc. above	25.00	50.00	100	225	—
1904Cn MH	1,554,000	15.00	16.50	25.00	75.00	—
1904Cn RP	Inc. above	50.00	100	150	350	—
1905Cn RP	598,000	25.00	50.00	100	250	—

KM# 410.2 PESO
1.6920 g., 0.8750 Gold 0.0476 oz. AGW **Obv:** Facing eagle, snake in beak **Obv. Legend:** REPUBLICA MEXICANA **Rev:** Value within 1/2 wreath **Mint:** Culiacan

Date	Mintage	F	VF	XF	Unc	BU
1873Cn P	1,221	75.00	100	150	250	—
1875Cn P	—	85.00	125	150	250	—
1878Cn G	248	100	175	225	500	—
1879Cn D	—	100	150	200	475	—
1881/0Cn D	338	100	150	200	475	—
1882Cn D	340	100	150	200	475	—
1883Cn D	—	100	150	200	475	—
1884Cn M	—	100	150	200	475	—
1886/4Cn M	277	100	150	225	500	—
1888/7Cn M	2,586	100	175	225	450	—
1888Cn M	Inc. above	65.00	100	150	265	—
1889Cn M Rare	—	—	—	—	—	—
1891/89Cn M	969	75.00	100	150	275	—
1892Cn M	780	75.00	100	150	275	—
1893Cn M	498	85.00	125	150	275	—
1894Cn M	493	80.00	125	150	275	—
1895Cn M	1,143	65.00	100	150	250	350
1896/5Cn M	1,028	65.00	100	150	250	350
1897Cn M	785	65.00	100	150	250	350
1898Cn M	3,521	65.00	100	150	225	325
1898Cn/MoM	Inc. above	65.00	100	150	250	350
1899Cn Q	2,000	65.00	100	150	225	325
1901Cn Q	Inc. above	65.00	100	150	225	325
1901/0Cn Q	2,350	65.00	100	150	225	325
1902Cn Q	2,480	65.00	100	150	225	325
1902Cn/MoQ/C	Inc. above	65.00	100	150	225	325
1904Cn H	3,614	65.00	100	150	225	325
1904Cn/Mo/ H	Inc. above	65.00	100	150	250	350
1905Cn P	1,000	—	—	—	—	—

Note: Reported, not confirmed

KM# 410.3 PESO
1.6920 g., 0.8750 Gold 0.0476 oz. AGW **Obv:** Facing eagle, snake in beak **Obv. Legend:** REPUBLICA MEXICANA **Rev:** Value within 1/2 wreath **Mint:** Guanajuato

Date	Mintage	F	VF	XF	Unc	BU
1870Go S	—	100	125	150	265	—
1871Go S	500	100	175	225	475	—
1888Go R	210	125	200	250	550	—
1890Go R	1,916	75.00	100	150	265	—
1892Go R	533	100	150	175	350	—
1894Go R	180	150	200	250	550	—
1895Go R	676	100	150	175	325	—
1896/5Go R	4,671	65.00	100	150	250	—
1897/6Go R	4,280	65.00	100	150	250	—
1897Go R	Inc. above	65.00	100	150	250	—
1898Go R	5,193	65.00	100	150	250	750

Note: Regular obverse

1898Go R	Inc. above	75.00	100	150	250	750

Note: Mule, 5 Centavos obverse, normal reverse

1899Go R	2,748	65.00	100	150	250	—
1900/800Go R	864	75.00	125	150	285	—

KM# 410.4 PESO
1.6920 g., 0.8750 Gold 0.0476 oz. AGW **Obv:** Facing eagle, snake in beak **Obv. Legend:** REPUBLICA MEXICANA **Rev:** Value within 1/2 wreath **Mint:** Hermosillo

Date	Mintage	F	VF	XF	Unc	BU
1875Ho R Rare	310	—	—	—	—	—

Date	Mintage	F	VF	XF	Unc	BU
1876Ho F Rare		—	—	—	—	—
1888Ho G/MoM Rare		—	—	—	—	—

KM# 410.5 PESO
1.6920 g., 0.8750 Gold 0.0476 oz. AGW **Obv:** Facing eagle, snake in beak **Obv. Legend:** REPUBLICA MEXICANA **Rev:** Value within 1/2 wreath **Mint:** Mexico City

Date	Mintage	F	VF	XF	Unc	BU
1870Mo C	2,540	50.00	65.00	95.00	185	250
1871Mo M/C	1,000	60.00	100	150	250	250
1872Mo M/C	3,000	50.00	65.00	95.00	185	300
1873/1Mo M	2,900	50.00	65.00	100	200	250
1873Mo M	Inc. above	50.00	65.00	95.00	185	250
1874Mo M	—	50.00	65.00	95.00	185	250
1875Mo B/M	—	50.00	65.00	95.00	185	250
1876/5Mo B/M	—	50.00	65.00	95.00	185	250
1877Mo M	—	50.00	65.00	95.00	185	250
1878Mo M	2,000	50.00	65.00	95.00	185	250
1879Mo M	—	50.00	65.00	95.00	185	250
1880/70Mo M	—	50.00	65.00	95.00	185	250
1881/71Mo M	1,000	50.00	65.00	95.00	185	250
1882/72Mo M	—	50.00	65.00	95.00	185	250
1883/72Mo M	1,000	50.00	65.00	95.00	185	250
1884Mo M	—	50.00	65.00	95.00	185	250
1885/71Mo M	—	50.00	65.00	95.00	185	250
1885Mo M	—	50.00	65.00	95.00	185	250
1886Mo M	1,700	50.00	65.00	95.00	185	250
1887Mo M	2,200	50.00	65.00	95.00	185	250
1888Mo M	1,000	50.00	65.00	95.00	185	250
1889Mo M	500	100	150	200	285	—
1890Mo M	570	100	150	200	285	—
1891Mo M	746	100	150	200	285	—
1892/0Mo M	2,895	50.00	65.00	95.00	185	250
1893Mo M	5,917	50.00	65.00	95.00	185	250
1894/3MMo	—	50.00	65.00	95.00	185	250
1894Mo M	6,244	50.00	65.00	95.00	185	250
1895Mo M	8,994	50.00	65.00	95.00	185	250
1895Mo B	Inc. above	50.00	65.00	95.00	185	250
1896Mo B	7,166	50.00	65.00	95.00	185	250
1896Mo M	Inc. above	50.00	65.00	95.00	185	250
1897Mo M	5,131	50.00	65.00	95.00	185	250
1898/7Mo M	5,368	50.00	65.00	95.00	185	250
1899Mo M	9,515	50.00	65.00	95.00	185	250
1900/800Mo M	9,301	50.00	65.00	95.00	185	250
1900/880Mo M	Inc. above	50.00	65.00	95.00	185	250
1900/890Mo M	Inc. above	50.00	65.00	95.00	185	250
1900Mo M	Inc. above	50.00	65.00	95.00	185	250
1901Mo M Small date	Inc. above	50.00	65.00	95.00	185	250
1901/801Mo M Large date	8,293	50.00	65.00	95.00	185	250
1902Mo M Large date	11,000	50.00	65.00	95.00	185	250
1902Mo M Small date	Inc. above	50.00	65.00	95.00	185	250
1903Mo M Large date	10,000	50.00	65.00	95.00	185	250
1903Mo M Small date	Inc. above	60.00	85.00	125	200	300
1904Mo M	9,845	50.00	65.00	95.00	185	250
1905Mo M	3,429	50.00	65.00	95.00	185	250

KM# 410.6 PESO
1.6920 g., 0.8750 Gold 0.0476 oz. AGW **Obv:** Facing eagle, snake in beak **Obv. Legend:** REPUBLICA MEXICANA **Rev:** Value within 1/2 wreath **Mint:** Zacatecas

Date	Mintage	F	VF	XF	Unc	BU
1872Zs H	2,024	125	150	175	275	—
1875/3Zs A	—	125	150	200	325	—

Date	Mintage	F	VF	XF	Unc	BU
1878Zs S	—	125	150	175	275	—
1888Zs Z	280	175	225	325	700	—
1889Zs Z	492	150	175	225	450	—
1890Zs Z	738	150	175	225	450	—

KM# 409.3 PESO
27.0730 g., 0.9030 Silver 0.7860 oz. ASW **Obv:** Facing eagle, snake in beak **Rev:** Radiant cap **Mint:** Zacatecas **Note:** Mint mark Zs. Varieties exist.

Date	Mintage	F	VF	XF	Unc	BU
1898Zs FZ	5,714,000	14.00	16.50	25.00	65.00	—
1899Zs FZ	5,618,000	14.00	16.50	25.00	70.00	—
1900Zs FZ	5,357,000	14.00	16.50	25.00	70.00	—
1901Zs FZ	Inc. above	15.00	16.50	20.00	55.00	—
1901Zs AZ	5,706,000	4,000	6,500	10,000	—	—
1902Zs FZ	7,134,000	15.00	16.50	20.00	55.00	—
1903/2Zs FZ	3,080,000	15.00	16.50	50.00	125	—
1903Zs FZ	Inc. above	15.00	16.50	20.00	65.00	—
1904Zs FZ	2,423,000	15.00	16.50	25.00	85.00	—
1904Zs FM	Inc. above	15.00	16.50	25.00	75.00	—
1905Zs FM	995,000	20.00	40.00	60.00	150	—

KM# 408.7 PESO
27.0730 g., 0.9030 Silver 0.7860 oz. ASW **Obv:** Facing eagle, snake in beak **Rev:** Radiant cap above scales **Mint:** San Luis Potosi **Note:** Varieties exist.

Date	Mintage	F	VF	XF	Unc	BU
1870Pi S	1,967,000	200	350	500	1,000	—
1870Pi S/A	Inc. above	200	350	550	1,200	—
1870Pi G	Inc. above	27.50	45.00	80.00	550	—
1870Pi H	Inc. above	—	—	—	—	—

Note: Contemporary counterfeits

1870Pi O/G	Inc. above	27.50	45.00	80.00	550	—
1870Pi O	Inc. above	22.50	35.00	105	400	—
1871Pi O/G	Inc. above	18.00	35.00	65.00	500	—
1871Pi O	—	18.00	35.00	65.00	500	—
1871/69Pi O	2,103,000	80.00	105	205	500	—
1872Pi O	1,873,000	18.00	35.00	65.00	500	—
1873Pi O	893,000	18.00	35.00	65.00	500	—
1873Pi H	Inc. above	18.00	35.00	65.00	500	—

KM# 408.8 PESO
27.0730 g., 0.9030 Silver 0.7860 oz. ASW **Obv:** Facing eagle, snake in beak **Rev:** Radiant cap above scales **Mint:** Zacatecas **Note:** Varieties exist.

Date	Mintage	F	VF	XF	Unc	BU
1870Zs H	4,519,000	15.00	35.00	45.00	220	—
1871Zs H	4,459,000	15.00	25.00	45.00	220	—
1872Zs H	4,039,000	15.00	25.00	45.00	220	—
1873/1Zs H	Inc. above	15.00	25.00	45.00	220	—
1873Zs H	1,782,000	15.00	25.00	45.00	220	—

KM# 409.1 PESO
27.0730 g., 0.9030 Silver 0.7860 oz. ASW **Obv:** Facing eagle, snake in beak **Rev:** Radiant cap **Mint:** Guanajuato **Note:** Varieties exist.

Date	Mintage	F	VF	XF	Unc	BU
1898Go/MoRS	Inc. above	22.50	30.00	60.00	125	—
1898Go RS	4,256,000	14.00	19.00	38.00	80.00	—
1899Go RS	3,207,000	14.00	19.00	33.00	80.00	—
1900Go RS	1,489,000	27.50	50.00	100	250	—

KM# 409.2 PESO
27.0730 g., 0.9027 Silver 0.7857 oz. ASW **Obv:** Facing eagle, snake in beak **Obv. Legend:** REPUBLICA MEXICANA **Rev:** Radiant cap **Mint:** Mexico City **Note:** Varieties exist.

Date	Mintage	F	VF	XF	Unc	BU
1898Mo AM	10,250,000	15.00	17.50	19.50	45.00	—

Note: Restrike (1949) - reverse with 134 beads

| 1898Mo AM | 10,156,000 | 15.00 | 17.50 | 21.50 | 65.00 | — |

Note: Original strike - reverse with 139 beads

1899Mo AM	7,930,000	15.00	17.50	23.00	75.00	—
1900Mo AM	8,226,000	15.00	17.50	23.00	75.00	—
1901Mo AM	14,505,000	16.00	16.50	23.00	75.00	—
1902/1Mo AM	16,224,000	150	300	500	950	—
1902Mo AM	Inc. above	15.00	16.50	20.00	70.00	—
1903Mo AM	22,396,000	15.00	16.50	20.00	70.00	—
1903Mo MA (Error)	Inc. above	1,500	2,500	3,500	7,500	—
1904Mo AM	14,935,000	15.00	16.50	20.00	70.00	—
1905Mo AM	3,557,000	16.50	25.00	55.00	125	—
1908Mo AM	7,575,000	15.00	16.50	20.00	60.00	—
1908Mo GV	Inc. above	15.00	16.50	18.50	40.00	—
1909Mo GV	2,924,000	15.00	16.50	18.50	40.00	—

KM# 410 PESO
1.6920 g., 0.8750 Gold 0.0476 oz. AGW **Obv:** Facing eagle, snake in beak **Obv. Legend:** REPUBLICA MEXICANA **Rev:** Value within 1/2 wreath **Mint:** Alamos

Date	Mintage	F	VF	XF	Unc	BU
1888AsL/MoM Rare	—	—	—	—	—	—
1888As L Rare	—	—	—	—	—	—

KM# 410.1 PESO
1.6920 g., 0.8750 Gold 0.0476 oz. AGW **Obv:** Facing eagle, snake in beak **Obv. Legend:** REPUBLICA MEXICANA **Rev:** Value within 1/2 wreath **Mint:** Chihuahua

Date	Mintage	F	VF	XF	Unc	BU
1888Ca/MoM Rare	104	—	—	—	—	—

KM# 411.3 2-1/2 PESOS
4.2300 g., 0.8750 Gold 0.1190 oz. AGW **Obv:** Facing eagle, snake in beak **Obv. Legend:** REPUBLICA MEXICANA **Rev:** Value within 1/2 wreath **Mint:** Guanajuato

Date	Mintage	F	VF	XF	Unc	BU
1871Go S	600	1,250	2,000	2,500	3,250	—
1888Go/MoR	110	1,750	2,250	2,750	3,500	—

KM# 411.4 2-1/2 PESOS
4.2300 g., 0.8750 Gold 0.1190 oz. AGW **Obv:** Facing eagle, snake in beak **Obv. Legend:** REPUBLICA MEXICANA **Rev:** Value within 1/2 wreath **Mint:** Hermosillo

Date	Mintage	F	VF	XF	Unc	BU
1874Ho R Rare	—	—	—	—	—	—
1888Ho G Rare	—	—	—	—	—	—

KM# 411.5 2-1/2 PESOS
4.2300 g., 0.8750 Gold 0.1190 oz. AGW **Obv:** Facing eagle, snake in beak **Rev:** Value within 1/2 wreath **Mint:** Mexico City

Date	Mintage	F	VF	XF	Unc	BU
1870Mo C	820	150	250	350	750	—
1872Mo M/C	800	150	250	350	750	—
1873/2Mo M	—	200	350	750	1,350	—
1874Mo M	—	200	350	750	1,350	—
1874Mo B/M	—	200	350	750	1,350	—
1875Mo B	—	200	350	750	1,350	—
1876Mo B	—	250	500	1,000	1,850	—
1877Mo M	—	200	350	750	1,350	—
1878Mo M	400	200	350	750	1,350	—
1879Mo M	—	200	350	750	1,350	—
1880/79Mo M	—	200	350	750	1,350	—
1881Mo M	400	200	350	750	1,350	—
1882Mo M	—	225	400	850	1,500	2,000
1883/73Mo M	400	200	350	750	1,350	—
1884Mo M	—	250	500	1,000	1,600	—
1885Mo M	—	400	850	1,750	3,000	—
1886Mo M	400	200	350	750	1,350	—
1887Mo M	400	200	350	750	1,350	—
1888Mo M	540	200	350	750	1,350	—
1889Mo M	240	150	300	525	950	—
1890Mo M	420	200	350	750	1,350	—
1891Mo M	188	200	350	750	1,350	—
1892Mo M	240	200	350	750	1,350	—

KM# 411.6 2-1/2 PESOS
4.2300 g., 0.8750 Gold 0.1190 oz. AGW **Obv:** Facing eagle, snake in beak **Obv. Legend:** REPUBLICA MEXICANA **Rev:** Value within 1/2 wreath **Mint:** Zacatecas

Date	Mintage	F	VF	XF	Unc	BU
1872Zs H	1,300	200	350	500	1,200	—
1873Zs H	—	175	325	475	900	—
1875/3Zs A	—	200	350	750	1,350	—
1877Zs S	—	200	350	750	1,350	—
1878Zs S	300	200	350	750	1,350	—
1888Zs/MoS	80	300	500	1,000	1,800	—
1889Zs/Mo Z	184	250	450	950	1,600	—
1890Zs Z	326	200	350	750	1,350	—

KM# 411 2-1/2 PESOS
4.2300 g., 0.8750 Gold 0.1190 oz. AGW **Obv:** Facing eagle,

snake in beak **Obv. Legend:** REPUBLICA MEXICANA **Rev:** Value within 1/2 wreath **Mint:** Alamos

Date	Mintage	F	VF	XF	Unc	BU
1888As/MoL Rare	—	—	—	—	—	—

KM# 411.1 2-1/2 PESOS
4.2300 g., 0.8750 Gold 0.1190 oz. AGW **Obv:** Facing eagle, snake in beak **Rev:** Value within 1/2 wreath **Mint:** Culiacan

Date	Mintage	F	VF	XF	Unc	BU
1893Cn M	141	1,500	2,000	2,500	3,500	—

KM# 411.2 2-1/2 PESOS
4.2300 g., 0.8750 Gold 0.1190 oz. AGW **Obv:** Facing eagle, snake in beak **Rev:** Value within 1/2 wreath **Mint:** Durango

Date	Mintage	F	VF	XF	Unc	BU
1888Do C Rare	—	—	—	—	—	—

KM# 412.2 5 PESOS
8.4600 g., 0.8750 Gold 0.2380 oz. AGW **Obv:** Facing eagle, snake in beak **Obv. Legend:** REPUBLICA MEXICANA **Rev:** Radiant cap above scales **Mint:** Culiacan

Date	Mintage	F	VF	XF	Unc	BU
1873Cn P	—	300	600	1,000	2,000	—
1874Cn P	—	—	—	—	—	—
1875Cn P	—	300	500	800	1,750	—
1876Cn P	—	300	500	800	1,750	—
1877Cn G	—	300	500	800	1,750	—
1882Cn Rare	174	—	—	—	—	—
1888Cn M	—	500	1,000	1,350	2,000	—
1890Cn M	435	250	500	750	1,600	—
1891Cn M	1,390	250	400	550	1,000	—
1894Cn M	484	250	500	750	1,600	—
1895Cn M	142	500	750	1,500	2,500	—
1900Cn Q	1,536	240	300	475	900	—
1903Cn Q	1,000	300	325	500	950	—

KM# 412.3 5 PESOS
8.4600 g., 0.8750 Gold 0.2380 oz. AGW **Obv:** Facing eagle, snake in beak **Obv. Legend:** REPUBLICA MEXICANA **Rev:** Radiant cap above scales **Mint:** Durango

Date	Mintage	F	VF	XF	Unc	BU
1873/2Do P	—	700	1,250	1,800	3,000	—
1877Do P	—	700	1,250	1,800	3,000	—
1878Do E	—	700	1,250	1,800	3,000	—
1879Do B	—	700	1,250	1,800	3,000	—
1879/7Do B	—	700	1,250	1,800	3,000	—

KM# 412.4 5 PESOS
8.4600 g., 0.8750 Gold 0.2380 oz. AGW **Obv:** Facing eagle, snake in beak **Obv. Legend:** REPUBLICA MEXICANA **Rev:** Radiant cap above scales **Mint:** Guanajuato

Date	Mintage	F	VF	XF	Unc	BU
1871Go S	1,600	400	800	1,250	2,250	—
1887Go R	140	600	1,200	1,600	3,000	—
1888Go R Rare	65	—	—	—	—	—
1893Go R Rare	16	—	—	—	—	—

KM# 412   5 PESOS
8.4600 g., 0.8750 Gold 0.2380 oz. AGW **Obv:** Facing eagle, snake in beak **Obv. Legend:** REPUBLICA MEXICANA **Rev:** Radiant cap above scales **Mint:** Alamos

Date	Mintage	F	VF	XF	Unc	BU
1875As L	—	—	—	—	—	—
1878As L	383	900	1,700	3,000	4,500	—

KM# 412.6   5 PESOS
8.4600 g., 0.8750 Gold 0.2380 oz. AGW **Obv:** Facing eagle, snake in beak **Obv. Legend:** REPUBLICA MEXICANA **Rev:** Radiant cap above scales **Mint:** Mexico City

Date	Mintage	F	VF	XF	Unc	BU
1870Mo C	550	240	400	600	1,500	—
1871/69Mo M	1,600	240	300	400	650	—
1871Mo M	Inc. above	240	300	400	650	—
1872Mo M	1,600	240	300	400	650	—
1873/2Mo M	—	240	400	550	850	—
1874Mo M	—	240	400	550	850	—
1875/3Mo B/M	—	240	400	550	950	—
1875Mo B	—	240	400	550	950	—
1876/5Mo B/M	—	240	400	550	1,000	—
1877Mo M	—	250	450	750	1,650	—
1878/7Mo M	400	240	400	550	1,250	—
1878Mo M	Inc. above	240	400	550	1,250	—
1879/8Mo M	—	240	400	550	1,250	—
1880Mo M	—	240	400	550	1,250	—
1881Mo M	—	240	400	550	1,250	—
1882Mo M	200	250	450	750	1,650	—
1883Mo M	200	250	450	750	1,650	—
1884Mo M	—	250	450	750	1,650	—
1886Mo M	200	250	450	750	1,650	—
1887Mo M	200	250	450	750	1,650	—
1888Mo M	250	240	400	550	1,650	—
1889Mo M	190	250	450	750	1,650	—
1890Mo M	149	250	450	750	1,650	—
1891Mo M	156	250	450	750	1,650	—
1892Mo M	214	250	450	750	1,650	—
1893Mo M	1,058	240	400	500	800	—
1897Mo M	370	240	400	550	1,000	—
1898Mo M	376	240	400	550	1,000	—
1900Mo M	1,014	240	300	400	650	1,000
1901Mo M	1,071	300	325	450	750	1,250
1902Mo M	1,478	300	325	450	750	1,250
1903Mo M	1,162	300	325	450	750	1,250
1904Mo M	1,415	300	325	450	750	1,250
1905Mo M	563	300	400	550	1,500	2,000

KM# 412.7   5 PESOS
8.4600 g., 0.8750 Gold 0.2380 oz. AGW **Obv:** Facing eagle, snake in beak **Obv. Legend:** REPUBLICA MEXICANA **Rev:** Radiant cap above scales **Mint:** Zacatecas

Date	Mintage	F	VF	XF	Unc	BU
1874Zs A	—	250	500	750	1,500	—
1875Zs A	—	240	400	500	1,000	—

Date	Mintage	F	VF	XF	Unc	BU
1877Zs S/A	—	240	400	550	1,000	—
1878/7Zs S/A	—	240	400	550	1,000	—
1883Zs S	—	175	300	450	750	—
1888Zs Z	70	1,000	1,500	2,000	3,000	—
1889Zs Z	373	240	300	500	850	—
1892Zs Z	1,229	240	300	450	750	1,250

KM# 412.1   5 PESOS
8.4600 g., 0.8750 Gold 0.2380 oz. AGW **Obv:** Facing eagle, snake in beak **Obv. Legend:** REPUBLICA MEXICANA **Rev:** Radiant cap above scales **Mint:** Chihuahua

Date	Mintage	F	VF	XF	Unc	BU
1888Ca M Rare	120	—	—	—	—	—

KM# 412.5   5 PESOS
8.4600 g., 0.8750 Gold 0.2380 oz. AGW **Obv:** Facing eagle, snake in beak **Obv. Legend:** REPUBLICA MEXICANA **Rev:** Radiant cap above scales **Mint:** Hermosillo

Date	Mintage	F	VF	XF	Unc	BU
1874Ho R	—	1,750	2,500	3,000	4,500	—
1877Ho A	Inc. above	650	1,100	1,750	2,750	—
1877Ho R	990	750	1,250	2,000	3,000	—
1888Ho G Rare	—	—	—	—	—	—

KM# 413.2   10 PESOS
16.9200 g., 0.8750 Gold 0.4760 oz. AGW **Obv:** Facing eagle, snake in beak **Obv. Legend:** REPUBLICA MEXICANA **Rev:** Radiant cap above scales **Mint:** Culiacan

Date	Mintage	F	VF	XF	Unc	BU
1881Cn D	—	460	600	1,000	1,750	—
1882Cn D	874	460	600	1,000	1,750	—
1882Cn E	Inc. above	460	600	1,000	1,750	—
1883Cn D	221	—	—	—	—	—
1883Cn M	Inc. above	460	600	1,000	1,750	—
1884Cn D	—	460	600	1,000	1,750	—
1884Cn M	—	460	600	1,000	1,750	—
1885Cn M	1,235	460	600	1,000	1,750	—
1886Cn M	981	460	600	1,000	1,750	—
1887Cn M	2,289	460	600	1,000	1,750	—
1888Cn M	767	460	600	1,000	1,750	—
1889Cn M	859	460	600	1,000	1,750	—
1890Cn M	1,427	460	600	1,000	1,750	—
1891Cn M	670	460	600	1,000	1,750	—
1892Cn M	379	460	600	1,000	1,750	—
1893Cn M	1,806	460	600	1,000	1,750	—
1895Cn M	179	500	1,000	1,500	2,500	—
1903Cn Q	774	600	700	1,000	2,000	—

KM# 413.3 10 PESOS
16.9200 g., 0.8750 Gold 0.4760 oz. AGW **Obv:** Facing eagle, snake in beak **Obv. Legend:** REPUBLICA MEXICANA **Rev:** Radiant cap above scales **Mint:** Durango

Date	Mintage	F	VF	XF	Unc	BU
1872Do P	1,755	455	500	800	1,250	—
1873/2Do P	1,091	455	500	850	1,350	—
1873/2Do M/P	Inc. above	455	550	900	1,450	—
1874Do M	—	455	550	900	1,450	—
1875Do M	—	55.00	550	900	1,450	—
1876Do M	—	470	750	1,250	2,000	—
1877Do P	—	455	550	900	1,450	—
1878Do E	582	455	550	900	1,450	—
1879/8Do B	—	455	550	900	1,450	—
1879Do B	—	455	550	900	1,450	—
1880Do P	2,030	455	550	900	1,450	3,750
1881/79Do P	2,617	455	550	900	1,450	—
1882Do P Rare	1,528	—	—	—	—	—
1882Do C	Inc. above	455	550	900	1,450	—
1883Do C	793	470	750	1,250	2,000	—
1884Do C	108	470	750	1,250	2,000	—

KM# 413.4 10 PESOS
16.9200 g., 0.8750 Gold 0.4760 oz. AGW **Obv:** Facing eagle, snake in beak **Obv. Legend:** REPUBLICA MEXICANA **Rev:** Radiant cap above scales **Mint:** Guadalajara

Date	Mintage	F	VF	XF	Unc	BU
1870Ga C	490	500	800	1,000	1,750	—
1871Ga C	1,910	475	800	1,250	2,250	—
1872Ga C	780	500	1,000	2,000	2,500	—
1873Ga C	422	500	1,000	2,000	3,000	—
1874/3Ga C	477	500	1,000	2,000	3,000	—
1875Ga C	710	500	1,000	2,000	3,000	—
1878Ga A	183	600	1,200	2,500	3,500	—
1879Ga A	200	600	1,200	2,500	3,500	—
1880Ga S	404	500	1,000	2,000	3,000	—
1881Ga S	239	600	1,200	2,500	3,500	—
1891Ga S	196	600	1,200	2,500	3,500	—

KM# 413.5 10 PESOS
16.9200 g., 0.8750 Gold 0.4760 oz. AGW **Obv:** Facing eagle, snake in beak **Obv. Legend:** REPUBLICA MEXICANA **Rev:** Radiant cap above scales **Mint:** Guanajuato

Date	Mintage	F	VF	XF	Unc	BU
1872Go S	1,400	2,000	4,000	6,500	10,000	—
1887Go R Rare	80	—	—	—	—	—

Date	Mintage	F	VF	XF	Unc	BU
Note: Stack's Rio Grande Sale 6-93, P/L AU realized, $12,650						
1888Go R Rare	68	—	—	—	—	—

KM# 413.6 10 PESOS
16.9200 g., 0.8750 Gold 0.4760 oz. AGW **Obv:** Facing eagle, snake in beak **Obv. Legend:** REPUBLICA MEXICANA **Rev:** Radiant cap above scales **Mint:** Hermosillo

Date	Mintage	F	VF	XF	Unc	BU
1874Ho R Rare	—	—	—	—	—	—
1876Ho F Rare	357	—	—	—	—	—
1878Ho A	814	1,750	3,000	3,500	5,500	—
1879Ho A	—	1,000	2,000	2,500	4,000	—
1880Ho A	—	1,000	2,000	2,500	4,000	—
1881Ho A Rare	—	—	—	—	—	—

Note: American Numismatic Rarities Eliasberg sale 4-05, MS-62 realized $34,500.

KM# 413.7 10 PESOS
16.9200 g., 0.8750 Gold 0.4760 oz. AGW **Obv:** Facing eagle, snake in beak **Obv. Legend:** REPUBLICA MEXICANA **Rev:** Radiant cap above scales **Mint:** Mexico City

Date	Mintage	F	VF	XF	Unc	BU
1870Mo C	480	500	900	1,200	2,000	—
1872/1Mo M/C	2,100	460	550	900	1,350	—
1873Mo M	—	460	600	950	1,450	—
1874/3Mo M	—	460	600	950	1,450	—
1875Mo B/M	—	460	600	950	1,450	—
1876Mo B Rare	—	—	—	—	—	—
1878Mo M	300	460	600	950	1,450	—
1879Mo M	—	—	—	—	—	—
1881Mo M	100	500	1,000	1,600	2,500	—
1882Mo M	—	460	600	950	1,450	—
1883Mo M	100	600	1,000	1,600	2,500	—
1884Mo M	—	600	1,000	1,600	2,500	—
1885Mo M	—	460	600	950	1,450	—
1886Mo M	100	600	1,000	1,600	2,500	—
1887Mo M	100	600	1,000	1,625	2,750	—
1888Mo M	144	460	750	1,200	2,000	—
1889Mo M	88	600	1,000	1,600	2,500	—
1890Mo M	137	600	1,000	1,600	2,500	—
1891Mo M	133	600	1,000	1,600	2,500	—
1892Mo M	45	600	1,000	1,600	2,500	—
1893Mo M	1,361	460	550	900	1,350	—
1897Mo M	239	460	600	950	1,450	—
1898/7Mo M	244	460	625	1,000	1,750	—
1900Mo M	733	460	600	950	1,450	—
1901Mo M	562	600	620	850	1,500	—
1902Mo M	719	600	620	850	1,500	2,500
1903Mo M	713	600	620	850	1,500	2,500
1904Mo M	694	600	620	850	1,500	—
1905Mo M	401	600	650	975	1,700	—

KM# 413.8   10 PESOS
16.9200 g., 0.8750 Gold 0.4760 oz. AGW **Obv:** Facing eagle, snake in beak **Obv. Legend:** REPUBLICA MEXICANA **Rev:** Radiant cap above scales **Mint:** Oaxaca

Date	Mintage	F	VF	XF	Unc	BU
1870Oa E	4,614	460	600	900	1,600	—
1871Oa E	2,705	460	600	950	1,650	—
1872Oa E	5,897	460	600	850	1,500	—
1873Oa E	3,537	460	600	850	1,500	—
1874Oa E	2,205	460	600	1,200	1,850	—
1875Oa E	312	475	750	1,400	2,250	—
1876Oa E	766	475	750	1,400	2,250	—
1877Oa E	463	475	750	1,400	2,250	—
1878Oa E	229	475	750	1,400	2,250	—
1879Oa E	210	475	750	1,400	2,250	—
1880Oa E	238	475	750	1,400	2,250	—
1881Oa E	961	460	600	1,200	2,000	—
1882Oa E	170	600	1,000	1,500	2,500	—
1883Oa E	111	600	1,000	1,500	2,500	—
1884Oa E	325	475	750	1,400	2,250	—
1885Oa E	370	475	750	1,400	2,250	—
1886Oa E	400	475	750	1,400	2,250	—
1887Oa E	—	700	1,250	2,250	4,000	—
1888Oa E	—	—	—	—	—	—

KM# 413.9   10 PESOS
16.9200 g., 0.8750 Gold 0.4760 oz. AGW **Obv:** Facing eagle, snake in beak **Obv. Legend:** REPUBLICA MEXICANA **Rev:** Radiant cap above scales **Mint:** Zacatecas

Date	Mintage	F	VF	XF	Unc	BU
1871Zs H	2,000	455	500	800	1,250	—
1872Zs H	3,092	455	500	750	1,150	—
1873Zs H	936	460	600	950	1,450	—
1874Zs H	—	460	600	950	1,450	—
1875/3Zs A	—	460	600	1,000	1,750	—
1876/5Zs S	—	460	600	1,000	1,750	—
1877Zs S/H	506	460	600	1,000	1,750	—
1878Zs S	711	460	600	1,000	1,750	—
1879/8Zs S	—	475	750	1,400	2,250	—
1879Zs S	—	475	750	1,400	2,250	—
1880Zs S	2,089	455	550	950	1,450	—
1881Zs S	736	460	600	1,000	1,750	—
1882/1Zs Z	—	460	600	1,000	1,750	2,500
1882Zs S	1,599	455	550	950	1,450	—
1883/2Zs S	256	400	600	1,000	1,750	—
1884/3Zs S	—	455	550	950	1,600	—
1884Zs S	—	455	550	950	1,600	—
1885Zs S	1,588	455	550	950	1,450	—
1886Zs S	5,364	455	550	950	1,450	—
1887Zs Z	2,330	455	550	950	1,450	—
1888Zs Z	4,810	455	550	950	1,450	—
1889Zs Z	6,154	455	500	750	1,250	—
1890Zs Z	1,321	455	550	950	1,450	—
1891Zs Z	1,930	455	550	950	1,450	3,250
1892Zs Z	1,882	455	550	950	1,450	—
1893Zs Z	2,899	455	550	950	1,450	—
1894Zs Z	2,501	455	550	950	1,450	—
1895Zs Z	1,217	455	550	950	1,450	—

KM# 413   10 PESOS
16.9200 g., 0.8750 Gold 0.4760 oz. AGW **Obv:** Facing eagle, snake in beak **Obv. Legend:** REPUBLICA MEXICANA **Rev:** Radiant cap above scales **Mint:** Alamos

Date	Mintage	F	VF	XF	Unc	BU
1874As DL Rare	—					
1875As L	642	600	1,250	2,500	3,500	—
1878As L	977	500	1,000	2,000	3,000	—
1879As L	1,078	500	1,000	2,000	3,000	—
1880As L	2,629	500	1,000	2,000	3,000	—
1881As L	2,574	500	1,000	2,000	3,000	—
1882As L	3,403	500	1,000	2,000	3,000	—
1883As L	3,597	500	1,000	2,000	3,000	—
1884As L Rare	—					
1885As L	4,562	500	1,000	2,000	3,000	—
1886As L	4,643	500	1,000	2,000	3,000	—
1887As L	3,667	500	1,000	2,000	3,000	—
1888As L	4,521	500	1,000	2,000	3,000	—
1889As L	5,615	500	1,000	2,000	3,000	—
1890As L	4,920	500	1,000	2,000	3,000	—
1891As L	568	500	1,000	2,000	3,000	—
1892As L	—					
1893As L	817	500	1,000	2,000	3,000	—
1894/3As L	1,658					
1894As L	Inc. above	500	1,000	2,000	3,000	—
1895As L	1,237	500	1,000	2,000	3,000	—

KM# 413.1   10 PESOS
16.9200 g., 0.8750 Gold 0.4760 oz. AGW **Obv:** Facing eagle, snake in beak **Obv. Legend:** REPUBLICA MEXICANA **Rev:** Radiant cap above scales **Mint:** Chihuahua

Date	Mintage	F	VF	XF	Unc	BU
1888Ca M	175	—	—	7,500		

KM# 414   20 PESOS
33.8400 g., 0.8750 Gold 0.9519 oz. AGW **Obv:** Facing eagle, snake in beak **Rev:** Radiant cap above scales **Mint:** Alamos

Date	Mintage	F	VF	XF	Unc	BU
1876As L Rare	276	—	—	—	—	—
1877As L Rare	166	—	—	—	—	—
1878As L	—	—	—	—	—	—
1888As L Rare	—	—	—	—	—	—

KM# 414.2   20 PESOS
33.8400 g., 0.8750 Gold 0.9519 oz. AGW **Obv:** Facing eagle,

snake in beak **Obv. Legend:** REPUBLICA MEXICANA **Rev:** Radiant cap above scales **Mint:** Culiacan

Date	Mintage	F	VF	XF	Unc	BU
1870Cn E	3,749	BV	925	1,200	2,500	—
1871Cn P	3,046	BV	925	1,200	2,500	—
1872Cn P	972	BV	925	1,200	2,500	—
1873Cn P	1,317	BV	925	1,200	2,500	—
1874Cn P	—	BV	925	1,200	2,500	—
1875Cn P	—	925	1,600	2,250	3,150	—
1876Cn P	—	BV	925	1,200	2,500	—
1876Cn G	—	BV	925	1,200	2,500	—
1877Cn G	167	925	1,350	1,900	3,750	—
1878Cn Rare	842	—	—	—	—	—
1881/0Cn D	2,039	—	—	—	—	—
1881Cn D	Inc. above	BV	925	1,200	2,500	—
1882/1Cn D	736	BV	925	1,200	2,500	—
1883Cn M	1,836	BV	925	1,200	2,500	—
1884Cn M	—	BV	925	1,200	2,500	—
1885Cn M	544	BV	925	1,200	2,500	—
1886Cn M	882	BV	925	1,200	2,500	—
1887Cn M	837	BV	925	1,200	2,500	—
1888Cn M	473	BV	925	1,200	2,500	—
1889Cn M	1,376	BV	925	1,200	2,500	—
1890Cn M	—	1,100	2,350	4,400	11,000	—
1891Cn M	237	BV	1,200	1,500	2,800	—
1892Cn M	526	BV	925	1,200	2,500	—
1893Cn M	2,062	BV	925	1,200	2,500	—
1894Cn M	4,516	BV	925	1,200	2,500	—
1895Cn M	3,193	BV	925	1,200	2,500	—
1896Cn M	4,072	BV	925	1,200	2,500	—
1897/6Cn M	959	BV	925	1,200	2,500	—
1897Cn M	Inc. above	BV	925	1,200	2,500	—
1898Cn M	1,660	BV	925	1,200	2,500	—
1899Cn M	1,243	BV	925	1,200	2,500	—
1899Cn Q	Inc. above	BV	1,200	1,500	2,800	—
1900Cn Q	1,558	BV	925	1,200	2,500	—
1901Cn Q	Inc. above	BV	1,250	1,350	2,750	—
1901/0Cn Q	1,496	—	—	—	—	—
1902Cn Q	1,059	BV	1,250	1,350	2,750	—
1903Cn Q	1,121	BV	1,250	1,350	2,750	—
1904Cn H	4,646	BV	1,250	1,350	2,750	—
1905Cn P	1,738	BV	1,300	1,500	2,950	—

KM# 414.3 20 PESOS
33.8400 g., 0.8750 Gold 0.9519 oz. AGW **Obv:** Facing eagle, snake in beak **Obv. Legend:** REPUBLICA MEXICANA **Rev:** Radiant cap above scales **Mint:** Durango

Date	Mintage	F	VF	XF	Unc	BU
1870Do P	416	1,100	1,650	2,500	3,150	—
1871/0Do P	1,073	1,100	1,950	2,800	3,450	—
1871Do P	Inc. above	1,100	1,650	2,500	3,150	—
1872/1Do PT	—	1,650	3,300	5,600	8,800	—
1876Do M	—	1,100	1,650	2,500	3,150	—
1877Do P	94	1,650	2,500	3,450	4,050	—
1878Do Rare	258	—	—	—	—	—

KM# 414.4 20 PESOS
33.8400 g., 0.8750 Gold 0.9519 oz. AGW **Obv:** Facing eagle, snake in beak **Obv. Legend:** REPUBLICA MEXICANA **Rev:** Radiant cap above scales **Mint:** Guanajuato

Date	Mintage	F	VF	XF	Unc	BU
1870Go S	3,250	BV	925	1,150	1,900	—
1871Go S	20,000	BV	925	1,150	1,900	2,750
1872Go S	18,000	BV	925	1,150	1,900	—
1873Go S	7,000	BV	925	1,150	1,900	—
1874Go S	—	BV	925	1,150	1,900	—
1875Go S	—	BV	925	1,150	1,900	—
1876Go S	—	BV	925	1,150	1,900	—
1876Go M/S	—	—	—	—	—	—
1877Go M/S Rare	15,000	—	—	—	—	—
1877Go R	Inc. above	BV	925	1,150	1,900	—
1877Go S Rare	Inc. above	—	—	—	—	—
1878/7Go M/S	13,000	950	1,750	2,500	3,500	—
1878Go M	Inc. above	950	1,750	2,500	3,500	—
1878Go S	Inc. above	BV	925	1,150	1,900	—
1879Go S	8,202	BV	1,100	1,500	2,900	—
1880Go S	7,375	BV	925	1,150	1,900	—
1881Go S	4,909	BV	925	1,150	1,900	—
1882Go S	4,020	BV	925	1,150	1,900	—
1883/2Go B	3,705	BV	1,050	1,450	2,800	—
1883Go B	Inc. above	BV	925	1,150	1,900	—
1884Go B	1,798	BV	925	1,150	1,900	—
1885Go R	2,660	BV	925	1,150	1,900	—
1886Go R	1,090	950	1,100	1,550	3,150	—
1887Go R	1,009	950	1,100	1,550	3,150	—
1888Go R	1,011	950	1,100	1,550	3,150	—
1889Go R	956	950	1,100	1,550	3,150	—
1890Go R	879	950	1,100	1,550	3,150	—
1891Go R	818	950	1,100	1,550	3,150	—
1892Go R	730	950	1,100	1,550	3,150	—
1893Go R	3,343	BV	925	1,250	2,500	—
1894/3Go R	6,734	BV	925	1,150	1,900	—
1894Go R	Inc. above	BV	925	1,150	1,900	—
1895/3Go R	7,118	BV	925	1,150	1,900	—
1895Go R	Inc. above	BV	925	1,150	1,900	—
1896Go R	9,219	BV	925	1,150	1,900	7,200
1897/6Go R	6,781	BV	925	1,150	1,900	—
1897Go R	Inc. above	BV	925	1,150	1,900	—
1898Go R	7,710	BV	925	1,150	1,900	—
1899Go R	8,527	BV	925	1,150	1,900	—
1900Go R	4,512	950	1,100	1,550	2,950	—

KM# 414.5 20 PESOS
33.8400 g., 0.8750 Gold 0.9519 oz. AGW **Obv:** Facing eagle, snake in beak **Obv. Legend:** REPUBLICA MEXICANA **Rev:** Radiant cap above scales **Mint:** Hermosillo

Date	Mintage	F	VF	XF	Unc	BU
1874Ho R Rare	—	—	—	—	—	—
1875Ho R Rare	—	—	—	—	—	—

SECOND REPUBLIC

Date	Mintage	F	VF	XF	Unc	BU
1876Ho F Rare	—	—	—	—	—	—
1888Ho g Rare	—	—	—	—	—	—

KM# 414.6 20 PESOS
33.8400 g., 0.8750 Gold 0.9519 oz. AGW **Obv:** Facing eagle, snake in beak **Obv. Legend:** REPUBLICA MEXICANA **Rev:** Radiant cap above scales **Mint:** Mexico City

Date	Mintage	F	VF	XF	Unc	BU
1870Mo C	14,000	BV	920	1,150	1,900	—
1871Mo M	21,000	BV	920	1,150	1,900	—
1872/1Mo M	11,000	BV	920	1,150	2,050	—
1872Mo M	Inc. above	BV	920	1,150	1,900	—
1873Mo M	5,600	BV	920	1,150	1,900	—
1874/2Mo M	—	BV	920	1,150	1,900	—
1874/2Mo B	—	BV	920	1,250	2,050	—
1875Mo B	—	BV	920	1,150	2,000	—
1876Mo B	—	BV	920	1,150	2,000	—
1876Mo M	—	—	—	—	—	—
Note: Reported, not confirmed						
1877Mo M	2,000	BV	1,150	1,400	2,500	—
1878Mo M	7,000	BV	920	1,150	2,000	—
1879Mo M	—	BV	920	1,150	2,200	—
1880Mo M	—	BV	920	1,150	2,200	—
1881/0Mo M	11,000	BV	920	1,150	1,900	—
1881Mo M	Inc. above	BV	920	1,150	1,900	—
1882/1Mo M	5,800	BV	920	1,150	1,900	—
1882Mo M	Inc. above	BV	920	1,150	1,900	—
1883/1Mo M	4,000	BV	920	1,150	1,900	—
1883Mo M	Inc. above	BV	920	1,150	1,900	—
1884/3Mo M	—	BV	920	1,150	2,000	—
1884Mo M	—	BV	920	1,150	2,000	—
1885Mo M	6,000	BV	920	1,150	2,200	—
1886Mo M	10,000	BV	920	1,150	1,900	—
1887Mo M	12,000	BV	1,150	1,900	3,150	—
1888Mo M	7,300	BV	920	1,150	1,800	—
1889Mo M	6,477	BV	1,150	2,050	4,700	—
1890Mo M	7,852	BV	920	1,150	1,950	—
1891/0Mo M	8,725	BV	920	1,150	1,950	—
1891Mo M	Inc. above	BV	920	1,150	1,950	—
1892Mo M	11,000	BV	920	1,150	1,900	—
1893Mo M	15,000	BV	920	1,150	1,900	—
1894Mo M	14,000	BV	920	1,150	1,900	—
1895Mo M	13,000	BV	920	1,150	1,900	—
1896Mo B	14,000	BV	920	1,150	1,900	—
1897/6Mo M	12,000	BV	920	1,150	1,900	—
1897Mo M	Inc. above	BV	920	1,150	1,900	—
1898Mo M	20,000	BV	920	1,150	1,900	—
1899Mo M	23,000	BV	920	1,150	1,900	—
1900Mo M	21,000	BV	920	1,150	1,900	—
1901Mo M	29,000	BV	1,100	1,250	2,000	—
1902Mo M	38,000	BV	1,100	1,250	2,000	—
1903/2Mo M	31,000	BV	1,100	1,250	2,000	—
1903Mo M	Inc. above	BV	1,100	1,250	2,000	—
1904Mo M	52,000	BV	1,100	1,250	2,000	—
1905Mo M	9,757	BV	1,100	1,250	2,000	—

KM# 414.7 20 PESOS
33.8400 g., 0.8750 Gold 0.9519 oz. AGW **Obv:** Facing eagle, snake in beak **Obv. Legend:** REPUBLICA MEXICANA **Rev:** Radiant cap above scales **Mint:** Oaxaca

Date	Mintage	F	VF	XF	Unc	BU
1870Oa E	1,131	1,000	2,050	3,150	6,300	—
1871Oa E	1,591	1,000	2,050	3,150	6,300	—
1872Oa E	255	1,000	1,750	3,750	8,800	—
1888Oa E	170	2,000	3,500	6,300	—	—

KM# 414.8 20 PESOS
33.8400 g., 0.8750 Gold 0.9519 oz. AGW **Obv:** Facing eagle, snake in beak **Rev:** Radiant cap above scales **Mint:** Zacatecas

Date	Mintage	F	VF	XF	Unc	BU
1871Zs H	1,000	3,500	6,500	8,800	11,500	—
1875Zs A	—	4,000	6,000	9,400	12,000	—
1878Zs S	441	4,000	6,000	9,400	12,000	—
1888Zs Z Rare	50	—	—	—	—	—
1889Zs Z	640	3,500	5,500	8,800	11,500	—

KM# 414.1 20 PESOS
33.8400 g., 0.8750 Gold 0.9519 oz. AGW **Obv:** Facing eagle, snake in beak **Rev:** Radiant cap above scales **Mint:** Chihuahua **Note:** Mint mark CH, Ca.

Date	Mintage	F	VF	XF	Unc	BU
1872CH M	995	BV	950	1,250	3,150	—
1873CH M	950	BV	950	1,250	3,150	—
1874CH M	1,116	BV	925	1,200	3,150	—
1875CH M	750	BV	950	1,250	3,150	—
1876CH M	600	BV	1,100	1,550	3,450	—
1877CH Rare	55	—	—	—	—	—
1882CH M	1,758	BV	925	1,200	3,150	—
1883CH M	161	950	1,350	1,900	3,750	—
1884CH M	496	BV	950	1,250	3,150	—
1885CH M	122	950	1,350	1,900	3,750	—
1887Ca M	550	BV	950	1,250	3,150	—
1888Ca M	351	BV	950	1,250	3,150	—
1889Ca M	464	BV	950	1,250	3,150	—
1890Ca M	1,209	BV	925	1,200	3,150	—
1891Ca M	2,004	BV	900	1,150	2,800	—
1893Ca M	418	BV	950	1,200	3,150	—
1895Ca M	133	950	1,350	1,900	3,750	—

ESTADOS UNIDOS
DECIMAL COINAGE
100 Centavos = 1 Peso

KM# 415 CENTAVO
3.0000 g., Bronze, 20 mm. **Obv:** National arms **Rev:** Value below date within wreath **Mint:** Mexico City **Note:** Mint mark Mo.

Date	Mintage	F	VF	XF	Unc	BU
1905 Narrow date	6,040,000	4.00	6.50	14.00	90.00	—
1905 Wide date	—	4.00	6.50	14.00	90.00	—
1906 Narrow date	Est. 67,505,000	0.50	0.75	1.25	14.00	25.00
Note: 50,000,000 pcs. were struck at the Birmingham Mint						
1906 Wide date	Inc. above	0.75	1.50	2.50	22.00	—

Date	Mintage	F	VF	XF	Unc	BU
1910 Narrow date	8,700,000	2.00	3.00	6.50	85.00	100
1910 Wide date	—	2.00	3.00	6.50	85.00	100
1911 Narrow date	16,450,000	0.60	1.00	2.75	22.50	—
1911 Wide date	Inc. above	0.75	1.00	4.00	35.00	—
1912	12,650,000	1.00	1.35	3.25	35.00	—
1913	12,850,000	0.75	1.25	3.00	35.00	—
1914 Narrow date	17,350,000	0.75	1.00	3.00	15.00	20.00
1914 Wide date	Inc. above	0.75	1.00	3.00	15.00	20.00
1915	2,277,000	11.00	25.00	67.50	250	—
1916	500,000	45.00	80.00	170	1,200	—
1920	1,433,000	22.00	50.00	115	400	—
1921	3,470,000	5.50	15.50	47.00	275	—
1922	1,880,000	9.00	17.00	50.00	250	—
1923	4,800,000	0.75	1.25	1.75	13.50	—
1924/3	2,000,000	65.00	170	275	525	—
1924	Inc. above	4.50	11.00	22.00	250	300
1925	1,550,000	4.50	10.00	25.00	220	—
1926	5,000,000	1.00	2.00	4.00	20.00	28.00
1927/6	6,000,000	30.00	45.00	70.00	175	—
1927	Inc. above	0.75	1.25	4.50	32.00	45.00
1928	5,000,000	0.75	1.00	3.25	16.50	45.00
1929	4,500,000	0.75	1.00	1.75	17.00	25.00
1930	7,000,000	0.75	1.00	2.50	20.00	—
1933	10,000,000	0.25	0.35	1.75	16.50	22.00
1934	7,500,000	0.25	0.95	3.25	40.00	—
1935	12,400,000	0.15	0.25	0.40	11.50	15.00
1936	20,100,000	0.15	0.20	0.30	9.00	—
1937	20,000,000	0.15	0.25	0.35	4.00	6.00
1938	10,000,000	0.10	0.15	0.30	2.00	3.00
1939	30,000,000	0.10	0.20	0.30	1.00	2.50
1940	10,000,000	0.20	0.30	0.60	5.50	8.50
1941	15,800,000	0.15	0.25	0.35	2.00	3.00
1942	30,400,000	0.15	0.20	0.30	1.25	2.00
1943	4,310,000	0.30	0.50	0.75	9.00	12.50
1944	5,645,000	0.15	0.25	0.50	6.00	8.50
1945	26,375,000	0.10	0.15	0.25	1.00	1.75
1946	42,135,000	—	0.15	0.20	0.60	1.50
1947	13,445,000	—	0.10	0.15	0.80	1.50
1948	20,040,000	0.10	0.15	0.30	1.10	2.25
1949	6,235,000	0.10	0.15	0.30	1.25	3.00

Note: Varieties exist

KM# 416 CENTAVO
1.5000 g., Bronze, 16 mm. **Obv:** National arms **Rev:** Value below date within wreath **Mint:** Mexico City **Note:** Zapata issue. Struck at Mexico City Mint, mint mark Mo. Reduced size. Weight varies 1.39-1.5g.

Date	Mintage	F	VF	XF	Unc	BU
1915	179,000	18.00	30.00	60.00	85.00	—

KM# 417 CENTAVO
2.0000 g., Brass, 16 mm. **Obv:** National arms, eagle left **Rev:** Oat sprigs **Mint:** Mexico City **Note:** Mint mark Mo.

Date	Mintage	F	VF	XF	Unc	BU
1950	12,815,000	—	0.15	0.35	1.65	2.25
1951	25,740,000	—	0.15	0.35	0.65	1.25
1952	24,610,000	—	0.10	0.25	0.40	0.85
1953	21,160,000	—	0.10	0.25	0.40	0.85
1954	25,675,000	—	0.10	0.15	0.85	1.50
1955	9,820,000	—	0.15	0.25	0.85	1.75
1956	11,285,000	—	0.15	0.25	0.80	1.75
1957	9,805,000	—	0.15	0.25	0.85	1.50
1958	12,155,000	—	0.10	0.25	0.45	0.75
1959	11,875,000	—	0.10	0.25	0.75	1.50
1960	10,360,000	—	0.10	0.15	0.40	0.65
1961	6,385,000	—	0.10	0.15	0.45	0.85
1962	4,850,000	—	0.10	0.15	0.55	0.90

Date	Mintage	F	VF	XF	Unc	BU
1963	7,775,000	—	0.10	0.15	0.25	0.45
1964	4,280,000	—	0.10	0.15	0.20	0.30
1965	2,255,000	—	0.10	0.15	0.25	0.40
1966	1,760,000	—	0.10	0.25	0.60	1.00
1967	1,290,000	—	0.10	0.15	0.40	0.75
1968	1,000,000	—	0.10	0.20	0.85	1.45
1969	1,000,000	—	0.10	0.15	0.65	0.85

KM# 418 CENTAVO
1.5000 g., Brass, 13 mm. **Obv:** National arms, eagle left **Rev:** Oat sprigs **Mint:** Mexico City **Note:** Reduced size.

Date	Mintage	F	VF	XF	Unc	BU
1970	1,000,000	—	0.20	0.40	1.45	2.25
1972	1,000,000	—	0.20	0.45	2.50	4.00
1972/2	—	—	0.50	1.25	3.50	5.00
1973	1,000,000	—	1.65	2.75	9.00	17.50

KM# 419 2 CENTAVOS
6.0000 g., Bronze, 25 mm. **Obv:** National arms **Rev:** Value below date within wreath **Mint:** Mexico City **Note:** Mint mark Mo.

Date	Mintage	F	VF	XF	Unc	BU
1905	50,000	150	300	500	1,200	1,350
1906 Inverted 6	9,998,000	30.00	55.00	120	375	—
1906 Wide date	Inc. above	5.00	11.00	28.00	95.00	110
1906 Narrow date	Inc. above	6.50	14.00	30.00	95.00	—

Note: 5,000,000 pieces were struck at the Birmingham Mint

1920	1,325,000	6.50	17.50	75.00	350	—
1921	4,275,000	2.50	4.75	15.00	100	—
1922	—	225	550	1,750	5,500	—
1924	750,000	8.50	27.50	75.00	450	—
1925	3,650,000	2.50	3.50	7.50	35.00	40.00
1926	4,750,000	1.00	2.25	5.50	40.00	—
1927	7,250,000	0.60	1.00	4.50	22.00	35.00
1928	3,250,000	0.75	1.50	4.75	25.00	35.00
1929	250,000	85.00	225	550	1,200	—
1935	1,250,000	4.25	9.25	65.00	225	275
1939	5,000,000	0.60	0.90	2.25	20.00	30.00
1941	3,550,000	0.45	0.60	1.25	18.00	28.00

KM# 420 2 CENTAVOS
3.0000 g., Bronze, 20 mm. **Obv:** National arms **Rev:** Value below date within wreath **Mint:** Mexico City **Note:** Zapata issue. Mint mark Mo. Reduced size. Weight varies 3-3.03g.

Date	Mintage	F	VF	XF	Unc	BU
1915	487,000	7.50	9.00	17.50	75.00	—

KM# 421 5 CENTAVOS
5.0000 g., Nickel, 20 mm. **Obv:** National arms **Rev:** Value

and date within beaded circle **Mint:** Mexico City **Note:** Mint mark Mo. Varieties exist.

Date	Mintage	F	VF	XF	Unc	BU
1905	1,420,000	7.00	10.00	28.00	325	375
1906/5	10,615,000	13.00	30.00	70.00	375	—
1906	Inc. above	0.75	1.35	3.25	55.00	75.00
1907	4,000,000	1.25	4.00	35.00	350	450
1909	2,052,000	3.25	10.00	50.00	360	—
1910	6,181,000	1.30	3.50	9.00	85.00	125
1911 Narrow date	4,487,000	1.00	3.00	7.00	95.00	135
1911 Wide date	Inc. above	2.50	5.00	9.00	110	170
1912 Small mint mark	420,000	90.00	100	230	725	—
1912 Large mint mark	Inc. above	70.00	95.00	200	575	—
1913	2,035,000	1.75	4.25	30.00	200	300

Note: Wide and narrow dates exist for 1913

| 1914 | 2,000,000 | 1.00 | 2.00 | 5.00 | 75.00 | 110 |

Note: 5,000,000 pieces appear to have been struck at the Birmingham Mint in 1914 and all of 1909-1911. The Mexican Mint report does not mention receiving the 1914 dated coins

KM# 422   5 CENTAVOS
9.0000 g., Bronze, 28 mm.   **Obv:** National arms **Rev:** Value below date within wreath **Mint:** Mexico City

Date	Mintage	F	VF	XF	Unc	BU
1914Mo	2,500,000	10.00	23.00	65.00	300	—
1915Mo	11,424,000	3.00	5.00	35.00	165	265
1916Mo	2,860,000	15.00	35.00	175	650	—
1917Mo	800,000	75.00	225	400	900	—
1918Mo	1,332,000	35.00	90.00	250	675	—
1919Mo	400,000	115	225	360	950	—
1920Mo	5,920,000	3.00	8.00	45.00	265	350
1921Mo	2,080,000	10.00	24.00	75.00	275	—
1924Mo	780,000	40.00	95.00	275	700	—
1925Mo	4,040,000	5.50	11.00	47.50	225	—
1926Mo	3,160,000	5.50	11.00	48.00	325	—
1927Mo	3,600,000	4.00	7.00	35.00	250	350
1928Mo Large date	1,740,000	11.00	18.00	65.00	250	325
1928Mo Small date	Inc. above	30.00	45.00	100	385	—
1929Mo	2,400,000	5.50	12.00	50.00	200	—
1930Mo	2,600,000	5.00	8.00	27.50	225	—

Note: Large oval O in date

| 1930Mo | Inc. above | 65.00 | 125 | 250 | 565 | — |

Note: Small square O in date

1931Mo	—	475	750	1,450	4,000	—
1933Mo	8,000,000	1.50	2.25	3.50	27.50	45.00
1934Mo	10,000,000	1.25	1.75	2.75	25.00	50.00
1935Mo	21,980,000	0.75	1.20	2.50	22.50	40.00

KM# 423   5 CENTAVOS
4.0000 g., Copper-Nickel, 20.5 mm.   **Obv:** National arms, eagle left **Rev:** Value and date within circle **Mint:** Mexico City

Date	Mintage	F	VF	XF	Unc	BU
1936M	46,700,000	—	0.65	1.25	7.50	8.50
1937M	49,060,000	—	0.50	1.00	7.00	8.00
1938M	3,340,000	—	4.00	10.00	80.00	200
1940M	22,800,000	—	0.75	1.25	8.00	10.00
1942M	7,100,000	—	1.50	3.00	35.00	50.00

KM# 424   5 CENTAVOS
6.5000 g., Bronze, 25.5 mm.   **Obv:** National arms, eagle left **Rev:** Head left **Mint:** Mexico City

Date	Mintage	F	VF	XF	Unc	BU
1942Mo	900,000	—	25.00	75.00	375	550
1943Mo	54,660,000	—	0.50	0.75	2.50	3.50
1944Mo	53,463,000	—	0.25	0.35	0.75	1.00
1945Mo	44,262,000	—	0.25	0.35	0.75	1.25
1946Mo	49,054,000	—	0.50	1.00	2.00	3.00
1951Mo	50,758,000	—	0.75	0.90	3.00	5.00
1952Mo	17,674,000	—	1.50	2.50	9.50	11.50
1953Mo	31,568,000	—	1.25	2.00	6.00	9.00
1954Mo	58,680,000	—	0.40	1.00	2.75	4.00
1955Mo	31,114,000	—	2.00	3.00	11.00	14.00

KM# 425   5 CENTAVOS
4.0000 g., Copper-Nickel, 20.5 mm.   **Obv:** National arms, eagle left **Rev:** Bust right flanked by date and value **Mint:** Mexico City

Date	Mintage	F	VF	XF	Unc	BU
1950Mo	5,700,000	—	0.75	1.50	6.00	7.00

Note: 5,600,000 pieces struck at Connecticut melted

KM# 426   5 CENTAVOS
4.0000 g., Brass, 20.4 mm.   **Obv:** National arms, eagle left **Rev:** Bust right **Mint:** Mexico City

Date	Mintage	F	VF	XF	Unc	BU
1954Mo Dot	—	—	10.00	50.00	300	375
1954Mo Without dot	—	—	15.00	35.00	275	325
1955Mo	12,136,000	—	0.75	1.50	9.00	12.50
1956Mo	60,216,000	—	0.20	0.30	0.75	1.25
1957Mo	55,288,000	—	0.15	0.20	0.90	1.50
1958Mo	104,624,000	—	0.15	0.20	0.60	1.00
1959Mo	106,000,000	—	0.15	0.25	0.75	1.25
1960Mo	99,144,000	—	0.10	0.15	0.50	0.75

Date	Mintage	F	VF	XF	Unc	BU
1961Mo	61,136,000	—	0.10	0.15	0.50	0.75
1962Mo	47,232,000	—	0.10	0.15	0.25	0.35
1963Mo	156,680,000	—	—	0.15	0.25	0.40
1964Mo	71,168,000	—	—	0.15	0.20	0.40
1965Mo	155,720,000	—	—	0.15	0.25	0.35
1966Mo	124,944,000	—	—	0.15	0.40	0.65
1967Mo	118,816,000	—	—	0.15	0.25	0.40
1968Mo	189,588,000	—	—	0.15	0.50	0.75
1969Mo	210,492,000	—	—	0.15	0.55	0.80

KM# 426a   5 CENTAVOS
Copper-Nickel, 20.5 mm. **Obv:** National arms, eagle left **Rev:** Bust right **Mint:** Mexico City

Date	Mintage	F	VF	XF	Unc	BU
1960Mo	—	—	250	300	375	—
1962Mo	19	—	250	300	375	—
1965Mo	—	—	250	300	375	—

KM# 427   5 CENTAVOS
2.7500 g., Brass, 18 mm. **Obv:** National arms, eagle left **Rev:** Bust right **Note:** Due to some minor alloy variations this type is often encountered with a bronze-color toning. Reduced size.

Date	Mintage	F	VF	XF	Unc	BU
1970	163,368,000	—	0.10	0.15	0.35	0.45
1971	198,844,000	—	0.10	0.15	0.25	0.30
1972	225,000,000	—	0.10	0.15	0.25	0.30
1973 Flat top 3	595,070,000	—	0.10	0.15	0.25	0.40
1973 Round top 3	Inc. above	—	0.10	0.15	0.20	0.30
1974	401,584,000	—	0.10	0.15	0.30	0.40
1975	342,308,000	—	0.10	0.15	0.25	0.35
1976	367,524,000	—	0.10	0.15	0.40	0.60

KM# 428   10 CENTAVOS
2.5000 g., 0.8000 Silver 0.0643 oz. ASW, 18 mm. **Obv:** National arms **Rev:** Value and date within 3/4 wreath with Liberty cap above **Mint:** Mexico City **Note:** Mint mark Mo.

Date	Mintage	F	VF	XF	Unc	BU
1905	3,920,000	—	6.00	8.00	40.00	50.00
1906	8,410,000	—	5.50	7.50	27.00	50.00
1907/6	5,950,000	—	50.00	135	325	375
1907	Inc. above	—	5.50	6.25	35.00	50.00
1909	2,620,000	—	8.50	13.00	80.00	110
1910/00	3,450,000	—	10.00	40.00	75.00	85.00
1910	Inc. above	—	7.00	15.00	25.00	40.00
1911 Narrow date	2,550,000	—	11.00	17.00	88.00	125
1911 Wide date	Inc. above	—	7.50	10.00	45.00	65.00
1912	1,350,000	—	10.00	18.00	130	175
1912 Low 2	Inc. above	—	10.00	18.00	115	155
1913/2	1,990,000	—	10.00	25.00	40.00	70.00
1913	Inc. above	—	7.00	10.00	33.00	45.00
1914	3,110,000	—	5.50	7.00	15.00	25.00

Note: Wide and narrow dates exist for 1914

KM# 429   10 CENTAVOS
1.8125 g., 0.8000 Silver 0.0466 oz. ASW, 15 mm. **Obv:** National arms **Rev:** Value and date within 3/4 wreath with Liberty cap above **Mint:** Mexico City **Note:** Mint mark Mo. Reduced size.

Date	Mintage	F	VF	XF	Unc	BU
1919	8,360,000	—	10.00	15.00	95.00	125

KM# 430   10 CENTAVOS
12.0000 g., Bronze, 30.5 mm. **Obv:** National arms **Rev:** Value below date within wreath **Mint:** Mexico City **Note:** Mint mark Mo.

Date	Mintage	F	VF	XF	Unc	BU
1919	1,232,000	—	25.00	85.00	475	550
1920	6,612,000	—	15.00	50.00	400	475
1921	2,255,000	—	35.00	95.00	650	800
1935	5,970,000	—	14.00	35.00	125	200

KM# 431   10 CENTAVOS
1.6600 g., 0.7200 Silver 0.0384 oz. ASW, 15 mm. **Obv:** National arms **Rev:** Value and date within wreath with Liberty cap above **Mint:** Mexico City **Note:** Mint mark Mo.

Date	Mintage	F	VF	XF	Unc	BU
1925/15	5,350,000	—	30.00	75.00	125	175
1925/3	Inc. above	—	20.00	40.00	125	175
1925	Inc. above	—	2.00	5.00	40.00	50.00
1926/16	2,650,000	—	30.00	75.00	125	175
1926	Inc. above	—	3.50	7.50	65.00	95.00
1927	2,810,000	—	2.25	3.00	17.50	25.00
1928	5,270,000	—	2.00	2.75	13.50	20.00
1930	2,000,000	—	3.75	5.00	18.75	28.00
1933	5,000,000	—	1.50	3.00	10.00	17.00
1934	8,000,000	—	1.75	2.50	8.00	16.00
1935	3,500,000	—	2.75	5.00	11.00	18.00

KM# 432   10 CENTAVOS
5.5000 g., Copper-Nickel, 23.5 mm. **Obv:** National arms, eagle left **Rev:** Value and date within circle **Mint:** Mexico City **Note:** Mint mark Mo.

Date	Mintage	F	VF	XF	Unc	BU
1936	33,030,000	—	0.75	2.50	10.00	12.00
1937	3,000,000	—	10.00	50.00	215	250
1938	3,650,000	1.25	2.00	7.00	70.00	85.00
1939	6,920,000	—	1.00	3.50	27.50	35.00
1940	12,300,000	—	0.40	1.25	5.00	7.00
1942	14,380,000	—	0.60	1.50	7.00	10.00
1945	9,558,000	—	0.40	0.70	3.50	5.00
1946	46,230,000	—	0.40	0.60	2.50	4.00

KM# 433   10 CENTAVOS
5.5000 g., Bronze, 23.5 mm. **Obv:** National arms, eagle left **Rev:** Bust left **Mint:** Mexico City **Note:** Mint mark Mo.

Date	Mintage	F	VF	XF	Unc	BU
1955	1,818,000	—	0.75	3.25	23.00	35.00
1956	5,255,000	—	0.75	3.25	23.00	32.00
1957	11,925,000	—	0.20	0.40	5.50	9.00
1959	26,140,000	—	0.30	0.45	0.75	1.25
1966	5,873,000	—	0.15	0.25	0.60	1.75
1967	32,318,000	—	0.10	0.15	0.30	0.40

 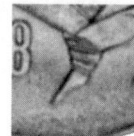

Sharp stem

KM# 434.1   10 CENTAVOS
1.5200 g., Copper-Nickel **Obv:** National arms, eagle left **Rev:** Upright ear of corn **Note:** Variety I- Sharp stem and wide date

Date	Mintage	F	VF	XF	Unc	BU
1974	6,000,000	—	—	0.35	0.75	1.00
1975	5,550,000	—	0.10	0.35	0.75	1.00
1976	7,680,000	—	0.10	0.20	0.30	0.40
1977	144,650,000	—	1.25	2.25	3.50	5.50
1978	271,870,000	—	—	1.00	1.50	2.25
1979	375,660,000	—	—	0.50	1.00	1.75
1980/79	21,290,000	—	2.45	3.75	7.00	9.00
1980	Inc. above	—	1.50	2.00	4.50	6.50

  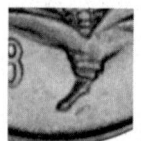

Blunt stem

KM# 434.2   10 CENTAVOS
1.5600 g., Copper-Nickel **Obv:** National arms, eagle left **Rev:** Upright ear of corn **Note:** Variety II- Blunt stem and narrow date

Date	Mintage	F	VF	XF	Unc	BU
1974	Inc. above	—	—	0.10	0.20	0.30
1977	Inc. above	—	0.15	0.50	1.25	2.25
1978	Inc. above	—	—	0.10	0.30	0.40
1979	Inc. above	—	0.15	0.35	0.85	1.50
1980	Inc. above	—	—	0.10	0.20	0.30

KM# 434.4   10 CENTAVOS
Copper-Nickel **Obv:** National arms, eagle left **Rev:** Upright ear of corn **Note:** Variety IV- Sharp stem and narrow date

Date	Mintage	F	VF	XF	Unc	BU
1974	—	—	—	—	1.50	2.50
1979	—	—	—	—	1.50	2.50

KM# 434.3   10 CENTAVOS
Copper-Nickel **Obv:** National arms, eagle left **Rev:** Upright ear of corn **Note:** Variety III- Blunt stem and wide date

Date	Mintage	F	VF	XF	Unc	BU
1980/79	—	—	—	—	7.00	9.00

KM# 435   20 CENTAVOS
5.0000 g., 0.8000 Silver 0.1286 oz. ASW, 22 mm.   **Obv:** National arms **Rev:** Value and date within wreath with Liberty cap above **Mint:** Mexico City **Note:** Mint mark Mo.

Date	Mintage	F	VF	XF	Unc	BU
1905	2,565,000	—	12.00	25.00	175	195
1906	6,860,000	—	9.00	16.50	60.00	85.00
1907 Straight 7	4,000,000	—	11.50	22.00	75.00	125
1907 Curved 7	5,435,000	—	7.50	15.00	70.00	120
1908	350,000	50.00	95.00	250	1,800	—
1910	1,135,000	—	11.00	16.00	90.00	110

Date	Mintage	F	VF	XF	Unc	BU
1911	1,150,000	12.00	15.00	40.00	145	175
1912	625,000	20.00	40.00	70.00	350	400
1913	1,000,000	—	14.50	30.00	100	125
1914	1,500,000	—	10.00	22.50	65.00	80.00

KM# 436   20 CENTAVOS
3.6250 g., 0.8000 Silver 0.0932 oz. ASW, 19 mm.   **Obv:** National arms **Rev:** Value and date within wreath with Liberty cap above **Mint:** Mexico City **Note:** Mint mark Mo. Reduced size.

Date	Mintage	F	VF	XF	Unc	BU
1919	4,155,000	—	30.00	65.00	200	275

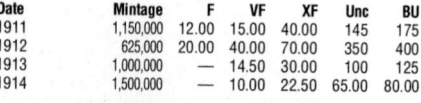

KM# 437   20 CENTAVOS
15.0000 g., Bronze, 32.5 mm.   **Obv:** National arms **Rev:** Value below date within wreath **Mint:** Mexico City **Note:** Mint mark Mo.

Date	Mintage	F	VF	XF	Unc	BU
1920	4,835,000	—	45.00	155	650	775
1935	20,000,000	—	6.00	10.00	95.00	145

KM# 438   20 CENTAVOS
3.3333 g., 0.7200 Silver 0.0772 oz. ASW, 19 mm.   **Obv:** National arms **Rev:** Value and date within wreath with Liberty cap above **Mint:** Mexico City **Note:** Mint mark Mo.

Date	Mintage	F	VF	XF	Unc	BU
1920	3,710,000	—	6.00	20.00	175	220
1921	6,160,000	—	6.00	14.00	100	150
1925	1,450,000	—	12.00	20.00	155	165
1926/5	1,465,000	—	20.00	70.00	350	375
1926	Inc. above	—	3.25	7.50	90.00	110
1927	1,405,000	—	3.50	8.00	95.00	115
1928	3,630,000	—	4.00	5.25	16.00	22.50
1930	1,000,000	—	5.00	8.00	25.00	35.00
1933	2,500,000	—	2.25	3.00	10.00	13.50
1934	2,500,000	—	2.25	4.00	11.00	16.50
1935	2,460,000	—	2.25	4.00	11.00	16.50
1937	10,000,000	—	1.75	2.25	4.00	6.00
1939	8,800,000	—	1.75	2.25	4.00	6.00
1940	3,000,000	—	1.75	2.25	3.50	6.00
1941	5,740,000	—	1.50	2.25	3.00	5.00
1942	12,460,000	—	1.50	2.25	3.25	5.50
1943	3,955,000	—	2.00	2.50	3.50	6.00

KM# 439 20 CENTAVOS
Bronze, 28.5 mm. **Obv:** National arms, eagle left **Rev:** Liberty cap divides value above Pyramid of the Sun at Teotihuacán, volcanos Ixtaccihuatl and Popocatepet in background **Edge:** Plain **Mint:** Mexico City **Note:** Mint mark Mo.

Date	Mintage	F	VF	XF	Unc	BU
1943	46,350,000	—	1.25	3.00	20.00	28.00
1944	83,650,000	—	0.40	0.65	8.00	12.00
1945	26,801,000	—	1.25	3.50	9.50	15.00
1946	25,695,000	—	1.10	2.25	6.00	9.00
1951	11,385,000	—	3.00	8.75	100	120
1952	6,560,000	—	3.00	5.00	25.00	35.00
1953	26,948,000	—	0.35	0.80	9.00	15.00
1954	40,108,000	—	0.35	0.80	9.00	15.00
1955	16,950,000	—	2.75	7.00	60.00	75.00

KM# 440 20 CENTAVOS
10.0400 g., Bronze, 28.5 mm. **Obv:** National arms, eagle left **Rev:** Liberty cap divides value above Pyramid of the Sun at Teotihuacán, volcanos Ixtaccihuatl and Popocatepet in background **Edge:** Plain **Mint:** Mexico City **Note:** Mint mark Mo.

Date	Mintage	F	VF	XF	Unc	BU
1955 Inc. KM#439	Inc. above	—	0.75	1.75	17.00	22.00
1956	22,431,000	—	0.30	0.35	3.00	5.00
1957	13,455,000	—	0.45	1.25	9.00	13.00
1959	6,017,000	—	4.50	9.00	75.00	100
1960	39,756,000	—	0.15	0.25	0.75	1.00
1963	14,869,000	—	0.25	0.35	0.80	1.00
1964	28,654,000	—	0.25	0.40	0.90	1.25
1965	74,162,000	—	0.20	0.35	0.80	1.00
1966	43,745,000	—	0.15	0.25	0.75	1.00
1967	46,487,000	—	0.20	0.50	1.00	1.25
1968	15,477,000	—	0.30	0.55	1.35	1.65
1969	63,647,000	—	0.20	0.35	0.80	1.00
1970	76,287,000	—	0.15	0.20	0.90	1.30
1971	49,892,000	—	0.30	0.50	1.25	2.00

KM# 441 20 CENTAVOS
Bronze, 28.5 mm. **Obv:** National arms, eagle left **Rev:** Liberty cap divides value above Pyramid of the Sun at Teotihuacán, volcanos Ixtaccihuatl and Popocatepet in background **Edge:** Plain **Mint:** Mexico City

Date	Mintage	F	VF	XF	Unc	BU
1971 Inc. KM#440	Inc. above	—	0.20	0.35	1.85	2.50

Date	Mintage	F	VF	XF	Unc	BU
1973	78,398,000	—	0.25	0.35	0.95	1.65
1974	34,200,000	—	0.20	0.35	1.25	2.00

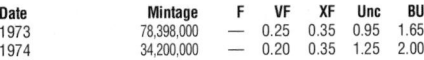

KM# 442 20 CENTAVOS
3.0600 g., Copper-Nickel, 20 mm. **Obv:** National arms, eagle left **Rev:** Bust 3/4 facing flanked by value and date **Mint:** Mexico City

Date	Mintage	F	VF	XF	Unc	BU
1974	112,000,000	—	0.10	0.15	0.25	0.30
1975	611,000,000	—	0.10	0.15	0.30	0.35
1976	394,000,000	—	0.10	0.15	0.35	0.45
1977	394,350,000	—	0.10	0.15	0.40	0.45
1978	527,950,000	—	0.10	0.15	0.25	0.30
1979	524,615,000	—	0.10	0.15	0.25	0.30
1979	—	—	1.25	2.00	4.00	8.00
Note: Doubled die obv. small letters						
1979	—	—	1.25	2.00	4.00	8.00
Note: Doubled die obv. large letters						
1980	326,500,000	—	0.15	0.20	0.30	0.40
1981 Open 8	106,205,000	—	0.30	0.50	1.00	2.00
1981 Closed 8, high date	248,500,000	—	0.30	0.50	1.00	2.00
1981 Closed 8, low date	—	—	1.00	1.50	3.50	4.25
1981/1982	—	—	40.00	75.00	175	195
Note: The 1981/1982 overdate is often mistaken as 1982/1981						
1982	286,855,000	—	0.40	0.60	0.90	1.10
1983 Round top 3	100,930,000	—	0.25	0.40	1.75	2.25
1983 Flat top 3	Inc. above	—	0.25	0.50	1.25	1.75
1983 Proof	998	Value: 45.00				

KM# 491 20 CENTAVOS
3.0000 g., Bronze, 20 mm. **Subject:** Olmec Culture **Obv:** National arms, eagle left **Rev:** Mask 3/4 right with value below **Mint:** Mexico City

Date	Mintage	F	VF	XF	Unc	BU
1983 Proof	53	Value: 185				
1983	260,000,000	—	0.20	0.25	1.25	1.75
1984	180,320,000	—	0.20	0.35	1.85	2.25

KM# 443 25 CENTAVOS
3.3330 g., 0.3000 Silver 0.0321 oz. ASW, 21.5 mm. **Obv:** National arms, eagle left **Rev:** Scale below Liberty cap **Mint:** Mexico City **Note:** Mint mark Mo.

Date	Mintage	F	VF	XF	Unc	BU
1950	77,060,000	—	0.60	0.80	1.60	2.00
1951	41,172,000	—	0.60	0.80	1.60	2.00
1952	29,264,000	—	0.75	1.10	1.75	2.25
1953	38,144,000	—	0.65	0.85	1.60	2.00

KM# 444 25 CENTAVOS
5.5000 g., Copper-Nickel, 23 mm. **Obv:** National arms, eagle left **Rev:** Bust 3/4 facing **Mint:** Mexico City

Date	Mintage	F	VF	XF	Unc	BU
1964	20,686,000	—	—	0.15	0.20	0.30

Date	Mintage	F	VF	XF	Unc	BU
1966 Closed beak	180,000	—	0.65	1.00	2.75	4.00
1966 Open beak	Inc. above	—	1.75	3.50	12.00	15.00

KM# 445 50 CENTAVOS
12.5000 g., 0.8000 Silver 0.3215 oz. ASW, 30 mm. **Obv:**
National arms **Rev:** Value and date within 3/4 wreath with
Liberty cap above **Mint:** Mexico City **Note:** Mint mark Mo.

Date	Mintage	F	VF	XF	Unc	BU
1905	2,446,000	12.50	20.00	35.00	175	250
1906 Open 9	16,966,000	—	6.00	10.00	45.00	70.00
1906 Closed 9	Inc. above	—	5.00	9.00	40.00	60.00
1907 Straight 7	18,920,000	—	5.00	9.00	30.00	35.00
1907 Curved 7	14,841,000	—	5.25	9.00	30.00	38.00
1908	488,000	—	80.00	190	550	675
1912	3,736,000	—	11.00	14.00	45.00	70.00
1913/07	10,510,000	—	40.00	90.00	250	300
1913/2	Inc. above	—	20.00	27.50	75.00	100
1913	Inc. above	—	5.50	8.50	27.50	35.00
1914	7,710,000	—	6.75	13.50	35.00	55.00
1916 Narrow date	480,000	—	60.00	85.00	250	350
1916 Wide date	Inc. above	—	60.00	85.00	250	350
1917	37,112,000	—	6.00	9.50	22.00	27.50
1918	1,320,000	—	70.00	135	300	400

KM# 446 50 CENTAVOS
9.0625 g., 0.8000 Silver 0.2331 oz. ASW, 27 mm. **Obv:**
National arms **Rev:** Value and date within 3/4 wreath with
Liberty cap above **Mint:** Mexico City **Note:** Mint mark Mo.
Reduced size.

Date	Mintage	F	VF	XF	Unc	BU
1918/7	2,760,000	—	525	700	1,450	—
1918	Inc. above	—	17.50	70.00	350	450
1919	29,670,000	—	10.00	25.00	150	180

KM# 447 50 CENTAVOS
8.3333 g., 0.7200 Silver 0.1929 oz. ASW, 27 mm. **Obv:**
National arms **Rev:** Value and date within 3/4 wreath with
Liberty cap above **Mint:** Mexico City **Note:** Mint mark Mo.

Date	Mintage	F	VF	XF	Unc	BU
1919	10,200,000	—	10.00	22.00	100	130
1920	27,166,000	—	8.00	17.00	75.00	90.00
1921	21,864,000	—	8.00	17.00	95.00	120
1925	3,280,000	—	17.50	35.00	145	185
1937	20,000,000	—	4.25	5.50	8.00	11.50
1938	100,000	—	50.00	95.00	245	350
1939	10,440,000	—	6.00	8.00	16.00	25.00
1942	800,000	—	6.00	9.00	18.00	22.00
1943	41,512,000	—	3.75	5.50	7.50	9.50
1944	55,806,000	—	3.75	5.50	7.50	9.50
1945	56,766,000	—	3.75	5.50	7.50	9.50

KM# 448 50 CENTAVOS
7.9730 g., 0.4200 Silver 0.1077 oz. ASW, 27 mm. **Obv:**
National arms **Rev:** Value and date within 3/4 wreath with
Liberty cap above **Mint:** Mexico City **Note:** Mint mark Mo.

Date	Mintage	F	VF	XF	Unc	BU
1935	70,800,000	—	2.50	3.50	6.00	8.00

KM# 449 50 CENTAVOS
6.6600 g., 0.3000 Silver 0.0642 oz. ASW, 26 mm. **Obv:**
National arms, eagle left **Rev:** Head with head covering right
Mint: Mexico City **Note:** Mint mark Mo.

Date	Mintage	F	VF	XF	Unc	BU
1950	13,570,000	—	1.50	1.85	3.50	5.50
1951	3,650,000	—	2.00	2.50	4.00	6.00

KM# 450 50 CENTAVOS
14.0000 g., Bronze, 33 mm. **Obv:** National arms, eagle left
Rev: Head with headdress left **Mint:** Mexico City **Note:** Mint
mark Mo.

Date	Mintage	F	VF	XF	Unc	BU
1955	3,502,000	—	1.50	3.00	80.00	40.00
1956	34,643,000	—	0.75	1.50	7.00	6.00
1957	9,675,000	—	1.00	2.00	6.50	8.00
1959	4,540,000	—	0.50	0.75	2.00	3.50

KM# 451 50 CENTAVOS
6.5000 g., Copper-Nickel, 25 mm. **Obv:** National arms, eagle
left **Rev:** Head with headdress left **Mint:** Mexico City

Date	Mintage	F	VF	XF	Unc	BU
1964	43,806,000	—	0.15	0.20	0.40	0.60
1965	14,326,000	—	0.20	0.25	0.45	0.65
1966	1,726,000	—	0.20	0.40	1.50	2.00
1967	55,144,000	—	0.20	0.30	0.75	1.25
1968	80,438,000	—	0.15	0.20	0.65	1.00
1969	87,640,000	—	0.20	0.35	0.80	1.25

KM# 452 50 CENTAVOS
6.5000 g., Copper-Nickel, 25 mm. **Obv:** National arms, eagle left **Rev:** Head with headdress left **Mint:** Mexico City **Note:** Coins dated 1975 and 1976 exist with and without dots in centers of three circles on plumage on reverse. Edge varieties exist.

Date	Mintage	F	VF	XF	Unc	BU
1970	76,236,000	—	0.15	0.20	0.80	1.35
1971	125,288,000	—	0.15	0.20	0.90	1.45
1972	16,000,000	—	1.25	2.00	3.50	5.50
1975 Dots	177,958,000	—	0.65	1.75	3.50	6.00
1975 No dots	Inc. above	—	0.15	0.20	0.75	1.25
1976 Dots	37,480,000	—	0.75	1.50	5.00	7.00
1976 No dots	Inc. above	—	0.15	0.20	0.50	0.90
1977	12,410,000	—	6.50	10.00	32.50	45.00
1978	85,400,000	—	0.15	0.25	0.50	1.20
1979 Round 2nd 9 in date	229,000,000	—	0.15	0.25	0.50	1.00
1979 Square 9's in date	Inc. above	—	0.20	0.40	1.60	2.25
1980 Narrow date, square 9	89,978,000	—	0.45	0.75	1.75	2.50
1980 Wide date, round 9	178,188,000	—	0.20	0.25	1.00	2.25
1981 Rectangular 9, narrow date	142,212,000	—	0.50	0.75	1.75	2.50
1981 Round 9, wide date	Inc. above	—	0.30	0.50	1.25	1.75
1982	45,474,000	—	0.20	0.40	1.95	1.75
1983	90,318,000	—	0.50	0.75	1.75	2.50
1983 Proof	998	Value: 45.00				

KM# 492 50 CENTAVOS
Stainless Steel, 22 mm. **Subject:** Palenque Culture **Obv:** National arms, eagle left **Rev:** Head with headdress 3/4 left **Mint:** Mexico City

Date	Mintage	F	VF	XF	Unc	BU
1983	99,540,000	—	—	0.30	1.50	2.50
1983 Proof	53	Value: 195				

KM# 453 PESO
27.0700 g., 0.9030 Silver 0.7859 oz. ASW, 39 mm. **Subject:**

Caballito **Obv:** National arms **Rev:** Horse and rider facing left among sun rays **Mint:** Mexico City **Designer:** Charles Pillet **Note:** Mint mark Mo.

Date	Mintage	F	VF	XF	Unc	BU
1910	3,814,000	—	45.00	50.00	200	275
1911	1,227,000	—	45.00	75.00	200	300

Note: Long lower left ray on reverse
| 1911 | Inc. above | — | 145 | 250 | 750 | 950 |

Note: Short lower left ray on reverse
1912	322,000	—	100	210	365	500
1913/2	2,880,000	—	45.00	75.00	300	450
1913	Inc. above	—	45.00	70.00	200	300

Note: 1913 coins exist with even and unevenly spaced date
| 1914 | 120,000 | — | 650 | 1,150 | 3,750 | — |

KM# 454 PESO
18.1300 g., 0.8000 Silver 0.4663 oz. ASW, 34 mm. **Obv:** National arms **Rev:** Value and date within 3/4 wreath with Liberty cap above **Mint:** Mexico City **Note:** Mint mark Mo.

Date	Mintage	F	VF	XF	Unc	BU
1918/7	—	250	350	—	—	—
1918	3,050,000	—	45.00	150	1,350	2,500
1919	6,151,000	—	25.00	125	950	1,750

KM# 455 PESO
16.6600 g., 0.7200 Silver 0.3856 oz. ASW, 34 mm. **Obv:** National arms **Rev:** Value and date within 3/4 wreath with Liberty cap above **Mint:** Mexico City **Note:** Mint mark Mo.

Date	Mintage	F	VF	XF	Unc	BU
1920/10	8,830,000	—	50.00	90.00	325	—
1920	Inc. above	—	10.00	35.00	195	350
1921	5,480,000	—	10.00	35.00	195	275
1922	33,620,000	—	BV	8.00	20.00	35.00
1923	35,280,000	—	BV	8.00	20.00	35.00
1924	33,060,000	—	BV	8.00	20.00	35.00
1925	9,160,000	—	8.00	10.00	60.00	85.00
1926	28,840,000	—	BV	8.00	25.00	40.00
1927	5,060,000	—	9.00	12.00	70.00	90.00
1932 Open 9	50,770,000	—	—	BV	8.00	12.00
1932 Closed 9	Inc. above	—	—	BV	8.00	12.00
1933/2	43,920,000	—	20.00	35.00	100	—
1933	Inc. above	—	—	10.00	8.00	12.00
1934	22,070,000	—	—	BV	10.00	18.00
1935	8,050,000	—	BV	8.00	11.50	20.00
1938	30,000,000	—	—	BV	8.00	10.00
1940	20,000,000	—	—	BV	8.00	10.00
1943	47,662,000	—	—	BV	8.00	10.00
1944	39,522,000	—	—	BV	8.00	10.00
1945	37,300,000	—	—	BV	8.00	10.00

KM# 456   PESO
14.0000 g., 0.5000 Silver 0.2250 oz. ASW, 32 mm. **Obv:**
National arms, eagle left **Rev:** Head with headcovering right
Mint: Mexico City **Note:** Mint mark Mo.

Date	Mintage	F	VF	XF	Unc	BU
1947	61,460,000	—	BV	3.50	6.00	10.00
1948	22,915,000	—	4.50	5.50	7.00	10.00
1949	4,000,000	—	—	1,200	1,600	2,500

Note: Not released for circulation
1949 Proof   — Value: 4,000

KM# 457   PESO
13.3300 g., 0.3000 Silver 0.1286 oz. ASW, 32 mm. **Obv:**
National arms, eagle left **Rev:** Armored bust 3/4 left **Mint:**
Mexico City **Note:** Mint mark Mo.

Date	Mintage	F	VF	XF	Unc	BU
1950	3,287,000	—	3.00	5.00	10.00	15.00

KM# 458   PESO
16.0000 g., 0.1000 Silver 0.0514 oz. ASW, 34.5 mm.
Subject: 100th Anniversary of Constitution **Obv:** National
arms, eagle left within wreath **Obv. Designer:** Manuel L.
Negrete **Rev:** Head left **Edge Lettering:** INDEPENDENCIA
Y LIBERTAD **Mint:** Mexico City **Note:** Mint mark Mo.

Date	Mintage	F	VF	XF	Unc	BU
1957	500,000	—	4.00	6.00	12.50	16.50

KM# 459   PESO
16.0000 g., 0.1000 Silver 0.0514 oz. ASW, 34.5 mm. **Obv:**
National arms, eagle left within wreath **Rev:** Armored bust

right within wreath **Edge Lettering:** INDEPENDENCIA Y
LIBERTAD **Mint:** Mexico City **Note:** Mint mark Mo.

Date	Mintage	F	VF	XF	Unc	BU
1957	28,273,000	BV	0.75	1.00	3.00	10.00
1958	41,899,000	—	BV	0.80	1.85	3.00
1959	27,369,000	BV	1.25	2.00	5.50	8.00
1960	26,259,000	BV	0.75	1.10	3.50	6.00
1961	52,601,000	—	BV	0.90	2.50	5.00
1962	61,094,000	—	BV	0.80	1.75	4.00
1963	26,394,000	—	BV	0.80	1.75	2.50
1964	15,615,000	—	BV	0.80	1.75	2.50
1965	5,004,000	—	BV	0.80	1.85	2.50
1966	30,998,000	—	BV	0.75	1.35	2.00
1967	9,308,000	—	BV	0.85	2.75	4.50

Tall date   Short date

KM# 460   PESO
9.0000 g., Copper-Nickel, 29 mm. **Obv:** National arms, eagle
left **Rev:** Head left **Mint:** Mexico City

Date	Mintage	F	VF	XF	Unc	BU
1970 Narrow date	102,715,000	—	0.25	0.35	0.65	0.80
1970 Wide date	Inc. above	—	1.25	2.50	7.50	10.00
1971	426,222,000	—	0.20	0.25	0.55	0.75
1972	120,000,000	—	0.20	0.25	0.40	0.65
1974	63,700,000	—	0.20	0.25	0.65	0.90
1975 Tall narrow date	205,979,000	—	0.25	0.45	1.00	1.35
1975 Short wide date	Inc. above	—	0.30	0.40	0.75	1.00
1976	94,489,000	—	0.15	0.20	0.50	0.75
1977 Thick date close to rim	94,364,000	—	0.25	0.45	1.00	1.25
1977 Thin date, space between sideburns and collar	Inc. above	—	1.00	2.50	8.50	16.50
1978 Closed 8	208,300,000	—	0.20	0.30	1.00	1.50
1978 Open 8	55,140,000	—	1.00	2.50	14.00	20.00
1979 Thin date	117,884,000	—	0.20	0.30	1.15	1.50
1979 Thick date	Inc. above	—	0.20	0.30	1.25	1.75
1980 Closed 8	318,800,000	—	0.25	0.35	1.00	1.25
1980 Open 8	23,865,000	—	0.75	1.50	8.00	15.00
1981 Closed 8	413,349,000	—	0.20	0.30	0.75	0.90
1981 Open 8	58,616,000	—	0.50	1.25	6.50	9.00
1982 Open 8	—	—	0.75	1.50	8.00	15.00
1982 Closed 8	235,000,000	—	0.25	0.75	2.25	2.50
1983 Wide date	100,000,000	—	0.30	0.45	3.00	3.50
1983 Narrow date	Inc. above	—	0.30	0.45	3.00	4.50
1983 Proof	1,051,000	Value: 38.00				

KM# 496   PESO
Stainless Steel, 24.5 mm. **Obv:** National arms, eagle left
Rev: Armored bust right **Mint:** Mexico City

Date	Mintage	F	VF	XF	Unc	BU
1984	722,802,000	—	0.10	0.25	0.65	1.45

Date	Mintage	F	VF	XF	Unc	BU
1985	985,000,000	—	0.10	0.25	0.50	1.25
1986	740,000,000	—	0.10	0.25	0.50	1.25
1987	250,000,000	—	0.10	0.25	0.50	1.25
1987 Proof; 2 known	—	Value: 1,000				

KM# 461   2 PESOS
1.6666 g., 0.9000 Gold 0.0482 oz. AGW, 13 mm. **Obv:** National arms **Rev:** Date above value within wreath **Mint:** Mexico City **Note:** Mint mark Mo.

Date	Mintage	F	VF	XF	Unc	BU
1919	1,670,000	—	BV	60.00	80.00	—
1920/10	—	BV	60.00	75.00	115	—
1920	4,282,000	—	BV	60.00	75.00	—
1944	10,000	BV	60.00	70.00	95.00	—
1945	Est. 140,000	—	—	—	BV+20%	—
1946	168,000	BV	60.00	70.00	125	—
1947	25,000	BV	60.00	70.00	95.00	—
1948 No specimens known	45,000	—	—	—	—	—

Note: During 1951-1972 a total of 4,590,493 pieces were restruck, most likely dated 1945. In 1996 matte restrikes were produced

KM# 462   2 PESOS
26.6667 g., 0.9000 Silver 0.7716 oz. ASW, 39 mm. **Subject:** Centennial of Independence **Obv:** National arms, eagle left within wreath **Rev:** Winged Victory **Mint:** Mexico City **Designer:** Emilio del Moral **Note:** Mint mark Mo.

Date	Mintage	F	VF	XF	Unc	BU
1921	1,278,000	—	40.00	65.00	425	650

KM# 463   2-1/2 PESOS
2.0833 g., 0.9000 Gold 0.0603 oz. AGW, 15.5 mm. **Obv:** National arms **Rev:** Miguel Hidalgo y Costilla **Mint:** Mexico City **Note:** Mint mark Mo.

Date	Mintage	F	VF	XF	Unc	BU
1918	1,704,000	—	BV	75.00	100	—
1919	984,000	—	BV	75.00	100	—
1920/10	607,000	—	BV	75.00	145	—
1920	Inc. above	—	BV	75.00	95.00	—
1944	20,000	—	BV	75.00	95.00	—
1945	Est. 180,000	—	—	—	BV+18%	—
1946	163,000	—	BV	75.00	95.00	—
1947	24,000	200	265	350	600	—
1948	63,000	—	BV	75.00	95.00	—

Note: During 1951-1972 a total of 5,025,087 pieces were restruck, most likely dated 1945. In 1996 matte restrikes were produced

KM# 464   5 PESOS
4.1666 g., 0.9000 Gold 0.1206 oz. AGW, 19 mm. **Obv:** National arms **Rev:** Miguel Hidalgo y Costilla **Mint:** Mexico City **Note:** Mint mark Mo.

Date	Mintage	F	VF	XF	Unc	BU
1905	18,000	125	175	245	600	—
1906	4,638,000	—	—	BV	150	—
1907/6	—	—	—	—	—	—
1907	1,088,000	—	—	BV	150	—
1910	100,000	—	—	BV	160	—
1918/7	609,000	—	—	BV	200	—
1918	Inc. above	—	—	BV	150	—
1919	506,000	—	—	BV	150	—
1920	2,385,000	—	—	BV	150	—
1955	Est. 48,000	—	—	—	BV+12%	—

Note: During 1955-1972 a total of 1,767,645 pieces were restruck, most likely dated 1955. In 1996 matte restrikes were produced

KM# 465   5 PESOS
30.0000 g., 0.9000 Silver 0.8680 oz. ASW, 40 mm. **Obv:** National arms, eagle left **Rev:** Head with headdress left **Mint:** Mexico City **Note:** Mint mark Mo.

Date	Mintage	F	VF	XF	Unc	BU
1947	5,110,000	—	—	BV	17.50	22.50
1948	26,740,000	—	—	BV	17.00	22.00

KM# 466   5 PESOS
27.7800 g., 0.7200 Silver 0.6430 oz. ASW, 40 mm. **Subject:** Opening of Southern Railroad **Obv:** National arms, eagle left **Rev:** Radiant sun flanked by palm trees above train **Edge Lettering:** COMERCIO - AGRICULTURA - INDUSTRIA **Mint:** Mexico City **Designer:** Manuel L. Negrete **Note:** Mint mark Mo.

Date	Mintage	F	VF	XF	Unc	BU
1950	200,000	—	22.50	40.00	55.00	65.00

Note: It is recorded that 100,000 pieces were melted to be used for the 1968 Mexican Olympic 25 Pesos

Date	Mintage	F	VF	XF	Unc	BU
1955	4,271,000	—	BV	8.00	9.00	10.00
1956	4,596,000	—	BV	8.00	9.00	10.00
1957	3,464,000	—	BV	8.00	9.00	10.00

KM# 467   5 PESOS
27.7800 g., 0.7200 Silver 0.6430 oz. ASW, 40 mm. **Obv:** National arms, eagle left **Rev:** Head left within wreath **Edge Lettering:** COMERCIO - AGRICULTURA - INDUSTRIA **Mint:** Mexico City **Note:** Mint mark Mo.

Date	Mintage	F	VF	XF	Unc	BU
1951	4,958,000	—	—	BV	13.50	16.00
1952	9,595,000	—	—	BV	13.00	15.00
1953	20,376,000	—	—	BV	13.00	15.00
1954	30,000	—	30.00	60.00	70.00	85.00

KM# 470   5 PESOS
18.0500 g., 0.7200 Silver 0.4178 oz. ASW, 36 mm. **Subject:** 100th Anniversary of Constitution **Obv:** National arms, eagle left **Rev:** Head left **Edge Lettering:** INDEPENDENCIA Y LIBERTAD **Mint:** Mexico City **Designer:** Manuel L. Negrete **Note:** Mint mark Mo.

Date	Mintage	F	VF	XF	Unc	BU
1957	200,000	—	8.50	9.50	13.50	16.00

KM# 468   5 PESOS
27.7800 g., 0.7200 Silver 0.6430 oz. ASW, 40 mm. **Subject:** Bicentennial of Hidalgo's Birth **Obv:** National arms, eagle left **Rev:** Half-length figure facing to right of building and dates **Edge Lettering:** COMERCIO - AGRICULTURA - INDUSTRIA **Mint:** Mexico City **Designer:** Manuel L. Negrete **Note:** Mint mark Mo.

Date	Mintage	F	VF	XF	Unc	BU
1953	1,000,000	—	BV	11.00	13.50	16.00

KM# 471   5 PESOS
18.0500 g., 0.7200 Silver 0.4178 oz. ASW, 36 mm. **Subject:** Centennial of Carranza's Birth **Obv:** National arms, eagle left **Rev:** Head left **Edge:** Plain **Mint:** Mexico City **Designer:** Manuel L. Negrete **Note:** Mint mark Mo.

Date	Mintage	F	VF	XF	Unc	BU
1959	1,000,000	—	—	BV	9.00	11.00

Small date   Large date

KM# 472   5 PESOS
14.0000 g., Copper-Nickel, 33 mm. **Obv:** National arms, eagle left **Rev:** Armored bust right **Edge Lettering:** INDEPENDENCIA Y LIBERTAD **Mint:** Mexico City **Note:** Small date, large date varieties.

Date	Mintage	F	VF	XF	Unc	BU
1971	28,457,000	—	0.50	0.95	2.50	3.25
1972	75,000,000	—	0.60	1.25	2.00	2.50
1973	19,405,000	—	1.25	2.00	4.50	5.50
1974	34,500,000	—	0.50	0.80	1.75	2.25

KM# 469   5 PESOS
18.0500 g., 0.7200 Silver 0.4178 oz. ASW, 36 mm. **Obv:** National arms, eagle left **Rev:** Head left **Mint:** Mexico City **Note:** Mint mark Mo.

Date	Mintage	F	VF	XF	Unc	BU
1976 Small date	26,121,000	—	0.75	1.45	3.25	4.00
1976 Large date	121,550,000	—	0.35	0.50	1.50	1.75
1977	102,000,000	—	0.35	0.50	1.50	1.75
1978	25,700,000	—	1.00	1.50	4.50	6.25

KM# 485   5 PESOS
Copper-Nickel, 27 mm. **Subject:** Quetzalcoatl **Obv:** National arms, eagle left **Rev:** Native sculpture to lower right of value and dollar sign **Edge Lettering:** LIBERTAD Y INDEPENDENCIA **Mint:** Mexico City **Note:** Inverted and normal edge legend varieties exist for the 1980 and 1981 dates.

Date	Mintage	F	VF	XF	Unc	BU
1980	266,899,999	—	0.25	0.50	1.75	2.25
1981	30,500,000	—	0.45	0.65	2.75	3.25
1982	20,000,000	—	1.50	2.35	4.25	5.25
1982 Proof	1,051	Value: 50.00				
1983 Proof; 7 known	—	Value: 1,200				
1984	16,300,000	—	1.25	2.00	4.75	6.00
1985	76,900,000	—	2.00	3.25	4.25	5.00

KM# 502   5 PESOS
Brass, 17 mm. **Subject:** Quetzalcoatl **Obv:** National arms, eagle left **Rev:** Date and value **Mint:** Mexico City **Note:** Circulation coinage.

Date	Mintage	F	VF	XF	Unc	BU
1985	30,000,000	—	—	0.15	0.35	0.50
1987	81,900,000	—	8.00	9.50	12.50	16.50
1988	76,600,000	—	—	0.10	0.25	0.35
1988 Proof; 2 known	—	Value: 600				

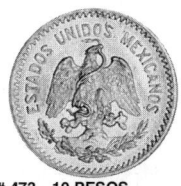 

KM# 473   10 PESOS
8.3333 g., 0.9000 Gold 0.2411 oz. AGW, 22.5 mm. **Obv:** National arms **Rev:** Miguel Hidalgo y Costilla **Mint:** Mexico City **Note:** Mint mark Mo.

Date	Mintage	F	VF	XF	Unc	BU
1905	39,000	—	BV	310	345	—
1906	2,949,000	—	BV	300	320	360
1907	1,589,000	—	BV	300	320	360
1908	890,000	—	BV	300	320	360
1910	451,000	—	BV	300	320	360
1916	26,000	—	BV	315	450	—
1917	1,967,000	—	BV	300	320	360
1919	266,000	—	BV	300	330	—
1920	12,000	—	BV	500	875	—
1959	Est. 50,000	—	—	—	BV+7%	—

Note: *During 1961-1972 a total of 954,983 pieces were restruck, most likely dated 1959. In 1996 matte restrikes were produced

KM# 474   10 PESOS
28.8800 g., 0.9000 Silver 0.8356 oz. ASW, 40 mm. **Obv:** National arms **Rev:** Head left **Mint:** Mexico City **Note:** Mint mark Mo.

Date	Mintage	F	VF	XF	Unc	BU
1955	585,000	—	—	BV	17.50	20.00
1956	3,535,000	—	—	BV	16.50	18.50

KM# 475   10 PESOS
28.8800 g., 0.9000 Silver 0.8356 oz. ASW, 40 mm. **Subject:** 100th Anniversary of Constitution **Obv:** National arms, eagle left **Rev:** Head left **Edge Lettering:** INDEPENDENCIA Y LIBERTAD **Mint:** Mexico City **Designer:** Manuel L. Negrete **Note:** Mint mark Mo.

Date	Mintage	F	VF	XF	Unc	BU
1957	100,000	—	16.50	27.50	45.00	50.00

KM# 476   10 PESOS
28.8800 g., 0.9000 Silver 0.8356 oz. ASW, 40 mm. **Subject:** 150th Anniversary - War of Independence **Obv:** National arms, eagle left **Rev:** Conjoined busts facing flanked by dates **Mint:** Mexico City **Designer:** Manuel L. Negrete **Note:** Mint mark Mo.

Date	Mintage	F	VF	XF	Unc	BU
1960	1,000,000	—	—	BV	16.50	20.00

ESTADOS UNIDOS MEXICANOS

KM# 477.1 10 PESOS
Copper-Nickel, 30.5 mm. **Obv:** National arms, eagle left **Rev:**
Miguel Hidalgo y Costilla **Shape:** 7-sided **Mint:** Mexico City
Note: Thin flan - 1.6mm

Date	Mintage	F	VF	XF	Unc	BU
1974	3,900,000	—	0.50	1.00	3.00	4.50
1974 Proof	—	Value: 650				
1975	1,000,000	—	2.25	3.25	7.50	8.50
1976	74,500,000	—	0.25	0.75	1.75	2.75
1977	79,620,000	—	0.50	1.00	2.00	3.00

KM# 477.2 10 PESOS
Copper-Nickel, 30.5 mm. **Obv:** National arms, eagle left **Rev:**
Head left **Shape:** 7-sided **Mint:** Mexico City **Note:** Thick flan
- 2.3mm

Date	Mintage	F	VF	XF	Unc	BU
1978	124,850,000	—	0.50	0.75	2.50	2.75
1979	57,200,000	—	0.50	0.75	2.50	2.75
1980	55,200,000	—	0.50	0.75	2.50	3.75
1981	222,768,000	—	0.40	0.60	2.25	2.75
1982	151,770,000	—	0.50	0.80	2.50	3.50
1982 Proof	1,051	Value: 45.00				
1983 Proof; 3 known	—	Value: 1,800				
1985	58,000,000	—	1.25	1.75	5.75	8.00

KM# 512 10 PESOS
3.8400 g., Stainless Steel, 19 mm. **Obv:** National arms,
eagle left **Rev:** Head facing with diagonal value at left **Mint:**
Mexico City **Note:** Date varieties exist.

Date	Mintage	F	VF	XF	Unc	BU
1985	257,000,000	—	—	0.15	0.50	0.75
1986	392,000,000	—	—	0.15	0.50	1.50
1987	305,000,000	—	—	0.15	0.35	0.50
1988	500,300,000	—	—	0.15	0.25	0.35
1989	—	—	0.20	0.25	0.75	1.50
1990	—	—	—	0.25	0.75	1.25
1990 Proof; 2 known	—	Value: 550				

KM# 478 20 PESOS
16.6666 g., 0.9000 Gold 0.4822 oz. AGW, 27.5 mm. **Obv:**
National arms, eagle left **Rev:** Aztec Sunstone with
denomination below **Edge:** Lettered **Edge Lettering:**
INDEPEDENCIA Y LIBERTAD **Mint:** Mexico City **Note:** Mint
mark Mo.

Date	Mintage	F	VF	XF	Unc	BU
1917	852,000	—	—	BV	620	—
1918	2,831,000	—	—	BV	620	—
1919	1,094,000	—	—	BV	620	—
1920/10	462,000	—	—	BV	620	—
1920	Inc. above	—	—	BV	650	—
1921/11	922,000	—	—	BV	620	—

Date	Mintage	F	VF	XF	Unc	BU
1921/10	—		—	—	—	—
1921	Inc. above	—	—	BV	650	—
1959	Est. 13,000	—	—	—	—	—

Note: During 1960-1971 a total of 1,158,414 pieces were
restruck, most likely dated 1959. In 1996 matte restrikes
were produced

KM# 486 20 PESOS
Copper-Nickel, 32 mm. **Obv:** National arms, eagle left **Rev:**
Figure with headdress facing left within circle **Mint:** Mexico
City

Date	Mintage	F	VF	XF	Unc	BU
1980	84,900,000	—	0.50	0.85	2.25	3.25
1981	250,573,000	—	0.60	0.80	2.25	3.25
1982	236,892,000	—	1.00	1.75	2.50	3.75
1982 Proof	1,051	Value: 50.00				
1983 Proof; 3 known	—	Value: 575				
1984	55,000,000	—	1.00	1.50	2.50	4.75

KM# 508 20 PESOS
6.0000 g., Brass, 21 mm. **Obv:** National arms, eagle left
Rev: Bust facing with diagonal value at left **Mint:** Mexico City

Date	Mintage	F	VF	XF	Unc	BU
1985 Wide date	25,000,000	—	0.10	0.20	1.00	1.50
1985 Narrow date	Inc. above	—	0.10	0.25	1.50	2.25
1986	10,000,000	—	1.00	1.75	5.00	6.00
1988	355,200,000	—	0.10	0.20	0.45	0.75
1989	—	—	0.15	0.30	1.50	2.00
1990	—	—	0.15	0.30	1.50	2.50
1990 Proof; 3 known	—	Value: 575				

Snake's tongue straight

KM# 479.1 25 PESOS
22.5000 g., 0.7200 Silver 0.5208 oz. ASW, 38 mm. **Obv:**
National arms, eagle left **Rev:** Olympic rings below dancing

native left, numeral design in background **Designer:** Lorenzo
Rafael **Note:** Type I, Rings aligned.

Date	Mintage	F	VF	XF	Unc	BU
1968	27,182,000	—	—	BV	10.00	12.00

KM# 479.2   25 PESOS
22.5000 g., 0.7200 Silver 0.5208 oz. ASW, 38 mm. **Subject:**
Summer Olympics - Mexico City **Obv:** National arms, eagle
left **Rev:** Olympic rings below dancing native left, numeral
design in background **Mint:** Mexico City **Note:** Type II, center
ring low.

Date	Mintage	F	VF	XF	Unc	BU
1968	Inc. above	—	BV	10.00	12.00	15.00

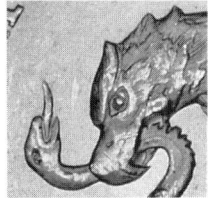

Snake's tongue curved

KM# 479.3   25 PESOS
22.5000 g., 0.7200 Silver 0.5208 oz. ASW, 38 mm. **Subject:**
Summer Olympics - Mexico City **Obv:** National arms, eagle
left **Rev:** Olympic rings below dancing native left, numeral
design in background **Mint:** Mexico City **Note:** Snake with
long curved or normal tongue. Type III, center rings low.

Date	Mintage	F	VF	XF	Unc	BU
1968	Inc. above	—	BV	10.00	13.00	16.00

KM# 480   25 PESOS
22.5000 g., 0.7200 Silver 0.5208 oz. ASW, 38 mm. **Obv:**
National arms, eagle left **Rev:** Bust facing **Mint:** Mexico City

Date	Mintage	F	VF	XF	Unc	BU
1972	2,000,000	—	BV	10.00	12.00	15.00

KM# 497   25 PESOS
7.7760 g., 0.7200 Silver 0.1800 oz. ASW **Subject:** 1986
World Cup Soccer Games **Obv:** National arms, eagle left **Rev:**
Value above soccer ball with date below **Mint:** Mexico City

Date	Mintage	F	VF	XF	Unc	BU
1985	354,000	—	—	—	—	7.50

KM# 503   25 PESOS
8.4060 g., 0.9250 Silver 0.2500 oz. ASW **Subject:** 1986
World Cup Soccer Games **Obv:** National arms, eagle left **Rev:**
Pre-Columbian hieroglyphs, ojo de buey, and soccer ball
Mint: Mexico City

Date	Mintage	F	VF	XF	Unc	BU
1985 Proof	277,000	Value: 12.00				

KM# 514   25 PESOS
8.4060 g., 0.9250 Silver 0.2500 oz. ASW **Subject:** 1986
World Cup Soccer Games **Obv:** National arms, eagle left **Rev:**
Value above soccer ball **Mint:** Mexico City

Date	Mintage	F	VF	XF	Unc	BU
1985 Proof	234,000	Value: 12.00				

KM# 519   25 PESOS
8.4060 g., 0.9250 Silver 0.2500 oz. ASW **Subject:** 1986
World Cup Soccer Games **Obv:** National arms, eagle left **Rev:**
Soccer ball within net, date and value to left **Mint:** Mexico City

Date	Mintage	F	VF	XF	Unc	BU
1986 Proof	—	Value: 12.00				

KM# 497a   25 PESOS
8.4060 g., 0.9250 Silver 0.2500 oz. ASW **Subject:** 1986
World Cup Soccer Games **Obv:** National arms, eagle left **Rev:**
Value above soccerball with date below **Mint:** Mexico City
Note: Without finess statement- reverse description

Date	Mintage	F	VF	XF	Unc	BU
1986 Proof	—	Value: 12.00				

KM# 481   50 PESOS
41.6666 g., 0.9000 Gold 1.2056 oz. AGW, 37 mm. **Subject:**
Centennial of Independence **Obv:** National arms **Rev:**
Winged Victory **Edge:** Reeded **Mint:** Mexico City **Designer:**
Emilio del Moral **Note:** During 1949-1972 a total of 3,975,654
pieces were restruck, most likely dated 1947. In 1996 matte
restrikes were produced. Mint mark Mo.

Date	Mintage	F	VF	XF	Unc	BU
1921	180,000	—	—	BV	1,650	3,000
1922	463,000	—	—	BV	1,500	1,700
1923	432,000	—	—	BV	1,500	1,700
1924	439,000	—	—	BV	1,500	1,700
1925	716,000	—	—	BV	1,500	1,700
1926	600,000	—	—	BV	1,500	1,700
1927	606,000	—	—	BV	1,500	1,700
1928	538,000	—	—	BV	1,500	1,700
1929	458,000	—	—	BV	1,500	1,700
1930	372,000	—	—	BV	1,500	1,700
1931	137,000	—	—	BV	1,500	1,700
1944	593,000	—	—	BV	1,500	1,700
1945	1,012,000	—	—	BV	1,500	1,700
1946	1,588,000	—	—	BV	1,500	1,700
1947	309,000	—	—	—	BV+3%	—
1947 Specimen	—	—	—	—	—	—

Note: Value, $6,500

KM# 482   50 PESOS
41.6666 g., 0.9000 Gold 1.2056 oz. AGW, 39 mm. **Obv:**
National arms **Rev:** Winged Victory

Date	Mintage	F	VF	XF	Unc	BU
1943	89,000	—	—	—	BV	1,600

KM# 481a   50 PESOS
Platinum APW **Subject:** Centennial of Independence **Obv:**
National arms **Rev:** Winged Victory **Edge:** Reeded **Mint:**
Mexico City

Date	Mintage	F	VF	XF	Unc	BU
1947Mo	Est. 5	—	—	—	—	13,000

KM# 490   50 PESOS
19.8400 g., Copper-Nickel, 35 mm. **Subject:** Coyolxauhqui
Obv: National arms, eagle left **Rev:** Value to right of artistic
designs **Edge:** Reeded **Mint:** Mexico City **Note:** Doubled die
examples of 1982 and 1983 dates exist.

Date	Mintage	F	VF	XF	Unc	BU
1982	222,890,000	—	1.00	2.50	5.00	6.50
1983	45,000,000	—	1.50	3.00	6.00	7.00
1983 Proof	1,051	Value: 55.00				
1984	73,537,000	—	1.00	1.35	3.50	4.50
1984 Proof; 4 known	—	Value: 750				

KM# 495   50 PESOS
Copper-Nickel, 23.5 mm. **Subject:** Benito Juarez **Obv:**
National arms, eagle left **Rev:** Bust 1/4 left with diagonal value
at left **Edge:** Reeded **Mint:** Mexico City

Date	Mintage	F	VF	XF	Unc	BU
1984	94,216,000	—	0.65	1.25	2.70	3.25
1985	296,000,000	—	0.25	0.45	1.25	2.25
1986	50,000,000	—	6.00	10.00	12.00	14.00
1987	210,000,000	—	0.25	0.45	1.00	1.25
1988	80,200,000	—	6.25	9.00	13.50	16.00

KM# 495a   50 PESOS
Stainless Steel, 23.5 mm. **Subject:** Benito Juarez **Obv:**
National arms, eagle left **Rev:** Bust 1/4 left with diagonal value
at left **Edge:** Plain **Mint:** Mexico City

Date	Mintage	F	VF	XF	Unc	BU
1988	353,300,000	—	—	0.20	1.25	1.75
1990	—	—	—	0.30	1.00	2.00
1992	—	—	—	0.25	1.00	2.75

KM# 504   50 PESOS
16.8310 g., 0.9250 Silver 0.5005 oz. ASW **Subject:** 1986
World Cup Soccer Games **Obv:** National arms, eagle left **Rev:**
Styilized athlete as soccer forerunner **Mint:** Mexico City

Date	Mintage	F	VF	XF	Unc	BU
1985 Proof	347,000	Value: 20.00				

KM# 515   50 PESOS
16.8310 g., 0.9250 Silver 0.5005 oz. ASW **Subject:** 1986
World Cup Soccer Games **Obv:** National arms, eagle left **Rev:**
Value to right of soccer player **Mint:** Mexico City

Date	Mintage	F	VF	XF	Unc	BU
1985 Proof	234,000	Value: 20.00				

ESTADOS UNIDOS MEXICANOS

KM# 498   50 PESOS
15.5520 g., 0.7200 Silver 0.3600 oz. ASW **Subject:** 1986
World Cup Soccer Games **Obv:** National arms, eagle left **Rev:**
Pair of feet and soccer ball **Mint:** Mexico City

Date	Mintage	F	VF	XF	Unc	BU
1985	347,000	—	—	—	—	8.50

KM# 523   50 PESOS
16.8310 g., 0.9250 Silver 0.5005 oz. ASW **Subject:** 1986
World Cup Soccer Games **Obv:** National arms, eagle left **Rev:**
Value to left of soccer balls **Mint:** Mexico City

Date	Mintage	F	VF	XF	Unc	BU
1986 Proof	190,000	Value: 20.00				

KM# 498a   50 PESOS
16.8310 g., 0.9250 Silver 0.5005 oz. ASW **Subject:** 1986
World Cup Soccer Games **Obv:** National arms, eagle left **Rev:**
Without fineness statement **Mint:** Mexico City

Date	Mintage	F	VF	XF	Unc	BU
1986 Proof	10,000	Value: 20.00				

KM# 532   50 PESOS
15.5500 g., 0.9990 Silver 0.4994 oz. ASW **Subject:** 50th
Anniversary - Nationalization of Oil Industry **Obv:** National
arms, eagle left **Rev:** Monument **Mint:** Mexico City

Date	Mintage	F	VF	XF	Unc	BU
ND(1988)	30,000	—	—	—	20.00	22.00

Low 7's

KM# 483.1   100 PESOS
27.7700 g., 0.7200 Silver 0.6428 oz. ASW, 39 mm.   **Obv:**
National arms, eagle left **Rev:** Bust facing, sloping right
shoulder, round left shoulder with no clothing folds **Edge:**
Reeded **Mint:** Mexico City

Date	Mintage	F	VF	XF	Unc	BU
1977 Low 7's	5,225,000	—	—	BV	10.00	12.50
1977 High 7's	Inc. above	—	—	BV	10.00	13.00

High 7's

KM# 483.2   100 PESOS
27.7700 g., 0.7200 Silver 0.6428 oz. ASW, 39 mm.   **Obv:**
National arms, eagle left **Rev:** Bust facing, higher right

shoulder, left shoulder with clothing folds. **Mint:** Mexico City
Note: Mintage inc. KM#483.1

Date	Mintage	F	VF	XF	Unc	BU
1977 Date in line	—	—	—	BV	10.00	12.00
1978	9,879,000	—	—	BV	10.00	12.50
1979	784,000	—	—	BV	10.00	12.50
1979 Proof	—	Value: 650				

KM# 493   100 PESOS
Aluminum-Bronze, 26.5 mm. **Obv:** National arms, eagle left
Rev: Head 1/4 right with diagonal value at right **Mint:** Mexico
City

Date	Mintage	F	VF	XF	Unc	BU
1984	227,809,000	—	0.45	0.60	2.50	4.00
1985	377,423,000	—	0.30	0.50	2.00	5.00
1986	43,000,000	—	1.00	2.50	4.75	7.50
1987	165,000,000	—	0.60	1.25	2.25	3.00
1988	433,100,000	—	0.30	0.50	2.00	2.75
1989	—	—	0.35	0.65	2.00	2.75
1990	—	—	0.15	0.40	1.50	2.50
1990 Proof; 1 known	—	Value: 650				
1991	—	—	0.15	0.25	1.00	2.50
1992	—	—	0.30	0.75	1.75	3.00

KM# 499   100 PESOS
31.1030 g., 0.7200 Silver 0.7200 oz. ASW **Subject:** 1986
World Cup Soccer Games **Obv:** National arms, eagle left **Rev:**
Value above artistic designs and soccer ball **Mint:** Mexico City

Date	Mintage	F	VF	XF	Unc	BU
1985	302,000	—	—	—	—	25.00

KM# 499a   100 PESOS
32.6250 g., 0.9250 Silver 0.9702 oz. ASW **Subject:** 1986
World Cup Soccer Games **Obv:** National arms, eagle left **Rev:**
Without fineness statement **Mint:** Mexico City

Date	Mintage	F	VF	XF	Unc	BU
1985 Proof	9,006	Value: 55.00				

KM# 505   100 PESOS
32.6250 g., 0.9250 Silver 0.9702 oz. ASW, 38 mm. **Subject:**
1986 World Cup Soccer Games **Obv:** National arms, eagle
left **Rev:** Without fineness statement **Mint:** Mexico City

Date	Mintage	F	VF	XF	Unc	BU
1985 Proof	9,006	Value: 50.00				

KM# 521   100 PESOS
32.6250 g., 0.9250 Silver 0.9702 oz. ASW **Subject:** 1986
World Cup Soccer Games **Obv:** National arms, eagle left **Rev:**
Without fineness statement **Mint:** Mexico City

Date	Mintage	F	VF	XF	Unc	BU
1986 Proof	208,000	Value: 55.00				

KM# 524   100 PESOS
32.6250 g., 0.9250 Silver 0.9702 oz. ASW **Subject:** 1986
World Cup Soccer Games **Obv:** National arms, eagle left **Rev:**
Without fineness statement **Mint:** Mexico City

Date	Mintage	F	VF	XF	Unc	BU
1986 Proof	190,000	Value: 55.00				

KM# 537 100 PESOS
32.6250 g., 0.7200 Silver 0.7552 oz. ASW **Subject:** World
Wildlife Fund **Obv:** National arms, eagle left **Rev:** Monarch
butterflies **Mint:** Mexico City

Date	Mintage	F	VF	XF	Unc	BU
1987 Proof	Est. 30,000	Value: 65.00				

KM# 533 100 PESOS
31.1030 g., 0.9990 Silver 0.9989 oz. ASW **Subject:** 50th
Anniversary - Nationalization of Oil Industry **Obv:** National
arms, eagle left **Rev:** Bust facing above sprigs and dates **Mint:**
Mexico City

Date	Mintage	F	VF	XF	Unc	BU
1988	10,000	—	—	—	35.00	50.00

KM# 539 100 PESOS
33.6250 g., 0.9250 Silver 0.9999 oz. ASW **Subject:** Save
the Children **Obv:** National arms, eagle left **Rev:** Child flying
kite, two others sitting and playing **Mint:** Mexico City

Date	Mintage	F	VF	XF	Unc	BU
1991 Proof	30,000	Value: 50.00				

KM# 540 100 PESOS
27.0000 g., 0.9250 Silver 0.8029 oz. ASW **Subject:** Ibero -
American Series **Obv:** National arms, eagle left within center
of assorted arms **Rev:** Maps within circles flanked by pillars
above sailboats **Mint:** Mexico City

Date	Mintage	F	VF	XF	Unc	BU
1991 Proof	50,000	Value: 85.00				
1992 Proof	75,000	Value: 80.00				

KM# 566 100 PESOS
31.1035 g., 0.9990 Silver 0.9990 oz. ASW **Subject:** Save
the Vaquita Porpoise **Obv:** National arms, eagle left **Rev:**
Swimming vaquita porpoise **Mint:** Mexico City

Date	Mintage	F	VF	XF	Unc	BU
1992 Proof	—	Value: 55.00				

KM# 509 200 PESOS
Copper-Nickel, 29.5 mm. **Subject:** 175th Anniversary of
Independence **Obv:** National arms, eagle left **Rev:** Conjoined
busts left **Mint:** Mexico City

Date	Mintage	F	VF	XF	Unc	BU
1985	75,000,000	—	—	2.00	3.50	5.50

KM# 510   200 PESOS
Copper-Nickel, 29.5 mm. **Subject:** 75th Anniversary of 1910
Revolution **Obv:** National arms, eagle left **Rev:** Conjoined
heads left below building **Mint:** Mexico City

Date	Mintage	F	VF	XF	Unc	BU
1985	98,590,000	—	—	2.00	4.00	6.00

KM# 525   200 PESOS
Copper-Nickel, 29.5 mm. **Subject:** 1986 World Cup Soccer
Games **Obv:** National arms, eagle left **Rev:** Soccer players
Edge: Reeded **Mint:** Mexico City

Date	Mintage	F	VF	XF	Unc	BU
1986	50,000,000	—	—	2.50	4.00	6.00

KM# 526   200 PESOS
62.2060 g., 0.9990 Silver 1.9979 oz. ASW **Subject:** 1986
World Cup Soccer Games **Obv:** National arms, eagle left **Rev:**
Value above 3 soccer balls **Mint:** Mexico City

Date	Mintage	F	VF	XF	Unc	BU
1986	50,000	—	—	—	60.00	70.00

KM# 500.1   250 PESOS
8.6400 g., 0.9000 Gold 0.2500 oz. AGW **Subject:** 1986
World Cup Soccer Games **Obv:** National arms, eagle left **Rev:**
Soccer ball within top 1/2 of design with value, date, and state
below **Mint:** Mexico City

Date	Mintage	F	VF	XF	Unc	BU
1985	100,000	—	—	—	—	325
1986	—	—	—	—	—	325

KM# 500.2   250 PESOS
8.6400 g., 0.9000 Gold 0.2500 oz. AGW **Subject:** 1986
World Cup Soccer Games **Obv:** National arms, eagle left **Rev:**
Without fineness statement **Mint:** Mexico City

Date	Mintage	F	VF	XF	Unc	BU
1985 Proof	4,506	Value: 325				
1986 Proof	—	Value: 325				

KM# 506.1   250 PESOS
8.6400 g., 0.9000 Gold 0.2500 oz. AGW **Subject:** 1986
World Cup Soccer Games **Obv:** National arms, eagle left **Rev:**
Equestrian left within circle **Mint:** Mexico City

Date	Mintage	F	VF	XF	Unc	BU
1985	88,000	—	—	—	—	320

KM# 506.2   250 PESOS
8.6400 g., 0.9000 Gold 0.2500 oz. AGW **Subject:** 1986
World Cup Soccer Games **Obv:** National arms, eagle left **Rev:**
Without fineness statement **Mint:** Mexico City

Date	Mintage	F	VF	XF	Unc	BU
1985 Proof	Est. 80,000	Value: 320				

KM# 501.1   500 PESOS
17.2800 g., 0.9000 Gold 0.5000 oz. AGW **Subject:** 1986
World Cup Soccer Games **Obv:** National arms, eagle left **Rev:**
Soccer player to right within emblem **Mint:** Mexico City

Date	Mintage	F	VF	XF	Unc	BU
1985	102,000	—	—	—	—	625
1986	—	—	—	—	—	625

KM# 501.2   500 PESOS
17.2800 g., 0.9000 Gold 0.5000 oz. AGW **Subject:** 1986
World Cup Soccer Games **Obv:** National arms, eagle left **Rev:**
Without fineness statement **Mint:** Mexico City

Date	Mintage	F	VF	XF	Unc	BU
1985 Proof	5,506	Value: 625				
1986 Proof	—	Value: 625				

KM# 507.1   500 PESOS
17.2800 g., 0.9000 Gold 0.5000 oz. AGW **Subject:** 1986
World Cup Soccer Games **Obv:** National arms, eagle left **Rev:**
Soccer ball within emblem flanked by value and date **Mint:**
Mexico City

Date	Mintage	F	VF	XF	Unc	BU
1985	—	—	—	—	—	625

KM# 507.2 500 PESOS
17.2800 g., 0.9000 Gold 0.5000 oz. AGW **Subject:** 1986
World Cup Soccer Games **Obv:** National arms, eagle left **Rev:**
Without fineness statement **Mint:** Mexico City

Date	Mintage	F	VF	XF	Unc	BU
1985 Proof	—	Value: 625				

KM# 513 1000 PESOS
17.2800 g., 0.9000 Gold 0.5000 oz. AGW **Subject:** 175th
Anniversary of Independence **Obv:** National arms, eagle left
Rev: Conjoined heads left below value **Mint:** Mexico City

Date	Mintage	F	VF	XF	Unc	BU
1985 Proof	—	Value: 650				

KM# 511 500 PESOS
33.4500 g., 0.9250 Silver 0.9947 oz. ASW **Subject:** 75th
Anniversary of 1910 Revolution **Obv:** National arms, eagle left
Rev: Conjoined heads left below building **Mint:** Mexico City

Date	Mintage	F	VF	XF	Unc	BU
1985 Proof	40,000	Value: 65.00				

KM# 527 1000 PESOS
31.1050 g., 0.9990 Gold 0.9990 oz. AGW **Subject:** 1986 World
Cup Soccer Games **Obv:** National arms, eagle left **Rev:** Value
above soccer ball and two hemispheres **Mint:** Mexico City

Date	Mintage	F	VF	XF	Unc	BU
1986	—	—	—	—	—	1,275

KM# 536 1000 PESOS
15.0000 g., Aluminum-Bronze, 30.5 mm. **Obv:** National
arms, eagle left **Rev:** Bust 1/4 left with diagonal value at left
Mint: Mexico City **Note:** Juana de Asbaje

Date	Mintage	F	VF	XF	Unc	BU
1988	229,300,000	—	0.85	2.00	4.25	5.75
1989	—	—	0.85	2.00	4.25	5.75
1990	—	—	0.85	2.00	4.00	5.50
1990 Proof; 2 known	—	Value: 550				
1991	—	—	1.00	2.00	3.00	7.00
1992	—	—	1.00	2.00	3.50	7.50

KM# 535 1000 PESOS
34.5590 g., 0.9000 Gold 0.9999 oz. AGW **Subject:** 50th
Anniversary - Nationalization of Oil Industry **Obv:** National
arms, eagle left **Rev:** Portrait of Cardenas **Mint:** Mexico City
Note: Similar to 5000 Pesos, KM#531.

Date	Mintage	F	VF	XF	Unc	BU
1988 Proof	—	Value: 1,275				

KM# 529 500 PESOS
Copper-Nickel, 28.5 mm. **Obv:** National arms, eagle left **Rev:**
Head 1/4 right **Mint:** Mexico City

Date	Mintage	F	VF	XF	Unc	BU
1986	20,000,000	—	—	1.00	3.25	4.00
1987	180,000,000	—	—	0.75	2.25	3.00
1988	230,000,000	—	—	0.50	2.25	3.00
1988 Proof; 2 known	—	Value: 650				
1989	—	—	—	0.75	2.25	3.50
1992	—	—	—	1.00	2.25	4.00

KM# 534 500 PESOS
17.2800 g., 0.9000 Gold 0.5000 oz. AGW **Subject:** 50th
Anniversary - Nationalization of Oil Industry **Obv:** National
arms, eagle left **Rev:** Monument **Mint:** Mexico City **Note:**
Similar to 5000 Pesos, KM#531.

Date	Mintage	F	VF	XF	Unc	BU
1988	—	—	—	—	—	650

KM# 528   2000 PESOS
62.2000 g., 0.9990 Gold 1.9977 oz. AGW **Subject:** 1986 World
Cup Soccer Games **Obv:** National arms, eagle left **Rev:** Value
above soccer ball and two hemispheres **Mint:** Mexico City

Date	Mintage	F	VF	XF	Unc	BU
1986	—	—	—	—	—	2,500

KM# 531   5000 PESOS
Copper-Nickel, 33.5 mm.   **Subject:** 50th Anniversary -
Nationalization of Oil Industry **Obv:** National arms, eagle left
Rev: Monument above dates with diagonal value at left **Mint:**
Mexico City

Date	Mintage	F	VF	XF	Unc	BU
ND(1988)	50,000,000	—	—	4.75	7.75	10.00

REFORM COINAGE

1 New Peso =
1000 Old Pesos

KM# 546   5 CENTAVOS
1.5900 g., Stainless Steel, 15.58 mm.   **Obv:** National arms
Rev: Large value **Edge:** Plain **Mint:** Mexico City

Date	Mintage	F	VF	XF	Unc	BU
1992	136,800,000	—	—	0.15	0.20	0.50
1993	234,000,000	—	—	0.15	0.20	0.50
1994	125,000,000	—	—	0.15	0.20	0.50
1995	195,000,000	—	—	0.15	0.20	0.50
1995 Proof	6,981	Value: 0.50				
1996	104,831,000	—	—	0.15	0.20	0.50
1997	153,675,000	—	—	0.15	0.20	0.50
1998	64,417,000	—	—	0.15	0.20	0.50
1999	9,949,000	—	—	0.15	0.20	0.50
2000Mo	10,871,000	—	—	0.15	0.20	0.50
2001Mo	34,811,000	—	—	0.15	0.20	0.50
2002Mo	14,901,000	—	—	0.15	0.20	0.50

KM# 547   10 CENTAVOS
2.0300 g., Stainless Steel, 17 mm.   **Obv:** National arms,
eagle left **Rev:** Value **Mint:** Mexico City

Date	Mintage	F	VF	XF	Unc	BU
1992	121,250,000	Value: 0.75				
1993	755,000,000	—	—	0.20	0.25	6.00
1994	557,000,000	—	—	0.20	0.25	0.60
1995	560,000,000	—	—	0.20	0.25	0.60
1995 Proof	6,981	Value: 0.50				
1996	594,216,000	—	—	0.20	0.25	0.60
1997	581,622,000	—	—	0.20	0.25	0.60
1998	602,667,000	—	—	0.20	0.25	0.60
1999	488,346,000	—	—	0.20	0.25	0.60
2000	577,546,000	—	—	0.20	0.30	0.75
2001	618,061,000	—	—	0.20	0.25	0.30
2002	463,968,000	—	—	0.20	0.25	0.30
2003Mo	378,938,000	—	—	0.20	0.25	0.30
2004	393,705,000	—	—	0.20	0.25	0.30
2005	488,773,000	—	—	0.20	0.25	0.30
2006	473,261,000	—	—	0.20	0.25	0.30
2007	473,261,000	—	—	0.20	0.25	0.30
2008	109,731,000	—	—	0.20	0.25	0.30
2009		—	—	0.20	0.25	0.30

KM# 548   20 CENTAVOS
Aluminum-Bronze, 19 mm.   **Obv:** National arms, eagle left
Rev: Value and date within 3/4 wreath **Shape:** 12-sided **Mint:**
Mexico City

Date	Mintage	F	VF	XF	Unc	BU
1992	95,000,000	—	—	0.25	0.35	1.00
1993	95,000,000	—	—	0.25	0.35	1.00
1994	105,000,000	—	—	0.25	0.35	11.00
1995	180,000,000	—	—	0.25	0.35	1.00
1995 Proof	6,981	Value: 0.75				
1996	54,896,000	—	—	0.25	0.35	1.00
1997	178,807,000	—	—	0.25	0.35	1.00
1998	223,847,000	—	—	0.25	0.35	1.00
1999	233,753,000	—	—	0.25	0.35	1.00
2000	223,973,000	—	—	0.25	0.35	1.00
2001	234,360,000	—	—	0.25	0.35	0.40
2002Mo	229,256,000	—	—	0.25	0.35	0.40
2003Mo	149,518,000	—	—	0.25	0.35	0.40
2004	174,351,000	—	—	0.25	0.35	0.40
2005	204,444,000	—	—	0.25	0.35	0.40
2006	234,263,000	—	—	0.25	0.35	0.40
2007	234,301,000	—	—	0.25	0.35	0.40
2008	59,778,000	—	—	0.25	0.35	0.40
2009		—	—	0.25	0.35	0.40

KM# 549   50 CENTAVOS
4.4000 g., Aluminum-Bronze, 22 mm.   **Obv:** National arms,
eagle left **Rev:** Value and date within 1/2 designed wreath
Shape: 12-sided **Mint:** Mexico City

Date	Mintage	F	VF	XF	Unc	BU
1992	120,150,000	—	—	0.45	0.85	1.75
1993	330,000,000	—	—	0.45	0.75	1.50
1994	100,000,000	—	—	0.45	0.75	1.50

Date	Mintage	F	VF	XF	Unc	BU
1995	60,000,000	—	—	0.45	0.75	1.50
1995 Proof	6,981	Value: 0.90				
1996	69,956,000	—	—	0.45	0.75	1.50
1997	129,029,000	—	—	0.45	0.75	1.50
1998	223,605,000	—	—	0.45	0.75	1.50
1999	89,516,000	—	—	0.45	0.75	1.50
2000	135,112,000	—	—	0.45	0.75	1.50
2001	199,006,000	—	—	0.45	0.75	1.00
2002	94,552,000	—	—	0.45	0.75	1.00
2003Mo	124,522,000	—	—	0.45	0.75	1.00
2004	154,434,000	—	—	0.45	0.75	1.00
2005	179,304,000	—	—	0.45	0.75	1.00
2006	234,142,000	—	—	0.45	0.75	1.00
2007	253,634,000	—	—	0.45	0.75	1.00
2008	79,760,000	—	—	0.45	0.75	1.00
2009	—	—	—	0.45	0.75	1.00

KM# 550   NUEVO PESO
3.9400 g., Bi-Metallic Aluminum-Bronze center in Stainless Steel ring, 22 mm. **Obv:** National arms, eagle left **Rev:** Value **Mint:** Mexico City

Date	Mintage	F	VF	XF	Unc	BU
1992	144,000,000	—	—	0.60	1.50	2.75
1993	329,860,000	—	—	0.60	1.50	2.75
1994	221,000,000	—	—	0.60	1.50	2.75
1995 Small date	125,000,000	—	—	0.60	1.50	2.75
1995 Large date	Inc. above	—	—	0.60	1.50	2.75
1995 Proof	6,981	Value: 2.75				

KM# 603   PESO
3.9500 g., Bi-Metallic Aluminum-Bronze center in Stainless-steel ring, 21.1 mm. **Obv:** National arms, eagle left within circle **Rev:** Value and date within circle **Mint:** Mexico City **Note:** Similar to KM#550 but without N.

Date	Mintage	F	VF	XF	Unc	BU
1996Mo	169,510,000	—	—	—	1.25	2.25
1997Mo	222,870,000	—	—	—	1.25	2.25
1998Mo	261,942,000	—	—	—	1.25	2.25
1999Mo	99,168,000	—	—	—	1.25	2.25
2000Mo	158,379,000	—	—	—	1.25	2.25
2001Mo	208,576,000	—	—	—	1.25	2.75
2002Mo	119,541,000	—	—	—	1.25	2.75
2003Mo	169,320,000	—	—	—	1.25	2.75
2004	208,611,000	—	—	—	1.25	2.75
2005	253,924,000	—	—	—	1.25	2.75
2006	289,834,000	—	—	—	1.25	2.75
2007	368,408,000	—	—	—	1.25	2.75
2008	99,687,000	—	—	—	1.25	2.75
2009	—	—	—	—	1.25	2.75

KM# 551   2 NUEVO PESOS
Bi-Metallic Aluminum-Bronze center in Stainless Steel ring, 23 mm. **Obv:** National arms, eagle left within circle **Rev:** Value and date within circle with assorted emblems around border **Mint:** Mexico City

Date	Mintage	F	VF	XF	Unc	BU
1992	60,000,000	—	—	1.00	2.50	4.00
1993	77,000,000	—	—	1.00	2.50	4.00
1994	44,000,000	—	—	1.00	2.50	4.00
1995	20,000,000	—	—	1.00	2.50	4.00
1995 Proof	6,981	Value: 6.00				

KM# 604   2 PESOS
5.2100 g., Bi-Metallic Aluminum-Bronze center in Stainless Steel ring, 23 mm. **Obv:** National arms, eagle left within circle **Rev:** Value and date within center circle of assorted emblems **Mint:** Mexico City **Note:** Similar to KM#551, but denomination without N.

Date	Mintage	F	VF	XF	Unc	BU
1996Mo	24,902,000	—	—	—	2.50	4.00
1997Mo	34,560,000	—	—	—	2.50	4.00
1998Mo	104,138,000	—	—	—	2.50	4.00
1999Mo	34,713,000	—	—	—	2.50	4.00
2000Mo	69,322,000	—	—	—	2.50	4.00
2001Mo	74,563,000	—	—	—	2.35	4.00
2002Mo	74,547,000	—	—	—	2.35	4.00
2003Mo	39,814,000	—	—	—	2.35	4.00
2004	89,496,000	—	—	—	2.35	4.00
2005	94,532,000	—	—	—	2.35	4.00
2006	144,123,000	—	—	—	2.35	4.00
2007	129,422,000	—	—	—	2.35	4.00
2008	49,801,000	—	—	—	2.35	4.00
2009	—	—	—	—	2.35	4.00

KM# 552   5 NUEVO PESOS
Bi-Metallic Aluminum-Bronze center in Stainless Steel ring, 25.5 mm. **Obv:** National arms, eagle left within circle **Rev:** Value and date within circle with bow below **Mint:** Mexico City

Date	Mintage	F	VF	XF	Unc	BU
1992	70,000,000	—	—	2.00	6.00	8.50
1993	168,240,000	—	—	2.00	6.00	8.50
1994	58,000,000	—	—	2.00	6.00	8.50
1995 Proof	6,981	Value: 25.00				

KM# 588   5 NUEVO PESOS
27.0000 g., 0.9250 Silver 0.8029 oz. ASW **Subject:** Environmental Protection **Obv:** National arms, eagle left within center of past and present arms **Rev:** Pacific Ridley Sea Turtle

Date	Mintage	F	VF	XF	Unc	BU
1994 Proof	20,000	Value: 50.00				

KM# 629   5 PESOS
27.0000 g., 0.9250 Silver 0.8029 oz. ASW **Subject:** Jarabe Tapatio **Obv:** National arms, eagle left within center of assorted arms **Rev:** Mexican dancers

Date	Mintage	F	VF	XF	Unc	BU
1997 Proof	20,000	Value: 350				
1998 Proof	—	Value: 350				

KM# 605   5 PESOS
Bi-Metallic Aluminum-Bronze center in Stainless Steel ring,
25.5 mm.   **Obv:** National arms, eagle left within circle **Rev:**
Value within circle **Mint:** Mexico City **Note:** Similar to KM#552
but denomination without N.

Date	Mintage	F	VF	XF	Unc	BU
1997Mo	39,468,000	—	—	3.00	6.00	8.50
1998Mo	103,729,000	—	—	3.00	6.00	8.50
1999Mo	59,427,000	—	—	3.00	6.00	8.50
2000Mo	20,869,000	—	—	3.00	6.00	8.50
2001Mo	79,169,000	—	—	3.00	5.00	7.50
2002Mo	34,754,000	—	—	3.00	5.00	7.50
2003Mo	54,676,000	—	—	3.00	5.00	7.50
2004	89,518,000	—	—	3.00	5.00	7.50
2005	94,482,000	—	—	3.00	5.00	7.50
2006	89,447,000	—	—	3.00	5.00	7.50
2007	123,382,000	—	—	3.00	5.00	7.50
2008	9,939,000	—	—	3.00	5.00	7.50
2009	—	—	—	3.00	5.00	7.50

KM# 631   5 PESOS
31.1800 g., 0.9990 Silver 1.0014 oz. ASW   **Subject:**
Millennium Series **Obv:** National arms, eagle left within center
of past and present arms **Rev:** Stylized dove as hand of peace
Rev. Designer: Omar Jiminez Torres

Date	Mintage	F	VF	XF	Unc	BU
1999-2000 Proof	75,000	Value: 50.00				

KM# 627   5 PESOS
31.1035 g., 0.9990 Silver 0.9990 oz. ASW   **Subject:** World
Wildlife Fund **Obv:** National arms, eagle left **Rev:** Wolf with pup

Date	Mintage	F	VF	XF	Unc	BU
1998 Proof	Est. 15,000	Value: 95.00				

KM# 632   5 PESOS
31.1800 g., 0.9990 Silver 1.0014 oz. ASW   **Subject:**
Millennium Series **Obv:** National arms, eagle left within center
of past and present arms **Rev:** Aztec bird design and value

Date	Mintage	F	VF	XF	Unc	BU
1999-2000 Proof	75,000	Value: 50.00				

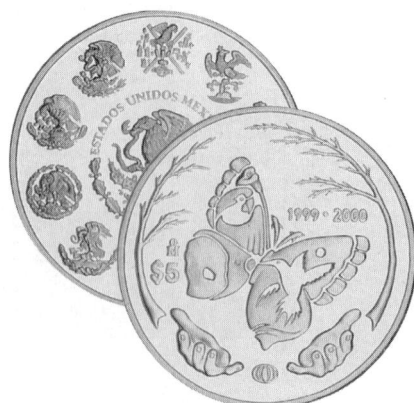

KM# 630   5 PESOS
31.1800 g., 0.9990 Silver 1.0014 oz. ASW   **Subject:**
Millennium Series **Obv:** National arms, eagle left within center
of past and present arms **Rev:** Butterfly flanked by sprigs
above hands **Rev. Designer:** Francisco Ortega Romero

Date	Mintage	F	VF	XF	Unc	BU
1999-2000 Proof	75,000	Value: 55.00				

KM# 635   5 PESOS
19.6000 g., 0.9250 Silver 0.5829 oz. ASW   **Subject:**
Millennium Series **Obv:** National arms, eagle left **Rev:** Naval
training ship Cuauhtemoc sailing into world globe

Date	Mintage	F	VF	XF	Unc	BU
1999	—	Value: 45.00				

KM# 640   5 PESOS
31.1030 g., 0.9990 Silver 0.9989 oz. ASW, 40 mm. **Subject:**
UNICEF **Obv:** National arms, eagle left **Rev:** Two children
flying kite **Edge:** Reeded **Mint:** Mexico City

Date	Mintage	F	VF	XF	Unc	BU
1999 Proof	—	Value: 60.00				

KM# 655   5 PESOS
31.1710 g., 0.9990 Silver 1.0011 oz. ASW, 40 mm. **Series:**
Endangered Wildlife **Subject:** Cocodrilo de Rio **Obv:** National
arms, eagle left within center of past and present arms **Rev:**
American Crocodile

Date	Mintage	F	VF	XF	Unc	BU
2000	50,000	—	—	—	40.00	50.00

KM# 656   5 PESOS
31.1710 g., 0.9990 Silver 1.0011 oz. ASW, 40 mm. **Series:**
Endangered Wildlife **Subject:** Nutria de Rio **Obv:** National
arms, eagle left within center of past and present arms **Rev:**
Neotropical River Otter

Date	Mintage	F	VF	XF	Unc	BU
2000	50,000	—	—	—	40.00	50.00

KM# 657   5 PESOS
31.1710 g., 0.9990 Silver 1.0011 oz. ASW, 40 mm. **Series:**
Endangered Wildlife - Berrendo **Obv:** National arms, eagle
left within center of past and present arms **Rev:** Peninsular
Pronghorn, giant cardon cactus in back

Date	Mintage	F	VF	XF	Unc	BU
2000	50,000	—	—	—	40.00	50.00

KM# 652   5 PESOS
31.1710 g., 0.9990 Silver 1.0011 oz. ASW, 40 mm. **Series:**
Endangered Wildlife **Subject:** Aguila Real **Obv:** National
arms, eagle left within center of past and present arms **Rev:**
Golden Eagle on branch

Date	Mintage	F	VF	XF	Unc	BU
2000	50,000	—	—	—	40.00	50.00

KM# 670   5 PESOS
27.0000 g., 0.9250 Silver 0.8029 oz. ASW, 40 mm. **Series:**
Ibero-America **Obv:** National arms, eagle left within center of
past and present arms **Rev:** Cowboy trick riding two horses
Edge: Reeded **Mint:** Mexico City

Date	Mintage	F	VF	XF	Unc	BU
2000 Proof	—	Value: 85.00				

KM# 653   5 PESOS
31.1710 g., 0.9990 Silver 1.0011 oz. ASW, 40 mm. **Subject:**
Aguila Arpia **Obv:** National arms in center of past and present
arms **Rev:** Crowned Harpy Eagle perched on branch

Date	Mintage	F	VF	XF	Unc	BU
2001	50,000	—	—	—	40.00	50.00

KM# 654   5 PESOS
31.1710 g., 0.9990 Silver 1.0011 oz. ASW, 40 mm. **Series:**
Endangered Wildlife **Subject:** Oso Negro **Obv:** National arms
in center of past and present arms **Rev:** Black bear, value
and date

Date	Mintage	F	VF	XF	Unc	BU
2001	50,000	—	—	—	40.00	50.00

KM# 658   5 PESOS
31.1710 g., 0.9990 Silver 1.0011 oz. ASW, 40 mm. **Series:**
Endangered Wildlife **Obv:** National arms in center of past and
present arms **Rev:** Jaguar, value and date

Date	Mintage	F	VF	XF	Unc	BU
2001	50,000	—	—	—	40.00	50.00

KM# 659   5 PESOS
31.1710 g., 0.9990 Silver 1.0011 oz. ASW, 40 mm. **Series:**
Endangered Wildlife **Obv:** National arms in center of past and
present arms **Rev:** Prairie dog, value and date

Date	Mintage	F	VF	XF	Unc	BU
2001	50,000	—	—	—	40.00	50.00

KM# 660   5 PESOS
31.1710 g., 0.9990 Silver 1.0011 oz. ASW, 40 mm. **Series:**
Endangered Wildlife **Obv:** National arms in center of past and
present arms **Rev:** Volcano rabbit, value and date

Date	Mintage	F	VF	XF	Unc	BU
2001	50,000	—	—	—	40.00	50.00

KM# 651   5 PESOS
31.1710 g., 0.9990 Silver 1.0011 oz. ASW, 40 mm. **Series:**
Endangered Wildlife **Obv:** National arms in center of past and
present arms **Rev:** Manatee, value and date **Edge:** Reeded
Mint: Mexico City

Date	Mintage	F	VF	XF	Unc	BU
2001	50,000	—	—	—	40.00	50.00

KM# 678   5 PESOS
27.0000 g., 0.9250 Silver 0.8029 oz. ASW, 40 mm. **Subject:**
Ibero-America: Acapulco Galleon **Obv:** National arms in
center of past and present arms **Rev:** Spanish galleon with
Pacific Ocean background and trading scene in foreground
Edge: Reeded **Mint:** Mexico City

Date	Mintage	F	VF	XF	Unc	BU
2003Mo Proof	5,000	Value: 90.00				

KM# 553   10 NUEVO PESOS
11.1300 g., Bi-Metallic 0.925 Silver center, .1667 oz. ASW
within Aluminum-Bronze ring, 27.95 mm. **Obv:** National arms
Obv. Legend: Estados Unidos Mexicanos **Rev:** Assorted
shields within circle **Edge:** Reeded **Mint:** Mexico City

Date	Mintage	F	VF	XF	Unc	BU
1992	20,000,000	—	—	6.00	10.00	14.00
1993	47,981,000	—	—	6.00	10.00	14.00
1994	15,000,000	—	—	6.00	10.00	14.00
1995 Proof	6,981	Value: 20.00				
1995	15,000,000	—	—	6.00	10.00	14.00

KM# 616   10 PESOS
10.3500 g., Bi-Metallic Copper-Nickel-Brass center within
Brass ring, 27.95 mm.   **Obv:** National arms **Obv. Legend:**
ESTADOS UNIDOS MEXICANOS **Rev:** Aztec design **Mint:**
Mexico City

Date	Mintage	F	VF	XF	Unc	BU
1997Mo	44,837,000	—	—	5.00	8.00	12.00
1998Mo	203,735,000	—	—	5.00	8.00	12.00
1999Mo	29,842,000	—	—	5.00	8.00	12.00

KM# 633   10 PESOS
62.0300 g., 0.9990 Silver 1.9922 oz. ASW **Subject:**
Millennium Series **Obv:** National arms, eagle left within center
of past and present arms **Rev:** Ancient and modern buildings
within circle

Date	Mintage	F	VF	XF	Unc	BU
1999-2000 Proof	75,000	Value: 50.00				

KM# 636   10 PESOS
10.3500 g., Bi-Metallic Copper-Nickel center in Brass ring,
28 mm.   **Series:** Millennium **Obv:** National arms **Obv.
Legend:** ESTADOS UNIDOS MEXICANOS **Rev:** Aztec
carving **Edge:** Lettered **Edge Lettering:** ANO and date
repeated 3 times **Mint:** Mexico City

Date	Mintage	F	VF	XF	Unc	BU
2000Mo	24,839,000	—	—	5.00	8.00	12.00
2001Mo	44,768,000	—	—	5.00	7.50	10.00
2002Mo	44,721,000	—	—	5.00	7.50	10.00
2004Mo	74,739,000	—	—	5.00	7.50	10.00
2005Mo	64,635,000	—	—	5.00	7.50	10.00
2006Mo	84,575,000	—	—	5.00	7.50	10.00
2007	89,678,000	—	—	5.00	7.50	10.00
2008	24,896,000	—	—	5.00	7.50	10.00
2009	—	—	—	5.00	7.50	10.00

KM# 561   20 NUEVO PESOS
16.9200 g., Bi-Metallic 0.925 Silver 16.9g, (.2500 oz. ASW)
center within Aluminum-Bronze ring, 31.86 mm.   **Obv:**
National arms **Obv. Legend:** ESTADOS UNIDOS

MEXICANOS **Rev:** Head of Hidalgo left within wreath **Edge:**
Reeded **Mint:** Mexico City

Date	Mintage	F	VF	XF	Unc	BU
1993Mo	25,000,000	—	—	6.00	12.00	15.00
1994Mo	5,000,000	—	—	6.00	12.00	15.00
1995Mo	5,000,000	—	—	6.00	12.00	15.00

KM# 641   20 PESOS
6.2210 g., 0.9990 Gold 0.1998 oz. AGW, 21.9 mm. **Subject:**
UNICEF **Obv:** National arms, eagle left **Rev:** Child playing
with lasso **Edge:** Reeded **Mint:** Mexico City

Date	Mintage	F	VF	XF	Unc	BU
1999 Proof	—	Value: 375				

KM# 637   20 PESOS
Bi-Metallic Copper-Nickel center within Brass ring, 32 mm.
Subject: Xiuhtecuhtli **Obv:** National arms, eagle left within
circle **Rev:** Aztec with torch within spiked circle

Date	Mintage	F	VF	XF	Unc	BU
2000	14,890,000	—	—	—	15.00	18.50
2001	2,478,000	—	—	—	16.00	18.00

KM# 638   20 PESOS
Bi-Metallic Copper-Nickel center within Brass ring, 32 mm.
Obv: National arms, eagle left within circle **Rev:** Head 1/4
right within circle

Date	Mintage	F	VF	XF	Unc	BU
2000	14,943,000	—	—	—	15.00	18.50
2001	2,515,000	—	—	—	16.00	18.50

KM# 571   50 NUEVO PESOS
34.1100 g., Bi-Metallic 0.925 Silver .5000 ASW center within

Brass ring, 38.87 mm. **Subject:** Nino Heroes **Obv:** National arms **Obv. Legend:** ESTADOS UNIDOS MEXICANOS **Rev:** Six heads facing with date at upper right, all within circle and 1/2 wreath **Edge:** Reeded **Mint:** Mexico City

Date	Mintage	F	VF	XF	Unc	BU
1993Mo	2,000,000	—	—	—	25.00	32.50
1994Mo	1,500,000	—	—	—	25.00	32.50
1995Mo	1,500,000	—	—	—	25.00	32.50

KM# 705   100 PESOS
33.7400 g., Bi-Metallic .925 Silver center in Aluminum-Bronze ring, 39 mm. **Subject:** 400th Anniversary of Don Quijote de la Manchia **Obv:** National arms **Obv. Legend:** ESTADOS UNIDOS MEXICANOS **Rev:** Sekeletal figure Horseback with spear galloping right **Edge:** Segmented reeding **Mint:** Mexico City

Date	Mintage	F	VF	XF	Unc	BU
2005Mo	726,833	—	—	—	25.00	32.00
2005Mo Proof	3,761	Value: 75.00				

KM# 730   100 PESOS
33.8250 g., Bi-Metallic .925 Silver 20.1753g center in Aluminum-Bronze ring, 39.9 mm. **Subject:** Monetary Reform Centennial **Obv:** National arms **Rev:** Radiant Liberty Cap divides date above value within circle **Edge:** Segmented reeding **Mint:** Mexico City

Date	Mintage	F	VF	XF	Unc	BU
2005Mo	49,716	—	—	—	40.00	45.00
2005Mo Proof	—	Value: 75.00				

KM# 731   100 PESOS
33.8250 g., Bi-Metallic .925 Silver 20.1753g center in Aluminum-Bronze ring, 39.9 mm. **Subject:** Mexico City Mint's 470th Anniversary **Obv:** National arms **Rev:** Screw press, value and date within circle **Edge:** Segmented reeding **Mint:** Mexico City

Date	Mintage	F	VF	XF	Unc	BU
2005Mo	49,895	—	—	—	40.00	45.00
2005Mo Proof	—	Value: 95.00				

KM# 732   100 PESOS
33.8250 g., Bi-Metallic .925 Silver 20.1753g center in Aluminum-Bronze ring, 39.9 mm. **Subject:** Bank of Mexico's 80th Anniversary **Obv:** National arms **Rev:** Back design of the 1925 hundred peso note **Edge:** Segmented reeding **Mint:** Mexico City

Date	Mintage	F	VF	XF	Unc	BU
2005Mo	49,712	—	—	—	40.00	45.00
2005Mo Proof	—	Value: 95.00				

KM# 764   100 PESOS
33.7000 g., Bi-Metallic .925 Silver 20.1753g center in Aluminum-Bronze ring **Subject:** 200th Anniversary Birth of Benito Juarez Garcia **Obv:** National arms **Rev:** Bust 1/4 left within circle **Mint:** Mexico City

Date	Mintage	F	VF	XF	Unc	BU
2006Mo	49,913	—	—	—	40.00	45.00

State Commemoratives

KM# 679   10 PESOS
31.1040 g., 0.9990 Silver 0.9990 oz. ASW, 39.9 mm. **Series:** First **Subject:** 180th Anniversary of Federation **Obv:** National arms **Obv. Legend:** ESTADOS UNIDOS MEXICANOS **Rev:** State Arms **Rev. Legend:** ESTADO DE ZACATECAS **Edge:** Reeded **Mint:** Mexico City

Date	Mintage	F	VF	XF	Unc	BU
2003Mo Proof	10,000	Value: 70.00				

KM# 680   10 PESOS
31.1040 g., 0.9990 Silver 0.9990 oz. ASW, 39.9 mm. **Series:** First **Subject:** 180th Anniversary of Federation **Obv:** National arms **Obv. Legend:** ESTADO UNIDOS MEXICANOS **Rev:** State arms **Rev. Legend:** ESTADO DE YUCATÁN **Edge:** Reeded **Mint:** Mexico City

Date	Mintage	F	VF	XF	Unc	BU
2003Mo Proof	10,000	Value: 70.00				

KM# 681   10 PESOS
31.1040 g., 0.9990 Silver 0.9990 oz. ASW, 39.9 mm. **Series:** First **Subject:** 180th Anniversary of Federation **Obv:** National arms **Obv. Legend:** ESTADOS UNIDOS MEXICANOS **Rev:** State arms **Rev. Legend:** ESTADO DE VERACRUZ-LLAVE **Edge:** Reeded **Mint:** Mexico City

Date	Mintage	F	VF	XF	Unc	BU
2003Mo Proof	10,000	Value: 70.00				

KM# 682   10 PESOS
31.1040 g., 0.9990 Silver 0.9990 oz. ASW, 39.9 mm. **Series:** First **Subject:** 180th Anniversary of Frederation **Obv:** National arms **Obv. Legend:** ESTADOS UNIDOS MEXICANOS **Rev:** State arms **Rev. Legend:** ESTADO DE TLAXCALA **Edge:** Reeded **Mint:** Mexico City

Date	Mintage	F	VF	XF	Unc	BU
2003Mo Proof	10,000	Value: 70.00				

KM# 683   10 PESOS
31.1040 g., 0.9990 Silver 0.9990 oz. ASW, 39.9 mm. **Series:** First **Subject:** 180th Anniversary of Federation **Obv:** National arms **Obv. Legend:** ESTADOS UNIDOS MEXICANOS **Rev:** State arms **Rev. Legend:** ESTADO DE TAMAULIPAS **Edge:** Reeded **Mint:** Mexico City

Date	Mintage	F	VF	XF	Unc	BU
2004Mo Proof	10,000	Value: 70.00				

KM# 684   10 PESOS
31.1040 g., 0.9990 Silver 0.9990 oz. ASW, 39.9 mm. **Series:** First **Subject:** 180th Anniversary of Federation **Obv:** National arms **Obv. Legend:** ESTADOS UNIDOS DE MEXICANOS **Rev:** State arms **Rev. Legend:** ESTADO DE TABASCO **Edge:** Reeded **Mint:** Mexico City

Date	Mintage	F	VF	XF	Unc	BU
2004Mo Proof	10,000	Value: 70.00				

KM# 685   10 PESOS
31.1040 g., 0.9990 Silver 0.9990 oz. ASW, 39.9 mm. **Series:** First **Subject:** 180th Anniversary of Federation **Obv:** National arms **Obv. Legend:** ESTADOS UNIDOS MEXICANOS **Rev:** State arms **Rev. Legend:** ESTADO DE SONORA **Edge:** Reeded **Mint:** Mexico City **Note:** Mexican States: Sonora

Date	Mintage	F	VF	XF	Unc	BU
2004Mo Proof	10,000	Value: 70.00				

KM# 686   10 PESOS
31.1040 g., 0.9990 Silver 0.9990 oz. ASW, 39.9 mm. **Series:**
First **Subject:** 180th Anniversary of Federation **Obv:** National
arms **Obv. Legend:** ESTADOS UNIDOS DE MEXICANOS
Rev: State arms **Rev. Legend:** ESTADO DE SINALOA **Edge:**
Reeded **Mint:** Mexico City **Note:** Mexican States: Sinaloa

Date	Mintage	F	VF	XF	Unc	BU
2004Mo Proof	10,000	Value: 70.00				

KM# 733   10 PESOS
31.1040 g., 0.9990 Silver 0.9990 oz. ASW, 39.9 mm. **Series:**
First **Subject:** 180th Anniversary of Federation **Obv:** National
arms **Obv. Legend:** ESTADOS UNIDOS MEXICANOS **Rev:**
State arms **Rev. Legend:** ESTADO DE QUERÉTARO
ARTEAGA **Edge:** Reeded

Date	Mintage	F	VF	XF	Unc	BU
2004 Proof	10,000	Value: 70.00				

KM# 687   10 PESOS
31.1040 g., 0.9990 Silver 0.9990 oz. ASW, 39.9 mm. **Series:**
First **Subject:** 180th Anniversary of Federation **Obv:** National
arms **Obv. Legend:** ESTADOS UNIDOS MEXICANOS **Rev:**
State arms **Rev. Legend:** ESTADO DE SAN LUIS POTOSÍ
Edge: Reeded **Mint:** Mexico City

Date	Mintage	F	VF	XF	Unc	BU
2004Mo Proof	10,000	Value: 70.00				

KM# 737   10 PESOS
31.1040 g., 0.9990 Silver 0.9990 oz. ASW, 39.9 mm. **Series:**
First **Subject:** 180th Anniversary of Federation **Obv:** National
arms **Obv. Legend:** ESTADOS UNIDOS MEXICANOS **Rev:**
State arms **Rev. Legend:** ESTADO DE PUEBLA **Edge:**
Reeded **Mint:** Mexico City

Date	Mintage	F	VF	XF	Unc	BU
2004Mo Proof	10,000	Value: 70.00				

KM# 735   10 PESOS
31.1040 g., 0.9990 Silver 0.9990 oz. ASW, 39.9 mm. **Series:**
First **Subject:** 180th Anniversary of Federation **Obv:** National
arms **Obv. Legend:** ESTADOS UNIDOS MEXICANOS **Rev:**
State arms **Rev. Legend:** ESTADO DE QUINTANA ROO

Date	Mintage	F	VF	XF	Unc	BU
2004 Proof	10,000	Value: 70.00				

KM# 739   10 PESOS
31.1040 g., 0.9990 Bi-Metallic 0.9990 oz., 39.9 mm. **Series:**
First **Subject:** 180th Anniversary of Federation **Obv:** National
arms **Obv. Legend:** ESTADOS UNIDOS MEXICANOS **Rev:**
State arms **Rev. Legend:** ESTADO DE OAXACA **Edge:**
Reeded **Mint:** Mexico City

Date	Mintage	F	VF	XF	Unc	BU
2004Mo Proof	10,000	Value: 70.00				

KM# 741   10 PESOS
31.1040 g., 0.9990 Silver 0.9990 oz. ASW, 39.9 mm. **Series:**
First **Subject:** 180th Anniversary of Federation **Obv:** National
arms **Obv. Legend:** ESTADOS UNIDOS MEXICANOS **Rev:**
State arms **Rev. Legend:** ESTADO DE NUEVO LEÓN **Edge:**
Reeded **Mint:** Mexico City

Date	Mintage	F	VF	XF	Unc	BU
2004Mo Proof	10,000	Value: 70.00				

KM# 796   10 PESOS
31.1040 g., 0.9990 Silver 0.9990 oz. ASW, 39.9 mm. **Series:**
First **Subject:** 180th Anniversary of Federation **Obv:** National
arms **Obv. Legend:** ESTADOS UNIDOS MEXICANOS **Rev:**
State arms **Rev. Legend:** ESTADO DE MICHOACÁN DE
OCAMPO **Edge:** Reeded **Mint:** Mexico City

Date	Mintage	F	VF	XF	Unc	BU
2004Mo Proof	10,000	Value: 70.00				

KM# 743   10 PESOS
31.1040 g., 0.9990 Silver 0.9990 oz. ASW, 39.9 mm. **Series:**
First **Subject:** 180th Anniversary of Federation **Obv:** National
arms **Obv. Legend:** ESTADOS UNIDOS MEXICANOS **Rev:**
State arms **Rev. Legend:** ESTADO DE NAYARIT **Edge:**
Reeded **Mint:** Mexico City

Date	Mintage	F	VF	XF	Unc	BU
2004Mo Proof	10,000	Value: 70.00				

KM# 747   10 PESOS
31.1040 g., 0.9990 Silver 0.9990 oz. ASW, 39.9 mm. **Series:**
First **Subject:** 180th Anniversary of Federation **Obv:** National
arms **Obv. Legend:** ESTADOS UNIDOS MEXICANOS **Rev:**
State arms **Rev. Legend:** ESTADO DE MÉXICO **Edge:**
Reeded **Mint:** Mexico City

Date	Mintage	F	VF	XF	Unc	BU
2004Mo Proof	10,000	Value: 70.00				

KM# 745   10 PESOS
31.1040 g., 0.9990 Silver 0.9990 oz. ASW, 39.9 mm. **Series:**
First **Subject:** 180th Anniversary of Federation **Obv:** National
arms **Obv. Legend:** ESTADOS UNIDOS MEXICANOS **Rev:**
State arms **Rev. Legend:** ESTADO DE MORELOS **Edge:**
Reeded **Mint:** Mexico City

Date	Mintage	F	VF	XF	Unc	BU
2004Mo Proof	10,000	Value: 70.00				

KM# 749   10 PESOS
31.1040 g., 0.9990 Silver 0.9990 oz. ASW, 39.9 mm. **Series:**
First **Subject:** 180th Anniversary of Federation **Obv:** National
arms **Obv. Legend:** ESTADOS UNIDOS MEXICANOS **Rev:**
State arms **Rev. Legend:** ESTADO DE JALISCO **Edge:**
Reeded **Mint:** Mexico City

Date	Mintage	F	VF	XF	Unc	BU
2004Mo Proof	10,000	Value: 70.00				

KM# 711   10 PESOS
31.1040 g., 0.9990 Silver 0.9990 oz. ASW, 39.9 mm. **Series:**
First **Subject:** 180th Anniversary of Federation **Obv:** National
arms **Obv. Legend:** ESTADOS UNIDOS MEXICANOS **Rev:**
State arms **Rev. Legend:** ESTADO DE HIDALGO **Edge:**
Reeded **Mint:** Mexico City

Date	Mintage	F	VF	XF	Unc	BU
2005Mo Proof	10,000	Value: 70.00				

KM# 708   10 PESOS
31.1040 g., 0.9990 Silver 0.9990 oz. ASW, 39.9 mm. **Series:**
First **Subject:** 180th Anniversary of Federation **Obv:** National
arms **Obv. Legend:** ESTADOS UNIDOS MEXICANOS **Rev:**
State arms **Rev. Legend:** ESTADO DE DURANGO **Edge:**
Reeded **Mint:** Mexico City

Date	Mintage	F	VF	XF	Unc	BU
2005Mo Proof	10,000	Value: 70.00				

KM# 710   10 PESOS
31.1040 g., 0.9990 Silver 0.9990 oz. ASW, 39.9 mm. **Series:**
First **Subject:** 180th Anniversary of Federation **Obv:** National
arms **Obv. Legend:** ESTADOS UNIDOS MEXICANOS **Rev:**
State arms **Rev. Legend:** ESTADO DE GUERRERO **Edge:**
Reeded **Mint:** Mexico City

Date	Mintage	F	VF	XF	Unc	BU
2005Mo Proof	10,000	Value: 70.00				

KM# 707   10 PESOS
31.1040 g., 0.9990 Silver 0.9990 oz. ASW, 39.9 mm. **Series:**
First **Subject:** 180th Anniversary of Federation **Obv:** National
arms **Obv. Legend:** ESTADOS UNIDOS MEXICANOS **Rev:**
Federal District arms **Rev. Legend:** DISTRITO FEDERAL
Edge: Reeded **Mint:** Mexico City

Date	Mintage	F	VF	XF	Unc	BU
2005Mo Proof	10,000	Value: 70.00				

KM# 709   10 PESOS
31.1040 g., 0.9990 Silver 0.9990 oz. ASW, 39.9 mm. **Series:**
First **Subject:** 180th Anniversary of Federation **Obv:** National
arms **Obv. Legend:** ESTADOS UNIDOS MEXICANOS **Rev:**
State arms **Rev. Legend:** ESTADO DE GUANAJUATO
Edge: Reeded **Mint:** Mexico City

Date	Mintage	F	VF	XF	Unc	BU
2005Mo Proof	10,000	Value: 70.00				

KM# 753   10 PESOS
31.1040 g., 0.9990 Silver 0.9990 oz. ASW, 39.9 mm. **Series:**
First **Subject:** 180th Anniversary of Federation **Obv:** National
arms **Obv. Legend:** ESTADOS UNIDOS MEXICANOS **Rev:**
State arms **Rev. Legend:** ESTADO DE CHIHUAHUA **Edge:**
Reeded **Mint:** Mexico City

Date	Mintage	F	VF	XF	Unc	BU
2005Mo Proof	10,000	Value: 70.00				

STATE COMMEMORATIVES

KM# 706   10 PESOS
31.1040 g., 0.9990 Silver 0.9990 oz. ASW, 39.9 mm. **Series:**
First **Subject:** 180th Anniversary of Federation **Obv:** National
arms **Obv. Legend:** ESTADOS UNIDOS MEXICANOS **Rev:**
State arms **Rev. Legend:** ESTADO DE CHIAPAS **Edge:**
Reeded **Mint:** Mexico City

Date	Mintage	F	VF	XF	Unc	BU
2005Mo Proof	10,000	Value: 70.00				

KM# 726   10 PESOS
31.1040 g., 0.9990 Silver 0.9990 oz. ASW, 39.9 mm. **Series:**
First **Subject:** 180th Anniversary of Federation **Obv:** National
arms **Obv. Legend:** ESTADOS UNIDOS MEXICANOS **Rev:**
State arms **Rev. Legend:** ESTADO DE CAMPECHE **Edge:**
Reeded **Mint:** Mexico City

Date	Mintage	F	VF	XF	Unc	BU
2005Mo Proof	10,000	Value: 70.00				

KM# 728   10 PESOS
31.1040 g., 0.9990 Silver 0.9990 oz. ASW, 39.9 mm. **Series:**
First **Subject:** 180th Anniversary of Federation **Obv:** National
arms **Obv. Legend:** ESTADOS UNIDOS MEXICANOS **Rev:**
State arms **Rev. Legend:** ESTADO DE COLIMA **Edge:**
Reeded **Mint:** Mexico City

Date	Mintage	F	VF	XF	Unc	BU
2005Mo Proof	10,000	Value: 70.00				

KM# 724   10 PESOS
31.1040 g., 0.9990 Silver 0.9990 oz. ASW, 39.9 mm. **Series:**
First **Subject:** 180th Anniversary of Federation **Obv:** National
arms **Obv. Legend:** ESTADOS UNIDOS MEXICANOS **Rev:**
State arms **Rev. Legend:** ESTADO DE BAJA CALIFORNIA
SUR **Edge:** Reeded **Mint:** Mexico City

Date	Mintage	F	VF	XF	Unc	BU
2005Mo Proof	10,000	Value: 70.00				

KM# 751   10 PESOS
31.1040 g., 0.9990 Silver 0.9990 oz. ASW, 39.9 mm. **Series:**
First **Subject:** 180th Anniversary of Federation **Obv:** National
arms **Obv. Legend:** ESTADOS UNIDOS MEXICANOS **Rev:**
State arms **Rev. Legend:** ESTADO DE COAHUILA DE
ZARAGOZA **Edge:** Reeded **Mint:** Mexico City

Date	Mintage	F	VF	XF	Unc	BU
2005Mo Proof	10,000	Value: 70.00				

KM# 722   10 PESOS
31.1040 g., 0.9990 Silver 0.9990 oz. ASW, 39.9 mm. **Series:**
First **Subject:** 180th Anniversary of Federation **Obv:** National
arms **Obv. Legend:** ESTADOS UNIDOS MEXICANOS **Rev:**
State arms **Rev. Legend:** ESTADO DE BAJA CALIFORNIA
Edge: Reeded **Mint:** Mexico City

Date	Mintage	F	VF	XF	Unc	BU
2005Mo Proof	10,000	Value: 70.00				

KM# 720 10 PESOS
31.1040 g., 0.9990 Silver 0.9990 oz. ASW, 39.9 mm. **Series:**
First **Subject:** 180th Anniversary of Federation **Obv:** National
arms **Obv. Legend:** ESTADOS UNIDOS MEXICANOS **Rev:**
State arms **Rev. Legend:** ESTADO DE AGUASCALIENTES
Edge: Reeded **Mint:** Mexico City

Date	Mintage	F	VF	XF	Unc	BU
2005Mo Proof	10,000	Value: 70.00				

KM# 718 10 PESOS
31.1040 g., 0.9990 Silver 0.9990 oz. ASW, 40 mm. **Series:**
Second **Obv:** National arms **Obv. Legend:** ESTADOS
UNIDOS MEXICANOS **Rev:** Facade of the San Marcos
garden above sculpture of national emblem at left, San
Antonio Temple at right **Rev. Legend:** AGUASCALIENTES
Edge: Reeded **Mint:** Mexico City

Date	Mintage	F	VF	XF	Unc	BU
2005Mo Proof	6,000	Value: 65.00				

KM# 757 10 PESOS
31.1040 g., 0.9990 Silver 0.9990 oz. ASW, 40 mm. **Series:**
Second **Obv:** National arms **Obv. Legend:** ESTADOS
UNIDOS MEXICANOS **Rev:** Rams head, mountain outline in
background **Rev. Legend:** BAJA CALIFORNIA - GOBIERNO
DEL ESTADO **Edge:** Reeded **Mint:** Mexico City

Date	Mintage	F	VF	XF	Unc	BU
2005Mo Proof	6,000	Value: 65.00				

KM# 761 10 PESOS
31.1040 g., 0.9990 Silver 0.9990 oz. ASW, 40 mm. **Series:**
Second **Obv:** National arms **Obv. Legend:** ESTADOS
UNIDOS MEXICANOS **Rev:** Outlined map of peninsula at
center, cave painting of deer behind, cactus at right **Rev.
Legend:** ESTADO DE BAJA CALIFORNIA SUR **Edge:**
Reeded **Mint:** Mexico City

Date	Mintage	F	VF	XF	Unc	BU
2006Mo Proof	6,000	Value: 65.00				

KM# 759 10 PESOS
31.1040 g., 0.9990 Silver 0.9990 oz. ASW, 40 mm. **Series:**
Second **Obv:** National arms **Obv. Legend:** ESTADOS
UNIDOS MEXICANOS **Rev:** Jade mask - Calakmul,
Campeche **Rev. Legend:** ESTADO DE CAMPECHE **Edge:**
Reeded **Mint:** Mexico City

Date	Mintage	F	VF	XF	Unc	BU
2006Mo Proof	6,000	Value: 65.00				

KM# 780 10 PESOS
31.1040 g., 0.9990 Silver 0.9990 oz. ASW, 40 mm. **Series:**
Second **Obv:** National arms **Obv. Legend:** ESTADOS
UNIDOS MEXICANOS **Rev:** Outlined map with turtle, mine
cart above grapes at center, Friendship dam above Christ of
the Nodas at left, chimneys above crucibles and bell tower of
Santiago's cathedral at right **Rev. Inscription:** COAHUILA
DE ZARAGOZA **Edge:** Reeded **Mint:** Mexico City

Date	Mintage	F	VF	XF	Unc	BU
2006Mo Proof	6,000	Value: 65.00				

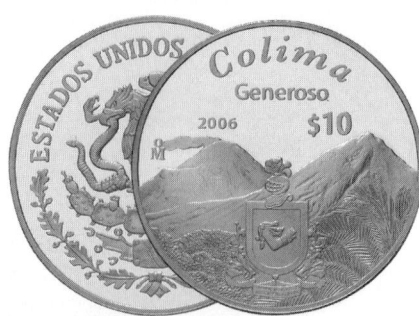

KM# 776   10 PESOS
31.1040 g., 0.9990 Silver 0.9990 oz. ASW, 40 mm. **Series:**
Second **Obv:** National arms **Obv. Legend:** ESTADOS
UNIDOS MEXICANOS **Rev:** State arms at lower center,
Nevado de Colima and Volcan de Fuego volcanos in
background **Rev. Legend:** *Colima* **Rev. Inscription:**
GENEROSO **Edge:** Reeded **Mint:** Mexico City

Date	Mintage	F	VF	XF	Unc	BU
2006Mo Proof	6,000	Value: 65.00				

KM# 772   10 PESOS
31.1040 g., 0.9990 Silver 0.9990 oz. ASW, 40 mm. **Series:**
Second **Obv:** National arms **Obv. Legend:** ESTADOS
UNIDOS MEXICANOS **Rev:** Head of Pakal, ancient Mayan
king, Palenque **Rev. Legend:** ESTADO DE CHIAPAS -
CABEZA MAYA DEL REY PAKAL, PALENQUE **Edge:**
Reeded **Mint:** Mexico City

Date	Mintage	F	VF	XF	Unc	BU
2006Mo Proof	6,000	Value: 65.00				

KM# 774   10 PESOS
31.1040 g., 0.9990 Silver 0.9990 oz. ASW, 40 mm. **Series:**
Second **Obv:** National arms **Obv. Legend:** ESTADOS
UNIDOS MEXICANOS **Rev:** Angel of Liberty **Rev. Legend:**
MÉXICO - ANGEL DE LA LIBERTAD, CHIHUAHUA **Edge:**
Reeded **Mint:** Mexico City

Date	Mintage	F	VF	XF	Unc	BU
2006Mo Proof	6,000	Value: 65.00				

KM# 778   10 PESOS
31.1040 g., 0.9990 Silver 0.9990 oz. ASW, 40 mm. **Series:**
Second **Obv:** National arms **Obv. Legend:** ESTADOS
UNIDOS MEXICANOS **Rev:** National Palace **Rev. Legend:**
DISTRITO FEDERAL - ANTIGUO AYUNTAMIENTO **Edge:**
Reeded **Mint:** Mexico City

Date	Mintage	F	VF	XF	Unc	BU
2006Mo Proof	6,000	Value: 65.00				

KM# 786   10 PESOS
31.1040 g., 0.9990 Silver 0.9990 oz. ASW, 40 mm. **Series:**
Second **Obv:** National arms **Obv. Legend:** ESTADOS
UNIDOS MEXICANOS **Rev:** Tree **Rev. Legend:** PRIMERA
RESERVA NACIONAL FORESTAL - DURANGO **Edge:**
Reeded **Mint:** Mexico City

Date	Mintage	F	VF	XF	Unc	BU
2006Mo Proof	6,000	Value: 65.00				

KM# 788   10 PESOS
31.1040 g., 0.9990 Silver 0.9990 oz. ASW, 40 mm. **Series:**
Second **Obv:** National arms **Obv. Legend:** ESTADOS
UNIDOS MEXICANOS **Rev:** State arms at center, statue of
Miguel Hidalgo at left, monument to Pípila at lower right **Rev.
Inscription:** *Guanajuato* **Edge:** Reeded **Mint:** Mexico City

Date	Mintage	F	VF	XF	Unc	BU
2006Mo Proof	6,000	Value: 65.00				

KM# 790   10 PESOS
31.1040 g., 0.9990 Silver 0.9990 oz. ASW, 40 mm. **Series:**
Second **Obv:** National arms **Obv. Legend:** ESTADOS
UNIDOS MEXICANOS **Rev:** Stylized portrait of Vicente
Guerrero at left, church of Taxco at upper center, Acapulco's
la Quebrada with diver above Christmas Eve flower and mask
Rev. Legend: GUERRERO **Edge:** Reeded **Mint:** Mexico City

Date	Mintage	F	VF	XF	Unc	BU
2006Mo Proof	6,000	Value: 65.00				

KM# 792 10 PESOS
31.1040 g., 0.9990 Silver 0.9990 oz. ASW, 40 mm. **Series:**
Second **Obv:** National arms **Obv. Legend:** ESTADOS
UNIDOS MEXICANOS **Rev:** Monument of Pachuca Hidalgo
Rev. Inscription: *RELOJ/MONUMENTAL/DE/PACHUCA
/HIDALGO - La/Bella/Airosa* **Edge:** Reeded **Mint:** Mexico
City

Date	Mintage	F	VF	XF	Unc	BU
2006Mo Proof	6,000	Value: 65.00				

KM# 831 10 PESOS
31.1040 g., 0.9990 Silver 0.9990 oz. ASW, 40 mm. **Series:**
Second **Obv:** National arms **Obv. Legend:** ESTADOS
UNIDOS MEXICANOS **Rev:** Four Monarch butterflies **Rev.
Legend:** ESTADO DE MICHOACÁN **Edge:** Reeded **Mint:**
Mexico City

Date	Mintage	F	VF	XF	Unc	BU
2006Mo Proof	6,000	Value: 65.00				

KM# 794 10 PESOS
31.1040 g., 0.9990 Silver 0.9990 oz. ASW, 40 mm. **Series:**
Second **Obv:** National arms **Obv. Legend:** ESTADOS
UNIDOS MEXICANOS **Rev:** Hospicio Cabañas orphanage
Rev. Legend: ESTADO DE JALISCCO **Edge:** Reeded **Mint:**
Mexico City

Date	Mintage	F	VF	XF	Unc	BU
2006Mo Proof	6,000	Value: 65.00				

KM# 832 10 PESOS
31.1040 g., 0.9990 Silver 0.9990 oz. ASW, 40 mm. **Series:**
Second **Obv:** National arms **Obv. Legend:** ESTADOS
UNIDOS MEXICANOS **Rev:** 1/2 length figure of Chinelo (local
dancer) at right, Palacio de Cortes in background **Rev.
Inscription:** ESTADO DE / MORELOS **Edge:** Reeded **Mint:**
Mexico City

Date	Mintage	F	VF	XF	Unc	BU
2006Mo Proof	6,000	Value: 65.00				

KM# 830 10 PESOS
31.1040 g., 0.9990 Silver 0.9990 oz. ASW, 40 mm. **Series:**
Second **Obv:** National arms **Obv. Legend:** ESTADOS
UNIDOS MEXICANOS **Rev:** Pyramid of la Loona (Moon)
Rev. Legend: ESTADO DE MÉXICO **Edge:** Reeded **Mint:**
Mexico City

Date	Mintage	F	VF	XF	Unc	BU
2006Mo Proof	6,000	Value: 65.00				

KM# 833 10 PESOS
31.1040 g., 0.9990 Silver 0.9990 oz. ASW, 40 mm. **Series:**
Second **Obv:** National arms **Obv. Legend:** ESTADOS
UNIDOS MEXICANOS **Rev:** Isle de Mexcaltitlán **Rev.
Legend:** ESTADO DE NAYARIT **Edge:** Reeded **Mint:**
Mexico City

Date	Mintage	F	VF	XF	Unc	BU
2007Mo Proof	6,000	Value: 65.00				

STATE COMMEMORATIVES

KM# 834   10 PESOS
31.1040 g., 0.9990 Silver 0.9990 oz. ASW, 40 mm. **Series:**
Second **Obv:** National arms **Obv. Legend:** ESTADOS
UNIDOS MEXICANOS **Rev:** Old foundry in Pargue Fundidora
(public park) at right, Cerro de la Silla (Saddle Hill) in
background **Rev. Legend:** ESTADO DE NUEVO LEÓN
Edge: Reeded **Mint:** Mexico City

Date	Mintage	F	VF	XF	Unc	BU
2007Mo Proof	6,000	Value: 65.00				

KM# 837   10 PESOS
31.1040 g., 0.9990 Silver 0.9990 oz. ASW, 40 mm. **Series:**
Second **Obv:** National arms **Obv. Legend:** ESTADOS
UNIDOS MEXICANOS **Rev:** Mask at left, rays above state
arms at center, Mayan ruins at right **Rev. Legend:** QUINTANA
ROO **Edge:** Reeded **Mint:** Mexico City

Date	Mintage	F	VF	XF	Unc	BU
2007Mo Proof	6,000	Value: 65.00				

KM# 835   10 PESOS
31.1040 g., 0.9990 Silver 0.9990 oz. ASW, 40 mm. **Series:**
Second **Obv:** National arms **Obv. Legend:** ESTADOS
UNIDOS MEXICANOS **Rev:** Teatro Macedonio Alcala
(theater) **Rev. Legend:** OAXACA **Edge:** Reeded **Mint:**
Mexico City

Date	Mintage	F	VF	XF	Unc	BU
2007Mo Proof	6,000	Value: 65.00				

KM# 838   10 PESOS
31.1040 g., 0.9990 Silver 0.9990 oz. ASW, 40 mm. **Series:**
Second **Obv:** National arms **Obv. Legend:** ESTADOS
UNIDOS MEXICANOS **Rev:** Acueduct of Querétaro at left,
church of Santa Rosa de Viterbo at right **Rev. Legend:**
ESTADO DE QUERÉTARO ARTEAGA **Edge:** Reeded **Mint:**
Mexico City

Date	Mintage	F	VF	XF	Unc	BU
2007Mo Proof	6,000	Value: 65.00				

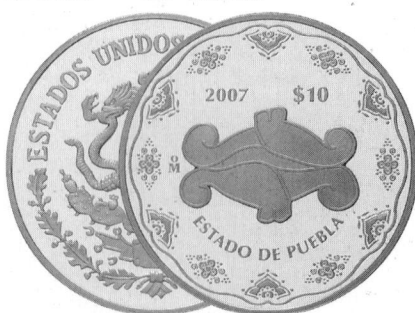

KM# 836   10 PESOS
31.1040 g., 0.9990 Silver 0.9990 oz. ASW, 40 mm. **Series:**
Second **Obv:** National arms **Obv. Legend:** ESTADOS
UNIDOS MEXICANOS **Rev:** Talavera porcelain dish **Rev.
Legend:** ESTADO DE PUEBLA **Edge:** Reeded **Mint:**
Mexico City

Date	Mintage	F	VF	XF	Unc	BU
2007Mo Proof	6,000	Value: 65.00				

KM# 839   10 PESOS
31.1040 g., Silver, 40 mm. **Series:** Second **Obv:** National
arms **Obv. Legend:** ESTADOS UNIDOS MEXICANOS **Rev:**
Facade of Caja Real **Rev. Legend:** • SAN LUIS POTOSÍ •
Edge: Reeded **Mint:** Mexico City

Date	Mintage	F	VF	XF	Unc	BU
2007Mo Proof	6,000	Value: 65.00				

KM# 840   10 PESOS
31.1040 g., 0.9990 Silver 0.9990 oz. ASW, 40 mm. **Series:**
Second **Obv:** National arms **Obv. Legend:** ESTADOS
UNIDOS MEXICANOS **Rev:** Shield on pile of cactus fruits
Rev. Legend: ESTADO DE SINALOA - LUGAR DE
PITAHAYAS **Edge:** Reeded **Mint:** Mexico City

Date	Mintage	F	VF	XF	Unc	BU
2007Mo Proof	6,000	Value: 65.00				

KM# 843   10 PESOS
31.1040 g., 0.9990 Silver 0.9990 oz. ASW, 40 mm. **Series:**
Second **Obv:** National arms **Obv. Legend:** ESTADOS
UNIDOS MEXICANOS **Rev:** Ridge - Cerro Del Bernal,
Gonzáles **Rev. Legend:** TAMAULIPAS **Edge:** Reeded **Mint:**
Mexico City

Date	Mintage	F	VF	XF	Unc	BU
2007Mo Proof	6,000	Value: 65.00				

KM# 841   10 PESOS
31.1040 g., 0.9990 Silver 0.9990 oz. ASW, 40 mm. **Series:**
Second **Obv:** National arms **Obv. Legend:** ESTADOS
UNIDOS MEXICANOS **Rev:** Local in Dance of the Deer at
left, cactus at right, mountains in background **Rev. Legend:**
ESTADO DE SONORA **Edge:** Reeded **Mint:** Mexico City

Date	Mintage	F	VF	XF	Unc	BU
2007Mo Proof	6,000	Value: 65.00				

KM# 844   10 PESOS
31.1040 g., 0.9990 Silver 0.9990 oz. ASW, 40 mm. **Series:**
Second **Obv:** National arms **Obv. Legend:** ESTADOS
UNIDOS MEXICANOS **Rev:** Basilica de Ocotlán at left, state
arms above Capilla Abierta, Plaza de Toros Ranchero Aguilar
below, Exconvento de San Francisco at right **Rev. Legend:**
ESTADO DE TLAXCALA **Edge:** Reeded **Mint:** Mexico City

Date	Mintage	F	VF	XF	Unc	BU
2007Mo Proof	6,000	Value: 65.00				

KM# 842   10 PESOS
31.1040 g., 0.9990 Silver 0.9990 oz. ASW, 40 mm. **Series:**
Second **Obv:** National arms **Obv. Legend:** ESTADOS
UNIDOS MEXICANOS **Rev:** Fuente de los Pescadores
(fisherman fountain) at lower left, giant head from the Olmec-
pre-Hispanic culture at right, Planetario Tabasco in
background **Rev. Legend:** TABASCO **Edge:** Reeded **Mint:**
Mexico City

Date	Mintage	F	VF	XF	Unc	BU
2007Mo Proof	6,000	Value: 65.00				

KM# 845   10 PESOS
31.1040 g., 0.9990 Silver 0.9990 oz. ASW, 40 mm. **Series:**
Second **Obv:** National arms **Obv. Legend:** ESTADOS
UNIDOS MEXICANOS **Rev:** Pyramid of El Tajín **Rev.**
Legend: • VERACRUZ • - • DE IGNACIO DE LA LLAVE •
Edge: Reeded **Mint:** Mexico City

Date	Mintage	F	VF	XF	Unc	BU
2007Mo Proof	6,000	Value: 65.00				

KM# 846   10 PESOS
31.1030 g., 0.9990 Silver 0.9989 oz. ASW, 40 mm. **Series:**
Second **Obv:** National arms **Obv. Legend:** ESTADOS
UNIDOS MEXICANOS **Rev:** Stylized pyramid of Chichén-Itzá
Rev. Legend: Castillo de Chichén Itzá **Rev. Inscription:**
YUCATÁN **Edge:** Reeded **Mint:** Mexico City

Date	Mintage	F	VF	XF	Unc	BU
2007Mo Proof	6,000	Value: 65.00				

KM# 847   10 PESOS
31.1040 g., 0.9990 Silver 0.9990 oz. ASW, 40 mm. **Series:**
Second **Obv:** National arms **Obv. Legend:** ESTADOS
UNIDOS MEXICANOS **Rev:** Cable car above Monumento al
Minero at left, Catedral de Zacatecas at center right **Rev.
Legend:** Zacatecas **Edge:** Reeded **Mint:** Mexico City

Date	Mintage	F	VF	XF	Unc	BU
2007Mo Proof	6,000	Value: 65.00				

KM# 688   100 PESOS
33.9400 g., Bi-Metallic .925 Silver 20.1753g center in
Aluminum-Bronze ring, 39.04 mm. **Series:** First **Subject:**
180th Anniversary of Federation **Obv:** National arms **Obv.
Legend:** ESTADOS UNIDOS MEXICANOS **Rev:** State arms
Rev. Legend: ESTADO DE ZACATECAS **Edge:** Segmented
reeding **Mint:** Mexico City

Date	Mintage	F	VF	XF	Unc	BU
2003Mo	244,900	—	—	—	40.00	50.00

KM# 696   100 PESOS
29.1690 g., Bi-Metallic .999 Gold 17.154g center in .999 Silver
12.015g ring, 34.5 mm. **Series:** First **Subject:** 180th
Anniversary of Federation **Obv:** National arms **Obv. Legend:**
ESTADOS UNIDOS MEXICANOS **Rev:** State arms **Rev.
Legend:** ESTADO DE ZACATECAS **Edge:** Segmented
reeding **Mint:** Mexico City

Date	Mintage	F	VF	XF	Unc	BU
2003Mo Proof	1,000	Value: 750				

KM# 689   100 PESOS
33.9400 g., Bi-Metallic .925 Silver 20.1753g center in
Aluminum-Bronze ring, 39.04 mm. **Series:** First **Subject:**
180th Anniversary of Federation **Obv:** National arms **Rev:** State arms
Rev. Legend: ESTADO DE YUCATÁN **Edge:** Segmented
reeding **Mint:** Mexico City

Date	Mintage	F	VF	XF	Unc	BU
2003Mo	235,763	—	—	—	40.00	50.00

KM# 697   100 PESOS
29.1690 g., Bi-Metallic .999 Gold 17.154g center in .999 Silver
12.015g ring, 34.5 mm. **Series:** First **Subject:** 180th
Anniversary of Federation **Obv:** National arms **Obv. Legend:**
ESTADOS UNIDOS MEXICANOS **Rev:** State arms **Rev.
Legend:** ESTADO DE YUCATÁN **Edge:** Segmented reeding
Mint: Mexico City

Date	Mintage	F	VF	XF	Unc	BU
2003Mo Proof	1,000	Value: 750				

KM# 690   100 PESOS
33.9400 g., Bi-Metallic .925 Silver 20.1753g center in
Aluminum-Bronze ring, 39.04 mm. **Series:** First **Subject:**
180th Anniversary of Federation **Obv:** National arms **Obv.
Legend:** ESTADOS UNIDOS MEXICANOS **Rev:** State arms
Rev. Legend: ESTADO DE VERACRUZ-LLAVE **Edge:**
Segmented reeding **Mint:** Mexico City

Date	Mintage	F	VF	XF	Unc	BU
2003Mo	248,810	—	—	—	40.00	50.00

KM# 698   100 PESOS
29.1690 g., Bi-Metallic .999 Gold 17.154g center in .999 Silver
12.015g ring, 34.5 mm. **Series:** First **Subject:** 180th
Anniversary of Federation **Obv:** National arms **Obv. Legend:**
ESTADOS UNIDOS MEXICANOS **Rev:** State arms **Rev.
Legend:** ESTADO DE VERACRUZ-LLAVE **Edge:**
Segmented reeding **Mint:** Mexico City

Date	Mintage	F	VF	XF	Unc	BU
2003Mo Proof	1,000	Value: 750				

KM# 691   100 PESOS
33.9400 g., Bi-Metallic .925 Silver 20.1753g center in Aluminum-Bronze ring, 39.9 mm.   **Series:** First **Subject:** 180th Anniversary of Federation **Obv:** National arms **Obv. Legend:** ESTADOS UNIDOS MEXICANOS **Rev:** State arms **Rev. Legend:** ESTADO DE TLAXCALA **Edge:** Segmented reeding **Mint:** Mexico City

Date	Mintage	F	VF	XF	Unc	BU
2003Mo	248,976	—	—	—	35.00	40.00

KM# 699   100 PESOS
29.1690 g., Bi-Metallic .999 Gold 17.154g center in .999 Silver 12.015g ring, 34.5 mm.   **Series:** First **Subject:** 180th Anniversary of Federation **Obv:** National arms **Obv. Legend:** ESTADOS UNIDOS MEXICANOS **Rev:** State arms **Rev. Legend:** ESTADO DE TLAXCALA **Edge:** Segmented reeding **Mint:** Mexico City

Date	Mintage	F	VF	XF	Unc	BU
2003Mo Proof	1,000	Value: 750				

KM# 693   100 PESOS
33.9400 g., Bi-Metallic .925 Silver 20.1753g center in Aluminum-Bronze ring, 39.04 mm.   **Series:** First **Subject:** 180th Anniversary of Federation **Obv:** National arms **Obv. Legend:** ESTADOS UNIDOS MEXICANOS **Rev:** State arms **Rev. Legend:** ESTADO DE TABASCO **Edge:** Segmented reeding **Mint:** Mexico City

Date	Mintage	F	VF	XF	Unc	BU
2004Mo	249,318	—	—	—	35.00	40.00

KM# 701   100 PESOS
29.1690 g., Bi-Metallic .999 Gold 17.154g center in .999 Silver 12.015g ring, 34.5 mm.   **Series:** First **Subject:** 180th Anniversary of Federation **Obv:** National arms **Obv. Legend:** ESTADOS UNIDOS MEXICANOS **Rev:** State arms **Rev. Legend:** ESTADO DE TABASCO **Edge:** Segmented reeding **Mint:** Mexico City

Date	Mintage	F	VF	XF	Unc	BU
2004Mo Proof	1,000	Value: 750				

KM# 692   100 PESOS
33.9400 g., Bi-Metallic .925 Silver 20.1753g center in Aluminum-Bronze ring, 39.04 mm.   **Series:** First **Subject:** 180th Anniversary of Federation **Obv:** National arms **Obv. Legend:** ESTADOS UNIDOS MEXICANOS **Rev:** State arms **Rev. Legend:** ESTADO DE TAMAULIPAS **Edge:** Segmented reeding **Mint:** Mexico City

Date	Mintage	F	VF	XF	Unc	BU
2004Mo	249,398	—	—	—	35.00	40.00

KM# 700   100 PESOS
29.1690 g., Bi-Metallic .999 Gold 17.154g center in .999 Silver 12.015g ring, 34.5 mm.   **Series:** First **Subject:** 180th Anniversary of Federation **Obv:** National arms **Obv. Legend:** ESTADOS UNIDOS MEXICANOS **Rev:** State arms **Rev. Legend:** ESTADO DE TAMAULIPAS **Edge:** Segmented reeding **Mint:** Mexico City

Date	Mintage	F	VF	XF	Unc	BU
2004Mo Proof	1,000	Value: 750				

KM# 694   100 PESOS
33.9400 g., Bi-Metallic .925 Silver 20.1753g center in Aluminum-Bronze ring, 39.04 mm.   **Series:** First **Subject:** 180th Anniversary of Federation **Obv:** National arms **Obv. Legend:** ESTADOS UNIDOS MEXICANOS **Rev:** State arms **Rev. Legend:** ESTADO DE SONORA **Edge:** Segmented reeding **Mint:** Mexico City

Date	Mintage	F	VF	XF	Unc	BU
2004Mo	249,300	—	—	—	35.00	40.00

KM# 702   100 PESOS
29.1690 g., Bi-Metallic .999 Gold 17.154g center in .999 Silver 12.015g ring, 34.5 mm.   **Series:** First **Subject:** 180th Anniversary of Federation **Obv:** National arms **Obv. Legend:** ESTADOS UNIDOS MEXICANOS **Rev:** State arms **Rev. Legend:** ESTADO DE SONORA **Edge:** Segmented reeding **Mint:** Mexico City

Date	Mintage	F	VF	XF	Unc	BU
2004Mo Proof	1,000	Value: 750				

KM# 695   100 PESOS
33.9400 g., Bi-Metallic .925 Silver 20.1753g center in
Aluminum-Bronze ring, 39.04 mm.   **Series:** First **Subject:**
180th Anniversary of Federation **Obv:** National arms **Obv.**
Legend: ESTADOS UNIDOS MEXICANOS **Rev:** State arms
Rev. Legend: ESTADO DE SINALOA **Edge:** Segmented
reeding **Mint:** Mexico City

Date	Mintage	F	VF	XF	Unc	BU
2004Mo	244,722	—	—	—	35.00	40.00

KM# 703   100 PESOS
29.1690 g., Bi-Metallic .999 Gold 17.154g center in .999 Silver
12.015g ring, 34.5 mm.   **Series:** First **Subject:** 180th
Anniversary of Federation **Obv:** National arms **Obv. Legend:**
ESTADOS UNIDOS MEXICANOS **Rev:** State arms **Rev.**
Legend: ESTADO DE SINALOA **Edge:** Segmented reeding
Mint: Mexico City

Date	Mintage	F	VF	XF	Unc	BU
2004Mo Proof	1,000	Value: 750				

KM# 736   100 PESOS
33.9400 g., Bi-Metallic .925 Silver 20.1753g center in
Aluminum-Bronze ring, 39.04 mm.   **Series:** First **Subject:**
180th Anniversary of Federation **Obv:** National arms **Obv.**
Legend: ESTADOS UNIDOS MEXICANOS **Rev:** State arms
Rev. Legend: ESTADO DE QUINTANA ROO **Edge:**
Segmented reeding **Mint:** Mexico City

Date	Mintage	F	VF	XF	Unc	BU
2004Mo	249,134	—	—	—	35.00	40.00

KM# 807   100 PESOS
29.1690 g., Bi-Metallic .999 Gold 17.154g center in .999 Silver
12.015g ring, 34.5 mm.   **Series:** First **Subject:** 180th
Anniversary of Federation **Obv:** National arms **Obv. Legend:**
ESTADOS UNIDOS MEXICANOS **Rev:** State arms **Rev.**
Legend: ESTADO DE QUINTANA ROO **Edge:** Segmented
reeding **Mint:** Mexico City

Date	Mintage	F	VF	XF	Unc	BU
2004Mo Proof	1,000	Value: 750				

KM# 803   100 PESOS
33.9400 g., Bi-Metallic .925 Silver 20.1753g center in
Aluminum-Bronze ring, 39.04 mm.   **Series:** First **Subject:**
180th Anniversary of Federation **Obv:** National arms **Obv.**
Legend: ESTADOS UNIDOS MEXICANOS **Rev:** State arms
Rev. Legend: ESTADO DE SAN LUIS POTOSÍ **Edge:**
Segmented reeding **Mint:** Mexico City

Date	Mintage	F	VF	XF	Unc	BU
2004Mo	249,662	—	—	—	35.00	40.00

KM# 806   100 PESOS
29.1690 g., Bi-Metallic .999 Gold 17.154g center in .999 silver
12.015 ring, 34.5 mm.   **Series:** First **Subject:** 180th
Anniversary of Federation **Obv:** National arms **Obv. Legend:**
ESTADOS UNIDOS MEXICANOS **Rev:** State arms **Rev.**
Legend: ESTADO DE SAN LUIS POTOSÍ **Edge:** Segmented
reeding **Mint:** Mexico City

Date	Mintage	F	VF	XF	Unc	BU
2004Mo Proof	1,000	Value: 750				

KM# 734   100 PESOS
33.9400 g., Bi-Metallic .925 Silver 20.1753g center in
Aluminum-Bronze ring, 39.04 mm.   **Series:** First **Subject:**
180th Anniversary of Federation **Obv:** National arms **Obv.**
Legend: ESTADOS UNIDOS MEXICANOS **Rev:** State arms
Rev. Legend: ESTADO DE QUERETARO ARTEAGA **Edge:**
Segmented reeding **Mint:** Mexico City

Date	Mintage	F	VF	XF	Unc	BU
2004Mo	249,263	—	—	—	35.00	40.00

KM# 808   100 PESOS
29.1690 g., Bi-Metallic .999 Gold 17.154g center in .999 Silver
12.015g ring, 34.5 mm.   **Series:** First **Subject:** 180th
Anniversary of Federation **Obv:** National arms **Obv. Legend:**
ESTADOS UNIDOS MEXICANOS **Rev:** State arms **Rev.**
Legend: ESTADO DE QUERÉTARO ARTEAGA **Edge:**
Segmented reeding **Mint:** Mexico City

Date	Mintage	F	VF	XF	Unc	BU
2004Mo Proof	1,000	Value: 750				

KM# 738   100 PESOS
33.9400 g., Bi-Metallic .925 Silver 20.1753g center in
Aluminum-Bronze ring, 39.04 mm. **Series:** First **Subject:**
180th Anniversary of Federation **Obv:** National arms **Obv.**
Legend: ESTADOS UNIDOS MEXICANOS **Rev:** State arms
Rev. Legend: ESTADO DE PUEBLA **Edge:** Segmented
reeding **Mint:** Mexico City

Date	Mintage	F	VF	XF	Unc	BU
2004Mo	248,850	—	—	—	35.00	40.00

KM# 809   100 PESOS
Bi-Metallic .999 Gold 17.154g center in .999 Silver 12.015g
ring, 34.5 mm. **Series:** First **Subject:** 180th Anniversary of
Federation **Obv:** National arms **Obv. Legend:** ESTADOS
UNIDOS MEXICANOS **Rev:** State arms **Rev. Legend:**
ESTADO DE PUEBLA **Edge:** Segmented reeding **Mint:**
Mexico City

Date	Mintage	F	VF	XF	Unc	BU
2004Mo Proof	1,000	Value: 750				

KM# 742   100 PESOS
33.9400 g., Bi-Metallic .925 Silver 20.1753g center in
Aluminum-Bronze ring, 39.04 mm. **Series:** First **Subject:**
180th Anniversary of Federation **Obv:** National arms **Obv.**
Legend: ESTADOS UNIDOS MEXICANOS **Rev:** State arms
Rev. Legend: ESTADO DE NUEVO LEÓN **Edge:**
Segmented reeding **Mint:** Mexico City

Date	Mintage	F	VF	XF	Unc	BU
2004Mo	249,199	—	—	—	35.00	40.00

KM# 811   100 PESOS
29.1690 g., Bi-Metallic .999 Gold 17.154g center in .999 Silver
12.015g ring, 34.5 mm. **Series:** First **Subject:** 180th
Anniversary of Federation **Obv:** National arms **Obv. Legend:**
ESTADOS UNIDOS MEXICANOS **Rev:** State arms **Rev.**
Legend: ESTADO DE NUEVO LEÓN **Edge:** Segmented
reeding **Mint:** Mexico City

Date	Mintage	F	VF	XF	Unc	BU
2004Mo Proof	1,000	Value: 750				

KM# 740   100 PESOS
33.9400 g., Bi-Metallic .925 Silver 20.1753g center in
Aluminum-Bronze ring, 39.04 mm. **Series:** First **Subject:**
180th Anniversary of Federation **Obv:** National arms **Obv.**
Legend: ESTADOS UNIDOS MEXICANOS **Rev:** State arms
Rev. Legend: ESTADO DE OAXACA **Edge:** Segmented
reeding **Mint:** Mexico City

Date	Mintage	F	VF	XF	Unc	BU
2004Mo	249,589	—	—	—	35.00	40.00

KM# 810   100 PESOS
29.1690 g., Bi-Metallic .999 Gold 17.154g center in .999 Silver
12.015g ring, 34.5 mm. **Series:** First **Subject:** 180th
Anniversary of Federation **Obv:** National arms **Obv. Legend:**
ESTADOS UNIDOS MEXICANOS **Rev:** State arms **Rev.**
Legend: ESTADO DE OAXACA **Edge:** Segmented reeding
Mint: Mexico City

Date	Mintage	F	VF	XF	Unc	BU
2004Mo Proof	1,000	Value: 750				

KM# 744   100 PESOS
33.9400 g., Bi-Metallic .925 Silver 20.1753g center in
Aluminum-Bronze ring, 39.04 mm. **Series:** First **Subject:**
180th Anniversary of Federation **Obv:** National arms **Obv.**
Legend: ESTADOS UNIDOS MEXICANOS **Rev:** State arms
Rev. Legend: ESTADO DE NAYARIT **Edge:** Segmented
reeding **Mint:** Mexico City

Date	Mintage	F	VF	XF	Unc	BU
2004Mo	248,305	—	—	—	35.00	40.00

KM# 812   100 PESOS
29.1690 g., Bi-Metallic .999 Gold 17.154g center in .999 Silver
12.015g ring, 34.5 mm. **Series:** First **Subject:** 180th
Anniversary of Federation **Obv:** National arms **Obv. Legend:**
ESTADOS UNIDOS MEXICANOS **Rev:** State arms **Rev.**
Legend: ESTADO DE NAYARIT **Edge:** Segmented reeding
Mint: Mexico City

Date	Mintage	F	VF	XF	Unc	BU
2004Mo Proof	1,000	Value: 750				

STATE COMMEMORATIVES

KM# 746   100 PESOS
33.9400 g., Bi-Metallic .925 Silver 20.1753g center in
Aluminum-Bronze ring, 39.04 mm.   **Series:** First **Subject:**
180th Anniversary of Federation **Obv:** National arms **Obv.**
Legend: ESTADOS UNIDOS MEXICANOS **Rev:** State arms
Rev. Legend: ESTADO DE MORELOS **Edge:** Segmented
reeding **Mint:** Mexico City

Date	Mintage	F	VF	XF	Unc	BU
2004Mo	249,260	—	—	—	35.00	40.00

KM# 813   100 PESOS
29.1690 g., Bi-Metallic .999 Gold 17.154g center in .999 Silver
12.015g ring, 34.5 mm.   **Series:** First **Subject:** 180th
Anniversary of Federation **Obv:** National arms **Obv. Legend:**
ESTADOS UNIDOS MEXICANOS **Rev:** State arms **Rev.**
Legend: ESTADO DE MORELOS **Edge:** Segmented reeding
Mint: Mexico City

Date	Mintage	F	VF	XF	Unc	BU
2004Mo Proof	1,000	Value: 750				

KM# 748   100 PESOS
33.9400 g., Bi-Metallic .925 Silver 20.1753g center in
Aluminum-Bronze ring, 39.04 mm.   **Series:** First **Subject:**
180th Anniversary of Federation **Obv:** National arms **Obv.**
Legend: ESTADOS UNIDOS MEXICANOS **Rev:** State arms
Rev. Legend: ESTADO DE MÉXICO **Edge:** Segmented
reeding **Mint:** Mexico City

Date	Mintage	F	VF	XF	Unc	BU
2004Mo	249,800	—	—	—	35.00	40.00

KM# 815   100 PESOS
29.1690 g., Bi-Metallic .999 Gold 17.154 center in .999 Silver
12.015 ring, 34.5 mm.   **Series:** First **Subject:** 180th
Anniversary of Federation **Obv:** National arms **Obv. Legend:**
ESTADOS UNIDOS MEXICANOS **Rev:** State arms **Rev.**
Legend: ESTADO DE MÉXICO **Edge:** Segmented reeding
Mint: Mexico City

Date	Mintage	F	VF	XF	Unc	BU
2004Mo Proof	1,000	Value: 750				

KM# 804   100 PESOS
33.9400 g., Bi-Metallic o.925 Silver 20.1763g center in
Aluminum-Bronze ring, 39.04 mm.   **Series:** First **Subject:**
180th Anniversary of Federation **Obv:** National arms **Obv.**
Legend: ESTADOS UNIDOS MEXICANOS **Rev:** State arms
Rev. Legend: ESTADO DE MICHOACÁN DE OCAMPO
Edge: Segmented reeding **Mint:** Mexico City

Date	Mintage	F	VF	XF	Unc	BU
2004Mo	249,492	—	—	—	35.00	40.00

KM# 814   100 PESOS
29.1690 g., Bi-Metallic .999 Gold 17.154g center in .999
12.015g ring, 34.5 mm.   **Series:** First **Subject:** 180th
Anniversary of Federation **Obv:** National arms **Obv. Legend:**
ESTADOS UNIDOS MEXICANOS **Rev:** State arms **Rev.**
Legend: ESTADO DE MICHOACÁN DE OCAMPO **Edge:**
Segmented reeding **Mint:** Mexico City

Date	Mintage	F	VF	XF	Unc	BU
2004Mo Proof	1,000	Value: 750				

KM# 750   100 PESOS
33.9400 g., Bi-Metallic .925 Silver 20.1753g center in
Aluminum-Bronze ring, 39.04 mm.   **Series:** First **Subject:**
180th Anniversary of Federation **Obv:** National arms **Obv.**
Legend: ESTADOS UNIDOS MEXICANOS **Rev:** State arms
Rev. Legend: ESTADO DE JALISCO **Edge:** Segmented
reeding **Mint:** Mexico City

Date	Mintage	F	VF	XF	Unc	BU
2004Mo	249,115	—	—	—	35.00	40.00

KM# 816   100 PESOS
29.1690 g., Bi-Metallic .999 Gold 17.154g center in .999 Silver
12.015g ring, 34.5 mm.   **Series:** First **Subject:** 180th
Anniversary of Federation **Obv:** National arms **Obv. Legend:**
ESTADOS UNIDOS MEXICANOS **Rev:** State arms **Rev.**
Legend: ESTADO DE JALISCO **Edge:** Segmented reeding
Mint: Mexico City

Date	Mintage	F	VF	XF	Unc	BU
2004Mo Proof	1,000	Value: 750				

KM# 717   100 PESOS
33.9400 g., Bi-Metallic .925 Silver center in Brass ring,
39.04 mm. **Series:** First **Subject:** 180th Anniversary of
Federation **Obv:** National arms **Obv. Legend:** ESTADOS
UNIDOS MEXICANOS **Rev:** State arms **Rev. Legend:**
ESTADO DE HIDALGO **Edge:** Segmented reeding **Mint:**
Mexico City

Date	Mintage	F	VF	XF	Unc	BU
2005Mo	249,820	—	—	—	35.00	40.00

KM# 817   100 PESOS
29.1690 g., Bi-Metallic .999 Gold 17.154g center in .999 Silver
12.015g ring, 34.5 mm. **Series:** First **Subject:** 180th
Anniversary of Federation **Obv:** National arms **Obv. Legend:**
ESTADOS UNIDOS MEXICANOS **Rev:** State arms **Rev.
Legend:** ESTADO DE HIDALGO **Edge:** Segmented reeding
Mint: Mexico City

Date	Mintage	F	VF	XF	Unc	BU
2005Mo Proof	1,000	Value: 750				

KM# 715   100 PESOS
33.9400 g., Bi-Metallic .925 Silver center in Brass ring,
39.04 mm. **Series:** First **Subject:** 180th Anniversary of
Federation **Obv:** National arms **Obv. Legend:** ESTADOS
UNIDOS MEXICANOS **Rev:** State arms **Rev. Legend:**
ESTADO DE GUANAJUATO **Edge:** Segmented reeding
Mint: Mexico City

Date	Mintage	F	VF	XF	Unc	BU
2005Mo	249,489	—	—	—	35.00	40.00

KM# 819   100 PESOS
29.1690 g., Bi-Metallic .999 Gold 17.154g center in .999 Silver
12.015g ring, 34.5 mm. **Series:** First **Subject:** 180th
Anniversary of Federation **Obv:** National arms **Obv. Legend:**
ESTADOS UNIDOS MEXICANOS **Rev:** State arms **Rev.
Legend:** ESTADO DE GUANAJUATO **Edge:** Segmented
reeding **Mint:** Mexico City

Date	Mintage	F	VF	XF	Unc	BU
2005Mo Proof	1,000	Value: 750				

KM# 716   100 PESOS
33.9400 g., Bi-Metallic .925 Silver center in Brass ring,
39.04 mm. **Series:** First **Subject:** 180th Anniversary of
Federation **Obv:** National arms **Obv. Legend:** ESTADOS
UNIDOS MEXICANOS **Rev:** State arms **Rev. Legend:**
ESTADO DE GUERRERO **Edge:** Segmented reeding **Mint:**
Mexico City

Date	Mintage	F	VF	XF	Unc	BU
2005Mo	248,850	—	—	—	35.00	40.00

KM# 818   100 PESOS
29.1690 g., Bi-Metallic .999 Gold 17.154g center in .999 Silver
12.015 ring, 34.5 mm. **Series:** First **Subject:** 180th
Anniversary of Federation **Obv:** National arms **Obv. Legend:**
ESTADOS UNIDOS MEXICANOS **Rev:** State arms **Rev.
Legend:** ESTADO DE GUERRERO **Edge:** Segmented
reeding **Mint:** Mexico City

Date	Mintage	F	VF	XF	Unc	BU
2005Mo Proof	1,000	Value: 750				

KM# 714   100 PESOS
33.9400 g., Bi-Metallic .925 Silver center in Brass ring,
39.04 mm. **Series:** First **Subject:** 180th Anniversary of
Federation **Obv:** National arms **Obv. Legend:** ESTADOS
UNIDOS MEXICANOS **Rev:** State arms **Rev. Legend:**
ESTADO DE DURANGO **Edge:** Segmented reeding **Mint:**
Mexico City

Date	Mintage	F	VF	XF	Unc	BU
2005Mo	249,774	—	—	—	35.00	40.00

KM# 820   100 PESOS
29.1690 g., Bi-Metallic .999 Gold 17.154g center in .999 silver
12.015g ring, 34.5 mm. **Series:** First **Subject:** 180th
Anniversary of Federation **Obv:** National arms **Obv. Legend:**
ESTADOS UNIDOS MEXICANOS **Rev:** State arms **Rev.
Legend:** ESTADO DE DURANGO **Edge:** Segmented
reeding **Mint:** Mexico City

Date	Mintage	F	VF	XF	Unc	BU
2005Mo Proof	1,000	Value: 750				

STATE COMMEMORATIVES

KM# 713   100 PESOS
33.9400 g., Bi-Metallic .925 Silver 20.1753g center in Brass
ring, 39.04 mm. **Series:** First **Subject:** 180th Anniversary of
Federation **Obv:** National arms **Obv. Legend:** ESTADOS
UNIDOS MEXICANOS **Rev:** Federal District arms **Rev.
Legend:** DISTRITO FEDERAL **Edge:** Segmented reeding
Mint: Mexico City

Date	Mintage	F	VF	XF	Unc	BU
2005Mo	249,461	—	—	—	35.00	40.00

KM# 821   100 PESOS
29.1690 g., Bi-Metallic .999 Gold 17.154g center in .999 Silver
12.015g ring, 34.5 mm. **Series:** First **Subject:** 180th
Anniversary of Federation **Obv:** National arms **Obv. Legend:**
ESTADOS UNIDOS MEXICANOS **Rev:** Federal District arms
Rev. Legend: DISTRITO FEDERAL **Edge:** Segmented
reeding **Mint:** Mexico City

Date	Mintage	F	VF	XF	Unc	BU
2005Mo Proof	1,000	Value: 750				

KM# 712   100 PESOS
33.9400 g., Bi-Metallic .925 Silver 20.1753g center in Brass
ring, 39.04 mm. **Series:** First **Subject:** 180th Anniversary of
Federation **Obv:** National arms **Obv. Legend:** ESTADOS
UNIDOS MEXICANOS **Rev:** State arms **Rev. Legend:**
ESTADO DE CHIAPAS **Edge:** Segmented reeding **Mint:**
Mexico City

Date	Mintage	F	VF	XF	Unc	BU
2005Mo	249,417	—	—	—	35.00	40.00

KM# 823   100 PESOS
29.1690 g., Bi-Metallic .999 Gold 17.154g center in .999 Silver
12.015g ring, 34.5 mm. **Series:** First **Subject:** 180th
Anniversary of Federation **Obv:** National arms **Obv. Legend:**
ESTADOS UNIDOS MEXICANOS **Rev:** State arms **Rev.
Legend:** ESTADO DE CHIAPAS **Edge:** Segmented reeding
Mint: Mexico City

Date	Mintage	F	VF	XF	Unc	BU
2005Mo Proof	1,000	Value: 750				

KM# 754   100 PESOS
33.9400 g., Bi-Metallic .925 Silver 20.1753g center in
Aluminum-Bronze ring, 39.04 mm. **Series:** First **Subject:**
180th Anniversary of Federation **Obv:** National arms **Obv.
Legend:** ESTADOS UNIDOS MEXICANOS **Rev:** State arms
Rev. Legend: ESTADO DE CHIHUAHUA **Edge:** Segmented
reeding **Mint:** Mexico City

Date	Mintage	F	VF	XF	Unc	BU
2005Mo	249,102	—	—	—	35.00	40.00

KM# 822   100 PESOS
29.1690 g., Bi-Metallic .999 Gold 17.154g center in .999 Silver
12.015g ring, 34.5 mm. **Series:** First **Subject:** 180th
Anniversary of Federation **Obv:** National arms **Obv. Legend:**
ESTADOS UNIDOS MEXICANOS **Rev:** State arms **Rev.
Legend:** ESTADO DE CHIHUAHUA **Edge:** Segmented
reeding **Mint:** Mexico City

Date	Mintage	F	VF	XF	Unc	BU
2005Mo Proof	1,000	Value: 750				

KM# 729   100 PESOS
33.8250 g., Bi-Metallic .925 Silver 20.1753g center in
Aluminum-Bronze ring, 39.04 mm. **Series:** First **Subject:**
180th Anniversary of Federation **Obv:** National arms **Obv.
Legend:** ESTADOS UNIDOS MEXICANOS **Rev:** State arms
Rev. Legend: ESTADO DE COLIMA **Edge:** Segmented
reeding **Mint:** Mexico City

Date	Mintage	F	VF	XF	Unc	BU
2005Mo	248,850	—	—	—	35.00	40.00

KM# 824   100 PESOS
29.1690 g., Bi-Metallic .999 Gold 17.154g center in .999 Silver
12.015g ring, 34.5 mm. **Series:** First **Subject:** 180th
Anniversary of Federation **Obv:** National arms **Obv. Legend:**
ESTADOS UNIDOS MEXICANOS **Rev:** State arms **Rev.
Legend:** ESTADO DE COLIMA **Edge:** Segmented reeding
Mint: Mexico City

Date	Mintage	F	VF	XF	Unc	BU
2005Mo Proof	1,000	Value: 750				

KM# 752 100 PESOS
33.9400 g., Bi-Metallic .925 Silver 20.1753g center in
Aluminum-Bronze ring, 39.04 mm. **Series:** First **Subject:**
180th Anniversary of Federation **Obv:** National arms **Obv.**
Legend: ESTADOS UNIDOS MEXICANOS **Rev:** State arms
Rev. Legend: ESTADO DE COAHUILA DE ZARAGOZA
Edge: Segmented reeding **Mint:** Mexico City

Date	Mintage	F	VF	XF	Unc	BU
2005Mo	247,991	—	—	—	35.00	40.00

KM# 825 100 PESOS
29.1690 g., Bi-Metallic .999 Gold 17.154g center in .999 Silver
12.015g ring, 34.5 mm. **Series:** First **Subject:** 180th
Anniversary of Federation **Obv:** National arms **Obv. Legend:**
ESTADOS UNIDOS MEXICANOS **Rev:** State arms **Rev.**
Legend: ESTADO DE COAHUILA DE ZARAGOZA **Edge:**
Segmented reeding **Mint:** Mexico City

Date	Mintage	F	VF	XF	Unc	BU
2005Mo Proof	1,000	Value: 825				

KM# 725 100 PESOS
33.9400 g., Bi-Metallic .925 Silver 20.1753g center in
Aluminum-Bronze ring, 39.04 mm. **Series:** First **Subject:**
180th Anniversary of Federation **Obv:** National arms **Obv.**
Legend: ESTADOS UNIDOS MEXICANOS **Rev:** State arms
Rev. Legend: ESTADO DE BAJA CALIFORNIA SUR **Edge:**
Segmented reeding **Mint:** Mexico City

Date	Mintage	F	VF	XF	Unc	BU
2005Mo	249,585	—	—	—	35.00	40.00

KM# 827 100 PESOS
29.1690 g., Bi-Metallic .999 Gold 17.154g center in .999 Silver
12.015g ring, 34.5 mm. **Series:** First **Subject:** 180th
Anniversary of Federation **Obv:** National arms **Obv. Legend:**
ESTADOS UNIDOS MEXICANOS **Rev:** State arms **Rev.**
Legend: ESTADO DE BAJA CALIFORNIA SUR **Edge:**
Segmented reeding **Mint:** Mexico City

Date	Mintage	F	VF	XF	Unc	BU
2005Mo Proof	—	Value: 750				

KM# 727 100 PESOS
33.9400 g., Bi-Metallic .925 Silver 20.1753g center in
Aluminum-Bronze ring, 39.04 mm. **Series:** First **Subject:**
180th Anniversary of Federation **Obv:** National arms **Obv.**
Legend: ESTADOS UNIDOS MEXICANOS **Rev:** State arms
Rev. Legend: ESTADO DE CAMPECHE **Edge:** Segmented
reeding **Mint:** Mexico City

Date	Mintage	F	VF	XF	Unc	BU
2005Mo	249,040	—	—	—	35.00	40.00

KM# 826 100 PESOS
29.1690 g., Bi-Metallic .999 Gold 17.154g center in .999 Silver
12.015g ring, 34.5 mm. **Series:** First **Subject:** 180th
Anniversary of Federation **Obv:** National arms **Obv. Legend:**
ESTADOS UNIDOS MEXICANOS **Rev:** State arms **Rev.**
Legend: ESTADO DE CAMPECHE **Edge:** Segmented
reeding **Mint:** Mexico City

Date	Mintage	F	VF	XF	Unc	BU
2005Mo Proof	1,000	Value: 750				

KM# 723 100 PESOS
33.9400 g., Bi-Metallic .925 Silver 20.1753g center in
Aluminum-Bronze ring, 39.04 mm. **Series:** First **Subject:**
180th Anniversary of Federation **Obv:** National arms **Obv.**
Legend: ESTADOS UNIDOS MEXICANOS **Rev:** State arms
Rev. Legend: ESTADO DE BAJA CALIFORNIA **Edge:**
Segmented reeding **Mint:** Mexico City

Date	Mintage	F	VF	XF	Unc	BU
2005Mo	249,263	—	—	—	35.00	40.00

KM# 828 100 PESOS
29.1690 g., Bi-Metallic .999 Gold 17.154g center in .999 Silver
12.015g ring, 34.5 mm. **Series:** First **Subject:** 180th
Anniversary of Federation **Obv:** National arms **Obv. Legend:**
ESTADOS UNIDOS MEXICANOS **Rev:** State arms **Rev.**
Legend: ESTADO DE BAJA CALIFORNIA **Edge:**
Segmented reeding **Mint:** Mexico City

Date	Mintage	F	VF	XF	Unc	BU
2005Mo Proof	1,000	Value: 750				

STATE COMMEMORATIVES

KM# 721   100 PESOS
33.9400 g., Bi-Metallic .925 Silver 20.1753g center in Aluminum-Bronze ring, 39.04 mm. **Series:** First **Subject:** 180th Anniversary of Federation **Obv:** National arms **Obv. Legend:** ESTADOS UNIDOS MEXICANOS **Rev:** Estados de Aguascalientes state arms **Rev. Legend:** ESTADO DE AGUASCALIENTES **Edge:** Segmented reeding **Mint:** Mexico City

Date	Mintage	F	VF	XF	Unc	BU
2005Mo	248,410	—	—	—	35.00	40.00

KM# 829   100 PESOS
29.1690 g., Bi-Metallic .999 Gold 17.154g center in .999 Silver 12.015g ring, 34.5 mm. **Series:** First **Subject:** 180th Anniversary of Federation **Obv:** National arms **Obv. Legend:** ESTADOS UNIDOS MEXICANOS **Rev:** State arms **Rev. Legend:** ESTADO DE AGUASCALIENTES **Edge:** Segmented reeding **Mint:** Mexico City

Date	Mintage	F	VF	XF	Unc	BU
2005Mo Proof	1,000	Value: 750				

KM# 758   100 PESOS
33.9400 g., Bi-Metallic .925 Silver 20.1753g center in Aluminum-Bronze ring, 39.04 mm. **Series:** Second **Obv:** National arms **Obv. Legend:** ESTADOS UNIDOS MEXICANOS **Rev:** Ram's head and value within circle **Rev. Legend:** BAJA CALIFORNIA - GOBIERNO DEL ESTADO **Edge:** Segmented reeding **Mint:** Mexico City

Date	Mintage	F	VF	XF	Unc	BU
2005Mo	—	—	—	—	25.00	30.00

KM# 863   100 PESOS
29.1690 g., Bi-Metallic .999 Gold 17.154g center in .999 Silver 12.015g ring, 34.5 mm. **Series:** Second **Obv:** National arms **Obv. Legend:** ESTADOS UNIDOS MEXICANOS **Rev:** Ram's head, mountain outline in background **Rev. Legend:** BAJA CALIFORNIA - GOBIERNO DEL ESTADO **Edge:** Segmented reeding **Mint:** Mexico City

Date	Mintage	F	VF	XF	Unc	BU
2005Mo Proof	600	Value: 750				

KM# 719   100 PESOS
33.8250 g., Bi-Metallic .925 Silver 20.1753g center in Aluminum-Bronze ring, 39.04 mm. **Series:** Second **Obv:** National arms **Obv. Legend:** ESTADOS UNIDOS MEXICANOS **Rev:** Facade of the San Marcos garden above sculpture of national emblem at left, San Antonio Temple at right **Rev. Legend:** AGUASCALIENTES **Edge:** Segmented reeding **Mint:** Mexico City

Date	Mintage	F	VF	XF	Unc	BU
2005Mo	149,705	—	—	—	25.00	30.00

KM# 862   100 PESOS
29.1690 g., Bi-Metallic .999 Gold 17.154g center in .999 Silver 12.015g ring, 34.5 mm. **Series:** Second **Obv:** National arms **Obv. Legend:** ESTADOS UNIDOS MEXICANOS **Rev:** Facade of the San Marcos garden above sculpture of national emblem at left, San Antonio temple at right **Rev. Legend:** AGUASCALUENTES **Edge:** Segmented reeding **Mint:** Mexico City

Date	Mintage	F	VF	XF	Unc	BU
2005Mo Proof	600	Value: 750				

KM# 762   100 PESOS
33.9400 g., Bi-Metallic .925 Silver 20.175g center in Aluminum-Bronze ring, 39.04 mm. **Series:** Second **Obv:** National arms **Obv. Legend:** ESTADOS UNIDOS MEXICANOS **Rev:** Outlined map of peninsula at center, cave painting of deer behind, cactus at right **Rev. Legend:** ESTADO DE BAJA CALIFORNIA SUR **Edge:** Segmented reeding **Mint:** Mexico City

Date	Mintage	F	VF	XF	Unc	BU
2005Mo	149,152	—	—	—	25.00	30.00

KM# 864   100 PESOS
29.1690 g., Bi-Metallic .999 Gold 17.154g center in .999 Silver 12.015g ring, 34.5 mm. **Series:** Second **Obv:** National arms **Obv. Legend:** ESTADOS UNIDOS MEXICANOS **Rev:** Outlined map of peninsula at center, cave painting of deer behind, cactus at right **Rev. Legend:** ESTADO DE BAJA CALIFORNIA SUR **Edge:** Segmented reeding **Mint:** Mexico City

Date	Mintage	F	VF	XF	Unc	BU
2006Mo Proof	600	Value: 750				

KM# 760   100 PESOS
33.9400 g., Bi-Metallic .925 Silver 20.1753g center in
Aluminum-Bronze ring, 39.04 mm. **Series:** Second **Subject:**
Estado de Campeche **Obv:** National arms **Obv. Legend:**
ESTADOS UNIDOS MEXICANOS **Rev:** Jade mask -
Calakmul, Campeche **Rev. Legend:** ESTADO DE
CAMPECHE **Edge:** Segmented reeding **Mint:** Mexico City

Date	Mintage	F	VF	XF	Unc	BU
2006Mo	—	—	—	—	25.00	30.00

KM# 865   100 PESOS
29.1690 g., Bi-Metallic .999 Gold 17.154g center in .999 Silver
12.015g ring, 34.5 mm. **Series:** Second **Obv:** National arms
Obv. Legend: ESTADOS UNIDOS MEXICANOS **Rev:** Jade
mask - Calakmul, Campeche **Rev. Legend:** ESTADO DE
CAMPECHE **Edge:** Segmented reeding **Mint:** Mexico City

Date	Mintage	F	VF	XF	Unc	BU
2006Mo Proof	600	Value: 750				

KM# 777   100 PESOS
33.9400 g., Bi-Metallic .925 Silver 20.1753g center in
Aluminum-Bronze ring, 39.04 mm. **Series:** Second **Obv:**
National arms **Obv. Legend:** ESTADOS UNIDOS
MEXICANOS **Rev:** State arms at lower center, Nevado de
Colima and Volcan de Fuego volcanos in background **Rev.
Legend:** Colima **Rev. Inscription:** GENEROSO **Edge:**
Segmented reeding **Mint:** Mexico City

Date	Mintage	F	VF	XF	Unc	BU
2006Mo	149,041	—	—	—	25.00	30.00

KM# 867   100 PESOS
29.1690 g., Bi-Metallic .999 Gold 17.154g center in .999 Silver
12.015 ring, 34.5 mm. **Series:** Second **Obv:** National arms
Obv. Legend: ESTADOS UNIDOS MEXICANOS **Rev:** State
arms at lower center, Nevado de Colima and Volcan de Fuego
volcanos in background **Rev. Legend:** Colima **Rev.
Inscription:** GENEROSO **Edge:** Segmented reeding **Mint:**
Mexico City

Date	Mintage	F	VF	XF	Unc	BU
2006Mo Proof	600	Value: 750				

KM# 781   100 PESOS
33.7000 g., Bi-Metallic .925 Silver 20.1753g center in
Aluminum-Bronze ring, 39.04 mm. **Series:** Second **Obv:**
National arms **Obv. Legend:** ESTADOS UNIDOS
MEXICANOS **Rev:** Outlined map with turtle, mine cart above
grapes at center, Friendship Dam above Christ of the Nodas
at left, chimneys above crucibles and bell tower of Santiago's
cathedral at right **Rev. Legend:** COAHUILA DE ZARAGOZA
Edge: Segmented reeding **Mint:** Mexico City

Date	Mintage	F	VF	XF	Unc	BU
2006Mo	—	—	—	—	25.00	30.00

KM# 866   100 PESOS
29.1690 g., Bi-Metallic .999 Gold 17.154g center in .999 Silver
12.015g ring, 34.5 mm. **Series:** Second **Obv:** National arms
Obv. Legend: ESTADOS UNIDOS MEXICANOS **Rev:**
Outlined map with turtle, mine cart above grapes at center,
Friendship dam above Christ of the Nodas at left, chimneys
above crucibles and bell tower of Santiago's cathedral at right
Rev. Inscription: COAHUILA DE ZARAGOZA **Edge:**
Segmented reeding **Mint:** Mexico City

Date	Mintage	F	VF	XF	Unc	BU
2006Mo Proof	600	Value: 750				

KM# 773   100 PESOS
33.9400 g., Bi-Metallic .925 Silver 20.1753g center in
Aluminum-Bronze ring, 39.04 mm. **Series:** Second **Obv:**
National arms **Obv. Legend:** ESTADOS UNIDOS
MEXICANOS **Rev:** Head of Pakal, ancient Mayan king,
Palenque **Rev. Legend:** ESTADO DE CHIAPAS - CABEZA
MAYA DEL REY PAKAL, PALENQUE **Edge:** Segmented
reeding **Mint:** Mexico City

Date	Mintage	F	VF	XF	Unc	BU
2006Mo	149,491	—	—	—	25.00	30.00

KM# 868   100 PESOS
29.1690 g., Bi-Metallic .999 Gold 17.154g center in .999 Silver
12.015g ring, 34.5 mm. **Series:** Second **Obv:** National arms
Obv. Legend: ESTADOS UNIDOS MEXICANOS **Rev:** Head
of Pakal, ancient Mayan king, Palenque **Rev. Legend:**
ESTADO DE CHIAPAS - CABEZA MAYA DEL REY PAKAL,
PALENQUE **Edge:** Segmented reeding **Mint:** Mexico City

Date	Mintage	F	VF	XF	Unc	BU
2006Mo Proof	600	Value: 750				

STATE COMMEMORATIVES

KM# 775   100 PESOS
33.9400 g., Bi-Metallic .925 Silver 20.1753g center in
Aluminum-Bronze ring, 39.04 mm. **Series:** Second **Obv:**
National arms **Obv. Legend:** ESTADOS UNIDOS
MEXICANOS **Rev:** Angel of Liberty **Rev. Legend:** MÉXICO
- ANGEL DE LA LIBERTAD, CHIHUAHUA **Edge:** Segmented
reeding **Mint:** Mexico City

Date	Mintage	F	VF	XF	Unc	BU
2006Mo	149,557	—	—	—	25.00	30.00

KM# 869   100 PESOS
29.1690 g., Bi-Metallic .999 Gold 17.154g center in .999 Silver
12.015g ring, 34.5 mm. **Series:** Second **Obv:** National arms
Obv. Legend: ESTADOS UNIDOS MEXICANOS **Rev:** Angel
of Liberty **Rev. Legend:** MÉXICO - ANGEL DE LA
LIBERTAD, CHIHUAHUA **Edge:** Segmented reeding **Mint:**
Mexico City

Date	Mintage	F	VF	XF	Unc	BU
2006Mo Proof	600	Value: 750				

KM# 787   100 PESOS
33.9400 g., Bi-Metallic .925 Silver 20.1753g center in Brass
ring, 39.04 mm. **Series:** Second **Obv:** National arms Obv.
Legend: ESTADOS UNIDOS MEXICANOS **Rev:** Tree **Rev.**
Legend: PRIMERA RESERVA NACIONAL FORESTAL -
DURANGO **Edge:** Segmented reeding **Mint:** Mexico City

Date	Mintage	F	VF	XF	Unc	BU
2006Mo	149,034	—	—	—	25.00	30.00

KM# 871   100 PESOS
29.1690 g., Bi-Metallic .999 Gold 17.154g center in .999 Silver
12.015g ring, 34.5 mm. **Series:** Second **Obv:** National arms
Obv. Legend: ESYADOS UNIDOS MEXICANOS **Rev:** Tree
Rev. Legend: PRIMERA RESERVA NACIONAL
RORESTAL - DURANGO **Edge:** Segmented reeding **Mint:**
Mexico City

Date	Mintage	F	VF	XF	Unc	BU
2006Mo Proof	600	Value: 750				

KM# 779   100 PESOS
33.9400 g., Bi-Metallic .925 Silver 20.1753g center in
Aluminum-Bronze ring, 39.04 mm. **Series:** Second **Obv:**
National arms **Obv. Legend:** ESTADOS UNIDOS
MEXICANOS **Rev:** National Palace **Rev. Legend:** DISTRITO
FEDERAL - ANTIGUO AYUNTAMIENTO **Edge:** Segmented
reeding **Mint:** Mexico City

Date	Mintage	F	VF	XF	Unc	BU
2006Mo	149,525	—	—	—	25.00	30.00

KM# 870   100 PESOS
29.1690 g., Bi-Metallic .999 Gold 17.154g center in .999 Silver
12.015g ring, 34.5 mm. **Series:** Second **Obv:** National arms
Obv. Legend: ESTADOS UNIDOS MEXICANOS **Rev:**
National palace **Rev. Legend:** DISTRITO FEDERAL -
ANTIGUO AYUNTAMIENTO **Edge:** Segmented reeding
Mint: Mexico City

Date	Mintage	F	VF	XF	Unc	BU
2006Mo Proof	600	Value: 750				

KM# 789   100 PESOS
33.9400 g., Bi-Metallic .925 Silver 20.1753g center in Brass
ring, 39.04 mm. **Series:** Second **Obv:** National arms Obv.
Legend: ESTADOS UNIDOS MEXICANOS **Rev:** State arms
at center, statue of Miguel Hidalgo at left, monument to Pipila
at lower right **Rev. Inscription:** *Guanajuato* **Edge:**
Segmented reeding **Mint:** Mexico City

Date	Mintage	F	VF	XF	Unc	BU
2006Mo	149,921	—	—	—	25.00	30.00

KM# 872   100 PESOS
29.1690 g., Bi-Metallic .999 Gold 17.154g center in .999 Silver
12.015g ring, 34.50 mm. **Series:** Second **Obv:** National arms
Obv. Legend: ESTADOS UNIDOS MEXICANOS **Rev:** State
arms at lower center, statue of Miguel Hidalgo at left,
monument to Pipila at lower right **Rev. Inscription:**
Guanajauto **Edge:** Segmented reeding **Mint:** Mexico City

Date	Mintage	F	VF	XF	Unc	BU
2006Mo Proof	600	Value: 750				

STATE COMMEMORATIVES

KM# 791   100 PESOS
33.9400 g., Bi-Metallic .925 Silver 20.1753g center in Brass
ring, 39.04 mm. **Series:** Second **Obv:** National arms **Obv.
Legend:** ESTADOS UNIDOS MEXICANOS **Rev:** Stylized
portrait of Vicente Guerrero at left, church of Taxco at upper
center, Acapulco's la Quebrada with diver above Christmas
Eve flower and mask **Rev. Legend:** GUERRERO **Edge:**
Segmented reeding **Mint:** Mexico City

Date	Mintage	F	VF	XF	Unc	BU
2006Mo	149,675	—	—	—	25.00	30.00

KM# 873   100 PESOS
29.1690 g., Bi-Metallic .999 Gold 17.154g center in .999 Silver
12.015g ring, 34.5 mm. **Series:** Second **Obv:** National arms
Obv. Legend: ESTADOS UNIDOS MEXICANOS **Rev:**
Stylized portrait of Vicente Guerrero at left, church of Taxco
at upper center, Acapulco's la Quebrada with diver over
Christmas Eve flower and mask **Rev. Legend:** GUERRERO
Edge: Segmented reeding **Mint:** Mexico City

Date	Mintage	F	VF	XF	Unc	BU
2006Mo Proof	600	Value: 750				

KM# 793   100 PESOS
33.9400 g., Bi-Metallic .925 Silver 20.1753g center in
Aluminum-Bronze ring, 39.04 mm. **Series:** Second **Obv:**
National arms **Obv. Legend:** ESTADOS UNIDOS
MEXICANOS **Rev:** Monument of Pachuca Hidalgo **Rev.
Inscription:** RELOJ / MONUMENTAL / DE / PACHUCA /
HIDALGO - La / Bella / Airosa **Edge:** Segmented reeding
Mint: Mexico City

Date	Mintage	F	VF	XF	Unc	BU
2006Mo	149,273	—	—	—	25.00	30.00

KM# 874   100 PESOS
29.1690 g., Bi-Metallic .999 Gold 17.154g center in .999 Silver
12.015g ring, 34.5 mm. **Series:** Second **Obv:** National arms
Obv. Legend: ESTADOS UNIDOS MEXICANOS **Rev:**
Monument of Pachuca Hidalgo **Rev. Inscription:** RELOJ /
MONUMENTAL / DE / PACHUCA / HIDALGO **Edge:**
Segmented reeding **Mint:** Mexico City

Date	Mintage	F	VF	XF	Unc	BU
2006Mo Proof	600	Value: 750				

KM# 795   100 PESOS
33.9400 g., Bi-Metallic .925 Silver 20.1753g center in Brass
ring, 39.04 mm. **Series:** Second **Obv:** National arms **Obv.
Legend:** ESTADOS UNIDOS MEXICANOS **Rev:** Hospicio
Cabañas orphanage **Rev. Legend:** ESTADO DE JALISCO
Edge: Segmented reeding **Mint:** Mexico City

Date	Mintage	F	VF	XF	Unc	BU
2006Mo	149,750	—	—	—	25.00	30.00

KM# 875   100 PESOS
29.1690 g., Bi-Metallic .999 Gold 17.154g center in .999 Silver
12.015g ring, 34.5 mm. **Series:** Second **Obv:** National arms
Obv. Legend: ESTADOS UNIDOS MEXICANOS **Rev:**
Hospicio Cabañas orphanage **Rev. Legend:** ESTADO DE
JALISCO **Edge:** Segmented reeding **Mint:** Mexico City

Date	Mintage	F	VF	XF	Unc	BU
2006Mo Proof	600	Value: 750				

KM# 802   100 PESOS
33.9400 g., Bi-Metallic .925 Silver 20.1753g center in
Aluminum-Bronze ring, 33.04 mm. **Series:** Second
Obv: National arms **Obv. Legend:** ESTADOS UNIDOS
MEXICANOS **Rev:** Pyramid de la Loona (moon) **Rev.
Legend:** ESTADO DE MEXICO **Edge:** Segmented reeding
Mint: Mexico City

Date	Mintage	F	VF	XF	Unc	BU
2006Mo	149,377	—	—	—	25.00	30.00

KM# 876   100 PESOS
29.1690 g., Bi-Metallic .999 Gold 17.154g center in .999 Silver
12.015g ring, 34.5 mm. **Series:** Second **Obv:** National arms
Obv. Legend: ESTADOS UNIDOS MEXICANOS **Rev:**
Pyramid de la Looona (moon) **Rev. Legend:** ESTADO DE
MEXICO **Edge:** Segmented reeding **Mint:** Mexico City

Date	Mintage	F	VF	XF	Unc	BU
2006Mo Proof	600	Value: 750				

KM# 785   100 PESOS
33.9400 g., Bi-Metallic .925 Silver 20.1753g center in
Aluminum-Bronze ring, 33.7, 39.04 mm. **Series:** Second
Obv: National arms **Obv. Legend:** ESTADOS UNIDOS
MEXICANOS **Rev:** Four Monarch butterflies **Rev. Legend:**
ESTADO DE MICHOACÁN **Edge:** Segmented reeding **Mint:**
Mexico City

Date	Mintage	F	VF	XF	Unc	BU
2006Mo	149,730	—	—	—	25.00	30.00

KM# 877   100 PESOS
29.1690 g., Bi-Metallic .999 Gold 17.154g center in .999 Silver
12.015g ring, 34.5 mm. **Series:** Second **Obv:** National arms
Obv. Legend: ESTADOS UNIDOS MEXICANOS **Rev:** Four
Monarch butterflies **Rev. Legend:** ESTADO DE
MICHOACÁN **Edge:** Segmented reeding **Mint:** Mexico City

Date	Mintage	F	VF	XF	Unc	BU
2006Mo Proof	600	Value: 750				

KM# 800　100 PESOS
33.9400 g., Bi-Metallic .925 Silver 20.1753g center in
Aluminum-Bronze ring, 33.7, 39.04 mm. **Series:** Second
Obv: National arms **Obv. Legend:** ESTADOS UNIDOS
MEXICANOS **Rev:** 1/2 length figure of Chinelo (local dancer)
at right, Palacio de Cortes in background **Rev. Inscription:**
ESTADO DE / MORELOS **Edge:** Segmented reeding **Mint:**
Mexico City

Date	Mintage	F	VF	XF	Unc	BU
2006Mo	149,648	—	—	—	25.00	30.00

KM# 878　100 PESOS
29.1690 g., Bi-Metallic .999 Gold 17.154g center in .999 Silver
12.015g ring, 34.5 mm. **Series:** Second **Obv:** National arms
Obv. Legend: ESTADOS UNIDOS MEXICANOS **Rev:** 1/2
length figure of Chinelo (local dancer) at right, Palacio de
Cortes in background **Rev. Inscription:** ESTADO DE /
MORELOS **Edge:** Segmented reeding **Mint:** Mexico City

Date	Mintage	F	VF	XF	Unc	BU
2006Mo Proof	600	Value: 750				

KM# 848　100 PESOS
33.9400 g., Bi-Metallic .925 Silver 20.1753 center in
Aluminum-Bronze ring, 39.04 mm. **Series:** Second **Obv:**
National arms **Obv. Legend:** ESTADOS UNIDOS
MEXICANOE **Rev:** Old foundry in Parque Fundidora (public
park) at right, Cerro de la Silla (Saddle Hill) in background
Rev. Legend: ESTADO DE NUEVO LEÓN **Edge:**
Segmented reeding **Mint:** Mexico City

Date	Mintage	F	VF	XF	Unc	BU
2007Mo	149,425	—	—	—	25.00	30.00

KM# 880　100 PESOS
29.1690 g., Bi-Metallic .999 Gold 17.154g center in .999 Silver
12.015g ring, 34.5 mm. **Series:** Second **Obv:** National arms
Obv. Legend: ESTADOS UNIDOS MEXICANOS **Rev:** Old
foundry in Parque Fundidora (public park) at right, Cerro de
la Silla (Saddle hill) in background **Rev. Legend:** ESTADO
DE NUEVO LEÓN **Edge:** Segmented reeding **Mint:** Mexico
City

Date	Mintage	F	VF	XF	Unc	BU
2007Mo Proof	600	Value: 750				

KM# 798　100 PESOS
33.9400 g., 33.8250 Bi-Metallic 0.925 Silver 20.1753g center
in Aluminum-Bronze ring 36.908 oz., 39.04 mm. **Series:**
Second **Obv:** National arms **Obv. Legend:** ESTADOS
UNIDOS MEXICANOS **Rev:** Isle de Mexcaltitlán **Rev.
Legend:** ESTADO DE NAYARIT **Edge:** Segmented reeding
Mint: Mexico City

Date	Mintage	F	VF	XF	Unc	BU
2007Mo	149,560	—	—	—	25.00	30.00

KM# 879　100 PESOS
29.1690 g., Bi-Metallic .999 Gold 17.154g center in .999
12.015g ring, 34.5 mm. **Series:** Second **Obv:** National arms
Obv. Legend: ESTADOS UNIDOS MEXICANOS **Rev:** Isle
de Mexcaltitlán **Rev. Legend:** ESTADO DE NAYARIT **Edge:**
Segmented reeding **Mint:** Mexico City

Date	Mintage	F	VF	XF	Unc	BU
2007Mo Proof	600	Value: 750				

KM# 849　100 PESOS
33.9400 g., Bi-Metallic .925 Silver 20.1753g center in
Aluminum-Bronze ring, 39.04 mm. **Series:** Second **Obv:**
National arms **Obv. Legend:** ESTADOS UNIDOS
MEXICANOS **Rev:** Teatro Macedonio Alcala (theater) **Rev.
Legend:** OAXACA **Edge:** Segmented reeding **Mint:** Mexico
City

Date	Mintage	F	VF	XF	Unc	BU
2007Mo	149,892	—	—	—	25.00	30.00

KM# 881　100 PESOS
29.1690 g., Bi-Metallic .999 Gold 17.154g center in .999 Silver
12.015g ring, 34.50 mm. **Series:** Second **Obv:** National arms
Obv. Legend: ESTADOS UNIDOS MEXICANOS **Rev:**
Teatro Macedonio Alcala (theater) **Rev. Legend:** OAXACA
Edge: Segmented reeding **Mint:** Mexico City

Date	Mintage	F	VF	XF	Unc	BU
2007Mo Proof	600	Value: 750				

KM# 850   100 PESOS
33.9400 g., Bi-Metallic .925 Silver 20.1753g center in
Aluminum-Bronze ring, 39.04 mm.   **Series:** Second **Obv:**
National arms **Obv. Legend:** ESTADOS UNIDOS
MEXICANOS **Rev:** Talavera porcelain dish **Rev. Legend:**
ESTADO DE PUEBLA **Edge:** Segmented reeding **Mint:**
Mexico City

Date	Mintage	F	VF	XF	Unc	BU
2007Mo	149,474	—	—	—	25.00	30.00

KM# 882   100 PESOS
29.1690 g., Bi-Metallic .999 Gold 17.154g center in .999 Silver
12.015g ring, 34.5 mm.   **Series:** Second **Obv:** National arms
Obv. Legend: ESTADOS UNIDOS MEXICANOS **Rev:**
Talavera porcelain dish **Rev. Legend:** ESTADO DE PUEBLA
Edge: Segmented reeding **Mint:** Mexico City

Date	Mintage	F	VF	XF	Unc	BU
2007Mo Proof	600	Value: 750				

KM# 852   100 PESOS
33.9400 g., Bi-Metallic .925 Silver 20.1753 center in
Aluminum-Bronze ring, 39.04 mm.   **Series:** Second **Obv:**
National arms **Obv. Legend:** ESTADOS UNIDOS
MEXICANOS **Rev:** Aqueduct of Querétaro at left, church of
Santa Rosa de Viterbo at right **Rev. Legend:** ESTADO DE
QUERÉTARO ARTEAGA **Edge:** Segmented reeding **Mint:**
Mexico City

Date	Mintage	F	VF	XF	Unc	BU
2007Mo	149,127	—	—	—	25.00	30.00

KM# 884   100 PESOS
29.1690 g., Bi-Metallic .999 Gold 17.154g center in .999 Silver
12.015g ring, 34.5 mm.   **Series:** Second **Obv:** National arms
Obv. Legend: ESTADOS UNIDOS MEXICANOS **Rev:**
Aqueduct of Querétaro at left, church of Santa Rosa de Viterbo
at right **Rev. Legend:** ESTADO DE QUERÉTARO ARTEAGA
Edge: Segmented reeding **Mint:** Mexico City

Date	Mintage	F	VF	XF	Unc	BU
2007Mo Proof	600	—	—	—	—	750

KM# 851   100 PESOS
33.9400 g., Bi-Metallic .925 Silver 20.1753g center in
Aluminum-Bronze ring, 39.04 mm.   **Series:** Second **Obv:**
National arms **Obv. Legend:** ESTADOS UNIDOS
MEXICANOS **Rev:** Mask at left, rays above state arms at
center, Mayan ruins at right **Rev. Legend:** QUINTANA ROO
Edge: Segmented reeding **Mint:** Mexico City

Date	Mintage	F	VF	XF	Unc	BU
2007Mo	149,582	—	—	—	25.00	30.00

KM# 883   100 PESOS
29.1690 g., Bi-Metallic .999 Gold 17.154g center in .999 Silver
12.015g ring, 34.5 mm.   **Series:** Second **Obv:** National arms
Obv. Legend: ESTADOS UNIDOS MEXICANOS **Rev:** Mask
at left, rays above state arms at center, Mayan ruins at right
Rev. Legend: QUINTANA ROO **Edge:** Segmented reeding
Mint: Mexico City

Date	Mintage	F	VF	XF	Unc	BU
2007Mo Proof	600	Value: 750				

KM# 853   100 PESOS
33.9400 g., Bi-Metallic .925 Silver 20.1753g center in
Aluminum-Bronze ring, 39.04 mm.   **Series:** Second **Obv:**
National arms **Obv. Legend:** ESTADOS UNIDOS
MEXICANOS **Rev:** Facade of Caja Real **Rev. Legend:** • SAN
LUIS POTOSÍ • **Edge:** Segmented reeding **Mint:** Mexico City

Date	Mintage	F	VF	XF	Unc	BU
2007Mo	148,750	—	—	—	25.00	30.00

KM# 885   100 PESOS
29.1690 g., Bi-Metallic .999 Gold 17.154g center in .999 Silver
12.015 ring, 34.5 mm.   **Series:** Second **Obv:** National arms
Obv. Legend: ESTADOS UNIDOS MEXICANOS **Rev:**
Facade of Caja Real **Rev. Legend:** • SAN LUIS POTOSÍ •
Edge: Segmented reeding **Mint:** Mexico City

Date	Mintage	F	VF	XF	Unc	BU
2007Mo Proof	600	Value: 750				

STATE COMMEMORATIVES

KM# 854   100 PESOS
33.9400 g., Bi-Metallic .925 Silver 20.1753g center in
Aluminum-Bronze ring, 39.04 mm. **Series:** Second **Obv:**
National arms **Obv. Legend:** ESTADOS UNIDOS
MEXICANOS **Rev:** Shield on pile of cactus fruits **Rev.**
Legend: ESTADO DE SINALOA - LUGAR DE PITAHAYAS
Edge: Segmented reeding **Mint:** Mexico City

Date	Mintage	F	VF	XF	Unc	BU
2007Mo	149,032	—	—	—	25.00	30.00

KM# 886   100 PESOS
29.1690 g., Bi-Metallic .999 Gold 17.154 center in .999 Silver
12.015g ring, 34.5 mm. **Series:** Second **Obv:** National arms
Obv. Legend: ESTADOS UNIDOS MEXICANOS **Rev:**
Shield on pile of cactus fruits **Rev. Legend:** ESTADO DE
SINALOA - LUGAR DE PITAHAYES **Edge:** Segmented
reeding **Mint:** Mexico City

Date	Mintage	F	VF	XF	Unc	BU
2007Mo Proof	600	Value: 750				

KM# 855   100 PESOS
33.9400 g., Bi-Metallic .925 Silver 20.1753g center in
Aluminum-Bronze ring, 39.04 mm. **Series:** Second **Obv:**
National arms **Obv. Legend:** ESTADOS UNIDOS
MEXICANOS **Rev:** Local in Dance of the Deer at left, cactus
at right, mountains in background **Rev. Legend:** ESTADO
DE SONORA **Edge:** Segmented reeding **Mint:** Mexico City

Date	Mintage	F	VF	XF	Unc	BU
2007Mo	149,891	—	—	—	25.00	30.00

KM# 887   100 PESOS
29.1690 g., Bi-Metallic .999 Gold 17.154g center in .999 Silver
12.015g ring, 34.5 mm. **Series:** Second **Obv:** National arms
Obv. Legend: ESTADOS UNIDOS MEXICANOS **Rev:** Local
in Dance of the Deer at left, cactus at right, mountains in
background **Rev. Legend:** ESTADO DE SONORA **Edge:**
Segmented reeding **Mint:** Mexico City

Date	Mintage	F	VF	XF	Unc	BU
2007Mo Proof	600	Value: 750				

KM# 856   100 PESOS
33.9400 g., Bi-Metallic .925 Silver 20.1753 center in
Aluminum-Bronze ring, 39.04 mm. **Series:** Second **Obv:**
National arms **Obv. Legend:** ESTADOS UNIDOS
MEXICANOS **Rev:** Fuente de los Pescadores (fisherman
fountain) at lower left, giant head from the Olmec-pre-Hispanic
culture at right, Planetario Tabasco in background **Rev.**
Legend: TABASCO **Edge:** Segmented reeding **Mint:** Mexico
City

Date	Mintage	F	VF	XF	Unc	BU
2007Mo	149,715	—	—	—	25.00	30.00

KM# 888   100 PESOS
29.1690 g., Bi-Metallic .999 Gold 17.154g center in .999 Silver
12.015g ring, 34.5 mm. **Series:** Second **Obv:** National arms
Obv. Legend: ESTADOS UNIDOS MEXICANOS **Rev:**
Fuente de los Pescadores (fisherman fountain) at lower left,
giant head from the Olmec-pre-Hispanic culture at right,
Planetario Tabasco in background **Rev. Legend:** TABASCO
Edge: Segmented reeding **Mint:** Mexico City

Date	Mintage	F	VF	XF	Unc	BU
2007Mo Proof	600	Value: 750				

KM# 857   100 PESOS
33.9400 g., Bi-Metallic .925 Silver 20.1753g center in
Aluminum-Bronze ring, 39.04 mm. **Series:** Second **Obv:**
National arms **Obv. Legend:** ESTADOS UNIDOS
MEXICANOS **Rev:** Ridge - Cerro Del Bermal, Gonzáles **Rev.**
Legend: TAMAULIPAS **Edge:** Segmented reeding **Mint:**
Mexico City

Date	Mintage	F	VF	XF	Unc	BU
2007Mo	149,776	—	—	—	25.00	30.00

KM# 889   100 PESOS
29.1690 g., Bi-Metallic .999 Gold 17.154g center in .999 Silver
12.015g ring, 34.5 mm. **Series:** Second **Obv:** National arms
Obv. Legend: ESTADOS DE MEXICANOS **Rev:** Ridge -
Cerro Del Bermal, Gonzáles **Rev. Legend:** TAMAULIPAS
Edge: Segmented reeding **Mint:** Mexico City

Date	Mintage	F	VF	XF	Unc	BU
2007Mo Proof	600	Value: 750				

KM# 858 100 PESOS
33.9400 g., Bi-Metallic .925 Silver 20.1753g center in
Aluminum-Bronze ring, 39.04 mm. **Series:** Second **Obv:**
National arms **Obv. Legend:** ESTADOS UNIDOS
MEXICANOS **Rev:** Basilica de Ocotlán at left, state arms
above Capilla Abierta, Plaza de Toros Ranchero Aguilar
below, Exconvento de San Francisco at right **Rev. Legend:**
ESTADO DE TLAXCALA **Edge:** Segmented reeding **Mint:**
Mexico City

Date	Mintage	F	VF	XF	Unc	BU
2007Mo	149,465	—	—	—	25.00	30.00

KM# 890 100 PESOS
29.1690 g., Bi-Metallic .999 Gold 17.154g center in .999 Silver
12.015g ring, 34.5 mm. **Series:** Second **Obv:** National arms
Obv. Legend: ESTADOS UNIDOS MEXICANOS **Rev:**
Basilica de Ocotlán at left, state arms above Capilla Abierta,
Plaza de Toros Ranchero Aguilar below, Exconvento de San
Francisco at right **Rev. Legend:** ESTADO DE TLAXCALA
Edge: Segmented reeding **Mint:** Mexico City

Date	Mintage	F	VF	XF	Unc	BU
2007Mo Proof	600	Value: 750				

KM# 860 100 PESOS
33.9400 g., Bi-Metallic .925 Silver 20.1753 center in
Aluminum-Bronze ring, 39.04 mm. **Series:** Second **Obv:**
National arms **Obv. Legend:** ESTADOS UNIDOS
MEXICANOS **Rev:** Stylized pyramid of Chichén Itzá **Rev.
Legend:** Castillo de Chichén Itzá **Edge:** Segmented reeding
Mint: Mexico City

Date	Mintage	F	VF	XF	Unc	BU
2007Mo	149,579	—	—	—	25.00	30.00

KM# 892 100 PESOS
29.1690 g., Bi-Metallic .999 Gold 17.154g center in .999 Silver
12.015g ring, 34.5 mm. **Series:** Second **Obv:** National arms
Obv. Legend: ESTADOS UNIDOS MEXICANOS **Rev:**
Stylized pyramid of Chichén-Itzá **Rev. Inscription:**
YUCATÁN **Edge:** Segmented reeding **Mint:** Mexico City

Date	Mintage	F	VF	XF	Unc	BU
2007Mo Proof	600	Value: 750				

KM# 859 100 PESOS
33.9400 g., Bi-Metallic .912 Silver 20.1753g center in
Aluminum-Bronze ring, 39.04 mm. **Series:** Second **Obv:**
National arms **Obv. Legend:** ESTADOS UNIDOS
MEXICANOS **Rev:** Pyramid of El Tajín **Rev. Legend:** •
VERACRUZ • - • DE ÍGNACIO DE LA LLAVE • **Edge:**
Segmented reeding **Mint:** Mexico City

Date	Mintage	F	VF	XF	Unc	BU
2007Mo	149,703	—	—	—	25.00	30.00

KM# 891 100 PESOS
29.1690 g., Bi-Metallic .999 Gold 17.154g center in .999 Silver
12.015g ring, 34.5 mm. **Series:** Second **Obv:** National arms
Obv. Legend: ESTADOS UNIDOS MEXICANOS **Rev:**
Pyramid of El Tajin **Rev. Legend:** • VERACRUZ • - • DE
IGNACIO DE LA LLAVE • **Edge:** Segmented reeding **Mint:**
Mexico City

Date	Mintage	F	VF	XF	Unc	BU
2007Mo Proof	600	Value: 750				

KM# 861 100 PESOS
33.9400 g., Bi-Metallic .925 Silver 20.1753g center in
Aluminum-Bronze ring, 39.04 mm. **Series:** Second **Obv:**
National arms **Obv. Legend:** ESTADOS UNIDOS
MEXICANOS **Rev:** Cable car above Monumento al Minero at
left, Cathedral de Zacatecas at center right **Rev. Legend:**
ZACATECAS **Edge:** Segmented reeding **Mint:** Mexico City

Date	Mintage	F	VF	XF	Unc	BU
2007Mo	148,833	—	—	—	25.00	30.00

KM# 893 100 PESOS
29.1690 g., Bi-Metallic .999 Gold 17.154g center in .999 Silver
12.015g ring, 34.5 mm. **Series:** Second **Obv:** National arms
Obv. Legend: ESTADOS UNIDOS MEXICANOS **Rev:** Cable
car above Monumento al Minero at left, Cathedral de
Zacatecas at center right **Rev. Legend:** Zacatecas **Edge:**
Segmented reeding **Mint:** Mexico City

Date	Mintage	F	VF	XF	Unc	BU
2007Mo Proof	600	Value: 750				

SILVER BULLION COINAGE
Libertad Series

KM# 542   1/20 ONZA (1/20 Troy Ounce of Silver)
1.5551 g., 0.9990 Silver 0.0499 oz. ASW **Obv:** National arms, eagle left **Rev:** Winged Victory **Mint:** Mexico City

Date	Mintage	F	VF	XF	Unc	BU
1991Mo	50,017	—	—	—	—	5.50
1992Mo	295,783	—	—	—	—	4.50
1992Mo Proof	5,000	Value: 10.00				
1993Mo	100,000	—	—	—	—	4.50
1993Mo Proof	—	Value: 10.00				
1994Mo	90,100	—	—	—	—	4.50
1994Mo Proof	10,000	Value: 10.00				
1995Mo	50,000	—	—	—	—	5.50
1995Mo Proof	2,000	Value: 12.00				

KM# 609   1/20 ONZA (1/20 Troy Ounce of Silver)
1.5551 g., 0.9990 Silver 0.0499 oz. ASW **Obv:** National arms, eagle left **Rev:** Winged Victory **Mint:** Mexico City

Date	Mintage	F	VF	XF	Unc	BU
1996Mo	50,000	—	—	—	—	10.00
1996Mo Proof	1,000	Value: 15.00				
1997Mo	20,000	—	—	—	—	10.00
1997Mo Proof	800	Value: 15.00				
1998Mo	6,400	—	—	—	—	15.00
1998Mo Proof	300	Value: 18.50				
1999Mo	8,401	—	—	—	—	12.00
1999Mo Proof	600	Value: 16.50				
2000Mo	63,750	—	—	—	—	12.00
2000Mo Proof	1,200	Value: 16.50				
2001Mo	23,750	—	—	—	—	12.00
2001Mo Proof	3,200	Value: 15.00				
2002Mo	55,000	—	—	—	—	8.00
2002Mo Proof	1,200	Value: 13.00				
2003Mo	35,000	—	—	—	—	8.00
2003Mo Proof	3,015	Value: 13.00				
2004Mo	35,000	—	—	—	—	8.00
2004Mo Proof	5,285	Value: 13.00				
2005Mo	16,525	—	—	—	—	8.00
2005Mo Proof	1,500	Value: 12.00				
2006Mo	20,000	—	—	—	—	8.00
2006Mo Proof	3,300	Value: 12.00				
2007Mo	—	—	—	—	—	8.00
2007Mo Proof	—	Value: 12.00				
2008Mo	—	—	—	—	—	8.00
2008Mo Proof	—	Value: 12.00				
2009Mo	—	—	—	—	—	8.00
2009Mo Proof	—	Value: 12.00				

KM# 543   1/10 ONZA (1/10 Troy Ounce of Silver)
3.1103 g., 0.9990 Silver 0.0999 oz. ASW **Obv:** National arms, eagle left **Rev:** Winged Victory **Mint:** Mexico City

Date	Mintage	F	VF	XF	Unc	BU
1991Mo	50,017	—	—	—	—	7.50
1992Mo	299,983	—	—	—	—	6.50
1992Mo Proof	5,000	Value: 12.00				
1993Mo	100,000	—	—	—	—	6.50

Date	Mintage	F	VF	XF	Unc	BU
1993Mo Proof	—	Value: 12.00				
1994Mo	90,100	—	—	—	—	6.50
1994Mo Proof	10,000	Value: 12.00				
1995Mo	50,000	—	—	—	—	7.50
1995Mo Proof	2,000	Value: 13.50				

KM# 610   1/10 ONZA (1/10 Troy Ounce of Silver)
3.1103 g., 0.9990 Silver 0.0999 oz. ASW **Obv:** National arms, eagle left **Rev:** Winged Victory **Mint:** Mexico City

Date	Mintage	F	VF	XF	Unc	BU
1996Mo	50,000	—	—	—	—	12.00
1996Mo Proof	1,000	Value: 17.50				
1997Mo	20,000	—	—	—	—	12.00
1997Mo Proof	800	Value: 17.50				
1998Mo	6,400	—	—	—	—	16.50
1998Mo Proof	300	Value: 22.50				
1999Mo	8,400	—	—	—	—	14.00
1999Mo Proof	600	Value: 20.00				
2000Mo	33,750	—	—	—	—	14.00
2000Mo Proof	1,300	Value: 20.00				
2001Mo	23,750	—	—	—	—	14.00
2001Mo Proof	3,200	Value: 18.00				
2002Mo	45,000	—	—	—	—	10.00
2002Mo Proof	1,200	Value: 15.00				
2003Mo	5,000	—	—	—	—	10.00
2003Mo Proof	3,500	Value: 15.00				
2004Mo	22,277	—	—	—	—	10.00
2004Mo Proof	3,500	Value: 15.00				
2005Mo	7,086	—	—	—	—	10.00
2005Mo Proof	2,500	Value: 14.00				
2006Mo	15,000	—	—	—	—	10.00
2006Mo Proof	3,000	Value: 14.00				
2007Mo	—	—	—	—	—	10.00
2007Mo Proof	—	Value: 14.00				
2008Mo	—	—	—	—	—	10.00
2008Mo Proof	—	Value: 14.00				
2009Mo	—	—	—	—	—	10.00
2009Mo Proof	—	Value: 14.00				

KM# 544   1/4 ONZA (1/4 Troy Ounce of Silver)
7.7758 g., 0.9990 Silver 0.2497 oz. ASW **Obv:** National arms, eagle left **Rev:** Winged Victory **Mint:** Mexico City

Date	Mintage	F	VF	XF	Unc	BU
1991Mo	50,017	—	—	—	—	9.00
1992Mo	104,000	—	—	—	—	7.50
1992Mo Proof	5,000	Value: 15.00				
1993Mo	86,500	—	—	—	—	7.50
1993Mo Proof	—	Value: 15.00				
1994Mo	90,100	—	—	—	—	7.50
1994Mo Proof	15,000	Value: 15.00				
1995Mo	50,000	—	—	—	—	9.00
1995Mo Proof	2,000	Value: 16.50				

KM# 611 1/4 ONZA (1/4 Troy Ounce of Silver)
7.7758 g., 0.9990 Silver 0.2497 oz. ASW **Obv:** National
arms, eagle left **Rev:** Winged Victory **Mint:** Mexico City

Date	Mintage	F	VF	XF	Unc	BU
1996Mo	50,000	—	—	—	—	15.00
1996Mo Proof	1,000	Value: 20.00				
1997Mo	20,000	—	—	—	—	15.00
1997Mo Proof	800	Value: 20.00				
1998Mo	6,400	—	—	—	—	20.00
1998Mo Proof	300	Value: 32.50				
1999Mo	7,400	—	—	—	—	18.00
1999Mo Proof	600	Value: 25.00				
2000Mo	21,000	—	—	—	—	18.00
2000Mo Proof	850	Value: 25.00				
2001Mo	23,750	—	—	—	—	18.00
2001Mo Proof	2,850	Value: 22.00				
2002Mo	45,000	—	—	—	—	13.50
2002Mo Proof	1,200	Value: 20.00				
2003Mo	7,000	—	—	—	—	13.50
2003Mo Proof	3,500	Value: 20.00				
2004Mo	30,000	—	—	—	—	13.50
2004Mo Proof	3,900	Value: 20.00				
2005Mo	1,901	—	—	—	—	13.50
2005Mo Proof	1,500	Value: 18.50				
2006Mo	15,000	—	—	—	—	13.00
2006Mo Proof	2,900	Value: 18.50				
2007Mo	—	—	—	—	—	13.00
2007Mo Proof	—	Value: 18.50				
2008Mo	—	—	—	—	—	13.00
2008Mo Proof	—	Value: 18.50				
2009Mo	—	—	—	—	—	13.00
2009Mo Proof	—	Value: 18.50				

KM# 545 1/2 ONZA (1/2 Troy Ounce of Silver)
15.5517 g., 0.9990 Silver 0.4995 oz. ASW **Obv:** National
arms, eagle left **Rev:** Winged Victory **Mint:** Mexico City

Date	Mintage	F	VF	XF	Unc	BU
1991Mo	50,618	—	—	—	—	12.00
1992Mo	119,000	—	—	—	—	10.00
1992Mo Proof	5,000	Value: 17.50				
1993Mo	71,500	—	—	—	—	10.00
1993Mo Proof	—	Value: 17.50				
1994Mo	90,100	—	—	—	—	10.00
1994Mo Proof	15,000	Value: 17.50				
1995Mo	50,000	—	—	—	—	10.00
1995Mo Proof	2,000	Value: 18.50				

KM# 612 1/2 ONZA (1/2 Troy Ounce of Silver)
15.5517 g., 0.9990 Silver 0.4995 oz. ASW **Obv:** National
arms, eagle left **Rev:** Winged Victory **Mint:** Mexico City

Date	Mintage	F	VF	XF	Unc	BU
1996Mo	50,999	—	—	—	—	20.00
1996Mo Proof	1,000	Value: 30.00				
1997Mo	20,000	—	—	—	—	20.00
1997Mo Proof	800	Value: 30.00				
1998Mo	6,400	—	—	—	—	30.00
1998Mo Proof	300	Value: 45.00				

Date	Mintage	F	VF	XF	Unc	BU
1999Mo	7,400	—	—	—	—	22.00
1999Mo Proof	600	Value: 35.00				
2000Mo	20,000	—	—	—	—	22.00
2000Mo Proof	700	Value: 35.00				
2001Mo	20,000	—	—	—	—	22.00
2001Mo Proof	1,000	Value: 30.00				
2002Mo	45,000	—	—	—	—	18.00
2002Mo Proof	2,800	Value: 25.00				
2003Mo	15,000	—	—	—	—	18.00
2003Mo Proof	3,000	Value: 25.00				
2004Mo	24,000	—	—	—	—	18.00
2004Mo Proof	4,300	Value: 25.00 ·				
2005Mo	8,126	—	—	—	—	18.00
2005Mo Proof	1,500	Value: 22.00				
2006Mo	15,000	—	—	—	—	18.00
2006Mo Proof	2,900	Value: 22.00				
2007Mo	—	—	—	—	—	18.00
2007Mo Proof	—	Value: 22.00				
2008Mo	—	—	—	—	—	18.00
2008Mo Proof	—	Value: 22.00				
2009Mo	—	—	—	—	—	18.00
2009Mo Proof	· —	Value: 22.00				

KM# 494.1 ONZA (Troy Ounce of Silver)
31.1000 g., 0.9990 Silver 0.9988 oz. ASW **Subject:** Libertad
Obv: National arms, eagle left **Rev:** Winged Victory **Mint:**
Mexico City

Date	Mintage	F	VF	XF	Unc	BU
1982Mo	1,049,680	—	—	—	BV	27.00
1983Mo	1,001,768	—	—	—	BV	37.00
1983Mo Proof	998	Value: 600				
1984Mo	1,014,000	—	—	—	BV	27.00
1985Mo	2,017,000	—	—	—	BV	27.00
1986Mo	1,699,426	—	—	—	BV	27.00
1986Mo Proof	30,006	Value: 35.00				
1987Mo	500,000	—	—	—	BV	50.00
1987Mo Doubled die	Inc. above	—	—	—	—	70.00
1987Mo Proof	12,000	Value: 50.00				
1988Mo	1,500,500	—	—	—	BV	55.00
1989Mo	1,396,500	—	—	—	BV	35.00
1989Mo Proof	10,000	Value: 85.00				

KM# 494.2 ONZA (Troy Ounce of Silver)
31.1000 g., 0.9990 Silver 0.9988 oz. ASW **Obv:** National
arms, eagle left **Rev:** Winged Victory **Edge:** Reeded **Mint:**
Mexico City

Date	Mintage	F	VF	XF	Unc	BU
1988Mo Proof	10,000	Value: 95.00				
1990Mo	1,200,000	—	—	—	BV	27.00
1990Mo Proof	10,000	Value: 80.00				
1991Mo	1,650,518	—	—	—	BV	42.00

KM# 494.5 ONZA (Troy Ounce of Silver)
31.1000 g., 0.9990 Silver 0.9988 oz. ASW **Subject:** Libertad
Obv: National arms, eagle left **Rev:** Winged Victory **Edge:**
Reeded edge **Mint:** Mexico City **Note:** Mule

Date	Mintage	F	VF	XF	Unc	BU
1991Mo Proof	10,000	Value: 75.00				

KM# 494.3 ONZA (Troy Ounce of Silver)
31.1000 g., 0.9990 Silver 0.9988 oz. ASW **Subject:** Libertad
Obv: National arms **Rev:** Winged Victory with revised design
and lettering **Edge:** Reeded edge **Mint:** Mexico City **Note:** Mule

Date	Mintage	F	VF	XF	Unc	BU
1991Mo	Inc. above	—	—	—	BV	45.00
1991Mo Proof	10,000	Value: 75.00				
1992Mo	2,458,000	—	—	—	BV	40.00
1992Mo Proof	10,000	Value: 75.00				

KM# 494.4 ONZA (Troy Ounce of Silver)
31.1000 g., 0.9990 Silver 0.9988 oz. ASW **Subject:** Libertad
Obv: National arms, eagle left **Rev:** Winged Victory with
revised design and lettering **Edge:** Reeded edge **Mint:**
Mexico City **Note:** Mule

Date	Mintage	F	VF	XF	Unc	BU
1993Mo	1,000,000	—	—	—	BV	30.00
1993Mo Proof	—	Value: 80.00				
1994Mo	400,000	—	—	—	BV	35.00
1994Mo Proof	10,000	Value: 75.00				
1995Mo	500,000	—	—	—	BV	35.00
1995Mo Proof	2,000	Value: 75.00				

KM# 613 ONZA (Troy Ounce of Silver)
33.6250 g., 0.9250 Silver 0.9999 oz. ASW **Obv:** National
arms, eagle left **Rev:** Winged Victory **Mint:** Mexico City

Date	Mintage	F	VF	XF	Unc	BU
1996Mo	280,001	—	—	—	—	38.00
1996Mo Proof	1,000	Value: 80.00				
1997Mo	119,999	—	—	—	—	48.00
1997Mo Proof	2,500	Value: 60.00				
1998Mo	67,000	—	—	—	—	125
1998Mo Proof	500	Value: 195				
1999Mo	95,000	—	—	—	—	40.00
1999Mo Proof	600	Value: 85.00				

KM# 639 ONZA (Troy Ounce of Silver)
31.1000 g., 0.9990 Silver 0.9988 oz. ASW **Subject:** Libertad
Obv: National arms, eagle left within center of past and present
arms **Rev:** Winged Victory **Edge:** Reeded **Mint:** Mexico City

Date	Mintage	F	VF	XF	Unc	BU
2000Mo	396,400	—	—	—	—	35.00
2000Mo Proof	2,000	Value: 70.00				
2001Mo	768,600	—	—	—	—	30.00
2001Mo Proof	4,100	Value: 70.00				
2002Mo	955,000	—	—	—	—	28.00
2002Mo Proof	1,700	Value: 75.00				
2003Mo	678,869	—	—	—	—	28.00
2003Mo Proof	5,000	Value: 65.00				
2004Mo	560,412	—	—	—	—	37.50
2004Mo Proof	5,300	Value: 65.00				
2005Mo	600,007	—	—	—	—	45.00
2005Mo Proof	1,500	Value: 75.00				
2006Mo	300,000	—	—	—	—	28.00
2006Mo Proof	4,000	Value: 70.00				
2007Mo	—	—	—	—	—	47.50
2007Mo Proof	—	Value: 75.00				
2008Mo	—	—	—	—	—	32.50
2008Mo Proof	—	Value: 75.00				
2009Mo	—	—	—	—	—	37.50
2009Mo Proof	—	Value: 75.00				

KM# 614 2 ONZAS (2 Troy Ounces of Silver)
62.2070 g., 0.9990 Silver 1.9979 oz. ASW, 48 mm. **Subject:**
Libertad **Obv:** National arms, eagle left within center of past
and present arms **Rev:** Winged Victory **Edge:** Reeded **Mint:**
Mexico City

Date	Mintage	F	VF	XF	Unc	BU
1996Mo	50,000	—	—	—	—	50.00
1996Mo Proof	1,000	Value: 85.00				
1997Mo	15,000	—	—	—	—	50.00
1997Mo Proof	1,500	Value: 70.00				
1998Mo	7,000	—	—	—	—	55.00
1998Mo Proof	400	Value: 225				
1999Mo	5,000	—	—	—	—	60.00
1999Mo Proof	280	Value: 3,530				
2000Mo	12,800	—	—	—	—	60.00
2000Mo Proof	650	Value: 90.00				
2001Mo	1,600	—	—	—	—	60.00
2001Mo Proof	1,350	Value: 80.00				

Date	Mintage	F	VF	XF	Unc	BU
2002Mo	9,000	—	—	—	—	55.00
2002Mo Proof	400	Value: 95.00				
2003Mo	9,000	—	—	—	—	55.00
2003Mo Proof	400	Value: 95.00				
2004Mo	11,349	—	—	—	—	50.00
2004Mo Proof	1,360	Value: 80.00				
2005Mo	1,200	—	—	—	—	50.00
2005Mo Proof	740	Value: 75.00				
2006Mo	5,800	—	—	—	—	50.00
2006Mo Proof	1,100	Value: 75.00				
2007Mo	—	—	—	—	—	50.00
2007Mo Proof	—	Value: 85.00				
2008Mo	—	—	—	—	—	55.00
2008Mo Proof	—	Value: 85.00				
2009Mo	—	—	—	—	—	55.00
2009Mo Proof	—	Value: 85.00				

Date	Mintage	F	VF	XF	Unc	BU
2004Mo Prooflike	500	—	—	—	—	1,200
2005Mo Prooflike	874	—	—	—	—	1,150
2006Mo Prooflike	—	—	—	—	—	1,100
2007Mo Prooflike	—	—	—	—	—	1,100
2008Mo Prooflike	—	—	—	—	—	1,100
2009Mo Prooflike	—	—	—	—	—	1,100

GOLD BULLION COINAGE

KM# 530 1/20 ONZA (1/20 Ounce of Pure Gold)
1.7500 g., 0.9000 Gold 0.0506 oz. AGW **Obv:** Winged Victory **Rev:** Calendar stone **Mint:** Mexico City

Date	Mintage	F	VF	XF	Unc	BU
1987Mo	—	—	—	—	—	275
1988Mo	—	—	—	—	—	—

KM# 589 1/20 ONZA (1/20 Ounce of Pure Gold)
1.5551 g., 0.9990 Gold 0.0499 oz. AGW **Obv:** Winged Victory **Rev:** National arms, eagle left **Mint:** Mexico City

Date	Mintage	F	VF	XF	Unc	BU
1991Mo	10,000	—	—	—	—	BV+30%
1992Mo	65,225	—	—	—	—	BV+30%
1993Mo	10,000	—	—	—	—	BV+30%
1994Mo	10,000	—	—	—	—	BV+30%

KM# 642 1/20 ONZA (1/20 Ounce of Pure Gold)
1.5551 g., 0.9990 Gold 0.0499 oz. AGW **Obv:** National arms, eagle left **Rev:** Native working **Mint:** Mexico City

Date	Mintage	F	VF	XF	Unc	BU
2000Mo Proof	—	Value: 75.00				

KM# 671 1/20 ONZA (1/20 Ounce of Pure Gold)
1.5551 g., 0.9990 Gold 0.0499 oz. AGW, 16 mm. **Obv:** National arms, eagle left **Rev:** Winged Victory **Edge:** Reeded **Mint:** Mexico City **Note:** Design similar to KM#609. Value estimates do not include the high taxes and surcharges added to the issue prices by the Mexican Government.

Date	Mintage	F	VF	XF	Unc	BU
2000Mo	5,300	—	—	—	—	BV+30%
2002Mo	5,000	—	—	—	—	BV+30%
2003Mo	300	—	—	—	—	BV+30%
2004Mo	6,318	—	—	—	—	BV+30%
2005Mo	1,520	—	—	—	—	BV+30%
2005Mo Proof	200	BV+35%				
2006Mo	3,200	—	—	—	—	BV+30%
2006Mo Proof	520	BV+35%				
2007Mo Proof	—	BV+35%				

KM# 615 5 ONZAS (5 Troy Ounces of Silver)
155.5175 g., 0.9990 Silver 4.9948 oz. ASW, 65 mm. **Subject:** Libertad **Obv:** National arms, eagle left within center of past and present arms **Rev:** Winged Victory **Edge:** Reeded **Mint:** Mexico City **Note:** Illustration reduced.

Date	Mintage	F	VF	XF	Unc	BU
1996Mo	20,000	—	—	—	—	115
1996Mo Proof	1,000	Value: 175				
1997Mo	10,000	—	—	—	—	115
1997Mo Proof	1,500	Value: 175				
1998Mo	3,500	—	—	—	—	200
1998Mo Proof	400	Value: 600				
1999Mo	2,800	—	—	—	—	110
1999Mo Proof	100	Value: 750				
2000Mo	5,080	—	—	—	—	110
2000Mo Proof	650	Value: 200				
2001Mo	3,120	—	—	—	—	110
2001Mo Proof	1,450	Value: 200				
2002Mo	5,500	—	—	—	—	110
2002Mo Proof	400	Value: 200				
2003Mo	5,500	—	—	—	—	100
2003Mo Proof	495	Value: 150				
2004Mo	6,324	—	—	—	—	100
2004Mo Proof	1,805	Value: 135				
2005Mo	790	—	—	—	—	125
2005Mo Proof	900	Value: 135				
2006Mo	3,000	—	—	—	—	100
2006Mo Proof	1,000	Value: 160				
2007Mo	—	—	—	—	—	100
2007Mo Proof	—	Value: 125				
2008Mo	—	—	—	—	—	125
2008Mo Proof	—	Value: 165				
2009Mo	—	—	—	—	—	135
2009Mo Proof	—	Value: 165				

KM# 677 KILO (32.15 Troy Ounces of Silver)
999.9775 g., 0.9990 Silver 32.116 oz. ASW, 110 mm. **Subject:** Collector Bullion **Obv:** National arms in center of past and present arms **Rev:** Winged Victory **Edge:** Reeded **Mint:** Mexico City

Date	Mintage	F	VF	XF	Unc	BU
2001Mo Prooflike	—	—	—	—	—	1,480
2002Mo Prooflike	1,100	—	—	—	—	1,150
2003Mo Prooflike	2,234	—	—	—	—	1,100

KM# 628 1/15 ONZA (1/15 Ounce of Pure Gold)
0.9990 Gold **Obv:** Winged Victory above legend **Rev:** National arms, eagle left within circle **Mint:** Mexico City

Date	Mintage	F	VF	XF	Unc	BU
1987Mo	—	—	—	—	—	275

KM# 541 1/10 ONZA (1/10 Ounce of Pure Gold)
3.1103 g., 0.9990 Gold 0.0999 oz. AGW **Obv:** National arms, eagle left **Rev:** Winged Victory **Mint:** Mexico City

Date	Mintage	F	VF	XF	Unc	BU
1991Mo	10,000	—	—	—	—	BV+20%
1992Mo	50,777	—	—	—	—	BV+20%
1993Mo	10,000	—	—	—	—	BV+20%
1994Mo	10,000	—	—	—	—	BV+20%

KM# 672 1/10 ONZA (1/10 Ounce of Pure Gold)
3.1103 g., 0.9990 Gold 0.0999 oz. AGW, 20 mm. **Obv:** National arms, eagle left **Rev:** Winged Victory **Edge:** Reeded **Mint:** Mexico City **Note:** Design similar to KM#610. Value estimates do not include the high taxes and surcharges added to the issue prices by the Mexican Government.

Date	Mintage	F	VF	XF	Unc	BU
2000Mo	3,500	—	—	—	—	BV+20%
2002Mo	5,000	—	—	—	—	BV+20%

Date	Mintage	F	VF	XF	Unc	BU
2003Mo	300	—	—	—	—	—
2004Mo	2,500	—	—	—	—	BV+20%
2005Mo	500	—	—	—	—	BV+20%
2005Mo Proof	200	BV+22%				
2006Mo	2,500	—	—	—	—	BV+20%
2006Mo Proof	520	BV+22%				
2007Mo	—	—	—	—	—	BV+20%

KM# 487   1/4 ONZA (1/4 Ounce of Pure Gold)
8.6396 g., 0.9000 Gold 0.2500 oz. AGW **Obv:** National arms, eagle left **Rev:** Winged Victory **Mint:** Mexico City **Note:** Similar to KM#488.

Date	Mintage	F	VF	XF	Unc	BU
1981Mo	313,000	—	—	—	—	BV+11%
1982Mo	—	—	—	—	—	BV+11%

KM# 590   1/4 ONZA (1/4 Ounce of Pure Gold)
7.7758 g., 0.9990 Gold 0.2497 oz. AGW **Obv:** Winged Victory above legend **Rev:** National arms, eagle left **Mint:** Mexico City

Date	Mintage	F	VF	XF	Unc	BU
1991Mo	10,000	—	—	—	—	BV+11%
1992Mo	28,106	—	—	—	—	BV+11%
1993Mo	2,500	—	—	—	—	BV+11%
1994Mo	2,500	—	—	—	—	BV+11%

KM# 673   1/4 ONZA (1/4 Ounce of Pure Gold)
7.7758 g., 0.9990 Gold 0.2497 oz. AGW, 26.9 mm. **Obv:** National arms, eagle left **Rev:** Winged Victory **Edge:** Reeded **Mint:** Mexico City **Note:** Design similar to KM#611. Value estimates do not include the high taxes and surcharges added to the issue prices by the Mexican Government.

Date	Mintage	F	VF	XF	Unc	BU
2000Mo	2,500	—	—	—	—	BV+12%
2002Mo	5,000	—	—	—	—	BV+12%
2003Mo	300	—	—	—	—	—
2004Mo	2,000	—	—	—	—	BV+12%
2004Mo Proof	1,000	BV+15%				
2005Mo	500	—	—	—	—	BV+12%
2005Mo Proof	1,800	BV+15%				
2006Mo	1,500	—	—	—	—	BV+12%
2006Mo Proof	2,120	BV+12%				
2007Mo	—	—	—	—	—	BV+12%

KM# 488   1/2 ONZA (1/2 Ounce of Pure Gold)
17.2792 g., 0.9000 Gold 0.5000 oz. AGW **Obv:** National arms, eagle left **Rev:** Winged Victory **Mint:** Mexico City

Date	Mintage	F	VF	XF	Unc	BU
1981Mo	193,000	—	—	—	—	BV+8%
1982Mo	—	—	—	—	—	BV+8%
1989Mo Proof	704	Value: 675				

KM# 591   1/2 ONZA (1/2 Ounce of Pure Gold)
15.5517 g., 0.9990 Gold 0.4995 oz. AGW **Obv:** Winged Victory above legend **Rev:** National arms, eagle left **Mint:** Mexico City

Date	Mintage	F	VF	XF	Unc	BU
1991Mo	10,000	—	—	—	—	BV+8%
1992Mo	25,220	—	—	—	—	BV+8%
1993Mo	2,500	—	—	—	—	BV+8%
1994Mo	2,500	—	—	—	—	BV+8%

KM# 674   1/2 ONZA (1/2 Ounce of Pure Gold)
15.5517 g., 0.9990 Gold 0.4995 oz. AGW, 32.9 mm. **Obv:** National arms, eagle left **Rev:** Winged Victory **Edge:** Reeded **Mint:** Mexico City **Note:** Design similar to KM#612. Value estimates do not include the high taxes and surcharges added to the issue prices by the Mexican Government.

Date	Mintage	F	VF	XF	Unc	BU
2000Mo	1,500	—	—	—	—	BV+8%
2002Mo	5,000	—	—	—	—	BV+8%
2003Mo	300	—	—	—	—	—
2004Mo	1,000	—	—	—	—	BV+8%
2005Mo	500	—	—	—	—	BV+8%
2005Mo Proof	200	BV+12%				

Date	Mintage	F	VF	XF	Unc	BU
2006Mo	500	—	—	—	—	BV+8%
2006Mo Proof	520	BV+12%				
2007Mo	—	—	—	—	—	BV+8%

KM# 489   ONZA (Ounce of Pure Gold)
34.5585 g., 0.9000 Gold 0.9999 oz. AGW **Obv:** National arms, eagle left **Rev:** Winged Victory **Mint:** Mexico City **Note:** Similar to KM#488.

Date	Mintage	F	VF	XF	Unc	BU
1981Mo	596,000	—	—	—	—	BV+3%
1985Mo	—	—	—	—	—	BV+3%
1988Mo	—	—	—	—	—	BV+3%

KM# 592   ONZA (Ounce of Pure Gold)
31.1035 g., 0.9990 Gold 0.9990 oz. AGW **Obv:** Winged Victory above legend **Rev:** National arms, eagle left **Mint:** Mexico City

Date	Mintage	F	VF	XF	Unc	BU
1991Mo	109,193	—	—	—	—	BV+3%
1992Mo	46,281	—	—	—	—	BV+3%
1993Mo	10,000	—	—	—	—	BV+3%
1994Mo	1,000	—	—	—	—	BV+3%

KM# 675   ONZA (Ounce of Pure Gold)
31.1035 g., 0.9990 Gold 0.9990 oz. AGW, 40 mm. **Obv:** National arms, eagle left **Rev:** Winged Victory **Edge:** Reeded **Mint:** Mexico City **Note:** Design similar to KM#639. Value estimates do not include the high taxes and surcharges added to the issue prices by the Mexican Government.

Date	Mintage	F	VF	XF	Unc	BU
2000Mo	2,730	—	—	—	—	BV+3%
2002Mo	15,000	—	—	—	—	BV+3%
2003Mo	500	—	—	—	—	BV+3%
2004Mo	4,810	—	—	—	—	BV+3%
2004Mo Proof	150	BV+5%				
2005Mo	2,000	—	—	—	—	BV+3%
2005Mo Proof	50	BV+5%				
2006Mo	4,000	—	—	—	—	BV+3%
2006Mo Proof	520	BV+5%				

PLATINUM BULLION COINAGE

KM# 538   1/4 ONZA (1/4 Ounce)
7.7775 g., 0.9990 Platinum 0.2498 oz. APW **Obv:** National arms, eagle left **Rev:** Winged Victory **Mint:** Mexico City

Date	Mintage	F	VF	XF	Unc	BU
1989Mo	704	Value: 500				

BULLION COINAGE
Pre-Columbian • Azteca Series

KM# 644   NUEVO PESO
7.7700 g., 0.9990 Silver 0.2496 oz. ASW, 26.8 mm. **Subject:** Eagle Warrior **Obv:** National arms, eagle left within D-shaped circle and dotted border **Rev:** Eagle warrior within D-shaped circle and dotted border **Edge:** Reeded **Mint:** Mexico City

Date	Mintage	F	VF	XF	Unc	BU
1993Mo	1,500	—	—	—	—	18.00
1993 Proof	900	Value: 30.00				

KM# 645   2 NUEVO PESOS
15.4200 g., 0.9990 Silver 0.4952 oz. ASW, 32.9 mm.
Subject: Eagle Warrior **Obv:** National arms, eagle left **Rev:**
Eagle warrior **Edge:** Reeded **Mint:** Mexico City

Date	Mintage	F	VF	XF	Unc	BU
1993Mo	1,500	—	—	—	—	18.00
1993 Proof	800	Value: 40.00				

KM# 646   5 NUEVO PESOS
31.0500 g., 0.9990 Silver 0.9972 oz. ASW, 40 mm. **Subject:**
Eagle Warrior **Obv:** National arms, eagle left **Rev:** Eagle
warrior **Edge:** Reeded **Mint:** Mexico City

Date	Mintage	F	VF	XF	Unc	BU
1993	2,000	—	—	—	—	35.00
1993 Proof	1,000	Value: 70.00				

KM# 647   5 NUEVO PESOS
31.0000 g., 0.9990 Silver 0.9956 oz. ASW, 40 mm. **Subject:**
Xochipilli **Obv:** National arms, eagle left within D-shaped circle
and flower blossom border **Rev:** Seated figure sculpture within
D-shaped circle and flower blossom border **Edge:** Reeded
Mint: Mexico City

Date	Mintage	F	VF	XF	Unc	BU
1993	2,000	—	—	—	—	35.00
1993 Proof	800	Value: 85.00				

KM# 649   5 NUEVO PESOS
31.0000 g., 0.9990 Silver 0.9956 oz. ASW, 40 mm. **Subject:**
Huchucteotl **Obv:** National arms, eagle left within D-shaped
circle and designed border **Rev:** Aztec sculpture within D-
shaped circle and designed border **Edge:** Reeded

Date	Mintage	F	VF	XF	Unc	BU
1993	5,000	—	—	—	—	30.00
1993 Proof	800	Value: 85.00				

KM# 648   5 NUEVO PESOS
31.0000 g., 0.9990 Silver 0.9956 oz. ASW, 40 mm. **Subject:**
Brasco Efigie **Obv:** National arms, eagle left within D-shaped
circle and designed border **Rev:** Sculpture within D-shaped
circle and designed border **Edge:** Reeded

Date	Mintage	F	VF	XF	Unc	BU
1993	2,000	—	—	—	—	50.00
1993 Proof	500	Value: 95.00				

KM# 650   10 NUEVO PESOS
155.3100 g., 0.9990 Silver 4.9881 oz. ASW, 64 mm.
Subject: Piedra de Tizoc **Obv:** National arms, eagle left **Rev:**
Warrior capturing woman **Edge:** Reeded **Mint:** Mexico City
Note: Illustration reduced, similar to 100 Pesos, KM# 557

Date	Mintage	F	VF	XF	Unc	BU
1992 Proof	—	Value: 300				
1993	1,000	—	—	—	—	110
1993 Proof	1,000	Value: 185				

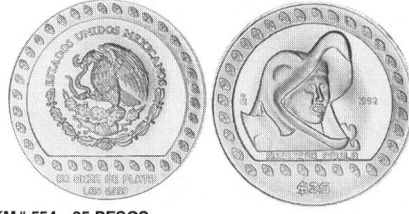

KM# 554   25 PESOS
7.7758 g., 0.9990 Silver 0.2497 oz. ASW **Obv:** National
arms, eagle left within D-shaped circle and designed border
Rev: Eagle warrior right within D-shaped circle and a designed
border **Mint:** Mexico City

Date	Mintage	F	VF	XF	Unc	BU
1992	50,000	—	—	—	18.00	—
1992 Proof	3,000	Value: 30.00				

KM# 555   50 PESOS
15.5517 g., 0.9990 Silver 0.4995 oz. ASW **Obv:** National

arms, eagle left within D-shaped circle designed border **Rev:**
Eagle warrior right within D-shaped circle and designed
border **Mint:** Mexico City

Date	Mintage	F	VF	XF	Unc	BU
1992	50,000	—	—	—	25.00	—
1992 Proof	3,000	Value: 40.00				

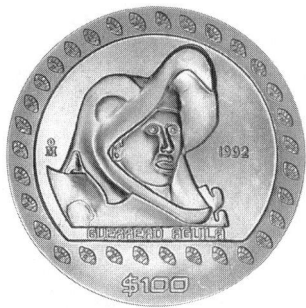

KM# 556   100 PESOS
31.1035 g., 0.9990 Silver 0.9990 oz. ASW **Obv:** National
arms, eagle left **Rev:** Eagle warrior **Mint:** Mexico City

Date	Mintage	F	VF	XF	Unc	BU
1992	205,000	—	—	—	35.00	47.50
1992	4,000	Value: 75.00				

KM# 562   100 PESOS
31.1035 g., 0.9990 Silver 0.9990 oz. ASW **Obv:** National
arms, eagle left within D-shaped circle and designed border
Rev: Seated figure sculpture within D-shaped circle and
designed border **Mint:** Mexico City

Date	Mintage	F	VF	XF	Unc	BU
1992 Proof	4,000	Value: 90.00				

KM# 563   100 PESOS
31.1035 g., 0.9990 Silver 0.9990 oz. ASW **Obv:** National
arms, eagle left within D-shaped circle and designed border
Rev: Brasero Efigie - The God of Rain within D-shaped circle
and designed border **Mint:** Mexico City

Date	Mintage	F	VF	XF	Unc	BU
1992 Proof	4,000	Value: 72.00				

KM# 564   100 PESOS
31.1035 g., 0.9990 Silver 0.9990 oz. ASW   **Obv:** National
arms, eagle left within D-shaped circle and designed border
Rev: Huehueteotl - The God of Fire within D-shaped circle
and designed border **Mint:** Mexico City

Date	Mintage	F	VF	XF	Unc	BU
1992 Proof	4,000	Value: 65.00				

KM# 558   250 PESOS
7.7758 g., 0.9990 Gold 0.2497 oz. AGW   **Subject:** Native
Culture **Obv:** National arms, eagle left within D-shaped circle
and designed border **Rev:** Sculpture of Jaguar head within
D-shaped circle and designed border **Mint:** Mexico City

Date	Mintage	F	VF	XF	Unc	BU
1992	10,000	—	—	—	—	325
1992 Proof	2,000	Value: 350				

KM# 559   500 PESOS
15.5517 g., 0.9990 Gold 0.4995 oz. AGW   **Subject:** Native
Culture **Obv:** National arms, eagle left within D-shaped circle
and designed border **Rev:** Sculpture of Jaguar head within
D-shaped circle and designed border **Mint:** Mexico City

Date	Mintage	F	VF	XF	Unc	BU
1992	10,000	—	—	—	—	625
1992 Proof	2,000	Value: 650				

KM# 560   1000 PESOS
31.1035 g., 0.9990 Gold 0.9990 oz. AGW   **Subject:** Native
Culture **Obv:** National arms, eagle left within D-shaped circle
and designed border **Rev:** Sculpture of Jaguar head within
D-shaped circle and designed border **Mint:** Mexico City

Date	Mintage	F	VF	XF	Unc	BU
1992	17,850	—	—	—	—	1,250
1992 Proof	2,000	Value: 1,300				

KM# 557   10000 PESOS
155.5175 g., 0.9990 Silver 4.9948 oz. ASW, 64 mm.
Subject: Piedra De Tizoc **Obv:** National arms, eagle left
within D-shaped circle and designed border **Rev:** Native
warriors within D-shaped circle and designed border **Mint:**
Mexico City **Note:** Similar to 10 Nuevo Pesos, KM#650

Date	Mintage	F	VF	XF	Unc	BU
1992	51,900	—	—	—	—	110
1992 Proof	3,300	Value: 275				

BULLION COINAGE
Pre-Columbian •
Central Veracruz Series

KM# 567   NUEVO PESO
7.7601 g., 0.9990 Silver 0.2492 oz. ASW   **Subject:** Bajo
relieve de el Tajin **Obv:** National arms, eagle left within D-
shaped circle and designed border **Rev:** Design within D-
shaped circle and designed border **Mint:** Mexico City

Date	Mintage	F	VF	XF	Unc	BU
1993	100,000	—	—	—	—	20.00
1993 Proof	3,300	Value: 35.00				

KM# 568   2 NUEVO PESOS
15.5516 g., 0.9990 Silver 0.4995 oz. ASW   **Subject:** Bajo
relieve de el Tajin **Obv:** National arms, eagle left within D-
shaped circle and designed border **Rev:** Design within D-
shaped circle and designed border **Mint:** Mexico City

Date	Mintage	F	VF	XF	Unc	BU
1993	100,000	—	—	—	—	25.00
1993 Proof	3,000	Value: 35.00				

KM# 569   5 NUEVO PESOS
31.1035 g., 0.9990 Silver 0.9990 oz. ASW   **Subject:** Bajo
relieve de el Tajin **Obv:** National arms, eagle left within D-
shaped circle and designed border **Rev:** Design within D-
shaped circle and designed border **Mint:** Mexico City

Date	Mintage	F	VF	XF	Unc	BU
1993	100,000	—	—	—	—	30.00
1993 Proof	3,000	Value: 70.00				

KM# 582   5 NUEVO PESOS
31.1035 g., 0.9990 Silver 0.9990 oz. ASW   **Subject:** Palma
Con Cocodrilo **Obv:** National arms, eagle left within D-shaped
circle and designed border **Rev:** Aerial view of crocodile within
D-shaped circle and designed border **Mint:** Mexico City

Date	Mintage	F	VF	XF	Unc	BU
1993	4,500	—	—	—	—	30.00
1993 Proof	2,650	Value: 75.00				

KM# 583 5 NUEVO PESOS
31.1035 g., 0.9990 Silver 0.9990 oz. ASW **Subject:** Anciano Con Brasero **Obv:** National arms, eagle left within D-shaped circle and designed border **Rev:** Kneeling figure sculpture within D-shaped circle and designed border **Mint:** Mexico City

Date	Mintage	F	VF	XF	Unc	BU
1993	2,650	—	—	—	—	30.00
1993 Proof	1,500	Value: 75.00				

KM# 584 5 NUEVO PESOS
31.1035 g., 0.9990 Silver 0.9990 oz. ASW **Subject:** Carita Sonriente **Obv:** National arms, eagle left **Rev:** Sculptured head **Mint:** Mexico City

Date	Mintage	F	VF	XF	Unc	BU
1993	4,500	—	—	—	—	30.00
1993 Proof	3,300	Value: 75.00				

KM# 570 10 NUEVO PESOS
115.5170 g., 0.9990 Silver 3.7101 oz. ASW, 64 mm.
Subject: Piramide Del El Tajin **Obv:** National arms, eagle left within flat shaped circle and designed border **Rev:** Pyramid within flat shaped circle and designed border **Note:** Illustration reduced.

Date	Mintage	F	VF	XF	Unc	BU
1993	50,000	—	—	—	—	110
1993 Proof	3,100	Value: 185				

KM# 585 25 NUEVO PESOS
7.7758 g., 0.9990 Gold 0.2497 oz. AGW **Subject:** Hacha Ceremonial **Obv:** National arms, eagle left **Rev:** Mask left **Note:** Similar to 100 New Pesos, KM#587.

Date	Mintage	F	VF	XF	Unc	BU
1993	15,500	—	—	—	—	325
1993 Proof	800	Value: 365				

KM# 586 50 NUEVO PESOS
15.5517 g., 0.9990 Gold 0.4995 oz. AGW **Subject:** Hacha Ceremonial **Obv:** National arms, eagle left **Rev:** Mask left **Note:** Similar to 100 New Pesos, KM#587.

Date	Mintage	F	VF	XF	Unc	BU
1993	15,500	—	—	—	—	625
1993 Proof	500	Value: 675				

KM# 587 100 NUEVO PESOS
31.1035 g., 0.9990 Gold 0.9990 oz. AGW **Subject:** Hacha Ceremonial **Obv:** National arms, eagle left **Rev:** Mask left

Date	Mintage	F	VF	XF	Unc	BU
1993	7,150	—	—	—	—	1,275
1993 Proof	500	Value: 1,350				

BULLION COINAGE
Pre-Columbian • Mayan Series

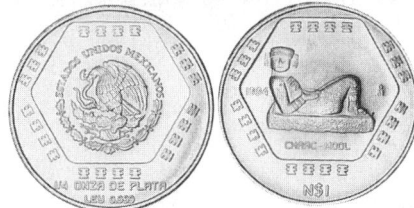

KM# 572 NUEVO PESO
7.7601 g., 0.9990 Silver 0.2492 oz. ASW **Subject:** Chaac Mool **Obv:** National arms, eagle left within six sided shield and designed border **Rev:** Reclining figure within six sided shield and designed border **Mint:** Mexico City

Date	Mintage	F	VF	XF	Unc	BU
1994 Matte	30,000	—	—	—	—	20.00
1994 Proof	2,500	Value: 35.00				

KM# 573 2 NUEVO PESOS
15.5516 g., 0.9990 Silver 0.4995 oz. ASW **Subject:** Chaac Mool **Obv:** National arms, eagle left within six sided shield and designed border **Rev:** Reclining figure within six sided shield and designed border **Mint:** Mexico City

Date	Mintage	F	VF	XF	Unc	BU
1994 Matte	30,000	—	—	—	—	25.00
1994 Proof	2,500	Value: 35.00				

KM# 574 5 NUEVO PESOS
31.1035 g., 0.9990 Silver 0.9990 oz. ASW **Subject:** Chaac Mool **Obv:** National arms, eagle left within six sided shield and designed border **Rev:** Reclining figure within six sided shield and designed border **Mint:** Mexico City

Date	Mintage	F	VF	XF	Unc	BU
1994 Matte	50,000	—	—	—	—	28.00
1994 Proof	3,000	Value: 70.00				

KM# 575 5 NUEVO PESOS
31.1035 g., 0.9990 Silver 0.9990 oz. ASW **Subject:** Chaac Mool **Obv:** National arms, eagle left within six sided shield and designed border **Rev:** Tomb of Palenque Memorial Stone within six sided shield and designed border **Mint:** Mexico City

Date	Mintage	F	VF	XF	Unc	BU
1994	4,500	—	—	—	—	28.00
1994 Proof	2,800	Value: 70.00				

KM# 577 5 NUEVO PESOS
31.1035 g., 0.9990 Silver 0.9990 oz. ASW **Subject:** Mascaron Del Dios Chaac **Rev:** Elaborately carved wall segment **Mint:** Mexico City

Date	Mintage	F	VF	XF	Unc	BU
1994	4,500	—	—	—	—	28.00
1994 Proof	2,500	Value: 70.00				

KM# 578 5 NUEVO PESOS
31.1035 g., 0.9990 Silver 0.9990 oz. ASW **Subject:** Dintel 26 **Obv:** National arms, eagle left within six sided shield and designed border **Rev:** Two seated figures wall carving within six sided shield and designed border

Date	Mintage	F	VF	XF	Unc	BU
1994	4,500	—	—	—	—	45.00
1994 Proof	2,600	Value: 75.00				

KM# 676 10 NUEVO PESOS
155.5175 g., 0.9990 Silver 4.9948 oz. ASW, 65 mm.
Subject: Piramide Del Castillo **Obv:** National arms, eagle left above metal content statement **Rev:** Pyramid above two-line inscription **Rev. Inscription:** PIRAMIDE DEL CASTILLO / CHICHEN-ITZA **Edge:** Reeded **Mint:** Mexico City

Date	Mintage	F	VF	XF	Unc	BU
1993Mo Proof	—	Value: 650				

KM# 576 10 NUEVO PESOS
115.5170 g., 0.9990 Silver 3.7101 oz. ASW, 64 mm.
Subject: Piramide del Castillo **Obv:** National arms, eagle left **Rev:** Pyramid **Note:** Illustration reduced.

Date	Mintage	F	VF	XF	Unc	BU
1994	20,000	—	—	—	—	120
1994 Proof	2,100	Value: 200				

KM# 579 25 NUEVO PESOS
7.7758 g., 0.9990 Gold 0.2497 oz. AGW **Subject:** Personaje de Jaina **Rev:** Seated figure

Date	Mintage	F	VF	XF	Unc	BU
1994	2,000	—	—	—	—	325
1994 Proof	500	Value: 365				

KM# 580 50 NUEVO PESOS
15.5517 g., 0.9990 Gold 0.4995 oz. AGW **Subject:** Personaje de Jaina **Rev:** Seated figure

Date	Mintage	F	VF	XF	Unc	BU
1994	1,000	—	—	—	—	625
1994 Proof	500	Value: 675				

KM# 581 100 NUEVO PESOS
31.1035 g., 0.9990 Gold 0.9990 oz. AGW **Subject:** Personaje de Jaina **Obv:** National arms, eagle left within six sided shield and designed border **Rev:** Seated figure within six sided shield and designed border

Date	Mintage	F	VF	XF	Unc	BU
1994	1,000	—	—	—	—	1,275
1994 Proof	500	Value: 1,350				

BULLION COINAGE
Pre-Columbian • Olmec Series

KM# 593 PESO
7.7750 g., 0.9990 Silver 0.2497 oz. ASW **Subject:** Senor De Las Limas **Obv:** National arms, eagle left within square and designed border **Rev:** Sitting figure facing within square and designed border **Mint:** Mexico City **Note:** Similar to 5 Pesos, KM#595.

Date	Mintage	F	VF	XF	Unc	BU
1996	4,000	—	—	—	—	20.00
1996 Proof	2,200	Value: 35.00				
1998 Matte	2,400	—	—	—	—	22.00

KM# 594   2 PESOS
15.5517 g., 0.9990 Silver 0.4995 oz. ASW **Subject:** Senor
De Las Limas **Obv:** National arms, eagle left within square
and designed border **Rev:** Sitting figure facing within square
and designed border **Mint:** Mexico City **Note:** Similar to 5
Pesos, KM#595.

Date	Mintage	F	VF	XF	Unc	BU
1996	4,000	—	—	—	—	25.00
1996 Proof	2,200	Value: 35.00				
1998 Matte	2,400	—	—	—	—	28.00

KM# 597   5 PESOS
31.1035 g., 0.9990 Silver 0.9990 oz. ASW **Subject:** El
Luchador **Obv:** National arms, eagle left **Rev:** El Luchador

Date	Mintage	F	VF	XF	Unc	BU
1996	4,500	—	—	—	—	30.00
1996 Proof	2,700	Value: 70.00				
1998 Matte	2,000	—	—	—	—	35.00

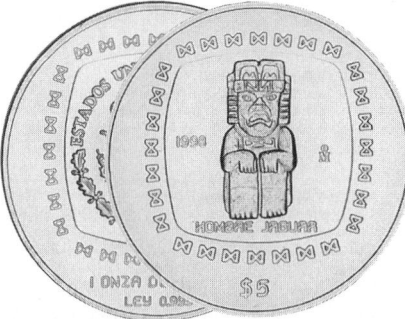

KM# 596   5 PESOS
31.1035 g., 0.9990 Silver 0.9990 oz. ASW **Subject:** Hombre
Jaguar **Obv:** National arms, eagle left within square and
designed border **Rev:** Statue facing within square and
designed border

Date	Mintage	F	VF	XF	Unc	BU
1996	1,500	—	—	—	—	110
1996 Proof	2,800	Value: 100				
1998 Matte	6,000	—	—	—	—	35.00
1998 Proof	4,800	Value: 75.00				

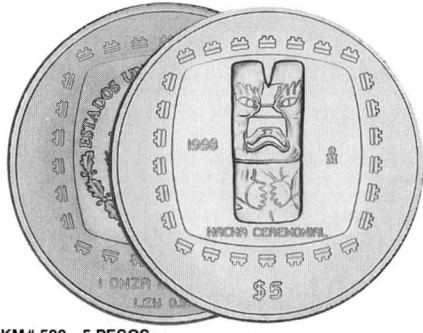

KM# 598   5 PESOS
31.1035 g., 0.9990 Silver 0.9990 oz. ASW **Subject:** Hacha
Ceremonial **Obv:** National arms, eagle left within square and
designed border **Rev:** Statue within square and designed
border

Date	Mintage	F	VF	XF	Unc	BU
1996	4,500	—	—	—	—	30.00
1996 Proof	2,700	Value: 70.00				
1998 Matte	2,000	—	—	—	—	35.00

KM# 595   5 PESOS
31.1035 g., 0.9990 Silver 0.9990 oz. ASW **Subject:** Senor
De Las Limas **Obv:** National arms, eagle left within square
and designed border **Rev:** Seated figure facing within square
and designed border

Date	Mintage	F	VF	XF	Unc	BU
1996	4,000	—	—	—	—	30.00
1996 Proof	3,000	Value: 70.00				
1998 Matte	3,400	—	—	—	—	32.00

KM# 599   10 PESOS
115.5170 g., 0.9990 Silver 3.7101 oz. ASW, 64 mm.
Subject: Cabeza Olmeca **Obv:** National arms, eagle left **Rev:**
Native mask **Note:** Illustration reduced.

Date	Mintage	F	VF	XF	Unc	BU
1996	2,000	—	—	—	—	115
1996 Proof	2,750	Value: 180				
1998 Matte	2,150	—	—	—	—	115

KM# 600 25 PESOS
7.7758 g., 0.9990 Gold 0.2497 oz. AGW **Subject:** Sacerdote
Obv: National arms, eagle left **Rev:** Sculpture **Note:** Similar
to 100 Pesos, KM#602.

Date	Mintage	F	VF	XF	Unc	BU
1996	500	—	—	—	—	350
1996 Proof	750	Value: 365				

KM# 601 50 PESOS
15.5517 g., 0.9990 Gold 0.4995 oz. AGW **Subject:**
Sacerdote **Obv:** National arms, eagle left **Rev:** Sculpture
Note: Similar to 100 Pesos, KM#602.

Date	Mintage	F	VF	XF	Unc	BU
1996 Proof	500	Value: 675				
1996	500	—	—	—	—	650

KM# 602 100 PESOS
31.1035 g., 0.9990 Gold 0.9990 oz. AGW **Subject:**
Sacerdote **Obv:** National arms, eagle left within square and
designed border **Rev:** Sculpture within square and designed
border

Date	Mintage	F	VF	XF	Unc	BU
1996	500	—	—	—	—	1,300
1996 Proof	500	Value: 1,350				

BULLION COINAGE
Pre-Columbian • Teotihuancan Series

KM# 617 PESO
7.7759 g., 0.9990 Silver 0.2497 oz. ASW **Subject:** Disco De
La Muerte **Obv:** National arms, eagle left within oblong circle
and designed border **Rev:** Sculpture within oblong circle and
designed border **Mint:** Mexico City

Date	Mintage	F	VF	XF	Unc	BU
1997	3,000	—	—	—	—	20.00
1997 Proof	1,600	Value: 35.00				
1998 Proof	500	Value: 45.00				
1998 Matte	2,400	—	—	—	—	25.00

KM# 618 2 PESOS
15.5517 g., 0.9990 Silver 0.4995 oz. ASW **Subject:** Disco
De La Muerte **Obv:** National arms, eagle left within oblong
circle and designed border **Rev:** Sculpture within oblong circle
and designed border **Mint:** Mexico City

Date	Mintage	F	VF	XF	Unc	BU
1997	3,000	—	—	—	—	25.00
1997 Proof	1,600	Value: 35.00				
1998	2,400	—	—	—	—	30.00
1998 Proof	500	Value: 50.00				

KM# 621 5 PESOS
31.1035 g., 0.9990 Silver 0.9990 oz. ASW **Subject:**
Teotihuacan - Vasija **Obv:** National arms, eagle left within
oval and designed border **Rev:** Seated woman joined to
pottery vase within oval and designed border

Date	Mintage	F	VF	XF	Unc	BU
1997	4,500	—	—	—	—	30.00
1997 Proof	Est. 1,800	Value: 75.00				
1998 Proof	500	Value: 150				
1998 Matte	2,000	—	—	—	—	35.00

KM# 622 5 PESOS
31.1035 g., 0.9990 Silver 0.9990 oz. ASW **Subject:**
Teotihuacan - Jugador de Pelota **Obv:** National arms, eagle left

Date	Mintage	F	VF	XF	Unc	BU
1997	4,500	—	—	—	—	30.00
1997 Proof	Est. 1,800	Value: 75.00				
1998 Proof	500	Value: 150				
1998 Matte	2,000	—	—	—	—	35.00

KM# 619 5 PESOS
31.1035 g., 0.9990 Silver 0.9990 oz. ASW **Subject:**
Teotihuacan - Disco de la Muerte **Obv:** National arms, eagle
left within oblong circle and designed border **Rev:** Sculpture
within oblong circle and designed border

Date	Mintage	F	VF	XF	Unc	BU
1997	3,500	—	—	—	—	30.00
1997 Proof	Est. 1,800	Value: 75.00				
1998	3,400	—	—	—	—	32.00
1998 Proof	500	Value: 150				

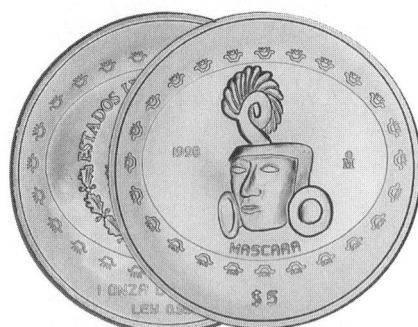

KM# 620   5 PESOS
31.1035 g., 0.9990 Silver 0.9990 oz. ASW **Subject:**
Teotihuacan - Mascara **Obv:** National arms, eagle left within
oblong circle and designed border **Rev:** Face sculpture within
oblong circle and designed border

Date	Mintage	F	VF	XF	Unc	BU
1997	4,500	—	—	—	—	30.00
1997 Proof	Est. 1,800	Value: 75.00				
1998	2,000	—	—	—	—	35.00
1998 Proof	500	Value: 150				

KM# 623   10 PESOS
155.5175 g., 0.9990 Silver 4.9948 oz. ASW, 64 mm.
Subject: Piramide Del Sol **Obv:** National arms, eagle left
within oblong circle and designed border **Rev:** Pyramid within
oblong circle and designed border **Note:** Illustration reduced.

Date	Mintage	F	VF	XF	Unc	BU
1997	1,500	—	—	—	—	110
1997 Proof	2,100	Value: 200				
1998 Matte	2,150	—	—	—	—	110

KM# 624   25 PESOS
7.7758 g., 0.9990 Gold 0.2497 oz. AGW **Subject:** Serpiente
Emplumada **Obv:** National arms, eagle left **Note:** Similar to
100 Pesos, KM#626.

Date	Mintage	F	VF	XF	Unc	BU
1997	500	—	—	—	—	350
1997 Proof	200	Value: 375				

KM# 625   50 PESOS
15.5517 g., 0.9990 Gold 0.4995 oz. AGW **Subject:**
Serpiente Emplumada **Obv:** National arms, eagle left **Note:**
Similar to 100 Pesos, KM#626.

Date	Mintage	F	VF	XF	Unc	BU
1997 Proof	200	Value: 700				
1997	500	—	—	—	—	650

KM# 626   100 PESOS
31.1035 g., 0.9990 Gold 0.9990 oz. AGW **Subject:**
Teotihuacan - Serpiente Emplumada **Obv:** National arms,
eagle left

Date	Mintage	F	VF	XF	Unc	BU
1997	500	—	—	—	—	1,300
1997 Proof	Est. 200	Value: 1,400				

BULLION COINAGE
Pre-Columbian • Tolteca Series

KM# 661   PESO
7.7759 g., 0.9990 Silver 0.2497 oz. ASW, 27 mm. **Subject:**
Jaguar **Obv:** National arms, eagle left **Rev:** Jaguar carving
Edge: Reeded **Mint:** Mexico City

Date	Mintage	F	VF	XF	Unc	BU
1998	6,000	—	—	—	—	20.00
1998 Proof	4,800	Value: 30.00				

KM# 662   2 PESOS
15.5517 g., 0.9990 Silver 0.4995 oz. ASW, 33 mm. **Subject:**
Jaguar **Obv:** National arms, eagle left **Rev:** Jaguar carving
Edge: Reeded **Mint:** Mexico City

Date	Mintage	F	VF	XF	Unc	BU
1998	6,000	—	—	—	—	25.00
1998 Proof	4,800	Value: 35.00				

KM# 663   5 PESOS
31.1035 g., 0.9990 Silver 0.9990 oz. ASW, 40 mm. **Subject:**
Jaguar **Obv:** National arms, eagle left within shield and
designed border **Rev:** Jaguar carving within shield and
designed border **Edge:** Reeded **Mint:** Mexico City

Date	Mintage	F	VF	XF	Unc	BU
1998	6,000	—	—	—	—	30.00
1998 Proof	4,800	Value: 75.00				

KM# 664   5 PESOS
31.1035 g., 0.9990 Silver 0.9990 oz. ASW, 40 mm. **Obv:**
National arms, eagle left **Rev:** Sacerdote sculpture **Edge:**
Reeded **Mint:** Mexico City

Date	Mintage	F	VF	XF	Unc	BU
1998	5,000	—	—	—	—	30.00
1998 Proof	4,800	Value: 75.00				

KM# 666 5 PESOS
31.1035 g., 0.9990 Silver 0.9990 oz. ASW, 40 mm. **Subject:**
Serpiente con Craneo **Obv:** National arms, eagle left **Rev:**
Large sculpture **Edge:** Reeded **Mint:** Mexico City

Date	Mintage	F	VF	XF	Unc	BU
1998	5,000	—	—	—	—	30.00
1998 Proof	4,800	Value: 75.00				

KM# 665 5 PESOS
31.1035 g., 0.9990 Silver 0.9990 oz. ASW, 40 mm. **Subject:**
Quetzalcoatl **Obv:** National arms, eagle left **Rev:** Quetzalcoatl
sculpture **Edge:** Reeded **Mint:** Mexico City

Date	Mintage	F	VF	XF	Unc	BU
1998	5,000	—	—	—	—	30.00
1998 Proof	4,800	Value: 75.00				

KM# 634 10 PESOS
155.7300 g., 0.9990 Silver 5.0016 oz. ASW **Subject:**
Atlantes **Obv:** National arms, eagle left within shield and

designed border **Rev:** Three carved statues within shield and
designed border

Date	Mintage	F	VF	XF	Unc	BU
1998	3,500	—	—	—	—	115
1998 Proof	4,200	Value: 185				

KM# 667 25 PESOS
7.7759 g., 0.9990 Gold 0.2497 oz. AGW, 23 mm. **Subject:**
Aguila **Obv:** National arms, eagle left **Rev:** Eagle sculpture
Edge: Reeded **Mint:** Mexico City

Date	Mintage	F	VF	XF	Unc	BU
1998 Proof	300	Value: 400				
1998	300	—	—	—	—	375

KM# 668 50 PESOS
15.5517 g., 0.9990 Gold 0.4995 oz. AGW, 29 mm. **Subject:**
Aguila **Obv:** National arms, eagle left **Rev:** Eagle sculpture
Edge: Reeded **Mint:** Mexico City

Date	Mintage	F	VF	XF	Unc	BU
1998	300	—	—	—	—	675
1998 Proof	300	Value: 725				

KM# 669 100 PESOS
31.1035 g., 0.9990 Gold 0.9990 oz. AGW, 34.5 mm.
Subject: Aguila **Obv:** National arms, eagle left within
designed shield **Rev:** Eagle sculpture within designed shield
Edge: Reeded **Mint:** Mexico City

Date	Mintage	F	VF	XF	Unc	BU
1998	300	—	—	—	—	1,350
1998 Proof	300	Value: 1,400				

MEDALLIC SILVER BULLION COINAGE

KM# M49a ONZA
33.6250 g., 0.9250 Silver 0.9999 oz. ASW **Obv:** Mint mark
above coin press

Date	Mintage	F	VF	XF	Unc	BU
1949	1,000,000	BV	16.50	20.00	25.00	40.00

BULLION • MEDALLIC

KM# M49b.1   ONZA
33.6250 g., 0.9250 Silver 0.9999 oz. ASW   **Obv:** Wide spacing between DE MONEDA **Rev:** Mint mark below balance scale **Mint:** Mexico City **Note:** Type I

Date	Mintage	F	VF	XF	Unc	BU
1978Mo	280,000	—	—	BV	17.50	25.00

KM# M49b.2   ONZA
33.6250 g., 0.9250 Silver 0.9999 oz. ASW   **Obv:** Close spacing between DE MONEDA **Rev:** Mint mark below balance scale **Mint:** Mexico City **Note:** Type II

Date	Mintage	F	VF	XF	Unc	BU
1978Mo	Inc. above	—	—	BV	18.50	28.00

KM# M49b.3   ONZA
33.6250 g., 0.9250 Silver 0.9999 oz. ASW   **Obv:** Close spacing between DE MONEDA **Rev:** Left scale pan points to U in UNA **Mint:** Mexico City **Note:** Type III

Date	Mintage	F	VF	XF	Unc	BU
1979Mo	4,508,000	—	—	BV	17.50	22.00

KM# M49b.4   ONZA
33.6250 g., 0.9250 Silver 0.9999 oz. ASW   **Obv:** Close spacing between U and N of UNA **Mint:** Mexico City **Note:** Type IV

Date	Mintage	F	VF	XF	Unc	BU
1979Mo	Inc. above	—	—	BV	17.50	22.00

KM# M49b.5   ONZA
33.6250 g., 0.9250 Silver 0.9999 oz. ASW   **Obv:** Close spacing between DE MONEDA **Rev:** Left scale pan points between U and N of UNA **Mint:** Mexico City **Note:** Type V

Date	Mintage	F	VF	XF	Unc	BU
1980/70Mo	Inc. above	—	—	BV	18.50	26.00
1980Mo	6,104,000	—	—	BV	17.50	22.00

MEDALLIC GOLD COINAGE

KM# M91a   10 PESOS
8.3333 g., 0.9000 Gold 0.2411 oz. AGW   **Subject:** 200th Anniversary - Birth of Hidalgo

Date	Mintage	F	VF	XF	Unc	BU
1953	—	—	—	—	BV	300

KM# M123a   10 PESOS
8.3333 g., 0.9000 Gold 0.2411 oz. AGW   **Subject:** Centennial of Constitution

Date	Mintage	F	VF	XF	Unc	BU
1957	Est. 73,000	—	—	—	BV	300

Note: Mintage includes #M122a

KM# M92a   20 PESOS
16.6666 g., 0.9000 Gold 0.4822 oz. AGW   **Subject:** 200th Anniversary - Birth of Hidalgo

Date	Mintage	F	VF	XF	Unc	BU
1953	—	—	—	—	BV	600

KM# M122a   50 PESOS
41.6666 g., 0.9000 Gold 1.2056 oz. AGW   **Subject:** Centennial of Constitution

Date	Mintage	F	VF	XF	Unc	BU
1957	—	—	—	—	BV	1,500

Note: Mintage included in total for KM#M123a

MEXICO-REVOLUTIONARY

AGUASCALIENTES

Aguascalientes is a state in central Mexico. Its coin issues, struck by authority of Pancho Villa, represent his deepest penetration into the Mexican heartland. Lack of silver made it necessary to make all denominations in copper.

FRANCISCO PANCHO VILLA

REVOLUTIONARY COINAGE

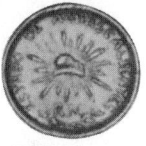 

KM# 601 CENTAVO
3.5500 g., Copper, 17 mm. **Obv:** Liberty cap **Rev:** Value within 3/4 wreath below date **Note:** Large date weight 3.55g.

Date	Mintage	VG	F	VF	XF	Unc
1915	—	30.00	60.00	100	130	—
Note: Small date, plain edge						
1915	—	250	350	450	—	—
Note: Large date, plain edge						
1915	—	30.00	60.00	100	200	—
Note: Large date, reeded edge						
1915	—	30.00	60.00	80.00	120	—
Note: Small date, reeded edge						

KM# 602.1 2 CENTAVOS
4.2800 g., Copper **Obv:** Liberty cap **Rev:** Value within 3/4 wreath below date

Date	Mintage	VG	F	VF	XF	Unc
1915	—	40.00	100	200	350	—
Note: Round front 2, plain edge						

KM# 602.2 2 CENTAVOS
3.3500 g., Copper, 19 mm. **Obv:** Liberty cap **Rev:** Value within 1/2 wreath below date

Date	Mintage	VG	F	VF	XF	Unc
1915	—	35.00	60.00	85.00	200	—
Note: Square front 2, reeded edge						
1915 Plain edge	—	50.00	90.00	200	325	—
Note: Square front 2						

KM# 603 5 CENTAVOS
Copper, 25 mm. **Obv:** National arms **Rev:** Liberty cap and value above sprigs

Date	Mintage	VG	F	VF	XF	Unc
1915 Plain edge; Rare	—	—	—	—	—	—
1915 Reeded edge	—	10.00	20.00	30.00	50.00	—

KM# 604.1 5 CENTAVOS
7.1300 g., Copper, 25 mm. **Obv:** National arms **Rev:** Vertically shaded 5 within sprigs

Date	Mintage	VG	F	VF	XF	Unc
1915	—	100	150	225	325	—
Note: Plain edge						
1915	—	20.00	40.00	50.00	100	—
Note: Reeded edge						

KM# 604.2 5 CENTAVOS
Copper, 25 mm. **Obv:** National arms **Rev:** Horizontally shaded 5 within sprigs

Date	Mintage	VG	F	VF	XF	Unc
1915	—	25.00	40.00	65.00	125	—
Note: Reeded edge						
1915	—	30.00	50.00	80.00	150	—
Note: Plain edge						

KM# 606 20 CENTAVOS
Copper, 29 mm. **Obv:** National arms **Rev:** Value below Liberty cap within sprigs

Date	Mintage	VG	F	VF	XF	Unc
1915 Reeded edge	—	10.00	20.00	50.00	80.00	—

KM# 605   20 CENTAVOS
Copper, 29 mm.   **Obv:** National arms **Rev:** Value below
Liberty cap within sprigs

Date	Mintage	VG	F	VF	XF	Unc
1915 Reeded edge	—	10.00	20.00	50.00	80.00	—

KM# 600   20 CENTAVOS
Copper   **Obv:** National arms **Rev:** Value below Liberty cap
within sprigs **Edge:** Reeded

Date	Mintage	VG	F	VF	XF	Unc
1915	—	15.00	20.00	35.00	65.00	—

Note: Varieties exist with both plain and milled edges and
many variations in the shading of the numerals

CHIHUAHUA

Chihuahua is a northern state of Mexico bordering the
U.S. It was the arena that introduced Pancho Villa to the world.
Villa, an outlaw, was given a title when asked by Madero to
participate in maintaining order during Madero's presidency.
After Madero's death in February 1913, Villa became a per-
suasive leader. Chihuahua was where he made his first coins -
the Parral series. The *Army of the North* pesos also came
from this state. This coin helped Villa recruit soldiers because
of his ability to pay in silver while others were paying in worth-
less paper money.

ARMY OF THE NORTH
Ejercito Del Norte

REVOLUTIONARY COINAGE

KM# 619   PESO
29.2700 g., Silver   **Obv:** National arms **Rev:** Liberty cap

Date	Mintage	VG	F	VF	XF	Unc
1915	—	20.00	35.00	65.00	185	500

KM# 619a   PESO
Copper   **Obv:** National arms **Rev:** Liberty cap

Date	Mintage	VG	F	VF	XF	Unc
1915	—	500	1,000	1,500	2,500	—

KM# 619b   PESO
Brass   **Obv:** National arms **Rev:** Liberty cap **Note:** Uniface
obverse

Date	Mintage	VG	F	VF	XF	Unc
1915 Rare	—	—	—	—	—	—

CONSTITUTIONALIST ARMY
Ejercito Constitucionalista

REVOLUTIONARY COINAGE

KM# 612   5 CENTAVOS
Copper   **Obv:** Liberty cap **Rev:** Value above date

Date	Mintage	VG	F	VF	XF	Unc
1914	—	25.00	45.00	80.00	125	—

KM# 613   5 CENTAVOS
6.6000 g., Copper, 25 mm.   **Obv:** Liberty cap **Rev:** Value
above date **Note:** Numerous varieties exist. Weight varies
6.3-6.93g.

Date	Mintage	VG	F	VF	XF	Unc
1914	—	1.00	2.50	4.00	10.00	—
1915	—	1.00	2.50	4.00	10.00	—

KM# 613a   5 CENTAVOS
Brass   **Obv:** Liberty cap **Rev:** Value above date **Note:**
Numerous varieties exist.

Date	Mintage	VG	F	VF	XF	Unc
1914	—	2.00	3.00	8.00	10.00	—
1915	—	2.00	3.00	8.00	10.00	—

KM# 613b   5 CENTAVOS
Cast Copper   **Obv:** Liberty cap **Rev:** Value above date

Date	Mintage	VG	F	VF	XF	Unc
1914	—	75.00	200	300	450	—

KM# 614a   5 CENTAVOS
Copper   **Obv:** National arms **Rev:** Value below date within
sprigs with solid V

Date	Mintage	VG	F	VF	XF	Unc
1915 Rare	—	—	—	—	—	—

KM# 614b   5 CENTAVOS
Copper   **Obv:** National arms **Rev:** Value above date **Note:**
Mule.

Date	Mintage	VG	F	VF	XF	Unc
1915	—	350	—	—	—	—

KM# 614c   5 CENTAVOS
Copper   **Obv:** National arms **Rev:** Liberty cap **Note:** Mule.

Date	Mintage	VG	F	VF	XF	Unc
1915 Rare	—	—	—	—	—	—

KM# 614   5 CENTAVOS
Copper   **Obv:** National arms **Rev:** Value below date within
sprigs with double-lined V

Date	Mintage	VG	F	VF	XF	Unc
1915 SS Unique	—	—	—	—	—	—

KM# 615   10 CENTAVOS
8.7900 g., Copper, 27.5 mm. **Obv:** Liberty cap **Rev:** Value
above date

Date	Mintage	VG	F	VF	XF	Unc
1915	—	1.25	2.50	3.50	5.00	—

KM# 615a   10 CENTAVOS
8.8900 g., Brass, 27.5 mm. **Obv:** Liberty cap **Rev:** Value
above date

Date	Mintage	VG	F	VF	XF	Unc
1915	—	5.00	10.00	30.00	50.00	—

Note: Many varieties exist

HIDALGO DEL PARRAL
Fuerzas Constitucionalistas

REVOLUTIONARY COINAGE

KM# 607   2 CENTAVOS
6.8500 g., Copper, 25 mm. **Obv:** Liberty cap within circle
flanked by sprigs **Rev:** Value flanked by sprigs within circle

Date	Mintage	VG	F	VF	XF	Unc
1913	—	5.00	10.00	15.00	25.00	—

KM# 607a   2 CENTAVOS
Brass **Obv:** Liberty cap within circle flanked by sprigs **Rev:**
Value flanked by sprigs within circle

Date	Mintage	VG	F	VF	XF	Unc
1913	—	95.00	150	200	350	—

KM# 608   50 CENTAVOS
12.6500 g., Silver **Obv:** Liberty cap **Rev:** Value flanked by
sprigs below Liberty cap **Edge:** Reeded

Date	Mintage	VG	F	VF	XF	Unc
1913	—	15.00	40.00	60.00	85.00	—

KM# 609   50 CENTAVOS
12.1700 g., Silver, 30 mm. **Edge:** Plain

Date	Mintage	VG	F	VF	XF	Unc
1913	—	50.00	70.00	95.00	125	—

KM# 610   PESO
30.0000 g., Silver **Obv:** Inscription **Rev:** 1 through PESO
and small circle above sprigs **Note:** Weight varies 29.18-
30.9g.

Date	Mintage	VG	F	VF	XF	Unc
1913	—	1,200	2,000	3,000	6,000	14,000

KM# 611   PESO
Silver, 38 mm. **Obv:** Inscription **Rev:** Value above sprigs
Note: Well struck counterfeits of this coin exist with the dot at
the end of the word Peso even with the bottom of the O. On
legitimate pieces the dot is slightly higher. Weight varies 27.3-
28.85g.

Date	Mintage	VG	F	VF	XF	Unc
1913	—	35.00	40.00	120	275	475

DURANGO

A state in north central Mexico. Another area of operation for Pancho Villa. The *Muera Huerta* peso originates in this state. The coins were made in Cuencame under the orders of Generals Cemceros and Contreras.

Cuencame

Muera Huerta (Death to Huerta)

REVOLUTIONARY COINAGE

KM# 620   PESO
Silver **Obv:** National arms **Rev:** Liberty cap with written value flanked by stars

Date	Mintage	VG	F	VF	XF	Unc
1914	—	1,000	2,000	3,000	5,000	9,500

KM# 621   PESO
23.2000 g., Silver, 39 mm. **Obv:** National arms with continuous border **Rev:** Liberty cap with continuous border

Date	Mintage	VG	F	VF	XF	Unc
1914	—	75.00	150	300	700	1,650

KM# 621a   PESO
Copper **Obv:** National arms with continuous border **Rev:** Liberty cap with continuous border **Note:** Varieties exist.

Date	Mintage	VG	F	VF	XF	Unc
1914	—	400	600	1,000	2,000	—

KM# 621b   PESO
Brass **Obv:** National arms **Rev:** Liberty cap

Date	Mintage	VG	F	VF	XF	Unc
1914	—	—	1,000	2,000	3,500	—

KM# 622   PESO
23.4000 g., Silver, 38.5 mm. **Obv:** National arms with dot and dash border **Rev:** Liberty cap with continuous border **Note:** The so-called 20 Pesos gold Muera Huerta pieces are modern fantasies. Refer to Unusual World Coins, 4th edition, ©2005, KP Books, Inc.

Date	Mintage	VG	F	VF	XF	Unc
1914	—	60.00	100	300	500	950

ESTADO DE DURANGO

REVOLUTIONARY COINAGE

KM# 625   CENTAVO
3.2900 g., Copper, 20 mm. **Obv:** Large date in center **Rev:** Value within wreath

Date	Mintage	VG	F	VF	XF	Unc
1914	—	2.00	4.00	8.00	12.00	—

KM# 625a   CENTAVO
Brass **Obv:** Large date in center **Rev:** Value within wreath

Date	Mintage	VG	F	VF	XF	Unc
1914	—	75.00	150	300	400	—

KM# 625b   CENTAVO
Lead **Obv:** Large date in center **Rev:** Value within wreath

Date	Mintage	VG	F	VF	XF	Unc
1914	—	20.00	40.00	65.00	90.00	—

KM# 625c   CENTAVO
Copper **Obv:** Large date in center **Rev:** Value within wreath

Date	Mintage	VG	F	VF	XF	Unc
1914	—	25.00	50.00	80.00	125	—

KM# 626a   CENTAVO
Brass **Obv:** Date **Rev:** Value within wreath

Date	Mintage	VG	F	VF	XF	Unc
1914	—	75.00	100	200	350	—

KM# 626b   CENTAVO
Lead **Obv:** Date **Rev:** Value within wreath

Date	Mintage	VG	F	VF	XF	Unc
1914	—	20.00	40.00	70.00	125	—

Note: Varieties in size exist

KM# 627 CENTAVO
Copper, 20 mm. **Obv:** Stars below date **Rev:** Value with retrograde N

Date	Mintage	VG	F	VF	XF	Unc
1914	—	6.00	10.00	20.00	30.00	—

KM# 627a CENTAVO
Lead, 20 mm. **Obv:** Stars below date **Rev:** Value with retrograde N

Date	Mintage	VG	F	VF	XF	Unc
1914	—	20.00	40.00	60.00	100	—

KM# 628 CENTAVO
Aluminum **Obv:** National arms within sprigs **Rev:** Value

Date	Mintage	VG	F	VF	XF	Unc
1914	—	0.65	1.00	2.00	4.00	10.00

KM# 624 CENTAVO
Lead **Obv:** Date **Rev:** Value within wreath **Note:** Cast.

Date	Mintage	VG	F	VF	XF	Unc
1914	—	45.00	75.00	100	200	—

KM# 626 CENTAVO
2.8000 g., Copper, 20 mm. **Obv:** Date **Rev:** Value within wreath **Note:** Weight varies 2.46-2.78g.

Date	Mintage	VG	F	VF	XF	Unc
1914	—	15.00	20.00	35.00	45.00	—

KM# 634b 5 CENTAVOS
6.8900 g., Copper-Nickel, 25.53 mm. **Obv:** National arms above sprigs **Obv. Legend:** REPUBLICA MEXICANA **Rev:** Value **Rev. Legend:** ESTADO DE DURANGO **Edge:** Plain

Date	Mintage	F	VF	XF	Unc	BU
1914	—	25.00	50.00	85.00	135	175

KM# 629 5 CENTAVOS
6.2000 g., Copper, 24 mm. **Obv:** Date above sprigs **Obv. Legend:** ESTADO DE DURANGO **Rev:** Value within designed wreath

Date	Mintage	VG	F	VF	XF	Unc
1914	—	2.00	3.00	6.00	12.00	—

KM# 630 5 CENTAVOS
Copper **Obv:** Date above sprigs **Obv. Legend:** E. DE DURANGO **Rev:** Value within designed wreath

Date	Mintage	VG	F	VF	XF	Unc
1914	—	125	275	375	600	—

KM# 631 5 CENTAVOS
5.0500 g., Copper, 23.5 mm. **Obv:** Date above sprigs **Obv. Legend:** E. DE DURANGO **Rev:** Value within designed wreath

Date	Mintage	VG	F	VF	XF	Unc
1914	—	1.25	3.00	6.00	15.00	—

KM# 631a 5 CENTAVOS
Brass **Obv:** Date above sprigs **Obv. Legend:** E. DE DURANGO **Rev:** Value within designed wreath

Date	Mintage	VG	F	VF	XF	Unc
1914	—	30.00	40.00	50.00	85.00	—

KM# 631b 5 CENTAVOS
Lead **Obv:** Date above sprigs **Obv. Legend:** E. DE DURANGO **Rev:** Value within designed wreath

Date	Mintage	VG	F	VF	XF	Unc
1914	—	45.00	70.00	100	180	—

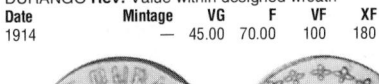

KM# 632 5 CENTAVOS
4.6100 g., Copper, 23.5 mm. **Obv:** Date above sprigs **Obv. Legend:** E. DE DURANGO **Rev:** Roman numeral value

Date	Mintage	VG	F	VF	XF	Unc
1914	—	4.00	8.00	15.00	35.00	—

KM# 632a 5 CENTAVOS
Lead **Obv:** Date above sprigs **Obv. Legend:** E. DE DURANGO **Rev:** Roman numeral value

Date	Mintage	VG	F	VF	XF	Unc
1914	—	50.00	75.00	100	150	—

KM# 634 5 CENTAVOS
Brass **Obv:** National arms above sprigs **Obv. Legend:** REPUBLICA MEXICANA **Rev:** Value **Rev. Legend:** ESTADO DE DURANGO

Date	Mintage	VG	F	VF	XF	Unc
1914	—	0.50	1.00	2.50	5.00	—

KM# 633 5 CENTAVOS
Lead **Obv:** Three stars below 1914 **Rev:** 5 CVS **Note:**
Counterfeits are prevalent in the market

Date	Mintage	VG	F	VF	XF	Unc
1914	—	—	600	2,000	—	—

KM# 634a 5 CENTAVOS
Copper **Obv:** National arms above sprigs **Obv. Legend:**
REPUBLICA MEXICANA **Rev:** Value **Rev. Legend:**
ESTADO DE DURANGO **Note:** There are numerous varieties
of these general types of the Durango 1 and 5 Centavo pieces.

Date	Mintage	VG	F	VF	XF	Unc
1914	—	75.00	125	175	250	—

GUERRERO

Guerrero is a state on the southwestern coast of Mexico.
It was one of the areas of operation of Zapata and his forces in
the south of Mexico. The Zapata forces operated seven different mints in this state. The date ranges were from 1914 to
1917 and denominations from 2 Centavos to 2 Pesos. Some
were cast but most were struck and the rarest coin of the
group is the Suriana 1915 2 Pesos.

EMILIANO ZAPATA
(General Salgado)

REVOLUTIONARY COINAGE

KM# 638 2 CENTAVOS
6.0000 g., Copper, 22 mm. **Obv:** National arms **Obv.
Legend:** REPUBLICA H MEXICANA **Rev:** Value within
wreath **Note:** Weight varies 5.4-6.03g.

Date	Mintage	VG	F	VF	XF	Unc
1915	—	75.00	125	175	250	—

KM# 635 3 CENTAVOS
Copper, 25 mm. **Obv:** National arms **Obv. Legend:**
REPUBLICA MEXICANA **Rev:** Value within wreath **Note:**
Weight varies 4.63-6.87g.

Date	Mintage	VG	F	VF	XF	Unc
1915	—	500	1,500	2,000	3,000	—

KM# 636 5 CENTAVOS
Copper, 26 mm. **Obv:** National arms **Rev:** Value within
wreath

Date	Mintage	VG	F	VF	XF	Unc
1915GRO	—	800	1,200	2,000	3,000	—

KM# 637.1 10 CENTAVOS
Copper, 27-28.5 mm. **Obv:** National arms, snake head ends
at L in REPUBLICA **Obv. Legend:** REPUBLICA MEXICANA
Rev: Date and value within wreath **Note:** Size varies.

Date	Mintage	VG	F	VF	XF	Unc
1915GRO	—	600	1,000	1,500	2,000	—

KM# 637.2 10 CENTAVOS
Copper, 27-28.5 mm. **Obv:** National arms, snake head ends
at C in REPUBLICA **Obv. Legend:** REPUBLICA MEXICANA
Rev: Value within wreath **Note:** Size varies.

Date	Mintage	VG	F	VF	XF	Unc
1915GRO	—	3.00	5.00	8.00	15.00	—

KM# 637.2a 10 CENTAVOS
8.2300 g., Brass, 26 mm. **Obv:** National arms, snake head
ends at C in REPUBLICA **Obv. Legend:** REPUBLICA
MEXICANA **Rev:** Value within wreath

Date	Mintage	VG	F	VF	XF	Unc
1915GRO	—	8.00	15.00	25.00	50.00	—

KM# 637.2b 10 CENTAVOS
Lead **Obv:** National arms, snake head ends at C in
REPUBLICA **Obv. Legend:** REPUBLICA MEXICANA **Rev:**
Value within wreath

Date	Mintage	VG	F	VF	XF	Unc
1915GRO	—	50.00	75.00	175	275	—

KM# 637.3 10 CENTAVOS
Copper **Obv:** National arms, snake head ends before A in
REPUBLICA **Obv. Legend:** REPUBLICA MEXICANA **Rev:**
Date and value within wreath

Date	Mintage	VG	F	VF	XF	Unc
1915.GRO	—	3.00	5.00	8.00	15.00	—

KM# 637.3a 10 CENTAVOS
Brass **Obv:** National arms, snake head ends before A in
REPUBLICA **Obv. Legend:** REPUBLICA MEXICANA **Rev:**
Value and date within wreath

Date	Mintage	VG	F	VF	XF	Unc
1915.GRO	—	12.00	20.00	50.00	100	—

KM# 639 25 CENTAVOS
7.5000 g., Silver, 25 mm. **Obv:** Liberty cap **Obv. Legend:** Mexicana REPUbLICA **Rev:** Value above date **Note:** Weight varies 7.41-7.5g.

Date	Mintage	VG	F	VF	XF	Unc
1915	—	125	300	500	900	—

KM# 640 50 CENTAVOS
14.8000 g., Silver, 34 mm. **Obv:** Liberty cap **Rev:** Date and value within beaded border **Note:** Weight varies 14.5-14.8g.

Date	Mintage	VG	F	VF	XF	Unc
1915	—	1,000	2,000	3,500	5,000	—

KM# 641 PESO (UN)
Gold With Silver, 29-31 mm. **Obv:** National arms **Obv. Legend:** REPUBLICA MEXICANA - H UN PESO **Rev:** Liberty cap and rays within sprigs **Rev. Legend:** "REFORMA LIBERTAD JUSTICIA Y LEY" **Rev. Inscription:** Oro:0,300 **Note:** Many die varieties exist. Size varies. Weight varies 10.28-14.84g. Coin is 0.30g fine Gold.

Date	Mintage	VG	F	VF	XF	Unc
1914GRO	—	15.00	25.00	35.00	75.00	—

KM# 642 PESO (UN)
Gold With Silver, 30.5-31 mm. **Obv:** National arms **Obv. Legend:** REPUBLICA MEXICANA - H UN PESO H **Rev:** Liberty cap and rays within sprigs **Rev. Legend:** "REFORMA.LIBERTAD.JUSTICIA Y LEY" **Rev. Inscription:** Oro:0,300 **Note:** Weight varies 12.93-14.66g. Coin is 0.300g fine Gold.

Date	Mintage	VG	F	VF	XF	Unc
1914GRO	—	50.00	75.00	100	180	—
1915GRO	—	600	1,000	1,500	1,850	—

KM# 643 2 PESOS (Dos)
Gold With Silver, 38.25-39.6 mm. **Obv:** National arms **Obv. Legend:** REPUBLICA MEXICANA **Rev:** Radiant sun face above high mountain peaks **Rev. Legend:** "REFORMA LIBERTAD, JUSTICIA Y LEY", **Rev. Inscription:** Oro:0,595 **Note:** Many varieties exist. Coin is 0.595g fine Gold.

Date	Mintage	VG	F	VF	XF	Unc
1914GRO	—	15.00	35.00	125	200	425

KM# 644 2 PESOS (Dos)
Gold With Silver, 39-40 mm. **Obv:** National arms **Obv. Legend:** REPUBLICA MEXICANA **Rev:** Radiant sun face above high and low mountain peaks **Rev. Legend:** "REFORMA, LIBERTAD, JUSTICIA Y LEY" **Rev. Inscription:** Oro:0,595 **Note:** Weight varies 21.71-26.54g. Coin is 0.595g fine Gold.

Date	Mintage	VG	F	VF	XF	Unc
1915GRO	—	65.00	85.00	160	250	550

KM# 644a 2 PESOS (Dos)
Copper **Obv:** National arms **Obv. Legend:** REPUBLICA MEXICANA **Rev:** Radiant sun face above high and low mountain peaks **Rev. Legend:** "REFORMA, LIBERTAD, JUSTICIA Y LEY"

Date	Mintage	VG	F	VF	XF	Unc
1915GRO	—	400	1,000	1,200	1,800	—

ATLIXTAC

REVOLUTIONARY COINAGE

KM# 645 10 CENTAVOS
Copper, 27.5-28 mm. **Obv:** National arms **Obv. Legend:** REPUBLICA MEXICANA **Rev:** Value within sprigs **Note:** Size varies. Weight varies 4.76-9.74g.

Date	Mintage	VG	F	VF	XF	Unc
1915	—	3.00	5.00	8.00	15.00	—

KM# 646   10 CENTAVOS
Copper, 27.55-28 mm.   **Obv:** National arms **Obv. Legend:**
REPUBLICA H MEXICANA **Rev:** Value within sprigs **Note:**
Size varies. Weight varies 6.13-7.94g.

Date	Mintage	VG	F	VF	XF	Unc
1915	—	3.00	5.00	8.00	15.00	—

CACAHUATEPEC

REVOLUTIONARY COINAGE

KM# 648   5 CENTAVOS
12.1900 g., Copper, 28 mm.   **Obv:** National arms **Obv.
Legend:** ESTADOS UNIDOS MEXICANOS **Rev:** Value
within wreath

Date	Mintage	VG	F	VF	XF	Unc
1917	—	12.00	25.00	40.00	75.00	—

KM# 649   20 CENTAVOS
Silver, 21-23.8 mm.   **Obv:** National arms **Obv. Legend:**
ESTADOS UNIDOS MEXICANOS **Rev:** Value within sprigs
below liberty cap and rays **Note:** Size varies. Weight varies
3.99-6.2g.

Date	Mintage	VG	F	VF	XF	Unc
1917	—	100	200	350	400	—

KM# 650   50 CENTAVOS
13.8000 g., Silver, 30-30.3 mm.   **Obv:** National arms **Obv.
Legend:** ESTADOS UNIDOS MEXICANOS **Rev:** Value and
date within sprigs below Liberty cap **Note:** Size varies. Weight
varies 13.45-13.78g.

Date	Mintage	VG	F	VF	XF	Unc
1917	—	20.00	60.00	150	375	—

KM# 651   PESO (UN)
Silver, 38 mm.   **Obv:** National arms **Rev:** Liberty cap **Note:**
Weight varies 26.81-32.05g.

Date	Mintage	VG	F	VF	XF	Unc
1917 L.V. Go	—	2,000	4,000	6,000	9,000	—

CACALOTEPEC

REVOLUTIONARY COINAGE

KM# 652   20 CENTAVOS
Silver, 22.5 mm.   **Obv:** National arms **Obv. Legend:**
ESTADOS UNIDOS MEXICANOS **Rev:** Date and value
within sprigs below Liberty cap and rays **Note:** Weight varies
3.89-5.73g.

Date	Mintage	VG	F	VF	XF	Unc
1917	—	1,000	1,800	3,000	5,000	—

CAMPO MORADO

REVOLUTIONARY COINAGE

KM# 653   5 CENTAVOS
4.3700 g., Copper, 23.5-24 mm.   **Obv:** National arms **Rev:**
Value within wreath **Note:** Size varies.

Date	Mintage	VG	F	VF	XF	Unc
1915 C.M.	—	9.00	15.00	22.50	35.00	—

KM# 654 10 CENTAVOS
Copper, 25.25-26 mm. **Obv:** National arms **Rev:** Value and date within wreath **Note:** Size varies. Weight varies. 4.48-8.77g.

Date	Mintage	VG	F	VF	XF	Unc
1915 C.M. GRO	—	6.00	10.00	20.00	30.00	—

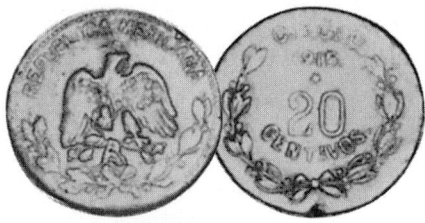

KM# 655 20 CENTAVOS
Copper, 28 mm. **Obv:** National arms **Rev:** Date above star and value within wreath **Note:** Weight varies 4.48-9g.

Date	Mintage	VG	F	VF	XF	Unc
1915 C.M. GRO	—	15.00	25.00	35.00	50.00	—

KM# 657a 50 CENTAVOS
Billon **Obv:** National arms **Rev:** Date and value within wreath **Note:** Regular obverse.

Date	Mintage	VG	F	VF	XF	Unc
1915 C.M. GRO	—	200	300	500	1,000	—

KM# 657 50 CENTAVOS
Copper, 30-31 mm. **Obv:** National arms **Rev:** Date and value within wreath **Note:** Regular obverse. Size varies. Weight varies 6.49-13.19g.

Date	Mintage	VG	F	VF	XF	Unc
1915 C.M. GRO	—	6.00	10.00	15.00	25.00	—

KM# 656 50 CENTAVOS
Copper, 29-31 mm. **Obv:** National arms **Rev:** Date and value within wreath **Note:** Size varies. Weight varies 9.81-16.77g.

Date	Mintage	VG	F	VF	XF	Unc
1915 C.M. GRO	—	12.00	20.00	30.00	60.00	—

KM# 658a PESO (UN)
Brass **Obv:** National arms **Rev:** Liberty cap

Date	Mintage	VG	F	VF	XF	Unc
1914 Co Mo Gro	—	—	—	—	—	—
Unique						

KM# 659 PESO (UN)
Gold With Silver, 30-31 mm. **Obv:** National arms **Rev:** Liberty cap within sprigs **Rev. Inscription:** Oro:0,300 **Note:** Weight varies 12.26-15.81g. Coin is 0.300g fine Gold.

Date	Mintage	VG	F	VF	XF	Unc
1914 CAMPO Mo	—	15.00	30.00	45.00	75.00	—

KM# 658 PESO (UN)
Gold With Silver, 32-32.5 mm. **Obv:** National arms **Rev:** Liberty cap **Rev. Inscription:** Oro:0,300 **Note:** Weight varies 12.42-16.5g. Coin is 0.300g fine Gold.

Date	Mintage	VG	F	VF	XF	Unc
1914 Co Mo Gro	—	500	600	1,000	1,200	—

KM# 660a 2 PESOS (Dos)
Copper **Obv:** National arms **Rev:** Sun over mountains

Date	Mintage	VG	F	VF	XF	Unc
1915 Co. Mo.	—	—	800	1,000	1,200	—

KM# 662a.1 2 PESOS (Dos)
Copper **Obv:** National arms **Rev:** Liberty cap

Date	Mintage	VG	F	VF	XF	Unc
1915 C. M. GRO	—	—	—	—	1,200	—

KM# 662a.2 2 PESOS (Dos)
Copper **Obv:** National arms **Rev:** Liberty cap

Date	Mintage	VG	F	VF	XF	Unc
1915 C. M. GRO	—	—	—	—	—	—
Unique						

KM# 661 2 PESOS (Dos)
29.4400 g., Gold With Silver, 39 mm. **Obv:** National arms **Rev:** Sun and mountains **Rev. Inscription:** Oro:0,595 **Note:** Coin is 0.595g fine Gold.

Date	Mintage	VG	F	VF	XF	Unc
1915 Co. Mo.	—	2,500	5,000	9,000	15,000	—

KM# 662   2 PESOS (Dos)
0.5950 g., 1.0000 Gold With Silver 0.0191 oz., 34.5-35 mm.
Obv: National arms **Rev:** Liberty cap **Note:** Size varies.
Weight varies 18.27-20.08g.

Date	Mintage	VG	F	VF	XF	Unc
1915 C. M. GRO	—	20.00	30.00	60.00	120	—

KM# 660   2 PESOS (Dos)
Gold With Silver, 38.9-39 mm. **Obv:** National arms **Rev:** Sun
over mountains **Rev. Inscription:** Oro:0,595 **Note:** Weight
varies 20.6-26.02g. Coin is 0.595g fine Gold.

Date	Mintage	VG	F	VF	XF	Unc
1915 Co. Mo.	—	12.00	20.00	35.00	75.00	425

CHILPANCINGO

REVOLUTIONARY COINAGE

KM# 663   10 CENTAVOS
2.5200 g., Cast Silver, 18 mm. **Obv:** National arms **Rev:** Sun
above value and sprigs

Date	Mintage	VG	F	VF	XF	Unc
1914	—	700	1,000	1,200	1,500	—

Note: Many counterfeits exist

KM# 664   20 CENTAVOS
4.9400 g., Cast Silver, 21.5 mm. **Obv:** National arms **Rev:**
Sun above value and sprigs

Date	Mintage	VG	F	VF	XF	Unc
1914	—	700	1,000	1,200	1,500	—

Note: Many counterfeits exist

SURIANA

REVOLUTIONARY COINAGE

KM# 665   2 PESOS (Dos)
22.9300 g., Gold With Silver, 39 mm. **Obv:** National arms
Rev: Sun over mountains **Rev. Inscription:** Oro:0,595 **Note:**
Coin is 0.595g fine Gold.

Date	Mintage	VG	F	VF	XF	Unc
1915 Rare	—	—	—	20,000	35,000	—

 Note: Ira & Larry Goldberg - Millenia sale, 5-08 AU-55 replica. Ponterio & Associates sale, 4-09 VF realized $17,000.
Spink America Gerber sale part 2, 6-96 VF realized $16,500

TAXCO

REVOLUTIONARY COINAGE

KM# 667   2 CENTAVOS
Copper, 25.25-26 mm. **Obv:** National arms **Obv. Legend:**
EDO.DE.GRO **Rev:** Value within sprigs **Note:** Size varies.
Weight varies 6.81-8.55g.

Date	Mintage	VG	F	VF	XF	Unc
1915 O/T	—	25.00	40.00	60.00	90.00	—

KM# 668   5 CENTAVOS
Copper **Obv:** National arms **Obv. Legend:** REPUBLICA H
MEXICANA **Rev:** Value within sprigs **Note:** Weight varies
7.13-7.39g.

Date	Mintage	VG	F	VF	XF	Unc
1915	—	10.00	20.00	30.00	50.00	—

KM# 669 10 CENTAVOS
Copper, 27-28 mm. **Obv:** National arms **Obv. Legend:**
REPUBLICA H MEXICANA **Rev:** Date and value within sprigs
Note: Size varies. Weight varies 7.51-8.67g.

Date	Mintage	VG	F	VF	XF	Unc
1915	—	9.00	20.00	35.00	50.00	—

KM# 670 50 CENTAVOS
5.4500 g., Copper, 27-28 mm. **Obv:** National arms with
legend in large letters **Rev:** Value within sprigs **Note:** Size
varies.

Date	Mintage	VG	F	VF	XF	Unc
1915	—	15.00	25.00	50.00	65.00	—

KM# 671 50 CENTAVOS
Silver, 27.6-28 mm. **Obv:** National arms **Rev:** Sun above
value and sprigs **Note:** Size varies. Weight varies 8.95-
10.85g.

Date	Mintage	VG	F	VF	XF	Unc
1915	—	25.00	40.00	60.00	100	—

KM# 672a PESO (UN)
Brass **Obv:** National arms **Rev:** Liberty cap within sprigs

Date	Mintage	VG	F	VF	XF	Unc
1915	—	200	300	450	600	—

KM# 672b PESO (UN)
Lead **Obv:** National arms **Rev:** Liberty cap within sprigs

Date	Mintage	VG	F	VF	XF	Unc
1915	—	50.00	100	200	350	—

KM# 672c PESO (UN)
Copper **Obv:** National arms **Rev:** Liberty cap within sprigs

Date	Mintage	VG	F	VF	XF	Unc
1915	—	200	300	400	650	—

KM# 673 PESO (UN)
11.6000 g., Gold With Silver, 30 mm. **Obv:** National arms
Rev: Liberty cap within sprigs **Rev. Inscription:** Oro:0,300
Note: Coin is 0.300g fine Gold.

Date	Mintage	VG	F	VF	XF	Unc
1915	—	250	400	500	800	—

KM# 674 PESO (UN)
Gold With Silver, 30 mm. **Obv:** National arms **Rev:** Liberty
cap within sprigs **Rev. Inscription:** Oro:0,300 **Note:** Weight
varies 10.51-12.79g. Coin is 0.300g fine Gold.

Date	Mintage	VG	F	VF	XF	Unc
1915	—	100	200	300	550	—

KM# 672 PESO (UN)
Gold With Silver, 30-31 mm. **Obv:** National arms **Rev:** Liberty
cap within sprigs **Rev. Inscription:** Oro:0,300 **Note:** Weight
varies 30-31g. Coin is 0.300g fine Gold.

Date	Mintage	VG	F	VF	XF	Unc
1915	—	12.00	20.00	30.00	50.00	—

JALISCO

Jalisco is a state on the west coast of Mexico. The few
coins made for this state show that the *Army of the North* did
not restrict their operations to the northern border states. The
coins were made in Guadalajara under the watchful eye of
General Dieguez, commander of this segment of Villa's forces.

GUADALAJARA

REVOLUTIONARY COINAGE

KM# 675 CENTAVO
Copper **Obv:** Liberty cap **Rev:** Value

Date	Mintage	VG	F	VF	XF	Unc
1915	—	9.50	15.00	20.00	30.00	—

KM# 675a CENTAVO
Brass **Obv:** Liberty cap **Rev:** Value

Date	Mintage	VG	F	VF	XF	Unc
1915	—	—	—	300	450	—

KM# A676 CENTAVO
Copper **Obv:** Liberty cap **Rev:** Retrograde value **Note:**
Varieties exist.

Date	Mintage	VG	F	VF	XF	Unc
1915	—	100	300	600	1,000	—

KM# 676.1   2 CENTAVOS
Copper, 20 mm.   **Obv:** Liberty cap **Rev:** Value

Date	Mintage	VG	F	VF	XF	Unc
1915	—	10.00	18.00	20.00	35.00	—

Note: Varieties exist.

KM# 676.2   2 CENTAVOS
Copper   **Obv:** Liberty cap **Rev:** Value

Date	Mintage	VG	F	VF	XF	Unc
1915	—	200	300	500	800	—

KM# 677   5 CENTAVOS
Copper, 24 mm.   **Obv:** Liberty cap **Rev:** Value

Date	Mintage	VG	F	VF	XF	Unc
1915	—	6.50	12.00	15.00	25.00	—

KM# 677a   5 CENTAVOS
Brass   **Obv:** Liberty cap **Rev:** Value

Date	Mintage	VG	F	VF	XF	Unc
1915 rare	—	—	—	—	—	—

KM# 678   10 CENTAVOS
Copper   **Obv:** Liberty cap above value and date **Rev:**
Crowned shield

Date	Mintage	VG	F	VF	XF	Unc
1915	—	—	—	3,000	5,000	—

KM# A678   PESO
Copper   **Obv:** Liberty cap above value and date **Rev:**
Crowned shield

Date	Mintage	VG	F	VF	XF	Unc
1915	—	—	—	—	17,000	—

MEXICO, ESTADO DE

Estado de Mexico is a state in central Mexico that surrounds the Federal District on three sides. The issues by the
Zapata forces in this state have two distinctions – the Amecameca pieces are the crudest and the Toluca cardboard piece
is the most unusual. General Tenorio authorized the crude
incuse Amecameca pieces.

AMECAMECA

REVOLUTIONARY COINAGE

KM# 679   5 CENTAVOS
12.5500 g., Brass, 24.5 mm.   **Obv:** Legend **Obv. Legend:**
EJERCITO CONVENCIONISTA **Rev:** Value above cent sign

Date	Mintage	VG	F	VF	XF	Unc
ND unique	—	—	—	—	—	—

KM# 680   5 CENTAVOS
12.7700 g., Brass, 24.6 mm.   **Obv:** National arms above RM
Rev: Value above cent sign **Note:** Hand stamped.

Date	Mintage	VG	F	VF	XF	Unc
ND	—	300	400	600	800	—

KM# 681a   10 CENTAVOS
Copper   **Obv:** National arms above RM **Rev:** Value above
cent sign **Note:** Hand stamped.

Date	Mintage	VG	F	VF	XF	Unc
ND	—	75.00	125	225	350	—

KM# 681   10 CENTAVOS
15.0000 g., Brass, 24.5-24.8 mm.   **Obv:** National arms above
RM **Rev:** Value above cent sign **Note:** Hand stamped.
Varieties exist. Size varies.

Date	Mintage	VG	F	VF	XF	Unc
ND	—	60.00	90.00	150	200	—

KM# 682 20 CENTAVOS
Brass, 24-25 mm. **Obv:** National arms above RM **Rev:** Value above cent sign **Note:** Hand stamped. Varieties exist. Size varies. Weight varies 11.34-12.86g.

Date	Mintage	VG	F	VF	XF	Unc
ND	—	15.00	22.50	35.00	60.00	—

KM# 682a 20 CENTAVOS
Copper **Obv:** National arms above RM **Rev:** Value above cent sign **Note:** Hand stamped.

Date	Mintage	VG	F	VF	XF	Unc
ND	—	25.00	50.00	175	250	—

KM# 683 20 CENTAVOS
Copper, 19-20 mm. **Obv:** National arms above A. D. J. **Rev:** Value **Note:** Size varies. Weight varies 3.99-5.35g.

Date	Mintage	VG	F	VF	XF	Unc
ND	—	7.50	12.50	20.00	35.00	—

KM# 683a 20 CENTAVOS
Brass **Obv:** National arms above A. D. J. **Rev:** Value

Date	Mintage	VG	F	VF	XF	Unc
ND	—	—	—	300	500	—

KM# 684 25 CENTAVOS
Brass **Obv:** Legend **Obv. Legend:** EJERCITO CONVENCIONISTA **Rev:** Value above cent sign

Date	Mintage	VG	F	VF	XF	Unc
ND unique	—	—	—	—	—	—

KM# 685 25 CENTAVOS
Copper, 25 mm. **Obv:** National arms above sprigs **Rev:** Large numeral value **Note:** Hand stamped. Many modern counterfeits exist in all metals. Weight varies 6.32-6.99g.

Date	Mintage	VG	F	VF	XF	Unc
ND	—	15.00	20.00	30.00	40.00	—

KM# 685a 25 CENTAVOS
7.9200 g., Brass, 25 mm. **Obv:** National arms above sprigs **Rev:** Large numeral value **Note:** Hand stamped.

Date	Mintage	VG	F	VF	XF	Unc
ND	—	—	—	100	300	—

KM# 685b 25 CENTAVOS
Silver **Obv:** National arms above sprigs **Rev:** Large numeral value **Note:** Hand stamped.

Date	Mintage	VG	F	VF	XF	Unc
ND	—	—	—	250	400	—

KM# 687 50 CENTAVOS
Copper, 23.5-29 mm. **Obv:** National arms above sprigs **Rev:** Large numeral value **Note:** Contemporary counterfeit, hand engraved. Size varies. Weight varies 8.8-10.8g.

Date	Mintage	VG	F	VF	XF	Unc
ND	—	12.00	30.00	50.00	80.00	—

Note: "¢" clears top of 5

KM# 686a 50 CENTAVOS
16.0400 g., Brass, 28.5 mm. **Obv:** National arms above sprigs **Rev:** Large numeral value **Note:** Hand stamped.

Date	Mintage	VG	F	VF	XF	Unc
ND	—	100	200	300	400	—

Note: Stem of "¢" above the 5

KM# 686 50 CENTAVOS
Copper, 28-28.5 mm. **Obv:** Eagle over sprays **Note:** Hand stamped. Size varies.

Date	Mintage	VG	F	VF	XF	Unc
ND	—	8.00	10.00	18.00	30.00	—

TENANCINGO, TOWN
(Distrito Federal Mexico)

REVOLUTIONARY COINAGE

KM# 688.1 2 CENTAVOS
Copper **Obv:** National arms **Rev:** Value within wreath without TM below value

Date	Mintage	VG	F	VF	XF	Unc
1915	—	—	—	800	2,000	—

KM# 688.2   2 CENTAVOS
Copper **Obv:** National arms **Rev:** Value within wreath with TM below value

Date	Mintage	VG	F	VF	XF	Unc
1915	—	—	400	800	2,000	—

KM# 689.1   5 CENTAVOS
Copper, 19 mm.   **Obv:** National arms **Rev:** Numeral value over lined C within wreath **Note:** Weight varies 2.83-2.84g.

Date	Mintage	VG	F	VF	XF	Unc
1915	—	10.00	20.00	30.00	50.00	—

KM# 689.2   5 CENTAVOS
Copper, 19 mm.   **Obv:** National arms **Rev:** Numeral value over lined C within wreath **Note:** Weight varies 2.83-2.84g.

Date	Mintage	VG	F	VF	XF	Unc
1915	—	100	300	500	900	—

KM# 690.1   10 CENTAVOS
Copper, 25.25 mm.   **Obv:** National arms **Rev:** Value over lined C within wreath below date **Note:** Weight varies 4.27-5.64g.

Date	Mintage	VG	F	VF	XF	Unc
1916	—	10.00	20.00	40.00	60.00	—

KM# 690.2   10 CENTAVOS
Copper, 25.25 mm.   **Obv:** National arms **Rev:** Value over lined C within wreath **Note:** Weight varies 4.27-5.64g.

Date	Mintage	VG	F	VF	XF	Unc
1916	—	100	200	400	600	—

KM# 691   20 CENTAVOS
Copper, 27.5-28 mm.   **Obv:** National arms **Rev:** Value and date above sprigs **Note:** Size varies. Weight varies 8.51-11.39g.

Date	Mintage	VG	F	VF	XF	Unc
1915	—	25.00	40.00	55.00	85.00	—

TOLUCA, CITY

(Distrito Federal Mexico)

REVOLUTIONARY COINAGE

KM# 692.1   5 CENTAVOS
Cardboard grey in color, 27-28 mm.   **Obv:** Crowned shield within sprigs **Rev:** Banner accross large numeral value **Note:** Size varies. Weight varies 1.04-1.16g.

Date	Mintage	VG	F	VF	XF	Unc
1915	—	15.00	30.00	50.00	85.00	—

KM# 692.2   5 CENTAVOS
Cardboard grey in color, 27-28 mm.   **Obv:** Crowned shield within sprigs **Rev:** Banner accross large numeral value **Note:** Size varies. Weight varies 1.04-1.16g.

Date	Mintage	VG	F	VF	XF	Unc
1915	—	15.00	30.00	50.00	85.00	—

COUNTERMARKED COINAGE

KM# 693.1   20 CENTAVOS
Copper, 20 mm.   **Countermark:** 20 within C **Obv:** National arms **Rev:** Numeral 20 within C and inner circle within sprigs **Note:** Countermark on 1 Centavo, KM#415. Varieties exist. Weight varies 2.65-2.95g.

CM Date	Host Date	Good	VG	F	VF	XF
ND(1915)	ND	—	20.00	40.00	55.00	95.00

KM# 693.2   20 CENTAVOS
Copper, 20 mm.   **Countermark:** 20 within C **Obv:** National

arms **Rev:** Numeral 20 within C and inner circle within 3/4 wreath **Note:** Countermark on 1 Centavo, KM#394.1. Weight varies 2.65-2.95g.

CM Date	Host Date	Good	VG	F	VF	XF
ND(1915)	1904	—	30.00	50.00	90.00	165

KM# 694 40 CENTAVOS
5.8600 g., Copper, 24.75-25 mm. **Countermark:** 40 within C **Obv:** National arms **Rev:** Numeral 40 within C and inner circle within wreath **Note:** Countermark on 2 Centavos, KM#419. Varieties exist. Size varies.

CM Date	Host Date	Good	VG	F	VF	XF
ND(1915)	ND	—	25.00	40.00	60.00	100

MORELOS

Morelos is a state in south central Mexico, adjoining the federal district on the south. It was the headquarters of Emiliano Zapata. His personal quarters were at Tlatizapan in Morelos. The Morelos coins from 2 Centavos to 1 Peso were all copper except one type of 1 Peso in silver. The two operating Zapatista mints in Morelos were Atlihuayan and Tlaltizapan.

EMILIANO ZAPATA
(Zapatista)

REVOLUTIONARY COINAGE

KM# 695 2 CENTAVOS
Copper, 23 mm. **Obv:** National arms **Obv. Legend:** E.L. DE MORELOS **Rev:** Value within wreath

Date	Mintage	VG	F	VF	XF	Unc
1915	—	1,000	1,400	1,800	2,750	—

KM# 696 5 CENTAVOS
9.0000 g., Copper, 25.9 mm. **Obv:** National arms **Rev:** Value within 3/4 wreath **Rev. Legend:** E. DE MOR. 1915

Date	Mintage	VG	F	VF	XF	Unc
1915	—	300	500	1,000	3,500	—

KM# 697 10 CENTAVOS
8.6900 g., Copper, 24 mm. **Obv:** National arms **Rev:** Value within lined C and wreath

Date	Mintage	VG	F	VF	XF	Unc
1915	—	12.00	20.00	30.00	40.00	—

KM# 699 10 CENTAVOS
Copper **Obv:** National arms **Rev:** Date and value within wreath **Rev. Legend:** E. DE MOR

Date	Mintage	VG	F	VF	XF	Unc
1915	—	1,000	2,000	3,000	5,000	—

KM# 698 10 CENTAVOS
Copper, 24-24.5 mm. **Obv:** National arms **Rev:** Value within lined C and wreath with date effaced from die **Note:** Size varies. Weight varies 4.83-6.8g.

Date	Mintage	VG	F	VF	XF	Unc
ND	—	12.00	20.00	35.00	55.00	—

KM# 700 10 CENTAVOS
Copper, 28 mm. **Obv:** National arms **Rev:** Date and value within wreath **Rev. Legend:** MOR **Note:** Weight varies 5.56-8.36g.

Date	Mintage	VG	F	VF	XF	Unc
1916	—	5.00	20.00	30.00	50.00	—

KM# 701 20 CENTAVOS
Copper, 23.75-24.75 mm. **Obv:** National arms **Rev:** Value

within lined C and 3/4 wreath **Note:** Size varies. Weight varies 3.88-4.15g.

Date	Mintage	VG	F	VF	XF	Unc
1915	—	9.00	15.00	25.00	35.00	—

KM# 702   50 CENTAVOS
Copper, 28.8 mm.   **Obv:** National arms with MOR beneath eagle **Rev:** 50C monogram

Date	Mintage	VG	F	VF	XF	Unc
1915	—	300	500	900	1,450	—

KM# 703a   50 CENTAVOS
Brass **Obv:** National arms above sprigs **Rev:** 50C monogram

Date	Mintage	VG	F	VF	XF	Unc
1915	—	100	200	400	600	—

KM# 706   50 CENTAVOS
Copper, 28 mm.   **Obv:** National arms **Rev:** Date above large numeral value **Rev. Legend:** REFORMA LIBERTAD JUSTICIA Y LEY

Date	Mintage	VG	F	VF	XF	Unc
1915	—	350	500	850	1,200	—

KM# 703   50 CENTAVOS
Copper, 28-29.5 mm.   **Obv:** National arms **Rev:** Numeral value within lined C and 1/2 wreath **Note:** This coin exists with a silver and also a brass wash. Size varies. Weight varies 5.73-13.77g.

Date	Mintage	VG	F	VF	XF	Unc
1915	—	12.50	17.50	30.00	50.00	—

KM# 704   50 CENTAVOS
Copper, 29-30 mm.   **Obv:** National arms with Morelos written below **Rev:** Value within wreath **Note:** Size varies. Weight varies 8.56-11.47g.

Date	Mintage	VG	F	VF	XF	Unc
1916	—	12.50	20.00	30.00	50.00	—

KM# 708   PESO (UN)
Silver   **Obv:** National arms **Rev:** Liberty cap within wreath

Date	Mintage	VG	F	VF	XF	Unc
1916	—	450	750	1,150	1,850	—

KM# 708a   PESO (UN)
10.0000 g., Copper, 30 mm. **Obv:** National arms **Rev:** Liberty cap within wreath

Date	Mintage	VG	F	VF	XF	Unc
1916	—	500	1,000	1,200	2,300	—

OAXACA

Oaxaca is one of the southern states in Mexico. The coins issued in this state represent the most prolific series of the Revolution. Most of the coins bear the portrait of Benito Juarez, have corded or plain edges and were issued by a provisional government in the state. The exceptions are the rectangular 1 and 3 Centavos pieces that begin the series.

PROVISIONAL GOVERNMENT

REVOLUTIONARY COINAGE

 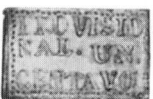

KM# 709   CENTAVO (UN)
Copper, 19 mm.   **Obv:** Legend within beaded rectangle **Rev:** Legend within beaded rectangle **Note:** Rectangular flan.

Date	Mintage	VG	F	VF	XF	Unc
1915	—	90.00	125	400	650	—

KM# 710   CENTAVO (UN)
Copper, 18 mm.   **Obv:** Bust left with date flanked by stars below **Rev:** Value within lined C and 1/2 wreath

Date	Mintage	VG	F	VF	XF	Unc
1915	—	12.00	17.50	25.00	40.00	—

KM# 710a   CENTAVO (UN)
Brass **Obv:** Head left with date flanked by stars below **Rev:** Value within lined C and 1/2 wreath

Date	Mintage	VG	F	VF	XF	Unc
1915	—	50.00	100	200	350	—

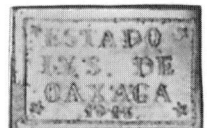 

KM# 711   3 CENTAVOS (Tres)
Copper, 24 mm.   **Obv:** Legend within rectangle with date below, stars in corners **Rev:** Legend within rectangle with

stars in corners **Rev. Legend:** PROVISIO... **Note:** Rectangular flan.

Date	Mintage	VG	F	VF	XF	Unc
1915	—	100	200	400	600	—

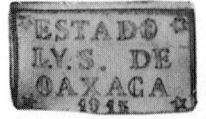 

KM# 712 3 CENTAVOS (Tres)
Copper **Obv:** Legend within rectangle with date below, stars in corners **Rev:** Legend within rectangle with stars in corners **Rev. Legend:** PROVISI... **Note:** Rectangular flan.

Date	Mintage	VG	F	VF	XF	Unc
1915	—	1,000	3,000	5,000	9,000	—

KM# 713.1 3 CENTAVOS (Tres)
2.2500 g., Copper, 20 mm. **Obv:** Bust left flanked by stars below **Rev:** Value above sprigs **Note:** Without TM below value

Date	Mintage	VG	F	VF	XF	Unc
1915	—	3.00	5.00	12.00	25.00	—

KM# 713.2 3 CENTAVOS (Tres)
2.2500 g., Copper, 20 mm. **Obv:** Bust left flanked by stars below **Rev:** Value above sprigs **Edge:** Plain **Note:** Without TM below value

Date	Mintage	VG	F	VF	XF	Unc
1915	—	—	—	70.00	100	—

KM# 713.3 3 CENTAVOS (Tres)
2.2500 g., Copper, 20 mm. **Obv:** Bust left flanked by stars below **Rev:** Value above sprigs **Note:** With TM below value

Date	Mintage	VG	F	VF	XF	Unc
1915	—	100	200	400	500	—

KM# 714 3 CENTAVOS (Tres)
Copper, 20 mm. **Obv:** Bust left **Rev:** Value above sprigs **Note:** Small 3

Date	Mintage	VG	F	VF	XF	Unc
1915	—	6.00	10.00	15.00	30.00	—

KM# 715 5 CENTAVOS
Copper **Note:** JAN. 15 1915. incuse lettering

Date	Mintage	VG	F	VF	XF	Unc
1915 Rare	—	—	—	—	—	—

KM# 716 5 CENTAVOS
Copper **Obv:** Bust facing within circle **Rev:** Value above sprigs

Date	Mintage	VG	F	VF	XF	Unc
1915	—	—	—	—	8,000	—

KM# 717 5 CENTAVOS
Copper, 22 mm. **Obv:** Low relief bust left with date flanked by stars below **Rev:** Value above sprigs **Note:** Low relief with long, pointed truncation

Date	Mintage	VG	F	VF	XF	Unc
1915	—	1.50	3.00	4.50	10.00	—

KM# 718 5 CENTAVOS
Copper, 22 mm. **Obv:** Raised bust left with date flanked by stars below **Rev:** Value above sprigs **Note:** Heavy with short unfinished lapels

Date	Mintage	VG	F	VF	XF	Unc
1915	—	1.50	2.50	4.00	10.00	—

KM# 719 5 CENTAVOS
Copper, 22 mm. **Obv:** Raised bust left with date flanked by stars below **Rev:** Value above sprigs **Note:** Curved bottom

Date	Mintage	VG	F	VF	XF	Unc
1915	—	1.50	2.50	4.00	10.00	—

KM# 720 5 CENTAVOS
Copper, 22 mm. **Obv:** Bust left with date flanked by stars below **Rev:** Value above sprigs **Note:** Short truncation with closed lapels

Date	Mintage	VG	F	VF	XF	Unc
1915	—	1.50	3.00	4.50	10.00	—

KM# 721 5 CENTAVOS
Copper, 22 mm. **Obv:** Bust left with date flanked by stars below **Rev:** Value above sprigs **Note:** Short curved truncation

Date	Mintage	VG	F	VF	XF	Unc
1915	—	1.50	2.50	5.00	10.00	—

KM# 722 10 CENTAVOS
Copper **Obv:** Low relief bust left with date flanked by stars below **Rev:** Value above sprigs **Note:** Low relief with long pointed truncation

Date	Mintage	VG	F	VF	XF	Unc
1915	—	1.50	2.50	5.00	10.00	—

KM# 723 10 CENTAVOS
Copper **Obv:** Bust left with date flanked by stars below **Rev:** Value above sprigs **Note:** Obverse and reverse legend retrograde.

Date	Mintage	VG	F	VF	XF	Unc
1915 Rare	—	—	—	—	—	—

KM# 724 10 CENTAVOS
Copper, 26.5 mm. **Obv:** Raised bust left with date flanked by stars below **Rev:** Value above sprigs **Note:** Bold and unfinished truncation using 1 peso obverse die of km#740

Date	Mintage	VG	F	VF	XF	Unc
1915	—	3.00	5.00	7.00	10.00	—

KM# 725 10 CENTAVOS
Copper, 26.5 mm. **Obv:** Bust left with date flanked by stars below **Rev:** Value above sprigs **Note:** Heavy with short unfinished lapels centered high

Date	Mintage	VG	F	VF	XF	Unc
1915	—	1.50	2.50	4.00	10.00	—

KM# 726 10 CENTAVOS
Copper **Obv:** Raised bust left with date flanked by stars below **Rev:** Value above sprigs **Note:** Curved bottom

Date	Mintage	VG	F	VF	XF	Unc
1915	—	1.50	2.50	4.00	10.00	—

KM# 727.1 10 CENTAVOS
Copper **Obv:** Raised bust left with date flanked by stars below **Rev:** Value above sprigs **Note:** Short truncation with closed lapels

Date	Mintage	VG	F	VF	XF	Unc
1915	—	1.50	2.50	4.00	10.00	—

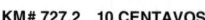

KM# 727.2 10 CENTAVOS
Copper **Obv:** Bust left with date flanked by stars below **Rev:** Value above sprigs **Note:** At present, only four pieces of this type are known. All are VF or better; T below bow with M below first leaf

Date	Mintage	VG	F	VF	XF	Unc
1915	—	—	—	400	550	—

KM# 727.3 10 CENTAVOS
Copper **Obv:** Raised bust left flanked by letters GV with date flanked by stars below **Rev:** Value above sprigs **Note:** This counterstamp appears on several different type host 10 cent coins.

Date	Mintage	VG	F	VF	XF	Unc
1915	—	100	200	300	450	—

Note: Letters GV correspond to General Garcia Vigil

KM# 730 20 CENTAVOS
Copper **Obv:** Bust left with date flanked by stars below **Rev:** Value above sprigs **Note:** 5th bust, heavy with short unfinished lapels using 20 Pesos obverse die

Date	Mintage	VG	F	VF	XF	Unc
1915	—	5.00	7.00	10.00	15.00	—

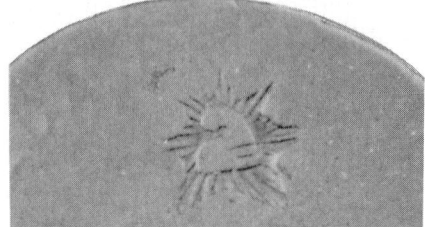

KM# 729.2 20 CENTAVOS
Copper **Counterstamp:** Liberty cap **Obv:** Bust left with date flanked by stars below **Rev:** Value above sprigs **Note:** Counterstamp: Liberty cap and rays with bold unfinished truncation using 1 peso obverse die

Date	Mintage	VG	F	VF	XF	Unc
1915	—	100	150	300	375	—

KM# 728   20 CENTAVOS
Silver, 19 mm.   **Obv:** Low relief bust left with date flanked by
stars below **Rev:** Value above sprigs **Note:** Low relief with
long pointed truncation

Date	Mintage	VG	F	VF	XF	Unc
1915	—	800	2,000	3,000	4,000	—

KM# 728a   20 CENTAVOS
Copper, 19 mm.   **Obv:** Bust left with date flanked by stars
below **Rev:** Value above sprigs **Note:** Low relief with long
pointed truncation

Date	Mintage	VG	F	VF	XF	Unc
1915 Rare	—	—	—	—	—	—

KM# 729.1   20 CENTAVOS
Copper   **Obv:** Raised bust left with date flanked by stars
below **Rev:** Value above sprigs **Note:** Unfinished truncation
using 1 peso obverse die

Date	Mintage	VG	F	VF	XF	Unc
1915	—	1.50	3.00	4.50	10.00	—

KM# 731.1   20 CENTAVOS
Copper, 31 mm.   **Obv:** Raised bust left with date flanked by
stars below **Rev:** Value above sprigs **Note:** Curved bottom

Date	Mintage	VG	F	VF	XF	Unc
1915	—	1.50	2.50	5.00	10.00	—

KM# 731.2   20 CENTAVOS
Copper   **Obv:** Raised bust left with date flanked by stars
below **Rev:** Value above sprigs **Note:** Similar to KM#731.1
but with fourth bust.

Date	Mintage	VG	F	VF	XF	Unc
1915 Unique	—	—	—	—	—	—

KM# 732   20 CENTAVOS
Copper   **Obv:** Raised bust left with date flanked by stars
below **Rev:** Value above sprigs

Date	Mintage	VG	F	VF	XF	Unc
1915	—	1.50	2.50	4.00	10.00	—

KM# 733   20 CENTAVOS
Copper   **Obv:** Bust left with date flanked by stars below **Rev:**
Value above sprigs **Note:** 7th bust, short truncation with
closed lapels

Date	Mintage	VG	F	VF	XF	Unc
1915	—	1.50	3.00	4.50	10.00	—

KM# 735   50 CENTAVOS
Silver, 22 mm.   **Obv:** Raised bust left with date flanked by
stars below **Rev:** Value above sprigs **Note:** Curved bottom

Date	Mintage	VG	F	VF	XF	Unc
1915	—	8.00	15.00	30.00	50.00	—

KM# 734   50 CENTAVOS
4.0700 g., Silver, 22 mm.   **Obv:** Raised bust left with date
flanked by stars below **Rev:** Value above sprigs **Note:** Heavy
with short unfinished lapels

Date	Mintage	VG	F	VF	XF	Unc
1915	—	10.00	20.00	50.00	100	—

KM# 739   50 CENTAVOS
Billon   **Obv:** Raised bust left with date flanked by stars below
Rev: Value above sprigs **Note:** Ninth bust, high nearly straight
truncation

Date	Mintage	VG	F	VF	XF	Unc
1915	—	—	—	—	4,000	—

KM# 739a   50 CENTAVOS
Copper   **Obv:** Raised bust left with date flanked by stars
below **Rev:** Value above sprigs **Note:** Ninth bust, high nearly
straight truncation

Date	Mintage	VG	F	VF	XF	Unc
1915	—	—	—	—	—	—

KM# 736   50 CENTAVOS
Silver   **Obv:** Bust left with date flanked by stars below **Rev:**
Value above sprigs **Note:** Short truncation with closed lapels

Date	Mintage	VG	F	VF	XF	Unc
1915	—	8.00	15.00	30.00	50.00	—

KM# 737   50 CENTAVOS
4.5400 g., Silver, 22 mm.   **Obv:** Bust left with date flanked
by stars below **Rev:** Value above sprigs **Note:** Short
truncation with pronounced curve

Date	Mintage	VG	F	VF	XF	Unc
1915	—	10.00	15.00	25.00	40.00	—

KM# 741   PESO (UN)
Silver   **Obv:** Raised bust with date flanked by stars below
Rev: Value above sprigs **Note:** Fifth bust, heavy with short
unfinished lapels, centered high

Date	Mintage	VG	F	VF	XF	Unc
1915	—	8.00	10.00	25.00	35.00	—

KM# 740.1   PESO (UN)
Silver, 26 mm.   **Obv:** Raised bust left with date flanked by
stars below **Rev:** Written value above sprigs **Note:** Fourth
bust with heavy unfinished truncation

Date	Mintage	VG	F	VF	XF	Unc
1915	—	5.00	10.00	20.00	35.00	—

KM# 740.2   PESO (UN)
Silver, 26 mm.   **Obv:** Raised bust left with date flanked by
stars below **Rev:** Written value above sprigs **Note:** Fourth
bust with heavy unfinished truncation w/TM.

Date	Mintage	VG	F	VF	XF	Unc
1915	—	150	300	400	650	—

KM# 743   PESO (UN)
Silver   **Obv:** Low relief bust left with date flanked by stars
below **Rev:** Value above sprigs **Note:** Seventh bust, short
truncation with closed lapels

Date	Mintage	VG	F	VF	XF	Unc
1915	—	10.00	20.00	30.00	50.00	—

KM# 743a   PESO (UN)
Silver   **Obv:** Low relief bust left with date flanked by stars
below **Rev:** Value above sprigs **Note:** Seventh bust, short
truncation with closed lapels

Date	Mintage	VG	F	VF	XF	Unc
1915	—	35.00	75.00	150	200	—

KM# 742   PESO (UN)
Silver   **Obv:** Low relief bust left with date flanked by stars
below **Rev:** Value above sprigs **Note:** Sixth bust; Curved
bottom line

Date	Mintage	VG	F	VF	XF	Unc
1915	—	10.00	15.00	30.00	50.00	—

KM# 742a   PESO (UN)
Copper   **Obv:** Low relief bust left with date flanked by stars
below **Rev:** Value above sprigs **Note:** Sixth bust; Curved
bottom line

Date	Mintage	VG	F	VF	XF	Unc
1915	—	—	—	—	500	—

KM# 744   2 PESOS (Dos)
Silver, 30 mm.   **Obv:** Raised bust left with date flanked by
stars below **Rev:** Value above sprigs **Note:** Fourth bust, using
1 peso obverse die

Date	Mintage	VG	F	VF	XF	Unc
1915	—	15.00	25.00	40.00	65.00	—

KM# 744a   2 PESOS (Dos)
Copper   **Obv:** Raised bust left with date flanked by stars
below **Rev:** Value above sprigs **Note:** Fourth bust, using 1
peso obverse die

Date	Mintage	VG	F	VF	XF	Unc
1915 Rare	—	—	—	—	—	—

KM# 745   2 PESOS (Dos)
Gold With Silver, 22 mm.   **Obv:** Low relief bust left with date
flanked by stars below **Rev:** Value above sprigs **Note:** 0.9020
Silver, 0.0100 Gold. Fifth bust, curved bottom 2 over pesos

Date	Mintage	VG	F	VF	XF	Unc
1915	—	12.00	20.00	40.00	60.00	—

KM# 745a   2 PESOS (Dos)
Copper   **Obv:** Low relief bust left with date flanked by stars
below **Rev:** Value above sprigs **Note:** Fifth bust, curved
bottom 2 over pesos

Date	Mintage	VG	F	VF	XF	Unc
1915	—	75.00	100	150	250	—

KM# A746 2 PESOS (Dos)
Copper **Obv:** Raised bust left with date flanked by stars below **Rev:** Balance scale below liberty cap **Note:** Seventh bust, short truncation with closed lapels

Date	Mintage	VG	F	VF	XF	Unc
1915 Unique	—	—	—	—	—	—

KM# 746 2 PESOS (Dos)
Silver **Obv:** Raised bust left with date flanked by stars below **Rev:** Balance scale below liberty cap

Date	Mintage	VG	F	VF	XF	Unc
1915	—	20.00	25.00	50.00	75.00	—

KM# A747 2 PESOS (Dos)
Silver **Obv:** Bust left with date flanked by stars below **Rev:** Balance scale below liberty cap **Note:** Obverse die is free hand engraved.

Date	Mintage	VG	F	VF	XF	Unc
1915	—	—	—	185	275	—

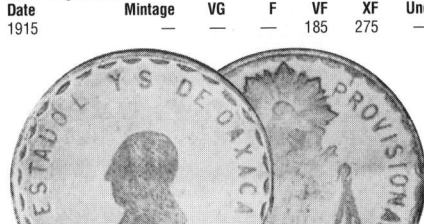

KM# 747.1 2 PESOS (Dos)
13.4400 g., Silver, 33 mm. **Obv:** Bust left with date flanked by stars below **Rev:** Balance scale below liberty cap

Date	Mintage	VG	F	VF	XF	Unc
1915	—	15.00	20.00	50.00	90.00	—

KM# 747.2 2 PESOS (Dos)
13.4400 g., Silver, 33 mm. **Obv:** Bust left with date flanked by stars below **Rev:** Balance scale below liberty cap

Date	Mintage	VG	F	VF	XF	Unc
1915	—	20.00	25.00	50.00	90.00	—

KM# 747.3 2 PESOS (Dos)
13.4400 g., Silver, 33 mm. **Obv:** Bust left with date flanked by stars below **Rev:** Balance scale below liberty cap

Date	Mintage	VG	F	VF	XF	Unc
1915	—	15.00	30.00	50.00	90.00	—

KM# 748 2 PESOS (Dos)
0.9020 Silver, 22 mm. **Obv:** Bust left with date flanked by stars below **Rev:** Value above sprigs

Date	Mintage	VG	F	VF	XF	Unc
1915	—	15.00	30.00	50.00	90.00	—

KM# 749 2 PESOS (Dos)
Silver **Obv:** Head left with date flanked by stars below **Rev:** Value above sprigs

Date	Mintage	VG	F	VF	XF	Unc
1915 Unique	—	—	—	—	3,000	—

KM# 751 5 PESOS
16.7700 g., Silver, 30 mm. **Obv:** Low relief bust left with date flanked by stars below **Rev:** Value above sprigs **Note:** Seventh bust, short truncation with closed lapels

Date	Mintage	VG	F	VF	XF	Unc
1915	—	50.00	80.00	175	275	—

KM# 751a 5 PESOS
Copper **Obv:** Low relief bust left with date flanked by stars below **Rev:** Value above sprigs **Note:** Seventh bust, short truncation with closed lapels

Date	Mintage	VG	F	VF	XF	Unc
1915	—	125	200	300	800	—

KM# 750 5 PESOS
0.1750 Gold, 19 mm. **Obv:** Bust left **Rev:** Value above sprigs **Note:** Third bust, heavy, with short unfinished lapels

Date	Mintage	VG	F	VF	XF	Unc
1915	—	150	200	300	500	800

KM# 750a 5 PESOS
Copper **Obv:** Bust left **Rev:** Value above sprigs **Note:** Third bust, heavy, with short unfinished lapels

Date	Mintage	VG	F	VF	XF	Unc
1915 Unique	—	—	—	—	—	—

KM# A752 10 PESOS
0.1500 Gold, **Obv:** Bust left with date flanked by stars below **Rev:** Value above sprigs

Date	Mintage	VG	F	VF	XF	Unc
1915 Rare	—	—	—	—	—	—

KM# 752   10 PESOS
0.1750 Gold, 23 mm. **Obv:** Bust left with date flanked by stars below **Rev:** Value above sprigs

Date	Mintage	VG	F	VF	XF	Unc
1915	—	200	300	400	600	1,000

KM# 752a   10 PESOS
Copper **Obv:** Bust left with date flanked by stars below **Rev:** Value above sprigs

Date	Mintage	VG	F	VF	XF	Unc
1915	—	800	1,500	2,000	4,000	—

KM# 753   20 PESOS
0.1750 Gold **Obv:** Bust left with date flanked by stars below **Rev:** Value above sprigs

Date	Mintage	VG	F	VF	XF	Unc
1915	—	400	500	800	1,000	1,500

KM# 754   20 PESOS
0.1750 Gold, 27 mm. **Obv:** Bust left with date flanked by stars below **Rev:** Value above sprigs

Date	Mintage	VG	F	VF	XF	Unc
1915	—	200	400	600	900	1,600

KM# A753   20 PESOS
0.1500 Gold **Obv:** Bust left with date flanked by stars below **Rev:** Value above sprigs **Note:** Fourth bust

Date	Mintage	VG	F	VF	XF	Unc
1915 Unique	—	—	—	—	—	—

KM# 755   60 PESOS
50.0000 g., 0.8590 Gold 1.3808 oz. AGW **Obv:** Head left within 3/4 wreath **Rev:** Balance scale below liberty cap **Edge:** Reeded

Date	Mintage	F	VF	XF	Unc	BU
1916 Rare	—	—	10,000	20,000	28,000	—

KM# 755a   60 PESOS
Silver **Obv:** Head left within 3/4 wreath **Rev:** Balance scales below liberty cap **Edge:** Reeded

Date	Mintage	F	VF	XF	Unc	BU
1916	—	—	—	—	1,800	—

KM# 755b   60 PESOS
Copper **Obv:** Head left within 3/4 wreath **Rev:** Balance scales below liberty cap **Edge:** Plain

Date	Mintage	F	VF	XF	Unc	BU
1916	—	—	—	1,000	1,800	—

PUEBLA

A state of central Mexico. Puebla was a state that occasionally saw Zapata forces active within its boundaries. Also active, and an issuer of coins, was the Madero brigade who issued coins with their name two years after Madero's death. The state issue of 2, 5, 10 and 20 Centavos saw limited circulation and recent hoards have been found of some values.

CHICONCUAUTLA
Madero Brigade

REVOLUTIONARY COINAGE

KM# 756   10 CENTAVOS
6.7300 g., Copper, 27 mm.   **Obv:** Date below national arms
Rev: Letters X and C entwined

Date	Mintage	VG	F	VF	XF	Unc
1915	—	7.50	12.50	17.50	25.00	—

KM# 758   20 CENTAVOS
Copper, 28 mm.   **Obv:** Date below national arms **Rev:** Value

Date	Mintage	VG	F	VF	XF	Unc
1915	—	2.50	4.00	6.50	12.00	—

KM# 757   20 CENTAVOS
Copper, 28 mm.   **Obv:** Date below national arms **Rev:** Value
Note: Varieties exist.

Date	Mintage	VG	F	VF	XF	Unc
1915	—	2.50	4.00	6.50	12.00	—

TETELA DEL ORO Y OCAMPO

REVOLUTIONARY COINAGE

KM# 759   2 CENTAVOS
Copper, 16 mm.   **Obv:** National arms above date **Rev:** Value

Date	Mintage	VG	F	VF	XF	Unc
1915	—	12.50	20.00	28.00	45.00	—
1915 Restrikes	—	—	1.00	1.50	2.00	—

KM# 760   2 CENTAVOS
Copper, 20 mm.   **Obv:** National arms within beaded circle
Rev: Value within beaded circle **Rev. Legend:** E. DE PU.

Date	Mintage	VG	F	VF	XF	Unc
1915	—	15.00	25.00	35.00	75.00	—

KM# 761   2 CENTAVOS
Copper, 20 mm.   **Obv:** National arms within beaded circle
Rev: Value within beaded circle **Rev. Legend:** E. DE PUE.

Date	Mintage	VG	F	VF	XF	Unc
1915	—	9.00	20.00	25.00	50.00	—

KM# 762   5 CENTAVOS
Copper, 21 mm.   **Obv:** National arms within beaded circle
Rev: Value within beaded circle

Date	Mintage	VG	F	VF	XF	Unc
1915	—	100	200	300	400	—

KM# 764   20 CENTAVOS
Copper, 24 mm.   **Obv:** National arms **Rev:** Value above sprigs

Date	Mintage	VG	F	VF	XF	Unc
1915	—	50.00	100	150	225	—

SINALOA

A state along the west coast of Mexico. The cast pieces of this state have been attributed to two people - Generals Rafael Buelna and Juan Carrasco. The cap and rays 8 Reales is usually attributed to General Buelna and the rest of the series to Carrasco. Because of their crude nature it is questionable whether separate series or mints can be determined.

BUELNA / CARRASCO

COUNTERMARKED COINAGE

Revolutionary

These are all crude sand cast coins using regular coins to prepare the mold. Prices below give a range for how much of the original coin from which the mold was prepared is visible.

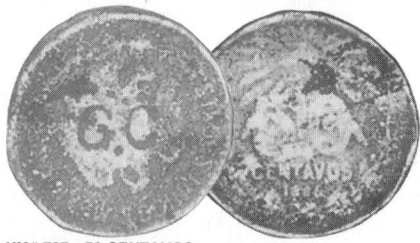

KM# 767   50 CENTAVOS
Cast Silver   **Countermark:** G.C. **Obv:** National arms with additional countermark **Rev:** Value and date within wreath with liberty cap above **Note:** Sand molded using regular 50 Centavos, KM#445.

CM Date	Host Date	Good	VG	F	VF	XF
ND	ND(1905-1918)	100	150	200	300	—

KM# 770   PESO
Cast Silver, 38.5 mm.   **Countermark:** G.C **Obv:** National arms with additional countermark **Rev:** Liberty cap with additional countermark **Note:** Sand molded using regular Peso, KM#409.

CM Date	Host Date	Good	VG	F	VF	XF
ND(ca.1915)	ND(1898-1909)	30.00	60.00	140	175	—

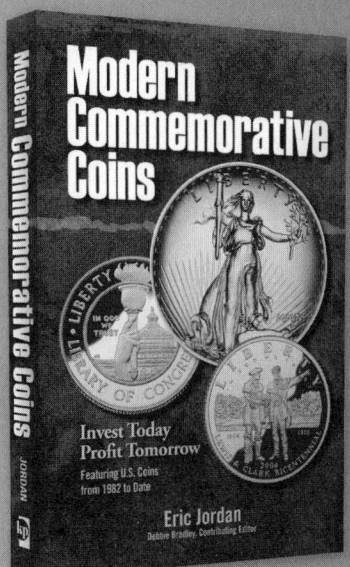
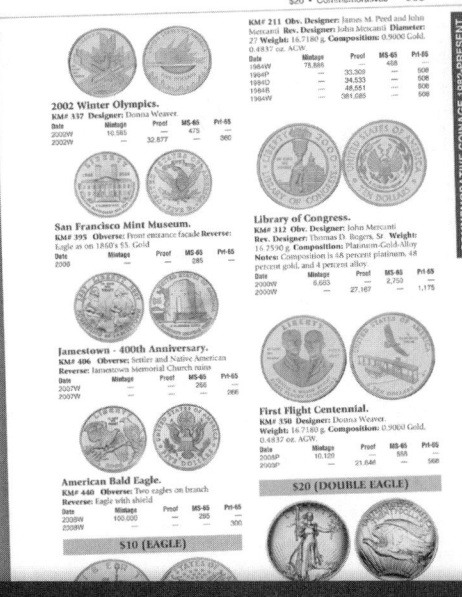

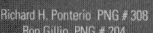